est be spoken Mandarin, classical philology, or one of the dialects.

Yuen Ren Chao is Agassiz Professor of Oriental Languages and Literature Emeritus at the University of California, Berkeley. This publication is the result of more than fifty years of distinguished research and teaching in both China and the United States.

# A GRAMMAR OF
# SPOKEN CHINESE

# A GRAMMAR OF
# SPOKEN CHINESE

By

Yuen Ren Chao

中國话的文法

趙元任

University of California Press

Berkeley and Los Angeles

1968

University of California Press
Berkeley and Los Angeles, California


Cambridge University Press
London, England

© 1968 by The Regents of the University of California.
This work was supported by a contract with the United States
Office of Education, Department of Health, Education, and Wel-
fare.

Library of Congress Catalog Card Number: 65-10576


Printed in the United States of America

To
MY WIFE

Whose inadvertencies
have furnished me
with many an apt example
of Spoken Chinese

# PREFACE

When I translated my *Cantonese Primer* into Mandarin—for that was what *Mandarin Primer* essentially was—I was going to use the same eight pages on grammar, except for some minor points in which Cantonese and Mandarin differ grammatically. But Fang-Kuei Li insisted that I write a fuller grammatical chapter, and so it was subsequently expanded to thirty-seven pages. No sooner, however, was *Mandarin Primer* published, in 1948, than Lien-Sheng Yang began to furnish me with additional materials and urged me to write a full-length book on the subject. For some time I had been jotting down notes and had written some articles on special topics in the grammar of spoken Chinese, but it was not until 1954, when I went to Europe on a John Simon Guggenheim Memorial Foundation Fellowship, that I decided to make a book project of it. Everybody laughed at my going to Europe for Chinese grammar. But when it was possible to exchange ideas with European students of modern Chinese, with men like Harry Simon, who were not only able to take part in but even conduct discussion groups in Chinese, with the whole paraphernalia of new terms, I found that going to Europe for Chinese grammar was, to change the figure a little, not entirely a matter of 东辕西辙.

Preoccupation with other, though related, matters delayed my progress on the book, but during my sojourn in the Orient in 1959 I was able to make profitable contacts, both in the way of theoretical discussion and in the collecting of raw material in the form of tape recording of live conversation.

Most of the actual writing of the book was, however, not begun until the fall of 1960, when the grammar project was given additional impetus by a grant under the National Defense Education Act of the Office of Education of the Department of Health, Education, and Welfare, under the terms of which I was able to obtain most of the needed assistance, linguistic and typographical

vii

as well as calligraphic, and to put the book finally in the present form.

The Chinese title of this book, 中 國 话 的 文 法 *Jonggwo Huah de Wenfaa*, is typical of the language under study, but very atypical as Chinese book titles go. Ordinarily one would call such a book 國 语 文 法 *Gwoyeu Wenfaa*, as Lii Jiinshi called his book, which title, though often criticized for its mixed figures, is perfectly good Chinese, because the mixture occurs at the level of bound morphemes. However, I am not using such a title, for the reason that *Gwoyeu* connotes Standard Mandarin, and my emphasis has been to de-emphasize the standard aspect of Mandarin, since, especially in matters of grammar, most of what is said here about Mandarin is true of all Chinese, even of a good part of the literary language. Another natural title would be 中 國 口 语 ‹ 法 *Jonggwo Koouyeu Yeufaa*. (Cf. Lii Rong's translation of chap. 3 of my *Mand Prim* as *Beeijing Koouyeu Yeufaa*.) This is free of mixed figures, but both *koouyeu* 'spoken language' and *yeufaa* 'grammar of speech' are newly coined learned terms and nobody would talk about *koouyeu* or *yeufaa* in conversation except in technical discussions. Likewise, the now frequently used title 汉 语 ‹ 法 *Hannyeu Yeufaa* (see bibliography) is a phrase of two words each of which is scientifically precise but not actually spoken except in contexts such as that of linguistic seminars. There is, to be sure, no necessity for naming a book in the language which is being described in the book, any more than a Chinese grammar has to be written in Chinese. But I prefer the present title because it sets the right tone for the subject matter of the book.

This is a discussion book and not an instruction book to learn Chinese grammar from. An attempt has, however, been made to use only examples which have been or can be said in real life. Special forms or styles, such as wenyan, written bairhuah, or dialects, will be so marked. As a discussion book, it is likely to raise more problems than it solves. I only invite the reader to consider problems with me as a fellow student of the subject. There is no editorial 'we', with its 'ourself' in the singular, but only the inclusive 'we', meaning you the reader and I the writer studying the subject together; in other words, the 'we' in the book is the 咱们 *tzarmen* 'we' rather than the 我们 *woomen* 'we'. When occasionally I do mean 'I', I say 'I'.

It is I, of course, who will now have the pleasant duty of acknowledging the help of all who have rendered moral support and linguistic sustenance in bringing this lengthy undertaking to a quasi-finished form—quasi-finished, because such a book is never finished but only considered as finished.

I have already referred to the early encouragements from Fang-Kuei Li and Lien-Sheng Yang, who also gave their time in going over the whole manuscript, with their helpful ideas, both theoretical and informational. With Fa-Kao Chou, the grammarian of classical Chinese, I have had much profitable exchange of views, especially regarding the comparison between the classical and the modern forms. Tsu-Lin Mei has been very helpful with his criticisms as logician-linguist. My daughter Rulan C. Pian stole a march on me by publishing her *Syllabus to Mandarin Primer* and I took my revenge by stealing back some of her examples without acknowledgment, taking them as common property. From Nicholas C. Bodman and Samuel E. Martin, who also waded through the whole thousand-page manuscript, I got much help and stimulation when they raised points of relevance which had escaped me as a native speaker, who took too much for granted. I wish also to acknowledge my debt to other writers on the subject, from Maa Jiannjong ( 馬建忠 ) down to my students and students' students, whose names are so numerous as to form practically an "open class", but they will appear in the bibliography and in the footnotes, not the least frequent of which refer to recalled conversations with the late Dr. Hu Shih on matters grammatical.

I must of course express my unreserved thanks to all who have at one time or another taken part in the actual preparation of the book: to Shih-Feng Yang for the initial calligraphic work and for making arrangements for recordings while I was in Taiwan; to Gari Ledyard, who summarized a large amount of published material for possible use; and to Jerry L. Norman, who rendered the greater part of the actual research assistance, ranging from calling to my attention new books and articles, to checking redundancies and inconsistencies in terminology, as well as in theory, in different parts of the book written years apart. To

Dorothy Lun Ballou thanks are due for the major part of the preparation of the manuscript, for the revision of the index, and for the calligraphy in the published book. The characters may look a little stiff in style, but I told her to make each one as near- ly square as possible—except the character — !—in order to pre- sent a more uniform printed appearance. Her calligraphy, if it had not been so restricted, would have shown to better advan- tage. Last but not least, thanks are due to the staff of the Univer- sity of California Press, especially to Grace W. Buzaljko, for un- dertaking so fussy, not to say so costly, a job for which I hope the result will give some justification.

A book of this length cannot but contain many errors of omission and commission, for which I alone am responsible and for the correction of which by readers I would be most apprecia- tive.

Yuen Ren Chao

# CONTENTS

Contents

# LIST OF TABLES

## USAGES OF THIS BOOK

1. Characters Used. Characters are used in citations of references and of illustrative examples.

(1) When necessary for clarity, titles of Chinese authors and works will be given in characters, for example, 陈澧, 切韵考 (Chern Lii, *Chieh Yunn Kao*), except well-known titles in English, for example *Shuo Wen*, *The Analects*, *Mencius*, and Hu Shih, *Collected Works*, ser. 1.

(2) Illustrative Examples. These are given in characters and in GR transcription, with an English gloss. The characters are included for the convenience of readers who feel more comfortable with them than with romanization. On abbreviated characters, see pp. xxv-xxvii.

Certain onomatopoeic and other words have no characters to write them. Fourteen are listed in *Conc Dict* (p. 251), of which the first one ☐ *bell* occurring in ☐ 棒 *bellbanq* 'very smart' probably comes from 倍儿 'doubly' and 棒 *banq* 'smart' (Peip. localism). The sixth word ☐ *geh* 'chafes' (for example, cinder in the eye) is probably a cognate of 梗, 哽, 鲠 *geeng* of the same semantic group. The others, such as ☐ *Pia!* 'Whack!' or 'Splash!', ☐ *Wo!* 'Giddap!', are morphemes without characters.

Somewhat different are cases where the usual spoken forms do not agree with the usual written forms. Since we are primarily concerned with the language as it is spoken and not so much with the way it is written, we are adopting, in the following cases, forms which reflect the speech better:

| Now Usually Written | Meaning | To Be Written in This Book | To Be Spelled in This Book | Remark |
|---|---|---|---|---|
| 他 | 'he' | | | |
| 她 | 'she' } | 他 | *ta* | |
| 它 | 'it' | | | |

| | | | | |
|---|---|---|---|---|
| 底<br>的<br>地 | (reverse) 'of'<br>''s, -tic,'etc.'<br>'-ly' | 的 | *de* | These new distinctions are not reflected in actual speech. On *de*, see sec. 5. 3. 6. 1. |
| 告想<br>告诉 | 'tells' | 告送 | *gaw.sonq* | Cf. 木 *mung* in Hupeh; also cf. 告诵 in *Shiyou Jih* ("Monkey"), Chap. 23. |
| (坐)在(这儿) | 'at, to' | (坐)得(这儿) | *(tzuoh) de (jell)* | Blend of 在 *tzay* and 到 *daw*. See sec. 5. 6. 3. |
| 早晨<br>早起 | 'morning' | 早晨 | *tzao.chin* | Blend of 晨 *chern* and 起 *chii*. |
| 这种 | 'this kind' | 这种 | *jey.tzoong* | Blend of 种 *joong* and 宗 *tzong*. |
| 这么 | 'so' | 这么 | *tzemme* | From analogy with 怎么 *tzeeme*. |

In the last example the forms *jehme* (with open vowel) and *jemme* (*with checked vowel*) are also spoken, though somewhat more formal in style than the more familiar *tzemme*.

For a fuller discussion of these points, see my 方言记錄中汉字的功用 ("The Function of Chinese Characters in the Recording of the Dialects"), *Annals of Academia Sinica* (Taipei, 1954), vol. 1, pp. 117-128.)

2. Glossing

(1) Degrees of Literalness and Idiomaticalness. Illustrative examples will be given in characters, followed by romanization and a gloss. A literal translation and an idiomatic translation,

if they differ, are marked by the insertion of a comma-dash ",—", as listed under the List of Symbols. Since literalness versus idiomaticalness is not a question of either-or, but a matter of degree, this sign can be used in succession, as in  这儿的 人 太多 . *Jell de ren tay duo.* 'This place's people too many,—The people here are too many,—There are too many people here.' In general only one point will be important in any given context, so that successive use of this sign is rarely necessary. Thus, if the point under discussion is the substantive nature of place words, then use the form 'this place's people,—the people here' while if it is about the predicative function of adjectives, then use the form '...too many,—...are too many'; in any case, the picture should not be blurred by adding unnecessary literal translations which do not illustrate the point being discussed.

(2) Principle of Immediate Semantic Constituents. In glossing a construction with more than one morpheme, the structural constituents should be glossed *at the stage at which they enter the construction* and not at a prior stage. For example, a literal glossing of 面生 *miann-sheng* should be 'face-unfamiliar' and not 'face-raw', since at the stage at which *sheng* enters the compound it has already gone beyond the meaning of 'raw'.

(3) Popular[1] or Correct Etymology? Since we are taking the language of the average educated person's speech as the subject of our study and not that of the classical scholar, we shall follow the popular etymology in analyzing compounds, even though it is known to be wrong by the scholar. For example, the compound 良心 *liang.shin* 'conscience' is popularly understood as the 'good heart', although in fact *liang* originally meant 'inborn' and 'conscience' was called *liang-shin* on the theory of man's nature being born good. Again, 'snake' is called 长虫 *charng.chorng* because *chorng* originally meant any animal. (Cf. the form 大虫 *dah-*

---

[1]A distinction is sometimes made between (1) popular etymology, or a popular interpretation of an etymology, and (2) folk etymology, by which a form is altered to make it meaningful. Thus 耳朵 *eel-duoo* 'ear-blossom,—ear', is changed, through metathesis, to *eel.dou*, which makes no sense, and then to 耳头 *eel.tou*, in analogy with 舌头 *sher.tou*, with -*.tou* taken as a suffix by folk etymology. See also p. 176 on descriptive etymology.

*chorng* 'tiger', used in old novels.) But now that *chorng* means only 'insect', *charng.chorng* is understood, at the descriptive level, as 'long insect,—snake'.

(4) Simplified Glossing. The relation between morphemes of different languages are more often that of n-to-n than 1-to-1. For example, the one morpheme 牛 *niou* corresponds to English 'ox', 'bull', 'cow', 'cattle', while to English 'cousin' there are 堂兄 *tarngshiong* or 堂房哥ㄦ *tarngfarng ge.ge* 'elder cousin on father's side', 堂弟 *tarngdih* or 堂房弟ㄦ *tarngfarng dih.dih* 'younger cousin on father's side' and numerous other forms according to age or sex, whether on father's or mother's side, whether as direct address or as a designative term. Since in most cases the disparity of semantic categories does not affect the grammatical analysis, we shall, except where the distinctions happen to be grammatically relevant, adopt simplified glosses, of which the following are some of the most common examples:

| Chinese Form | | Simplified Gloss | Strictly |
|---|---|---|---|
| 人 | *ren* | man, people | man, woman, person, people, etc. |
| 二位 | *ell-wey* | you two gentle-men | you two gentlemen, you two ladies, you sir and you lady |
| 哥ㄦ | *ge.ge* | brother | older brother, older male cousin |
| 姐ㄦ | *jiee.jiee* | sister | older sister, older female cousin |
| 叔ㄦ | *shu.shu* | uncle | uncle on father's side younger than father |
| 筆 | *bii* | pen | pen, pencil, brush |
| 诗 | *shy* | poetry, poem | poetry, poem of equal length of lines |
| 牛 | *niou* | ox | ox, bull, cow, cattle |

| 桌子 | *juotz* | table | table, desk |
| 江 | *jiang* | river | the Yangtze River; large river |
| 河 | *her* | river | the Yellow River; river |
| 打牌 | *daa-pair* | plays mahjong | plays mahjong, dominoes, or cards. |
| 下棋 | *shiah-chyi* | plays chess | plays chess or *go* |
| 酒 | *jeou* | wine | wine, liquor |

Verbs will be glossed in the infinitive form, without 'to', for example, 去 *chiuh* 'go', except in case of ambiguity, for example, 种 *jonq* 'to plant'.

(5) Style. Other things being equal, an attempt will be made to make the glosses comparable in style with the forms glossed, for example, 真糟糕! *Jen tzaugau!* 'What a mess!' but 真是不幸! *Jensh bushinq!* 'How unfortunate!' but not vice versa. Comparability in style, however, is not as important as comparability in structure, which is after all our chief concern here.

3. List of Symbols

(1) Special Punctuation Marks

A>B        A changed into B historically: 心 *sim* > *shin*.

A<B        A is derived from B historically: 心 *shin* < *sim*.

A → B      A changes into B synchronically: 今日 *jinryh* → 今ㄦ *jiel*.

A←B        A is derived from B synchronically: 今ㄦ *jiel* ← 今日 *jinryh*.

'A,—B'      Literally A, idiomatically B: 再見 *tzayjiann* 'see (you) again,—goodbye'.

A—          Drawl on last sound or sounds: 我想 —*Woo sheang*—, with *a* and *ng* prolonged. (May also indicate the usual functions of dashes.)

A ∼ B      A alternates with B: 扔 *rheng* ∼ *reeng*.

°A           The form °A does not occur: °第兩 °*dihleang* for 'second'.

A°, A°       See section (3) below.

A B C  Coordinate items which are grammatically separate but usually spoken without pause, as 風花雪月 *feng hua sheue yueh* 'winds, flowers, snow, the moon'.

.A  A is in the neutral tone. (For convenient identification of morphemes the etymological tone is still indicated in the spelling: 服侍 *fwu.shyh* (instead of *fwu.shy*) 'waits on'.

₀A  Optional neutral tone in A: 不知道 *bujy₀daw* 'don't know'.

○  Item zero.

▢  Character does not exist, or exists but need not be specified.

[   ]  Symbols enclosed are phonetic.

/   /  Symbols enclosed are phonemic.

{   }  Symbols enclosed are morphophonemic.

, or  An 'or' preceded by a comma is synonymous with 'i.e.', as in '2 + 1, or 3', but an 'or' unpreceded by a comma joins real alternatives, as in '3 or 4'.

A hyphen is used between highly versatile elements of compounds, and in A-N or V-O constructions, where A and N or V and O are both monosyllabic, whether free or bound, except that a pronoun object is written without a hyphen.

'  (a) An apostrophe separates a syllabic ending from a following bound syllable beginning with a vowel: 興安 *Shing'an* 'Hing An (Mountains)' vs. 心肝 *shingan* 'heart and liver,—darling'.

(b) Entering tone: — *ie'* Wu dialects, where an Entering Tone ends in a glottal stop if final and is simply very short when followed by another syllable.

(2) Phonetic Symbols

(a) IPA. The forms of IPA used here follow those in the back page of issues of *Le Maître Phonétique*, for example, that of no. 124, 3rd ser., 1965. American usage differs slightly from that of IPA in using *y* for [j], *ü* for [y], and single letters for affricates: *c* for [ts], and *š* for [ ʃ ], and in using ▢ for syllabicity: m̩ for IPA [m], whereas [m̥] in IPA means voiceless [m].

(b) Additional Symbols. For the purposes of the present book, we shall add the following symbols:

[ ʅ ]    Dental apical vowel, as in 絲 *sy* [s ʅ ] ( = [sz̩] of IPA).

[ ʅ ]    Retroflex apical vowel, as in 詩 *shy* [ʂ ʅ ] ( = [ʂʐ̩] or [ʂɻ̩]
         of IPA).

[ A ]    Medium *a*, between front [a] and back [ɑ].

[ E ]    Medium *e*, between [e] and [ɛ].

The first two were adapted from Karlgren's notation (*Phonologie*
295, Ch tr 197), the third is from Jespersen[2], and the last one was
my proposal.[3] For convenience of printing, Greek gamma, chi,
and other letters are given without serifs, which are supposed to
be attached to free ends of most of the IPA letters.

Occasional citations of dialectal forms will be mainly in IPA,
except that Cantonese will be in the system used in *Cant Prim*
and the Wu dialects will mainly follow the forms used in my
*Studies in the Modern Wu Dialects*, (Peking, 1928).

(c)    Modifiers and Glides. We shall set up a rule that a
superscribed letter will be an additive glide and a subscribed
letter will be an adjectival modifier. For example [a$^n$] means
[a] followed by an incompletely formed [n], or by [ã], while
[a$_n$] is taken as [a] nasalized throughout its duration, synonymous
with [ã]. Similarly [ə$_r$] = [ɚ], but [ə$^r$] = [əɹ] or [əɚ̌].

(3)  Prosodic Elements

(a)    Stress. Stress will be marked thus:

ˈ☐        normal stress

ˌ☐        secondary stress

ₙ☐        tertiary stress

ₙ☐        contrastive stress

.☐        weak, or zero stress

As to what stresses are distinctive, see the section on Phonology
(sec. 1.3.6).

(b) Tone Marks. Besides the tonal spelling in GR (see table
inside back cover) tones in general are expressed by a set of tone
letters consisting of time-pitch graphs attached to the left of a
vertical reference line divided into four intervals by five points.
These can be used for any dialect. For Mandarin they are as
shown in the table on this page. A neutral tone (at various

---

[2]Otto Jespersen, *Lehrbuch der Phonetik*, Leipzig, 1904, p. 157.

[3]"E" for Middle e, *Le Maître Phonétique*, no. 46, 23-24 (1931).

heights) is indicated by a dot, as in 他 的 *ta.de* ㄱ ⌐ .

| Tone Letter | Code | Tone |
|:---:|:---:|:---:|
| ㄱ | 55: | 1st Tone |
| ㄱ | 35: | 2nd Tone |
| ㄥ | 214: | 3rd Tone |
| ㄥ | 51: | 4th Tone |
| ㄥ | 21: | 5th Tone |

Alternatively the same graphs, without a vertical reference line, can be used over letters or characters,[4] as in 陰, 陽, 上, 去.

(c) Tone Classes. When only class membership is to be indicated, regardless of actual tone values, Mandarin tones are to be indicated by superscribed figures, as in the Wade system, for example, 衣$^1$, 移$^2$, 以$^3$, 意$^4$; the traditional tone classes by semicircles, for example, 平, 上, 去, 入; and subdivisions of these classes according to (ancient) voicing, indicated thus: 研, 平, 賞, 養, 去, 具, 涅, 十. Semicircles solidly attached to the characters, however, are to be regarded as part of variant characters, usually with more then mere difference in tone: 重 *jonq:* 重 *chorng,* 長 *charng:* 長 *jaang.* The semicircles, whether attached or detached, are not used for tonal distinctions of limited geographical and/or historical validity; for example, 雌 *tsyr* < *ts'ie* is not to be marked as 雌, but as 雌$^2$ or 雌. In particular, a new value of the Entering Tone, from redistribution over one of the other tones, is not to be marked with a semicircle. For example, 鉄 *tiee* < *t'iet* is not to be marked as 鉄, but as 鉄$^3$ or 鉄.

---

[4]I proposed these time-pitch graphs to be used in connection with the National Phonetic Letters, as for example in my 新 國 语 嘅 声 片 课 本, 甲 种 (Textbook for New Records of the National Language, Version Jea), Shanghai, 1935, which were later adopted by George Kennedy into the Yale System of romanization. Such time-pitch graphs differ in principle from, and are preferable to, the type of tone signs in which acute "´" means high, grave "`" means low, "ˆ" means falling and "ˇ" means rising, such as used in the *BEFEO* system of romanization. This latter type is mathematically more sophisticated, since it represents the first derivative, or *rate of change* of pitch in time rather than pitch simply, and is therefore not as easily imaginable, or *anschaulich*, as the time-pitch type of graphs.

Tone-class spelling follows the GR system (pp. 00-00) and goes by analogy with the GR system for the dialects, except that for Cantonese a doubled vowel means a long vowel, -x and -g ( = -ng) indicate Rising Tone, and -q ( = -ng) indicates Going Tone.

The *pinn'iam*, or changed tones, of Cantonese are shown by □° for the first tone (phonetically [55:]) and □° for the second (phonetically [25:]).

4. Abbreviated Characters. Following is a partial list of abbreviated characters used in the citations in this book. They do not include those common simplified characters which are either better known among students of Chinese than the full characters such as 闩 for 檊 *shuan* 'bolt' and 针 for 鍼 *jen* 'needle', or equally well known, such as 宝 for 寶 *bao* 'treasure' and 双 for 雙 *shuang* 'double'. Most of the abbreviated characters used in the book are found in 刘復,李家瑞, 宋元以来俗字谱 (Liou Fuh and Lii Jiaruey, *Sonq Yuan Yiilai Swutzyh Puu*, Shanghai: Academia Sinica, 1930). Of the newest abbreviations, such as those listed in Ronald Hsia and Peter Penn, *Dictionary of Simplified Chinese*, Hong Kong, 1959, relatively few are used here, since they are not so well known and it is not one of the purposes of this book on spoken Chinese to teach such characters in order to facilitate the reading of current publications.[5] Characters are included in citations, as noted above, primarily for the convenience of those who can follow the examples more comfortably in characters than in transcription. The abbreviated characters listed below are in the order of their *apparent* radicals and residual strokes. Those which have no clear apparent radicals are grouped at the end of the list in the order of total numbers of strokes. When a character is followed by "etc." the simplified form is applicable analogously to other characters of which it forms a part; for example, " 劲 = 勁 , etc." means also 径 = 徑 , even though the latter case is not listed.

---

[5]For an objective discussion of the problems of abbreviated characters, see 周法高,中國语文论从 (Fa-Kao Chou, *Essays on Chinese Language and Writing*), Taipei, 1963, pp. 169-179.

## By Apparent Radicals

| | | | | |
|---|---|---|---|---|
| 世 = 世 , etc. | | 尽 = 盡 , etc. |
| 旧 = 舊 | | 属 = 屬 , etc. |
| 从 = 從 or 叢 | | 歲 = 歲 |
| 传 = 傳 | | 岩 = 巖 |
| 会 = 會 | | 帅 = 帥 |
| 价 = 價 | | 师 = 師 |
| 体 = 體 | | 干 = 乾 'dry' |
| 党 = 黨 | | 应 = 應 |
| 兴 = 興 | | 床 = 牀 |
| 写 = 寫 , etc. | | 庄 = 莊 |
| 几 = 几 or 幾 | | 庙 = 廟 |
| 刘 = 劉 | | 昇 = 異 |
| 劝 = 勸 | | 弃 = 棄 |
| 办 = 辦 | | 执 = 執 , etc. |
| 劲 = 勁 , etc. | | 怀 = 懷 |
| 势 = 勢 , etc. | | 报 = 報 |
| 区 = 區 , etc. | | 荅 = 答 , etc. |
| 医 = 醫 | | 搁 = 擱 , etc. |
| 压 = 壓 | | 齐 = 齊 , etc. |
| 听 = 聽 , etc. | | 斋 = 齋 |
| 虽 = 雖 | | 断 = 斷 , etc. |
| 啚 = 圖 | | 时 = 時 |
| 营 = 營 , etc. | | 权 = 權 |
| 坚 = 堅 , etc. | | 条 = 條 |
| 坏 = 壞 | | 枟 = 檀 |
| 变 = 變 , etc. | | 样 = 樣 |
| 处 = 處 | | 梹 = 檳 |
| 妇 = 婦 | | 欢 = 歡 |
| 娇 = 嬌 , etc. | | 齿 = 齒 , etc. |
| 学 = 學 , etc. | | 汉 = 漢 |
| 宝 = 寶 | | 湾 = 灣 , etc. |
| 实 = 實 | | 灶 = 竈 |
| 寿 = 壽 , etc. | | 炉 = 爐 |
| 当 = 當 , etc. | | 点 = 點 |

爱 = 愛

犹 = 猶

独 = 獨

献 = 獻

畄 = 留 , etc.

盐 = 鹽

县 = 縣

碍 = 礙

种 = 種

称 = 稱

稳 = 穩 , etc.

窃 = 竊

绳 = 繩

续 = 續

总 = 總

罗 = 羅 , etc.

联 = 聯

腊 = 臘

芦 = 蘆

蚕 = 蠶

蝇 = 蠅

蝎 = 蠍

蜡 = 蠟

观 = 觀

誉 = 譽

译 = 譯 , etc.

读 = 讀

辞 = 辭

边 = 邊

迁 = 遷

过 = 過

这 = 這

还 = 還

郑 = 鄭

钟 = 鐘

关 = 關

难 = 難 , etc.

鬥 = 鬪

鸡 = 鷄

By Strokes:

呙 = 咼

讠 = 訁

门 = 門

问 = 問

么 = 么 or 麼

专 = 專 , etc.

义 = 義 , etc. ( ≠ 又 )

与 = 與

氵 = 氵

纟 = 糹

无 = 無 , etc.

云 = 雲

书 = 書

宦 = 官 , etc.

卒 = 卒 , etc.

车 = 軋

饣 = 飢

头 = 頭

东 = 東 , etc.

归 = 歸

乐 = 樂

尊 = 尊 , etc.

龙 = 龍 , etc.

乔 = 喬 , etc.

丝 = 絲

皃 = 貌 ( ≠ 兒 )

单 = 單 , etc.

丧 = 喪

举 = 舉

发 = 發

忧 = 憂 , etc.

临 = 臨

## 5. Abbreviated References to Frequently Cited Works

| | |
|---|---|
| *BEFEO* | *Bulletin de l'École Française de l'Extrême Orient* |
| *BIHP* | 中央研究院歷史语言研究所集刊<br>*Bulletin of the Institute of History and Philology, Academia Sinica* (called "CYYY" in *HJAS*) |
| Bloomfield, *Lg* | Leonard Bloomfield, *Language*, New York, Henry Hold, 1933 |
| *BMFEA* | *Bulletin* [of the] *Museum of Far Eastern Antiquities* |
| *BSOAS* | *Bulletin of the School of Oriental and African Studies*, University of London |
| *Cant Prim* | Yuen Ren Chao, *Cantonese Primer*, Cambridge, Mass.: Harvard University Press, 1947 |
| *Conc Dict* | Yuen Ren Chao and Lien Sheng Yang, *Concise Dictionary of Spoken Chinese*, Cambridge, Mass.: Harvard University Press, 1947 |
| Dragunov | A. A. Dragunov, *Issledovanija po Grammatike Sovremennogo Kitaiskogo Jazyka, Chasti Rechi*, Moscow, 1952<br>Chinese transl.: 龙果夫，現代汉语之法研究，第一卷，词類，郑祖慶译，Peking, 1958 |
| *HJAS* | *Harvard Journal of Asiatic Studies* |
| Hockett, Course | Charles F. Hockett, *A Course in Modern Linguistics*, New York: Macmillan, 1958 |
| Hockett, Peip Morphoph | Charles F. Hockett, "Peiping Morphophonemics", *Language*, 26:23-85 (1950) |
| Hockett, Peip Phon | Charles F. Hockett, "Peiping Phonology", *JAOS*, 67:253-267 (1947) |
| Hwu-Wen, Tannsuoo | 胡附、文鍊，現代汉语之法探索<br>(Hwu Fuh and Wen Liann, *Researches in the Grammar of Present-Day Chinese*), Shanghai, 1955 |
| *IJAL* | *International Journal of American Linguistics* |

| | |
|---|---|
| *JAOS* | *Journal of the American Oriental Society* |
| Jespersen, *Anal Synt* | Otto Jespersen, *Analytic Syntax*, London: George Allen and Unwin, 1937 |
| Karlgren, Gram Ser Rec | Bernhard Karlgren, "Grammata Serica Recensa", *BMFEA*, 29:1-332 (1957) |
| Karlgren, *Phonologie* | Bernhard Karlgren, *Etudes sur la Phonologie Chinoise*, Leyden and Stockholm, 1915-1923 Chinese transl.: 高本汉著，中國音韵学研究，趙元任、罗常培、李方桂合译，Shanghai, 1948 |
| Leu, *LWJyi* | 吕叔湘，汉语ㄥ法论文集 (Leu Shwu-shiang, *Essays in Chinese Grammar*), Peking, 1955 |
| Leu, *S and O* | 吕冀平等，汉语的主语賓语问题 (Leu Jihpyng, *et al.*, *Problems of the Subject and Object in Chinese*), Peking, 1958 |
| Li Jiinshi, *GYWF* | 黎錦熙，新著國语文法 (Li Jiinshi, *New Grammar of the National Language*), Shanghei, 1924; rev. ed., 1933 |
| Li-Liou, *Jiawtsair* | 黎錦熙，刘世儒，中國语法教材 (Li Jiinshi and Liou Shyhru, *Teaching Materials in Chinese Grammar*), Peking, vol. 1, 1953; vols. 2-4, 1954; vols. 5-6 and suppl., 1955 |
| Luh, *GTFaa* | 陸志韋等，汉语的构词法 (C. W. Luh *et al.*, *The Structure of Chinese Words*), Peking, 1957 |
| Malmqvist, Sïch'uanese | Göran Malmqvist, "The Syntax of Bound Forms in Sïch'uanese", *BMFEA*, 33: 125-199 (1961) |
| *Mand Prim* | Yuen Ren Chao, *Mandarin Primer*, Cambridge, Mass.: Harvard University Press, 1948 |
| Mullie, *Struct Princ* | Joseph Mullie, *The Structural Principles of the Chinese Language*, English transl. by A.C. Versichel, Peiping, 1932, 2 vols. |
| *Phonog Course* | Yuen Ren Chao, *A Phonograph Course in the Chinese National Language*, Shanghai, 1925 |

| *PMLA* | *Publications of the Modern Language Association of America* |
| *Shin Gwoyeu* | 趙元任，新國语 出声片 课本 (Yuen Ren Chao, *Textbook for New Records of the National Language*), Shanghai, 1935 |
| Simon Subst Complexes | H. F. Simon, "Two Substantival Complexes in Standard Chinese", *BSOAS*, 15:327-355 (1953) |
| Simon, Verb Complex | H. F. Simon, "Some Remarks on the Structure of the Verb Complex in Standard Chinese", *BSOAS*, 21:553-577 (1958) |
| *Studies in Wu* | 趙元任，現代吳语的研究 (Yuen Ren Chao, *Studies in the Modern Wu Dialects*), Peking: Tsing Hua University, 1928 |
| *TP* | *T'oung Pao* |
| Wang Leaui, *Outline* | 王了一 [ = 王力 ]，汉语ㄓ法纲要 (Wang Leaui, *Outline of Chinese Grammar*), Shanghai, 1957 |
| Wang Lih, *Liiluenn* | 王力，中國语法理论 (Wang Lih, *Theory of Chinese Grammar*), 2 vols., Shanghai, 1947 |
| Wang Lih, *Yeufaa* | 王力，中國現代语法 (Wang Lih, *Modern Chinese Grammar*), 2 vols., Shanghai, 1947 |
| *YYYJ* | 语言研究 (Studies in Linguistics) |
| *ZGYW* | 中國语文 *Zhongguo Yuwen* (Chinese Language and Writing) (monthly) |

6. Abbreviations for Frequently Occurring Morphemes and Grammatical Terms

| A | adjective | d | demonstrative |
| *a* | the particle 啊 .*a* | *de* | particle or suffix 的 .*de* |
| B | bound | dial. | dialect(al) |
| *ba* | the particle 吧 or 罢 .*ba* | F | free |
| *bu* | the adverb 不 *bu, bwu, buh* | g | 个 $_0$*geh* general classifier |
| C | consonant | GR | Gwoyeu Romatzyh |
| Cant | Cantonese | | (National Romanization) |
| D | determinative | H | adverb |

I!  interjection

*i*  the numeral 一 *i, yi, yih*

*ia*  the particle 呀 *.ia*

IC  immediate constituent

IPA  International Phonetic Alphabet

J  conjunction

*j*  the suffix 着 -*.jy* ～ -*.je*

K  preposition

L  (1) literary (wenyan)
   (2) localizer

*le*  particle or suffix 了 *.le*

*ma*  interrogative particle 嗎 *.ma*

M  measure

Mand  Mandarin

*me*  (1) suffix 么 -*.me*
   (2) particle 嚜 *.me*

*men*  plural suffix 们 -*.men*

N  noun

Np  place word

Nr  proper name

Nt  time word

n  numeral

*ne*  particle 呐 *.ne*

O  object

P  (1) pronoun
   (2) predicate

p  particle

R  complement

S  subject

*sh*  是 $_o$*shyh*

*tz*  suffix 子 -*.tzy*

V  (1) verb
   (2) vowel

V *bu* V  V *.bu* $_o$V

Vi  intransitive verb

Vt  transitive verb

Vx  auxiliary verb

Wu  Wu dialects

# 1.Grammar

## 1.1.1. *Scope of Present Work*

(1) Wider and Narrower Senses of Grammar. A grammar in the wider sense is the total description of a language, including and often emphasizing its phonology, as well as other aspects of its structure. For example, Jakob Grimm of "Grimm's law" called his work *Deutsche Grammatik*, which was a comparative study of the Germanic languages. Textbooks for learning foreign languages are also often called grammars of such and such, even including lesson by lesson reading material. In the present work we shall take grammar in the narrower sense of the study of the structure of spoken Chinese above the level of phonology. Since, however, phonology is often relevant to the discussion of larger structures, we shall, for convenient reference, devote a section of this chapter to a brief resume of Mandarin phonology.

(2) Synchronic and Diachronic Studies. The present study is a description of Mandarin Chinese of the present time, approximately the language of the middle of the twentieth century. Frequent reference will, however, be made to earlier stages of the language, often reflected in older forms or older distinctions in other dialects, whenever it is relevant to the description of the present. The idea of a purely synchronic stage of a language is methodologically comparable to the idea of velocity or of acceleration at a given instant. The instantaneous value is defined as the limit of average values over a length of time, including the instant, as the length vanishes. In a sense, then, it is a scientific fiction set up for methodological convenience.

A distinction is often made between synchronic and historical studies of a language. Logically, one can study the language of one period, say that of the language of Ch'angan around 600 A.D., which will be both synchronic and historical. There is also

1

lack of logic in the opposition sometimes set up between synchronic and descriptive studies, since diachronic studies of a language can be pursued through various stages from a descriptive point of view.

(3) Descriptive and Prescriptive Grammars. School grammars usually prescribe what is correct and what is incorrect, what is grammatical and what is ungrammatical. A descriptive grammar, on the other hand, is concerned with stating the facts of the language without passing any value judgment on them. However, the difference is rather one of form of statement and relative emphasis than one of content. For example, to say "Don't say 'like I do', but say 'as I do'" is a prescriptive statement, while "people of certain educational or economic class say one and people of another class say the other" is a descriptive statement. One is translatable into the other. The prescriptive statement is a categorical imperative, while the other, if stated in the form "if you want to be classed as a member of a certain class, you must say such and such" is a hypothetical imperative. Moreover, the statement that Keats said: "They raven down scenery like children do sweetmeats"[1] is both a historical and a descriptive statement. There is usually no issue in the arguments between descriptivists and prescriptivists if they explicate what they are talking about.

(4) Classificatory and Structural Grammars. Much of grammatical description has to do with classifications of linguistic forms. Conceivably, if classification were thorough and complete enough, it would contain enough information about the structure of the language to tell what does and what does not occur and would give what has recently been called a generative grammar. In practice, however, the usual classificatory categories found in grammars neither give all the essential facts of structure nor enable one to produce all those and only those forms which are grammatical in the language analyzed. As Wang Lih has said, "Whether we regard English 'than' as a conjunction or a preposition, or, with Jespersen, as a particle, these are all unimportant questions. What is important is to tell people under what conditions it is to be followed by the nominative case and under what conditions by the objective case, or whether either is possible.

---

[1]Quoted by *Word Study*, 38:4.5 (April, 1963).

Our responsibility ends when we can make a foreigner to the language use the word 'than' without error. As for the argument over what to call it, it is as trivial as whether the chicken gets a chance at the worm." (*Liiluenn*, I, 4).

Grammatical structure can be studied by analyzing it into hierarchical structure of immediate constituents, or ICs [see sec. 1.1.2 (2)] by predicting new forms from given forms, such as attributive from predicative, passive from active, interrogative from declarative, negative from affirmative, and other new forms by the now well-known process of transformation; and by additional processes which together with transformations will serve to generate all those and none but those forms which will be grammatical in the language.[2] Since no transformational or generative grammar has as yet been fully worked out for any language, we shall, for the purposes of the present work, take the conservative position of using hierarchies of ICs as the main approach to structure (Chomsky's "phrase structure grammar"[3]), but will make such use of transformations or rules of generation as will be useful. Statements to the effect that you can say this and you can't say that will be fairly frequent, but no attempt will be made here to build a system of generative grammar of Chinese.

*1.1.2. Grammar and Form*

(1) Linguistic Forms. A form[4] in the widest sense is any fraction of a language, be it a word or any succession of words. In practice, however, the smallest units, such as phonemes, features of a phoneme, say voicelessness, or very large units, such as a whole lecture of a play, are not forms as object of grammatical

---

[2] On these various approaches, see for example Wells, "Immediate Constituents"; Chomsky, *Syntactic Structures*; and Victor H. Yngve, "A Model and an Hypothesis for Language Structure", *Proc. of the Amer. Philos. Soc.*, 104:444-466 (1960).

[3] Chomsky, chap. 4.

[4] It is an awkward discrepancy in usage between Chinese and Western writers that Chinese 形 *shyng* 'form (of characters)' is contrasted with 音 *in* 'sound' and 义 *yih* 'meaning', while 'form' in Western usage corresponds really to *in* and not to *shyng*. The confusion is compounded when recent Chinese writers translate 'morphology' as 形态 *shyngtay* 'form-state' and when recent Western writers go further and use 'shape' for a particular phonemic make-up of a form. However, one can usually tell what an author means, given the context of use.

analysis. Only the smallest unit that has meaning, the morpheme, and the largest unit between pauses, the sentence,[5] and units of intermediate sizes have generally been included in grammatical analysis. Forms usually occur in succession, except for a relatively small number of simultaneous or overlapping forms, such as an interrogative intonation over a whole sentence, which can be considered a morpheme having a meaning but residing parasitically on the other forms, the words in the sentence. Forms which are worth considering in grammar have a certain unity such that they will recur with similar forms in similar contexts. Such forms are then constituents, as distinguished from any fraction of a larger form, cut out arbitrarily, which makes up a string but not necessarily a constituent. For example, in 说中國话 *shuo Jong-.gwohuah* 'speak Chinese', each of the syllables, which is also a morpheme, is a constituent. Furthermore, *shuo, Jong.gwohuah, Jong.gwo*, and *huah* are constituents, but *shuo Jong* and *.gwohuah* are not constituents. In other contexts *shuo Jong.gwo* 'speaks of China' could be a constituent, but it is not one in *shuo Jong-.gwohuah*. It goes without saying that a fractional part of a morpheme plus whatever follows or precedes will make up a string but not a constituent.

(2) Immediate Constituents. When a complex form is cut up into its constituents, the results of the first cut are its immediate constituents, or ICs for short.[6] Thus, in the example given above, the ICs are *shuo* and *Jong.gwohuah;* the latter in turn consists of ICs *Jong.gwo* and *huah;* and *Jong.gwo* has *Jong* and *.gwo* as ICs, so that the whole hierarchy of these ICs can be diagrammed as follows:

说　中　國　话
*shuo Jong.gwohuah*　　　or:　　*shuo Jonq .gwo huah*

---

[5]A beginning, however, has been made in the formal study of larger units by Zellig S. Harris, in his "Discourse Analysis", *Language*, 28:1-30, and "Discourse Analysis: A Sample Text", *Language*, 28:474-494 (1952).

[6]See Wells, *op. cit.*

In most cases a complex form breaks into two ICs, for example, subject and predicate, verb and object, modifier and modified, root and suffix, phrase and particle. In a minority of cases, however, there are more than two ICs. Typical among these are coordinate forms spoken in a string (with or without pauses in between) as they usually are in Chinese, for example, 天地人 *tian dih ren* 'heaven, earth, man'. 他不抽烟，不喝酒，不打牌。 *Ta bu chou-ian, bu he-jeou, bu daa-pair.* 'He doesn't smoke, doesn't drink, doesn't play cards'.

(3) Form as Type Rather than Token. Let us take an actual historical instance of a form being uttered, as when Mencius went to see King Huey of the state of Liang, who began with addressing him: " 叟 ! *Soou!* 'Sir!' " That was a token of the type 叟 *soou*, which occurred many times both before and after that particular instance. If we are interested in the particular occurrence as a historical event, with its linguistic as well as nonlinguistic circumstances, that constitutes a philological study. On the other hand, if we are interested in the *soou* as a type and the conditions under which it does or does not occur, especially in relation to contexts made up of other types, then it is a linguistic problem. Thus, philology is the study of tokens, and linguistics is the study of types.

(4) Grammar as the Study of Form Classes in Slots. In particular, grammar is the study of groups or classes of forms as regards their occurrence in frames or slots constituted by other classes. All forms which behave alike in this respect are members of a form class. For example, 吃了饭 *chyle fann* 'have eaten (one's) meal', 打过球 *daa.guo chyou* 'have played ball', and 骑着马 *chyij maa* 'riding a horse' are all of the class of verbal expressions, and within each of them, *chy, daa,* and *chyi* are all of the class of transitive verbs, *-le, -.guo* and *-j* are all of the class of verbal suffixes, and *fann, chyou,* and *maa* are all of the class of nouns, which, among other things, can fill the frame or slot of objects after verbs. Note that, since a form is a class of tokens, a form class is a class of classes.[7]

---

[7]This characterization is sufficient for our present purposes. On closer analysis of the situation, especially when modern means of communication and recording are considered, the relations are more complicated, on which

(5) Circularity of Form Classes: Selection. If form classes
are defined in terms of the frames in which they occur and the
frames themselves consist of form classes, wouldn't that be defining in a circle, since one wouldn't know when and where to begin
with the first form classes and first frames? To answer this, we
have to resort to what Bloomfield (*Lg*, 164-165) calls "selection".
There are many complicated phases of the grammatical concept
selection, but the essential idea is the fact that certain forms
arbitrarily behave alike in one way and certain others behave
alike in another. To make selection applicable in grammar, however, it would be necessary to have a complete lexicon of the
language with the form classes all marked. In fact, most grammarians grant the necessity of including the whole lexicon in
order to have a complete grammar of a language. Otherwise
there is no way to set up grammatical rules in order to know, to
use Bloomfield's examples, that 'prince', 'author', 'sculptor' take
the suffix -ess, while 'king', 'singer', 'painter' do not. A lexicon of
the language, with all form classes of the entries properly indicated, is the ultimate answer to the question of selection.

(6) Class Meaning, or Grammatical Meaning. In practice,
however, we make short cuts by resorting to consideration of
meaning and see what forms of similar meanings are also formally
similar. On the whole, nouns are names of persons and things,
verbs are words expressing events and actions, and so on. Such
loose definitions will of course not stand rigorous formal scrutiny,
and exceptions are very easy to find. But through the general
trend of meanings some formal features may be found to serve as
more rigorous definitions. For example, since most names of
persons and things have the formal feature of being modifiable by
a D-M compound, that is, a determinative plus a measure, such
as — 种 *i-joong* 'a kind (of)', + 双寸 *shyr-duey* 'ten pairs (of)', we
can turn around and define a noun as whatever can be modified
by a D-M compound, and then the class of nouns so defined will
include not only most names of persons and things but whatever
will satisfy the definition, for example, — 种 习 惯 *i-joong shyiguann* 'a kind of habit', which will make *shyiguann* a noun,

---

see my study of "The Logical Structure of Chinese Words", *Language*,
22:5-8 of 4-13 (1946).

though it denotes neither a person nor an event or action. The meaning or set of meanings for the majority of cases of a given grammatical category is called the class meaning, or grammatical meaning of that category. Once a form class or any other grammatical category is defined formally, then its class meaning (which has often served to suggest the formal definition) will be useful only as a convenient reminder and no longer used as a real criterion.

(7) Open Classes and Lists. Most form classes, even not counting phrases, are of unlimited membership, short of complete enumeration through the whole lexicon of the language. At the other extreme, a form class may have only one member, such as the subordinative particle *de*. Between the two extremes there are the relatively short lists[8] such as the class of simple numerals, personal pronouns, auxiliary verbs, and aspect suffixes, which can be exhaustively enumerated or even memorized. In the preceding example of a noun being defined as that which can be modified by a D-M compound, we were defining an open class in terms of (closed) lists, namely, determinatives (D) and measures (M). Proceeding thus from the listables to the unlistables, we can define the unknown by the known and thus break the circularity we were concerned about above. This does not eliminate the usefulness of going to meaning, but will free the study of form from dependence on the study of meaning. But grammatical meaning does have a positive correlation with real meaning, since linguistic forms, after all, have evolved out of their use in life. [But see also sec. 1.1.3 (3) on skewed relations.]

*1.1.3. Further Methodological Considerations*

(1) Elements of Arrangement. Bloomfield (*Lg*, 163-165) speaks of four ways of arranging linguistic forms that constitute the grammar of language: (a) order, (b) modulation, (c) phonetic modification, and (d) selection. Although these are applicable to all languages, the parts they play in Chinese are of very unequal importance. In modern Chinese, modulation and phonetic modification are of minor importance, while order and selection bear the main burden of grammatical arrangement. As we have already discussed selection in the preceding section, and as order

---

[8]See F. W. Householder, Lists.

of the type like 狗咬人, 人咬狗. *Goou yeau ren, ren yeau goou.* 'Dog bites man, man bites dog.' is too well known to need elaboration, we need only give a few examples of the other two elements.

Modulation consists of differences in stress, juncture, and intonation. For example, 鸡, 肉 *ji, row* 'chicken, meat', with a pause in between, is a coordinate construction of two nouns, whereas 鸡肉 *jirow* 'chicken meat', with no pause, is a subordinate construction, where *ji* modifies *row*. ⸝煎 '饼⸝*jian* '*biing* 'fries cake', with main stress on *biing*, is a verb-object (V-O) construction, but '*jian.biing* 'fried cake', with stress on *jian* and neutral tone on *biing*, is a subordinate compound.

Phonetic modification as a grammatical process is no longer active. Examples are 長 : 長 *charng : jaang* 'long : grows (becomes long)', 刷:涮 *shua* ( < *ṣwat*) : *shuann* ( < *ṣwan*ʾ) 'scours : rinses'. Since the tones are part of the phonemic make up of words, changes of tone corresponding to grammatical differences are phonetic modification and not modulation. Thus, 卷³ : 卷⁴ *jeuan : jiuann* 'to roll : a roll', 好³ : 好⁴ *hao : haw* 'good : finds good, i.e., likes' are cases of phonetic modification.

Note that mere phonetic difference is not phonetic modification in the grammatical sense. Thus, there is phonetic modification in 'man : men', 'send : sent', but not in 'bad : bed' or 'feed : feet', any more than between 'cabbages' and 'kings'. Similarly, there is mere phonetic difference in 包 *bau* 'wraps' and 跑 *pao* 'runs', in 槍 *chiang* 'spear, gun' and 倉 *tsang* 'storehouse', or for that matter in 風 *feng* 'wind', 馬 *maa* 'horse', and 牛 *niou* 'cow'. They are simply phonetically different. But even when there is true phonetic modification, for practical purposes they can be treated more conveniently as arbitrary lexical facts of phonetic difference. One cannot say, for instance, that a 4th Tone changes a noun into a verb. The moment one gets such an impression from a few cases like 种³ *joong* 'seed' 种⁴ *jonq* 'to plant', there comes an opposite case like 处⁴ *chuh* 'place' 处³ *chuu* 'to be placed, live with'. The situation is not only so in modern Chinese but was so in historical times. (Cf. sec. 3.7.4 on "split readings".)

(2) Overt and Covert Categories.[9] In inflected languages, form classes and their relations in a sentence can often be told from overt markers such as endings for plural nouns or tense forms of verbs. To a very limited extent Chinese also has overt markers, such as *-tz* for nouns, *-le* for verbs, but in most cases the total grammatical behavior of form classes is not revealed except in certain frames; otherwise it remains implicit, or covert. We shall cite two sets of examples, one in English and one in Chinese, as they form very similar covert categories. Of substantives in English, the names of countries and cities form a covert class in that one cannot use 'it' or 'her' after the prepositions 'in, at, to, and from'. Thus, one can say 'That is a large house. He lives in it.' But after 'That is San Francisco.', one cannot say 'He lives in it.', but must say 'He lives there.' Similarly, the substantives 上海 *Shanqhae* 'Shanghai', 王家 *Wang.jia* 'the Wangs' (house)', 桌子 *juotz* 'table', and 你 *nii* 'you' seem to be all alike, but when preceded by 到 *daw* 'goes to', the noun *juotz* and the pronoun *nii* must be suffixed by the localizer 那儿 *-.nall* to form place words before they can be objects of the preposition *daw*, thus: 这是上海，我喜欢上海，我到上海去。那是王家，我喜欢王家，我到王家去. *Jeh sh Shanqhae, woo shii-.huan Shanqhae, woo daw Shanqhae chiuh. Nah sh Wang.jia, woo shii.huan Wang.jia, woo daw Wang.jia chiuh.* 'This is Shanghai, I like Shanghai, I go to Shanghai. That is the Wangs' (house), I like the Wangs, I go to the Wangs.' But, with common nouns and pronouns, we have 这是摇椅，我喜欢摇椅，我到摇椅那儿去。那是你，我喜欢你，我到你那儿去. *Jeh sh yauyii, woo shii.huan yauyii, woo daw yauyii.nall chiuh. Nah sh nii, woo shii.huan nii, woo daw nii.nall chiuh.* 'This is a rocking chair, I like rocking chairs, I go to the rocking chair. That is you, I like you, I go to you.' Thus, the distinction between place words and nouns, like most other grammatical categories in Chinese, is a covert and not an overt one.

(3) Parallelism, Asymmetry, and Skewed Relations. The search for system and symmetry, especially in social phenomena, such as language is, is useful methodology, provided that it is not carried

---

[9]See Benjamin Lee Whorf, "Grammatical Categories", *Language*, 21:1-19 (1945).

too far. For example, in listing the Mandarin initials, we find four retroflexes as in 知 *j-*, 吃 *ch-*, 诗 *sh-*, 日 *r-*, but only three dental sibilants 兹 *tz-*, 此 *ts-*, 四 *s-*, and no ☐ *z-*. This lack of symmetry disturbs the phonologist, and, in order to gain symmetry, it has been proposed to consider the retroflexes as complexes of *tz-*, *ts-*, or *s-*, plus *-r-* regarded as medial or semivowel, so that phonemically *j* = /tzr/, *ch* = /tsr/, and *sh* = /sr/, and *r-* is not regarded as an initial consonant, but as a medial, like *y* and *w*. But this gain of symmetry is at a cost. The initial *sh*, phonetically [ ʂ ], is a homogeneous simple consonant. By analyzing it as a succession of phonemes /s/ and /r/, we are taking the drastic step of treating simultaneous distinctive features as a succession of "segmental" phonemes. Whether the gain is worth the cost in this particular case is a matter to be decided by over-all considerations, and we are not specially concerned with the merits of the case at present. The methodological point to be emphasized here is simply that there is much room for give and take in the search for symmetry and system.

Coming closer to grammatical examples, take the often quoted passage 庖 有 肥 肉, 廐 有 肥 馬, 民 有 飢 色, 野 有 餓 莩. *Paur yeou feir row, jiou yeou feir maa, min yeou ji seh, yee yeou eh peau.* L 'Kitchens have fat meat, stables have fat horses, the people have hungry looks, the wilds have starved corpses.' (*Mencius*, III 2.9.9 滕 文 下). The translation of *yeou* as 'have' in all instances brings out the construction as S-V-O (subject-verb-object), which is the best grammatical analysis of these clauses. But if translated into modern colloquial, the four subjects will have to be place words 厨 房 裡 *chwufarng.lii* 'in the kitchens', 馬 号 裡 *maahaw.lii* 'in the stables', 百 姓 的 臉 上 *bae.shinq de lean.shanq* 'on the people's faces', and 野 地 裡 *yeedih.lii* 'in the wilderness', where the third subject is out of step, since one cannot say ° 百 姓 上 °*bae.shinq.shanq* 'on the people'. Moreover, if we use transformations here, we can say 肥 肉 在 厨 房 裡 *Feirrow tzay chwufarng.lii* 'Fat meat is in the kitchens', and so on, but not, except in written bairhuah, 餓 的 樣 子 在 百 姓 的 臉上。 *Eh de yanqtz tzay bae.shinq de lean. shanq.* 'Hungry looks are on the people's faces.'[10] Thus, by further scrutiny, we find that, although the four clauses are all of the S-V-O type, the *yeou* in the third clause is of a different, though covert, form (sub)class from the *yeou* in the other cases. In sum, although the search for parallelism and symmetry is very helpful for analysis, it must be supplemented by other approaches.

While looking for symmetry we should always be on guard for what I call skewed relations, namely relations which are regular and symmetrical in some cases but irregular or asymmetrical in others. We find, for example, that in verb-noun sequences like 吃饭 *chy-fann* 'eats meal' and 看报 *kann-baw* 'reads newspapers', with the main stress on the second syllable, the noun is object to the verb, whereas in cases like 煎饼 *jian.biing* 'fried cake', 劈柴 *pii.chair* 'split wood,—kindling wood', with the stress on the verb, the verb modifies the noun. But further examination will show that, while in true verb-object construction the stress is always on the object, the converse is not always true; for example, 炒饭 *chao-fam* 'fries rice' ⁓ 'fried rice' and 烙饼 *law-biing* 'bakes cake' ⁓ 'baked cake' are grammatically ambivalent: the verb may either take the noun as object or modify it. The relationship is further skewed in that, as verb modifying noun, *law-₀biing* has an optional neutral tone but, as verb-object, it has no neutral tone. Equally skewed is the case of 反正 *faan₀jenq* 're-verse or right,—anyway', an adverb; but *faan-jenq*, without neutral tone, 'returns to the right side (after a rebellion or mutiny)', is a verb-object compound. All such cases will be taken up when we come to syntax and compounding in chapters 5 and 6. For a longer example of skewed relationships, take the matter of potential (that is, intermittently occurring) pauses, such as those occurring between subject and predicate. Once my wife asked: 你 花[11] 么 的水够 不 够? said without pause or open juncture between any of the syllables. I understood 花么 as 花椒

---

[10]Legge's translation has prepositional phrases except in the third clause with 'their people have'.

[11]In her dialect, with a background of Southern Mandarin, 花 *hua* 'flower' does not usually take the diminutive suffix 儿 *-l*.

*huajiau* 'fagara' or 'Szechwan pepper' and wondered what it was all about. But on repetition, she inserted a subject-predicate pause (without *nii*) and said: 花，浇 的 水 夠 不 夠 ？ *Hua, jiau de shoei gow.bu.gow?* 'As for the flowers, was the water poured over them enough,—did you put enough water on the flowers?' Thus, the juncture between parts of compounds and between subject and predicate is not a simple yes-or-no or a simple closed or open one, but one is of one kind and the other is potentially both. All such cases will be taken up when we come to them in the following chapters. The point to emphasize here is that, in matters grammatical, skewed relationships are almost as common as straight rules.

# 1.2 Spoken Chinese

## 1.2.1. Dialects and Styles Studied

(1) What Is Spoken Chinese? By Spoken Chinese, as used in the title of this book, I mean the dialect of Peiping in the middle of the twentieth century, spoken in an informal, sometimes known as casual, style. This gives a general idea of the kind of language we are describing, but as a definition it is both too wide and too narrow. It is too wide because (1) Peiping is so large that there is noticeable variation, at least in pronunciation, between extreme localities of the city; (2) during the period considered there is already noticeable change in the speech of the same individuals; and (3) even if we specify the style of language studied, there is still considerable variation according to the age group and the social and educational background of the speaker. Strictly speaking, the only thing specifically identifiable is the idiolect of one person at one time. On the other hand, the definition given above is too narrow in that, even if the dialect of Peiping is taken in a broad sense, what is true of that dialect, especially in matters of grammar, is usually true of all the northern dialects, and very often true of all the dialects. This is in fact the justification for the ambitious title in which the dialect of Peiping is taken to represent the whole of Spoken Chinese.

(2) National and Local Aspects of the Peiping Dialect. State-

ments about various aspects of the Peiping dialect will have varying degrees of validity when applied to other dialects. Most of
its phonological characteristics are shared by most of the Northern
Mandarin dialects, such as redistribution of the Entering Tone
into the other tones, the distinguishing of *-in* from *-ing* and *-en*
from *-eng*, the lack of distinction between two mid-vowel phonemes, so that both 阁 and 格 are *ger*, instead of *gor* and *ger* as in
Southern and Southwestern Mandarin. In matters of vocabulary,
there is remarkable uniformity in the personal and demonstrative
pronouns, even including those of Southwestern and Southern
Mandarin. But there are two extremes in vocabulary as regards
geographical spread. In science and politics, because the vocabulary is new, most words have a national status, apart from pronunciation. At the other extreme there are local words for
certain terms of address, especially terms of direct address, and
names of many small plants and small animals, especially insects,
for which not only the Peiping forms are local in nature, but for
which there are no words in any dialect which have a national
status. There are, to be sure, literary and scientific equivalents
for the localisms, but then they are outside the range of everyday
speech, which is the style we are studying.

   Third, it is in matters of grammar that the greatest degree of
uniformity is found among all the dialects of the Chinese language. Apart from some minor divergencies, such as indirect object before direct object in the Wu dialects and Cantonese—for
which Mandarin (like English) has the opposite order, and slight
differences in the order of the negative in potential complements
in some of the southern dialects, and so on, and apart from differences in suffixes and particles for which, however, fairly close
equivalents can be set up between dialects, one can say that there
is practically one universal Chinese grammar. Even taking wenyan into consideration, we shall find that the only important differences are that wenyan has more free monosyllabic words and
less use of compounds and that its prepositional phrases of locality
and origin can follow instead of always preceding the main verb.
Otherwise it has substantially the same grammatical structure
as, not only the dialect of Peiping, but any dialect. Thus there is
even a stronger claim for calling the *grammar* of the Peiping dialect the *grammar* of spoken Chinese than calling the Peiping

dialect spoken Chinese. Nevertheless, to make it clear that all unqualified citations are possible forms for the Peiping dialect, non-Peiping forms will be marked as such, for example, "L" for wenyan, "Wu" for Shanghai, Ningpo, and so on, "Cant" for Cantonese, "dial." for unspecified dialects, and also "local" for Peiping localisms. The wenyan and dialectal forms are occasionally cited to make a contrast or to illustrate a point which can be well exemplified in these other forms.

(3) Styles Studied. The main style to be studied is that of everyday speech, with occasional reference, for purposes of comparison, to wenyan, formal style such as that of public speeches, children's language, and so on. It is the style of speech an invisible observer would observe in the talk between Chinese speakers of Chinese. It is definitely not the style of speech a foreigner is expected to use in talking to a native speaker of Chinese. Rightly or wrongly, reasonably or unreasonably, a native speaker is often surprised or even disconcerted when a foreigner talks exactly as he does instead of talking more stiffly, preferably with a little accent, accenting syllables that are usually slurred, giving a full tone when it should be neutral, and so on. Professor André Martinet used to make his Columbia University students feel ill at ease when he spoke in pure Brooklynese. It is okay for American students, but not for a famous professor from Paris. It's unhöid of.

Since this book is intended to be a factual study of an important style of the Chinese language, it is to be described as closely as possible as it is actually spoken. As to the question of what style of language is best to teach a beginning foreigner in the language, there is room for variation of approach according to circumstances: an academic course, an army course, or courses for business, diplomacy, or other careers. As an experiment, I once started a small beginning course in pure wenyan, treating it like a conversational class, out of which has come one of the leading American scholars in Chinese studies.

1.2.2. *Sources of Citations.* In studying the grammar of a given work, say *Mencius*, of a given period at a given place, say the dialect of Ch'angan under the T'ang dynasty, or any specified amount of material, we have a closed corpus from which our task is to find and formulate concisely and completely the structure of whatever is given. On the other hand, if the object of study is a living language, we should not only try to account for what happens to have been observed, but should also go out of our way to look for examples and find out what can or cannot be said. The difference is similar to but not quite the same as that between ordinary and generative grammar. By studying *Mencius* closely enough, one could produce a generative grammar from which sentences or whole discourses could be generated that would agree entirely with the grammar of the corpus known as *Mencius*. As a matter of fact, this is very much what has actually been done, since current wenyan, which is still a living language, is modeled more closely after *Mencius* than after any other of the classical works.

The sources of citations belong to the following categories:

(1) Made-up Examples. These are mostly short examples which I have made up in the double capacity of linguist-informant. Since, however, I lived in Peiping only at the ages of 1, 17, 32-39, and 41 and in various other districts of Hopei Province from 0-9, and since, moreover, I studied all the classics in the pronunciation of a Wu dialect,[12] I cannot claim native-like infallibility as an informant. I have therefore had my examples checked by other informants in cases where I had doubts. Interestingly enough, however, where my examples were not of the pure Peiping dialect, nine cases out of ten were questions of vocabulary rather than grammar, which is simply a corollary of the preceding observation that grammar has less dialectal variation than have phonology and vocabulary.

(2) "Chinese Grammar Cases". These are on-the-spot jottings over the years of what I have heard or overheard from actual conversations and found grammatically worth noting. Much of this category of data is in non-Peiping or even non-Mandarin dialects. If an example of this kind illustrates the same point as in Mandarin, I usually do not bother to translate it into Mandarin and only indicate the fact that it is dialectal.

(3) Disc and Tape Recordings of Conversations in Mandarin. Some of the recordings used were made long ago for other purposes. Others were made in recent years as source material to

---

[12]See my *Mand Prim*, Lesson 23, which is largely autobiographical.

select from for the present work. All material under this category
was of the unrehearsed kind. This does not, therefore, include
such recordings as I have made from my books, which belong to
heading (1) above. In true free conversation, in which one thinks
as one talks, or very often doesn't think as one talks, certain constructions, such as redundant demonstratives before and after long
clause modifiers, are quite common, but would not usually occur
in composed texts.

One important feature of recordings from free conversation is
the inclusion of prosodic elements, which are rarely or very
sketchily indicated in composed texts. While the present work
does not include a detailed treatment of suprasegmental elements,
note will be taken of them when they are grammatically relevant.[13]

(4) Composed Texts Intended to Represent Present-Day
Speech. These are dialogues from contemporary plays and novels,
such as those by 曹禺 Tsaur Yeu and 老舍 Lao Shee (Lao Shaw).
I have also drawn from my translations of Lewis Carroll, A.A.
Milne, and others. These do not belong to category (1), since I
made them with no idea of using them for illustrations in a grammar to be written thirty or forty years afterwards.

(5) Texts Representing Other Periods. Some writers, for example, Wang Lih, draw freely from works like 红楼梦 (*Hornglou
Menq*), and 兒女英雄传 (*Erlneu Ingshyong Juann*), where the
language is noticeably different from contemporary Mandarin but
provides excellent illustrations of points of grammar which are
still valid today. We shall, however, not make much use of such
sources except in quoting other grammarians who quote them.

(6) Current Written Bairhuah. Last and least we shall make
relatively little use of current written bairhuah, with its Euro-
peanisms and other neologisms. Note will, however, be taken of
them when occasionally people are heard to talk that way, and,
if they keep talking like that, the usage will become part of
spoken Chinese, whether we conservatives like it or not.

---

[13]Thus, James Sledd, in his review of C. C. Fries' *What Is Correct English?* in *Language* 31:340-341 (1955), notes that the reason Fries found the
headline 'Vandenberg Reports Open Forum' ambiguous was the lack of the
necessary stress marks.

*1.2.3. Types of Discourse.* Speech is a form of behavior, and its occurrence is normally interposed between or superposed upon other forms of behavior, while long connected discourse is the exception. It is an illusion on our part as linguists to handle extended text most of the time and thus give the impression that monologues or continuous dialogues represent the typical form of language in use. This was, in fact, the mistake of scenario writers in the early days of the "talkies", in which there was talking going on all the time, as if to make up for lost time during all those years of the silent movie. Only gradually did they realize that talking was needed as only one of the happenings in the story, and, with the freedom of the film technique, less talking was needed than with the limited resources of action and scenery on the stage.

The following list of types of dicourse is in the order of connectedness, from the more artificially composed to the actual bits of speech as used in daily living:

(1) Monologues read stiffly from manuscript, such as a learned lecture given by a professor over the radio.

(2) Dialogues of a play written realistically but read stiffly by inexperienced students.

(3) Extempore speeches from very sketchy notes or no notes at all.

(4) Connected conversation, such as the dialogues in the early plays by Ding Shilin ( 丁 西 林 ) à la Oscar Wilde, or the late-morning telephoning between two ladies.

(5) Monologues with interposed action and/or event influencing or determining what to say next, as in a demonstration lecture.

(6) Dialogues under the same conditions as above.

(7) Occasional remarks made during action and/or event, such as playing a game of mahjong, watching a sport, or attending a dinner party, especially just after a new course has been served.

(8) Things said in response to some situation or to something in the stream of consciousness, such as 对 了 *!Dueyle!* 'Oh, yes!', when something important that has been forgotten suddenly comes to mind and must be said at once before it slips the mind again.

It should be noted that the different types of discourse make more difference in sentence structure and in the expressive elements than in other aspects of grammar. For example, in saying 你 你 弄 ˋ ˎ 回 头 弄 坏 了 !! *Nii jiin nonq jiin nonq hweitour* NONQ-HUAYLE!! 'You keep playing and playing with it and by and by you're GOING TO SPOIL IT!!! to a child playing improperly with a toy or with something he is not supposed to play with, the crescendo starts because he is doing worse as the sentence progresses. Again, while inspecting a window which had been hit, my wife started to say, 他 把 玻 璃 ( 打 破 了 ) *Ta baa bo.li (daa-pohle)* 'He (the cat) broke the glass', but before she finished the sentence, she found that it had not been broken and so just continued on without pause, and the sentence actually came out as 他 把 玻 璃 没 打 破. *Ta baa bo.li mei daa-poh.* 'He did not break the glass.' If it had been planned and composed it would of course have to read: *Ta mei baa bo.li daa-poh.* (For further details, see section 2.14 on planned and unplanned sentences.)

Many other problems of general grammatical import have not been touched upon in the preceding discussions. They will be deferred until they come up in the individual chapters, where they will mean more than in this introductory context. The preceding, it is hoped, will serve to indicate the general drift and tone of the book.

# 1.3. Phonology

*1.3.1. Syllabic Structure.* Traditional Chinese phonology divides the syllable into an initial and a final. The initial is the way a syllable begins, usually with a consonant. For example, *s* in 蘇 *su, l* in 蘭 *lan, tz* in 走 *tzoou,* and *ts* in 倉 *tsang.* The last, an aspirated affricate, is the nearest to a consonant cluster in modern as well as ancient Chinese for at least the past 1500 years. One can therefore tell at once that syllables like *blah, spu, fran* cannot be Chinese. A small number of syllables, such as 安 *an,* and 啊 *a,* do not begin with a consonant. They are said to begin with the initial zero (or the "zero initial").[14]

---

[14]See Sec. 1.3.2 on the phonetic value of the zero initial.

The final of a syllable is the syllable minus the initial. For example, in 他 *ta*, 七 *chi*, 今 *jin*, 窗 *chuang*, the finals are *-a*, *-i*, *-in*, and *-uang*, respectively. The longest form of a final consists of three parts: a medial, or semivowel; a main vowel, or head vowel; and an ending, or, in the case of retroflex suffixes, sometimes two endings, as in 明儿 *miengl* 'tomorrow' [cf. table 5, sec. 1.3.8 (2)]. Thus, in the final *-iau*, *-i-* is the medial, *-a-* the head vowel, and *-u* the ending. There may be no medial or ending, but there must be at least a main vowel[15] (*sh* for 是 $_o$*shyh* and *j* for 着 *.jy* ~ *.je* are simply graphical abbreviations).

In addition to an initial and a final, every syllable has as an essential component a tone, which is primarily the pitch pattern of the voiced part of the syllable, so that, if the initial is voiced, the tone begins with the initial and spreads over the whole syllable, while, if the initial is voiceless, the tone is spread over the final only.[16]

---

[15]Hockett (Peip Phon, p. 262), in agreement with Chinese usage, treats syllables like 兹 *tzy*, 差 *tsy* (as in 参差 *tsentsy* 'uneven'), and 思 *sy* as "semiconsonants", which can be vocalized by vocalizing, or buzzing, the last part of the consonant to carry the syllable. In the National Phonetic Letters such syllables are written ㄗ, ㄘ, ㄙ, exactly as they are written when occurring as initials. In the GR system we are using here, a dummy vowel letter *y* is written. If written in the IPA system, the corresponding syllable carrier would be written as a syllabic *z*, thus: 思 *sy* [sz̩]. For the retroflex initials, the same notational situation obtains for the National Phonetic Letters, the GR, and the IPA.

[16]In the Ancient Chinese of 601 A.D., as represented in 切韵 *Chieh Yunn*, the tone was included as part of the final, and the pronunciation of each syllable was given by a glossing process known as 反切 *faanchieh*, consisting of taking two other characters, one with the same initial and the other with the same final as the syllable to be glossed. For example, 荒 *huang* is given as 呼 *hu* + 光 *guang*, that is, *h*(*u* + *g*)*uang*, taking the initial of the first character and the final of the second. Similarly, 爰 *chiann* is glossed as 去 *chiuh* + 劔 *jiann*, that is, *ch*(*iuh* + *j*)*iann*. Note that in the ancient conception of the final, the tone is included as a part of it. The examples are given in modern Mandarin for illustrative purposes. Actually the first example meant $\chi$(*uo* + $_c$*k*)*uâng* = $_c$$\chi$*uâng*, which is pretty much the modern pronunciation, but the second example did not mean what it

*1.3.2. Initials and Consonants.* Initials, as we have seen, are consonants, except for the initial zero. This initial, in the majority-type pronunciation, does have a slight consonantal-type obstruction in the form of a frictionless velar or uvular voiced continuant, [ɣ] or [ʁ], which is the reason why in 棉襖 *mian'ao* 'wadded jacket' the *n* does not link with *ao*, as one would link English *ran out*.[17] The only exceptions are interjections such as 啊 *a!* and particles such as 啊 *a* and 哎 *ou*, which have true vocalic beginnings and do not resist linking. A (large) minority of speakers use a glottal stop or a pure vocalic beginning for all words with a zero initial. A very small minority of speakers begin such words with a consonantal *ng-* (again excepting interjections and particles). For the purpose of teaching English-speaking students of Chinese, the simplest way is to pronounce the zero initial with a true vowel or with a glottal stop, with the warning not to link it with a preceding terminal -*n*, but to slur the -*n* instead.

The only consonantal endings in Mandarin are -*n*, -*ng*, and -*l*, the last being the GR notation for the American 'curled' *r*, as in 'err' and 'art'. There are some marginal cases of an apparent consonantal ending -*m*, on which see section 1.3.9 (2).

In the list of initials given in table 1, the term 'gutturals' is

---

seems to mean now, since it originally meant *k'(įwo + k)įɒmˀ = k'įɒmˀ*. Both examples have been chosen from the small proportion of cases where either the pronunciation of all three of the characters has not changed much or has changed parallelly, so that the a + b = c relation still holds. In a great many cases, however, the old *faanchieh* does not work for modern pronunciation. For example, the gloss 东 德 红 切, that is, ₂*tung* = *tɜk* + ₂*ɣ ung* worked perfectly for Ancient Chinese, but read in Mandarin, *d(er* + *h)orng* would give °*dorng*, a nonexistent syllable, instead of *dong* for 东, since the makers of the *faanchieh* could not have foreseen that a thousand years hence 东, with a voiceless initial, and 红, with a voiced initial, would have developed into two different tones 1st and 2nd Tones, respectively.

[17]See Y. R. Chao, "The Voiced Velar Fricative as an Initial in Mandarin", *Le Maître Phonétique*, 63:2-3 (1948). In the case of a final beginning with a semivowel (2nd, 3rd, and 4th rows in table 2), there is with some speakers a (non-distinctive) slightly more consonantal articulation, i.e. [j. w. ɥ]; some speakers even use a non-frictional dentilabial [ʋ] instead of [w], though this last phonetic feature is more common in Tientsin than in Peiping.

to include both velars, *g, k, (ng)*, and sounds further back, *h*, (which is a uvular [$\chi$]), and Ø (which is either a uvular [ʁ] or a glottal stop or a vowel, as described above). Note also that in the GR transcription, the letters *b, d, g*, etc., are used to represent unaspirated voiceless sounds (to be equated with [ḇ, ḏ, g̊] because of their lenis nature, resulting in true voiced [b, d, g] in intervocalic positions), while *p, t, k*, etc., represent the corresponding aspirates. A striking distributional aspect of Mandarin is that the palatals are in complementary distribution with the dental sibilants, retroflexes, and velars, in that the palatals occur only before *i* and *iu* (Row-*i* and -*iu*) and the others only before other vowels (Row-*a* and -*u*) in table 2. Historically the palatals have come from the dentals and the velars, as reflected in many present-day dialects and in the *BEFEO* system of romanization. The "feeling of the native"[18] seems to favor the velars. Most English-speaking learners of Chinese favor the retroflexes (they usually pronounce them too palatally, anyway, thus making them sound like palatals to start with). By considering the total systematic distribution of the palatals with the three competing candidates, Hartman decided that they should be identified phonemically with the dental sibilants, so that not only 西 *shi* ( < *si siei*) is phonemicized as /si/, but 希 *shi* (hi < $\chi i\partial i$) also as /si/. But Hartman's solution, as can be seen from his table of comparison,[19] was practically a photo finish of the three competing sets

---

[18]This appears in two symptoms: (1) There is a form of "pig Latin" in Peiping in which a syllable CV is given as *Cei-gV*, for example, *ta ⇒ tei-ga*. When the final is in Row-*i* or Row-*iu*, for example, in *nii*, then there is free variation between *neei-gii* and *neei-jii*. (2) In vivid reduplications of the $X_1$-*lhi*-$X_2$-*lhu* type (sec. 4.2.2.1), there is often an alternation between palatals and velars, as in 叽哩咕噜 *ji₀lhigulhu* 'grunts and grumbles', 唏哩呼噜 *shi₀lhihulhu* 'slurp slurp', where the alliterations could be put on a phonemic basis, or else they would involve more complicated morphophonemics. This idea and the examples were suggested to me by Fa-kao Chou.

See also Samuel E. Martin, "Problems of Hierarchy and Indeterminancy in Mandarin Phonology", *BIHP*, 29:223-224 of 209-229 (1958).

[19]Lawton Hartman III, "The Segmental Phonemes of the Peiping Dialect", *Language*, 20:39 of 28-42 (1944). His actual notation is /sji/, his /i/ being a generalized high vowel, which is phonetically [i] after the semivowel /j/.

of allophones.  In the GR system we are using, it is in the tradition of the Wade system and other systems,[20] except that the Wade has the luxury spelling of *hs* for palatal *sh*, instead of letting the palatalization be implied by the following *i* or *iu* (*ü* of Wade). The subscripts in $j_r$, $j_i$, and so on in table 1 are used only when the retroflex and palatal initials are mentioned in isolation, since there is no ambiguity when the final is spelled out.

Table 1.  Initials

1(a)  In G. R.

| Place \ Manner | Unaspirated Stops | Aspirated Stops | Nasals | Fricatives | Voiced Continuants |
|---|---|---|---|---|---|
| Labials | b | p | m | f | |
| Dentals | d | t | n | | l |
| Dental sibilants | tz | ts | | s | |
| Retroflexes | $j_r$ | $ch_r$ | | $sh_r$ | r |
| Palatals | $j_i$ | $ch_i$ | | $sh_i$ | |
| Gutturals | g | k | (ng) | h | $\varnothing$ |

1(b)  In IPA

| Place \ Manner | Unaspirated Stops | Aspirated Stops | Nasals | Fricatives | Voiced Continuants |
|---|---|---|---|---|---|
| Labials | b̥ | $p^h$ | m | f | |
| Dentals | d̥ | $t^h$ | n | | l |
| Dental sibilants | ts | $ts^h$ | | s | |
| Retroflexes | tʂ | $tʂ^h$ | | ʂ | ɹ |
| Palatals | tɕ | $tɕ^h$ | | ɕ | |
| Gutturals | g̊ | $k^h$ | ( ŋ ) | χ | ʁ ~ $\varnothing$ |

---

[20]Among them that of Douglas M. Beach, in his (unpublished) Ph.D. thesis at the University of London in 1923, entitled "The Phonetics of Pek-

*1.3.3. Finals and Vowels.* A final consists of one of the four medials: Ø, *i, u,* or *iu* ( = [y] as in German *Süd*), one of the vowels: *a, e,* or *o,* and one of the six endings: Ø, *-i, -u, -n, -ng,* and *-l* (phonetically -r). This gives rise to 4 x 2 x 6 = 48 possible finals (since *e* and *o* can count as one, as we shall see below). Actually there are 37 (if finals involving retroflex suffixes of table 5 are not counted). This shows an extremely high phonological load for all the variables involved; in other words, any little difference will make a great difference, and mispronouncing a word will very likely result in saying another word.

In table 2, finals of the same medial are in the same (horizontal) row, those in the same box of columns have the same ending, and those of the same main vowel phoneme are in the same (vertical) column; that is, *y* (zero), *i, u,* and *iu* in column 1 are considered as one general high vowel phoneme with allophones according to the medial (Hartman, pp. 32-33). For the practical purpose of the GR orthography they will be written as different vowels. The vowel in column 3, table 2(b) is given as [ ɛ ] after the high front medials *i* and *iu,* and as [ ɤ ] after zero and *u;* this is reflected in GR by writing *e* for the first vowel and *o* for the second. (Compare Wade- *ê, ieh, (u)o, üeh.*) Actually the vowel is more consistently a central-back vowel than is usually represented. In a very narrow transcription, the four finals would have the values: [ ɤˆ, iɛˆ, uoˆ], and [yɛˆ]. Note that in the morphophonemic alternation between 天 *tian* [tʻiɛn], with [ ɛ ], and 天ㄦ *tial* [tʻia_r], with [a], as in table 5, p. 62, the [ ɛ ] in the former is definitely not retracted as in 贴 *tie* [tʻiɛˆ ]. In the box for the ending *-ng* in table 2(a), there seems to be a minimal contrast between *e* and *o* in *eng* and *ong,* as in 登 *deng* and 东 *dong.* This is, however, more orthographic than phonemic. The vowel in *ong* and *iong* is an open *u* ([ʊ], or [ ɷ ]), and the medial in *iong* is slightly rounded, so that the two finals can be considered as *ung* and *iung* phonemically, as indeed they are so treated in the National Phonetic spelling ㄨㄥ and ㄩㄥ, literally *u* +

## Table 2. Finals

### 2(a)  In G. R.

| Medial \ Ending (Column) | Open Ending | | | -i | | -u | | -n | | -ng | | | -l |
|---|---|---|---|---|---|---|---|---|---|---|---|---|---|
| | 1 | 2 | 3 | 4 | 5 | 6 | 7 | 8 | 9 | 10 | 11 | 12 | 13 |
| Row-a | y | a | e | ai | ei | au | ou | an | en | ang | eng | ong | el |
| Row-i | i | ia | ie | iai | | iau | iou | ian | in | iang | ing | iong | |
| Row-u | u | ua | uo | uai | uei | | | uan | uen | uang | ueng | | |
| Row-iu | iu | | iue | | | | | iuan | iun | | | | |

### 2(b)  In IPA

| Medial \ Ending (Column) | Open Ending | | | -i | | -u | | -n | | - ŋ | | | - ɹ |
|---|---|---|---|---|---|---|---|---|---|---|---|---|---|
| | 1 | 2 | 3 | 4 | 5 | 6 | 7 | 8 | 9 | 10 | 11 | 12 | 13 |
| Row-a | z̩,ɹ̩* | A̲ | ɤ | ai | ei | au | ou | an | ən | aŋ | ʌŋ | ɔŋ | ɚ |
| Row-i | i | iA̲ | iɛ | iai | | iau | iou | iɛn | in | iaŋ | iŋ | iɔŋ | |
| Row-u | u | uA̲ | uɤ | uai | uei | | | uan | uən | uaŋ | uʌŋ | | |
| Row-iu | y | | yɛ | | | | | yan | yn | | | | |

°Karlgren invented the symbols ɿ and ʅ for these apical vowels,
as he calls them. See his *Phonologie*, pp. 295-297, Chinese transl.,
pp. 197-199.

(e)ng and *iu* + (e)ng. Both *ong* and *ueng* are given as ㄨㄥ, but there is no conflict, since *ong* is always preceded by a consonantal initial and *ueng* (as in 翁) always has the zero initial. Other features of the finals will come out in table 2(b) in phonetic transscription.

*1.3.4. Tones*

(1)    Nature of Tones. Mandarin has four tones, usually numbered as 1st, 2nd, 3rd, and 4th Tones. These are not to be confused with the four classical tones of 平, 上, 去, 入, *Pyng, Shaang* (or *Shanq*), *Chiuh,* and *Ruh,* usually translated as 'Even, Rising, Going, and Entering'. In most modern dialects the Even Tone is split into two different tones according as the ancient initial was voiceless or voiced, thus giving rise to Mandarin 1st and 2nd Tones. Ancient Rising Tone corresponds roughly to Mandarin 3rd, Ancient Going Tone to 4th, and Ancient Entering Tone, which ended in *-p, -t,* or *-k,* has lost the consonantal endings and is redistributed over the modern four tones in most of the northern dialects.    For    example, 七, *tsʻiet* > *chi*[1], 十, *źiəp* > *shyr*[2], 百, *pɒk bae*[3], 六, *liuk* > *liow*[4].

Every stressed syllable has a tone, spread, as we have noted, over the voiced part of the syllable. For example, in *nian* the tone begins with *n,* but it *tyan,* it does not begin until *y.* If we divide the range of a speaker's voice into four equal intervals, marked by five points, 1 low, 2 half-low, 3 middle, 4 half-high, and 5 high, then practically any tone occurring in any of the Chinese dialects can be represented unambiguously by noting the beginning and ending points, and, in the case of a circumflex tone, also the turning point; in other words, the exact shape of the time-pitch curve, so far as I have observed, has never been a necessary distinctive feature, given the starting and ending points, or the turning point, if any, on the five-point scale. On the average the five reference points can roughly be identified, in the tonic sol-fa system, with *do, re mi, fi, si* or, when enlarged, with *do, me, fi, la, dó* of the diminished seventh chord.

For graphical representation, a vertical reference line (instead of the usual horizontal line for abscissa) extending from points 1 to 5 is set up, to which a simplified tone graph is attached, as shown here.[21]

| Tone | Chinese Name | Description | Pitch | Graph |
|------|-------------|-------------|-------|-------|
| 1st Tone | 陰平 *Inpyng* | High-level | 55: | ˥ |
| 2nd Tone | 陽平 *Yangpyng* | High-rising | 35: | ˦ |
| 3rd Tone | 上声 *Shaangsheng* | Low-dipping | 214: | ˩ |
| 4th Tone | 去声 *Chiuhsheng* | High-falling | 51: | ˥ |

Both the actual intervals and the absolute pitch are relative to the individual voice and the key and mood at the moment of speaking. Imagine a five-line musical staff on which overlies a set of tone graphs drawn on an elastic transparent sheet. Stretching the sheet vertically or letting it shrink will vary the pitch range of the tones; doing the same horizontally will make the syllables longer or shorter; moving the sheet up or down as a whole will raise or lower the absolute pitch; and moving the sheet to the left or right will simply mean speaking earlier or later. On the average, for clear but casual speech to a person a few feet away, the pitch for simple syllables spoken in the four tones is approximately as in the figure. The reason that the pitch given here seems to be rather low (one octave lower than written for

8 va  - -    -  -  -  -  -

Average shapes of tones.

women, and two octaves for men) is that a person's speaking voice is normally centered around the lowest part of his or her voice range, as against the best range for singing, which is in the upper middle portion. The tail end of the 4th Tone, for instance, trails to a near grunt, since it touches or seems to try to go beyond the lower limit of one's voice.

(2) Tone Sandhi. When tones come together, certain allophonic and phonemic changes occur, known as tone sandhi. In

---

[21]See Y. R. Chao, "A System of Tone Letters", *Le Maître Phonétique*, 45:24-27 (1930).

Mandarin, as well as in other Chinese dialects, the tone of a syllable is affected much more by the tone of the following syllable than by a preceding one. Fortunately for students of Mandarin, its tone sandhi is among the simplest of all the dialects.

(a) The most frequently occurring change is that of the 3rd Tone into the $\frac{1}{2}$ 3rd Tone, which takes place when a 3rd Tone is followed by any tone except another 3rd. The $\frac{1}{2}$ 3rd Tone has the pitch 21: ⌐, which is the full 3rd Tone minus its terminal rising part.

(b) When a 3rd Tone is followed by another 3rd, the first one changes into a 2nd Tone. For example, 着火 *jaur-huoo* ⌐⌐ 'catches fire' is originally 2nd + 3rd, but 找火 *jao* + *huoo* ⌐ + ⌐ 'looks for fire' changes to ⌐⌐, and is thus homophonous with *jaur-huoo*. Similarly, the surnames 许 *Sheu* and 徐 *Shyu* are ⌐ and ⌐, respectively, but when spoken together with a given name, say 宝 *Bao*, then 许宝 and 徐宝 will both be pronounced with the tones ⌐⌐. Since the 2nd Tone is itself a separate phoneme, it does not constitute an allophone of the 3rd Tone, as does the $\frac{1}{2}$ 3rd Tone, and the sandhi is thus morphophonemic in nature.[22]

(c) A tone sandhi of minor importance has to do with the change of the 2nd to a 1st Tone in three-syllable groups. If in a three-syllable word or phrase ABC, A is in the 1st or 2nd Tone, B in the 2nd Tone, and C in any except the neutral tone (to be described below), then B changes into the 1st Tone for speech at

---

[22]This amounts to saying that all the so-called 3rd Tone morphemes have two alternate phonemic make-ups, one with the 3rd Tone, with its two allophones 214: and 21:, and the other with the 2nd Tone. Thus, there are some morphemes exclusively in the 2nd Tone, but no morphemes exclusively in the 3rd Tone (except possibly interjections like 咦?! *Yee?!* = 'How strange!' where the 214: is really an intonation). An alternate analysis is to treat the 2nd Tone from an alternative 3rd Tone as an intersecting allophone, which is not a very neat treatment either. In any case we shall write such a tonal morphophoneme in the 3rd Tone form (see below on tonal spelling) in order to gain a constant shape for the same morpheme. Thus, we shall spell 马 'horse' always as *maa* whether in 骑马 *chyi maa* ⌐⌐ 'rides a horse', or in 马头 *maatour* ⌐⌐ 'horse's head', or in 马脚 *maajeau* ⌐⌐ 'horse's feet'.

conversational speed, but does not change at a more deliberate speed. For example, the name 梅蘭芳 *Mei Lanfang* is ˧˥ ˥ ˥ at slow speed, but ˥ ˥ ˥ at conversational speed.[23] Following are all the possibilities with three such syllables:

| 121 | ˥˥˥ → ˥˥˥ | 西洋參 | *shiyangshen* '(occidental) ginseng' |
| 122 | ˥˥˥ → ˥˥˥ | 三年级 | *sannianjyi* '3rd-year grade' |
| 123 | ˥˥˥ → ˥˥˥ | 葱油饼 | *tsongyou-biing* 'onion oil cake' |
| 124 | ˥˥˥ → ˥˥˥ | 东河沿ㄦ | *Dong Heryall* 'East Riverside' |
| 133 | ˥˥˥ → ˥˥˥ | 分水嶺 | *fenshoei-liing* 'watershed' |
| 221 | ˥˥˥ → ˥˥˥ | 谁能飛? | *Sheir neng fei?* 'Who can fly?' |
| 222 | ˥˥˥ → ˥˥˥ | 还没完 | *hair mei wan* 'not yet finished' |
| 223 | ˥˥˥ → ˥˥˥ | 油炸烩 | *youjar-goei* 'fried hollow dough-nut' |
| 224 | ˥˥˥ → ˥˥˥ | 隆福寺 | *Longfwu Syh* 'Lung Fu Temple' |
| 233 | ˥˥˥ → ˥˥˥ | 寒暑表 | *harnshuubeau* 'thermometer' |
| 333 | ˥˥˥ → ˥˥˥ | 好几种 | *haojii-joong* 'quite a few kinds' |

   (d) I used to set up another rule of tone sandhi to the effect that a 4th Tone followed by another 4th does not fall to the bottom; that is, ＼＼ → ˑ＼ or 51: + 51: → 53: 51:, as in 大樹

---

[23]Nicholas C. Bodman called my attention to the more "staccato" (or with open juncture) and phonemically identical stress on 还没来 *hair mei lai* 'hasn't come yet' than 联合國 *Lianhergwo* 'The United Nations', which is more "legato" (or with close juncture). I think, however, that the difference is rather one of degree, as a result of relative frequency of occurrence and *hair mei lai* does sometimes occur 'legato' in the form ˧˥ ˥ ˧˥ , while *Lianhergwo* in more deliberate speech also occurs as ˧˥ ˧˥ ˧˥ ˧˥ .

*dah shuh* 'big tree'. But since stress will enlarge the range and length of a tone and since a two-syllable compound or phrase will have a slightly greater stress on the second syllable, unless it is in the neutral tone, a succession of two 4th Tones is more accurately represented as a small graph " ╲ " followed by a bigger one than as represented above. Moreover, this is true of any combination of tones; for example, a 3rd Tone in second position will dip lower than a ½ 3rd Tone, and, since this is true in general, there is no need of using two sets of bigger and smaller tone graphs.

(3) Tonal Spelling. In the National Romanization, or GR used in this book, tones are built-in in the spelling of the syllables. Following are the rules of tonal spelling:

1st Tone:

Rule 1. Use basic form, as given in table 2 above: 他 *ta*, 说 *shuo*, 天 *tian*, 高 *gau*.

2nd Tone:

Rule 2. Add *r* after vowel for Row-*a* finals: 茶 *char*, 河 *her*, 才 *tsair*, 陈 *chern*.

Rule 3. In Row-*i*, Row-*u*, and Row-*iu*, change the medials *i, u, iu* into *y, w, yu*, respectively: 祥 *shyang*, 滑 *hwa*, 情 *chyng*, 圓 *yuan*. Note, however, that as complete finals, *i* is changed into *yi* (not *y!*) and *u* into *wu* (not *w!*): 旗 *chyi*, 胡 *hwu*, 夷 *yi*, 吾 *wu*.

3rd Tone:

Rule 4. Single vowel letters, as well as *e* next to *i* (i.e., in *ei* and *ie*) and *o* next to *u* (i.e., in *ou* and *uo*), are doubled: 纸 *jyy*, 打 *daa*, 请 *chiing*, 给 *geei*, 姐 *jiee*, 手 *shoou*, 火 *huoo*.

Rule 5. Change the medial or ending *i, u, iu* into *e, o, eu*, respectively: 讲 *jeang*, 滚 *goen*, 捲 *jeuan*, 買 *mae*, 好 *hao*. But if the medial is changed, the ending is left unchanged: 小 *sheau* (not *sheao* or *shiao*), 柺 *goai* (not *goae* or *guae*).

4th Tone:

Rule 6. Change endings zero, *-i, -u, -n, -ng, -l* into *-h, -y, -w, -nn, -nq, -ll*, respectively: 住 *juh*, 卖 *may*, 夠 *gow*, 慢 *mann*, 上 *shanq*, 二 *ell*.

Supplementary rules:

Rule 7. Insert *h* after *m, n, l, r* for the 1st Tone: 媽 *mha*, 捏
*nhie*, 拉 *lha*, 扔 *rheng*, but use the basic form for the 2nd Tone, as
麻 *ma*, 年 *nian*, 来 *lai*, 人 *ren*.

Rule 8. In finals in Row-*i*. Row-*u*, and Row-*iu* with zero
initial, ADD the letter *y-*, *w-*, *y-*, respectively, for the 3rd Tone:
有 *yeou* (cf. 酒 *jeou*), 碗 *woan* (cf. 莞 *goan*). But the final *-iee* is
CHANGED into *yee* (not *yiee*), and *-uoo* into *woo* (not *wuoo*).

Rule 9. In the same finals with zero initial for the 4th Tone,
CHANGE *i-*, *u-*, *iu-* into *y-*, *w-*, *yu-*, respectively: 要 *yaw* (cf. 叫
*jiaw*, 问 *wenn* (cf. 睏 *kuenn*). But ADD *y* or *w* to the four finals
*-ih, -uh, -inn, -inq* to form 意 *yih*, 霧 *wuh*, 印 *yinn*, 硬 *yinq*.

Table 3 gives the finals in all the tones resulting from the application of the preceding rules. The rows headed by "-3" and
"-4" are finals used only when the initial is not zero. In Row-*u*,
column 3, there is a special form for labial initials, namely, 波 *bo*,
坡 *po*, 摸 *mho*, 脖 *bor*, 婆 *por*, 摩 *mo*, 佛 *for*, etc. This is only graphical, and the actual pronunciation is still *buo*, *puo*, and so on.
Forms in parentheses are rare, and blank spaces are for possible finals not represented by actual morphemes. Column 13 gives
only single morphemes. On syllabic types like 今儿 *jiel* 味儿 *well*, etc.,
see sec. 1.3.8(3), on the morphophonemics of the retroflex suffix,
and table 5.

*1.3.5. Syllabic Types.* Not every initial combines with every
final, their combination being conditioned by the place of articulation of the initial and the medial of the final. We already noted
the complementary distribution of the palatals in Row-*i* and Row-
*iu*, as against the dentals, retroflexes, and the gutturals in Row-*a*,
and Row-*u*. The complete list of types of combinations is shown
in table 4. Each syllable stands for a series with homorganic initials (that is, in the same row in table 1); for example, 官 *guan*
stands for *guan, kuan, huan, uan* in any tone. As far as possible
the examples are chosen from unaspirated stops in the 1st Tone;
otherwise they are marked with intial and/or tone. For instance,
there being no °*din*, 林 *is* chosen, superscribed *l'*. Onomatopoeic
morphemes with no characters are given as " ☐ !". For readers
who do not use characters, each character may be read as ' + ',
meaning 'exists'.

Table 3. Finals in All Tones

| Row | Tone | Zero | | | -i | | -u | | -n | | -ng | | | -l |
|---|---|---|---|---|---|---|---|---|---|---|---|---|---|---|
| | | 1 | 2 | 3 | 4 | 5 | 6 | 7 | 8 | 9 | 10 | 11 | 12 | 13 |
| a | 1 | y | a | e | ai | ei | au | ou | an | en | ang | eng | ong | el |
| a | 2 | yr | ar | er | air | eir | aur | our | arn | ern | arng | erng | orng | erl |
| a | 3 | yy | aa | ee | ae | eei | ao | oou | aan | een | aang | eeng | oong | eel |
| a | 4 | yh | ah | eh | ay | ey | aw | ow | ann | enn | anq | enq | onq | ell |
| i | 1 | i | ia | ie | (yai) | | iau | iou | ian | in | iang | ing | iong | |
| i | 2 | yi | ya | ye | | | yau | you | yan | yn | yang | yng | yong | |
| i | -3 | ii | ea | iee | | | eau | eou | ean | iin | eang | iing | eong | |
| i | -4 | ih | iah | ieh | | | iaw | iow | iann | inn | ianq | inq | ionq | |
| i | 3 | yii | yea | yee | | | yeau | yeou | yean | yiin | yeang | yiing | yeong | |
| i | 4 | yih | yah | yeh | | | yaw | yow | yann | yimn | yanq | yinq | yonq | |

Table 3.  Finals in All Tones  (Continued)

| Row | Tone | Zero | | | -i | | -u | | -n | | -ng | | -l | |
|---|---|---|---|---|---|---|---|---|---|---|---|---|---|---|
| | | 1 | 2 | 3 | 4 | 5 | 6 | 7 | 8 | 9 | 10 | 11 | 12 | 13 |
| u | 1 | u | ua | uo | uai | uei | | | uan | uen | uang | ueng | | |
| | 2 | wu | wa | wo | wai | wei | | | wan | wen | wang | | | |
| | -3 | uu | oa | uoo | oai | oei | | | oan | oen | oang | | | |
| | -4 | uh | uah | uoh | uay | uey | | | uann | uenn | uanq | | | |
| | 3 | wuu | woa | woo | woai | woei | | | woan | woen | woang | (woeng) | | |
| | 4 | wuh | wah | woh | way | wey | | | wann | wenn | wanq | wenq | | |
| iu | 1 | iu | ieu | | | | | | iuan | iun | | | | |
| | 2 | yu | yue | | | | | | yuan | yun | | | | |
| | -3 | eu | eue | | | | | | euan | eun | | | | |
| | -4 | iuh | iueh | | | | | | iuann | iunn | | | | |
| | 3 | yeu | | | | | | | yeuan | yeun | | | | |
| | 4 | yuh | | yueh | | | | | yuann | yunn | | | | |

Table 4. Syllabic Types

| Medial | Initial | y | a | e | ai | ei | au | ou | an | en | ang | eng | ong | el |
|---|---|---|---|---|---|---|---|---|---|---|---|---|---|---|
| Zero | b  p  m  f | | 巴 | 么ᵐ | 扮 | 碑 | 包 | 谋ᵐ | 班 | 奔 | 邦 | 崩 | | |
| | d  t  n  l | | 搭 | 的 | 獃 | 得 | 刀 | 兜 | 单 | 嫩ⁿ' | 当 | 登 | | |
| | tz  ts  s  r | 貲 | 咂 | 則 | 災 | 賊 | 糟 | 鄒 | 簪 | 簪 | 臓 | 增 | 宗 | |
| | j  ch  sh  r | 知 | 扎 | 遮 | 齋 | 這 | 招 | 周 | 沾 | 真 | 張 | 争 | 中 | |
| | g  k  h  ○ | | 喝 | 哥 | 該 | 給 | 高 | 鉤 | 干 | 根 | 剛 | 庚 | 工 | 兒ᵉˡ |

| Medial | Initial | i | ia | ie | iai | iau | iou | ian | in | iang | ing | iong |
|---|---|---|---|---|---|---|---|---|---|---|---|---|
| -i | b  p  m  - | 逼 | | 憋ᵖ | | 標 | 谬ᵐ | 边 | 賓 | | 氷 | |
| | d  t  n  l | 低 | | 爹 | | 刁 | 丢 | 顛 | 林ⁿ' | 娘ⁿ' | 丁 | |
| | j  ch  sh  ○ | 鸡 | 家 | 接 | 崖 | 交 | 揪 | 尖 | 今 | 將 | 紅 | 扃 |

Table 4. Syllabic Types  (Continued)

| Medial | Initial | Final | | | | | | | | |
|---|---|---|---|---|---|---|---|---|---|---|
| | | u | ua | uo | uai | uei | uan | uen | uang | ueng |
| -u | b p m f | 不 | | 波 | | | | | | |
| | d t n l | 都 | | 多 | | 堆 | 端 | 敦 | | |
| | tz ts s | 租 | | 嘬 | | 堆 | 鑽 | 尊 | | |
| | j ch sh r | 朱 | 抓 | 桌 | 摔sh | 追 | 专 | 诗 | 庄 | |
| | g k h | 姑 | 瓜 | 锅 | 乖 | 归 | 官 | 滚 | 光 | 翁° |

| Medial | Initial | Final | | | |
|---|---|---|---|---|---|
| | | iu | iue | iuan | iun |
| -iu | – – n l | 女nˇ | 略ˋ | 孪ˊ | 淋ˊ |
| | j ch sh | 居 | 噘 | 捐 | 均 |

*1.3.6. Stress.* Stress in Chinese is primarily an enlargement in pitch range and time duration and only secondarily in loudness. Thus, when a 3rd Tone is stressed it is dipped lower, and when a 4th Tone is stressed it starts higher and falls lower. Stress, there-fore, can be pictured by stretching the tone graph on an elastic background, as described above [sec. 1.3.4(1)]. There are physic-ally many perceptible degrees of stress, but phonemically we have found it best to set up no more than three degrees of stress: normal, contrastive, and weak.

(1) Normal Stress. All syllables that have neither weak nor contrastive stress are said to have normal stress. Actually, se-quences of normally stressed syllables without intermediate pause, whether in a phrase or in a compound word, are not all of the same degree of phonetic stress, the last being the strongest, the first next, and the intermediate being least stressed, as in 好人 ₁*hao* ˈ*ren* 'good man', 注意 ₍₎*juh*ˈ*yih* 'pays attention', 山海関 ₁*Shan*‖*hae* ˈ*Guan* 'Shanhaikuan', 我没懂。*Woo* ‖*mei* ˈ*doong.* 'I did not understand.', 东南西北 ₁*Dong-*‖*Nan-*‖*Shi-*ˈ*Beei* 'East, South, West, and North', 人乞都想去。₁*Ren*‖*ren*‖*dou*‖*sheang* ˈ*chiuh* (or with ₁*dou* if spoken as two phrases). 'Everyone wants to go there.' Since these degrees of stress are predictable by position, they are all allophones of one phonemic stress.

(2) Contrasting Stress. The contrasting stress is distinct from normal stress and has a wider pitch range and longer duration, usually with associated increase in loudness. For example, there is normal stress (with the usual allophones according to position) in the name 黄种强 ₁*Hwang* ‖*Joong*ˈ*chyang.* But if someone misheard *Hwang* as *Wang*, then in correcting him one would say 不是王种强, 是黄种强。*Bush* ‖ˈ*Wang Joongchyang, sh* ‖ˈ*Hwang Joongchyang.* 'It is not ‖ˈWang Joongchyang, it is ‖ˈHwang Joongchyang', where the stress is shifted to the syllables contrasted, with more than normal stress.

(3) Weak Stress: the Neutral Tone. In weak stress, the tone range is flattened to practically zero and the duration is rela-tively short. Most cases of weak stress occur enclitically, that is, closely following a stressed syllable, whose tone determines the pitch of the weakly stressed syllable. In the relatively few cases when the weak stress precedes a closely following stressed sylla-

ble, usually a pronoun or one of a few conjunctions such as 或者 ₀huoh₀jee 'or' it is then a proclitic and the pitch is about average, or 3:, on the scale of five points. Because the tone is flattened to zero, I have called it the neutral tone. Almost any morpheme in one of the four regular tones can be in the neutral tone under certain conditions, there being only a very small number of morphemes, such as suffixes and particles, which are always in the neutral tone and do not belong to any one of the four tones. The pitch of the neutral tone is:

| ⌐ half-low | after 1st Tone: | 他 的 | *ta.de* 'his' |
| ⌐ middle | after 2nd Tone: | 黄 的 | *hwang.de* 'yellow one'[24] |
| ⌐ half-high | after 3rd Tone: | 你 的 | *nii.de* 'yours' |
| ⌐ low | after 4th Tone: | 大 的 | *dah.de* 'big one' |

For practical purposes, it is sufficient to remember the neutral tone as being high after a $\frac{1}{2}$ 3rd Tone and (relatively) low after the other tones.

The neutral tone affects the consonants and vowels in the syllable in the following ways. Unaspirated stops (column 1 of table 1) which are voiceless when stressed are voiced in the neutral tone, as in 籬笆 *li.ba* 'fence', with a voiced [b], as against the voiceless [b̥] in 第八 *dihba* 'number eight', Similarly, we have 知道 *jy.daw* 'knows', 西瓜 *shi.gua* 'watermelon', 看見 *kann.jiann* 'see', where the *d*, *g*, and *j* are all true voiced sounds, though they would be voiceless in stressed positions. The affricate *tz*, however, is usually not fully voiced in the neutral tone except that the noun suffix *-.tzy* (which we abbreviate as *-tz*) is pronounced by many speakers as [zə]; for example, 兔子 *tuhtz* 'rabbit' is usually pronounced [tʰutsz̩ ⌐ ⌐ ], but by many speakers as [tʰuzə ⌐ ⌐ ].

Vowels in the neutral tone tend to become mid. Thus, the second syllables in 棉花 *mian.hua* 'cotton', 窗户 *chuang.huh* 'window', and 快活 *kuay.hwo* 'happy' all sound like *-.huo*, with

---

[24]Some speakers use the pattern ⌐ ⌐ , especially in 谁 的? *sheir.de?* 'whose?', 什 么? *sherme?* 'what?', and so on, perhaps from the interrogative intonation. Hockett (Peip Morphoph, 76) treats *sherme* as having two syllables, but one miscrosegment, carrying one 2nd Tone.

a mid main vowel. After a 4th Tone, a high vowel in a neutral-tone syllable with *f*, *ts*, *s*, *ch*, or *sh* tends to be voiceless, as in 丈夫 *janqfu* 'husband' [-fu̥], 意思 *yih.sy* 'meaning' [-sz̥], 阔气 *kuoh.chih* 'swanky' [-t ɕ 'i̥], and 送去 *sonq.chiuh* 'sends over' [-t ɕ 'y̥]. For further examples, see section 3.1.2.

In rapid speech, weakened initials tend to become voiced continuants; retroflex *j*, *ch*, *sh* all becoming *r*, and palatal *j*, *ch*, *sh* all becoming *i*, as in 王先生 *Wang .Shian.sheng → Wang .ian.reng* 'Mr. Wang', 报上 *baw.shanq → baw.ranq → baw-*[ã_r] 'on the,—in the newspaper'.

The following changes are on a somewhat different basis in that they do not occur with all or even similar cases. One is the loss of distinction between aspirated and unaspirated consonants in the neutral tone, for example, 板凳 *baan.denq~baan.teng* 'bench', 折腾 *je.terng~je.denq* 'shifts restlessly'. The other is the metathesis of *uo* into *ou*, as in 拾掇 *shyr.duoh → shyr.dou* 'tidy up'. Sometimes both factors come into play, as in 耳朵 *eel.duoo → eel.dou → eel.tou* 'ear', influenced by analogy with 舌头 *sher-.tou* 'tongue'. These are not always operative under the same conditions and should therefore be regarded as lexical cases of allomorphs of certain morphemes. Thus, because *baan.denq* alternates with *baan.teng* one cannot generalize and assume that 胳臂 *ge.bey* 'the arm' alternates with °*ge.pey*, which does not exist (although it does in the dialect of Paoting).

(4) Medium Stress? Some writers (for example, Hockett Peip Phon, 256) set up a medium degree of stress between the normal and the weak. For instance, in 这不是苦瓜，也不是甜.瓜，就是一种甜瓜。 *Jeh bush ˌkuuˈgua, yee bush tyan.gua, jiow sh i-joong ˈtyan ˌgua.* 'This is not bitter-melon (*Momordica charantia*), nor sweetmelon (*Cumumis melo*), it's just a kind of sweet melon.', where apparently the second *tyan* has normal stress and the second *gua*, though less stressed, is not completely neutral and weak and the pattern of ˈ☐ ˌ☐ does not fit the preceding analysis of the two degrees of stress as allophones of one phonemic normal stress, which should be in the order ˌ☐ ˈ☐ . My treatment of such cases is to regard ˈtyan ˌgua 'sweet melon' as having contrasting stress: ‖*tyan* ˈ*gua*. Since stress is relative,

putting a contrasting stress is often physically equivalent to putting an average normal stress on the syllable to be contrasting-stressed and reducing the degree of other normal stresses, in other words $[\,{}'\square\,{}_{\mid}\square\,] \; = \; /{}''\square\,{}'\square\,/$.

Another example, in which a medium stress seems to be called for is 芝蔴大的燒餅 *jy.ma dah de shau.biing:* (1) with ${}_{\mid}jy.ma\;{}'dah$ ..., it means 'hot biscuits on which the sesame seeds are large', (2) with ${}'jy.ma\;{}_{\mid}dah$ ..., it means 'sesame-size hot biscuits (tiny little biscuits)'. An alternate analysis is to treat (1) as having normal stresses throughout (applying the rule that the first of two stressed syllables in a phrase is predictably less stressed) and (2) as having contrastive stress: ${}''jy.ma\;{}'dah$ ..., thus needing no phonemic medium stress.

Apart from the possibility of the treatment of the medium stress as stated above, another reason for not recognizing a phonemic medium stress is the difficulty of obtaining agreement among native speakers of Peiping in a significant proportion of cases tested, as against the occurrence of the neutral tone, on which there is a good degree of agreement.[25]

(5) Occurrence of the Neutral Tone. Geographically speaking, the neutral tone has a much heavier phonological load in the Peiping dialect than in the other dialects. In some dialects, such as Cantonese, there is no neutral tone in which the stress is completely weak. Grammatically, the neutral tone in the Peiping dialect occurs in suffixes, particles, pronouns as objects (except when in contrastive stress), and verbs reduplicated as cognate objects. Interjections are in the neutral tone but are not always unstressed and may have intonations, some of which may happen to sound like some of the four tones. An object of a verb (other than a pronoun) is never in the neutral tone unless the whole expression is used exocentrically as something other than verb-object, for example, 酦麵 *fa-miann* 'raises dough' (in non-slang sense), but *fa.miann* 'raised dough'. Most literary expressions, new terms about modern life, and scientific terms do not contain the neutral tone. Of what remains, namely colloquial expressions of old standing, one would like to be able to say that they all have

---

[25]*Putonghua Qingshengci Huibian,* Peking: Commercial Press, 1963.

neutral tones, but actually some do and some don't, and the facts about the neutral tones are purely lexical data that have to be recorded individually in the dictionary.

In some cases (including half-new expressions and translation borrowings on the way to being naturalized as everyday expressions) there is alternation between a form with and the same without the neutral tone. Such forms are said to have an optional neutral tone, marked by a circle before the syllable in question. For example, 希望 $shi_0wanq$ 'hope', noun or verb, 不知道 $bujiy_0daw$ 'doesn't know' (but $jy.daw$ 'knows'), 江蘇 $Jiang_0su$ 'Kiangsu' (and other province names of long standing),[26] 好像 $hao_0shianq$ 'seems as if', 苞保 and $_0goan_0bao$ 'I am sure, I bet', conjunction (but 保苞 $baogoan$ 'keeps custody of', verb). There is always a neutral tone on the $bu$ and an optional neutral tone on the second V in V-not-V questions, and the symbols for these can be omitted; for example, $lai bu lai$ is short for $lai.bu_0lai$.

*1.3.7. Intonation.* The question has often been raised as to how Chinese can have sentence intonation if words have definite tones. The best answer is to compare syllabic tone and sentence intonation with small ripples riding on large waves (though occasionally the ripples may be "larger" than the waves). The actual result is an algebraic sum of the two kinds of waves. Where two pluses concur, the result will be more plus; when a plus meets a minus, the algebraic addition will be an arithmetical subtraction. For example, in 你姓王，我姓陸。*Nii shinq Wang, woo shinq Luh.* 'Your name is Wang, my name is Luh.', the rising intonation in the further referring clause will make the rising 2nd Tone *Wang* rise higher than usual and the falling intonation on the falling 4th Tone *Luh* fall lower than usual (or, in this par-

---

[26] A very interesting case is the history of the province name 台湾 'Taiwan'. In my school days, not long after the cession of Taiwan to Japan, people still spoke of *Tair.uan*, an old and familiar name. Now, after a lull of half a century, when people in China begin to talk about the place again, it is more often spoken of as *Tair'uan*, without a neutral tone, just like the new province names 寧夏 *Ningshiah* 'Ninghsia' and 西康 *Shikang* 'Hsikang', and few people outside those of my age group remember that Taiwan was ever called *Tair.uan* 乁 ·| .

ticular instance, since a 4th Tone falls to near the limit of the voice, the falling intonation will make it start lower and squeeze it narrower). But in *Woo shinq Luh, nii shinq Wang.*, *Luh* will be pitched higher as a whole, but still with a 4th Tone contour, and *Wang* will be pitched lower as a whole, but still with a 2nd Tone contour, without losing the identity of the tones, as a foreigner sometimes does when he lets the intonation mask the tone completely and thus seems to be saying 我姓盧，你姓望。*Woo shinq Lu, nii shinq Wanq.*

The main types of intonation described below are found not only in Mandarin, but in almost all the dialects.[27] In some respects, intonation varies less even from language to language. It is, however, never safe to assume that any given type of intonation in one language will have the same function in another language; for example, the echo question for confirmation with a high rising intonation in American English will have a low, almost breathy intonation in Chinese: ↑ 'This one you mean?' (Did I hear you right?)' = ↓ 这个啊? *Jeyg'a?* As for cases of English intonation translatable into Chinese particles, such as function (6) of 啊 *a* = 'falling-rising intonation in English', they will be treated under particles, section 8.5.

Below is a list and brief description of some of the most important varieties of Chinese intonation. Some modifications of voice quality will be included, but we shall not be able to go fully into this subject, which has more to do with stylistics than with grammar proper.

(1) Normal Intonation. Ordinary statements are in normal intonation. In short sentences of three or four syllables, there is no special intonational modification. In longer sentences, there is a slight tendency for the pitch to trail off to a lower key toward the end. For example, in 那个人我叫了他半天他也不来。*Neyg ren woo jiawle ta banntian ta yee bu lai.* 'I called that man a long time and he wouldn't come.' and in 他会中文,

---

[27]For further details see Y. R. Chao, "A Preliminary Study of English Intonation (with American Variants) and Its Chinese Equivalents", *BIHP*, Ts'ai Yüan-p'ei Anniversary Vol. (1933), pp. 105-156. There are also phonograph records which accompany my *Shin Gwoyeu* G. R. version, pp. 30-35 on intonation.

日文，英文，法文四國的语言文字。*Ta huey Jongwen, Ryhwen, Ing'wen, Fahwen syh-gwo de yeuyan wentzyh.* 'He knows the language and writing of four countries, Chinese, Japanese, English, and French.', the last few syllables are in a slightly lower key than the preceding. However, the difference is slight and may be partly attributable to the contrasting effect of *banntian* and *syh-gwo* in the examples. On the whole, therefore, normal intonation is simply a succession of the tones.

(2) Suspense-Conclusion Intonation. A phrase or a first clause in a composite sentence is in a slightly higher key than a concluding phrase or clause. Examples are: 说起浮水耒啊，我忘了带浮水衣了。 ↑*Shuo.chii fuh-shoei .lai a,* ↓*woo wanqle day fuh-shoei-i le.* 'Speaking of swimming, I've forgotten to bring my bathing suit.' 天儿这么冷，咱们得隆点儿炉子。↑*Tial tzemm leeng,* ↓*tzarmen deei long deal lutz.* 'It's so cold, we'll have to start a fire.' 你还不快齐行李．回头就趕不上火車了。 ↑*Nii hair bu kuay chyi shyng.lii,* ↓*hweitour jiow gaan.bu-shanq huooche le.* 'If you don't hurry and pack up, you won't be able to catch the train.' Such a difference in pitch differs from a similar difference in English in two respects: first, the difference in Chinese is slight, and, secondly, the difference is one of key and not an upward and downward sweep, as is often the case with English.[28]

(3) Accelerated Tempo in the Last Few Syllables: Simple Questions, Simple Commands. In a simple question or a simple command, with no special implications, there is a slight acceleration toward the end of the sentence. Examples are: 问话的时候儿，是不是这么樣子问的？ *Wenn huah de shyr.howl, sh bush tzemm yanqtz wenn de?* 'When you ask a question, is it to be asked like this?' 世界上什么东西最便宜？ *Shyh.jieh-.shanq sherm dong.shi tzuey pyan.yi?* 'What is the cheapest thing in the world? 你把那边儿那双筷子遞给我！ *Nii bae*

---

[28]For example, in 'It's ten o'clock [ , ], I have to go home [ . ]' (Bloomfield, *Lg*, 171), the phonemic comma is phonetically realized in an upswing on the second syllable of the word 'o'clock', and the phonemic period in a down swing on the word 'home'. (Note that Bloomfield's *Lg* was written before the use of the slashes to mark phonemes.)

*neybial ney-shuang kuaytz dih .geei woo!* 'Hand me that pair of chopsticks over there!'

Since the main stress in a phrase is the last non-neutral sylla-ble and stress is realized by magnification in time and pitch range, a slight acceleration toward the end of a question or a command will have the effect, on the average, of canceling the magnification in time. The impression of a slight acceleration, or a kind of promptness in ending the sentence, is therefore in relation to the expected lengthening rather than in relation to other parts of the sentence.

(4) Extra Wide Range: Airy, Breezy Expression; Complaining Expression. 还 早 呐, 请 坐 会儿 再 走 啊! ↑*Hair tzao ne, chiing tzuoh .hoel tzay tzoou a!* 'It's still early, please sit a while before you go!' 嗐! 这么 重 的 礼, 我 简直 不 好意思 收! ↑*Hai! Tzemm jonq de lii, woo jeanjyr buhaoyih.sy shou!* 'Oh, such a large gift, I am simply too embarrassed to accept!' 我 到 处 找 也 找 不 着你! ↕*Woo dawchuh jao yee jao.bu-jaur nii!* 'I looked for you everywhere and couldn't find you!' The difference between the two is that in the airy, breezy expression the pitch is higher and the voice quality is smoother, while in the com-plaining expression the key is average in height and the voice quality is more creaky (as indicated by the wavy line in " ↕ "). In either case, the widened range gives no effect of stress, since there is no increase in length or loudness.

(5) High Pitch, Quiet: Taking Things Lightly; Asking Ques-tions a Second Time. 也 不 一 定 啊, 爱 怎么 办 就 怎 么 办。 ↑*Yee buidinq a, ay tzeem bann jiow tzeem bann.* '(With falling-rising intonation in each of the following clauses:) Not necessarily, do as you like!' 他 姓 什么 来着? *Ta shinq sherm .laij?* 'What did you say his name was?'

(6) Falsetto: Impatience, Strong Disapproval. This is often accompanied by stuttering, as in: 这 ₹ ₹ 这 幹 麻 ?! *Jeh jeh jeh jeh gann ma?!* 'Wha-wha-what's this all about?!' 你 ₹ 你 安 ₹ 頓 ₹ 的 坐 得 那儿 敪 ! *Nii nii nii an'anduennduennde tzuoh de nall sha!* 'You just sit there quietly and properly, won't you!'

(7) Low Pitch: Seriousness, Praise, Great Feeling. 诸君，咱们到现在还不努力啊, 那就没有希望了。↓*Jujiun, tzarmen daw shianntzay hair bu nuulih a, nah jiow meiyeou shiwang le.* 'Gentlemen, if by this time we still fail to exert ourselves, then there is no hope.' ↓唉, 真可憐! *Hhai, jen kee-lian!* 'Oh, it's really pitiful!' (Cf. the insincere form, with Particle 28, function 6, sec. 8.5.5.) An automatic feature of low pitch is the narrowness of the range, since, as we have noted, the lower limit of the speaking voice is the lower limit of the voice, and if the key is low the range will have be narrowed.

(8) Low, Often Breathy: Questions of Confirmation ('Did I hear you right?'). This usually goes with the particle 啊 *a*. For examples of this intonation and the particle, see sec. 1.3.7.

(9) Low and Fast: Parenthetical Insertions. 他那位親戚啊 — 我这只是对你说咔 — 恐怕有点儿靠不住。*Ta ney-wey chin.chi a—woo jeh jyysh duey nii shuo d'a—koongpah yeoudeal kaw.bu-juh.* 'That relative of his—I am telling this only to you—I'm afraid is a little unreliable.' '谈起國貨耒啊,'他说, '咱们应该先提倡國医,'他说. *Tarn.chii gwohuah .lai a,' ta shuo, 'tzarmen inggai shian tyichang gwoi,' to shuo.* '"Talking about national products," he said, "we should first of all promote national (herb) medicine," he said.' For further details on digressions and interpolations, see sec. 2.14.2.

(10) Negative Pause: Words Trying to Catch Up with Thoughts. Since words are slower than thought (or sketchy innervations of articulation, or whatever thought is, in behavioristic terms), it often happens that a speaker already knows what to say next before he has finished with what he is saying. In such cases, he will not only omit the usual pause for a comma or period, but will hurry with the next sentence (often associated with reduced pitch range in the direction of the neutral tone), so that what would normally be a pause becomes a negative pause, symbolized by " ← ". Examples follow: 那么索性就等他耒了再定吧←要是他耒的话。*Nemme swoshing jiow deeng ta laile tzay shuo ba ← yawsh ta lai de huah.* 'Well, then we might as well wait until he comes before we decide ← if

he comes.' In doing figures aloud, for example, the progress in speech is often out of step with the progress of the arithmetic, as in: 八塊, 八塊十六塊, 十六 的 十 六 三 十 二 塊 ← 也 我 这 么 樣算对 吧 ? *Ba-kuay, ba-kuay shyrliow-kuay, shyrliow de shyrliow sanshyrell-kuay ← è woo tzemmyanq suann duey ba?* 'Eight dollars, and eight is sixteen, sixteen and sixteen is thirty-two ← say, am I doing these figures right?' Sometimes, a sentence is given up before it is finished, as if to hurry on to the next before it is forgotten. In the example before the last, one could have stopped, say, with 再 *tzay* (omitting *shuo ba*) and gone on to the afterthought clause. For additional examples, see section 2.14 on planned and unplanned sentences.

(11-12) Rising and Falling Endings. There are two types of pitch changes, the rising ending ⌐ and the falling ending ⌐, which I used to treat as forms of intonation. But since these do not affect any except the last syllable of the sentence and are added after the tone of even that syllable, I treat these as Particles 27 and 28, on which see section 8.5.5.

(13) Random Loudness: Anger or Impatience. We noted that stress is primarily a matter of pitch range and length and is only secondarily associated with loudness. There is, however, a type of hammer-like loudness which is applied to most of the syllables in a sentence, sometimes even over neutral tones, and express anger or impatience. We are not including this under types of stress, as it has more to do with expressive intonation than with the structure of words or phrases. Examples are: 瞎说! *Shiǎshuó!* 'Nonsense!' 这简直要命! *Jeh jeǎnjyr yǎwmǐnq!* 'This simply gets your life,—is unbearable!' 你好不好别弄那个 怪声音! *Nii hǎo bu hǎo byě nǒnq neyg guǎy shěng.ïn* ⌐ ! 'Will, you, stop, making, that, infernal, noise!' where even the neutral tone is loud and carries a falling ending. In none of these examples is the pitch range or length increased, as it is in contrastive stress.

*1.3.8 Morphophonemics*

(1) Morphophonemic Tone Sandhi. Of the forms of tone sandhi mentioned above [sec. 1.3.4(2)], that of the $\frac{1}{2}$ 3rd Tone is usually treated as a matter of allophones. But when a tonal variant is the same as an allophone of another phoneme, then a mor-

phophonemic problem arises. Thus, the sandhi of the 3rd Tone that occurs before another 3rd Tone is not an allophone, since it is the same as the 2nd Tone: 買 馬 *mae maa* 'buys a horse' and 埋 馬 *mai maa* 'buries a horse', other things being equal, are homophonous. Likewise, when a 2nd Tone changes into a 1st if preceded by a 1st or 2nd and followed by any except the neutral tone (including the case of a 2nd Tone derived from an original 3rd Tone followed by another 3rd), it is a case of morphophonemic change. For examples of all the possible combinations, see section 1.3.4 (2). It should be repeated that such changes occur only at ordinary conversational speed. Slower speech or special stress on the second syllable would bring back the 2nd Tone.

There are four morphemes which have tonal alternations depending upon tonal environment: 一 *i* 'one', 不 *bu* 'not', 七 *chi* 'seven', and 八 *ba* 'eight'. They are in the 1st Tone before pause, but 不 *bu* 'not' is more usually pronounced *buh* even in this position. In other positions, they are in the 2nd Tone before a 4th Tone and are in the 4th Tone before other tones. A substantial minority of speakers use the 1st Tone for *chi* and *ba* in all positions. For this reason, it is perhaps advisable for students of the language to use the same tone in all positions for these two numerals. But the tone sandhi of *i* and *bu* is obligatory. In the spelling adopted in this book we shall use the morphophonemic forms *i* and *bu* without change, though some teachers find it easier for the student to spell them differently according to pronunciation.[29]

(2) Alternation of 啊 *a* with 呀 *ia*. We have seen (sec. 1.3.2) that the particles 啊 *a*, 七 *è*, and 呕 *ou* begin with true vowels, and that, unlike other morphemes which seem to begin with a vowel but really have a lenis consonant [ ɤ ] and resist linking with the endings of preceding endings, these particles do link with them, as in  这 儿 没 人 ＿啊 ? *Jell mei ren ＿ a?* 'Is there nobody here?'  那 不 行＿七 ! *Nah bushyng ＿ è!* 'That won't

---

[29]For example, in Walter Simon's books: Simon and C. H. Lu, *Chinese National Language (Gwoyeu) Reader*, London: Percy Lund, Humphries, 1957; and Simon, *A Beginner's Chinese-English Dictionary of the National Language*, London: Percy Lund, Humphries, 1957.

do, you know!'   太 晚 了＿呕 ! *Tay woan l'ou!* 'Mind you, it's
too late now!' We shall take no notice of this in our spelling except in the case of 啊*a* after an open vowel, when a medial *i* is
inserted to break the hiatus which would otherwise result. Thus,
in 耒啊! *Lai a!* 'Come!' the auditory-articular effect of a linked
*ia* is allowed to result automatically, though writers often do
write the character 呀 in such cases; but in 他 呀, *ta ia*, 'as for
him', the 呀 *ia* is an allomorph of the morpheme 啊*a* and we
shall write it phonemically 呀*ia* rather than morphophonemically
啊*a*.[30]

(3) Morphophonemics of the Retroflex Ending. The retroflex
suffix 儿 -*l*, or rather three homophonous suffixes derived from 裡
-.*lii* 'therein', 日 *ryh* 'day' B, and 兒 *erl* 'child' B,[31] is the only nonsyllabic morpheme in Mandarin. It involves a set of rather complicated morphophonemic changes in the final of the root morpheme, which should best be given by giving the entire list of
finals with the retroflex ending. The general principle of change
follows what I call the "simultaneity of compatible articulations,"
namely, the tendency for articulations to be telescoped together if
they are not incompatible. Thus, *al* is pronounced like *ar* in
Middle Western American 'art', where the vowel and retroflexion
are for the most part simultaneous. The same is true of *ul*, with
simultaneous retroflexion in *u*, since the vowel calls for raising
the back of the tongue and lip-rounding, but leaves the tip of the
tongue free to be retroflexed at the same time. The high front
vowels *i* and *iu*, however, with the tongue flat, are incompatible
with retroflexion; therefore they must be followed by a retroflexed midvowel, thus: 鸡 *ji* + 儿 -*l* → 鸡儿 *jiel* 'chicks'. The
endings -*i*, -*n*, also incompatible with retroflexion, are simply
dropped, thus: 今 *jin* + 儿 -*l* → 今儿 *jiel* 'today', consequently
homophonous with 鸡儿 *jiel*. With the back nasal ending -*ng*,
a compromise is followed by having the preceding vowel both
nasalized and retroflexed, thus: 声 *sheng* + 儿 -*l* → 声儿 *shengl*

---

[30]In the Huai'an, Kiangsu dialect, which is a variety of Southern Mandarin, it is *ta 儿 ua 儿*, with the medial *u* to break the hiatus.

[31]For examples of use, see sec. 4.4.3.

Table 5.  Retroflex Finals

5(a)  Finals

| Row | Tone | ○ | | | -i | | -u | | -n | | -ng | | |
|---|---|---|---|---|---|---|---|---|---|---|---|---|---|
| | | 1 | 2 | 3 | 4 | 5 | 6 | 7 | 8 | 9 | 10 | 11 | 12 |
| a | 1 | el | al | e'l | al | el | aul | oul | al | el | angl | engl | ongl |
| | 2 | erl | arl | er'l | arl | erl | aurl | ourl | arl | erl | arngl | erngl | orngl |
| | 3 | eel | aal | ee'l | aal | eel | aol | ooul | aal | eel | aangl | eengl | oongl |
| | 4 | ell | all | ehl | all | ell | awl | owl | all | ell | anql | enql | onql |
| i | 1 | iel | ial | ie'l | | | iaul | ioul | ial | iel | iangl | iengl | iongl |
| | 2 | yel | yal | ye'l | yal | | yaul | youl | yal | yel | yangl | yengl | yongl |
| | -3 | ieel | eal | ieel | | | eaul | eoul | eal | ieel | eangl | ieengl | eongl |
| | -4 | iell | iall | iell | | | iawl | iowl | iall | iell | ianql | ienql | ionql |
| | 3 | yeel | yeal | yeel | | | yeaul | yeoul | yeal | yeel | yeangl | yeengl | yeongl |
| | 4 | yell | yall | yell | | | yawl | yowl | yall | yell | yanql | yenql | yonql |

Root Ending / Column n / Tone / Row

Table 5. Retroflex Finals (Continued)

5(a) Finals

| Root Ending / Column / Tone, Row | | ○ | | | -i | | -u | | -n | | -ng | | |
|---|---|---|---|---|---|---|---|---|---|---|---|---|---|
| | | 1 | 2 | 3 | 4 | 5 | 6 | 7 | 8 | 9 | 10 | 11 | 12 |
| u | 1 | ul | ual | uol | ual | uel | | | ual | uel | uangl | uengl | |
| | 2 | wul | wal | wol | wal | wel | | | wal | wel | wangl | | |
| | -3 | uul | oal | uool | oal | oel | | | oal | oel | oangl | | |
| | -4 | ull | uall | uoll | uall | uell | | | uall | uell | uanql | | |
| | 3 | wuul | woal | wool | woal | woel | | | woal | woel | woangl | woengl | |
| | 4 | wull | wall | woll | wall | well | | | wall | well | wanql | wenql | |
| iu | 1 | iuel | | iue'l | | | | | iual | iuel | | | |
| | 2 | yuel | | yue'l | | | | | yual | yuel | | | |
| | -3 | euel | | euel | | | | | eual | euel | | | |
| | -4 | iuell | | iuell | | | | | iuall | iuell | | | |
| | 3 | yeuel | | | | | | | yeual | yeuel | | | |
| | 4 | yuell | | yuell | | | | | yuall | yuell | | | |

Table 5. Retroflex Finals (Continued)

5(b)  Examples in Characters*

| Row | Tone | ○ (1) | ○ (2) | ○ (3) | -i (4) | -i (5) | -u (6) | -u (7) | -n (8) | -n (9) | -ng (10) | -ng (11) | -ng (12) |
|-----|------|------|------|------|------|------|------|------|------|------|------|------|------|
| a | 1 | 丝 | 疤 | 歌 | 呆 | 杯 | 刀 | 兜 | 班 | 根 | 当 | 声 | 盅 |
| a | 2 | 词 | 把 | 盒 | 牌 | "培" | 桃 | 头 | 盘 | 盆 | 房 | 绳 | 虫 |
| a | 3 | 子 | 马 | 揩 | 色 | "北" | 袄 | 口 | 板 | 本 | 挡 | 等 | 种 |
| a | 4 | 事 | 把 | 个 | 盖 | 倍 | 泡 | 豆 | 半 | 份 | 当 | 缝 | 种 |
| i | 1 | 鸡 | 家 | 街 |  |  | 腰 | 揪 | 尖 | 今 | 腔 | 星 | 兄 |
| i | 2 | 席 | 匣 | 鞋 |  |  | 条 | 球 | 弦 | "琴" | "祥" | 形 | 熊 |
| i | -3 | 几 | 卡 | 姐 | 崖 |  | 鸟 | 绺 | 点 | "引" | "养" | "影" | "迥" |
| i | -4 | 粒 | 下 | "列" |  |  | 叫 | 救 | 线 | 印 | "样" | "应" | "用" |
| i | 3 | 尾 | "雅" | "野" |  |  |  |  |  |  |  |  |  |
| i | 4 | "意" | "硬" | 叶 |  |  |  |  |  |  |  |  |  |
| u | 1 | 插 | 花 | 锅 | 乖 | 灰 |  |  | 官 | 昏 | 光 | 翁 |  |
| u | 2 | 核 | 华 | 活 | 怀 | 回 |  |  | 玩 | 魂 | 黄 |  |  |

Table 5.  Retroflex Finals  (Continued)

5(b)  Examples in Characters*

| Root Ending / Column / Tone | | O | | | -i | | | -u | -n | | -ng | | |
|---|---|---|---|---|---|---|---|---|---|---|---|---|---|
| Row | Tone | 1 | 2 | 3 | 4 | 5 | 6 | 7 | 8 | 9 | 10 | 11 | 12 |
| u | -3 | 鼓 | 瓜 | 果 | 柺 | 鬼 | | | 叟 | 滾 | "廣" | | |
| u | -4 | 樹 | | 畫 "碩" | 塊 | 桂 | | | 串 | 棍 | 悞 | | |
| u | 3 | "五" | 包 | "我" | "咼" "外" | "委" | | | 碗 "穩" | "門" | "往" | "淌" | |
| u | 4 | "霧" | 襪 | 臥 | | 味 | | | 腕 | "望" | | 纏 | |
| iu | 1 | 鬚 | 靴 | | | | | | 圈 | "勛" | | | |
| iu | 2 | 橘 | 學 | | | | | | 園 | 雲 | | | |
| iu | -3 | "許" | 雪 | | | | | | 卷 "絹" | "窘" | | | |
| iu | -4 | 趣 | "要" | | | | | | 絹 "訓" | | | | |
| iu | 3 | 雨 | 月 | | | | | | 遂 "允" | | | | |
| iu | 4 | 玉 | | | | | | | 院 "韵" | | | | |

*The status of the characters, whether free or bound when suffixed, can be found in the Conc Dict. Characters not found there are rare characters.  Characters in quotes, when suffixed, are possible familiar forms of proper names.  For simplicity ' 儿 ' has been omitted after each character.

= [ ş ɔ̌ ]. If the root already ends in a retroflex, then no further retroflex suffix is added. The only common root morphemes
ending in -l are 兒 *erl* 'child' B, 耳 *eel* 'ear' B, and 二 *ell* 'two' B,
and none of them takes such a suffix.

A complication, involving differences between different generations today, has to do with the treatment of the midvowels.
Take the roots 果 *guoo* 'fruit' B, 鬼 *goei* 'ghost', and 滾 *goen* 'to
roll'. When -l is suffixed to these and the ending -i and -n are
dropped, as expected, the results are *guool, goel, goel*. The older
generation distinguishes the first from the rest, but not 鬼儿 *goel*
from 滾儿 *goel*. The new generation pronounces 果儿 *goel* also,
thus making all three alike. When no medial *u* is involved, the
corresponding differences of treatment are found in, say, 歌儿
*ge'l* (with a longer and back vowel) 'song', as against 根儿 (*gen*
+ -l →) *gel* (with a shorter and central vowel) 'root', both of
which the new generation pronounce as *gel*. A further complication is that of the effect of the 3rd and 4th Tones vs. the 1st and
2nd Tones in the finals *ie* and *iue*. It is true in general that there
is some phonetic difference between the vowels in these two sets
of tones: higher vowels in the 1st and 2nd Tones and slightly
lower vowels in the other tones. In the case of the final *i, iu, in,
iun*, which all become *iel* or *iuel* with the retroflex suffix, they
contrast with the retroflexed form derived from *ie* and *iue* in the
1st and 2nd Tones, but not in the 3rd or 4th Tones.[32] Thus, 小 鸡儿
*sheau-jiel* 'little chicks' ≠ 小 街儿 *sheau-jie'l* 'little street', but
几儿 *jieel* 'what day (of the month)' and 姐儿 *jieel* 'sister, maiden'
are homophonous. Hence the asymmetry in these finals in table
5(a). It should be noted in passing that the distinction, as represented by the 根儿 : 歌儿 *gel : ge'l* contrast and the 鸡儿 : 街儿

*jiel : jie'l* contrast,[33] is disappearing fast, but my daughter
Rulan C. Pian is keeping it up because she has to teach Americans

---

[32] This was the conclusion arrived at, after I had lengthy discussions
with the late Bair Dyijou 白 滌 洲 during the 1920's, as representing the
typical pronunciation of those finals at that time.

[33] For a different treatment of these distinctions, involving vowel clusters,
see Søren Egerod, *The Lungtu Dialect*, Copenhagen, 1956, p. 26.

Chinese and we both agree to include the maximum distinctions, so long as they are still alive with some speakers.

*1.3.9 Marginal Phonemes.* In most languages there are a few phonemes that carry a very light burden, or phonological load. A well-known example is the contrast between / ө / and / ә / in English. As there are very few minimal pairs involving this contrast, such as 'thigh' and 'thy', there is little chance of confusion if written alike, as indeed they are, with the digraph *th*. This pair has been treated as distinct by all who analyze English phonemes, for two reasons. One is that the number of morphemes in which they occur is very large and their textual occurrence is extensive. Secondly, the feature that distinguishes them is that of voiced vs. voiceless, a feature that pairs off many other consonants, such as /s/:/z/, /p/:/b/, into different phonemes; in other words, the distinction fits systematically into the pattern of English phonology. On the other hand, if in a language a phoneme has a very light phonological load and does not fit well into the general phonemic pattern, then it forms what may be called a marginal phoneme. In Mandarin the following are the chief important marginal phonemes:[34]

(1) The Midvowel or Vowels. In the Yangtze Valley dialects, down to and including that of Nanking, there are two midvowel phonemes /o/ and /e/. For example, 阁合蛾莫 , etc., belong to the /o/-type and 格核額墨 , etc., belong to the /e/-type, but in Northern Mandarin both types are pronounced *ger, her, er, m(u)oh*, etc., without distinction, the phonetic difference between *e* and *o* being allophonic and determined by the medial, as can be seen from table 2 (a and b), column 3. There are, however, three marginal cases in which there seem to be more than one midvowel phoneme.

(a) One is the contrast between a long and a short midvowel

---

[34]See also Samuel E. Martin, "Problems of Hierarchy," *BIHP*, 29:209-229 (1958).

[35]Hockett (Peip Phon, 259-260) phonemicizes the short *e* as in *gel* as /eir/, since it has a more central quality than the back vowel *e* in *ge'l*. He also sets up a parallel contrast between /par/ as in 耙ᵣrake' (derived from /-a/) and /pair/ as in 盤ᵣ'tray' (derived from /-an/) or 牌ᵣ'board' (derived

such as that between 歌儿 *ge'l* and 根儿 *gel* or between 街儿 *jie'l* and 今儿 *jiel*,[35] as we have already noted.

(b) Second, there seems to be a marginal phonemic difference between the two qualities of the first *e* in 这是水 *Jeh sh shoei* 'This is water' : in one case with [ ɤ ] in *jeh*, as given in table 3, and alternatively with a more fronted, shorter [ə], as in the final *en*. In other words, the following initial *sh* is treated as if it were an ending to form a syllable with the *e*, thus making it a "checked vowel" instead of an open vowel that requires the back quality of [ ɤ ]. There is a similar difference between the rare *jeh.me*, with open [ ɤ ] for 这 么 'so, thus, this (adv.)' and the more common *jemme*, with checked [ə] (even more commonly *tzemme*). In the case of 那 么 'so, thus, that (adv.)', the open form °*nah.me*[36] does not even exist and it is always *nemme*. If *nah* is used as 'in that case', it has no suffix. The interrogative adverb 怎 么 ? *tzeeme?* 'how?' has only the checked form with [ə]. But the interrogative pronoun 什 么 ? *sherme?* 'what?' has two forms. With checked vowel [ə], where the *m* belongs to both syllables (cf. *m* in English 'summer'), it is the ordinary way of saying 'what?' But with the open vowel [ ɤ ], then it has a sarcastic sense. Thus, 这 是 什 么 ?! *Jeh sh sher-me?!* 'Whatever is this (queer) thing?!' is almost[37] homophonous with 这是蛇吗? *Jeh sh sher .ma?* 'Is this a snake?' Since this verges on matters of voice qualifier and expression, it has to be considered marginal with respect to the phonemic system.

(c) The allophone è [ɛ] is conditioned on the medial *i* or *iu*,

---

from /-air/), the last two being supposed to have a more fronted quality. This analysis makes the /er/ : /eir/ contrast less lonely, but the greatest difficulty is that I have not found much confirmation from native informants. The midvowel contrast, as we have noticed, is already going out with the new generation. The low-vowel contrast proposed to keep the mid-vowels company, if it ever was active, must have been obsolescent in the North by the time I was born.

[36]Except in 那 嘿... *Nah me* ... 'In that case, then ...', where *nah* is a conjunction and *me* is a particle, synonymous with 那 樣 嘿... *nahyanq me* ... 'if it is like that, then ...'.

[37]On a subtle distinction between the two, see sec. 7.11.5.2.

and the allophone *o* [oᴧ] is conditioned on the medial *u*. But as particles and interjections, which often go outside the regular phonemic system, they occur as if they were Row-*a* finals, in a distinct column from column 3, table 3. For examples, see Particle 9 廿 *è* (sec. 8.5.5); Interjections 2-7 廿 È (in various tones), and 14-17, 哦 etc., *o* (in various tones) (sec. 8.6.4). Interjections, of course, often contain marginal phonemes in any language.

(d) Most, though not all, speakers distinguish 油 井 *youjiing* [iu ˧ tɕi ŋ  ˨˩] 'oil well' and 有 井 *yeou-jiing* [iou ˧ tɕi ŋ   ˨˩ ] 'has a well', where *yeou* ˨˩ raised to the 2nd Tone ˧ does not coalesce with 油 *you* ˧ since it retains the usually lower (that is, more open) vowel of the original 3rd Tone. There are several possible ways of treating this, none of which, however, is satisfactory. One is to regard an original 2nd Tone as having a closer main vowel than the 2nd Tone derived from a 3rd, thus: 油 井 /ieu/-*jiing* 'oil well' as against 有 井 /iou/*jiing* 'has a well'. This involves setting up more than one midvowel phoneme, which we have avoided, except for the interjections *e* and *o*, as noted above. Another analysis is to regard the original 2nd Tone as /iu/, either as a vowel cluster, as a descending diphthong *iᵘ*, or an ascending diphthong *ⁱu*. This is unsatisfactory, since 油 *you* rhymes with 楼 *lou* and not with 盧 *lu*, which is unlike English 'you' rhyming with 'true'. However, since Chinese (popular as well as classic) rhymes can pair off 金 *jin* : 針 *jen*, or 京 *jing*: 爭 *jeng*, then by analogy, 流 *liou*/li*ᵘ*/ and 楼 *lo*ᵘ are also a plausible pair. Finally, one can set up a 5th Tone in 有 井 *yeou*[5] *jiing*. For reasons stated below, this is not a satisfactory treatment. We shall, however, have no practical difficulty in distinguishing these forms, as the GR spelling is morphophonemic in this respect: 油 井 *youjiing* : 有 井 *yeou-jiing*. The same remarks apply to similar examples, such as 谁 長 了 ? *Shwei jaangle?* 'Who has grown?': 水 漲 了。 *Shoei jaangle.* 'The water has risen.'

(2) The Low Vowel or Vowels. The low vowel-phoneme *a* has a medium quality in open syllables, a fronted quality before front endings (*-i*, *-n*) and a back quality before back endings (*-u*, *-ng*). But in a pair like 您 不 秉 *Tan bu lai* 'He (honorif.) is not com-

ing' and 他们不来 *Tamen bu lai* 'They are not coming', spoken at conversational speed, the *-n* in *tan* will be assimilated to the following *b* as *-m* and the *men bu* elided as *m bu*, so that both sound like *Tam bu lai*. But in the *tam* from *tan* the vowel is a fronted *a*, while in the *tam* from *ta.men* it is an open and therefore more central or back *a*. To avoid setting up two *a*-phonemes (as one has to in French *moi* vs. *mois*), we can, as in the case of the midvowel problem, make the vowel quality be conditioned on syllabication. In 您*tam* ( ← *tan*) it is one syllable and the *a* is checked. In 他们 *tam* ( ← *ta.men*), it is two syllables *ta.m*, where the *a* has a zero ending and therefore has another allophone. The cost of this analysis is the necessity of setting up a syllabic *m*. However, there is space for it in the upper left corner of table 4 for Syllabic Types, where it is left blank. To keep company with it, there is the 3rd Tone syllabic *mm*, familiar form for 我们 *woomen* '(exclusive) we', as in 我们不要。*Mm buyaw.* 'We don't want it'. (See also sec. 3.1.2.)

(3) The "Fifth Tone". When a 3rd Tone morpheme is followed by a neutral-tone morpheme originally in the 3rd Tone, the first syllable may be in the $(\frac{1}{2})$ 3rd Tone, as before any other neutral tone, or go up to a 2nd, as before any stressed 3rd Tone. On the whole, if the two morphemes are in one word, the result will be in the first pattern, namely ⌐ ꞌ, as in 癢ꞏ *yeang.yeang* 'itches', 姐ꞏ *jiee.jiee* 'older sister', 宝ꞏ *bao.bao* 'baby', 椅子 *yiitz* 'chair', and other nouns with a root in the 3rd Tone with suffix *-tz* ($<$*tzyy*). If the two morphemes form a phrase or a reduplicated verb, as in 咬你 *yeau .nii* 'bites you', 買点儿 *mae .deal* 'buys some', 養ꞏ(儿) *yeang.yeang(l)* 'nurses a little (plants, animals, etc.)', 想ꞏ(儿)*sheang.sheang(l)* 'gives a little thought to', then the first syllable goes up, as a 3rd Tone before another 3rd does, but in this stress pattern it does not usually become quite homophonous with a 2nd Tone, as it retains a little of the glottal stricture of the 3rd Tone dip, and the value is 325: ⌒ rather than a simple 35: ⌐,[38] and it can be regarded as an allophone of the

---

[38]Except when there is contrastive stress, in which case there is, at least with some speakers, a glottal stricture and even a dip in the 2nd Tone, too.

3rd Tone. Apart from committing the so-called Pike's heresy[39] in presupposing grammatical categories before completing the phonology—a difficulty which I believe one can get around by considerations of selection classes and frames—there are two other difficulties. One is that a neutral tone is a neutral tone and would not act as a 3rd Tone to the preceding syllable unless it is slightly stressed, and this would involve an intermediate degree of phonemic stress, which we have avoided setting up. The other difficulty is that some of this pattern involves compounds rather than phrases, as in 打掃 *daa.sao* 'dusts and cleans,—tidies up', 火把 *huoo$_0$baa* 'fire bunch,—a torch'. To take care of such cases, Hockett (Peip Phon, 257) sets up a 5th Tone, distinct from the 3rd or the phonemic 2nd derived from the 3rd. Martin (*op. cit.* 215-216) recognizes Hockett's 5th Tone, but observes rightly its marginal morphophonemic nature. Two cases, however, can be explained away. In the word 小姐 *shyau.jiee* 'little miss,—miss (as term of address)' it is a real 2nd Tone *shyau* ㄋ, though it has the usual phonemically distinct allomorph *sheau*. In the case of 麻煩 *ma.farn* 'troublesome' cited by Hockett, where the 5th Tone *ma* is not followed by an original 3rd Tone, the vocal constriction is a voice quality associated with the feeling of annoyance when the word is spoken and is therefore not a part of the phonemics. But there still remains the problem of the raised 3rd Tone in the other cases, and, as I have done in the *Conc Dict*, the ambiguity is only resolved by giving the actual tone graphs. So in this tone of uncertainty we shall end the discussion of phonology, perhaps to illustrate the often unneat nature of the subject matter of Chinese grammar and all grammars.

---

[39]Kenneth S. Pike, "Grammatical Prerequisites to Phonemic Analysis", *Word*, 3:155-172 (1947), and "More on Grammatical Prerequisites", *Word*, 8:106-121 (1952).

**CHAPTER 2**
**THE SENTENCE**

## 2.1. General Observations

*2.1.1. The Sentence as a Unit.* The sentence is the largest language unit that is important for grammatical analysis. A sentence is often defined as a segment of speech bounded at both ends by pauses. Since in actual speech there may be interruptions or other external factors which will leave only a fraction of a sentence uttered between periods of silence, the pauses should be understood as deliberate pauses made by the speaker and not simply as physical silence.

A sentence has a start and an end. If it has only one word, the starting word and the end word will be the same, as: 好! *Hao!* 'All right!' If it has only one sound, the starting sound and the end sound will be the same, as: せ!*É!* [ ε ㄱ ], interjection of sudden surprised interest. In most cases, a sentence contains more than one word and therefore different starting and ending words or sounds.

A sentence is a free form, since it is bounded by pauses at both ends. If what could be a sentence is joined to another form without pause, then it ceases to be a sentence and the enlarged form may form a sentence. Thus, 我不知道. *Woo bu jydaw.* 'I don't know.' is a sentence, but *Woo bu jydaw le.* 'I don't know any more.' is an enlarged sentence of which *Woo bu jydaw* forms only a part. Again:他 不 耒. 我 不 去. *Ta bu lai. Woo bu chiuh.* 'He is not coming. I am not going.' are separate sentences. But if the pause between *lai* and *woo* is omitted, then the whole thing is one sentence meaning 'If he doesn't come, I won't go'.

*2.1.2. Sentence Identity.* We shall find it convenient to use the term "utterance" for an instance of the occurrence of a sentence,[1] so that the same sentence can occur in different utterances. In the language of communication theory, a sentence is a "type", while an utterance is a "token" of the type.

In working with written texts, it is common practice to treat as "the same sentence" whatever is written alike. But since most systems of writing omit indication of significant prosodic elements, one should always remember that the same sequence of words may not represent the same sentence. For example: 他 走 不 好. (1) *Ta tzoou* (,) *bu hao.* 'That he goes is not good, —he had better not go.': (2) *Ta tzoou.bu-hao.* 'He cannot walk well.' Here, the full tone on *bu* (*buh*) and the optional pause between *Ta tzoou* and *bu hao* in sentence (1) make it a different sentence from sentence (2), in which *tzoou.bu-hao* is one word, with no possibility of any break within.

When the segmental phonemes (including tones) and the prosodic elements are all specified, they usually determine only one sentence. Exceptionally, however, two or more different sentences can still have exactly the same phonemic make up and thus are homophonous sentences. This happens, of course, when there is a word in the sentence which is homophonous with another which can fill the same position in the sentence. Sometimes no homophonous words are involved, but a different structuring of the parts, not necessarily reflected in the prosodic elements, gives rise to different sentences. For example: 我 要 切糕。 *Woo yaw chie-gau.* (1) 'I want to cut cake.' (2) 'I want cut cake (a special kind of cake).'

*2.1.3. Sentence Values.* In connected discourse, most sentences are in the form of (1) declarative sentences, while sentences in the form of (2) commands, (3) questions, (4) vocative expressions, and (5) exclamations are much less frequent. In two-way conversation or speech interposed with action or events, on the other hand, forms (2) to (5) are much more common than in connected discourse. Each of these five forms of sentences has what we may call sentence values.

(1) A declarative sentence is true or false and thus has truth value.

---

[1]This is not the usage among all writers, some of whom use the term "utterance" for a unit which is sometimes larger than a sentence.

(2) A command (in the broad sense, to include request, plea, suggestion, and so on) is either complied with or refused and has compliance value. Thus, 送他这三本书！ *Sonq ta jeh san-been shu!* 'Send him these three books!' and *Bae jeh san-been shu sonq geei ta!* 'Send these three books to him!' have the same compliance value, but *Sonq ta san-been shu* 'Send him (any) three books' does not have the same compliance value as the first two commands, since it is not satisfied by quite the same action.

(3) A question has information value. Two questions which will be satisfied by the same information have the same information value. Thus the sentences (1) *Nii jii-suey?* 'How old are you?' and (2) *Nii shyrjii-suey?* 'How umpteen years old are you?' do not have the same information value, since the ranges of information for them are different. Pragmatically, a question may be regarded as a species of command and can usually be so reworded as such formally, such as: 告送我 ... *Gaw.sonq woo ...* 'Tell me, ... '.

(4) A vocative expression has attention value: 妈！ *Mha!* 'Ma!' 各位！ *Gehwey!* 'Ladies and gentlemen!' In Chinese 'Good morning' or 'How do you do?' takes the form of a vocative, using whatever is the proper term of direct address.

(5) An exclamation has expressive value. Two exclamations giving the same degree and kind of affective reaction in both speaker and hearer have the same expressive value. This is usually hard to determine, and such values can only be described in a general way, though in a limited number of cases the conditions of occurrence can be stated (see list of interjections, sec. 8.6.4).

*2.1.4. Sentence and the Use of a Sentence.* Under types of discourse (sec. 1.2.3), we noted that much of language is spoken not only in a linguistic context, but also in nonlinguistic contexts. A major part of language contains morphemes and longer forms with variable references, which will make a difference in the sentence values. Pronouns, relative time and place words, and even inflected forms, such as 'is' vs. 'was', will yield different sentence values in which they occur, according to the values of the variables. For example, the sentence 'The King of France is wise.' spoken by a Frenchman living during the reign of Louis XIV and the same sentence spoken by a Frenchman during the reign of

Louis XV will have different truth values.[2] Thus the sentence value is not so much tied up with a sentence as a type, but rather with its use. This does not, however, limit sentence values to individual utterances, or tokens, since many sentences do not contain variables which affect their values, such as the declarative sentence: 'Twice two is four.' or the command: 'Go to China!'

## 2.2.  Minor Sentences

Sentences may be classified, from the point of view of structure, into full and minor sentences. A full sentence consists of two parts, a subject and a predicate, and is the commonest type in connected discourse. It is in this sense the favorite sentence type in Chinese, as it is in many other languages. A minor sentence is not in the subject-predicate form. It occurs more frequently in two-way conversation and in speech interposed or accompanied by action than it does in connected discourse. The full sentence is more likely to be used in declarative sentences and questions, while a minor sentence is more likely to be used for commands, vocatives and responses, and exclamations. The correlation is, however, not absolute and all the five pragmatic values of sentences can be of either the full or the minor type. Thus, 你别来! *Nii bye lai!* 'Don't you come!' is a full-sentence command, while 下雨了。*Shiah-yeu le.* 'It is raining.' is a minor declarative sentence.

Most minor sentences are either verbal expressions or nominal expressions. Interjections, though forming only a small proportion of minor sentences, are, however, minor sentences par excellence.

*2.2.1. Verbal Expressions as Declarative Sentences.* A declarative sentence may be made by a verbal expression, that is, a verb or a verbal phrase, as 对.*Duey.* 'Correct.' 行.*Shyng.* 'Okay.' 有. *Yeou.* 'There is.' 摔! *Shuai!* '(Mind you, you will) fall down!' 燙! *Tanq!* '(It's) hot!' 有人.*Yeou ren.* 'There are people.' or

---

[2]The example, with slight modification, was given to me by Tsu-Lin Mei, who also called my attention to P. F. Strawson's distinction between the sentence and the use of a sentence in "On Referring", *Mind*, 59:320-344 (1950).

'There is someone.', used, for example, as a sign over a rest room. 讨厭! *Taoyann!* 'Invites loathing,—what a nuisance!' 气人！ *Chih-ren!* 'Angers one,—how provoking!' 要坏! *Yaw huay!* 'Will (go) bad!', said when an unavoidable accident is about to happen. 着火了！ *Jaur-huoo le!* 'Catches fire,—there is a fire!' 从来没听見过这种事。 *Tsornglai mei ting.jiann- .guoh jeh.tzoong shyh.* 'Never heard of such a thing.' 想起来了. *Sheang.chii.lai le.* '(I have) just thought,—it has just occurred to me,—by the way.' 可以查ㄓ電话簿子. *Keeyii char.char diannhuah-buhtz.* '(One) can consult the telephone book.'

Although it is possible to supply subjects to such verbal expressions, as seen in some of the translations, they should be regarded as sufficient by themselves, because (a) there is not always one specific form of a subject that can be supplied, and (b) sometimes no subject can be supplied. Take, for example, the sentence *Duey* 'Correct'. It is possible sometimes to treat it as abbreviated from 你说的对。 *Nii shuo de duey.* 'What you say is correct.', but there is no reason to deny that it could also be an abbreviation of 你说的话对。 *Nii shuo.de huah duey.* 'The words you said were right.' or *Nii shuo .de neyg duey.* 'The one you mentioned was right.' and there are various other hypothetical possibilities which never occurred to the speaker when he said *Duey*. Moreover, the statement may not even be applied to any linguistic form in the first place. For instance, if a pupil of music or painting does something following the instruction of his teacher, and the latter says *Duey*, it would be a case of speech interposed with non-speech, which, as we have seen, is one of the most productive conditions for the occurrence of minor sentences.

*2.2.2. Verbal Expressions as Commands.* Like commands in many other languages, a command in Chinese usually does not contain the actor word, and thus takes the form of a minor sentence.[3] Examples are: 来！ *Lai!* 'Come!' 走吧！ *Tzoou ba!* 'Let's go!' 请坐！ *Chiing tzuoh!* 'Please sit,—please have a seat!' 干杯！ *Gan-bei!* '(Let's) dry the cups,—bottoms up!' 别打岔！ *Bye daa-chah!* 'Don't interrupt!' 请有事！ *Chiing yeou-shyh!*

---

[3]Although Bloomfield (*Lg,* 172) regards commands as full sentences.

'Please have business,—please don't bother to stand up!' (said at the end of a business interview: Central Yangtze dialect). As noted above, a command may sometimes include the subject, and such a form, though less frequent than the minor sentence form, is relatively more frequent than in English. It goes without saying that for stylistic and other reasons commands may be implied by sentences in declarative form, whether as a full or a minor sentence, as: 不准抽烟! *Bu joen chou ian!* 'Don't permit smoking,—no smoking permitted!' 招贴即撕。 *Jau tie jih sy.* L 'Bills posted will be torn off at once, —post no bills'.

2.2.3. *Verbal Expressions in Questions and Answers.* Verbal expressions as questions are relatively less common than as answers. Examples of questions are: 怎么了? *Tzeem le?* 'How now,—what's the matter?' 为什么呐? *Wey sherm ne?* 'For what, then,—then why?' 出了什么事了? *Chule sherm shyh le.* 'Happened what matter,—what has happened?' 行不行? *Shyng.bu.shyng?* 'Will it do?' 有人没有? *Yeou-ren .mei.yeou?* 'Is there anybody?' In general, any statement in the form of a verbal expression becomes a question by changing a part of it into an interrogative word X or by putting the verb into the V-not-V form of a question. Conversely, when a question is asked in such a minor-sentence form, the answer will, of course, also be in the same form when a value is substituted for the unknown X, or when a choice is made between V and not-V. For example, Qu: 是谁啊? *Sh sheir a?* 'Who is it?' Ans: 是我。 *Sh woo.* 'It's me.' Qu: 来不来? *Lai bu lai?* 'Are you coming?' Ans: 来。 *Lai.* 'Yes.'

When, however, a question is asked in the form of a full sentence, the answer may be either a full sentence or a minor sentence. For example, Qu: 你认得那个人吗? *Nii renn.de neyg ren ma?* 'Do you know that man?' Ans: 认得。 *Renn.de.* '(I) do.' Qu: 你干麻不出去? *Nii gannma bu chu.chiuh?* 'Why don't you go out?' Ans: 因为太冷。 *Inwey tay leeng.* 'Because it's too cold.'

Note that when an answer is a minor sentence, it is preferably in the form of a predicate, and if the question has an interrogative word X in the subject, the verb is preferably given in the answer anyway. For example, Qu: 谁 在 屋 裡 ? *Sheir tzay u.lii?* 'Who is in the room?' Ans: 老 王 在 屋 裡。 *Lao Wang tzay u.lii.* 'Wang is in the room.' with the whole predicate, or, with a changed form of the predicate, Ans: 是 老 王。 *Sh Lao Wang.* 'It's Wang.' Qu: 哪儿 的 气 候 最 好? *Naal de chih.how tzuey hao?* 'The climate of where is best?' Ans: 昆 明 的 气候 最 好。 *Kuenming de chih.how tzuey hao.* 'The climate of Kunming is best.', or *Jell tzuey hao.* 'Here is best (as to climate).' If the question has an interrogative X in the predicate other than the main verb, the verb is preferably given anyway. For example, Qu: 他 要 吃什么 ? *Ta yaw chy sherme?* 'What does he want to eat?' Ans: 要 吃 肉。 *Yaw chy row.* 'Wants to eat meat.', or at least 吃肉。 *Chy row.* 'Eat meat.' Qu: 你 叫 什么 呐 ? *Nii jiaw sherm ne?* 'What are you calling?' Ans: 我 叫 茶 房。 *Woo jiaw char.farng.* 'I am calling the waiter.' Qu: 他 几 时来 ? *Ta jii-.shyr lai?* 'When is he coming?' Ans: 初 三 来。 *Chusan lai.* '(He) is coming on the third.' Qu: 你 最 喜 欢 跟 谁 下 棋 ? *Nii tzuey shii.huan gen sheir shiah-chyi?* 'Whom do you like best to play chess with?' Ans: *Tzuey shii.huan gen nii shiah.* '(I) like most to play with you.'

It is only in special cases, such as answers to riddles and intentionally blunt or pert answers, that the minimum substitute for the interrogative is given without a full predicate. For example, Qu: 什 么 最 便 宜 ? *Sherm tzuey pyan.yi?* 'What is most cheap?' Ans: 水。 *Shoei.* 'Water.' Qu: 你 什么 时候儿 回 家 ? *Nii sherm shyr.howl hwei-jia?* 'When do you go home?' Ans: 三 点 钟。 *San-dean jong.* 'Three o'clock.' Qu: 你 猜 我们 貓 爱 吃 什 么 ? *Nii tsai woom mhau ay chy sherme?* 'Guess what our cat loves to eat?' Ans: 香 瓜儿。 *Shianggual.* 'Musk-melon.' In all these examples it would be more usual to answer with the fulll predicate, or at least a verbal predicate.

*2.2.4. Nominal Expressions as Predicates.* In speaking about things present to the speaker, the subject and verb *Jeh sh* 'This is' or *Nah sh* 'That is' is often not used and the predicative nominal expression can be used as a minor sentence. Thus, when a child sees an object gliding along in the sky, he may say: 飛 机。

*Feiji.* '(It's) an airplane.', but when he sees it fla⁊ its wings, he says.' 不是，是个鸟儿。 *Bush, sh g neaul.* 'No, (it) is a bird.', with a full verbal predicate. In introducing a person, one either (1) begins with subject and verb: *Jeh sh* 'This is' or *Jeh-wey sh* 'This gentleman (or lady) is' or (2) merely mentions the proper term of address: 李先生。 *Lii .Shian.sheng.* 'Mr. Lii.' The latter form (minus title, of course) is always used when introducing oneself, rather than saying *Woo sh* 'I am', as: 張天才。 *Jang Tian-.tsair.* '(My name is) Jang Tiantsair.' Since, however, monosyllabic surnames are not free words, it will not be possible to say *Jang* alone and one will say 姓張 *Shinq Jang* or *Woo shinq Jang* (where *shinq* 'have the name of' is a transitive verb), if one does not bother to give one's full name.

A slightly different type of nominal minor sentence is used, not for contrasting one kind of predicate with another, but for calling attention to the existence of something. For example, water carriers warning pedestrians call out: 水！ *Shoei!* '(Look out for) water!' 火車！ *Huooche!* 'Train (coming)!' Nominal sentences of this type need not be exclamatory. Thus, announced headings like: 问。*Wenn.* 'Question.', 答。*Dar.* 'Answer.', and 第一条。*Dih'i Tyau.* 'Article one.', where the English translations are usually spoken with a falling intonation, are nominal sentences, calling attention to the existence of things.

2.2.5. *Nominal Predicate Sentences with Modifiers.* Like verbal-predicate sentences containing modifiers, such as 快下雨了。 *Kuay shiah-yeu le.* 'It will rain soon.', nominal-predicate sentences for calling attention to things may also contain modifiers. Thus, one can warn a child playing with a bottle and say: 毒药！ *Dwu-yaw!* 'Poisonous chemical,—poison!' This type of minor sentence is extremely common in poetry, where the writer often wishes only to set the scene without necessarily saying explicitly how things are or what is going on. For example, in the two lines:

啼莺舞燕，   *Tyi-ing wuu-yann,* 'Crying orioles, dancing swallows,

小桥流   *Sheau-chyau liou-*   Little bridge, flowing water,
　水飞红。   *shoei fei-horng.*   flying reds.'

there are five nominal sentences. In each of them the words could be reversed and made into full sentences: *Ing tyi.* 'Orioles cry.', and so on, but they would not be the same sentences and the resulting language would then be pedestrian rather then dancing. This form of minor sentence is also extremely common for chapter headings in novels.

*2.2.6. Labels.* Written labels, though not language proper, are like minor sentences in nominal predicative form so far as communicative function is concerned, as if to say: 'This is so and so'. They include (1) titles of books, plays, and so on: 红楼夢 *Horng lou Menq* 'Red-Chamber Dream' (but 火烧红蓮寺 *Huoo Shau Hornglian Syh* 'Fire Burns Red-Lotus Temple', cf. 'Mr. Smith Goes to Washington'); (2) street signs: 大街 *Dah Jie* 'Main Street', 单行路 *Danshiangluh* 'One Way Street', 大学之道 *Dahshyue jy Daw* 'The Way to Great Learning,—University Avenue' (sign over the entrance road to Kwangsi University); (3) signs at stations, on buildings, stores, etc.: 蘇州 *Sujou* 'Soochow', 文庙 *Wen Miaw* 'Temple of Letters,—Confucian Temple', 當 *Danq* 'Pawn', 酱 *Jianq* 'Sauce,—Pickles', the last two, especially *Jianq*, often occupying a whole wall measuring 20 feet wide by 30 feet high. Sometimes there is a slight difference between the usual label and the usual way a place is called. For example a theater is called 戲園 *shihyuan*, lit. 'play-garden,' but the usual sign over a theater is such-and-such 戲院 *shihyuann*, lit. 'play-house.' Note that the title of the play *Huoo Shau Hornglian Syh*, even though in subject-predicate form, is not quite a full sentence, but an S-P clause, because, other things being equal, it is usually spoken faster than a sentence, and because an actual full sentence would have an aspect particle, for example, *Huoo shaule Hornglian Syh le.* 'Fire has burned down the Red Lotus Temple.' It goes without saying that the English translation (at least before the ",—" sign) given here, as elsewhere in the book, is given in order to reflect as closely as possible the structural point under discussion and is often not the most idiomatic equivalent. For example, the written sign: 此路不通 *Tsyy Luh Bu Tong L* 'This road does not go through' is a full sentence, but (1) the English equivalent 'No Thoroughfare' is a nominal predicate sentence with modified, (2) the American equivalent 'Not a Through Street' is a quasi-verbal expression, while (3) the Chinese equivalent, as such a street is actually called 死胡同儿 *syy-hwutonql* 'deadend alley', is also a nominal predicate sentence with modifier.

2.2.7. *Commands in the Form of Things Desired.* Somewhat different from nominal expressions merely specifying something with an implied *Sh ...* or calling attention to the existence of something with an implied *Yeou ...* , a nominal expression is also used to imply *Woo yaw* 'I want', *Na.lai* 'Bring here', and so on. Thus, a street vendor may announce the existence of: 豆腐脑儿! *Dow.fu naol!* 'Beancurd junket!' (a specially tender form of beancurd, sold on the streets hot and ready to serve), and a buyer will also call: *Dow.fu naol!* Similarly, one calls 茶! *Char!* 'Tea!' 車子! *Chetz!* 'Cab!' 兩張大人，一張小孩儿。 *Leang-jang dah.ren, i-jang sheauharl.* '(Tickets for) two adults and one child.' (spoken at the ticket window).

2.2.8. *Vocative Expressions.* Vocative expressions are nominal expressions used to get the listener's attention before or without turning his attention to the nature or existence of anything. Examples are: 媽! *Mha!* 'Ma!' 大哥! *Dah Ge!* 'Big Brother!' 老王啊! *Lao Wang a!* 'Wang!' 茶房! *Char.farng!* 'Waiter!' 伙计! *Huoo.jih!* 'Waiter!' 先生! *Shian.sheng!* 'Sir!' 卖豆腐脑儿的! *May dow.funaol de!* '(You) who are selling beancurd junket!' 修洋傘的! *Shiou yangsaan de!* '(You) who repair umbrellas!'

A formal difference between vocative and other kinds of nominal expressions is that a vocative has reduced pitch range (including zero) while the other kinds have normal or contrastive (widened) range. Thus, in a full sentence: 这是我二姐 *Jeh sh woo Ell Jiee* 'This is my Second Sister', *Ell* has a full falling 4th Tone and *Jiee* a full dipping-rising 3rd Tone. In a vocative form, on the other hand, *Ell Jiee!* has a greatly narrowed range of pitch; sometimes practically zero, differing from an ordinary neutral tone *.Ell.Jiee* only in not being shortened or weakened. Vocatives often have a trailing falling intonation, which is really a final particle (P 28, sec. 8.5.5), just like the particle *a*, after terms of direct address. When, however, a name is mentioned with great contrastive stress, as when one is surprised to find someone when least expected, then there will be an exaggerated pitch range, as: *Yee! Ell Jiee!* 'Why, *if it isn't Ell Jiee!*', since it is no longer a vocative, but a predicate.

*2.2.9. Interjections.* Interjections are minor sentences par excellence. They are like vocatives in being stressed and yet atonal, but unlike them, they do not as a rule enter into constructions in other contexts. For details on interjections, see chapter 8.

## 2.3 Structure of the Full Sentence

*2.3.1. Formal Features of the Full Sentence.* The full sentence has two ICs: a subject and a predicate, separated from each other by a pause, a potential pause, or one of the four pause particles: *a* ($\sim ia$), *ne*, *me*, and *ba*. Thus, the sentence: 我 有 水。*Woo yeou-shoei.* 'I have water.' may be spoken in various ways as follows:

(1) With no pause      *Woo yeou-shoei.* ⌐ ⌐ ⌐ ( ← ⌐ ⌐ ⌐ [4])

(2) With a slight pause  $\frac{1}{2}$ *Woo yeou-shoei.* ⌐ ⌐ ⌐

(3) With pause          *Woo, yeou-shoei.*   ⌐,⌐ ⌐

(4) With particle (a)    *Woo ia, yeou-shoei.*

        (b)    *Woo ne, yeou-shoei.*

        (c)    *Woo me* — , *yeou-shoei.*

        (d)    *Woo ba, yeou-shoei.*

where the pause particles may be translated as 'as for (me, I) ...'.[5] The difference between no pause and a potential pause can be seen by comparing a full sentence construction with a compound word of otherwise identical tone and stress pattern. Take 北九 水 *Beei Jeoushoei* 'North Nine Waters', a resort near Tsingtao. It is just like form 1 for the sentence *Woo yeou-shoei*, but since it has no potential pause, this is the only form in which the name is

---

[4]See sec. 1.3.4 (2).

[5]In example 4d, a noun subject, say 水果 *shoeiguoo* 'fruit' would go more naturally with the particle *ba* than would a pronoun like *woo*.

spoken, and neither form 2 nor 3, not to mention 4, is available for the name *Beei Jeoushoie.* Again, take the sentence: 他 跑 的 快. *Ta pao de kuay.* 'The way (speed, manner, and so on) he runs is fast,—he runs fast.' is completely homophonous with 他 跑 得 快. *Ta pao.de kuay.* 'He can run fast.' but while the latter admits of a pause only after *Ta,* the former admits of a pause or a pause particle also after *pao de* as a subject before the predicate *kuay.*

The importance of the (potential) pause between subject and predicate is reflected in the Chinese usage with regard to punctuation. It is true that most of the older books were not punctuated, but of the minority of books that were, it was the universal practice to punctuate after a subject that was three or four syllables long, sometimes even after one- or two-syllable subjects. For example, 大 学 之 道. 在 明 明 德。 *Dah-shyue jy daw* (punctuation) *tzay ming ming-der* (punctuation). 'The way of the great learning (*subject*) lies in illuminating the illustrious virtues (*predicate*).'

Contrasted with the Chinese usage, a subject and verb in a sentence in written English are never separated by punctuation.[6] Too much, however, should not be inferred from features of the writing system to the language itself. The absence of punctuation in most Chinese books does not of course prove that most Chinese authors don't pause for breath when writing their books. While a German does not pause at commas before restrictive relative clauses, an English speaker does pause or use a further-referring intonation after a long subject. In fact the conception of potential pause between subject and predicate is implied in the way homophonous sentences can be distinguished in the case of: 'The sun's rays meet.' and 'The sons raise meat.'[7]

---

[6]For an excellent example of this usage, note the use and especially non-use of punctuation in the following: "An efficient translating machine that can operate whenever required, can continue when its human partner is fatigued, can instruct its partner without the wearisome labor of consulting dictionaries and grammars, and can retire quietly into the background when the human partner desires to exercise his powers unaided [no punctuation!] qualifies in considerable measure as a good companion." R. H. Richens, "Programming for Mechanical Translation," *MT*, 3:20 (July, 1956).

[7]Kenneth S. Pike, "Taxemes and Immediate Constituents," *Language*, 19:78 (1943).

*2.3.2. Inverted Sentences.* Although the normal order of the ICs of a sentence is that of subject-predicate, it can be reversed in exceptional cases. This happens when, after a minor sentence has been spoken, a subject is supplied as an afterthought. For example, 進來吧,你! *Jinn.lai ba, .nii!* 'Come in, you!' 要睡了,我。*Yaw shuey le, .woo.* 'Want to sleep, I (do).' 可笑極了,这个人! *Keeshiaw-jyile, .jeyg .ren!* 'Awfully funny, this man!'[8] That the phrase after the pause is not the predicate can be seen from the fact that a predicate is always fully stressed, while the afterthought phrases in the examples above are always in the neutral tone, often said in a hurried tempo, as afterthought additions are likely to be. Another way to tell an inverted sentence is that it can be changed back into the straight order, with the subject repeated in the neutral tone as a redundant reminder. Thus the preceding examples can be changed, without affecting any of the sentence values, into: *Nii jinn.lai ba, .nii! Woo yaw shuey le, .woo. Jeyg ren keeshiaw-jyile, jyg .ren!* Once I heard one of my daughters say: 黑貓吃,黑貓。*Hei-mhau chy, .hei.mhau.* 'The black cat eats (the food given it), the black cat (does).', and she refused to find it funny when her sister repeated intentionally *Hei-mhau chy hei-mhau.* 'The black cat eats the black cat!' since that wasn't what she had said.

On inverted objects, see section 5.4.7.2. On inverted subjects in a different sense, see section 8.1.2.2(4).

# 2.4  The Grammatical Meaning
## of Subject and Predicate

2.4.1. Subject and Predicate as Topic and Comment.[9] The grammatical meaning of subject and predicate in a Chinese sentence is topic and comment, rather than actor and action. Actor and action can apply as a particular case of topic and comment,

---

[8]Cf. the L examples in 君子哉若人!尚德哉若人! *Jiuntzyy tzai ruoh ren! Shanq der tzai ruoh ren!* 'How princely, that man! How virtue-minded, that man!' *The Analects*, XIV, 6 憲问.

[9]Note that we are using the terms "topic" and "comment" as semantic terms and not as grammatical terms as used by many writers in discussing Chinese grammar.

as in: 狗咬人. *Goou yeau ren.* 'Dog bites man.' and the percentage of applicability of the actor-action meaning to sentences in many languages is so high as to make it a good enough semantic characterization of the full sentence for such languages. When such subject-predicate relation is called "grammatical action", so as to include predicates of the types 'is ...-ed by ...', 'suffers ...-ing', 'is a ...', then it is possible to save 'actor-action' as the grammatical meaning of the subject-predicate form. But in Chinese, the proportion of applicability of the actor-action meanings, even after making such adjustments as illustrated above, is still very low, perhaps not much higher than 50 per cent, and the wider conception of topic and comment is much more appropriate. The subject is literally the subject matter to talk about, and the predicate is what the speaker comments on when a subject is presented to be talked about. Thus what is expressed by the subject need not be the performer of the action in an action verb; it need not be equatable to what comes after equational verbs like *sh* 'is'; nor need it have the quality named in a predicative adjective. It may do all these, but it need not do so, so long as there is some general relationship of topic and comment between subject and predicate. For example, in 这件事早荙表了. *Jeh-jiann shyh tzao fabeaule.* 'This matter has long been published.', we are translating *fabeau* by the passive verb form 'has been published', but in the Chinese there is no marker for received action (被 *bey* 'by', '-ed' would not be appropriate here), and a closer structural translation would be: '(As for) this matter, (one) has long published (it).' Again in: 这瓜吃着很甜. *Jeh gua chyj heen tyan.* 'This melon eating very sweet,—tastes very sweet.', *chyj* 'eating' seems to be an active verb used passively, but a nearer rendering of the structure of the sentence is: 'This melon, (when one is) eating (it), is very sweet.' All such renderings in English, however, are limited by the exigencies of English grammar requiring a clear actor-action relation, at least in the grammatical sense, thus entailing a number of parenthetical devices which never were in the Chinese, which simply said: 'This matter has long ago published.' 'This melon eating very sweet.'

Sometimes, ellipsis results in a looseness of subject-predicate relation which would be ungrammatical in another language. A very common form consists of the use of a substantive when its possessive followed by another substantive would be the fuller form, as: 他是个日本女人. *Ta sh g Ryhbeen neu.ren.* 'He is a Japanese woman.', when the speaker meant 他的用人是… *Tade yonq.ren sh … .* 'His servant is … .' 他是一个美國丈夫. *Ta sh ig Meei.gwo janq.fu.* 'She is (a case of being married to) an American husband.' 你(的鞋)也破了. *Nii (de shye) yee poh le.* 'You(r shoes) are also worn through.' 我(的肉丸子)掉得你勺儿裡了. *Woo (de rowwantz) diaw de nii shaurl.lii le.* 'I have,——my meatball has fallen into your spoon.' 我(的鉛筆)比你(的)尖. *Woo(de chianbii) bii nii(de) jian.* 'I am (my pencil is) sharper than you(rs).' 你(的小松樹)要死了找我. *Nii(de sheau songshuh) yaw syyle jao woo.* 'If you(r little pine tree) should die, look me up.' 这劏煤的人(的口吻)不是工人的口吻. *Jeh chaan-mei de ren(de koouwoen) bush gongren de koouwoen.* '(The language of) this coal stoker is not the language of a workman.' All except the last example were recorded from actual speech. A purist, especially one who knows some Occidental language, is likely to correct his children or students when he hears such sentences, but goes on using them when not listening to himself—as who does?

There are times, however, when the relation between subject and predicate is so general that there is no specific word or words that can be considered omitted or understood. Thus in: 人家是丰年. *Ren.jia sh fengnian.* 'Those people are a bumper year,—(as for) those people (who are living comfortably, they) have had a bumper year.', any filling out like: *Ren.jia sh g fengnian de ren-jial* or: *Ren.jia de nian sh fengnian* would sound artificial, and since the forms filled out are not uniquely determined, they cannot be considered as "understood".

The topical meaning of the subject is very often met with in poetry. Thus, Li Po (Lii Bor)'s well known line: 雲想衣裳花想容. *Yun sheang ishang hua sheang rong.* is usually translated as 'Clouds remind one of her garments and flowers remind one of her face.', but the word *sheang* 'thinks' is never used anywhere else in a causative sense. While one should grant that a literary translation may aptly use the word 'remind', it should be remembered that the subjects *yun* and *hua* only set the scene and the actor is simply shifted somewhere else: 'Looking at the clouds, one thinks, and so on.' Again, in the couplet 琴臨秋水弹明月；酒近 东山酌白雲 *Chyn lin chioushoei tarn mingyueh; jeou jinn dongshan jwo bair-yun* 'The lute, over the autumn waters, (one?) plays (is played?) (to? under?) the bright moon; wine, near the eastern mountains, (one?) sips (is sipped?) (to? under?) the white clouds,' where the relations expressed by the words supplied in the translation are not specifically understood in the original.

*2.4.2 Direction of Action in Predicates.* A corollary to the topic-comment nature of predication is that the direction of action in an action verb in the predicate need not go outward from subject to object. One can ask: 酒喝不喝？ *Jeou he bu he?* '(As for) wine, does it (do you) drink?' and answer: 酒不喝，烟抽. *Jeou bu he, ian chou.* 'Wine (I) don't drink, (but) tobacco (I) smoke.' Even in a N-V-N' sequence, such as 狗咬人.*Goou yeau-ren.* 'Dog bites man.' it is not always certain that the action goes outward from N to N'. For example, in: 我老鬧病.*Woo lao naw-binq.* 'I all the time disturb sickness,—I am bothered by sickness all the time.', the action of *naw* is directed inward. Take the sentence 这鱼不能吃了. *Jeh yu buneng chy le.*, if one is talking about the freshness of prepared fish, it meant 'This fish cannot be eaten any more', while if the question is concerned with the health of goldfish one is feeding, then it means 'This fish cannot eat any more (it is so sick)'.[10] Other examples are: 十个人吃 两磅肉. *Shyrg ren chy leang-banq row.* 'Ten people eat two pounds of meat.': *Leang-banq row chy shyrg ren.* 'Two pounds of meat eats,—feeds, ten people.' 四个人坐一条板凳. *Syhg ren tzuoh i-tyau baan.denq.* 'Four people sit on one bench.': *I-tyau baan.denq tzuoh syhg ren.* 'One bench seats four people.' 这地方儿使人菢臙. *Jeh dih-fangl shyy ren fa-nih.* 'This place

---

[10]While finite verbs in English have a definite voice, infinitives in a grammatically active form are ambivalent as to the direction of action. Hence the possibility of stories like the following:

"Daddy, is a trout big enough to eat when it is three inches long?"

"No, my boy."

"Then how does it grow up, Daddy?"

makes one feel bored.' has a verb with action directed outward. In 这地方儿能住. *Jeh dih.fangl neng juh.* '(At) this place (one) can live,—this place can be inhabited.', the action seems to be directed inward, but if *neng juh* is translated as 'habitable', then it would be in grammatically "active" form again. In the saying: 哀莫大于心死. *Ai moh dah yu shin syy.*L '(Of) calamities none is greater than that the heart dies.', *syy* seems to be directed outward from *shin*, but in *Ta syyle shin le.* 'He has killed the idea,—he has let go dead, given up, the idea.', *syy* is directed outward from *ta.* Similarly, in 他父親死了. *Ta fuh.chin syyle.* 'His father died.': *Ta syyle fuh.chin.* 'He has lost his father.' 我的腿麻了. *Woode toei ma le.* 'My legs feel numb.': *Woo male toei le* 'I have benumbed my legs.' (Headline:) 南韓八百万人毁家 *Nan Harn Babae Wann Ren Hoei Jia* 'South Korea 8 Million People (see, allow, suffer to be) Destroyed (their) Homes': (explanation:) *Nan Harn babae-wann ren de jia hoeile.* 'South Korea 8 Million People's Homes (have been) Destroyed.' In all these the direction of action is not clear except that the translation one way or the other makes it seem so. In Chinese, as in any other language, it is of course always possible to make things clearer if the speaker notices any possibility of ambiguity. The following sentence, from an actual conversation, is a case in point: 彬ㄦ应该告送他. *Binbin* [potential but no actual pause] *inggai gaw-.sonq ta—woode yih.sy sh shuo inggai gaw.sonq Binbin.* '(To) Binbin (one) ought to tell—I mean (one) ought to tell Binbin.'

Since the subject need not represent the actor, it can, among other things, represent the place at, place to, object for, and so on, which may be grouped under the general idea of locative meaning. Thus, 这地方儿可以溜氷. *Jeh dih.fangl keeyii lhiou-bing.* '(At) this place (one) can skate.' 中國常ㄗ去信. *Jong.gwo charngcharng chiuh-shinn.* '(To) China (one) often sends letters.' 这花ㄦ得澆水了. *Jeh hual deei jiau-shoei le.* '(On) these flowers (one) must pour water,—these flowers must be watered.' 这樹能軋枝, *Jeh shuh neng yah-jy,* '(Of or for) this tree (one) can put down branches (into the soil to grow new trees),' 可是得先上肥. *keesh deei shian shanq-feir.* 'but must first put on fertilizers.'

In the preceding examples the verbs do have a direction of action, even though not explicitly indicated. With many verbs there is even no clear and definite direction from the nature of the action. In: 他 掉 淚ㄦ了。 *Ta diaw-lell le.* 'He dropped tears.', the question whether the dropping is performed or suffered by the tears does not arise for the speaker. My former colleague Li Jiinshi calls verbs so used 半被性 *bann-bey-shing* 'semi-passive' (Leu, S & O, 67). Another way to look at it is to compare it with the middle voice in Greek, or with English verbs with neutral direction like 'looks, sounds, feels, tastes, smells'. What is special in Chinese is that verbs which behave this way are much more numerous. The verb 叫 *jiaw* may be used for 'calls (someone or something)', but also for 'is called', for which German has a verb in the formally active form *heissen.* Thus: 你 叫 誰? *Nii jiaw sheir?* 'Whom are you calling?' 我 叫 王 二 呐。 *Woo jiaw Wang Ell ne.* 'I am calling Wang Ell.' 你 叫 什 么? *Nii jiaw sherme?* 'What are you called?' '*Wie heissen Sie?*' *Woo jiaw Wang Ell.* 'I am called Wang Ell.' *Nii jiaw sherme?* 'What are you calling?' 我 叫 " 救命 !" *Woo jiaw "Jiow Ming!"* 'I am calling "Help!" '

In Chinese, as in any other language, ambiguities do exist and communication does sometimes fail. Thus, in a conversation about the French vote on joining the North Atlantic Treaty Organization in 1954, one speaker said: 法 國 委 員 会 十六 对 十五 通 过 了 , 德 國 还 不 知 道 呐. *Fah.gwo woeiyuan-huey shyr-liow duey shyrwuu tongguoh le, Der. gwo hair bu jydaw ne.* 'The French committee passed it by a vote of sixteen to fifteen, (as for) Germany (one) does not know yet.', to which the hearer wondered: 德 國 怎 么 会 不 知 道 ? 报 上 都 有 了 嚜 ! *Der.gwo tzeem huey bu jydaw? Baw.shanq dou yeoule me!* 'How is it possible that Germany doesn't know? It's even in the papers!' and the first speaker had to expand: 我 是 要 说 ... *Woo sh yaw shuo Der.gwo tongguoh bu tongguoh hair bujydaw.* 'I mean whether Germany passes it or not (one) still doesn't know.', thus removing the ambiguity. But the interesting thing here is that the ambiguity is not removed by giving the direction of the transitive verb *jydaw*, but by expanding the context so that the direction of action can be inferred from it.

There is available to the speaker, when desired, an explicit way to specify the direction of action by the use of the pretransitive verbs 把 *bae*, for direction outward, and 被 *bey*, for direction inward. Thus, the sentence: 鱼吃了. *Yu chyle*. can mean (1) 'The fish has eaten.' or (2) 'The fish has been eaten' but with pretransitives the meaning is clearer: 鱼把食吃了. *Yu bae shyr chyle*. 'The fish has eaten the feed.': 把鱼吃了! *Bae yu chyle!* 'Eat the fish!': 鱼被貓吃了. *Yu bey mhau chyle*. 'The fish has been eaten by the cat.' 鱼食被鸟儿吃了。 *Yushyr bey neaul chyle*. 'The fish feed has been eaten by the bird.' The pretransitives *bae* and *bey* are, however, not exclusively markers of direction of action. Along with the directionally neutral pretransitive *geei* 'for', their occurrence in the sentence has other uses, such as definite reference, implications of interest or harm. In fact, even the use of *bae* does not guarantee that the direction is outward. For example, in: *Tzeeme! Ta bae g fuh.chin syyle!* 'How come! he had a father die (on him)!', where *bae* has not the remotest association with any idea of patricide, but means only that he suffered such a thing to happen to him.

The ambivalence of verbs as to direction of action is usually resolved either by the linguistic context or the situational context and thus does not necessarily lead to ambiguity. The sentence: 你就写他偷車的事情. *Nii jiow shiee ta tou che de shyh-.shyng.*, out of context, would certainly seem to mean 'You just write about the incident of his stealing the car.' But because the hearer knew what the speaker was talking about, it was correctly understood as 'You just write about the incident of her bicycle having been stolen.', and it was because the speaker knew that the hearer knew about the incident that he did not bother to put it more explicitly. It is only to the linguist, who works mostly with isolated sentences out of context, that those sentences seem to be poorly constructed. There is, on the whole, probably no more and no less ambiguity in spoken Chinese than in most other languages spoken.[11]

---

[11]On this and other types of ambiguity in Chinese, see my article in *Studia Serica Bernhard Karlgren Dedicata*, Copenhagen, 1959, pp. 1-13.

*2.4.3. Definite and Indefinite Reference.* Since the subject sets
the topic of the talk and the predicate gives the information by
adding something new, the subject is likely to represent the
known while the predicate introduces something unknown: *the
thing we are already familiar with has a feature which the speaker
wants to bring out in his comment.* Thus there is a very strong
tendency for the subject to have a definite reference and the object to have an indefinite reference.[12]   For example: 水 闹 了.
*Shoei kaile.* 'The water (we have set on the stove) is boiling.':
苦 水 了. *Fa-shoei le.* '(There has) developed water,—there is a
flood.' 火 着 了. *Huoo jaurle.* 'The fire (we are trying to start) is
lit.': 着 火 了 ! *Jaur-huoo le!* '(There has) started a fire,—there is a
fire!' 我 看 完 了 书 了. *Woo kann-wanle shu le.* 'I have finished
reading (for example, bedtime reading, of any book).': 书 看 完
了 吗 ? *Shu kann-wanle ma?* 'Have you finished reading the book
(I lent you, you said you wanted to read, etc.)?' or 'Have you done
your reading (as you said you were going to)?'     哪儿 有 书 ? *Naal
yeou shu?* 'Where are (some) books?'    书 在 哪儿 ? *Shu tzay naal?*
'Where are the books,—where is the book department (in the
store)?' 我 要 请 客. *Woo yaw chiing-keh.* 'I want to invite (some)
guests,—I want to give a party.': 客 来 了. *Keh Laile.* 'The guests
(I invited) have come', but *Lai keh le.* '(There) have come some
(unexpected) guests,—we have some visitors.'

It is, of course, always possible to say *jeyg* 'this', *neyg* 'that',
etc., for definite reference, and *ig* 'a', etc., for indefinite reference.
For example:   你 写 完 了 那 封 信 了 没 有 ? *Nii shiee-wanle
ney-feng shinn le meiyeou?* 'Have you finished writing that letter?': 一 个 卖 刷 子 的 在 门 口儿 呐. *Ig may shuatz de tzay
menkooul ne.* 'A brush peddler is at the door.' But the preferred,
that is, more frequently occurring, forms would be: *ney-feng shinn
shiee-wan.le meiyeou?* 'That letter have (you) finished writing,—
has that letter been written yet?': *Menkooul yeou g may shuatz
de.* 'The doorway has a brush peddler.'

It is, however, not so much the subject or object function that

---

[12]On this point see Mullie, *Struct Princ*, I, 160-168. It was brought out
still more explicitly by Lien-Sheng Yang in a conversation with the author.

goes with definite or indefinite reference as position in an earlier
or later part of the sentence that makes the difference. Thus, by
the use of the pretransitive, an object is moved farther ahead and
is made more suggestive of a definite reference: *Nii bae ney-feng
shinn shiee-wanle meiyeou?* 'Have you taken that letter and written (it) to a finish,—have you finished writing that letter?' Instead
of starting a sentence with *ig, i-jiann, etc.*, the preferred form for
indefinite reference is *yeou ig, yeou g,* or even just *yeou* 'there is
a … which … ', as: *Yeou ren laile.* 'There is someone (who) has
come,—someone has come.' For 些 *shie* 'an amount, a number of',
a sentence never starts with *i-shie*, it is always *yeou i₀shie* or *yeou
₀shie* 'there is (are) some', so much so that *₀shie* practically is
enclitic to *yeou*. Thus, *Yeou.shie* has become practically a compound, meaning 'some', as: *Yeou.shie ren bu chy suann.* 'There-
are-a-number-of,—some, people don't eat garlic.' *Yeou ren lai kann
nii.* 'Somebody has come to see you.' Likewise, *yeou₀shyr.howl*
'there are times.—sometimes', *yeou₀dih.fangl* 'there are places,—
somewhere'. Thus, the way in which "particular propositions"
involving the idea of 'some' are expressed in Chinese turns out to
agree with the post-Aristotelian position that such propositions
always entail existence; that is, 有 *yeou* 'there is' or *yeoude* 'that
which there is'.

Reference to every member of a class, as 个ㄜ儿人 *gehgehl
ren* 'everybody', 件ㄜ事 *jiannjiann shyh* 'every affair,' is considered definite reference and must be in the forward position, as:
双ㄜ鞋都穿破了。 *Shuangshuang shye dou chuan-poh le.*
'Every pair of shoes has been worn through.' With pretransitive:
他苩人ㄜ都叫老朋友。 *Ta goan renren dou jiaw lao perng-
.yeou.* 'He takes everybody and calls (him) old friend,—he calls
everybody old friend.' Similarly, reference to any arbitrary member of a whole class in the form of a stressed interrogative word,
followed by *dou* or *yee* in a later part of the sentence, also occurs
in a foward position, as: 他们什么都吃. *Tamen sherm dou
chy.* 'They eat anything.' 他哪儿也不去. *Ta naal yee bu chiuh.*
'He doesn't go anywhere.' The sentence: 这个人谁都不信.
*Jeyg ren sheir dou bu shinn.* means either (1) 'This man doesn't
believe anybody.' or (2) 'Nobody believes this man.' The latter
can be changed to *Sheir dou bu shinn jeyg ren.* and made unam-

biguous at the expense of putting *jeyg ren* (with definite reference) at the end of the sentence. But meaning (1) can only be in
the order given, unless paraphrased in more bookish language as:
这 个 人 不 相 信 任 何 人。 *Jehg ren bu shiangshinn rennher
ren.* 'This man does not believe whatever person.' Note that
while *jeyg, neyg,* and so on *can* come last, and *ig* and so on *can*
come first, the two types of forms: (1) the reduplicated distributive and (2) the stressed interrogative plus *dou* (~*yee*) never
comes last. There is no ° 他 懂 件 ˄ 事。 °*Ta doong jiannjiann
shyh.* for 'He understands everything,' while   他们 都 吃什么 ?
*Tamen dou chy sherme?* though possible, would be a different
sentence, meaning: 'What do they all eat?' For further examples,
see section 4.2.3. (3).

# 2.5. The Logical Predicate

*2.5.1. Logical and Grammatical Predicates.* We have seen that
the point of the message in a sentence is normally located in the
predicate. Thus, in the sentence: 我 穷。*Woo chyong.* 'I am poor.',
*chyong* is the point of the message, or the logical predicate, as
well as the grammatical predicate. Often, however, for stylistic
reasons, or merely from ineptitude of expression, the logical predicate is located in any part of the sentence, in the subject, or part
of the predicate, as well as the whole predicate. Thus, in: 我 有
个 虫 牙。*Woo yeou g chorngya.* 'I have a decayed tooth.', the
logical predicate is not the verb *yeou*, nor primarily the whole
predicate *yeou g chorngya*, but the object *chorngya*. Such is the
point of the story in which the guide said: 'We are now passing
the oldest winery in this region' and the tourist asked: 'Why?'
Translated into Chinese:    咱们 現 在 走 过 的 是 这 一 带 最
老 的 酒 坊 了。*Tzarm shianntzay tzoou-guoh de sh jey-i-day
tzuey lao de jeoufang le.* 'The one we are passing now is the
oldest winery of this region.', the point of the joke would be lost.
In general, if in a sentence of the form S-V-O the object O is the
logical predicate, it is often recast in the form S-V *de sh* O
'what S-V's is O', thus putting O in the center of the predicate.

Adjectives and adverbs in attributive position often serve as logical predicates. Thus, a sentence in a governmental regulation says: 'The minimum salary for the classification should be requested.', where the logical predicate 'minimum' should better be placed in a more central position. Quite normal and acceptable are English sentences of the type: 'There are too many people here.', the Chinese for which would be in the form: 这儿 的 人 太 多. *Jell de ren tay duo.* 'The people here are too many.' But current writing, partly because of Occidental influence, already has sentences of the type: 愈 来 愈 多 的 人 要 研 究 科 学 了. *Yuh lai yuh duo de ren yaw yan.jiou keshyue le.* 'More and more people are studying science.', for which it would be more usual to say: *Yan.jiou keshyue de ren yuh lai yuh duo le.* 'Those who study science are becoming more and more numerous.'

It may of course happen that the speaker does not want to make his point explicit and purposely drops a hint into an obscure corner, as name droppers do when dropping names. Thus, instead of 'I know so and so.', with the predicate in plain message, one would    say: 我 从 前 在 爱 因 斯 坦 家 吃 饭 的 时 候儿 啊, ... *Woo tsorngchyan tzay Ayinsytaan jia chy-fann de shyr.howl a,* ... 'When I was dining at Einstein's house, ...'

*2.5.2. Stress as a Marker of the Logical Predicate.* Besides casting the sentence so as to bring the point of the message into a prominent place, namely in the position of the grammatical predicate, the objective can also be attained by contrastive stress, that is, by magnified length and pitch range and, less importantly for Chinese, increased loudness. For example, with ordinary predication, when logic and grammar go together, the point of the sentence: 我 的 名 字 是 约 翰. *Woode mingtz sh Iuehann.* is that 'My name is John (and not James).' whereas *Iuehann sh woode mingtz.* means that John is my name and not any title or nickname. But by displacing the chief stress to the subject, leaving the rest of the sentence at a reduced time and pitch scale — to neutral tone as a limit in extreme cases — the logical predicate can be shifted to the grammatical subject, so that: *Woode "mingtz sh Iuehann.* means 'My *name* (and not my title or nickname) is John.', while *"Iuehann sh woode mingtz.* means 'John (and not James) is my name.' Similarly, the riddle, 鸟儿 为 什 么 望 南 飞? 因 为 走 太 远    *Neaul weysherme wanq nan fei?*

*Inwey tzoou tay yeuan* "Why do birds fly south? Because it is too far to walk' would lose its point if stress marks were placed on *nan* 'south' or *fei* 'fly' to resolve the ambiguity. (See Bennett Cerf, *Book of Riddles*, New York, Random House, 1960, for this and other similar riddles.) In general, one can make almost any full word in a sentence the logical predicate by giving it a contrasting stress.

Incidentally, one can test whether a morpheme or group of morphemes is free or not by its capability of receiving a contrasting stress. For examples, see section 3.3.3 on contrasting stress on words.

Since speech is clearer when it makes one point at a time, it is not usual to find two or more points of prominence in the same sentence. For example, the sign on some trains which says: 'Flush toilet EACH time EXCEPT when at station,' sounds rather schizophrenic and gives the impression that the management did not quite know its own mind as to what to emphasize. If two points are to be made, the normal way to do it is to make them separately. For example, 这事情得做，得小心点儿 做 *Jeh shyh.chyng deei tzuoh, deei sheau.shin.deal tzuoh.* 'This thing must be done, and must be done carefully.'[13] It should be noted, however, that contrastive stress, which is actualized by time and pitch magnification, with little or no increase in loudness, should be distinguished from emotional stress, which is actualized by greater loudness, often of the *sforzando* type, sometimes accompanied by raising of the pitch, but with little magnification in time value or pitch range. In the case of emotional stress, there is no limit to the number of times one hammers on words, as in: 'Will, you, stop, making, that, infernal, noise!' (p. 56). When one is feeling schizophrenic, one is not likely to be very logical.

---

[13]D. L. Bolinger, in discussing contrastive points in adverbs, says: "We are not likely to combine two orders in one. Thus in Do it carefully, the do it part is almost certainly resumptive, carefully being the only new datum. If the do it is also a new term, the dual command will probably take some such shape as Do it, and be careful about it." "Linear Modification," *PMLA*, 57:1124 (1952).

## 2.6. Subject and Predicate as Question and Answer

*2.6.1. Pause Particles and Interrogative Particles.* When we examine the four pause particles *a*, *ne*, *me* and *ba* which can occur after a subject, we find that they all occur as interrogative particles at the end of questions: (1) 这个人啊，一定是个好人。 *Jehg ren a, idinq sh go hao ren.* 'This man (as for), must be a good man.' Cf: 他是哪儿的人啊? *Ta sh naal de ren a?* 'Where is he from?' (2) 他自己的小孩儿呐，也不大听他的话。 *Ta tzyhjii de sheauharl ne, yee bu dah ting tade huah.* 'His own children (if it is a question of), do not listen to him much, either.' Cf: 小孩儿都上哪儿去了呐? *Sheauharl dou shanq naal chiuh le ne?* 'Where have all the children gone to, then?' (3) The hesitation pause particle 么 *me* [mə] after a subject has a less open vowel than the interrogative particle 吗 *ma* [mɐ] for agreement and disagreement. Thus: 他辞職的意思么，已竟打消了。 *Ta tsyr-jyr de yih.sy me, yiijinq daashiaule.* 'His idea of resigning (as for), has already been canceled.' Cf: 你知道他要辞職了吗? *Nii jy.daw ta yaw tsyr-jyr le ma?* 'Do you know that he is going to resign?' But the vocalic difference is dependent on position in the sentence, probably also as a result of sentence intonation. (4) The particle *ba* is really two: one (P 10, sec. 8.5.5) is the advisative or tentative particle as a reduction of the verb 罢 *bah* 'finishes,—do that and call it a day,—let's'; the other 吧(P11, sec. 8.5.5) is a fusion of *bu* and *a* for questions and tentative statements. The two have practically blended into one for most speakers and writers, who will as soon write one character as the other. As a pause particle, the tentative meaning is nearer. Thus: 丈夫吧，找不着事儿；孩子们吧，又不肯念书。*Janq.fu ba, jao.bu-jaur shell; hairtzmen ba, yow bukeen niann-shu.* 'The husband (if you consider him), can't find a job; the children (if you consider them), won't study, either.' Cf: 我们问々他的丈夫吧? *Woomen wenn.wenn tade janq.fu ba?* 'Shall we ask her husband?'

*2.6.2. Subject as Question and Predicate as Answer.* The close parallel between the pause particles and the interrogative particles is no mere accident, but derives from the nature of the subject as a question and the predicate as an answer. Imagine a man going into the dining room and finding that dinner is not ready. He asks: 饭 呐? *Fann ne?* 'Dinner, as to,—where's dinner?' and his wife, not having heard him clearly, or merely stalling for time, says: 饭啊? *Fann a?* 'Dinner, you mean?' He grunts:嗯.*Ng.* 'Yes.', and she says: 还 没 得 呐。*Hair mei der ne.*[14] 'Not done yet.' Or, when he is looking for a second helping and finds the pot empty, he asks: *Fann .ne?* '(Where's) the rice?' and his wife says: 都 吃 完 了。*Dou chy-wanle.* 'It is all eaten.' Thus, we have the following degrees of integration between questions and answers: (1) two-way conversation, (2) posing a question in the subject and answering it oneself in the predicate, and (3) combining question and answer into one continuous full sentence without pause. For instance:

(1) *Fann a?  Hair mei der ne.  Fann ne?  Dou chy-wanle.*
(2) *Fann a,  hair mei der ne.  Fann ne,  dou chy-wanle.*
(3) *Fann      hair mei der ne.  Fann      dou chy-wanle.*

# 2.7. The Full Sentence as Made Up of Minor Sentences

*2.7.1. Subject and Predicate as Minor Sentences.* We have considered the subject in a full sentence as the topic and as the question, and the predicate as the comment on the topic and as the answer to the question. Now we have seen that among minor sentences, some serve to present or to call attention to things, while others have more to say and are more in the nature of comments, although the thing commented upon is in the situation and not expressed in words. But if you put the two minor sen-

---

[14]This particle for continuing state, which appears in some dialects and in old novels as 哩.*li* is different from the homophonous particle for questions for specific points, which appears in the corresponding dialects as 呢 .*ni* or .*gni* [ ȵi ]. See sec. 8.5.5 on particles P 6 and P 7.

tences together, then you get exactly the makeup of a full sentence: topic and comment, expressed as subject and predicate. Thus we have arrived at the surprising, and yet obvious, conclusion that a full sentence is a complex sentence consisting of two minor ones.

*2.7.2. Primacy of Minor Sentences.* Now if, as we have previously observed, the full sentence is the favorite Chinese sentence type, why go to the trouble of explaining the usual in terms of the unusual? The answer is that the full sentence is the favorite sentence type only in deliberate connected discourse. In daily life, speech and non-speech are thoroughly interposed and minor sentences are normal and adequate when full sentences are not necessary. From the point of view of the pragmatics of speech, therefore, minor sentences are more primary than full sentences and it does help the understanding of sentence structure to analyze a full sentence as made up of minor sentences, both genetically and ontogenetically in the life of the speaker. This will make intelligible the almost unlimited variety of forms in the structure of subjects and predicates: nominal expressions, verbal expressions, subject-predicate clauses, and what not, as we shall see in the next sections.

## 2.8. Types of Subjects

*2.8.1. Nominal Expressions.* The commonest type of subject is that of nouns, pronouns, or other nominal expressions, as: 水开了. *Shoei kaile.* 'The water is boiling.' 这儿的山很高. *Jell de shan heen gau.* 'The mountains here are very high.' 他们上哪儿? *Tamen shanq naal?* 'Where are they going?' *Nah sh, nah sh.* 'That's right, that's right.' 请来的人还没到呐. *Chiing.lai de ren hair mei daw ne.* 'Those invited have not yet arrived.' 知识, 经验, 资格是三样必须的条件. *Jy.shyh, jing₀yann, tzy.ger sh san-yang bihshiu de tyaujiann.* 'Knowledge, experience, and standing are three necessary conditions.'

*2.8.2. Verbal Expressions.* Verbs and phrases with verbal centers can be subjects, as: 走行, 不走也行. *Tzoou shyng, bu tzoou yee shyng.* 'To go is all right, not to go is also all right.'

走了就好了. *Tzooule jiow hao le.* '(For one or for it) to have gone would be good.' 光说没用。*Guang shuo mei yonq.* 'Just saying it has no use.' 说比做容易. *Shuo bii tzuoh rong.yih.* 'Talking is easier than doing.' 知难行易. *Jy nan shyng yih.* L 'Knowing is difficult, doing is easy.' (Sun Yat-sen's motto in support of science). 打是疼，骂是爱. *Daa sh terng, mah sh ay.* 'To spank is to care, to scold is to love.' 站着不动很难. *Jannj bu donq heen nan.* 'Standing without moving is very difficult.' 说出来(了)也不要紧. *Shuo.chu.lai (le) yee buyawjiin.* 'To say it out does not matter either.' 老做事不休息可以把人累死. *Lao tzuoh-shyh bu shiou.shi keeyii bae ren ley.syy.* 'Working all the time and not resting can tire one to death.'

Sometimes a verbal subject may specify a time, place, or condition, as: 吃饭得使筷子. *Chy-fann deei shyy kuaytz.* 'Eating a meal must use chopsticks.' 买票请排队. *Mae-piaw chiing pair-duey.* 'Buying tickets please line up.', where one may supply ... $de_o shyr.howl$ 'when eating ...'; ... $de_o dih.fangl$ 'where one buys tickets'; or ... *de ren* 'those who buy tickets'; but since what could be supplied is indeterminate, these should be analyzed as verbal subjects, and subjects in general do introduce time, place, and condition, anyway.

Adjectives being a species of verbs, they can also be subjects, as: 高好；低了太热. *Gau hao; dile tay reh.* '(For the ceiling to be) high is good; (to be) low is too hot.' 慢不碍事；太快会弄错了的. *Mann bu ay.shyh; tay kuay huey nonq-tsuohle de.* '(To be) slow doesn't hinder matters; (to be) too fast can go wrong.'

*2.8.3. Time, Place, and Condition Expressions.* Take the sentences:今儿冷.*Jiel leeng.* 'Today is cold.' 这儿是哪儿？*Jell sh naal?* 'Where is here?' 他死了的话简直不堪设想了. *Ta syyle de huah jeanjyr bukan shehsheang le.* 'The supposition that he should die is simply unthinkable.' Here, the subjects are nominal expressions of topics on which the predicates make ordinary types of comments. Now consider the following three sentences:今儿不去了.*Jiel bu chiuh le.* '(We are, one is, etc.) today not going any more.' 这儿不能说话. *Jell buneng shuo-huah.* 'Here (one) can't talk.' 他死了的话，就不容易

解决了. *Ta syyle de huah, jiow bu rong.yih jieejyue le.* '(In the) event of his death, (things) will be very difficult to settle.' In each case, the translation will have to supply a subject as the actor while the time, place, or condition expression becomes an adverb. Since, however, the Chinese subject only serves to introduce the topic of the discourse, the actor need not appear unless needed in case of ambiguity. So far as grammatical form is concerned, there is therefore no difference between the two sets of examples of *jiel* 'today', *jell* 'here', and ... *de₀huah* '(in) the case of ... '.[15]

We have so far treated the actor word as a special case of the topic word, on a par with time and place words. An interesting converse of this is the treatment of an actor word as if it were a time word in the dialects of southern Hopeh and Shansi. Thus, in addition to the usual optional pause and pause particles, these dialects can also use, as another alternative, the form ... *de₀shyr-.how* 'the time when ... ', not only after expression for real time, but after any kind of subject. It is especially frequent in a public speech, when the speaker stalls for time. For example: 大 家 的 时 候 ... *Dahjia de .shyr.how* ... (dial.), 'All of us, then, ...' (not 'everybody's time', which would have full stress on *shyr*); 他 道 歉 的 时 候 , 我 们 就 算 了. *Ta daw-chiann de .shyr.how, woomen jiow suann le.* 'When,—if, he apologizes, we will let it go.' (cf. German *wenn* 'if'). 这 问 题 的 时 候 , 就 等 下 次 再 谈 吧. *Jeh wenntyi de .shyr.how, jiow deeng shiah-tsyh tzay tarn ba* (dial.). 'As for this problem, wait for next time to talk about it.'

2.8.4. *Actor Subject Introduced by a Preposition.* We have suggested that the subject is but a minor sentence. As such it can take, among other forms, the form of a preposition and an object. This occurs when an actor is made explicit by being preceded by *you* 'through' or *guei* 'up to, for ... to'. Similarly, *lian* 'including, even' can be used to introduce an actor in the subject. Examples are: 由 主 席 召 集 会 议. *You juushyi jawjyi hueyyih.* '(It is) through the chairman (who) convenes the

---

[15]On a striking example of place words as subjects in a passage in *Mencius*, see sec. 1.1.3 (3).

meeting.' 归 各人 自己 料理. *Guei gehren tzyhjii liaw₀lii*. (It
is) up to each one to manage it himself.' 连 我 都 不 知 道.*Lian
woo dou bu jydaw*. 'Including me don't know,—even I don't
know.' Even the marker of passive action *bey* can introduce as
its object a subject-actor, as: 被 这 几 文 钱 把 这 小 人 瞒 过.
*Bey jeh jii-wen chyan bae jeh sheau-ren man-guoh*. '(It was) by
this little cash (that) fooled this small man.' That this is not
unique with Chinese can be seen from the example in French,
cited from Jespersen (*Anal Synt*, 32) by Leu Shwushiang (*LWJyi*,
123): *Jusqu'aux enfants furent massacrés.*, which can be paralleled by a perfectly natural Chinese translation: 连(~ 一 直 到 )
小 孩 子 们 都 被 屠 杀 了.*Lian ( ~ ijyr daw) sheauhairtzmen dou
bey twushale*. 'Including (or up to) the children were massacred.'

 *2.8.5. Other Prepositional Phrases*. Phrases like *jusqu'aux
enfants* or *lian sheauhairtzmen* would not seem so strange as
subjects if we remember that by the term "subject" we simply
mean whatever starts the topic, what some grammarians call
起 词 *chiitsyr* 'starting expression'. Similarly, then, other prepositional phrases starting a sentence, which are commonly regarded as adverbial phrases, are also subjects in this broad sense,
for example, 为 了 这 事 情 我 真 苦 愁.*Weyle jeh shyh.chyng
woo jen fa-chour*. 'On account of this I am really worried.' 在 一
年 裡 我 只 病 了 一 次. *Tzay i-nian.lii woo jyy binqle i-tsyh*.
'In one year I was sick only once.' In both sentences the prepositions can be omitted and the resulting sentences will have ordinary substantive subjects. In these cases of double subjects, the
subjects can be reversed, with a change of emphasis and change
of construction. If the prepositions are retained, we have verbal
expressions in series (sec. 5.5), in which the first expression is
subordinated to the second. But the fact that there is no subordinative particle *de* in such constructions shows that the first
expression is still not quite an ordinary adverbial expression.

 *2.8.6. S-P Subjects*. A full sentence with subject and predicate
can be the subject of another predicate, thus forming an S-P
clause subject. For example: 貓 比 狗 凶 是 会 的. *Mhau bii
goou shiong sh huey de*. 'That a cat is fiercer than a dog is
possible.' 他 不 来 也 成.*Ta bu lai yee cherng*. 'That he will

not (or may not) come is all right, too.' 他信了你这话才怪呐！ *Ta shinnle nii jeh huah tsair guay ne!'* 'That he should believe this word of yours would be strange indeed!' 物价涨的这么高，把生活弄的这么苦。 *Wuhjiah jaang de tzemm gau, bae sheng.hwo nonq de tzemm kuu.* '(The situation that) prices have risen so high renders life so hard.' 我不能说中國话很好。 *Woo buneng shuo Jong.gwohuah heen hao.* 'That I can't speak Chinese is very good.' The last was a student's sentence by which he meant to say: 'I cannot speak Chinese very well.', but, since an adverb cannot follow the verb it modifies, the sentence turned out to mean something else. 东西扔得地下不好。 *Dong.shi rheng.de dih.shiah bu hao.* 'That things are thrown on the ground is not good.' has an S-P subject, but *Dong.shi rheng.de dih.shiah de bu hao.* 'The things, those that are thrown on the ground, are not good.' has a nominal subject.

## 2.9. Types of Predicates

*2.9.1. Verbal Predicates.* The commonest type of predicate has a verb as the center, as: 我认得他。 *Woo renn.de ta.* 'I know him.' 他会。 *Ta huey.* 'He can.' 这个人到过中國。 *Jeyg ren daw.guo Jong.gwo.* 'This man has been to China,' 那个消息早菱表了。 *Neyg shiau.shyi tzao fabeaule.* 'That news has long been published.' 人々都知道这件事。 *Renren dou jy.daw jey-jiann shyh.* 'Everybody knows about this affair.'

Most Chinese grammarians divide full sentences into narrative sentences, descriptive sentences, and judgment sentences, corresponding approximately to sentences with verbal, adjectival, and nominal predicates, respectively. The correspondence, however, is not complete. Thus, predicates like 怕冷 *pah-leeng* 'minds the cold', 信教 *shinn-jiaw* 'believes in a religion', and 在礼 *tzay-lii* 'is at rite,—does not smoke or drink' are verbal predicates but would form descriptive rather than narrative sentences.

A formally more relevant distinction, which cuts across the preceding classification of sentences, has to do with the nature of the predication as to whether it is (1) contrastive, (2) assertive, or (3) narrative,[16] as exemplified below.

(1) In the sentence: 我現在说话. *Woo shianntzay shuo-huah.* 'I am now talking.', the verb *shuo-huah* is contrasted with other things I might be doing, such as 睡覚 *shuey-jiaw* 'sleeping', 吃东西 *chy dong.shi* 'eating things 玩儿 *wal* 'playing', and what not. If the contrast is emphasized, it receives extra contrastive stress, which in Chinese is actualized by greater time value and pitch range and less importantly by increased loudness. If a contrastive verb is preceded by *sh*, *sh* is always less stressed than the contrastive verb and may even be in the neutral tone, as: *Woo shianntzay* ₀*sh shuo-huah* ( 不是打架 *bush daa-jiah*). 'I am now talking (and not quarreling).'

(2) In the assertive function, a verbal predicate is not contrasted with some other verbal predicate or predicates, but with its total contradictory, as: *Woo shianntzay* "*shuo-huah, woo shianntzay* '*sh shuo-huah* (*bush bu shuo-huah*). 'I am talking now (and not being silent).'

(3) When a verb narrates some progress in the story, when something is happening, then the inchoative particle *le* is used at the end of the sentence, as: *Woo shianntzay shuo-huah le* ( 剛才 *gangtsair mei-yeou*). 'I am talking now (I wasn't talking a while ago).'

*2.9.2. Adjectival Predicates.* Adjectives in Chinese being a species of verbs, they can be used as full predicates and do not need any 'copula' *sh* 'is' to make them predicates, as: 今儿天涼. *Jiel tian liang.* 'Today the weather is cool.' 菜很鹹. *Tsay heen shyan.* 'The dish is very salty.' 我热. *Woo reh.* 'I am hot.' 你那儿舒服点儿. *Nii.nall shu.fwu.deal.* 'Your place is more comfortable.'

Like other verbs, adjectives also have three modes of predication, as follows:

---

[16]Lien-Sheng Yang called my attention to the fact that type 3 also cuts across 1 and 2, as in 他昨儿回"家了. *Ta tzwol hwei-"jia le.* 'He went *home* yesterday.': *Ta tzwol sh hwei-jia le.* 'He did go home yesterday.' In most cases, however, type 3 involves neither 1 nor 2.

(1) Contrastive:这 瓜 甜。*Jeh gua tyan.* 'This melon is sweet.' In this mode of predication the adjective can take $_osh$ followed by the subordinate suffix *de* as a nominalizer, as *Jeh gua $_osh$ tyande* (*bush* 酸 的 *suande,* 苦 的 *kuude,* etc.). 'This melon is a sweet one (not a sour one, a bitter one, etc.).'

Like action verbs, an adjective used contrastively can have an auxiliary verb before it or a complement after it, and when used in a quasi-quotation, it requires the verb $_osh$, since it will then become nominalized. Thus, with auxiliary verb: 你 得 快 , 也 得 小 心. *Nii deei kuay, yee deei sheau.shin.* 'You must (be) quick, also must (be) careful.'; with complement: 可 是 我 快 不 了 嘿 ! *Keesh woo kuay.bu-leau me!* 'But I can't (be) quick!'; in quasi-quotation: 最 要 紧 的 是 快. *Tzuey yawjiin de $_osh$ kuay.* 'The most important thing is (to be) quick.'

(2) Assertive mode, which does not contrast one adjective with another, but with its total contradictory, as: *Jeh gua tyan., Jeh Guah 'sh tyan* (*bush bu tyan*). 'This melon is sweet, it *is* sweet (not not-sweet).' In this assertion it can take *sh* with full tone or with contrastive stress.

(3) Narrative mode: *Jeh gua tyan le* ( 先 前 没 熟 *shianchyan mei shour*). 'This melon is sweet now (previously it wasn't ripe).' In general, an adjectival predicate with particle *le* or a verb with an adjectival complement and *le* often has the meaning of 'becomes', 'begins to be', whence the frequent use of A *le* to express an excessive degree, as: 这 屋 子 黑 了 ( 漆 的 太 黑 了 ). *Jeh utz hei le* (*chi de tay hei le*). 'This room is (too) dark (painted too dark).' 鞋 ( 买 ～ 做 ) 小 了. *Shye* (*mae* or *tzuoh*) *sheau le.* 'These shoes are (have been bought *or* made) (too) small.' 这 话 差 远 了。*Jeh huah chah-yeauan le.* 'This remark misses by (too) far.' The force of the particle *le* is to imply that the quality in question was increasing and now it is excessive.

Note that while the verb *sh* 'is' is not required in order to make predicates out of adjectives, it can be used with predicative adjectives both for the assertive and the contrastive functions, but with this formal difference: When used for assertion, it is stressed, with enlarged time value and pitch range, but in the contrastive function, it is the adjective that receives the magnification in length and pitch range, while *sh* is not only not magnified, but is reduced, sometimes to zero, that is, to the neutral tone. In this respect the use or non-use of *sh* is no different from the case of verbs of action.

*2.9.3 Nominal Predicates.* In 这 个 人 好 人. *Jeyg ren hao-ren.* 'This man, a good man.', *hao-ren* is a nominal predicate. In *Jeyg ren sh hao-ren.* 'This man is a good man.', *sh hao-ren* 'is a good man' is a verbal predicate, with *sh* as its center, although *hao-ren* is still the logical predicate. Note, however, that the verb *sh* has many special properties which make it a class by itself, on which see section 8.1.8.

A nominal predicate, like the verbal (including adjectival) predicates, can also have the three modes of predication: (1) contrastive: 今儿 礼 拜. *Jiel Liibay.* 'Today (is) Sunday (not Monday, etc.).; (2) assertive: *Jiel 'Liibay.* (with displaced stress) 'Today *is* Sunday (not non-Sunday).'; (3) narrative: *Jiel liibay le.* 'Today is Sunday (again).' Under (2) it is more usual to add a stressed '*sh*, thus making it a verbal predicate.

Cutting across these three modes of predication, a nominal predicate can (a) represent a class to which the subject is subsumed, (b) call attention to the existence or extent of something, or (c) express a process or event.

(a) Subsumption is the commonest type of nominal predication. It is the epsilon (ε) function of formal logic, when a member is subsumed under a class. In *Jeyg ren hao-ren.*, *jeyg ren* is a member of the class of *hao-ren*. Other examples are 孔 子 鲁 人. *Koong Tzyy Luu-ren.* (biographical style) 'Confucius (was a) native of (the State of) Luu.' 他 太 ㄟ 美 国 人. *Ta tay.tay Meeigworen.* 'His wife an American.' 我(,) 傻 子? *Woo (,) shaatz?* 'I (,) a fool?' 四 川 好 地 方儿 也! *Syh.chuan hao dih.fangl é!* 'Szechwan a nice place, you know!' 今儿初一. *Jiel chu'i.* 'Today is the first of the month.'

A very common subtype of the above is the phrase ending in the nominalizing particle *de* [sec. 5.3.6.5 (2)], as: 他 从 英 国 来 的. *Ta tsorng Ing.gwo lai de.* 'He is one who comes from England,—he comes from England.', where *de* stands for *de ren.* 我 八 点 到 的. *Woo ba-dean daw de.* 'I am one who arrived at

eight,—it was at eight that I arrived.' 他 的 身 材 很 高 的。
*Tade shen₀tsair heen gau de.* 'His stature is a very tall one'.

A nominal predicate can be modified by an adverb, as:
那 个 人 简 直 骗 子 嘿! *Neyg ren jeanjyr pianntz me!* 'That
man simply a swindler!' 一 定 好 消 息! *Idinq hao shiau.shyi!*
(minor sentence) 'Certainly good news!', where *idinq* modifies the
predicate as a whole, since otherwise *de* would be needed after
*hao.* 这 个 人 真 君 子。*Jeyg ren jen jiuntzyy.* 'This man truly a
gentleman.', where *jen* is not an attributive adjective, but an
(exclamatory) adverb. In this respect the verb *sh* behaves in some
ways like one of the adverbs above.[17] In enclitic positions, it becomes an adverbial suffix, as in 倒 是 *daw.sh* 'surprisingly', 真 是
*jen.sh* 'really', 原 是 *yuan.sh* 'originally', 正 是 *jenq.sh* 'precisely',
都 是 *dou.sh* 'in all cases'.

Quite different from adverbs before a nominal predicate, an
attributive adjective forms part of a nominal predicate and often
carries the point of the message. We have noted that a minor
sentence may take the form of an attributive adjective and a noun
(sec. 2.2.5), commonly met with in poetry, as: 青 山 绿 水。*Ching-
shan, liuh-shoei.* 'Blue mountains and green waters.' Since a
predicate is a minor sentence, such constructions can also serve as
predicates, as: *Jeh dih.fangl ching-shan liuh-shoei.* 'This place
(has) blue mountains and green waters.' Further examples are:
那 个 姑 娘 大 眼 睛 小 嘴 儿。*Neyg gu.niang dah-yean.jing
sheau-tzoel.* 'That girl (has) big eyes and a small mouth.' 那 个
人 怪 樣 子。*Neyg ren guay-yanqtz.* 'That man (has) a queer
look.' 这 个 孩 子 坏 脾 气。*Jeyg hairtz huay-pyi.chih.* 'This
child (has a) bad temper.' 这 个 人 大 舌 头。*Jeyg ren dah-sher-
.tou.* 'This man is big-tongued,—he lisps.'

The negation of a nominal predicate takes the form of *bush*
rather than a simple *bu*, as with verbs, as: 他 不 是 北 方 人。*Ta
bush beeifang-ren.* 'He is not a northerner.' 我 不 是 三 十 九
岁。*Woo bush sanshyrjeou-suey.* 'I am not 39 years old (maybe 38,
maybe 40).' 我 不 是 这 儿 生 的。*Woo bush jell sheng de.*

---

[17]While Wang Lih (*Liiluenn*, I, 229) does not call *sh* an adverb, he does
emphasize its relation to the predicate as a whole.

'I was not (one who was) born here.'

In the quoting of a list of nominal predicates, we often find examples of the type: 君 ₹, 臣 ₹, 父 ₹, 子₹.*Jiun jiun, chern chern, fuh fuh, tzyy tzyy.* (*Analects*, 12.11 顏 淵 ) 'The king is kingly, the minister is ministerly, the father is fatherly, and the son is filial.' But in a later passage (*loc. cit.*) one finds *Jiun bu jiun, chern bu chern, fuh bu fuh, tzyy bu tzyy.* 'The king is not kingly, ... ' Since the normal L-style equivalent for *bush* is *fei* and not *bu* (as in 白 馬 非 馬 *Bair maa fei maa.* 'A white horse is not [just] a horse.'), and such predicative use of *jiun, chern, fuh,* and *tzyy* is hardly met with again, the passage cited should be considered a *tour de force* and not as ordinary examples of the nominal predicate. With equal grammatical self-consciousness, one says  他 画 的 馿 不 馿 , 馬 不 馬. *Ta huah de liu bu liu, maa bu maa.* 'He draws so that donkeys are not donkey(-like) and horses not horse(-like).' (Cf. 非 馿 非 馬 *fei-liu-fei-maa* 'nondescript', an L-cliché in which *fei* is a verb.)

(b) A nominal predicate calling attention to the existence or extent of something almost always has a quantity expression, such as a numeral followed by a classifiier, with or without a following noun, as: 文 王 十 尺. *Wen Wang shyr-chyy.* 'King Wen was ten (ancient) feet (tall).'  我 们 兩 个 男 孩儿 一 个 女 孩儿。  *Woomen leangg nanharl ig neuharl.* 'We two boys and a girl.', which, spoken by one of the children themselves would be of the subsumption type and mean 'We are two boys and a girl.', but spoken by their parents would be of the existential type and mean 'We have two boys and a girl.' In the former case one can insert an optional *sh* and in the latter, an optional *yeou*. Other examples are: 屋 裡 ( 有 ) 許 多 蚊 子。*U.lii (yeou) sheuduo wentz.* 'The room-inside many mosquitoes,—there are many mosquitoes in the room.'  房 頂儿 上 ( 有 )一 个 老 鴣。*Farngdieengl.shanq (yeou) ig lao.gua.* 'The roof top a crow,—(there is) a crow on the roof.'

Note that *yeou* has the further function of expressing quantity 'as much as', 'not less than'. Thus, 这 小 孩儿 四 岁。*Jeh sheauharl syh-suey* or *sh syh-suey.* 'This child is four years old (not three or five years old).', but *Jeh sheauharl yeou syh-suey.* 'This child is (as old as) four years old.' the contrary being: *Ta mei.yeou syh-suey.* 'He is not as old as four (i.e., less than four).' [See sec. 8.1.3 (1.1).]

Following our principle of minimum assumption of words understood, we shall consider the following sentences as having nominal predicates: 这 本 书 两塊錢. *Jey-been shu leang-kuay chyan.* 'This book (sells for, costs, etc.) two dollars.' 一个人一塊錢. *Ig ren i-kuay chyan.* 'One person (puts out, gets, has, etc.) one dollar,—one dollar per person.'

(c) Nominal predicates announcing or expressing a process or event: 昨儿夜裡大風暴。 *Tzwol yeh.lii dah-fengbaw.* 'Last night great storm.', where the gratuitous addition of *yeou* 'there was' would make the sentence much weaker, in any event a different sentence. 今儿下午体操。 *Jiel shiahwuu tiitsau.* 'This afternoon physical exercise.', where it cannot be determined as to whether a verb *yeou* 'there will be' or *shanq* 'takes up' (as a class hour) or *jiau* 'teaches', or what was being understood. 这个人一定腥红热. *Jeyg ren idinq shinghorngreh.* 'This man must (be having, be a case of) scarlet fever.' 他肺炎. *Ta feyyan.* 'He has pneumonia.' 去年大選. *Chiuh.nian dahsheuan.* 'Last year great election.' 我们快軍训了. *Woomen kuay jiunshiunn le.* 'We (shall) soon military training.', where the insertion of a verb *shanq* 'takes up', *show* 'receive', *yeou* 'have', and so on is not uniquely determinable. Such nominal predicates have a way of becoming full-fledged verbs, as *tiitsau* has, at least in student language, when they are treated like separable verb-object compounds. More on that when we take up the ionization of pseudo-V-O compounds (sec. 6.5.8).

Naturally, not every succession of two nominal expressions makes a full sentence of subject and predicate. Thus, 聰明法子好法子。 *Tsong.ming fartz hao fartz.* means ambiguously either (1) 'The clever way is a good way.' or (2) 'clever ways and good ways'. Similar ambiguities exist in headline English such as 'Actress Mother', which looks like a subordinate NN' construction, but turns out, from the news itself, to be subject and predicate. In this instance the Chinese would have 女演員母親了。 *Neu-yeanyuan muu.chin le.* 'Actress (is) mother now.', with the new-situation particle *le* to mark the whole construction as a sentence (though not in Chinese journalistic style). But such ambiguities both in English and Chinese, are textual rather than linguistic, since stressing the second nominal expression would bring out its predicate function.

We have seen that, although a nominal subject and a verbal predicate is the commonest combination of subject and predicate, there is practically no limit to the form class of either constituent of the full sentence. Is it then possible to have a verbal subject with a nominal predicate? If only single verbs and single nouns are considered, then I have so far been able to find only one doubtful example: 逃偬头 *Taur tsann.tou*, which seems to say 'To run away is coward.' The suffix *-.tou* seems to mark *tsann.tou* as a noun, but *tsann.tou* can be modified not only by 真 *jen* 'truly' and 实在 *shyrtzay* 'really', which may be considered to modify the predication, but also by intensives such as 很 *heen* 'very' and 太 *tay* 'too', from which we shall have to regard *tsann.tou* as 'cowardly' rather than 'coward'. If, however, longer verbal and nominal expressions are also considered, we can have sentences like: (他) 不死一百岁了. *(Ta) bu syy ibae suey le.* 'If he had not died, he would have been 100 years old.'; 不下雨已经三个月了. *Bu shiah-yeu yii.jing san'g yueh le.* 'Not rain already three months,—it has been three months since it rained.' In the following example a subject-predicate pause is required in each of the clauses: 编,贾波林; 出演,贾波林 ;導演,贾波林; 演,贾波林. *Bian, Jeabolin; chuyean, Jeabolin; daoyean, Jeabolin; yean, Jeabolin.* 'Writing, Chaplin; producing, Chaplin; directing, Chaplin; acting, Chaplin.'[18] Note that, although the verbs are translated as gerunds, the Chinese forms, especially the monosyllables *bian* and *yean*, cannot be regarded as nouns by any stretch of terminology.

## 2.10. Full Sentence (S-P) Predicates

*2.10.1. The S-P Predicate as a Generalized Full Sentence.* We have seen that a full sentence can be treated as a complex of two

---

[18]This and a few other examples of the same kind were suggested to me by Leo Chen.

minor sentences. Under types of subjects we have seen that a full sentence can also serve as a clause subject. There remains, then, the possibility of a full sentence serving as a clause predicate or S-P predicate. This is indeed a very rich type.[19] Its relation to the subject, like other types of predicates, can be any kind of comment, including description and narration as special cases; the subject of an S-P predicate is sometimes described as an 'absolute', as it is set apart from the predicate clause as a whole, rather than specifically related to its (small) predicate. Such absolutes are not unknown in English, though they do not occur nearly as frequently as in Chinese. For example: *The last game we went to, why were you cheering for the visiting team all the time?* *But long run, the outlook is not so bad.* Such subjects, especially when they are time, place, and condition expressions, often translate into adverbial phrases beginning with a preposition: 'at the last game', 'in the long run', and so on. When there is no particular relation calling for a particular preposition, such a subject can always be translated with 'as for', as: 我谁知道? *Woo sheir jydaw?* 'As for me, who knows?,—How should I know?'

*2.10.2. Relation of Main Subject to the Clause Subject.* The main subject of a sentence may be closely or loosely related to the S in the S-P clause predicate. It is close when it is that of owner and owned, whole and part, class and member; it is loose when the main subject is that of time, place, condition, or other extrinsic topics. For examples of close relations, we have 这个人耳朵软. *Jeyg ren eel.dou roan.* '(As for) this man, the ear is soft,—is gullible.' 十个梨五个烂了。 *Shyrg li wuung lann le.* '(Of) ten pears, five have spoiled.' 朋友旧的好，衣裳新的好。*Perng.yeou jiow de hao; i.shang shin de hao.* '(Of) friends, old ones are best; (of) clothes, new ones are best.' These can be transformed into simple S-P by the use of *de* or *-.lii(.tou)de*, though it may either change the style or even the sentence value. Thus, while *Ta eel.dou roan.* always means 'He is gullible.', *Tade*

---

[19]The first mention of the S-P predicate, as far as I am aware, was by 陈承泽 Chern Cherngtzer, when he said, 得以句为说明语("One can take a sentence as the predicate.") 学艺 (Shyueyih) *Wissen und Wissenschaft*, no. 2 (1921).

*ell.dou roan.* may mean either (1) 'He is gullible.' or (2) 'His ear is (physically) soft.' As examples of a loose relation between the two subjects, the following sentences have been taken from conversations: 電影儿我看报了，没什么好的。*Diannyeenql woo kann-baw le, mei sherm haode.* '(As for) movies, I have looked over the papers, there aren't any good ones.' 我结婚的总送这个。*Woo jye-huen de tzoong sonq jeyg.* '(As for) me, (to) those getting married (I) always give this.' Following are further subtypes of S-P predicates:

*2.10.3. S-P as State, Characteristic, or Event About the Main Subject.* The commonest subtype of an S-P predicate is one which describes the state or characteristic, less commonly an event, about the main subject. A personal subject may have an S-P predicate in which the subject represents a part of the body and the (small) predicate some physiological or psychological condition or property. Thus, any one of the small subjects 头 *tour* 'head', 脚 *jeau* 'foot', 腿 *toei* 'leg', 腰 *iau* 'Waist, back', 肚子 *duhtz* 'belly', 牙 *ya* 'tooth', 嗓子 *saangtz* 'throat', etc., can be predicated by any of the following: 疼 *terng* 'hurts, aches', 痒 *yeang* or *yeang-.yeang* 'itches', 痠 *suan* 'sore', 麻 *ma* 'feels numb', giving rise to sentences: *Woo tour terng.* 'As for me, the head aches,—I have a headache.' *Woo toei ma le.* 'I the legs feel numb,—my legs feel numb.' *Nii jiel hair iau suan bu iau suan l'a?* 'Do you still the waist feels sore today?,—Does your waist still feel sore today?'

When an S-P predicate denotes a characteristic of the subject, usually a personality trait, the main predication can be translated as 'such that', as: 我性子急。*Woo shinqtz jyi.* 'I am such that the temperament is impatient,—I have an impatient temperament.' Other examples of predicates expressing personality traits are: 脾气好,坏,燥,慢 *pyi.chih hao, huay, tzaw, mann* 'temper good, bad, quick, slow'; 心好,坏,软 *shin hao, huay, roan* 'heart good, bad, soft'; 心眼儿直 *shinyeal jyr* 'heart straight,—frank'; 心眼儿毒 *shinyeal dwu* 'heart poisonous,—ruthless'; 胆儿大,小 *daal dah, sheau* 'gall bladder big, small,—bold, timid'; 记心(～性)好,坏 *jih.shin(q) hao, huay* 'memory good, bad'; 手巧 *shoou cheau* 'hand skillful'; 臉嫩 *lean nenn* 'face tender,—diffident'; 臉皮厚 *leanpyi how* 'face skin thick,—brazen-faced'.

Application to characteristics of nonpersonal subjects is slightly less frequent than to those of personal subjects. For examples of nonpersonal subjects: 这棵树葉子大，花儿少。 *Jey-ke shuh yehtz dah, hual shao.* '(As for) this tree, the leaves are large, flowers few.' 中國地大物博。 *Jong.gwo dih dah wuh bor.* L 'China (is such that) the land is great and resources are comprehensive.' 百事头难。 *Bae shyh tour nan.* (proverb) 'All things (are such that) the beginning is difficult.'

It is of course always possible to have nonpersonal subjects refer to personal subjects by metaphor, as: 牆上芦葦，头重脚轻根底淺 : 山尖竹筍，嘴尖皮厚腹中空。 *Chyangshanq luwoei, tour jonq jeau ching gendii chean: Shan-jian jwusoen, tzoei jian pyi how fuh-jong kong.*[20] The reeds on the walls, tops heavy, feet light, roots shallow: the bamboo shoots in the mountains, mouth sharp, skin thick, inside the body empty.', where *fuh*, literally 'abdomen', is traditionally regarded as the seat of learning.

As events about, including action by, the subject, we have: 我心跳。 *Woo shin tiaw.* 'I the heart jumps,—I have a paliptation of the heart.' 他肚子又大了。 *Ta duhtz yow dah le.* 'She the abdomen is big again,—she is pregnant again.' 他手拿着一把佛盤劍。 *Ta shoou naj i-baa forparn jiann.* 'He hand taking a vorpal sword,—He took his vorpal sword in hand.' 你怎么眼睛看着他摔了也不荄。 *Nii tzeeme yean.jing kannj ta shuaile yee bu goan?* 'Why do you eyes see him fall,—see him fall under your eyes, and do nothing about it?'

*2.10.4. The S de S' Form as a Simple Subject.* We have seen that, when the main subject S and the clause subject S' are in close relation, it is possible to use the subordinate particle *de* and make S *de* S' into one simple subject. This transformation is always possible, but it may not result in an equipollent sentence; that is, the transformation may not leave the sentence value undisturbed. In general, the form with *de* is more likely to be taken literally, while the S-P predicate (i.e., without *de*) often has a specialized or a figurative meaning. For example, both (1) *Ta duhtz*

---

[20]Leu, *Talks*, 20.

*dah le.* and (2) *Tade duhtz dah le.* may mean either (a) 'She is pregnant.' or (b) 'Her abdomen has become big (for any reason).' but form 1 is more likely to go with meaning a and form 2 with meaning b than the other way around. Thus, we have here another case of what I have called skewed relations between form and meaning. Structurally, the S *de* S' form admits no other insertion than *de*, while between a main subject and the S'-P' clause one can usually insert adverbs that modify predicates. Thus, 我 的 胆儿 小。*Woode daal sheau.* 'My courage is small,—I am timid.' has *woode daal* as an unexpandable subject, but between *woo* and *daal sheau* in *Woo daal sheau.*, one can insert various adverbs, resulting in forms like: *Woo hair daal sheau.* 'I am still timid.' *Woo bu daal sheau le.* 'I am not timid any more.' *Nii tzeem tzemm daal sheau?* 'How come you are so timid?' The following are from children's speech, which, though slightly unusual, reflects the process of their learning the use of the S-P predicate: 我 们 也 门铃儿 不响了。*Woomen yee menliengl bu sheang le.* 'We, too, the doorbell doesn't ring.' 我 老 鞋 带儿 洒了. *Woo lao shyedall saale.* 'I all the time the shoelaces have spilled.' (from confusion with 散 *saan* 'come loose'). From the topic-comment point of view, the speaker meant to say that it was the well-known doorbell failure that happened to *us*, rather than that it was a failure that happened to our doorbell, or, again, it was the shoelace loosening that is troubling *me* all the time, rather than the coming loose that keeps happening to my shoe laces.

*2.10.5. Characteristics Expressed by A-N Predicates.* Since a minor sentence may take the form of an attributive adjective and a noun (sec. 2.5.5) and a full sentence is simply predicating one minor sentence of another, we can have an A-N construction as a nominal predicate. Thus, instead of using the S-P predicate, made up of N + A, to express a characteristic, the reverse form A + N is also frequently used with a similar effect. Compare, for example: 这个人脾气强。 *Jeyg ren pyi.chih jianq.* 'This man (is such that his) temperament is stubborn.': *Jeyg ren jianq pyi.chih.* 'This man (is) stubborn temper(ed).' 这个人脑筋简单。 *Jeyg ren naojin jeandan.* 'This man (is such that his) mind is simple.': 这个人 太死心眼儿. *Jeyg ren tay syy-shinyeal.* 'This man is too fixed idea(ed).' Similarly, A-N constructions like: 沙 嗓 子 *sha-saangtz* 'sandy throat(ed),—raspy-voice(d)', 小 心 眼 ㄦ *sheau-shinyeal* small-mind(ed)', 大 舌 头 *dah-sher.tou* 'big-tongue(d),—lisping', and 急 性 子 *jyi-shinqtz* 'quick-temper(ed)' are all frequently used as nominal predicates expressing characteristics.

    *2.10.6. Bound S-P Predicates.* An S-P predicate may be a compound in which one or both parts are bound or the predicate may be in the neutral tone, or the whole compound may be used exocentrically, such as a transitive verb or an auxiliary verb. For example, in: 他 眼 睛 看 着 你 吶. *Ta yean.jing kannj nii ne.* 'He, the eyes are looking at you.' and 他 眼 睛 並 不 看 着 我. *Ta yean.jing binq bu kannj woo.* 'He, the eyes are, as a matter of fact, not looking at me.', we have the usual S-P clause with free S and P in it. But in: 你 怎 么 眼 看 着 不 荚 ? *Nii tzeem yean-kannj bu goan?* 'Why do you, (with) eyes looking, not do anything about it?', *yean* is bound and does not admit any insertion before *kannj*. In 他 心 滿 意 足 了. *Ta shin-maan yih-tzwu le.* 'He, the heart is full and intention satisfied.', *maan* in the sense of 'satisfied' is only L and therefore bound, and *yih* is also bound. In 情 願 *chyng₀yuann* 'the feeling is willing' both parts are bound and the compound is used as an auxiliary verb as in 情 願 放 棄 了 *chyng₀yuann fanqchih le* 'would rather give up'. In 头 眩 *tour.shiuann* 'head dizzy,—dizzy', *-shiuann* is bound. *Tour* 'head' and 疼 *terng* 'aches' are both free and *tour terng* is a common S-P caluse, but there is an optional neutral tone in *tour₀terng*, which is more and more being used exocentrically as a transitive verb, as in: 我 实 在 头 疼 这 件 事. *Woo shyrtzay tour₀terng jey-jiann shyh.* 'I really headache this thing,—I find this thing a real headache.' Similarly, 心 疼 *shin terng* 'the heart (literally) aches', but *shin.terng* 'hates to part with (money, etc.)' or 'is solicitous for'. The predicate 性 子 急 *shinqtz jyi* 'the temperament is quick,—quick-tempered' has free S and P and can be modified by insertion of *bu* 'not', *tay* 'too', and so on, as: *shinqtz bu jyi* 'the temperament is not quick', *shinqtz tay jyi* 'the temperament is too quick', but in *shinqjyi* 'quick-tempered' *shinq* is bound and can only be modified in the forms *bu shinqjyi, tay* *shinqjyi*, and so on. Similarly, 面善 *miannshann* 'face kindly,— looks familiar' has both parts bound, and 面生 *miannsheng* 'face unfamiliar,—unfamiliar' has a bound subject. 这个人年纪很 轻.*Jeyg ren nian.jih heen ching*. 'This man, the age is very light, —is very young.' has free subject *nian.jih* and free predicate *heen ching*, but *Jeyg ren heen nianching*. 'This man is very years-light, —young.' has a bound subject *nian*. In the following examples: 我見了他就头大． *Woo jiannle ta jiow tour-dah*. 'Whenever I see him I feel head-swollen,—he is a nuisance.' 他看見了那 么些錢也不眼儿热． *Ta kann.jiann le nemm shie chyan yee bu yeal-reh*. 'He sees so much money and yet does not eyes hot, —is not covetous for it.' 你打算路过哪些城？ *Nii daa- .suann luh-guoh neei.shie cherng?* 'Which cities are you planning to road-pass,—to pass through on your way?'—in all these exam- ples the S and P are otherwise free but admit of no insertions. Thus while one could, with a free S-P predicate, say either: (1) 我不肚子疼了． *Woo bu duhtz terng le*. or (2) *Woo duhtz bu terng le*. 'I no longer have a belly ache.', one can only say: (1) 你路过不路过盧山？ *Nii luhguoh bu luhguoh Lu Shan?* but not (2) °*Nii luh guoh bu guoh Lu Shan?* for 'Are you going to pass Lu Shan on your way?' One could recast the sentence in the S *de* S′ form and say: *Nii de luh* 经过 *jingguoh bu jingguoh Lu Shan?* 'Does your way pass through Lu Shan?' where the point of the question is differently placed. Note that in: 他姓 王.*Ta shinq Wang*. 'His surname is Wang.', *shinq Wang* is not an S-P predicate. While one can say: *Woo bu luhguoh Lu Shan*. (with bound S-P) or *Woo bu duhtz terng le*. (with free S-P) as well as *Woo bu shinq Wang*., one cannot use the perfective suffix *le* and say °*luhle* or °*duhtzle* as one can with real verbs, as in 我姓 了王才怪呐！ *Woo shinqle Wang tsair guay ne!* '(If) I were named Wang, then it would be strange!' *Shinq* in *shinq Wang* is therefore a transitive verb 'has the name of' used in the predicate and not a noun used as the small subject.

2.10.7. *Time, Place, Conditon in Main Subject*. When the main subject sets the scene by giving the time, place, condition, and the like, the second subject is more loosely related to it and the S *de* S′ change will not generally be available. Thus, although: 今儿天好. *Jiel tian hao.* 'Today, the weather is good.' could be changed to *Jiel de tian hao.* 'Today's weather is fine.', the more general case like: 今儿王先生来. *Jiel Wang .Shian-.sheng lai.* 'Today Mr. Wang is coming.' cannot be changed to: *Jiel de Wang .Shian.sheng lai.* 'Today's Mr. Wang, etc. 'It has been claimed (Hwu-Wen, 137-138) that, treating *Ta jiel lai.* as having *ta* as subject and *Jiel ta lai.* as having *jiel* as subject would be a *reductio ad absurdum* of the theory that the first part of the sentence before the major break is the subject. This would be so if the subject were still understood as the actor expression. But if the subject is the main topic that sets the scene, then that is precisely the difference of interest expressed by the different word order. In: *Jiel ta lai.* 'Today he is coming.' we are talking about the program of the day and in: *Ta jiel lai.* 'He comes today.' we are talking about him and his date of coming. Other things being equal, there is in Chinese a slight preference for time to come before place, but no special preference as to the position of the actor expression,[21] as we have seen in the preceding sentence.

---

[21]俞敏 (Yu Miin), ZGYW, no. 61, 7-10 (1957), has a time-place-line-nucleus scheme of sentence structure, illustrated by the sentence:

| | | |
|---|---|---|
| 昨儿响午呀, | *Tzwol shaang.huo ia,* | 'Yesterday noon,' (time) |
| 德勝门外头啊, | *Dersheng Men-way.tou ua,* | 'outside Dersheng Men,' (place) |
| 一个老头儿啊, | *ig laotourl a,* | 'an old man,' (line) |
| 釣上来了一条 | *diaw.shanq.laile i-tyau* | 'fished up a ten-catty |
| 十斤重的鱼. | *shyr-jin-jonq de yu.* | fish.' (nucleus) |

While this formula fits many, perhaps most, of the cases, it is far from being a universal rule of Chinese word order. Yu Miin does, however, make the following important observations: (1) that in wenyan the place expression usually comes last; (2) that in dialects with complicated tone sandhi, as in Amoy, each of these four units ends in a pre-pause tone but has progressive (non-pause) tones within each unit; (3) that the "line" tells only with whom the phenomenon in the "nucleus" is concerned, while the direction of action is left to other methods of distinction.

Further examples of time and place expressions for the main subject are: 清明时節雨纷ㄟ. *Chingming shyrjye yeu fenfen.* (poet.) 'Chingming (about Easter) time, the rain freely falls.' 八月十五家ㄟ儿吃月饼。 *Bayueh shyrwuu jiajial dou chy yueh.biing.* 'The fifteenth of the eighth moon, every family eats mooncakes.' 那回大火, 幸虧消防隊到的早. *Ney-hwei dahhuoo, shinq.kuei shiaufarng-duey daw de tzao.* 'The fire that time, fortunately, the fire department arrived early.' 美國芒菓貴，因為美國芒菓都不是美國芒菓. *Meei.gwo mang-guoo guey, inwey Meei.gwo mangguoo dou bush Meei.gwo mang-guoo.* '(In) America, mangoes are expensive, because (in) America, mangoes are none of them American mangoes.', where insertion of *de* is not possible in the first *Meei.gwo mangguoo*, is possible in the second, with resulting change of construction, and is possible in the third, without affecting the construction. 中國冬菇从前都是日本来的. *Jong.gwo donggu tsorngchyan dou sh Ryhbeen lai de.* '(In) China, the (dried) mushrooms formerly all came from Japan.'

Following are examples of very general and loose relations between the two subjects: 留学的事情政府早規定了办法了. *Lioushyue de shyh.chyng, jenqfuu tzao gueidinqle bann$_0$faa le.* '(With regard to) the matter of studying abroad, the government made regulations of procedure long ago.' 中國话'cigarette' 怎么说？ *Jong.gwohuah 'cigarette' tzeeme shuo?* '(In) Chinese "cigarette" is said how,—how do you say "cigarette" in Chinese? (I know how to say "cigar").' 'Cigarette' *Jong.gwo-huah tzeem shuo?* '(As for) "cigarette", the Chinese is said how,—how do you say "cigarette" in Chinese? (I know how to say it in French.)' 你浮水学会了没有？ *Nii fuh-shoei shyue-hueyle mei-.yeou?* 'Have you learned how to swim (among other things)?' 浮水你学会了没有？ *Fuh-shoei nii shyue-hueyle mei.yeou?* '(Speaking of) swimming, have you learned (it)?' 你不能功课不做完啊！ *Nii buneng gong$_0$keh bu tzuoh-wan a!* 'You mustn't the-lesson-isn't-finished,—you mustn't leave your lesson unfinished!' 邪[1]俗耶. *Ye$_1$ swu ye$_2$.* '(As for the character) ye$_1$, the vulgar form is $ye_2$.[22] This last example is in common lexicographical style, when $ye_2$ is a nominal predicate in the predicate clause. It was cited by Giles[23] to show that Chinese was *supra grammaticam,* since an apparently parallel form 耶 俗 邪 字 *Ye₂ swu ye₁-tzyh* would mean exactly the reverse: 'Ye₂ is the vulgar(ized) $ye_1$ character'. It means the opposite because the longer sentence has a different, and simpler, construction, in which *swu ye₁-tzyh* 'vulgar $ye_1$ character' is a nominal predicate in the whole sentence. It goes without saying that a correct analysis of a sentence is not necessarily the whole story of its meaning, but there is nothing paradoxical about $ye_1$ *swu* $ye_2$ having one construction and *Ye₂ swu ye₁ -tzyh* having another, with a difference in meaning. Note that the shorter sentence, with its S-P predicate, is a more complicated sentence than the longer sentence, with only a nominal predicate.

*2.10.8. Subject or Inverted Object?* A sentence like: 我 酒 現 在 不 喝 了。 *Woo jeou shianntzay bu he le.* 'I am not going to drink wine now.' is often analyzed as having *jeou* as object of *he,* but placed in inverted word order for greater emphasis or prominence than the V-O order: *Woo shianntzay bu he jeou le.* But since the direction of a verb can go either outward from, or inward to, the subject, *jeou* can very well be the subject of *he:* 'As for me, wine is not going to be drunk now.' and the emphasis, if desired, is made equally effective by *jeou* being in the subject position in the S-P caluse. If the goal word is placed in the main subject position, still greater prominence is attained, as: 晚 报 老 三 拿 去 了。 *Woanbaw Lao San na.chiuh le* '(As for) the evening paper, Lao San took (it) away.' Similarly, the following sentences, often analyzed as having inverted objects, can be analyzed as having S-P predicates: 我 头 也 不 回， 汗 也 不 擦。 *Woo tour yee bu hwei, hann yee bu tsa.* 'I, neither the head turns, nor the sweat is wiped,—I neither turn my head nor

---

[22]This is also the character for the adjective *shye* 'heretical, diabolical', which is not the word under discussion. *Ye,* written with either character, is a final particle of wenyan, used in rhetorical questions.

[23]Herbert A. Giles, *A Chinese-English Dictionary,* London and Shanghai, 1892, p. xi.

wipe my sweat.' 你 小 題 大 做 嘜! *Nii sheau-tyi dah-tzuoh me!* 'You, a little problem, big ado!' 大 洞 大 貓 鑽, 小 洞 小 貓 鑽. *Dah-donq dah-mhau tzuan, sheau-donq sheau-mhau tzuan.* 'Big hole big cat goes through, little hole little cat goes through'; 大 貓 大 碗 餵, 小 貓 小 碗 餵. *Dah mhau dah-woan wey, sheau-mhau sheau-woan wey.* 'Big cat big bowl feeds, little cat little bowl feeds.' (Cf. 'It *feeds* on fish.')

It may be objected that the transitives verbs *hwei* 'turns', *tsa* 'wipes', etc., will be left dangling without object if *tour* 'head', *hann* 'sweat', etc., are made their subjects instead of their objects. The answer is that there are many verbs in which the direction of action is not clear to begin with (sec. 2.6.2): Does my head turn, or do I have to turn it before it turns? And even with verbs which do have directed actions, it is the usual practice with Chinese transitive verbs to omit the object if the goal of action has been mentioned in a near context, even in a separate sentence, as: *Jeh sh woode baw; nii yaw kann ma?* 'This is my paper; do you want to read (it)?' If an object *ta* 'it' were added, it would have a totally different connotation: 'Do you want to read that kind of stuff?' (See end of 5.4.5 on omission of objects.)

# 2.11 Compound Sentences

*2.11.1. Simple and Composite Sentences.* Two or more sentences may come into close combination to form a composite sentence. A composite sentence may be compound or complex according as the component sentences are in coordinate or non-coordinate relation. For example, 你 不 認 得 我, 我 也 不 認 得 你. *Nii bu rennde woo, woo bu rennde nii.* 'You don't know me and I don't know you either.' is a compound sentence, consisting of two parallel sentences, but 你 要 是 看 不 起 他, 他 就 看 不 起 你. *Nii yawsh kann.bu-chii ta, ta jiow kann.bu-chii nii.* 'If you look down upon him, he will look down upon you.' is a complex sentence, consisting of a dependent clause marked by *yawsh* 'if' followed by the principal clause.

Since we have treated the full sentence as consisting of two minor sentences, and since the subject-predicate relation is not a coordinate relation, it follows that a full sentence is a complex sentence of two minor sentences. In ordinary usage, however, such a sentence is called a simple (full) sentence and there will be no danger of confusion so long as we understand that a complex sentence of the lowest degree is just the simple (full) sentence with a subject and a predicate.

Most Chinese grammarians[24] distinguish between (1) complex sentences (proper), consisting of a dependent clause and a principal clause, each complete in itself and (2) pregnant sentences, or mother-and-child sentences, in which the mother sentence contains, kangaroo fashion, a child sentence as one of its essential constituents.

*2.11.2. Compound Minor Sentences.* A succession of two minor sentences does not necessarily make a full sentence. They may be two separate sentences if each has a conclusive sentence intonation, as: 这 个 人！ 也 不 跟 朋 友 打 招 呼！ *Jeyg ren! Yee bu gen perng.yeou daa jau.hu!* 'What a man! Doesn't even say hello to his friends!' Two minor sentences of parallel form may form a compound minor sentence instead of a full sentence of subject and predicate. For example: 下 雨 了， 冒 泡ㄦ 了 ；王 八 带 了 草 帽ㄦ 了。 *Shiah-yeu le, maw-pawl le; wang.ba dayle tsaomawl le.* 'It is raining, it is bubbling; the turtle is wearing a straw hat.' (nursery rhyme) consists of two (verbal) minor sentences forming a compound sentence, separated by a concluding intonation and pause (indicated by ";") from the full sentence that follows.

*2.11.3. Compound Sentence or Separate Sentences?* Since a compound sentence consists of clauses each of which is complete in itself, how can one tell whether any given succession of sentences are parts of a compound sentence or simply separate sentences? This depends upon several factors: (1) prosodic elements, such as pause and intonation, (2) adverbs or conjunctions as markers, (3) parallelism of the sentences. Thus, in: 天 气 很 好。但 是 我 不 能 出 去。 *Tian.chih heen hao / . / Dannsh woo buneng chu.chiuh / . /* 'The weather is very fine / . / But I cannot go out / . /' *hao* has a full 3rd Tone, followed by a full pause, and

---

[24]See Leu, *LWJyi,* 114; ZGYW, no. 60:9-13 (1957); no. 62:20-24 (1957).

we have two sentences. But if *hao* has a drawl on a full or half 3rd Tone, then we have one compound sentence. An interesting sidelight on the use of compound sentences is reflected in the greater use of commas (or whatever punctuation signs correspond to commas) in Chinese writing, where a similar passage or a translation in English would have periods for some of the commas.

Repeated or correlative adverbs bind clauses into compound sentences, as: 你也不认得我，我也不认得你。 *Nii yee bu rennde woo, woo yee bu rennde nii.* 'Neither do you know me, nor do I know you.', where *yee ... yee* 'also ... also' are adverbs. 風又冷，雨又大，我又没有車。 *Feng yow leeng, yeu yow dah, woo yow meiyeou che.* 'The wind is cold, the rain is heavy, too, and I have no car, either.' 他一头儿跑，我一头儿追。 *Ta itourl pao, woo itourl juei.* 'He runs on the one hand, I give chase on the other,—I chase him as he runs.' 不但朋友们来找他，而且(～ 並且 )生人也来找他。 *Budann perng-.yeoumen lai jao ta, erlchiee* (or *binqchiee*) *shengren yee lai jao ta.* 'Not only do friends come to look him up, but strangers also come to look him up.'

Single conjunctions as 但是 *dannsh* 'but', 可是 *keesh* 'but', and 況且 *kuanqchiee* 'moreover' can also join clauses in a compound sentence, but, since they can also begin new sentences after a preceding sentence is concluded, such conjunctions alone are not unambiguous markers of coordinate sentences. The other factors may have to be considered.

Parallelism is often a mark of compound sentences, as: 一个人付錢，一个人收錢。 *Ig ren fuh chyan, ig ren shou chyan.* 'One pays, another receives.' 初等学生上初等科，中等 ... ，高等 ...。 *Chudeeng shyue.sheng shanq chudeengke, jongdeeng shyue.sheng shanq jongdeengke, gaudeeng shyue.sheng shanq gaudeengke.* 'Elementary students take elementary courses, intermediate students take intermediate courses, and advanced students take advanced courses.' In 上船的上船，上岸的上岸！ *Shanq-chwan de shanq-chwan, shanq-ann de shanq-ann!* 'All aboard that's going aboard, all ashore that's going ashore!', the suspense-conclusion intonation [sec. 1.3.7 (2)] binds the two coordinate clauses into one sentence.

Of the three factors mentioned above, those of prosodic elements are the most important and are often sufficient to determine a compound sentence. Since ordinary writing, whether in characters or in some form of transcription, never marks all the prosodic features, there is often possibility of textual ambiguity where there is really no ambiguity in the actual speech, as was the case with the first example in this section.

*2.11.4 Coordinate Subjects and Predicates.* A subject can be a construction consisting of two or more coordinate constituents, as: 你 我 他 一 塊儿 去 吧! *Nii woo ta ikuall chiuh ba!* 'You (and) I (and) he go there together, let's!' 吃 饭 睡 觉 都 在 一 间 小 屋 子 裡。 *Chy-fann shuey-jiaw dou tzay i-jian sheau-utz.lii.* 'Eating and sleeping are both in one small room.' 四 书 五 经 没 全 念 完。 *Syh-shu Wuu-jing mei chyuan niann-wan.* 'The Four books and the Five Classics were not all read through.' Likewise, a predicate can also consist of two or more coordinate constituents, as: 我 又 睏 又 饿。 *Woo yow kuenn yow eh.* 'I am both sleepy and hungry.' 维 持 生 活，得 有 的 吃 ， 有 的 穿 ， 有 的 住。 *Weichyr sheng.hwo, deei yeou de chy, yeou de chuan, yeou de juh.* 'Maintaining life needs to have something to eat, something to wear, and somewhere to live.' Or, both subject and predicate can have two or more coordinate parts, as: 红、绿、 黄、青、蓝、紫，既 不 是 國 旗 的 颜 色 ，又 不 是 分 光 谱 的 七 色。*Horng liuh hwang ching lan tzyy, jih bush gwochyi de yan-.shae, yow bush fenguangpuu de chi-seh.* 'Red, green, yellow, blue-green, blue, purple are neither the colors of the national flag, nor the seven colors of the spectrum.' Note that in none of these examples is it possible to split the subject into separate subjects of a compound sentence without resulting either in nonsense or in a sentence of a different sentence value. Thus, *Woo ikuall chiuh* 'I go together' would be nonsense; *Syh-shu mei chyuan niann-wan, Wuu-jing mei chyuan niann-wan* 'The Four Books were not all read through and the Five Classics were not all read through' has obviously a different sentence value from that of the original sentence with one (coordinate) subject, since one could finish reading all the Four Books, but not all the Five Classics, in which case the simple sentence with the compound subject would be true but the compound sentence would be false.

If, on the other hand, separation of a compound subject or a compound predicate results in no change of sentence value, then either analysis will be possible, but, since supplying unexpressed forms is always gratuitous when it is not necessary, the simplest analysis is to treat all such cases as simple sentences with compound subjects and/or predicates. Examples follow: 四书五经是好书. *Syh-shu (sh hao-shu,) Wuu-jing sh hao-shu.* 'The Four Books (are good books) and the Five Classics are good books.' 人人都得做工，都得休息。*Renren dou deei tzuoh-gong, (renren) dou deei shiou.shyi.* 'Everyone must work, (everyone) must rest.' 哥哥弟弟姐姐妹妹一天到晚在这儿吃，一天到晚在这儿玩儿。 *Ge.ge dih.dih jiee.jiee mey.mey i-tian-daw-woan tzay jell chy, i-tian-daw-woan tzay jell wal.* 'The older brothers, the younger brothers, the older sisters, and the younger sisters eat here all day and play here all day.' It would obviously be artificial to analyze the last simple sentence as an abbreviation of, even though it is of the same truth value as, the conjunction of, the eight clauses: (1) *Ge.ge i-tian-daw-woan tzay jell chy,* (2) *Ge.ge i-tian-daw-woan tzay jell wal,* (3) *dih.dih i-tian-daw-woan tzay jell chy,* ... (8) *mey.mey i-tian-daw-woan tzay jell wal.*

## 2.12. Complex Sentences

*2.12.1. "Pregnant" Sentences and Complex Sentences.* As we have noted, most Chinese grammarians make a distinction between pregnant, or mother-and-child, sentences and other complex sentences. The two types of sentences differ in at least three respects: (1) there is usually no pause or pause particle between the mother clause and the child clause, while between a dependent and a principal clause there is the same potential pause or pause particle as between a subject and its predicate, as: 我没想到你忘了。 *Woo mei sheang.daw nii wanqle.* 'I didn't think that you would forget.' which has no pause, whereas: *Woo (yawsh) mei sheang.daw a* (or *me, ne,* or zero), *nii jiow wanqle.* 'If I hadn't thought of it, you would have forgotten.' has an optional pause or pause particle. (2) A dependent clause is often introduced by a conjunction, whereas a child clause is never introduced in this way.[25] (3) The child clause being a constituent of the sentence, the mother clause is incomplete without it, as: 我盼望明儿不下雨。*Woo pann.wanq miengl bu shiah-yeu.* 'I hope it won't rain tomorrow.', where *Woo pann.wanq* 'I hope' would be left dangling without an object. However, there are many intermediate cases which make the explanation of these three tests uncertain, and it is a matter of terminology as to whether a complex sentence is of one type or another so long as the functions of its parts are analyzable, as detailed below.

2.12.2. *Clause (S-P) Subjects and Predicates.* Under types of subjects and predicates we have already examined cases where the subject or predicate is in the form of a full sentence, or S-P form. Further examples of SP-P: 狗拿耗子，多管闲事。*Goou na hawtz, duo goan shyan-shyh.* 'That a dog catches rats is meddling with none of his business.' 你光说那个没用。*Nii guang shuo neyg mei yonq.* 'That you merely say it is of no use.' 妈々的宝贝把菠菜吃完了乖。 *Mha.mha de bao.bey bae bortsay chy-wanle guai.* '(That) Mama's darling has finished eating the spinach is being a good boy.' S-SP: 这个人命苦。*Jeyg ren minq kuu.* 'This man (is such that his) luck is hard.' SP-SP (both the subject and the predicate in S-P form in the same sentence): 他死了我真难受。 *Ta syyle woo jen nanshow.* 'That he should have died (is something about which) I feel awfully bad.'

2.12.3. *Clause Objects.* When a clause is the whole subject or the whole predicate, it is one of the immediate constituents of the sentence. When, however, a clause forms only a part of the subject or the predicate, then it is a constituent of a lower level and is not separated by a pause from the rest of the subject or predicate. Thus, in: 我说钱的事儿不要紧。*Woo shuo chyan de shell buyawjiin.* 'I say that the matter of money is not important.', the clause object to *shuo* 'say' is joined on without

---

[25]This is of course not necessarily true of languages other than Chinese: 'I know *that* I must ask him.'

pause, while if the particle *ia* and a pause / , / were inserted
after *shuo*, then the sentence would mean 'I say (i.e., listen to
me), the matter of money is not important.' and the second clause
would be actually asserted as a coordinate sentence and not as a
grammatical object to *shuo*. Other examples of clause objects are:
他 就 想 不 起 来 谁 来 拜 望 他 来 着。 *Ta jiow sheang.bu-
chiilai sheir lai bay.wanq ta laij.* 'He just can't recall who came
to call on him.' 我 知 道 我 不 知 道 的 人 也 许 知 道 我。
*Woo jy.daw woo bu jy.daw de ren yeesheu jy.daw woo.* 'I know
that people I don't know of may know of me.' 你 说 那 个 没
用。*Nii shuo neyg mei yonq.* 'You say that that is of no use.'
(Cf. supra.)

Exceptionally, however, if a clause object is very long, a
pause and/or pause particle may be inserted after the verb, as in:
我 们 都 以 为 啊 ， 他 又 是 一 个 人 拿 了 本 小 说儿 躲
得 那儿 看 去 了。 *Woomen dou yiiwei a, ta yowsh ig ren nale
been sheaushuol duoo de nall kann .chiuh le.* 'We all thought,
that he had again taken hold of a novel and hid in a corner to
read away all by himself.'[26]

Clause objects typically occur after verbs of thought and perception, the most important of which are: 想 *sheang* 'think';
知道 *jy.daw* 'knows'; 以 为 *yiiwei* 'takes it (that)'; 当 着 *daangj*
(sic), 当 是 *danqsh* 'thought (mistakenly that)'; 怕,恐 怕 *pah,
koong$_o$pah* 'afraid (that), perhaps'; 说 *shuo* 'says'; 听 说 *ting shuo*,
听 见 *ting.jiann*, 听 见 说 *ting.jiann shuo* 'has heard (that)'; 看
*kann*, 看 见 *kann.jiann* 'sees (that)'; 告 送 *gaw.sonq* 'tells (that)';
盼 望 *pann.wanq*, 希 望 *shiwanq* 'hopes (that)'; 指 望 ( 着 ) *jyy-
.wanq(j)* 'expects (that)'; 答 应 *da.ying* 'promises (that)'; 记 着 *jihj,
记 得 *jihde* 'remembers (that)'; 记 住 *jih.juh* 'keeps in mind (that)';
忘 了 *wanqle,* 忘 记 *wanq.jih* 'forgets (that)'; and their negatives
with *bu* 'not' or *mei(.yeou)* 'did not', 'have not'.

With an S-P subject or S-P predicate, there is of course the
possibility of a clause object after the verb in one of the clauses,

---

[26]The possibility of such a pause was called to my attention by Tsu-Lin
Mei, who also furnished the above example.

as: 你 不 知 道 水 銀 会 凝 固 真 奇 怪。 *Nii bujy.daw shoeiyn huey ningguh jen chyiguay.* 'That you don't know that mercury can solidify is really strange.' 那 回 大 火，人 々 都 以 为 電 線 走 了 電. *Ney-hwei dah huoo, renren duo yiiwei diannshiann tzooule diann.* 'That time big fire, everyone thought that the wires had had the electricity run away,—had had a short circuit'.

2.12.4. *Adjectival Clauses.* A clause can modify any nominal expression by adding the subordinative particle *de*. The simplest form of such a clause consists of a subject and a verbal expression, as in 他 说 的 话 *ta shuo de huah* 'he said *de* words,—the words he said,—what he said', 我 信 的 教 *woo shinn de jiaw* 'the religion I believe in'. The adverb 所 *suoo* 'actually' is often added for emphasis, as in *ta suoo shuo de huah* 'the words he actually said', whence also 'all the words he said'.[27] Similarly, 所 有 的 人 *suoo yeou de ren* 'all the people (that there are),—all the people'.

Since *de* indicates modification in a very general way, it can be used where the relations would have to be specified if translated into English, as in the italicized words in the following examples: 耳 朵 聋 的 人 最 苦. *Eel.dou long de ren tzuey kuu.* 'One *whose* ear is deaf is most miserable.' 脾 气 坏 的 人 不 识 玩. *Pyi.chih huey de ren bu shyh-wan.* 'People *whose* temper is bad can't take a joke.' 这 是 他 睡 觉 的 地 方儿. *Jeh sh ta shuey-jiaw de dih.fangl.* 'This is the place *where* he sleeps.' 我 遇 見 过 很 多 烟 卷儿 不 離 手 的 人. *Woo yuh.jiann.guo heen duo ianjeual bu li shoou de ren.* 'I have met many people

---

[27]Because of the occurrence of *suoo* in subordinative clauses, it is often equated to English 'which, whom, that', which may be a valid analysis for wenyan, as it has other cases of objects before verbs, but in the modern language *suoo* occupies the position of an adverb, namely between the subject and the verb. There is also a Peiping localism in which *suoo* is an intensive adverb, as in 他 所 阔 呐! *Ta suoo kuoh ne!* 'He is awfully rich!' The function of *suoo* in wenyan, in which there is frequent occurrence of preverbal pronominal objects, is a different story, on which see 周 法 高，"所" 字 之 性 質 Fa-Kao Chou, "On the Nature of the Word *suoo*", 中 央 研 究 院 院 刊 *Annals of Academia Sinica*, III:221-276 (1956).

*whose* cigarettes never left *their* hands.' Note that the subordinate particle *de* is always applicable between the modifier and the modified, whatever the specific relation is between them. Thus, 我写字的纸笔 *woo shiee-tzyh de jyy-bii* 'the paper I write on and the pen I write with'; 我喝水的杯子 *woo he shoei de beitz* 'the cup I drink out of'; 我跳的井 *woo tiaw de jiing* 'the well I jump into (or over)'; 我来的地方儿 *woo lai de dih-.fangl* 'the place I came from'; 我去的地方儿 *woo chiuh de dih.fangl* 'the place I go to'. It is possible, when necessary for clarity, to specify the relation and say 我从那儿来的地方儿 *woo tsorng nall lai de dih.fangl* 'I from there come's place—the place I come from', but such constructions are considered awkward and are rarely needed. (Cf. the L form 余所自来 *yu suoo tzyh lai.* 'I where from come,—where I came from.' Similarly, a construction like 我对他说了多谢的那个人 *woo duey ta shuole 'duoshieh' de neyg ren* 'the man to whom I said "many thanks" ' is also awkward, but is nevertheless sometimes heard.

A very frequent and important use of the adjectival clause is that of modifying a word for time, place, or condition, thus forming a subject expression of time, place, or condition, often translatable into an adverbial clause, as: 我昨儿晚上上床的时候儿, 客人还没全走. *Woo tzwol woan.shanq shanq-chwang de* $_0$*shyr.howl, keh.ren hair mei chyuan tzoou.* 'When I went to bed last night, the guests had not all gone.' 大家用功的地方儿, 你不能大声儿说话. *Dahjia yonq-gong de dih.fangl, nii buneng dahshengl shuo-huah.* 'Where everybody is studying, you must not talk loudly.' 他一定要去的话, 我也没法儿拦阻他. *Ta idinq yaw chiuh de* $_0$*huah, woo yee meifal lantzuu ta.* '(In) the event that he insists on going, I have no way of stopping him, either'. So frequently, however, is the modified noun in the neutral tone that the subordinative particle *de*, together with a noun for time, place, or condition, practically forms with it a compound particle, marking the clause as a dependent clause, so that ... *de.shyr.howl* can be equated with the subordinate conjunction 'when', ... *de.dih.fangl* to 'where', and ... *de.huah* to 'in case'. Note, however, that the change from a sentence S plus *de shyr.howl* 'the time of S' into S + enclitic *de.shyr.howl* 'when S' is only a change from a nominal subject with a clause modifier into a clause subject introduced by a (compound) particle. The whole resulting form, though translatable into an adverbial clause, is, in our analysis, still the large subject.

*2.12.5. Adverbial Clauses as Subjects.* We have seen that a dependent clause in a pregnant sentence can be a subject, an object, or an adjectival modifier. These three kinds of clauses are, however, not entirely on a par with each other, since a subject is always capable of being followed by a pause before the predicate, while verb-object and adjective-noun constructions admit of no pause. Now what about an adverb-verb or adverbial clause-principal clause construction? As a matter of fact, these two are quite different things. In 很好 *heen hao* 'very good', 快跑 *kuay pao* 'runs fast', or even *kuaykualde pao* 'runs rapidly', there is no pause between adverb and verb. But all grammarians agree that dependent clauses with 虽然 *sweiran* 'although', 要是 *yawsh* 'if', and so on can, and in fact usually do, have a pause before the principal clause and that this is one of the criteria for distinguishing a complex sentence proper from a pregnant sentence. A dependent clause is usually taken as modifying the principal clause as a whole instead of merely modifying the verb in it and is thus detachable without leaving the principal clause incomplete.

The main types of adverbial clauses most commonly recognized are those expressing: (1) concession, (2) cause or reason, time, and place, or (3) condition. Because (a) such clauses are usually followed by the same pause or pause particles as after subjects, (b) they occur at the beginning of a sentence unless they are an afterthought, (c) the so-called subordinate conjunctions can *always* follow the subject and modify the verb in the clause, (d) complex sentences shade into compound sentences or simple sentences with complex predicates—for all these reasons we prefer to treat a dependent clause simply as a clause subject and the principal clause as the predicate.

*2.12.6. Subordinate Conjunctions or Adverbs?* A rather striking characteristic of the so-called subordinate conjunctions like 虽然 *sweiran* 'although', 因为 *inwey* 'because', and 假如 *jearu* 'if is that all of them, as noted above, *can* follow the subject of the dependent clause. Thus, one can say either: 雖然我想發財, ... *Sweiran woo sheang fa-tsair*, ... 'Although I wish to get rich, ...' or: *Woo sweiran sheang fa-tsair*, ... . Whether such a word precedes or follows the subject usually depends upon whether the two clauses have different subjects or the same subject. Thus, of the forms below:

(1) *Sweiran woo sheang fa-tsair*,     'Although I want to get rich,

    可是你不讓我
    *keesh nii bu ranq .woo.*        yet you don't let me.'

(2) *Woo sweiran sheang fa-tsair*,    'I although want to get rich,

    可是不敢冒險
    *keesh bugaan maw-shean.*     yet don't dare to take risks.'

(3) *Sweiran woo sheang fa-tsair*,    'Although I want to get rich,

    *keesh bugaan maw-shean.*     yet don't dare to take risks.'

(4) *Woo sweiran sheang fa-tsair*,     'I although want to get rich,

    *keesh nii bu ranq .woo.*        yet you don't let me.'

all four are possible, but forms 1 and 2 are much more common than forms 3 and 4. A few adverbs in complex sentences never precede the subjects; *jiow* 'then', *hair* 'still', etc., and most of the correlative adverbs in sec. 2.12.8 below are of this type. For example, in: 要是我遲了,你就甭等. *Yawsh woo chyr le, nii jiow berng deeng.* 'If I am late, you (then) don't need to wait.', *jiow* cannot come before *nii*, as 'then' could and normally does, if used at all, before 'you' in English. Note, however, that the wenyan equivalent of *jiow*, namely 則 *tzer*, more often precedes than follows the subject. But exceptionally, in 要是兩个包,就一个是你們的, 一个是他們的;要是一个包,就全是你們的. *Yawsh leangg bau, jiow ig sh niimende, ig sh tamende; yawsh ig bau, jiow chyuan sh niimende.* 'If it's two packages, then one is yours and the other is theirs; if it's one package, then it's all yours.', the first *jiow* does precede the subject.

    *2.12.7. Types of Subordinate Clauses.* With the understanding that subordinate clauses can be analyzed as subjects, we shall give illustrations of their use below:

(1) Concession is expressed by *sweiran ... keesh* ( ~ *dannsh*) 'although ... yet' or *guhran ... dannsh* (~ *keesh*) 'to be sure ... but', as: 虽然打雷, 可是不下雨. *Sweiran daa-lei, keesh bu shiah-yeu.* 'Although it thunders, (yet) it doesn't rain.' 世界上好人固然不少, 但是坏人更多. *Shyh.jieh.shanq hao-ren guhran bu-shao, dannsh huay-ren genq duo.* 'There are many good people in the world, to be sure, but there are still more bad people.'

(2) Cause or reason is expressed by $in_0wey ... suoo_0yii$ 'because ... therefore', *jihran ... jiow* 'since (or inasmuch as) ... then', as: 他因为太太病了, 所以不能来. *Ta $in_0wey$ tay.tay binq le, $suoo_0yii$ buneng lai.* 'Because his wife is sick, (therefore) he cannot come.' 既然大家都没预备好, 那事情就下次再谈吧. *Jihran dahjia dou mei yuh.bey-hao, nah shyh.chyng jiow shiah-tsyh tzay tarn ba.* 'Since everybody is unprepared, (then) the matter had better be discussed next time.'

Besides $in_0wey$ 'because', which can be followed by either a verbal expression or a full S-P clause, there are two overtly verbal forms *weyle* 'because of' and *weyj* 'owing to, due to' which can also take a nominal expression, as: 他为了 (~ 为着) 钱去做坏事. *Ta weyle* (~*weyj*) *chyan chiuh tzuoh huay-shyh.* 'He, on account of money, goes to do evil deeds.', but not: °*Ta $in_0wey$ chyan chiuh tzuoh huay-shyh.* With $in_0wey$, one can say: *Ta $in_0wey$ yaw chyan, suoo.yii ... .* 'He because (he) wants money, ... .'

A reason or cause clause cannot come as the second clause except (a) as a nominal predicate ending in 的缘故 *de .yuan.guh* 'the reason that' or (b) as an afterthought. Thus, one can say: 他因为下雨, 所以不来了. *Ta $in_0wey$ shiah-yeu, suoo.yii bu lai le.* 'Because it is raining, he is not coming.', but *Ta (suoo.yii) bu lai, sh ($in_0wey$) shiah-yeu de $_0yuan.guh$.* '(That) he is not coming, is (for) the reason that it is raining.' Note that the *de* here is the appositional *de* 'the reason, namely, that it is raining'. It is the same *de* in definitions such as: 獃就是不走的意思. *'Dai' jiowsh 'bu tzoou' de yih.sy.* ' "To stay" is just "not to leave" that meaning,—"To stay" means "not to leave".' For a fuller discussion of this appositional, or equational *de*, see section 5.3.6.5.

As an afterthought, the consequent clause is spoken with a concluding intonation /./ and the afterthought clause fails to be a separate sentence only by the *piu mosso* tempo (marked by '←') in its first few words, characteristic of afterthought expressions, as: *Ta bu lai le* /./ ← *inwey shiah-yeu le.* 'He is not coming /./ 'cause it's raining.' The preceding discussion does not concern questions of scope of the negative in: 'He is not staying away because it's raining, but because ... .' which in Chinese would take the form: *Ta bush inwey shiah-yeu le bu lai, sh inwey ... .* Here it is a question of ICs and involves nothing new as to forms of expressing reason or cause.

(3) Condition or supposition is expressed by the following 'if'-words: 要是 *yawsh* (etym. the same as *ruohsh*), *yaw,* 假如 *jearu,* 若是 *ruohsh* (如 *ru* and *ruoh* limited to wenyan), 倘若 *taangruoh,* 假若 *jearuoh,* 假使 *jeashyy,* 倘使 *taangshyy,* and 设若 *shehruoh,* in approximately descending order of (a) frequency of occurrence, as well as (b) the likelihood of the supposition, so that the later ones are more apt to go with suppositions contrary to fact. The consequent clause usually has the adverb *jiow* 'then' in the predicate. Examples are: 要是你不会，我可以教你。 *Yawsh nii buhuey, woo kee.yii jiau nii.* 'If you don't know how, I can teach you.' 倘若你早警告了他们，那次出事或者就能避免了. *Taangruoh nii tzao jiinggawle tamen, ney-tsyh chu-shyh huohjee jiow neng bihmean le.* 'If you had warned them early, that accident could perhaps have been avoided.' As noted before, *jiow* must follow the subject; all the 'if'-words can either precede or follow the subject in the clause, except that *yaw* as 'if' must follow.

A conditional clause can occur without an 'if'-word by merely having the adverb *jiow* 'then' in the consequent clause or by having negatives in one or both clauses, depending upon the sense, as: 你打電話给他，我就不用写信了。 *Nii daa-diann-huah geei ta, woo jiow buyonq shiee-shinn le.* 'If you telephone to him, I won't need to write.' 你不来( , )我不去. *Nii bu lai* (with zero or /, /) *woo bu chiuh.* 'If you don't come, I don't go.', as contrasted with: *Nii bu lai* (with / ; / or / . /)

*woo bu chiuh.* 'You don't come; I don't go.'[28]   东西不好，你
不一定得買. *Dong.shi bu hao, nii bu idinq deei mae.* '(If) the
thing is not good, you don't necessarily have to buy it.' Since
condition and time are sometimes quite similar (cf. German
*wenn*), the same perfective suffix *-le* can also be used in conditional clauses. Thus when an aged parent says in a (verbal) will:
我死了丧事从简.   *Woo syyle sangshyh tsorng-jean.* 'When I
die, the funeral should be simple.', it is a time relation, while if a
young husband says: 我死了你頂好再嫁. *Woo syyle nii
diing hao tzay jiah.* 'If I die, you'd better marry again.' it is a
conditional.

A necessary condition[29] is given by using in the dependent
clause 非,得`,非得`,除非,除了 *fei, deei, feideei, chwufei,
chwule* (the last, in this sense, before subject only), and in the
consequent clause *bu* or *tsair. Fei* is the L form for *bush* 'is not',
but in speech it can mean either 'unless' or 'necessarily', depending upon the context. Thus, 你非去不行. *Nii fei chiuh bu
shyng.* 'Unless you go, it won't do.', but 你非去才行. *Nii fei
chiuh tsair shyjg.* 'You must go, only then will it do,—you must
go before it will do.' *Chwufei,* like *fei* and *feideei,* is now used
for 'unless' or 'necessarily', as:   除非西天出了太陽，我也
不会改主意的.   *Chwufei shi-tian chule tay.yang, woo yee
buhuey gae jwu.yih de.* 'Unless the sun should rise in the west, I
wouldn't change my mind.' ... , 我才会改主意呐.   ... , *woo
tsair huey gae jwu.yih ne.* '(Only if the sun should rise in the
west), would I change my mind.' In old-style speech, however,
*chwufei* is limited to afterthought in dependent sentences, as:
他不会答应的—除非你劝得動他.   *Ta buhuey da.yinq
de—chwufei nii chiuann.de-donq ta.* 'He won't agree unless you

---

[28]Translating this as: 'You don't come and I don't go.' would still be
ambiguous, since with 'come' in a rising intonation, 'and' would practically
be equivalent to *jiow.* Cf. 'Spare the rod and spoil the child.'

[29]In popular usage, as distinguished from mathematical usage, both for
English and for Chinese, a necessary condition expressed by 'only if', 'not
unless', etc., and their Chinese equivalents is usually understood to be both
necessary and sufficient.

could persuade him.'[30] This afterthought use of *chwufei* is still the only form available in Cantonese—unless it be Cantonese influenced by Mandarin.

The combination *bush ... jiowsh* 'if not ... then' is commonly used for its logical equivalent: *huohjee ... huohjee* or *huohsh ... huohsh* 'either ... or', as: 不是 我 来，就是 你 去。 *Bush woo lai, jiowsh nii chiuh.* 'If it isn't I come, it's you go,—either I come or you go.' Whenever a disjunction is to be expressed, then the *bush ... jiowsh* form is much more frequently used than the *huohjee ... huohjee* or the *huosh ... huohsh* form.

So far we have been speaking of the conditional clause in conventional terms. Just as concessive clauses can be taken as clause subjects, so can a conditional clause be regarded as a clause subject. After every conditional clause one can supply *de ₀huah* 'the supposition that, the case that, the matter of', as: 要是 不肯 的 话，那就算了。 *Yawsh ta bukeen de huah, nah jiow suann le.* 'If (it is a matter of) his not willing, then let it go.' To illustrate further the close parallel between pause particles after conditional clauses and ordinary subjects, we have:

| | | |
|---|---|---|
| 要是下起雨来，咱们就甭出去了。 | *Yawsh shiah.chii yeu.lai, tzarmen jiow berng chu.chiuh le.* | 'If it starts to rain, we'd better not go out.' |
| ... 噢，让我看怎么办。 | *Yawsh shiah.chii yeu.lai me, ranq woo kann tzeem bann.* | 'If it starts to rain (hesitation), let me see what shall we do.' |
| ... 呐，那也不要紧。 | *Yawsh shiah.chii yeu .lai ne, nah yee buyawjiin.* | 'If it is (a question of) starting to rain, that won't matter.' |
| ... 吧，咱们就坐车吧。 | *Yawsh shiah.chii yeu .lai ba, tzarmen jiow tzuoh-che ba.* | 'If it is (the alternative of) starting to rain, we will take a car.' |
| ... 啊，那就糟糕了。 | *Yawsh shiah.chii yeu .lai a, nah jiow tzaugau le.* | 'If it should start to rain, that would be a mess.' |

---

[30] See 黄 诚 一，说 " 除非 " (Hwang Cherngi, "On 'Chwufei' "), ZGYW, no. 55:11 (1957).

A further point of contact between the conditional clause as a subject and the subject as a question is that not only do subjects, questions, and conditional clauses have the same pause or pause particles, but they are even paralleled by the old-style conditional clause in English which uses an inverted word order instead of 'if', as: 'Should it rain tomorrow (/ , / ~ / ? /) that would be too bad.', where / , / and / ? / are usually phonetically indistinguishable. The same ambivalent intonation and particle of the above applies to the Chinese equivalent: *Miengl shiah.chii yeu lai ne* (/ , / ~ / ? /) *nah jiow huay le.*

(4) Time clauses are marked by ... *de* $_o$*shyr.howl* 'time when, —when ...', ... *yiichyan* 'before ...', and *yiihow* 'after ...'. We have seen (sec. 2.12.4) that a clause ending in *de* $_o$*shyr.howl* is really an adjectival clause modifying the noun *shyr.howl* forming an ordinary substantive subject. The same applies to time before and after. For one can say: 大家 吃 饭 的 前 头 , 你 别 吃 点 心. *Dahjia chy-fann de chyan.tou, nii bye chy-dean.shin.* 'Don't you eat any snack before we all have dinner.' Where *de chyan-.tou* can be compared with the colloquialism in 'ten minutes in front of six' for 'ten minutes of (~ to) six'. The corresponding L-forms are 之 先 *jy shian* (more frequently than 之 前 *jy chyan*) and 之 後 *jy how.*

For more explicit time relations, there is *dang* 'being right at' or *tzay* 'being at' used before ... *de* $_o$*shyr.howl*, and *tzay* before ... *yiichyan* (~ *de chyan.tou*) 'before' and ... *yiihow* (~ *de how.tou*)[31] 'after'. But 'before' and 'after' usually take (with or without *tzay*) the redundant forms of 'before something has *not* happened' and 'after something has *already* happened'. For example: 他 还 没 到 家 以 前 就 累 的 走 不 動 了. *Ta hair mei daw-jia yiichyan jiow ley de tzoou.bu-donq le.* 'He was too tired to walk before he (hadn't) reached home.' 他 已 竟 到 了 家 以 後 才 知 道 有 多 累. *Ta yiijinq dawle jia yiihow tsair jy.daw yeou dwo ley.* 'He began to realize how tired he was after he (had already) got home.'

---

[31] Some speakers use *de chyan.tou* and *de how.tou* mainly, and some exclusively, in the spatial sense.

Time relation can also be indicated in the dependent clause by the perfective suffix -le for 'after' and its corresponding negative mei (.yeou) for 'before', as: 我 吃 完 了 你 吃. Woo chy-wanle nii chy. 'You eat after I have finished eating.' 票 还 没 買 你 不 能 上 船. Piaw hair mei mae, nii buneng shang-chwan. 'Before you have bought your ticket you can't board the ship.' Note that if these examples have a full pause with concluding intonation, they would be compound sentences or separate sentences: 'I have finished eating; (now) you eat.'; 'Your ticket hasn't been bought yet (usually with ne); you can't board the ship.', where the truth values are obviously very different.

(5) Place clauses, usually ending in de ₀dih.fang(l) 'where ...', are, even more explicitly than time clauses, nominal subjects with a modifier. Besides ... .de chyan.tou 'before, in front of' and ... de how.tou 'after, behind', there are of course other spatial relations, but they are rarely modified by a full S-P clause. In modern learned and journalistic styles one can say: 言 论 自 由 不 自 由 的 方 面, 他 们 还 没 有 什 么 表 示. Yanluenn tzyh-you bu tzyhyou de fangmiann, tamen hair mei.yeou sherm beau-shyh. 'The aspect of whether speech is free,—as for whether speech will be free, they have not yet expressed themselves.', where the spatial word fangmiann is of course taken in a purely abstract sense and is usually preceded by tzay 'at, on, in, or 关 于 guanyu 'with regard to'.

In sum, all the concessive, causal, conditional, temporal, and spatial clauses are in the last resort subjects, whether S-P subjects, or S-P subjects modifying a nominal expression, or a verbal expression consisting of tzay, dang, and so on with an S-P clause subject. When the modified nominal expression like (de) .shyr-.howl is reduced to an enclitic it behaves like a compound final particle. When the initial verb or preposition such as .tzay, .deeng.daw is reduced to a proclitic,[32] it behaves like a conjunction. In both such cases, the S-P modifier and the S-P object acquire the full status of an S-P subject to the whole sentence and that is why it is usually called an adverbial clause.

---

[32]An enclitic (or a proclitic) is a form which is phonetically attached to the preceding (or following) word, but grammatically attached to a longer preceding (or following) construction.

*2.12.8. Correlative Clauses.* The mere fact that apparently corresponding parts of two sentences make a pair which are in parallel, in contrast, or in some other close relation does not make one a dependent clause on the other. Thus: *Woo bu lai; nii bu chiuh.* 'I don't come; you don't go.' are just two parallel sentences, without any relation except that one comes after the other and has very similar and parallel parts to the other. But in: 你 越 大 声儿 说 话，我 越 听 不 懂. *Nii yueh dahshengl shuohuah, woo yueh ting.bu-doong.* 'The more loudly you talk, the less I can understand (you).', the correlative adverbs *yueh ... yueh* make it impossible for the clauses to be independent sentences. If two coordinate *yueh*-forms are to be correlated with another, such 2 + 1 structure is indicated by the suspended intonation (higher ending) and/or pause particle, and/or use of 'if' - 'then' words such as *yawsh ... jiow,* or adverbs such as *yow, yee,* since the use of any 'and'-word between (the first two) clauses is not available between clauses, as in: 嗓 子 越 大，话 说 的 ( 又 ) 越 长，人 就 越 不 听. *Saangtz yueh dah, huah shuo de (yow) yueh charng, ren jiow yueh bu ting.* 'The louder the voice and the longer the talk, the less people will listen.[33]

The form *yueh ... yueh* (~ *yuh ... yuh*) must go with two verbs, the second being one capable of degrees, as: 你 越 说 他 越 不 信. *Nii yueh shuo ta yueh bu shinn.* 'The more you talk, the less he believes (you).' 風 越 颳 越 大. *Feng yueh gua yueh dah.* 'The wind blew harder and harder.' If no specific action can be ascribed to the first verb, a dummy verb, *lai* 'comes', *biann* 'changes', or *guoh* 'as (one) lives' or 'as (time) passes' is used to complete the formula, as: 他 越 耒 越 傻 了. *Ta yueh lai yueh shaale.* 'He is getting sillier and sillier.' 你 越 过 越 糊 塗 了. *Nii yueh guoh yueh hwu.du le.* 'You are getting more and more muddle-headed.'

One common type of correlative is in the form of repeated interrogative-indefinites, as in: 谁 先 耒 谁 先 吃. *Sheir shian lai*

---

[33]Cf. the more Chinese-style construction in: "The more complex our problems become, the more dangerous they become, then the more they must be explained to the people." James B. Reston, in *Atlantic Monthly,* 185:40 (April, 1950).

*sheir shian chy.* 'Whoever comes first eats first' 哪儿 舒 服 哪儿 睡. *Naal shu.fwu naal shuey.* 'Sleep wherever it's comfortable.'

Correlative words need not be, and usually are not, the same word in repetition. Thus, we have *dwo ... yee* in: 事 情 多 难 你 也 得 做 完 了 他. *Shyh.chyng dwo nan, nii yee deei tzuoh-wanle ta.* 'No matter how hard the job, you must finish it (, too).' Preference is expressed by the correlatives *yeoude ... buru* or *yeuchyi ... buru* 'rather than ... , better ... ', as: 有 的 (～ 与 其 ) 费 工 夫儿 写 信 , 不 如 打 个 電 报 去. *Yeoude (～yeuchyi) fey gong.ful shiee-shinn, buru daa g diannbaw .chiuh.* 'Rather than spend the time to write a letter, better send a telegram.' For further discussion and illustration of correlatives, see sections 5.2.2 and 8.4.2.

2.12.9. *Truth Values of Dependent Clauses.* Referring back to the correlative adverbs like *yee ... yee* 'both ... and' as markers of compound sentences (sec. 2.11.3), they seem to be rather similar to markers of complex sentences like *dwo ... yee* 'no matter how ... too'. Why is the sentence: 錢 固 然 是 少 , 可 是 事儿 好 做.*Chyan guhran sh shao, keesh shell hao-tzuoh.* 'The pay is little, to be sure, but the job is easy.' a compound sentence, while a quite similar sentence: 錢 虽 然 ... *Chyan sweiran shao, keesh shell hao-tzuoh.* 'Although the pay is little, the job is easy.' a complex sentence? The answer is: Why indeed? There is really no formal difference between the semantically slightly different adverbs *guhran* 'to be sure' ('freilich') and *sweiran* 'although', and the difference in translation reflects only the difference of behavior between the English words. One should not, however, conclude that there is no difference between compound and complex sentences in Chinese. A workable criterion for a sufficient condition for a complex sentence can be stated in terms of its truth value: In a compound sentence the truth value of the whole is a conjunction of the truth values of its constituent coordinate clauses; while the truth value of a complex sentence is taken as a whole and the constituent clauses may have different truth values from that of the whole sentence or may not even make sense as to truth value. Thus, the mother clause in a pregnant sentence is not complete even as a clause, while a time clause, even with *de.shyr.howl* reduced to an enclitic compound particle, is incapable of being true

or false, and the child clause in sentences like 'It is false that ... '
obviously has a truth value opposite to that of the whole sentence.

When this criterion is applied to composite sentences of various types we have considered so far, we shall find that the division
between compound and complex sentences still agrees, in most
cases, with the constructions in their English translation. But
there are some notable exceptions. Thus, clauses containing 虽 然
*sweiran* 'although' and 既 然 *jihran* 'since' will have to be regarded as coordinate clauses, though they are regarded in English
as dependent clauses.

In this connection, a very interesting case of translation borrowing has been noticed on the ambivalent 'if' (1) 'in the case
of' and (2) 'since it is true that', which in ordinary Chinese would
be, respectively, (1) *jearu*, giving rise to a conditional (dependent)
clause, and (2) *jihran*, giving rise, according to our new definition,
to a coordinate clause. In the new style, with the translation
borrowing of *jearu* in meaning 2, it passed unnoticed for some
time until attention was called to its foreign origin.

*2.12.10. Compressed Sentences.* In sentences like: (1) 我 说
做 就 做. *Woo shuo tzuoh jiow tzuoh.* '(As soon as) I say (I'll) do
it, (I) do it.'; (2) 我 问 他 也 不 答 应. *Woo wenn .ta yee bu da-
.yinq.* 'I asked him (and he) wouldn't reply, either,'; (3) 饭 催
了 才 坐 下 来 吃. *Fann tsueile tsair tzuoh.shiah.lai chy.* 'The
meal (we) asked to hurry up before (people) sat down to eat.', the
predicates seem to form one compound predicate, but do not all
belong to the same subject, if supplied. Hence these should be
regarded as separate clauses in compressed form.[34] The important
characteristics of compressed sentences are: (1) There is no pause
between the parts which in expanded full clause form could admit
of pauses; and (2) The second predicate does not have a subject,
and, even if one is supplied, it may be different from that of the
first predicate.

A compressed sentence may have one or two correlative adverbs, but it does not always have them nor are they excluded
from occurrence elsewhere. Sentences with such adverbs are: 我

---

[34]For details, see 向 若, 紧 缩 句 (Shianq Ruoh, *Jiinsuo Jiuh*), Shanghai,
1958.

一气 就 头疼. *Woo i chih jiow tour.terng.* 'Anytime I get angry, (then) I have a headache.' 咱们再大声儿一点儿叫他 也听不見. *Tzarmen tzay dahsheangl.i.deal jiaw ta yee ting.bu-jiann.* 'No matter *how* loudly we call him, he can't hear us, either.' In cases where the first clause can form the subject of a predicate, it is of course not necessary to assume that anything has been left out by compression, as: 你赔不是也没用. *Nii peir bush yee mei yonq.* '(Even if) you apologize, it's no use, either.', where *Nii peir bush* is the subject 'Your (possible) apologizing'. Further examples are: 你派了我(我)也不能去. *Nii payle woo (woo) yee buneng chiuh.* 'Even if you appointed me, I couldn't go either.' 下午最高(ʒ)到九十度. *Shiah-wuu tzuey gau (gau) daw jeoushyr-duh.* In the afternoon the highest temperature was as high as 90°.'

A marginal case of a compressed sentence is one in which the relation of subordination is implied by the absence of a pause between clauses. For example, in 票还没買/X/你不能上 船.*Piaw hair mei mae /X/ nii buneng shanq-chwan.*, if there is a complete pause at /X/, it is two sentences: 'The tickets haven't been bought yet. You can't go on board.' If there is a drawl on *mae* in a ($\frac{1}{2}$) 3rd Tone, or if there is no pause at all and *mae* goes into a raised 3rd Tone, going on to *nii* without pause, then one would like to be able to say that it is a compressed conditional sentence with *yawsh* 'if' and/or *jiow* 'then' omitted, meaning 'You can't go on board without first buying tickets.', but, as is often the case, the relation between form and meaning is a skewed one: with full pause, it is two statements. In the compressed form, it may be either a conjunctive statement or a conditional. If it is desired to make the conditional meaning clear, one could of course always say *yawsh* and/or *jiow*.

## 2.13.  Pivotal Constructions

*2.13.1 Pivotal Constructions and Object Clauses.* A pivotal construction consists of a succession of a verbal expression $V_1$, a nominal expression, and another verbal expression $V_2$, with the nominal expression serving at once as object of $V_1$ and subject of

V$_2$, as: 我们 派 他 做 代 表. *Woomen pay $_0$ta tzuoh daybeau.*
'We delegate him to be representative.', where *ta* is object of *pay*
and subject of *tzuoh daybeau.* 他 请 你 帮 忙. *Ta chiing $_0$nii
bang-mang.* 'He asks you to help.', where *nii* is object of *chiing*
and subject of *bang-mang.* A pivotal construction is a mixed construction, where the pivot has an ambiguous position, as reflected
in the optional neutral tone if it is a pronoun, since an object
pronoun is normally in the neutral tone, while a subject pronoun
is normally not. In: 我 请 你 就 走. *Woo chiing nii jiow tzoou.*
'I ask you to go right away.', it is obviously not *Woo chiing nii.*
'I invite you.' It may look like a case of clause object *nii jiow
tzoou* 'that you go right away' to the verb *chiing* 'request (that
you go)'[35] but such constructions behave rather differently from
other, more clear, cases of clause objects, such as: *Woo shuo nii
jiow tzoou.* 'I say that you go right away.' With 'say, think' types
of verbs (see sec. 8.1.5.3) it is possible to add as afterthought
forms: *Nii jiow tzoou, woo shuo.* 'You must go right away, I say.'
But it would be nonsense to say: °*Nii jiow tzoou, woo chiing.*
Similarly, one can say either: 你 想 我 怎 么 办 呐? *Nii sheang
woo tzeem bann ne?* or *Woo tzeem bann ne, nii sheang?* 'What do
you think I should do about it?' but *Nii jiaw woo tzeem bann ne?*
'What are you going to tell me to do?' cannot be turned around
into °*Woo tzeem bann ne, nii jiaw?* That the pivot itself is also
the object of the first verb can be seen when it is repeated and
put back in again in the afterthought form, and the sentence is
all right again, as: *Nii deei tzoou, woo chiing nii.* 'You must go, I
ask you.' *Woo tzeem bann ne, nii jiaw woo?* 'What shall I do, you
tell me?'

A pivotal sentence is also to be distinguished from a compressed sentence. Thus, *Woo chiing ta (, ta) yee bu lai.* 'I asked
him (and he) wouldn't come, either.' is a compressed sentence,
which is capable of being expanded by the insertion of / , / and
*ta*, while *Woo chiing ta bye lai.* 'I asked him not to come.' is a
pivotal sentence, which cannot be so expanded.

*2.13.2. Pre-Pivotal Verbs.* In general, pre-pivotal verbs, or
link verbs, are of the 'cause to' type, whereas verbs with clauses

---

[35]This is in fact Jespersen's treatment of English when he marks 'him
run' in 'We saw him run.' as subject-predicate. See Jespersen, *Anal Synt*, 55.

as objects, or think verbs, are of the 'think, say' type. Typical pre-pivotal verbs are:

| | | | |
|---|---|---|---|
| 叫 ~ 教 | jiaw 'causes, tells' | 派 | pay 'dispatches' |
| 使 | shyy 'causes' | 帮 (着) | bang(j) 'helps' |
| 让 | ranq 'lets' | 陪 (着) | peir(j) 'keeps company' |
| 准,许, 准 许 | joen, sheu, joen-sheu 'permits' | 带 (着) | day(j) 'takes along' |
| 要 | yaw 'wants' | 领 (着) | liing(j) 'leads' |
| 请 | chiing 'requests' | 扶 (着) | fwu(j) 'supports' |
| 劝 | chiuann 'persuades, advises' | 送 | sonq 'sends' |
| 催 | tsuei 'urges, hurries' | 约 | iue 'makes an agreement with' |
| 逼 | bi 'compels' | 找 | jao 'gets (someone) to ...' |
| 引 | yiin 'induces' | | |
| 鼓動 | $guu_0donq$ 'incites' | 怪 | guay 'blames' |
| 慫恿 | $soong_0yeong$ 'incites' | 怕 | pah 'is afraid' |
| | | 喜 欢 | shii.huan 'likes' |
| 認 | renn 'recognizes' | 埋.怨 | $mai_0yuann$ (~ $man_0yuann$) 'complains' |
| 選,举,選 举 | sheuan, jeu, sheuan-jeu 'elects' | 禁 止 | jinnjyy 'prohibits' |

The so-called sign of the passive 被,给,叫,讓 bey, geei, jiaw, ranq, and 归,由,有 guei, you, yeou, which we treated as prepositions introducing actors, are also pre-pivotal verbs, as: 他讓强盗抢了. Ta ranq chyang.daw cheang le. 'He let bandits rob,—he was robbed by bandits.' 这錢归我付. Jeh chyan guei woo fuh. 'This money is for me to pay.' This is quite a different thing from Jeh chyan guei woo. 'This money goes to me.'

The division of verbs taking clause objects and pre-pivotal verbs is not absolute, and there is some overlapping. Thus, 我看見他在那儿写信. Woo kann.jiann $_0$ta tzay.nall shiee-shinn. can mean either (1) 'I saw that he was writing a letter.' or (2) 'I saw him write a letter.' Similarly, 我願意你别那么樣儿聋. Woo yuan.yih nii bye nemmyanql long. can mean

(1) 'I wish you were not quite so deaf.' or (2) I wish you to be not quite so deaf.' With a greater difference in truth value is the example: 我听見他唱的很好. *Woo ting.jiann ta chanq de heen hao* (1) 'I hear that he sings very well.' or (2) 'I hear him sing very well.' Also (1) 我告送你我不抽烟. *Woo gaw.sonq nii woo bu chou-ian.* 'I tell you I don't smoke.' or (2) 我告送你别抽烟. *Woo gaw.sonq nii bye chou-ian.* 'I tell you not to smoke.' In such cases the prosodic elements may sometimes serve to differentiate the two: (1) a full tone on *ta* will mark off a clause object; (2) a neutral tone on *ta* will mark it as a pivot. This distinction is brought out even more strikingly in the dialect of Tongyuan of Haeyan District, which has a postverbal form and a free form for the first and third person singular pronouns: [ƒio no] 'I', [-u] 'me', [ji nei] 'he', [-i] 'him', so that it is possible to distinguish between 'I saw that he was writing a letter.' and 'I saw him write a letter.'[36]

*2.13.3. Direction of Action of Post-Pivotal Verbs.* We have seen that the direction of action of verbs in predicates may go either way, and this is true of course for verbs after a pivot, ... : Thus, a student will say: 我找不着先生教. *Woo jao.bu-jaur shian.sheng jiau.* 'I can't find a teacher to teach (me).', while a teacher says: *Woo jao.bu-jaur shyue.sheng jiau.* 'I can't find students to teach (to be taught).' 他不少事做. *Ta bu shao shyh tzuoh.* 'He does not lack work to do (to be done.' 你幹麻找

了事情煩心 ? *Nii gannma jaole shyh.chyng farn-shin?* 'Why have you looked for things to trouble your mind?' Just as with main predicates, some post-pivotal verbs have no basically clear direction of action, as: 他让(～给)水洒(～潑)的滿身. *Ta ranq (or geei) shoei saa (or po) de maan-shen.* 'He let water splash (be splashed?) all over him.'

When there is a double pivot consisting of a direct object and an indirect object, the direction of action is of course different in relation to each of the object-subjects, as: 我给他饭吃. *Woo geei ta fann chy.* 'I give him food to eat.' Note that, while the

---

[36] 胡明揚, 海盐通圈方言的代词 Hwu Mingyang, "Pronouns in the Dialect of Haeyan Tongyuan." ZGYW no. 60:17-18 (June, 1957).

normal order in a simple sentence is to have the indirect object first (except in Cantonese and Wu dialects), either order is possible in a pivot, as: *Woo geei fann ta chy.* 'I give food to him to eat.'

2.13.4. *Chain Pivots.* If the nature of the actions permits, a chain reaction can be set up with pivots as the links, as: 我请 你叫他 找人 寄这 封信. *Woo chiing nii jiaw ta jao-ren jih jey-feng shinn.* 'I request you to tell him to find so.neone to mail this letter.' 东家叫 掌櫃的 讬人 请个 大师傅 教徒 弟们做菜. *Dong.jia jiaw jaanggueyde tuo ren chiing g dah.shy-.fu jiaw twu.dih.men tzuoh-tsay.* 'The proprietor tells the manager to entrust someone to engage a chef to teach apprentices to cook.'[37]

2.13.5. *Post-Pivotal Predicates with de.* In the pivotal construction: 我坐 过一 辆公共汽車老停ʔ ₹. *Woo tzuoh.guo i-lianq gonggonq-chihche lao tyng lao tyng.* 'I have been in a bus which kept stopping.', the second predicate *lao tyng lao tyng* is not a causative result of the first verb *tzuoh*, but simply a further predication of the pivotal word *gonggonq-chihche*. As such it often takes a final particle *de* as a nominalizer 'one who', 'that which', etc: 'I have been in a bus, one that kept stopping.' In the following three forms: (1) 我看見过许多 人用左手 写字. *Woo kann.jiann.guo sheuduo ren yonq tzuoo-shoou shiee-tzyh.* 'I have seen many people write with their left hands.' (2) *Woo kann.jiann.guo sheuduo ren yonq tzuoo-shoou shieh-tzyh de.* 'I have seen many who write with their left hands.' (3) *Woo kann.jiann.guo sheuduo yonq tzuoo-shoou shiee-tzyh de ren.* 'I have seen many left-handed writers.', the constructions are all different: (1) is a pivotal construction; (2) is a simple sentence, with a nominal clause in apposition with the object: 'I have seen people, people who write, ...', (3) is subject-verb-object, with a

---

[37]An example of a similar construction in English is: 'I imagined him listening to the announcer reporting Bill catching Tom stealing third base.', quoted by Victor Yngve, "Computer for Translation", *Scientific American*, June, 1962, p. 72.

clause modifier for the object. The nature of the difference is similar to that between the continuative and restrictive relatives in languages which have relative clauses, the former corresponding approximately to (1) and (2), the latter to (2) and (3). For another example:

我 昨儿 看 見 了 一 个 人 会 对 眼儿。

(1) *Woo tzwol kann.jiannle ig ren huey duey-yeal.*
(2) *Woo tzwol kann.jiannle ig ren huey duey-yeal de.*
(3) *Woo tzwol kann.jiannle ig huey duey-yeal de ren.*

(1) and (2) 'I saw a man yesterday, who (= and he) could cross his eyes.'; (2) and (3) 'Yesterday I saw a man who could cross his eyes.' It should be remembered, as usual, that it is the different structures that form our topic of study, and the use of translation is only to provide suggestions for the formal analysis.

*2.13.6. Other Post-Pivotal Predicates.* More generally, any type of predicate can occur post-pivotally.[38] Thus, with a nominal predicate (other than in V-*de* form): 買 了 个 桌 子 三 条 腿 *maele g juotz san-tyau toei* 'bought a table (which had) three legs'. With adjectives (which we treat as a species of verbs): 原 谅 他 小 ! *Yuanlianq ta sheau!* 'Forgive him (being so) young!' With S-P predicates: 祝 你 们 生 意 兴 隆 ! *Juh niimen shengyih shinglong!* 'Wish you (your) business prosper!'

## 2.14 Planned and Unplanned Sentences

A sentence may be planned, at least in its main parts, before it is begun, or it may get started and take shape as it goes along, or it may be planned one way and be actually finished another way. In written texts, in which the writer usually has a chance to revise his sentences, all sentences will be in a deliberately planned form, the only exceptions being realistic dialogues in

---

[38]A good treatment of this and related problems is found in 陈 建 民, 论 兼 语 式 和 一 些 有 关 句 子 分 析 法 的 问 题 Chern Jiannmin, "On Pivotal Constructions and Some Problems Concerning Sentence Analysis", ZGYW, no. 93:101-106 (1960), from which I have borrowed some examples.

drama and fiction and texts of actual speech recorded for scientific or legal purposes. Even materials prepared for foreign language instruction tend to be in the completely planned style, and the learner is usually expected to learn about the other style if and after he gets abroad, usually carrying over the forms of hems and haws and intonations which are native to his own language but foreign to the language he is learning.

*2.14.1. Full Stops and Half Stops.* A full stop /;/ , /./ , /?/, or /!/ is the pause between sentences or coordinate clauses and is realized in a longer period of silence and/or a slight acceleration in the tempo of the last syllables and/or a slight lowering of the key of the voice in statements and raising of the key in questions, or one of the exclamatory intonations (sec. 1.3.7). A half stop consists of a relatively short pause /,/, and/or a drawl on the last syllable /——/, and/or one of the pause particles *a, ne, me, ba* and/or no pause / $\emptyset$ /, as a special case. As we have seen, whether there is a full or a half stop often makes the difference between two sentences and a composite sentence. If we let {,} represent any of the half stops and {.} represent any of the full stops, the following will have different sentence values according to the kind of pauses involved:

(1) 不是二妹说的. *Bush Ellmey shuo de* /X/ 一定是三妹说的. *idinq sh Sanmey shuo de.* (a) /X/ = {.}: 'It wasn't Second Sister who said it; it must have been Third Sister who said it.' (b) /X/ = {,}: 'If it wasn't Second Sister who said it, then it must have been Third Sister who said it.'

(2) 你不认得路 *Nii bu rennde luh* /X/ 我教你怎么走. *woo jiau nii tzeem tzoou.* (a) /X/ = {.}: 'You don't know the way; I'll show you how to get there.' (b) /X/ = {,}: 'If you ... , I'll ... .'

(3) 人家要赔钱 *Ren.jia yaw peir-chyan* /X/ 你怎么办? *nii tzeem bann?* (a) /X/ = {.}: 'They want you to pay for the damages; what are you going to do about it?' (b) /X/ = {,}: 'If they ... , what ... ?'

(4) 房子着火了 *Farngtz jaur-huoole* /X/ 你得快去叫消防队啊! *nii deei kuay chiuh jiau shiaufarng-duey a!* (a) /X/ = {.}: 'The house is on fire! You must hurry up and call

the fire department!' (b) /X/ = {,}: 'If the house ... , you will have to ... .'

(5) 你 上 哪儿 *Nii shanq naal* /X/ 他 上 哪儿? *ta shanq naal* {.}. (a) /X/ = {.}: 'Where are you going? Where is he going?' (b) /X/ ={,}: 'Wherever you go, there he goes.' Here {,} usually takes the form / ∅ /.

The interrogative-plus-*dou* (or *yee*) form with distributive function is never used with {.}. Thus, in: 他 变 成 了 什 么 樣 子 我 都 认 得。 *Ta bianncherngle sherm yanqtz* /X/ *woo dou rennde.*, /X/ is always {,}, usually in the form of / ∅ /: 'No matter how he has changed, I can recognize him.'

*2.14.2. Digressions and Interpolations.* If a sentence is interrupted by a cough, a sneeze, a sudden noise, or some accident, it may be left incomplete at any part of the sentence and may not even be resumed after the interrupting event is over. If it is resumed, the speaker may start with the beginning of the unfinished sentence, phrase, or word, but not the middle of a polysyllabic word. In fact, we use the place of resumption after an interruption as one of the markers of word boundaries, as: 喂! ㄕ( 刷!), ㄕ ㄈ-( ㄆㄧㄚ!), 书 房 裡 有 个 马 蜂 我 给 打 死 了! *Uai! Shu-* (*shua!*), *Shuf-* (*pia!*), *shufarng.lii yeou g maa.feng woo geei daa.syyle!* 'Heh! There's a wasp in the st- (swish!), in the stud- (swat!), in the study I have killed!'

If the speech is interrupted when the speaker wishes to insert something he did not intend when beginning the sentence, either as a sudden thought, or to take account of a new event, then the insertion is made after the completion of a phrase or at least a syntactical word, and either the resumption will continue from there or the unfinished half will be repeated, as: 一 个 偏 見 太 深 的 人 啊—我 这 不 是 说 你, 啊!—— 没 法 子 跟 他 说 理 的。 *ig pianjiann tay shen de ren a——woo jeh bush shuo nii, a!* ——*mei fartz gen ta shuo-lii de.* 'A person who is too deeply prejudiced——I am not talking about you, mind you!—— you can't talk reason with him.' 一 百 年 以 後 的 世 界—— 要 是 还 有 个 世 界 的 话 —— 一 定 有 许 多 更 新 奇 的 苔 明。 *Ibae-nian yiihow de shyh.jieh——yawsh hair yeou g shyh- .jieh de huah——idinq yeou sheuduo genq shinchyi de faming.*

'The world of a hundred years hence——if there is still going to be a world——will certainly have many more wonderful inventions.' For an example of a new situation: 这么大的光圈 —— 别動!—— 我得把遠近对準了. *Tzemm dah de guangchiuan——bye donq!——woo deei bae yeuanjinn dueyjoenle.* 'With such a large aperture——don't move!——I'll have to adjust the distance correctly.'

While an interpolation may come after a pause, it is more likely to come after a negative pause; that is, there is not only no pause, but the break is marked by a faster tempo, a *piu mosso* on the interpolated part. For the decision to interpolate comes either before, at, or after the end of the preceding part, and the chance of its coming right at the moment is, in the nature of the case, always very small. If it is much later, then the original sentence would have continued before an interpolation set in. So the most likely moment is shortly before the break, and the speaker is likely to hurry on to the new material. Such hurrying, as we have seen (sec. 3.7) is indicated by reversed arrows ← , as: 他跟他太ₓ ← 你可别告送人啊！—— 昨ㄦ吵了一架. *Ta gen ta tay.tay ← nii kee bye gau.sonq ren a!——tzwol chaole i-jiah.* 'He and his wife ← don't you tell anybody!——had a quarrel last night.'

*2.14.3. Afterthought Forms.* If an unplanned part is added to a sentence which has already been completed, then it is an afterthought form. Afterthought forms have the same likelihood of faster tempo as interpolations and for the same reasons. But what goes before an afterthought can stand as a complete sentence without it, as: 你简直没規矩, 越来越. *Nii jeanjyr mei guei-.jeu, yueh lai yueh.* 'You are simply without manners, more and more.' 我今ㄦ不去看戏了 —— 因为天ㄦ太热. *Woo jiel bu chiuh kann-shih le——inwey tial tay reh.* 'I am not going to the show today, for the weather is too hot.' This is quite different from the planned sentence: *Inwey tial tay reh, suooyii woo bu chiuh kann-shih le.* 'Because the weather is too hot, I am not going to the show today.' Similarly, with afterthought: 我实在没法ㄦ帮他的忙—— 虽然他是个老朋友. *Woo shyrtzay meifal bang tade mang——sweiran ta sh g lao-perng-.yeou.* 'I really have no way of helping him, although he is an old friend.'; with planned qualification: *Ta sweiran sh g lao-perng-.yeou, keesh woo hairsh meifal bang tade mang.* 'Although he is an old friend, I still have no way of helping him.'

In Europeanized Chinese, however, one does not limit post-posed dependent clauses exclusively to afterthoughts. In this style it is quite usual to put 'if'- and 'although' - clauses after the principal clause. Since, however, such construction is chiefly on paper and has not been generally adopted in everyday speech, one cannot record objectively any pause or intonation between the clauses. Since, moreover, what goes onto paper is always planned, it is read without the change of tempo noted above and in this way sounds foreign or learned. This limitation to the written language does not include conditional clauses ending in *de huah* '(if it is) a question of ... ', which is very commonly used in afterthought clauses and, if found in written text, is expected to be read (i.e., acted) with the usual faster tempo, as: 錢甭存了← 要是就要用的话. *Chyan berng tswen le ← yawsh jiow yaw yonq de huah.* 'The money does not need to be deposited, ← if it's to be used right away.'

A reason-cause clause at the end is not necessarily an afterthought clause, but can also be a predicate in a planned sentence, as: 我不去看戏, 是因為天儿热(～ 天儿热的缘故). *Woo bu chiuh kann-shih, sh inwey tial reh* (or *tial reh de $_0$yuan-.guh*). 'That I am not going to the show is because (*or* for the reason that) the weather is hot.' (Cf. sec. 2.12.7).

*2.14.4. Planned Interpolations.* In planned interpolations there is no pause before and after: 他看得出是个学生. *Ta kann-.de-chu sh g shyue.sheng.* 'He (one) can see is a student.' 他不晓得 哪儿去了. *Ta busheaude naal chiuh le.* 'He (one) doesn't know has gone where,—I wonder where he's gone to.'[39] Such comments added at the end, however, are almost always unplanned afterthoughts. Thus (1) 不知道他玩儿的是什么把戏？ *Bujydaw ta wal de sh sherm baa.shih?* '(I) wonder what trick he is up to?' and (2) *Ta bujydaw wal de sh sherm baa.shih?* 'He (I) wonder is up to what trick?' contain planned interpolations without pause. But (3) *Ta wal de sh sherm baa.shih, .bu.jy.daw?*

---

[39]Examples from Malmqvist, Sïch'uanese, 155.

'What trick is he up to, I wonder?' is likely to have a pause (or a negative pause / ← /) before the afterthought comment. When occurring very frequently, such comments become enclitics or proclitics, as discussed below.

*2.14.5. Proclitic and Enclitic Clauses.* 我 包 你 这 買 実 不 賠 錢. *Woo bau nii jeh mae.may bu peir-chyan.* 'I guarantee you that this business won't lose money.' is a clear case of the pregnant sentence, in which *woo* is the main subject and *bau* the main verb, with *jeh* ... as object-clause. The same will be the case if 担保 *danbao* 'guarantees', a synonym of *bau*, is used instead. But 苫保 *₀guan₀bao*, with an optional neutral tone, is used so much as a hyperbole that it is no stronger than 'I bet' and it usually introduces a clause when the speaker wishes to weaken, rather than strengthen, its probability, as: 屋子裡 这 么 冷！苫 保 是 炉子 滅 了. *Utz.lii tzemm leeng! ₀Guan₀baosh lutz mieh le.* 'It's so cold in the room! I bet the stove is out.' Similarly, 我 怕 *woo pah* 'I am afraid that ... ' is usually taken literally, though weakened, while 恐怕 *₀koong₀pah* has degenerated into a conjunction with very little of the *pah* 'afraid' idea, and is now used as 'probably', applicable to eventualities that the speaker feels only mildly or not at all concerned about. Such change of role of principal and dependent clause into conjunctions and main setence may be compared with the difference between *I think that* ... , which takes a clause object, and the now obsolete *methinks*, which is only a conjunction to the sentence which follows. Expressions introducing a direct quotation like *ta shuo* 'he says' get worn down into neutral tone forms and further reduced phonetically, thus: *ta shuo > .ta.shuo > .t'.ruo > .tʳuo*, a very frequently used filler in telling a story, as if quoting from someone else. Children often use a liberal sprinkling of *.tʳuo*'s in their stories, though the form is by no means limited to children's speech. As often happens with features of informal speech, a speaker often refuses to admit that he talks this way until confronted with a tape recording.

The other side of the reduction of an initial principal clause to a proclitic is the reduction of the predicate of a clause subject to an enclitic final particle. Thus, to the clause subject 咱 们 今

天 歇 ㄗ. *Tzarmen jin.tian shie .shie* 'That we take a rest today' we can add the predicate 也 罢 *yee bah* 'will be a (good) way to finish, too,—will be okay, too'. But if 罢 *bah* is reduced to 吧 *ba* or *be*, it becomes an advisative final particle and the subject clause becomes the main sentence: *Tzarmen jin.tian shie.shie ba.* 'Let's take a rest today.' Similarly, *jiow sh le* 'that's it' is the main predicate in: 你要找青年会，看 見那个有三角ㄦ招牌 的 就是了。 *Nii yaw jao Chingnian Huey, kann.jiann neyg yeou sanjeaul jau.pair de jiow sh le.* 'If you want to find the YMCA, when you see that building with the triangular sign, then that's it.' But when reduced to enclitic form *.jiowshle*, it is appended to the main sentence as final particle, meaning 'that's all (there is to it)', as: 没什么讲究的畫案，就画一个三 角形 就是了. *Mei sherm jeang.jiou de twuann, jiow huah ig sanjeaul-shyng .jiowshle.* 'There is no elaborate design, they just draw a triangular form, that's-all-there-is-to-it.' A synonym of *.jiowshle* is *.bale* or *.bele*, reduced from 罢 了 *bahleau* and *bahle* 'let's', but is quite equivalent to *.jiowshle* in expressing a limitation: 'that's all there's to it' or in commands, 'that's all you need to do', as: 你去 罢 了! *Nii chiuh bele!* 'You just go! (why hesitate?)' Its occurrence in Northern Mandarin is, however, much less frequent than in the other dialects.

Sometimes both a proclitic conjunction and an enclitic particle are present, as: 难道 我非赔你錢不成？ $_0$*Nan$_0$daw woo fei peir nii chyan bu.cherng?* 'Do you mean to say that I have got to pay you money for the damage?' Where $_0$*nan$_0$daw* 'hard to say' is no longer used as a verb and only introduces a rhetorical question with or without the final particle *bu.cherng*, which in full tones means 'it won't do (unless ... )'.

# 3.1 General

Not every language has a kind of unit which behaves in most (not to speak of all) respects as does the unit called "word" when we talk or write *in* English about the subunits *of* English. It is therefore a matter of fiat and not a question of fact whether to apply the word "word" to a type of subunit in the Chinese sentence which has so many points in common with, and so few points divergent from, the English word "word" as to warrant the use of that term without danger of serious misunderstanding. As we shall see when we come to actual cases, we shall meet various types of word-like units which can claim to be called the word, which overlap to a great extent, but which do not have quite the same scope. As usual, I shall prefer to use a familiar term, with a warning against making unwarranted inferences, in preference to using unfamiliar terms, which, though safe from being misunderstood, are often also safe from being understood.

*3.1.1. The Sociological Word.* By the "sociological word" I mean that type of unit, intermediate in size between a phoneme and a sentence, which the general, nonlinguistic public is conscious of, talks about, has an everyday term for, and is practically concerned with in various ways. It is the kind of thing which a child learns to say, which a teacher teaches children to read and write in school, which a writer is paid for so much per thousand, which a clerk in a telegraph office counts and charges so much per, the kind of thing one makes slips of the tongue on, and for the right or wrong use of which one is praised or blamed. Thus it has all the social features of the common small change of every day speech which one would call a "word" in English.

The Chinese sociological equivalent of the word is called 字 *tzyh*. Examples are 上 *shanq* 'up', 大 *dah* 'large', 人 *ren* 'man', 孔

136

*Koong* common surname, 乙 *Yii* the second heaven's stem, used like 'B' for counting items, 己 *jii* 'self'. Like the popular conception of the word in English, it is usually not clear in the mind of its user whether it is the spoken unit or the written character that is referred to when one uses the term *tzyh*. It is sometimes one, sometimes the other, sometimes both, and half the time either one or the other without making any difference. That it is often the linguistic rather than the graphic unit that is referred to comes out from the fact that an illiterate person can, just as naturally as a literate person, say, 你敢说一个"不"字！ *Nii gaan shuo ig "bu" tzyh!* '(Don't) you dare say the word "no"!'; that is, 'I won't take "no" for an answer.', or 他对那件事一个字没提。 *Ta duey ney-jiann shyh ig tzyh mei tyi.* 'He did not mention a single word about that matter.' Because of the close sociological equivalence between *tzyh* and "word", practically all Chinese students of English refer to the unit of Chinese writing as a word and never as a character. They feel puzzled, as I did before being corrected time after time, why one should take the trouble of using a long name for such a simple everyday item? If one looks in Webster's for an unfamiliar word in English, why shouldn't one look in the *Kangshi* for an unfamiliar word in Chinese, but must say "character" instead? This undifferentiated concept of *tzyh* as either spoken or written and its social importance was recognized by Western Sinologists, and in order to avoid misunderstanding about the structural properties of the *tzyh* at least one writer, W. E. Soothill, left it untranslated in the title of his dictionary *The Student's Four Thousand* 字, London, 1899; 3rd ed., 1902. One cataloguer in a university library listed it as *The Student's Four Thousand*, apparently taking the *tzyh* "字" as a decoration on the title page!

The difference between the sociological word and the linguistic word can be illustrated further by a similar difference in usage in the names of citrus fruits. There are at least ten different names for as many common citrus fruits, of which by far the commonest in China is 橘子 *jyutz* 'tangerine'. Among speakers of Mandarin in America, however, it is the custom to say *jyutz* not only for 'tangerine' but also for 'orange', and 橘子汁 *jyutzjy* or

橘子水 *jyutzshoei* for 'orange juice', even though they know perfectly well that the botanically correct name for 'orange' is 橙子 *cherntz*.[1] The term *jyutz* is therefore the sociological equivalent for 'the citrus fruit for everyday use.'

Whatever conception of the syntactic word we shall find scientifically justifiable to define, it plays no part in the Chinaman of the street's conception of the subunits of the Chinese language. Thus, if one wishes to ask what the syntactic word *shianntzay* 'now' means, one would say: "现在"这两个字是什么意思？ *"Shianntzay" jey leanngg tzyh sh sherm yihsy?* 'What is the meaning of these two *tzyh "shianntzay"?'* Instead of calling it (or them?) *leangg tzyh*, one could also call it 这个话 *jeyg huah* 'this saying', 这个话语 *jeyg huahyeu* 'this expression', or 这个名词(儿) *jeyg mingtsyr ~ -tserl* 'this term', since *mingtsyr*, although it means 'noun' in technical grammar, means in popular usage (any) 'expression'. The spirit of saying *shianntzay jey leangg tzyh* has been very well expressed by a radio comedian, when he said: "I'll tell you what I'll do in just two words—re-sign." Nobody but a Western-trained linguistician would say *"Shianntzay" jeyg tsyr sh sherm yihsy?*, since 词 *tsyr* in the sense of the syntactic word is a new usage which was introduced only a few decades ago. In older usage, *tsyr* meant 'diction, wording', as in 措词不当 *tsuoh-tsyr budanq* L 'improperly worded'.

*3.1.2. The Morpheme in Chinese: Monosyllabism.* The nearest equivalent to *tzyh* as a linguistic unit is the morpheme,[2] which is usually defined as the smallest unit in the language which has a

---

[1]Speakers of Cantonese in America, however, do say 橙 *jhaang*° and 橙汁 *jhaangcap*, since oranges are common in the Kwangtung province. In fact, another northern term for 'orange' is 廣橘 *Goangjyu* 'Cantonese tangerine'.

[2]The morpheme, as applied to the Chinese language, has been called the logoid by Carr (49). Boodberg (333, n. 7) uses the term "phonosemanteme", though it is not limited to the synchronic sense. Current Chinese writers use the term 词素 *tsyrsuh* '(prime) element of words', though usages still differ as to whether a *tsyrsuh* is limited to a bound morpheme which is not a complete word or is applied to all morphemes, whether bound or free.

meaning. This is the sense in which Chinese has been called, and to a large extent is, a monosyllabic language—a language in which every syllable has a meaning. The so-called "monosyllabic myth" is in fact one of the truest myths in Chinese mythology. Exceptions in which it takes more than a syllable to represent a minimum meaningful unit are relatively few. Examples are: 蜈蚣 *wu.gong* 'centipede', 玫瑰 *meiguey* 'rose', 踌躇 *chour$_0$chwu* 'hesitates', □ □ □ *hah.shymaa* 'Kirin frog', 菩薩 *pwu$_0$sah* bodhisattva', 仿佛 *faang$_0$fwu* 'apparently'. The predominance of monosyllabism is so great that a speaker or writer tends to read meaning into single syllables when there was none originally. Thus, *pwu.taur* 'grapes' a foreign borrowing written with the separately meaningless characters 葡萄 has also been written as 葡桃 with the suggestion that it is some kind of *taur* 桃 'peach' (cf. 'cranberry' as some kind of 'berry', although 'cran-' is nothing). In the Shanghai streetcar system, the last car on a line at night is known as 賴四卡 *lahsyhka*, being the Shanghaized form of English 'last car'. Since the car before the last car is also of importance to the riding public and since what comes before 四 *syh* 'four' is 三 *sɛ* 'three' (Mand. *san*), they call the penultimate car *lahsɛka*.[3] In the technical terms derived from foreign borrowings, there is a strong tendency, whenever there is a chance, to read Chinese monosyllabic meanings into foreign polysyllables or even consonant clusters. Thus a trust, in the sense of a monopoly, is 讬賴斯 *tuolaysy*, literally 'entrust, rely on this'. A tractor is half transliterated (with meanings) and half translated as 拖拉机 *tuolhaji*, literally 'drag-pull machine', where *tuo* and *lha* transliterate the *t-* and *-ra-*, and *-ji* 'machine' translates the suffix *-or*. Which all goes to show that completely meaningless monosyllables in Chinese are always felt as something of an anomaly.[4]

---

[3]I did not come across this expression when I was in Shanghai. It was Dr. Chiang Monlin, who lived there longer than I did, who gave me this information.

[4]For additional examples, analyzed into subtypes, see Edward H. Schafer, "Preliminary Remarks on the Structure and Imagery of the Medieval Period", *TP*, 50:259-261 of 257-264 (1963).

Cases of morphemes less than a syllable are even rarer than polysyllabic morphemes. The only important ones are the non-syllabic retroflex suffix *-l* (phonetically [-əɹ], [-r], or an *r*-coloring of the preceding sound or sounds) and the suffix *m*. That the retroflex *-l* is nonsyllabic comes out from such constrasts as be-tween:

他 编 了 一 个 曲 ㄦ .    *Ta bian.le ig cheul.* 'He has made up a song.'

and

他 添 了 一 个 女兒 .    *Ta tian.le ig neu.erl.* 'He has added (to his family) a daughter.'

In the second sentence *neu.erl* is a compound 'female child,— daughter', in which *.erl*, even though in the neutral tone, still oc-cupies a separate syllable, whereas *cheul* is all one syllable.[5] The difference is also found in the slight divergence between the speech of the Manchus in Peiping and the rest of the inhabitants of the city. Among other things there is a tendency in the Manchu style of speech to give the diminutive suffix a separate syllable. For example, 兔兒爺 'the rabbit in the moon' (instead of the man in the moon) is called *tuh.erl-ye* by the Manchus, but *tull-ye* by the non-Manchus. Since the Republican Revolution of 1911, after which the Forbidden City was opened to the public and persons of Manchu origin found it advantageous to adopt non-Manchu names, there has been complete mobility of residence in all parts of the city. The difference between the Manchu style and the general style of Peiping pronunciation has all but disap-peared.

---

[5]In ordinary orthography it is not possible to tell whether the 兒 in 曲 兒 'song' and 女 兒 'daughter' is syllabic. I have proposed the use of the National Phonetic letter ㄦ for the nonsyllabic ending and the regular charac-ter 兒 for the syllabic form—a usage which has gained some currency. But in recent linguistic publications ㄦ has been used for both the syllabic *erl* and nonsyllabic *-l*.

The case of the nonsyllabic *m* is in a different category. In the first place, whenever there is an *m* there is always an alternate form with a vowel, forming with it a clearly separate syllable. For example, *tam~tamen* 'they', *dwom~dwome* 'how, to what extent'. Moreover, even when there is no vowel, it is not certain that the *m* is not occupying the position of a syllable in the neutral tone, somewhat like the syllabic status of the nasal syllable in Japanese, commonly romanized as *n*. A test may be set up by inquiring into the tonal behavior of the element in question. With *niimen yeou* 'you (pl.) have' the usual expected tonal pattern will be $\frac{1}{2}$ 3rd + neutral + (full) 3rd: ⌐ ˈ⅃ . In *niim yeou*, if the *m* is nonsyllabic, the pattern should be 2nd (⌐ 3rd) + 3rd: ⌐Ⅎ . Actually, however, the pattern is still ⌐ ˈ⅃, with *m* acting like a neutral-tone syllable. This seems to prove the syllabic status of the *m*. The evidence, however, is not conclusive, for in a quite similar form *tzeem tzoou* 'how to go' both tonal patterns are possible, with perhaps a slight perference for ⌐Ⅎ , which would make the *m* nonsyllabic. Thus we shall have to regard such *m*, whether as a plural ending or as a modal suffix, as an intermediate case of a subsyllabic morpheme.

There are a few other apparent cases of nonsyllabic morphemes when a neutral tone with a fricative initial occurs after a 4th Tone, as in 豆腐 *dow.fu* 'beancurd', 妹夫 *mey.fu* 'younger sister's husband', 气死了 *chih.syyle* 'angered to death', 意思 *yih.sy* 'meaning', which sound almost like *dowf, meyf, chiss, yiss*. The second parts of these words should be regarded as neutral-tone syllables with their vowels [pronounced] voiceless as a result of following a 4th Tone, which normally ends in a *perdendosi* pitch. It is quite similar to the voiceless syllables in Japanese *chi* (/ti/), *shi* (/si/), and so on, which are often voiceless but occupy syllabic positions. The vowels in these morphemes are quite voiced when following other than the 4th Tone, as in 姐夫 *jiee.fu* 'older sister's husband'.

*3.1.3. Recognition of Morphemes.* A much more difficult theoretical problem is that concerning the status of polysyllabic forms which are reducible or not reducible to meaningful subunits, varying individually with the speaker. To every speaker, literate or illiterate, 樹林子 *shuhlintz* 'tree-grove-*noun suffix,—*

woods' is three morphemes, and 玫瑰 *meiguey* 'rose', whether spoken or written, is one morpheme. But between the two extremes the intermediate cases are much more frequent. Thus, 如果 *ruguoo* for some speakers is just 'if', while for others it is compounded of *ru* 'if, as' and *guoo* 'indeed', even though they use the compound as 'if' and not as 'if indeed' (for which the spoken form is 假如果然 *jearu guooran*). Likewise, for some 麻煩 *ma.farn* is simply 'troublesome', while others analyze it into *ma* 'confused (like snarled hemp)' and *farn* 'annoying'. Similarly with 組織 *tzu(u).jy* 'gather together' + 'weave' ⟶ 'organize, -ization', 警察 *jiingchar* 'warn(ing)' + 'scrutinize, -y' ⟶ 'police', 廣播 *goangboh* 'broad' + 'cast' ⟶ 'broadcast' (of which even most speakers of English forget its original agricultural meaning), and so on. Because of the greater chance of arriving at a convergent answer from different speakers, it is more practical to lean on the analysis by literate persons. To be sure, a literate person is apt to read meanings into characters that are not there or misinterpret the semantic history. However, we are investigating the present status of the language as it is used and folk etymologies are to be recorded as facts, plus the true etymologies, if known and important enough to be noted. For example, 利害 *lihhay* 'profit (able) and harm(ful)', when pronounced *lih.hay* means 'which can be profitable or harmful,—powerful'. From this, which was originally a compound of antonyms, it gets to be written as 厲害 'fierce-harmful'—a compound of synonyms.

Without completely equating the morpheme to the character or to the *tzyh*, it is on the whole advisable to take the maximum analysis of literate speakers, since there will be a better chance of arriving at more convergent results than if we followed the analysis in varying degrees by speakers of varying degrees of literacy. It is true that linguistic units do not necessarily correspond to units of writing. But if writing has had a stabilizing effect on the use of the language, then it is proper to record such usage.

We are taking the morpheme as the smallest unit that has a meaning. As to units larger than a morpheme forming morpheme complexes of various levels, they also have meanings which may or may not be predictable from the meanings of the parts. Even when the meaning of the whole can be gotten from the meanings of the parts, it is by no means certain that in actual use the speaker or hearer is thinking of (read "reacting to", in behavioristic terms) the meaning of the parts even if he can tell what the parts mean if asked. In fact, it is quite certain that the user of language is not always fully aware and often does not know the meaning of the parts. This constitutes therefore another reason that the morpheme should be the end result from analysis of meaningful units. As to when a morpheme is the same and when a different one, we shall leave the discussion to a later section (sec. 3.7) under the problem of word and morpheme identity.

*3.1.4. Syntagmatic and Paradigmatic Aspects.* The word unit may be considered from the point of view of concatenation of morphemes in the sentence: the question of where they go together to form words and where they are separate words. This is the syntagmatic aspect of word analysis. On the other hand, a word is a word in that it behaves like other morphemes or morpheme complexes in filling corresponding positions in the sentence. This is the paradigmatic aspect of word analysis. Roughly speaking, the first is a question of size and the latter a question of kind. In the following discussions, sections 3.2 and 3.3 have to do with the syntagmatic aspects, sections 3.6 and 3.7 with the paradigmatic aspects, and sections 3.4, 3.5, and 3.8 have to do with both aspects.[6]

## 3.2  Free and Bound Forms

A morpheme which can be uttered alone is free (F), and one which always occurs without pause with another morpheme in an utterance is bound (B). For example, to the question 'What is this?' one can answer 这是梨. *Jeh sh li.* 'This is a pear.' or simply *Li.* 'A pear.' Therefore *li* 'pear' is free. But the morpheme *taur* occurs in 桃花儿 *taurhual* 'peach blossom', 桃园 *tauryuan*

---

[6]Richard S. Pittman, in his "On Defining Morphology and Syntax", *IJAL*, 25:199 (1959), calls these sequence relations and list relations. We shall, however, use the term *list* in a narrower sense: listables are those which can be listed in a book on grammar, for example, pronouns and auxiliary verbs; and unlistables are those which can only be listed in a dictionary, for example, nouns and verbs. Pittman's "list" includes both.

'peach garden', 櫻 桃 *ing.taur* 'baby-peach,—cherry', *taurtz* 'a
peach', but never *taur* alone. Therefore *taur* is bound. Note that
a free morpheme like *li* also occurs in combinations like *lihual*
'pear blossom', 鳳 梨 *fenqli* 'phoenix-apple,—pineapple', and 梨
園 *liyuan* 'pear garden; the theatrical world'. Almost all free
morphemes except interjections can enter into such close combinations with other morphemes. Consequently, when we say a
morpheme is free we mean it is sometimes free, whereas if a
morpheme is bound it is always bound.

According to Bloomfield's definition (*Lg*, 178), a word is a
minimum free form, whether it is one morpheme (*li*) or more than
one morpheme (*taur-l*). But if we begin to apply this definition,
we shall find that the idea of free and bound will admit of various
interpretations.[7]

*3.2.1. Start-Free, Start-Bound, End-Free, End-Bound.* A morpheme or a complex of morphemes may be free or bound at its
beginning or at its end, resulting in the following types of beginnings and ends with respect to F and B.

(1) B-: Start-Free but End-Bound. This includes prefixes such
as 第 *dih-*, prefix for ordinal numbers, 初 *chu-*, prefix for the first
ten days of the month, as 初 三 *chusan* 'the 3rd (of the month)'.
The form *gwojih-* 'international' is used in compounds such as
國 際 法 *gwojihfaa* 'international law', and when used predicatively, it has to be bound with a suffix, as  这 个 问 题 是 國 際
的. *Jehg wenntyi sh gwojihde.* 'This problem is international' or ...
是 國 際 性 的  *sh gwojihshinqde.* ' ... is international in nature.'
Similarly, *Jonghwa-* 'China' is used only in compounds such as
中 華 民 國  *Jonghwa Mingwo* 'Republic of China', the free form
for 'China' being *Jong.gwo.* Proper names abbreviated from longer,
full forms are of course a different matter, as 國 際（ 飯店 ）的
菜 好. *Gwojih (Fanndiann) de tsay hao.* 'The food at the International (Hotel) is good.'  这 书 是 中 華（ 书局 ）出 版 的。*Jeh
shu sh Jonghwa (Shujyu) chubaan de.* 'This book was published

---

[7]See Lien-Sheng Yang, "The Concept of 'Free' and 'Bound' in Spoken
Chinese", *HJAS*, 12:462-469 (1949), and Robert A. Hall, Jr., "A Note on
Bound Forms", *Journ. of Eng. and Germ. Philology*, 45:450 (Oct., 1946).

by Chung Hwa (Book Company)', where the forms in parentheses are often omitted in speech.

Most modal adverbs are start-free but end-bound, as 就 *jiow* 'then', 最 *tzuey* 'most', 还 *hair* 'still', 更 *genq* 'still more', 多么 *dwome* 'how, to what extent?', 一 *i* 'as soon as', 简直 *jeanjyr* 'simply, just'. Conjunctions, however, are not end-bound, since one can always pause or add pause particles after them, as, 假如 啊, ...*Jearu a,* ... 'If, ...', 可是啊, ... *Keesh a,* ... 'However, ...'!

(2) -B: End-Free but Start Bound. Under this category, we find suffixes: -*de* for subordination, -*le* perfective suffix, -*j* progressive suffix, -*tz*, -*l*, -.*ba*, -.*tou* noun suffixes, -*me* modal suffix, -*men* plural suffix; final particles bound to phrases or larger units; *ne, me, a,* interrogative particles, *ne, ma, a,* declarative particles; and translations of suffixes in new terms as -*huah* '-ize, -fy-' as in 机械化 *jishiehhuah* 'mechanize', 科学化 *keshyuehhuah* 'to make scientific', -*shinq* '-ity', as in 可能性 *keenengshinq* 'possibility', 弹性 *tarnshinq* 'elasticity'. As these will be treated in the next chapter, we shall not go into further details here.

(3) (-)B(-): Start-Free or End-Free, but Not Both. The great majority of morphemes entered in a dictionary of single characters belong to this category. All numerals are of this type, as *san-* in *sanshyr* 'thirty', -*san* in *shyrsan* 'thirteen'; most measures, as -*jiann* 'article' in 一件事 *i-jiann shyh* 'an item of business', *jiann-* in *jiann.tou* 'article, part (of machine)'; the cardinal directions, as *dong-* in 东南 *dongnan* 'southeast', 廣东 *Goangdong* 'Kwangtung (province)'; the seasons of the year, as *chuen-* in 春天 *chuen.tian* 'spring days,—the Spring', -*chuen* in 立春 *Lihchuen* 'establish-spring' (one of the 24 sections of the solar year, beginning on or about February 5); monosyllabic names, as *Wang-* in 王家 *Wang-.jia* 'Wang-family,—the Wangs', -*Wang* in 老王 *Lao Wang*[8] 'Old Wang', where prefixing *Lao-* has the effect of dropping "Mr."

3.2.2. *Root Words.* All these (-)B(-) forms are bound forms, since they are bound at least at one end. It is useful to distinguish here between those bound forms which will become free by the

---

[8]We are adopting the convention of omitting hyphens where a string of capitalized forms is understood to be one compound.

addition of an affix and those which occur only in combination
with other root morphemes. The first kind consists of roots to
form primary derived words or root words. Examples are: 椅子
*yiitz* 'chair', 襪子 *wahtz* 'sock, stocking' (cf. the Cantonese cognate *maat*, which is free without any suffix), *wey + -l → 味儿
well* 'taste, odor', 石头 *shyr.tou* 'stone', 托着 *tuoj* 'holds up with
one's palm', *dihsyh* 'fourth'. The other is a much larger class,
consisting of bound morphemes occurring in compounds. Examples
are 男 *nan* 'man, male', 女 *neu* 'woman, female', 力 *lih* 'strength',
畧 *liueh* 'outline, approximate', 謠 *yau* 'rumor', 结 *jye* 'to knot, to
conclude'.

(4) -B-: Both Ends Bound. Morphemes which are always sim-
ultaneously bound at both ends are rare. Examples are -.*li*- in 糊
哩糊塗 *hwu.li-hwutwu* or *hwu.li-hwudu* 'quite muddled', 小哩
小气的 *sheau.li-sheauchih de* 'small and stingy', -.*bu*- in 直不
扰绕的 *jyr.bu-loongtoong de* 'stiff and straight', 酸不溜ᵌ
(儿) 的 *suan.bu-lhioulhiou (l) de* 'sourish', and so on. If the -.*de*-
in 看得見 *kannde-jiann* 'can see' and the -.*bu*-in 看不見 *kann-
.bu-jian* 'cannot see' are regarded as being in construction with
**kann.jian** 'sees', then the infixed -.*de*- and -.*bu*- are also such
doubly bound morphemes.

(5) F: Both Ends Free. Finally, the second largest class of
morphemes next to those which are free at either end, but not at
both ends, namely (-)B(-), is the class of those which are simultane-
ously free at both ends. Examples are: 来 *lai* 'comes', 天 *tian* 'sky',
有 *yeou* 'has', 大 *dah* 'large', 喂! *Uai!* 'Hello!', 你 *nii* 'you (sing)',
分 *fen* 'divides', 帅 *shuay* 'smart, chic', 城 *cherng* 'city'.

## 3.3. Prosodic Aspects

*3.3.1. The Word as a Phonological Unit.* The definition of a
word as a minimum free form (free at both ends) has often been
felt to be too drastic, and weaker conditions have been proposed
instead.[9] In languages with clear and regular phonological mark-

---

[9]Bloomfield (*Lg*, 179-180) himself has to show the word status of 'the'
by comparing it with the syntactically parallel forms 'this' and 'that'.

ers, it is fairly simple to find word boundaries without trying to find an isolated occurrence of the word as an independent utterance. For example, words in Latin can in most cases be marked off by the penultimate and antepenultimate stress rules. In the Wu dialects, compound words are recognizable from their tone sandhi, which are different within words from the tone sandhi between words. Thus, in the Soochow dialect, if Tone ∨ is followed by Tone ⌐ in a phrase, the result is ∨⌐ , involving relatively little change from the tones in isolation. But if Tone ∨ is compounded with Tone ⌐ to form one word, then the result is ⌐∨ , which is quite a drastic sandhi change. Examples are 放參 *fonq-sen* ∨⌐ 'puts in ginseng' (Mand *fanq-shen*, or more idiomatically 搁參 *ge-shen*), but 放生 *fonq-sen* ⌐∨ 'sets free a living being (for religious or similar reasons)' (Mand *fanq-sheng*). In the Mandarin equivalents the tonal patterns are the same, in fact with no sandhi change at all. There is some difference in the stress patterns, but they are secondary in the Wu dialects.

In Mandarin, stress and tonal patterns can sometimes be used to mark off words, but potential pauses are more generally available for this purpose.

*3.3.2 Stress and Tone as Word Markers.* In Chapter 1 we considered various types of stress and tone combinations in Mandarin. Apart from various degrees of stress and intonation in sentence prosody, we have worked with four tones and two degrees of stress (or three degrees if we count the contrastive stress). A syllable is either stressed, in which case it has a tone, or unstressed and in the neutral tone. In a group of two, three, or four syllables of which none is in the neutral tone, the last has the loudest stress, the first next, and the inside syllables least loud. If one or more syllables are in the neutral tone, then the last stressed syllable has the main stress. Since all these different degrees of stress between syllables not in the neutral tone are predictable, the differences are not distinctive.

The great majority of polysyllabic forms which are generally regarded as words are dissyllables.[10] These are either iambs[11] or trochees. Examples are:

| IAMBS | | TROCHEES | |
|---|---|---|---|
| 天下 | *tianshiah* 'under heaven, —the world' | 知道 | *jy.daw* 'knows' |
| 起初 | *chiichu* 'at first' | 本事 | *been.shyh* 'ability' |
| 同事 | *torngshyh* 'colleague' | 待会儿 | *dai.hoel* 'after a while' |
| 拒绝 | *jiuhjyue* 'rejects' | 琢磨 | *tzwo.mo* 'thinks over' |
| 袖口 | *shiowkoou* 'sleeve-opening' | 鄉下 | *shiang.shiah* '(down) in the country' |
| 代筆 | *daybii* 'substitutes-pen, —ghostwrites, -er' | 明白 | *ming.bair* 'clear, understands' |

Although the preceding examples are obviously syntactic words, the mere fact that they are iambs or trochees cannot be a sufficient condition for their being so. Thus, the iambs:

先嫁 *shian jiah* 'marries (of a woman) first'

你输. *Nii shu.* 'You lose.'

红痣 *horng jyh* 'red wart'

去学 *chiuh shyue* 'go and learn'

就走 *jiow tzoou* 'leaves right away'

带筆 *day bii* 'takes along a pen'

With identical finals and tones as above, are obviously phrases or sentences, so that other criteria will have to be used to distinguish compound words from phrases. As to tone sandhi in Mandarin, the only significant change in iambs is the raising of a 3rd-Tone syllable to the 2nd Tone before another 3rd Tone. The following compound words and phrases are of this tonal pattern:

---

[10]See, for example, the word count reported in 郑林義，从一种统计看汉语词彙 (Jenq Linshi, "Looking at the Lexicon of Chinese from a Certain Statistic") in 汉语的词儿和拼写法 (*Chinese Words and Their Spellings*); Collection I, Peking, 1955, p. 33 of pp. 31-39.

[11]Strictly, they are iambs in an extended sense, since the first syllable in Chinese is only less stressed than the second, but not completely unstressed.

| WORD | PHRASES OR SENTENCES |
|---|---|
| 许久 *sheujeou* 'for a long time' | 举手 *jeu-shoou* 'raises the hand' |
| 粉笔 *feenbii* 'chalk' | 很挤 *heen jii* 'very crowded' |
| 火酒 *huoojeou* 'fire-wine, —alcohol' | 我有. *Woo yeou.* 'I have.' |
| 酒鬼 *Jeougoei* 'wine-fiend, —an alcoholic' | 有水. *Yeou-shoei.* 'There is water.' |
| 理想 *liisheang* 'ideal' | 你讲. *Nii jeang.* 'You explain.' |
| 保守 *baoshoou* 'conserves' | 老走 *lao tzoou* 'keeps going' |

Thus the 3rd-Tone sandhi for stressed syllables applies equally within a word and between words and is therefore not available, as tone sandhi is in the Wu dialects, for use as a word marker.

In a trochee, the second syllable is in the neutral tone and is closely attached to the first syllable. In the majority of cases a trochee is a syntactical word, as cited in the trochaic examples above. The neutral-tone syllables may be any one of a relatively short listable class of morphemes, namely (1) suffixes, (2) pronouns in object position, (3) final particles, or it may be (4) one of an open, or unlistable, class of syllables.

(1) Suffixes will be treated in detail in chapter 4. Here we shall give only a few examples to illustrate different types of suffixed words. With free root morphemes, we have 瓶子 *pyngtz* 'a jar', 盖子 *gaytz* 'a lid', 砖头 *juan.tou* 'brick', 认得 *renn.de* 'can recognize, knows', 坐着 *tzuohj* 'is sitting'; with bound root morphemes, we have 法子 *fartz* 'method, way', 石头 *shyr.tou* 'stone', 觉得 *jyue.de* 'feels', 觉着 *jyuej* 'feels'.

(2) Pronoun objects are usually in the neutral tone without forming part of a word with the preceding verb. Examples are 问他 *wenn ta* 'asks him', 叫我们 *jiaw woomen* 'calls us'.

(3) Particles are enclitics (unstressed final syllables) which are in construction with a preceding phrase or sentence, though phonetically closely attached to the syllable immediately preceding it. Thus, in 他决定今天不回家了. *Ta jyuedinq jin.tian bu hwei-jia le.* 'He decides not to go home today.', the *le* is as closely attached to *jia* as the suffix *-.tou* is attached to the root word *guann* in 罐头 *guann.tou* 'a can', but is actually in construction

with the rest of the whole predicate, if not the whole sentence. In 他是一个心眼儿很直的人。 *Ta sh ig shinyeal heen jyr de ren.* 'He is a man with a very straightforward heart.', *de* is phonetically closely attached to *jyr*, but it is not *jyr de ren* 'a straight man' nor *heen jyr de ren* 'a very straight man', but *shinyeal heen jyr de ren* 'a man whose heart is very straightforward'. A particle, though always start-bound, can be in construction with a phrase, clause, or sentence, and is thus not part of a word, as a suffix is. That is one reason why Chinese grammarians have always treated particles as words, forming a separate part of speech.[12]

(4) What remains then consists of an unlistable open class of neutral-tone syllables which form polysyllabic words with one or more preceding syllables. A very small proportion of these are submorphemic syllables forming polysyllabic morphemes with what precedes, as 纥缝 *ga.da* 'a knot', 疙瘩 *ge.da* 'a wart', 螞螂 *mha.lang* 'dragonfly'. In the great majority of cases, the neutral-tone syllable is a whole morpheme bound to the preceding syllable or syllables to form a polysyllabic word, constituting most of the trochaic entries in a dictionary of the *tsyrdean* type. Examples are:

扁担 *bean.dann* 'flat-load,—(flat) carrying pole'
拾掇 *shyr.dou* 'pick up-tidies,—tidies up'
反正 *faan.jenq* 'reverse-right,—anyway'
托盤 *tuo.parn* 'hold up-tray,—tray'
干淨 *gan.jinq* 'dry-clean,—clean (including liquids)'
意見 *yih.jiann* 'idea-view,—opinion'
通条 *tong.tyau* 'poke-rod,—a poker'
棉花 *mian.hua* 'cotton-flower,—cotton'

*3.3.3. Contrasting Stress on Words.* In general a word can be given a contrasting stress, while sub-word morphemes cannot normally be stressed. Thus, in: 他没到山东去，他到山西去了。 *Ta mei daw "Shan.dong chiuh, ta daw "Shan.shi chiuh le.* 'He did not go to Shantung, he went to Shansi.', the whole contrasting word is stressed instead of the contrasting parts *.dong* and

---

[12]Cf. similar treatment of Japanese particles, as discussed in Rulon S. Wells, "Immediate Constituents", *Language*, 23:102 of 81-117 (1947).

.shi. In: 你 以 為 他 看 不 見 啊 ? 他 其 实 看 得 見. *Nii yii-wei ta kann.bu-* '*jiann a? Ta chyishyr* "*kann.de-jiann.* 'You think he can't see? He can see, as a matter of fact.', the stress is displaced, though illogically, from -*jiann* to *kann-*, instead of being applied to the contrasted parts .*bu* and .*de*. Note, however, that children of pre-grammatical age sometimes speak correct logic, but wrong grammar, as in 爹 ˋ 抱 "得 動, 媽 ˋ 抱 "不 動. *Die.die baw-*"*der-donq, Mha.mha baw-* "*buu-donq.*, as if to say 'Daddy CAN hold (me), Mommy can'T hold (me).'

When, however, a morpheme or even a phoneme is in quotes or in quasi-quotation, then it tends to acquire the status of a word and can be contrasted by stress, as: *Woo shuo de sh Shan* "*dong, bush Shan* "*shi.* 'What I said was *Shan* "*tung,* not *Shan* "*si.*' This is similar to the word-chewing practice sometimes heard in: 'I meant princi"pal [pæl], not princi"ple [pl].'

*3.3.4. Pause and Potential Pauses as Word Markers.* If there are actual pauses before and after a form, then it satisfies the requirement of F at both ends. But it will be more convenient not to require actual pauses but only potential or facultative pauses.[13] Take, for example, the sentence: 今 天 我 要 上 理 髮 鋪 去 理 髮. *Jin.tian woo yaw shanq liifahpuh chiuh lii-fah.* 'Today I want to go to the barbershop to have a haircut.' Between the words there are various possible pauses, pause particles, and sounds of hesitation. As a case of extreme hesitancy, one might say the sentence thus: *Jin.tian a, woo ia, yaw—shanq —, .ne.ge .ne.ge—liifah—, liifahpuh—, chiuh lii—lii—lii-fah.* Hesitant as the sentence may sound, it is by no means completely inarticulate, and the forms of hesitation follow patterns which few learners of Chinese as a foreign language will be able to use without keen observation and prolonged practice. Thus, after the time-word subject *jin.tian* or the actor subject *woo*, one can have a simple pause /,/ or one of the pause particles *a(~ia), .me, ne,* less commonly, *ba.* Within a subject or a predicate, consisting of more than one word, a pause takes the form of a prolongation of the

---

[13] "It is more fruitful to define Words initially as minimum facultative pause-groups than as minimum free forms." *Ibid.,* 115, n. 58. "A word is . . . any segment of a sentence bounded by successive points *at which pausing is possible.*" Hockett, *Course,* 167.

last sound at the pitch at which the tone ends (low in the case of the 3rd Tone), here indicated by a dash. Before a substantive expression, the filler word, in neutral tone, *.ne.ge .ne.ge* or *.je.ge .je.ge* 'the, the' is sometimes inserted. The essential point to note here is that if a speaker hesitates in the midst of a polysyllabic work, then, before going on, he starts over again so as to have the whole word repeated without pause, as in the cases of *lii-fahpuh* and *lii-fah*. The verb-object compound *lii-fah* consists of two bound morphemes *lii-* 'to put in order' and *-fah* 'the hair (of the head)'. Contrast this with the phrase of free syntactic words *leu tour.fah*, where *leu* is the free and colloquial equivalent of *lii*, in fact written with the same character 理, and *tour.fah* is the free form for 'hair', so that if one hesitates at *leu*, one can resume at *tour.fah* without starting back from *leu*, thus: *Woo yaw leu—, leu—, leu i-leu—, (woode) tour.fah.* 'I want to comb (straighten, pat, etc.), to comb, to give (my) hair a combing.' To be sure, one could choose to resume from the beginning and repeat the whole phrase, or even repeat the whole sentence if one wanted to. But in the case of *lii-fah*, the repetition of *lii* after a hesitation is obligatory,[14] since *fah* is a bound morpheme of the (-) B (-) type.

The use of a potential pause as a word marker can resolve ambiguity in word division in an otherwise identical pattern or even in an identical succession of morphemes. Take for example the succession of three 3rd-Tone morphemes 比 *bii* 'than', 我 *woo* 'I', 小 *sheau* 'small', which at normal speed would be pronounced ㄅ ㄋ ㄋ 'younger than I' (see sec. 1.3.4.2). This has the

---

[14]Only very rarely does one resume with a bound form like *-fah* without repeating *lii-*. Cf. the unusual form in English: 'Only an hour [1-second pause]'s drive away' (heard on the Evangeline Baker program, KNBR, San Francisco, September 13, 1962). The following is another plausible, though a made up, example of literally broken English:

Lady Kitty: ... The Church is so wise to take its stand on the indi— indi—

Elizabeth: Solu—

Lady Kitty: Bility of marriage.

From W. Somerset Maugham, *The Circle*, Act III.

same tone sandhi and resulting pattern as in *beei* 'north', *jeou* 'nine', *shoei* 'water' in the name of the mountain resort of Tsing-tao, 北 九 水 *Beeijeoushoei*, pronounced ˊ ˉ ˊ . But whereas *bii woo sheau* allows hesitation and the low ½ 3rd-Tone drawl at *bii* and *woo*, with possibility of a full 3rd-Tone on *woo*, *Beeijeou-shoei* allows no such pause or drawl, and in case of hesitation the full name would be resumed, as *Woo sheang sh tzay* ½ *beei—*, ½ *beei—, Beeijeoushoei* ˊ ˉ ˊ . 'I think it was at North—, North—, Northninewater.'

As an example of an identical succession of morphemes, 雪 *sheue* 'snow', 裡 *.lii* 'in', 红 *horng* 'red', 燒 *shau* 'cooks', 肉 *row* 'meat' spoken together can be understood as either (1) *sheue.lii-horng* (also called, by some, *shiue-*) 'red-in-snow,—mustard green' + *shaurow* 'cooked (with) meat' or (2) *sheue.lii* 'in snow' + *horng-shaurow* 'red-cooked meat (a well-known dish-', i.e., 'red-cooked meat in snow', which is a somewhat fanciful idea, though the phrase is perfectly grammatical. To resolve the ambiguity, one could insert pauses or drawls at the places of the "+" signs. But in normal speech at average speed one does not make such pauses or drawls. Hence the desirability of taking potential pauses and not actual pauses as word markers.

We noted (sec. 3.2) that free meant sometimes free and that bound meant always bound. Now if we have a succession of free morphemes, how can we tell whether they are in that context free or bound? There the potential pause will often be useful in de-ciding whether the free forms make a compound a word or a phrase. If it is a trochee, it will be one word except when the neutral tone is a pronoun (*kann .ta*) or a particle (*Tzoou .ba*) or the not-V part of a V-not-V question (*Lai .bu .lai?*). If it is iambic, then stress and tone will not be decisive. Thus, 没 山 *mei shan* 'has no hill' is two words, but the identically pronounced 煤 山 *meishan*[15] 'coalhill' is one word. However, in the former it is pos-sible to drawl on *mei* and then say *shan*, while in the latter, if

---

[15]Some claim to hear a special stress at the end of such compounds, but I fail to find the stress any different from that in a phrase.

one hesitates at *mei-*, one will probably resume and say *meishan* together.

A distinction should be made between pauses, sounds of hesitation, and so on, which are part of the language behavior, and interruptions in speech which are nonlinguistic. A cough, a sneeze, or a telephone ringing could interrupt a sentence, a polysyllabic word, or even the middle of a phoneme, as when one is interrupted after the stop and before the fricative part of the last phoneme in 'I want eac(h of you to ...)'. If the speaker has changed his mind or forgotten where he was before the interruption, that would of course not make the part before the interruption end-free in the usual sense. (See also sec. 2.14.2 for other examples.)

A word should be said about the question of the identity of a sentence spoken with different prosodic features. If there is a difference in the stress pattern, it is often not the same sentence and the division of words in it may also not be the same. For example, 小 心 打 手! *Sheau.shin daa-'shoou!* 'Be careful (the machine, or whatever, may) hit your hand!': *Sheau.shin 'daa.shoou* 'Beware of thugs!' But the insertion of pauses, while it will obviously make a stylistic difference and would constitute a different rendition for dramatic purposes, should in general not be considered to result in a different sentence; otherwise it would lead to the recognition of too many different sentences to be useful for purposes of grammatical analysis. We should therefore consider the 'haircut' sentence above as the same sentence whether in straightforward utterance or with many hesitations, except perhaps for the insertion of such filler words as *.je.ge .je.ge.*

To summarize the phonological aspects of the syntactic word, we have found that tone sandhi in Mandarin offers no help in distinguishing compounds from phrases in most cases, as it does in the Wu dialects. Where no neutral tone is involved, the degrees of stress in a string of syllables are predictable and independent of word structure. If a neutral tone occurs, it will form part of a word with the preceding syllable, except in the cases of object pronouns, the not-V part of V-not-V questions, and final particles. In the case of particles, it is bound with the preceding phrase as a whole. Stress and tone are therefore relatively unimportant in marking out syntactic words. Potential pauses, on the other hand, are good tests for word boundaries: if for any reason a speaker hesitates in the middle of a polysyllabic word, he does not continue from there, but repeats himself by starting from the beginning of the word, so as to say the whole polysyllabic syntactic word without interruption.

## 3.4. Substitution and Separation

*3.4.1. Versatile and Restricted.* There is a difference between the conception of free vs. bound and that of versatile and restricted.[16] A form is free if it can occur as an utterance (including an answer to a question), and is bound when it cannot. A form is restricted if it occurs only when one or a very small number of other forms occur in a near context, and versatile if its occurrence is not so limited. There is, to be sure, a fair degree of correlation between freedom and versatility, but there are also cases when the two are not parallel, as shown in the following examples:

(1) Free and Versatile: *ren* 'man, person', *yeou* 'has, there is', *dah* 'large', *Uai!* 'Hello!'

(2) Free and Restricted: *mian* in 我从来没知道蚕眠. *Woo tsornglai mei jydaw tsarn mian.* 'I never knew that silkworms stop-feeding-for-a-while-after-feeding-for-a-few-days.' This verb *mian* as a free verb in sericultural terminology occurs only when *tsarn* 'silkworm' occurs in the near context, although in other respects it behaves like any other free form in the sentence. Sim-

---

[16]Murray B. Emeneau, in his *Studies in Vietnamese Grammar*, Berkeley and Los Angeles, Calif., 1951, p. 44, uses the terms "free" and "restricted". To avoid confusion, I am using "versatile" here for his "free". Overlapping and similar to versatility is the notion of productivity. "The productivity of any pattern—derivational, inflectional, or syntactical—is the relative freedom with which speakers coin new grammatical forms by it. Thus the formation of English noun-plurals with /z s əz/ is highly productive. The addition of -*ly* to produce an adverbial is fairly productive; the addition of -*dom* to form a noun is quite restricted." (Hockett, Course, 307-308.) Thus productivity has more to do with the pattern as a whole, while versatility is here applied to the morphemes in a pattern.

ilarly, the verb 磕 *keh* (not *ke*) 'cracks open with one's front teeth' is restricted to contexts when one talks about 瓜子儿 *guatzeel* 'melon seeds' and the like; the noun 賍 *tzang* 'spoils, loot' is restricted chiefly to *fen* 'divides'. Nothing happens *au fur* unless also *à mesure*, and none is one's kith but is also one's kin. But forms which are both free and restricted in Chinese, rare as they are compared with the other three combinations, are by no means such curiosities as *fur* and 'kith'.

(3) Bound and Versatile: This is a very large class. For example, affixes are typically bound morphemes and are extremely versatile. The prefix *dih-* for ordinal numbers goes with any numeral, the suffixes *-l* and *-tz* form thousands of nouns, and the aspect suffix *-j* '-ing' goes with all action verbs and many adjectives. Many root morphemes occur only bound but in a great variety of combinations, as one can see in any medium-sized Chinese dictionary. Examples are 杏 *shinq* 'apricot' B; 桌 *juo* 'table' B; 外 *way* 'out' B, as in 外头 *way.tou* 'outside', 外國 *way.gwo* 'foreign country', *gwoway* 'abroad', ... 除外 *chwuway* 'outside of,— excepting ...', and so on; and 数 *shuh* 'number' B, as in 数目 *shuh-.muh* 'number', 代数 *dayshuh* 'substitutes numbers, — algebra', 数学 *shuhshyue* 'number science,—mathematics', 数论 *shuh-luenn* 'theory of numbers', 亐数的 *wushuhde* 'without number, —countless', etc.

(4) Bound and Restricted: Morphemes which are both bound and restricted form the bulk of a dictionary, although the frequency of occurrence of any one of them in actual speech or running texts will be low. Examples are *aw* 'haughty' in 驕傲 *jiauaw* 'haughty, conceited' and 傲慢 *awmann* 'haughty in manner', *shyr* 'eclipse' in 日蝕 *ryhshyr* 'solar eclipse', 月蝕 *yuehshyr* 'lunar eclipse', 蚕蝕 *tsarnshyr* 'silkworm-eats,—encroaches upon (politically)'; *tzwu* in 民族 *mintzwu* 'people-tribe,—nation'.

3.4.2. *Substitution by Isotopes.* In his *Vocabulary of Chinese Monosyllabic Words*,[17] C. W. Luh sets up a test for words by what he calls substitution by isotopes. For example, in:

---

[17] Luh Jyhwei ( 陆志韦 ), *Hannyeu Dan'intsyr Tsyrhuey*, Peiping, 1936 (see also Selected Bibliography).

说话 *shuo huah* 'says words'          说话 *shuo huah* 'says words'
听话 *ting huah* 'listens to words'   说梦 *shuo menq* 'tells one's
                                                                      dreams'
谈话 *tarn huah* 'talks words'        说书 *shuo shu* 'talks book,
                                                              —tells stories'

*shuo*, *ting*, and *tarn* occupy the same position in the left-hand column and are therefore isotopes. Likewise, *huah*, *menq*, and *shu* in the righthand column are also isotopes. If such an isotopic table of substitution can be constructed, then *shuo* and *huah* are, by this test, words. As to whether certain forms are or are not isotopic, that is to be left to the feeling of the native speaker to decide. Thus, in 费话 *fey huah*[18] 'wasted words' *fey* is not isotopic with *shuo* in *shuo huah;* and in 说笑 *shuo shiaw* 'talks (and) laughs,—banters' *shiaw* is not isotopic with *huah* in *shuo huah*. This dependence on the secondary judgment or reflective judgment of the speaker, though usually to be avoided for general methodological reasons, is no great objection here, as one does usually get convergent answers with regard to isotopy. The difficulty with the test lies in that it works too well. If applied to English words, one could get tables like this:

|           |           |
|-----------|-----------|
| *warmly*  | *warmly*  |
| *warmish* | *coldly*  |
| *warmest* | *badly*   |

from which not only *warm*, but also *ly* would be a word. As Luh himself admits in the preface to the 1956 printing of his *Vocabulary* (p. 11), what substitution by isotopes does is to indicate where to mark out morphemes rather than words.

Another problem arising from the substitution working too well is that in paradigms like:

| 这 | 这儿 | *jeh* | *jell* |
|-----|-------|-------|--------|
| 那 | 那儿 | *nah* | *nall* |
| 哪 | 哪儿 | *naa* | *naal* |

---

[18]I am writing these morphemes separately without hyphens or spelling them together in order to be noncommittal as to their status as words or phrases.

it would seem that one could extract words, or at least morphemes, 止- *j-* for near reference, 那- *n-* for distant reference, 4th Tone for demonstratives, and 3rd Tone for interrogatives. This is quite similar to the analysis of:

| 'this' | 'here' |
|--------|--------|
| 'that' | 'there' |
| 'what' | 'where' |

into *th-* for demonstratives, *wh-* for interrogatives, and so forth. While it is possible to extract meanings from these elements, they are always bound and highly restricted. Moreover, as phonemic shapes, they are swamped by frequently occurring and totally unrelated morphemes, such as 債 *jay* 'debt', 耐 *nay* 'endure', 乃 *nae* 'thereupon'. Bloomfield (*Lg.* 245) calls such partially analyzable forms "*root-forming morphemes* of vague signification". For an account of the Chinese lexicon or grammar it is simpler just to list *jeh, nah, naa,* without further analysis (though 儿 *-l* 裡 *-lii,* because of its high versatility, should be analyzed as a morpheme). We are citing these examples to show that substitution by isotopes does not always result in words.

3.4.3. *Free Utterance and Free Use.* We have seen that to be free as an independent utterance is too drastic a requirement for a word and that added potential pause is an admissible test for a word. Luh Jywei proposes the conception of independent use ( 独用 ) or free activity( 自 由 活 動 ) to supplement the stricter requirement of independent occurrence ( 独立 ). For example, 旗 *chyi* 'flag' is bound, though the form *chyitz* is free, but one says 一面旗 *i-miann chyi* 'a flag' when the classifier *miann* is used. 市 *shyh* 'market' is bound, in the compound 上 市 *shanq-shyh* 'comes up on the market,—is in season', but in *shanq-.guoh shyh* 'has come up on the market,—has been in season' *shyh* has a certain degree of freedom in use.[19] Since, however, *chyi* and *shyh* do not fill the slots for frames *Jeh sh* ... , *Nah sh* ... , etc., they are not (free syntactic) words. (Cf. secs. 3.5.2 and 3.5. 2.1.)

---

[19]*ZGYW*, no. 54:3 (Dec., 1956), and Luh, *GTFaa* 1, chap. 1.

*3.4.4. Ionized Forms.* In the example *shanq-shyh* 'comes up on the market', *shyh* is not free and yet can be separated from *shanq* by the aspect suffix *-.guoh*. One can still say that *shanq.guoh-shyh* is a compound word analyzed either as *shanq-shyh* plus an infix *-.guoh-*, or better, as a suffixed verb *shanq.guoh* plus *shyh*. In the case of potential verb-complement compounds, such as *kann-.de-jiann* 'can see' and *kann.bu-jiann* 'cannot see', it is better to treat them as consisting of *kann.jiann* 'sees' plus the potential infix *-.de* or *-.bu-*. The two types of constructions differ in several respects: The former can be put in the V-not-V interrogative form either by repeating the whole compound or by repeating the verb *shanq*, as *Shanq.guoh-shyh mei shanq.guoh-shyh?*, or *Shanq.guoh-shyh.mei.yeou?* or *Shanq-mei-shanq.guoh-shyh?* With the potential form, on the other hand, the only interrogative form is *Kann-.de-jiann ₀kann.bu₀jiann?* (apart from the ... ma? form, which is possible for both types). Only in Cantonese can one break up a potential and say 睇唔睇得見? *Thae-m(u)-thae-tak-kinn?* Another difference is that, while any V-R compound can take the potential form by the insertion of *-de-* or *-bu-*, only certain V-O compounds are ionizable.

There are various degrees and types of separation of morphemes which are usually bound to each other. One general condition, however, is that the parts must be in the same sentence or at least in a near context. Because of the similarity of a part of a chemical compound floating around in the same solution with its partners, for example $H_2^{++}$ and $SO_4^{--}$ or $Na^+$ and $OH^-$, the separated morphemes have been described as being ionized.[20] We regarded *lii-fah* 'had a haircut' as one word by applying the pause test. But one cannot only add suffixes *liij-fah ne* 'is having a haircut' and *tzay nall lii.guoh-fah* 'has had a haircut there before', but also *lii-wanle i-tsyh fah* 'has finished

---

[20]For a number of years I attributed the idea of ionization to the late George Kennedy. When asked about the source of this term, he said that he had got the idea from Fang-Kuei Li. But when I asked Li, he said: "I got the idea from you." It probably happened during the 1930's, when Li and I had offices on the same floor in Academia Sinica in Nanking, and the idea must have been floating around in the corridors, as ideas often do in academic corridors.

having one haircut'. Similarly 组阁 *tzuu-ger* 'organizes a cabinet', a compound of bound morphemes, as contrasted with the phrase of two free words 组织内阁 *tzuujy neyger* 'organizes a cabinet', can be ionized as in *tzuule jii-tsyh de ger* 'has several times organized a cabinet'. As with most analogies, they go only so far and should not be pushed farther. Thus, it is possible to repeat one of the ions without repeating the other, as in *Nii tzuu-ger bu tzuu?* 'Are you going to organize a cabinet?' as a king might ask his premier. Here the chemical analogy breaks down, of course. The opposite of having an extra ion is having one ion present and the complementary ion lacking, or only present implicitly. For example, I have heard, in connection with applying a lotion to stop itching, the advice 你一擦就止了. *Nii i tsa jiow jyy le.* 'Once you apply it and (the itching) will stop.', where *jyy* 'stops' is normally a bound morpheme. Here the speaker was holding a bottle of 止痒的药水儿 *jyy-yeang de yaw-shoel* 'itch-stopping lotion', but did not actually name it aloud, so that the other ion *yeang* was not heard in the near linguistic context.

The order of bound morphemes can be changed when ionized. For example, 升旗 *sheng-chyi* 'raises the flag' (as a ceremony) can be inverted in the ionized form *chyi hair mei sheng* 'the flag has not yet been raised' (as a ceremony). If free words *chyitz* 'flag' and *sheng.chii.lai* or *sheng.shanq.chiuh* 'is raised up' are used, as in *chyitz hair mei sheng.chii.lai*, then it means literally 'the flag has not yet been raised' (whether as a ceremony of flag-raising or not).

Sometimes a dissyllabic compound of the iambic type is ionized as verb and object, even though the morphemes are not in such relation. For examples of such pseudo V-O constructions, see section 6.5.8.

## 3.5 Words in Functional Frames

*3.5.1. Answers to Questions and Syntactical Frames.* Instead of requiring a word to be the smallest unit which can be uttered in isolation, we can recognize words as the smallest unit which can fill the place of certain functional frames, which in fact is an explication of Luh's "free in use". In terms of frames an isolated utterance such as: *Hao!* 'Okay!. will then be a special limiting case, when the frame is zero. Intermediate between the zero frame and frames of syntactical constructions is the case of answers to questions and other forms of minor sentences in two-way conversation. Both in answers to questions and positions in frames, different parts of speech will have different types of questions to answer or different positions to fill.[21]

*3.5.2. Frames for Substantives.* A substantive can be tested by the question: *Jeh (∼nah) sh sherme?* 'What is this (∼that)?' or the to-be-completed sentence *Jeh (∼nah) sh ...* [with a prolongation on *sh (yh)*] 'This (∼that) is ...' and the answer can start either with *Jeh (∼nah) sh* or simply give the answer word as a one-word (minor) sentence,[22] be it 玫瑰 *meiguey* 'a rose (∼roses)', 內人 *ney₀ren* 'my wife', 客厛 *kehting* 'the living room', 绅子 *chourtz* 'silk', or 稻 *daw* 'rice (plant)'.

Quoted forms may also function as substantives and are free. In proper names monosyllables are bound and polysyllables are free, so that one can talk about 欧陽 *Ouyang* or 司徒 *Sytwu* as persons with those family names, but must say 老張 *Lao Jang*, comparable in style to (plain) 'Smith', or 王先生 *Wang Shiansheng* 'Mr. Wang', since monosyllabic names *Jang* and *Wang* are not free. That is why newspapers like to transliterate monosyllabic foreign names with two characters, for example, the English name *Dean* with two characters 第安 *Dih'an* or the German place name *Bonn* as 波昂 *Bo'arng*, just as one can say 保定 *Baoding* 'Paoting', but 定県 *Dingshiann* 'Ting Hsien,—the district Ting', since one cannot say °我生在定。 °*Woo sheng tzay Ding.* 'I was born in (the district) Ting.'

However, to the question: 您貴姓？ *Nin Gueyshinq?* or *Gueyshinq?* 'What is your name, please?' or *Gueyshinq sh—*

---

[21]See L. S. Yang, op. cit., 464-466 (see n. 7 above), and 俉子东，词类的区分和辨认 ("On the Differentiation and Recognition of the Parts of Speech", ZGYW, no. 51:14-16 of 11-16 (Sept., 1956).

[22]On the stylistic difference here, see sec. 2.2.4.

'Your name is—' it is possible to reply either *Woo shinq Wang.*
'I am named Wang.' (*shinq* being here a transitive verb meaning
'have the name of') or simply *Wang.* In the case of *shinq Wang*
we can still regard *Wang* as bound, since a free verb is very often
bound with a bound object to form a V-O compound, like 吃斋
*chy-jai* 'eats (religious) fast,—observes a vegetarian diet', 开春
*kai-chuen* 'opens spring,—spring begins', and so on. But in the
simple answer *Wang* it is of course free by definition. The reason this is possible is that the form is more or less in quotes:
'My name is "Wang".', and any form in quotes may be considered as equivalent to something like 'the word so-and-so'. Thus,
not only can monosyllabic names 張, 王, 李, 趙 *Jang, Wang, Lii,
Jaw* be used as free words, but practically anything, even a submorphemic element, can be used. Thus, one can say:  这是 X
音. *Jeh sh* [u]-*in.* 'This is the sound [u]'.' To be sure, one can
still consider [u]-*in* as a compound, as close apposition in Chinese is in most cases, but to the question 这个字是– *Jeyg tzyh
sh*— 'This character is—' one can very naturally pronounce the
characters 天, 地, 日, 月 *tian* (F), *dih* (F), *ryh* (B), *yueh* (B),
irrespectively of their being free or bound, since they are treated
as being in quotes and therefore equivalent to '*tian*' -*tzyh*, '*dih*'
-*tzyh*, and so on.[23]  More or less quoted are also morphemes for
units and standards following *luenn* 'by the, according to', as in
论斤卖 *luenn jin may* 'sold by the catty', and in 巴黎也是
论区的. *Bali yeesh luenn chiu de.* 'Paris (voltage) also varies
according to locality.', where *chiu* is ordinarily not free. Of similar status are also numerals *i, ell, san,* ... on the faces of dice or
as spoken when counting, and abstract counters 甲, 乙, 丙, 丁,
*Jea, Yii, Biing, Ding,* and so forth. Marginal is the case of counting off at a military drill, where it may be questioned whether
the activity involved is speech behavior.

   *3.5.3. Frames for Verbs.* A free verb can occupy the frame

---

[23]One of my children, when first taught to read, used to say *tian-tzyh,
dih-tzyh, ryh-tzyh, yueh-tzyh,* instead of *tian, dih, ryh, yueh,* apparently feeling that some of the items are bound and therefore finding it unnatural to
say them separately.

V-not-V in a question, the negative being *bu* or *mei*, the latter being the negative for the verb *yeou* 'has, there is'. Thus, 你 知道不知道? *Nii jy.daw bujy.daw?* 'Do you know?' *Jy.daw.* 'Yes, I do.' 打算不打算去? *Daa.suann bu daa.suann chiuh?* 'Are you planning to go?' *Daa.suann.* or *daa.suann chiuh.* 'Yes, I am.' In Cantonese the first syllable can be repeated alone, even though bound, as: 你听唔听得見佢? *Nee theang-mu-theang-tak-kinn ghoe?* 'Can you hear him?' (In Mandarin, if the question takes the V-not-V form, it must be 你听得見听不見他? *Nii ting.de-jiann ting.bu-jiann ta?*, since both *ting.de-jiann* and *ting.bu-jiann* are words.) This is possible in Cantonese even if it does not make good sense, as 你肚唔肚饿? *Nee dhoo-mu-dhoongoh?* 'Are you hungry?', where *dhoongoh* means literally 'stomach hungry'. In Mandarin the verb in a dissyllabic verb-object construction can be so repeated, whether free or bound (and thus ionized). For example, 你们放假不放? *Niimen fanq-jiah bu fanq?* 'Do you have a holiday (or vacation)?', where *fanq* 'lets go free' is free and *jiah* 'vacation, holiday' is bound, though ionized. But if the second syllable is not an object, as in the case of 打算 *daa.suann* above, then the compound cannot[24] be so ionized (as it can in Cantonese), even though the first syllable is free in other contexts. Other examples are 参加不参加? *Tsanjia bu tsanjia?* '(Will you) take part in (it)?' 相信不相信他? *Shiangshinn bu shiangshinn ta?* '(Do you) believe him?' In the last example, though *shinn* is free, *shiang* is bound.

*3.5.4. Frames for Adjectives.* Adjectives being a species of verbs in Chinese, they also fit the frame of V-not-V, as: 新鲜不新鲜? *Shin.shian bu shin.shian?* 'Is it fresh?' 糟糕不糟糕? *Tzaugau .bu tzaugau?* 'Is(n't) it a mess?' In addition, adjectives[25] can take adverbs of degree like *heen* 'very' and *tzuey* 'most' and can be compared in the frame *bii* N ... '... -er than N'. For ex-

---

[24]Except in recent Cantonized Mandarin by way of structural borrowing, as in *Nii daa bu daa.suann chiuh?* 'Are you planning to go?'

[25]Malmqvist (Sïch'uanese, pp. 138-140) calls them comparative adjectives. Cf. sec. 8.1.3.1.

ample, 很憋忸 *heen bieh.neou* 'very awkward', 最知己 *tzuey jyjii* 'most knows-me,—most intimate', 比我精明 *bii woo jing-.ming* 'smarter than I', 比水泥结实 *bii shoeini jie.shyr* 'more solid than concrete'.

It may seem strange that the adjective-noun frame is not always available for testing free adjectives or nouns. There is 大狗 *dah goou* 'big dog(s)', 好菜 *hao tsay* 'good dish(es)', but not °多人 °*duo ren* for 'many people' or °糟糕事 °*tzaugau shyh* for 'messy business', for which a subordinative particle *de* has to be inserted. The words 多 *duo* and 少 *shao*, to be sure, have certain special behaviors, such as having the putative function, as in 多了我 *duole woo* 'finds me (one too) many,—finds me in the way' and 少了他不行 *shaole ta bushyng* 'lacking him it won't do,—can't do without him'. But the general explanation of the lack of complete free and versatile A-N phrasing is that adjectives in Chinese are verbs and one is not always sure of A-N forms for the same reason that one is not always sure of V-N forms: 流水 *liou-shoei* 'flowing water', but not 潑水 *po shoei* except as verb-object construction, while 'spilled water' is *po de shoei* or *pole de shoei*.

*3.5.5. Other Frames.* Other parts of speech, except interjections, are free in use and free in admitting pauses, but not free in zero frame—in other words, not F in the Bloomfieldian sense of isolated utterance. Thus adverbs 就 *jiow* 'then, just', 还 *hair* 'still', 也 *yee* 'also', 非常 *feicharng* 'unusually,—extremely', conjunctions like 假如 *jearu* 'if', 虽然 *sweiran* 'although', 可是 *kee.sh* 'but' always occur in included position and are not used even as a supplementary, or completing answers to questions, though conjunctions can be followed by pauses or pause particles. Interjections are free words par excellence. Prepositions are transitive verbs which are always in first position in verbal expressions in series and are therefore always in included position. While one can answer the question: 你抽烟不抽？ *Nii chou-ian bu chou?* 'Do you smoke?' with *Chou.* 'I do.', one cannot answer the question: 你望东不望东走？ *Nii wanq dong bu wanq dong tzoou?*

'Are you going toward the east?' with just °*Wanq*. 'Toward.', but must say *Wanq dong tzoou.* or *Wanq dong.*[26]

A distinction should be made between (1) adverbs of time, such as 就 *jiow* 'then, right away', 快 *kuay* 'soon', 已经 *yii_ojinq* 'already', and (2) time words like 今天 *jin.tian* 'today', 現在 *shianntzay* 'now'. Time words are substantives and therefore F, while monosyllabic adverbs of time are not. Thus, one can say: *Woo shianntzay jiow chiuh.* 'I go right now.' *Shianntzay a?* 'Now?' *Dueyle, shianntzay.* 'Yes, now.' But one cannot say °*Jiow a?* 'Right away?' °*Dueyle, jiow.* 'Yes, right away.' The substantive nature of time words is also seen in that they can be objects in verb-object or preposition-object frames, as in 到現在 *daw shianntzay* 'down to the present'.

*3.5.6. Frames for Form Classes and Frames for Word Classes.* It should be remembered that the test frames described above will work for word classes only on condition that the form being tested is the smallest in question; otherwise they would also work for phrases in the same functions. Thus, the frame *Jeh sh* 'This is' works not only for *ren* 'a man', but also for 昨儿来吃晚饭 的那个人 *tzwol lai chy-woanfann de neyg ren* 'the man who came to dinner yesterday'. Without this limitation, the tests will then only constitute necessary but not sufficient conditions for words. In fact, they give the lower limit of words but not the upper limit. What they yield are substantives, or nominals, instead of nouns and pronouns, verbal expressions, or verbals, instead of verbs, adjectivals instead of adjectives, and adverbials instead of adverbs.

*3.5.7. Generalized Frames Through Transformations.* On the basis of Householder's treatment of words as forms which are transformationally productive,[27] Tsu-Lin Mei, in commenting on an early draft of this chapter, proposed a generalization of functional frames, as follows:

---

[26]Children of pregrammatical age ($\leq 3$) sometimes answer, to the question 你跟我出去吗? *Nii gen woo chuchiuh ma?* 'Are you going out with me?' simply 跟.*Gen.* 'With.'

[27]Fred W. Householder, "On Linguistic Primes", *Word*, 15:231-239 (1959).

Instead of recognizing the smallest unit that can fill the place of certain functional frames as a word, we can require a word to fill the place of several transformationally related frames; e.g., an adjective (i.e., a quality verb) can fill the place of (A) N V, (B) V de N, and others like 很 *heen* ... , 最 *tzuey* ... , 比 *bii* N ... , etc. For a word-like unit to occur in (A) means that it can occur in (B), for these two are transformationally related. For example, 春 *chuen* [sec. 3.8.2] is not transformationally versatile, because, although it occurs in 春 天 *chuen.tian* 'spring', 春分 *chuenfen* 'vernal equinox', there is no such form as °天春了. °*Tian chuenle.* or °分春了. °*Fen chuen le.* Hence *chuen* is not a word. On the other hand, 天 *tian* 'sky', 眠 *mian* 'stops feeding ...', 磕 *keh* 'cracks open with the front teeth', 賍 *tzang* 'spoils' N [sec. 3.4.1] are all syntactical words in this sense since each of them occur in several transformationally related functional frames.

It would exceed the scope of the present admittedly "phrase-structure" grammar to work out all the transformational frames for all the form classes, which is, however, a fruitful line of attack, as pursued by Mei himself and William S-Y. Wang and others.

## 3.6 The Word as a Unit of Meaning

*3.6.1. Word as Idea.* We noted that the conception of *tzyh* is the Chinese sociological equivalent of 'word', but it often takes more than one *tzyh* to make a word in the syntactical sense; we also noted that such a concept is not represented in the ordinary language and that recent grammarians have used the term *tsyr* for it. The most commonly used definition of a word or *tsyr* is "that which expresses an idea."[28] The difficulty of applying such a definition is of course in deciding what is one idea. It is true that in many cases, perhaps even in a majority of cases, one can agree as to whether an expression of one, two, or three syllables expresses one idea, as 人 *ren* 'man', 馬 *maa* 'horse', 红 *horng* 'red',

---

[28]Li Jiinshi, *GYWF* (main), p. 2. Wang Lih, *Yeufaa*, pp. 15-16 supplements this with the test of separability.

来 *lai* 'comes', 鹦鹉 *ingwuu* 'parrot', 老头子 *laotourtz* 'old man', 便宜 *pyan.yi* 'cheap', 分付 *fen.fuh* 'gives order to'.[29] But in a great many cases, even if a minority of cases, the idea of an idea is not such a simple idea. It is easy enough to tell that *ing*- or -*wuu* in *ingwuu* represents less than an idea and that it takes *ingwuu* to give the idea of 'parrot', in other words, that *ingwuu* is one dissyllabic morpheme. However, even what is ordinarily regarded as a polysyllabic morpheme can often be analyzed as a complex of morphemes, thanks to the genius of the Chinese language to read meaning into every syllable. Thus, the popular name for 'parrot' is 鹦哥儿 *ing.gel*, literally 'brother parrot', parallel with 八哥儿 *ba.gel* 'brother mynah,—a mynah', thus making the otherwise meaningless syllable *ing*- attain the morphemic status of at least 'cran-' or 'cranberry'. But apart from such marginal cases, the general question as to when a complex of morphemes represents one idea is not one which can be answered from linguistic considerations. Is 河马 *hermaa* 'river horse, —hippopotamus' one idea or two? How about 海象 *haeshianq* 'sea elephant,—walrus'? 绑票 *baangpiaw* 'ties up (as a) ticket, —kidnaps'? 例如 *lihru* 'example as,—e.g.'? 寒暑表 *harnshuubeau* 'colt-hot-meter,—thermometer'? 羊肉 *yangrow* 'sheep meat, —mutton'? Why is *laotourtz* 'old-head-*suffix*,—old man' one idea and not a complex of two or three ideas? If, as we often say, a whole sentence or even a whole speech may express some one central idea and if a word is that which expresses an idea, it will have to be an idea of a more unitary nature. Without going too far afield into problems of methodology, suffice it to say that the only workable approach to the unity of the word is through unity of the structure, as discussed in other sections. The idea of an idea can at best only give some useful suggestions for the recognition of the syntactical word.

*3.6.2 The Lexical Unit.* While it is hard to count ideas, it is relatively easy to count morphemes, especially since almost all Chinese morphemes are monosyllables. The question is then often asked whether a given string of morphemes has the same meaning as the sum of their meanings or a new meaning of the whole

---

[29]To use Li's examples, p. 3.

which cannot be gathered from the meanings of the parts. Thus, 黑纸 *hei-jyy* 'black paper' is simply black paper, but 黑板 *hei-baan* 'black board' is a blackboard, which nowadays is often green; 肥肉 *feir-row* 'fat meat' is just fat meat, but 肥料 *feirliaw* 'fat material' is not any fat material, but fertilizer. This is a perfectly good test for inclusion or exclusion as an entry in a dictionary. But so far as novelty of meaning is concerned, a dictionary can very well, and often does, include entries which are more as well as those which are less than a syntactic word. Without even including proverbs, a medium-sized dictionary will usually contain compounds and phrases with meanings which cannot be obtained from the meanings of the constituent words, in other words, idioms. For example, 死胡同儿 *syy hwutonql* 'dead lane-*suffix*, deadend street', 冰糖胡盧儿 *bingtarng hwu.lul* 'crystal-sugar gourd,—sugar-glazed fruits strung on a stick (shish kebab fashion)', 碰钉子 *penq dingtz* 'bumps against a nail,—gets rebuffed', 半斤八两 *bann-jin ba-leang* 'half a catty (and) eight tael,—six and half a dozen'. The first two examples are compounds, and the other two are phrases whose meanings could not be guessed by putting together the meanings of their parts and must therefore be considered proper entries in a dictionary of the 词典 *tsyrdean* type, the scope of inclusion depending upon the size of the dictionary. These are quite analogous to the case of *red tape*, which is a lexical phrase and is therefore found in most dictionaries, as opposed to *red cape*, which is not found in any dictionary. On the other hand, *redcap* is a compound word, not because it is spelt together, but because it has the trochaic stress pattern, characteristic of English compound words.

*3.6.3. Bound Entries in Dictionaries and Transient Words.* In the opposite direction from phrases are those entries in dictionaries which are less than a syntactical word, namely, bound morphemes, less frequently morpheme complexes. They include the determinatives (*jeh-* 'this', *nah-* 'that', *san-* 'three', *jii-* 'several, how many'), measures (个 *-g* individualizing classifier, 双 *-shuang* 'pair', 寸 *-tsuenn* 'inch'), affixes (第 *dih-* '-th', *-j* '-ing') particles (*ma* interrogative particle), and root words, that is, bound morphemes which underlie primary derived words (桌 *juo-* 'table' for *juotz* 'table'). Although all except root words are listable, their unrestricted combinations will add up to a very large number, and the meanings of the combinations will in most cases be the combinations of the meanings. Thus, there is little reason for including as dictionary entries such syntactical words as 兩天 *leang-tian* 'two days', 十七塊 *shyrchi-kuay* 'seventeen dollars', 看着 *kaanj* 'is looking at' (in addition to *kann* 'looks at'). Although these are words in the syntactic sense, they are of no lexical import. They are transient words (Bloomfield, *Lg*, 173, 200), of which the number is almost unlimited. Occasionally a transient word does have a special meaning and thus qualifies for an entry in addition to the entries as parts. For example, 半天 *bann-tian*, in addition to the literal meaning of 'half a day', is also a hyperbole for 'for a long time', or 半夜 *bann-yeh* 'midnight' in addition to 'half a night'. In Cantonese 第九 *daykao* (Mandarin *dihjeou*) 'number nine' is an epithet for an unwanted person, since eight people make just the right number for a square dinner table.

*3.6.4 Correlation Between Semantic Units and Formal Features of a Word.* We have so far emphasized the difference between semantic units, which are proper items to enter in a dictionary, and the syntactic word as a unit of certain formal features, and have cited cases where the two do not go together. However, by and large, the syntactic word does tend to be associated with a meaning, difficult as it sometimes is to tell when an idea is one idea. On the whole there is a certain degree of correlation between unity or specialization of meaning and unity of formal features. Thus, the contrast between the phrase 打手 *daa-shoou* 'hits the hand' and the word *daa.shoou* 'thugs' has parallels such as 扶手 *fwu-shoou* 'supports (by the) hand': *fwu.shoou* 'a hand support,—railing, etc.' (cf. Fr. *appuimain*), 小心 *sheau-shin* 'a small heart(-shaped object)': *sheau.shin* 'is careful', 甜瓜 *tyan-gua* '(any) sweet melon': *tyan.gua* 'muskmelon'. This correlation explains partly the popularity of the definitions of the word by meaning, which work in many cases, but cannot be entirely depended upon as working definitions. Thus, 開水 *kai-shoei*, with the same ⬚'⬚ stress pattern, is either (1) 'turns on the water' or (2) 'boiling water', where the relation between form and meaning as well as function is skewed (cf. sec. 1.1.3).

# 3.7. Word Identity and Morpheme Identity

*3.7.1. Size and Kind.* Our discussion so far has been chiefly concerned with the question of how long a stretch of speech can be marked apart as one word. This is the question of size. A different, though not unrelated, question is the question of kind: when is a word the same word and when a different word? The same question can be asked about the morpheme. To the general literate person, the unit and form of writing will be the answer to both questions and the result is the sociological word, both as to size and kind. We noted that in the case of Chinese if it is one character it is one word. Likewise, if it is the same character, it is the same word.

*3.7.2. Sameness of Character.* The question of the sameness of a character is not so simple as that of the oneness of one character. Not counting seal characters and cursive characters and limiting ourselves to regular characters, we must first recognize the usual variants which are entered in dictionaries and which do not affect the identity of characters. Recent accelerated introduction of simplified variants adds further complication to the picture. Another aspect of the variations in characters which bothers learners of Chinese has to do with those graphic variations which Chinese users of characters are hardly conscious of as variants. Native writers overlook common conventional alternations of strokes such as (1) with ╲, as in ㇏ with ㇏, (2) with ⺌, as in 糸 with 糸, and (3) isolated variations like that of 為 with 爲.[30] They overlook such variations by very much the same psychology as native speakers of English unconsciously use aspirated *p* in 'peak' and unaspirated *p* in 'speak', or, better, unaspirated (unreleased) *-k* or aspirated (released) *k* in both words in free variation without noticing the difference, since the difference there "makes no difference".

*3.7.3. Skewed Differentiation.* Sometimes, however, significant and nonsignificant variations are not paralleled in character and in word. Take the very word for '(syntactic) word' *tsyr*. It is written

---

[30]See *Mand Prim*, p. 68, for the principal typical variations.

either as (1) 辭 or as (2) 词 as graphic variants. But no. 1 is also
the character for the verb 'declines, resigns', and *tsyr* written with
no. 2 means also a type of verse characterized by strict require-
ments of internal tones as well as tones in rhymes (features shared
by metric verse, or verse of the 律诗 *liuhshy* type) and by the
fact that the lines are mostly of unequal lengths, whence the
popular name for it 長短句 *charngdoan-jiuh* 'long-and-short-
sentences'. In these meanings 1 and 2 are not interchangeable, at
least not since 楚辭 *Chuutsyr* of the classical times. Again, *yeh*
as 'leaf (of a plant)' is written (1) 葉 , while *yeh* as 'leaf (of a
book),—page or double page' is written either as (1) or, more frequently, as (2) 頁 .[31]

*3.7.4. Homographs.* It will take but a cursory look through
any dictionary of characters to find at least one on every page
with which one can write any one of two or more different syllables. In a very few cases the character is a free variation of the
same morpheme, as 森 *sen~shen* 'forest' B, 期 *chi~chyi* 'period
of time' B, where the same character is pronounced in either of
the variant forms without any difference in meaning or grammatical function. A fairly large number of cases have to do with the
so-called literary vs. colloquial pronunciation of the same characters, mostly involving morphemes derived from ancient forms
ending in -*k*. For example 白 *b'ɒk* > *bor* ~ *bair* 'white', 北 *pɒk*
> *boh* ~ *beei* 'north' B, 鶴 *γâk* > *heh* ~ *haur* 'the crane' B, 熟
*źiuk* > *shyu* ~ *shour* 'familiar, cooked, ripe'. Both the free variations and the literary and colloquial pronunciations can be regarded as cases of alternation between different forms of the same
morpheme, since there is in the majority of cases no difference in
meaning or grammatical function. These, then, are not true
homographs.

A few cases border on difference of morphemes. Thus, 得

---

[31]The character 頁 should be regarded as a homograph of two etymons:
(a) originally γ*iet* 'head', with a theoretical Mand *shye* and Cant *yit*, obsolete
in both dialects; 頁 occurs only as part of characters such as 頭 *tour* 'head';
(b) now as 'page', being an allograph of 葉 'leaf, page' *iap* > Mand *yeh*
and Cant *yip* (not *yit!*).

(*tək* >): (1) *der* 'gets, obtains'; (2) .*de* suffix or infix for possibility, as in 吃得 *chy.de* 'can eat' or 'can be eaten' and 跑得快 *pao-.de-kuay* 'can run fast'; and (3) *deei* 'must'. The semantic connection can still be seen (cf. 'you've *got* to'), but *der* and *deei* are quite different both in meaning and function.

The majority of cases of one character with several pronunciations are the so-called 破读 *pohdwu* 'split readings', in which through some process of phonetic modification (including tones), long since unproductive as a process, a character has a different meaning and/or function with a different pronunciation. Examples are: 長 *charng* 'long': *jaang* 'becomes long,—grows' or 'senior (in age)' B; 降 *jianq* 'descends': *shyang* 'surrenders'; 曲 *chiu* 'crooked, bent' B: *cheu* 'melody, piece of music' B; 惡 *eh* 'evil, bad' B: *wuh* 'finds bad,—hates' B. [32] Such cases had their origin at a very early stage of the language and are reflected in most of the dialects in parallel, if not phonetically identical, ways. Less important are those of more recent origin, which are consequently more restricted in geographic spread. Thus, the distinction between 曲 *chiu* 'crooked, bent' B and *cheu* 'melody, piece of music' B, or that between *tuu* 'spits' and *tuh* 'vomits', is limited to Northern Mandarin, while that between 错 *tsuoh* 'wrong' and *tsuoo* 'uneven, staggered' is only made in Southern Mandarin. The distinctions in Maa Yng's *List*, on the other hand, are found throughout the country. We should include as regular cases where the split readings considered national happen to be neutralized as a result of regular phonetic change. For example, the same character for ancient 易 *iäk* 'changes': *i'* 'easy' has the split pronunciations *yek* and *yih* in Cantonese and *ye'* and *yih* in Shanghai, but in Mandarin, since ancient words beginning with *i̯-* go into the 4th Tone and final -*k* is lost, both *i̯äk* and *i'* fall together into modern *yih*.

3.7.5. *Homophones*. The reverse of homographs is homophones, different words pronounced alike. The Chinese language is of course well known for its abundance in homophones, or

---

[32] For further examples, see 馬瀛, 破音字舉例 (Maa Yng, *List of Split Readings*), Shanghai, 1923, and 傅東華, 北京音異读字的初步探讨 (Fuh Donghwa, *Preliminary Studies in Split Readings in Peking Pronunciation*), Peking, 1958.

homonyms. The words for both 'book' 书 and 'defeated (in games, etc.' 输 are pronounced *shu*,[33] though written in different characters; the words for 道 'way', 稻 'rice plant', and 到 'arrives (at)', just to cite free forms, are all *daw*. In fact one could construct whole stories by playing changes on four tones of the same syllable if one made use of the literary idiom. Such stories are quite intelligible to the modern eye, would have been intelligible to the ancient ear, but are quite unintelligible to the modern ear, since the modern cognates now sound quite ambiguous.[34]

Note that a homophone as a linguistic concept is the same sound or sounds representing two or more different words, which may or may not be written alike. In Chinese writing, most homophones are written with different characters. But there are also homophones which are at the same time also homographs. Thus both *bye* 'other' B, as in *bye.ren* 'others' and *bye* 'don't!' are written with the same character 别.

*3.7.6. The Etymon and the Word Family.* Cutting across the identity of characters are the conceptions of the etymon and the word family, both of which have to do with historical linguistics and will therefore be touched upon only briefly here. An etymon is a class of different words or morphemes which were historically related. For example, 見 *jiann* (< *kien* < *kian*) 'sees' and 現 *shiann* (< γien < g'*ian*) 'becomes seen,—appears' belong to the same etymon. Again, 長 *charng* (< *đ'*iang < d'*iang*) 'long' and 長 *jang* (< *t̬iang* < *t̬iang*) 'extends, opens' belong to the same etymon. But since voicing-unvoicing and aspiration-nonaspiration have for most of historical time ceased to be active processes in word formation, the forms *jiann* 'sees' and *shiann* 'appears' as well as *charng* 'long' and *jang* 'extends, opens' are best treated, on the descriptive plane, as separate morphemes.

---

[33]Hence the Cantonese popular euphemism 读 胜 *dok sheq* 'reads victorious' instead of the normal 读 书 *dok-shu* 'reads books', which is homophonous with 读 输 'reads defeated'.

[34]For examples see my articles on the Chinese language in the *Encyclopaedia Britannica*, 1960, for the story in the syllable *shy* and in 1962 for the story in *ji;* in *Collier's Encyclopedia*, 1962, for the story in the syllable *i;* and in my *Language and Symbolic Systems*, 1967, for the story in *shi*.

Still wider in scope and more interesting historically is the word family, consisting of a large class of typical quasi-morphemes, usually in the form of homorganic initials and endings, with related meanings. Thus, in the outline form *k-ng*, there is a family of words having to do with brightness or light:

景 *kiäng* > *ˊkiɒng* > *jiing* 'bright, light, scenery, etc.'
鏡 *kiäng* > *kiɒngˋ* > *jinq* 'mirror'
光 *kwâng* > *ˌkuâng* > *guang* 'light, brightness'
煌 *g'wâng* > *ˌɣuâng* > *hwang* 'bright, to blaze'
晃 *g'wâng* > *ˋɣuâng* > *hoang* 'bright'
旺 *giwang* > *jiwangˋ* > *wanq* 'bright, burning brightly'
螢 *g'iweng* > *ˌɣiweng* > *yng* 'glowworm, firefly'
赫 *xăk* > *xɒk* > *heh* 'burning, brilliant'
旭 *xiuk* > *xiuk* > *shiuh* 'brightness'
熙 *xiəg* > *ˌxi* > *shi* 'bright'
曉 *xiog* > *ˋxieu* > *sheau* 'dawn, light'[35]

From our point of view, that of present-day spoken Chinese, all these forms are separate morphemes, whether written with the same or with different characters.

*3.7.7. Descriptive Synchronic Etymology.* To the general user of the language, the sociological word from the point of view of size is the monosyllable and, from the point of view of identity, as a first approximation, is the character. But if we abstract our consideration from historical derivation, or etymology, and from that of the proper characters, and raise the question of what is the same word or morpheme on a purely synchronic plane, that is, in a description of the present, then the question is less easy to settle.

Obviously, slight extensions of meaning and most figures of speech do not affect the identity of words. The various meanings of the verb 看 *kann* 'looks at', 'reads (silently)', 'thinks ( the way one looks at the matter)', 'goes to see (the doctor, a friend)', and so on, are all extensions of one basic meaning and come under one

---

[35]These were chosen from a list of examples given by Bernhard Karlgren in his Word Families in Chinese, *BMFEA*, vol. 5 (1933), p. 60, Chinese translation by 張世祿 (Jang Shyhluh), Shanghai, 1936, p. 111.

identical word *kann*. The adjective *kuu* 'bitter' also occurs in 苦
笑 *kuu-shiaw* 'bitter laugh' and 吃苦 *chy-kuu* 'suffers hardship'.
In the case of 结菓子 *jie guootz* 'bears fruit' and 结果 *jyeguoo*
'result', 'consequently', the identity of *guoo* in the two cases is less
clear. In fact, in the figurative use, the original character 果, the
picture of a fruit on the tree, is used, whereas in the literal sense
the word *guoo* is written, in present-day usage, with the enlarged
character 菓.

In general, when intermediate stages of semantic extension
have ceased to be represented in active use and only apparently
unrelated extremes remain, then it has become a case of homophony, even though historically related and/or written with the
same character. Thus, the etymon *yuan* (< *ngiwɒn*) has meanings
(1) 'plateau, plain' written 原, (2) 'source, spring' written 原,
usually enlarged as 源, and (3) 'source, origin, originally' written
原 or 元, and (4) 'primary' written only as 元. The connection
between 2, 3, and 4 is fairly obvious, but that between these and
1 is much less clear, and so it seems practical to set up two morphemes: (1) *yuan* 'a plain' and (2) *yuan* 'origin(ally)'.

Again, *shy*, though written with the same character 师, has
the meanings 'division (of an army)' and 'teacher', where the
semantic connection is obscure. The compound 师长 *shyjaang*
means therefore either 'division commander' or 'teachers and
elders,—faculty (in relation to the students)' and thus constitutes
a pair of homophonous compounds.

The etymon *tsair* (< ᵤ*dz* ˆ*ai*) 'sprout' is now differentiated into
(1) 才 'talent', (2) 材 'material', (3) 财 'wealth', and (4) 纔 'just, then-
and-only-then' (< 'budding, beginning'). In the last meaning as an
adverb, the more complicated character is popularly regarded as
the "correct" character and character 1 is regarded as a "simplified" loan character for 4, whereas actually character 1 is the
original by a semantic extension which has been forgotten by the
average speaker-writer. For purposes of a practical lexicon, then,
it would be best to set up two morphemes under the same
etymon with 1, 2, and 3 as three related meanings and 4 as a separate homophonous morpheme.

The identification and differentiation of morphemes on the

basis of present-day usage has been called descriptive etymology,[36] as contrasted with etymology in the usual sense, which traces the identity of morphemes or words in history and may be tautologically called historial etymology. The possibility of descriptive etymology is of course based on the assumption that members of the speech community will agree when a word is the same and when a different word, apart from the identity or difference of the character—an assumption which works most of the time, but sometimes breaks down when native speakers begin to argue in the form of secondary judgments about the language, which can easily happen with questions of etymology.

3.7.7.1. *The Descriptive Etymon.* If there is descriptive etymology, then there should also be descriptive etymons (with or without differences in phonemic or morphophonemic make up). Thus,

| | | |
|---|---|---|
| *tour* | N | morpheme 1 in function 1, as in *ig tour* 'a head' |
| *-tour* | M | morpheme 1 in function 2, as in *i-tour niou* 'a head of cattle' |
| *-.tou* | -x | morpheme 2 suffix, as in *shyr.tou* 'stone' |

all belonging to the same etymon. A descriptive etymon is usually, though not always, written with the same character, 頭 in the preceding case.

3.7.7.2. *Marginal Morphemes.* For finding about such identification and differentiation, Charles Hockett sent out a questionnaire in 1948 to a number of informants, including the present writer and Fang-Kuei Li, in which Hockett gave about sixty dissyllabic Chinese words and asked them to mark them as to whether they were one or two morphemes. Most of the examples were trochees and fell under three types: (1) 似乎 *syh.hu* 'seems to' analyzed as *syh* 'similar' and *hu* 'to', 舒服 *shu.fwu* 'comfortable', analyzed as *shu* 'relaxed' and *fwu* 'fitting, snug', (2) 尾巴 *woei.ba* 'tail', 下巴 *shiah.ba* 'chin', consisting of a root morpheme

---

[36]I am following the terminology of Fred W. Householder, who defines descriptive etymology as the "analysis of non-productive types of [formations and their alternants] which are like productive ones". See his review of Zellig S. Harris, *Methods in Structural Linguistics in IJAL*, 18: 266 of 260-268 (1952).

and a suffix, and (3) 玻璃 *bo.li* 'glass', 蛤蟆 *har.ma* 'frog', unanalyzable morphemes. Different informants, however, differed considerably as to which words belonged to which type.

A lexically much more frequent type of polysyllabic, mostly
dissyllabic, words, which Hockett did not include in his questionnaire, consists of parts which are free and/or versatile in wenyan,
but bound and restricted in the spoken language. Examples are:

> 履歷 *leulih* 'walks' L + 'passes through' B → 'curriculum
> vitae
>
> 侮辱 *wuuruh* 'insults' L + 'shames' L → 'insults'
>
> 規矩 *guei.jeu* 'compasses' B + '(carpenter's) square' → 'true
> (e.g., of carpentry)'; 'a rule'; 'well-behaved'
>
> 纖維 *shianwei* 'fine' B + 'holds together' → 'tissue' (biol.)
>
> 範疇 *fannchour* 'scope' B + 'tally', 'scheme' B → 'category'

Note that while all these words are fairly frequent in the spoken
language, the meanings of the parts, *as parts*, which I have put
down more or less by ear, are quite subject to dissent from my
fellow users of the words, even though the characters are never
in question. All of this shows that the morphemic status of the
parts is quite marginal[37] and shifts with the background of the
speaker. As noted above (sec. 3.1.3), we thought it more condu-
cive to convergent results to take the maximum analysis of literate speakers.

*3.7.8. Dialect Influence on Morpheme Differentiation or Blend-
ing.* Although, from the descriptive point of view of one dialect
at one time, what other dialects do or other periods did should
not be decisive factors in the identity or difference of words,
they do have an influence on the feeling of the native in many
cases. For the homogeneous speech community of the Peiping
dialect is a scientific fiction, whereas the heterogeneous and in-
tercommunicating speech community of the Chinese language is
a national reality. Let us look at a few sets of examples:

---

[37]I borrow the adjective *marginal* from Richard S. Pittman, who, in his
"On Defining Morphology and Syntax", *IJAL*, 25:3.199 (1959), describes
those morphemes as being marginal whose substitution possibilities are
strictly limited, or in Emeneau's terms, restricted.

(1) The two morphemes $jyue_1 < kiwet$ 決 'decides' B, occurring in $bu\text{-}jyue_1$, 'undecided', $jyue_1\text{-}bu$ 'decidedly not', and $jyue_2 < dz'iwät$ 绝 'cuts short' B, 'absolutely' B, occurring in $bu\text{-}jyue_2$ 'incessantly', $jyue_2\text{-}bu$ 'absolutely', are homophonous and nearly synonymous. Some speakers of Mandarin write $jyue_1\text{-}bu$ and $jyue_2\text{-}bu$ almost interchangeably. Yet, since they are not homophonous in all the major dialects, it is possible to say $jyue_1\text{-}jyue_2$ 'decisive to an absolute degree'—a verb-complement compound, which a native speaker of Mandarin would never form spontaneously and would never use if he had not read or heard the compound used by southerners, such as $khütdzüt$ in Cantonese or, for that matter, as $jyue\text{-}tzyue$ only about a hundred miles south of Peiping.

(2) In the case of $dinq_1 < d'ieng'$ 定 'definite'; 'makes definite,—decide, order (goods, etc.)' and $dinq_2 < tieng'$ 订 'makes formal agreement on (dinner, marriage, treaty, etc.)', they are different and nonhomophonous morphemes in the Wu and Cantonese dialects,[38] and it is possible to say, as a verb-complement construction in these dialects, $dinq_2\text{-}dinq_1$ 'makes definite an agreement,—finalizes', with a difference in initial voicing and/or tone register according to the dialect. At the same time, speakers of Mandarin, who constantly communicate orally with speakers with southern accents and who see such a phrase written with two different characters, also come to regard these as different words, although they are homophonous and nearly synonymous.

(3) In the case of (a) $lian_1 < ljän_1$ 連 'joins' and (b) $lian_2 < ljän_2$ 聯 'joins, combines', even $Shuo\ Wen$ gives 連 as a first gloss for 聯. Now in the Peiping dialect there is for $a$ a modified pronunciation $lhian$ and a modified meaning 'connected', occurring usually with the suffix $-j$, as in: 非 洲 跟 亚 洲 本 来 是 連 着 的. $Feijou\ gen\ Yahjou\ beenlai\ sh\ lhianj\ de.$ 'Africa and Asia originally were connected.' Thus it becomes a new morpheme,

---

[38]There was in 廣 韵 $Goang\ Yunn$ an alternate ancient form for $dinq_1$, with a voiceless initial, which is, however, not reflected in modern dialects and does not concern us here. Possibly this was an early instance of subsequent large-scale surdation or unvoicing. See Paul B. Denlinger, "Chinese Historical Linguistics: the Road Ahead", $JAOS$, 81:6-7 of 1-7 (1961).

although obviously the same etymon. On the other hand, Cantonese has *lin* for *a* and *lün* for *b*, thus making the two even more distinct in sound and meaning.

(4) There are four homophonous morphemes forming two homophonous words *yih₁yih₂* 意義 'idea significance,—meaning' and *yih₃yih₄* 异議 'different opinion,—dissent'. These compounds would never have been made on the basis of Mandarin alone and would even be difficult to maintain in oral usage if not constantly being reinforced by dialect distinctions such as found in the Shanghai or Cantonese dialects.

(5) The determinative 各 *geh₁* 'each, the various ... s', Cantonese *koak*, is homophonous with the general classifier 个 *geh₂* (abbr. as *g*), Cantonese *koh*. Without dialectal support, it would be hard to keep in use pairs like 各人 *geh₁-ren*, Cantonese *koak-yan* 'each person': 个人 *geh₂ren*, Cantonese *kohyan* 'individual person' or 各个 *geh₁-geh₂*, Cantonese *koak-koh* 'each piece, each one': 个个（儿）*gehgeh(l)*, Cantonese *kohkoh* 'everyone'.

(6) A headline in a San Francisco Chinese newspaper reported about the 绖 技 合 作, obviously abbreviated from 绖 济 技 術 合作 'economic and technical cooperation', between two countries. The editor, being probably of Cantonese origin, must have been saying to himself *kenggey haptzoak* as abbreviated from *kengtzay-geyzöt haptzoak*. A Mandarin-speaking city editor would probably have thought twice before abbreviating *jingjih₁-jih₂shuh hertzuoh* into *jingjih₂ hertzuoh*, as 绖 技 'econo-technical' would be completely homophonous with 绖 济 'economic'.

Following are examples in which ancient and/or dialectal distinctions are losing out and etymologically different near-synonyms are on the way to be blended into one morpheme.

(7) The difference between 垫 *diann₁* < *tien*ʼ 'cushion' and 簟 *diann₂* < ʻ*dʼiem* 'mat' is now more and more regarded as extensions of meaning of the same morpheme, even in Cantonese, in which a theoretical *dhimx* for *diann₂* is becoming obsolescent and *dimm* is used for both, except in some trade terms.

(8) All but disappeared is the distinction between 併 *binq₁* < ʻ*piäng* 'combines, keeps together' and 並 *binq₂* < ʻ*bʼiweng* 'paral-

lel, side by side, together'. As in the case of 定 $dinq_1$: 订 $dinq_2$, the Wu and Cantonese dialects treat these as different words with different pronunciations and slightly different meanings. In Mandarin, however, the distinction, as in the case of $dinq$, is no longer kept and both are often written, in simplified character, as 并 for both 'combines' and 'side by side'. They are generally regarded as extensions of meaning that do not affect the identity of the morphemes, especially as 并, by a graphic accident, happens to look like 並 minus the bottom stroke. Here, then, is another case where the leveling has taken place in Mandarin in disregard of distinctions existing in the dialects.

3.7.9. *The General Word.* To take into account the dialectal divergences and usages of characters, it will probably be useful to set up a conception of the general word (or morpheme) in Chinese, based on combining under one word (or morpheme) all extensions of meaning, so long as they belong to the same etymon *and fall under the same pronunciation* in all the major dialects. Thus, the various forms of ₍$ngiwɒn$ > $yuan_1$ 'plain, origin, etc.' would be one general word, but 園 ₍$jiwɒn$ > $yuan_2$ 'garden' must be separate, since $yuan_1$ in the Wu dialects has a nasal initial $ng$- or $ń$- and $yuan_2$ has only a semivocalic initial $y$-. Similarly, 燬 *hoei* 'destroys by fire' could be subsumed under 毀 *hoei* 'destroys (in general)'.[39] Again, under 支 *jy* 'branch, props up with a branch' we can subsume 枝 *jy* 'branch of plants' and 肢 *jy* 'branch of animals,—limb', and under 申 *shen* 'extends, (fig.)' we can subsume 伸 *shen* 'extends (lit.)'. Historically, 身 *shen* 'the body (that which extends)' is under the same etymon. But since few present speakers recognize the connection, it should, according to descriptive etymology, be treated as an unrelated homophone of the preceding. By thus combining graphic enlargements under the same etymon, the lexicon of the language can be reduced to a much smaller number of morphemes than is usually recognized when characters are counted. It will of course be the job of the lexicographer, possibly also workers on normatively oriented pro-

---

[39]This is at the present descriptive level. Historically 燬 *hoei* is probably more primary. Cf. 火 ͨ*hui* ˧ 'fire' in the Foochow dialect.

jects, to work out this kind of descriptive etymology for the whole of the language, possibly as a cooperative undertaking by a committee of linguists and informants, much as 切韵 *Chieh Yunn* was done in 601 or 廣韵 *Goang Yunn* in 1007. Here we have only indicated the possibility and probable usefulness of constructing a lexicon of general words by the kind of analysis and synthesis suggested above. The idea of the general word is in fact simply the descriptive etymon on a national or at least a large regional scale. Because of the greater geographic spread, it will in actual application approach the historical etymon, or simply etymon.

*3.7.10. The Morpheme in a Function:* The Lexical Gloss. I. A. Richards once said[40] that to find out whether a word is translated by the same word or different words, just look it up in a dictionary and in the majority of cases each numbered gloss will correspond to a different word in the target language. This is of course intended only as a first approximation, since it all depends upon how the monolingual dictionary is compiled and what translating language is involved. It is, however, very useful to set up under the same descriptive etymon different lexical glosses, especially those which differ in their functional status, so that the unit as a learning item will be the morpheme in a function. Thus, 分 *fen* 'divides' F is a transitive verb, and *fen* 'a division', 'tenth', 'minute', etc. B is a measure and thus constitutes at least a separate learning item. Similar differences in function are found in 包 *bau* 'wraps' F, Vt, vs. 'package' F, N or M; 套 *taw* 'enwraps' F, Vt, 'a case, set' B, M; 理 *lii* reason' F, N, 'takes notice of' F, Vt, 'cut (the hair)' B, '-ics, -ology' B; 老 *lao* 'old' F, A, 'keeps ... -ing' B-, H; 要 *yaw* 'wants, will' F, Vt, or Vx, 'important' B, as in 要人 *yawren* 'VIP'; 出 *chu* 'goes ( ∼ comes) out' B, Vi, 'causes to go ( ∼ comes) out,—issues, produces' F, Vt, 'a coming out onto the stage,—a scene, act, or play' B, M, the last usually written 齣 instead of 出 used in the other senses. To make clear which kind of unit we are talking about, Harris distinguishes between classed and unclassed morphemes. 'Thus, he says, "if we want to keep in view the connection between (*a*) *table* and (*to*) *table*, we have to

---

[40]In a conversation with the author.

speak of classed and unclassed morphemes, and say that the unclassed morpheme *table* appears both in the N class and in the
V class."[41]  It is the unclassed morpheme that is meant, when
Nida puts the 'run' in (1) 'a run in her stocking' N, (2) 'They run
away.' Vi, and (3) 'They run the office.' Vt under the same morpheme.[42]  The inclusion of grammatical function is also found in
the much quoted definition by A. Meillet: "Un mot résulte de
l'association d'un sens donné à un ensemble donné de sons sus-
ceptible d'un emploi grammatical donné."[43]  This definition will
of course also apply to larger units than morphemes and words,
as has been noted by Finngeir Hiorth.[44]

## 3.8.  Definitions and Tests for the Syntactic Word

*3.8.1. Syntagmatic Definitions.*  Having considered the word
both from the point of view of size and from the point of view of
kind, we shall now try to formulate a working definition of the
syntactic word in Chinese. We found that Bloomfield's definition
of the word as a minimum free form—free in the sense of isolated
utterance—too drastic, and added pause and potential pause and
versatility or free use as supplementary tests. Starting with defining the syntactical word as a minimum pause group, we have to
add at once that final particles like *a, ne, ma,* though not detachable from the preceding syllable, are bound with a whole phrase
or sentence. Thus, Bloch says that, if a form has as its immediate
constituents a phrase of two or more words on the one hand and
an element which does not occur alone as a pause-group, the
latter is a word.[45]  This gets around the difficulty of having to

[41]Zellig Harris, "Discourse Analysis", *Language*, 28:13 (1952).

[42]Eugene A. Nida, "The Identification of Morphemes", *Language*, 24:
435 of 414-441 (1948).

[43]*Revue de Métaphysique et de Morale*, 21:11 (1913).

[44]Finngeir Hiorth, "On Defining the 'Word' ", *Studia Linguistica*, 12:9
of 1-26 (1958).

[45]Bernard Bloch, "Studies in Japanese II, Syntax", *Language*, 22: 205 of
200-248 (1946).

consider a whole long phrase or sentence as a compound simply
because of the occurrence of a final particle, as in 英 國 的 國
王 的 女 兒  *Inggwo de gwowang de neu.erl* 'the King of England's daughter', where neither does the second *de* make one word
of *Inggwo de gwowang* nor does the apostrophe *s* make 'the King
of England' a compound word.[46]

   *3.8.2. Paradigmatic Definition: Bound Words.* If we make
exceptions of such elements as final particles in the definition of a
word by pause groups, what are the general considerations from
which to decide on the word status of bound forms? Here the
factor of versatility (which is not necessary for free but restricted
words like 嗑 *keh* 'cracks open between one's front teeth' and 眠
*mian* 'stops feeding . . .') becomes an important criterion. As a
first approximation to a paradigmatic definition, we can define a
(bound or free) word as a minimum form which has unlimited
versatility in combination with a certain form class or form classes.
For example, 天 *tian* 'sky, heaven' F is a noun and can be followed
by any verb or preceded by any adjective or transitive verb. As
'day' it is a measure and bound, but it can follow any determinative, that is, a demonstrative or a numeral, as 那 天 *ney-tian* 'that
day', 三 百 六 十 五 天  *sanbae liowshyrwuu tian* '365 days'.
Hence *tian* in either meaning and function is a word in this sense.
On the other hand, 春 *chuen* 'spring' B occurs in 春 天 *chuen.tian*
'spring', 春 分 *chuenfen* 'vernal equinox', 春 風 *chuenfeng* 'spring
wind', 春 宮 *chuengong* 'pornographic painting', 春 不 老 *chuen-
.bulao* '(in) spring-not-tough,—a vegetable like mustard green', 立
春 *lihchuen* 'establish-spring,—one of the 24 seasons of the solar
year, beginning on or about February 5', 開 春 *kai-chuen* 'when
spring opens,—next New Year'. It is versatile, but not unlimitedly
so, and its occurrence has to be lexically defined. On the other
hand, 完 *wan* 'finishes' F can follow any substantive as a predicative verb, as in 他 还 没 完 吶. *Ta hair mei wan ne.* 'He hasn't
finished yet.', in contrast with 畢 *bih* 'finishes' B, which occurs

----

[46]See also Robert A. Hall, Jr., "A Note on Bound Forms", *Journ. of Eng.
and Germ. Philology*, 45:450 (Oct., 1946).

only in 畢業 *bihyeh* 'finishes course of study,—graduates', 畢竟 *bihjinq* 'finally', 完畢 *wanbih* 'is completed', and a very few other compounds. The criterion of versatility will apply to final particles, which have unlimited combination with phrases and sentences of certain types and, as we have seen (sec. 3.3.2) a separate part of speech, which by definition is a class of words of a certain function.

It should be noted that our concern is only with grammar and not with logic or truth. What is grammatical may not always be true or even be consistent or make sense, as in the much-quoted example by Chomsky of the grammatical sentence: *Colorless green ideas sleep furiously.* Similarly, 水还没掰呐. *Shoei hair mei bai ne.* 'The water has not yet (been) pried.' is just as grammatical as 水还没闹呐. 'The water has not yet boiled,' Thus, in applying the criterion of absolute vs. restricted versatility we should take it only in the grammatical and not in a logical sense.[47]

*3.8.3. Other Criteria.* Besides the two essential criteria of pause and absolute versatility and the other important criteria discussed above, there are some criteria for testing the word which, though not always applicable from a strictly grammatical point of view, have often been used and may be useful and suggestive.

(1) Translational Equivalent. 猪肉 *Jurow* is one word because it translates into one word 'pork', 睡觉 *shuey-jiaw* is one word because it translates into one word 'sleeps'. So are 种田 *jonqtyan* 'plants field,—to farm', 圖书馆 *twushugoan* 'library', 无恶不作 *wu-eh-bu-tzuoh* 'there is no evil (he) does not do,—unscrupulous', 无家可归 *wu-jia-kee-guei* 'has no home to return to,—homeless', 耳朵软 *eel.dou roan* 'ear soft,—gullible'. Apart from the obvious question as to what language we are translating Chinese into, there is also the question of alternative translations in different word structures in the same language. Thus 好看

---

[47]See, however Tsu-Lin Mei, "The Logic of Depth Grammar", *Philosophy and Phenomenological Research*, 24:97-105 (1963) in which it was shown that with sufficient further structural analysis logical distinctions often turn out to be grammatical distinctions.

*haokann* can be translated by one word 'beautiful' or 'pretty', a compound word 'good-looking', or a phrase 'good to look at' or the slang phrase 'easy on the eyes', since *hao* also means 'easy to'. 羊腿 *Yangtoei* is 'leg of lamb', a phrase, but 羊肉 *yangrow* is 'mutton', one word. 蟹肉 *Shiehrow* must be one word, since *shieh* 'crab' is both bound and restricted, but either the word *shiehrow* or the phrase 螃蟹的肉 *parngshieh de row* will translate into the compound word 'crabmeat'. The consideration of word units in a translational target language is therefore of no use in recognizing words in the source language and would not have to be mentioned if it were not so often invoked, whether avowedly or implicitly.

(2) Independent Intelligibility. Many grammarians[48] use the criterion of independent intelligibility as a criterion for the syntactical word. From the point of view of a word as an F form, something that can be uttered alone, intelligibility will of course be a necessary condition, since normal speech heard clearly is expected to be understood. But intelligibility is influenced by a number of factors which cut across the conditions of a form's being free or being versatile: (a) frequency of occurrence, (b) absence of homophones, (c) comparable or unequal relative frequencies of homophones, (d) linguistic and situational contexts—all these affect intelligibility. Thus (a) *ren* 'man', *maa* 'horse', *dah* 'large', *yeou* 'has', are free as well as frequent and are immediately intelligible when spoken. (b) Of the 1277 syllables of Mandarin listed in 國音常用字彙 *Gwoin Charngyonq Tsyrhuey*, 261 or 20% have no homophones and are thus presumably intelligible, irrespective of whether they are free or bound: *shoei* 'water' F, *sheir* 'who?' F, *che* 'vehicle' F, *chou* 'pulls, draws' F, *pao* 'runs' F, *tong* 'goes through' F, *tii* 'body' B,[49] *sherng* 'rope' B, *sen* 'forest', *reng* 'still' B. It is, however, true that the F forms are more often easier to understand than the B forms. (c) If one hears *chyong*, he is more likely to understand it as 窮 'poor' F than as

---

[48]For example, Li-Liou, vol. 1, p. 9.

[49]Except as a philosophical term 'substance' F, but terms in reflective discourses as in philosophy and linguistics are often of a quasi-quoted status and anything quoted is free, as explained above (sec. 3.5.2).

the bound part of the place name 瓊州 *Chyongjou* or 瓊山 *Chyongshan,* the principal city of Hainan Island. On the other hand, *syh* brings to mind at once the bound form 四 'four', and not the much less frequently heard free form 寺 'monastery'. If homophones occur with comparable frequencies, then isolated utterance will not be intelligible: *chi* 七 'seven' B, 漆 'lacquer' F, 沏 'steep (tea)' F, 妻 'wife' L or B; *dih* 地 'earth, ground' F, 弟 'younger brother' B, 帝 'emperor' B, 遞 'hand over' B, 第 prefix for ordinal number, B; *jiau* 交 'hand over' B, 'interchange' B, 'have sexual intercourse' F, 礁 'reef' F, 教 'teach' F, 驕 'haughty' B; *lii* 理 'reason' F, *lii* 礼 'ceremony' B, 'gift' F, 李 'plum' B, 裡 'inside' B; 里 '*li*' unit of distance B; *charng* 長 'long' F, 常 'frequent, constant' B, 嘗 'have a taste of' F, 償 'reward, compensate' B. (d) In most contexts, *ta* will be understood as 他 'he' but if one is talking about a house in a tornado then *ta* will be understood as 塌 'collapse'. A single utterance *yaw* in most contexts will be understood as 要 'want,—I will'. But if a hospital nurse holds a bottle and says *yaw* to a patient, he will hear it as 药 'medicine'. Independent intelligibility therefore is at best a supplementary test and has a certain degree of positive correlation with the word unit, but cannot be an essential part in the definition of a syntactic word.

(3) Unit of Spelling. In the popular mind, for English- as for Chinese-speaking people, a word is that which is written as one unit. According to Webster's *International,* 2d edition, 'fingerprint' is one word, but 'finger mark' is two words; 'doorkeeper' is one word, 'door opener' is two words, and 'door-roller' is a hyphenated word, although all these forms have the same stress pattern and their meanings are synthesizable or specialized to approximately the same degree. With recent activities in devising an alphabetic system of writing for Chinese, the problem of what is a syntactic word, to be written as an orthographic word, becomes very important.[50] Much of the discussion is normatively oriented, which is of course not our primary concern

---

[50]Li Jiinshi started in the 1920's the slogan of 词类连书 *tsyrley lianshu* L 'words to be written connectedly'. Among recent publications may be mentioned 林汉达 Lin Hanndar *et al.,* 汉语的词儿和拼写法

here. For example, 林逴肯 Lin Dyekeen asks (p. 81 in the second work cited), should 緊隨 *jiin swei* 'closely follows' be written *jin suei*, or *jin-suei*, or *jinsuei* (there being no tonal indication in the system being considered)? And his answer is, don't say *jiin swei*, but say instead 緊ㄓ地跟着 (spelled *jinjindi genje*), which is of course changing the language and not writing it. Li Jiinshi's advocacy of writing words together is unquestionably a sound approach to the problem of alphabetic writing. But it is rather grammatical analysis that will be of value to the practical problem of orthography, and considerations of orthography will be of little help for grammatical analysis.

As a practical convention, we spell separately (1) free and versatile and (2) free and restricted morphemes, both being words. We spell solid (3) complexes of bound versatile morphemes if they are (a) derived words (roots with affixes) or (b) versatile but not unlimitedly so, as 独立 *dwulih* 'alone-stand,—independent', but no ° 独走 °*dwutzoou* for 'go alone'; we spell them hyphenated if (c) they have unlimited versatility, thus forming transient words: 几回 *jii-hwei* 'several times', 整年 *jeeng-nian* 'the whole year'; we spell solid (4) bound and restricted morpheme complexes, as 自由 *tzyhyou* 'free(dom)', 貢献 *gonqshiann* 'offer-present,—contribute, offer'. In general, solid compounds, whether under 3b or under 4, are those whose formation cannot safely be trusted to a (Chinese) college sophomore. Both end-bound adverbs such as 就 *jiow* 'then' and 还 *hair* 'still' and start-bound particles such as *ma, le, ne* will be spelled separate. In compound proper names and place names the hyphen or solid spelling will be implied in the capitalizations, as 李斯 *Lii Sy*, 盐湖城 *Yanhwu Cherng* 'Salt (-)Lake City', 中華书局 *Jonghwa Shujyu* 'Chung Hwa Book Company'.

---

(*Chinese Words and How to Spell Them*), 2nd ed., Shanghai, 1955; 文字改革出版社 (Society for Writing Reform), 拼音文字写法資料選例(*Selected Sources on the Orthography of Alphabetic Writing*), Peking, 1957.

## 3.9 Synoptic Tables of Word-Like Units

Tables 6 and 7 summarize word-like units of various types, with two or more examples of each type. In order to save space, some forms which are lexically rare are not tabulated. Thus the diminutive suffix -*l* is the only morpheme which is subsyllabic, and so no column for subsyllabic morphemes is set up.[51] Monosyllabic morpheme complexes consisting of one syllabic and one subsyllabic element are, however, included, as in columns 8, 9, and 10, table 7. Polysyllabic suffixes like -.*buji*, as in 酸 ㄅㄨ ㄐㄧ *suan.buji* are lexically also very limited in number and are not tabulated. Untabulated, too, are the few cases where a polysyllabic morpheme has no meaning but the word with which it forms a compound and the compound as a whole do have meanings. Thus, in *bor.leng-gall* or *bor.le-gall* 'knee-cap, the knee', 盖ㄦ *gall* has the meaning 'a cover, lid', but *bor.leng-* or *bor.le-* has no meaning except that of the compound minus that of *gall*. Again, in *yeh-.leng-gall* 'forehead', *yeh.leng-* has no meaning. It is probably etymologically 額 *er*[52] 'forehead' and 稜 *leng* 'edge, protruding part of a solid'. Cf. *cauli-* in *cauliflower*, which, from the point of view of English, has no meaning except that of *cauliflower* minus that of *flower*.

Estimated frequencies of occurrence are indicated by the grades a, b, c, d, the top ones in each table having to do with lexical frequency, the lower ones with frequency in running text —text in the sense of speech rather than printed text. Grade a is of the order of 50% or more; b 10% or more; c 1% or more; and d below 1%. In column 12, table 7, since transient words have no lexical status, the lexical frequency is marked zero.

The line between column 13, lexical compounds, and column 14, unanalyzed compounds, is a shifting one. It has to do with the problem raised in the Hockett questionnaire mentioned above. Since we are not mainly concerned with the word as a unit,

---

[51]On the marginal nature of a syllabic *m*, see sec. 1.3.9.

[52]The alternation of *er* ~ *yeh* < *ngvk* is quite similar to *ger* ~ *jieh* < *kɛk* 'separated from', as in 隔壁 *gerbih* ~ 隔壁ㄦ *jiehbieel* 'separated-by-a-waller, — the house next door'.

rather than its internal structure, we shall postpone detailed discussion of the morphological structure of words, including forms
of compounding, until chapters 4 and 5. For the present we shall
regard a word as a lexical compound (column 13) if most of those
who use it will agree on the meanings of its parts, and as an unanalyzed compound (column 14) if they do not agree on the
meanings of its parts or do not read meanings into its parts, in
which case it approaches the status of polysyllabic morphemes
(column 7). The examples *Sanyean Jieengl* in column 9 and *ban-*
*.budaol* in column 13 are strictly decompounds (sec. 4.4.1). Because of their low lexical frequency, we are not setting up a
separate column for decompounds. The last examples in columns
7 and 13 illustrate the rare cases where one character (as a much
rarer alternative form) writes two syllables. In the case of 丼 *Pwu-*
*.sah* 'bodhisattva' (usually written 菩薩) it is a dissyllabic morpheme. In the case of 圕 *twushugoan* 'charts-books-institution,—
library' (usually written 圖書館) it is a three-morpheme compound.

For convenient reference between the Chinese forms and
their translations into English, they are grouped by fours, with
lines between the groups.

Table 6. Morphemes

| | | Root Morphemes | | | | |
|---|---|---|---|---|---|---|
| | | Bound | | FREE: Syntactic Words | | |
| | | | | Monosyllabic | | Polysyllabic |
| Affixes, Particles | Root Words | Versatile | Restricted | Versatile | Restricted | Versatile |
| (1) | (2) | (3) | (4) | (5) | (6) | (7) |
| d<br>b | c<br>c | c<br>a | a<br>a | b<br>a | d<br>d | d<br>d |
| chu–<br>dih–<br>–tz<br>–.tou | jin(tz)<br>yn(tz)<br>taur(l)<br>shinq(l) | wuu–<br>neei–<br>meei–<br>bann– | (–)tzer(–)<br>(–)uei(–)<br>(–)meng(–)<br>(–)shye(–) | yu<br>men<br>huei<br>sheir | (tsarn) mian<br>keh (guatzeel)<br>(yeu) shaw<br>chyr (yu) | luo.bo<br>pwu.taur<br>wu.gong<br>chou.chwu |
| –.ba<br>–j<br>–huah<br>–de | shyr(.tou)<br>how(.tou)<br>woei(.ba)<br>tuo(j) | –g<br>–tyau<br>–jang<br>–chian | (–)lih(–)<br>(–)lau(–)<br>(–)woang(–)<br>(–)wuu(–) | liuh<br>hao<br>kuay<br>fen | bih (yean.jinq) | ningmeng<br>luojih<br>piee.la<br>pwu.sah |
| a<br>ma | shianq(j) | jiow<br>gang<br>hair<br>wanq | (–)sheh(–) | fei<br>shyng<br>neng<br>bu | | |
| –th (of month)<br>–th<br>N sufx<br>N sufx | gold<br>silver<br>peach<br>apricot | five<br>which<br>each<br>half a | charge<br>prestige<br>treaty<br>united | fish<br>door<br>dust<br>who | (silkworm) sleeps<br>cracks (seeds)<br>(rain) spatters<br>scales (a fish) | radish<br>grape<br>centipede<br>hesitates |

| N sufx / -ing / -ize / subord. part.; pause part. / interr. part. | stone / the rear / tail / holds on palm; favors the side of | general M / strip / sheet / thousand; just, then / just / still / toward | strength / toil / goes toward / military; society | green / good / quick / divides; flies / O.K. / can / not | closes (eyes) | lemon / logic / kohlrabi / bodhisattva |
|---|---|---|---|---|---|---|
| 初 第 子 头 | 金 银 桃 杏 | 五 哪 每 半 | 青 威 盟 协 | 鱼 门 灰 谁 | (蚕) 眠 / 磕 (瓜子儿) / (雨) 淅 / 遥 (鱼) | 萝 卜 / 葡 萄 / 蜈 蚣 / 跻 蹰 |
| 巴 着 化 的 | 石 後 尾 托 | 个 条 张 千 | 力 劳 往 武 | 绿 好 快 分 | 闭 (眼睛) | 檬 样 / 逻 辑 / 苤 蓝 / 菩 薩 ~艹 |
| 啊 吗 | 向 | 就 刚 还 望 | 杜 | 飞 行 能 不 | | |

Table 7. Morpheme Complexes

| Bound | | FREE: Syntactic Words | | | | |
| Versatile | Restricted | Syntactic Words | Bound | Transient Words | Lexical Compounds | Unanalyzed Compounds |
| | | | | | Polysyllabic | |
| (8) | (9) | (10) | (11) | (12) | (13) | (14) |
| c | d | c | d | o | a | a |
| c | d | b | d | b | a | b |
| -ball<br>-hoel<br>tzemm<br>dwom | (Sanyean) Jieengl<br>(huh.nonq) -jyuel | tial<br>kooul<br>well<br>wal | wujenqfuu-(juuyih)<br>Jonghwa-(Mingwo) | wuu-piann<br>san-wann<br>meei-been<br>tamen | beenlai<br>nanshow<br>haokann<br>howhoei | jy.daw<br>miauǫtyau<br>ba.jie<br>jen.jwo |
| | | | gwojih-(faa)<br>tzemme<br>dwome | na.chu.lai | yiijinq<br>pialltang<br>ban.budaol<br>tsanguan | tzwo.mo<br>dow.fu<br>muhdih<br>gueifann |
| | | | | | kaoliuh<br>twushugoan | |
| half<br>moment<br>so<br>how (much) | (Three-hole) Well (Street)<br>(makeshift) situation | weather<br>opening<br>odor, taste<br>plays | anarch-(ism)<br>Chinese (Republic) | five slices<br>30,000<br>each<br>volume<br>they | originally<br>feels bad<br>good-looking<br>regrets | knows<br>slender<br>flatters<br>thinks over |

Monosyllabic

| | | international (law)<br>so<br>how (much) | take out | already<br>doughsheet soup<br>roly-poly visits<br><br>deliberates<br>library | estimates<br>beancurd<br>objective<br>norm |
|---|---|---|---|---|---|
| | | 号政府（主義）<br>中華（民國） | 五片<br>三万<br>每本<br>他们 | 本来<br>难受<br>好看<br>後悔 | 知道<br>苗条<br>巴结<br>斟酌 |
| | | 國際（法）<br>这么<br>多么 | 拿出来 | 巳竟<br>片儿汤<br>搬不倒儿<br>参观 | 琢磨<br>豆付<br>目的<br>规范 |
| | | | | 考虑<br>画书的饭<br>~画 | |
| | 天儿<br>口儿<br>味儿<br>玩儿 | | | | |
| | （三 眼）井儿<br>（糊 弄）局儿 | | | | |
| | 半儿<br>会儿<br>这么<br>多么 | | | | |

# CHAPTER 4
# MORPHOLOGICAL TYPES

## 4.1. General

*4.1.1. Morphology and Syntax.*[1] Morphology is usually defined as the study of the internal structure of words, and syntax as the study of the relations between words. Thus, the distinction between morphology and syntax in a language is clear insofar as the word unit can be clearly marked in that language. In classical Chinese, if we do not count the few unproductive morphological processes, such as changing the tone of a syllable or voicing a consonant to form a causative verb (see sec. 1.1.3), most morphemes are also words. Hence the common saying among Western scholars that all Chinese grammar is syntax.

In modern Chinese, however, words have become largely dissyllabic (see sec. 3.3.2) or polysyllabic, and many formerly free monosyllabic morphemes—in other words, words—now occur only as bound morphemes in compounds. Furthermore, a small number of bound forms in compounds have lost their meanings as root morphemes and acquired the status of affixes which serve to mark the functions of the words of which they form a part, thus resulting in derived words of various types. We shall deal with the latter, the morphological types, first. As for the formation of compounds from root morphemes, since the relations involved are mostly analogous to those in syntactic constructions, we shall delay its consideration until chapter 6, after dealing with syntax in chapter 5.

*4.1.2. Item-and-Process (IP) and Item-and Arrangement (IA) Grammars.* Grammatical analysis can be done by considering

---

[1] For discussions from a more general point of view, see Charles F. Voegelin, "Meaning Correlations and Selections in Morphology—Syntax Paradigms", *BIHP*, 29:91-111 (1957), and Richard S. Pittman, "On Defining Morphology and Syntax", *IJAL*, 25:199-201 (1959).

various items as being put together by certain processes, or, alternatively, by considering everything as consisting only of items in a certain arrangement.[2] For example, by the item-and-process analysis (IP), *boys* is formed by the process of plural suffixation to the stem *boy*, whereas by the item-and-arrangement (IA) analysis, *boys* consists of the stem *boy-*, followed by the bound morpheme for plural number *-s*. Although in most cases it is possible to translate IP and IA statements of the same facts into each other, it is often more convenient or efficient to adopt one treatment rather than the other for any given language or any aspect of the language. Thus, by the IP treatment, it is simple enough to say that the past of *sing* is formed by the process of vowel change from *i* to *a*, while the equivalent IA statement that *sang* consists of *sing* plus the item $i \rightarrow a$ is awkward and almost amounts to begging the question. For Chinese, it may be useful to apply the IP analysis to very early stages of the language, but for most historical periods, including modern Chinese, the IA analysis is on the whole more convenient.

*4.1.3. Full and Empty Morphemes.* Of the two terms 实字 *shyrtzyh* and 虚字 *shiutzyh*, commonly translated as 'full word' and 'empty word', respectively, the latter, often in the more colloquial form 虚字眼儿 *shiutzyhyeal*, has always been a concern of schoolteachers and pupils in traditional China. To avoid the terminological ambiguity of *tzyh*, the terms 实词素 *shyr-tsyrsuh* 'full morpheme' and 虚词素 *shiu-tsyrsuh* 'empty morpheme' have recently come into use.[3] Thus, among the forms listed in tables 6 and 7, most of those under columns 1 and 3 are empty morphemes, and the others are full morphemes or morpheme complexes in which at least one is a full morpheme.

*4.1.4. Meaning, Infrequency, Listing, and Stress.* The usual characterization of the difference between full and empty morphemes is that full morphemes are full of meaning, while empty morphemes are devoid of meaning and only serve to mark the

---

[2]Charles F. Hockett, "Two Models of Grammatical Description", *Word*, 11:210-234 (1954).

[3] 張寿康，畧论汉语构词法 (Jang Showkang, "A Sketch of Chinese Word Formation"), *ZGYW*, no. 60:3 of 1-8 (1960).

grammatical functions of the full morphemes. For example, 擦 *tsa*, a full morpheme, has a clear meaning 'wipe', while the empty morpheme *-tz* in *tsatz* 'wiper' has no meaning of its own, but only makes an instrument noun out of the verb; similarly, *-j* has no meaning in *tsaj* 'to be wiping', except that it marks the verb as being in the progressive aspect.

Since meaningfulness is a matter of degree,[4] it follows that fullness and emptiness of morphemes also admit of differences of degree. Thus there are borderline cases where the same morpheme or same class of morphemes may be regarded as being either full or empty. Modal adverbs 就 *jiow* 'then', 还 *hair* 'still', 刚 *gang* 'just', and so on are usually classed as empty words by Chinese grammarians. Directional complements like *-.lai* in 拿 来 *na.lai* 'brings here', *-.shanq* in 关上 *guan.shanq* 'closes up', and localizers like *-.lii* in 书裡 *shu.lii* 'in the book', *-way* in 门 外 *men-way* 'outside the door' are also intermediate types, which we regard as full morphemes by listing all of them in chapter 6 on compounds. Sometimes the same morpheme will be full or empty according to slightly different functions. Thus, in 吃 过了饭了 *chy-guohle fann le* 'has already finished eating one's meal', *-guoh* (just like 完 *-wan* in *chy-wanle fann le*) is a full complement, while in 没吃过中國饭 *mei chy.guoh Jong.gwo fann* 'has never eaten Chinese food', *-.guoh* is an aspect suffix for verbs, indicating 'ever once before' (sec. 4.4.5.(4) ).

The degrees of fullness and emptiness of morphemes are correlated with degrees of infrequency and frequency of occurrence. This is quite in consonance with the general theory of measurement of information. What is repeated often doesn't mean so much. In Chinese, as in other languages, a relatively small number of morphemes occurs with high frequency, while the bulk of the items in a dictionary occur with very low frequency.[5] On the

---

[4] 趙元任，语言成分裡意义有旡的程度问題 (Y. R. Chao, "Degrees of Meaningfulness in Language Constituents"), *Tsing Hua Journal*, 2: 1-17 (1961).

[5] See George K. Zipf, *The Psycho-Biology of Language*, Boston, 1935, esp. pp. 257 ff.

whole the high-frequency morphemes are the empty morphemes and are listable, while the low-frequency ones are the full morphemes, which cannot be listed short of a dictionary of the whole language. For example, affixes, particles, determinatives, pronouns, measures, and modal adverbs are mostly regarded as empty morphemes, can be listed, and occur with high frequency, whereas the rest, the bulk, of the lexicon consists of full morphemes.

Stress is another factor which is correlated positively with infrequency and fullness of morphemes. Affixes are mostly in the neutral tone, that is, unstressed. But translations of foreign affixes in the so-called new terms such as 化 -*huah* '-ize, -fy' 準 *joen-* 'quasi-', and 非 *fei-* 'non-' are not in the neutral tone. Measures, including classifiers, are usually not in the neutral tone, but the most frequently used measure, the individualizing classifier 个 *geh*, is usually unstressed, which is one of the reasons we have adopted for it the abbreviation g. Associated with stress are also the factors of length and clearness of articulation. Full and therefore relatively infrequent morphemes are more clearly articulated and occupy more time than empty morphemes. Take, for example, 我 想 咱 们 顶 好 还 是 把 理 论 研 究 完 了 再 考 虑 应 用 吧. (*Prestissimo:*) *Woo sheang tzarmen diing hao hairsh* (*andante:*) *bae liiluenn yanjiow-wanle tzay kaoliuh yinqyonq ba.* 'I think we'd better finish studying the theory before considering applications.' The first part, being words and phrases of high frequency and relatively empty meaning, is spoken extremely fast and underarticulated, as compared with the full words that follow.

*4.1.5. Plan of This Chapter.* Referring to the 14 columns in tables 6 and 7, we shall treat columns 4, 8, 9, and 11 through 14 in chapter 6, since they have to do with compounds or root morphemes for forming compounds. Columns 5 through 7 are morpheme words; they are of lexical and syntactic import and do not involve morphology except for their membership in parts of speech, which will be treated in chapter 8. Column 3 consists of bound morphemes of unlimited versatility, which will be treated in chapters 6 through 8.

It remains then to treat in this chapter columns 1, 2, and 10, which have to do with affixation and derivation, except that final particles under column 1 will be treated under parts of speech, in chapter 8.

If this meager fare for Chinese morphology does not seem to do justice to the richness of the language, it is because the formation of words of more than one morpheme is a relatively new phenomenon and one does not have to stretch scientific objectivity to prove the superiority of the Chinese language by attributing to it the virtues of morphology over syntax, as some writers have done. It was not so long ago that Jesperson put out of date the notion that the then reputedly isolating Chinese language was backward and that highly inflected languages were the more highly advanced.[6]

# 4.2 Reduplication

*4.2.1. Reduplication as Process or Affix.* Of the various morphological processes, phonetic modification plays a very minor part in modern Chinese. As for reduplication, although the term sounds more like a process, it is treated by Bloomfield (*Lg*, 218) as an affix, except that, instead of being an affix of a given form, it assumes the form or a part of whatever form it is affixed to.[7]

Mere repetition of the same morpheme does not necessarily constitute reduplication. Thus, 鎖 ᛪ *suoo suoo* 'locks a lock', 註 ᛪ *juh juh* 'writes a (foot)note', and 夢 ᛪ *menq menq* 'dreams a dream' (dial.) just happen to have the same form for the verb and its noun object. In 三ᛪ 制 *sansan-jyh* 'the three-three system' it happens that both the junior high and the senior high courses are each three years in length. Reduplication proper is involved only when a repetition (or partial repetition) is regularly associated with a grammatical function.

*4.2.2. Forms of Reduplication.* We shall first consider the various forms of reduplication before taking up their grammatical functions and meanings. The two aspects, as usual, are rather highly correlated.

*4.2.2.1. Syllabic and Morphemic Patterns.* The simplest reduplication is of course in the form of a repetition of a monosylla-

---

[6]Otto Jesperson, *Language, its Nature, Development and Origin*, New York, 1922, pp. 367-373.

[7]Hockett's "chameleons", Peip Morphoph, 79-80.

bic morpheme, as *ren* 'man': *renren* 'everyman'. In *uang'uang* 'bow-wow-, *uang* is not a free form and only the reduplicated form is.

When different syllables are involved, there are various possibilities: XYXY, XXYY, XXY, XYY, XYXZ, XZYZ, and, with infixes, X.*li*XY, and X.*bu*YY. Examples are:

XYXY 叮当〻〻 *dingdang dingdang* 'dingdong, dingdong'
琢磨〻〻 *tzwo.mo.tzwo.mo* 'thinks over a little' [cf. sec. 4.2.3.(5)]

XXYY 零〻碎〻 *linglingsueysuey* 'odds and ends'
家〻户〻 *jiajiahuhhuh* 'every house and home'

XXY 崩〻脆 *bengbeng-tsuey* 'crackling crisp'
濛〻雨 *mengmeng-yeu* 'drizzly-drizzly rain'

XYY 冷冰〻 *leeng-bingbing* 'cold as ice'
红希〻 *horngshishi* 'reddish'

XYXZ 有条有理(的) *yeoutyau-yeoulii*(*de*) 'with articles and reasons, — systematical(ly), 大天大亮 *dahtian-dahlianq* 'in big broad daylight'

XZYZ 七岔八岔的 *chichah-bachahde* 'seven interrupting eight interrupting,—with all sorts of interruptions (or digressions)' 買空卖空 *maekong-maykong* 'buys empty, sells empty,—speculates on margin'

X.*li*XY 傻哩傻气 *shaa.li-shaachih* 'simple and silly'
纥哩纥络的 *ge.ligedade* 'with knots and gnarls'

X.*bu*YY 酸不溜〻儿的 *suan.bulhioulhioulde* 'sourish'
滑不济〻(儿)的 *hwa.bujiji*(*el*)*de* 'slimy and slippery'

A more complicated syllabic pattern consists of the partial reduplication in which only the finals of the syllables are repeated:

$XlV_xYlV_y$ 叽哩咕噜 *ji.ligulhu* 'grunts and grumbles' (see however, sec. 1.3.2)
叮呤当啷 *dinglhing-danglhang* 'jingling-jangling'

4.2.2.2. *Tone and Stress.* When a single syllable is reduplicated, it either takes the iambic form XX or the trochaic form X.X, that is, with a neutral tone on the second syllable. There is no change in tone in the XX type except in vivid reduplicates, as described below (sec. 4.2.4). We shall not regard the usual 3rd Tone sandhi as a change in tone, since it will be there, irrespectively of whether the two syllables are the same or different. Thus, there is nothing special about 本々 *beenbeen* 'every volume' being pronounced *bernbeen*, as compared with 很稳 *heen woen* 'very steady' being pronounced *hern woen*, so far as tone sandhi is concerned.

Longer reduplicated forms follow the usual subphonemic, or non-distinctive, grades of stress in polysyllabic forms, namely, loudest stress on the last syllable which is not in the neutral tone, next loudest on the first syllable, and weakest on the inside syllables, though not necessarily in the neutral tone. For example, ₁*ley-* ₁₁*uang'uangde* 'tears a-welling', ₁*yuan* ₁₁*yuan*₁*been'beende* 'from origins and sources'.

*4.2.3. Functional Types: Nouns and Action Verbs.* Reduplicated forms resulting in nouns and action verbs do not have special vivifying effects as do adjectives and adverbs, which will be treated separately (sec. 4.2.4.3).

(1) Terms of Address. Terms of address, especially terms of direct address, often take the reduplicated form X.X, where the root form X is sometimes free and sometimes bound. Thus, in 哥々 *ge.ge* 'older brother', *ge* is B; in 爸々 *bah.bah* 'papa' *bah* is F but rare, while 媽々 *mha.mha* 'mama' and *mha* 'ma' F are equally common. Other reduplicated terms of relationships are: 爺々 *ye.ye* 'grandpa' (on father's side), 奶々 *nae.nae* 'grandma' (on f.s.), 姥々 *lao.lao* 'grandma' (on m.s.), 舅々 *jiow.jiow* 'uncle' (on m.s.), 姑々 *gu.gu* 'aunt' (on f.s.), 姐々 *jiee.jiee*[8] 'older sister', 妹々 *mey.mey* 'younger sister', 弟々 *dih.dih* 'younger brother', 公々 *gong.-gong* 'father-in law' (of a woman), 婆々 *por.por* 'mother-in-law' (of a woman). That there are a number of obvious lacunae in the preceding list is due to the fact that some terms of address do not take the reduplicated form. Thus, the word for 'grandpa' (on

---

[8]All these 3rd Tone reduplicates *nae.nae, lao.lao,* and *jiee.jiee* follow the pattern ⅃ ⅃ . See sec. 1.3.9 (3).

m.s.) is, *lao.ye* and the word for 'aunt' (on m.s.) is 姨儿 *yel*, derived from the root form *yi* B plus diminutive suffix -*l*.[9]

Terms of relationship, especially terms of direct address, are of rather varying geographical spread. The forms *bah.bah* and *mha.mha* have a national or even an international status.[10] The forms *ge.ge*, *dih.dih*, *jiee.jiee*, and *mey.mey* are still nearly national, but the others might be marked as "*Peip.*" or at any rate only current in the Hopei region. (See sec. 1.2.1.) In other dialects the reduplicated forms are rather differently applied. For example, 爹 *die* 'dad', 娘 *niang* 'mother' are free in Peiping, but *die.die* and *niang.niang* do not occur except in other dialects. The dialects have 伯儿 *bor.bor* 'uncle' (father's older brother) and 叔儿 *shu.shu* 'uncle' (father's younger brother). While *shu.shu* is sometimes heard in Peiping, *bor.bor* is always called 大爺 *dah.ye* (≠ *dahye*, as in *tzuoh dahye* 'acts like a gentleman of leisure'). The reduplicated forms apply only to persons of an older or equal generation, although in my own dialect of Changchow, Kiangsu, 女兒 *neu.erl* is spoken of as [ɲʏɲʏ˥˥]. On the whole there is no complete set of terms of direct address of national standing, as there is for the corresponding designative and the learned terms.

The only non-kinship terms of address in reduplicated form are 太儿 *tay.tay* 'Mrs.' and 少奶儿 *shawnae.nae* 'young Mrs.' The latter is becoming absolete, as it was used to distinguish the young wife from the senior lady of the house, when two or three generations lived in the same household. Now *tay.tay* has acquired national status as the designative term for "wife" as well as the term of direct address "Mrs."

(2) Other Nouns. Reduplicated nouns other than terms of address are of somewhat miscellaneous nature. They are all trochees, that is, in the form X.X, often with the suffix -*l*. Examples are 蛐儿 *chiu.chiuel* 'cricket', 蝈儿 *guo.guol* 'large green cricket', 蛛儿 *jwu.ju* 'spider' (alternating with the less colloquial name 蜘蛛 *jyju*), 猩儿 *shing.shing* 'ape', 回儿 *Hwei.hwei* 'a Mos-

---

[9]I have given a detailed treatment of this topic in "Chinese Terms of Address", *Language* 32:212-241 (1956).

[10]See Roman Jakobson, "Why 'Mama' and 'Papa'?" *Perspectives in Psychological Theory*, pp. 124-134 (1960).

lem' (term not used in his presence),  宝ㄦ *bao.bao* 'baby',  娃ㄦ
*wa.wa* 'baby' (dial.)  洋娃ㄦ *yang-wa.wa* 'foreign-baby,—doll,'
星ㄦ  *shing.shing* '(real) star' (less colloquially, *shing*),  兜ㄦ *dou.-
dou* (< 兜肚 *dou-duh*) 'hold belly,—(a baby's) stomacher or belly
band'. These nouns are rather limited in number, except in children's language, or rather what grown-ups regard as children's
language and teach the child to say, for example, 吃饭ㄦ *chy
fann.fann* 'eat your rice-rice',  穿鞋ㄦ *chuan shye.shye* 'put on
your shoe-shoe', which is quite productive in this type of artificial
language. Usually, a growing child discards this language as soon
as he notices that grown-ups don't talk that way to each other.
A rather productive reduplication does exist in the dialect of
Kunming, Yunnan, and some Szechwan dialects, where reduplication has the class meaning of 'small object of obvious shape' for
example, 球ㄦ *chyou.chyou* 'small ball, bead',[11] 茛ㄦ *goæ.goæ*
(= Mandarin °*goangoan*) 'a tube-like thing'. That is why outsiders
get the wrong impression that people in Yunnan sometimes
talk like babies.[12]

(3) Distributive Reduplicates. When a measure M, less often
a noun, is reduplicated with no neutral tone, usually with the
retroflex suffix -*l*, it has the meaning of 'every'. This form is applicable to almost all monosyllabic M's. Examples are 个ㄦ
*gehgehl* 'every one', 张ㄦ *jangjang* 'every sheet', 天ㄦ *tiantial*
'every day', 寸ㄦ *tsuenntsuenn* 'every inch', 处ㄦ *chuhchull*
'everywhere', 回ㄦ *hweihwel* 'every time'.

Nouns as a rule are not reduplicated as a distributive form
with the exception of *renren* 'everybody'. In 山ㄦ出老虎.
*Shanshan chu laohuu.* 'Every mountain produces tigers.', 事ㄦ
如意. *Shyhshyh ruyih.* 'Every affair is as one wishes,—everything
satisfying.', and 他说的头ㄦ是道. *Ta shuo de tourtour sh*

---

[11]Cf., however, *chyouchyoudanndannde* (sec. 4.2.4.2).

[12]That one does not get the same impression from similar forms in the
Foochow dialect, such as 扣ㄦ *kou-kāu* 'button' and 瓶ㄦ *bing-bing* 'vase'
is probably because by the time an outsider has learned to understand such
a different dialect from Mandarin he will have also learned the proper use of
such reduplicates.

*daw.* 'He talks as if every heading is a good reason.', we have fixed phrases from which *shanshan, shyhshyh,* and *tourtour* cannot be extracted to form parts of other sentences or phrases. Other apparent nouns as distributive reduplicates are cases of class overlap of the same morpheme occuring sometimes as noun, sometimes as M. Thus, with *men* 'door (way to learning)' as M for subjects of study, one can say 大考 时候儿门ᷟ考了 个甲 *dahkao.shyr.howl menmen kaole g Jea* 'at the finals got an A in every subject', but not ° 把门ᷟ都开了 °*bae menmen dou kaile* 'has opened every door', for which one must use the M 扇 *shann* for *men* as a noun and say *bae shannshann men dou kaile.* The word 水 *shoei* can be a noun as 'water' or M as 'a washing', as 洗了三水衣裳, 水ᷟ洗的干淨 *shiile san-shoei i.shang, shoeishoei shii de gan.jinq* 'did three washings of clothes, every washing washed clean'. But there is no ° 火 ᷟ °*huoohuoo* for 'firings in an oven or a kiln', since *huoo* is only a noun (or a verb in L), and only rarely an M, as in 一 火, 二 火 *i-huoo, ell-huoo* 'first firing, second firing'. As another example of the same morpheme occurring both as noun and M with comparable frequency, one can say 一家(儿)人家儿 *i-jia(l) renjial* 'a household'. Perhaps *ren* can also be regarded as a case of N ∼ M overlaps, since it can also follow a determinative, as in 每人 *meei-ren* 'each person', 一人一塊 *i-ren i-kuay* 'one piece for each person'.

A limitation on reduplication of M's is that dissyllables cannot be reduplicated. Thus, 每加侖 *meei-jialuen* 'every gallon', but not °*jialuenjialuen;* 每米突 *meei-miituh* or *meeig-miituh* 'every meter' (the latter form with *miituh* as a noun, taking -g as its M), but not °*miituhmiituh.* Even monosyllables, if they are new M's of foreign origin, cannot be reduplicated. Thus, there is no °*miimii* 'every meter' or ° 克ᷟ °*kehkeh* 'every gram', and ° 秒 ᷟ °*meaumeau* 'every second' is rare. Some new M's of high frequency of occurrence have been naturalized enough to be reduplicated, as: 買了五磅肉, 磅ᷟ新鲜 *maele wuu-banq row, banqbanq shin.shian* 'bought five pounds of meat, every pound fresh'.

An important syntactic feature of distributive reduplicates is that, since they refer to a whole class of things and thus have definite reference, they must occupy an early portion rather than a late portion in the sentence (sec. 2.4.3). One can say: 人ィ都 来了. *Renren dou laile.* 'Everybody has come.' 棵ィ儿樹的 枝子上有花儿。 *Keke'l shuh de jytz.shanq yeou hual.* 'On every tree's branches there are flowers.' 他把个ィ儿人都 得罪了. *Ta bae gehgehl ren dou der.tzuey le.* 'He has offended everybody.' The sentence: 那个先生记得个ィ儿学生的 名字。 *Neyg shian.sheng jih.de gehgehl shyue-.sheng de mingtz.* That teacher remembers every student's name.' is possible, but not so good as: *Neyg shian.sheng, ta gehgehl shyue.sheng de mingtz dou jih.de.* A distributive reduplicate never occurs at the end of a sentence. Thus, instead of: °他认得个ィ儿学生。 °*Ta renn.de gehgehl shyue.sheng.* 'He knows every student.', one must say: *Ta gehgehl shyue.sheng dou renn.de.*

(4) Miscellaneous Compound Nouns and Verbs. A few nouns are formed of reduplicates which do not exist separately, as 毛ィ 虫 *mau.mauchorng* 'hairy-hairy-bug,—caterpillar', 捻ィ转儿 *nean.neanjuall* 'twirl-twirl-turner,—a top', 嘎ィ枣儿 *gar.ga-tzaol* 'jujube (the kind with a rhombus longitudinal section)'. In 打哈ィ *daa-ha.ha* 'banters', *ha.ha* is not used as a free noun, and, when used as an interjection, it has no neutral tone. The simple verb 哼 *heng* and its reduplicate *heng.heng* 'grunts, groans, hums (a tune)' do not differ much even in connotation. 嚷 *Raang* 'shouts' is *Vi* or *Vt*, while *rhang.rang* 'shouts noisily' is mostly used intransitively. In 痒ィ *yeang.yeang* 'it itches' the morpheme *yeang* is not free (except in some dialects). The common feature, if a negative feature, of these miscellaneous examples is the lack of any vivifying or other expressive effects. (Cf. sec. 4.2.4 below.)

(5) Tentative Aspect of Verbs. An action verb repeated in the neutral tone can be regarded as one of its aspects, along with its progressive aspect, perfective aspect, and so on. Thus, *kannj* 'looking', *kannle* 'looked', *kann.kann* 'just look'.[13] This last form,

---

[13]Jang Showkang, *op. cit.*, p. 6. (See n. 3.)

however, is closely connected with the syntactic construction of verb plus cognate object: *kann i-tsyh* 'look once', *kann$_o$i$_o$kann* 'take a look', whence *kann.kann* 'just look'. We shall regard the tentative aspect as a borderline case between morphological and syntactic constructions. It is symptomatic of the looser juncture in the tentative form in that a 3rd Tone verb is raised instead of staying low: 想ㄷ *sheang.sheang* ( ㄱ·| ) 'just think', as compared with *yeang.yeang* ( 」·| ) 'it itches'. In fact, one says: 这花ㄦ 得養ㄷ ₍ㄦ₎ 才会開呐。 *Jeh hual deei yeang.yeang(l)* ( ㄱ.| ) *tsair huey kai ne.* 'This flower must be cultivated a little before it will blossom.' Note that the tentative reduplicate does not take an (optional) *-l* in verbs of motion, for example, 坐 ㄷ ₍ㄦ₎ *tzuoh.tzuoh(l)* 'sits a while', 歇ㄷ ₍ㄦ₎ *shie.shie(l)* 'rests a little', but 跳ㄷ *tiaw.tiaw* 'jumps a little', 跑ㄷ *pao.pao* 'runs a little'.

*4.2.4. Functional Types: Vivid Reduplicates.*

*4.2.4.1. Further Details on Tone and Stress.* Vivid forms of reduplicates, or vivid reduplicates for short, are like distributive reduplicates in having an optional retroflex suffix *-l*, usually followed by the subordinative suffix *-de*. They differ from distributive reduplicates in having the tone of the second syllable usually changed to the 1st Tone, if it is not already in the 1st Tone. For example, in 高ㄷㄦ的 *gaugaulde* 'good and high' *gau* is an original 1st Tone, but in 吃的饱ㄷㄦ的 *chy de baobaulde* 'has eaten good and full' the morpheme *bao* is changed to *bau* on repetition. This tonal change is somewhat limited in geographical spread. Thus, 重ㄷㄦ的打 *jonqjonglde daa* 'hits good and hard' is pronounced *jonqjonqdi daa*, with no change in tone, in Southern Mandarin. This tonal change is also absent in reduplicated forms which are felt to be L in style, in which the retroflex suffix *-l* is also absent. Examples are 往ㄷ ( 的 ) *woangwoang (de)* 'frequently', as opposed to 常ㄷㄦ( 的 )*charngchangl(de)* 'often'. In borderline cases, the same morpheme undergoes a tonal change in informal style, but no change in a more formal style, as: 他漸ㄷㄦ 懂了。 *Ta jiannjial doongle.* 'He gradually understands.': 他漸 ㄷ 了解了。*Ta jiannjiann leaujieele.* 'He gradually comprehends.'

When a vivid reduplicate is longer than just one syllable

repeated, it may be of the pattern XYY or XXYY, rarely XXY, and never XYXY. For example, we have 直挺ㄥ的 *jyrtiingtiingde* 'straight and stiff', 普ㄥ通ㄥ的 *puupuutongtongde* 'common and ordinary', while 壁ㄥ直 *bihbihjyr* is less common than *bihjyr* 'straight as a wall' and 撲通ㄥ ㄥ *putong putong* 'splash splash! ... is an onomatopoeic reduplicate, which is quite a different thing from a vivid reduplicate. (See sec. 4.2.5 below.)

The main stress in XYY and XXYY, as noted above, is on the last syllable, even if the basic form is a trochee: X.Y. For example, from 荒張 *huang.jang* 'flustered' the usual vivid form is ₁*huang₀huang* ₁*jang'jang.de* and much less frequently ʹ*huang-.huang.jang.jangde* 'ruffled and flustered'. When a neutral tone is restressed, it either takes the 1st Tone, as in the case of vivid reduplicates from monosyllables (*haohaulde*) or, for literate persons, goes back to the etymological tone of the character, whether it is the proper character or not. Thus, 快活 *kuay.hwo* 'happy': *kuay .kuayhwohuolde* 'happy and cheerful'; 清楚 *ching.chuu* 'clear': *chingchingchuuchuude* or *chingchingchuuchude* 'perfectly clear'; 規矩 *guei.jeu* 'rule', 'well-behaved':*guei.guei.jeu.jeude* or *guei.guei.jeujiude* 'well behaved and well mannered'. The form *gueigueijeujeude* is rare, since few speakers, even literate persons, analyze *guei.jeu* into *guei* 'compasses' and *jeu* ʹ(carpenter's) square'.[14] Sometimes a speaker wavers between different possible original strong forms for a given weak form -.Y. For example, 糊塗 *hwu.du* 'muddled' is reduplicated sometimes as₁*hwu.li* ₁*hwu'du*, sometimes as ₁*hwu.li₁hwu'twu* 'muddled and addled', since a *twu* in a neutral tone may lose its aspiration and thus be indistinguishable from *du*, both resulting in -.*du* in *hwu.du*.

*4.2.4.2. Underlying Forms in Vivid Reduplication.* The root morpheme X in a vivid reduplicate XX may be free or bound, and when it is free the reduplication often has a suffix -*l*, as: 遠 *yeuan* 'far' F: 遠ㄥ儿(的) 来了一个人。 *yeuan'iual(de) laile ig ren.* 'There comes a man from afar.'; 僅 *jiin* 'mere' B: 僅ㄥ三五

---

[14]The phrase 循規蹈矩 *shyun-guei daw-jeu* 'follows the rule and toes the line,—is well behaved' is completely L in style and is on a different plane.

个 人 *jiinjiin san-wuug ren* 'a mere handful of men'. All mono-syllabic adjectives can form vivid reduplicates. Vivid reduplicates usually connote favorable meanings; however, they may be derived from words with pejorative meanings, for example, *luann* 'confused, disorderly': 把头髮弄的乱ㄦ的 *bae tour.fah nonq de luannlhualde* 'had her hair well mussed up (as intended)'.

With the pattern XXY and XYY, the ICs are XX-Y and X-YY and XY is not a constituent. Thus even though both 崩脆 *beng-tsuey* and *bengbeng-tsuey* 'crackling crisp' exist, the latter form consists of *beng* reduplicated plus *tsuey* rather than X + XY. If, however, the ICs are X + XY, then no reduplication is involved, as in 小ㄦ孩ㄦ *sheau-sheauharl* 'small child'. In most cases of XYY, there is usually no such form as XY. For example, 冷冰ㄖ *leeng-bingbing* 'icy cold' but no *leeng-bing*, except as a phrase 'cold ice', which is quite something else.

With the pattern XXYY, sometimes XY occurs as a word, and sometimes XY is limited to the reduplicated form. Thus 结ㄖ实ㄖ 的 *jiejieshyrshyrde* 'strong and solid' from *jie.shyr* 'solid', 平ㄖ 常ㄖ的 *pyngpyngcharngcharngde* 'quite usual and ordinary' from *pyngcharng* 'usual(ly)'. On the other hand, there is 哭ㄖ啼ㄖ的 *kukutyityide* 'with sobs and tears', but no such a compound as °*kutyi* (except in L); there is 鬼ㄖ祟ㄖ的 *goeigoeisueysueyde* 'sly and stealthy', but no °*goeisuey* (except in L). These, then, are primary derived words, which exist as reduplicates in the first place, while the former kind are secondary derived words, which already exist in the unreduplicated form. The forms 汤ㄖ水ㄖ的 *tangtangshoeishoeide* 'full of soup and juice' and 球ㄖ弹ㄖ的 *chyouchyoudanndannde* 'full of balls and beads' also belong to the latter category.

*4.2.4.3. Syntactic Limitations of Vivid Reduplicates.* Whether or not the base of a vivid reduplicate exists separately and, if it does, whatever its usual grammatical class, the reduplicated form is always limited to adjectives and adverbs, with or without the addition of the suffix -*de*.[15] Thus, from 婆 *por* 'old lady' B and 妈

---

[15]It is common practice to write -*de* as 的 for the adjectival ending and

*mha* 'ma', we have *porpormhamhade* 'womanish', from *san* 'three'
B and *leang* 'two' B, we have  三ㄥ两ㄥ的不断的来     *sansan-
leangleangde buduannde lai* 'come continually by two's and
three's'. In 客气 *keh.chih: kehkehchihchihde* 'courteous and cordial', it is from adjective to adjective (or adverb), as *keh.chih*
'guest-air,—polite' is not a noun but an adjective. The same holds
for the adjectives 大气 *dah.chih* 'generous' and 小气 *sheau.chih*
'small, mean, stingy', and their reduplicates.

Vivid reduplicates seem to occupy all the usual positions of
adjectives and adverbs: (1) attributive: 胖ㄥ儿的身材  *panqpangl-
de shen.tsair* 'fat and plump stature', 和ㄥ气ㄥ的声音    *herher-
chihchihde sheng.in* 'a cordial and kindly voice'; (2) predicative:
你怎么 老那么 糊 哩 糊 塗 的？ *Nii tzeem lao nemm hwu-
.lihwutwude?* 'How come you are always so muddle-headed?'

你 瞧这天儿又混哩混沌的了. *Nii chyau jeh tial yow hoen-
.lihoenduennde le.* 'Look, this weather is getting foggy and smog-
gy again!' (3) adverbial: 早ㄥ儿睡, 晚ㄥ儿起 , 又省灯油又省
米。*Tzaotzaul shuey, woan'ual chii, yow sheeng dengyou yow
sheeng mii.* 'Early to bed and late to rise, saves lamp oil and
saves rice! (proverb); (4) predicative complement: 打的乒ㄥ乓ㄥ的
*daa de pingpingpangpangde* or *daa de pinglhing-panglhangde*
'strikes banging and slamming', 磨的亮光ㄥ的 *mo de lianq-
guangguangde* 'polished smooth and bright';[16] and (5) commands
in the form of adjectives or adverbs, as 快ㄥ儿的！ *Kuaykualde!*
'Hurry up!' which is more relaxed than *Kuay!* 'Quick!' used in
emergencies,    好ㄥ儿的 ！ *Haohaulde!* 'Be good!' as compared
with *Hao!* 'Okay!', which is never used as a command.[17]

There are, however, some respects in which vivid reduplicates
are more limited in function than other adjectives and adverbs. A

---

as 地 for the adverbial ending, but there is no linguistic basis for this distinction except in the dialects. See sec. 4.4.6.

[16]For additional examples of 1 to 4, see 朱德熙, 现代汉语形容
词的研究 (Ju Dershi, "Studies in Modern Chinese Adjectives"), *Yeuyan
Yanjiou*, 1:107-108 of 83-111 (1956).

[17]Except by implication, as in: 倒, 倒, 再倒一点儿 ！好! *Daw, daw,
tzay daw .i.deal! Hao!* 'Back, back, back a little more! Okay!'

vivid reduplicate does not usually take adverbs of degree; for example, one can say: 他做的太慢ᴣ□ᴣ的了. *Ta tzuoh de tay mannmann-tengtengde le.* 'His work is too slow and sluggish.' But as a rule one does not use forms like °很亮晶ᴣ的 °*heen lianqjingjingde* 'very glittering and glimmering'.[18] The negative *bu* is available only in contrastive predication and not in assertive predication (sec. 2.9.1). Thus, one cannot say: °这料子綠油 ᴣ的不綠油ᴣ的？不, 不綠油ᴣ的. °*Jeh liawtz liuhyouioude bu liuhyouioude? Bu, bu liuhyouioude.* 'Is this material sort of greenish? No, it isn't greenish.' But one can say '*Jeh liawtz sh bush liuhyouioude? Bu, bush liuhyouioude,* 是红希ᴣ的. *sh horngshishide.* 'Is this material sort of greenish? No, it is not greenish, it's sort of reddish.' A vivid reduplicate admits of no degree of comparison. There is no °*genq horngshishide* 'more reddish' or °*Jeyg bii neyg dahdalde.* 'This is bigger than that.', for which the correct form is *Jeyg bii neyg dah.* or *Jeyg bii ney dah .i.deal.* Here, again a contrastive predication is possible, as: 这屋子更是黑漆ᴣ的了. *Jeh utz genqsh heichiuhchiude le.* 'This room is all the more darkish (after repainting, rearrangement, and so on).'

*4.2.4.4. Class Meanings of Vivid Reduplication.* Besides the general meaning of liveliness and connotations of much ado expressed by much asaid, various syllabic types have somewhat varied implications. The type XX *(l)de* usually has a favorable connotation, as 短ᴣ儿下裸, 高ᴣ儿的裉 *doandualde shiah$_o$bae, gaugaulde kenn* 'nice and short-length skirt, with nice and high slits', a form of description which one would not use if one did not approve of such dresses. Even words normally of unfavorable meanings will have an opposite effect when reduplicated, as 坏 ᴣ的使个主意, 故意把臉上弄的髒ᴣ的 *huayhuayde*[19] *shyy g jwu.yih, guh.yih bae lean.shanq nonq de tzangtzangde* 'mischievously used a ruse and purposely made her face good and dirty' (Ju Dershi, *op. cit.*, p. 110).

---

[18]Malmqvist, Sïch'uanese, 140.

[19]This is only transcribing the original text in characters. One would usually say *huayhualde*.

With type XXYY, the meaning may be favorable, as 大ㄟ方ㄟ
的 *dahdahfangfangde* 'in good taste, unassuming', or neutral, as
接ㄟ連ㄟ 的 *jiejielianliande* 'one after another, continually', or
unfavorable, as 扭ㄟ捏ㄟ的 *neouneounhienhiede* 'coy and sheep-
ish'.

The same is true of type XYXZ, as 大明大白 *dahming-
dahbair* 'greatly clarified', 不清不楚 *buching-buchuu* 'muddled
and confused'.

Type X.*li*XY always has a pejorative meaning, as 小哩小气
的 *sheau.lisheauchihde* 'small and stingy', as contrasted with
XXYY in 大ㄟ气ㄟ的 *dahdahchihchihde* 'great and generous'.

4.2.5. *Functional Types: Onomatopoeic Reduplicates.* Onomatopoeic reduplicates differ in several ways from vivid reduplicates.
In syllabic type, they usually take XYXY and less often XXYY. For
example, 普ㄟ通ㄟ的 *puupuutongtongde* 'common and ordinary'
is a vivid reduplicate, while 撲通ㄟㄟ! *putong putong!* 'splash,
splash' is an onomatopoeic reduplicate. Of the two partial reduplications X.*li*XY and X*lV*xY*lV*y, the former, always with pejorative
meaning, is a vivid form, for example, 啰哩啰唆的 *lhuo.lilhuo-
suode* 'fussy and wordy', and the latter is always onomatopoeic,
with no pejorative meaning, as 唏哩呼噜 的喝 *shilhihulhude*
*he* 'drinks slurp, slurp'. (Cf. sec. 1.3.2. n. 18.) While vivid reduplicates can be used in the imperative: 慢ㄟ儿的 !*Mannmhalde!*
'Take it easy!' onomatopoeic reduplicates are not so used. On the
other hand, when a vivid reduplicate is not used alone as an imperative or, rather rarely, as a predicate sentence, it is always in
construction with another part of the sentence, while an onomatopoeic reduplicate, whether also a vivid form or not, often occurs
as an absolute, as: 你听那钟，叮噹，ㄟㄟ! 一会儿就得上
课 3. *Nii ting nah jong, dingdang, dingdang! ihoel jiow deei*
*shanq-keh le.* 'Listen to the bell, dingdong, dingdong! You will
have to go to class in a moment.' Note that XYXY for sound effects usually has a potential pause and can be extended as XYXY
XY ... , so that it really forms a phrase of two words, and thus is
properly a syntactic repetition rather than a morphological reduplication.

# 4.3. Prefixes

*4.3.1. Compounding and Affixation.* We have noticed a certain degree of positive correlation (a) among the meaningful, the infrequent, the stressed, the clearly articulated, and the unlistable full morphemes, on the one hand, and (b) among the meaningless, the frequent, the unstressed, the phonetically more neutral, and the listable empty morphemes on the other. But, since all these features admit of differences of degree, there are intermediate cases with combinations of different degrees of the various factors. Thus, there is (1) the stressed verb 起来 *chii.lai* 'rises', as in 我想起来了. *Woo sheang chii.lai le.* 'I want to get up now.'; (2) the unstressed directional complement -.*chii.lai* 'up(ward)' (lit. or fig.), as in *lha.chii.lai* 'pulls up' and 我想起来了. *Woo sheang-.chii.lai le.* 'I have just thought of it (up from below the threshold of memory),—I remember it now.' 我想不起来了. *Woo sheang.bu-chiilai.* 'I cannot recall it.'; (3) the inchoative aspect suffix -.*chii.lai*, which is never stressed, as in 哭起来了 *ku.chii-.lai le* 'starts to cry', 想起来了... *Sheang.chii.lai le ...* 'It has just occurred to me, —by the way ...' We shall now examine both the empty morphemes, which are more typically prefixes and suffixes, and the fuller morphemes, which ordinarily go under the names of prefixes and suffixes but are really versatile components of compounds, the detailed treatment of which will be taken up in the sections on localizers (secs. 6.4.4 and 7.10) and directional complements (sec. 6.6.6).

*4.3.2 Versatile First Morphemes in Compounds.* We speak casually of prefixing the title of "Mr." to a proper name (actually in apposition to it), and it is in such a broad sense that many versatile elements in compounds have come to be called prefixes.

Before verbs (some of which are L), we have 禁 *jin-*[20] 'stands, endures', as in 禁使 *jin-shyy* 'stands use', 禁用 *jin-yonq* 'stands use', 禁穿 *jin-chuan* 'stands wearing', 禁看 *jin-kann* 'stands reading (without being boring or finished too soon)'; 可 *kee-* 'worth

---

[20]The character 禁 for *jin-* is also used for *jinn* 'prohibits' B. In Cantonese *jin-* is *kham-* and *jinn* is *kamm*.

. . . -ing, -able', as in 可爱 *keeay* 'lovable, lovely', 可恶 *keewuh* 'hateable, detestable', 可怜 *keelian* 'pitiable', 可笑 *keeshiaw* 'laughable', 可靠 *keekaw* 'reliable', 可疑 *keeyi* 'doubtful', 'suspicious', by analogy, with nouns, as in 可口 *keekoou* 'palatable', 可人 *keeren* (rare) 'personable', 可身儿 (的衣裳) *keeshel(de i.shang)* '(body) fitting clothes'; *hao-* 'good to', 'easy to', as in 好吃 *haochy* 'good to eat', 好闻 *haowen* 'good to smell, fragrant', 好看 *haokann* 'pretty', 好听 *haoting* 'sounds good', 好受 *haoshow* 'feels good, comfortable', 好做 *haotzuoh* 'easy to do', 好办 *haobann* 'easy to manage', 好说话 *haoshuohuah* 'easy to talk with, good-natured'; 难 *nan-* 'bad to', 'hard to', as in 难吃 *nanchy* 'tastes bad', 难闻 *nanwen* 'smells bad', 难看 *nankann* 'ugly', 难听 *nanting* 'sounds bad', 难受 *nanshow* 'feels bad, miserable', 难做 *nantzuoh* 'hard to do', 难说话 *nanshuohuah* 'hard to talk with, hard to get along with'. In the Central dialects, *hao* is also used as a free auxiliary verb 'may, it's okay to', as in 好不好看電影儿去? 好. *Hao bu hao kann diannyeengl chiuh? Hao.* 'May I go see a movie? Yes, you may.' In the case of compounds, one will have to repeat the whole word, as in 那電影儿好看不好看? *Nah diannyeengl haokann bu haokann?* 'Is that movie good?' whereas *hao* the auxiliary verb, being a free word, can be repeated alone in the V-not-V form of a question. The bound morpheme 自 *tzyh-* 'self, auto'- precedes the verb with which it is bound as a relic of ancient grammar in which *tzyh* as a reflexive pronoun regularly preceded the verb (cf. Fr. *se*). In modern Chinese *tzyh* is often regarded as a prefix, which for the reasons given above we regard as versatile first morphemes. Examples are: 自由 *tzyhyou* 'follows self, —free(dom), liberty', 自治 *tzyhjyh* 'governs self, —self-governing, —ment, 自命 *tzyhminq* 'ordains self, —self-styled', 自殺 *tzyhsha* 'kills self, —(commits) suicide', or with *tzyh* as the actor in newer forms, as in 自動 *tzyhdonq* 'self-moving,—automatic, of one's own accord', 自转 *tzyhjoan* 'self-turning,—rotation (of planets, etc.)', as opposed to 公转 *gongjoan* 'public turning,—revolution (of planets, etc.)'.

In polite speech, there is a whole set of honorific and humble bound forms which are commonly said to be "prefixed" to terms of address, one's house, and so on, in place of first and second person possessive pronouns or, less frequently, in addition to third person possessive pronouns. With relationship terms referring to relatives older than oneself, 家 *jia-* 'home' is used, as in 家父 *jiafuh* 'my father', 家姊 *jiajiee* 'my elder sister'. For relatives younger than oneself 舍 *sheh-* 'house, hut' is used, as in 舍弟 *shehdih* 'my younger brother'. In older style speech 先 *shian-* '(gone) before' replaces *jia-* when a deceased person is referred to; in like manner 亡 *wang-* 'lost' replaces *sheh-*, whereas in current speech one would use the neutral form *woode* or *woo*, as *jia-* and *sheh-* are available only for living persons.

To 姓 *shinq* 'surname', 处 *chuh* 'place (of origin)', and 国 *gwo* 'country', one may add 敝 *bih-* 'dilapidated' for 'my'. As in the case of honorific forms, these humble forms displace the possessive pronouns, so that there is no °我的敝处 °*woode bihchuh* 'my hometown', since *bihchuh* already means 'my hometown'. The plural form is, however, sometimes used, by way of redundancy, as in 我们敝处 *woomen bihchuh* 'our hometown'. With 姓 *shinq* the prefix 贱 *jiann-* 'mean, lowly' may occur, but it does not occur with *chuh*. Formerly one often referred to one's own wife as 贱内 *jiannney* 'the lowly one of the interior,—my wife'; nowadays 内人 *ney$_o$ren* 'the interior one' is heard more frequently in this sense. The nonpolite form is 我的太太 *woode tay.tay*. In referring to one's own works an author uses the term 拙著 *juojuh* 'my clumsy composition'.

The "prefix" 贵 *guey-* 'noble, esteemed' may be used with 姓 *shinq* F, 处 *chuh* B, and 国 *gwo* F, to mean 'your', as in 贵姓 *gueyshinq*, which is used either as a noun or as a complete question 'What's your name, please?' Because of the preponderance of Chinese-speaking Japanese over other foreigners in China in recent decades, there is a curious association of 贵国 *gueygwo* 'your honorable country' and 敝国 *bihgwo* 'my humble country' with the Japanese, so that 贵国人 *gueygworen*, less frequently 敝国人 *bihgworen*, has become a slang term for 'Japanese'. Actually, except on very formal occasions, the plain forms 中国 *Jong.gwo*

'China' and 美國 *Meei.gwo* 'America', and so on are much more common in ordinary speech.

'Your father' is often referred to as 尊大人 *tzuen-dah.ren* 'respected great man'; the form 尊姓 *tzuenshinq* 'your surname' (less frequent than 貴姓 *gueyshinq*) is also found. With many relationship terms 令 *linq-* 'excellent' is used for 'your', as in 令 叔 *linqshwu* 'your uncle (father's younger brother)', 令兄 *linq-shiong* 'your elder brother', 令姪 *linqjyr* 'your nephew'. When someone's parents or sons or daughters are referred to with the prefix *linq-*, special forms are used, as in 令尊 *linqtzuen* 'excellent respected one,—your father', 令堂 *linqtarng* 'excellent lady in the hall,—your mother', 令郎 *linqlang* 'excellent young man,—your son', 令愛 *linqay* 'excellent loved one,—your daughter'. The tek-nonymous term 世兄 *shyhshiong* 'older brother of the generation' is occasionally used for a friend's sons. The prefix 世 *shyh-* is short for *shyhjiau* 'friendship of the older generation or generations'.

The honorific form for the third person is used chiefly in the presence of the person, as for example in introducing a person, as in   这是王先生的世兄。 *Jeh sh Wang.shian.sheng de shyh-shiong.* 'This is Mr. Wang's son.' (said in the presence of Mr. Wang and his son).[21]

*4.3.3. Modern "Prefixes".* Translations of foreign prefixes are also versatile first morphemes in compounds. They are called pre-fixes because they are prefixes in the foreign language. What makes some of them different from ordinary compounds is that they often play different functions from those in other contexts. For example, *bu* 'not' is an adverb, but in 不科学 *bukeshyue* 'unscientific' and 不道德 *budawder* 'immoral', 科学 *keshyue* 'science' and 道德 *dawder* 'morality' are nouns. Occasionally a noun becomes an adjective by back formation, for example from 不名譽 *buming$_o$yuh* 'disreputable' *ming$_o$yuh* 'reputation, fame' is also used in *heen ming$_o$yuh* 'quite reputable', especially when *buming$_o$yuh* is in the near context. Similarly, there is *heen*

───────────────

[21]For a full discussion of Chinese relationship terminology, see Yuen Ren Chao, "Chinese Terms of Address", *Language*, 32:217-241 (1956).

*keshyue* 'quite scientific' to contradict or forestall a possible *buke-shyue*. In the case of 不規則 *buguei$_o$tzer* 'irregular', *guei$_o$tzer* 'a rule' has become a full-fledged adjective (in addition to being a noun) without having to have *buguei$_o$tzer* in the near context.

Some very common modern prefixes are:

单 *dan-* 'single, mono-, uni-', as in 单方面 *danfangmiann-* 'unilateral', 单细胞 *danshihbau-* 'unicellular' B-, 单向路 *danshiaqluh* 'one-way street'.

多 *duo-* 'many, poly-, multi-', as in 多元论 *duoyuanluenn* 'pluralism', 多音節 *duoinjye-* 'polysyllabic' B-. 汎 *fann-* 'pan-', as in 汎心论 *fannshinluenn* 'panpsychism', 汎美洲 *Fann Meeijou-* 'Pan-American' B-, 汎太平洋 *Fann Taypyngyang-* 'Pan-Pacific' B-.

準 *joen-* 'quasi-', as in 準学者 *joen-shyuejee* 'quasi-scholar', 準白话的 *joen-bairhuahde* 'quasi-colloquial'. But in 準时候儿到 *joen-shyrhowl daw* 'arrives on time', *joen* 'accurate' is an adjective in an A-N compound, used here adverbially.

偽 *wey-* 'pseudo', as in 偽政府 *wey-jenqfuu* 'pseudo-government, puppet government', 偽君子 *wey-jiuntzyy* 'pseudo-government, puppet government', *wey-jiuntzyy* 'pseudo-gentleman, hypocrite'.

不 *bu* 'not, un-', as in 不逻辑 *buluojih* 'illogical', 不民主 *buminjuu* 'undemocratic'. Cf. old term 不通 *butong* 'ungrammatical, illogical'.

兮 *wu-* 'without, -less', as in 兮線電 *wushiann-diann* 'without-wire electricity,—wireless', 兮政府主义 *wu-jenqfuu-juuyih* 'without-government-ism,—anarchism', 兮条件的 *wu-tyaujiannde* 'unconditional(ly)'.

非 *fei-* 'is not,—non-', as in 非物質的 *fei-wuhjyrde* 'non-physical', 非戰鬥員 *fei-janndowyuan* 'a non-combatant'.

親 *chin-* 'pro-', as in 親美 *chin-Meei* 'pro-American', 親共 *Chin-gonq* 'pro-Communist', rather unproductive as compared with a different and more productive *chin-* of the same etymon, meaning 'of one's own, by one's own', as in

親眼看見 *chin-yean kann-jiann* 'sees with one's own eyes'. The second type of *chin-* is of much older standing. 反 *faan-* 'anti-, counter-', as in 反猶太 *faan-Youtay-* 'anti-Semitic', 反宣傳 *faan-shiuanchwan* 'counterpropaganda 反革命 *faan-germinq* 'counter-revolutionary', 反間諜 *faan-jianndye* 'counterespionage', 'counterspy'.

Note that these modern prefixes are more frequently attached to polysyllables than to monosyllables. In a form like 偽足 *weytzwu* 'pseudopodium' it is felt to be more like a compound: 'false-foot'.

*4.3.4. Prefixes Proper.* Chinese prefixes form a rather small class. They are short of being completely empty in that, except for *ah-*, they are also full morphemes in other functions and are not in the neutral tone, since there is no initial neutral tone except in sentence prosody, and prefixed words are iambs of the usual quasi-iambic type.

(1) Prefix 阿 *ah-*. The prefix *ah-* is the only prefix which is not also used as a full morpheme as a word or part of a compound word. Its occurrence is, however, extremely rare both lexically and textually. About the only word with this prefix is the term of address 阿哥 *ahge* 'older brother', used as a title at the court of the Manchu dynasty. Otherwise its occurrence is limited to forms quoted from dialects, in some of which the prefix is productive. For example, in the Shanghai dialect 'older brother' is 阿哥 *a' ku* (Mandarin *ge.ge*), and 'older sister' is 阿姐 *a'tzea* (Mandarin *jiee.jiee*), the prefix being in the entering tone. In Cantonese the prefix *ah-* is used with monosyllabic surnames with the same effect as prefixing 老 *lao-* (see below), as 亞王 *Ah*[22] *Woang°* = Mandarin 老王 *Lao Wang*.

(2) Prefix 老 *lao-*. The morpheme *lao* is a full word as an adjective 'old', 'tough (of vegetables and fruits)', as an adverb 'all the time, keeps ... -ing', and as a surname. In the phrase ˌ*lao* ˈ*shian.sheng* 'old gentleman', *lao* is an adjective, whereas in the

---

[22]The character 阿 commonly used in Mandarin and Wu-dialect texts for this prefix is pronounced *o* in Cantonese. The usual character for this prefix in Cantonese texts is 亞, which would be *yah* in Mandarin, as in 亞細亞 *Yahshihyah* 'Asia'.

compound, as a close apposition, *'Lao.Shian.sheng* 'Mr. Lao', *Lao* is a surname. In *lao.tz* ( ⌐ˑl ) 'the old man' (colloq. for 'father'), *lao* is the root morpheme with suffix-*tz*. In *,Lao 'Tzyy* ( ⼈⼈ ) 'Philosopher Lao,—Laotze' *Lao* is a proper noun. In 老玉米 *laoyuh.mii* '(Indian) corn' and 老酒 *laojeou*, '(old) wine' (dial.) *lao* enters as part of lexical compounds.

As a prefix, *lao*-occurs:

(a) In names of animals: 老虎 *lao₀huu* 'tiger', 老鼠 *laoshuu* 'rat', 'mouse', 老鷹 *laoing* 'eagle', where *huu* 'tiger' and *shuu* 'rat', 'mouse' are bound and *ing* 'eagle' is free. These words apply to the animals irrespectively of age, as in 小老虎 *sheau laohuu* 'little tiger,—cub'.

(b) In kinship terms to indicate order of seniority: 老大 *lao-dah* 'number one (among brothers and/or sisters)', where *dah* is the usual form for 'first' when designating persons, 老二 *laoell* 'number two', 老三 *laosan* 'number three', … 老幺 *laoiau* 'number little' (for the youngest). This prefix is not used with polysyllabic numerals, there being no °老十一 °*laoshyri* 'number 11', the siblings younger than number ten being called 十一弟 *shyridih* 'brother 11' or 十三妹 *shyrsanmey* 'sister 13', and so on.

(c) In terms of address before monosyllabic surnames, and so on: 老王 *Lao Wang* 'Wang', 老李 *Lao Lii* 'Lii'. The prefixing of *lao* to a surname has the same social effect as dropping of 'Mr.' when the degree of acquaintance no longer requires the use of titles but is not advanced to the use of 號 *haw* 'courtesy name', corresponding roughly to the use of first names in English. In the few dissyllabic surnames which are current, dropping of 'Mr.' consists simply of dropping 先生 *Shian.sheng*, but since monosyllabic proper names are not free, a prefix is required.

The antonym of *lao*, namely 小 *sheau*, has not yet attained the status of a prefix insofar as loss of its original meaning is concerned. Thus *laosan* means no more than third in seniority, while *sheausan*, usually in the diminutive form *sheausal*, though a common enough appellation for the third of siblings, still retains much of the original meaning of 'Little Number Three'.

With surnames, as in 小張 *Sheau Jang*, the form is often used to distinguish a son from his father or a younger brother from his older brother.

(3) Prefix 第 *dih-*. The morpheme *dih* '(serial) order' B is not productive as a full morpheme. There is 门第 *mendih* 'door and mansion,—social position', 次第 *tsydih* (a compound of synonyms) 'order'. As a prefix, it forms ordinal numbers with the numerals: 第一 *dihi* 'first', 第二 *dih'ell* 'second', 第三 *dihsan* 'third', etc. There is no °第百 °*dihbae* 'hundredth', ° 第千 °*dihchian* 'thousandth', or ° 第万 °*dihwann* 'ten thousandth' because *bae*, *chian*, and *wann* are not numerals, but measures (M). On the other hand 一百 *ibae* 'one hundred', etc., are numerals, and so one can say 第一百 *dih-ibae* as 'the one-hundredth', etc. For 'the last' there is 第末拉 *dihmohlha*, less commonly, 第末 *dihmoh*. The youngest of siblings is sometimes spoken of as being 第老 *dihlao*, used antonymously for a theoretical °第小 °*dihsheau* 'number little'. When one is being very mathematical, one sometimes says 第零 *dihling* 'number zero'.

Sometimes 头一 *touri* is regarded as an equivalent alternative form of 第一 *dihi*, so that *tour* looks like a prefix for ordinal numbers. However 头一 *touri-* is always bound, whereas *dihi* is free. For example, 考了个第一 *kaole g dihi* 'got a number one at an examination', but with *touri* it must be followed by an M as in 考了个头一名 *kaole g touri-ming*. In fact one can also say 考上了头十名 *kao-shanqle tour-shyrming* 'qualified among the first ten names', quite like 前十名 *chyan-shyrming* 'the fore(most) ten names'. Thus *tour* 'the first' is in construction with *i-ming* or *shyr-ming* and should better be treated as the first full morpheme in a compound rather than as a prefix.

(4) Prefix 初 *chu-*. As a full morpheme, *chu* is bound and means 'beginning', as in 起初 *chiichu* 'at first', 初等 *chudeeng* or 初级 *chujyi* 'first grade, elementary grade', 月初 *yuehchu* 'month's beginning', 初次 *chu-tsyh* 'for the first time'. As a prefix it is used for the days of the month: 初一 *chui* 'the 1st', 初二 *chu'ell* 'the 2nd', 初三 *chusan* 'the 3rd', ... 初十 *chushyr* 'the

10th', after which the days are called by numbers, 十 一 *shyri*
'the 11th', etc., without prefix. When the Gregorian calendar
was first used in China in 1912, the days of the month were
called such and such 号 *haw* 'number', while dates called by *chu-*
or by plain numerals above ten were applied to the lunar calendar only. However, the old terms are more and more used for
the Gregorian calendar, too, gradually displacing the new term
一 号 *ihaw,* 二 号 *ellhaw, ... .* As for the M 日 *ryh* 'day' in dates,
it is never used in speech, except when one is talking bookishly.

## 4.4 Suffixes

*4.4.1. General.* A suffix in Chinese is an empty morpheme,
mostly in the neutral tone, which occurs at the end of a word
and characterizes its grammatical function. It differs from a prefix not only in position but in being in the neutral tone, in the
case of the retroflex suffix -*l,* non-syllabic. Suffixes are both lexically more numerous and textually more frequent than prefixes.
A word suffix, or simply suffix, differs from a phrase suffix, or
particle, in that the former is a part of a word, whereas the latter can only be in construction with a phrase or a sentence. In a
few cases the same syllable is sometimes a suffix and sometimes a
particle, as in 吃了饭了 *chyle fann le* 'has eaten one's meal',
where the first *le* is the perfective suffix and the second *le* is a
particle indicating occurence of an event. Again, in *woode* 'my',
*de* is a possessive suffix, while in 一定不会下雨的 *idinq
buhuey shiah-yeu de* 'will certainly not rain', *de* is a particle, having the force of 'the fact is such that'. On the whole, however,
suffixes and particles belong to classes with quite separate mem-
berships. We shall consider particles in detail in chapter 8.

Very frequently, a suffixed word has a meaning other than
simply the addition of the meaning of the root and the grammatical meaning of the suffix. These will then become items of lexical import. Following are some examples:

抱 *baw* 'holds (as baby)'          *bawde* '(is an) adopted (one)'
乏 *far* 'inferior, of poor quality' *farle* 'fatigued'
驚 *jing* 'frighten(ed)' B          *jingle* 'run away (of a horse)'

瓶 *pyng* 'vase'                    *pyngtz* '(any) bottle'

耗 *haw* 'wastes, consumes' B        *hawtz* 'waster,—rat, mouse'

                                   *hawj* 'wasting,—up against
                                       each other in a deadlock'

指 *jyy* 'points to'                *jyyj* 'depends upon ... for', as
                                       in  指着他養家  *jyyj ta
                                       yeang-jia* 'depends upon
                                       him to support the family'

Sometimes the root form is not a free word but occurs only in the suffixed form, for example, 托着 *tuoj* 'to support (from below, as on the palm, on a tray, etc.)', 忘了 *wanqle* 'forget'.

It is sometimes useful for pedagogical purposes to consider root words as having a zero suffix. Thus, along with sufixes -*l*, -*tz*, and -.*tou*, which form nouns with a root morpheme, some roots otherwise similar to those with such suffixes are free nouns, and one can very well regard such unsuffixed nouns on a par with suffixed nouns. Thus, we have 貓 *mhau* 'cat', 狗 *goou* 'dog', but 騾子 *luotz* 'mule', 狮子 *shytz* 'lion'; 梨 *li* 'pear', 藕 *oou* 'lotus stem', but 桃儿 *taurl* 'peach', 杏儿 *shienql* 'apricot'; 飯 *fann* 'rice', 麵 *miann* 'noodles', but 饅头 *man.tou* 'steamed bun'; 饺子 *jeautz* '(Chinese) ravioli'; 嘴 *tzoei* 'mouth', but 舌头 *sher.tou* 'tongue'. With verbs of action, an unsuffixed form has the special function of indicating 'habitual action' or 'near future action', which therefore constitutes the class meaning of the zero suffix, just as 'completed action' is the class meaning of the suffix -*le*, and so on, as will be detailed below (sec. 4.4.5).

If a suffix is attached to a morpheme complex as a whole rather than to the last morpheme, then the result is a decompound (Bloomfield, *Lg*, 210), as 搬不倒儿 *ban.budaol* 'push can't topple,—a roly-poly', 捻㇏转儿 *nean.neanjuall* 'twirl, twirl and it spins *suffix*, —a top'.

As with prefixes, there are many intermediate types of end morphemes in words which are not completely empty, but are often called "suffixes". We shall consider these in the following order: sec. 4.4.2: versatile end morphemes in compounds; 4.4.3: modern suffixes; 4.4.4: noun suffixes; 4.4.5: verbal suffixes; 4.4.6:

the subordinative suffix -*de*; 4.4.7: other suffixes. On the whole, the first three categories, although most of them are versatile, are lexically limited, while the last three are generally of very high versatility with respect to roots of given form classes.

4.4.2. *Versatile End Morphemes in Compounds*

(1) 者 -*jee* 'one who, -er'. As a word in L it is of unlimited versatility, but in speech it is somewhat limited. Thus there is 译者 *yihjee* 'translator', but no ° 抄者 °*chaujee* 'copier', for which the word is 抄錄員 *chauluhyuan* 'copying member,— copyist'; there is 学者 *shyuejee* 'student' or more frequently 'scholar, savant', but no ° 教者 °*jiaujee* or °*jiawjee* 'teacher', for which the word is 教員 *jiaw$_0$yuan* or 教师 *jiawshy*. In general, purely non-L verbs do not combine with -*jee*, and that is why there is no ° 跑者 °*paojee* 'runner', ° 打者 °*daajee* 'beater', ° 吃者 °*chyjee* 'eater', or ° 喝者 °*hejee* 'drinker', for which one has to say 跑的 *pao de* or 跑的人 *pao de ren*, etc. That there is 说者 *shuojee* is not an exception, since *shuojee* is used in L in the special sense of 'those who have been discussing the subject' rather than 'one who says'. For the rest, that is, verbs which are L or general in style, one cannot predict or list the -*jee* forms except in a dictionary. Further examples are: 作者 *tzuohjee* 'the writer', 著者 *juhjee* 'author', 筆者 *biijee* 'the penner,—the (present) writer', 编者 *bianjee* 'compiler', 记者 *jihjee* '(news) correspondent', 读者 *dwujee* 'the reader', 耒者 *laijee* 'whoever comes', 長者 *jaangjee* 'elder, senior person', 前者 *chyanjee* 'recently', 'the former', 後者 *howjee* 'the latter', 当事者 *dangshyhjee* 'person(s) concerned' 好事者 *hawshyhjee* 'one who likes business,—busybody', 劳動者 *laudonqjee* 'toiler,—one of the working class'.

(2) 然 -*ran* '-like, -ly'. As a word in L it means 'thus, so'. In the conjunction 不然 *buran* '(if) not so,—otherwise' it is still taken in that sense. But in the following words, -*ran* only makes an adverb of the resulting form and differs from other suffixes in not being in the neutral tone: 忽然 *huran* 'suddenly', 顯然 *sheanran* 'obviously', 公然 *gongran* 'publicly', 当然 *dangran* 'of course', 果然 *guooran* or 居然 *jiuran* 'indeed (to my pleasant

surprise)', 固然 *guhran* 'to be sure, it's true that ...', 徒然 *twu-ran* 'in vain', 枉然 *woangran* 'in vain', 断然 *duannran* 'determinedly', 突然 *tuhran* 'abruptly', 自然 *tzyhran* 'naturally' or 'of course', 天然 *tianran* 'naturally', 虽然 *sweiran* 'although' ( $\neq$ *swei ran* L 'although it is so'). Some of these can be made into adjectives or adverbs by adding *de*, namely, *sheanrande* 'obvious', *dangrande* '(as a matter) of course', *twurande* or *woangrande* 'forlorn', *tzyhrande* 'natural', *tianrande* 'natural (not artificial)'. *Tzyhran* is also a noun for 'Nature', with a capital N, and as a school subject.

(3) 来 *-lai* 'coming (down in time)' forms adverbs 本来 *been-lai* or 原来 *yuanlai* 'originally', 近来 *jinnlai* 'coming from near, —recently', 後来 *howlai* 'afterwards', 向来 *shianqlai* 'hitherto', 从来 *tsornglai* 'ever' (mostly in the negative), 素来 *suhlai* 'so far always, habitually', 自来 *tzyhlai* 'so far always', 歷来 *lihlai* 'so far in all cases', 生来 *shenglai* 'ever since (one was) born'.

Somewhat different from the preceding is the *-lai* after numerals in *i-lai* 'in the first place', *ell-lai* or *ell-i-lai* 'in the second place.' Although there is no limit to the number to which this can be suffixed, one rarely goes beyond the third or fourth place. Other synonymous expressions, such as 第一層 *dihi-tserng* 'first layer (of reasoning, etc.)' or 第一点 *dihi-dean* 'the first point', and so on, are used more often for higher numbers, especially with *dean*, which is a translation borrowing from 'point'.

Still a third use of *-lai*, with optional neutral tone $-_olai$, is after round numbers for an additional small fraction of the round number. For example, 十来块钱 $shyr_olai$-*kuay chyan* 'around ten dollars', as distinguished from 十几块钱 *shyrjii-kuay chyan* 'umpteen dollars' (11 to 19 incl.), 百十来里地 $baeshyr_olai$-*lii dih* '110 *li* of distance or thereabouts'.

The following are versatile end morphemes which are in the neutral tone:

(4) 人 *-.ren* '-man, -er', as in 工人 *gong.ren* 'workman', 中人 *jong.ren* 'middle man,—witness (to a transaction)', 证人 *jenq.ren* 'prove man,—witness (of an event)', 媒人 *mei.ren* 'go-between, matchmaker', 夫人 *fu.ren* 'lady, Mrs.' (honorif. form), 丈人 *janq-*

.*ren* 'father-in-law (of a man)', 举人 *jeu.ren* '(old style) second academic degree' (comparable to M.A.), 大人 *dah.ren* 'an adult', also 'esquire' (old-style term of address).

(5) 师 -$_o$*shy* 'master, teacher', as in 教师 *jiawshy* 'teacher', 牧师 *muh$_o$shy* 'pastor', 律师 *liuh$_o$shy* 'lawyer', 技师 *jihshy* 'technician', 讲师 *jeangshy* 'lecturer'.

(6) 士 -$_o$*shyh* 'scholar, professional person', as in 进士 *jinn-.shyh* '(old style) advanced degree' (comparable to Ph.D.), 学士 *shyue$_o$shyh* 'bachelor', 硕士 *shuoh$_o$shyh* 'master', 愽士 *bor$_o$shyh* 'doctor', 教士 *jiaw.shyh* 'minister', 护士 *huh$_o$shyh* '(medical) nurse', 女士 *neu$_o$shyh* 'miss' (often also applied to a married woman, as in English).

(7) 親 -.*chin* 'next of kin', only in 父親 *fuh.chin* 'father and 母親 *muu.chin* 'mother'.

(8) 夫 -.*fu* 'man', as in 丈夫 *janq.fu* 'husband', 姐夫 *jiee.fu* 'older sister's husband', 妹夫 *mey.fu* 'younger sister's husband', 車夫 *che.fu* 'vehicle driver' (but *chihchefu* 'chauffeur'), 馬夫 *maa$_o$fu* 'groom', 轿夫 *jiaw$_o$fu* 'sedan chair carrier', 農夫 *nong$_o$fu* 'farmer'. In 姑夫 *gu.fu* and 姨夫 *yi.fu* 'husband of aunt on father's and mother's side, respectively', polite epistolary usage has 父 *fuh* 'father, i.e., person of senior generation to myself rather than 夫 *fu* 'husband', both sounding alike in the neutral tone. In the Wu dialects however, *fuh* 'father' would be pronounced *vuh*, which is not their pronunciation in the terms of address for husbands of aunts. On the other hand, in *shy.fuh* 'master tutor,— master', always written 师傅, the second morpheme has always had a voiceless initial and yet it is *syvuh* in the Wu dialects. This can only be described as a compound of different etymons, the second etymon being that for 'father' in the Wu dialects.

The words 工夫 *gong.fu* 'time, time spent at work', 豆付(～ 荳腐) *dow.fu* 'beancurd', 皮膚 *pyi.fu* 'skin', 衣服 *i.fwu* 'clothes', and 舒服 *shu.fwu* 'comfortable' can be regarded as morpheme words, or, if they are analyzed as compounds, the second parts should be regarded as unrelated homophones of *fu* 'man'.

(9) 家 -.*jia* ~ .*jie* 'home, the so-an-so's, as in 張家 *Jang.jia* 'the

Jangs', 王家 *Wang.jia* 'the Wangs', 自家 *tzyh.jia* 'oneself', 咱家
*tzarn.jia* 'ourselves', 谁家 *sheir.jia* 'whose family', 姑娘家
*gu.niang.jia* 'young womenfolk', 小孩子家 *sheau-hairtz.jia*
'young folks', 行家 *harng_0 jia* 'those in the line,—professionals'.
This is to be distinguished both from the adverbial suffix -*.jia* ∼
*.jie* (4.4.7.2) and from the full-toned modern suffix -*jia* '-ist' (4.4.3.
11).

(10) 心 -*.shin* 'heart, mind', as in 良心 *liang.shin* 'conscience',
恶心 *ee.shin* 'nauseating, nauseated', 耐心 *nay.shin* 'patience';
but 忠心 *jongshin* 'faithful heart,—loyal', 同情心 *torngchyng-shin* 'sympathy', 自信心 *tzyhshinnshin* 'self-confidence', and the
like, with full tone on *shin*, should be regarded as regular com-
pounds of full morphemes.

(11) 性 -*.shinq* 'nature, temperament', as in 记性 *jih.shinq*
'memory', 常性 *charng.shinq* 'constancy, perseverance', 耐性
*nay.shinq* 'patience'.[23]

(12) 錢 -*.chyan* 'money', as in 价錢 *jiah.chyan* 'price money,
—price', 本錢 *been.chyan* 'cost (in trade)', 利錢 *lih.chyan*
'profit money,—interest', 租錢 *tzu.chyan* 'rent', 房錢 *farng.chyan*
'rent (for a house)', 酒錢 *jeou.chyan* 'pourboire,—tip'. In 榆錢
(ル) *yu.chyan* ∼ *yu.chyal* 'elm seeds (which are supposed to look
like coins)' it is *chyan* in the sense of 'coin'.

(13 气 -*.chih* 'air, essence', as in nouns: 天气 *tian_0 chih*
'weather', 脾气 *pyi.chih* 'temperament, temper', 勇气 *yeong-_0 chih* 'courage', 骨气 *gwu_0 chih* 'backbone' (fig.), 才气 *tsair_0 chih*
'talent', 习气 *shyi.chih* 'bad taste, mannerism'; adjectives: 客气
*keh.chih* 'polite, courteous', 俗气 *swu.chih* 'common, vulgar', 丧
气 *sanq.chih* 'in bad luck', 小气 *sheau.chih* 'small, stingy', 大气
*dah.chih* 'generous, in good taste' (last two often also written
with 器 'untensil, capacity, ability'); nouns and adjectives: 福气

---

[23]In the Central dialects, which do not distinguish between -*in* and -*ing*,
there are still more overlapping cases of (10) and (11). Hence the popular
belief that eating chicken's heart (鸡心 *jishin*) improves the memory (记
性 *jih.shinq*), especially in the Soochow dialect, in which tone sandhi makes
both *jih* and *ji* high level (sec. 3.3.1).

*fwu.chih* 'good luck, lucky', 運气 *yunn.chih* 'luck (good or bad), lucky', 晦气 *huey.chih* 'bad luck, unlucky', 神气 *shern.chih* 'expression', also, as a borrowing from the Wu dialects, 'expressive, lively'.

(14) 和 -.*hwo* 'nice and', as in 暖和 *noan.hwo* 'nice and warm', 软和 *roan.hwo* 'nice and soft', 温和儿 *uen.hwol* 'lukewarm', 快活 *kuay.hwo* 'happy', the last written 活, but sometimes felt as the same morpheme as in the other words.

(15) 腾 -.*teng* 'with quick and repeated activity', as in 翻腾 *fan.teng* 'upsets and stirs up', 折腾 *je.teng* or *je.deng* 'changes and overturns', 搗腾 *daur.teng* 'stirs and upsets', 宣腾 *shiuan-.teng* 'makes noises and stirs', 鬧腾 *naw.teng* 'disturbs and makes noises', 叨腾 *dau.teng* 'talks and fusses'. The writing of *teng* with 腾 *terng* 'rises, rears, soars' is probably folk etymology.

(16) 是 -.*sh(yh)* 'is', as in 但是 *dann.sh* 'but', 可是 *kee.sh* 'but', 就是 *jiow.sh* 'namely, even if', 要是 *yaw.sh* 'if', 若是 *ruoh.sh* 'if', 倒是 *daw.sh* 'is indeed (contrary to expectation)', 凡是 *farn.sh* 'in all cases', 老是 *lao.sh* 'all the time, always', 总是 *tzoong.sh* 'in all cases, always', 横是 *herng.sh* (一横竖 *herng-shuh*) 'horizontal or vertical,—anyway'. Dragunov (38, Chinese transl., 29) notes that in the Kansu-Shensi dialects *sh* (pron. *syh*) is also a particle for the subject position, as in 这个人是不是工人. *Jehg ren-syh bu-syh gongren.* 'This man *subject marker* is not a workman.'

*4.4.3. Modern Suffixes.* Modern suffixes are not in the neutral tone and are mostly, though not exclusively, nouns or bound nouns (i.e., nouns in L or centers in compound nouns), and thus no different from other cases of centers of subordinate compounds. They are called suffixes because they often come from translating foreign suffixes, as 论 *luenn* '-ism' 'theory', in 惟心论 *weishinluenn* 'only-mind theory,—idealism', 炎 *yan* 'inflammation, -itis' in 盲腸炎 *mangcharngyan* 'blind-intestine inflammation,—appendicitis'. By analogy these suffixes are used also in words not corresponding to any foreign word with a suffix. Thus, there is 科学化 *keshyuehuah* 'makes scientific', but Merriam-

Webster (2d ed.) marks 'scientize' as "Rare". Following are the commonest modern suffixes:

(1) 化 -*huah* '-ize, -ify', as in 机械化 *jishiehhuah* 'mechanize', 工業化 *gongyehhuah* 'industrialize', 合理化 *herliihuah* 'rationalize', 美化 *meeihuah* 'beautify', 美國化 *Meeigwohuah* 'Americanize', 具体化 *jiuhtihuah* 'become or make concrete', 软化 *roanhuah* 'soften', 腐化 *fuuhuah* 'become corrupt', 赤化 *chyhhuah* 'make or become red (communist)', 恶化 *ehhuah* 'worsen', 尖鋭化 *jianrueyhuah* 'become acute'; '-ide', as in 氯化 鈉 *liuhhuah-nah* 'sodium chloride', 硫化氫 *liouhuah-ching* 'hydrogen sulfide'.

(2) 的 -*dih* '-tic, -al', as in 科学的 *keshyuedih* 'scientific', 政 治的 *jenqjyhdih* 'political'. This -*dih* is written with the same character 的 as the general subordinative suffix *de*, which has a reading pronunciation *dih* < *tiek*, Cantonese *tek*, and so transliterates very well English '-tic'. This was much used during the first quarter of this century, when most writing was in wenyan, and so it was possible to distinguish between 技術的问題 *jihshuhdih wenntyi* 'a technical question' and 技術之问題 *jihshuh jy wenntyi* 'a question of technique'. Now that most writing is in the spoken style and the particle *jy* becomes -*de*, with the same character 的 , this difference will have to come out of the context, unless one goes into rewordings such as *jihshuhshinqde* 'technical in nature', as under (3) below. On other uses of *dih* vs. *de*, see section 4.4.6 below.

(3) 性 -*shinq* '-ity, -ness', as in 可能性 *keenengshinq* 'possibility', 必然性 *bihranshinq* 'necessity', 普遍性 *puubiannshinq* 'universality', 弹性 *tarnshinq* 'elasticity', 伸缩性 *shensuoshinq* 'elasticity, flexibility', 嚴重性 *yanjonqshinq* 'gravity, seriousness', 片面性 *piannmiannshinq* 'onesidedness', 重要性 *jonqyawshinq* 'importance', 酸性 *suanshinq* 'acid(ity)', 鹼性 *jeanshinq* 'alkaline, -ity'. This modern suffix, which is never in the neutral tone, should be distinguished from its less productive cognate -.*shinq* 'nature, temperament' under 4.4.1 (11) above.

(4) 論 -*luenn* 'theory, -ism', as in 惟心論 *weishinluenn* 'idealism', 惟物論 *weiwuhluenn* 'materialism', 一元論 *iyuanluenn*

'monism', 多元论 *duoyuanluenn* 'pluralism', 天演论 *tianyean-luenn* 'theory of evolution', 相对论 *shiangdueyluenn* 'theory of relativity', 方法论 *fangfaaluenn* 'methodology'.

(5) 观 *-guan* '(point of) view, outlook', as in 主观 *juuguan* 'subjective', 客观 *kehguan*         'objective', 人生观 *renshengguan* 'philosophy of life, *Lebensanschauung*', 宇宙观 *yeujowguan* 'universe outlook, *Weltanschauung*', 乐观 *lehguan* 'optimism, -istic', 悲观 *beiguan* 'pessimism, -istic'.

(6) 率 *-liuh* 'rate of', as in 速率 *suhliuh* 'velocity', 效率 *shiawliuh* 'effect-rate,—efficiency, 生產率 *shengchaanliuh* 'rate of production'.

(7) 法 *-faa* 'method', as in 分析法 *fen.shifaa* 'method of analysis', 演绎法 *yeanyihfaa* 'deduction', 归纳法 *gueinahfaa* 'induction', 十進法 *shyrjinnfaa* 'decimal system', 比较法 *bii-jeaufaa* 'comparative method'. (Cf. *-.fa* sec. 4.4.5.7).

(8) 界 *-jieh* 'the world of', as in 教育界 *jiaw$_o$yuhjieh* 'the educational world', 政界 *jenqjieh* 'the political circles', 金融界 *jinrongjieh* 'the financial circles'.

(9) 炎 *-yan* 'inflammation, -itis', as in 盲腸炎 *mangcharng-yan* 'appendicitis', 腦膜炎 *naomohyan* 'meningitis', 肺炎 *feyyan* 'pneumonia', 扁桃腺炎 *beantaurshiannyan* 'tonsilitis'.

(10) 学 *-$_o$shyue* '-ology, -ics', as in 数学 *shuh$_o$shyue* 'mathematics', *huah$_o$shyue* 'chemistry', 医学 *i$_o$shyue* 'medicine', 哲学 *jer$_o$shyue* 'philosophy'. If there is more than one syllable preceding *shyue*, then the suffix is optional, as 物理学 *wuhliishyue* 'physics', more commonly *wuhlii*, but it is usually included if there is possible ambiguity, as 動物 *donq.wuh* 'animal': *donq.wuhshyue* 'zoology', 心理 *shinlii* '(the) psychology (of something)': *shinliishyue* 'psychology (as a subject)'.

(11) 家 *-jia* '-ist', as in 作家 *tzuohjia* '(professional) writer', 科学家 *keshyuejia* 'scientist', 理论家 *liiluennjia* 'theorist', 天文学家 *tianwenshyuejia* 'astronomer', 教育家 *jiaw$_o$yuhjia* 'educator', 政治家 *jenqjyhjia* 'political scientist', 'statesman', 体育家 *tii$_o$yuhjia* 'physical educationist', 運動家 *yunn$_o$donqjia* 'ath-

lete'. This *jia* with full tone is to be distinguished from *.jia* ~ *.jie* (secs. 4.4.2.9 and 4.4.7.2.)

(12) 員 *-yuan* 'member of a group', as in 教員 *jiawyuan* 'instructor', *jyryuan* 'member of an administrative staff', 人員 *renyuan* 'personnel', 教職員 *jiawjyryuan* 'faculty and staff', 海員 *haeyuan* 'seamen', 飛行員 *feishyngyuan* 'flier, pilot', 议員 *yihyuan* 'legislator', 僱員 *guhyuan* 'employee'.

*4.4.4. Noun Suffixes.* By far the most numerous noun suffixes, lexically as well as textually, are zero, *-l*, and *-tz;* the others, *-.tou, -.ba,* and *-.men,* are much less frequent.

(0) Zero. As stated above, we have found it convenient to regard unsuffixed morpheme words as having a suffix zero. In general there is no special class meaning associated with the zero suffix for nouns, but two exceptions are worth special mention: (a) As has been noted above, monosyllabic family names are not free, so that a person with the family name of 張 *Jang* and personal name of 飛 *Fei* will have to be called either (1) *Jang Shian.sheng* or (2) *Lao Jang* or (3) *Jang Fei,* but not °*Jang*. However, his mother or his wife can call him *Fei*. The reason is that *Fei* is free, with a zero suffix whose class meaning is that of endearment or intimacy, and this is applicable to all monosyllabic personal names, or monosyllabic abbreviations of dissyllabic personal names. (b) Very often, a polysyllabic verbal expression V can stand for 'one who V's, thus making zero an agent suffix. One can of course form agent nouns with the suffixes *-jee* and *de,* as in 卖 柑者 *mayganjee* L 'tangerine vendor', or 看门的 *kanmende* 'watch door -er, —doorman'. But in 司馬 *Symaa* 'Tends horses, —chevalier', a common family name both in Chinese and in French, we have zero suffix for the (Chinese) agent word. Similarly: 编辑 *bian.jih* 'compile, edit' and 'editor'; 幹事 *gannshyh* 'execute affairs' and 'executive secretary'; 跑街 *paojie* 'run the streets' and 'messenger boy'.

(1) *-l* is the only suffix which is nonsyllabic. It is often regarded as a diminutive suffix, but actually the *-l* forms have come from three different etymons: (a) the localizer 裡 *-lii* 'in', forming with demonstratives place words, (b) 日 *ryh* 'day' B forming names

of days with reference to the present, and (c) 兒 *erl* 'child', which has become the diminutive suffix proper.[24]

(a) The strong forms of the place words 这裡 *jeh.lii* 'here', 那裡 *nah.lii* 'there', and 哪裡 *naa.lii* 'where', which are very formal in style, are normally spoken as 这儿 *jell* (or *jall*), 那儿 *nall* (or *nell*), and 哪儿 *naal*, respectively. When used as compound postpositions, *jell* and *nall* are further weakened into the neutral tone, as in *woo.jell* 'where I am, *chez moi*', *nii.nall* 'where you are, *chez vous*'.

(b) In the strong forms, 今日 *jinryh* 'today' is L, but when *ryh* is reduced to -*l* (which in our GR orthography stands for [ ɹ ][25], we have *jin* + -*l* → *jiel*,which is the everyday word for 'today'. Similarly, we have 昨儿 *tzwol* 'yesterday', 明儿 *miengl* 'tomorrow', 前儿 *chyal* 'day before yesterday', 後儿 *howl* 'day after tomorrow', 大前儿 *dahchyal* 'day before day before yesterday', 大後儿 *dahhowl* 'day after day after tomorrow', and 几儿 *jieel* 'what day of the month'. There are of course also the alternate names of the days with 天 -.*tian* in *jin.tian, tzwo.tian, ming-.tian, chyan.tian, how.tian, dahchyan.tian,* and *dahhow.tian,* which are neutral in style and slightly less informal than the words ending in -*l*.

(c) The suffix -*l* < *erl* has been regarded as a diminutive suffix because its original meaning is 'child', whence 'smallness', but

---

[24] 徐知白, 释'兒'与'子'(Shyu Jybair, "On *Erl* and *Tzyy*") 中和月刊 (*Jongher Yuehkan*), 1:68 (1940), quotes Duh Fuu's lines:

细雨鱼兒出, *Shih yeu yu erl chu,*
微風燕子斜. *Wei feng yann tzyy shye.*
'Fine rain, and the fish come out.
'Light breeze, and swallows slant (their wings).'

and comments on the fact that neither *erl* nor *tzyy* means 'child' but both are suffixes. This is no doubt true as to function and meaning, but the position of *erl* filling an Even Tone syllable in the meter also shows that it was phonologically quite full.

[25]The closeness of the syllable *ryh* and the suffix -*l* is even greater in the dialect of Sian, Shensi, in which *ryhtz* 'date' and *erltz* 'son' are both pronounced *erltz*.

as actually used now it usually serves to mark a form as a noun. The only exceptions are a few verbs of which only one is in ordinary language, as shown in the table:

| Verb | | Style | Approximate Equivalent |
|---|---|---|---|
| 玩儿 | *wal* | ordinary | 'to play' |
| 火儿了 | *huoolle* | slang | 'got mad' |
| 颠儿了 | *dialle* | slang | 'beat it, scram' |
| 蔼儿了 | *geelle* | slang | 'died, kicked the bucket' |
| 皮儿了 | *pyelle* | slang | ditto |
| 狠儿 | *heel* | children's language | 'makes (for fun) a fierce sound' |
| 闷儿 | *mhel* | children's language | 'says "mhel!"',—peekaboo' |

Semantically, the diminutive suffix starts from the idea of smallness and shades off through the speaker's attitude of regarding the thing as small and thence to almost nothing but a change of grammatical function with or without change of meaning from that of the root morpheme. Examples of various types of meanings of the suffix *-l* are:

(c.1) Smallness, as in 球儿 *chyoul* 'globule': *chyou* 'ball', 绳儿 *sherngl* 'cord': *sherngtz* 'rope'.

(c.2) Lightness of tone or style, that is, regarded by speaker as small or trivial, as in 官儿 *gual* 'an official (who cares?)': *guan* 'an official'; 弦儿 *shyal* 'string (of a popular musical instrument)': *shyan* 'string (of a classical musical instrument, such as the 琴 *chyn* 'zither')': *shyantz* 'string (of any instrument)' or 'three-stringed plucked instrument', also called 三弦 *sanshyan*.

(c.3) Various extensions of meaning, as in 天 *tian* 'sky' or 'weather': *tial* 'weather', 肠子 *charngtz* 'intestine': *charngl* 'intestines as food, —sausage', 信 *shinn* 'letter': *shiell* 'message, news'.

More important and more amenable to consistent analysis are the various structural types of the *-l* forms. It should be noted that the occurrence of this suffix is a lexical matter and that, however versatile it is, the versatility is not unlimited. The lexical facts, however, must be gathered from the recording of actual speech as heard or at least from realistic dialogues rather than the usual bairhuah texts, since much of what is written by non-native speakers of Mandarin seems to be the result of a liberal sprinkling of handfuls of *erl*'s on the pages, rather than the writing of speech.[26] In the following examples, types 1.1 and 1.6 are simple suffixed words. Types 1.7 through 1.14 are either suffixed compounds (decompounds) or compounds in which at least one constituent is a suffixed word.

(1.1) Type $N_B$ -*l* → N. This is the commonest type, consisting of a bound monosyllabic morpheme plus -*l*. Since the root is bound, it belongs to no part of speech, for example, in 伴 *bann* + -*l* → *ball* 'companion', is *bann* being used as the verb 'accompanies' or as noun 'companion'? Sometimes one can refer to wenyan and say that *bann* L does occur as a noun. In most cases one can also refer to compounds in which the root in question occurs as the center of a nominal compound or as the object and thus decide that it is nominal. For example, *parn* occurs as center in 棋盤 *chyiparn* 'chessboard', and hence the *parn* as root in *parl* or *parntz* 'tray' can also be regarded as nominal. Sometimes one can apply the definition of a noun as the name of a person or thing in such roots as 猴 *hour* in *hourl* 'monkey', 花 *hua* in *hual* 'flower', 繩 *sherng* in *sherngl* 'cord', though it is never safe to depend upon semantic definitions. Following are some more examples of $N_B$ -*l* → N.

Nouns with -*l* only: 核儿 *hwul* 'stone (of a fruit)', 谜儿 *mell* 'riddle', 鸟儿 *neaul* 'bird', 瓤儿 *rangl* 'pulp', 味儿 *well* 'odor, taste'. Some polysyllabic roots in iambs: 胡同儿 *hwutonql* 'lane' (in names of streets in Peiping, the form is in neutral tone without suffix, as in 元宝胡同 *Yuanbao .Hwu.tonq* 'Ingot Lane'), 蝴蝶儿 *huhtieel* 'butterfly' (reading pron. *hwudye*), 旮旯儿 *galal* 'nook', 犄角儿 *jijeaul* 'corner' (cf. *ji.jeau* 'horn'), 靠不輪儿 *kaw.buluel* 'press against-*infix*-wheel-er, —clutch (of an automobile)' (half-transliteration, half-translation of the British term 'coupler'). Roots in trochees: 胍肭儿 *gu.dul* 'bud' (Conc Dict, 176), 轂轆儿 *gu.lul*

---

[26]The Chao-Yang *Conc Dict* seems to be the only place where the use of the suffixes zero, -*l*, and -*tz*, based on observation of the Peiping dialect, has been recorded for all the common morphemes of the language.

'wheel', 蜘蛛儿 *ji.liaul* 'cicada'. There are the adjective□□儿 *u.tul* 'lukewarm' and the verb (打) 出溜 *chu.lioul ~ daa-chu.lioul* 'slides', but most polysyllables in *-l* are nouns.

Nouns with *-l* or *-tz* with the same meaning except for a slight diminutive effect in the *-l* forms: 虫儿 *chorngl~chorngtz* 'insect', 豆儿 *dowl~dowtz* 'bean', 座儿 *tzuoll~tzuohtz* 'stand, base' (cf. *tzuoll* 'seat' above, which has no *-tz* form), 影儿 *yeengl~yiingtz* 'shadow' (but 電影儿 *diannyeengl* 'movie', a decompound).

Nouns with *-l* different in meaning from those with *-tz*: 本儿 *beel* 'cost (in trade)', but *beel~beentz* 'booklet', 鼻儿 *byel* 'noselike object' ≠ *byitz* 'nose', 頂儿 *dieengl* 'top (of anything)' ≠ *diingtz* 'knob (Mandarin buttons on official hats to indicate rank)', 苗儿 *miaul* 'shoots, sprouts', ≠ *Miautz* 'the Miao people'.

(1.2) Type N-*l* → N. A free noun may take the suffix *-l* with or without a change in meaning. We shall also compare these with the *-tz* forms.

Nouns with suffix zero, *-l*, or *-tz* with no difference except lightness of tone in *-l*: 魂 *hwen~hwel* 'soul, spirit', 盆 *pern~perl~perntz* 'basin', 事 *shyh~shell* 'event, business, job', 字 *tzyh~tzell* 'word, character'.

Nouns in which adding *-l* and/or *-tz* makes an important difference: 水 *shoei* 'water' ≠ *shoel* 'watery part, juice', 板 *baan* 'board' or 'beat (in music)', but *baal~baantz* 'board' (only), 烟 *ian* 'smoke (in general) or '(tobacco) smoke' ≠ *ial* 'smoke (in general)', but 烟煤子 *ianmeitz* 'soot' and 鍋烟子 *guoiantz* 'soot on pots', 瓶 *pyng* 'vase' ≠ *pyngtz* 'jar, bottle' ~ *pyengl* 'bottle', 词 *tsyr* 'verse of unequal lines' or 'word (in linguistic sense)' ≠ *tserl* 'words (of a song or a play)', ≠ *tsyrtz* (obsolescent) 'verse of unequal lines'.

(1.3) Type M-*l* → N. Classfiers, or M's for individual physical objects suffixed with *-l*, become nouns, with the class meaning of 'size, shape, or quality (of the thing)', as in 个 *g* (i.e., *-geh*) general individualizing M: *gehl~-tz* 'size, stature'; 塊 *kuay* 'piece, lump': *kuall* 'size, shape of piece'; 条 *tyau* 'strip': *tyaul* 'length, thickness (of strip)'; 片 *piann* 'slice': *piall* 'size, thickness of slice'; 粒 *lih* 'granule': *liell* 'size, roundness of granule'; 張 *jang* 'sheet': *jangl* 'size or thickness of sheet', 張 *jang* M for mahjong, domino, or card pieces: *jangl* (more commonly *jangtz*) 'quality of piece for the particular hand'. Note that this is not applicable to units of measure or quasi-measures, there being no ° 里 儿 °*lieel* for 'mileage' or ° 课 儿 °*kehl* for 'quality or length of a lesson'.

(1.4) Type M-*l* → M. Certain M's have an optional suffix -*l* without any difference in meaning. In these cases, even the lightness in tone is minimal. Examples are: 分 *fenn* ～ *fell* 'share', 剳 *dar*～*darl* 'stack, pad', 本 *been*～*beel* 'volume (of books, etc.)', 朶 *duoo*～*duool* 'blossom', 節 *jye*～*jyel* 'section', 对 *duey*～ *duell* 'pair', but 一个对子 *ig dueytz* 'a couplet': 一付对子 *i.fuh dueytz* 'a pair of scrolls'.

(1.5) Type V-*l* → N. Nouns for the action: 唱 *chanq* 'sing': *chanql* 'song', 印 *yinn* 'to print' or 'a seal': *yell* 'imprint, mark', 缝 *ferng* 'sew': *fenql* (with change of tone) 'seam', also 'a crack'.

Nouns for goals of action: 包 *bau* 'to wrap': *baul* 'package' ≠ *bautz* 'bun with stuffing'; 掛 *guah* 'hang': 褂儿 *guall* 'garment hung from shoulder,—(unlined) coat'; 画 *huah* 'draw': *huall* 'picture'; 賺 *juann* 'earn': *juall* 'earning'.

Nouns for agent or instrument of action: 塞 *sai* 'stop up': *sal* ～*saitz* 'stopper'; 盖 *gay* 'to cover': *gall*～*gaytz* 'lid'.

(1.6) Type A-*l* → N. Nouns of quality: 亮 *lianq* 'bright': *lianql* 'light'; 好 *hao* 'good', *haol*, as in 带个好儿给... *day g haol geei* ... 'give my regards to ...', 落了一个好儿 *lawle ig haol* 'got praised', 叫好 (儿) *jiaw hao(l)* 'says "bravo!"', i.e., to express applause by calling *Hao!* 空 *konq* 'vacant, free': *konql* 'vacancy, leisure'; 弯 *uan* 'bent': *ual* 'a bend', 'a corner in the road'; 方 *fang* 'square': *fangl* 'a square' ≠ *fangtz* 'a prescription'.

Nouns for things with the quality: 黃 *hwang* 'yellow': *hwangl* 'yolk'; 单 *dan* 'single': *dal*～*dantz* 'sheet, tablecloth' or 'items arranged on one sheet, —a list'.

From the following type 1.7 on, as noted before, there are at least two morphemes besides the suffix -*l*. In a combination X-Y -*l* it is sometimes uncertain whether the ICs are X + Y-*l* (a compound) or XY + -*l* (a suffixed compound, i.e., a decompound). In principle, if neither XY nor Y-*l* occurs as a word, then XY should be treated as a bound compound and is free only when suffixed. In practice, however, it is often a matter of degree. For example, 瓜 - 子儿 *guatzeel* 'melon seeds' is *gua* + *tzeel*, since *tzeel* is a word and there is no such compound as °*guatzyy*. But 酒窩儿 *jeouuol* 'wine vortex,—dimple' seems to be a decompound XY + -*l*, since there is neither °*jeouuo* nor *uol*. On the other hand, there are 热 - 窩儿 *rehuol* 'warm nest, cozy place' and 動窩儿 *donq-uol* ~ 挪 - 窩儿 *nuo-uol* 'move (from one's) nest' (lit. or fig.), where *uol* is versatile enough to be the center of an A-N or an object of a V-O construction.

The matter of lexical or idiomatic meaning is, as usual, not invariably paralleled by structure, for example, 小馬儿 *sheau-maal* '(just any) small horse', but 小脚儿 *sheau-jeaul* '(any) small feet' or 'bound feet'. The following are of the compound or decompound types.

(1.7) Type A + X-*l* → N. This construction is very productive, with or without lexical specialization, as 後院儿 *how-yuall* 'backyard', 老头儿 *laotourl* ~ *laotourtz* 'old man', 老婆儿 *laoporl* 'old woman' ( ≠ *lao.por* 'the woman, wife'), 小燕儿 *sheauyall* 'swallow' (cf. 大雁 *dahyann* 'swan' or 'wild goose'), 小孩儿 *sheauharl* ~ *sheauhairtz* 'child', 雜拌儿 *tzarball* 'miscellaneous mixture, —mixed candies, nuts, etc.' If X is a free noun N, then *Sheau-N-l* is of unlimited productivity, as 小人儿 *sheaurel* 'little man', 小樹儿 *sheaushull* 'little tree', sometimes with lexical specialization, as 小米 $sheau_omii$ ~ $sheau_omieel$ 'millet'.

(1.8) Type N + X-*l* → N. This is another very productive form (though not of unlimited productivity), whether X is free or bound. We are taking the initial N in the wide sense of a nominal morpheme [see (1.1) above]. Examples are: 杏仁儿 *shinqrel* 'apricot kernel,—almond', 门口儿 *menkooul* 'doorway', 狗牙儿 *goouyal* 'dog-teeth,—serration', 被窩儿 *bey'uol* 'made-up bed' ( ≠ *bey.uo* 'bedding'), 鬼臉儿 *goeileal* 'mask', 桑椹儿 *sangrell* 'mulberry berry', 眼鏡儿 *yeanjienql* ~ *yeanjinqtz* 'eyeglasses', 餅干儿 *biinggal* 'biscuit, cracker', 葡萄干儿 *pwu-.taurgal* 'grape dry-let,—raisin', 飯館儿 *fanngoal* ~ *fanngoantz*

~ *goantz* 'restaurant', 字纸篓儿 *tzyhjyylooul* 'wastepaper basket', 栀子花儿 *jytz₀hual* 'gardenia', 走之儿 *tzoooujel* '(radical which means) "walks" (and looks like the L particle) 之 *jy*, —radical 162', 嘎儿枣儿 *gar.gatzaol* 'jujube with rhombus vertical section'. Cases with X as a verb are less common. Examples are 锅贴儿 *guotiel* 'pot stick -er,—baked (not boiled) wrappling', 脚印儿 *jeauyell* 'footprint'.

A minority of this type has the last syllable in the neutral tone, as 笛膜儿 *dyi.moll* '(Chinese) flute membrane (over one hole, giving it a reedy timbre)', 媳妇儿 *shyi.fel* 'daughter-in-law' or 'wife'. Demonstratives followed by 边儿 -.*bial* 'side', 会儿 -.*hoel* 'moment', and □儿-.*hel* 'place or moment' are of unlimited productivity, though the total list is quite short, as *jeh.hoel* 'this moment', *neei.hel* 'where (abouts)?'

(1.9) Type V + X-*l* → N. This type is found in 别针儿 *bye-jel* 'pin', 玩意儿 *wanyell* 'toy', 顶针儿 *diing₀jel* 'push needle -er,—thimble', 拨鱼儿 *boyuel* 'push fish -er, —boiled soft dough (pushed into boiling soup like little fish)', 围嘴儿 *weitzoel* ~ -*tzoeitz* 'bib', 围脖儿 *weiborl* 'muffler' (clothing), ( 洋 ) 取灯儿 (*yang*-) *cheudengl* '(foreign) get light -er,—matches', 跑堂儿 (的) *paotarngl* ~ -*de* '(one who) runs in the hall,—waiter'.

(1.10) Type V + X-*l* → V + O. If X-*l* is a free noun then any transitive verb may take it as an object, resulting in a verb-object phrase, as 看画儿 *kann-huall* 'look at pictures', often with idiomatic meaning, as 起头儿 *chii-tourl* 'begin', 拐湾儿 *goai-ual* 'turn a corner', 挑眼儿 *tiau-yeal* 'pick an opening,—find fault', 找碴儿 *jao-charl* 'look for cracks,—find fault'. If X-*l* is not free, then the result is a V-O compound, though, as usual, always ionizable. Examples are 摸黑儿 *mhohel* 'grope in the dark', 抓阄儿 *jua jioul* or 捻阄儿 *nhian jioul* 'draw lot', 抓周(儿) *jua jou(l)* 'grab (at things on) first birthday' (first thing touched tells baby's future profession), 包原儿 *bauyual* 'buy up remainder of the stock', 打雜儿 *daatzarl* 'do sundry things (mainly outdoors)', also used as 'one who does ...'.

(1.11) Type X-*l* + Y. As first part in a compound, -*l* forms are rare. With second part as noun, resulting in a noun, we have 片儿湯 *pialltarng* '(thin dough) slices soup', 毛儿戲 *maulshih* 'play with an all-woman cast (impersonating men when needed)', 猴儿筋 *hourljin* ~ 猴筋儿 *hourjiel* 'monkey muscle,—rubber band'. There is an optional *-l* in 哈吧(儿)狗 *ha.be(l)goou* 'bulldog' varying also with *haa.bagooul, balgoou*. I used to say *ba.erlgoou* (in three syllables), which was probably due to influence of Paoting, where I lived for a time as a child.

There is of course no limit to a form with X-*l* as subject followed by a predicate. Some of these, however, have idiomatic meanings and are often used as an SP predicate. Examples are 眼儿热 *yeal reh* 'eyes hot, —envious', also as a transitive verb 'to covet', 胆儿大 *daal dah* ~ *danntz dah* 'brave', 胆儿小 *daal sheau* ~ *daantz sheau* 'timid', 子儿衝 *tzeel chonq* (slang) 'pennies gushing, —has plenty of dough'.

(1.12) Type X-*l* + Y-*l*. This is extremely rare. The only examples I have come across are 娘儿们儿 *niangl.mel* 'womenfolk' and, less frequently, 爺儿们儿 *ye'l.mel* 'menfolk'. The form 哥儿俩儿 *ge'l-leal* 'the brothers two' or 'the two fellows' is not as common as the shorter *ge'l-lea*. The form 華儿ʾ²! *hwal hwal...!* 'kitty, kitty,...!' should be regarded as a simple X-*l* repeated as separate words and so does not belong here.

(1.13) Type *i*-X-*l*. With *i* 'one, a' and an M with -*l*, we have a few idiomatic compounds, as 一会儿 *ihoel* 'a while', 一点儿 *ideal* 'a little', and an unlimited number of transient words, as 一片儿 *i-piall* 'a slice', 一根儿 *i-gel* 'a stick of', 一樣儿 *i-yanql* ~ zero 'a kind of' (note that the adjective *iyang* 'same' always has zero suffix).

A few of such forms are adverbs: 一早儿 *itzaol* 'from morning', 一塊儿 *ikuall* 'together', 一順儿 *ishuell* 'in the same direction', 一送儿 *isonql* 'one way (trip)', 一头儿 *itourl...itourl* 'on the one hand,...at the same time on the other hand', 一死儿 *iseel* 'all the way to death, —insistently'.[27]

---

[27]Because the usual procedure in compiling dictionaries is to go to published sources only, the volume on *i*,   王雲五，  中山大辞典一字

(1.14) Type XX-*l*. Under this there are the distributive forms, as 回ㄹㄦ *hweihwel* 'every time' and vivid forms as 嚴ㄹㄦ (的) *yan'ial* (*de*) 'good and tight'. As these have been discussed under reduplication (sec. 4.2.4), we shall not repeat the details here.

(2) Suffix -*tz*, like suffix -*l*, is also cognate with a full morpheme meaning 'child', in this case 子 *tzyy*. As a full morpheme it can be a noun, as in 这个鱼没子. *Jeyg yu mei tzyy*. 'This fish has no eggs', or can form compounds, as 原子 *yuantzyy* 'prime particle, —atom', 質子 *jyrtzyy* 'fundamental particle', 子弹 *tzyydann* 'cartridge'. It can even be in the neutral tone as in 孟子 *Menq.tzyy* 'Mencius (as a school text)', *Menq Tzyy* 'Mencius (the man or the book)'. It can also take the diminutive suffix -*l* and form *tzeel* 'seed' or 'penny' or 'money' (slang), which also enters in compounds as in 鸡子ㄦ *jiitzeel* 'hen's eggs'. In Southern Mandarin there is even 子ㄹ *tzyytz* 'granules'.

As a suffix -*tz* is similar to -*l* in many respects, both in form and in meaning, but it also differs from it in some important respects. Although it means 'child' etymologically, it has no diminutive effect or lightness of tone, its chief function being to nominalize. There are a few broad statistical tendencies, as Dragunov has observed (secs. 60-69), such as -*l* for part (盖ㄦ *gall* 'lid') and -*tz* for whole ( 剪子 *jeantz* 'scissors'), -*l* for the abstract (魂ㄦ *hwel* 'soul') and -*tz* for the concrete ( 身子 *shentz* 'body'), -*l* for the generic ( 鸟ㄦ *neaul* 'bird') and -*tz* for the specific ( 鸽子 *getz* 'pigeon'), but these observations do not exclude a considerable number of contrary cases, such as concrete 门ㄦ *mel* 'door' and abstract 门子 *mentz* 'pull, influence', concrete 面ㄦ *miall* 'surface' or 'powder' and abstract *mianntz* 'face (the kind you save or lose)'.

As the structural types of the -*tz* forms are quite similar to those of the -*l* forms, we shall number the subtypes with the same numbers. The lexical occurrence with the root forms will of course be very different.

---

長编 (Wang Yunwuu, ed., *The Sunyatsen Dictionary: Long Section on I*), Hong Kong, 1938, 478 pp., has no *iseel*, although it contains 5,474 entries with *i*.

(2.1) Type N$_B$-*tz* → N. This and the next type are quite similar to, but lexically richer than, the corresponding -*l* types. As in the case of -*l*, some -*tz* forms are no more than merely nominalized while others have quite specialized meanings. Examples are: 棒子 *banqtz* '(Indian) corn' ≠ F 'rod, club', 妻子 *chitz* 'wife' ≠ *chitzyy* 'wife and children' L, 厨子 *chwutz* 'cook', 凳子 *denqtz* ' stool', 对子 *dueytz* 'couplet, pair of scrolls', 肚子 *duhtz* 'abdomen', 肚子 *duutz* 'stomach (as food), tripe', 兒子 *erltz* 'child', 方子 *fangtz* 'prescription (for drugs)', 房子 *farngtz* 'house', 菓子 *guootz* 'fried puffy doughnuts' ≠ 水菓(儿) *shoeiguoo(l)* 'fruit', 鬍子 *hwutz* 'mustache, beard', 腰子 *iautz* 'the waist, kidney' ≠ *iaul* 'kidney (as food)', 糨子 *jianqtz* 'paste, mucilage', 卷子 *jiuanntz* 'examination paper' ≠ *jiuann* M 'fascicule' ≠ 馓子 *jeuantz* '(steamed) roll', 金子 *jintz* 'gold', 桌子 *juotz* 'table', 筷子 *kuaytz*[28] 'chopsticks', 料子 *liawtz* '(yard) material', 栗子 *lihtz* 'chestnut', 李子 *liitz* 'plum', 麥子 *maytz* 'wheat', 片子 *pianntz* '(calling) card' ≠ *piall* 'slice' (homophonous with 騙子 *pianntz* 'swindler' under Type V-tz → N below), 嫂子 *saotz* 'older brother's wife', 骰子 ( ～色子 ) *shaetz* 'dice' ≠ 色儿 *shaal* 'color', 扇子 *shanntz* 'fan', 身子 *shentz* 'body', 靴子 *shiuetz* 'boots', 孙子 *suentz* 'grandson (on son's side)', 梯子 *titz* 'ladder', 屋子 *utz* 'room', 襪子 *wahtz* 'socks, stockings', 万子 *wanntz* 'character (of mahjong)' ≠ *wann* M '10,000', 胰子 *yitz* 'soap', 椅子 *yiitz* 'chair', 銀子 *yntz* 'silver', 院子 *yuanntz* 'courtyard' ≠ -*yuall* B.

(2.2) Type N-*tz* → N. This type is found in 布子 *buhtz* 'small cloth for casual use' ≠ *buh* 'cloth in general', 刀子 *dautz*～*daul*～ *dau* 'knife', ( 洋 )鬼子 *goeitz*～*yanggoeitz* 'foreign devil, ≠ *goei* 'ghost', ( 火 )鍋子 *guotz*～*huooguotz*～-*l* 'fire pot (soup surrounding fire served on the table)', 海子 *haetz* 'lake, pond' ≠ *hae* 'sea', 烟子 *iantz* 'soot' ≠ *ial* 'smoke' ≠ *ian* 'smoke' or 'tobacco smoke',

---

[28]We are treating 筷 *kuay* as N$_B$ because even though it is etymologically the same as 快 *kuay* 'fast', as a euphemism for the now obsolete 箸 *juh* 'chopsticks', homophonous with 'stay, becalmed', it has long acquired the status of the morpheme for 'chopsticks', as in 象牙筷 *shianqyakuay* 'ivory chopsticks'.

例子 *lihtz~lih* 'example', 路子 *luhtz* 'pull, influence' ≠ *luh* 'way', 腦子 *naotz* 'brain, brains' ≠ *naol* 'brain (as food)', 票子 *piawtz* 'ticket' or 'paper money', but *piaw* 'ticket'.

(2.3) Type M-*tz* → N. As in the case of M-*l*, nouns from M-*tz* also have the class meaning of 'size, shape, or quality', but the -*tz* forms are not nearly as common as the -*l* forms. Examples are: 个子 *gehtz* 'stature', 張子 *jangtz* 'quality of piece in a game of cards, etc.', 份子 *fenntz* 'gift', as in 一份儿份子 *i-fell fenntz* 'a gift'.

(2.4) Type M-*tz* → M. While type 1.4, M-*l* → M, such as *been-l* → *beel* 'volume (of books)', is quite common, the addition of -*tz* to an M still resulting in an M is rare, except in temporary measures. Thus, there is 一担米 *i-dann mii* ' (standard) pole-load of rice (usually 100 catties, *dann* being often written 石, the same character as for *shyr* 'stone'), but 一担子米 (not °石子 ) *i-danntz mii* would be literally 'a pole-load (of any weight or size) of rice'.

(2.5) Type V-*tz* → N. Nouns for the action, as 拍 *pai* 'to beat': *paitz* 'time beat', as in 四拍子 *syh-paitz* '4/4 time', 印 *yinn* 'impresses': *yiintz* 'imprint'.

Nouns for goals of action: 釣 *diaw* 'suspend': *diawtz* 'kettle (suspended over the fireplace)'; 呈 *cherng* 'memorialize, petition': *cherngtz* 'a memorial, a petition'; 挑 *tiau* 'carry loads on two ends of a pole on the shoulder': *tiautz* 'a pair of such loads'; 摊 *tan* 'to spread: *tantz~tal* 'bazaar spread on the street'.

Nouns for agents or instruments of action: 騙子 *pianntz* 'swindler', 拐子 *goaitz* 'kidnapper', 探子 *tanntz* 'detective', 耗子 *hawtz* 'waster,—rat, mouse', 卡子 *cheatz* 'clip', 起子 *chiitz* 'raiser, leaven', 垫子 *dianntz* 'cushion', 划子 *hwatz* 'rower,—rowboat', 夾子 *jiatz* 'folder', 'clip', 扣子 *kowtz* 'buttoner,—button', 拍子 *paitz* 'flyswatter, rugbeater, etc.' (cf. above), 刷子 *shuatz* 'brush', 问子 *wenntz* 'asker,—repeater (the projection on a striking watch which one presses to find the time)', 引子 *yiintz* 'introduction to a book, prologue to a play, fuse to a firecracker', 药引子 *yaw-yiintz* 'medicine chaser'.

(2.6) Type A-*tz* → N. Note that while there are no special implications in names of things, the form A-*tz* applied to persons, with the exceptions of 老子 *laotz* 'the old man,—father' and 小子 *sheautz* 'the young one,—boy', always has pejorative meanings (Dragunov, sec. 67). In the case of 明子 *mingtz* 'a seeing person', the word is not used without 瞎子 *shiatz* 'blind person' in the near context.

Nouns for things: 淺子 *cheantz* 'shallow dish', 光子 *guangtz* 'lenses of spectacles', 辣子 *lahtz* 'hot stuff, such as pepper sauce', 缺子, 豁子 *chiuetz, hetz* 'a broken part (as in a cup or a wall)', 乱子 *l(u)anntz* 'riot'. The form 七寸子 *chitsuenntz* 'seven-incher, a kind of snake' is more of the type A-*tz* → N than M-*tz* → N.

Nouns for persons: 老子 *laotz* 'father', 小子 *sheautz* 'boy', 傻子 *shaatz* 'fool', 痴子 *chytz* 'fool' (dial.), 呆子 *daitz* 'imbecile', 瘋子 *fengtz* 'insane person', 哼子 *koatz* 'speaker with a substandard accent, usually with reference to tone', 瘦子 *showtz* 'a skinny', 胖子 *panqtz* 'fatty', 麻子 *matz* 'person with pockmarks', 矮子 *aetz* 'shorty', 禿子 *tutz* 'baldy', 瞎子 *shiatz* 'blind person', 聾子 *longtz* 'deaf person', 啞子 *yeatz* 'deaf-mute' (dial., = Mandarin 啞巴 *yea.ba*).

(2.7) Type A + X-*tz* → N. This type is very productive and we can, as usual, only cite examples: If X-*tz* is a free word, then the form is a phrase and almost unlimited, with or without idiomatic meaning, as in 旧椅子 *jiow yiitz* 'old chair', 生柿子 *sheng shyhtz* 'unripe persimmon'. With bound X-*tz*, the result is a compound. Most of such compounds happen to be words for persons: 大伯子 *dahbaetz* 'husband's older brother', 小姨子 *sheauyitz* 'wife's younger sister', 大舅子 *dahjiowtz* 'wife's older brother' (≠*dahjiow* or *dahjiow.jiow* 'mother's number one brother'), 新娘子 *shinniangtz* 'bride', 老媽子 *laomhatz* 'maidservant', 左撇子 *tzuoopieetz* 'southpaw', 小大子 *sheaudahtz* 'young maidservant' (S. Mand). The form 老花子 *laohuatz* 'beggar' consists of *huatz* prefixed by *lao-*, *huatz* itself being an abbreviated form of 叫花子 *jiawhuatz*, from 叫化 *jiawhuah* 'calls for alms', with tonal modification *huah* > *hua*.

(2.8) Type N + X-*tz* → N. Compared with the corresponding -*l* type (1.8), there are more cases of suffixed verbs with *tz*. With agent words: 馬販子 *maa-fanntz* 'horse-trader', 夜遊子 *yeh-youtz* 'night roamer,—night owl (person)'. With instrument words: 鞋拔子 *shyebartz* 'shoe-puller,—shoehorn', 耳挖子 *eelwatz* 'eardigger' (*wa* being a phonetic modification of *ua* 'dig'), 牙刷子 *yashuatz ~ shuayatz ~ yashua ~ yashual* 'toothbrush', 電滾子 *dianngoentz* 'electric roller,—motor', 螺丝起子 *luo$_0$sychiitz* 'screw raiser,—screwdriver' (cf. Ger. *Schraubzieher*), 灯罩子 *dengjawtz* 'lampshade'. With X as non-verbs, 书架子 *shujiahtz ~ shujiah* 'bookshelf', 飯碗子 *fannwoan(tz)* 'rice bowl (fig.),—job' ≠ *fannwoan* 'rice bowl (lit.)', 樹林子 *shuhlintz* 'woods', 地窖子 *dihyinntz* 'basement', 蝎(□)虎子 *shiehuutz ~ shie.le-huutz* 'scorpion's tiger,—lizard (which is supposed to eat scorpions)'.

(2.9) Type V + X-*tz* → N. This is found in 圍嘴子 *wei-.tzoeitz ~ weitzoel* 'bib', 刷牙子 *shuayatz* 'toothbrush' [see (2.8)]. This type is not numerous, and the ICs are VX and *tz*, that is, a decompound.

(2.10) Type V + X-*tz* → V + O. As in the case of -*l* forms, if X-*tz* is a free noun, then any transitive verb can form with it a phrase without limitation, as 買帽子 *mae mawtz* 'buy a hat', 吃餃子 *chy jeautz* 'eat wraplings (boiled Chinese ravioli)'. Following are either compounds or idiomatic phrases: 过日子 *guoh ryhtz* 'pass one's days, lives', 有身子 *yeou shentz* 'has a body,—is pregnant', 拿(~摆)牌子(~架子) *na (~ bae) pairtz (~ jiahtz)* 'put on airs', 拜把子 *bay-baatz* 'to make sworn brothers', 抽冷子 *chou-leengtz* 'pull a fast one', 串门子 *chuann-mentz* 'call around for chatting', 打摆子 *daa-baetz* 'have malaria', 带尾子 *day-woeitz* 'carry a (foreign) accent', 吊膀子 *diaw-baangtz ~ diaw-banqtz* 'flirt, make a pass', 发瘧子 *fa-yawtz* 'have malaria', 光膀子 *guang-baangtz* 'stripped to the waist', 光眼子 *guang-yeantz* 'go naked',[29] 扎猛子 *ja-meengtz* 'dive'.

---

[29]In the last two examples, *guang* is the verb 'bares' rather than the adjective 'bare, smooth', as one can say *guangj baangtz, guangj yeantz* in the progressive form.

(2.11) Type X-*tz* + Y→ N. This is a little more common than the corresponding *-l* form: 棒子面儿 *banqtz-miall* 'cornmeal', 底子钱 *diitz*$_0$*chyan* 'servants' commission on purchases', 肥子子儿 *feirtz-tzeel* 'soap pod seeds', *feirtz* being a reduction of 肥皂 *fair*$_0$*tzaw* 'soap plant' (*Gleditschia sinensis*), 亭子间 *tyngtz-jian* 'backstairs apartment (Shanghai style)', 様子间 *yanqtz-jian* 'sample room, showroom', 面子事儿 *mianntz-shell* 'a matter of face'.

(2.12) Type X-*tz* + Y-*tz*. Any two nouns ending in *-tz* may form a compound with or without idiomatic meaning as 橘子挤子 *jyutzjiitz* 'orange squeezer'. But it is more usual to have one suffix or to alternate between different suffixes, as 椅垫子 *yii-dianntz* or 椅子垫儿 *yiitzdiall* 'chair cushion' in preference to 椅子垫子 *yiitzdianntz,* 呢料子 *niliawtz* ~ *nitzliawtz* 'woolen material', but 房子様子 *farngtz-yanqtz* 'model for a house'.

(2.13) Type *i*-X-*tz*. There is no limit to *i* followed by any M which has *-tz,* or any noun used as a temporary M, as 一屋子 *i-utz* 'a whole roomful'. Other forms of this type are: 一輩子 *i-beytz* 'a generation-ful,—all one's life', 一家子 *i-jiatz* 'the whole household'.

(2.14) Type XX-*tz*. There is no distributive or vivid reduplication with *-tz,* as there is with *-l.* The only case of XX-tz I know is the quasionomatopeic word □□子 *chu.chutz* I learned as a child in central Hopei. It is the name of a fictitious animal or insect to frighten children when they are not good. Some northern dialects also have forms like 小罐〻子 *sheau-parn.parntz* for *sheau-parl* 'little tray', 小盤〻子 *sheau-guann.guanntz* for *sheau-guall* 'little jar'.

(3) 头 *-.tou* is much less productive than the preceding suffixes. As a full word *tour* 'head' it can take a suffix and enter into compounds, as 头子 *tourtz,* less common than *tourl,* 'head, chief, leader' or '(either) end', 头脑 *tournao* 'head and brain,—mind', 钟头(儿) *jongtour* (*l*) (not **jong.tou*) 'clock head, —hour', 滑头 *hwatour* 'slippery head,—a sly person' or 'sly' (a borrowing from Shanghai), 镜头 *jinqtour* 'len's head,—a (camera) shot', 窩头

*uotour* 'wigwam-shaped cornbread', 舌头 *shertour* 'tongue-tip', as in: 端透定泥舌头音. *Duan tow dinq ni shertour-in.* '*Duan, tow, dinq, ni* (i.e., *t, t', d', n* of Ancient Chinese) are tongue-tip sounds.'

As suffix, -.*tou* occurs in the following types:

(3.1) Type N + .*tou* → N. 骨头 *gwu.tou* (from *guu* B) 'bone', 饅头 *man.tou* 'steamed bun', 木头 *muh.tou* 'wood', 舌头 *sher-.tou* 'tongue' ≠ *shertz* 'tongue-like part of an object', 石头 *shyr-.tou* 'stone, rock', 芋头 *yuh.tou* 'taro'.

A textually very frequent class consists of place words with -.*tou*: 前头 *chyan.tou* 'front', 後头 *how.tou* 'back', 裡头 *lii.tou* 'inside', 外头 *way.tou* 'outside', 上头 *shanq.tou* 'above', 下头 *shiah.tou* 'below'. The last, however, is not as commonly used as its synonym 底下 *dii.shiah*.

(3.2) Type A + .*tou* → N. 準头 *joen.tou* 'certainty', 甜头 *tyan.tou* 'sweetness,—advantage, profit', 少头 *shao.tou* 'shortage', also 'discount, reduction'.

(3.3) Type V + .*tou* → N. 念头 *niann.tou* 'thought, idea', 楦头 *shiuann.tou* ~ *shiuanntz* 'stretcher (for hat, shoes, etc.)', 姘头 *pin.tou* 'get together -er,—paramour, mistress'.

A formula of unlimited productivity consists of the verb *yeou* or *mei* (.*yeou*) followed by any action verb with suffix -.*tou*, usually with -*l*, with the meaning of 'it is worth V-ing' or 'there is no point in V-ing', as 有吃头儿 *yeou chy.tourl* 'worth eating', 有什么看头儿? *yeou sherm kann.tourl?* 'what is there worth seeing?' 没听头儿 *mei ting.tourl* 'not worth listening', 跟他没说头儿 *gen ta mei shuo.tourl* 'there is no point in talking with him'.

Because in the neutral tone the distinctions between aspirated and unaspirated initials and between *uo* and *ou* and between *au* and *ou* are often neutralized, we get the following -.*tou* forms for words usually written otherwise. For example, what would be written 耳朵 *eelduoo* 'ear lobe,—ear' is usually called *eel.tou* 'ear', which, by a back formation and folk etymology, is sometimes called 耳道 *eel.daw* 'ear passage,—ear'. What in characters 觔斗 looks like *jindoou* 'a tumble' is actually called *gen.tou*.

(4) 巴 -.*ba*. As a full morpheme, *ba* occurs in 巴住 *ba.juh* 'clings to', 巴结 *ba.jie* 'courts favor with', 巴望 *ba₀wang* 'hopes anxiously'. As a suffix, it has the general meaning of 'attached, adhering, appended, and so on', as in 尾巴 *woei.ba* ∼ *yii.ba* 'tail', 泥巴 *ni.ba* 'mud, clay', 鍋巴 *guo.ba* 'pot clinger,—rice toast', □ 巴 *ga.ba* 'shoe-side (made from pasted cloth)', 籬巴 *li.ba* 'fence', 鸡巴 *ji.ba* 'penis', 结巴 *jie.ba* 'stutter(er)' 哑巴 *yea.ba* 'deaf mute'.

In 枇杷 *pyi.ba* (*pyi.par* L) 'loquat' or 琵琶 *pyi.ba* (*pyipar* L) '(Chinese) guitar', it is better to treat -.*ba* as part of a dissyllabic morpheme, as it contains no meaning similar to that of the suffix -.*ba*. In the verb 眨巴 *jaa.ba* 'blinks' we have one of the few cases of an older final labial consonant developing into an additional syllable: *tsạp* > *jaa* as reading pron., but *jaa.ba* in the colloquial. This is quite similar to *ẓịạm* > *shenn* (read. pron.) 'very', but *sherme* 'what' in the colloquial.

(5) 们 -*men*, -*me*, -*m*. This so-called plural suffix is actually pronounced -.*men* or -.*me* or -.*m*. In older texts, as in edicts in 永乐大典 (*Yeongleh Dahdean*), it was in fact written with the character 每 *meei*. As to which of the three alternate forms it takes, it depends upon the speed of utterance and the nature of the following sound. For instance, before a labial, it is more likely to take the form -*m* than -*men* or -*me*. In the case of *woo-men* 'we', it has, besides the usual alternants *woome* and *woom*, also *weem* and the very informal *mm* (syllabic [m̩] in the 3rd Tone). (Cf. sec. 7.11.4.)

With pronouns, this suffix is a pure pluralizer: *woomen* 'we', *tzarmen∼tzarmmen* '(inclusive) we' (also used rhetorically as a very exclusive 'we'), *niimen* 'you', there is no *Ninmen* except in epistolary style, *tamen* (not applicable to inanimate objects, for which *ta* is the only form used, whether referring to one or more things). There is no °*sheirmen* 'who', since *sheir* is applicable to one or more persons anyway.

With nouns the suffix -*men* makes a collective noun of words for persons,[30] as *shian.shengmen* 'the gentlemen', *shiong₀dihmen*

---

[30] In the dialect of Kaocheng, near Shihchiachuang, the suffix -*men* is also

'brothers'. Since the result is a collective noun, it cannot be preceded by specific numbers. Instead of °两个强盗们 °*leangg chyang.dawmen* 'two bandits', one must say *leangg chyang.daw*. But one can say 那些强盗们 *ney₀shie chyang.dawmen* 'those bandits (as a gang)'. Incidentally, in the form 娘儿们儿 *nianglmel* the collective force of -*men* is lost in its diminutive form -*mel*, so that one can also say *san'g nianglmel* 'three women'. Occasionally a phrase for groups of persons can be suffixed by -*men*, as 先生跟学生们 *shian.sheng- gen shyue.shengmen* 'teachers and students'.

4.4.5. Verbal Suffixes. We are limiting ourselves to the consideration of aspect suffixes of verbs. Suffix-like morphemes such as -.*lai*, -.*chiuh*, and so on, will be considered versatile complements and will be treated in detail under directional complements (sec. 6.6.6). The aspect suffixes differ from the nominal suffixes in that they are unlimitedly productive and that there are relatively few lexical forms in proportion to those which are not. Almost any verb can take any of the aspect suffixes. Some verbs, such as auxiliary verbs, lack certain aspects, for example, there is no °*nengj* progressive aspect of 'can'. These will be detailed later under parts of speech (chap. 8).

(0) We set up suffix zero for verbs of action because it has characteristic class meanings: (1) habitual action, (2) near future action, (3) non-narrative predication (sec. 2.9.1). For example: (1) 他难受的时候儿不哭，他笑. *Ta nanshow de .shyr.howl bu ku, ta shiaw.* 'When he feels sad, he does not cry, he laughs.' (1) or (2) 你抽烟不抽? *Nii chou-ian ·bu chou?* 'Do you smoke (as a rule)?' or 'Are you going to have a smoke?' 抽.*Chou*. 'Yes, I do.' or 'Yes, I am (going to).' (3) 他 (是) 吃药，不是不 吃药（不喝酒）. *Ta (sh) chy-yaw, bush bu chy-yaw* or (*bu*

---

applicable to animals and inanimate things, as 小鸡们 *sheaujimen* 'little chickens', 树们 *shuhmen* 'trees', 衣裳们 *i.shangmen* 'clothes', 肉们 *rowman* 'meats', as reported in 楊耐思、沈士英，藁城方言里的"们" (Yang Naysy and Sheen Shyhing, "*Men* in the Dialect of Gaocherng"), ZGYW, no. 72:278 (June, 1958). Dragunov (59, Chinese transl., 50) reports similar examples in other northern dialects.

*he-jeou).* 'He is taking medicine, not not-taking medicine *or* (not drinking wine).', as compared with the narrative predicate in 他現在吃着药呐。 *Ta shianntzay chyj yaw ne.* 'He is taking medicine now.'

(1) 了 *-le,* the perfective aspect. This suffix has the class meaning of 'completed action', as in:  辞了行再動身！*Tsyrle shyng tzay donq-shen!* 'After having taken leave, (and only then) depart,—Don't depart without having taken leave!' 怎么碰了 杯子也 不喝？ *Tzeem penqle beitz yee bu he?* 'How come, having touched glasses, you don't drink?'

Although *-le* expresses completed action, there are of course other ways of expressing the same idea. For example, one can omit the *-le* in 这是去年完成（了）的房子。 *Jeh sh chiuh- .nian wancherng (le) de farngtz.* 'This is a house that was completed last year.', where *wancherng* already says 'complete(d)'. In the verb 忘了 *wanqle* 'have forgotten', the dialects have 忘记 *wanq.jih* 'forget (to) remember' with optional *-le* or its equivalent. The complement 掉 $-_0diaw$ 'off, away', with optional addition of *-le,* is used more frequently in the Central dialects in verbs where Mandarin has a simple *-le,* as in 扔了 *rhengle* 'throws away' instead of $rheng_0diaw(le),$ 丢了 *dioule* 'have lost' instead of $diou-_0diaw(le).$

This suffix *-le,* which is a weakened form of the verb 了 *leau* 'finish' and can be suffixed to it like any other verb, as in 了了 一件事 *leaule i-jiann shyh* 'have finished a business', should be distinguished from a homophonous particle *le,* probably a weak form of *lai* 'comes',[31] with various meanings such as

---

[31]Two pieces of evidence for this etymology are: (1) in the Ningpo dialect the verb 'comes' and the particle in question are both pronounced [le]. (2) In certain old texts 耒 occurs where a modern 了 would be expected, as in: 百丈 一 日问师：" 什么处去耒？"曰：" 大雄山下採菌子 耒." *Baejanq i-ryh wenn Shy: "Sherme chuh chiuh lae?" Iue: 'Dahshyong Shan shiah tsae jiunntz lai."* 'One day, disciple Baejanq asked Master [Monk 希運 Shiyunn]: "Where go *lai?*" He replied: "To the foot of Dahshyong Mountain to pick mushrooms *lai.*"' From 景 德 传 灯 錄 *Records of the*

'new situation', 'progress in the story', and so on (see sec. 8.5.5, P 2). The difference is more striking in Cantonese and the Wu dialects. For example, 傷了風了 *shangle feng le* 'has caught cold' is in Cantonese 傷咗風咯 *sheung-cox fong lhoh* and in Shanghai 傷仔風哉 *sang-z fong ze*. In Cantonese it is even possible to have the suffix followed immediately by the particle, as in 已经去咗咯 *yixkeng xöy-cox lhoh* 'has already gone it-has-happened'. In such cases Mandarin always avoids a repetition of the same syllable by way of haplology: *-le le → -le*, ° 已竟走了 了 °*yiijinq tzooule le → yiijinq tzooule*. As a consequence of this haplology, there is possible ambiguity in the sentence: 你把这 个杯子洗干淨了．*Nii bae jeyg beitz shii-gan.jinqle.* If the *-le* is understood as one *-le*, it is a command 'Wash this cup clean!' But if it is understood as *-le le*, then it is a statement 'You have washed this cup clean.' This haplology also explains why Northern Mandarin has *syyle* 'has died' for the 死掉了 *syy-diawle* or 死脱哉 *sii-te'ze* 'has died off,—has died' of other dialects, since Northern Mandarin already has the perfective suffix *-le* for *diaw* and so on, and an additional particle *le* will simply be absorbed into the first *le*.[32]

Note that the suffix *-le* is attached to verbs and not to objects of verbs. Thus, although *chubaan* 'issues printing, —publishes' is V-O in form when used as a transitive verb as a whole, it is followed by *-le*, as in 出版了一部书 *chubaanle i-buh shu* 'have published a book'. But in 出了一种雑誌 *chule i-joong tzarjyh* 'issued a magazine' *chu* is the verb and is therefore immediately

---

*Transmission of the Lamp*, compiled during the Ching-te era (1004-1007), *Ssu-pu-Ts'ung-k'an* 9.6A. In giving me the above example, Lien-Sheng Yang commented that these two occurrences of *lai* had very much the same force of modern 未着 *laij*. Actually, *lai* and *le* are very close in sound and *le* would fit very well in this context.

[32]In connection with the haplology of *li li → li* of Southwest Mandarin, which is equivalent to *de de → de* of Northern Mandarin, Malmqvist (Sïch-'uanese, 162) cites Knud Togeby (*Structure*, 126), who analyzes the *le* in *le plus beau paysage* as being really *le le*, the first being the article for the whole phrase and the second being the mark of the superlative degree of the adjective.

followed by *le*. This perfective suffix is obligatory after a verb for past action if it has a quantified object, as: 我 昨儿 碰見 了 一 个 老 朋友，他 请 我 吃了 一 頓 飯. *Woo tzwol penq.jiannle ig lao perng.yeou, ta chiing woo chyle i-duenn fann*. 'Yesterday I met an old friend and he invited me to a dinner.'

(2) 着 *-j* (i.e., *-.jy ~ -.je*), the progressive suffix. The etymon *djak* has split into various verbs and complements, as in 着地 *jaur dih* 'touch ground', 着凉 *jau-liang* 'catch cold', 碰着 *penqo-jaur* 'meet with (by accident)', 这 一 着 *jey-i-jau* 'this step (taken)', etc., all of which also has the reading pron. of *jwo* or *juo*.[33]

The weakest form is *-.jy ~ -j* '-ing', the suffix for the progressive aspect. In a main predicate the sentence usually ends with the particle *ne*, which, either alone or in conjunction with *-j*, also indicates progressive action, as: 他 幹 麻 吶？ *Ta gann ma ne?* 'What is he doing?' 他 打 着 電 话 吶. *Ta daaj diannhuah ne.* 'He is telephoning.'

Adjectives being verbs, they can also take the progressive suffix *-j*, as: 还 早 吶，太 陽 还 斜 着 吶. *Hair tzao ne, tay.yang hair shyej ne.* 'It is still early; the sun is still at a slant.' 这 棍儿 老 得 正着. *Jeh guell lao deei jenqj.* 'This stick must always (stay) upright.'

A special intensive form for adjectives (sec. 8.1.3) and other verbs admitting of degrees (sec 8.1.6) consists in the addition of *jne* (sec. 8.5.5, P 18), as in *hao jne* 'awfully good', the idea being 'it is (not only good, but actually being) good'. In a verb-object construction, the progressive suffix *-j* goes with the verb, but as an intensive *jne* comes after the object. For example: 他 捧着 他 吶. *Ta peengj ta ne.* 'He is holding her up (e.g., in a circus).', but 他 捧 他 着 吶. *Ta peeng ta jne.* 'He is plugging for her.' 我 想 着 你 吶. *Woo sheangj nii ne.* 'I am thinking of you (favorably, unfavorably, or indifferently).', but 我 想 你 着 吶. *Woo sheang nii jne.* 'I miss you terribly.'

By way of class overlap, a few adjectives can be used as transitive verbs and, since there is no distinction of voice in Chinese

---

[33]For further details, see Chao-Yang, *Conc Dict*, 151-152.

and any verb can be used in a passive sense, the form A *jne* can mean either 'very A' or 'is being made A'. For example: 湯热 着呐. *Tang rehj ne.* 'The soup is being heated.': *Tang reh jne.* 'The soup is awfully hot.' (The difference in spacing only marks the ICs and is of no phonological significance; in other words, the sentences are completely homophonous.) 酒凉着呐. *Jeou liangj ne.* 'The wine is being cooled.': *Jeou liang jne.* 'The wine is very cool.' Since causative adjectives are cases of class overlap, they are lexical facts. Most adjectives are not used causatively. Thus: 鞋黑着呐. *Shye hei jne.* 'The shoes are pretty black.', not 'The shoes are being blacked', since the adjective *hei* is not also a causative verb.

The *-j* forms can also be used in commands. With action verbs: 拿着! *Naj!* 'Hold on to it!' 记着! *Jihj!* 'Remember!' 等着! *Deengj!* 'Wait!' 坐着! *Tzuohj!* 'Be sitting,—remain seated!' 戴着帽子! *Dayj mawtz!* 'Wear a hat!' *Mawtz dayj!* 'Keep your hat on!' With adjectives: 慢着! *Mannj!*    慢ㄦ着! *Mannmhalj!*   慢着点ㄦ! *Mannj.deal!* 'Slow! Be good and slow! More slowly!' In the reduplicated form, we have seen that the suffix *-de* can be used instead of *-j*, as *Mannmhalde!* 轻ㄦ着! *Chingchienglj!* ~ *-de* 'Take it lightly!'

The adverbs of manner *tzemme* 'in this way', *nemme* 'in that way and *tzeeme?* 'how?' can take the suffix *-j* without much change in meaning, except that as pro-verbs the longer forms are preferred: 他老那么走路. *Ta lao nemm tzoou-luh.* in preference to *Ta lao nemmj tzoou-luh.* 'He always walks like that.', but *Ta lao nemmj.* in preference to *Ta lao nemme.* 'He keeps acting that way.'

The form 来着 *.laij~.leij* (sec. 8.5.5, P 19) with the meaning of 'recent past' or 'was...-ing' is not a suffix to verbs but a double particle and occurs after an object if there is one. (For examples of use, see Particle 19.)

Like any other verbal expression, a *-j* form can occur in first position and is thus subordinated to the second expression, in which case there is no *ne* unless it happens to be used in the sentence for other reasons. For example, 龇着牙笑 *tzyj ya shiaw* 'laugh with teeth showing', 骑着马找马 *chyij maa jao-maa*

'look for a horse while riding a horse, —look for a job while holding on to a job'. In: 闲着眼睛呐，就看不見东西了．
*Bihj yean.jing ne, jiow kann.bu-jiann dong.shi le.* 'If one keeps one's eyes closed, then one can't see things.', the *ne* is a pause particle which translates into the upswing in the English intonation and has nothing to do with the suffix *-j*, which indicates continued closing of the eyes. In some dialects the pause particle has *n-*, while the progressive particle which is associated with *-j* or its equivalent has *l-*. In old novels they appear as 呢 and 哩, respectively.

A special meaning of a V-*j* form in subordinate position is 'so far as V-ing is concerned', 'when one V's', and so on. For example: 这事儿看着好做．*Jeh shell kannj hao tzuoh.* 'This job, when you look at it, is easy to do.'   这橘子闻着香，可是吃起来酸．*Jeh jyutz wenj shiang, keesh chy.chii.lai suan.* 'This tangerine, when you smell it, is sweet, but, when you start eating it, is sour,—this tangerine smells sweet, but tastes sour.'

We noted that a few adjectives are also used causatively as transitive verbs, as *reh* 'hot' or 'to heat' *bing* (besides being a noun 'ice') 'icy' or 'to ice'. We also noted that these are cases of class overlap and that what words do or do not have class overlap is a matter of lexical fact. However, many adjectives, without becoming causative verbs in general, can be used causatively when suffixed by *-j* and placed, together with an object, in subordinate position to a following verbal expression. For example, *yinq* 'hard': 硬着心腸做 *yinqj shin$_0$charng tzuoh* 'hardening one's heart, do it,—act with a hardened heart,—act mercilessly', 斜着眼儿看人   *shyej yeal kann-ren* 'look at people slanting the eyes,—look at people askance', 歪着嘴笑 *uaij tzoei shiaw* 'smile with mouth awry,—give a wry smile'.

As in the case of the perfective suffix, there are a few verbs which occur with *-j*, but not with zero suffix, as 托着 *tuoj* 'hold up on the palm', 向着 *shianqj* 'favor (the side of), to be pro- ...', 衝着 *chonqj* 'face (the direction of)', 记着 *jihj* 'remember'.[34] In

---

[34]This is the usual word for 'remember' in the pure Peiping dialect, with *jihde* as a less frequent form, with the connotation of 'can remember'.

some cases, although the zero form does occur, the suffixed form has a special idiomatic meaning, as *na* 'take, hold', *naj* 'holding', but also 'holding (oneself) as a ... and yet', as in: 拿着个科学家，还信神信鬼呐！ *Naj g keshyuejia, hair shinn-shern shinn-goei ne!* Holding (yourself as) a scientist, you still believe in gods and ghosts!'

(3) 起来 *-.chii.lai,* the inchoative aspect. Besides being a compound verb and a compound directional complement [sec, 6.6.6 (3.5)], *-.chii.lai* is also an aspect suffix, meaning 'starts to', as in: 他们玩着〻〻忽然哭起来了。 *Tamen walj walj huran ku.chii.lai le.* 'They were playing and playing and suddenly started to cry.' 那回事情，你一提起来我就生气。 *Ney-hwei shyh.chyng, nii i-tyi.chii.lai woo jiow sheng-chih.* 'Every time you (start to) mention that incident, I get angry.' 他胖起来了。 *Ta panq.chii.laile.* 'He has started to get fat.' 这孩子渐〻儿懂事起来了。 *Jeh hairtz jiannjial doong-shyh.chii.lai le.* 'This child gradually begins to understand things.' 说起来啊，... *Shuo.chii.lai a, ...* 'Starting to talk about it, ..., —by the way, ... '.

(4) 过 *-guoh,* the indefinite past aspect. As a verb, *guoh* 'passes' is also used as a directional complement, as in 走过了 *tzoou-guohle* 'has passed (the place)', 说过了就算了 *shuo-guohle jiow suannle* 'having said (one's) say, let it go at that'. In 吃过了飯了 *chy$_0$guohle fann le* 'have had one's meal', the *-$_0$guoh* is still a complement, which can take a perfective suffix. In the neutral-tone syllable *-.guoh,* however, it is a pure suffix, with the class meaning of 'happened at least once in the past, —ever'. Examples are: 你吃过鱼翅没有？ *Nii chy.guoh yuchyh meiyeou?* 'Have you ever eaten shark's fin?' A direct answer to the question is 吃过。*Chy.guoh.* 'Yes, I have.' But *Nii chy$_0$guohle yuchyh (le) meiyeou?* 'Have you eaten the shark's

---

However, with increasing southern influence, *jihde* and *jihj* are now used almost interchangeably. Both, however, are different from 记住 *jih.juh* 'keep in mind'.

fin? (Are you ready for the next course?)' *Chy.le.* ~ *Chy₀guoh-.le.* 'Yes, I have.' Other examples: 没出过洋 *mei chu.guoh yang* 'has never gone out across the ocean,—has never been abroad'. 今年草莓还没上过市呐. *Jin.nian tsaomei hair mei shanq.guoh shyh ne.* 'Strawberries have not yet been on the market this year.' 这东西我上过当的。 *Jeh dong.shi woo shanq.guoh danq de.* '(About) this thing, I have been gypped before.'

(5) Reduplication as a tentative aspect. If we consider reduplication as an affix, then the reduplication of a verb to express a tentative notion, 'just', 'make a try', can be regarded as another aspect affix. For details, see section 4.2.3(5) under reduplication.

(6) 下去 -.*shiah.chiuh*, the successive aspect, as in    你那樣做下去，结果一定不好。    *Nii nahyanq tzuoh.shiah.chiuh, jyeguoo idinq buhao.* 'If you go on doing (it) like that, the result will certainly be bad.' This is to be distinguished from the directional complement, as in: 滚下去 *goen.shiah.chiuh* 'roll down (away)'.[35]

(7) 法（子）-.*fa*~-.*fatz* 'way' looks like a noun, but a verb followed by it can be modified by one of the three adverbs *tzemme* 'so, this', *nemme* 'so, that', and *tzeeme* 'how, in what way, to what extent'. For example: 这话得这么说法。 *Jeh huah deei tzemm shuo.fa.* 'This thing must be said this way.' 天气那么冷法子， 你们那儿怎么过法子呐？ *Tian.chih nemm leeng.fatz, niimen nall tzeem guoh.fatz ne?* 'The weather was so cold, how did you people live there?' 这话不知道该怎么问他法子. *Jeh huah bujydaw gai tzeem wenn ta .fatz.* 'Wonder how I should ask him this.', which is an interesting form in that the verb is separated from .*fatz* by the object *ta.* Some nominal effect is seen from the possibility of inserting g or ig, as in: 这事儿是这么一个办法。 *Jeh shell sh tzemm ig bann-.faa.* 'This matter is to be done this way.'

The last example is an intermediate case between -.*fa* as an

---

[35]Wang Lih (*Liiluenn*, I, 284) seems to have been the first to set up this aspect under the term 继续兒 *jihshiuhmaw.*

empty morpheme, with unlimited versatility after verbs of action, and *faa* as a root word, which can occur in compounds, with lexically limited occurrence. With *faa* in the sense of 'method', we have 好办法 *hao bann$_0$faa* 'a good method to deal with it', 分身法 *fenshenfaa* 'divide oneself method,—magic by which to be at different places at the same time', 书法 *shufaa* 'writing method,—calligraphy'. As a modern suffix, which is of course only a versatile second morpheme, we have 归纳法 *gueinahfaa* 'inductive method', 出版法 *chubaanfaa* 'copyright law'. To this intermediate type belongs also *shuo$_0$faa* 'theory', as in 他这 说法一点根據都没有。 *Ta jeh shuo$_0$faa ideal genjiuh dou meiyeou.* 'This theory of his has no basis at all.'

*4.4.6. Subordinative Suffixes: Varieties of de.* We have seen the modern suffix 的 *dih* ' ⸗tic, -al' and the more general empty morpheme 之 *jy*, the L equivalent of *-de*. In the written bairhuah of the 1910's and 1920's, a differentiation of *-de* into three functions, written with three different characters, presumably with different pronunciations, was advocated and much used during those decades: (1) 底 reading pronunciation *dii*, the possessive particle '(reversed) of, apostrophe-s', as in 马底头 *maa dii tour* 'Horse's head', 科学底分析 *keshyue dii fen.shi* 'the analysis of sciences'; (2) 的 reading pron. *dih* ($<$ *tiek*, Cantonese *tek*), the adjectival ending ' ⸗tic, -al', as in 野蛮的举動 *yeeman dih$_1$ jeudonq* 'barbarous behavior', 科学的分析 *keshyue dih$_1$ fen.shi* 'scientific analysis'; and (3) 地 reading pronunciation *dih$_2$* ($<$ *d'i'*, Cantonese *dey°*), as in 慢ㄟ地 *mannmanndih$_2$* 'slowly', 科学地分析 *keshyuedih$_2$ fen.shi* 'analyzes scientifically'. Although these distinctions are somewhat artificial, they do have some basis in the dialects and in history. In the Changsha, Hunan dialect, it is *dii* (i.e., the same syllable as the word for 'bottom') for all the three functions. In the Shanghai dialect (1) and (2) are *ke'* and (3) is *-kjaw*; in Cantonese (1) and (2) are 嘅 *keh* and (3) is 哋 *-dey°*. Historically *dii* was used for both (1) and (2), and 地 *dih$_2$* for (3).[36] But in the normal speech of Peiping everything is *-.de*,

---

[36]For further details and examples, see Leu, *LWJyi*, 90.

not counting -.*de* as a weak form of 得 *der* < *tǝk* 'gets'.[37]

It should be noted that, while in cases of *woode, niide, ...sheir-de* 'my, yours,..., whose' the -*de* is typically a suffix for the possessive form of pronouns and in 要 飯ㄦ的 *yawfallde* 'beggar', 送 信 的 *sonqshinnde* 'messenger' the -*de* looks like a suffix for agent nouns, in most cases the subordinated construction before -*de* is a phrase, thus making *de* a phrase enclitic, in other words a particle. That is why Chinese grammarians have often marked *de*, or its near equivalent in L 之 *jy*, as a 介词 *jiehtsyr*, a term applied mostly to prepositions; since, however, *jieh* 'introduces, relates' implies nothing about 'pre-' vs. 'post-', *jiehtsyr* could perhaps be translated 'introducer'; in any case, *de* or *jy* is usually regarded as a word, if an empty word. A good case for taking this point of view is the form 卖 书 的 人 *may-shu de ren* 'sell book *de* person, —one who sells books', whence *may-shu de* 'book seller'. But why is the Chinese order 'sell book -er', while the English order is 'book seller'? The answer is that '-er' is a word suffix, while *de* is a phrase suffix, so that one cannot say °*shu may de*. On the other hand, -*tz* is a word suffix and so *fanntz* 'dealer' is a word and 书 贩子 *shu-fanntz* 'book dealer' is a compound word and one does not say °*fannshutz*. In a very few cases we have de-compounds in which -*tz* is suffixed to the V-O construction. For examples of these, see (2.9) above.

On the various other types of constructions with *de*, see section 5.3.6.

### 4.4.7 Miscellaneous Suffixes.

(1) The modal suffix -*men, -me, -m*. The modal suffix used with demonstrative adverbs and interrogative adverbs and pronouns is a near homophone of the plural suffix which has the same three alternative forms, depending upon speed of utterance and upon whether the following sound is a labial. The slight difference is that here the form *men* is less common than in the plural ending, possibly under the influence of the fact that in current usage (but not always in older books) the reading pronunciation of the plural ending is们*men* and that of the modal suffix is 麼

---

[37]For the potential -.*de* 'able' and .*de* in predicative complements, see sec. 6.6.5(3) and sec. 5.6.4., respectively.

( 么 ) *mho* or *moo*. For simplicity we shall use the form *-m(e)*, unless there is a special reason to do otherwise.

The words ending in the modal suffix are: 什么 *sherme* 'what', 怎么 *tzeeme* 'how', 哪么 *neeme* 'how', 这么 *tzemme* 'in this manner, to this degree, —so', 那么 *nemme* 'in that manner, to that degree, —so', 多么 *duome*~*dwome* 'to what degree, how'. Note that there is no °*naa.me* or °*nah.me*. The form *jemme* is more formal and less frequent than *tzemme*.

(2) Adverbial suffix *-.jia* or *-.jie* (written variously as 家 *jia*, 價 *jiah*, or 价 *jiah*). 别 *Bye!* 'Don't!': *Bye.jie!* 'Don't!' (in a milder tone); *Bu.* 'No.': *Bu.jie.* 'Not so.'; *Hao.* 'All right': *Hao.jie!* 'Goodness!'; 成天玩儿 *cherng-tian wal* 'plays all day': *cherng-tian.jie wal* 'plays all day'; 更 *genq* 'still more': *genq.jie* 'all the more'. The last example is probably a reinforced blend of *genq* plus this suffix with the compound *genq*$_o$*jia* 'more-additionally', as the *jia* in the neutral tone can very well become *.jie*. This suffix is of very limited versatility.

(3) *-g* after words for days ending in *-l*. To the names of days *jiel*, *miengl*, etc., may be suffixed, as *jielg* 'today', *mienglg* 'tomorrow' The slightly longer form adds nothing to the meaning, but is used more often before verbs of action than other verbs or nominal predicates, as in 今儿个来 *jielg lai* 'comes today', but *jiel* is used more often than *jielg* in 今儿是他生日. *Jiel sh ta sheng.ryh.* 'Today is his birthday.' 今儿比昨儿冷. *Jiel bii tzwol leeng.* 'Today is colder than yesterday.'

(4) 于 *-.hu* ← *hu* 'to, at, in' L. Closest to the original wenyan preposition is the *hu* in 近于 *jinn.hu* 'near to, approaches, resembles' and 在于 *tzay.hu* 'is in' from which 'sets one's heart in, —cares for'. The conjunction 于是于 *yushyh*$_o$*hu* 'thereupon', though rather L in style, is nevertheless quite part of the spoken language, as it can be followed by the pause particle *me* in *yushyh*$_o$*hu me* 'thereupon ⟋', where *me* is translated by the rising intonation ' ⟋ '. In the following, *hu* serves only as an adverbial suffix: 纯乎 *chwen.hu* 'purely', 確乎 *chiueh.hu* 'authentically, factually', 幾乎 *ji*$_o$*hu* 'well-nigh'; *jiji*$_o$*hu* 'almost'.

(5) 的慌 *-de.huang* ~ *de.heng*. From the predicative comple-

ment (5.6.4) *de huang* as in 他嚇的慌了. *Ta shiah de huang le.* 'He was so frightened as to be flustered!, comes the much weakened form *de.huang* or further weakened to *-de.heng* as a slightly intensifying suffix for undesirable qualities, as in 累 *ley* 'to tire, tired': *leyde.huang* '(feel) tired'. Other examples of words which take *-de.huang* are: 暈 *iun* 'dizzy', 麻 *ma* 'numb, got the pins and needles', 疼 *terng* 'painful', 鬧 *naw* 'noisy', 急 *jyi* 'nervous', 擠 *jii* 'crowded', 悶 *mhen* 'stuffy', 冤 *iuan* 'feel wronged, gypped', 冷靜 *leeng$_0$jinq* 'lonesome', 癢ㄟ *yeang.yeang* 'to itch'. This suffix is of unlimited productivity. Even *hao.de.huang* is possible if one wants to say 'it's too good to stand'.

(6) The polysyllabic suffix 不唧的 *.bujide* '-ish- does not have a standard way of writing in characters. It is used with adjectives for liquid and semi-liquid things, tastes, and their figurative extensions, always with undesirable meanings, as in 滑... *hwa.bujide* 'slippery', 黏... *nhian.bujide* 'sticky (of things or temperaments)', 酸... *suan.bujide* 'sourish', 甜... *tyan.bujide* 'sweetish (where it shouldn't be sweet)'; with special idiomatic meaning: 冷... *leeng.bujide* 'suddenly, without warning' (cf. slang 'cold'). The suffix is not applicable to 大 *dah* 'large', 長 *charng* 'long', and most positive qualities, nor to polysyllabic adjectives, as 軟和 *roan.hwo* 'soft', although there is *roan.bujide* (of things that shouldn't be soft).

For reduplicated suffixes such as 黑漆ㄟ的 *hei.chiuhchiude* 'dark and dim', 冷不唧ㄟ的 *leeng.bujijide* 'cold and clammy' (≠ *leeng.bujide* above), see under vivid reduplication (sec. 4.2.4).

(7) 唏ㄟ(的) *-shishide* '-ish'. With polysyllabic morphemes or morpheme groups *-shishide* '-ish' is more often used than *-.bujide*, though by no means limited to polysyllabic forms, as 紅唏ㄟ的 *horngshishide* 'reddish', 驕傲唏ㄟ的 *jiauawshishide* 'proud and haughty'.

# 4.5 Infixes

There are few infixes in Chinese. The infix -.*li*- as in 糊哩 糊塗的 *hwu.lihwudude* 'good and muddled' and -.*bu*- in 酸不 溜ㄧ（儿）的 *suan.bulhioulhiou(l)de* 'good and sour' have been mentioned under vivid reduplication. The -.*de*- and -.*bu*- in *kann-.de-jiann* 'can see' and *kann.bu-jiann* 'cannot see' will be taken up under potential complements (sec. 6.6.5).

# CHAPTER 5
## SYNTACTICAL TYPES

## 5.1 Expressions and Constructions

*5.1.1. Words, Phrases, and Expressions.* When we noted at the beginning of chapter 4 that syntax is the study of the relations tions between words, the statement should be made more precise in two respects. From the point of view of size of units, syntax includes the relations, not only between single words, but also between phrases. For example, 打柴火 *daa chair.huoo* 'gather fuel' consists of the words *daa* and *chair.huoo* in the relation of verb and object or V-O. But in 先... *shian daa chair.huoo* 'first gather fuel', we have an adverb *shian* modifying a V-O phrase *daa chair.huoo.* Again, in ...後煮水 *shian daa chair.huoo how juu-shoei* 'first gather fuel, then boil water' we have two phrases in coordination, each of which is of the adverb-modifying-V-O type. Further, in: ...才行。 *Shian daa chair.huoo how juu-shoei tsair shyng.* 'It is necessary to gather fuel first and then boil water.', the complex coordinate phrase is now in the relation of subject to *tsair shyng* as predicate. Since syntax has to do with either words or phrases, it will be convenient to speak of "expressions" to cover either words or phrases. Thus, the term "expression" is narrower than "constituent", which also includes expressions and units less than words, such as bound morphemes and phonemes.

*5.1.2. Expressions and Constructions.* From the point of view of kinds of units, syntax is not primarily concerned with expressions in their capacities as lexical items, but with types of constructions into which expressions of various types enter. The classes of expressions that enter into various positions in constructions are, however, not the same thing as the parts of speech. In the first place a part of speech is a class of words and not of phrases. Secondly, the same place in a construction may be filled by different parts of speech and vice versa. More on this will be considered in the subsequent sections and chapters 7 and 8.

*5.1.3. Endocentric and Exocentric Constructions.* In most constructions it is possible to locate the words in phrases which would play the same parts as the whole phrases. For example, 煮 开 了 一 壺 沏 茶 的 水 *juu-kaile i-hwu chi-char de shoei* 'have boiled to boiling point a kettle of water for making tea' consists of verb *juu-kaile* and object *i-hwu chi-char de shoei*, so that *juu* is the center of the verbal expression and *shoei* the center of the object expression. Such constructions, then, are endocentric constructions. On the other hand, 春 不 老 *chuen.balao* '(in) spring doesn't get tough,—mustard green (*Brassica juncea*)' is the name of a vegetable (the unexpressed center) which does not get tough in the spring and is thus exocentric. A synonym of it, used more often in the Central dialects, is 雪 裡 红 *sheue-.liihorng* 'turn red in snow', the name of a vegetable which does this and is thus also an exocentric expression. The phrase 二 把 刀 *ell-baa dau* 'second knife,—assistant chef' admits of two alternative analyses: (1) Taken as '(one who) handles the second knife', it is exocentric. (2) If *dau* is taken as a metaphor for 'cook', then it is endocentric. Which is the better analysis depends upon the frequency of occurrence of the constituent in the form class being considered. In this case, since *dau* is rarely used as a person, analysis 1 is better. On the other hand, 好 手 *hao shoou* 'good hand,—an expert' should better be analyzed as endocentric (by synecdoche), since *shoou* is used often elsewhere as person, as in 兇 手 *shiong$_0$shoou* 'evil hand,—murderer', 打 手 *daa.shoou* 'striking hand,—hired rioter', 助 手 *juh$_0$shoou* 'helping hand,—an assistant', 水 手 *shoei$_0$shoou* 'water hand,—sailor' (cf. 'all hands on deck'), and so on. By contrast, 扶 手 *fwu.shoou* 'support the hand,—a hand support (e.g., a doorknob or a balustrade)' is an exocentric construction, since it functions neither like *fwu* 'support' nor like *shoou* '(lit. or fig.) the hand', but is transformable as 扶 着 手 的 东 西 *fwuj shoou de dong.shi* 'something which supports, or with which to support, the hand'. The majority of constructions in Chinese are of the endocentric type, and thus it is possible to illustrate most syntactical constructions with center words representing whole expressions.

Exocentric constructions are more common in compound words than in phrases (cf. sec. 6.1.3). Sometimes an endocentric phrase becomes a compound when used exocentrically. For example, 跑街 *pao-jie* 'run the streets,—run errands' is an endocentric phrase, with *pao* as center, but the entirely homophonous *paojie* 'run the streets,—errand boy' is an exocentric compound. One can say: 我不能给你跑街，因為我不是个跑街也！ *Woo buneng geei nii pao-jie, inwey wo bush g paojie .é!* 'I can't run errands for you, because I am not an errand boy, you know!' For further examples, see chapter 6.

*5.1.4. Word Order in Constructions.* It is often said that all Chinese grammar is syntax, all Chinese syntax is word order, and therefore all Chinese grammar is word order. We have already disposed of part of the problem of syntax and morphology in chapter 4. As to word order, it does play a very important part, as shown by such stock examples as 好人 *hao-ren* 'good man' vs.: *Ren hao* 'The man is good.'; 狗咬人. *Goou yeau-ren.* 'Dog bites man.' vs.: *Ren yeau-goou.* 'Man bites dog.' But, as we have seen in chapter 1, the factors of phonology, prosody, and, above all, selection are also important in syntactical constructions. For example, the verb-object construction must always have the stress on the object unless it is a pronoun, so that 煎饼 *jian-biing,* 'fries cake' with stress on *biing,* is a verb-object phrase, while *jian-.biing* 'fried cake' is a compound. In: 他明年才三岁. *Ta "ming.nian tsair san-suey.* 'Not until next year will he be three years old.': *Ta ming.nian tsair "san-suey.* 'Next year he will be only three years old.', the position of the contrasting stress makes a difference in having *tsair* go with the preceding or the following word.

The most important syntactical factor besides word order is selection [cf. sec. 1.1.2(5)], which means that certain classes of forms combine with certain classes of forms to make certain kinds of syntactical constructions. Some of these classes are listable, others are not listable except in a dictionary. Thus, *hao-ren* 'good man' is modifier-modified, but 找人 *jao-ren* 'looks for someone' is verb-object, simply because *hao* belongs to one selection, that is, class, of words, while *jao* belongs to another selection.

5.1.5. *Empty Words as Markers.* In: 吃 跟 喝 都 得 给 钱. *Chy gen he dou deei geei-chyan.* 'Both eating and drinking must be paid for.', the phrase *chy gen he* can be analyzed in one of two ways. One is to treat it as consisting of three consituents, two full words *chy* and *he*, joined by the coordinate conjunction *gen*. This is the item-and-arrangement (IA) analysis. The other is to treat the phrase as consisting of two constituents *chy* and *he*, with a coordinative empty morpheme or marker *gen*, which does not count as a constituent. This is the item-and-process (IP) analysis (cf. sec. 4.1.2). The two points of view are equivalent descriptions of the same facts and are usually mutually translatable. In the case of syntactical constructions the IP analysis will yield fewer types and is simpler, in this respect, than the IA analysis. Thus, all the three forms (1) *chy gen he*, (2) *chy, he* and (3) *chy he* can be regarded as a coordinate phrase of two words with optional conjunction *gen*∼pause / , / ∼ zero as marker, whereas if *gen* is counted as an item, we shall have to have three ICs in *chy gen he* as compared with two ICs in *chy he*.

For other examples of empty morphemes, we have: 把 桌 子 擦 干 淨 了 *bae juotz tsa-gan.jinqle* 'wipes the table clean', where *bae* marks *juotz* as a goal object (see sec. 5.5.4 on pre-transitives); 气 的 糊 塗 了 *chih de hwu.dule* 'so angry as to be confused', where *de* marks a predicative complement; 快 走 吧! *Kuay tzoou ba!* 'Hurry up and go!' where *ba* marks an advisative form of a command.

5.1.6. *Classification of Syntactical Types.* In the present chapter we shall consider various basic syntactical types. The principal syntactical division in a sentence is between subject and predicate, forming the S-P construction. This has already been considered in chapter 2 and need not be repeated here. It remains then to consider smaller constructions within the sentence, namely: 5.2. Coordination, 5.3. Subordination, 5.4 Verb-Object (V-O) Constructions, 5.5. Verbal Expressions in Series (V-V), and 5.6. Verb-Complement (V-R) Constructions. These basic constructions can be iterated and/or combined to form more complex constructions, just as composite sentences can be formed from simple sentences, but nothing new in principle will be involved and only such cases as may be of special interest will be noted, such as phrases becoming compounds or vice versa.

# 5.2. Coordination

*5.2.1. Definition of a Coordinative Construction.* A coordinative construction is an endocentric construction with two or more centers, each of which has approximately the same function as the whole construction. For example, in: 他们实桌子椅子. *Tam may juotz yiitz.* 'They sell tables and chairs.', *juotz* and *yiitz* form a coordinative compound object of *may* in: 殺人放火 都有罪. *Sha-ren fanq-huoo dou yeou tzuey.* 'Killing people and setting fires are both criminal.', *sha-ren* and *fanq-huoo* are two verbal expressions forming a coordinate compound subject; in: 他有时候儿哭，有时候儿笑. *Ta yeou shyr.howl ku, yeou shyh .howl shiaw.* 'He sometimes cries and sometimes laughs.', we have two coordinate verbal expressions forming a coordinate compound predicate to *ta*. As examples of more than two centers in coordination, we have: 甜酸苦辣的东西他都吃，就是不 吃鹹的. *Tyan suan kuu lah de dong.shi ta dou chy, jiowsh bu chy shyan de.* 'He eats sweet, sour, bitter, or hot things, only (he) doesn't eat anything salty.', where *tyan suan kuu lah* (usually without pause) are coordinate adjectives modifying *dong.shi*. The class meaning of coordination is 'and/or', in other words, items presented jointly or alternatively. On the logical aspects of coordinate constructions, see section 2.11.4.

*5.2.2. Markers of Coordination*

(1) Zero and pauses. The simplest and most frequent marker of coordination is zero; in other words the coordinated expressions occur in simple succession, as in the examples just cited, where not even pauses are used between items. Alternatively, pauses may be inserted in those examples, such as *juotz, yiitz* or *tyan, suan, kuu, lah.* It is significant that, when Western punctuation is used in Chinese, the old pear-shaped symbol " ", which was used for shorter divisions than sentences, is now often

used along with Western symbols as a smaller division than the
comma, and one of its uses is to mark out coordinate expressions,
as in *tyan、suan、kuu、lah*. It is called 頓号 *duennhaw* 'pause
sign', but in practice the pause is more hypothetical than actual,
either in speaking or in reading.

(2) Particles mark off coordinate expressions with special implications of liveliness or impressiveness. The particle *a*, with its
alternant *ia* after mid- and low vowels, has a neutral or favorable connotation, while the particle 咧 *le* (≠ 了 !) has a neutral
or slightly unfavorable connotation. For example: 花呀，草啊，
貓啊，狗啊，什么都有。 *Hua ia, tsao a, mhau a, goou a,
sherm dou yeou.* 'Flowers, grasses, cats, and dogs, there's everything.' 他们天ㄦ打球咧，浮水咧，跳舞咧，什么
的，可是我一樣ㄦ都不会。 *Tamen tiantial daa chyou
le, fuh shoei le, tiawwuule, shermde, keesh woo iyanql dou buhuey.* 'Every day they play ball, swim, dance, and so on, but I
don't know how to do any of those things.' These particles, being
enclitics, belong to the preceding words and do not join, but instead separate them from, the following item. They are therefore
not like English *and*, but like Japanese *to*. For this reason, the
last item is followed by a particle just as the preceding ones,
whereas a conjunction can only come between the expressions
joined.

(3) The falling ending, symbolized " ⌉ ", consisting of an
added falling of the pitch at the end of the last syllable of a
phrase, sounds like a feature of sentence intonation, but functions
like a particle. It differs from an ordinary particle in that it has
no segmental phonemes of its own but dwells parasitically on a
lengthened last phoneme of the phrase to which it is attached,
with the falling intonation on this prolongation. It is not a feature of intonation of the preceding phrase, since it occurs after
it in time. The meaning of this falling ending is like that of a
condescending attitude toward the person spoken to or the thing
spoken of. More formal and semantic details will be given in
chapter 8 (Particle 27). Here we are interested in the falling ending as a marker of coordination. Examples are: 他会画鸟ㄦ，
花ㄦ，樹，房子，就是不会画人。 *Ta huey huah neaul ⌉,*

*hual* ↘, *shuh* ↘, *farngtz* ↘, *jiowsh buhuey huah ren.* 'He can draw birds, and flowers, and trees, and houses, only he can't draw people.' 鸡, 羊, 狗, 馬, 駱駝, 都不肯走。*Ji* ↘, *yang* ↘, *goou* ↘, *maa* ↘, *lou.two* ↘, *dou bukeen tzoou.* 'Chickens, sheep, dogs, horses, and camels are all unwilling to move.' (from a school reader).

(4) Conjunctions as markers of coordinate constructions are not as common as one would gather from reading translations of foreign languages or from writings in the style of such translations, where *and* is equated to 和 *her* (or one of its homographic synonyms) and *or* is equated to 或者 *huoo₀jee* (or one of its synonyms) or to 还是 *hairsh*. In ordinary speech, zero is the commonest marker of coordination. The commonest spoken 'and'-word is 跟 *gen*, which, on account of its having too many strokes and on account of its relatively restricted geographical spread, has not become as widely used in writing as 和. The morpheme *gen* is primarily a verb which means 'follows', as in 跟师傅学本事 *gen shy.fuh shyue been.shyh* 'follows a master and learns a skill', 跟着他跑 *genj ta pao* 'following him runs,—runs after him'. In: 我要跟你说话。*Woo yaw gen nii shuo-huah.* 'I want to talk with you.' and in: 你得跟他一塊儿走。*Nii deei gen ta ikuall tzoou.* 'You must go with him.', *gen* is in first position in verbal expressions in series, which, as often happens, is translatable by a preposition, in this case by 'with'. In fact this rule applies equally to the other so-called 'and'-words *her, hann, hay,* and to the Central and Southern dialectal 同 *torng,* for example, 我要同你说话。*Woo yaw torng nii shuo-huah.* (dial.) 'I want to talk with you.' That the L equivalents 与 *yeu* and 及 *jyi* cannot be used here is simply because of the conflict of styles. If the whole phrase is in L then it will be quite normal again, as in 与子偕行 *yeu tzyy jie shyng,* which is equivalent, word for word, to *gen nii ikuall tzoou* 'with you together goes,—goes with you'. In: 先生跟学生在课堂裡上课呐。*Shian.sheng gen shyue.sheng tzay kehtarng.lii shanqkeh ne.* 'The teacher *gen* the students are having a class in the classroom.', the *gen* may

be translated either as 'with' or as 'and'. In: 現在我要做的 兩件事是吃飯跟睡覺. *Shianntzay woo yaw tzuoh de leang-jiann shyh sh chy-fann gen shuey-jiaw.* 'The two things I want to do now are eating and sleeping.', *gen* is more naturally translated as 'and' though 'together with' is also possible. Thus there seems to be no primarily coordinate conjunction of the English 'and'-type which simply joins two expressions in logical conjunction. In the last example, the most natural way of expressing the coordination is to say *chy-fann shuey-jiaw*, with zero marks. (On the use of *de* for 'and' between expressions of quantity see S 5.3.6, p. 390.)

For the 'or'-words in Chinese, it makes a difference whether it is a disjunctive 'or' (the 'or' of 'whether or') or an alternative 'or' (the 'or' of 'either or'). In the former case the word usually regarded as the equivalent conjunction to 'or' is 还是 $_0$*hairsh*, for example: 你在那儿做事还是玩儿? *Nii tzay.nall tzuoh shyh hairsh wal?* 'Are you working or playing?' In the latter case the equivalent to 'or' is 或者 $_0$*huoh.jee* or 或是 $_0$*huohsh* and their weaker forms *.he.je, .hesh:* 做事或者玩儿都行. *Tzuoh-shyh .he.je wal dou shyng.* 'It's all right to either work or play.' As in the case of the 'and'-words, it is also common practice to use zero for disjunction of alternation, as in: 你吃 饭吃麵? *Nii chy-fann chy-miann?* 'Will you eat rice or eat noodles?' ... 没关係. *Chy-fann chy-miann mei guan.shih.* 'Eating rice or eating noodles makes no difference.', where it is possible, but not necessary, to insert *hairsh* in the first example and *hairsh* or *huohjee* in the second example. As we shall see below, these 'or'-words are not simple conjunctions but are also adverbial in function.

(5) A set of two or more correlative markers or repeated markers often serves to mark out coordinate constructions. For example: 你不来,我不去. *Nii bu lai, woo bu chiuh* could be a coordinate sentence 'You don't come and I don't go' or a conditional sentence 'If you don't come, I won't go'. But in 你也 不来,我也不去。 *Nii yee bu lai, woo yee bu chiuh.* 'Neither do you come, nor do I go.' and: 不但..., 並且 ... *Budann nii bu lai, binqchiee woo yee bu chiuh.* 'Not only you don't come, but

I don't go, either', the adverbs *yee* 'also' and *budann ... binqchiee* 'not only ... but also' make it clear that the constructions are coordinate. Again, when a bandit says: 你 要 錢 要 命 ? *Nii yaw-chyan yaw-minq?* 'Do you want your money or your life?' it is a disjunctive coordinative construction, and if the traveler is quick enough to disarm the bandit, he can reply 我 也 要 錢 也 要 命 . *Woo yee yaw-chyan yee yaw-minq.* 'I want both my money and my life.'

It is common practice in language teaching to equate such pairs as *you...yow* or *yee...yee* to conjunctions 'both...and' and to equate pairs like *huohjee... huohjee* to 'either... or' and *hairsh... hairsh* to 'whether... or', as found in the preceding examples. But note that one does not say ° 也 亞 洲 也 歐 洲 在 赤 道 以 北 . °*Yee Yahjou yee Oujou tzay Chyhdaw yiibeei.* for: 'Both Asia and Europe are to the north of the Equator.' Instead one has to say *Yahjou Oujou dou tzay Chyhdaw yiibeei.*, or, if *yee* is to be used, it will in the form: *Yahjou yee tzay Chyhdaw yiibeei, Oujou yee tzay Chyhdaw yiibeei.* Nor does one say ° 你 要 看 还 是 戏 还 是 電 影 儿 ? °*Nii yaw kann hairsh shih hairsh diannyeengl?* for 'Do you want to see a show or a movie?' Instead, it will be in the form: *Nii hairsh yaw kann-shih, hairsh yaw kann diannyeengl?* or: *Nii yaw kann de hairsh shih hairsh diannyeengl?* The reason for these limitations is very simple. These apparent correlative conjunctions for coordination are not conjunctions, but adverbs (*yee, yow,* etc.) or verbs (*hairsh,* lit., 'still is, after all is') and must be placed where such words are normally placed; adverbs before verbs (*yee tzay*) and not before nouns (°*yee Yahjou*). All the correlative words do is to bring into relief the already parallel coordinate construction marked by zero or pause marks. They are therefore not to be regarded as conjunctions in spite of the fact they often translate into English conjunctions. For further examples of correlative words, see chapter 8.

*5.2.3. The "A, B, and C" Rule for Coordinative Markers.* In current writing, many writers use markers like 和 *her* (etc.) 'and' and 或 者 *huohjee* 'or' before the last item, but only punctuation marks between the other items, if there are more than two items in coordination. This usage, though by no means unknown in old writing, has no doubt been reinforced by foreign influence. But in everyday speech, as distinguished from a lecture, the commonest form of using markers is either to have zeros throughout or a marker word repeated between all items, as in *nii woo ta* 'you, I, he' or *nii gen woo gen ta* 'you and I and he'. Some interesting studies showed that the "A, B, and C" form was used quite early, but it certainly is not, and has never been, the general rule for any period or style.[1]

*5.2.4. Order and Reversibility in Coordination.*[2] The order of items in coordination is grammatically reversible, though sometimes idiomatically irreversible. Things in a natural order are of course usually mentioned in that order, such as numbers, days of the week, seasons of the year, and so on. Other items can be given in any order, as in 他老喜欢打人骂人，可是骂人打人不好。 *Ta lao shii_o huan daa-ren mah-ren, keesh mah-ren daa-ren bu hao.* 'He always like to strike people and abuse people, but to abuse people and (/or) to strike people are (/is) not good.' In 買了些又酸又苦又涩的沙菓儿 *maele shie yow suan yow kuu yow seh de shaguool* 'bought some both sour and bitter and astringent crabapples', the three adjectival phrases can be in any order and will result in an equally idiomatic compound adjectival phrase.

In many cases, however, only one order is idiomatic, as in 殺人放火 *sha-ren fanq-huoo* 'kill people and set fires,—commit murder and arson', 新的旧的 *shinde jiowde* 'the new and the old', 老的少的 *laode shawde* 'the old and the young', 父親母親 *fuh.chin muu.chin* 'father and mother', 先生学生 *shian- .sheng shyue.sheng* 'teacher and student', 有吃有穿 *yeou-chy yeou-chuan* 'have (things to) eat and have (things to) wear', 天地 *tian dih* 'heaven and earth', 快慢 *kuay mann* 'fast and (/or) slow', 大風大雨 *dah-feng dah-yeu* 'big wind and big rain', 吃

---

[1]See discussion between 斯尔忠 (Sy Eeljong) and 蕭斧 (Shiau Fuu) in ZGYW, no. 55:49 (1957).

[2]See also Yakov Malkiel, "Studies in Irreversible Binominals," *Lingua*, 8:113-160 (1959).

喝嫖賭 *chy he pyau duu* 'eating (opium), drinking (liquor), wenching, and gambling', 金木水火土 *jin muh shoei* ( ㄌ or ㄱ ) *huoo* ( ㄱ ) *tuu* 'metal, wood, water, fire, and earth' (the traditional five elements). In all such cases it is grammatical to change the order of the terms, but the resulting phrase will sound unusual. Stylistically the changed order may either sound queer, as *muu.chin fuh.chin* 'mother and father', *shyue.sheng shian.sheng* 'student and teacher', or more fresh and interesting than the usual order, as *yeou-chuan yeou-chy* 'have (things to) wear and (things to) eat', *dah-yeu dah-feng* 'big rain and big wind', *shoei huoo muh jia tuu* 'water, fire, wood, metal, and earth'.

In the case of a coordinate phrase of two monosyllabic words, however, an idiomatic order is not reversible unless a pause or a marker word is used. Thus one can say: 快慢都一樣。*Kuay mann dou iyanq.* 'Fast and slow are both the same.', but not: °*Mann kuay dou iyanq.* However, it is possible to say: *Mann a, kuay a, dou iyanq,* or: *Mann gen kuay dou iyanq.* Similarly, with *tian dih,* it is possible to say *dih a, tian a* or *dih huohjee tian; dih, tian* is not so common; and °*dih tian,* without pause, does not occur. The reason for this, as we shall discuss in more detail in chapter 6, is that two monosyllabic words in succession tend to form compounds and that parts in coordinate compounds are normally not reversible in order. Thus in: 飯菜都夠吃。*Fann tsay dou gow chy.* 'Both rice and other dishes are enough to eat.', *fann tsay* is the usual order for this phrase, while *tsay-fann* would form a subordinate compound meaning 'rice cooked with vegetables'. Similarly, 筆墨 *bii moh* 'brush and ink', but *moh-bii* 'ink writing-instrument (brush or pen, as against pencil or chalk)'. In most cases, only one order occurs, to the exclusion of the reversed order. Examples are: 手脚 *shoou jeau* 'hands and feet', 水火 *shoei huoo* 'water and fire', 風雨 *feng yeu* 'wind and rain, —storm', 书报 *shu baw* 'books and periodicals', 推拉 *tuei lha* 'pushes and/or pulls', 買賣 *mae may* 'buys and/or sells', 好坏 *hao huay* 'good and/or bad', 遠近 *yeuan jinn* 'far and/or near', 多少 *duo shao* 'much (~many) and/or little (~few)', 濃淡 *nong dann* 'strong and/or weak (of colors or tastes)', 干濕 *gan shy* 'dry and/or wet', and many others. The reverse of these do not occur except when marked by a pause or some other marker of coordination. It should be noted here that we are considering the order of free words in a coordinate phrase and not of parts in compounds. Thus, *shoou.jeau* '(degree of) agility', *duo.shao ~ dwo-.shao* 'how much (~ many)', and *mae.may* 'trade' are trochaic compounds and not phrases, nor are we considering compounds in which one or both morphemes are ever-bound, as in 升降 *shengjianq* 'rise and/or fall', 来往 *laiwoang* 'coming and/or going,—intercourse (social, financial, etc.)', which cannot be re-versed even with coordination markers, since one or both parts would not be free. In a limited number of cases the reverse order also occurs, with or without a difference in meaning or style, in both compounds and phrases. For example, *woanglai* 'intercourse' does occur, excluding, however, the meaning of intercourse in the sense of deposits and withdrawals at a bank. Of reversible phrases we have 大小 *dah sheau* 'large and/or small', 長短 *charng doan* 'long and/or short', 硬软 *yinq roan* 'hard and/or soft', 貓狗 *mhau goou* 'cats and/or dogs', of which the reversed forms do occur, with a slight effect of freshness in style because of their relative infrequency, though the difference in frequency between *yinq roan* and *roan yinq* is rather small. Since reversibility is rather limited, the cases should be regarded as lexical and re-corded in a dictionary. As to compounds in which one or both morphemes are bound, the reversible cases will of course enter automatically into a dictionary containing compounds.

*Order in Disjunctive Questions.* In disjunctive questions of the 'A or B' type, as in 你吃飯吃麵? *Nii chy fann chy miann?* 'Are you going to eat rice or noodles?' the order of the alternatives is reversible. But in the particular case of V-not-V questions where V and its contradictory are the alternatives, the order is fixed,[3] except when there are markers such as *hairsh* or *sh* 'or'. For example, 好不好? *Hao bu hao?* 'Is it all right?' not °*Bu hao hao?* 来不来? *Lai bu lai?* 'Are you coming?' not °*Bu lai lai?* One can, however, say 你不来, 还是来? *Nii bulai, hairsh lai?* 'Are you not coming, or are you coming?' Note

---

[3]Malmqvist, Sïch'uanese, 127.

that in the irreversible form there is a neutral tone on *bu* and an optional neutral tone on the verb on repetition.

*5.2.5. Types of Expressions in Coordination.* Terms in coordination must of course be expressions of comparable functional classes, besides being in the relation of coordination. In the first place, words forming centers of phrases in coordination are normally of the same part of speech, unless of course one is talking about words or even bound morphemes, in which case everything is in quotes and is thus treated as a noun, as in: *"Lai", "sheir", "shian" sh san'g tzyh.* ' "Come", "who", "first" are three words'. When nouns and pronouns are in coordination, there must be a pause or some other marker, as:  我，媽，坐得这儿；你，爸ㄝ，坐 得.那儿。 *Woo, Mha, tzuoh .de jell; nii, Bah.bah, tzuoh .de nall.* or: *Woo gen Mha ... Nii gen Bah.bah... .* 'I and Ma sit here; you and Papa sit there.' If there were no pause or *gen, woo mha* would mean 'my ma' and *nii bah.bah* would mean 'your papa'.

Another characteristic of coordinate expressions is that they have parallel constructions or at least the same number of syllables. If not, a marker is required to set the expressions apart. For example the usual translation of the Occidental traditional elements is 火，空气，水,地 *huoo, kongchih, shoei, dih* 'fire, air, water, and earth'. Since the second expression *kongchih* is structurally different as well as longer than the other three, the four elements are always mentioned with pauses, whereas the five Chinese traditional elements 金木水火土 *jin muh shoei huoo tuu* are usually mentioned without pause, as shown by the tone sandhi on *shoei* and *huoo*. To show that this is not a matter of foreign vs. Chinese examples, take the case of the absent-minded sheriff who had to stop at an inn overnight with a prisoner, who was a monk, on their way to a distant prison. The sheriff had been instructed to keep constantly in mind three things: 文书， 和尚，我 *wen.shu, her.shanq, woo* 'briefcase, monk, me'. According to the story, the monk shaved the sheriff's hair and escaped. Next morning, the sheriff felt his head and was reassured that the *her.shanq* was still there.[4] So was the *wen.shu*, but he wondered whatever had become of *woo*. As items to memorize one could

---

[4]Chinese monks always have shaven heads.

even regard all three as in quasi-quotation, but the disparity in syllables as well as parts of speech makes it necessary to have pauses whenever the story is told.

Between longer expressions, it is necessary to have a coordination marker, though the lengths need not be equal. Since the expressions must be comparable in structure, it is not good to have a nominal phrase and a clause in coordination, as in the sentence: 这一次分开教学 的成功是由于校方的大力协助和 教师充分備课。 *Jeh i-tsyh fenkai jiaushyue de cherggong sh youyu shiawfang de dahlih shyejuh hann jiawshy chongfenn bey-keh.* 'The success of the separately carried out instruction this time was due to (1) the strong support on the part of the school administration and (2) the teachers adequately prepared their lessons'., which Shyu Jonqhwa[5] quoted as an example of ungrammatical coordination, since *hann* is being used to join a nominal phrase and an S-P clause.

*5.2.6. Loose Apposition as a Species of Coordination.* When two expressions in succession refer to the same thing, the relation is one of apposition. Since reference to the same thing is a semantic conception, it may actually involve different formal features. As a matter of fact, there are (1) close apposition, (2) loose apposition, and (3) interpolated apposition, and only (2) is a coordinative construction.

(1) As examples of close apposition, we have 王家 *Wang-.jia* 'Wang family,—the Wangs', 李大夫 *Lii Day.fu* 'Doctor Lii', ㄨ-音 *'u'-in* 'the sound "u"', 天字 *'tian'-tzyh* 'the word "tian"', 科学雜志 *Keshyue Tzarjyh* 'the magazine *Science*', 吳县 *Wu Shiann* 'the district Wu,—Soochow', 你懂不懂'豈 有此理' 这个话? *Nii doong bu doong 'chii yeou tsyy lii!' .jeyg .huah?* 'Do you understand this expression "how ridiculous!"?' As a rule, close appositions are subordinate phrases or compounds, such that the first part modifies the second: the Wang family, as distinguished from other families; the 'u' sound, not the 'a' sound; *Science* magazine and not some other magazine; the 'how ridicu-

---

[5] 徐仲华,词类 (Shyu Jonqhwa, *Tsyrley* [*Parts of Speech*]), Paoting, 1957, p. 89.

lous' expression, and so on. It is the specific modifying the general.

(2) In loose apposition the expressions are in coordination without pause, as in 我的朋友江一 *woode perng.yeou Jiang I* 'my friend Jiang I', 文学院長陈方伯 *Wenshyue Yuannjaang Chern Fangbor* 'Dean of College of Letters Chern Fangbor', 东西交通的孔道 蘇彝士運河 *Dong-Shi jiautong de koongdaw Suyishyh Yunnher* 'passage between the East and West, the Suez Canal', 我有个八哥儿会说话的。 *Woo yeou g ba.gel huey shuo huah de.* 'I have a mynah bird, one that can talk.' (cf. 4.23 on pivotal constructions).

(3) An expression in interpolated apposition is not in construction with the rest of the sentence except as an insertion or afterthought and can be omitted and still leave the sentence complete. For example, in: 江一,(是)我的一个朋友,要来见你。 *Jiang I, (sh) woode ig perng .yeou, yaw lai jiann nii.* 'Jiang I, (who is) a friend of mine, wants to come to see you.', omitting *woode ig perng.yeou* still leaves *Jiang I yaw lai jiann nii* a complete sentence. Other examples are: 他们(是)外國人不会吃瓜子儿。 *Tamen (sh) way.gwuoren buhuey chy guatzeel.* 'They (being) foreigners don't know how to eat melon seeds.' 他做了一套新洋服,挺漂亮的一套洋服。 *Ta tzuohle i-taw shin yangfwu, tiing piawlianq de i-taw yangfwu.* 'He had a new suit made, quite a smart suit.' In all these examples the interpolations are predicates, before which it is possible to add an equational verb like *sh* 'is' or *jiowsh* 'is namely', and therefore they should not be regarded as in coordination with the preceding expression.[6]

In this connection it may be noted that neither (a) expressions of the type 三張纸 *san-jang jyy* 'three sheets of paper', 两条

---

[6]L. S. Yang seems to have been the first to have noticed the difference between (2) and (3). In a letter to me, he cites 你们父子俩 *niimen fuh-tzyy lea* 'you two, father and son' as an example of ordinary apposition, and 我,一个学生,能做什么呐? *Woo, ig shyue.sheng, neng tzuoh sherm ne?* 'What can I, (being merely) a student, do?' as an afterthought apposition.

鱼 *leang-tyau yu* 'two fish', nor (b) expressions of the type 肉二
斤 *row ell-jin* 'meat two catties', 白菜兩棵 *bairtsay leang-ke*
'cabbages two heads' are coordinate constructions. Type (a) is a
subordinate construction, where *san-jang* modifies *jyy*. Type
(b) is an S-P construction. In an itemized list, the item *row ell-
jin* says: *Row sh* ('is') or *yeou* ('has') *ell-jin*. A housewife reading
such a list aloud even supplies *"sh"* where it is not written on the
invoice or shopping list. In ordinary speech one never uses the
word order of *row ell-jin* as a subject or in a predicate. This form
occurs only in a very formal style, as in 定造戰鬥机五百
架 *dinqtzaw janndowji wuubae-jiah* 'orders to be built fighter
planes five hundred', or in poetic style, as in: 小孩儿三个靠
着枕, *Sheauharl san'g kawj jeen*, which was my free translation of Lewis Carroll's 'Children three shall nestle near' (*Shin
Gwoyeu*, 75). In ordinary speech it is of course *wuubae-jiah
janndowji* 'five hundred fighter planes' and *San'g sheauharl* 'three
children'.

Type (b) is not to be confused with forms like *tamen san-wey*
'They three (gentlemen)'. This is loose apposition, type (2), since
位 *-wey* here is not a measure for *tamen*, but for *shian.sheng*
understood and one can just as well say *tamen san-wey shian-
.sheng*.

## 5.3. Subordination

*5.3.1. Modification and Subordination.* Subordination has
been taken by some writers in the wide sense to apply to any
endocentric construction, so as to include forms like (a) 桌子
*juotz* 'table', with root *juo-* as center, with suffix *-tz* subordinated
to it, (b) 喝酒 *he-jeou* 'drinks wine', with object *jeou* subordinated to the center *he*, (c) 查出來 *char.chu.lai* 'finds out', with
complement *-.chu.lai* subordinated to *char* as center, as well as
(d) 羊肉 *yangrow* 'sheep meat,—mutton', with *yang* subordinated
to *row* as center, and (e) 你的书 *niide shu* 'your book', with

*niide* subordinated to *shu.*[7] In this usage the center of an endocentric construction is also called the head.

Instead of following this usage, we shall find it more convenient to limit subordination to constructions like *yangrow* and *woode shu*, in which the first part modifies the second, thus making subordination synonymous with modification.

5.3.2. *What Is Modification?* An expression X is said to modify another expression Y when XY is an endocentric construction and Y, but no X, is the center. X is called the *attribute* or modifier, and Y the *head* or the modified part. Thus in 中國銀行 *Jonggwo Ynharng* 'China Bank,—Bank of China', *Jonggwo* modifies *Ynharng* as attribute and head. Similarly, in 深綠 *shen-liuh* deep green,—dark green' *shen* modifies *liuh* as attribute and head.

If Y in XY is not the only center in the construction, then XY is not an attribute-head construction and X does not modify Y. This happens with the following possibilities:

(a) If both X and Y are centers, then we have a coordinate construction. Examples are: 桌子板凳 *juotz bann.denq* 'tables (and) benches', 干淨漂亮 *gan.jinq piaw.lianq* 'clean (and) nice'.

(b) If X is the center, there are two possibilities. One is a V-O construction, as 寫信 *shiee-shinn* 'writes letters', with *shiee* as center, 看戲 *kann-shih* 'sees a show,—goes to a show', with *kann* as center. The other possibility is:

(c) A V-R construction, as 走遠了 *tzoou-yeuanle* 'has walked far', 說對了 *shuo-dueyle* 'has said correctly', in which *tzoou* and *shuo* are centers and *yeuanle* and *dueyle* are complements. In the English translations 'far' and 'correctly' are sometimes regarded as modifiers of the preceding verbs, but that is from the point of view of English grammar. In the Chinese constructions *yeuan* and *duey* are complements and not modifiers.

Sometimes it is possible for the same two expressions to occur in one order as modifier-modified (specifically as adverb-verb, or

---

[7]For instance, Eugene Nida, in "The Analysis of Grammatical Constituents", *Language*, 24:173-174 of 168-177 (1948), gives as examples of subordinative forms 'mannish' (a), 'shot him' (b), 'greenhouse' (d), and 'my friend' (e).

H-V) or in the reverse order as verb-complement, or V-R, with a slight difference in emphasis. For example: 你 刚 才 那 段 话 多 说 了. *Nii gangtsair ney-duann huah duo shuo le~...shuo-duole.* 'Those words of yours just now were needlessly said~... said needlessly.' 快 点儿走! *Kuay.deal tzoou!* 'Hurriedly go,—hurry up and go!'~*Tzoou-kuay .deal!* 'Go (so that the result will be) faster,—go faster!' 你 错 听 了 他 的 话 了. *Nii tsuoh-tingle tade huah le.* 'You wrongly heard his words.'~*Nii ting-tsuohle tade huah le.* 'You heard his words wrong. But this reversal, resulting in different types of constructions with differences in meaning, is possible only in a relatively small number of combinations. Thus, there is 说 完 了 *shuo-wanle* 'said to a finish,—finished saying', but there is no °*wan-shuole;* there is 煮 开 了 *juu-kaile* 'heat until it boils', but no °*kai-juule.* In the case of 治 好 了 *jyh-haole* 'healed (with the result) well,—cured', the reversed form *hao jyh le* 'easy to cure now' or 'can cure (~be cured) now' involves an auxiliary verb *hao* and a particle *le* for 'new situation'.

(d) Finally, in an S-P construction, neither X nor Y is the center, as: 这 个 小 孩儿 聪 明. *Jeyg sheauharl tsong.ming.* 'This child is clever.' 你 要 什 么? *Nii yaw sherme?* 'What do you want?' In the case of predicative adjectives, the predicate 'clever' is sometimes said to modify the subject 'this child'. This is sometimes a useful point of view, especially in describing inflected languages, where the subject and a predicative adjective must agree in number and gender. But in Chinese, it is better to treat the adjective as a species of verb and, if it is predicated of a subject, then it does not modify it in the sense in which we are using the term here.

There are a few apparent exceptions to the rule that the modifier always precedes the modified, as required by our definition. In addition to the usual phrase 生 鱼 *sheng-yu* 'raw fish' there is a Cantonese dish called *yusheng* (Cant *yushang*), as if to say 'fish raw'. Actually, the adjective *sheng* is being used nominally, so that the construction is really that of 'fish raw-dish', which therefore still follows the regular order of modifier-modified. For further examples of this type, see section 6.4.6. (1.2b) on N-A compounds.

*5.3.3. Order and Hierarchy.* Problems of order and hierarchy arise when there are two or more modifiers to one modified: $X_1X_2Y$. In 红黑帽 *hornghei-maw* 'red and black hat (worn by members of a magistrate's retinue during recent imperial times), and in 糖醋鱼 *tarngtsuh-yu* 'sugar-vinegar fish,—sweet and sour fish' we have $X_1X_2$ as coordinate modifiers of Y; in 黑皮鞋 *hei-pyishye* 'black leather shoe,—black shoe' (since Occidental style shoes are called *pyishye*) and 醬黄瓜 *jianq-hwang.gua* 'pickled cucumber' it is $X_1$ modifying $X_2Y$, in which $X_2$ modifies Y. In general, if the whole or part of the construction is a compound, the internal structure is a matter of lexical data and cannot be determined by rule.

When an adjective or a verb is modified by more than one adverb it is usually in hierarchical structure, while adverbs in unmarked coordination are relatively rare. Thus 不很好 *bu heen hao* 'not very good': *heen bu hao* 'very not good,—very bad' 一定先去 *idinq shian chiuh* 'certainly first go,—certainly will go first': *shian idinq chiuh* '(at) first certainly will go (perhaps change one's mind later)', 馬上就不高兴 *maashanq jiow bu gaushinq* 'at once not pleased,—at once displeased': *bu maashanq jiow gaushinq* 'not at once pleased (possibly pleased later)'. In the last example *maashanq* and *jiow* are synonyms in coordination, usually occurring in that order, though *jiow maashanq* also occurs.

In forms like 老年的男人跟女人 *lao-niande nan.ren gen neu.ren* 'old men and women', the same ambiguity of ICs exists in Chinese and English. There are of course always ways of rewording to clarify the scope of modification, such as use or non-use of pauses, markers like *gen*, or the subordinative particle *de* to mark the larger divisions. In this particular example it is also possible to use the compound form *nanneu*, so that *lao-nian de nanneu* 'men-and-women who are old' can have only one structure, while *lao-nian de nan.ren, gen neu.ren* 'old men, and women', with both pause and *gen*, can only have the other structure.

When a string of modifiers admits of various analyses into ICs, ambiguity can also be resolved by the use of pauses, or rather change of tempo and by the particle *de*. Thus, in 少年的研究生的導师 *shawnian de₁ yanjiousheng de₂ daoshy* 'young research student adviser', if there is a slower tempo before *de₁*, it is (1) 'young adviser to research students', while if there is a fast tempo before *de₂*, it is (2) 'adviser to young research students'. A common practice, both in writing and in speech, is to leave the smaller units unmarked and mark the larger units with *de*, thus: (1) *shawnian de yanjiousheng daoshy* 'young adviser to research students', but (2) *shawnian yanjiousheng de daoshy* 'adviser to young research students'.

*Displaced Modifiers.* Sometimes, because of resistance of compounds to separation, preference for frequently occurring compounds or phrases, or other factors, a modifier occupies a position which is not what seems to be the logical one. For example, in 再(～还)写々清楚! *Tzay (～hair) shiee.shiee ching.chuu!* 'Write still more clearly!' *tzay* or *hair* 'still more' seems to modify the verb *shiee*, whereas it has more to do with *ching.chuu*. The reason for this order is that *shiee-ching.chuu* or *shiee-.shiee-ching.chuu* is a V-R compound and resists separation, and so the adverb *tzay* or *hair* will have to modify the compound as a whole. In the case of predicative complements (sec. 5.6.4), since a predicate is easily separated from its subject, we can say 我現在写的更清楚了。 *Woo shianntzay shiee de genq ching.chuu le.* 'I write more clearly now.', with *genq* immediately before *ching.chuu*. Again, 同鄉 *torngshiang* 'same locality,—from the same locality or one who is from the same locality' is a compound of the FB type. If someone comes from the same large locality, say a province, then he is a 大同鄉 *dah-torngshiang*, while if he is from the same small locality, say a town or a .village, then he is a 小同鄉 *sheau-torngshiang*. One does not use the apparently more logical form °*torng-dahshiang* and °*torng-sheaushiang*, mainly because one hears the word *torngshiang* all the time and hesitates to break it up and coin new compounds. In the case of 请客 *chiing-keh* 'invite guests,—give a party', the words 大 *dah* and 小 *sheau* can be placed before *chiing* meaning 'in a big way' and 'on a small scale', but one also speaks of *chiing dah-keh* and *chiing sheau-keh* meaning either 'invite big (prominent) guests' and 'invite small (children or ordinary people) guests' or, with displaced modifiers, 'give a big party' and 'give a small party'.

5.3.4. *Subordinative Phrase and Subordinative Compound.* In the preceding discussion we have cited both phrases and compounds, so long as they satisfy the definition of subordinative constructions. To take a closer view of the difference between subordinative phrases and compounds, consider the following possibilities: If one or both parts are bound, the result is of course a compound, as: 厨房 *chwufarng* BB 'kitchen room,—kitchen', 國際法 *gwojih-faa* BB 'international law', 洋灰 *yanghuei* BF 'foreign dust,—cement', 月餅 *yueh.biing* BF 'moon cake', 大概 *dahgay* FB 'great outline,—probably', 保險箱 *baosheanshiang* FB 'insurance box,—a safe'. If both parts are free and the head is in the neutral tone, then it is a compound, as 客人 *keh.ren* 'guestman,—guest', 大人 *dah.ren* 'big person,—an adult', 元宝胡同 *Yuanbao .Hu.tong* 'Ingot Lane' FF.

What remains then will be cases where there is no neutral tone and both the attribute and the head are free words, FF. In such cases, are the combinations phrases or compound words? Take 好书 *hao-shu* 'good book', 酸蘋菓 *suan pyngguoo* 'sour apple'. These are evidently A-N phrases. Take 油纸 *youjyy* 'oil paper', 城牆 *cherngchyang* 'city wall', 湯勺儿 *tangshaurl* 'soup spoon', 保險公司 *baoshean gongsy* 'insurance company', 中國銀行 *Jong.gwo Ynharng* 'Bank of China'. In such cases a common reaction on the part of both native speakers and grammarians is to ask whether there is any specialization of meaning. If there is, it is a compound; if not, a phrase. A less justifiable approach is to ask whether it is one word or a phrase when translated into a foreign language, English being usually the unconsciously assumed target language. For example, 小米(儿) *sheaumii* or *sheaumieel* 'small rice,—millet', with special meaning, is one word, but 新米 *shin-mii* 'new rice' just any rice which is new, is a phrase. If, however, 牛肉 *niourow* 'beef' is one word because it is one word in English, then 馬肉 *maarow*, which is quite like *niourow* in construction, would be two words because it is two words 'horse meat' in English.

Here a phonological feature will be of help in recognizing a compound in English, but not for Chinese. In an English subordinative phrase, the main stress is on the head and there is a secondary stress or no stress on the attribute, so that ˌfresh 'fish is a phrase and 'freshman is a compound word; ˌred 'tape is a phrase and 'redˌcap is a compound word. But in spite of the differences in conventional orthography the three forms 'fireˌfly, 'fire¬god and 'fire ˌengine have the same stress pattern and are all compound words in the grammatical (as against orthographical) sense. Now the question remains: what is the status of Chinese nouns modifying nouns (when the head is not in the neutral tone)? The simplest way to deal with such cases is to treat them as compounds with or without specialization of meaning, whether or not translatable into one word in a foreign language, whether spelled solid, with a hyphen, or with a space when written in an alphabetic orthography. This is of course a matter of grammatical terminology: when a nominal expression modifies another nominal expression, whether with the main stress on the attribute or with the main stress on the head, the result is a compound. We shall revert to this point when we take up the subordinate forms with .de (sec. 5.6.3).

*5.3.4.1. Distribution of Coordinate Modifiers in Phrases and Compounds.* In section 5.3.3, we considered hierarchies of modification. Now if we have coordinate attributes $X_1X_2$ modifying head Y, we can ask (1) whether the form $X_1YX_2Y$ is also possible, and (2) if possible, whether the sentence containing $X_1X_2Y$ has the same truth value if it is changed to $X_1YX_2Y$. On the whole, if $X_1$, $X_2$, and Y are free forms, distribution into $X_1YX_2Y$ is possible, while if $X_1X_2Y$ is a compound, then distribution is not possible. For example in: 他说了许多有意思跟没意思的话. *Ta shuole sheuduo yeou yih.sy gen mei yih.sy .de huah.* 'He made many interesting and uninteresting remarks.', the head *huah* 'remarks' can be repeated and we get: *Ta shuole sheuduo yeou yih.sy de huah gen mei yih.sy de huah.* and the truth value will be the same. But with: 他有许多有时候好有时候吵的朋友. *Ta yeou sheuduo yeou shyr.howl hao yeou shyr-.howl chao do perng.yeou.* 'He has many friends with whom he is sometimes on good terms and sometimes quarrels.', it is still grammatical to say: *Ta yeou sheuduo yeou shyr.howl hao de*

*perng .yeou gen yeou shyr.howl chao de perng.yeou.* 'He has
many friends with whom he is sometimes on good terms and
many friends with whom he sometimes quarrels.', but the distrib-
uted form obviously has a different truth value. If in the last
example *sheuduo* 'many' is changed into *ig* 'a', then the coordinate modifiers cannot be split at all without changing the sentence into a radically different one.

In compounds, it is usually not possible, even grammatically,
to distribute the modifiers. For example, 寒暑表 *harnshuubeau*
'cold-hot-meter,—thermometer', 红黑帽 *horngheimaw*      'red-
black-cap' cited above, 耒往户头 *laiwoang-huhtour* 'coming-
going account,—on-demand account (at a bank)', 華英字典
*Hwa-Ing-dzyhdean* 'Chinese-English dictionary'.[8]

*5.3.4.2. Postpositions and Directional Complements.* In 牆上
*chyang.shanq* 'on the wall', 天下 *tianshiah* 'under heaven,—the
world', 城裡 ( 头 ) *cherng₀lii(.tou)* 'in the city, down town', which
are translatable into prepositional phrases, the postpositions or
localizers -*.shanq*, -*shiah*, and so on are really heads to which
the preceding parts are attributes, so that *cherng₀lii* (*.tou*), for
instance, is structurally 'city's inside'. These are subordinative
compounds and will be treated in detail under compounds in
chapter 6 (sec. 6.4.4).

In 闩上 *guan.shanq* 'shuts up', 拿耒 *na.lai* 'brings here',
掉下去 *diaw.shiah.chiuh* 'drops down (away)', the -*.shanq*,
-*.lai*, etc., are directional complements, which will be treated in
chapter 6. It should be noted that in spite of a few cases of
class overlap (-*.shanq*, -*shiah*), directional complements are not
heads, and not even centers, since in such compound verbs it is
the first verb which is the center of the construction.

*5.3.5. Class Meaning of Modification.* The meaning of the

---

[8]For more examples of distribution of modifiers in phrases, see 吳 競
存 , 论 向 心 式 Wu Jinqtswen, ("On Endocentric Forms"),     语言学
论 从 *Yeuyanshyue Luenntsorng,* Shanghai, 1957, pp. 135-139 of 130-148.
Wu says that syntactic subordination differs from subordinative compounding in that in the former each of several coordinate modifiers can directly
modify the center. He does not, however, add the warning that the result,
although grammatical, may not always have the same truth value.

modifier to the modified is that of species to genus or special to
the general. As usual, the class meaning of a given grammatical
form is only the meaning of most of the cases under that form,
and some cases do not fit in semantically. In the following examples both compounds and phrases are included. The semantic
categories are set up, not so much to aim at completeness, as to
show the impossibility of covering all varieties of meaning under
a given form. It will be seen that the compounds, as usual, are
more likely to have specialized meanings than the phrases.

(1) Class A modifying class B, resulting in the logical product
AB: 女演員 *neu-yeanyuan* 'woman actor,—actress', *neude yean-
yuan* 'actor who is a woman,—actress'. Since a logical product
is commutative, that is, reversible without affecting the truth
value of the sentence in which it occurs, one would expect AB to
be equivalent to BA. But in matters linguistic, this is so, if and
only if BA exists. Thus there is *neu-yeanyuan* or its synonym 女
戲子 *neu-shihtz*, but there is no °*yeanyuan-neu* or °*yeanshih-
neu*. In the form of phrases we have the logically equivalent
forms *neude yean-shih de* 'woman play-performer' and *yean-shih
de neu.ren* 'play-performing woman'.

(2) Origin, nationality, and so on, as modifier: 井水 *jiing-
shoei* 'well water', 泉水 *chyuan₀shoei* 'spring water', 吕宋 烟
*leu.sonq-ian* 'Luzon smoke,—cigar'. 西洋參 *shiyang-shen* 'Occidental *shen*,—ginseng', 中國人 *Jong.gworen* 'Chinese person,—
a Chinese', 廣東銀行 *Goangdong Ynharng* 'Kwangtung bank,
—Bank of Canton'. Phrase: *Goangdong de ynharng* 'Kwangtung
(province)'s (any) bank'.

(3) Quantity modifying thing: In the form of a numeral modifying a measure (n-M), it is a compound, as 一年 *i-nian* 'year',
多半儿 *duoball* 'greater half', 少数 *shaoshuh* 'few-number,—
minority'. When n-M modifies a noun, we have a phrase: 一个
人 *ig ren*, 几条河 *jii-tyau her* 'several (strips) rivers', 三件行
李 *san-jiann shyng.lii* 'three pieces of luggage'. A limited number of quantitative words can modify nouns directly, as 许多东
西 *sheuduo dong.shi* 'a lot of things'.

(4) Determiner modifying the determined: 这些 *jeh₀shie*

'this amount' or 'these', 哪边儿 *neei-bial* 'which side'. Phrase:
那位先生 *ney-wey shian.sheng* 'that gentleman'.

(5) Person modifying person: 君子人 *jiuntzyy ren* 'gentle-
man(ly) person', *tade bah.bah ~ ta bah.bah* 'his papa', 我们（的）
先生 *woo.men (de) shian.sheng* 'our teacher' *woomen shian.sheng*
(without *de*) 'our (household's) husband,—my husband'.

(6) Person modifying thing: 谁家? *sheir.jia?* 'who, what
family?' 你们（的）学校 *niimen (de) shyueshiaw* 'your school',
咱们的钱 *tzarmen de chyan* 'our money', 我国 *woo gwo* L
'our country', 我军 *woo jiun* L 'our troops'.

(7) Whole modifying part: 狗尾巴 *goou-yii.ba* 'dog's tail',
人心 *renshin* 'human heart (~ mind)', 年底 *niandii* 'year's
bottom,—year's end', 月初 *yuehchu* 'month's beginning, first of
the month', 週末 *joumoh* 'weekend' (transl. borrowing, or calque).
Phrases: 人的身子 *ren de shentz* 'man's body', 桌子的腿
*juotz de toei* 'the leg(s) of a table'.

(8) Quality modifying thing: 白菓 *bairguoo* 'white-fruit,—
gingko'. 臭虫 *chow.chorng* 'stink-bug,—bedbug'. Phrases: 好人
*hao-ren* 'good man', 大樹 *dah-shuh* 'big tree', 红衣裳 *horng
i.shang* 'red garment', 便宜的布 *pyan.yi de buh* 'cheap cloth'.

(9) Material modifying thing: (a) whole: 粉筆 *feenbii* 'powder
writing-instrument,—chalk', 金鐲子 *jinjwotz* 'gold bracelet', 鋼
骨 *gangguu* 'steel bone,—steel bars (for reinforced concrete)';
(b) part: 鋼筆 *gangbii* 'steel pen', 鉛筆 *chianbii* 'lead pencil';
(c) operating part: 火車 *huooche* 'fire vehicle,—train', 汽車 *chihche* 'gas vehicle,—automobile', 電机 *diannji* 'electric machine,—
motor'; (d) changed material: 烟灰 *ianhuei* 'cigarette (etc.)
ashes', 水汽 *shoeichih* 'water gas,—steam'. Under this heading,
phrases, such as 真金的首飾 *jenjin de shoou.shyh* 'jewelry of
real gold', are not as common as compounds.

(10) Thing modifying container: 水缸 *shoeigang* 'water vat',
粉盒儿 *feenher'l* 'powder box,—compact', 酒杯（儿）*jeou-
bei (~ - bel)* 'wine cup'.

(11) Action modifying goal: 薰鱼 *shiunyu* 'smoked fish', 燒
饼 *shau.bing* 'baked cake,—sesame hot biscuit', 敬菜 *jinqtsay*

'presented dish,—complimentary dish (on the house)'. Phrases: 写的字 *shiee de tzyh* 'written words', 炒的饭 *chao de fann* 'fried rice'.

(12) Purpose modifying thing: 靠椅 *kawyii* 'reclining chair', 炒锅 *chaoguo* 'frying pot', 洗澡水 *shiitzao-shoei* 'take-bath water'. Phrases: 喝酒的杯子 *he jeou de beitz* 'cup for drinking wine', 我写大字的纸 *woo shiee dah-tzyh de jyy* 'paper on which I write large characters', 我睡的床 *woo shuey de chwang* 'the bed I sleep in', 我住的地方儿 *woo juh de dih-.fangl* 'the place where I live'.

(13) Action modifying actor: 来人 *lairen* 'come-man,—messenger (from receiver's point of view)', 飛机 *feiji* 'flying machine,—airplane', 流水 *lioushoei* 'flowing water'. Phrases: 来的人 *lai de ren* '(any) person that comes', 捱了一顿打的人 *airle i-duenn daa de ren* 'man who has received a beating' (action-actor in form only).

(14) Goal modifying actor or instrument: 书贩子 *shu-fanntz* 'bookdealer', 牙刷儿(～子) *yashual (～-tz)* 'toothbrush', 手套儿 *shooutawl* 'hand-coverer,—glove', 螺丝起子 *luo.sychiitz* 'screw puller,—screwdriver', which can be compared with 'woman hater' and 'lady killer' (in the usual sense).

(15) Thing modifying locality: 桌儿上 *juol.shanq* 'table-topside, —on the table', 家裡 *jia.lii* 'home-inside,—in the home', 陛下 *bihshiah* 'imperial court steps' below,—below the imperial steps, —Your (～ His) majesty'. Phrases: 桌子的底下 *juotz de dii-.shiah* 'table's below,—under the table', 你的旁边儿 *niide parngbial* 'your lateral-side,—beside you'.

(16) Locality modifying thing: 上房儿 *shanqfarngl* 'upper rooms,—master's rooms', 下房儿 *shiahfarngl* 'servants' quarters', 底下人 *dii.shiah₀ren* 'below man,—servant'. Phrases: 这儿的人 *jell de ren* 'here's people,—the people here', 底下的人 *dii.shiah de ren* 'the people down below' (not necessarily, and usually not, servants).

(17) Thing-locality modifying thing: 门外汉 *menway-hann* 'outside-the-door man,—man who is outside the field,—amateur-

ish man, dabbler', 梁上君子 *liangshanq jiuntzyy* 'gentleman (hiding) on the girder,—burglar'. Phrases: 报上的新闻 *baw-.shanq de shinwen* 'news in the newspaper', *tzay baw.shanq de shinwen* 'news which is in the newspaper', 登在报上的 新闻 *deng tzay baw.shanq de shinwen* 'news which is published in the newspaper'.

(18) Event modifying time: 雨前 *yeuchyan* 'before the rain, —(hence, exocentrically, green) tea picked before spring rain', 饭 後 *fannhow* 'after meal'. Phrases: 下雨以前 *shiah-yeu yii-chyan* 'before it rains (literally)', 写大字的时候儿 *shiee dah-tzyh de shyr.howl* 'time of or for writing large characters'.

(19) Modality modifying quality or event: Phrases: 还好 *hair hao* 'rather good', 不要 *buyaw* 'does not want', 大概会 *dahgay huey* 'probably can', 一定来 *idinq lai* 'will certainly come', 也 许行 *yeesheu shyng* 'possibly all right'.

(20) Manner modifying action: Phrases: 这么做 *tzemm tzuoh* 'do this way', 怎么说 *tzeem shuo* 'how say it?', 好儿的走 *haohaulde tzoou* 'walks properly'.

(21) Degree modifying quality: Phrases: 这么好 *tzemm hao* 'so good', 多宽? *dwo kuan?* 'how wide?' (or '!'), 太小 *tay sheau* 'too small', 非常奇怪 *feicharng chyiguay* 'extremely strange', 侭量的发展 *jiinlianqde fajaan* 'develops to the fullest extent'.

It will be noted that the preceding headings are neither exhaustive nor mutually exclusive. Take the compound 水泥 *shoeini* 'water clay,—cement' or the phrase 主要的原因 *juuyaw de yuan'in* 'principal cause'. They do not fit very clearly in any of the preceding headings. The class meaning of modification as species to genus has to be quite vague, and the only thing about modification that is clear and constant is that there is only one center[9] and it is in second position. In other words, only form is clear and well defined, while the actual meanings under

---

[9]In the case of forms like *laonian de nanneu* 'old-aged men-and-women', although *nanneu* is two centers in a coordinate compound, it is one center in the larger, subordinative construction.

the form are always shifting in scope, as is to be expected (cf. sec. 1.1.2.6).

*5.3.6. The Particle de*

*5.3.6.1. The Particle de as a Marker of Explicit Modification.* In discussing suffixes in chapter 4 (sec. 4.4.6), we examined briefly the various kinds of *de* which in recent written bairhuah have been written and read as 底 *dii* for 'of' or '-'s', as 的 *dih* for '-(t)ic, -al', and as 地 *dih* for '-ly', features which are partly reflected in some Central and Southern dialects. In spoken Peiping, however, everything is *de*.

In the examples of various meanings of modification in the preceding section, it may be noted that those with *de* are always phrases, while most of those without *de* are compounds. Various writers have noticed the explicit prominence given to the modifier by *de*. Without *de* the attribute is an inherent part of the thing modified, as 黑鹅 *hei-er* 'black goose', which is just an item of which the blackness is taken for granted, while *hei de er* 'black kind of goose' is contrasted with geese which are white. In: 我爱青山绿水. *Woo ay ching-shan liuh-shoei.* 'I love blue mountains and green waters.', *ching-shan* and *liuh-shoei* are just parts of the landscape, but with *de* inserted after the adjectives it makes explicit my preference for those colors over other colors.[10] The same point has been made by Dragunov (secs. 155 ff.), who makes the further point that attributive adjectives without *de* are like nouns, as in 好书 *hao-shu* 'good book', 要紧话 *yawjiin huah* 'important words', to be compared with 铁箱子 *tiee shiangtz* 'iron box', 木头桌子 *muh.tou juotz* 'wood table, —wooden table', whereas *yawjiin de huah* 'words that are important', *heen hao de shu* 'very good book' are more like verbal modifiers such as 昨天来的人 *tzwo.tian lai de ren* 'the man who came yesterday', 我念的书 *woo niann de shu* 'the book I read'.

This bringing into explicit prominence by the particle *de* can

---

[10]Examples from 陈瓊瓚, 修饰语和名词之间的"的"字的研究 (Chern Chyongtzann, "Study of the Word *de* Between Modifiers and Nouns"), *ZGYW*, no. 40:22-27 (1955).

be viewed as another way of implying a logical predicate, when
it does not coincide with the grammatical predicate. In chapter
2 (sec. 2.5.2) we noted that logical predicate can be expressed by
putting a contrasting stress on it. Here we find that a similar but
slightly weaker effect is attained by the use of *de*. In: 我 要
找 一 个 空 碗. *Woo yaw jao ig kong-woan.* 'I am looking for an
empty bowl.', the predicate is in the verbal expression as a whole.
But in: *Woo yaw jao ig kong de woan.* 'I am looking for a bowl
that's empty.', there is a secondary logical predicate contained in
*kong de* 'that's empty'. If a contrasting stress is placed on *kong*
in either form of the sentence, then the logical predicate is entirely in the stressed part.[11] The predicative nature of the *de*-
forms is probably more important than the verbal nature that was
noted by Dragunov. Thus, with nominal attributes there is still
the difference between *tiee shiangtz* 'iron box' and *tiee de shiangtz*
'box (made) of iron', where *tiee de* can be regarded as an implied (nominal predicate).

 *5.3.6.2. Restrictive and Descriptive Uses of* de. Although *de*
marks explicit modification, it has less logical force when used
descriptively than when used restrictively. For example, in:
可 怜 的 孩 子! 饿 了 也 没 的 吃! *Keelian de hairtz! Ehle yee
mei de chy!* 'Poor child! He's hungry and has nothing to eat!'
*keelian de* only describes *hairtz* rather than distinguishing it from
other *hairtz*. If there is a demonstrative D-M modifier and another modifier, the order determines whether it is restrictive or
descriptive. For example: (a) 那 位 戴 眼 镜 儿 的 先 生 是 谁?
*Ney-wey day yeanjienql de shian.sheng sh sheir?* 'Who is that
gentleman (who incidentally is) wearing glasses?': (b) *Day yeanjienql de ney-wey shian.sheng sh sheir* 'Who is the gentleman
who is wearing glasses (not the one who is not wearing glasses)?'
But if a contrasting stress is placed on a modifier, it is used restrictively, so that if *day yeanjienql* in (a) is contrastively stressed,
the sentence will have the same restrictive sense as in (b).

 The same may be said of adverbial modifiers. For example,
in (a) 来 回 的 这 样 看 *laihwei de jehyanq kann* 'to look thus

---

 [11]The examples are adapted from Dwight L. Bolinger, "Linear Modification", *PMLA*, 67:1122-1123 of 1117-1144 (1952).

back and forth (and not straight ahead)', but (b) *jehyanq laihwei de kann* 'to look thus, i.e., back and forth'. With contrasting stress, the stressed modifier acquires restrictive status: "*jehyanq (bu nahyanq) laihwei de kann* 'to look back and forth in this manner (not in that manner)': *jehyanq "laihwei de kann (bu ijyr kann)* 'to look lack and forth (not straight ahead)'.

In both the adjectival and adverbial modifiers, the same effect of restrictive modification can be achieved by downgrading the stresses one peg, that is, ordinary stress for contrasting stress and neutral tone for ordinary stress (and neutral tone). (Cf. sec. 1.3.6.)

A somewhat weaker effect of the order of demonstratives has to do with permanent as against temporary characteristics in the modifier. For example, 那个爱说话的人 *neyg ay shuo-huah de ren* 'the man who loves to talk,—that talkative man', but 穿黑大衣的那个人 *chuan hei-dahi de neyg ren* 'that man (who happens to be) wearing a black overcoat'. Another effect of a postposed demonstrative is liveliness: 見了书就買 的那个人 *jiannle shu jiow mae de neyg ren* 'the man who buys any book he sees' is more lively than *neyg jiannle shu jiow mae de* (with or without a second *neyg*) *ren*.[12]

*5.3.6.3. de as a Marker of Nonlexical Phrases.* Although compounds are likely to have idiomatic or lexical meanings and phrases are likely to have meanings which are synthesizable from the meanings of the parts, the opposite is sometimes also possible. For instance, 三天 *san-tian* 'three days', 水裡 *shoei.lii* 'in the water', 刀把儿 *dauball* 'knife handle' are transient-word compounds with no meaning other than those of the parts put together, while the phrase 蓝青友话 *lanching Guanhuah* 'blue and green Mandarin' has the special meaning of Mandarin spoken with a provincial accent. If, however, the attribute is marked with *de*, the resulting phrase is more likely to be taken literally. Thus ( 老 ) 玉米 *lao-yuh.mii ~ yuh.mii* '(Indian) corn': *lao de yuh-.mii* or *lao de lao-yuh.mii* 'corn which has grown tough'; 来人 *lairen* 'messenger': *lai de ren* '(any) person that comes'; 中國銀 行 *Jong.gwo Ynharng* 'Bank of China': *Jong.gwo de ynharng* '(any)

---

[12]Examples from a letter from Lien-Sheng Yang, who also called my attention to the effects of the differences in word order.

bank in or of China'; 廣东銀行 *Goangdong Ynharng* 'Bank of Canton': *Goangdong de ynharng* 'Cantonese bank' or 'bank in Kwangtung province'; 美國銀行 *Meei.gwo Ynharng* 'Bank of America'; *Meei.gwo de ynharng* 'an American bank'; 德國飯店 *Der.gwo Fanndiann* '(name of hotel in Peiping which calls itself) "Hotel du Nord"': *Der.gwo de fanndian* '(any) German hotel'; 烙餅 *lawbiing* 'baked (non-sweet) cake about 1 inch thick and 1 foot in diameter': *law de biing* 'baked (non-sweet) cake of any size'; 薄餅 *baurbiing* 'Chinese tortillas': *baur de biing* '(any non-sweet) cake that is thin'; 大麥 *dah$_o$may* 'big wheat,—barley': *dah de maytz* 'large wheat plant'; 小米 *sheau$_o$mii* 'little rice,—millet': *sheau de mii* 'small-grain rice'; 小孩儿 *sheauharl* 'small-child,—child (large or small)': *sheau-sheauharl* ~ *sheau de sheau-harl* 'small child'. In many cases, of course, the insertion of *de* only serves to make the modification more explicit and involves no change of meaning. Examples are: 保險公司 *baoshean gongsy* 'insurance company': *baoshean de gongsy* 'company for insurance'; 樹頂儿 *shuhdieengl* 'treetop': *shuh de dieengl* 'top of a tree'.

5.3.6.4. *Zero and de as Markers of ICs*. In general, a zero marks smaller constituents and *de* marks larger constituents. For example, of the four forms:

| | | | |
|---|---|---|---|
| (1) 好　学生的宿舍 | *hao* | *shyue.sheng* | *de suhsheh* |
| (2) 好的学生　宿舍 | *hao de shyue.sheng* | | *suhsheh* |
| (3) 好　学生　宿舍 | *hao* | *shyue.sheng* | *suhsheh* |
| (4) 好的学生的宿舍 | *hao de shyue.sheng* | | *de suhsheh* |

(1) means 'dormitory for good students', (2) 'good dormitory for students', (3) is ambiguous, with greater likelihood of being the same as (1), and (4) is ambiguous. Exceptionally, because of the resistance to breaking up a compound, an IC construction of the form (A *de* B) + C is sometimes found. I have heard, for example, 整的草莓糕 *jeeng de tsaomeigau*, apparently meaning 'strawberry cake which is whole', whereas it actually meant 'strawberry cake with whole strawberries', which with a clearer but less convenient way of phrasing would be 整(个儿)草莓的 草莓糕 *jeeng(gehl) tsaomei de tsaomeigau*.

*5.3.6.5. Types of Constructions with de.* We shall now give examples of types of constructions in which the modifier is introduced by *de:* (1) Nominal expressions with a nominal head; (2) attributes nominalized by a final *de* without a following nominal head; and (3) adverbial attributes modifying an adjectival or verbal head. They correspond approximately to the artificially differentiated (1) 底 *dii* and 的 $dih_1$, (2) 的 $dih_1$, and (3) 地 $dih_2$ (sec. 4.4.6).

(1) Nominal Expressions

(1.1) Type N *de* N → N. After any pronoun: 我 的 书 *woode shu* 'my book', 他们的东西 *tamende dong.shi* 'their things', 谁 的 话 ? *sheirde huah?* 'whose words?' After nouns: 象的 鼻子 *shianq de byitz* 'elephant's trunk', 後门的鑰匙 *howmen de yaw.shyr* 'the key to the back door', 人類的命運 *renley de minq₀yunn* 'the destiny of man', 牙的刷子 *ya de shuatz* 'brush for the teeth'. After personal pronouns *de* is usually omitted before nouns for personal relations (unless the modification is to be made specially explicit), as 我父親 *woo fuh.chin* 'my father', 他先生教他作文儿 , *Ta shian.sheng jiau ta tzuoh-wel,* 'His teacher teaches him composition,' *keesh woode shian.sheng bu* 'but my teacher does not'.

If the center is a place word, the result is also a place expression, e.g., *chyan.tou* 'the front': 桌子的前头 *juotz de chyan.tou* 'the front of the table', *dong.bial* 'the east': 美國的 东边儿 *Meei.gwo de dong.bial* '(in or to) the east of the United States'. If the first N is a place word, it usually translates into a prepositional phrase in English, as 屋裡的人 *u.lii de ren* 'the people in the room', 國外的新闻 *gwoway de shinwen* 'news from outside the country,—foreign news'.[13] Like the case of personal relations, a pronoun before a place word often has the *de* omitted, as in 我左边儿 *woo tzuoo.bial* 'my left', 你上头 *nii shanq.tou* 'your above'.

If the subordinate part consists of a D-M compound, no *de* is inserted if the M is an individual classifier, or if the D is a

---

[13]For details on place words, see sec. 7.3.3.

demonstrative, as 两条蛇 *leang-tyau sher* 'two snakes', but no °*leang-tyau de sher:* there is 那磅肉 *ney-banq row* 'that pound of meat' but no °*ney-banq de row.* With a numeral and a measure, then the *de* is optional, as *leang-banq (de) row* 'two pounds of meat'. With a temporary measure, a *de* is usually, though not absolutely, required, as 一 地 ( 的 ) 水 *i-dih (de) shoei* 'a floorful of water', 一屋 子 ( 的 ) 人 *i-utz (de) ren* 'a roomful of people', 一 身 ( 的 ) 汗 *i-shen (de) hann* 'a bodyful of perspiration'.

There is an equational or appositional use of *de* in which, although it is formally a subordinative relation, involves two terms for what in fact are the same thing. In ㄆㄧ ㄆㄚˊ ˋ 的声音 *pipapipa de sheng.in* 'the sound of pitapat' the sound is namely 'pitapat' which is a different kind of relation from 琵琶 *pyi.ba de sheng.in* 'the sound of the (instrument called) pipa'. In " 坏 " 是 " 不好 "的意思. *"Huay" sh "buhao" de ₀yih.sy.* ' "Bad" means "not good".', the force of *de* is to say that *buhao* 'not good' is namely the *yih.sy* 'meaning'. With the usual subordinative *de* one would say *"Huay" de yih.sy sh "buhao"*, 'The meaning of *"huay"* is *"buhao"*, i.e., 'The meaning of "bad" is "not good" ', but, though more logical and equally grammatical, it is not the usual formula for giving the meaning of a word.

Quite analogous to *sh... de ₀yih.sy* 'means...' is the formula 是 ... 的 缘 故 *sh... de ₀yuan.guh* 'because...'. Now there are three synonyms, *yuan.guh* 'reason, cause', *yian'in* 'cause', *liiyou* 'reason, ground'. All can be used after *de* in the ordinary subordinative sense, as 我来晚了的 缘 故 (～原因) 是因为瘪了 车胎了. *Woo lai-woanle de yuan.guh (～yuan'in) sh inwey bieele chetai le* 'The reason for (or cause of) my arriving late was because I had a flat tire'. 我不去的理由是因为我不 应该去. *Woo bu chiuh de liiyou sh inwey woo bu inggai chiuh.* 'The reason I am not going is that I ought not to go'. But in the equational sense, *de* can be used with *yuan.guh* (rarely with *yuan'in* and *liiyou*) as 'the reason, namely...', as: *Woo lai-woanle sh bieele chetai le de ₀yuan.guh* 'I came late for the reason that I had a flat tire'. An optional *inwey* can be inserted after *sh*, as: *Woo bu chiuh sh inwey woo bu inggai chiuh de ₀yuan.guh* 'That I am not going is because I ought not to go (: that's the reason).'

This equational use of *de*, which applies to onomatopoeia, to definitions, and to clauses for reason or cause, can be compared to a similar use of 'of' in English where the two expressions before and after it refer to the same thing, as in *'the state of California,—the* state, namely, California', no more, no less—as contrasted with the 'of' in 'the state of the Union', which has the usual kind of 'of'.[14]

Similar to the equational *de* is the use of *de* between two quantity words in the sense of 'and' or 'plus', as in 二 十 的 三 十 是 五 十。 *Ellshyr de sanshyr sh wuushyr.* 'Twenty's thirty is fifty,—20 + 30 = 50.' Another similar (optional) *de* is used in doing sums on the abacus, as in 三 塊 三 毛,（的）一 个 五 *san-kuay san-mau, (de) ig wuu* 'three dollars thirty cents, and a five (cents)', where the *de* and *ig* are time fillers while the fingers are getting ready to push the next bead.

A special possessive use of *de* is to express a person's part in some setup, so that X *de* Y is short for X *tzuoh de sh* Y 'What X does (~ did) is (~ was) (the part as) Y'. For example: 今儿是 我 的 东. *Jiel sh woode dong.* 'Today is my (part as) host.' 太陽说: " 世界上是 我 的 主人 啊，怎么 会 是 你 的 主人 呐？" *Tay.yang shuo: "Shyh.jieh.shanq sh woode juu.ren a, tzeem huey sh niide juu.ren ne?"* 'The Sun said (to the North Wind): "It is my (part to be) master in the world, how can it be your (part to be) master?"' 昨儿 请 客是 老 張 的 大师傅，老 李 的 二 把 刀。 *Tzwol chiing-keh sh Lao Jang de dah.shy.fuh, Lao Lii de ellbaadau.* 'For yesterday's party, Jang was chef, Lii was assistant chef.'

The last subtype of N *de* N which deserves special mention is what I call "possessive objects". For example: 打岔 *daa-chah* 'strike interruption,—interrupt': *daa tade chah* 'strikes his interruption,—interrupts him', 挑眼儿 *tiau-yeal* 'pick loopholes—find fault': 挑别人 的眼儿 *tiau bye.ren de yeal* 'pick on other people's loopholes,—find fault with others', 帮 忙 *bang-mang* 'help in getting busy': *bang ren de mang* 'help people's being busy,— helps people'. In all these cases the real goal of the action, which

---

[14]See also sec. 2.12.7 on *de* ₀*yuan.guh.*

is a person, is in the subordinate form with *.de,* while the formal object is only part of the V-O idiom. For brevity I call the goal word in possessive form the "possessive object" (secs. 5.4.6.6 and 6.5.7(4).[15]

(1.2) Type N *de* A → N. This is infrequent: 我的窮是人 ㄥ知道的。 *Woode chyong sh renren jy.daw de.* 'My (being) poor is what everyone knows.' More commonly the adjective is put in the predicate form, without *de,* so that *Woo chyong* will be a clause subject 'That I am poor is...'

An interesting example of the two preceding types of *de* from written bairhuah is the following: 因為从那裡面， 看見了被压迫者的善良的灵魂，的心酸，的爭執 ... *Inwey nahliimiann, kann.jiannle beyiapohjee de shannliang de linghwen, de shinsuan, de jengjyr ...*[16] 'Because from there one saw the oppressed ones' good soul, 's bitter(ness), 's struggl-(ing) ...'. This is of course not normal speech, but besides exemplifying the nominalizing of a verb or adjective after a *.de,* it also shows Luu Shiunn's feeling for the bound morpheme *.de* struggling to become free—not only to be end-free, which it already is, but also to be start-free, for which this is, to my knowledge, still a *hapax legomenon.*[17]

(1.3) Type N *de* V → N. This form is not very common in speech. Examples are: 他的说谎是个習慣. *Tade shuo-hoang sh g shyiguann.* 'His lying is a habit.' 你信他的不懂! *Nii shinn tade bu doong!* '(Don't) you believe his not understanding (you)!' In wenyan (with *jy* instead of *de*) and in written bairhuah, this form is fairly common, as 王之不王 *wang jy bu wanq* L 'the king's not ruling in a kingly manner', 政客们的 爭权夺利 *jenqkehmen de jeng-chyuan dwo-lih* 'the politicians'

---

[15]This construction is just the opposite of the German usage in which what might be a possessive pronoun is more idiomatically put in the dative form, as in: *Wehmut schleicht mir ins Herz hinein* 'Sadness steals to me into the heart,—into my heart'; *aufs Haupt dir legen* 'on the head to you lay, —lay on your head'.

[16]鲁迅(Luu Shiunn), quoted in Luh, *GTFaa,* 136, punctuation as in original.

[17]See English example of 'an hour [pause]'s drive away', chap. 3, n. 14.

wrangling over power and fighting for advantage', 英语的学习 *Ingyeu de shyueshyi* 'the learning of the English language'.

(1.4) Type A *de* N → N. This is of course a very productive type, as 深的水 *shen de shoei* 'deep water', 大的國家 *dah de gwojia* 'a large country', 淡青的布 *dannching de buh* 'light blue cloth', 麻煩的事情 *ma.farn de shyh.chyng* 'troublesome business'. It would seem that any adjective could be in attributive position before any noun without any marker like *de*. Actually the versatility of A + N is much less than that of A *de* N. Thus, while there is both 白紙 *bair-jyy* and *bair de jyy* for 'white paper', there is no °窄紙 °*jae-jyy* for which one says *jae de jyy* 'narrow (kind of) paper'. There is no °辛苦工人 °*shin₀kuu gong₀ren*, but *shin₀kuu de gong₀ren* 'hard-working (kind of) workmen', no °聰明小鳥儿 °*tsong.ming sheauneaul*, but *tsong.ming de sheauneaul* 'clever little birds'. In the case of an adjective modified by an adverb, *de* is always required. Thus there is 闊人 *kuoh-ren* 'rich man', but no °很闊人 °*heen kuoh ren* 'very rich man', for which one must say *heen kuoh de ren*. An apparent exception is 特別快車 *tehbye* + *kuay* + *che* 'specially fast train', but the correct ICs are *tehbye* 'special' and *kuay-che* 'fast train'.[18]

Adjectives, with or without *de*, do not as a rule modify pronouns. A form like 一个无産无業无家可归的我 *ig wu-chaan wu-yeh wu-jia-kee-guei de woo* 'a propertyless, jobless, and homeless I' is definitely only seen in print and never used in speech. The only comparable expression that is sometimes spoken is 可憐的我 *keelian de woo* 'poor me', which, however, is not as common as a different construction without *de*, as in: 可憐他在那儿一个人都不认得. *Keelian ta tzaynall ig ren dou bu rennde.* 'Pity him, not knowing a single person there.'

(1.5) Type V *de* N → N. Since *de* marks the general relation of subordination, there may be several different ways in which V can modify N. In 来的人 *lai de ren* 'the man who comes', 回去的船 *hwei.chiuh de chwan* 'the ship which goes back', N is

---

[18]For further details on adjectives, see chap. 8.

agent of the action V. In 吃的东西 *chy de dong.shi* 'things to eat', 穿髒了的衣裳 *chuan-tzangle de i.shang* 'clothes which have been worn dirty', N is the goal of the action V. In 下的 雨 *shiah de yeu* 'the rain which is falling', 閞着的水 *kaij de shoei* 'the water which is boiling', 经营的方法 *jing'yng de fangfaa* 'the method of managing', the relation of V to N is more general and there is no clear actor or goal.

(1.6) Type V-O *de* N → N. A common type of action is expressed by the V-O construction, which may be related to a following noun as agent, goal, or one of a number of relations often expressed in English by prepositions. Examples are: 走道儿 的人 *tzoou-dawl de ren* 'man who is walking', 学工程的学 生 *shyue gong₀cherng de shyue.sheng* 'students who are studying engineering', 買菜的老媽子 *mae-tsay de laomhatz* 'maidservant who buys provisions', 刷牙的刷子 *shua-ya de shuatz* 'the brush which brushes or with which to brush teeth', 掃地的条 帚 *sao-dih de tyau.joou* 'the broom which sweeps or with which to sweep the floor', 学工程的資格 *shyue gong₀cherng de tzy.ger* 'qualifications for studying engineering', 買菜的錢 *mae tsay de chyan* 'money for buying provisions', 打字的纸 *daa-tzyh de jyy* 'paper for typing', 退烧的药 *tuey-shau de yaw* 'drug for reducing or which reduces fever'. Note that the alternate translations are purely a matter of English grammar and there is nothing in the Chinese forms that is two-valued either in form or in meaning.

If there is a demonstrative *jeyg, neyg,* and so on, its position before or after the modifying phrase depends on such factors as whether the phrase is restrictive or descriptive, whether it expresses a temporary or permanent characteristic, and whether it is a lively or plain modifier. For examples, see section 5.3.6.2.

(1.7) Type S-P *de* N. When a clause in the form of a subject and predicate modifies a noun, a simple *de* is sufficient to indicate the relation, as 我写的信 *woo shiee de shinn* 'the letter I write', 他喝湯的勺儿 *ta he-tang de shaurl* 'the spoon he eats soup with'. As these forms have been described fully in chapter 2, under subordinate clauses, we shall not go into them further.

(2) *de* as Nominalizer. We shall consider the nominalizing *de*

as a morpheme in a different function from the subordinative *de* (corresponding approximately to *dih₁*). This form X *de* acquires a nominal status when Y is omitted from X *de* Y. But once *de* acquires the status of a nominalizer, it can be so used even though no particular nominal expression can be specified as having been omitted or understood, as in types 2.2 to 2.7 below.

(2.1) Type X *de* Y → X *de*. 这是我的书. *Jeh sh woode shu.* 'This is my book': *Shu sh woode.* 'The book is mine.'; 很紧的门 *heen jiinde men* 'a very tight door': *Jey-shann men sh heen jiin de.* 'This door is a (or the) tight one.' 这是喝的水。 *Jeh sh he de shoei.* 'This is drinking water.': *Jeh shoei sh he de.* 'This water is for drinking.'; 他是从中国来的人。 *Ta sh tsorng Jong.gwo lai de ren.* 'He is a man who comes from China.': *Ta sh tsorng Jong.gwo lai de.* 'He is one who comes from China.'; 他是卖酒的人。 *Ta sh may-jeou de ren.* 'He is a man who sells wines.': *Ta sh may-jeou de.* 'He is one who sells wines.' Thus *de* acquires the status of a nominalizer when the noun itself is understood.

(2.2) Type V (-O)-*de* as '-er', or regular agent. We have seen that, in formal or L style, agent or profession is often expressed by 者 *-jee*, as in 译者 *yihjee* 'translator', 吊者 *diawjee* 'mourner' L. In ordinary speech *de* is used, as in 掌櫃的 *jaanggueyde* 'control counter -er, —owner or manager of an old-style store', 要饭儿的 *yawfallde* 'asks for food -er, —beggar', 打杂儿的 *daatzarlde* 'does sundries -er, —general-purpose servant (outdoors)'. Note that while the type 2.1 *de* can be equated in most cases to 之 *jy* in L, this agent *de* of type 2.2 cannot be equated to *jy*, but to *jee*, which is one of the reasons for considering type 2.2 as a morpheme in a different function from type 2.1.

While it is possible to add a word like *ren* after the agent *de*, it sometimes changes a specialized agent into a more general one, as 做饭的 *tzuoh-fann de* 'prepare meal -er,—cook', but *tzuoh fann de ren* 'one who (incidentally) prepares a meal'; 掃街的 *saojie de* 'sweep street -er, —street cleaner': *sao jie de ren* 'man who sweeps the street (possibly just the part in front of his house)'.

(2.3) Type *de* expressing result or extent. Result or extent is sometimes expressed by a blend of 到 *daw* and *de*, usually weakened to *de*, as in: 收音机闹的我听不見你说话了。 *Shouinji naw de woo ting.bu-jiann nii shuo-huah le.* 'The radio is so loud that I can't hear you talk.' When the result is not actually expressed, then the *de* acquires a nominal status, as in: 你看你洒的！ *Nii kann nii saa de!* 'You look at what (the result) you have splashed!' 头疼是苃烧苃的。 *Tour$_0$terng sh fa-shau fa de.* 'The headache was the result of having a fever.' 他病了是想你想的。 *Ta binq le sh sheang nii sheang de.* 'That he got sick was the result of missing you (badly).' 一个人得近視眼多半儿是看书看的。 *Ig ren der jinn.shyh-yean duoball sh kann-shu kann de.* 'A person gets myopia mostly from reading.' (Cf sec. 5.6.3.2.)

(2.4) Situational *de.* Sometimes the *de* refers to the whole situation with the meaning of 'such is the case', 'this is the kind of situation' and no particular noun is understood or can be supplied rather than some other noun. For example: 他是跟你闹玩笑的。 *Ta sh gen nii kai wanshiaw de.* 'He was just joking with you that-was-what-he-was-doing.' If *ren* were supplied after *de*, it would mean 'He (and not someone else) is the man who...' 你不能走了就算完事的。 *Nii buneng tzooule jiow suann wan-shyh de.* 'You can't just go away and consider the business done that's-the-situation.', where no noun could be supplied after *de* that would fit the construction. Because this *de* is in construction with the whole preceding clause, it is properly a sentence particle (sec. 8.5.5, P 1).

A special idiom with this type of *de* consists of *sh*, followed by the clause with *de*, predicated by an adjective. For example, 我想是先说的（法子，办法，...)好。*Woo sheang sh shian shuo de (fartz, bannfaa, etc.) hao.* 'I think (the method, the alternative, etc.) to say it first is better,—I think better say it first.' 还是不理他的（法子，办法，...) 聰明。 *Hairsh bu lii ta de (fartz, bannfaa, etc.) tsong.ming.* 'After all, it's wiser not to pay any attention to him.'

(2.5) *de* for specification. With *sh* and *de* a sentence often

throws the logical predicate to some other part than the verb
(sec. 2.5.1), with the force of 'it is... that...'. For example: 他是
要去休息ˢˢ的. *Ta sh yaw chiuh shiou.shyi.shiou.shyi de.*
'It is (∼was) to take a rest that he is going (∼went).' 他是从
日本来的. *Ta sh tsorng Ryhbeen lai de.* 'It was from Japan
that he came.'   您是来看房子咑? *Nin sh lai kann farngtz
d'a?* 'You came to look at the house? (It was to look at the house
that you came?)'

(2.6) Type V-O *de* → V *de* O. There is a specially Northern
usage in which a specifying *de* involving an object, which ordinarily calls for the form V-O *de*, takes the form V *de* O instead. For
example, without any specifying *de*, one says: 我昨儿去看戏
了. *Woo tzwol chiuh kann-shih le.* 'I went to see a play yesterday.' In the specifying form, one could say: 我是昨儿去看
戏的. *Woo sh tzwol chiuh kann-shih de.* 'It was yesterday that
I went to see a play.' But the usual way is to say: *Woo sh tzwol
chiuh kann de shih.* This actually means the same thing, but
seems to be saying 'I was the play which was seen yesterday.',
which of course would not make sense. When, however, such an
interpretation does make sense, it leads to genuine homophony,
as in: 他是去年生的小孩儿. *Ta sh chiuh.nian sheng de
sheauharl.* (1) with specifying *de:* 'It was last year that she gave
birth to a child'; (2) with ordinary restrictive *de:* 'He (or she) is
a child who was born last year.' 他是昨儿考的博士. *Ta sh
tzwol kao de borshyh.* (1) with specifying *de*, direction of action
outward: 'It was yesterday that he (the professor) gave an examination for the degree of Ph.D.; (2) with specifying *de*, direction
of action inward: 'It was yesterday that he was examined for the
degree of Ph.D.'; (3) with ordinary restrictive *de:* 'He is the Ph.D.
who took his examination yesterday.' Following are further examples of the specifying *de:*   那个電影儿是谁買的票?
*Neyg diannyeengl sh sheir mae de piaw?* 'Who was it who bought
the ticket(s) for that movie?' (Cf. *Jeh sh sheir mae de piaw?* 'This
is a ticket ∼ these are tickets bought by whom?')   那房子
是張先生画的圖, 王先生包的工, 李先生出的錢.
*Neh farngtz sh Jang .Shian.sheng huah de twu, Wang .Shian.-
sheng bau de gong, Lii .Shian.sheng chu de chyan.* 'About that

house, it was Mr. Jang who drew the plans, Mr. Wang who contracted for the job, and Mr. Lii who put up the money.'

(2.7) Type *de de* → *de*. Just as *le le* is telescoped into *le* by haplology (sec. 4.4.5), the same thing happens when two *de*'s come together. For example, to the question: 这 是 谁 的 筐 子 ? *Jeh sh sheirde kuangtz?* 'Whose basket is this?' one may answer: 是 那 个 卖 菜 的。*Sh neyg maytsayde.*, which seems to say 'It's the vegetable vendor.', which would not be answering what is being asked. If one wishes to answer 'It's that vegetable vendor's.', it would seem that, since *-or* in 'vendor' is usually equivalent to *de* and *'s* is also equivalent to *de*, one would have to say: °*Sh neyg maytsayde de*, and yet nobody says *de de* ever in any context. A natural speaker of Mandarin refuses to say it even when he sees *de de* in print. This happened when I tried to teach my two oldest daughters Li Jiinshi's *Gwoyeu Muofann* (sic) *Dwubeen* (National Language Model Reader), Shanghai, 1928, where it says (p. 27) 打 猎 的 的 槍 *daaliehde de chiang* (actually spelt *-di di*) 'the hunter's gun', the first *de* ( 的 ) being the *-er* in 'hunter' and the second *de* ( 底 ) the *'s*. But correct them as I would, they kept saying *daaliehde chiang*, which would seem to say 'hunting gun'. But their feeling for the language would not allow *de de* any more than it would allow *le le*, logic or no logic. However, if a pause occurs, whether in a very deliberate discussion or through an accidental interruption (cf. sec. 3.3.3), then the two *de*'s do get untelescoped, as in *Jeh sh maytsayde* (cough) *de kuangtz.*, but not with a single nominalizing *de*, as in °*Jeh kuangtz sh maytsayde* (cough) *de.*

(3) Adverbial *de*. We noted that, in the new style of writing, *dih₂* ( 地 ) should be used for endings of adverbial expressions and that the distinction between *dih₁* and *dih₂* is reflected in the dialects, such as 嘅 *keh* and 哋 *dey°* in Cantonese. The following types of adverbial *de* may be recognized:

(3.1) *de* in vivid adverbs. Under vivid reduplicates we met forms like 好 ㄠ ㄦ 的 做 *haohaulde tzuoh* 'do it properly and well', 慢 ㄠ ㄦ 的 走 *mannmhalde tzoou* 'walk good and slow', 重 ㄠ ㄦ 的 打 *jonqjonglde daa* 'hit good and hard'. This *de* is optional.

(3.2) *de* in distributive reduplicates. This *de* is also optional:

天ㄜㄦ（的）苦愁 *tiantial (de) fa-chour* 'worry every day', 处ㄜㄦ
（的）找 *chuhchull (de) jao* 'look for everywhere'. It occurs less
frequently than in the vivid adverbs.

(3.3) *de* in adverbs of manner. 一句ㄗㄗ的解释 *i-jiuh i-
jiuh de jiee.shyh* 'explain sentence by sentence', 一五一十的
数 *i-wuu i-shyr de shuu* 'count by fives'.

(3.4) Quasi-quotations.[19]  ㄆㄧㄚ！的一声！ *pia! de i-sheng!*
'with the sound of a whack!', 乌都ㄗㄗ的叫 *'udu udu' de jiaw*
'to whistle "toot toot"',    咱爹不咱爹的，倒不挑你。*'Tzarn
die' bu 'tzarn die' de, daw bu tiau nii.* 'I don't care whether you
say "our dad" or not, I am not picking on you.[20] 刷锅洗碗的，
哪ㄦ有空ㄦ茇那个？ *Shua guo shii woan de, naal yeou konql
goan neyg?* 'What with scouring pots and washing dishes, where's
the time to bother with that?' As usual, such quasi-quoted forms
tend to be in an absolute position instead of being closely attached to a modified word or phrase.

In both types 3.3 and 3.4 a resumptive adverb *nemme*, less
often *tzemme*, can be added to, or used instead of, the *de*, as
" 兹ㄦㄗㄗ" （的）那么叫 *"tzel tzel" (de) nemm jiaw* 'to sound
"squeak, squeak!" (-like)' (cf. sec. 5.3.6.2).

(3.5) Type V + *de* → H. In ordinary language not many verbs
take a suffix *de* to form adverbs. There are 不住的害病
**bujuhde hay binq** 'constantly troubled with sickness', 不停的
哭 **butyngde ku** 'cry incessantly', 消息不断的来。*Shiau.shi
buduannde lai.* 'News comes continually.' Most of these can
have a resumptive ₀*nemme* in apposition, as in *butyngde nemm
hay-binq.* (Cf. sec. 8.3.2(2) ). In current written bairhuah, how-

---

[19]The term is borrowed from W. V. Quine, *Mathematical Logic*, New
York, 1940, pp. 33 ff. Although Quine himself has given up the term, I have
found it useful to apply to linguistic forms which are more language-
consciously used than in their ordinary occurrences. For a fuller discussion
of the nature of quotation marks, see H. S. Sorensen, "An Analysis of Linguistic Signs Occurring in *Suppositio Materialis* or the Meaning of Quotation
Marks and Their Phonetic Equivalents", *Lingua*, 10:174-189 (1961).

[20]Leu, *LWJyi*, 167, quoting 石玉崑，三侠五义 (Shyr Yuhkuen,
*Sanshya Wuuyih*), Yahdong ed., 80.11.

ever, the adverbial suffix $dih_2$, presumably pronounced *de*, is used without restriction for any adverb of manner, including those formed with verbs. Thus in ordinary speech, 用心 *yonq-shin* 'use mind, —to be careful' can be used adjectivally with a noun, as in 用心的事情 *yonq-shin de shyh.chyng* 'work on which one must use one's mind, —concentrated work'. But used adverbially, it either takes the first position in verbal expressions in series without *de*, as in 用心做 *yonq-shin tzuoh* 'work carefully' or in vivid reduplication with *de: yonq.yonq-shinshinde tzuoh*, or with a progressive aspect suffix -*j*, as in *yonq-shinj tzuoh*. The form *yonq-shinde* ($dih_2$) *tzuoh*, however, is new style, and only beginning to be used in speech.

5.3.7. *Displaced Modifiers*. A subordinative expression modifying another expression may, for reasons of rhythm, idiom, and so on, be placed inside it so that it seems to be modifying a part of it. For example, in 下半旗 *shiah bann-chyi* 'lower a half-flag, —have the flag at half-mast', *bann* formally modifies *chyi*, but semantically modifies *shiah-chyi*, since it is the lowering of the flag that is done half-way. Similarly, in 費大事 *fey dah-shyh* 'take big trouble,—much ado', *fey-shyh* is the usual expression for 'take trouble' and *dah-shyh* 'big affair' is not the usual expression for 'big trouble'. In this particular case one can also say *dah fey-shyh* and then there is no discrepancy between the formal and the semantic analyses. In the case of 吃長素 *chy charng-suh* 'eat a permanent vegetarian diet (usually as a religious practice)', *charng-suh* as an A-N construction occurs practically always in the near context of *chy*. The reason that one does not say °長吃素 °*charng chy-suh* 'permanently eat a vegetarian diet' is that it would be homophonous with 常吃素 'often eats a vegetarian diet', since 常 *charng* as an adverb in modern speech means 'often' and not 'constantly, always', as it does in compounds or in wenyan.

5.3.8. *Verbal Expressions in Series*. A very productive type of syntactical construction consists of two verbal expressions, usually with an object after the first verb, in which the order is irreversible and the second expression has approximately the same function as the whole and therefore functions as a head of which the first expression is a modifier. In translation into English, the first expression often comes out as a prepositional phrase as 拿筷子 吃饭 *na kuaytz chy fann* 'take chopsticks and eat one's food, —eat with chopsticks'. As there is a rich variety of forms and meanings under this form, we shall defer its detailed treatment to a later section (sec. 5.5.).

## 5.4 Verb-Object (V-O) Constructions

*5.4.1. Definition of a Verb-Object Construction.* A verb-object (V-O) construction is an endocentric construction with a verbal expression as the center in first position and a (usually) nominal expression, in second position, as its object. The verbal expression is sometimes said to govern the object, and the relation between verb and object is sometimes known as that of government. Examples are: 种菜 *jonq-tsay* 'to plant vegetables', 做怕 梦 *tzuoh pah-menq* 'have a nightmare', 打定了一个主意 *daa-dinqle ig jwu.yih* 'decided upon an idea', 关心时事 *guan-shin shyrshyh* 'pay attention to current events', 参观联合国 *tsanguan Lianher Gwo* 'visit the United Nations', 喜欢阔 *shii-.huan kuoh* 'like to be rich'. Rather than include all the characteristics of the V-O relation in a long definition, we shall enumerate and illustrate its other formal features as we come to them.

Another type of verbal expression with center in the first constituent is the verb-complement (V-R) construction in which the second constituent is not a nominal, but a verbal expression, as in 写倒了 *shiee-dawle* 'write upside down', 拿走 *na-tzoou* 'take-go,—take away', 说的对 *shuo de duey* 'say correctly'. This type of construction will be the subject of section 6.7.

Some Chinese grammarians use the term 補(足)语 *buuyeu* or *buutzwuyeu*, and F. K. Li in his lectures has used the term "complement", to include both the object as defined above and the V-R forms just mentioned. One important reason is that an object in Chinese is less regularly tied up with the meaning of the goal of action (cf. 5.4.4) than it is in other languages. Thus, 李人 鑑 (Lii Renjiann), in his 賓语这个术语能不能取消？

("Can the Term 'Object' Be Abolished?"), answers his own question in the affirmative and proposes to use 補 语 *buuyeu* 'complement' instead.[21]  On the other hand, 定 國 (Dinq Gwo, apparently a pen name) notes that Chinese translators from the Russian have been influenced by the literal meaning of *dopolnenie* and call it *buuyeu*, with the misleading effect of making it comparable to English [resultative] complement, and he prefers the usage of writers who equate *dopolnenie* to 賓 语 *binyeu* 'object'.[22] In any case, it is necessary on formal grounds to distinguish between the post-center constituents in 拿东西 *na dong.shi* 'take things' and 拿走 *na-tzoou* 'take away', and we are now using object and complement in the narrow senses, since there are relatively few occasions to mention together the two quite differently behaving second constituents in verbal expressions.

5.4.2. *Formal Features of the V-O Construction.* V-O constructions, besides having as first constituent a verbal center, followed by an object (usually a nominal expression) nearly always have these formal features also:

(1)   Except for pronouns, the object is never in the neutral tone.   Thus, 搌 布 *jaan.buh* 'wiping cloth,—kitchen cloth' is a subordinate construction in which *buh* 'cloth' is the center; so is 绑腿 *baang.toei* '(cloth with which to) bind the leg,—legging', an exocentric construction in which neither *baang* nor *toei* is the center.   One can in fact say *yonq baang.toei baang-toei* 'uses legging to bind one's legs', where the second *baang* is the verbal center, and the second *toei*, with full tone, is the object in the V-O construction *baang-toei*.   Pronoun objects, however, are as a rule in the neutral tone, unless contrastively stressed.   Thus: *Chiing .nii gaw.sonq .woomen.* '(1) request you to tell us, —please tell us.'; but: *Gaw.sonq "woomen, bye gaw.sonq "tamen.* 'Tell "us, don't tell "them.'   Although a noun object is stressed, an indefinite quantity modifier like *(i)g a* and *.leangg* 'a couple of' is unstressed, as in 吃个梨 *chy g li* 'eat a pear', 叫碗湯 *jiaw .woan tang* 'order a bowl of soup', 買兩本儿书 *mae .leang.beel shu* 'buy a

---

[21]Leu, S & O, 201-203.

[22]ZGYW, no. 67:  47 (1958).

couple of books', but *mae* (¹)*leang-beel shu* 'buy (exactly) two books'.

To say that the object is not in the neutral tone is not to say that, conversely, a second constituent not in the neutral tone must be the object to a preceding verb. Thus, 逃兵 *taurbing* is not 'escape from soldiers', but 'escaped soldier,—deserter', 弹簧 *tarnhwang* is not 'spring a spring' but 'springing spring,—elastic spring'. In some cases, the same sequence may be ambivalently either a subordinative or a V-O construction. For examples of such ambivalence, see sec. 1.1.3 on skewed relations.

(2) Between V and O, one cannot insert the particle *de* without changing it into a subordinate construction. For example, 看报 *kann-baw* 'read the newspaper': *kann de baw* 'newspaper to be read'; 干杯! *gan-bei!* 'dry the cup, —bottoms up!'; *gan de beitz* 'a dry cup'; 喜欢那个人 *shii.huan neyg ren* 'like that person': *shii.huan de neyg ren* (a) 'the person who is liked', (b) 'the person who is glad'. In the apparent exceptions with *de* in V-O constructions, such as 认字 *renn-tzyh* 'learn (to recognize the characters)': 认得字 *renn.de tzyh* 'know the characters, —is literate', and 记账 *jih-janq* 'keeps accounts': 记得账 *jih.de janq* 'remembers the accounts', all of which are V-O constructions, the *.de* is not the subordinative particle, but a different, homophonous particle or potential suffix, which makes *renn.de* 'know, be acquainted with' a different verb from *renn* '(try to) recognize' and makes *jih.de* 'remember' a different verb from *jih* 'to record, note down'. In fact, it is also possible to use the verbs, with or without the potential suffix -.*de*, in attributive position with the subordinative particle *de*, as in: 这是那小孩儿要认的字，那是他已经认得的字。 *Jeh sh nah sheauharl yaw renn de tzyh, nah sh ta yiijinq renn.de de*[23] *tzyh.* 'These are the characters the child is going to learn, those are the characters he already knows.' In the Wu and Cantonese dialects the potential suffix and the subordinative particle are quite different syllables, for ex-

---

[23]We noticed (2.7 above) the resistence to saying two *de*'s in succession when both represent the subordinative particle. Here, with two different, though homophonous, *de*'s, the succession seems easier to say, though in both instances it is easy enough to say .*de*(,) *de*, with a slight pause.

ample, Cant 識得嘅字 *shektak keh dzih* for Mand *renn.de de tzyh*. In characters the potential *.de* and the subordinative *de* are of course written 得 and 的, with reading pronunciations *der* and *dih*, respectively.

(3) A V-O construction can usually[24] be separated by the insertion of a suffix after the verb. If both V and O are free, there is of course no problem of insertion. But even if either or both V and O are bound forms, one can still insert a suffix after the verb, as: FB 拜寿 *bay-show* 'greet birthday': 拜过寿 *bay.guoh-show* 'have greeted birthday'; 带孝 *day-shiaw* 'wear mourning': *dayj-shiaw* 'wearing mourning'; 鞠躬 *jyu-gong* 'bend body,—make a bow': *jyule-gong .jiow tzoou* 'leave right after having made a bow'. Forms of the BF type are relatively infrequent, as 阅兵 *yueh-bing* 'review the troops': *yuehj bing ne* 'is reviewing the troops'; 译书 *yih-shu* 'translate books': 从来没译过书 *tsornglai mei yih.guo shu* 'have never translated books'.

(4) A V-O construction can be separated by the insertion of a determinative modifier before the object. In 费了您的许多精神 *feyle Ninde sheuduo jing.shern* 'spent your much energy,—gave you a lot of trouble', we have FF in which *jing-.shern* takes a determinative modifier *Ninde sheudeo* 'a lot of your'. But in *fey-shern*, which is FB, it is also possible to say *feile Ninde sheuduo shern* 'gave you a lot of trouble', where *shern* (in the sense of 'energy') is otherwise not free. With 攜手 *shi-shoou* 'joins hands', which is BF, it is possible to say: 德國跟俄國曾经攜过一次手. *Der.gwo gen Eh.gwo tserngjing shi.guoh i-tsyh shoou.* 'Germany and Russia once joined hands.', with *i-tsyh* 'once' in attributive position before *shoou*, although in effect it modifies *shi-shoou*. With the BB form *jyu-gong* 'bend body' cited above, one can say: 你得对他鞠三个躬. *Nii deei duey ta jyu san g gong.* 'You must make three bows to him.', which is different in structure from: *Nii deei duey ta sanjyugong* 'You must do the (ceremony of) three bows to him.', where *sanjyugong* is one inseparable compound verb. Note that when a modifier, as

---

[24]Except for solid V-O compounds, on which see sec. 6.5.6.

opposed to a governing verb, precedes a determinative expression, a *de* is required, as 逮着了那隻老虎 *dae-jaurle ney-jy laohuu* 'caught that tiger': *dae-jaurle de ney-jy laohuu* 'the tiger which was caught'.

The insertion of a verbal suffix and/or a determinative modifier sometimes serves, besides their usual functions, to indicate more clearly the V-O nature of the construction. For example, 红臉 *horng-lean* can be (1) a subordinative construction 'red face' or a V-O construction 'redden the face, —— (a) to blush, (b) get angry'. In 从来没跟他红过臉 *tsornglai mei gen ta horng.guo lean* 'have never been angry with him', it is V-O. In 雪耻 *shiueh-chyy* 'wash-away a shame,—avenge a wrong', we have a BB and L expression. In order to make the V-O nature more explicit, one can say *shiueh jeyg chyy* 'avenge this wrong'. In the much cited 水其田 *shoei chyi tyan* L 'water their fields', the determinative *chyi* makes it clear that it is a V-O construction, while *shoei-tyan* would very likely be taken to be, and in modern speech always is, a subordinative construction 'water fields,—wet fields (e.g., rice paddies)'.

*5.4.3 Free and Bound Verbs and Objects.* We have found, in the preceding examples of free and bound verbs and objects, that verbs which are otherwise bound may take verbal suffixes and that objects which are otherwise bound may be modified by determinative modifiers. When, however, a verb or an object is described as free, it is not only separable in the ways just stated, but free in many other contexts. The V-O construction in 弯腰 *uan-iau* 'bend the waist' is FF because *uan* is a free verb, such that one can say: 这棍儿你不能弯他，弯了会断的. *Jeh guell nii buneng uan ta, uanle huey duann de.* 'This stick you mustn't bend; if you bend it, it may break'; and *iau* is a free noun, such that one can say: 你看他那腰真细，跳起舞来老把腰那么扭来扭去的. *Nii kann ta nah iau jen shih, tiaw.chii-wuu .lai lao bae iau nemm neoulai-neouchiuh de.* 'Look what a slender waist he (or she) has, when he (or she) dances, the waist is twisting this way and that way all the time.' On the other hand, *jyu-gong* 'bend the body, —make a bow' can only be separated in the ways prescribed above, and neither

*jyu* nor *gong* is free in other respects. (See also sec. 8.5.6 on forms
of expansion and ionization.)

5.4.3.1. *Syllabicity and Freedom.* Among monosyllables the
numbers of free verbs and objects and that of bound verbs and
objects are of the same order of magnitude, though in terms of
lexical frequency there are more bound verbs and objects than
free ones. When, however, a verb or an object has two or more
syllables, it is not only almost always free, but its partner, whether
or not monosyllabic, will also be free. For example, 換錢
*huann-chyan* 'change money' is FF, 兌現 *duey-shiann* 'exchange
cash,—honor a paper,—to be negotiable' is BB, 兌(換)現欵
*duey shiannkoan* or *dueyhuann shiannkoan* 'exchange cash-
money,—exchange for cash' is FF, but there is no °*dueyhuann
shiann,* since *dueyhuann* is a dissyllabic free verb and *shiann* in
the sense of 'cash' is bound and therefore cannot be the object of
the dissyllabic verb *dueyhuann.* Again, 祭祖 *jih-tzuu* FB, 祭祖
宗 *jih tzuu.tzong* FF, and 祭祀祖宗 *jih₀syh tzuu.tzong* FF all
mean 'offer sacrifice to one's ancestor', but there is no °*jih.syh
tzuu,* since *jih.syh* is a dissyllabic free verb and *tzuu* is bound and
therefore cannot be its object.

Further examples of FF V-O's in which one or both of V and
O are polysyllabic are: 想主意 *sheang jwu.jih* 'think up an idea',
吃螃蟹 *chy parng.shieh* 'eat crabs', 拜望人 *bay.wanq ren* 'call
on people', 製造船 *jyh.tzaw chwan* 'manufacture ships', 注意
书 *juhyih shu* 'pay attention to books', 打听消息 *daa.ting
shiau.shyi* 'hunt for news', 掃干淨了地 *sao-gan.jinqle dih*
'swept the floor clean', 打破了一个杯子 *daa-pohle ig beitz*
'broke a cup'.

5.4.3.2. *Restricted and Idiomatic V-O.* In discussing free and
bound forms in general (sec. 3.4.1), we considered phrases like
磕瓜子儿 *keh guatzeel* 'crack (between one's teeth) melon
seeds', where *keh* is like other free verbs except that it is almost
always restricted to taking *guatzeel* as its object. Similarly, 沏 *chi*
'steep, infuse' only takes 茶 *char* 'tea' as object. In 買米 *mae-mii*
'buy rice', on the other hand, both O and V are completely versatile. There are, however, a great many cases of intermediate
degrees of restrictedness and versatility. Thus in 做夢 *tzuoh-*

*menq* 'do a dream, —to have a dream' *tzuoh* is very versatile, but *menq* as object is restricted to such contexts as *tzuoh-menq*, 緣夢 *yuan-menq* '(give the) origin (of) a dream,—interpret a dream', 说夢 *shuo-menq* 'tell a dream' or 'tell about dreams', 讲夢 *jeang-menq* 'explains dreams' and very few other verbs take *menq* as object. In 防贼 *farng-tzeir* 'guard against thieves' *tzeir* is completely versatile, but *farng* is restricted to such objects as 火 *huoo* 'fire', 水 *shoei* 'water', 乱 *luann* 'disorder', and in the phrase 防君子不防小人 *farng jiuntzyy bu farng sheauren* 'guard against gentlemen, but not against mean men' (said of makeshift guards which a determined burglar could break through),[25] *farng* is of relatively restricted occurrence. The progressive form *farngj*, however, is more versatile in that it can be followed by any S-P clause, as in 不用防着半夜鬼来打门 *buyonq farngj bannyeh goei lai daa-men* 'don't need to guard against ghosts coming at midnight knocking at your door'. This is quite similar to the case of 记着 *jihj* 'remember' being more versatile than *jih* 'remember, note', or, 认得 *renn.de* 'know, to be acquainted with' being more versatile than *renn* 'tell apart, learn to recognize'.

Idiomatic or lexical V-O's are different from, though positively correlated with, restricted V-O's. A V-O construction is lexical if its meaning is more specialized or generalized than, or in some way different from, what can be gathered from the meanings of the parts. Examples are: 认床 *renn-chwang* FF 'tell apart beds, —cannot sleep in a strange bed', 认生 *renn-sheng* FF 'recognize the unfamilar,—to be shy of strangers (said of children)', 破产 *poh-chaan* FB 'break up property,—go bankrupt', 打字 *daa-tzyh* FF 'strike characters,—to type (on a typewriter)', 排字 *pair-tzyh* FF 'arrange (in a row) characters,—set (printer's) type', 掛賬 *guah-janq* FF 'hang account,—charge on a charge account', 掛失 *guah-shy* FB 'enter a loss (in a lost and found department', 敲竹杠 *chiau jwu₀ganq* FF (borrowing from Wu) 'beat the bamboo pole,—defraud, extort' (as a hyperbole), 'to overcharge'.

---

[25]In dicitionaries such as R. H. Mathews, *A Chinese-English Dictionary*, Shanghai, 1931; Amer. ed., Cambridge, Mass., 1943, p. 263, there are a few additional V-O forms with *farng* which are either obsolete or L only.

In a dictionary, those V-O forms in which either part is bound should of course be entered as compounds. Of the FF forms only the idiomatic phrases need be entered, as there is no point in entering the other cases. That is from the point of view of theoretical lexicography, as in a Chinese-Chinese dictionary. In a bilingual dictionary, a V-O form, whether the parts are free or not, will have to be entered, if it translates into one single word in the other language, as 睡觉 *shuey-jiaw* 'to sleep', 认生 *renn-sheng* 'shy', 说话 *shuo-huah* 'speak'.

*5.4.4. Class Meaning of the V-O Construction.* The grammatical meaning, that is, the most frequently met with meaning, of the V-O construction is that of action and goal, with typical examples such as 打靶子 *daa-baatz* 'shoot a target', 吃东西 *chy dong.shi* 'eat things', 放火 *fanq-huoo* 'set fire', 掷色子 *jy shaetz* 'throw dice'. There are, however, a great many instances where the action and goal relation is either vague or clearly reversed. For example in: 我流血了. *Woo liou-shiee le.* 'I am bleeding.', if *liou* is regarded as my action 'I let flow (blood).', it seems to be action and goal; if *liou* is regarded as 'there flows out (blood)', then *shiee* is actor rather than goal. Similarly, 刮风 *gua-feng* 'blow wind', and 下雨 *shiah-yeu* 'fall rain,—it rains' are V-O constructions simply because they have the usual formal feature of V-O constructions.

A second and secondary part of the grammatical meaning of the V-O construction is that an object has indefinite reference, whereas a subject has definite reference. For example, 写完了 信 *shiee-wanle shinn* 'have finished writing a letter': 信写完 了 *shinn shiee-wanle* 'the letter (I planned to write) has been finished' or 'the letter writing (I planned to do) has been finished'. As these points have already been discussed and illustrated in detail (sec. 2.4.3), we shall not dwell on them further.

Various classifications of verb-object relations have been made,[26] such as: (a) causative: 跑马 *pao-maa* 'run horses,—cause

---

[26]For example, by 李人鑑 (Lii Renjiann), pp. 201-203, and 任铭善 Ren Mingshann), p. 229, in Leu, S & O. See also Malmqvist, Sïch'uanese,

horses to run,—do horse-racing', 来 饭! *Lai-fann!* (said to a waiter) 'cause rice to come!—bring some rice!', 去 髒 *chiuh-tzang*
'cause to go the dirt,—remove dirt', 红 着 脸 *horngj lean* 'red-
dening the face,—blushing', 丰 富 词 彙 *fengfuh tsyrhuey* a
recently coined V-O phrase for 'enrich one's vocabulary'. (b) in-
strumental: 我 睡 大 床. *Woo shuey dah-chwang.* 'I sleep on the
big bed.' 他 吃 小 碗. *Ta chy sheau-woan.* 'He eats with the
small bowl.' (c) causing to or letting something come into or out
of existence: 写 字 *shiee-tzyh* 'write characters', 生 小 孩 儿
*sheng sheauharl* 'give birth to a child', 丢 了 东 西 *dioule dong-
.shi* 'have lost something'. There is practically no limit to such
categories of classifying the meanings of action-goal, once we start
setting them up. They not only overlap, but the meaning of the
V-O relation varies also with what we regard as part of the verb
and what as in the V-O relation. Take the verb *chy* 'eat'. Without even going into its numerous metaphorical meanings, there
are the various uses as in (a) 吃 肉 *chy-row* 'eat meat', (b) 吃 大
碗 *chy dah-woan* 'eat (out of a) big bowl', (c) 吃 馆 子 *chy-
goantz* 'eat (in a) restaurant', or even 吃 女 招 待 *chy neu-
jauday* 'eat (where there are) waitresses', (d) 吃 晌 午 *chy shaang-
.huo* 'eat lunch'.[27] In such cases one can either (1) regard the V-
O relation as having four meanings (a) direct action on goal, (b)
instrument, (c) place, (d) time, or (2) regard the verb and/or object as having different meanings in different contexts (a) direct
action 'eat', (b) 'eat with', (c) 'eat in', (d) 'eat at time of'. As to
which analysis to follow, it depends upon the frequency of use. If
the meaning is restricted to one or a very few O's for a given V,
or vice versa, as in *gan-bei* 'dry the cup,—bottoms up!' (since *gan-
woan* 'a dry bowl' is not V-O and °*shy-bei* 'wet cup' does not
exist), then it is a lexical V-O which should be a dictionary entry.
If the special meaning or meanings of V or O are of moderate
versatility, then they should be entered as additional glosses under

---

141. See also Nicholas C. Bodman, *Spoken Amoy Hokkien*, Kuala Lumpur,
1955, pp. 205-206, on *siōu kuê* 'to roast chicken' or 'roasted chicken'.

[27]In the Wenchow dialect, one eats daybreak, daytime, and dusk. See
my *Studies in Wu*, 117.

each part in the dictionary. Thus, in 请客 *chiing-keh* 'invite guests', and 请酒 *chiing-jeou* the latter need not be considered an abbreviation of 请人吃酒席 *chiing ren chy jeoushyi*, 'invite guests to a wine feast', but *chiing* can be given a second gloss as 'invite guests to'.

Simple V-O Used in a Causative Sense. A very frequent causative meaning of transitive verbs is that of having something done by someone else than what is expressed in the subject. Thus, when a mechanic says 我得修车了. *Woo deei shiou-che le.* 'I must repair cars now.' *shiou-che* is taken in an ordinary action-goal sense, but when a customer says the same words, it means 'I must have my car repaired now.' It is possible to use a transformed pivotal sentence such as 叫人修车 *jiaw ren shiou-che* 'have someone repair the car', but when no ambiguity is involved, the simple V-O form is used. Similarly, 洗衣裳 *shii i.shang* 'wash clothes' ~ 'have the clothes washed', 刷鞋 *shua-shye* 'shine the shoes' ~ 'have one's shoes shined'. This causative use of the V-O construction is so much taken for granted that it is usually very difficult to teach a Chinese learner of English to use the have-something-done construction, as distinguished from the simple do-something construction.

*5.4.5. Types of Verbs Which Take Objects.* (1) Transitive verbs (Vt) take almost any object. With verb *he* 'drinks' there is not only 喝茶 *he-char* 'drinks tea', or 喝西北风 *he shibeei-feng* 'drinks the northwest wind,—suffers privation', but *he-shu* 'drinks books', in describing a voracious reader like an alcoholic, would be so fanciful as to be barely grammatical. In 逞个早 *gaan g tzao* 'makes a try at being early', 图个快活 *twu g kuay.hwo* 'do something for the sake of (being) happy', 吃过香 *chy.guoh shiang* 'has eaten the flavorous,—has been in favor' we have adjective objects. In verbs of the 想 *sheang* 'thinks', 知道 *jy.daw* 'knows' type, or think verbs we often have S-P clauses as objects (see secs. 2.12.3 and 8.1.5.3).

A limited number of transitive verbs take place words as objects, as 到了家 *dawle jia* 'arrived home', 到过西湖 *daw.guoh Shi Hwu* 'have been to West Lake', *tzay ta.nall* 'to be at his place'. These verbs do not take ordinary nominal expressions as objects.

Certain verbs, such as 给 *geei* 'give', 送 *sonq* 'send, make a present of', 赏 *shaang* 'bestow, reward', 罚 *far* 'punish, fine', can take one object or a direct and an indirect object. For example, 送礼 *sonq-lii* 'send gifts', 送他一份儿礼 *sonq ta i-fell lii* 'send him a gift'. For details, see section 5.4.6(3) below.

On verbs of the type 叫 *jiaw* 'make, cause to', 请 *chiing* 'request', 劝 *chiuann* 'persuade', 催 *tsuei* 'urge', which often takes a pivotal object, as in 催他回来 *tsuei ta hwei.lai* 'urge him to come back', see secs. 2.13.1 and 8.1.5.3 on pre-pivotal, or link verbs.

(2) Intransitive verbs (Vi) and adjectives (A) are not verbs which do not take objects, but verbs which can take only cognate objects, for example, *shiaw i-shiaw* 'smile a smile', *charngle san-tsuenn* 'too long or longer by three inches'. For further details see sec. 5.4.6, part (1).

(3) Defective verbs. A few verbs lack some of the formal features of verbs with objects. The modal auxiliary verbs 能 *neng* 'can', 願意 *yuann.yih* 'is willing to', 要 *yaw* 'will, want to', etc., cannot take aspect suffixes and can only take verbs as objects. In isolated cases like 会水 *huey-shoei* 'can water,—can swim' (cf. Ger. *Können Sie Deutsch?*), *huey* should be regarded as an ordinary transitive verb by way of class overlap. That an auxiliary verb is still the center, as required in the definition of a V-O construction, can be tested by the V-not-V frame: 你要去不要 ? *Nii yaw chiuh bu yaw?* or *Nii yaw bu yaw chiuh?*, but not °*Nii yaw chiuh bu chiuh?* 'Do you want to go?', and the answer will be: *Yaw*, or: *Yaw chiuh*, while: *Chiuh* 'I am going (whether I want to or not)', though grammatical as a one-word sentence, would not be answering the question. On the other hand, with 还 *hair* 'still', an adverb, a question will take the form: 还下不下啦 ? *Hair shiah bu shiah l'a?* Is it still raining (or snowing, etc.) now?', and the answer will be: *Shiah* or: *Hair shiah*, but not: °*Hair*.

The verb 有 *yeou* 'have' is defective in that it can take *le*, but not, except in recent written bairhuah, *j*. We noted that 到

*daw* 'arrive at, go to' and 在 *tzay* 'to be in' must take time and place words as objects; moreover, *daw* can only take *le* and *.guoh*, but cannot take *j*, while *tzay* can take none of the aspect suffixes. The verb *sh* 'is', like *tzay*, also takes no aspect suffix. In the following sentence, spoken by a man denying that he had ever been anybody's man (in a political sense): 我从来没是 过谁的人. *Woo tsornglai mei sh.guoh sheirde ren.*, it should be regarded as a quasi-quoted *sh* in objecting to someone's saying that he 'was' somebody's man.

*Omission of Objects.* A transitive verb does not become intransitive by not having an object. In general an object to a transitive verb is omitted if it has occurred in a near context, whether or not as object to the verb in question. For example: 我看完了报了。你要看吗？ *Woo kann-wanle baw le. Nii yaw kann ma?* 'I have finished reading the newspaper. Do you want to read it?', where the object *it* is required in the English, but normally omitted in Chinese. If *ta* is expressed: *Nii yaw kann ta ma?* it may even have the implication: 'Do you want to read that kind of stuff?' In the following example, the understood object is not even an object in the preceding context: *Jiel de baw lai le. Nii yaw kann ma?* 'Today's paper has come. Do you want to read it?'

*5.4.6. Special Types of Objects*

*5.4.6.1. Cognate Objects.*[28] Intransitive verbs, as we have seen, can only take cognate objects, while transitive verbs take both cognate and other kinds of objects. A cognate object may consist of an expression for (a) the number of times of an action, (b) its duration (c) its extent, (d) the course of locomotion, or, less often, its destination (cf. sec. 3.1.2.2).

(a) The commonest cognate objects for the number of times of an action are 回, 次, 番 *-hwei, -tsyh, -fan* (in descending order of frequency) as general M's for number of times, 趟 *tanq* 'trip', and 遍 *-biann* 'once through' (over a course, a text, a series of items, and so on). Examples are: 他们吵了两回了. *Tamen chaole leang-hwei le.* 'They have quarreled twice.' 你跟他见

---

[28]Note that the usual adjective 'cognate' for this type of object has nothing at all to do with 'cognate' as applied to etymological relatedness.

过几次就熟了. *Nii gen ta jiann.guoh jii-tsyh jiow shour le.*
'After you have met him a few times, you will be better acquainted.' 跟他解释了一番, 他懂了. *Gen ta jiee.shyhle
i-fan, ta doongle.* 'After it was talked over with him once, he
then understood.' 那儿我已竟跑了许多趟了. *Nall woo
yiijinq paole sheuduo-tanq le* 'I have already made quite a few
trips there.' 这小说看了三遍也不腻. *Jeh sheaushuol kann-
le san-biann yee bu nih.* 'One doesn't get tired of this novel
even after reading it (through) three times.' Some cognate objects are more specifically associated with the verbs, as in 打两
下 (儿) *daa leang-shiah* (~ *shiall*) 'strike a couple of strokes', 说
一声 (儿) *shuo i-sheng* (l) 'say a voice, —make a mention', 看了
两眼 *kannle leang-yean* 'looked two eyes, —gave two glances'
得睡一大觉 *deei shuey i-dah-jiaw* 'must sleep a big nap, —
must have a good sleep', 踢一脚 *ti i-jeau* 'kick a footful, —give
a kick', 打一拳 *daa i-chyuan* 'hit a fistful, —give a blow of the
fist', 拍一巴掌 *pai i-ba.jaang* 'slap a palmful, —give a slap',
吃三顿 *chy san-duenn* 'eat three meals', 骂一顿 *mah i-duenn*
'scold a spell, —give a scolding', 咬一口 *yeau i-koou* 'bite a
mouthful, —make a bite', 会来两手儿 *huey lai leang-shooul*
'can (cause to) come a couple of hands, —can play a few hands,
—can do a few tricks'.

The number of times an action is taken may be expressed by
a repetition of the verb itself, the number being usually *i* 'one,
a' and only rarely more than one: 看一看 *kann i-kann* 'take a
look', 讲一讲 *jeang i-jeang* 'explain a little', 跳三跳 *tiaw san-
tiaw* 'jump three jumps'. In some non-Mandarin dialects the
cognate object 下 *shiah* 'stroke', which in Mandarin is limited to a
very few verbs of the 打 *daa* 'strike' type, is used instead of repeating the verb itself. In Cantonese, for example, *Kann i-kann*
'look a look' will appear as 睇吓 *thae hax*, and *shyh i-shyh* 'try
a try' as 试吓 *shih hax*, whose literal translation into Mandarin
would be 看一下儿 *kann i-shiall* and 试一下儿 *shyh i-shiall*, both
of which are possible, but not nearly as common as the reduplicated forms.

(b) Examples of cognate objects of duration are: 住了三年

*juhle san-nian* 'lived (there) for three years', 等了半天 *deengle bann-tian* 'waited for a long time', 坐一会儿 *tzuoh ihoel* 'sit for a while', 走了一个钟头 *tzooule ig jongtour* 'have walked for an hour'. The last example is to be distinguished from: *Ta tzooule (yeou) ig jongtour le,* which is ambivalently either (1) 'He has been walking for fully an hour', or (2) 'It has been fully an hour since he left.' In the latter case, *ta tzooule* is an S-P subject clause, with *ig jongtour* as predicate instead of object.

As to whether duration is taken literally as being actually continuous or intermittent within a period, it has the same ambiguity in Chinese as in English. For example, in: "Dorothy Hayworth Rigner wants to thank all the members of the class who responded so generously last year to 'the call' for Annual Giving. She says it makes all the work worth while! She has vacationed in Nassau for six years now.',[29] the last sentence could be translated as 他在拿婆歇了六年的暑假了。 *Ta tzay Nassau shiele liow-nian de shuujiah le.* and only the *shuu* in *shuujiah* 'summer vacation' makes it improbable that the vacation was six years long.

(c) Extent or quantity, as in: 长了三寸 *jaangle san-tsuenn* 'has grown three inches', 大十倍 *dah shyr-bey* 'bigger by ten times', 可惜慢了一步 *keeshi mannle i-buh* 'unfortunately too late by one step', 大不了多少 *dah.bu-leau duoshao* 'cannot exceed by much', 只大了一点儿 *jyy dahle ideal* 'have exceeded by only a little'.

(d) Course or destination of locomotion, as in: 走路 *tzoou-luh* or 走道儿 *tzoou-dawl* 'walk (one's) way,—walk', 走江湖 *tzoou-jianghwu* 'go the rivers and lakes,—go adventuring', 跑街 *pao-jie* 'run the streets, —run errands', 走粤汉铁路 *tzoou Yueh-Hann Tieeluh* 'go by the Canton-Hankow Railway', 飞太平洋 *fei Taypyng Yang* 'fly the Pacific', 开上海 *kai Shanqhae* 'run or fly to Shanghai'.

When a cognate object for number of times, duration, and extent is weakened to the neutral tone, usually with omission of *i*, it loses its status as object and becomes a suffix, thus putting the

---

[29]Quoted by *The New Yorker*, June 15, 1963, p. 98.

verb of action into a tentative form and, in the case of adjectives, a comparative form. For example, 坐（一）会儿 *tzuoh .i.hoel* or *tzuoh.hoel,* or 坐ㄗ儿 *tzuoh.tzuoll* 'sit a while, just sit', 獃 会儿 耒 *dai.hoel lai* 'wait a while before coming,—come later', 大（一）
点儿 *dah.i.deal* or *dah.deal* 'large by a little,—larger', 看ㄗ *kann.kann* 'look a look,—take a look' 等 ㄗ 儿 *deeng.deengl* 'wait a waiting,—just wait' [cf. sec. 4.2.3(5)].

(1.1) Cognate Object and Complement of Extent. When a verb (including adjectives) is followed by a cognate object, as in 寛三尺 *kuan san-chyy* 'wide three feet', there is sometimes ambiguity as to whether it means 'three feet wider or too wide' or 'three feet wide'. the ambiguity can be resolved by using the perfective particle -*le* for the former and changing the construction to the V-R form by using the verb $_0$*daw* 'as far as'. For example, 过重了五磅 *guohjonqle wuu-banq* 'have exceeded (in weight) by five pounds', but 高到六尺 *gau daw liow-chyy* 'tall to six feet,—as tall as six feet'. If the content is clear enough, then a speaker often does not use the precisive forms with -*le* or *daw*.

(1.2) Cognate Object and Goal Object. If besides a cognate object there is also an object expressing the goal of an action, then the goal object usually comes first if it is a pronoun and last if it is a noun, for example, 看过他三次 *kann.guoh ta san-tsyh* 'have seen him three times', but 看过三次戏 *kann.guoh san-tsyh shih* 'have been to a show three times'.

*5.4.6.2. Objects of Auxiliary Verbs.* We noted above that auxiliary verbs are defective in that they lack certain aspect forms. They are further limited in that they take only verbs as objects, though not restricted in any way as to the kinds of verbs as objects. Thus, we have as objects transitive verbs in 肯说 *keen shuo* 'to be willing to say (it)', intransitive verbs in 要休息 *yaw shiou.shyi* 'want to rest', adjectives in 会胖 *huey panq* 'can be fat', and another auxiliary verb in 会肯 *huey keen* 'may be willing to', 应该敢 *inaggai gaan* 'ought to dare to'. While objects of transitive verbs can have determinative modifiers, as in 买一本儿书 *mae i-beel shu* 'buy a book', objects of auxiliary verbs, being themselves verbs, can only take adverbial modifiers, as 要 先 去 *yaw shian chiuh* 'want to go first', 肯 不 去 *keen bu chiuh* 'to be willing not to go'. An auxiliary verb can take a noun as object by class overlap. Thus 喜 欢 *shii.huan* 'like to' is an auxiliary verb in 喜 欢 看 電 影ﾉ *shii.huan kann diann-yeengl* 'like to see movies', but a transitive verb in *shii.huan diannyeengl* 'to like movies'. Similarly, 怕 *pah* 'to fear' is a transitive verb in 怕 鬼 *pah-goei* 'fear ghosts', but an auxiliary verb in 怕 做 事 *pah tzuoh-shyh* 'to be afraid to work'. (See chap. 8, Vx 12 and 13.)

5.4.6.3. *Indirect and Other Multiple Objects.* A limited number of verbs can take two objects, an indirect object, representing the person affected, and a direct object, representing the thing acted on, as in 给 他 一 点ﾉ 錢 *geei ta ideal chyan* 'give him some money', 拿 了 我 两 本ﾉ 书 *nale woo leang beel shu* 'took (from) me two books'. These are obviously different from one object consisting of coordinate and therefore grammatically reversible parts, as in 画 山 水 人 物 *huah shanshoei renwuh* 'paint landscape and human figures', which can be reversed into *huah renwuh shanshoei*. The latter order, though less usual, is perfectly grammatical. On the other hand, the order of indirect-direct objects is fixed, though it is not the same for all dialects. Thus, in Cantonese and the Wu dialects the order is regularly the opposite of that of Mandarin. In the movie 三 个 母 親 "San'g Muuchin" (Three Mothers), there was a sentence: 谢ㄟ 奶ㄟ 给 粥 我 吃 ! *Shieh.shieh Nae.nae geei jou woo chy!* 'Thank you grandma, for giving congee me to eat!' and the audience murmured: "That's Shanghai dialect!"[30] Again, in Cantonese, 俾 啲 錢 佢 *pee ti°dsin° ghoe* 'give some money him' would have to be, in Mandarin, 给 他 点ﾉ 錢 *geei ta deal chyan* 'give him some money'. Apparent contrary examples are such constructions as 送 一 份ﾉ 礼 给 他 *song i-fell lii $_0$geei ta* 'send a gift to him', 卖 一 本ﾉ 书 给 我 *may i-beel shu $_0$geei woo* 'sell a book to

---

[30]Reported by 刘 新 友, 关 于 電 影 裡 的 方 言 (Liou Shinyeou, "On Dialects in the Movies"), *ZGYW*, no. 90:590 (1959).

me'. Here we have no longer cases of one verb with two objects, but two verbs, each with an object to itself.

It is, however, a different matter when *geei* is joined enclitically to a preceding verb, in which case the same indirect-direct object order is followed as with simple verbs, as in *song$_0$geei ta i-fell lii* 'send-to him a gift'. In general, verbs of the 'send', 'give' type take (a) an obligatory or (b) an optional bound *geei;* (c) verbs like 'take (from)', 'ask (of)', and 'call' do not take *geei;* and (d) other verbs take or do not take *geei* according to the direction to or from the indirect object. Following are the commonest verbs with or without *geei* which take indirect objects.[31] (Cf. sec. 5.6.3. below.)

(a) Verbs in which -$_0$*geei* is obligatory before an indirect object: 传 *chwan* 'pass on' (usually fig.), 交 *jiau* 'hand over', 遞 *dih* 'pass on' (usually lit.), 许 *sheu* 'promise', 寄 *jih* 'mail', 卖 *may* 'sell', 输 *shu* 'lose (in a bet, game, etc.)'.

(b) Verbs with optional -$_0$*geei* before an indirect object: 送 *songq* 'send, present', 教 *jiau* 'teach', 赏 *shaang* 'bestow', 讬( 付) *tuo ~ tuofuh* 'entrust', 告送 *gaw.songq* 'tell', 还 *hwan* 'return (a loan, etc.)'. The form 教 给 *jiau$_0$geei* 'teach', especially in the sense of showing how, is limited to the Peiping region and is homophonous with 交 给 *jiau$_0$geei* 'hand over'. Outside this local usage, *jiau* 'teach' does not take -$_0$*geei*. Note that 告 *gaw* 'sue, accuse' takes a personal direct object and if the action accused of is expressed, it is in the form of a post-pivotal verbal expression, rather than a direct object, as in 告 他偷东西 *gaw ta tou dong.shi* 'accuse him of stealing things'. In L style *gaw* means 'tell', but, unlike colloquial 告送 *gaw.songq*, it takes the person told as direct object and adds another verb 以 *yii* 'take' before the thing told, as in 告之以故 *gaw jy yii guh* L 'tell him tak-

---

[31]Most of the examples are from 胡竹安 , 動词後的"给"的词性和双賓语问题 Hwu Jwu'an, ("The nature of the Word *Geei* after Verbs and the Problem of Double Objects"), *ZGYW*, no. 95:222-224 (1960). Cf. also 向若 ,关于"给"的词性 (Shianq Ruoh, "On the Nature of *Geei* as a Word"), *ZGYW*, no. 92:64-65 (1960), and 楊欣安 , 说"给"(Yang Shin'an, "On *Geei*"), ibid., 66-68.

ing the reason,—tell him with the reason,—tell him the reason' = 告送他缘故 *gaw.sonq ta yuan.guh* and in 以此告之 *yii tsyy gaw jy* L 'take this tell him,—tell him this' = 把这个告送他 *bae jeyg gaw.sonq ta.*

Note that in all the compound forms with -$_o$*geei*, it is possible to rephrase the V-O$_1$-O$_2$ into V-O$_1$ *geei*-O$_2$ in series, as in 许给他一个女兒 *sheu$_o$geei ta ig neu.erl* 'promise him a daughter' ~ *sheu ig neu.erl .geei ta* 'promise a daughter to him', except that the Peiping verb 教给 *jiau$_o$geei* 'teach' cannot be so rephrased. Thus, 交一课书给他 *jiau i-keh shu .geei ta* can only mean 'hand over a lesson to him', with the 'hand over' 交 *jiau.*

(c) Verbs which never take -$_o$*geei* before an indirect object: 问 *wenn* 'ask, query', 请教 *chiingjiaw* 'ask, inquire (respectfully)', (麻)烦 *farn* or *ma.farn* 'trouble (someone with something)', 吃 *chy* 'eat', 喝 *he* 'drink', 抽 *chou* 'smoke', 收 *shou* 'receive', 用 *yonq* 'use', 赚 *juann* 'earn', 赢 *yng* 'win (in a bet, etc.), 抢 *cheang* 'rob', 偷 *tou* 'steal', 佔 *jann* 'occupy', 罚 *far* 'fine'. With these verbs, it is sometimes possible to change the indirect object into a possessive form, thus making it a modifier of the direct object, resulting in a simple V-O form. Thus, 他骗了我许多钱. *Ta piannle woo sheuduo chyan.* 'He swindled of me a lot of money.', or *Ta piannle woode sheuduo chyan.* 'He swindled a lot of my money.' which is of course a differently constructed sentence.

Of verbs of the 'call' type there are: 叫 *jiaw* 'call', 骂 *mah* 'call (names)', 当 *danq* 'take as', 封 *feng* 'enfeoff'. Thus, 骂他坏蛋 *mah ta huay-dann* 'call him a bad egg', 当他好人 *danq ta hao-ren* 'take him for a good man'.

The verb 给 *geei* 'give' itself does not take -$_o$*geei* 'to', though it is not of the 'take (from)' type of meaning. It is, however, quite common to have two verbal expressions in series using *geei* in both expressions, as in 给钱给他 *geei chyan $_o$geei ta* 'give money to him'.

(d) Verbs in which the use or non-use of -$_o$*geei* before an indirect object makes a difference in the direction of the action: 拿 *na* 'take', 买 *mae* 'buy', 租 *tzu* 'rent', 借 *jieh* 'loan', 分 *fen* 'share', as in 借了我三塊錢 *jiehle woo san-kuay chyan* 'borrowed three dollars from me': 借给了我三塊錢 *jieh$_o$geeile woo san-kuay chyan* 'lent me three dollars', 分我一点儿責任 *fen woo ideal tzerrenn* 'share some of my responsibilities': 分给我一点儿責任 *fen$_o$geei woo ideal tzerrenn* 'share with me some (of your) responsibilities'. Note, however, that in the classical style the direction of action is sometimes just the opposite of that in modern speech. For example, in the well-known passage in *Shyyjih* where Shianq Yeu was holding the future Hann Gautzuu Liou Bang's father as hostage and threatened to kill and cook him, Gautzuu said: If you do, 幸分我一杯羹 *shinq fen woo i-bei geng* 'kindly divide (for) me a cup of the soup',[32] which in the modern language would require -$_o$*geei* after *fen;* otherwise the direction of the sharing would be reversed.

*5.4.6.4. Goals of V-O Constructions.* An action expressed by a V-O construction may naturally have effects on other things, and such effects may be expressed in various grammatical forms. For example, 闹刀 *kai-dau* FF 'operate knife,—operate (surgically)': 给病人闹刀 *geei binqren kai-dau* 'operate on a patient'; 革職 *gerjyr* BB 'remove office,—remove from office': 革他的職 *ger tade jyr* (by ionization) 'remove his office,—remove him from office'. In a few cases the V-O form has acquired the status of a transitive verb and takes a direct object. Thus 得罪 *der$_o$tzuey* FB 'get offense' is no longer a V-O as 獲罪 *huoh tzuey* in 獲罪於天 *huoh tzuey yu tian* L 'get offense from heaven', but as a transitive verb 'offend', as in 得罪了人 应该賠不是 *der$_o$tzueyle ren inggai peir bush* 'having offended people, one ought to apologize'. Similarly, 注意 *juhyih* BB 'pour mind,—pay attention' though still ionizable as V-O as in *juh deal yih* 'pay some attention', is also used as a transitive verb, as in 得注意你自己的身体 *deei juhyih nii tzyhjii de shentii* 'must pay attention to your own health'. With most V-O's which affect other goals, it is necessary to use another verb *geei* or a possessive modifier to express the relation, as *bao-shean* 'guarantee (against)

---

[32] 項羽本纪(*Shinq Yeu Beenjih*), fasc. 7, p. 32A, Kaiming ed.

danger,—insure': 给他保险 *geei ta bao-shean* or 保他的險
*bao tade shean* 'insure him'; *daa-tzyh* 'strike characters,—type':
*geei ney-pian wen.jang daa-tzyh* 'for that article type characters,
—type that article'.

When, however, the goal word is in the subject position, then
the V-O expression can be used as predicate without any special
indication of the action-goal relation, since, as we have seen (sec.
2.4.2), the direction of action in a predicate need not be specified.
Thus, one can say: 这信还没打字呐. *Jeh shinn hair mei
daa-tzyh ne.* 'This letter has not yet been typed.', just like 还没
写呐 *hair mei shiee ne* 'has not yet been written'. 車应該保
險.*Che inggai bao-shean.* 'The car ought to be insured.' 我好
久没理髮了. *Woo haojeou mei lii-fah le.* 'I haven't had my
hair cut for a long time.', (or, said by a barber) 'I haven't done
any haircutting for a long time.' 这个和同还没簽字，可
是那个合同倒是簽了字了. *Jehg hertorng hair mei
chian-tzyh, keesh neyg hertorng dawsh chianle-tzyh le.* 'This contract has not yet been signed, but that contract already has.'
(*chian-tzyh* 'sign word,—sign one's signature' being a V-O construction).

*5.4.6.5. Mock Object.* We have noted that verbs and adjectives can be objects, as in 怕说话 *pah shuo-huah* 'afraid to
talk', 喜欢快 *shii.huan kuay* 'like (to be) fast'. But as a result
of a verb of action, an adjectival expression is usually in the form
of a complement, as in *shuo-ming.bairle* 'explain clearly', *he de
tonq.kuay* 'drink so as to be thoroughly satisfied'. Sometimes,
however, an adjectival expression in object position is treated as
nominal expression by being modified by the determinative *ig* or
*g*, and even preceded by a dummy indirect object *ta*, actually
referring to nothing specific except the total situation. Thus, besides the simple 说明白了 *shuo-ming.bairle* in V-R form, there
is the more lively V-O form: *Nii deei shuo g ming.bair* 'You have
to explain it to a clearness'. Similarly, there is: 我要喝他个
痛快. *Woo yaw he ta g tonq.kuay.* 'I want to drink to a thorough
satisfaction of it.', 哭的个不得了 *ku de g buderleau* 'wept to
an endlessness,—wept like anything', 哭他有什么用呐？
*Ku ta yeou sherm yonq ne?* 'What's the use of crying over it?'

*5.4.6.6. Possessive Objects and Other Special Modifiers of Objects*

(a) Possessive Objects. The grammatical modifier of an object sometimes does not modify the object semantically, but represents something else. When an apparent possessive modifier, instead of the object, represents the goal, I call it "possessive object". For example, in: 別 闹 他 的 玩 笑 ! *Bye kai tade wanshiaw!* 'Don't make his fun,—don't make fun of him!', it is not his fun, but your fun that you are told not to make of him, so that the real goal is the *ta* of *tade*. Sometimes, though not in all cases, the construction can be rephrased as verbal expressions in series (V-V series), with the verb *gen* 'with' or *geei* 'gives, for', etc., in first position, as 跟 他 闹 玩笑 *gen ta kai-wanshiaw* 'with him make fun,—make fun of him'. Other V-O constructions with possessive objects which are convertible to V-V series are: 打 他 的 岔 *daa tade chah* ~ *gen ta daa-chah* 'interrupt him'; 借 您 的 光 *jieh Ninde guang*~*gen Nin jieh-guang*~*jieh Nin guang* '(may I) borrow your light,—may I trouble you?', the *Nin* in the last form being an indirect object; 赌 我 的 气 *duu woode chih*~*gen woo duu-chih* 'hold a grudge against me'; 搗 他 的 乱 (~ 蛋 ) *dao tade luann (~-dann)*~*gen ta dao-luann (~-dann)* 'make trouble for him'; 帮 我 的 忙 *bang woode mang*~*geei woo bangmang* 'help my busyness,—help me'; 多 他 的 心 *duo tade shin* ~*duey ta duoshin* 'toward him have superfluous ideas,—suspect him', where the *shin* is not his, but somebody else's. Note that in 见 他 的 面 *jiann tade miann*~*gen ta jiann-miann* 'meet with him' the object *miann* is B and the phrase does not mean literally 'see his face', for which one has to say 看 見 他 的 臉 *kann.jiann tade lean*.

Sometimes a V-O construction with a possessive object cannot be rephrased in the V-V form, as 拆 我 的 枱 *chai woode tair* 'dismantle my platform,—spoil my plans'; 摊 我 的 枱 *tan woode tair* 'collapse my platform,—make me lose face'. Unlike *jiann tade miann*~*gen ta jiann-miann*, the V-O compound 见 情 *jiann-chyng* 'to be appreciative or grateful' only takes a possessive object, as in 我 不 是 不 見 情， 我 很 見 他 的 情 啊 ! *Woo bush bu jiann-chyng, woo heen jiann tade chyng a!* 'I am not un-grateful, I am quite appreciative of his kindness!' Sometimes, the rephrased V-V form will have a different sentence value, as 说 他的闲话 (〜坏话) *shuo tade shyanhuah (〜huayhuah)* 'talk his gossip (〜bad words),—gossip against him', but *gen ta shuo shyanhuah (〜huayhuah)* 'talk with him gossiping (about 〜 against someone else)'; 搞他的鬼 *dao tade goei* 'tell on him', but *gen ta dao-goei* 'whisper to him'; 告他的状 *gaw tade juanq* 'sue him' or 'tell on him', but *gen ta gaw-juanq* 'inform him (against someone else)'. For further examples of possessive objects, see section 6.5.7.4.

(b) *Sherme* as Modifier of Objects. In addition to the ordinary use of *sherme* as an interrogative adjective, as in: 什么花儿顶 香? *Sherm hual diing shiang?* 'What flower smells the sweetest?' and: 你要买什么书? *Nii yaw mae sherm shu?* 'What book do you want to buy?', there is a rhetorical use of the adjectival *sherme* before objects, with the intention of contradicting a state-ment. For example, if an illiterate person says that he wants to buy a book, one may say: 你连字都不认得，还买什么 书呐? *Nii lian tzyh dou bu rennde, hair mae sherm shu ne?* 'You don't even know any characters, what books are you going to buy?' This usage is similar to, but not quite the same as, the colloquial '*What* books?!' with stress on 'what', whereas the *sherme*, though syntactically modifying the object, refers to the V-O construction as a whole: 'What is the point in talking about buying books?' and *sherme* is often said in the netural tone. (Cf. 'Out sherm side', sec. 6.5.8.) With intransitive verbs, *sherme* in the same rhetorical sense is used as the object instead of modify-ing another object, as in: 那还去什么呐? *Nah hair chiuh sherm ne?* 'In that case what's the point of still going there?' or more colloquially 那还去个什么劲儿呐? *Nah hair chiuh g sherm jiell ne?*, where *sherm jiell* has the effect of something like 'what sort of a deal?'

(c) Other Special Modifiers of objects. Other cases of formal modifiers of objects which in fact refer to the V-O constructions as wholes are as follows: In analogy with 说了半天的话 *shuole banntian de huah* 'talked half a day's words,—talked for a long time', one also says 罵了几个钟头的人 *mahle jiig jongtour de ren* 'scolded several hours of people', where it is the scolding, and not the people, that is measured in hours. Similarly, in 拔了两塊錢的草 *barle leang-kuay chyan de tsao* 'pulled two dollars' worth of weeds', 戒了五年的酒 *jiehle wuu-nian de jeou* 'swore off five years' wine', 得请几十塊錢的客 *deei chiing jiishyr-kuay chyan de keh* 'have to entertain umpty dollars' worth of guests', all the quantitative modifiers of the objects really modify the V-O constructions as wholes: *bar-tsao* 'weeding', *jieh-jeou* 'swearing off drinking', *chiing-keh* 'entertaining'. This form of asemantic analysis is by no means limited to Chinese. A sign in an American library says: "Please shelve your own books!" which presumably does not imply that the library has an unusually acquisitive department of aquisition, but simply that readers should do their own shelving of the library books.

(d) Finally, there is a special use of a possessive modifier which does not represent the goal, nor does it function as a possessive determinative normally does in limiting the reference, but is added only for rhetorical emphasis, usually in command form. In general, possessive modifiers are not used in Chinese if the reference is not ambiguous, as: 他戴了帽子就上路了。 *Ta dayle mawtz jiow shanq-luh le.* 'He put on his hat and went on his journey.' But with this special rhetorical possessive, one can say: 戴上你那破帽子，快点儿滚你的蛋！*Day-shanq nii nah poh mawtz, kuah.deal goen niide dann!* 'Put on that broken hat of yours, hurry up and tumble you (like an egg) out of here!'

5.4.7. *"Inverted Subjects" and "Inverted Objects"*

5.4.7.1. *"Inverted Subjects".* We discussed (sec 2.3.2) the case of a subject coming after the predicate when it is added as an afterthought, as in: 好听極了，这个音樂！ *Haoting-jyile, jeyg inyueh!* 'Sounds very beautiful, this music!' Another type of construction which has often been regarded as involving an inverted subject is of the type like: 下雨了。*Shiah-yeu le.* 'It is raining.', 耒了三隻大狗。*Laile san-jy dah-goou.* 'There came three big dogs.' So far as our definition of the V-O construction is concerned, examples of the latter type satisfy the definition and must therefore be analyzed as verb-object, even though the object is the agent word. Sometimes it is not clear in which direction the action of the verb goes. Thus, in 起霧了 *chii-wuh le* 'there rises a fog' *wuh* 'fog' seems to be the agent, while in 闹船了 *kai-chwan le* 'start ship,—the ship is sailing now' *chwan* 'ship' seems to be what the pilot operates and therefore the goal. But in 这个船闹香港。 *Jeyg chwan kai Shianggaang.* 'This ship sails for Hong Kong.', *kai* 'sails' seems to be what the ship is doing. Rather than inquiring into the often unclear direction of action, the only consistent way of recognizing a grammatical object is simply to ask whether it is in the V-O form, as in 下过 三天的大雨。 *Shiah.guoh san-tian de dah-yeu.* 'It has rained three days big rain.', 他从小儿就死了父親。 *Ta tsorngsheaul jiow syyle fuh.chin.* 'He since childhood has-been-bereaved-of his father.' As has been noted by Mullie, such verbs can even take the pretransitive *bae*, as transitive verbs typically can, in 他把 个娘们儿死了。 *Ta bae g niang.mel syyle.* 'He had one of his womenfolks die (on him).'[33]

5.4.7.2. *"Inverted Objects"*. Here we shall only look at a few special types. Take the sentences: (a) 这个人不讲理。 *Jeyg ren bu jeang-lii.* 'This man does not talk reason.', (b) 这个人一点 儿道理都不讲。 *Jeyg ren ideal daw.lii dou bu jeang.* 'This man does not talk any reason at all.', (c) 这个人什么东西都 不吃。 *Jeyg ren sherm dong.shi dou bu chy.* 'This man does not eat anything.', (d) 这种东西谁都不吃。 *Jey.tzoong dong-.shi sheir dou bu chy.* 'Nobody eats this kind of thing!' Sentence (a) is in the usual straightforward S-V-O order. In sentences (b) to (d) we have the interrogative-indefinite plus *dou* (or *yee*) for 'any and every' (or 'none' in negative forms), which always comes before the verb. In (b) and (c) the usual treatment is to regard them as S-O-V, and (d) as O-S-V, with inverted object before the verb and before the subject. Our treatment is simply to regard all such cases as straightforward order and regard the "inverted object" as subject: as the small subject of an S-P predicate in the case of (b) and (c) and as the main subject in (d), in which *sheir*

---

[33]Mullie, *Struct Princ*, I, 184. See also sec. 5.5.4.2.

is the small subject, the direction of action being implied in the nature of the words involved.

Sometimes, real ambiguity exists in such a sentence as: (c) 这 个 人 谁 都 不 认 得。 *Jeyg ren sheir dou bu renn.de.* With the direction of action going one way, it means: 'Nobody knows this man', while with the direction of action going the other way, it means: 'This man does not know anybody.' Ambiguities can of course always be resolved by recasting the sentence, resulting in a more or less different structure. Thus, *Jeyg ren, ta sheir dou bu renn.de.* in the first meaning adds another subject stage, while *Jeyg ren sheir dou bu renn.de ta.* adds an object, which normally is not expressed if the goal word is in the near context.

While it is usually unsafe to depend upon the secondary judgments of an informant, it is not without significance that in sentence (b), which was made up by a student in a grammar class, the clause *idean daw.lii dou bu jeang* was regarded by him as 结 合 很 紧 的 一 个 东 西    *jyeher heen jiin de ig dong.shi* 'a tightly formed one thing' which as a unit was predicated of the subject.[34]

# 5.5 Verbal Expressions in Series[35]

*5.5.1. Verbal Expressions in Series and Other Syntactical Constructions*

(1) Coordinate Constructions. Verbal expressions in series (V-V series) form an intermediate type between coordinate and subordinate constructions, but are nearer the latter than the former. A V-V series is like a coordinate phrase in that both parts are verbal expressions, usually with an object after the first verb. However, whereas coordinate verbal expressions are reversible without affecting the value of the sentence of which they form a part, a V-V series, when reversed, often has a different sentence

---

[34]Reported by 祝 孔 嘉(Juh Koongjia) in Leu, *S & O*, 222.

[35]The term "verbal expressions in series" was suggested to me by Fang-Kuei Li and I appropriated it, without acknowledgment, in *Mand Prim*, 38, for which my apologies. The idea may have been in the air, but its crystallization in these words was definitely Li's.

value. Thus, to borrow Li's examples, in the coordinate construction in: 他天ㄈㄦ写信会客. *Ta tiantial shiee-shinn huey-keh.* 'He writes letters and receives callers every day.', the two verbal expressions can be reversed as *huey-keh shiee-shinn* 'receives callers and writes letters' without affecting the sentence value. But the two sentences: *Deeng i.hoel chiuh!* 'Wait a while (before you) go!' and: *Chiuh deeng i.hoel!* 'Go and wait a while!' obviously call for different actions to comply with the command. Thus a V-V series is like a coordinate construction in that it can usually be reversed and remain grammatical, but differs from it in not being reversible without involving a probable change in the sentence value.

(2) Subordinative Constructions. A V-V series is like a subordinative construction in that the second expression has approximately the same function as the whole and is thus the center to which the first verbal expression is a modifier, often translatable by a prepositional phrase. For example, 拿筆写字 *na-bii shiee-tzyh* 'take pen write characters,—write characters with a pen', 在屋裡睡觉 *tzay u.lii shuey.jiaw* 'being in the room, sleep,—sleep in the room'. A V-V series, however, rarely takes the subordinative particle *de* (*dih₂*) after the first verbal expression and is in this respect different from ordinary adverbial expressions.

(3) Verb-Complement (V-R) Constructions. A V-V series differs from a V-R construction in having its center in the second constituent, whereas a V-R construction has its center in the first constituent. For example, in 在揚州住家 *tzay Yang.jou juh-jia* 'in Yangchow dwell house,—live in Yangchow' has *juh-jia* as center, with *tzay Yang.jou* as modifier, while *juh ₀tzay Yang.jou* 'live in Yangchow' has *juh* as center and *₀tzay Yang.jou* as resultative complement. Again, 给他送信 *geei ta sonq-shinn* 'send a letter for him' is a V-V series, but in *sonq-shinn ₀geei ta* 'send a letter to him', *₀geei ta* is a complement. When a verb has both an object and a complement, as 吃完了饭 *chy-wanle fann* 'eat to a finish meal,—have finished eating one's meal', the verb is often repeated to form a V-V series, especially if the V-O either has bound parts or is a very common idiom, which the speaker does not like to separate, as 做寿做完了 *tzuoh-show tzuoh-*

*wanle* '(in) celebrating (someone's) birthday, have finished celebrating, have finished celebrating someone's birthday.'

(4) Pivotal Constructions. A V-V series differs from a pivotal
construction (sec. 2.13), in which an object is followed by another
verb with the object as its subject, whereas in a V-V series the
two verbs have the same subject. Thus: 我要他来。 *Woo yaw ta*
*lai.* 'I want him to come.' is a pivotal construction; 我買份儿
礼送人。 *Woo mae fell lii sonq ren.* 'I buy a gift to give to
someone.' is V-V series. The pre-pivotal verbs are limited to a
small listable number, whereas possible first verbs in V-V series
are unlistable. Here, as elsewhere, there may be isolated cases of
ambiguous construction such as 我要找一个人谈话。 *Woo*
*yaw jao ig ren tarn huah.* 'I want to find someone to have a talk.'
If it is taken as ... *gen woo tarn huah* 'to have a talk with me',
then it is a pivotal construction. If it is taken as ... *gen ta tarn*
*huah*, there are still two possibilities: (a) If *ta* refers to the same
*ren*, then it is '... to talk to' and it is a V-V series; (b) if *ta* refers
to a different person: 'I want to find someone to talk with him',
then it is still a pivotal construction.

(5) S-P Subjects. A subject S with a $V_1$-$V_2$ as predicate is to
be distinguished from S-$V_1$ as subject with $V_2$ as predicate. In
the former, the main break between the ICs, often reflected in a
pause or a particle, is after S, while in the latter it falls after the
S-$V_1$ as an S-P subject. Thus, in: 他(呀,)开車走了。 *Ta (ia,)*
*kai-che tzoou le.* 'He drove the car and left', the break is after
*ta*, while in: ...是一件怪事。 *Ta kai-che (ia,) sh i-jiann guay-*
*shyh.* 'That he drives a car is a strange thing.' Here, again, ambiguity is possible if both analyses make sense, as in: 他跟你
很好。 *Ta gen nii heen hao.*, as S + $V_1V_2$: 'He is very good to
you', and as $SV_1$ + $V_2$: 'That he follows you is very good', with
S-P subject. In this particular example, a third analysis is possible, namely, with *ta gen nii* as a coordinate subject, resulting in:
'He and you are very good (or are friendly with each other)'.

Verbal Expressions or Predicative Expressions in Series? In a
detailed and well-documented discussion of the subject, Wang
Fwutyng[36] questioned the propriety of the term "verbal expres-

---

[36] 王福庭,"連動式"还是"連谓式"? (Wang Fwutyng, "Verb-

sions in series" and proposed to change it to "predicative expressions in series". Among other examples, he cited nominal expressions as one member of the series, as: 我 一隻手 打 不过 你。 *Woo i-jy shoou daa.bu-guoh nii.* 'I, being one-handed, cannot beat you.' or 'I, using only one hand, cannot beat you.' In: 我 肚子疼 不 出 去了。 *Woo duhtz terng bu chu.chiuh le.* 'I, having a stomach-ache, am not going out.', *duhtz terng* is an S-P predicate. These cases are not only relatively infrequent compared with actual verbal expressions, but are also amenable to alternate analysis. Thus, in the first example, one can take *woo* as the main subject and *i-jy shoou* as the small subject in an S-P predicate. In both examples, it is better to treat the predicates as coordinate rather than in series, since they can have a pause inside and can be reversed without changing the sentence value. Thus, with pause: *Woo i-jy shoou, daa.bu-guoh nii. Woo duhtz terng, bu chiuh le.* With reversal: *Woo daa.bu-guoh nii, i-jy shoou me.* 'I can't beat you, one hand, you see.' *Woo bu chiuh le, duhtz terng.* 'I am not going, stomach-ache.' But my main objection to treating V-V series as P-P series is that they often do not consist of predicates. For example, frequently an auxiliary verb applies to both expressions and not merely to the first one. Thus, in 得 脱了 鞋 进去 *deei tuole shye jinn.chiuh* 'must remove your shoes to go in' one could claim that *deei* applies to *tuole shye*, since you don't have to go in, but in 不能光着头 出去。 *Buneng guangj tour chu.chiuh.* 'You can't go out bareheaded.', *buneng* applies to the V-V series as a whole and forms with it one simple predicate, since it neither says 'You can't go out' nor says 'You can't bare your head.' Again, in: 脱了 鞋 进去 才行。 *Tuole shye jinn.chiuh tsair shyng.* 'Only removing your shoes before going in will it do.', or: 光着头出去会 惹起伤風耒。 *Guangj tour chu.chiuh huey ree.chii shang-feng .lai.* 'Going out bare-headed may cause a cold.', the V-V series in each case is the subject and not the predicate.

*5.5.2. Formal Patterns of V-V Series*

(1) Chain V-V Series. Most V-V series consist of two expres-

_____

al in Expressions in Series" or "Predicative Expressions in Series?") ZGYW, no. 96:281-284; and no. 100:339-349 (1960).

sions. In a minority of cases more than two verbal expressions form a series in a chain, which, however, can usually be grouped hierarchically into two ICs and are thus still analyzable as two expressions. Thus, in 写信对他拜年 *shiee-shinn duey ta bay-nian* 'write a letter to give New Year greetings to him' *shiee-shinn* is in series with *duey ta bay-nian* as a whole, which is itself a V-V series. In 告假坐飛机回國省親 *gaw-jiah tzuoh feiji hwei-gwo shiing-chin* 'take a leave to take a plane to return to his country to visit his parents', there are various possibilities in cutting the series into ICs, though $V_1 + (V_2V_3 + V_4)$ seems to make the best sense.

(2) Objects of the Verbs. In a V-V series, the first verbal expression has an object in most cases, but the second verbal expression has or does not have an object, with relative frequencies of the same order of magnitude as other verbal expressions. Thus, 拿着扇子跳了一个舞 *naj shanntz tiawle ig wuu* 'holding a fan danced a dance' and 打开窗户说亮话 *daa.okai chuang.huh shuo lianq-huah* 'open the window to say lighted words,—call a spade a spade' have objects after both verbs; 拿着绳子跳 *naj sherngtz tiaw* 'holding a rope, jump' and 打开了窗户呼吸 *daa.kaile chuang.huh hu.shi* 'opened the window to breathe' have no objects after the second verbs; in 去做事 *chiuh tzuoh-shyh* 'go to do work' and 坐着看报 *tzuohj kann-baw* 'sitting, read the newspaper' the first verbs have no objects; in 来玩 *lai wal* 'come to play' and 哭着出去了 *kuj chu.chiuh le* 'crying, went out', both verbs are without objects. Where the first verb has no object, it is usually a verb of the *lai* 'comes' and *chiuh* (goes) type or, if another verb, it must have an aspect suffix or a complement, as *kuj* 'crying' in the last example, or in 睡完了起来 *shuey.wanle chii.lai* 'having finished sleeping, get up'.

In general, when two monosyllabic verbs come in succession, even though both are free, they do not form a V-V series, but tend to form a compound, as 说笑 *shuoshiaw* 'talk-laugh,—to banter', 出去 *chu.chiuh* 'exit-go,—go out', 走动 *tzoouodonq* 'walk -move,—walk about'. This can be compared with the tendency of a monosyllabic adjective to form a compound with a monosyllabic noun when there is no subordinative particle *de* to make them a phrase.

(3) Omission of Objects After First Verbs. In the preceding examples, when a first or second verb has no object, it simply has no object to begin with. But with certain typically first-position verbs, the object is sometimes present and sometimes omitted without much difference in meaning. They are: (a)把 *bae*, (b) 被 *bey*, (c)给 *geei*, (d)叫 *jaw*, (e) 在 *tzay* and the L verbs (f)以 *yii*, (g)为 *wey*, (h) 因 *in*, (i)从 *tsorng*, and (j)将 *jiang*.

(a) With *bae*, the pretransitive (sec. 5.5.4.1):　我 告送 他 别 把 玩 意ㄦ 弄 坏 了，他 偏 把 他 弄 坏 了. *Woo gaw.sonq ta bye bae wanyell nonq-huayle, ta pian bae ta nonq.huayle.* 'I told him don't take that toy and spoil it and he *would* take hold of it and spoil it.' With the last *ta* omitted, the second clause will read: *ta pian bae nonq-huayle* 'he *would* take hold and spoil it', where *bae* puts into prominence the active 'go-ahead-and' effect.

(b) With *bey:*[37] 我 被 他 骗 了. *Woo bey ta piann le.* 'I was fooled by him.': *Woo bey ren piann le.* 'I was fooled by someone (or by people).': *Woo bey piann le.* 'I was fooled.' In the last sentence, *bey* is not a full-fledged verb, since, as Ozaki observes (ibid., p. 81), one cannot ask: ° 哦? 你 被 了 ? °*Or? nii bey le?* 'Is that so? You were?' or answer ° 被 了. °*Bey le.* 'I was.' In other words, *bey* is used only in first position and not as a main verb. By contrast, 捱 *air* 'suffers' and 受 *show* 'receives' are not limited to first-position verbs, as: 他 捱 了 一 顿 打. *Ta airle i-duenn daa.* 'He suffered a spell of beating.', and 他 受 了 上 师 的 申 斥. *Ta showle shanq.shy de shenchyh.* 'He received a reprimand from his superior.'

(c) The verb *geei* is often used alone, as in 给 了 钱 了 *geeile chyan le* 'have given money,—have paid'. As the first verb, with omissible object, in a V-V series, it is sometimes used like *bae*, with direction of action outward, sometimes like *bey*, with direc-

---

tion of action inward, but it also has the force of giving benefit or harm, somewhat like the dative of interest, as in German. It is like *bae* in: 信写完了，请你给（～把）（他）抄了寄走吧。*Shinn shiee-wanle, chiing nii geei ( ～ bae) (ta) chaule jih-tzoou ba.* 'The letter is finished, please copy it and mail it off.' 这裂缝儿不要紧，我给（～把）（他）補起未就好了。*Jeh liehfenql bu yawjiin, woo geei (～bae) (ta) buu-.chiilai jiow hao le.* 'This crack doesn't matter, it will be all right when I give it a mending (up).' It is like *bey* in  你眼睛怎么了？给（～被）（人）打了一拳头。*Nii yean.jing tzeem le? Geei (～bey) (ren) daale i-chyuan.tou.* 'What's the matter with your eye? It was given a blow of the fist by someone,—it was hit by someone.' 我那枝鋼筆给（～被）孩子们玩了好久，後未给（～被）（他们）玩儿丢了。*Woo ney-jy gangbii geei (～bey) hairtzmen walle haojeou, howlai geei (～bey) (tamen) wal-dioule.* 'That pen of mine was played with by the children for a good while, afterwards it was lost by them.' As a verb of interest by way of benefit or harm, *geei* is used in  我不懂外國话，请你给（我）翻译。*Woo budoong way.gwohuah, chiing nii geei (woo) fan.yih.* 'I don't understand any foreign language, please interpret for me.' In  这是他頂好的杯子，别给（他）打破了。*Jeh sh ta diing hao de beitz, bye geei (ta) daa-pohle.* 'This is his best cup, don't you go and break it for him.'', if *ta* stands for the person it means 'don't break it, to his loss', but if it stands for the cup, then 给他 *geei ta* ～ 把他 *bae ta* is simply the pretransitive 'taking hold of'. Sometimes it is possible to have both in a chain V-V series with *bae* or *bey* for the direction of action and *geei* for interest, as in: 别把杯子给（我）打破了。*Bye bae beitz geei (woo) daa-pohle.* 'Don't take the cup and break it for me.' 房子被火给燒了。*Farngtz bey huoo geei shaule.* 'The house was burned by fire.', where *geei* indicates 'to its harm' or 'to the owner's loss'.

It is quite possible to have the three uses of 给 *geei:* (a) 'give', (b) 'taking hold of' or 'by', and (c) 'to someone's benefit (or harm)' occurring in the same sentence. For instance, 这东西我叫他别给人， 东西哪去了？— 他给他给给了。*Jeh dong.shi woo jiaw ta bye geei ren, dong.shi naal chiuh le?* —*Ta geei ta geei geei le.* 'I told him not to give this thing away, but where is the thing now? ...' after which the answer containing *geei* three times can still have two alternative analyses: (1) 'He took it and, to someone's benefit (or harm), gave it away.'; (2) 'It was by him, to someone's benefit (or harm), given away.'[38]

In the sense of interest, especially in the sense of advantage, the Central dialects use 替 *tih* 'substitutes, acts as proxy for', which in Northern Mandarin is used only in the narrower, literal sense. Thus, in: 我不能去，你替我去吧！ *Woo buneng chiuh, nii tih woo chiuh ba!* 'I can't go, you'd better go as my substitute!', *tih*, or the compound of synonyms 代替 *daytih*, is used in such a sentence in both Northern Mandarin and the Central dialects. But in the general sense of interest, when it is *geei* in Northern Mandarin, it is *tih* (but not *daytih*, which is always taken literally), as in: 我得罪了他，你也不肯替我解释ㄝㄝ. *Woo der.tzueyle ta, nii yee bukeen tih woo duey ta jiee.shyh .jiee.shyh.* 'I have offended him, and you won't explain it to him on my behalf.' 这东西很不结实，不要替我搞坏了。 *Jeh dong.shi heen bu jie.shyr, buyaw tih woo gao-huayle.* 'This thing is very fragile, don't spoil it for me.' In both examples, Northern Mandarin would have *geei* for *tih* (and, incidentally, 别...弄坏了 *bye...nonq-huayle* for 不要...搞坏了 *buyaw ... gao-huayle*).

(d) The verb 照 *jaw* 'shines upon, reflects', besides being a main verb, as in: 太陽照在大海上. *Tay.yang jaw .tzay dahhae.shanq.* 'The sun was shining on the sea.', is often used in first position in the sense of 'following, according to', as in 照着 这个法子办 *jawj jeyg fartz bann* 'perform according to this

---

[38]Dragunov (sec. 104) gave the example 给他给给了 *geei ta geei geei le* without context and said that the sentence was not possible outside the dialects of Kansu and Shensi. Actually, with the context as given above, it is quite possible in many other dialects, including that of Peiping. The ambiguity involved could be resolved by the use of the character 他 for 'he' or 'him' and 它 for 'it', but such distinctions are of course not reflected in actual speech in any dialect.

method', 照我的意見不行 *jaw woode yih.jiann bu shyng* 'according to my view won't do'. When so used, as the first verb in a V-V series, it can omit its object, as in 照办 *jaw bann* 'manage accordingly', 得照抄 *deei jaw chau* 'must copy as is', 已竟照准了 *yiijinq jaw joen le* 'already approved as petitioned'. This use of *jaw*, however, is not of unlimited versatility. Note that *jaw joen* as V-V series is not the same as the V-R construction: 用手電灯照準了 *yonq shoou-dianndeng jaw-joenle* 'aim accurately with the flashlight', where *jaw* is used as a main verb.

(e) The verb *tzay* 'to be at', like *geei*, is used either alone or as first verb, with omissible object, in a V-V series. In: 他在家裡 *Ta tzay jia.lii* 'He is at home', it is a main verb. In 在家裡歇着呐 *tzay jia.lii shiej ne* 'to be resting at home', it is in first position in a V-V series. The only object after *tzay* that is often omitted is 那儿 *.nall* in $_0$*tzay.nall* 'right there' used in connection with the progressive aspects of a verb or its equivalent, as in 他在那儿吃着饭呐。 *Ta $_0$tzay.nall chyj fann ne.* 'He is right there eating meal,—he is eating his meal.', where *.nall* is often omitted, giving rise to the form *tzay chyj fann* 'is at eating meal', which seems to suggest the English form *a-eating*. But actually the *tzay* here is really a first verb in a V-V series with an omitted object. This form is used more often in the Central dialects and has now spread over Northern Mandarin, where it is fairly commonly spoken and is practically standard in written bairhuah. But in everyday speech, the form: 他在那儿说话呐。 *Ta $_0$tzay.nall shuo-huah ne.* is still much more frequently heard (often realized phonetically as ... [zār] ... ) than the form *Ta $_0$tzay shuo-huah ne.*

(f) The verbs *yii* L 'takes' is one of the five wenyan verbs with omissible objects which we shall cite for purposes of comparison. In 以此告之 *yii tsyy gaw jy* L, translatable as: 拿这个告送他 *na jeyg gaw.sonq ta* 'take this and tell him,—tell him this', we have the usual V-V series with objects after both verbs. But in 遂以告之 *suey yii gaw jy* 'thereupon take (this) and tell him', the object of *yii* is omitted and since *yii* is used very frequently in this way, it becomes equivalent to *yii tsyy* or *yii jy* 'therewith'. Note that while *yii* is one of the typical first verbs with omissible objects, its spoken counterpart 拿 *na* in such a position never omits its object. Thus one can say: 这秘密别给告送了人. *Jeh mih.mih bye geei gaw.sonqle ren.* 'This secret mustn't be told people.', one cannot say: °*Jeh mih.mih bye na gaw.sonqle ren.*

(g) The L verb *wei* 'do, act as, to be in the capacity of, to be', has a phonetic modification *wey* 'to be for', often used in first position in a V-V series, as in 为我一询 *wey woo i-shyun* L (epistolary style) 'for me one inquire,—make an inquiry for me'. But, for reasons of rhythm, often an important factor in modern wenyan, the object is omitted in 祈为一询 *chyi wey i-shyun* L 'please for (me) one inquire,—please make an inquiry for (me)'. While *wey* 'to be for' is very much alive as a verb in modern speech, as in: 我谁也不为. *Woo sheir yee bu wey.* 'I am not for anybody (in particular).', 为什么不来? *Wey sherm bu lai?* 'For what don't come,—why don't you come?', the object is never omitted after *wey* when in first position in a V-V series. This, in: 请别为(～ 为了 ,～ 为着 ) 我麻煩! *Chiing bye wey* (～weyle～weyj) *woo ma.farn!* 'Please don't take trouble on my account!', *woo* cannot be omitted, as it could in wenyan.

(h) Similar to *yii* L and *wey* L, is the use of *in* L 'because of' with omitted object. Thus, 因恶之 *in wuh jy* is short for 因是恶之 *in shyh wuh jy* 'because of that hated him,—consequently hated him'. We have thus the apparently paradoxical result that *in* L sometimes means 'because' and sometimes means 'therefore', according to the context.

(i) Much less common is the use of *tsorng* 'follow, from' as a verb in L without object, as in: 欲从而帝之 *yuh tsorng erl dih jy* L 'wanted to follow from (that event) and king him—thereupon wanted to make him king', 又从而殺之 *yow tsorng erl sha jy* L 'moreover following (that event) killed him,—thereupon killed him'. In modern spoken style, there is the form: 我从不做这种事. *Woo tsorng bu tzuoh jeh-tzoong shyh.* 'I never do such things.', where *tsorng* is short for *tsornglai* 'hitherto,—ever before', which in turn probably came from 从本来 *tsorng beenlai* 'from original', 从 向 来 *tsorng shianqlai* 'from hitherto', or 从 古 以 来 *tsorng guu yiilai* 'from ancient hitherto'. Apart from this use of *tsorng*, which always goes with a negative *bu* or *mei* (*yeou*), it is not used without an object.

(j) The L verb *jiang* 'take' is the most interesting first verb with omissible objects (see sec. 6.5.8). As a pretransitive first verb, it is still used in modern Cantonese, in the form of *tzeung*, as an equivalent of Mandarin *bae*. Thus, 将 佢 食 哂 *tzeung ghoe zek-saay* = 把 他 吃 完 了 *bae ta chy-wanle* 'finish eating it'. But *jiang* L in first position in a V-V series very often occurs without object, as in: 牛 何 之 ? ... 将 以 釁 钟。 *Niou her jy?* ... *Jiang yii shinn jong.* 'Where is the ox going? Taking (it) using (it) to smear the bell (with sacrificial blood)'.[39] Here we have a chain V-V series in which both the first and the second verbs have their objects *jy* 'it' omitted. But in the case of *jiang*, it started with the idea of 'with it', 'therewith', 'withal' and ended up with the effect of 'what next?' so that *jiang* becomes a mark of near-future action. Note that the modern *word jianglai* '(in) the future' is a noun or an adverb, whereas the *phrase jiang lai*, which is L only, is a verbal expression: 'will come'. (Cf. Fr. *avenir* < *à venir*.)

(4) Prepositions and Coverbs. Verbs differ in the frequency with which they function as first verb in a V-V series. (a) Most transitive verbs occur as first verb only occasionally. (b) A listable number of verbs occur as first verbs with at least the same order of frequency as in other positions and are thus called coverbs[40] or prepositions, since they translate readily into prepositions when used in first position. Examples are: *tsorng* 'follow, from', 朝 *chaur* 'face, facing', 在 *tzay* 'to be at, at' as in: 你 得 从 这 儿。*Nii deei tsorng jell.* 'You must (go) this way.': *Nii deei tsorng jell tzoou.* 'You must go this way'. 这 屋 子 朝 东。*Jeh utz chaur dong.* 'This room faces the east.': *chaur dong tzoou* 'go eastward'. 他 在 外 国。*Ta tzay way.gwo.* 'He is in a foreign country, —he is abroad.': *Ta tzay way.gwo niann-shu.* 'He is studying in a foreign country.'

---

[39]*Mencius*, I, 7 ( 梁 惠 王 上 ).

[40]For example, by John de Francis, *Beginning Chinese*, New Haven, 1963, p. 76; see also Simon, Verb Complex, 565-567.

(c) Very few first verbs in a V-V series occur exclusively in that position and are thus prepositions par excellence. Even the L preposition 於 *yu*, which normally is not used as a main verb in modern wenyan, is acquiring main-verb status in the new-style date line in prefaces, as in 於北平 *Yu Beeipyng* 'At Peiping', instead of the more traditional 序於北平 *Shiuh yu Beeipyng* 'Prefaced at Peiping'.[41]

5.5.3 *Class Meaning of V-V Series.* The over all class meaning of V-V series is 'order of events' or 'circumstances of events', as contrasted with that of coordinate constructions which is 'and/or'. As the more specific meanings hinge mainly on what the first verbal expression says, they will be given in terms of the first verbal expression.

(1) First in Time Order. 我起來穿了衣裳. *Woo chii-.lai chuanle i.shang.* 'I got up and put on my clothes.': *Woo chuanle i.shang chii.lai.* 'I put on my clothes and got up'; 進去買了票 *jinn.chiuh maele piaw* 'went in and bought the ticket': *maele piaw jinn.chiuh* 'bought the ticket and went in'; 坐火車上北平 *tzuoh huooche shanq Beeipyng* 'take a train to go to Peiping': *shanq Beeipyng tzuoh huooche* 'go to Peiping to take a train'.[42] The time order idea in a V-V series is not unlike that expressed by: 'You can have your cake and eat it, but you can't eat your cake and have it'.

(2) Time When. Besides nominal subjects in the form of time words, such as 今天 *jin.tian* 'today', 这会儿 *jeh.hoel* 'this moment', 那时候儿 *nah shyr.howl* '(at) that time', time when is often expressed by a first verb 在 *tzay* 'at', *tsorng* 'from'. 到 *daw* 'reaching to,—by', as in 在年轻的时候儿做过这事 *tzay*

---

[41]In classical times, however, both 於 *yu* < *iwo* and 于 *yu* < *jiu* were used as main verbs. See Bernhard Karlgren, "The Authenticity and Nature of the *Tso Chuan*", *Göteborgs Högskolas Arsskrift*, 32:41-49 of 1-65, Gothenburg (1926). Further examples of prepositions will be given in sec. 8.2 on prepositions.

[42]On the difference between 去買菜 *chiuh mae tsay* 'go marketing' and *mae tsay .chiuh* 'go off marketing', see sec. 6.6.8(7).

*nianching de shyr.howl tzuoh.guoh jeh shyh* 'at youthful time did this thing,—did this when young', 从一大早就不舒服了 *tsorng i-dahtzao jiow bushu.fwu le* 'has not been feeling well since early morning', 到下午再谈吧 *daw shiahwuu tzay tarn ba* 'let's talk about it (not until) this afternoon'. Note that duration, as opposed to time when, is not expressed by a first verbal expression or time word, but by a nominal expression, either as subject or, more frequently, as object, as: 三个月没下雨了. *San g yueh mei shiah yeu le.* 'It's been three months it hasn't rained—since it rained.' 我昨儿晚上只睡了四个钟头. *Woo tzuol woan.shanq jyy shueyle syhg jonqtour.* 'I slept only four hours last night.' Time until is also not expressed by a first verbal expression, but by a complement with ₀*daw*, as in 说到 天亮 *shuo ₀daw tianlianq* 'talk until (reaching) dawn' (cf. sec. 2.12.3). We can summarize the above as follows:

| Time | | Expressed by |
|------|---|------|
| at, from, by | (when) | 1st verbal expression |
| (up) to | (when) | complement |
| for | (how long) | subject or object |

(3) Place Where. The uses and limitations of place words with regard to V-V series are quite parallel to those of time words. For 'place at', we have 在北平生長 *tzay Beeipyng sheng-jaang* 'was born and grew up in Peiping', 在屋裡做活 *tzay u.lii tzuoh-hwo* 'do (needle) work in the room', 在黑板上写 字 *tzay heibaan.shanq shiee-tzyh* 'write on the blackboard', 我在 字典裡找不着这个字. *Woo tzay tzyhdean.lii jao.bu-jaur jeyg tzyh.* 'I can't find this word in the dictionary.' Here the first verb *tzay* 'to be at' may apply either to the whole actor, as in the first two examples, or only to the action, as in the other two examples. For 'place from': 从中國来 *tsorng Jong.gwo lai* 'come from China', 打这儿走 *daa jell tzoou* 'go by way of here, —go by here', 离他太遠 *li ta tay yeuan* 'too far from him', where *li* is limited to static distance from. For 'place toward': 望

西 走 *wanq*[43] *shi tzoou* 'toward the west', 对 他 说 话 *duey ta shuo huah* 'speak to him', 对( 着 ) 敵 人 放 槍 *duey(j)dyiren fanq chiang* 'shoot at the enemy', 向 前 走 *shianq chyan tzoou* 'go forward'. Examples of *duey* used figuratively are: 对 他 道 歉 *duey ta daw-chiann* 'apologize to him', 对 他 道 谢 *duey ta daw-shieh* 'say thanks to him', 对 他 解 释 *duey ta jiee.shyh* 'explain to him'. Like time elapsed, distance covered is not expressed by a verbal expression in first position, but by a nominal expression, usually as object, as in 跑 了 一 百 碼 *paole ibae maa* 'ran a hundred yards', 長 了 三 寸 *charngle san-tsuenn* '(too) long (or lengthened) by three inches', 長 了 三 寸 *jaangle san-tsuenn* 'have grown three inches'. Corresponding to 'time (up) to', expressions for 'place arrived at' are also in the form of complements, as 回 到 家 裡 *hwei$_0$daw jia.lii* 'return to home'. The same verbal expressions may be in series or in V-R relation according to this order. Thus, 在 水 裡 扔 球 *tzay shoei.lii rheng chyou* 'throw balls (while) in water' (e.g., when playing water polo) is a V-V series, with *tzay shoei.lii* for 'place where'; *bae chyou rheng $_0$tzay shoei.lii* 'throws the ball into the water' is a V-R construction, with *tzay shoei.lii* for 'place arrived at'. Likewise, 在 北 平 住 *tzay Beeipyng juh* 'live in Peiping' has *tzay Beeipyng* for 'place where', but *juh $_0$tzay Beeipyng* 'live in Peiping' has *tzay Beeipyng* as complement. Note that in the V-R constructions, *tzay* has an optional neutral tone, and when the main verb has no object, *tzay* alternates with *.de* as a blend of *tzay* and *daw*. Thus one can say 坐 得 地 下 *tzuoh .de dih.shiah* 'sit on the floor', but not °*.de dih.shiah tzuoh*.[44]

---

[43]There is an optional local Peiping usage by which *wanq* assimilates to a following dental initial, as *wann dong* 'toward the east', *wann nan* 'toward the south', but it remains *wanq* before non-dentals. I prefer to write 望 instead of the more usual 往 because the former agrees better with the other dialects.

[44]See also sec. 5.6.3.1 on the blend of *tzay* and *daw*. For further examples of these types with *tzay* see 王 渙 , 说 " 在 " (Wang Huann, "On 'Tzay' "), *ZGYW*, no. 56:25-26 (1957).

(4) Interest and Benefit. We found that interest, benefit, and so on could be expressed in the form of an indirect object. Alternatively, one can express the same thing with the verbs *geei* or *tih* in first position in a V-V series, as in 给他補衣裳 *geei ta buu i.shang* 'mend clothes for him', 替(∼给) 我说几句好话 *tih (∼geei) woo shuo jii-jiuh hao-huah* 'say a few good words for me (on my behalf)', 给我对他请安 *geei woo duey ta chiing an* 'give him my regards', 给我滚! *G'woo goen!* 'Get out of here (for my benefit)!' The verb 衝着 *chonqj* 'facing toward' is used for 'place toward', under (3) above, but in the special use for 'on behalf of' it is a first verb expressing interest, as in: 那么我衝着你父親的面子就算了吧. *Nemme woo chonqj nii fuh.chin de mianntz jiow suannle ba.* 'Well, as favor to your father, I'll let it go.'

(5) Purpose, Reason, and/or Cause. The verb *wey* 'to be for' is mainly used in first position in a V-V series and is thus translatable as 'for', though occasionally it is used as a main verb, as in: 你为的是什么吶? *Nii wey de sh sherm .ne?* 'What was it that your (action) was for?' 什么也不为, 谁也不为, 就为了你. *Sherm yee bu wey, sheir yee bu wey, jiow weyle nii.* 'It wasn't for anything (in particular), nor for anyone (in particular), it was just on account of you.' But more typically, *wey* is used in first position, as in 为了錢做坏事 *weyle chyan tzuoh huay-shyh* 'do evil deeds for money', 为着害怕没去 *weyj hay-pah mei chiuh* 'on account of fear, did not go', 为嘴傷身 *wey-tzoei shang-shen* 'injure the body on account of the mouth (eat injudiciously)', 为什么来? *weysherm lai?* 'for what come,—why come?'

(6) Means to End. 倒碗茶喝 *daw $_o$woan char $_o$he* 'pour a cup of tea to drink', 借点儿錢用 *jieh .deal chyan $_o$yonq* 'borrow some money to use', 打水洗澡 *daa-shoei shii-tzao* 'bring water to take a bath', 跳绳子玩儿 *tiaw sherngtz $_o$wal* 'jump rope to play', 开会讨論 *kai-huey taoluenn* 'hold a meeting to discuss (it)'. Sometimes a $_o$*lai*, or less often a $_o$*chiuh*, is inserted between the two verbal expressions, thus forming a chain series,

as 打水去洗澡 *daa-shoei ₀chiuh shii-tzao* 'bring water to go to take a bath', 倒碗茶来喝 *daw ₀woan char ₀lai ₀he* 'pour a cup of tea to come to drink', where *₀lai* or *₀chiuh* is practically a particle like English *to* in the infinitive verb, which expresses the purpose. This type differs from the preceding in that the order of purpose and means is reversed and in that the second verb is often in the neutral tone. [Cf. sec. 6.6.8 (7) on *lai* and *chiuh* as particles of purpose.]

(7) Manner. Manner is one of the most frequent meanings of the first verbal expression. Examples are 拿筷子吃 *na kuaytz chy* 'eat with chopsticks', 拿纸糊窗户 *na jyy hwu chwang.huh* 'paste up windows with paper', 張(着)嘴大笑 *jang (j) tzoei dah shiaw* 'laugh greatly with the mouth open', 騎着馬找馬 *chyij maa jao-maa* 'look for a horse while riding a horse,—look for a job while holding onto a job, *or* do something absent-mindedly', 隨手一翻 *swei shoou i-fan* 'follow the hand, turn over once,— turn (it) over casually', 趁早走 *chenn-tzaol tzoou* 'go while (still) early'. Some of these verbal expressions of manner become compounds, and as adverbs they can take an optional subordinative suffix *de (dih₂)*, as in 用心(的)做 *yonqshin (de) tzuoh* 'do (it) by using the mind,—do (it) carefully', 使劲(的)拉 *shyy-jinn (de) lha* 'use strength to pull,—pull hard', 趕快(的)買 *gann-kuay (de) mae* 'hurry up and buy'. When the first verb has the progressive suffix *-j*, it is sometimes followed by an optional resumptive adverb *nemme* or *tzemme*, as 瞪着眼睛(那么)看 *denqj yean- .jing (nemm) kann* 'staring (the eyes), like that, look,—look, star- ing', 跟着我(这么)走 *genj woo (tzemm) tzoou* 'following me, like this, walk,—walk after me'. Note that while most V-O con- structions, whether the parts are free or bound, are ionizable, they do not have vivid reduplication, except certain cases of very high frequency of occurrence in first position. Thus, both 用心 *yonq-shin* 'use one's mind,—carefully' and 留心 *liou-shin* 'keep one's mind (on the subject),—carefully, cautiously' occur in first position, but there is, with some speakers, *yonqyonqshinshinde tzuoh* 'do (it) good and carefully', while *lioushin* is never so re- duplicated.

(8) Comparison. The verb 比 *bii* 'compare' is often used as a main verb in second position, as: 这个不能跟那个比. *Jeyg buneng gen neyg bii.* 'This can't compare with that.' When used in first position, it is the equivalent of 'than', as in: 你比他高. *Nii bii ta gau.* 'You are taller than he.' 他写的信一回比一回長. *Ta shiee de shinn i-hwei bii i-hwei charng.* 'The letters he writes become longer and longer each time.' 他们一个比一个嚷的响. *Tamen ig bii ig raang de sheang.* 'They shout, each louder than the other.' In first position, *bii* takes no aspect suffix and cannot be used alone in answers. But that is still felt as a verb is revealed in such children's neologisms as, in reply to a question: 你比他大嗎? *Nii bii ta dah ma?* 'Are you older than he?'比. *Bii.* 'Than.', where in adult language the answer would be: 比他大. *Bii ta dah.* For other degrees of comparison, see section 8.1.3.2

(9) Association in General. We noted [sec. 5.2.2(4)] that the so-called 'and'-words *gen, her* (~*hann, hay*), the dialectal *torng,* the L forms *yeu, jyi,* and so on are primarily first-position verbs and that completely symmetrical coordination with one of these as markers is a relatively new usage. Thus, in: 他跟我做朋友. *Ta gen woo tzuoh perng-.yeou.* looks like: 'He and I make friends.', but from the forms: *Ta bu gen woo tzuoh perng.yeou.* 'He does not make friends with me.' and *Ta ia, but gen woo tzuoh perng.yeou.* 'As for him, (he) does not make friends with me.', the lack of symmetry on both sides of *gen* becomes very obvious. Again: 水跟火不一樣. *Shoei gen huoo bu iyanq.* may be translated as: 'Water and fire are not the same.', but in: ... 可是跟酒有点儿像. *Shoei bu gen huoo iyanq, keesh gen jeou yeoudeal shianq.* 'Water is not the same as fire, but a little like wine.', *gen* corresponds more to 'as' than to 'and'. Other examples of *gen* to express association in general are: 跟他商量 *gen ta shang.liang* 'talk over with him', 跟他翻臉 *gen ta fan-lean* 'turn over the face with him,—get into a scrap with him', 跟他好 *gen ta hao* 'to be friendly with him', 跟他要好 *gen ta yaw-hao* 'make friends with him', 跟他订婚, 结婚, 离婚 *gen ta dinq-huen, jye-huen, li-huen* 'to be engaged to, married to,

divorced from him', 跟他不对 *gen ta buduey* 'make an enemy
of him', 跟他过不去 *gen ta guoh.bu-chiuh* 'with him cannot
go across,—make it unpleasant for him', 跟他打架 *gen ta daa-jiah* 'quarrel or fight with him',[45] 跟他打岔 *gen ta daa-chah*,
'with him strike interruption,—interrupt him'.

(10) *Action on Action.* The idea of action on action could be
expressed in a variety of forms, as in 禁止抽烟 *jinnjyy chou-ian* 'prohibit smoking' (V-O), 叫他快走 *jiaw ta kuay tzoou* 'tell
him to go in a hurry' (pivotal construction), and so on. Here we
consider cases of V-V series, where the first verbal expression
represents some action on that of the second expression. Examples are: 起头儿做事 *chiitourl tzuoh-shyh* 'start to do things',
闹始工作 *kaishyy gongtzuoh* 'commence to work', 罚咒不
去 *far-jow bu chiuh* 'swear not to go', 接着说下去 *jiej shuo-.shiah.chiuh* 'continue to talk on'. Some of these examples look
like manners of action, but are really not. Thus, in 拿手打人
*na-shoou daa-ren* 'use hand hit people' or 動手打人 *donq-shoou daa-ren* 'move hand hit people', both *na-shoou* and *donq-shoou* are first verbal expressions of manner 'with one's hand'.
But *donq-shoou* is also used for action on action in 動手預備
大考 *donq shoou yuh.bey dahkao* 'set about to prepare for a
final examination'. One even says: 我的脚已经動手麻了.
*Woode jeau yii.jing donq-shoou ma le.* 'My feet move their hands
to feel numb,—my feet have already started to feel numb.'[46]

*5.5.4. Pretransitive Constructions.* A special form of the V-V
series has a first verb, the pretransitive, and an object, which
ordinarily would be the object of the V-V series. For this reason
this object of the pretransitive is often regarded as a form of the
inverted object.[47] For example, with pretransitive: 别把鑰匙

---

[45]In Southern Mandarin *daa-jiah* is limited to physical fighting, while
架 *chao-jiah* or 吵 *chao-tzoei* is used for quarreling.

[46] 陈铨, 野玫瑰 [Chern Chyuan, *Yee Meiguey* (*The Wild Rose*)],
Shanghai, 1935, Act 4, p. 91. As this is a line spoken at a solemn moment,
it sometimes makes the audience, when they notice the mixed metaphor,
laugh at the wrong time.

[47]As, for example, by Leu Shwushiang in his excellent treatment of the

忘了！ *Bye bae yaw.shyr wanqle!* 'Don't take the key and forget (it)!' and in simple V-O form: *Bye wanqle yaw.shyr!* 'Don't forget the key!'

5.5.4.1. *Variant Forms of Pretransitives.* Besides *bae,* there is a less frequently used free variant *bay,* and the more formal *baa,* the last form also occurring as a main verb, as in: 他老把着门，也不许人过去． *Ta lao baaj men, yee bu sheu ren guoh-.chiuh.* 'He is holding the door all the time, and won't permit people to pass.' All three forms are written with the character 把.[48] In wenyan and Cantonese, as we have noted, the general pretransitive is 将 *jiang* (Cant *tzeung*). When the second verb is 叫 *jiaw* 'call (by some name)', the pretransitive used is 菱 *goan,* which as a main verb means 'control, take charge of'. In other dialects, the verb *jiaw* is used twice in both positions. For example, *goan ta jiaw bah.bah* is in the dialects *jiaw ta jiaw bah.bah* 'in calling him, call him papa'. Of course, *jiaw* as a main verb is not necessarily preceded by a pretransitive; for example, the form *jiaw ta bah.bah* 'call him papa' is used both in Mandarin and in many other dialects.

5.5.4.2. *Definite Reference in the First Object.* In discussing sentence structure we noted that an early part in a sentence is likely to have a definite reference and a later part an indefinite reference. In particular, the subject of a sentence or the object of a pretransitive has a definite reference, whereas the object in an ordinary V-O construction has indefinite reference, unless it has specific definite modifiers such as *jeyg* or *neyg.* As these points have been fully illustrated earlier (sec. 2.4.3), we need not add further examples here.

Attention should, however, be drawn to a class of apparent cases of indefinite reference consisting of a pretransitive with *ig* or *g* before the object, where something quite definite is referred

---

subject in Leu, *LWJyi,* 125-144. Among others on the subject may be mentioned: Li Jiinshi, *GYWF* 35-37 (as preposition); Wang Lih, *Liiluenn,* vol. 1, 174 (as coverb "juhdonqtsyr"); Henri Frei; and Willem A. Grootaers.

[48]Although *bae* is the form actually used in the Peiping dialect, it is usually cited, in oral discussions, as *baa,* just as the definite article in English is pronounced, before consonants, *thuh* in actual use, but referred to as *thee.*

to. Thus: 他把个皮包丢了. *Ta bae g pyibau dioule.* 'He has lost his wallet.' *Ta dioule g pyibau.* 'He has lost a wallet.' 他把个丈夫死了，可是不久又嫁了个丈夫.    *Ta bae g janq.fu syyle, keesh bujeou yow jiahle g janq.fu.* 'She (suffered) her husband to die (on her),—she lost her husband, but before long she married another husband.' Thus, the advanced position of the object, brought about by the pretransitive, has a stronger effect than the presence of the word *g* or *ig* in deciding the definiteness of reference. As Leu Shwushiang (*LWJyi*, 129-130) has noted, there is no reason why forms like *g* or *ig* in Chinese should be limited to indefinite reference because *a* or its equivalent in other Indo-European languages is the indefinite article. (Cf. sec. 5.4.7.1.)

5.5.4.3. *Meanings of the Second Verb.* The primary meaning of 把 *baa* as a main verb is 'take hold of, grasp', but in the pretransitive form *bae* little is left of the original meaning and only the form of the construction is there. Thus one can just as well say: 把那首诗全忘了 *bae ney-shoou shy chyuan wanqle* 'got hold of that poem and forgot (it) completely,—completely forgot that poem',     把一身的筋肉放鬆下來 *bae i-shen de jinrow fanq-song.shiah.lai* 'take hold of the whole body's muscles and loosen (them) down,—relax all the muscles of the body', where the second verbs are practically exact antonyms of the verb *baa.*

As a generalized meaning of the second verb after a pretransitive, Wang Lih (*Yeufaa*, I, 160) described it as that of disposal ( 处置式 *chuujyh-shyh*). But unless taken in a very broad sense, including disposal in an abstract sense, it will hardly be wide enough to apply to all cases. It is true that the defective verbs 有 *yeou* 'have', 是 *sh* 'be', 像 *shianq* 'be like', 在 *tzay* 'be at', and certain verbs of motion, 來 *lai* 'come', 去 *chiuh* 'go' 進 *jinn* 'enter', 出 *chu* 'go out', 回 *hwei* 'return', 到 *daw* 'arrive at, go to', do not, as a rule, take pretransitives. But exceptions occur, as: 他把这儿的学校都進过了，一个学校也没毕业。
*Ta bae jell de shyueshiaw dou jinn.guohle, ig shyueshiaw yee mei bihyeh.* 'He took and entered every school here, but did not

graduate from any one of them.' Verbs of nondirected motion take the pretransitive even more readily, as: 把椅子坐塌了 *bae yiitz tzuoh-tale* 'has collapsed the chair, sitting on it', 把路 走错了 *bae luh tzoou-tsuohle* 'have taken the wrong road', 把 地方跑熟了 *bae dih.fangl pao-shourle* 'have familiarized one-self with the place, running about in it', 把腿站累了 *bae toei jann-leyle* 'have fatigued the legs, standing on them'.

The second verb usually has its goal of action in the object of the pretransitive, which is the main reason for considering it an inverted object. But in many cases it is actually the actor of the second verb, as in 把个贼跑了 *bae g tzeir paole* 'allowed the burglar to escape', 把他急死了 *bae ta jyi.syyle* 'made him worry to death', 把我忙的手忙脚乱 *bae woo mang de shoou mang jeau luann* 'kept me so busy, that my hands and feet were all confused', where the pretransitive has the form of 'causes to' or 'allows to'. (Cf. *bae g fuh.chin syyle.*) In the example *bae ta jyi.syyle*, it is even doubtful what the direction of action is in *jyi:* does one worry to death, or is one worried to death?

### 5.5.4.4. *Forms of the Second Verbal Expression*
(1) Monosyllables or Polysyllables? The one feature that is common to all the second verbal expressions after pretransitives is their polysyllabicity. For example, there is: 我恨这个人. *Woo henn jeyg ren.* 'I hate this man.', but there is no: °*Woo bae jeyg ren henn.* It is only in traditional plays or novels in verse form of the 弹词 *tarntsyr* type (popularly known as 七字唱儿 *chitzyh-chanql*) that monosyllables are used after a pretransitive\ V-O. Thus in the play 汾河湾 *Fernher Uan (The Bend in River Fen)* there is the line with double pretransitives: 将身且把 窑门来进 *jiang shen chiee baa yaumen lai jinn* 'took his (own) person just took the gate to the hovel entered (it)'.[49] Again, in 滴水珠 *Dishoeiju (Dropping Water Pearls)*, there are lines like: 爹々在家把兒训。 *Die.die tzay jia baa erl shiunn.* 'Daddy at

---

[49] 程寅伯编，平劇歌谱初集 (Cherng Ynbor, ed., *Peiping Plays*), with scores, Collection I, Taipei, 1954, p. 204.

home took (me) the child and disciplined (him).', and: 莫非丙
郎把他害? *Mohfei Biinglan baa ta hay?* 'Could it be that
Biinglan took him and killed (him)?'[50] In modern speech the
phrases in question would be ... 進了窖門 ...*jinnle yaumen,* ...
把兒子教训一頓 ...*bae erltz jiaw.shiunn i-duenn,* and ...
把他害了 ...*bae ta hayle.* Sometimes, in a long sentence,
where the pretransitive construction is not the whole of the predicate, one may find something like: 你学会了字, 得天ㄦ把
他用. *Nii shyue-hueyle tzyh, deei tiantial bae ta yonq.* 'You must
take the words you have learned and use them every day.' But
even here it would be better to say ...*tiantial bae ta lai yonq* or
*tiantial bae ta na.lai yonq* or, without the pretransitive, *tiantial
na.lai yonq.* The general philosophy of the polysyllabicity of the
second verb seems to be that, since a pretransitive is employed to
advance the position of the object and get it out of the way,
something more elaborate is presumably meant to be said than
can be expressed by just one morpheme, which would have the
effect of an anticlimax.

(2)   With Suffix or Complement. The minimum addition to
a second verb is an aspect suffix, as 把东西捧着 *bae dong.shi
peengj* 'holding the thing (with both hands)', 把房子烧了 *bae
farngtz shaule* 'burnt the house' or 'allowed the house to be
burnt'. With complements: 把门关上 *bae men guan.shanq*
'shut up the door', 把他叫醒了 *bae ta jiaw-shiingle* 'have
waked him up (by calling)', 把他说信了 *bae ta shuo-shinnle*
'have spoken to him so that he believes,—have convinced him',
把事情诲明白了 *bae shyh.chyng jeang-ming.bairle* 'have
clarified matters'. With predicative complements: 把事情看
的太认真 *bae shyh.chyng kann de tay rennjen* 'take things
too seriously', 把我气的眼睛直莈火 *bae woo chih de
yean.jing jyr fa-huoo* 'angered me so much that my eyes kept
emitting fire?'.

While most of these complements represent what happens to
the object, occasionally they apply to the subject of the whole

[50]Quoted by Wang Leaui, *Outline,* 106.

V-V construction. For example, in: 你把饭煮烂了。 *Nii bae fann juu-lannle.* 'You have cooked the rice soft.', *lann* 'soft' is the resulting state of *fann* 'rice', while in: 你把饭吃饱了。 *Nii bae fann chy-baole.* 'You have eaten the rice full.', it is you who are full. In: 你把那些话说的太大意了。 *Nii bae ney.shie huah shuo de tay dah.yih le.* 'You have said those words too carelessly.', the predicative complement applies more to the subject than to the object.

Note that while the whole second verbal expression, including the complement, can take the first object as its object (when not using a pretransitive), the second verb alone often cannot do so. Thus, one can say either 嚷哑了嗓子 *raang-yeale saangtz* or *baa saangtz raang-yeale* 'has shouted one's throat hoarse', but there is no such a V-O construction as °*raang saangtz*. Other examples of the kind are: 把手绢儿哭湿了 *bae shooujiuall ku-shyle* 'have cried the handkerchief wet', 把眼睛看累了 *bae yean.jing kann-leyle* 'read until the eyes got tired', 把地板跳穿了 *bae dihbaan tiaw-chuanle* 'jumped the floor through,— made a hole in the floor by jumping' (≠ *tiaw de chuan-guohle dihbann* 'jumped through the floor').

Since a resultative complement normally takes the suffix *-le* (sec. 6.6.1.3) and a pretransitive will throw the V-R construction toward the end of the phrase, this suffix will often be telescoped with the phrase particle *le* [secs. 4.4.5(1) and 8.5.5, P 2], as 你得把条件说清楚了。 *Nii deei bae tyau$_0$jiann shuo-ching.chuule.* (with *-le* only) 'You must state the conditions clearly.': 我把条件说清楚了。 *Woo bae tyau$_0$jiann shuo-ching.chuule.* (with *-le le → -le*) 'I have stated the conditions clearly.' The form *Nii bae tyau$_0$jiann shuo-ching.chuule* is ambiguous. With a suffix *-le* only, it is a command: 'State the conditions clearly!' With two *le*'s, telescoped into one, it is a statement: 'You have stated the conditions clearly.'

We have seen examples of the pretransitive with resultative complements and predicative complements. Potential complements, however, do not go with the pretransitive. Instead, the potentiality is expressed by the auxiliary verb 能 *neng* if a pre-transitive is used. For example: 我能把他说信了. *Woo neng bae ta shuo-shinnle.* 'I can convince him.' ... 完全相信我. *Woo neng bae ta shuo de wanchyuan shiangshinn woo.* 'I can talk to him so he believes me completely.', but not: °我把他 说得信. °*Woo bae ta shuo.de-shinn.* for 'I *can* convince him.' In: 我能把他说的信. *Woo neng bae ta shuo de shinn.* 'I can talk to him so that he believes.', it is a case of the predicative and not the potential complement.

(3) Adverb-Verb (H-V) Constructions. While one cannot say °把酒喝 °*bae jeou he,* one can say 把酒不停的喝 *bae jeou butyngde he* 'drink the wine continually'. Similarly, one can say: 别把东西乱扔! *Bye bae dong.shi luann rheng!* 'Don't throw things around!', but not: °*Bye bae dong.shi rheng!* Since in a V-V series the first verbal expression is subordinated to the second and thus modifies it adverbially, a second verbal expression in a pretransitive can consist of a V-V series, thus resulting in a chain V-V series. For example, in 把字纸到处扔 *bae tzyhjyy dawchuh rheng* 'take waste paper and to everywhere throw,—throw waste paper all over the place' and 把宝玉 的襖儿往自己身上拉 *bae Baoyuh de aol wanq tzyhjii shen-.shanq lha* 'took Baoyuh's jacket and onto herself pulled,—pulled Baoyuh's jacket over herself',[51] the second verbal expressions are not the monosyllables *rheng* and *lha*, but *dawchuh rheng* and *wanq tzyhjii shen.shanq lha*, respectively.

(4) Polysyllabic Verbs. Polysyllabic verbs which do not consist of V-O or H-V compounds serve only infrequently as second verbal expressions after pretransitives. For example: 你得先把 情形调查, 再把问题分析, 然後才能把计画進 行. *Nii deei shian baa chyng$_0$shyng diawchar, tzay baa wenntyi fen.shi, ranhow tsair neng baa jih$_0$huah jinnshyng.* 'You must first investigate the conditions, next analyze the problem, only then can you proceed with the project.' However, it would even be

---

[51]*Hornglou Menq*, Renmin Wenshyue, ed., Peking, 1957, p. 870, quoted by Leu, *LWJyi*, 143.

more natural to add something after the first two dissyllabic verbs such as *diawshar .diaw.char* 'investigate a little' and *fen.shi .i.shiall* 'analyze once'.

The demonstrative pro-verbs *tzemme* 'do this' and *nemme* 'do that' and the interrogative pro-verb *tzeeme* 'do what?' can be used as a second verb after a pretransitive without adding anything further. For example: 把你这么，你也不喜欢　把你那么，你也不喜欢，那么你要我把你怎么呐？ *Bae nii tzemme, nii yee bu shii.huan, bae nii nemme, nii yee bu shii.huan, nemme nii yaw woo bae nii tzeem ne?* 'I do this to you and you don't like it, I do that to you and you don't like it, what do you want me to do to you, then?'

(5) Second Verbs with Objects. Instead of—or in addition to —a complement, a second verb may take an object other than the object of the pretransitive, as illustrated below.

(a) With Cognate Object. A cognate object, as we have seen, may consist of the verb itself, or the number of times, extent, or duration of the action. Examples are: 把衣裳燙一燙！ *Bae i.shang tanq .i.tanq!* 'Give the clothes an ironing!', whence the tentative aspect in the form of reduplication: *Bae i.shang tanq-.tanq!* 'Just iron the clothes!' Sometimes, instead of V.V for V-i-V, the first verb is omitted, resulting in *i*-V, as in 把眼睛一翻 *bae yean.jing i-fan* instead of *bae yean.jing fan.i.fan* 'roll the eyes once,—just roll the eyes'. With number of times: 他把全文读了一遍. *Ta bae chyuan-wen dwule i-biann.* 'He read the whole text once through.' With extent: 得把这摞纸轧着点儿 *deei bae jey-luoh jyy yahj .deal* 'must cover (with a paperweight, etc.) this pile of paper a little', 把袖子放三寸 *bae shiowtz fanq san-tsuenn* 'let out the sleeves by three inches'. With duration: 把水煮了好半天 *bae shoei juule hao banntian* 'have boiled the water a good long time', 把他骗了十年 *bae ta piannle shyr-nian* 'deceived him for ten years'.

(b) With Indirect Object. The second verb may take an indirect object when the normal direct object becomes the object of the pretransitive, as in 把事情都告送了他　*bae shyh.chyng dou gaw.songle ta* 'have told him everything'. 你把那份儿礼送了（给）谁了？ *Nii bae ney-fell lii sonqle (geei) sheir le?*

'Whom did you send that gift to?' The reverse order is not possible, there being no construction like °把人告送事情 °*bae ren gaw.sonq shyh.chyng* for *bae shyh.chyng gaw.sonq ren* 'tell the thing to people'.

(c) V-O Compounds and Idioms. Certain V-O compounds and V-O phrases with idiomatic meanings represent action on goals, and such goals may be represented in the object of the pretransitive, but not as direct object of the V-O construction. For example, 免職 *mean-jyr* FB 'removes from office' occurs in *bae ta mean-jyr* 'remove him from office', but not °*mean-jyr ta*, 殺头 *sha-tour* FF 'kills head,—beheads' occurs in *bae ta sha-tour* 'behead him', but not °*sha-tour ta*, 轧肥 *yah-feir* 'put down fertilizer' occurs in 把这棵菓樹轧了肥 *bae jey-ke guooshuh yahle feir* 'have put in fertilizer for this fruit tree', but not °*yah-feirle jey-ke guooshuh* (unless *feir* 'fat' is made an adjectival complement, which would mean something else. A V-O compound takes a direct object without a pretransitive only with certain compounds listed in a dictionary as transitive verbs (irrespective, of course, of translational equivalents), as 抱怨 *baw.yuann* 'hold a grudge' Vt: *baw.yuann ta* 'hold a grudge against him,—blame him (for something)'. With *gannma* FB for *gann sherme* 'do what?', we have: 你把我借你的那本书幹麻了? *Nii bae woo jieh nii de ney-been shu gannma le?*[52] 'What did you do with that book I lent you?' Here *gannma* implies action of a disposing nature.

# 5.6  Verb-Complement Constructions

*5.6.1. Free and Bound Complements.* The typical cases of complements we shall consider are free, predicative complements, as in 他走的很慢. *Ta tzoou de heen mann.* '(The way, the speed, etc.) he walks is very slow.', and bound verb-complement (V-R) compounds, as in 我吃飽了. *Woo chy-baole.* 'I have eaten full,—I am full from eating.' We shall defer the detailed

---

[52]Example from H. Frei, *op. cit.,* p. 35. See n. 47.

treatment of V-R compounds until we take up compounds (sec. 6.6), and will consider here only predicative complements and certain bound phrase complements. But before doing so we must consider the distinction between complements and objects.

*5.6.2. Complements and Objects.* We noted that the term "complement" has been used in a wide sense, so as to include objects (sec. 5.4.1), as in 我看书. *Woo kann shu.* 'I read books.', 狗咬人. *Goou yeau ren.* 'Dog bites man.', where *shu* and *ren* are complements in this very wide sense. However, there are certain special cases of objects which have been regarded as complements (e.g., Li Jiinshi, *GYWF*, 55), even though objects in general are not included as a species of complements. These special objects occur after equational verbs or in pivotal constructions.

Objects after equational verbs are called complements because in traditional English grammar a pronoun after the copula is supposed to be in the nominative form instead of the objective form. Since there is no formal category of case in Chinese pronouns, not to speak of nouns, this reasoning does not apply. There is thus no reason why the *woo* in: 那是我. *Nah sh woo.* 'That is I.' and 他像我. *Ta shianq woo.* 'He resembles me.' should be treated differently, both being grammatical objects to the verb *sh*. In fact, even in English the colloquial *me* after the copula is displacing the more formal *I* in such constructions. (Cf. Fr. C'est *moi*.)

As for the fact that the *sh* takes no aspect suffixes and *shianq* cannot take the pretransitive *bae*, that is because *sh* is one of the defective verbs and *shianq* is not one of those verbs of disposal. Neither circumstance is a reason why the following nominal expression cannot be an object. Even *sh* occasionally does take an aspect suffix -.*guoh*, as in the example *sh.guoh sheirde ren* 'has been anybody's man' [sec. 5.4.5(3)].

According to the same usage (Li Jiinshi, *GYWF*, 56), in expressions like 认他为父 *renn ta wei fuh* 'recognize him as father', 称他为先生 *cheng ta wei shian.sheng* 'address him as sir', 娶他为妻 *cheu ta wei chi* 'marry her as wife', 升他做上将 *sheng ta tzuoh shanqjiang* 'promote him to be full general', 举他做总统 *jeu ta tzuoh tzoongtoong* 'vote for (~elect) him for president', and so on, the nominal expression after the second verb is considered an objective complement. Since we have treated the nominal expression after *sh* as object, we shall treat the same also as object after *wei, tzuoh* 'acts as, is in the capacity of' as object. The only thing that is special in such examples is that a preceding verb 认 *renn,* 称 *cheng,* 娶 *cheu,* 升 *sheng,* or 举 *jeu* makes the object *ta* a pivot, resulting in a pivotal construction $V_1$-N-$V_2$, where N is the object of $V_1$ and the subject of $V_2$.

*5.6.3. Bound Phrase Complements.* We shall now consider an intermediate type between free and bound complements. We noted that in a V-V series the first verbal expression often denotes place where, while the second expression often the place arrived at or the result. Now, when the first verb has no object immediately following and the second verb is used for place arrived at, the latter is usually in the neutral tone, thus being attached enclitically to the first verb, with no possibility of pause or insertion in between (except *le*). For the second verbs *.tzay* and *.daw,* the object has to be a time-place expression. For $_0$*cherng* and $_0$*geei* it may be any expression. Examples are: 睡在床上 *shuey .tzay chwang.shanq* 'sleep on the bed', 坐在地下 *tzuoh .tzay dih-.shiah* 'sit on the ground', ( 好就 ) 好在这个上 (*hao* $_0$*jiow*) *hao .tzay jeyg.shanq* '(as for being good) the good point lies in here'; 走到张家 *tzoou .daw Jang.jia* 'walk to the Jangs', 说到天亮 *shuo .daw tianlianq* 'talk till daybreak'; 切成三块 *chie* $_0$*cherng san-kuay* 'cut into three pieces', 变成了一个鬼 *biann* $_0$*cherngle ig goei* 'change into a ghost', 打成一片 *daa* $_0$*cherng i-piann* 'beat into one slice,—weld into one unit'. With $_0$*geei* it is possible to have both an indirect and a direct object, as in 扔给他一莄笔 *rheng .geei ta i-goan bii* 'throw [to] him a pen', 寄给他一封信 *jih .geei ta i-feng shinn* 'mail [to] him a letter', 借给他许多钱 *jieh .geei ta sheuduo chyan* 'lend [to] him a lot of money'. (Cf. sec. 5.4.6.3 above.)

Note that V $_0$*tzay,* V $_0$*daw,* and so on are not end-free, because, unlike directional V-R compounds such as 出去 *chu.chiuh* 'go out' and 掉下去 *diaw.shiah.chiuh* 'drop down', they must have objects of destination, even though the objects themselves are usually free expressions. Thus, we have in such constructions a verb plus a V-O phrase bound with it through the enclitic status of the second verb. Compare:

(a) *tzay chwang.shanq shuey* 'sleep on the bed': V-V phrase

(b) *shuey .tzay chwang.shanq* 'sleep in bed': bound V-R phrase

Form b is a verb bound with a V-O phrase as its complement. There is nothing more unusual about a verb being bound to a whole phrase following it than a final particle being bound to a whole phrase preceding it, as is common.[53]

*5.6.3.1. The Form .de as a Blend of .tzay and .daw.* The complements for destination *.tzay* and *.daw* have a blended alternant *.de,* which occurs with even greater frequency than either. In most of the examples given above, the *.tzay* and *.daw* can be changed to *.de* and the resulting phrase will be even more natural: 別 就 那 么 坐 得 那儿 ! *Bye jiow nemm tzuoh .de .nall!* 'Don't just sit there like that!'; 他 搬 得 哪儿 去 了 ? *Ta ban .de naal .chiuh le?* 'Where has he moved (away) to?'; 头 髮 掉 得 地 下 了. *Tour.fah diaw .de dih.shiah le.* 'Your hair has dropped on the floor.'; 住 得 外 國 不 便 宜. *Juh .de way.gwo bu pyan-.yih.* 'It is not cheap to live abroad.' The form *.de* here is probably a reduced form of *daw.* That it also assumes the function of *tzay* is probably due, at least partially, to the influence of dialects where the aspect suffix *-j* takes the form of *-daw* or *-dao,* which, when reduced, will also become *.de.* Whether it is *daw, dao, dih,* or *der* ( 到 , 到 , 的 , 得 ) cannot be judged by examining any written or printed material, since, except in artificially prepared material (e.g., in *Mand Prim,* 293, line 1, and the four sentences above) the form *.de* is practically never written and the "proper" character for *tzay* or *daw* occurs instead, though neither *tzay* nor *daw* is spoken nearly as frequently as *.de* in such constructions.

Dragunov (secs. 46 and 84) has an interesting analysis of this spoken *.de* in place of the written *tzay* or *daw* for 'place arrived

---

[53]For a discussion of similar constructions, with a slightly different set of first verbs and second verbs, see section on "postverb phrases" in Malmqvist, Sīch'uanese, 171-172.

at'. Among his examples are: 包袱掉的⁵⁴ 河裡 *Bau.fu diaw .de her.lii.* 'The bundle drops into the river.', 別睡的地下！ *Bye shuey de dih.shiah!* 'Don't sleep on the ground!, 你住的 哪儿? 我住的北京. *Nii juh de naal? Woo juh de Beeijing.* 'Where do you live? I live in Peking.' He treated the whole expression ending with *.de* as a nominal subject to which the following nominal expression is predicated: 'The place where the bundle falls is the river-inside.' 'The place where you shouldn't sleep is the ground.' 'The place where you live is Peking.'

Apart from my "feeling of the native" that this does not seem natural, there is also the formal reason that the usual pause or pause particle between a subject and its predicate is not possible here. Thus, while one could say: 他睡咘, 很遲. *Ta shuey .d'a, heen chyr.* 'He sleeps (pause) very late.', one cannot say: °*Ta shuey .d'a, dih.shiah.* If a pause has to be made, it will have to be in the form of: 他呀, 睡得地下. *Ta ia, shuey .de dih.shiah.* or 他睡覺啊, 睡得地下. *Ta shuey-jiaw a, shuey .de dih- .shiah.*

Another reason against this S-P analysis is that it fits badly the corresponding constructions in other dialects. Thus, the equivalent for: 这个人坐得桌子上. *Jeyg ren tzuoh .de juotz. shanq.* 'This man sits on the table.' is in Soochow and Canton, respectively: 该格人坐喇枱子郎. *Kéke' nyen zew la' détzyy- lànq.*, and: 呢个人坐喺枱°处. *Nhi°koh yan dsox xae dhoai°- shuh.*, where it is not possible to pause after *la'* or *xae*. There is, to be sure, no reason why the same construction in Mandarin should always translate into the same structural pattern in other dialects. But taken together with the other reason, this will count as a reason against such an analysis, since, by and large, the dialects of China do have very closely similar structural patterns.

5.6.3.2. *Use of ₀daw or .de for 'extent'.* From the use of ₀*daw* or *.de* for 'reaches, arrives at, to' in space or time, comes another use for 'to' as applied to extent or degree. For example,

---

⁵⁴The choice of the character 的 rather than 得 is of course that of the translator, 郑祖慶 (*Jenq Tzuuchinq*).

说到嘴干 *shuo* ₀*daw tzoei gan* 'talk until the mouth is dry'
expresses both time and degree and 累到走不動了 *ley* ₀*daw
tzoou.bu-donq le* 'tired to the extent that one can't walk,—so
tired one can't walk any more' can only express degree or extent.

A variety of constructions can occur after this use of ₀*daw* or
.*de*. S-P: 吵得人家睡不着 *chao .de ren.jia shuey.bu-jaur*
'make so much noise that others cannot sleep'. V-O: 慢得急
人 *mann .de jyi-ren* 'so slow as to make people impatient', 冷
得要命 *leeng .de yaw-minq* 'so cold as to demand your life,—
terribly cold', 好得不得了 *hao .de buderleau* 'so good as not
to get to an end,—good no end,—awfully good'. V-R: 遠得看
不見了 *yeuan .de kann.bu-jiann le* 'so far as to be invisible'.
Coordinate verbal expressions: 气得又要哭又要笑 *chih .de
yow yaw ku how yaw shiaw* 'so angry as to want to both cry and
laugh'.

A special complement of extent is .*de huang* 'so ... as to be
flustered'. In an S-P form it is possible to say: 你老叫, 叫得
我心慌. *Nii lao jiaw, jiaw .de woo shin huang.* 'You keep calling, it makes me nervous.' A nursery rhyme has the line (According to L. S. Yang): 碗底儿盪得手心儿慌啊! *Woandieel
danq .de shoooushiel huang a!* 'The bottom of the bowl sways so,
(It makes) my palm nervous!' From this pattern, with the stress
on the complement, comes the reduced form -.*de.huang* ~ .*de-
.heng*, which is used merely as an intensive suffix to adjectival
expressions for unpleasant or strong sensations, as in 鬧得慌
*naw.de.huang* '(annoyingly) noisy', 挤得慌 *jii.de.huang* '(too)
crowded'. (See sec. 4.4.7 for other examples.)

*5.6.4. Predicative Complements.* We shall now take up the
case of the free complement as exemplified in: 他唱的好听.
*Ta chanq de hoating.* 'He sings beautifully.', 我昨儿晚上睡
的不舒服. *Woo tzwol woan.shanq shuey de bu shu.fwu.* 'Last
night I slept uncomfortably.'[55] This *de* is both different from the

---

[55]In Chao-Yang, *Conc Dict*, the expression after the .*de* was called
"descriptive complement", as contrasted with potential complements, with
a footnote saying: "The origin of such construction is probably that of sub-

blend of *.tzay* and *.daw* in 站得这ル *jann .de jell* 'stand here' and from the *.de* as weakened *.daw* for expressing extent in 站得腿疼了 *jann .de toei suan le* 'stand (so long) that the legs are sore'. It is also different from the infixed *.de* in potential complements as in 看得見 *kann.de-jiann* 'can see' which is an infix to the V-R construction.

Formal features of predicative complements:

(1) There can be a pause or a pause particle after *de*, as is the case after other kinds of subjects. For example: 他唱哫, 好听. *Ta chanq d'a, haoting.* '(The way, the voice, etc.) he sings (is) beautiful.' 你唱的嚜,—太响. *Nii chanq de me,—tay sheang.* 'As for (the way) you sing, (it is) too loud'. The only two cases where there is no pause before a predicative complement are (a) 多 *duo* after a comparative, as in 好的多 *hao de duo* '(the extent of being) better is much,—much better' and 好的多的多 *hao de duo de duo* 'much much better' (with ICs 1 + 2); (b) 很 *heen*, as in 好的很 *hao de heen* 'good so as to be very,—very good', where *duo* and *heen* do not often occur as single-morpheme predicates. [See also sec. 8.1.3.2(2.2).]

(2) Adverbs may be added before the complement, as in 我唱的不大好听. *Woo chanq de budah haoting.* '(The way) I sing (is) not very beautiful.' 他写的又快又清楚. *Ta shiee de yow kuay yow ching.chuu.* '(The way, the characters, the style, etc.) he writes (is) both fast and clear.'

(3) A V-not-V form of the question starts with the complement (after the *de*) and not with the verb before the *de*, as in 你走的快不快? *Nii tzoou de kuay bu kuay?* '(The manner, speed, etc.) you walk (is) fast or not,—do you walk fast?' as contrasted with the bound potential complement 走得快 *tzoou-.de-kuay* 'can walk fast' which is not separable and must be placed

---

ject and predicate. 他喫.的快 < 他喫.的法.子 (or 樣.子, etc.)快 *Ta chy .de kuah < Ta chy .de fartz (yanqtz,* etc.) *kuay* 'the way (or manner) in which he eats is fast.' " In *Mand Prim*, I followed the position of that footnote and treated such constructions as subject and predicate. Because most writers in China call such predicated *buuyeu* (complements), I now use, following F. K. Li's suggestion, the term "predicative complement".

next to its negative as a whole in: 你走得快走不快? *Nii tzoou.de-kuay tzoou.bu-kuay?* 'Can you walk fast?' Similarly, with (free) predicative complement 这个探海灯照的远不远? *Jeyg tannhaedeng jaw de yeuan bu yeuan?* 'Does this searchlight shine far?' With (bound) potential complement 这个探海灯照得远照不远? *Jeyg tannhaedeng jaw.de-yeuan jaw.bu-yeuan?'* 'Can this searchlight shine far?'

   In the non-interrogative and non-negative form, it is not possible to distinguish the predicative complement in 他走得快. *Ta tzoou de kuay.* 'He walks fast.' from the potential complement in 他走的快. *Ta tzoou.de-kuay.* 'He can walk fast.', since the artificial spaces in the former, as contrasted with the connected spelling in the latter, only indicates an optional break between subject and predicate and corresponds to nothing in the way it is usually said. As for the character involved being 的 (*dih*₁) or 得 (*der*), there is no uniformity of usage. In a statistical survey of the usages of three novels Hu Shih found[56] that *Shoeihuu Juann* used 的 in both the predicative and the potential cases, and that *Hornglou Menq* and *Rulin Wayshyy* used 得 in the potential cases, but principally 得 in the predicative cases, with a relatively small number of "exceptions". In my *Mand Prim*, Character Text, I have followed the latter usage without exception.

   *5.6.4.1. The ICs in Sentences with Predicative Complements.* In rendering 你唱的好听. *Nii chanq de haoting.* as 'The way, manner, etc. you sing is beautiful.', the translation seems to commit the IC analysis to *Nii chanq de* + *haoting*, and yet the feeling of the native seems to prefer the analysis: *Nii* + *chanq de haoting* with possible pauses such as *Nii a, chanq de haoting*. The solution to this difficulty was suggested, in a letter to me, by Fang-Kuei Li, who simply treated the sentence as of the $S_1$ + $S_2P$ type, so that *Nii* remains as the first IC and, within the second IC, *chanq de haoting*, the small subject is *chanq de*, with *haoting* as its predicate. A structural translation will then be: 'As for you, the way of singing is beautiful'.

   It should be noted, however, that, while this IC analysis is

---

[56]Collected Works, Ser. 1, Vol. 3, pp. 689-701.

the best in most cases, it does not preclude the other analysis
being the suitable one in special cases. For example: A: 我買
的这书很貴。 *Woo mae de jeh shu heen guey.* B: 乜! 我買
的便宜嘿! *È! Woo mae de pyan.yih me!* A: 'This book I
bought was very expensive.' B: 'Say! The one I bought was
cheap!' But in   我買书总是買的太貴; 怎么你总是
買的那么便宜? *Woo mae shu tzoong sh mae de tay guey;
tzeeme nii tzoong sh mae de nemm pyan.yih?* 'I, when buying
books, always buy too dear; how come you always buy them so
cheap?' the IC division given above (after *woo*) is the natural one.

One further problem. In the sentences:

(1) 你摆歪了! *Nii bae-uaile!* 'You have set it crooked!'

(2) 我摆不正嘿! *Woo bae.bu-jenq me!* 'But I can't set it
straight!'

(3) 那么他怎么摆得正呐? *Nemme ta tzeem bae.de-
jenq ne?* 'Then how come he can set it straight?'

(4) 那么他怎么摆的正呐? *Nemme ta tzeem bae de
jenq ne?* 'Then how come he sets it straight?'

In (1), *bae-uai.le* 'have set it crooked' is a V-R construction of the
usual resultative type (which will be treated in chap. 6). In (2)
*bae.bu-jenq* 'cannot set it straight' is in the usual potential form.
As for (3) and (4), they are homophonous, and the graphical difference in the romanization is not reflected either in speech or in
a character text (not by all writers, in any case). Taken as 'can
set straight', *bae.de-jenq* is a potential V-R compound, as in (2).
But if taken as '(did) set straight' and treated as a S-P predicate
'the way you set it was straight', it would seem to spoil the parallelism of construction in the four sentences. The answer to
that, as in other cases when facts fail to fall into a neat pattern,
is simply "So what?" There is nothing incredible about parallel
ideas not being paralleled by their linguistic expressions.

# 的 CHAPTER 6
# COMPOUNDS

## 6.1. Nature and Classification of Compounds

*6.1.1. Wide and Narrow Sense of "Compound".* A compound is a combination of two or more words bound together to form one word. For example,好 *hao* 'good' and 看 *kann* 'look at' are compounded to form *haokann* 'good-looking'; 買 *mae* 'buy' and 卖 *may* 'sell' are compounded to form *mae.may* 'trade'. Instead of requiring the constituents of a compound to be free words, we shall take compounds in a wide sense so as to include those in which the parts are bound morphemes other than affixes. For example, units of measure such as 尺 *chyy* 'foot' and 寸 *tsueen* 'inch' are bound morphemes and can be compounded, with phonetic modification, into the word *chyr.tsuenn* 'size'. Words like 桌子 *juotz* 'table' and 站着 *jannj* 'is standing', however, are not compounds, but derived words, since *-tz* and *-j* are affixes and not parts of compounds.

The term "compound" as used by Sinologists represents a rather broader concept. Practically any word written with two or more characters is a compound in this sense. Thus, not only are *juotz* and *jannj* compounds, but 这儿 *jell* 'here' and 桃儿 *taurl* 'peach', with nonsyllabic suffix, are also compounds, as are poly-syllabic (and therefore polygraphic) morphemes like *har.ma* (蛤蟆) 'toad', *meiguey* (玫瑰) 'rose'. We shall, however, restrict the term only to cases where the constituents are roots or root words. In this sense, decompounds [sec. 4.4.4 (2.9)] such as 刷牙子 *shuayatz* 'brush-tooth -er,—toothbrush' are also com-pounds, although only *yashuatz* and *yashual* are compounds in the sense in which we are using the term.

*6.1.2. Compound and Phrase.* In chapter 3 we discussed the various criteria for what makes one word, as summarized in tables 6 and 7 at the end of the chapter. Columns 12-14 of table 7 give examples of compounds. In the present chapter we shall consider the various dimensions in which compounds may be classified and then give detailed examples of compounds under the syntactical dimension. Most of the examples given here are taken from a 10,000-word vocabulary of Mandarin (unpublished) which I prepared during the 1940's. Supplementing those, I have drawn largely from the very rich store of illustrations in Luh, *GTFaa*. The latter source, being based mainly on written material, had to be used selectively, since we are limiting our scope to what is actually spoken.

    *6.1.3. Multidimensional Classification.* The principles by which compounds may be classified are to a large extent mutually independent and thus form several dimensions of cross-classification. For example, between the dimensions of freedom and versatility, there are compounds whose parts are free and versatile, free and restricted, bound and versatile, and bound and restricted. As it will not be practicable, nor always useful, to exhibit all the possible multidimensional combinations of factors in the formation of compounds, we shall only state and illustrate the various dimensions singly and then choose the most important of them, namely the syntactical dimension, and consider compounds in detail under this head, while referring to the other dimensions whenever any of them becomes specially relevant.

    We shall consider in turn the following dimensions of classification: (a) stress pattern, (b) freedom or bondage of parts, (c) versatility or restrictedness of parts, (d) whether synthesizable or lexical, (e) whether simple or complex, (f) whether endocentric or exocentric, (g) whether syntactic or asyntactic, and (h) functional classes of constituents.

    (a) Stress Pattern. From the rules of relative stress (sec. 1.3.6), it follows that a compound has the main stress on the last non-neutral syllable. For example, 進 士 *jinn.shyh* 'advanced scholar,—highest degree under the imperial systems', 博 士 ,*bor-ˈshyh* 'comprehensive scholar,—(modern) Ph.D.', 屋裡 ˈ*u.lii* 'room's inside,—in the room', 城 外 ,*cherng* ˈ*way* 'city's outside, —suburb'. In this respect, compounds do not differ from phrases, which may end on a pronoun or a particle in the neutral tone, otherwise with the main stress on the last syllable. For example, 看他们 '*kann .ta.men* 'look at (or calls on) them', 看信 ,*kann-*'*shinn* 'read letters'. It is sometimes claimed that a compound has a final stress (before final neutral tones, if any) which unifies it more closely than a final stress in a phrase unifies the phrase. For example, 城外,*cherng* '*way* 'suburb' is somehow felt as a closer unit than 能实 ,*neng*'*may* 'can sell'. This is, however, hard to test objectively, and the feeling of unity probably comes from the readiness of the speaker or hearer to relate the compound structurally and semantically to other parts of the sentence in dimensions other than stress pattern, such as lexical meaning, exocentric function, and expandability.

(b) Freedom of Parts. Each part of a compound may be free or bound, for example:

FF: 火車 *huooche* 'fire-vehicle,—train', 铁路 *tieeluh* 'iron-road,—railroad', 小心 *sheau.shin* 'small (detail)-mind,—careful', 火烧 *huoo.shau* 'fire-bake,—a kind of hot biscuit'.

FB: 飛机 *feiji* 'fly-machine,—airplane', 打仗 *daa-janq* 'fight-battle,—carry on war', in which *janq* is a measure and therefore bound, 長虫 *charng.chorng* 'long-insect,[1]—snake', 工友 *gongyeou* 'work-friend,—workman, janitor'.

BF: 柿饼 *shyhbiing* 'persimmon-cake,—dried persimmon', 媒人 *mei.ren* 'go-between-person,—matchmaker', 房客 *farng₀keh* 'house-customer,—tenant', 承认 *cherng₀renn* 'receive-recognize, —admit, recognize'.

BB: 校友 *shiawyeou* 'school-associate,—alumnus', 委員 *woei-₀yuan* 'delegated-member,—committee member', 驱逐 *chiujwu* 'drive-pursue,—chase away', 國際法 *gwojihfaa* 'international law', in which both *gwojih* and *faa* are bound.

When one of the parts is bound, the whole construction cannot of course be a phrase. But when both parts are free, the resulting FF form may be either a phrase or a compound, depending upon various conditions: It is a compound (1) if there is

---

[1]This literal translation is on the basis of descriptive etymology. Originally, *chorng* meant '(any) animal'. (See page xxii.) Cf. *dahchorng* L 'tiger'.

a neutral tone,[2] as in 煎餅 *jian.biing* '(a kind of) fried cake', 挑剔 *tiau.ti* 'pick and flip,—find fault with'; (2) if it is not expandable without a substantial change of meaning, as 橡皮 *shianq-pyi* 'rubber' ≠ *shianq de pyi* 'elephant's skin', (a popular analysis of the BF compound *shianqpyi* from 橡樹的皮 *shianq-shuh de pyi* 'rubber tree's bark'), except that a (V-R) compound may take an infix *-de-* or *-bu-* to form a potential V-R construction, as 上去 *shanq.chiuh* 'goes up': *shanq.bu-chiuh* 'cannot go up'; (3) if the construction is exocentric, as 填房 *tyan-₀farng* 'fill the room,—one who fills the room,—a second wife (to a widower)', 笑話 *shiaw.huah* 'laugh-word,—laugh at' in: *Bye shiaw.huah ta!* 'Don't laugh at him!' Sometimes the same succession of free words forms a phrase or a compound with a skewed relationship to meaning. Thus: (a) 他心跳. *Ta shin-tiaw*, or *Ta shin tiaw*. 'He has a palpitation of the heart.', (b) *Ta bu shintiaw le*, or *Ta shin bu tiaw le.₁* 'He no longer has a palpitation of the heart.', but *Ta shin bu tiaw le.₂* or *Tade shin bu tiaw le.* 'His heart no longer beats.' The above does not exhaust the cases of FF compounds, and the remaining possibilities will be dealt with under the syntactical types below.

(c) Versatility or Restrictedness of Parts. The dimension of versatility-restrictedness, as we have seen (sec. 3.4.1), cuts across, but is positively correlated with, that of F and B. In the list below, the constituents are marked as F or B at the stage at which they enter the compound; in the first example, although *kong* 'empty' is free, it enters the compound as an abbreviated compounding form of 航空 *harngkong* 'aviation' and is therefore bound.

Versatile-versatile: 空運 *kongyunn* BF 'air transport', 有意 *yeouyih* FB 'have-intention,—intentionally, intend to', 半天 *banntian* BF 'half a day,—quite a while', 牛肉 *niourow* FF 'beef'.

Versatile-restricted: 酒麴 *jeouchiu* FF 'wine leaven', 考慮 *kaoliuh* FB 'think-deliberate,—consider', 空襲 *kongshyi* BB 'air raid', 特殊 *tehshu* BB 'special-outstanding,—outstanding'.

---

[2]With the usual exceptions of particles and pronoun objects.

Restricted-versatile: 蠹鱼 *duhyu* BF 'grub-fish, — the silver fish (*lit.*, bookworm)', 矫情 *jeauchyng* BB 'dissemble-feeling,— affected, disingenuous', also pron. *jyau.chyng* 'sly, crafty', 怠工 *daygong* BF 'idle (on) work,—go on slow-down or sit-down strike', 恶心 *ee.shin* BF 'nauseated-heart,—nauseated'.

Restricted-restricted: 遭遇 *tzauyuh* BB 'meet-happen,— viscissitudes', 奉承 *fenq.cherng* BB 'offer-receive,—flatter', 鞠躬 *jyugong* BB 'bend-body,—make a bow', 继续 *jihshiuh* BB[3] 'succeed-continue,—continue to'.

The restricted forms, like the bound forms, are often relics of wenyan words, but the resulting compounds are not always L in style, for if they were we should not be citing them as examples.

(d) Synthesizable or Lexical Meaning. In discussing the structure of words, we noted (sec. 3.6) that the meaning of a phrase or a compound is either (1) synthesizable from the meanings of the parts or (2) lexical, that is, given in a dictionary as additional information. On the whole, most phrases are synthesizable, for example, 有衣裳 *yeou i.shang* 'have clothes' and 一杯茶 *i-bei char* 'a cup of tea' have no meaning beyond what can be gathered from the words. Only a small minority, though of course very numerous in absolute numbers, of phrases are lexical and thus form idioms, for example, 有意思 *yeou yih.sy* 'have meaning,—interesting', 半瓶醋 *bann-pyng tsuh* 'half a bottle of vinegar,—dabbler, dilettante'. On the other hand, most compounds are lexical in nature, as 大衣 *dah-i* 'big garment,—overcoat', 光阴 *guang*$_o$*in* 'light and shadow (from the sun),—time elapsed'. Only those compounds which are formed from certain special types of morphemes are synthesizable and thus form transient words, as 三天 *san-tian* 'three days' (numeral-measure, or n-M), 跳出来 *tiaw.chu.lai* 'jump out' (verb-directional complement). We have thus a fair degree of correlation between compounding and specialization of meaning, or lexicality, as shown in table 8.

---

[3] 续 *shiuh* is F only in the very special sense of 'replenish' (e.g., a teapot with hot water)'.

## Table 8
### Correlation Between Compounding and Lexicality

|            | Synthesizable  | Lexical        |
|------------|----------------|----------------|
| Phrases    | Most phrases   | Idioms         |
| Compounds  | Transient words | Most compounds |

As usual, we find skewed, or asymmetrical, relations between form and meaning, for both phrases and compounds, with regard to their being synthesizable or lexical. For example, *bann-pyng tsuh*, besides the idiomatic meaning given above, can also mean literally 'half a bottle of vinegar'. On the other hand, a few idioms are never or rarely used in the literal sense, for example, 用水 *yonq-shoei* 'use water', which a careful speaker of the older generation avoided using, because it was a euphemism for ablution on the part of a woman. With compounds, the potential form 拿不出去 *na.bu-chuchiuh* 'cannot be taken out' is sometimes taken in the literal sense, but also has the lexical meaning of 'unpresentable (in deportment, speech, etc.)'. It is of course the job of a lexicographer to include all compounds of a lexical nature, but it is also important to note whether the simple synthesized meaning is or is not still possible under the compounds in question.

(e) Simple or Complex Compounds. While most compounds consist of two morphemes, many compounds, especially subordinative compounds, are in the form of a hierarchy of several morphemes, or in a few cases (sec. 6.3.3 below) in a string of items in coordination. Thus, 鱼子 *yutzyy* 'fish roe' is a simple compound of two morphemes, as contrasted with 鸡子儿 *jitzeel* 'hen's eggs', in which the second constituent *tzeel* is a derived word with root *tzyy* + *-l*. In 葡萄干儿 *pwu.taur-gal* (raisin) the first constituent *pwu.taur* 'grape' is a dissyllabic morpheme, and the second constituent is derived from *gan* 'dry' + nominal suffix *-l*, resulting (with phonetic modification) in *-gal*. In 山楂膏 *shan-.ja-gau* 'hawthorn jelly' the first constituent is itself a compound of *shan* 'mountain' + *ja* 'hawthorn-like plant'. In 軍事委員会 *jiunshyh-woeiyuanhuey* 'committee (or commission) on military affairs', *jiunshyh* modifies *woeiyuanhuey*, and *jiunshyh* in turn

consists of *jiun* 'army' modifying *shyh* 'affairs', and *woeiyuanhuey*
consists of *woeiyuan* 'delegated member(s)—committee member(s)'
modifying *huey* 'group, organization'. While the majority of complex compounds consists of subordinative compounds, other types
of construction (cf. sec. 6.5 below) are also quite common. Thus
切菜刀 *chietsay-dau* 'cut-vegetables knife,—cutting knife' consists of *chie-tsay* 'cut vegetables', which is a V-O construction,
modifying *dau*. In 联合國教育科学文化组织 *Lianher
Gwo Jiawyuh Keshyue Wenhuah Tzuujy* 'United Nations Education Science Culture Organization,—UNESCO', we have *Lianher
Gwo* modifying the rest of the construction, in which *Tzuujy*, a
compound of coordinate synonyms, is the center, modified by
three modifiers in coordination: *Jiawyuh, Keshyue,* and *Wenhuah,*
while *Lianher* 'join-combine,—unite(d)' is a coordinative compound verb modifying *gwo* 'country, nation(s)' as its center'.

(f) Endocentric or Exocentric Compounds. A compound,
like any other construction, is endocentric or exocentric (sec.
5.1.3) according as it functions similarly to one of its constituents,
the center, or differently from any one of them. Examples of
endocentric compounds are: 鸡蛋 *jidann* 'hen's egg', with *dann*
'egg' as center; 鸡蛋糕 *jidanngau* 'cake with egg as an ingredient,—sponge cake', with *gau* 'cake' as center; 劳驾 *lau-jiah* '(may
I) bother (your) chariot,—may I trouble you', a V-O compound,
with the transitive verb as center; and 存欵 *tswen-koan* (1) 'deposit money', with *tswen* as center, (2) 'deposited money,—a
deposit', with *koan* as center. Examples of exocentric compounds
are 本分 *been.fenn* 'original parts,—(one who) does not exceed
one's proper parts,—well-behaved'; 外行 *wayharng* 'outside line,
—(one who) is outside the profression,—amateurish'; 四海
*syh.hae* 'four seas,—sociable (Peip.); and 買卖 *mae.may* 'buy-sell,
—trade', which can take a classifier such as 筆 *bii* in *jey-bii mae-
.may* 'this business deal', whereas *bii* is not applicable to the verb
*mae* or *may*. The word 枕头 *jeen.tour* 'a pillow' is of ambivalent
structure: (1) as a V-O construction for '(that with which to)
pillow the head', it is an exocentric compound; (2) as the root
*jeen* with noun suffix *.tou*, it is not a compound, but a derived

word. One cannot argue conclusively against its V-O nature on the ground that the verb is *jenn* rather than *jeen*, since in present day Mandarin the verb is either *jeen* or *jenn*, with *jeen* as the more usual form.

(g) Syntactic or Asyntactic Compounds. In inflected languages, compounds are often formed of words in other than normal syntactic relations and are thus asyntactic in construction. For example, in 'cry-baby', a normal subordinate verb would be in the form 'crying'; in German *Geburtstag* the *-s* is not the usual ending for a feminine noun like *geburt;* in French *boîtes-à-lettres,* the normal syntax would require *aux lettres* or *pour les lettres.* In Chinese most compounds are syntactic and only the relatively few cases of obscure relationships between the parts in compounds can be considered asyntactic. Of the 40,000 compounds examined, Luh found only about 100 which he considered obscure (*GTFaa*, 13). Examples are: 知道 *jy.daw* 'know and say (?),—know'; 丁香 *ding.shiang* 'lilac', from *ding* ( 丁 )-shaped flower or, according to 本草綱目 *Beentsao Gangmuh,* named after the man *Ding*(?); *daur.chy* 'keep adorning herself', usually written 刀尺 (*dau* 'knife', *chyy* 'foot'), which does not make sense either syntactically or semantically; 月亮 *yueh.lianq* 'moon bright,—the moon'; and 工夫 *gong.fu* 'work + man(?),—length of time (for work or leisure)'. It is of course quite possible for historical research to disclose the origin of these words, but at the descriptive level they are asyntactic compounds, bordering on "unanalyzed compounds" (column 14 of table 7).

(h) Functional Classes of Parts. While it is a simple matter to determine the form class of a compound as a whole, the form classes of its constituents are not always clear or determinate and consequently sometimes their syntactical relation is unclear or ambiguous. This is a reservation we have to make in all the headings and subheadings of the syntactic compounds detailed below. In classifying the form classes of the constituents of compounds Luh goes into great detail in labeling headings such as A-A → N 空白 *konqbair* 'empty-plain,—a blank', VV → A 保守 *baoshoou* 'preserve-keep,—conservative'. To be sure, Luh admits (*GTFaa*, 104) that some cases are obscure, as N-V → A 風流 *feng₀liou* 'wind-flow,—romantic, amorous, etc.', in which it is not clear whether *liou* enters as a verb 'to flow' or as a noun 'current'. But in many cases he assigns functions to parts about which one can still raise questions on the immediate analysis given. Thus under V-V → N he gives 吃食 *chy.shyr* 'eat-eat,—food, diet' marked as FB. But *shyr* is not only B 'eats', but also F 'food', as in: 这猫得喂他点儿食了。 *Jeh mhau deei wey ta deal shyr le.* 'This cat has to be fed some food.' It is therefore more natural to analyze *chy.shyr* as 'eating-food,—diet'. Again, under N-A → A, there is 名贵 *mingguey* BF 'name-valuable,—valuable, prized'. But since there is 名人 *mingren* 'famed person,—famous person', 名脚儿 *mingjeaul* 'famous actor (∼ actress)', it seems that in the compounding of *ming* with *guey*, *ming* enters, not directly as the root noun 'name' (as in *mingtz*), but as 'famed, famous' B before it combines with *guey*.

 6.1.4. *Principle of Immediate Analysis.* The preceding arguments may look like a conflict of the feeling of one native with that of another—Chao vs. Luh—something that may happen between any two informants and which may not be of particular significance in any given case. After all, such divergent analyses of compounds occur only in a small minority of cases.

 But what is of methodological import here is the principle of immediate analysis. One should ask, at any stage of analysis of a complex, what is the grammatical and semantic status of each constituent at the stage at which it enters the complex. Thus the compound 工合 *Gongher* for 'indusco', has been translated as 'work together', apparently very apt and accurate equivalents of the two morphemes, though contrary to the normal syntactical order of modifier-modified. But an immediate analysis will reveal that *gong* enters as an abbreviated and bound form of 工业 *gong-yeh* 'industry, industrial' and *her* as an abbreviated and bound form of 合作 *hertzuoh* 'together work,—cooperative', so that *gongher* 'Industrial Cooperatives' is still modifier-modified, as opposed to *work together*, which is modified-modifier, an impossible syntactical order for Chinese. In general, when the principle of immediate analysis is observed, the probability of convergent results by different informants will be greatly increased.

# 6.2. Subject-Predicate (S-P) Compounds

Taking the syntactical relations of parts as the main dimension of classification, we shall now consider in some detail compounds of various syntactical types, noting features of F or B of the parts and features in the other dimensions, especially with regard to exocentricity, whenever they are relevant.

The first type of syntactic compounds are S-P compounds, which we have already described briefly insofar as they occur as predicates (sec. 2.10.6). We shall now consider S-P compounds in all their functions. Like S-P sentences and clauses, an S-P compound is always exocentric; that is, it functions neither like its first constituent, nor like its second. For example, 兵变 *bing-biann* FF 'troop revolts,—a mutiny' is a noun, but does not have *bing* or *biann* as center.

(a) S-P → N. A nominal S-P compound, like other nouns, can always be modified by a D-M compound like 这个 *jeyg* 'this', 一种 *i-joong* 'a kind of'. Names of certain natural phenomena and of five of the twenty-four sections of the solar year take this form, as 天亮 *tianlianq* FF 'day brightens,—dawn', 地震 *dihjenn* FB 'the earth quakes,—an earthquake', 海啸 *haeshiaw* FB 'the sea screams,—a tidal wave', 春分 *chuenfen* BF 'the spring divides,—vernal equinox', 秋分 *chioufen* BF 'autumnal equinox', 夏至 *shiahjyh* BB 'the summer (is at its) extreme,—summer solstice', 冬至 *dongjyh* BB 'winter solstice', 霜降 *Shuangjiang* 'frost descends,—section falling on or about October 23'. In the sentence 今天霜降了。 *Jin.tian Shuangjianq le.* 'Today is the season of "Frost Descends".', it is to be analyzed exactly like: 今天礼拜日了。 *Jintian Liibayryh le.* 'Today is Sunday.', where *Shuangjianq* or *Liibayryh* is a nominal predicate, with the phrase particle *le* 'it has come to be'. In other words, the ICs are *Shuangjianq* + *le* and not °*shuanq* + *jianqle* 'frost has descended', since *jianq* as applied to frost is not a free word, and *Shuangjianq* as a compound is not separable. Unlike *Shuangjianq*, 天亮 *tian* (#) *lianq* can be either (1) a phrase, as in 天还没亮。 *Tian hair mei lianq.* 'The sky has not yet become bright (because it is not yet day or because the sun has not yet come out from behind the clouds), or (2) a compound, as in 还没天亮。 *Hair mei tianlianq.* 'It is not yet dawn.'

Another common type of S-P compound noun has to do with ailments of the body, as 气喘 *chihchoan* FF 'the breath pants,—asthma', 头疼 *tour₀terng* FF 'headache', 耳鸣 *eelming* BB 'ear-ringing', 陽萎 *yangwoei* BB 'male fades,—impotence', 脑出血 *naochusheue* BFF 'brain bleeds,—brain hemorrhage'.

Title of novels, plays, and other literary works sometimes take the form of a full sentence, as 三娘教子 *San-niang Jiaw Tzyy* 'Third Mother Educates the Son', 火烧红莲寺 *Huoo Shau Hornglian Syh* 'Fire Burns Red Lotus Temple'. While it is doubt-ful whether it is possible to find any prosodic distinction, in the case of dissyllabic quasi-iambs, between phrases like 有毒 *yeou-dwu* 'have poison,—poisonous' and compounds like 酒壶 *jeouhwu* FF 'wine bottle', there is probably a quicker tempo in com-pounds. There is also in some cases a difference in the suffixes and particles between a compound and a phrase or sentence. Thus, a sentence would take the form: *Huoo shaule Hornglian Syh le.* 'Fire has burned down the Red Lotus Temple.', while the name of the play is, at a faster tempo and without suffix or par-ticle, *Huoo Shau Hornglian Syh* 'Fire Burns Red Lotus Temple'. (Cf. the title *Mr. Smith Goes to Washington*, with no prosodic difference from the sentence: 'Mr. Smith goes to Washington.')

(b) S-P → V. Like other verbs, verbal S-P compounds can take modal adverbs, aspect suffixes, and enter into the V-not-V form of questions. For example, *luhguoh* FF 'Road passes,—go by way of' occurs in 你来的时候儿路过没路过洛机山? 我路过了没在意。 *Nii lai de shyr.howl luhguoh mei luhguoh Luohji Shan? Woo luhguohle mei tzayyih.* 'When you came here, did you go by way of the Rocky Mountains? I did but did not notice them.'

Intransitive verbs in S-P form, if we do not include adjectives, are not so common as transitive verbs. Examples are: 声張 *shengjang* BB 'noise opens up,—make a noise (about it),—an-nounce it', 这儿常儿儿地震。 *Jell charngchangl dihjenn.* 'Here it often earthquakes.', where *dihjenn*, sometimes a noun, is also a verb by way of class overlap. Unlike *dihjenn*, however, *Shuang-jianq* 'Frost Descends' can only be a noun, so that one cannot say °*Jell charngchangl shuangjianq* (unless one wanted to say 'It's often October 23 here'), but must say 这儿常ㄦ下霜.*Jell charngchangl shiah-shuang.* 'There is often frost here.' In wenyan there are S-P verbs as in 为之髮指 *wey jy fahjyy* L 'on account of it hairstands,—one's hair stands on end on account of it,—to be greatly angered by it', 为之神往 *wey jy shernwoang* L 'on account of it fancy goes,—to be attracted by it'. If these were phrases instead of compounds, the order would be *fah wey jy jyy* and *shern wey jy woang*, which are possible, but not the usual expressions used.

Whether an S-P construction is a compound often depends upon frequency of occurrence. Thus, 门铃儿不响. *Menliengl bu sheang.* 'The doorbell does not ring.' is normally not a compound, and a modal adverb such as 也 *yee* 'also', 又 *yow* 'again' would come between the subject *menliengl* and the verbal expression *bu sheang.* But when the S-P form is heard often enough, then it begins to acquire the status of a compound and so one hears: *Woomen yee menliengl bu sheang le.* 'We also the-door-bell-doesn't-ring.' instead of *Woomen menliengl yee bu sheang le.* '(As for) us, the doorbell doesn't ring either.'

S-P compounds functioning as transitive verbs are fairly common. Besides the examples given before (sec. 2.10.6), other examples are 手拿着 *shoounaj* FF 'hand holding,—holding in one's hand', 嘴说 *tzoeishuo* FF, 'mouth speaks,—promise with the mouth only'.

(c) S-P → A. Adjectives, or quality intransitives, take the form of S-P compounds more frequently than action verbs. Besides sharing with other verbs the possibility of using modal adverbs like 也 *yee* 'also' and 还 *hair* 'still' and entering into V-not-V forms of questions, they can also take adverbs of degree like 很 *heen* 'very', 太 *tay* 'too (excessively)', and so on. Besides 头眩 *tour.shiuann* FB 'dizzy', 头疼 *tour$_0$terng* FF 'have a headache', 性急 *shinqjyi* BF 'quick-tempered', 年轻 *nianching* BF 'youthful' cited before, other examples are 这么胆儿小 *tzemm daalsheau* FF 'so courage-small,—so timid', 真胆儿大 *jen daaldah*

FF 'how courage-large,—how brave', 真肉麻 *jen rowma* 'how flesh-creeping,—how (nauseatingly) sentimental', and 太手鬆 *tay shoousong* FF 'too hand-loose,—too easy in spending', also in uncompounded form: *shoou tay song.* In the popular "Fenqyang Flower Drum Song", the first and second stanzas begin respectively with: 我命苦，我真命苦．*Woo minqkuu* (FF), *woo jen minqkuu.* 'I luck-hard, I very luck-hard.' and 我命薄，我真命薄．*Woo minqbor* (FF), *woo jen minqbor.* 'I luck-thin, I very luck-thin.'

As in the S-P constructions with other functions, the same words may in some cases alternatively form either a compound or a phrase, with or without a difference in meaning. For example: (1) 一个人心不煩最舒服．*Ig ren shin bu farn tzuey shu.fwu.* = (2) *Ig ren bu shinfarn tzuey shu.fwu.* '(When) a man is not troubled in his mind, he is most at east.', where *shin (bu) farn* in (1) is a clause, while *shinfarn* in (2) is a compound. On the other hand, 你这么手硬．*Nii tzemm shoouyinq.* 'You have such a hard hand.' is always used in a figurative sense, but *Nii shoou tzemm yinq.* with S-P (clause) predicate, can be taken either in a literal or figurative sense, while *Niide shoou tzemm yinq.*, a simple sentence, is more likely to be taken in the literal sense.

(d) S-P in other functions than those given above are rare and unclear as to their construction. The compound 势必 *shyhbih* BB 'the situation (looks that it) must (be that) ... ,—unavoidably' is an adverb, as it occurs between the subject and the predicate, as in: 这个局面势必要惡化了．*Jeyg jyumiann shyhbih yaw ehhuah le.* 'The state of affairs will unavoidably worsen.' The compounds 例如 *lihru* BB and 譬如 *pihru* BB 'example as,—e.g.' are conjunctions introducing subjects, as in: 陰曆初一总是新月，例如年初一是新月．*Inlih chui tzoongsh shin-yueh, lihru Nianchui sh shin-yueh.* 'The first of the lunar month is always new moon, e.g., New Year's Day is new moon.[4]

---

[4]For further examples of obscure S-P compounds, see Luh, *GTFaa*, 99.

# 6.3 Coordinate Compounds

A coordinate compound is one in which the immediate constituents are in coordinate construction. It differs from a coordinate phrase in that apart from a few exceptions it cannot be reversed, and differs from a subordinate compound in that each
constituent is a center while in a subordinate compound only the
second constituent is the center.

*6.3.1. Composition of Coordinate Compounds by Form Classes.*
The constituents in coordination are normally of the same form
class and if one or both parts are bound, then we will have to go
by meaning or their functions in L, which are often inconclusive.
The greater part of the examples below are from Luh, *GTFaa*,
except that examples of doubtful analysis have not been included.

(1) Nouns

(a) N-N → N. 书报 *shubaw* FF 'books and periodicals,—
reading matter, collectively', 灯火 *denghuoo* FF 'lamps and fires,
—illumination (of a place at night)', 車馬 *chemaa* FF 'vehicles
and horses,—traffic'.

(b) M-M → N. 行列 *harnglieh* BB 'columns and rows,—for-
mat, formation', 条件 $tyau_ojiann$ BB 'articles and items,—stipu-
lations, conditions', 斤兩 *jin.leang* BB 'catty and tael,—weight'.

(c) A-A → N. 莊嚴 *tzuenyan* BF 'dignified and stern,—digni-
ty', 煩惱 *farnnao* FF 'vexed and angry,—vexation'.

(d) V-V → N. This form may be nouns for the actions themselves or, exocentrically, for person or things associated with the
type of action or actions: 告白 *gawbair* BB[5] 'tell and say (plainly),
—announcement,—advertisement', 長進 $jaang_ojinn$ FB 'grow and
advance,—progress, improvement' (also 'to progress'), 呼吸
*hu.shi* FF 'expire-inspire,—breath' (also 'breathe'); exocentric
cases: 教授 *jiawshow* FB 'teach and transmit,—professor' (less
frequently, 'teach'), 开关 *kaiguan* FF 'open and shut,—a switch',[6]

---

[5]Note that *gaw* 'sue' is F but in the sense of 'tell' it is B. Similarly, *bair*
'white' is F but in the sense of 'tell plainly' it is B.

[6]Note that, since *kai* means 'put in operation', *kai deng* is 'turn on the
light' and *guan deng* is 'turn off the light'.

编辑 *bian.jih* FB 'compile and collocate,—editor' (also 'edit'),
提调 *tyi$_0$diaw* FF 'bring up and arrange,—director, dean' (old
term).

(e) H-V → N. 廣告 *goanggaw* 'broad announce,—advertisement', 廣播 *goangboh* 'broad cast,—broadcast' (N or V),
*shian.sheng* 'first born,—sir, Mr., teacher, doctor, husband'.

(2) Adjectives

(f) A-A → A. 貴重 *guey.jonq* FF 'valuable and important,—
valuable', 懶惰 *laan$_0$duoh* FB 'lazy-indolent,—lazy', 新鮮 *shin-
.shian* FF 'new and fresh,—fresh', 奇怪 *chyiguay* FF 'strange-
strange,—strange'. Cf. free forms: *chyi* 'remarkable, strange (in
good sense)', *guay* 'queer, strange (in bad sense)'.

(g) N-N → A. 矛盾 *mau$_0$duenn* FB 'spear and shield,—contradictory, inconsistent', 窩囊 *uo.nang* FB 'nest and bag,—cozy;
sycophantic', 江湖 *jiang$_0$hwu* FF '(adventuring on the) rivers and
lakes,—world-wise, adventuresome', 勢利 *shyh.lih* BB '(attentive
to) influence and advantage,—snobbish'.

(h) V-V → A. 踴躍 *yeongyueh* 'skip and leap—enthusiastic',
保守 *baoshoou* 'keep and watch,—conservative' (also 'conserve,
preserve').

(3) Verbs

(i) V-V → V. 鋪排 *pu$_0$pair* FF 'spread out and arrange,—
supervise arrangements for', 依靠 *ikaw* 'follow and lean on,—
rely on', 失敗 *shybay* BF 'lose and be defeated,—fail'.

If a verb is compounded of parts one or both of which are
obviously non-verbs, an immediate analysis usually reveals that it
is something else which has changed into or has added the function of a verb. Thus, 滿足 *maantzwu* FF 'full and sufficient' is
an adjective 'satisfied' and more recently (though less often) a
transitive verb 'satisfy', as in 滿足他的慾望 *maantzwu tade
yuh$_0$wanq* 'satisfies his desire(s)'. In 短少 *doanshao* FF 'short
and few (~ little),—lack', both *doan* and *shao* are also transitive
verbs 'be short of' or 'be short by', so that the verb *doanshao*
should be immediate-analyzed as a compound of verbs. In 犧牲
*shisheng* BB 'sacrificial animal and domestic animal,—sacrifice'
the morpheme *shi* is limited to this one compound, so that

*shisheng* may as well be left unanalyzed. Be that as it may, *shisheng* is still used as a noun as well as a verb, and the verbal use can more simply be taken as a causative verb formed from a noun 'make a sacrifice of'. The compound 希罕 *shi.haan* FB 'sparse and rare' is a compound adjective meaning 'rare', and when used putatively it is a transitive verb meaning 'find rare, regard as valuable'. In current written bairhuah the noun 意味 *yih.wey* BB 'meaning and flavor,—significance, connotation' sometimes appears as a verb with a progressive suffix: *yih.weyj* 'connoting', which is another case of the compound noun used alternatively as a verb, rather than a verb compounded directly of two nouns.

(4) Adverbs

(j)  H-H → H. 剛才 *gangtsair* BB 'just just,—just now, a moment ago', 互相 *huhshiang* BB 'mutually mutually,—mutually', 全都 *chyuandou* BB 'completely all,—in all cases'.

(k)  There is a variety of other formations of adverbs: 反正 *faan₀jenq* FF 'right or reverse,—anyway', 橫竪 *herng.shuh* FF (more commonly *herng.sh*) 'horizontal or vertical, — anyway', 左 □ *tzuoo.yi* BB (< 左右 *tzyoo-yow*) 'right or left, anyway' (Central dial.), 早晚 *tzaowoan* FF 'sooner or later', 始終 *shyyjong* BB 'begin-end,—to the end, in the end', 彼此 *biitsyy* BB 'that and this,—mutually', 再三 *tzaysan* BB 'again and a third time, —over and over again', 根本 *genbeen* BB 'root-root,—basically', 日夜 *ryhyeh* BB 'day and night', 千万 *chianwan* (BB) ... ! '1000-10000,—by all means ... !', 絲毫不 *sy-haur* (BB) *bu* ... '0.00001-0.0001 not ... ,—not a bit ... ', 從來 *tsornglai* FF 'from (before) coming (to now)' ~ 向來 *shianqlai* BF 'toward coming (to now), —ever', *tsornglai bu* ~ *shianqlai bu* 'never'.

*6.3.2. Composition of Coordinate Compounds by Meaning.* Grammatical coordination includes not only semantic synonymy, but also antonymy as well as some general parallelism in meaning.

(a) Compounds of Synonyms. The term "synonymous compound" is often used by writers on Chinese to describe a compound whose *parts* are synonyms. We met examples of them in the preceding subsection. Further examples are: 租稅 *tzushuey*

FF 'levies and taxes', 艰难 *jian*₀*nan* BF 'hardships and difficulties,—hardships', 告示 *gaw.shyh* BB 'tells and manifests,—proclamation', 声音 *sheng.in* BB 'noise and tone,—sound', 意思 *yih.sy*
BB 'idea and thought,—meaning', also 'intention', 多馀 *duoyu*
FB 'extra and remaining,—excessive, extra', 乖巧 *guai*₀*cheau* FF
'shrewd and clever,—crafty', 爽快 *shoang.kuay* BF 'brisk and
quick,—straightforward', 周到 *jou.daw* BF 'around and reaching,
—thoughtful, hospitable', 活动 *hwo.donq* FF 'lively and moving,—
active', also 'loose and move,—works loose (of screws, teeth, etc.)',
清楚 *ching.chuu* FB 'clear and distinct,—clear', 明白 *ming.bair*
BF 'clear and plain,—clear', also used putatively: 'understand',
拾掇 *shyr.dou* FB ( ← *shyr-duoh*) 'pick and gather up,—tidy
up', 颠掇 *dian.dou* FB 'heft and pick up,—heft', 摩蹭 *mo*₀*tsenq*
FF 'rub and graze,—abrade', 摩擦 *mo*₀*tsa* FF 'rub and scrape,—
scrape', also 'friction', 打击 *daa.ji* FB 'strike and hit,—set back',
also 'a setback', 想像 *sheangshianq* FB 'think and imagine,—
imagine, 凑和 *tsow.hwo* FB 'piece together and mix together,—
make a temporary expedient', 分散 *fensann* FF 'divide and
scatter,—disperse', 消停 *shiau.tyng* FF 'subside and stop,—quiet
down', 分析 *fen.shi* FB 'divide and separate,—analyze', also
'analysis', 走动 *tzoou*₀*donq* FF 'walk and move,—to be up and
about', 存在 *tswentzay* BF 'exist and be there,—exist ( ≠ *tswen*
*.tzay~de*, as in 存在银行裡 *tswen .tzay ynharng.lii* 'deposited in a bank'), 言语 *yuan.yi* BB (from metathesis of *yanyeu*
'speech and talk,—language'[7]) 'say a word, make a remark'.

(b) Compounds of Antonyms. With free adjectives of opposite
qualities in coordination, as in: 人分好坏. *Ren fen hao huay.*
'People are divided into good and bad.', it is simpler to treat the
pair of adjectives as forming a phrase. The same applies to 大小
*dah sheau* 'large or small,—size', 长短 *charng doan* 'long or
short,—length', 高低 *gau di* 'high or low,—height', 高矮 *gau ae*
'tall or short,—stature', 厚薄 *how baur* 'thick or thin,—thickness
(of surfaces)', 粗细 *tsu shih* 'thick or thin,—thickness (of length-

---

[7]The current learned term for 'language' is *yeuyan*, but *yanyeu*, in the
form of *gengo*, is still the term in Japanese.

wise things)', 软硬 *roan yinq* soft or hard', 冷热 *leeng reh* 'cold
or hot', 鹹淡 *shyan dann* 'salty or bland', 濃淡 *nong dann*
'strong (concentrated) or weak (dilute)'. These paired antonyms
can be modified by the adverbs 这么 *tzemme* 'to this degree',
那么 *nemme* 'to that degree', 多么 *dwome* 'to what degree',
一样(的) *iyanq (de)* 'to the same degree', and 同样(的)
*torngyanq (de)* 'equally', but not by other adverbs of degree like
很 *heen* 'very', 多 *dwo* 'how, to what degree', which can take one
of a pair of antonyms, but not the pair. For example, there is
*dwom tsu shih?* 'how thick or thin?', *dwo tsu?* 'how thick?' or
*dwo shih?* 'how thin?', but not °*dwo tsu shih?* This shows that
such pairs, apart from their ready translation into simple words in
English, share some properties of a phrase and some properties
of a compound word, and it is for this reason that designers of
romanized writing for Chinese often prefer to spell them together.

When one or both constituents are bound and/or there is a
neutral tone and/or exocentric function, then the pair of antonyms forms a compound. Thus, *biitsyy* BB 'that this,—mutually',
as in: 他们彼此不通信. *Tamen biitsyy bu tong shinn.* 'They
do not write to each other.', where *bii* and *tsyy* are L and B and
the result is an adverb. In: 買賣都一樣价錢嗎? *Mae may
dou iyanq jiah.chyan ma?* 'Is it all the same price, buying or selling?' we have a phrase *mae may*, but in 一筆好買賣 *i-bii hao
mae.may* 'a good deal (in trade)', *mae.may* 'trade' is a noun. In
鋪盖 *pu.gay* FF 'spread-cover,—bedding' we have two verbs in
trochaic rhythm used exocentrically for 'that with which one
spreads and covers'. In 多少 *duo_oshao* ~ *dwo_oshaw* FF 'much-
little, many-few,—how much, how many', there is an optional
neutral tone on *shao*.[8] In the start-bound compounds 上下
-_oshanq_oshiah 'up or down,—or thereabouts' and 左右 -_otzuoo-
_oyow 'right or left,—or thereabouts', there is an optional neutral
tone on both parts. The compound 利害 *lih.hay* 'strong, powerful',
has had an interesting folk etymology. As 'profit or harm' BB, it

---

[8]The phrase *duo shao* ~ *dwo shao*, without neutral tone, 'how little,
how few' is adverb and adjective, which is quite something else from the
compound in question.

is used exocentrically as an adjective for 'capable of influencing profit or harm,—strong, powerful'. But in Mandarin both 利 B 'profit' and 厲 B 'fierce' are pronounced *lih*, hence the compound of antonyms gets to be written and interpreted as 'fierce and harmful' and thus becomes a compound of synonyms instead of antonyms.

(c) Parallel Compounds. Parallel compounds are those whose constituents are grammatically similar so as to be coordinate, but not near enough to be synonymous, nor so directly opposite as to be antonymous. Examples of nouns are 山水 *shanshoei* FF 'mountain and water,—landscape (itself or a painting)', 風水 *feng.shoei* FF 'wind and water,—geomancy', also 'geomantic quality of a site for a house, a tomb, etc.', 手腳 *shoou$_0$jeau* FF 'hands and feet,—agility' (vs. phrase *shoou jeau* 'hands and feet'), 薪水 *shin$_0$shoei* BF 'fuel and water,—salary', 錢糧 *chyan.liang* FB 'money and grains,—taxes' (old term), 板眼 *baan$_0$yean* BB 'rhythm in music',[9] 皮毛 *pyimau* FF 'skin and hair,—superficial aspects of a subject or skill', 風雨 *fengyeu* FF 'wind and rain, —rain storm', 云雨 *yunyeu* BF 'cloud and rain,—sexual intercourse', 尺寸 *chyr.tsuenn* BB 'feet and inches,—size', also 'tempo (in music)', 分寸 *fen$_0$tsuenn* BB '0.1-inches and inches,—measure, moderation'. Nouns formed exocentrically from verbs: 裁縫 *tsair.ferng* FF '(one who) cuts and sews,—tailor', 告示 *gaw.shyh* 'tells, proclaims,—proclamation'. Nouns from adjectives: 生冷 *shengleeng* 'raw or cold (things)' (foods a patient is often ordered to avoid, according to traditional medicine), 細軟 *shihroan* 'fine and soft (articles),—valuables (to save in emergencies)'. Collective nouns are often formed of correlative terms of address, as 父母 *fuhmuu* BB 'father and mother,—parents', 子女 *tzyyneu* BB 'sons and daughters,—children', 兄弟 *shiong$_0$dih* BB 'elder brothers and younger brothers,—brothers', 姊妹 *jiee$_0$mey* BB 'elder sisters and younger sisters,—sisters', 夫婦 *fufuh* BB 'husband and wife',

---

[9]So-called because $\frac{4}{4}$ time is said to have 一板三眼 *i-baan san-yean* 'one beat of the clappers and three empty beats' and $\frac{2}{4}$ time is said to have *i-baan i-yean*. Triple time is rare in Chinese music.

*jour.lii* BB 'wives of brothers'.[10] These cannot be used as terms for individuals, except that *shiong.dih* is used as a synonym of *dih.dih* 'younger brother'. For example, one cannot say: °*Jeh sh woo.de jieemey.* for 'This is my sister.' If one has occasion to speak of a man's sister without knowing whether she is older or younger than he, one will have to say: *Jey sh ta ⁺iee.jiee heje mey.mey.* 'This is his older-sister or younger-sister.'

Examples of adjectives are: 干淨 *gan.jinq* FB 'dry and clean, —clean', as in: 水干淨嗎？ *Shoei gan.jinq ma?* 'Is the water clean?', 白淨 *bair.jinq* FB 'white and clean,—clean and neat', 热鬧 *reh.naw* FF 'hot and noisy,—full of life'.

Examples of verbs are: 招呼 *jau₀hu* FB 'beckon and call,— greet; entertain; take care of', 打掃 *daa.sao* FF 'dust and sweep, tidy up', 斟酌 *jen.jwo* FB 'pour and decant,—deliberate', 琢磨 *tzwo.mo* BF 'carve and grind,—deliberate over' (≠ 琢磨 *jwomo* L 'carve and grind'), 打算 *daa.suann* FF 'set about and reckon,— plan to', 打發 *daa.fa* FF 'set out and send out,—dispatch', 打听 *daa.ting* 'set out and listen,—make inquiries about', 划算 *hwa-.suann* BF 'sketch and reckon,—estimate', also 'advantageous,—it pays to ... '.

*6.3.3. Polymers.* A list of coordinate morphemes one or more of which are bound roots is often mentioned without pause and functions as a collective noun. Because of its similarity to a long string of atoms forming a molecule, such a string of morphemes may be called a polymer. The order of parts, as in compounds with two parts, is fixed, either by the natural order of the things concerned, as in 春夏秋冬 *Chuen-Shiah-Chiou-Dong* 'spring, summer, autumn, and winter,—the four seasons' or by convention, as in 士農工商 *shyh-nong-gong-shang* 'scholars, farmers, workers, and merchants'. Other examples of polymers are 东南西北 *Dong-Nan-Shi-Beei* 'east, south, west, and north,—the cardinal directions', 酒色財气 *jeou-seh-tsair-chih* 'wine, women, wealth, and woe' (answers to drawing one's luck), 鸡鸭鱼肉

---

[10]For further details, especially on various meanings of *shiongdih*, see the articles concerned in Chao-Yang, *Conc Dict*, and Y. R. Chao, "Chinese Terms of Address", *Language*, 32:217-241 (1956).

*ji-ia-yu-row* 'chicken, duck, fish, and meat,—animal foodstuff', 亭
台楼阁 *tyng-tair-lou-ger* 'pavilions, terraces, upper stories, and
raised    alcoves,—elaborate    architecture', 加减乘除 *jia-jean-
cherng-chwu* 'add, subtract, multiply, divide,—arithmetic', 声光
化電 *sheng-guang-huah-diann* 'acoustics, optics, chemistry, and
electricity,—the physical sciences', 金銀銅鉄錫 *jin-yn-torng-
tiee-shyi* 'gold,silver, copper, iron, and tin,—the five metals', 金
木水火土    *jin-muh-shoei-huoo-tuu* 'metal, wood, water, fire,
and earth,—the five (traditional) elements', 天地君親师 *tian-
dih-jiun-chin-shy* 'heaven, earth, the sovereign, parents, and
teachers,—the five objects of reverence', 宋齐梁陈隋 *Song-
Chyi-Liang-Chern-Swei* 'The Southern Dynasties', 梁唐晋汉
周 *Liang-Tarng-Jinn-Hann-Jou* 'The Five Dynasties', 唐宋元
明清 *Tarng-Song-Yuan-Ming-Ching* 'The recent dynasties', 甲
乙丙丁戊己庚辛壬癸    *Jea-Yii-Biing-Ding   Wuh-Jii-Geng-
Shin-Ren-Goei* 'the Heaven's Stems', 子丑寅卯辰巳午未
申酉戌亥    *Tzyy-Choou-Yn-Mao   Chern-Syh-Wuu-Wey   Shen-
Yeou-Shiu-Hay* 'the Earth's Branches'. (For the meanings of the
last two polymers, see *Mand Prim*, p. 201, n. 40.)

Among the examples given above, more than half the morphemes are bound. In *shyh-nong-gong-shang*, the morpheme *gong*
'work' is free, but as '(the class) labor' it is bound, as in 工会
*gonghuey* 'labor union' (not to be immediate-analyzed as 'work
union'). For most of the bound morphemes there are longer free
forms. Thus, the full words for the seasons of the year are
*Chuen.tian, Shiah.tian, Chiou.tian, Dong.tian*. The words for the
cardinal directions are formed by adding the localizer 边(儿)
*-.bian~-.bial*. For the names of the sciences, the versatile end
morpheme is 学 *-shyue* 'leaning, -ology, -ics', so that even though
*guang* is free as 'light', it is bound as an abbreviation for *guang-
shyue* 'optics'. Of the names of the traditional lists of metals and
elements, *jin-* and *yn-* take the suffix *-tz*, *muh-* takes *-.tou*, and
*shyi-* takes the rare suffix 拉 *-.la.*[11] Of the names of the dynasties,

_____

[11]This is of course according to the forms used in everyday speech. In
technical language the name of every chemical element is free.

the bound morpheme to add is 朝-.*chaur*, the word for 'dynasty' being 朝代 *chaur$_0$day*. The Heaven's Stems and Earth's Branches are different from the other lists in two respects. One is the tendency to break too long a string into arbitrary phonological phrases regardless of any other grammatical break. Since a group of five syllables, unless it is the whole list, tends to give a sing-song effect, as if making a line of verse, the usual breaks are 4 + 6 for the Heaven's Stems and 4 + 4 + 4 for the Earth's Branches. The other point is that as abstract counters, those units are quasi-quoted and thus function as free nouns. As names of the old-style double hour, however, the Earth's Branches are bound and the full words are 子时 *Tzyyshyr* 'Tzyy-hour,—midnight', 午时 *Wuushyr* 'Noon-hour,—noon- (homophonous with 五十 *wuu$_0$shyr* 'fifty') and so on.

A polymer is a closer unit than a list of free words and a looser unit than an ordinary compound. It is closer in allowing no pauses (except as noted above) or insertions, whereas a list of free words such as *jintz, yntz, torng, tiee, shyi.la* can have insertions of pauses and/or one of the 'and'- words such as *gen* between the items. It is closer also in that the order is fixed, as in *Dong-Nan-Shi-Beei*, whereas a list of free words can be in any order and equally grammatical, if not always equally idiomatic. No eyebrows would be raised if one said *Beei.bial, Nan.bial, Dong.bial, Shi.bial,* following the usual order in English. To be sure, one does say *Dong-Shi-Nan-Beei* as a second most frequent order and *Nan-Beei-Dong-Shi,* as in the school "Song of the Earth," as a third, though rare, order. But considering all the 4! (= 24) possible permutations of four things, the limitation to two or three patterns makes the order far from being completely random.

On the other hand, a polymer is looser than an ordinary compound because the separate meanings are never lost to the same extent as in ordinary compounds. Thus 尺寸 *chyr.tsuen* 'feet and inches,—size' may be measured in meters or any unit and 薪水 *shin$_0$shoei* 'fuel and water,—salary' is paid by check or currency, whereas polymers are taken more nearly literally. Moreover, a polymer often has a generic word which does not enumerate its members and which can occur in apposition with it or in its stead. This, one can say (1) *Chuen-Shiah-Chiou-Dong,* or (2) *Chuen-Shiah-Chiou-Dong syh-jih,* or (3) 四季 *shy-jih* 'the four seasons'. Similarly, (1) *jin-muh-shoei-huoo-tuu,* or (2) *jin-muh-shoei-huoo-tuu wuu-shyng,* or (3) 五行 *wuu-shyng* 'the five elements'.

# 6.4 Subordinative Compounds

*6.4.1. Résumé on Subordination.* Since we have discussed both subordinative compounds and subordinative phrases in the preceding chapter, we shall devote the main part of the present chapter to illustrating in detail the various types of subordinative compounds and limit general discussions to a brief résumé.

As we have noted (sec. 5.3.4), if either the attribute or the center or both are bound, or if the center is in the neutral tone, it is a compound. If both parts are free (FF) and the center is not in the neutral tone, then the factors of separability (expandability), specialization of meaning, and exocentricity of function will have to be considered. We also noted (sec. 5.3.6.3) that the particle *de* always marks a subordinative phrase and never a compound. In this respect the particle *de* behaves differently from English 'of', which is otherwise equivalent to *de* with the terms on both sides of it reversed. Thus, there are no Chinese compounds of the 'man-of-war' or 'jack-in-the-pulpit' type. 等号 *Deenghaw* BB 'equality sign' is a compound; 相等的符号 *shiangdeeng de fwuhaw* 'sign of equality' is a phrase.

In marking the F or B status of the constituents of a compound, it is to be remembered that we always operate on the principle of immediate analysis (sec. 6.1.4); that is, an attribute or a center is marked F or B in the sense and in the function in which it enters the compound and not according to what it might mean or do or even usually means or does elsewhere. For simplicity, cases of FF will be left unmarked in the examples cited below, unless it is important to note the fact.

We shall now consider the following types of form classes forming subordinative compounds: 6.4.2. Compounds with nouns as centers; 6.4.3. Compounds with determinatives and measures;

6.4.4. Compounds with localizers; 6.4.5. Compounds with *bu-*. In most cases a subordinative compound is of the same form class as that of the center, except in the case of exocentric compounds, which will be indicated as such or implied in the translation.

### 6.4.2. Compounds with Nouns as Centers

(1) N-N Compounds. Subordinative compounds with nominal constituents are more numerous than any of the other types. A large proportion of them are lexical, and a rather small number of them are exocentric. As we have seen the form N *de* N is a phrase, with synthesizable meaning, while N-N is a compound, very likely with lexical meaning. For example, 城牆 *cherng-chyang* 'city wall' and *cherng de chyang* 'the wall of a city' mean the same thing. As to 牛肉 *niourow* 'beef' and *niou de row* 'the flesh of cattle', the two forms seem to refer to the same thing, but: 牛的肉長老了不好吃。 *Niou de row jaang-laole bu hao chy.* 'When the flesh of cattle has grown tough, it is not good to eat.' cannot be changed to: *Niourow ... ,* from which it can be seen that the apparently synthesizable 牛肉 *niourow* is somewhat specialized: 'the flesh of cattle cut up for food'. In 龙头 *longtour* 'dragon head', there are (1) the zero-grade meaning of 'dragon's head', as in a painting of a dragon or the head of a real dragon —the kind that fifty or a hundred people carry and dance with through the streets at festivals, (2) 'locomotive' (old popular term), (3) 'postage stamp' (under the Manchu dynasty), and (4) 'faucet', also called 水龙头 *shoei-longtour*. In 鸡眼 *ji.yean* FB 'chicken-eye,—corn on the toe', 冬天 *Dong.tian* BB 'winter-days, —winter', 電車 *diannche* 'electric car,—trolley car', the zero-grade meanings are no longer available and will have to be expressed, when necessary, by phrases such as 鸡的眼睛 *ji de yean.jing* 'chicken's eye', 冬天的日子 *Dong.tian de ryhtz* 'days of winter' (or, if *-.tian* is to be descriptive-etymologized as 'weather', then 'winter weather' will have to be phrased as 冬天的天气 *Dong.tian de tian.chih*), and 用電走的車 *yonq diann tzoou de che* 'vehicles which run by electricity (such as those using batteries)'. 賬房(儿) *janqfarng(l)* FB 'accounts room' is either 'cashier's office', or exocentrically, 'cashier'. 茶房 *char-.farng* FB 'tearoom' is always exocentric: 'waiter'; for 'teahouse'

one will have to say 茶館儿 *chargoal* FB 'tea establishment' or 茶室 *charshyh* FB 'tearoom'.

(2) A-N Compounds. As is the case with other compounds, if one or both constituents are bound, the result is a compound, as in 善人 *shannren* BF 'kindly person', 香料 *shiangliaw* FB 'fragrant material,—spice', 秘诀 *mihjyue* BB 'secret formula, secret method'. If the center is in the neutral tone, it is a compound, as in 良心 *liang.shin* BF 'good heart,[12]—conscience', 大人 *dah.ren* FF 'big person,—an adult', also old term of address for a high official. If an A-N combination functions exocentrically as an adjective, an action verb, and so on, it is a compound. For example, 热心 *rehshin* 'hot heart,—enthusiastic; devotes oneself to' occurs in: 他热心慈善事业，可是对政治一点儿不热心. *Ta rehshin tsyrshann shyhyeh, keesh duey jenqjyh ideal bu rehshin.* 'He devotes himself to charitable undertakings, but is not at all interested in politics.' Most exocentric cases of A-N compounds have one or both constituents bound and/or a neutral tone, as 虚心 *shiushin* BF 'empty mind,—unprejudiced mind,—modest, unassuming', 强调 *chyangdiaw* FB 'strong accent,—emphasizes' (semantic calque from English 'stress'), 霸道 *bah-.daw* BB 'oppressive ways,—domineering', also 'potent (of drugs)'.

For cases of FF without neutral tone or exocentricity, expansion by the insertion of *de* is the most important test. Relatively few cases of FF cannot be so expanded.[13] The test for what remains will then consist in asking whether there is any radical difference in meaning between FF and F *de* F. 黄油 *Hwangyou* 'yellow oil,—butter', but *hwang de you* '(any) oil that is yellow', 黄酒 *hwangjeou* 'yellow alcoholic drink,—Chinese rice

---

[12]The concept of *liang.shin* really came from *liang* 'original, inborn' + *shin* 'heart', being based on the theory that human nature is originally good. At the descriptive level, however, most users of the word *liang.shin* immediate-analyze it simply as 'good heart'.

[13]Compounds like 白铁 *bairtiee* 'white iron,—sheet iron' and 鹹盐 *shyanyan* 'salty salt,—table salt' (dial.), are apparently not expandable, as there is no such thing as *bair de tiee* 'iron that is white', and *shyan de yan* 'salt that is salty' seems unnecessarily redundant. However, arguments about

wine', but *hwang de jeou* '(any) alcoholic drink that is yellow', as in: 勃蘭地是一種黃的酒. *Borlandih sh i-joong hwang de jeou.* 'Brandy is a kind of yellow liquor.'; 大門 *dahmen* 'big door,—the front door (which may actually be small)', but *dah de men* '(any) door that is large'; 黑板 *heibaan* 'blackboard (which may be black or green)', but *hei de baan* 'a board which is black'. In special cases of A-N compounds, it is possible to tell a compound because the adjective is no longer taken literally, so that it can be modified by a redundant or even a contradictory modifier, as in 小孩儿 *sheauharl* 'little child,—child', but 小 ( 的 ) 小孩儿 *sheau (de) sheauharl* 'small (or young) child', 大 ( 的 ) 小孩儿 *dah (de) sheauharl* 'big (older) child'. Sometimes, the compound A-N, which formally denotes a species of the object denoted by N by virtue of the class meaning of subordination, is semantically not a species of N. For example 野鸡 *yeeji* 'wild chicken—pheasant' is not a kind of *ji* 'chicken', and 淡菜 *danntsay* 'flat (tasting) vegetable,—mussel' is not a kind of vegetable, but a mollusk. Apart from such special types, the general test, as proposed by Luh (*GTFaa*, 33), is expandability by *de*.

As usual, when two words are contrasted, they are contrasted as wholes and the original stressed syllables will receive contrasting stress, while, if two phrases are contrasted, only the contrasted words receive contrasting stress (cf. sec. 3.3.3). Thus, in: 我以為我買的是本儿新书，结果是本旧书. *Woo yiiwei woo mae de sh beel "shin ₁shu, jyeguoo sh beel "jiow ₁shu.* 'I thought I had bought a new book, but it turned out to be an old book.', where the A-N constructions would ordinarily be of the pattern ₁□ '□ if not in contrast. But with compounds, the second syllables in trochees would receive the contrasting stress, even though it is only the first syllable that is actually different,

---

the truth of statements are not arguments about grammar, as it is perfectly grammatical to say: 世界上沒有白的鐵. *Shyh.jieh.shanq meiyeou bair de tiee.* 'There is no such thing as white iron in the world.' and: 这盒儿盐不鹹，鹹的盐在那个蓝纸盒儿裡. *Jey-her'l yan bu shyan, shyan de yan tzay neyg lan-jyyher'l.lii.* 'This box of salt is not salty, the salty kind is in that blue paper box.'

as in: 我叫你買斤白菓，你怎么買了一斤青菓来
了？ *Woo jiaw nii mae jin ˌbair "guoo, nii tzeem maele i-jin
ˌching"guoo .lai le?* 'I told you to buy a catty of gingkos, how
come you bought a catty of olives instead?' However, when it is
the verbal aspect that is being considered, then the contrasted
words are being hypostatized and one can say: 我说的是白
菓，我没说青菓。 *Woo shuo de sh "bair ˌguoo, woo mei shuo
"ching ˌguoo!* 'What I said was "*bair ˌguoo*, I didn't say "*ching
ˌguoo*.'

Further examples of A-N compounds are: 白板 *bairbaan*
'white board,—the White Dragon in mahjong', 白梨 *bairli* 'white
pear,—a small, round variety of pear of the Peiping locality', 白
薯 *bairshuu* 'white potato,—sweet potato, yam',[14] 白菜 *bairtsay*
'white vegetable,—celery cabbage', 白话 *bairhuah* 'colloquial language', 長城 *Charngcherng* 'long wall,—the Great Wall', 長工
*charnggong* 'long work,—man engaged on a farm for long periods',
長江 *Charngjiang* 'long river,—the Yangtze River', 青茶 *ching-
char* 'green tea', 青草 *chingtsao* '(ordinary green) grass', 青鱼
*chingyu* 'green (blue) fish,—the buffalo carp', 大便 *dahbiann*
'great convenience,—feces, defecate', 大車 *dahche* 'great vehicle,
—two-wheeled cart', 大烟 *dahian* 'great smoke,—opium', 大麥
*dah₀may* 'great wheat,—barley', 大蒜 *dahsuann* 'great garlic,—
garlic', 大菜 *dahtsay* 'great dishes,—Occidental-style dinner', 大
意 *dahyih* FB 'great ideas,—main ideas, main theme', 大意 *dah-
.yih* 'great ideas (to the neglect of details),—negligent, inadvertent',
高等 *gaudeeng-* FB 'high class', 高祖 *gautzuu* 'high ancestor,
—great-great-grandfather, also posthumous title of first emperors
of the Han, T'ang, and some minor dynasties', 高足 *gautzwu*
'high foot,—your pupil (honorif.)', 空气 *kongchih* 'air in empty
space,—air', 空口 *kongkoou* FB 'empty mouth,—with mere

---

[14]So-called because, according to one etymology, it ripens in 100 days,
hence, 百薯 *baeshuu*, which by the usual tone sandhi is homophonous with
*bairshuu*. According to another theory, '(yellow) sweet potato' is called 白
薯 *bairshuu* to contrast with 红薯 *horngshuu* 'a red-dish variety of yam'.
Irish potatoes are called 山药蛋儿 *shan.yawdall*.

words', also 'without something to go with it (while eating or drinking something)', 空手 *kongshoou* 'empty-handed', 空话 *konghuah* 'empty words', 美观 *meeiguan* FB 'beautiful view,— good appearance', 美人 *meei₀ren*[15] FF 'beautiful person,— beautiful woman', 美術 *meeishuh* FB 'beautiful art,—fine art', 小便 *sheaubiann* 'minor convenience,—urine, urinate', 小賬 *sheaujanq* 'small account,—tips', 小麥 *sheau₀may* 'small wheat, —wheat', 小人 *sheauren* 'small man,—mean person', 小心 *sheau.shin* 'small (detailed) mind,—careful', 小数 *sheaushuh* FB 'small number,—decimal', 小学 *sheaushyue* 'lesser learning,— study of words and characters; primary school', 小时 *sheaushyr* L 'small hour ($\frac{1}{24}$ of day)', as contrasted with 时辰 *shyr.chern* '(old-style) hour ($\frac{1}{12}$ of day)', 粗工 *tsugong* 'rough work; unskilled labor', 粗活 *tsuhwo* 'rough work', 粗话 *tsuhuah* 'coarse language, obscene language', 粗人 *tsuren* 'coarse person, uncouth person, 粗心 *tsushin* 'coarse (grained) mind,—careless'.

(3) V-N Compounds. Since the normal syntactical relation of a verb and a noun in that order is that of verb and object, the only subordinative relation in a V-N sequence will be that of a subordinative compound. The action of the verb may have many kinds of relationships to what the noun stands for, so that V-N may mean (a) N which V's, (b) N which is V-ed, (c) N with which one V's, or (d) N having some general relation with the action of V. Sometimes the difference between the categories is not very clear; for example, in 飛机 *feiji* 'fly-machine,—airplane', one could take it as a machine which flies, which the pilot flies, or by means of which the passengers fly. In 噴壺 *penhwu* 'sprinkling pot (for watering plants', is it the pot which spouts water or the pot with which one sprinkles the plants? Most of the cases, however, are clear enough.

(a) N which V's.— 打手 *daa.shoou* 'striking hands,—hired rioters', 導師 *daoshy* BB 'guiding master,—(academic) adviser', 動物 *donq.wuh* BB 'moving thing,—animal', 犯人 *fann.ren*

---

[15]To be distinguished from *Meeiren* BF 'America person,—an American', which is the L form for *Meei.gworen*. Both *Meeiren* and *Meei.gworen* are N-N compounds rather than A-N compounds.

'offending person,—criminal, convict', 飛船 *feichwan* 'flying boat,—blimp, dirigible', 飛馬 *feimaa* 'Pegasus', 飛鱼 *feiyu* 'flying fish', 观众 *guanjonq* BB 'beholding multitude,—spectators', 听众 *tingjonq* FB 'listening multitude,—audience', 教师 *jiawshy* FB 'teaching master,—instructor',[16] 教員 *jiaw₀yuan* FB 'teaching member,—instructor', 進欵 *jinnkoan* BF 'incoming fund,—income', 進項 *jinn.shianq* 'incoming item,—income', 开水 *kaishoei* 'boiling water', 来人 *lairen* 'come man, —messenger (who has come)', 流水 *lioushoei* 'flowing water', 牧童 *muhtorng* BB 'shepherd boy,—shepherd', 入欵 *ruhkoan* BF 'entering fund,—income', 学生 *shyue.sheng* 'learning (young) person,—student', 逃兵 *taurbing* 'escaped soldier,—deserter'.

(b) N which is V-ed.— 包車 *bauche* 'regularly hired vehicle,—carriage, taxi, etc., hired by the month', 包饭 *baufann* 'regular boarding meals', 包工 *baugong* 'contracted work', 包廂 *baushiang* FB 'engaged box,—box (in a theater)', 插畵 *chatwu* 'inserted illustrations (in a book or periodical)', 抽屉 *chou.tih*,~ *-.tiell* 'draw tier,—drawer', 摁扣儿 *ennkowl* 'press button,—snap button', 摁钉儿 *enndiengl* 'press nail,—thumbtack', 進步 *jinn-₀buh* FB 'advance steps,—progress' N or V, 賠欵 *peirkoan* 'indemnify fund,—indemnity', 劈柴 *pii.chair* BF (← 劈 *pi* 'split' + 柴火 *chair.huoo* 'fuel wood') 'kindling wood', 退步 *tuey₀buh* FB 'retreat step,—retrogression' N (less frequently used as V than *jinn-₀buh*), 貼边 *tiebian* 'attached border,—hem on dress', 存欵 *tswenkoan* 'deposited fund,—deposit', also as V-O phrase 'deposit money', 提琴 *tyichyn* 'held-by-the-hand stringed-instrument,—violin', 委員 *woei.yuan* BB 'delegated member,—committee member', 遺囑 *yijuu* 'left-behind enjoinment,—a will'. Verbs for cooking form V-N compounds with great versatility, as in 拌黄瓜 *bann-hwang.gua* 'mixed (with sauces) cucumber,—cucumber salad', 炒饭 *chao-fann* 'fried rice', 燉鸡 *duenn-ji* 'simmered chicken', 溌麵 *fa₀miann* 'raised dough', 醃肉 *ian-row* 'salted

---

[16]The term 教士 *jiaw.shyh* BB 'minister, preacher' is better to be immediate-analyzed as an N-N compound 'religion-scholar', rather than as 'teaching scholar'.

meat', 炸虾 *jar-shia* 'deep-fried shrimp', 蒸饭 *jeng-fann* 'steamed rice', 煎饼 *jian.biing* 'baked cake,—a very thin large pancake', 煎鸡子儿 *jian-jitzeel* 'fried eggs', 煮白薯 *juu-bairshuu* 'boiled sweet potatoes', 烙饼 *lawbiing* 'baked cake,—very thick, large unsweetened cake', 泡菜 *paw-tsay* 'steeped (in brine) vegetables (Szechwan style)', 烧饼 *shau.biing* 'baked cake,—hot biscuit with sesame seeds on top', 薰鱼 *shiunyu* 'fumigated fish,—smoked fish'.

(c) N with which one V's.— 補靪 *buu.ding* FB 'mending patch', 别针儿 *byejel* 'fastening needle,—pin', 唱本儿 *chanqbeel* 'singing booklet,—songbook', 炒锅 *chaoguo* 'frying pan', 请帖 *chiingtiee* FB 'invitation card', 敦布 *duenbuh* 'stomping cloth, —mop', 渡船 *duhchwan* 'ferryboat', 搌布 *jaan.buh* BF 'mopping cloth,—kitchen cloth', 斩刀 *jandau* ( ← *jann-*) 'chopping knife', 蒸笼 *jenglong* FB 'steaming cage,—steamer (for food)', 蒸屉 *jengtih* FB 'steaming tier,—steamer (for food)', 夹钳 *jiachyan* FB 'pinching pliers,—pliers', 夹镊子 *jianiehtz* 'pincers, forceps', 住宅 *juhjair* FB 'living residence,—residence', 支票 *jypiaw* 'cashing ticket,—cheque', 烙铁 *law.tiee* 'branding iron,—flatiron', 跑道 *paodaw* (translation borrowing for) 'runway', 跑鞋 *paoshye* 'running shoes,—track shoes', 片刀 *pianndau* 'slicing knife', 聘书 *pinnshu* 'appointment letter', 玩意儿 *wanyell* BB 'playing idea, —toy', 卧車 *wohche* BF 'sleeping car', 熨斗 *yunn.doou* BF 'ironing pot,—hot iron'.

(d) N related to V in a general way. 把根 *baagen* 'take-hold root,—inch-length bunch of hair held at the base with yarn before winding the rest of the hair to form a woman's hairdo', 唱针 *chanqjen* 'singing needle,—phonograph needle', 唱片(儿) *chanqpiann*~*-pial* (sic) 'singing plate,—phonograph record', 防线 *farngshiann* 'defense line', 飞机 *feiji* FB 'flying machine,—airplane', 来由 *laiyou* FB 'reason for coming', 漏洞 *lowdonq* 'leaking hole,—loophole', 拼法 $pin_o faa$ FB 'spelling method,—spelling, orthography, 笑话 $shiaw_o huah$ 'laughing word,—joke', also 'laugh at', 收条 *shoutyau* FB 'receiving slip,—receipt', 跳棋 *tiawchyi* 'skipping chess,—Chinese checkers'.

*6.4.3. Compounds with Determinatives and Measures*

(1) D-M Compounds. A determinative (D) and a measure normally make a compound with unlimited versatility and form a transient word of no lexical import. Thus, out of the list of demonstratives (d) and numerals [sec. 7.8 (1 and 3)], and the list of measures (table 16), almost any combination will form a possible compound,[17] as 那个 *neyg* 'that (one)' (d-M), 三条 *san-tyau* 'three strips' (n-M), 几年 *jii-nian* 'how many years' or 'several years'. Of the demonstratives, 各 *geh* ( < *kâk*) 'each, the various' occurs only in 个人 *geh-ren* 'each person' [homophonous with 各人 *geh-ren* (< *kâ-ńźiĕn*) 'individual person'], 各处 *geh-chuh* 'various places', 各种 *geh-joong*, 各樣 *geh-yanq* 'various kinds', 各國 *geh-gwo* 'various countries', and so on, but is not applicable to units of measure, for example, 每寸 *meei-tsuenn* 'each inch', not °*geh-tsuenn*. The wenyan form 诸 *ju* 'the various' is extremely restricted and occurs only in a few forms like 诸位 *juwey* 'the various gentlemen and/or ladies,—ladies and gentlemen' and 诸公 *jugong* 'you gentlemen', 诸君 *jujiun* 'ladies and gentlemen', 诸侯 *juhour* '(ancient) feudal lords', 诸等 *judeeng* 'the various categories,—weights and measures, as a branch of school arithmetic'. Of the numerals, 二 *ell* 'two' is rarely used with a foreign measure or a polysyllabic measure, whereas the synonymous 两 *leang* can be used for all measures, as 二斤 *ell-jin* ~ 两斤 *leang-jin* 'two catties' but 两磅 *leang-banq* '2 lbs.' and not °*ell-banq*, 两加侖 *leang-jialuen* 'two gallons', and not °*ell-jialuen*.[18] This limitation does not apply to compound numerals ending in *ell*,

---

[17]The versatility would be much more limited if, besides demonstratives and numerals, determinatives were to include "specific determinatives" like 上 *shanq* 'top', 前 *chyan* 'front', 裡 *lii* 'inside', and so on, which we treat as localizers (sec. 7.10). See Simon, Subst Complexes, 335.

[18]A practice among the new generation is to write the character 二, where the writer and reader will obviously read *leang*, in order to save strokes in the character 两. This may prove to be the initial stage for the morpheme *leang* to acquire an alternate and new graph, but it is not yet general usage outside the context of writing familiar letters.

where the alternative form *leang* does not occur, as:　十二先令 *shyr'ell shianling* 'twelve shillings'.

(1.1) Lexical and Exocentric D-M Compounds. Out of the thousands of possible transient words in the form of D-M compounds, only a small handful have lexical meanings and/or other than nominal functions. This is especially so with demonstratives (d-M), of which the following are the only lexical cases.

The d-M compound 这会儿 *jeh.hoel*, besides the synthesizable meaning[19] of 'this moment' also means 'this place, here'. In the latter sense there is an alternate form 这□儿 *jeh.hel*. There is also a Peiping localism 这点儿 *jey.deal* for 'here' or 'now' in addition to the general usage in which *jey.deal* means 'this (small) amount'.[20] The d-M compound 这个 *jeyg* 'this (one)', with neutral tone on both syllables *.je.ge* in repeated form is a common filler during hesitation. The far-pointing d-M compound 那个 *neyg* 'that (one)' is used in a similar way, but keeps more of its demonstrative function and is thus not as fully exocentric as *.je.ge*. For example, in: 你认得不认得那个，ᵛ ₂,ᵛ ₂, 老爱说话的那个人? *Nii renn.de bu renn.de neyg, neyg, neyg, lao ay shuo-huah de neyg ren?* 'Do you know the, the, the, the man who loves to talk all the time?', *neyg* is still the usual d-M compound, though its repetition expresses hesitation. On the other hand, in 我想你啊，你简直是这个——，这个ᵛ ₂ᵛ ₂——，简直不讲理! *Woo sheang nii .a, nii jeanjyr sh .je.ge—, .je-ge.je.ge.je.ge—, jeanjyr bu jeanglii!* 'I think you, you are simply uh—, uh uh uh—, simply unreasonable!', *.je.ge* is no more than a sound of hesitation and can be followed by a verb, an adjective, or anything else. The d-M compound 那个 *nahg*, with the full vowel *a* and full tone on *nah*, is hardly ever used in the general

---

[19]All except one or two of the special d-M compounds cited here retain their synthesizable meanings; the special meanings are acquired as additions rather than displacements.

---

[20]The form *jey.deal* may be derived from 这地儿 *jey-diell ← jey-dih-l* 'this place', which is phonetically identical with *jey.deal* with its neutral tone and midvowel. Since this is never written in characters, there is no usage to help in deciding what the derivation is.

sense of 'that', for which *neyg* ( ~ ₀*nehg*) is the usual form. Instead, *nahg* (less frequently *neyg*, too) is used mostly as a substitute for adjectives which for some reason the speaker does not want to state explicitly, as: 我父親的脾气有时候儿很那个。*Woo fuh.chin de pyi.chih yeou.shyr.howl heen nahg.* 'My father's temper is sometimes quite that way.' (avoiding saying 坏 *huay* 'bad'). In this usage it is exocentrically an adjective. As a substantive, the object of the verb 幹 *gann* 'does' or 做 *tzuoh* 'does' is even more specialized. While 很那个 *heen nahg* means 'quite (unmentioned adjective)', 幹那个 *gann nahg* means 'do that (unmentionable thing)' and thus serves as a euphemism for doing whatever cannot be said in polite company. This is the only case where the zero-grade meaning of a D-M compound is not available. As a result, in order to say 'do that' a pro-verb, *nemme* [sec. 7.12(3)] is usually preferred, as in: 我没知道你要那么。*Woo mei jy.daw nii yaw nemme.* 'I didn't know you wanted to do that.' Similarly, 这么 *tzemme* 'thus; do this' and 怎么? *tzeeme?* 'how; do what?'. In the latter cases, the V-dM form is still available: 做这个 *tzuoh jehg* 'do this' and 做什么? *tzuoh sherme?* 'do what?'

Lexical and exocentric D-M compounds of the n-M (numeral-measure) type are slightly more numerous than those of the d-M type. 三角儿 *sanjeau(l)* 'triangle' is a lexical compound, as contrasted with the phrases 三个犄角儿 *san g jijeaul* 'three corners' and 三个角度 *san g jyue₀duh* 'three angles'. The hyperbole *banntian* 'half a day' means any time longer than expected, from a few seconds to, in children's language, days and weeks. For example, 我问了你的话，你怎么半天不回答我？ *Woo wenn nii de huah, nii tzeem banntian bu hweidar woo?* 'I asked you a question, how come you don't answer me?' (perhaps for 5 seconds). 咱们半天没看電影儿了. *Tzarm banntian mei kann diannyeengl le.* 'We haven't been to a movie for a long time.' As adverbs of degree there are *shyrfen* 'ten tenths,—100 per cent', as in 十分願意 *shyrfen yuann₀yih* '100 per cent willing'; *ibae ellshyrsyhg* '124 times (or per cent)' (as a hyperbole), as in 一百二十四个相信他 *ibae'ellshyrsyhg shiangshinn ta* 'believes him 124%'; *n-cherng* 'n tenths', as 九成新 *jeoucherng shin* 'nine-tenths new'. The n-M compounds *ideal* 'a dot,—a little' and *ihoel* 'a moment' should be considered synthesizable. They are not adverbs but express degree by being a cognate object of adjectives or verbs, as 大一点儿 *dah ideal* 'large by a little,—larger', 等一会儿 *deeng ihoel* 'wait a while'.

The adverb *chianwann* 'by all means' is not a subordinative compound but a coordinative compound, as in 你千万别去! *Nii chianwann bye chiuh!* 'A thousand times and ten thousand times don't go there.', rather than '1,000 × 10,000 don't go there.' The compound *wann'i* 'one chance in ten thousand,—if by any chance' is asyntactic, being abbreviated from 一万分之一 *iwann-fenn jy i*.

While an ordinal number with the prefix *dih-* is a free word and can form a transient word with any measure, such as 第二本 *dih'ell-been* 'second volume', 第三块 *dihsan-kuay* 'third piece', 第十年 *dihshyr-nian* 'tenth year', and so on, unprefixed numerals taken in the ordinal sense form n-M compounds with great restriction. The twelve months of the year are named 一月 *I.yueh* (~ 正月 *Jeng.yueh*), 二月 *Ell.yueh*, ... 十二月 *Shyr 'ell.yueh*. The side streets in Peiping are often named 头条胡同, 二条胡同 *Tourtyau .Hu.tung, Ell-tyau .Hu.tung*, and so on, but are usually abbreviated to *Ityau, Elltyau*, and so on, especially when modified by the name of the section of the city. The n-M compound 二回 *ell.hwei* 'second time,—next time,—perchance', as in: 二回他不信你了。 *Ell.hwei ta bu shinn nii le.* 'Maybe he won't believe you any more.', functions exocentrically as a conjunction and not like *dih'ell-hwei* 'second time', which is a nominal expression, like other D-M compounds. On the whole, compounds with numerals in the ordinal sense are restricted to those which are recognized in the lexicon and cannot be made up at will.

The adverb 一块儿 *ikuall* 'together' should be analyzed as *i-kuay* 'one piece' and '-l' suffix to change the nominal to an adverbial expression. It is therefore a decompound (sec. 6.7.4 below), and no longer a compound. It is equivalent in function and meaning to the 一道 *ie'daw* 'one way,—together' of the Wu dialects, where it is a compound, since its structure is not complicated by the addition of a suffix.

(1.2) nM-N Compounds. The nM-N construction is normally a phrase, consisting of the n-M (a species of D-M) compound modifying a noun, as 几斤肉 *jii-jin row* 'a few catties of meat', 两桌菜 *leang-juo tsay* 'two tables of dinner', 四口井 *syh-koou jiing* 'four wells', and so on. In a relatively small number of cases, though much more numerous than cases of n-M cited above under (1.1), the result is a compound noun and is thus capable of taking another D-M in front of it. For example, 一口钟 *i-koou jong* 'a (large) bell' can be taken literally as a phrase, where *koou* is the usual (old-fashioned) classifier for *jong* '(large) bell', but *ikooujong* 'a-large-bell (-shaped garment),—cape' is a compound noun since it, in its turn, takes the classifier for garments *jiann*, so that one has to say 一件一口钟 *i-jiann ikooujong* for 'a cape'. Similarly, in (1) 这张桌子只有三条腿 *Jey-jang juotz jyy yeou san-tyau toei.* 'This table has only three legs.', and (2) *Jey-jang juotz sh g san-tyau toei de.* 'This table is one with three legs.', *san-tyau toei* is a phrase. But in (3) *Jey-jang juotz sh g (~ ig) santyautoei.* 'This table is a three-leg(ger).', *santyautoei* is a compound, since it takes *ig* or the abbreviated *g* for *its* D-M modifier. The sentence (4) *Jey-jang juotz san + tyau + toei.* or *Jey-jang juotz sh san + tyau + toei.* is ambivalent in structure, since a nominal predicate or complement to *sh* can be either a phrase or a single noun (without a preceding D-M modifier). Probably taking sentence 4 as containing a phrase *san-tyau toei* is the better analysis. Other examples are *ityaulong* 'one dragon,—three suits 1-2-3, 4-5-6, and 7-8-9 in mahjong', as in 他胡了两个一条龙。 *Ta hwu.le leangg ityaulong.* 'He won two onedragons.' Titles of books, poems, songs, and other works, whatever the original grammatical structure, function as nouns, and the form nM-N is a very common one, as 十杯酒 *Shyrbei Jeou* 'Ten Cups of Wine' (a popular ballad), 八匹马! *Bapi Maa!* 'Eight Horses!' (formula for calling the number eight in the finger-guessing game), 十面埋伏 *Shyrmiann Mai-*

*.fwu* 'Ten Sides of Ambuscade' (name of a piece for the pipa).

Ordinal numbers in nM-N compounds are rare. One example is 二把刀 *ellbaa-dau* 'number two knife,—one who handles the number two knife,—an assistant chef'.

The great majority of nM-N combinations, however, are non-lexical phrases which neither have special meanings nor function as single words.

(2) n-N Compounds. The form n-N is of rather limited productivity. When N is bound, which happens more often than not, the nominal nature is of course to be established indirectly, as we judge the form class of other bound forms. Thus, in 八仙 *Bashian* 'the Eight Immortals', *shian* is $N_B$ because it is coordinate with 神 *shern* F 'spiritual being, a god' in *shern.shian* 'gods and immortals,—gods', because it is the object in the V-O compound 成仙 *cherng-shian* 'become an immortal', because it is a noun in L, and, last and least, because it means 'an immortal'. 八仙 *Bashian* is a compound formally, because it is BB, and lexically, because *Bashian* is the group of eight specific immortals, while the phrase *bag shian₀ren* is applicable to '(any) eight immortals'. In general, n-N compounds, whether n is a cardinal or an ordinal number, have to do with various numerical traditions and are therefore lexical in nature. Further examples are: 三朝 *sanjau* 'third morning (of the birth of child)' ( 做三朝 *tzuoh sanjau* 'celebrate the third morning'), 五金 *wuujin* 'the (traditional) five metals' (vs. 五樣金属 *wu-yanq jinshuu* '(any) five kinds of metals'), 一品, 二品, 三品 ... 九品 *ipiin, ellpin, sanpiin, ... jeoupiin* 'first rank, second rank, third rank, ... ninth rank (of officials under the dynasties)', 一月, 二月, ... 十二月 *I.yueh, Ell.yueh ... Shyr'ell.yueh* 'January, February, ... December' (cited above under D-M, since *yueh* functions either as M as in 下月 *shiah₀yueh* 'next month' or as N as 这个月 *jeyg yueh* 'this month').

nN-N Compounds. Unlike nM-N forms, nN-N forms do not form phrases and the compounds they form are lexical in nature. Examples are: 八仙桌 *bashian-juo* 'eight-immortals table,— table seating eight', 百葉窗 *baeyeh-chuang* 'hundred-leaf win-

dow,—Venetian blind', 五金店 *wuujin-diann* 'five-metals store,
—hardware store', 四眼儿狗 *syhyeal-goou* 'four-eyed dog,—dog
with two spots over the eyes' 三角架 *sanjeau-jiah* 'three-foot
frame,—tripod', 三眼儿井 *sanyeal-jiing* 'three-holed well,—well
with three openings',[21] 三点儿水 *sandeal shoei* 'three-dot water'
(popular name for Radical 85 when it appears in the form " 氵 "),
两点儿水 *leangdeal shoei* (popular name for Radical 15 " 冫 ").
The last examples, in which *deal* 'dot' is a noun, should be distinguished from the nM-N phrase 一点儿水 *ideal shoei* 'a little
water', in which *deal* is a measure. Note that the M or V for
'drop' is *di*, as in 滴了三滴水 *dile san-di shoei* 'has dripped
three drops of water'.

(3) N-n Compounds. Subordinative compounds with a numeral as centers are not very productive. There are the abbreviated forms *dah'i* for 大学一年 *dahshyue inian* 'college first
year,—freshman', *chusan* for 初中三年 *chujong sannian*
'junior high third year', the names of the days of the week 礼拜
一 *Liibay'i* 'week-one,—Monday', 礼拜二 *Liibay'ell* 'Tuesday',
... 礼拜六 *Liibayliow* 'Saturday' and their secular synonyms
星期一，星期二，... 星期六 *Shingchi'i, Shingchi'ell, ... Shingchiliow*. In the game of 天九 *Tianjeou* played with dominoes,
combinations of two pieces have various powers, named 天九
*Tianjeou* 'Heaven-nine' (whence the name of the game 打天九
*daa Tianjeou*), 地八 *Dihba* 'Earth-eight', and so on. In the game
of chance with dominoes called 推牌九 *Tuei Pairjeou*, one form
of scoring consists of taking the sum of a drawing of two pieces
minus 10, the worst hand being 10, which counts as zero under
the name of 憋十 *Bieshyr* 'Stopped-up Ten'. We have noted that
a monosyllabic surname is not free. When it is not prefixed by
老 *Lao-* or compounded with the given name, it can be com-

---

[21]To be distinguished from 三眼井儿 *Sanyean Jieengl* '(name of) street
where there is such a well', which is not a compound, but a decompound,
with *-l* suffixed to *sanyean-jiing*, that is, the street is a 'three-weller'. In
*Mand Prim*, 110, item 333, the first edition had the common-noun form and
the second edition had the proper-noun form, to agree with the recording.

pounded with a numeral indicating rank among brothers, so that
the third brother of the Jangs can be familiarly called (by those
outside the family) 張三 *Jang San.* Similarly 李四 *Lii Syh,* 王
二 *Wang Ell.* Conceivably the eighth brother of the Chiou ( 丘 )
family may be called 丘八 *Chiou Ba,* which, however, is pre-
ëmpted by the slang 丘八 *chiouba* 'GI', since the character 兵 for
*bing* 'soldier' is made up of *chiou* on top and *ba* at the bottom.

(4) N-M Compounds. A noun followed by its individual
classifier can usually form a collective noun or a noun for the
quality of the collection. Thus, from 一張纸 *i-jang jyy* 'a sheet
of paper', there is *jyy$_0$jang* 'stationery'. Similarly, 钟点 *jongdean*
'hours (as points of time), schedule', 布疋 *buhpii* 'yard goods',
車辆 *che.liang* 'vehicles (collectively)', 馬匹 *maapi* 'horses
(collectively)', 书本(儿) *shubeen, -l* 'books and things', 花朵
*huaduoo* 'florification', 船隻 *chwanjy* 'fleet of ships', 灯盏 *deng-
$_0$jaan* 'illumination, lighting equipment'. Not every noun and its
classifier form such a compound; for example, there is 信件
*shinnjiann* 'letters, correspondence, mail' but not °*shinnfeng* for
'letters (collectively)' although there is a compound *shinnfeng(l)*
'letter sealer,—envelope' where *feng* does not enter as a classifier
at the immediate compounding stage. Compounds with units of
measure such as      銀兩     *yn$_0$leang* 'quantity ( ~ -ies) of silver'
are rare.

(5) M-N Compounds. The succession of M and N does not
normally form a compound. In constructions like 買斤肉 *mae
jin row* 'buy a catty of meat' and 唱个歌儿 *chanq g ge'l* 'sing a
song', *jin* is short for *i-jin* and *g* is short for *ig*,[22] and *jin row* or

---

[22]This is limited to M + N as objects. In Cantonese, which also had this
M used as an abbreviated form of D-M, it also appears in the subject position, and, since the subject position has definite reference, the M translates
also into 'the' instead of 'a'. Thus, we have:

For:         'Call a man'.                              'The man won't come'.
Cant: 叫个人 . *Kiw koh yan.* 个人唔肯嚟. *Koh yan muxag lai.*
Mand: 叫个人. *Jiaw g ren.*    人不肯来。—*Ren bukeen lai.*

For definite reference Mandarin cannot use the classifier *g* for 'the', but has
to use demonstrative *nah, neh, neyg,* or zero, with definite reference implied
by position.

*g ge'l* does not form a compound. In the case of 一点钟 *i-dean jong* 'one o'clock', 几点钟 *jii-dean jong* 'what o'clock', and so on, it is no different from the usual DM-N construction, with *i-dean* in construction with *jong*, rather than *i* with *dean jong*, even though *dean jong* can be equated in translation with 'o-clock', which is itself a somewhat peculiar kind of IC. In one case, however, that of the MN 年级 *nianjyi* 'school grade (standing)', there is good syntactical justification for treating it as a compound. Thus, one can not only speak of a schoolboy as being in 一年级 *i-nian jyi* 'first-year grade', and so on, just like *i-dean jong*, but can also say: 他的年级很高。*Tade nianjyi heen gau.* 'His standing (e.g., junior, senior) is very high.', with *nianjyi* as a noun.

### 6.4.4. *Compounds with Localizers*

(1) N-L Compounds. Compounds formed from a noun and a localizer are not as numerous lexically as N-N compounds, since localizers form a listable class but localizers contain certain cases of unlimited versatility. For this reason localizers are often regarded as forming a part of speech as postpositions. We shall give the list of localizers in chapter 7 (sec. 7.10) and limit our discussion here to the ways in which a noun can be compounded with a localizer.

All monosyllabic localizers are bound: 上 *shanq* 'up', 下 *shiah* 'down', 裡 *lii* 'inside', 内 *ney* 'inside', 外 *way* 'outside', 前 *chyan* 'front, before', 後 *how* 'back, after', 左 *tzuoo* 'left', 右 *yow* 'right', 中 *jong* 'middle', 东 *Dong* 'East', 南 *Nan* 'South', 西 *Shi* 'West', 北 *Beei* 'North'. With a noun as attribute and one of the localizers as center, the result is a nominal compound and a place (or time) word, that is, a word which can be direct object of the verbs 在 *tzay* 'to be at', and 到 *daw* 'go to, arrive at'. For example, 屋裡 *u.lii* 'room('s) inside,—the inside of the room,—in the room' is a nominal compound which can be subject or object, as in 屋裡太冷。*U.lii tay leeng.* 'The room's inside is too cold,—it's too cold in the room.', 走到屋裡 *tzoou daw u.lii* 'walk to the room's inside,—walk into the room'. With the understanding that N-L compounds are nominal in nature, we shall dispense with the literal translation in the examples to be cited and give the semantic equivalent in prepositional phrases.

Note that the versatility of *shanq* and *lii* is almost unlimited, while their respective antonyms *shiah* and *way*, and the synonym of *lii*, namely *ney*, are not nearly as versatile. Thus, we have 街上 *jie.shang* 'on the street', 门上 *men.shanq* 'on the door', 身上 *shen.shanq* 'on the person', 心上 *shin.shanq* 'on one's mind' etc. etc.,[23] while compounds with *shiah* are always lexical and cannot be made up at will, as in 天下 *tianshiah* 'under heaven,—the world', 舍下 *shehshiah* 'under my abode,—my (humble) home', 里下 *hei.shiah* 'under darkness,—evening, night', 鄉下 *shiang-.shiah* '(down) in the country, countryside', but no ° 海下 °*hae-shiah* for 'under the sea' or ° 心下 °*shinshiah*, which conceivably might be but is not the actual translation-borrowing form for 'the subconscious', for which the word is 意识下 *yihshyhshiah*, although a more common and literal translation is *shiahyihshyh*. With *lii*, there are 家裡 *jia.lii* 'in the home', 字典裡 *tzyhdean-.lii* 'in the dictionary', 鋪子裡 *puhtz.lii* 'in the store (shop)', 碗裡 *woan.lii* 'inside the bowl', 國裡 *gwo.lii* 'in the country (nation)', 心裡 *shin.lii* 'in the mind', etc., etc.; but with *way*, there are only 海外 *haeway* 'outside the seas,—overseas', 城外 *cherng-way* 'outside the city', 郊外 *jiauway* 'outside the city limits,—suburbs', 例外 *lihway* 'outside the (regular) examples,—exception', 此外 *tsyyway* 'outside of this (or these)', and a few other compounds. There is 國內 *gwoney* 'within the country (not international)' but no ° 屋外 °*uway* or ° 屋子外 °*utzway* for 'outside the room', or ° 碗外 °*woanway* for 'outside the bowl', or ° 茶壺外 °*charhwuway* for 'outside the teapot' or ° 此內 °*tsyyney* for 'within this (or these)'. In this respect *ney* 'inside' is more like *way* than like *lii*.

When we say that *shanq* and *lii* are versatile and form almost without restriction transient words with attributive nouns, it does

---

[23]Note, however, that 皇上 *hwang.shanq* BB 'the emperor' is not an N-L compound, but a coordinate compound of synonyms, 上 *shanq* being an old term for 'the emperor', as often used in the dynastic histories.

not imply conversely that all N-L compounds with *shanq* and *lii* are transient and synthesizable. A considerable proportion of them, comparable in absolute numbers to those of compounds with *shiah* and *way* and *ney*, have lexical meanings, as in 馬上 *maa$_o$shanq* 'on horse,—at once, right away', also lit. 'on horseback' as in 騎在馬上 *chyi tzay maa.shanq* 'rides astride the horse', 府上 *fuu.shanq* 'on (your) mansion,—your home; your family', 堂上 *tarngshanq* 'up in the hall,—the mother' (usually in the honorific sense of 'your mother'), which can be compared with 閣下 *gershiah* 'under your studio,—you (honorif.)', 陛下 *bihshiah* 'under the imperial steps,—Your (or His∼Her) Majesty'. With *lii*, there are very few lexical compounds. The noun 夜裡 *yeh.lii* 'in the night, nighttime' is practically synthesizable, since the N-L compound is already nominal in function. Similarly, 日 裡 *ryh.lii* 'in the day, daytime'.

When these localizers are used in extended and abstract senses, as for example when *.shanq* is used as 'with respect to', then it is simpler to regard this as an additional meaning of the localizer than to take all the compounds formed with it as lexical compounds. For example, instead of entering in a dictionary entries like 政治上 *jenqjyh.shanq* 'with regard to politics, politically', 経済上 *jingjih.shanq* 'with regard to economics, economically', 國防上 *gwofarng.shanq* 'with regard to national defense', 歷史上 *lihshyy.shanq* 'historically', 理論上 *liiluenn-.shanq* 'theoretically', 実際上 *shyrjih.shanq* 'practically', 表面 上 *beaumiann.shanq* 'superficially', 方法上 *fangfaa.shanq* 'methodologically', and so on without end, it will be simpler to give as one of the meanings of the localizer *shanq* 'with regard to, with respect to, -ically' and illustrate its use with a few examples. From the Chinese point of view this extended but regular use of *shanq* is quite different from the true lexical compounds like *mae$_o$shanq* 'at once' and *fuu.shanq* 'your family'.

When a localizer is used in an extended, abstract sense, there is less certainty which preposition it will translate into in a language with prepositions such as English. Thus, in 书裡的 故事 *shu.lii de guh.shyh* 'the stories in the book', *lii* corresponds to 'in', as expected, but in 书上说的 *shu.shanq shuo de* 'what is said in the book', *shanq* is also translated as 'in'. Similarly, 报上 *baw.shanq* 'in the newspaper', 天上 *tian.shanq* 'in the sky', 世界上 *shyh.jieh.shanq* 'in the world', with the idea of 'on the surface of the earth (whether round or flat)', but 世间 *shyhjian* 'among the world (of people and things),—in the world', which is a Buddhistic term for the mundane world.

For examples of the remaining localizers mentioned above, we have 眼前 *yeanchyan*~ 目前 *muhchyan* BB 'before the eyes, now, in the near future', 背後 *beyhow* FB 'behind the back, in the rear', 饭後 *fannhow* 'after a meal', 江左 *Jiangtzuoo* 'left bank of the (Yangtze) River,—old name for lower left bank of the Yangtze', (N-L compounds with 右 *-yow* 'right' are rare), 关中 *Guanjong* 'In the Harnguu Pass ( 函谷关 ),—the Northwest, Shensi', 夢中 *menqjong* (more commonly, *menq.lii.tou*) 'in the dream', 路东, 路南 *luhdong, luhnan*, etc. 'east, south, ... side of the road' (in identifying locations of houses on a street), 山东 *Shan$_o$dong* 'Mountain East,—Shantung', 河南 *Her$_o$nan* '(Yellow) River South,—Honan', 江西 *Jiang$_o$shi* '(Yangtze) River West,—Kiangsi', 湖北 *Hwubeei* '(Tungting) Lake North,—Hupeh'.

(2) d-L Compounds. The demonstratives 这 *jeh* 'this', 那 *nah* 'that', and 哪 *naa* 'which?' take the localizer *-lii* and form place words 这裡 *jeh.lii* 'this place,—here', 那裡 *nah.lii* 'that place,— there' and 哪裡 *naa.lii* 'what place,—where?' These are somewhat formal in style. In everyday speech the localizer *lii* is weakened to the nonsyllabic suffix *-l* (pronounced [ɹ] or coloring the preceding vowel with retroflexion) with the resulting forms 这儿 *jell* 'here', 那儿 *nall* 'there' and *naal* 'where?' Since the final *-el* has a very open vowel in the 3rd and 4th Tones, analogical formations are facilitated, resulting in alternate forms *jell*~*jall* and *nall* ~*nell*. *Neel*, however, is rare.

(3) Compounds with Free Place Words as Centers. Noting the lack of symmetry between *shanq* and *shiah* and between *lii* and *way*, one might fairly ask how then does one say those things for which the supposed forms °*haeshiah* 'under the sea' °*woanway* 'outside the bowl', etc., do not exist? The answer is that these

things can be said by changing the localizers into free place words through the addition of suffixes or, in a few cases, through some other change, resulting in a dissyllabic word. Thus, corresponding to bound localizers *shiah* and *way*, there are the place words 底下 *dii.shiah*[24] and 外头 *way.tou*, respectively, so that one can say 海底下 *hae-dii.shiah* 'under the sea' and 碗外头 *woan-way.tou* 'outside the bowl'. If the attribute is a free noun, then it is also possible to use the particle *de* and form phrases, as *hae de dii.shiah* and *woan de way.tou*. As usual, the phrase form is more likely to be taken in a literal sense and the compound apt to be taken in extended senses. For example, 墙上(头) *chyang-.shanq* or *chyang.shanq.tou* 'on the wall', but *chyang de shanq.tou* 'above the wall'; 山裡(头) *shan.lii* or *shan.lii.tou* 'in the mountains, among the hills', but *shan de lii.tou* 'further in behind the mountains; inside the (rocks of the) mountains', 雨前 *yeuchyan* 'before the rain,—(brand of) green tea (picked before the spring rains)', but *shiah-yeu de chyan.tou* or, more usually, *shiah-yeu yiichyan* 'before it rains', 面子上(头) *mianntz.shanq (.tou)* 'with regard to face (courtesy, protocol, etc.),—on the face of it', but *mianntz de shanq.tou* 'on the upper facing', as in 你行被窝的时候儿，别在面子的上头(～面儿上)露出針脚来. *Nii harng bey.uo de shyr.howl, bye tzay mianntz de shanq-.tou (～ miall.shanq) low.chu jen.jeau .lai.* 'When you sew lines in the quilt (to keep the wadding from shifting), do not let the stitches show on the facing.' The localizer *jong* 'middle' is rather restricted, as compared with *shanq* and *lii*. The corresponding free place words 中间儿 *jongjial(l)*, 当间儿 *dangjiall*, and 当中 *dangjong* (in that order of frequency of occurrence) 'midst, among, between' can be compounded or form a phrase with any noun, as 屋子中间儿 *utz-jongjiall* 'in the middle of the room', 两间屋子的中间儿 *leang-jian utz de jongjiall* 'between the two rooms'. When there is no specific direction of locality, a noun can be changed into a place word by being com-

---

[24] 下头 *Shiah.tou* is rare in Mandarin. In the Wu dialects, however, *shiah.tou* (in their cognate forms, e.g., *hhohdeu* in Shanghai) is the usual equivalent of *dii.shiah*. In Cantonese, it is 下便 *hahbinn*.

pounded with the general place word *nall*, with neutral tone. Thus, 墙 *chyang* 'wall': *chyang.nall* 'where the wall is', 他那儿 *ta.nall* 'where he is,—*chez lui*'. The place word *jell* is not so used except after *woo*, *woomen*, and *tzarmen*, as in 我这儿 *woo.jell* 'where I am,—*chez moi*'. The general place word is not used with place names, since they are already place words without the addition of *nall*. Thus, 生在中國 *sheng tzay Jong.gwo* 'was born in China', but not °*sheng tzay Jong.gwo.nall*. In 上海 那儿冬天也冷吗 ? *Shanqhae nall Dong.tian yee leeng ma?* 'Is it cold there in Shanghai in winter, too?' *Shanqhae nall* 'there in Shanghai' is not a compound, since a pause is possible in between.

Bound nouns are rarely compounded with free place words. Thus, *u.lii*, *utz.lii*, and *utz.lii.tou* 'in the room' and *utz de lii.tou* 'inside the room' are equally common, *u.lii.tou* is less common, *u* being bound and *lii.tou* being free, while °*u de lii.tou* does not occur.

(4) NL-N Compounds. While phrases of the form N-L *de* N can be formed without restriction, as 家裡的事情 *jia.lii de shyh.chyng* 'affairs in the home', 山上的樹 *shan.shanq de shuh* 'tree(s) on the hill(s)', NL-N compounds are limited to lexical cases. Examples are 鄉下人 *shiang.shiah₀ren* 'country people, peasants', 底下人 *dii.shiah.ren* 'down-below-man,—servant' (old term), 门外汉 *menway-hann* 'man outside the door,—amateurish person, dabbler in a subject he is ignorant about', 甕中鱉 *wenqjong-bie* 'turtle in the urn,—something (or someone) as good as caught', 府右街 *Fuuyow Jie* 'street to the right of the mansion,—street name in Peiping', 馬後炮 *maahowpaw* 'the cannon after the horse (is gone),—something that came too late'. The compounds 雪裡红 *sheue.lii-horng* 'red in snow,—mustard green' and 门前清 *menchyan-ching* 'clear in front of the door,—a game of mahjong completed without any laid-down pieces' are not NL-N compounds, but S-P compounds, with place-word subjects and adjectival predicates. The proverb 聰明人不吃眼前虧。 *Tsong.ming ren bu chy yeanchyan-kuei.* 'A clever man does not suffer an immediate wrong.' (of one who yields to duress out of

prudence), contains the V-O compound *chy-kuei* FB 'suffer damage' which is ionized with the N-L compound *yeanchyan* 'in front of the eyes' compounded with *kuei*. As examples of this form in wenyan, there are 空中楼阁 *kongjong-louger* 'castles in the air', 月下老人 *yuehshiah-laoren* 'the old man under the moon,—matchmaker'. The form 屋裡人 *ue'lii-nyen* 'the person in the home,—wife' is a term used in Soochow, among other dialects.

*6.4.5. Compounds with Verbal Centers*

(1) N-V Compounds. Subordinative N-V compounds may be a noun, a verb, or both, as: 步行 *buhshyng* BB 'footstep-go,—go on foot'; 槍斃 *chiangbih* FB 'gun-kill,—execute by gunfire'; 電燙 *dianntanq* 'electricity curling,—permanent wave; give or get a permanent'; 風行 *fengshyng* 'wind(like) goes,—to be all the fashion'; 鬼混 *goeihuenn* 'devil(like) vagabonding,—go around vagabonding'; 規定 *gueidinq* BF '(by) rule determines,—regulate, set rules for'; 口试 *kooushyh* BB 'mouth examine,—oral examination'; 利用 *lihyonq* BF '(for) profit to use,—make use of'; 路祭 *luhjih* FB '(on) road sacrifice,—offer sacrifices to a moving funeral procession'; 夢想 *menqsheang* 'dream think,—dream of, fancy'; 面谈 *mianntarn* BF 'face (to face) discuss'; 水泻 *shoeishieh* 'water(like) having diarrhea,—have diarrhea'; 手谈 *shooutarn* 'hand talk,—play mahjong' (originally 'play chess'); 醋溜 *tsuhlhiou* 'vinegar cooked'; 瓦解 *woajiee* 'tile(like) unfasten,—come apart' (lit. or fig.); 意料 *yihliaw* 'idea foresee,—foresee'; 油炸 *youjar* 'oil fry,—to deep fry'; 油印 *youyinn* 'oil print,—make multigraph of'. On the whole, the N-V form of subordinative compounds is only moderately productive.

(2) A-V Compounds. Adjectives do not normally modify verbs and when some of them do, it is simpler to treat them as cases of class overlap between adjective and adverb (cf. sec. 8.3.5). For example, there is 大书 *dah-shu* 'large book', 大字 *dah-tzyh* 'large character', 大事情 *dah shyh.ching* 'large affair', and so on, as A-N phrases, but also 大跑 *dah-pao* 'run with great strides', 大笑 *dah-shiaw* 'laugh heartily', 大吃 *dah-chy* 'eat voraciously', 大罵 *dah-mah* 'scold strongly', 大玩儿 *dah-wal* 'play in a big way,—have a great time', 大鬧 *dah-naw* 'make a great dis-

turbance', where *dah* is also an adverb with high versatility with respect to verbs it can modify. That this comes from the adjective-adverb class overlap of *dah* and not from a general possibility of any adjective modifying any verb is easily seen from the fact that the grammatically parallel antonym of *dah*, namely *sheau* 'small', can only be used as an adjective without restriction in 小书 *sheau-shu* 'small book', 小字 *sheau-tzyh* 'small (written) character', 小事情 *sheau shyh.chyng* 'small affair', but., but there is no °*sheau pao*,[25] °*sheau shiaw*, °*sheau chy* (but see below), °*sheau mah* or °*sheau naw*. In this respect 快 *kuay* 'fast' is like *dah* rather than *sheau*, since we have both 快車 *kuay-che* 'fast vehicle', 快嘴 *kuay-tzoei* 'fast mouth', 快刀 *kuay-dau* 'fast knife,—sharp knife', and so on, and 快来 *kuay-lai* '(please) come quickly; will soon come', 快说 *kuay-shuo* '(please) say it fast; will soon say', 快跑 *kuay-pao* 'run fast', and so on. On the other hand, 慢 *mann* 'slow' is somewhere between *dah* and *sheau* in that it is quite versatile as adjective, but somewhat limited as adverb, as in 慢車 *mann-che* 'slow vehicle', 慢人 *mann-ren* 'slow man' vs. 慢用 *mann-yonq* '(please) eat slowly' (polite expression used by one who finishes eating first), 慢走 *mann-tzoou* '(please) go slowly' (said to a departing guest).

In the case of compounding, however, not only *sheau* and *mann* but many other adjectives can enter in attributive position and, since their occurrence is mostly lexically limited, there is no point in considering them as having changed into adverbs.

Most of the A-V compounds cited below, unless marked otherwise, are themselves verbs: 轻看 *chingkann* 'look upon lightly,—look down upon'; 轻视 *chingshyh* FB 'look upon lightly,—look down upon' (cf. V-R compound *kannching* 'look upon as being light,—look down upon', but no °*shyhching*); 重視 *jonqshyh* FB 'look upon as weighty,—regard as important' [(°) *jonqkann* and V-R compound (°) *kannjonq* less common than the predicative V-R *kann .de jonq* 'regard as important']; 複写 *fuhshiee* 'duplicate write,—duplicating'; 複印 *fuhyinn* 'duplicate print,—multigraphing', N or V; 干炸 *ganjar* 'dry fry,—deep fry' A or V; 公布

---

[25]Except as a term in physical exercises, meaning a trot.

*gongbuh* 'public announce,—announce publicly'; 公举 *gongjeu* 'public elect,—elect on the part of a group'; 公转 *gongjoan* 'public turning,—revolution (of a planet)' N; 公立 *gonglih-* 'publicly established (schools, etc.)'; 公卖 *gongmay* 'publicly sell,—sold by the city, etc.'; 假哭 *jeaku* 'false cry,—pretend to cry'; 假笑 *jeashiaw* 'pretend to laugh, laugh insincerely'; 近視 *jinn.shyh* 'near-sighted'; 苦笑 *kuushiaw* 'bitter laugh,—laugh bitterly'; 凉拌 *liangbann* 'cold mixed (of salad, etc.)' A or V; 傻笑 *shaashiaw* 'silly laugh,—laugh sillily'; 傻吃 *shaachy* 'silly eat,—eat immoderately'; 生嗆 *shengchianq* 'raw steeped,—steeped in wine sauce without cooking (of crabs, shrimps, etc.)'; 小吃 *sheauchy* 'little eat,—refreshment; hors d'oeuvres' N; 小看 *sheaukann* 'small look upon,—despise'; 小说(儿) *sheaushuo(l)* 'small talk,—a novel' N; 速成 *suhcherng-* BF 'rapid completing,—rapid (of courses of study)'; 私立 *sylih-* 'private established,—private (of schools, etc.)'; 私卖 *symay* 'private sell,—sold privately; sold illegally'; 遠視 *yeuan$_o$shyh* FB, 'distant sight,—farsighted (of eyes)'. In the cases of *jinn.shyh* and *yeuan$_o$shyh*, an alternate analysis is to regard *shyh* as a bound noun 'view, vision', since there is 電視 *diannshyh* 'electric vision,—television'.

(3) H-V Compounds. A monosyllabic adverb is normally end-bound and, if it is of unlimited versatility, it should be considered a word (see sec. 3.8.2) and is separable from the verb it modifies, as in 还来 *hair lai* 'still come': 还这么早来 *hair tzemm tzao lai* 'still come so early', 先生 *shian sheng* 'to be born first; give birth to first (e.g., a girl)', 快到 *kuay daw* 'will soon arrive'. These are obviously phrases and not compounds. Other examples with adverbs of unlimited versatility are: 不跑 *bu pao* 'do not run', 更怕 *genq pah* 'fear all the more', 就是 *jiow sh* 'namely is', 睖要 *lenq yaw* 'insistingly wants,—insist on'.

Few H-V compounds consist of attributes which are exclusively adverbs, but a number of words function as adverbs by class overlap and should be so noted in dictionaries, since whether a given word does or does not function both as an adjective or as an adverb cannot be deduced from the behavior of its synonym or antonym. Thus, we saw that *dah* is adjective or adverb, with unlimited versatility, while *sheau* is only adjective and modifies verbs only in a few compounds, as in 小看 *sheaukann* 'belittle'; again, 硬 *yinq* 'hard' is either adjective or adverb with unlimited versatility, as in 硬麵包 *yinq miannbau* 'hard bread', 硬说 *yinq shuo* 'insist on saying, assert dogmatically', while the synonymous adverb 睖 *lenq* is not used as an adjective.[26] Other such pairs which are functionally asymmetrical in varying degrees are: 先 *shian* 'first beforehand' and 後 *how* 'after, afterwards', as in 先卖 *shian may* 'sell first', 先睡 *shian shuey* 'sleep first', and other H-V phrases without limit, but as adjective limited to a few compounds, as 先父 *shian-fuh* 'former father,—my deceased father' (limited to use in terms of indirect address of deceased senior relatives), 先天 *shiantian* 'first nature,—inherited physique, constitution', 先鋒 *shianfeng* 'front edge (of the sword),—vanguard'; *how* is also more versatile as adverb than as adjective, as in 後来 *how lai* 'come afterwards', 後请 *how chiing* 'invite after (someone else)', 後说 *how shuo* 'say after (someone else says or after saying something else)', and so on, but as adjective only in a few compounds such as 後门 *howmen* 'rear door', 後娘 *howniang* 'stepmother', 後事 *howshyh* 'after-affairs,—funeral affairs; sequel to a story', 後人 *howren* 'posterity'. Of the pair of synonyms 瞎 *shia* 'blindly, at random' and 胡 *hwu* 'at random', the former is of unlimited versatility as well as having a class overlap in that it also functions as an adjective 'blind', while *hwu* is always of limited versatility and modifies only a few verbs. Thus, *shia* occurs as adjective in 眼睛瞎了。*Yean.jing shiale.* 'The eyes have become blind.', 瞎貓碰着了个死老鼠。 *Shia-mhau penq.jaurle g syy-laoshuu.* 'A blind cat has come upon a dead mouse.' (of a lucky gain made without ability or effort), 你把绳子弄瞎了。 *Nii bae sherngtz nonq-shiale.* 'You have made the cord blind,—you have snarled up the cord', and as adverb in 瞎说 *shia shuo* 'talk at random,—talk nonsense', 瞎

---

[26]The adjective *lenq* as in 发睖 *fa-lenq* 'to be at a loss, absent-minded', although written with the same character 睖, is better regarded as an unrelated homograph-homophone of the adverb *lenq* 'insistently'.

鬧 *shia naw* 'make noise at random,—act unreasonably', 瞎聊 *shia liau* 'chat at random,—have a bull session', 瞎吃 *shia chy* 'eat immoderately' (usually applied to eating between meals), etc.; but 胡 *hwu* is limited to a few verbs as 胡说 *hwushuo* 'talk at random,—talk nonsense', 胡谒 *hwutzou* 'make up (stories) at random', 胡鬧 *hwunaw* 'make noises at random, act heedlessly', 胡搞 *hwugao* 'act heedlessly'. In compounds, 相 *shiang-* and 自 *tzyh-* should be regarded as adverbs, though originally these are not adverbs. Thus, 相对 *shiangduey* 'mutually facing or opposing,—relative (to)' ( 相对论 *shiangduey-luenn* 'theory of relativity'); 相好 *shianghao* 'mutually befriend,—make friends with; close friend'; 相信 *shiangshinn* 'mutually believe,—believe' (originally Wu dialect, now also borrowed into Mandarin); 相罵 *shiangmah* 'mutually scold,—quarrel' (Wu dial.); 相打 *shiangdaa* 'mutually fight,—fight' (Wu dial.). The literal translations given here as 'mutually' are based on the face-value immediate analysis from the point of view of modern Mandarin. In wenyan, *shiang* serves as a preverbal object pronoun, somewhat like French *me, te, le, se,* etc., so that some grammarians regard *shiang* as pronoun and others regard it as adverb.[27] The compounds beginning with *tzyh* 'self, auto-' correspond even more closely to *se* in French, as in 自治 *tzyhjyh* 'regulate oneself,—self-government, self-control' V or N; 自殺 *tzyhsha* 'kill self,—suicide, commit suicide'; 自由 *tzyhyou* 'follow self,—free(dom)'; 自修 *tzyhshiou* 'cultivate oneself,—(do) homework (of school)' V or N. Once *tzyh* is used as the modifier in a H-V compound, there is no further need for it to be limited to the function of preverbal object as in wenyan or like *se* in French, and thus it acquires the status of a versatile bound adverb or "prefix," translatable as 'auto-' as in 自動 *tzyhdonq* 'move of its own accord,—automatic; on one's own initiative'; 自转 *tzyhjoan* 'self-turning,—rotation (of planets)' (cf. 公转 *gongjoan* 'revolution' under A-V compounds, sec. 6.4.5).

Lexical H-V Compounds. While an adverb may be of un-

---

[27]See Leu, *LWJyi,* 相字偏指示例 ("On the Unidirectional Reference of the Word *Shiang*"), 36-45.

limited versatility, it is not precluded from forming compounds with bound verbs, and/or with verbs in the neutral tone, and/or forming exocentric and/or lexical compounds. Thus besides *shian sheng* 'was born first; gave birth to first', there is the exocentric compound 先生 *shian.sheng* 'one who was born first,—gentlemen; sir; you, sir; teacher; (medical) doctor; husband'; besides 先進來 (~ 去) *shian jinn.lai* (~-.*chiuh*) 'come (go) in first', there is the exocentric compound 先進 *shianjinn* FB 'first advanced,—senior generation (of scholars and the like)'; besides *how lai* 'come later', there is the compound adverb 後來 *how₀lai* 'afterwards', as in 後來就去了 *how.lai jiow chiuh .le* 'then went there afterwards'; besides *how sheng* 'was born later; gave birth to later', there is the compound 後生 *how.sheng* 'born later,—youthful'. With bound verbs there is 後悔 *how₀hoei* FB 'regret afterwards,—regret'; 後進 *howjinn* FB 'advanced afterwards,—later comer, new generation' ( ≠ the D-M compound *how-jinn* 'rear row (of rooms in a house with more than one row)'.

*6.4.6. Compounds with Adjectival Centers*

(1) N-A Compounds. N-A subordinative compounds are adjectives or, less frequently, nouns.

(1.1) As adjectives, N-A compounds usually have the meaning 'as A as N'. Most of the N-A adjectives are also limited in one way or another in their functions as adjectives, as illustrated below:

(a) Very few N-A adjectives are of the comparative type.[28] Examples are 膚淺 *fuchean* BF 'skin shallow,—superficial' and *tianjen* 'nature true,—natural, childlike'. One can say *tay fuchean* 'too superficial', and 比他更天真 *bii ta genq tianjen* 'still more natural than he'. None of the following types are comparative.

(b) A few N-A adjectives are limited to attributive positions with *de*, as 火急 *huoojyi* 'fire-urgent,—extremely urgent'; 豆心大

---

[28]Malmqvist, Sìch'uanese, 134, distinguishes between comparative and noncomparative adjectival expressions. The great majority of adjectives are of the former type.

*dowldah* 'bean-sized,—small'; 芝蔴大 *jy.madah* 'sesame seed-sized,—tiny, trivial'; 天大 *tiandah* 'sky-sized,—big'. Thus, one cannot say: °这事儿芝蔴大。 °*Jey shell jy.madah.*, nor: °*Jey shell sh jy.madah de.*, but only *Jeh jyy sh i-jiann jy.madah de shell.* 'This is only a trivial matter.' Since these are FF compounds, it is possible to expand this in the form of *shianq* N *nemm* A or *yeou* N *nemm* A 'as A as N', in which case the phrase can be in predicative position (as well as in attributive position), as in 那弹瓦只有豆儿那么大。 *Neh dannwan jyy yeou dowl nemm dah.* 'That bullet is only as big as a bean (or pea).' As usual, the expanded form is more likely taken in the literal sense.

(c) The majority of N-A adjectives can occur predicatively as well as attributively (with *de*), but, as usual, they are not comparative. Examples are: 氷冷(～ - 涼 ) *bingleeng* (*～ -liang*) 'ice-cold'; 漆黑 *chiuhhei* (← *chi-hei*) 'lacquer-black,—pitch-black; pitch-dark'; 粉碎 *feensuey* 'powder-smashed, — smashed to smithereens'; 碧綠 *bihliuh* 'jade-green,—very green'; 屁輕 *pihching* 'breakwind-light,—as light as air'; 神勇 *shernyeong* 'gods-brave,—heroically brave'; 雪白 *shiuehbair* (← *sheue-bair*) 'snow-white'; 鉄硬 *tieeyinq* 'iron-hard'; 賊亮 *tzeirlianq* 'thief-bright,—shiny'. These (except perhaps *shernyeong*) cannot take adverbs, or complements of degree such as 很 *heen* 'very', 太 *tay* 'too', 更 *genq* 'still more', ... 極了 ... *-jyile* 'awfully ...', ... 的很 ... *de heen* 'very ...', but can take modal adverbs, as in 简直粉碎 *jeanjyr feensuey* 'simply broken to smithereens'. When used with *tzemme* or *nemme* they are rather in apposition than modified as to degree, as in 那么雪白的臉 *nemm shiuehbair de lean* 'such a snow-white face as that' rather than 'so snow-white a face'. There are a few other noncomparative adjectives of similar construction, except that their first member is not nominal: 通红 *tonghorng* 'red through and through', 鲜红 *shianhorng* 'fresh red', 蒼黄 *tsanghwang* 'hoary yellow', 飛快 *feikuay* 'flying fast', 飛薄 *feibaur* 'flying thin'.

(1.2) N-A compounds resulting in nouns are of two types:

(a) A few N-A colors are named after the things having those colors. Since they are nouns, they cannot be used predicatively as adjectival predicates or take adverbs of degree. They are: 茶绿 *charliuh* 'tea-green,—pea green'; 墨绿 *mohliuh* 'ink-green,—a dark green'; 雪青 *sheueching* 'snow-blue,—a pale mauve'; 藤黄 *ternghwang* 'vine-yellow,—gamboge'; 天青 *tianching* 'sky-blue,— a very dark (almost black) red' (so-called to avoid the somber-sounding word 黑 *hei* 'black'); 月白 *yuehbair* 'moon-white,—a very pale blue'. The pigment for gamboge is called *terng.hwang* (with neutral tone). One can say 我顶爱墨绿. *Woo diing ay mohliuh.* 'I love dark green most.'; 这件衣裳是墨绿的. *Jey-jiann i.shang sh mohliuh de.* 'This dress is a dark green one.'; but not °这件衣裳墨绿. °*Jey-jiann i.shang mohliuh.* or ° 太墨绿了. °*tay mohliuh le.*

(b) The other type of nouns from N-A consist of the A-quality (incl. color) substances coming from the N-material. Much speculation has been entertained about the Cantonese names of dishes 鱼生 *yusheng* (Cant *yushang.*) 'fish raw' and 鱼滑 *yuhwa* (Cant *yuwaat°*) 'fish slippery' as to the possibility of structural borrowing from the southwestern border languages, where the usual word order is modified-modifier.[29]  However, one need not look far afield to find the same constructions in Mandarin.  Thus, besides documented but now obsolete forms like 蛤蜊生 *geelihsheng* 'clams raw' and 江蟯生 *jiangyausheng* 'scallops raw' (武林旧事 *Wuulin Jiowshyh*, fasc. 9), there are still many common forms, such as 鱼白 *yubair* 'fish('s) white,—fish sperm, as food'; 蛋白(儿) *dannbair* (~ *-barl*) 'egg-white,—albumen'; 蛋黄(儿) *dannhwangl* (~ *-hwang*) 'egg-yellow,—yolk'; 血青 *sheueching* 'blood clear,[30]—serum'; 糖稀 *tarngshi* 'sugar thin,

---

[29]For example, the late V. K. Ting (Ding Wenjiang), an extensively traveled geologist, offered this explanation.

[30]Although the usual character is 青, it probably means the clear (清) part of the blood.

—treacle, syrup'; 口红 *koouhorng* 'mouth red,—lipstick'. All these adjectival centers are therefore being used in the sense of the substances with the qualities represented by the respective adjectives: 'mouth red' means 'the red stuff used for the mouth', and so on. Thus the adjectives *sheng* 'raw', *shi* 'thin', and so on may be regarded as bound nouns meaning 'raw stuff', 'thin stuff', and so on. In the case of *bair* 'white (of an egg)', it is also a free noun, as in: 这个鸡蛋的白是生的。*Jeyg jidann de bair sh sheng de.* 'This egg's white is raw.' In N-A compounds with the suffix *-l*, the nominal nature of the second constituent is even more obvious, as in 饼干儿 *biinggal* 'cake-dry,—crackers, cookies', 豆付干儿 *dow.fugal* 'beancurd-dry,—(firm) pressed beancurd', 葡萄干儿 *pwu.taurgal* 'grapes-dry,—raisins', just as in the compound 白干儿 *bairgal* 'white-*sec*,—distilled sorghum', where *gal* is the nominal center. Thus we have here perfectly regular cases of the modifier-modified order in subordinative compounds, and there is no need to explain the known by the unknown by postulating borrowing from foreign grammar.

In the preceding examples a semantic distinction could be made between those in which the second element represents the first in a different state, as 肉鬆 *rowsong* 'meat (in a) loose (state)' or a part of the first thing, as 蛋黄 *dannhwang* 'egg('s) yellow (part)'. However, no formal difference is involved here.

(2) V-A Compounds. V-A subordinative compounds result mostly in vivid, noncomparative adjectives. Examples are 飛薄 *feibaur* 'flying thin (of two-dimensional things)', 飛快 *feikuay* 'flying fast'; 滚热, 滚燙 *goenreh, goentanq* 'boiling hot'; 焦黄 *jiauhwang* 'scorching yellow'; 噴香 *pennshiang* (← *pen* + *shiang*) 'puffing fragrant'; 鲜红 ~ 通红 ~ 鲜通红 *shiuanhorng~tonghorng~shiuantonghorng* 'fresh (and/or) piercing red,—red through and through';[31] 透鲜 *towshian* 'piercing savory,—extremely savory'. The form 透明 *towming* 'piercing bright,—transparent'

---

[31]In the form *shianhorng* (with *-i-*)鲜红 is literally 'fresh-red', with no vivifying effect, while *shiuanhorng* is only taken in the vivid sense. In some dialects, such as those of Hupeh,鲜 is *shiuan* in both senses, so that *shiuanhorng* means either (1) 'fresh-red' or (2) 'red through and through'.

is comparative, as in: 这个玻璃不很透明. *Jeyg boli bu heen towming.* 'This glass is not very transparent.' The non-comparative V-A adjectives, like the N-A adjectives, admit of lively reduplication, as in 滚ㄥ烫 *goengoentanq* 'boiling, boiling hot', 透鲜ㄥㄥ *towshian-towshian* 'delicious through and through' like 冰(冷)冰冷 *bingbingleeng* or *bingleeng-bingleeng* 'ice-ice-cold'. But there is no °*towtowming*, which shows that *towming*, being a comparative adjective, is a different kind of compound from *towshian*.

(3) H-A Compounds. A free adverb and a free adjective usually form a phrase, while if one of the constituents is bound the result is of course a compound. The same bound adverbs *shiang-* and *tzyh-* which form H-V compounds also form H-A compounds, as in 相近 *shiangjinn* BF 'near'; 相等 *shiangdeeng* BB 'equal'; 相称 *shiangchenn* BF 'fitting, suitable'. While *shiang* retains some of the meaning of 'mutually', the compound must occur after a verbal expression in first position in series if what the adjective applies to is expressed, as in 跟他相近 *gen ta shiangjinn* 'near to him (in some quality)'; 跟那个相等 *gen neyg shiangdeeng* 'is equivalent to that'; 鞋跟袜子颜色不相称. *Shye gen wahtz yan.shae bu shiangchenn.* 'The shoes and socks do not match in color.' With *tzyh-* there are 自私 *tzyhsy* 'self selfish,—selfish'; 自足 *tzyhtzwu* 'self-sufficient'; 自满 *tzyh-maan* 'self full,—self-satisfied'. In the case of 自尊 *tzyhtzuen* 'self-dignified', 自新 *tzyhshin* 'self-renew(ed)', 自苦 *tzyhkuu* 'self miserable,—make oneself suffer', it is not certain that the center is an adjective, since one says 尊孔 *tzuen-Koong* 'respect Confucius', 苦了我了 *kuule woo le* 'have made me suffer'. (Cf. *tzyh-* as Fr. *se* in sec. 4.3.2.) Other examples of bound adverbs with adjectives are 至多 *jyhduo* 'most much ( ~ many),—at most', 至少 *jyhshao* 'most little ( ~ few),—at least',[32] 绝妙 *jyuemiaw* 'absolutely wonderful'.

---

[32]A recent semantic translation borrowing of 'at least' is the use of *jyhshao* in the sense of 'in any case', which was not so used in the early part of the present century, when it only meant 'at the least'.

*6.4.7. Compounds with bu-.* Like the other versatile adverbs which occasionally form special compounds, the very versatile adverb *bu* forms a rich variety of compounds *bu*-X, in which: (a) X has a different function from *bu*-X, (b) X has a different meaning in *bu*-X, (c) X occurs less frequently than *bu*-X, and (d) X does not occur free.

(a) X has a different function from *bu*-X in 不道德 *budawder* 'not-morality,—immoral', 不規則 *buguei$_0$tzer* 'not-rule,—irregular', *buming.yuh* 'not-fame,—infamous, scandalous', 不科学 *buke$_0$shyue* 'not-science,—unscientific'. In: 这車过 不过市塲? 不过. *Jeh che guoh bu guoh shyhchaang? Bu guoh.* 'Does this car go past the market? No, it doesn't.', *bu guoh* 'does not pass' has the zero-grade function and meaning, but in addition there is also $_0bu_0guoh$ 'not past,—only, but, however' as a conjunction which can occur before a subject. In 精神不足 *jing.shern bu tzwu* 'energy is not sufficient', *bu tzwu* has zero-grade function and meaning, but in 不足跟他辩论 *butzwu gen ta biannluenn* 'not worthwhile to argue with him', *butzwu* is an auxiliary verb 'is not worth V-ing'. The verb 不成 *bu cherng* 'won't do, not okay' has zero grade. In addition, in *Nandaw ... $_0bu_0cherng$?* 'Do you mean to say that ... (or else it won't do)!', $_0bu_0cherng$ is a compound particle.

(b) X has a different or a more specialized meaning in *bu*-X, as 不答应 *bu da.yinq* zero grade: 'do not reply, comply, or promise + 'take offense at'; 不依 *bu i* 'do not do accordingly, —take offense at' (the positive form being *ij* 'following, according to'); 不至于 *bujyh$_0$yu* 'not reaching to,—not as bad as' (*jyh$_0$yu* as to, as for'); 不止 *bujyy* 'not stopping at,—more than' (*jyy* 止 'stop', near synonym of a homonym *jyy* 只 'only'); 不要紧 *buyawjiin* zero grade: 'not important' + 'it doesn't matter, that's all right!'; 不要臉 *buyawlean* 'do not want face,—shameless' (*yawlean* 'care about matters of face'). That the plain meaning of *bu yaw-lean* is no longer available comes out from the fact that when my wife started to say 不要臉的人 *bu yaw-lean de ren*, she had to correct herself and say   不是特別要臉的人

*bush tehbye yaw-lean de ren* 'people who don't specially care about matters of face ...'.

(c) X occurs less frequently than *bu*-X in 不成话 *bucherng-huah* 'do not form (reputable) words,—scandalous'; 不得巳 *buderyii* 'cannot help it'; 不高兴 *bugaushinq* 'not glad (to)'; 不菅 *bugoan* zero grade: 'do not control, do not take charge of' + 'no matter whether ... , regardless of ... '; 不论 *buluenn* 'no matter whether ... , regardless of ...'; 不見得 *bujiann.de* 'can't see that,—probably not'; 不耐煩 *bunayfarn* 'do not endure annoyance,—impatient; bored'; 不配 *bupey* 'do not match, —not qualified to'.

(d) X does not occur free in 不便 *bubiann* 'not convenient, —it will not be tactful or opportune to'; 不必 *bubih* 'not must, —need not'; 不但 *budann* 'not only'; 不貳价 *bu elljiah* 'not second price,—no bargaining'; 不凡 *bufarn* 'not ordinary, uncommon'; 不妨 *bufarng* 'not hinder,—there is no harm to'; 不中 *bujong* 'not middle,—not up to the mark'; 不住的 *bujuh-de*, 不停的 *butyngde* 'incessantly'; 不及 *bujyi* 'not reach,—inferior to'; 不離儿 *buliel* 'not separated from (a norm),—about right, not bad'; 不如 *buru* 'not as good as,—inferior to' V; *buru* '(other alternatives are) not as good as,—we had better ... ' J; 不屑 *bushieh* 'do not deign to'; 不外乎 *buway.hu* 'not outside of,—nothing but, merely'; 不亚于, 不亚似 *buyah$_0$yu, buyah$_0$syh* 'not second to,—not inferior to'; 不由得 *buyou.de* 'not following (one's will),—involuntarily, unconsciously'.

Some of the positive forms have acquired new functions or free status by back information, usually first in A-not-A questions and rhetorical questions, and finally in independent positive form. For example, from *bupey* there is: 他配说那种话嗎？我想不配吧。*Ta pey shuo nah-joong huah ma? Woo sheang ta bupey ba.* 'Is he qualified to say that? I don't think he is.' 今天不見得会下雨。你怎么見得会哪？ *Jin.tian bu-jiann.de huey shiah-yeu. Nii tzeem jiann.de huey ne?* 'It doesn't look as if it's going to rain. What makes you think that it's going to?' In the case of 規則 *guei$_0$tzer* 'rule': *buguei$_0$tzer* 'irregular':

*guei$_o$tzer* 'regular', the positive back formation has acquired full adjectival status; 名誉 *ming$_o$yuh* 'reputable' has acquired less status, and 科学 *ke$_o$shyue* only in such contexts as: 你说我 不科学，我觉着我很科学嚜! *Nii shuo woo buke$_o$shyue, woo jyuej woo heen ke$_o$shyue me!* 'You said I am unscientific, I feel that I am quite scientific!'

*6.4.8. Other Subordinative Compounds.* Besides the preceding, there are a number of other types of subordinative compounds resulting in adverbs, conjunctions, and other parts of speech, as cited in Luh, *GTFaa*, 73-75. Examples are V-H → H 想必 *sheangbih* 'think must,—presumably', A-A → H 老早 *laotzao* 'good and early', H-J → H 反而 *fann'erl* 'reversely, contrariwise', J-V → J 若使 *ruohshyy* 'if let,—if', and N-M → M 市斤 *shyhjin* 'city catty,—unit of weight = ½ kilogram'. These are neither very productive as types nor very numerous as compared with those under each of the preceding main types.

## 6.5. Verb-Object (V-O) Compounds

A V-O construction is a compound under one or more of the following conditions: (1) one or both of the constituents being bound, (2) neutral tone in the object,[33] (3) exocentricity of the construction as a whole, (4) lexicality (specialization) of meaning, and (5) inseparability of the constituents. Since we have already discussed the general aspects of both V-O compounds and V-O phrases (secs. 5.4.2-5.4.5), we shall devote most of the present section to giving examples of types of V-O compounds under the various conditions.

*6.5.1. F or B Status of the Constituents.* If either the verb or the object is bound, the result is a compound. If both are free, then the other factors will have to be considered. As usual, the status of a constituent to be considered is that at which it enters the compound. For example, 保险 *baoshean* 'insures insurance' is FB because, even though *shean* is F as 'dangerous', it is here

---

[33]Except pronoun objects, which, though normally in the neutral tone, do not form compounds with the preceding verbs.

used as 'insurance' B, as there is not only 火險 *huooshean* 'fire insurance' but also 壽險 *showshean* 'longevity insurance,—life insurance', which cannot very well be interpreted as 'danger to longevity'.

(1) FB Compounds. 起鬨 *cl.ii-honq* 'raise disturbance,—start something for fun'; 出差 *chu-chai* 'go out on an (official) errand'; 出神 *chu-shern* 'there goes out the spirit,—being absent-minded'; 打獵 *daa-lieh* 'go hunting'; 打閃 *daa-shaan* 'strike flash,—there is lightning' (cf. 打雷 *daa-lei* FF 'strike thunder,—there is thunder,—it thunders'); 打嚏 *daa-tih* 'strike sneeze,—to sneeze' ( ~ 打嚏噴 *daa tih.fenn* FF); 打雜儿 *daa-tzarl* 'do miscellany,—do general (outdoor) work'; 動身 *donq-shen* 'move person,—start on a journey'; 放学 *fanq-shyue* 'let-out school,—the school is out' (cf. 放假 *fanq-jiah* FF 'let out (on a) holiday or vacation,—there is a holiday or vacation'); 告状 *gaw-juanq* 'accuse (on a) case,—bring suit' (although *gaw* 'tell' is B and *juanq* 'the brief for a lawsuit' is F); 开端 *kai-duan* 'open an end,—set a precedent (usually in a bad sense)'; 开学 *kai-shyue* 'open school' (cf. 开学校 *kai shyueshiaw* FF 'open (for the first time) a school'; 誇口 *kua-koou* 'boast mouth,—boast'; 寬衣 *kuan-i* 'loosen clothes,—take off (outer) garment (e.g., overcoat)'; 注册 *juh-tseh* 'enter notes (in a) record book,—register (e.g., when school opens)'; 排隊 *pair-duey* 'arrange groups,—form rows, columns, etc.'; 破例 *poh-lih* 'break (regular) examples,—break precedent'; 入神 *ruh-shern* 'enter into the spirit,—go into a trance, fascinated, absent-minded' (cf. *chu-shern*); 入伍 *ruh-wuu* 'enter the ranks,—volunteer for military service'; 上市 *shanq-shyh* 'come up to the market,—begin to be in season' (cf. 上城 *shanq-cherng* FF 'go up to the city,—go downtown'); 下鄉 *shiah-shiang* 'go down into the country' (cf. 下獄 *shiah-yuh* FF 'go to prison'); 洗澡 *shii-tzao* 'wash bath,—take a bath' (cf. 洗臉 *shii-lean* FF 'wash the face'); 送终 *sonq-jong* 'send the end,—arrange funeral affairs' or 'to be present at someone's death'; 辞職 *tsyr-jyr* 'resign from office,—resign'.

(2) BF Compounds. That V-O compounds appear much less

often as BF than as FB is probably because the tendency toward dissyllabism is much stronger in nouns than in verbs, especially in transitive verbs. Examples of BF are 告假 *gaw-jiah* 'take a leave of absence' where *gaw* 'accuse' is F, but *gaw* 'tell; announce; request' is B, as also in 告老 *gaw-lao* 'announce old age, —retire' and 告辞 *gawtsyr* 'request leave,—say (formal) good-by'; 忌嘴 *jih-tzoei* 'guard the mouth (from eating the wrong things, —to be on a diet because of sickness)'; 纳税 *nah-shuey* 'enter tax, —pay tax'; 歎气 *tann-chih* 'sigh air,—to sigh'.

(3) BB Compounds. 布景 *buh-jiing* 'display scenes,—design or set (stage) scenery; stage scenery'; 去世 *chiuh-shyh* 'depart from[34] the world,—die'; 革職 *gerjyr* 'remove from office'; 革命 *germinq* 'remove the (divine) mandate (to rule),—overthrow the ruling regime,—start a revolution', 值日 *jyrryh* 'to be on duty for the day'; 值班 *jyrban* 'take a turn on duty'; 投机 *tourji* 'rush toward an opportunity,—being opportunist; take chances'; 作揖 *tzuo'i* 'make a (Chinese) bow (with both hands)' [cf. 作 *tzuoh* 'make (in general)' F]; 厭世 *yannshyh* 'tired of the world —cynical; pessimistic'.

*6.5.2. Neutral Tone in the Object.* Since a V-O phrase must have the stress on the object, a V-O construction must be a compound if the object is in the neutral tone, as in 修行 *shiou.shinq* 'cultivate conduct,—become a Buddhist'; 得罪 *der.tzuey* 'get offense,—offend' Vt; 抱怨 *baw.yuann* 'hold grudge,—blame (someone for something)'; 護书 *huh.shu* 'protect documents,— portfolio'; 盖火 *gay.huoo* 'cover the fire,—stove lid'.

*6.5.3. Exocentric V-O Compounds.* A V-O construction functions as a whole as an intransitive verb; when it behaves otherwise, it is an exocentric compound. Since we have defined V-O

---

[34]The verb *chiuh* as (1) 'go' as in 到中國去 *daw Jong.gwo chiuh* 'go to China', as (2) 'remove', as in 去皮儿 *chiuh pyel* 'remove the skin', and as (3) a recent borrowing from Cantonese into Mandarin, as 'go to', as in 去 中國 *chiuh Jong-gwo* 'go to China' are all F. However, as (4) 'go away from, leave', as in 孔子去衛 *Koongtzyy chiuh Wey* 'Confucius leaves (the state of) Wey', *chiuh* is L and when it occurs in speech as in 去世 *chiuh-shyh* cited here, it should be considered B.

construction as an endocentric construction with a verbal center, and since in an exocentric V-O compound the V is no longer the center, the compound can be analyzed as V-O only indirectly in the same way other compounds are analyzed, namely by analogy with other compounds in which the constituents are free, and, less dependably, by functions in L and by meaning.

A sufficient but not necessary condition for exocentricity is a neutral tone in the object, which is also a sufficient condition for a V-O construction to be a compound, as in 得罪 *der.tzuey* 'get offense,—offend' (cf. sec. 5.4.6.4). The converse of course does not hold (cf., however, sec. 6.5.8 on pseudo-V-O), since an iambic stress pattern is compatible with many other types of constructions. Thus, although both 傷風 *shang-feng* and 傷寒 *shangharn* are iambic, *shang-feng* 'hurt by the wind,—catch cold' is endocentric as in 傷了很利害的風 *shangle heen lih.hay de feng* 'have caught a bad cold', but *shangharn* 'hurt by the cold,— typhoid fever' is asyntactic and therefore exocentric, as it is an inseparable noun, as in 害了一塲很利害的傷寒 *hayle i-chaang heen lih.hay de shangharn* 'had a siege of very severe typhoid fever'.

A V-O compound is exocentric if it functions as (1) transitive verb, (2) noun, (3) adjective, (4) adverb, or (5) interjection.

(1) V-O Compounds as Transitive Verbs. Most V-O Compounds which can function as Vt can function alternately as Vi: *hwaiyi* BB 'harbor doubt,—skeptical', as in: 我对于你那个说法很怀疑。*Woo dueyyu nii neyg shuo₀faa heen hwaiyi.* 'I am very doubtful about your theory': *Woo heen hwaiyi nii neyg shuo₀faa.* 'I very much doubt your theory.'; *juhyih* 'pour (one's) mind,—pay attention', as in: 很小的东西，谁也不注意。*Heen sheau de dong.shi, sheir yee bu juhyih.*[35] 'A tiny little thing, nobody pays any attention (to it).': 他从来不注意这一類的事。*Ta tsornglai bu juhyih jeh-i-ley de shyh.* 'He never pays any attention to such things.'; 留心 *liou-shin* FF 'leave one's mind (on the matter)' ~ 留神 *liou-shern* FB 'leave one's spirit

[35]Hu Shih (Hwu Shyh), "Lehguan" (September 20, 1919), *Charngshyh Jyi*, Yahdong ed., p. 65.

(on the matter)', as in: 可惜我没留心(～留神)。 *Kee.shi woo mei liou-shin* (～*liou-shern*). 'It's a pity I didn't pay any attention.'; 留心(～留神)地下的冰！ *Lioushin* (～ *lioushern*) *dih.shiah de bing!* 'Look out for the ice on the ground!' Some V-O compounds are used transitively in very recent usage, as 出版 *chu-baan* FB 'issue an edition,—publish; to be published', as in: 那书快出版了。 *Nah shu kuay chu-baan le.* 'That book will soon be published.': 他们出版了一部新书。*Tamen chubaanle i-buh shin-shu.* 'They published a new book.', for which the old and still more common form is simply: *Tamen chule i-buh shin-shu.* Similarly, there is *tsuei-mian* 'hasten sleep, —induce hypnosis', as in:他会催眠. *Ta huey tsuei-mian.* 'He knows how to induce hypnosis.': 他催眠了一屋子的人. *Ta tsueimianle i-utz de ren.* 'He hypnotized a roomful of people.' Exclusively transitive verbs in V-O forms are much less common. An example is 提议 *tyiyih* 'bring up proposal,—make a motion to', as in 提议一个新办法 *tyiyih ig shin bannfaa* 'propose a new way to do it', where *tyiyih* is Vt and not Vi, although, like most other dissyllabic verbs, it can also be a noun as 'proposal, motion', as in: 我有个新(的)提议. *Woo yeou g shin (de) tyiyih.* 'I have a new proposal.'

(2) V-O Compounds as Nouns. A nominal exocentric V-O compound may represent the agent, instrument, action, or goal of the verb.

(2.1) V-O as Agent. While a subordinate V-N compound functions as V *de* N 'N which V's', an agent or instrument V-$N_1$ compound functions as V-$N_1$ *de* $N_2$. Examples of agent compounds are: 当局 *dangjyu* FB 'to be right at the situations,—those who are in charge of affairs,—the authorities' (cf. 当局者 *dangjyu-jee* L); 当道 *dangdaw* FB 'to be right at the roadway, —the present regime'; 当差 *dang-chai* FF (～*dang-chaide*) 'to be at orders,—messenger, servant'; 董事 *doong₀shyh* 'arrange affairs, —member of board'; 跟班(儿)(的) *genbal* (～ *genban* ～ *-de*) 'follow the retinue,—servant in a yamen'; 校书 *jiawshu* 'proofread the documents,—(title of an ancient high official)', also (modern— L) euphemism for 'prostitute'; 知己 *jyjii* 'know self,—know me,

—one who knows me,—an intimate friend', also 'intimate' [see (3) below]; 領事 *liing*₀*shyh* 'lead affairs,—consul (in foreign service)'; 续绐 *shiuh-shyan* 'continue with a (new) string (of the musical instrument),—remarries (after the death of the first wife)' [cf. sec. 6.5.6 (part 2)], also '(such a) second wife'; 听差 *tinqchai* ( ~ *ting-*) 'listen to orders,—janitor'; 通事 *tong.shyh* 'put through matters, —(language) interpreter' (old term) (cf. endocentric subordinative compound 通条 *tong.tyau* 'rod which goes through,—poker'); 参事 *tsan*₀*shyh* 'take part in affairs,—counselor (in foreign service or other governmental service)'; 填房 *tyan.farng* 'fill the room,—second wife (after death of first wife)' (not used as a verb, as *shiuh-shyan* is).

(2.2) V-O as Instrument. This form functions as V-N₁ *de* N₂, 'N₂ with which one V's the N₁'. Examples are: 点心 *dean.shin* 'dot the heart,—stay the stomach,—refreshments'; 滴水 *di.shoei* 'drip water,—drip-tile'; 挖耳 *ua*₀*eel* 'dig the ear,—earpick' ~ *eelwatz*.

(2.3) V-O as Action or Process. 代数 *dayshuh* 'substitute numbers,—the science of substituting numbers (with letters),—algebra'; 排行 *pairharng* 'arrange in a column (according to seniority among siblings)'; 行政 *shyngjenq* 'carry out governmental affairs, —governmental affairs, administration'; 衛生 *weysheng* 'protect life,—hygiene; hygienic'. Note that almost any polysyllabic verb, either in the form of a V-O phrase compound or otherwise, can be the subject or object of another verb without being exocentric in a nontrivial sense, as in: 我喜欢打球；打球好玩。*Woo shii.huan daa-chyou; daa-chyou haowal.* 'I like to play ball; playing ball is fun.' We shall consider a V-O compound for an action to be exocentric only when it has the formal features of a noun, such as modifiability by a D-M compound, as in: 他教两堂 代数，一堂衛生。*Ta jiau leang-tarng dayshuh, i-tarng weysheng.* 'He teaches two classes of algebra and one class of hygiene.'

(2.4) V-O as the O which is V-ed. This form is rare; examples are: *jaw-shianq* 'take pictures': 照了几張照相 *jawle jii-jang jawshianq* 'have taken a few pictures'; 描红 *miau-horng* 'trace the red (model characters with a black brush, by beginners)', also 'the model characters in red', as in 買了几張描红 *maele jii-jang miauhorng* 'have bought several sheets of models in red'; 写(~描)描红 *shiee* (~*miau*) *miauhorng* 'practice (~trace) calligraphy on models with red characters'.

(3) V-O Compounds as Adjectives. Since many transitive verbs express qualities and admit of differences of degree, such verbs with objects do not necessarily become adjectives exocentrically by thus admitting difference of degree. Thus, 出名 *chu-ming* 'come out with a name,—famous' not only occurs in 很出名 *heen chu-ming* 'very famous', 出名極了 *chu-ming-jyile* 'extremely famous', 出名的很 *chu-ming de heen* 'awfully famous', but also in 出过一次名 *chu.guoh i-tsyh ming* 'has been famous once'. On the other hand, 讨厭 *taoyann* 'invite loathing —being a nuisance' cannot take any aspect suffixes after *tao-* and, like other adjectives, can only have degrees of intensity, as in 讨厭極了 *taoyann-jyile* 'being very much of a nuisance' or, if particles are to be used they occur after the whole compound, as in: 先不讨厭,後耒讨厭了 *shian bu taoyann, howlai taoyann le* 'not troublesome at first, but became troublesome afterwards!'. In the exclamatory sentence: 这事儿才讨厭着呐！ *Jeh shell tsair taoyann jne!* 'This business is an awful nuisance!', *jne* is not an aspect suffix but a compound sentence particle, since it also occurs in: 他信你着呐。 *Ta shinn nii jne.* 'He believes in you very much indeed.' We shall consider those V-O compounds as being exocentrically adjectives which admit of degrees of intensity and which either do not admit aspect suffixes between the verb and the object or, if they do, take such suffixes more often after than before the object. Thus, 失望 *shywanq* BB 'lose expectation,—to be disappointed', occurs in the form 从耒没失望过 *tsornglai mei shywanq.guoh* 'has never been disappointed before' much oftener than *tsornglai mei shy.guoh-wanq*, which sounds purposely ionized. Following are examples of adjectives formed exocentrically from V-O compounds which are normally not separable: 缺德 *chiueder* 'lack virtue', (understatement for) 'mean, malicious'; 吃力 *chylih* 'absorb strength,—fatiguing' (in

the Wu dialects also 'fatigued'); (很) 到 家 (*heen*) *dawjia* '(quite) at home (in a subject),—professional' (also zero grade: 'reach home', not an adjective); 得意 *deryih* 'obtain the idea, get what was intended,—self-satisfied, proud'; 知己 *jyjii* 'know self,— intimate', also under (2.1) above, 'intimate friend'; 耐煩 *nayfarn* 'endure annoyance,—patient'; 呕气 *owchih* 'distressed with anger'; 入味 *ruhwey* 'enter into (the right) taste,—properly cooked'; 守 旧 *shooujiow* 'keep to the old,—conservative'; 有限 *yeoushiann* 'have limits,—limited'.

(4) V-O Compounds as Adverbs. A V-O construction may modify a verbal expression without necessarily becoming exo-centrically an adverb. This happens when the V-O expression is the first constituent in a V-V series. Thus, in 用手打人 *yonq shoou daa ren* 'use the hand hit people,—hit people with the hand', *yonq shoou* is still an endocentric verbal expression and not an adverb, even though such first verbal expressions often translate into prepositional phrases functioning adverbially in English. But in 用心做事 *yonqshin tzuoh shyh* 'use mind do work,—works carefully', *yonqshin* is an adverb. Such adverbs have one or more of the following characteristics which are not in general shared by such verbal expressions as *yonq shoou*: (a) modifiable by adverbs of degree, as in 太认真 *tay rennjen* 'rec-ognize the real too much,—too seriously, too earnestly', (b) capable of taking an optional *de*, as in 照樣(的)做 *jawyanq* (*de*) *tzuoh* 'follow the pattern do,—do likewise'; 拼命的跑 *pinminqde pao* 'stake one's life run,—run like mad'; (c) capable of vivid reduplication, as (with some speakers)  用 ᷅ 心 ᷅ 的 写 *yonqyonqshinshinde shiee* 'write good and carefully'; (d) un-expandable by suffixes to the verb or modifiers to the object, as 当时 *dangshyr* 'right at that time'; 当时 *danqshyr* 'immediately at the time,—right away'; 当真 *danqjen* 'take as real,—seriously'; 到底 *dawdii* 'reach bottom,—at bottom,—basically, after all'; 照常 *jawcharng* 'follow the usual,—as usual'; 照旧 *jawjiow* 'follow the old,—as usual'; 照例 *jawlih* 'follow the examples,— regularly'; 转眼 *joanyean* 'turn the eyes,—at a turn of the eyes,

—before long';　轧根儿　*yahgel* 'pressing to the root (of the matter),—to start with, in the first place (i.e., basically)'.

(5) V-O Compounds as Interjections. Some interjections take the form of V-O compounds. Thus, 费心 *fey-shin* 'spend mind, —take trouble' and 劳驾 *lau-jiah* 'bother (your) carriage,— bother you,—will you please', besides being verbs and thus endocentric, are also used as interjections, often in reduplicated form and neutral tones, as: .*Fey.shin.fey.shin!* and .*Lau.jiah.lau.jiah!* as polite expressions for either favor promised or favor done: 'Much obliged!' The V-O compound 混帐 *huenn.janq* 'mix accounts,[36]—vile, scandalous' is an adjective, but often used as an interjection, in this case, not only without neutral tone on the second syllable, but with full tones and emotional stress on both syllables: *Huennjanq!~Huenn.janq!*

6.5.4. *Lexicality or Specialization of Meaning.* We noted that if neither constituent of a V-O construction is bound, then, whether it is a V-O compound will depend upon other factors. We found that a neutral tone in the object or exocentricity of the construction is a sufficient condition for it to be a compound. Lexicality or specialization of meaning, however, is a criterion which is not only non-structural in nature, but also more difficult to apply, since it is a factor which admits of differences of degree. Extreme cases are easy enough to distinguish. For example, 吃梨 *chy-li* 'eat pear(s)'; 找猫 *jao-mhau* 'look for cat(s)'; 買鞋 *mae-shye* 'buy shoes'; 洗鍋 *shii-guo* 'wash pot(s)' mean just what the parts say. At the other extreme, 親嘴 *chin-tzoei* 'caress mouth,—to kiss'; 发财 *fa-tsair* 'develop wealth,—get rich'; 算命 *suann-minq* 'calculate destiny,—tell fortune'; ( 跟他 ) 翻臉 (*gen ta*) *fan-lean* 'turn face,—become angry (with him)' are definitely lexical and their meanings will have to be given as wholes

---

[36]Now written 混賬. According to one etymology it was originally a euphemism for 混帐 'mixed tents,—practice promiscuity', an etymology no longer known to most users of the expression. It is therefore quite proper language, though still regarded as a strong epithet, especially in the phrase *Huenn.janq dong.shi!* 'Vile thing,—the scoundrel!' Note, however, that the character for accounts was formerly also written with Rad. 50.

in addition to the meanings of the parts. Intermediate between these are cases like 做活 *tzuoh-hwo* 'do work'; 背书 *bey-shu* 'recite book,—recite lessons'; 断奶 *duann-nae* 'break milk,—stop milk,—to be weaned'; 开車 *kai-che* 'operate a vechicle,—drive a car; start the train (or bus)', where the meanings can be given either as additional wholes or as special meanings of the parts in those particular contexts or a limited number of contexts. Thus, instead of regarding *tzuoh-hwo* 'work at his job' as having a lexical meaning 'do work', we can give *hwo* the additional lexical gloss of 'work', since it occurs in: 我的活遺得楼上了. *Woode hwo lah de lou.shanq le.* 'My (needle or knitting) work is left upstairs.' and 这个木匠的活不貴. *Jeyg muh.jiang de hwo bu guey.* 'This carpenter's work is not expensive.' Or, take 下 *shiah* 'move downward' as occurring in 下麵 *shiah-miann* 'put down (in boiling soup) noodles,—cook noodles', but in 下蛋 *shiah-dann* 'lay eggs', *shiah* is 'lay (as of a hen)', while 'put eggs down in hot soup,—poached eggs' is 卧鸡子儿 *woh jitzeel* or 卧果儿 *wohguool*.

### 6.5.5. Frequency of Association

6.5.5.1. *With Nouns.* A frequently associated V-O construction tends to acquire a neutral tone or an exocentric function or a lexical meaning and thus become a compound. But frequency alone, like lexicality alone, is a matter of degree and cannot be decisive in marking out compounds. Thus *chy-li* 'eat pear(s)' is of a much lower order of frequency of occurrence than *chy-fann* 'eat rice; eat a meal', where *fann* 'rice' is also 'meal', since there is also 做饭 *tzuoh-fann* 'prepare a meal'. Again, *ban chwang* 'move the bed' occurs much less often than 搬家 *ban-jia* 'move house' or than 上床 *shanq-chwang* 'go up the bed,—go to bed'. Other examples of frequently associated V-O compounds are: 扯谎 *chee-hoang* 'pull lies, tell lies'; 出门 *chu-men* 'go outside the door,—go out (of the house); get married (on the part of a woman)'; 出家 *chu-jia* 'go outside the home,—renounce the home (to become a monk)'; 放火 *fanq-huoo* 'set fire'; 放心 *fanq-shin* 'let down the mind,—relax, feel relieved'; 拐弯儿 *goai-ual* 'turn a bend,—turn a corner'; 开饭 *kai-fann* 'set out the meal,—start serving the meal'; 闹账 *kai-janq* 'open an account; make out the bill'; 算命 *suann-minq* 'calculate the destiny,—tell fortunes'; 谈天 *tarn-tian* 'talk about the weather,—chat'; 做夢 *tzuoh-menq* 'make dream,—have a dream'.

*6.5.5.2. With Non-Nominal Objects.* When the object is an adjective or a verb, the chance of frequent association, usually with lexicality of meaning, is much greater than with nouns, although phrases with zero-grade meanings are by no means rare, as in: 我喜欢短. *Woo shii.huan doan.* 'I like (it, *or* things, to be) short.', 他怕摔. *Ta pah shuai.* 'He is-afraid-of falling down.' Following are examples of compounds with non-nominal objects.

(1) With Adjectival Objects. 起早 *chii-tzao* 'rise early' not a verb modified by an adverb, but V-O, as it is expandable into 起了一个大早 (儿) *chiile ig dah-tzao(l)* 'get up a big early,—got up good and early'; 吃香 *chy-shiang* 'eat the delicious,—to be in favor, popular'; 发麻 *fa-ma* 'feel numb' 发睖 *fa-lenq* 'look absent-minded'; 发狂 *fa-kwang* 'get (literally) mad,—get frenzied'; 搁淺 *ge-chean* 'shelved shallow,—to be aground'; 害臊 *hay-saw* or 害羞 *hay-shiou* 'to be bothered with being bashful,—shy'; 卖俏 *may-chiaw* 'sell cute,—show off being cute'; 卖好 *may-hao* 'sell good,—sell a favor,—give a favor for something in return'; 拿翘 *na-chyau* 'hold the warped,—hold out (against something),—being uncooperative'; 耐久 *nay-jeou* 'endure long, —can last'; 耐煩 *nay-farn* 'endure being annoyed,—patient'; 怕羞 *pah-shiou* 'fear bashful,—shy'; 怕痒 *pah-yeang* 'fear tickle,—ticklish'; 认真 *renn-jen* 'take for real,—being serious' (also 'seriously', reduplicable, as in *rennrennjenjende shuo* 'say (it) with great seriousness'); 认生 *renn-sheng* 'recognize the unfamiliar,—shy of strangers'; 入迷 *ruh-mi* 'enter into being fascinated,—become fascinated (with a game, etc.)'; 受凉 *show-liang* 'suffer cold,—suffer a chill'; 受热 *show-reh* 'suffer hot,—suffer from the heat'.

(2) With Verbal Objects. V-O Compounds with verbal objects are not as frequent as with adjectival objects. Examples are: 捱打 *air-daa* 'suffer beating,—get beaten up (as punishment or in a fight)'; 捱罵 *air-mah* 'suffer scolding,—get scolded'; 认输 *renn-*

*shu* 'recognize losing,—admit defeat'; 上算 *shanq-suann* 'come up to accounting,—advantageous, it pays'.

*6.5.6. Forms of Expansion and Ionization.* A phrase can be expanded and varied in many ways. A compound can be expanded in a limited number of ways, provided its constituents remain in the near context. We have called such limited forms of expansion "ionization". For the good reason that expandability is a formal feature and thus admits of easier handling, Luh (*GTFaa*, 90-92) prefers this to all other factors. Since, however, there are various types of expansion and some V-O constructions satisfy some of them and not others, the problem of degree still cannot be completely eliminated.

We shall consider in turn (1) solid V-O compounds (compounds which are never ionized under any circumstances), (2) V-O compounds admitting of suffixes and complements to the verb, (3) those admitting of modifiers to the object, (4) inversions, and (5) separation in questions and answers.

(1) Solid V-O Compounds. The lowest, or zero, degree of expandability is that of solid V-O compounds, which are not expandable in any manner. In such a case the V-O nature of the constituents can only be determined by their functions as words in wenyan, by their meanings, or by analogical formations. Examples are 厭世 *yannshyh* BB 'loathe the world,—tired of the world,—pessimistic; cynical'; 分娩 *fenmean* FB 'separate at childbirth,—to have parturition; parturition', 屏風 *pyng₀feng* 'screen the wind,—a standing screen',[37] 跑街 *paojie* FF 'run the streets,—errand boy', which, however, is also used as a verb 'run the streets' and is then expandable, as in 跑了一趟街 *paole i-tanq jie* 'have done an errand in the city'. On the whole, V-O compounds with FF constituents are rarely solid except in exocentric cases.

(2) V-O Compounds with Suffixes and Complements to the Verb. Most endocentric V-O compounds admit of suffixes and complements after the verb. Thus, we have 斷絃 *duann-shyan*

---

[37]Actually it was *biing feng* 'shut out the wind,—that which shuts out the wind,—a screen', but with the character 屏 *biing* mispronounced in the nominal form *pyng* it is now commonly understood as 'screen the wind'.

'break string,—have one's (lute) string broken,—one's wife dies' and 续弦 *shiuh-shyan* 'continue with a string,—have one's lute restrung,—remarry (after the death of the first wife)': 他断了 弦就一直没续过弦。 *Ta duannle shyan jiow ijyr mei shiuh-.guoh shyan.* 'After his wife died he has never remarried.'; 磕头 *ke-tour* 'knock the head,—kowtows':[38] 磕着头祷告 *kej tour dao$_o$gaw* 'pray while kowtowing'; 作揖 *tzuo-i* 'make the Chinese bow (with palms together): 作ㄗ揖 *tzuo.tzuo-i* just make a bow', 作完了揖就走了 *tzuo-wanle-i jiow tzoou le* 'having made a bow, then left'; 组阁 *tzuu-ger* 'organize a cabinet' (BB form for the phrase 组织内阁 *tzuujy neyger*): 我不知道他 组没组阁。*Woo bu jydaw ta tzuu mei tzuu-ger.* 'I don't know whether he has organized his cabinet', with a possible reply: 阁 倒是组成了。 *Ger dawsh tzuu-cherngle.* 'The cabinet, to be sure, has been formed.', or: 他组了好久的阁还组不成。 *Ta tzuule haojeou de ger hair tzuu.bu-cherng.* 'He has (tried to) organize a cabinet for a long time and still cannot get one organized.' Ionized forms like V *mei* V-O, however, occur more frequently in the Southern than in the Northern dialects.

(3) V-O Compounds with Modifiers of the Objects. An object in a V-O compound can usually be modified by determinative modifiers. Other modifiers are of more limited occurrence. Thus, we have *juhyih* BB: 注（一)点儿意 *juh ideal yih~juh .deal yih* 'pay a little attention'; *sheeng-shyh* FF 'save labor': 省许 多事 *sheeng sheuduo shyh* 'save a lot of labor'; *day-shiaw* FB 'wear mourning': 得戴三年的孝 *deei day san-nian de shiaw* 'must wear three years' mourning'; *fey-shern* FB 'spend energy': 费了您（的)许多神 *feyle Nin(de) sheuduo shern* 'have spent a lot of your energy,—have given you a lot of trouble'; *shiueh-chyy* 'wash away the shame,—avenge a wrong': 你得雪这个 耻。*Nii deei shiueh jeyg chyy.* 'You must avenge this wrong.'

When a bound object is a quasi-measure, it can take a num-

---

[38]Webster 2,3 gives the etymology for English *kowtow* as "Pek. k'o¹- t'ou²", i.e., *ke-tour*. Actually English *kowtow* was from the more formal near synonym 叩头 *kow-tour* and not from 磕头 *ke-tour*.

eral as modifier. Examples are: *daa-janq* 'fight battles,—fight a war': 打一仗 *daa i-janq* 'fight a battle'; *daa-jiah* 'fight': 打一架 *daa i-jiah* 'fight once (with individuals)', also 'quarrel' (Peip.); *hua-chyuan* 'let out the fist,—play the finger-guessing game': 花几拳 *hua jii-chyuan* 'play several calls of the f.g. game'; *shanq-keh* 'take up lessons,—go to class (of teacher or student)': 上这一课 *shanq jey-i-keh* 'give or take this lesson'; *shuey-jiaw* 'sleep naps,—sleep': 睡两觉 *shuey leang-jiaw* 'sleep a couple of times'.

(4) Inversions of V and O in Compounds. A V-O phrase can always be inverted, as: *chy-gau* 'eat cake': 糕还没吃呐。*Gau hair mei chy ne.* 'The cake has not yet been eaten.'; *daa-pair* 'play mahjong (or dominoes, cards, etc.)': 牌都打完了。*Pair dou daa-wanle.* 'The game of mahjong has been played (to a finish).' Some compounds can be inverted and others cannot. Thus, we have *dao-luann* BB 'stir confusion,—stir trouble': 这乱搅的不小。*Jeh luann dao de bu sheau.* 'This trouble was stirred in a big way.', where *luann* as N is B, although as A 'disordered' is F; *kai-shyue* FB 'open school', *juh-tseh* BB 'register (in the registration) books,— register (as a student)': 学还没开。*Shyue hair mei kai.* 'The school has not yet opened.', but not: ° 册还没注。°*Tseh hair mei juh.*; *shuey-jiaw* FB 'sleep nap,—sleep': 你的觉得睡足了。 *Niide jiaw deei shuey-tzwule.* 'Your sleep should be slept sufficiently,—you should have enough sleep.'; *poh-ann* FB 'break the case': 这个案早破了。*Jehg ann tzao pohle.* 'This case was broken long ago.', where the word for 'case' in contexts without *poh* would be in the suffixed form *anntz.* On the other hand, *poh-chaan* 'break property,—go bankrupt', though it can occur in 破了产 *pohle chaan* 'have gone bankrupt' cannot be inverted as ° 产都破了   °*chaan dou pohle,* nor from *donq-shen* 'moves person,—starts on a journey' can one say: ° 身还没動。°*Shen hair mei donq.* In general, though not invariably, if the object is bound, inversion is not so frequently possible as when it is free.

(5) V-O Compounds in Questions and Answers. A V-O compound can occur in one or more of the following forms of questions and answers, with various degrees of freedom:

| | | | | |
|---|---|---|---|---|
| (a) | V-O *bu* V-O? V-O. | | (a′) | V-O *bu* V-O? V. |
| (b) | V-*bu*-V O?      V-O. | | (b′) | V-*bu*-V O?      V. |
| (c) | V-O *bu* V?      V-O. | | (c′) | V-O *bu* V?      V. |
| (d) | V sherme?        V-O. | | (d′) | V sherme?        O. |

Obviously a solid compound can only occur in form (a), and answers V or O alone (all the primed forms) can occur only if V or O is free, respectively. These are necessary but not sufficient conditions, and what forms do or do not occur depend very much upon the other factors mentioned above. Thus, with 打字 *daa-tzyh* FF 'type characters,—do typing', we have (a) *Daa-tzyh bu daa-tzyh? Daa-tzyh.* (a′) *Daa.* (b) *Daa-bu-daa-tzyh? Daa-tzyh.* (b′) *Daa.* (c) *Daa-tzyh bu daa? Daa-tzyh.* (c′) *Daa.* (d) *Daa sherme? Daa-tzyh.* But not (d′) *Daa Sherme? °Tzyh.* There are two reasons for this. One is that *daa-tzyh*, being the verb for a special type of action 'do typing' and no longer 'strike letters', the question: *Daa sherme?* is really asking what is being done rather what is being struck, so that the answer: *Tzyh.* 'Letters.' or 'Characters.' will not be answering the question. This is usually the case when the V-O construction is lexical even though it is in the form of FF, as in the case of *daa-tzyh*. The other reason, as has been noted before (sec. 2.2.3), is that except for certain special cases, such as answers to riddles, a verbal expression in the V-O form is preferred to the object alone in a minor-sentence answer to a question. Thus, to the question: 喝什么? *He sher-me?* 'What to drink?' the answer is: 喝湯(茶, 酒, ...) *He-tang* (*char, jeou,* etc.) 'Drink soup (tea, wine, etc.)' rather than: *Tang* (*char, jeou,* etc.), even though *he* and *tang* are both free and *he-tang* is completely synthesizable in meaning. To get around this difficulty, we can modify one of Luh's separability test frames thus. Instead of:

V *sherme?* O.

make it read:

V *de sh sherme?* (sh) O.

In this modified form, with *sh*, it will be giving the whole predicate, or with O alone, it will sound less like playing a game or answering a quiz than in the original form.

6.5.7. *Goals of V-O Compounds.* In the vast majority of V-O compounds the object represents the goal of action. But if there

is a goal which is not represented in the object, it has to appear
in some other form than as object to the verb, as we have noted
in connection with V-O phrases (secs. 5.4.6.4 through 5.4.7.2).
Further examples, with V-O compounds, are as follows:

(1) With exocentric V-O as Vt. *dang-shin* 'put-right-there the
mind,—be careful with': 当心火燭 *dang-shin huoo$_0$jwu* 'be
careful with fires and candles,—be careful with fire'; 起草一个
憲法 *chii-tsao ig shiannfaa* 'make-draft a constitution,—draft a
constitution' (rather new usage).

(2) With V-V series in which the first verbal expression consists of the coverbs *gen, geei,* and so on, and the goal word. Thus
while either 出版一部书 *chubaan i-buh shu* or 给一部书
出版 *geei i-buh shu chu-baan* is possible for 'publish a book',
one cannot say °*daatzyh jeyg shinn* for 给这个信打字 *geei
jeyg shinn daa-tzyh* or 把这个信打了字 *bae jeyg shinn
daale tzyh* 'type this letter'. Similarly, *luhin:* 'record sound': 得
先给那个演说錄音 *deei shian geei neyg yeanshuo luhin*
'must first record that speech'; *jaw-shianq* 'take photograph'; 给
大家照相 *geei dahjia jaw-shianq* 'take a photograph of everybody'; *chin-tzoei* 'caress mouth': 跟他親嘴 *gen ta chin-tzoei*
'kiss him (~ her)'.

(3) With "inverted objects". This, as we have seen, is a short
way of saying that the goal word is placed in the subject position,
with or without a redundant object afterwards. Thus, though one
cannot say °*Deei shian luhin neyg yeanshuo.* for 'You must first
record that speech.', it is perfectly normal to say: *Neyg yeanshuo
deei shian luhin.* '(As for) that speech (one) must first record-
sound,—the speech must first be recorded'. Alternatively it can
also take a redundant V-V series form with *geei ta* 'for it' in first
position: *Neyg yeanshuo deei shian geei ta luhin.* '(As for) that
speech (one) must record-sound for it.' Note that *geei ta* can also
be shortened to *geei* (sec. 5.5.2, part 3c).

(4) With "possessive objects". As we have seen, some V-O
constructions with possessive objects alternate with V-V forms
(sec. 5.4.6.6), as in *chiingshyh* FB 'ask for instructions': 请他的
示 *chiing tade shyh* 'ask for his instructions' ~ 跟他请示 *gen
ta chiingshyh* 'ask of him for instructions'. In the following ex-

amples of V-O compounds with possessive objects, those which
can take V-V forms are marked, in parentheses, with the appropriate first verb or verbs, while unmarked ones do not have such
alternates. Examples follow: *chiing-keh* 'invite guests,—entertains':
你得请我的客。 *Nii deei chiing woode keh.* 'You must invite
me.', also, with zero-grade meaning, 'You must invite my guests.';
*fey-shin* 'spend mind,—take trouble,—trouble (someone with a
favor)': 费您的心 *fey Ninde shin* '(may I) trouble you' (also
exocentrically, *feyshin Nin*); *gawmih* 'tell secret':   告他的密
*gaw tade mih* 'tell his secret,—inform the authorities on him';
*germinq* 'start a revolution' [secs. 6.5.1 (3) and 6.6.5 (3)]. 革他
的命 *ger tade minq* 'revo- his -lution,—start a revolution against
him' (～ 对他革命 *duey ta germinq*); *ruyih* BB 'follow wish,—
as you like it,—satisfying': 如了他的意了 *rule tade yih le*
'have satisfied his wish' (～*geei ta ruyih le*); *shanq-danq* FB 'go
on (the counter of a) pawn (shop),—get gypped': 上他的当
*shanq tade danq* 'to be gypped by him'; (but *geei ta shanq-danq*
'gyp him'); *shanq-suann* 'come up in the reckoning,—get an advantage': 上他的算 *shanq tade suann* 'take advantage of him';
*sheng-chih* 'grow anger,—angry'; 生他的气 *sheng tade chih*
(～*gen ta*,～*duey ta sheng-chih*), 'angry with him; *sonq-shyng* FB
'send journey,—see off; give a farewell party': 送他的行 *sonq
tade shyng* 'see him off; give him a farewell party' (～*geei ta
sonq-shyng*, in second meaning only).

   6.5.8. *Ionization of Pseudo-V-O Compounds.* Because a true
V-O construction, whether with free or bound parts, always has
the stress on the object, there is a strong tendency to treat any
iambic verbal expression as V-O and ionize it, even though it is
quite something else. The classic, or rather solecistic, example of
such analysis is 体操 *tiitsau* BB 'bodily exercise', the usual term
for a required school subject. To say 'had a period of gym work'
should then, and often does, take the form:   上了一堂体操
*shanqle i-tarng tiitsau*. But *tiitsau* is also used as a verb 'take
physical exercise', as in   现在得体操了 *shianntzay deei tiitsao
le* 'must take some physical exercise now'. Since one can say 上
了一堂课   *shanqle i-tarng keh* 'had a class', why not also say

体了一堂操 *tiile i-tarng tsau?* From the meanings of the morphemes, °*tsaule i-tarng tii* 'exercised a class of the physical' would seem far more logical. But as usually happens, phonological factors outweigh logical factors: the mere iambic rhythm of the V-O construction forces *tii* into the role of the verb and *tsau* into the role of the object, logic or no logic. Thus, *tiile i-tarng tsau* has become regular student language. I even heard, during my high school days, the V-not-V form—not only *Nii tii bu tii-tsau?* but also *tii bu tii* separated from *tsau* or *tiitsau* by two or three sentences, but never °*Tii* as an answer (form b′ above). In recent student language (1956) the subordinate compound 軍训 *jiunshiunn* 'military training' has been ionized, as in the following sentences: 九月十二 軍训 *Jeouyueh shyr'ell jiunshiunn.* 'September 12th (there will be) military training' [cf. sec. 2.9.3 (c)]. 軍完了训以後才可以去请護照。 *Jiun-wanle shi-unn yiihow tsair keeyii chiuh chiing huhjaw.* 'Only after having military-ed your training can you begin to apply for a passport.', which was said[39] without a smile or apology. In 取消 *cheushiau* 'take and cancel,—cancel' we have a verb complement (V-R) compound, which has been ionized, as spoken by a Peiping janitor, as 取了消了 *cheule shiau le*, as if it were V-O. In the dialogue of a play[40] there is a sentence: 我先提你个醒。*Woo shian tyi nii g shiing.* 'I'll first give you a reminder.', where *tyi-shiing* 'make (you) aware' is also a V-R, ionized as V-O. Adjective-noun constructions are sometimes also used as V-O. I have heard the command: 再左一点儿手! *Tzay tzuoo ideal shoou!* 'A little more with your left hand!', which was said after several instructions 左手! 右手!*Tzuoo shoou! Yow shoou!* in connection with some fine adjustments with the right and left hands. Similarly, a mother has been heard to say, about helping her baby to go to the bathroom, 我给他小一点儿便。*Woo geei ta sheau ideal biann.* 'I will "minor a little convenience" for him.' where the A-N compound *sheau-biann* 'minor convenience,—urine or

---

[39]By Beverly Hung (Fincher) on her first day in America.

[40] 曹禺, 雷雨 (Tsaur Yu, *Leiyeu*), *Thunderstorm*, Shanghai, prefaced 1936, Act I, p. 38.

urinate' is ionized as V-O. One of the latest is the ionization of the translit-translation of 幽默 *ioumoh* 'humor(ous)' in the phrase 还幽了他一默，说 *hair ioule ta i-moh, shuo* 'and *hu*-ed him a *mor*, saying,—and made a joke with him, saying' (*Central Daily News*, Taipei, Nov. 9, 1963).

Such pseudo-V-O analysis works not only on the grammatically wrong elements, but often also on elements which are not even morphemes. Thus, 慷慨 *kaangkae* 'generous' is one dissyllabic morpheme. But to say: 'He is generous with other people's goods', there is a very common phrase 慷他人之慨 *kaang taren jy kae*, as if to say 'He is gen- with other people's -erous'. If the parts are homophonous with real words, the attraction is even stronger. Thus 滑稽 *hwaji* 'comic', for which authorities differ as to etymology and even as to pronunciation (*hwaji* or *guuji*?), has been analyzed as V-O in the now often used facetious phrase 滑天下之大稽 *hwa tianshiah jy dah ji*,[41] 'become the biggest joke of the world', presumably on purpose to make it sound like 'make a slip with the biggest chicken of the world'. Quite on a par with analyzing the unanalyzable is the ionization of foreign loan words as V-O. In student language, again, when a referee says 'Outside!', a student who objects will say 'Out sherm side?!' as if to say: 'What side did we out?!' Here, again, the iambic pattern must be a contributing factor to the forced V-O analysis. In Cantonese one not only says: *Nee ci-m(u)-citow?* 你知唔知到？for Mandarin: *Nii jydaw.bu-jydaw?* 你知道不知道？'Do you know?', but also: *Nee gua-mu-guarantee?*, where a speaker of Mandarin borrowing the English word would probably say: *Nii guarantee.bu-guarantee?*

A case of pseudo-V-O becoming a true V-O is the expression 出恭 *chu-gong* 'have a bowel movement'. Originally, during the civil service examinations under the Mings, a candidate who wanted to go to the outhouse had to obtain from the proctor and hold up a card with the words 出恭入敬 *Chu gong ruh jinq* L 'Go out respectfully and come in deferentially'; one could not

---

[41] 冯友兰，新事论 (Ferng Yeoulan, *Shin Shyh Luenn*), *On New Affairs*, Shanghai, 1940, p. 67.

leave his place without proper authorization, whence the euphemism 出恭 *chu gong* for 'have a bowel movement'. But, as time went on, the euphemism wore thin and meanwhile it had acquired the status of an ionizable pseudo-V-O compound, as in 出完了一次恭 *chu-wanle i-tsyh gong* 'have finished having a bowel movement'. But this pseudo-V-O becomes a true V-O when one part begins to appear without the other in the near context, as in the now plain-spoken compounds 恭桶 *gongtoong* 'soil-pail,—commode' and 结恭 *jye-gong* 'harden soil,—have constipation, constipated'. The V-O analysis was reinforced in this case by the fact that *chu* 'go out (of the examination hall)' could also be used as a transitive verb in the causative sense. As usual, new euphemisms will have to be substituted, such as 洗手去 *shii-shoou chiuh* 'go to wash one's hands'. (Cf. *lavatory*, which is now practically obsolete.)

The most beautiful example of a pseudo-V-O, which nevertheless was originally a true V-O, is in the chess term 将军! *Jiangjiun!* 'Check!' from *Jiang jiun* L, which meant 'take command of an army', whence the exocentric compound *jiang$_0$jiun* 'one who takes command of an army,—a general', just like 幹事 *gannshyh* FF 'manage affairs,—executive secretary'. By phonetic modification we have also the form *jianq* 'general', the character for which 将 also appears on the chessman which corresponds in function to 'king' in Occidental chess. But when a player calls 'Check!' he says *Jiangjiun!* 'Your general is in peril!' or 'Look out for your general!' and that is a noun used as an interjection. The verb 'to check' is *jiang*, and the object of this verb is normally the name of the opponent and less often the name of his main piece. But *jiangjiun* is also used as a dissyllabic verb 'to check', and, since iambic verbs are likely to be ionized as V-O or Pseudo-V-O, we get forms like 将他一军 *jiang ta i-jiun* 'give him a "check"', or in possessive form *jiang tade jiun*. Thus we started with a V-O construction *jiang jiun* L 'command an army' and through *jiang$_0$jiun* 'a general', *jiangjiun!* 'check!', and finally, by an asemantic ionization, we have come back to a V-O construction *jiang-jiun* again, but lost the semantic contents of both *jiang* and *jiun* on the way.

# 6.6 Verb-Complement (V-R) Compounds

*6.6.1. Formal Features of V-R Compounds.* In section 5.6 we
discussed complements as a syntactical type, as in 别坐得地
下 ! *Bye tzuoh de dih.shiah!* 'Don't sit on the floor (or ground)!'
and 他唱的好听。 *Ta chanq de haoting.* 'He sings beautifully.'
In the present section we shall consider complements which are
bound to and follow the verb and express the result of the action
of the verb in ways more close than the *.de*-forms expressing
place whereto and degree to which. The parts of a V-R compound may be F or B, solid or expandable, versatile or restricted;
the complement may be stressed or unstressed; and the compound
may be synthesizable or lexical. These features are, however, not
without a considerable degree of positive correlation. Thus, the
features of being bound, restricted, lexical, and solid are more
likely to go together, while cross-combinations with the opposites,
though by no means rare, are less frequent. For example, 弄好
*nonq-hao* 'make good,—put in good shape' has both parts free
and versatile and the compound is synthesizable and expandable,
as in 弄不好 *nonq.bu-hao* 'cannot fix it' and 弄的很好 *nonq
de heen hao* 'makes a good job of it'. Such compounds then form
transient words. On the other hand, in 克服 *kehfwu* 'conquer to
submission,—subdue' both parts are bound and restricted and the
compound is solid, there being no such form °*keh de heen fwu.*
In such cases even the syntactic relation between the parts may
not be so clear as in compounds with versatile and/or free parts.
In this particular example one could also make a case of analyzing *kehfwu* as 'conquer and subdue', thus making it a coordinate
compound. Many cases are, however, between these extremes.
Thus, in 革新 *gershin* '(radically) change (into) new,—innovate',
the first verb *ger-* is B and restricted, the complement *shin* is F
and versatile, and the compound is solid; in 改良 *gaeliang* 'alter
(into) good,—improve', the first verb *gae* is F and versatile, the
complement *liang* is B and moderately restricted, and the compound is also solid.

We shall now consider the formal features of V-R compounds
in the following order: phonological features, expandability, and
occurrence of *-le* after complements.

### 6.6.1.1. Phonological Features

(1) Stress and Neutral Tone. As a rule, the complement receives the main stress, as: 变坏 *biann-huay* 'change (into) bad, —become bad'; 延長 *yancharng* 'extend long,—prolong'. If a dissyllabic complement has a neutral tone on the second syllable, the stress falls on the first, but otherwise on the second, as: 掃 干淨 *sao-'gan.jinq* 'sweep clean', but 变回头 *biann-hwei ' tour* 'change back'.

Directional complements (sec. 6.6.6) are among the few complements which are in the neutral tone, as: 关上 *guan.shanq* 'to close up'; 走進来 *tzoou.jinn.lai* 'walk in here'. Besides these there are a very limited number of complements in the neutral tone, as: 看見 *kann.jiann* 'look, so as to perceive,—see', 摸着 *mho.jaur* 'feel, so as to get at,—touch (by hand)'. In the potential form (sec. 6.6.5), however, a neutral-tone complement recovers its full tone, as: 走不進来 *tzoou.bu-jinnlai* 'cannot walk in', 看 得見 *kann.de-jiann* 'can see'.

The rule about the optional unstressing of a repeated verb in the V-not-V form of questions applies to V-R compounds like any other verbal expression, as:　这合同还延長不延長？ *Jeh hertorng hair yancharng .bu $_0$yan$_0$charng?* 'Will this contract be renewed?' It applies equally to stressed potential directional complements. Thus, it is  neutral tone for ordinary directional complement: 飛起来 *fei.chii.lai* 'fly up'; full tones for potential (directional) complement: 飛得起来 *fei.de-chiilai* 'can fly up'; (optional) neutral tone again as repeated verbal expression in a V-not-V question: 你飛得起来飛不起来？ *Nii fei.de-chii-lai $_0$fei.bu$_0$chii$_0$lai?* 'Can you fly up?'

(2) Syllabicity of the Constituents. As in the cases of A-N and V-O constructions, a monosyllabic verb and a monosyllabic complement (not counting suffix *le*) tend to form a close unit, such that on repetition after hesitation or interruption the whole combination will be resumed instead of being continued from there, as 你得吃，吃，吃，吃饱了. *Nii deei chy, chy, chy, chy-baole.* 'You must eat, eat, eat, eat-enough.' When both the verb and the complement are polysyllabic and the complement is not

in the neutral tone (as with directional complements), then there is no such limitation, as 你得打听 — 嗯 — 清楚了。*Nii deei daa.ting—ng—ching.chuule* 'You must find out about it—uh —clearly.', although the full repetition is still more usual than the continued form.

*6.6.1.2. Expandability*

(1) Solid V-R Compounds. A solid V-R compound takes no infix, nor any other inserted element. Besides 革新 *gershin* and 改良 *gaeliang* cited above, there is 規定 *gueidinq* 'regulate to a decision, prescribe', but no °*guei.de-dinq* or °*guei.de heen dinq;* there is 说破 *shuopoh* 'say broken,—tell explicitly' (cf. 'break the news'), but no °*shuo.de-poh* or °*shuo.bu-poh.* There is a differ- ence between the solid V-R compound 養活 *yeang.hwo* 'keep alive,—support (the livelihood of, e.g., a family)' and the expand- able V-R compound *yeang-'hwo* 'keep (and succeeds in keeping) alive (e.g., a pet)'. The former can take the suffixes *-le* or *-j,* while the latter can take only *-le.* If a solid compound has bound and restricted parts, how can one tell that they are V-R rather than other compounds? Take 解除 *jieechwu* 'unfasten remove,— release, relieve', which has occurred in a published list of ex- amples of V-R compounds. It would make as good sense to regard it as a V-R compound 'unfasten *so as to* remove'. Like- wise listed is 搗毀 *daohoei* 'knock destroy,—ravage', which could be taken either as 'knock and destroy' or 'knock until destroyed'. As is usual in such cases, one has to go to indirect evidence such as wenyan function, meaning, and analogy. It is, however, an empirical fact that most Chinese speakers, including the present writer, do agree, in most cases,[42] in analyzing a compound as being V-R, A-N, V-O, and so on.

(2) Infixable V-R Compounds. An intermediate type of V-R compound consists of those which admit insertion of *-.de-* 'can' or *-.bu-* 'cannot' as infix, resulting in potential V-R compounds, but no other insertion. For example, for 看破 *kann-poh* 'see

---

[42]Disagreements do occur, as in the case of 凝固 *ningguh* BB 'congeal solid,—solidify', which I analyze as V-R, while others have regarded it as consisting of 'congeal and solidify it', so that *ningguh* would then be regarded as a coordinate compound.

break,—see through,—to be disillusioned about' there is *kann.de-poh* 'can be unconcerned about', *kann.bu-poh* 'cannot be uncon-cerned about'.

Since this is a very productive construction, the force of analogy is sometimes so strong as to make V-R compounds out of otherwise non-V-R compounds. Thus the compound 完成 *wan-cherng* 'to complete, to form,—to complete' is probably a coor-dinate compound of synonyms. But in current writing one finds the form *wan.bu-cherng* 'cannot complete'. Since this is rare and still felt as rather forced, it should be regarded as a neologism and not as a normal part of the style of language we are de-scribing. Such forced analogical analysis is in fact by no means limited to analysis into V-R, but is also often applied to other constructions, such as V-O, as we have just seen.

(3) Expandable V-R Compounds. When the verb and comple-ment are both free, they usually allow insertions to form phrases. Thus from 吃饱 *chy-bao* 'eat full' one can form 吃的太饱 *chy de tay bao* 'eat too full', 吃的不很饱 *chy de bu heen bao* 'eat not very full', and so on. From 攆跑 *nean-pao* 'drive run,—drive away' one can have 攆的他直跑 *nean de ta jyr pao* 'drive him (so as to) keep (him) running'.

Note that when a V-R compound is expandable, it does not mean that it remains a compound when actually expanded. Thus *chy de tay bao* is a predicative-complement construction (sec. 5.6.4), with *chy de* '(the extent to which one) eats' as subject and *tay bao* 'is too full' as predicate.

A V-R compound, like other compounds, may be expandable when taken in the literal sense, but solid when taken in an idi-omatic or lexical sense. For example, *lha-dao* is separable in 这树我拉不倒. *Jeh shuh woo lha.bu-dao.* 'This tree I can't pull down.' But in the sense of 'let things be', 'give up the idea', or 'then don't, as you please' ( ← 'pull down the stage that was set for action'?), it is solid, as: 你不肯去拉倒. *Nii bu keen chiuh lhadao.* 'If you are not willing to go there, then don't'.

*6.6.1.3. Occurrence of Suffix -le in Complements.* Resultative complements take the perfective suffix *-le* in normal use, as: 你把画儿掛歪了. *Nii bae huall guah-uaile.* 'You have hung the picture crooked.' 再等一个钟头就等膩了。 *Tzay deeng ig jongtour jiow deeng-nihle.* '(If one) waits another hour, (one) will get tired of waiting.' Following are the conditions under which the suffix *-le* is not used.

(1) Negatives. Since the negative of perfective *le*-forms take *mei* or *meiyeou*, which replaces *-le*, the complement usually appears without *-le*. For example: 这门没闗紧. *Jeh men mei guan-jiin.* 'This door was not shut tight.'; 他们应该把他闗紧了. *Tamen inggai bae ta guan-jiinle.* 'They should have shut it tight.' 这个事儿没打听清楚(了)不行. *Jeyg shell mei daa.ting-ching.chuu (le) bu shyng.* 'About this thing, it won't do not to have found out clearly.'; or *Bu daa.ting-ching.chuu (le) bu shyng.* 'It won't do not to find out clearly.'

(2) Progressives. The progressive form of a V-R compound with suffix *-j* can occur without suffix *-le*. For example, 他会睁开着眼睛老不眨巴. *Ta huey jeng-kaij yean.jing lao bu jaa.ba.* 'He can keep his eyes open and not blink at all.' In such cases the perfective suffix *-le* can also be used, with a slightly different emphasis: *Ta huey jeng-kaile yean.jing lao bu jaa.ba.* 'He can open his eyes [opened] and not blink at all.' But the *le*-form is much more frequent than the *j*-form, even though the meaning is still obviously of continu*ing* action, just as it is more natural in English to speak of continu*ed* action here.

(3) Indefinite Past. The suffix *-.guoh* for the indefinite past aspect has a similar but different function from that of the perfective suffix *-le* and takes the place of *-le* in complements. For example, 我摔断过腿. *Woo shuai-duann.guoh toei.* 'I broke my leg once (but it has healed since).', as contrasted with *Woo shuai-duannle toei le.* 'I have broken my leg (and it is still in a cast).' Similarly, 我跟他閙翻过臉的. *Woo gen ta naw-fan.guoh lean de.* 'I fell out with him once (but we have made up).', as against *Woo gen ta naw-fanle lean le.* 'I have quarreled with him.'

(4) Commands. Commands with V-R complements usually take *-le* just as in statements. For example, 洗干淨了! *Shii-gan.jinq-le!* 'Wash (it) clean!' 问清楚了! *Wenn-ching.chuu-le!* 'Find out clearly!' 拿稳了! *Na-woen-le!* 'Hold (it) steady!' But

when the V-R compound in a command has a reduplicated verb
or a cognate object, then the suffix -le is not used. For example,
*Shii.shii-gan.jinq!* 'Wash (a) wash clean,—give it a clean washing!
拿稳一点儿! *Na-woen.i.deal!* 'Hold steady a little,—hold it
steadier!'

(5) Directional Complements. These do not require the suffix
-le, as: 他天ㄦ回去。*Ta tiantial hwei.chiuh.* 'He goes back
every day.' 我下午就把钱取出来。*Woo shiahwuu jiow bae
chyan cheu.chu.lai.* 'I will take out the money in the afternoon.'
昨儿我很晚才起来。*Tzwol woo heen woan tsair chii.lai.*
'Yesterday I did not get up until very late.' This, however, does
not exclude the use of -le, as: *Ta yiijinq tzoou-chu-le dah-men le.*
'He has already walked outside the front door'.

(6) Potential Complements. These cannot take suffix -le, as:
看不見人 *kann.bu-jiann ren* 'cannot see people'; 逃得出来
*taur.de-chulai* 'can escape [out]'. The form 他逃得出来了。
*Ta taur.de-chulai le.* 'He can escape now.' looks like an exception, but the le here is not a suffix to the verb but a particle
(phrase suffix) to the whole sentence, expressing a new situation.
Thus, if there is an object, the sentence particle le is not attached
to the V-R compound, but comes after the object, as 看不見
人了 *kann.bu-jiann ren le* 'cannot see people any more'.

(7) Attributive V-R Compounds. In a V-R compound used
attributively in a subordinative position, the suffix -le is optional
if the center is the goal but is not used as a rule if it is the actor
or instrument. Thus, 放大(了)的照相 *fanq-dah (le) de jaw-
shianq* 'enlarged photograph', but 放大的照相机 *fanq-dah
de jawshianqji* 'enlarging camera'; 写错(了)的字 *shiee-tsuoh
(le) de tzyh* (better with *le*) 'words which are written wrong', 写
错(了)的学生 *shiee-tsuoh (le) de shyue.sheng* (better without
*le*) 'students who write wrongly', whereas with *le* it is more likely
to mean 'students whose names have been written wrongly'.

(8) Considered Forms. In a considered form, as if by way of
quotation, the suffix le is optional, as: 说轻(了)说重(了)都不
大好。*Shuo-ching (le) shuo-jonq (le) dou bu dah hao.* '(Either)
putting it lightly (or) putting it strongly will be rather bad.' This
includes cases of V-R compounds after auxiliary verbs and certain

adverbs of time, as in 世！你得捻紧（了）那个螺丝！ *Èh! Nii deei nean-jiinle neyg luo.sy!* 'Say, you must turn that screw tight!'     我说了半天才说清楚（了）。*Woo shuole banntian tsair shuo-ching.chuule.* 'I talked a long time before I made it clear.'

(9) Quoted Forms.[43] In actually quoted forms, such as in a dictionary, the suffix *-le* is not included. The only exceptions are where the *le*-form is overwhelmingly more frequent than cases without suffix. Examples of lexical compounds are: 说破 *shuopoh* 'speak in plain words,—tell explicitly', 串通 *chuann$_o$tong* 'collude with', 打倒 *daa-dao* 'knock down', commonly used in slogans for 'down with....' But the intensive complements *-jyile* 'extremely, —awfully', 透了 *-towle* 'through,—thoroughly' are listed with the suffix *-le* attached, if included in a dictionary at all. Note that even in the attributive position such *-le* is included, as in: 一个 坏透了的人 *ig huay-towle de ren* 'a thoroughly bad man'. On the other hand, when *tow* 'go through' occurs as an ordinary complement, the *-le* is optional, as in: 已经泡透（了）的菜 *yiijinq paw-tow (le) de tsay* 'vegetable that has been steeped through'.

Apart from the cases outlined above, all forms of ordinary complements occur with the perfective suffix *-le*.

### 6.6.2. *Common First Verbs and Complements*

(1) Common First Verbs. While complements tend to fall into certain types, as we shall see, the first verb can be almost any verb, including of course any adjective. Naturally, verbs of very general meaning can have a greater variety of complements than very specific verbs. Thus, 弄 *nonq* 'do with', 搞 *gao* 'do with', 拿 *na* 'take', 做 *tzuoh* 'do, make', 打 *daa* 'strike' (with versatility comparable to German *schlagen*), and 变 *biann* 'change' take as complements adjectives such as 好 *hao* 'good' and 坏 *huay* 'bad', and directional complements such as 出来 *-.chu.lai* 'out (toward the speaker', 进去 *-.jinn.chiuh* 'in (away from the speaker)' where 'the speaker' in both cases is taken in the general sense to include

---

[43]On quoted forms in general see Peter Lackowski, "Words as Linguistic Primes", *Language*, 39:211-215 (1963).

the point of interest or point of reference, as in telling a story. Verbs of locomotion and physical action naturally can take directional as well as other complements. Adjectives as first verbs mostly take complements of degree as, 好極了 *hao-jyile* 'good to an extreme,—awfully good', 坏透了 *huay-towle* 'bad through and through,—thoroughly bad'. Nouns naturally cannot take complements, nor can a nominal predicate contain a complement as an immediate constituent. The verb 意识到 *yih.shyh-daw* 'become conscious of' looks like noun 'consciousness' followed by a complement 'arrived at', but, as this is a newly made-up expression, the first part should be regarded as a verb rather than as a noun, just as in another translation borrowing, 意味着 *yih.weyj* 'meaning-ing,—meaning' (the participle) F, where *yih.wey* should be regarded as a verb by way of class overlap.

The first verb need not of course be of one morpheme. If it is complex it may be a derived word, a coordinate compound, a subordinate compound, a V-O compound, or even a V-R compound itself. Thus we have a suffixed verb *tiawle* in 跳了下去 *tiawle.shiah.chiuh* 'have jumped down'; a coordinate verb compound *daa.sao* in 打掃干淨 *daa.sao-gan.jinq* 'dust and sweep clean,—tidy up'; a subordinative verb compound *gongbuh* in 公布完了 *gongbuh-wanle* 'publicly-spread to a finish,—finished announcing publicly'; a V-O compound *deryih* in 得意極了 *deryih-jyile* 'got at (one's) desire to an extreme,—extremely satisfied,—awfully proud'; and a potential V-R compound *kao.bu-cheu* in 他考不取定了. *Ta kao.bu-cheu-dinqle.* 'He is examined-unpassable to a certainty,—it is certain that he will fail (*or* has failed).' It is doubtful whether phrases or S-P clauses can form compounds with a complement. In 你又"之乎者也"起来了. *Nii yow "jy hu jee yee"-.chii.laile.* 'You are starting to show off (the literary particles) *jy hu jee yee* again.', the phrase *jy hu jee yee* is in quotes and should be regarded as a verb, with an inchoative aspect suffix -.*chii.lai* 'start to' [sec. 4.4.5(3)], rather than as a directional complement. In 他又心跳起来了. *Ta yow shintiaw-.chii.laile.* 'He again starts to the-heart-jumps,—he has a palpitation of the heart again.', *shintiaw* is an S-P verb compound 'have a palpitation', with inchoative aspect suffix -.*chii.lai* just as in (a differently constructed sentence): *Ta shin yow tiaw-.chii.laile* (or *yow tiaw le*) '(As for) him, the heart starts to beat again',—(1) 'He is having a palpitation again'; (2) 'His heart is beating again' (as said by a lifeguard, for instance).

(2) Ordinary Resultative Complements. Since the grammatical meaning of a complement is result, there is probably a larger proportion of adjectives than of action verbs. Some complements look like adverbs, as in 差多了 *chah-duole* 'inferior by far'; 餓很了就头疼。 *Eh-heenle jiow tourterng.* '(If one) is hungry very much, (one) will have a headache.' But it will be simpler to regard such cases as adjectives rather than adverbs, as there is no apparent adverbial complement that cannot also be an adjective in another context. Even the typical adverb of degree *heen*, usually written 很, is the same word as the word *heen* 'fierce', written 狠, not only historically, but also on the basis of descriptive etymology. Nouns are never used as resultative complements. Apparent exceptions are 输鉄了 *shu-tieele* 'has lost (a game as firmly as) iron' (Luh, *GTFaa*, 76) and 養家了 *yeang-jiale* 'have (~have been) domesticated'. Rather than create a category of noun complements with very few instances, it is systematically much simpler to regard this occurrence of *tiee* simply as an adjective by class overlap, which is a common enough occurrence, as in 他真木。 *Ta jen muh.* 'He is awfully wood(en),—dense.' In the case of *yeang-jiale* it can take the potential form *yeang.bu-jia* 'cannot domesticate (~be domesticated)'.

We shall proceed to examine the more frequent types of complements. Leaving some special kinds of complements to the next subsections, we have here a representative, though far from complete, list[44] of common resultative complements. Unless otherwise noted, they combine with *nonq*, *tzuoh*, and *biann*, as 弄好 *nonq-hao* 'make good,—put in good condition'; 做对

---

[44]For a list of frequencies of occurrence of common complements as well as first verbs, see 周遲明, 汉语的使動性複式動词(Jou Chyrming, "Causative Compound Verbs in Chinese"), in 山东大学之报 (Journal of Shantung University), 1957, pp. 196-198. Jou's lists differ somewhat from mine, as they were based on printed sources.

*tzuoh-duey* 'do or make right'; 变长 *biann-charng* 'change (into) long'. Note that verbs are translated in participial rather than infinitive forms, as the former is more natural for resultative compounds.

### List of Common Complements

好 -*hao* 'good'
坏 -*huay* 'bad'
对 -*duey* 'correct'
错 -*tsuoh* 'wrong'
早 -*tzao* 'early'
遲 -*chyr* 'late'

晚 -*woan* 'late'
快 -*kuay* 'fast; sharp (e.g., of knives)'
慢 -*mann* 'slow'
久 -*jeou* 'long (time)'
    as: *deeng-jeou.le* 'have waited long'
遠 -*yeuan* 'far'
近 -*jinn* 'near'
長 -*charng* 'long'
短 -*doan* 'short'
高 -*gau* 'high'
低 -*di* 'low'
矮 -*ae* 'short (of stature)'
大 -*dah* 'large'
小 -*sheau* 'small'
寬 -*kuan* 'broad, wide'
窄 -*jae* 'narrow'
深 -*shen* 'deep'
淺 -*chean* 'shallow'
彎 -*uan* 'bent'
直 -*jyr* 'straight'
平 -*pyng* 'level'

勻 -*yun* 'even (distribution)'
齊 -*chyi* 'even (height, length); completed'
正 -*jenq* 'right, correct (side)'
反 -*faan* 'reverse'

翻 -*fan* 'turned over'
擰 -*niing* 'twisted'
倒 -*daw* 'upside down'
倒 -*dao* 'toppled'
斜 -*shye* 'slant'
歪 -*uai* 'crooked, awry'
方 -*fang* 'square'
圓 -*yuan* 'round'
扁 -*bean* 'flat'
鈍 -*duenn* 'blunt'
空 -*kong* 'empty'
滿 -*maan* 'full'
粗 -*tsu* 'thick (in diam.); coarse'
細 -*shih* 'fine' (opp. of 'coarse')
厚 -*how* 'thick (of solid things)'
薄 -*baur* 'thin'
光 -*guang* 'smooth; up' (as in 'eat up')
毛 -*mau* 'rough'
透 -*tow* 'gone through'
穿 -*chuan* 'pierced through'

通 -*tong* 'gone through'
塞 -*sai* 'stuffed up'
散 -*sann* 'scattered'
散 -*saan* 'loose, apart'
鬆 -*song* 'loose, lax'
緊 -*jiin* 'tight, tense'
輕 -*ching* 'light'
重 -*jonq* 'heavy'
脆 -*tsuey* 'brittle; crisp'
僵 -*jiang* 'uncrisp; stiff; deadlocked'
硬 -*yinq* 'hard'
軟 -*roan* 'soft'
結實 -*jie.shyr* 'solid'
強 -*chyang* 'strong' (fig.)
弱 -*ruoh* 'weak' (fig.)
破 -*poh* 'broken (to pieces)'
斷 -*duann* 'broken (to sections)'
碎 -*suey* 'broken (to bits)'
爛 -*lann* 'pulped'
干 -*gan* 'dry'
溼 -*shy* 'wet'
潮,潮溼 -*chaur*, -*chaur₀shy* 'damp'
热 -*reh* 'warm, hot'
冷 -*leeng* 'cold'
涼(快) -*liang(.kuay)* 'cool'
暖和 -*noan.hwo* 'warm'
凍 -*donq* 'frozen'
化 -*huah* 'melted'
煳 -*hwu* 'scorched'
清 -*ching* 'clear'
渾 -*hwen* 'muddy'
生 -*sheng* 'raw; green; unfamiliar'

熟 -*shour* 'cooked; ripe'
熟 -*shour, -shwu* 'acquainted'
紅 -*horng* 'red'
綠 -*liuh* 'green'
黃 -*hwang* 'yellow, brown'
青 -*ching* 'blue-green'
藍 -*lan* 'blue'
紫 -*tzyy* 'purple'
粉 -*feen* 'pink'
黑 -*hei* 'black'
白 -*bair* 'white; pale'
甜 -*tyan* 'sweet'
酸 -*suan* 'sour'
苦 -*kuu* 'bitter'
辣 -*lah* 'hot'
鹹 -*shyan* 'salty'
鮮 -*shian* 'savory'
香 -*shiang* 'fragrant; good-tasting'
臭 -*chow* 'bad (of odor or taste)'
肥 -*feir* 'fat'
胖 -*panq* 'stout'
瘦 -*show* 'thin, slim'
餓 -*eh* 'hungry'
飽 -*bao* 'full (from eating)'
渴 -*kee* 'thirsty'
疼 -*terng* 'painful'
痒痒 -*yeang.yeang* 'itching'
麻 -*ma* 'numb; pins and needles'
痠 -*suan* 'sore'
新 -*shin* 'new'
旧 -*jiow* 'old'
貴 -*guey* 'expensive'

賤 -*jiann* 'cheap'

便宜 -*pyan.yih* 'inexpensive'

多 -*duo* 'much, many'

少 -*shao* 'little, few'

够 -*gow* 'enough'

足 -*tzwu* 'adequate'

没(有)-*mei (yeou)* 'disappeared'

整齐 -*jeeng.chyi* 'orderly'

乱 -*luann* 'disorderly'

亮 -*lianq* 'bright'

暗 -*ann* 'dark'

黑 -*hei* 'dark'

干淨 -*gan.jinq* 'clean'

髒 -*tzang* 'dirty'

清楚 -*ching.chuu* 'clear'

糊塗 -*hwu.du* 'muddled'

明白 -*ming.bair* 'clear, under-standing'

明 -*ming* 'explicit'

定 -*dinq* 'determined, definite'

重(復) -*chorng(.fuh)* 'redundant'

動 -*donq* 'moved'

活動 -*hwo.donq* 'loosened'

成 -*cherng* 'become; com-pleted'

真 -*jen* 'true'

假 -*jea* 'false'

老 -*lao* 'old; touch (e.g., of vegetables)'

少 -*shaw* 'youthful'

巧 -*cheau* 'smart (clever)'

笨 -*benn* 'dumb, obtuse'

窮 -*chyong* 'poor'

闊 -*kuoh* 'wealthy'

慣 -*guann* 'habituated; spoiled'

迷 -*mi* 'infatuated; astray'

煩 -*farn* 'bored, peeved'

气 -*chih* 'angry'

瘋 -*feng* 'raving'

膩 -*nih* 'tired (of) ...'

惡心 -*ee.shin* 'nauseated'

病 -*binq* 'sick'

死 -$_0$*syy* 'dead'

活 -*hwo* 'alive'

*6.6.3. Phase Complements and Aspect Suffixes.* There are a few complements which express the phase of an action in the first verb rather than some result in the action or goal. Some of them have the neutral tone and sometimes suffer vocalic reduction and become aspect suffixes. Following are the most important phase complements, most of which, as will be seen, also occur as ordinary resultative complements.

(1) 着 -$_0$*jaur.* The complement -*jaurle* 'hit the mark, touched the essential point', with full tone and the usual suffix -*le*, is an ordinary resultative complement, as: 猜着了 *tsai-jaurle* 'have guessed just right', 说着了 *shuo-jaurle* 'have predicted correctly',

碰着了　*penq-jaurle* 'have met just the right (person or thing)'
点着了（～　点焙了）*dean-jaurle* 'light so as to catch (fire),—have kindled'. As an ordinary complement, it requires the suffix *-le*, barring, as usual, the exceptions listed above (sec. 6.6.1.3).

However, the complement 着 -$_o$*jaur* 'touched, got at, successful after an attempt', is a phase complement, as: 貓逮着（了）个耗子.*Mhau dae$_o$jaur (le) g hawtz.* 'The cat has caught [hold of] a rat.' 我碰着（了）一件怪事。*Woo penq.jaur (le) i-jiann guay-shyh.* 'I met (lit., bumped) with a strange thing.' As phase complement, -$_o$*jaur* has an optional suffix *-le*. Note that 睡着了 *shuey-jaurle* is ambiguous; (1) with *-jaur* as an ordinary complement it means 'have fallen asleep'; (2) with the phase complement -$_o$*jaur*, when the full-tone option *-jaur* is taken, it means 'have succeeded in sleeping (after at first failing to find a place, get permission, etc., to sleep)'.

Both this phase complement -$_o$*jaur* and the ordinary complement *-jaur* should of course be distinguised from the cognate *-je* '-ing', suffix for the progressive aspect, as 他睡着呐，可是还没睡着。*Ta shueyj ne, keesh hair mei shuey-jaur.* 'He is sleeping (= lying down), but has not yet fallen asleep.' As this suffix has been treated in detail [sec. 4.4.5(2)], we shall not elaborate on it here.

(2)到 -.*daw*. The full-toned complement *-daw* 'arrive at, reach' is a directional complement (type 4a), as 咱们居然趕到了。*Tzarmen jiuran gaan-dawle.* 'We have actually hastened and arrived.' 这事情我早料到了。*Jeh shyh.chyng woo tzao liaw-dawle.* 'I foresaw (guessed at) this thing long ago.'

With neutral tone and optional suffix *-le*, the complement -.*daw* is a phase complement, with a very similar function to that of -.*jaur (le)*, as 我碰到（了）一件怪事。 *Woo penq.daw (le) i-jiann guay-shyh.* 'I met with a strange event.'

(3)見 -.*jiann*. The verb *jiann* 'see, meet (a person)' is only rarely used as an ordinary resultative complement, as 讓我来引見你.*Ranq woo lai yiin-jiann nii.* 'Let me introduce you [to see] (him).' As a phase complement -.*jiann (le)* to verbs of perception and the like, it is extremely frequent. Thus, we have

看見 *kann.jiann* 'look, so as to perceive,—see'; 听見 *ting.jiann* 'listen, so as to perceive,—hear'; 闻見 *wen.jiann* 'smell at, so as to perceive,—smell'; 夢見 *menq.jiann* 'dream of'; 碰見 *penq-.jiann* 'bump, so as to perceive,—meet with'; 遇見 *yuh.jiann* 'meet with'. The form 想見 *sheangjiann* 'think, so as to see, infer' is rather literary and should be regarded as an ordinary V-R compound, as it has full tone on *jiann* and is not separable by the potential infix -*.de*- or -*.bu*, as are the other forms with -*.jiann*, with full tone -*jiann* after -*.de* and -*.bu*.

A necessary condition for the use of -*.jiann* is that the first verb be for an event which happens to the "actor" without his volition. Thus, there is no ° 摸見 °*mho.jiann* 'feel (by hand) for, so as to feel,—feel', since the act of feeling with one's hand is considered more active than the reception of the distant senses. (The word for 'feel' in a passive sense is 覺着 *jyue.jaur*, 覺着 *jyuej*, or 覺得 *jyue.de*.) As to 夢見 *menq.jiann* 'dream of', a dream is supposed to occur to the dreamer without his conscious volition.[45] One should be reminded, however, that the grammatical meaning of a form is only a summary of the majority type meanings under that form. Whether any given verb 摸 *mho* 'feel' or 夢 *menq* 'dream' is a verb for passive perception or active volition depends upon whether it takes -*.jiann* and -*.daw* (which follow verbs of either type). This circularity of definition is in the very nature of formal grammar and is not vicious so long as there is correlation with other formal features.

(4) 到 -*dao* (dial.). In the dialects of the central, western, and southern provinces, there is a very common complement, usually written with the same character 到 as number 2 above, but pronounced -*dao*, that is, in the tone of the dialect concerned that is cognate with Mandarin 3rd Tone. Its function is very broad. Depending upon the dialect in question, it serves either as -*jaur*, -*daw*, or -*jiann* (usually without *le*), or as suffix -*.j*. Thus, 我 碰

---

[45]An interesting psychological sidelight comes from the common practice of sprinkling the phrases 说呀 *shuo ia* and 说是 *shuo sh* 'it is said' in every sentence or two in narrating a long dream, as if the story were told by someone else, quite beyond the control of the dreamer.

到一个朋友. *Woo penq-dao ig perngyeou.* 'I came across a friend.', where Standard Mandarin would have -.*jaur(le)*, -.*daw(le)*, or -.*jiann(le)* and never -*dao*. But if having literally knocked down a friend were meant, then -*dao* (written 倒) would be an ordinary single resultative complement and, as in Standard Mandarin, take the suffix -*le* 我碰倒了一个朋友. *Woo penq-daole ig perng-.yeou.* For an example of -*dao* as suffix, those dialects have 请你坐到! *Chiing nii tzuoh-dao!* 'Request you be sitting,—please (keep) be(ing) seated!' while Standard Mandarin would have *Chiing nii tzuohj!*

A factor which has contributed to the confusion is the fact that in most parts of the SW Mandarin regions (Szechwan, Yunnan, Kweichow, and parts of Kwangsi, Hupeh, and Hunan) the pitch pattern of the class of etymons corresponding to Standard Mandarin 3rd Tone is middle falling (:42 ⌄ ) and thus sounds like the Standard 4th Tone (:51 ⌄ ). But when the south-westerners learn the northern 3rd Tone and change their middle falling to a low rising pitch, the whole class, including this special case, changes, and so they say *jao.bu-dao* for *jao.bu-jaur* or *jao.bu-daw* 'cannot find', whereas they would do it more nearly right if they kept their original falling pitch on the complement. But that is not the usual way people learn to shift (tonal) gears when they learn other dialects by ear.

(5) 完 -*wan*, etc. The general idea of completion can be expressed by complements 完 -*wan* 'completed, finished', 好 -*hao* 'good, finished' (Wu dial.), 得 -*der* 'done' (Peip.), and 了 -*leau* 'finished', as 做完了事 *tzuoh-wanle shyh* 'have finished doing some business'; 吃好仔饭 *kie'-hao-z vaeh* (Shanghai dial.) 'have finished eating one's meal'; 做得了一件衣裳 *tzuoh-derle i-jiann i-shang* 'have finished making a garment'; 办了了差事 *bann-leaule chai.shyh* 'have finished doing an (official) errand'. Since these are always stressed and take the suffix -*le*, they are still ordinary complements rather than phase complements.

But the much reduced form -*le* from *leau* is practically a different morpheme. The difference is so great that both can occur as complement plus suffix just like any other suffix. The perfective suffix still has the general meaning of 'completion', but is no longer a full complement and does not take any further perfective suffix, as do ordinary complements.[46]

As for the suffix or infix 得 .*de*, semantic connection with 得 *-der* 'done' is made indirectly through the meaning of 'get, obtain', which is primary to both the other meanings. We shall take this up again in the next subsection on Potential Complements.

(6) 过 *-₀guoh*. The verb *guoh* 'passes' in the spatial sense can be used as a directional complement, as in 世, 你走过了! *Èh, nii tzoou-guohle!* 'Say, you have walked past it!' In the temporal sense, *-₀guohle* is a phase complement, as in 我吃过了饭就走。 *Woo chy₀guohle fann jiow tzoou.* 'I will go as soon as I have finished my dinner.' 你错过了一个好机会。 *Nii tsuoh-₀guohle ig hao-ji.huey.* 'You erred past,—missed a good opportunity.' But in 我也吃过法國饭(的)。 *Woo yee chy.guoh Fah.gwo fann. (de)* 'I have eaten French food, too.', the neutral-tone *-.guoh* is a suffix for the indefinite past aspect and is incapable of taking another suffix *-le*. Both this phase complement and the aspect suffix can occur in the same sentence, as: 他从来没错过好机会过。 *Ta tsornglai mei tsuoh₀guoh hao-ji.huey-.guoh.* 'He never missed a good opportunity.' 哪儿啊？他错过过! *Naal a? Ta tsuoh₀guoh.guoh!* 'Who said he hasn't? He has!'

6.6.4. *Intensifying Complements.* Intensification is usually expressed by preposed modifiers, as 極好 *jyi hao* 'extremely good', 死僵 *syy-jianq* 'dead-stubborn', or by way of predicative complements, as 我冷的要死。 *Woo leeng de yaw syy.* 'I am cold to death.' A few intensifiers, however, are in the form of V-R compounds:

(1) 極了 *-jyile*. The complement *-jyile*, literally 'extremely'

---

[46]Note that this discussion does not concern the inchoative sentence particle 了 *le*, which is different from both the complement 了 *-leau* and the word suffix 了 *-le*. Thus, three different things are involved in: 我做了了一件事了。 *Woo tzuoh-leaule i-jiann shyh le.* 'I have finished doing an item of business.', which in Cantonese appears as: 我做完咀一件事咯。 *Ngox dzow-yun-cox iat-ginn zih lhoh.*

is a somewhat exclamatory intensifier and corresponds in style much closer to 'awfully' than to 'extremely', which is stylistically as well as semantically equivalent to the preposed adverbial *jyi*. For example, 好看極了 *haokann-jyile* 'awfully good-looking', but 極美的景緻 *jyi meei de jiing.jyh* 'extremely beautiful scenery'. In the case of 衣服溼透了 *i.fwu shy-towle* 'the clothes wet through', both meanings can be present.

(2) 透了 *-towle*. The intensive complement *-towle* 'thoroughly' is also somewhat exclamatory, as 坏透了 *huay-towle* 'thoroughly bad' or 'bad through and through'. It also occurs as an ordinary resultative complement in the primary sense of going through, as in 穿透了一道牆 *chuan-towle i-daw chyang* 'has pierced through a wall'; 煮透了 *juu-towle* 'cooked through'.

(3)很 *-heen*. The rather weak intensive adverb *heen* is less weak when occurring as a complement, as in 我累很了就睡不着。 *Woo ley-heenle jiow shuey.bu-jaur.* 'Every time I am tired excessively I can't sleep.', where *heen ley* 'very tired' would be too weak.

(4) 多 *-duo*. While the adverb *duo* or *dwo* 'how...!' is an exclamatory intensive, as in 那多好! *Nah duo hao!* 'How nice that would be!', *-duo* as a complement (not alternating with *-dwo*) is an intensive for the comparative degree, as 那好多了。 *Nah hao-duole.* 'That would be much better.' On the use of *duo* as in *hao .de duo* 'much better' [see sec. 8.1.3.2(2.2)].

(5)死 $-_0$*syy*. The verb *syy* 'died, dead' is used as an hyperbole in the form of an intensive complement *-.syyle*, as in 我热死了。 *Woo reh.syyle.* 'I am hot to death.'; 我乐死了。 *Woo leh-.syyle.* 'I am thrilled to death.' As an ordinary resultative complement taken in the literal sense, it is usually still in the neutral tone, as 淹死了 *ian.syyle* 'drowned (to death)'; 气死了 *chih-.syyle* (1) 'angered (actually) to death', (2) 'angered to death (*as hyperbole*)'. But the negative of *-syy* as a resultative complement in the literal sense may have full tone by way of contrasting stress, as 没打死 *mei daa.syy* 'did not beat to death (perhaps did not beat at all)', as against *mei daa-syy* '(did beat but) did not beat to death'. In the extended sense of 'firm, secure, fixed', *syy* is an ordinary complement and has full stress, as *ding-syyle* 'has nailed firmly', as against the intensifying complement in 这蚊子叮死了。 *Jeh wentz ding.syyle.* 'These mosquitoes are stinging (me) to death (as hyperbole).' Or: 他把问题想死了. *Ta bae wenntyi sheang-syyle.* 'He thinks of the problem in a (too) fixed way.', as against 我想你想死了。 *Woo sheang nii sheang-.syyle.* 'I miss you and miss you terribly.'

### 6.6.5. *Potential Complements*

(1) General Cases. A potential complement compound is one in which an infix is inserted between the first verb and the complement to express possibility or impossibility of the result. Possibility is expressed by 得 -.*de-*, and impossibility by 不 -.*bu-*, as: 趕得上 *gaan.de-shanq* 'can catch up', 趕不上 *gaan.bu-shanq* 'cannot catch up'. The potential form is available to any V-R compound from free parts, so long as it makes sense. But even if it does not make sense, as 流不脆 *liou.bu-tsuey* 'cannot flow brittlely', it is still grammatical. If either part is bound, then the existence of a potential form is a matter of lexical fact and cannot be taken for granted. As we have seen, such cases are often solid compounds, which implies that no infix can be inserted, as: 改善 *gaeshann* FB 'improve' with no potential form. If the compound is a lexical one, it may not necessarily retain the idiomatic meaning when infixed. Thus 修正 *shioujenq* 'revise right (correct),—revise' is solid and therefore has no potential form. But with the literal meaning of 'whittle straight', one can say: 这棍儿我修不正. *Jeh guell woo shiou.bu-jenq.* 'This stick I can't whittle straight.' 请你给我修正了吧！ *Chiing nii geei shiou-jenqle ba!* 'Will you please whittle it straight!', though one would more usually say 直 *jyr* than *jenq* here for 'straight'.

Since a potential complement is stressed, there is a tendency for a stressed final syllable to be ionized as a complement, so much so that it occurs even in borrowed foreign words. An extreme case has been reported by Dr. Ta-Yu Wu, who in his school days at Nankai University heard in a class in geometry 这两条线 coin-不-cide. *Jey leang-tyau shiann* coin-*bu*-cide.

'These two lines (try to) coin- (but) cannot -cide'. [Cf. the ionization of pseudo-V-O compounds (sec. 6.5.8)].

A complement in the neutral tone recovers its tone when occurring in potential form. Thus, 看見 *kann.jiann* 'see', but *kann.de-jiann* 'can see'; 碰着 *penq.jaur* 'meet (or collide) with', but *penq.bu-jaur* 'cannot meet (or collide) with'. There is, however, no potential form for 遇着 *yuh.jaur* or 遇見 *yuh.jiann*, since *yuh-* is not free, but one can say (不)会遇着(～見) (*bu*)-*huey yuh.jaur* (～ *-.jiann*) 'can(not) meet with'. The only neutral-tone complement which does not recover full tone in potential form is *-.de-* itself, as: 要不得 *yaw.bu.de* 'cannot be wanted,—undesirable'. (See below on *-.de*.) A polysyllabic complement with a neutral tone, that is, in trochaic form, retains its neutral tone in simple or potential form, as: 听清楚 *ting-ching.chuu* 'hear clearly', *ting.bu-ching.chuu* 'cannot hear clearly'. In the case of polysyllabic directional complements, however, both the neutral-tone complements recover their full tones, as: 拿出来 *na.chu.lai* 'take out', but *na.bu-chulai* 'cannot take out'.

(2) Dummy Potential Complements. There are two common potential complements 了 *-leau* 'finish' and 来 *-lai* 'come' which have, as complements, very little specific meaning and serve as a kind of dummy complement, thus making the potential form available. For example: 这事太难，我做不了(～来)。*Jeh shyh tay nan, woo tzuoh.bu-leau* (or *-lai*). 'This thing is too hard, I can't do it.' Since in other contexts these words are used as single verbs and as complements with full meaning, there can be possible ambiguities, which can be resolved only in a larger context. Thus *chy.de-leau* is ambiguous: (1) 这么些饭，我三天也吃不了. *Tzemm shie fann, woo san-tian yee chy.bu-leau.* 'Such a lot of rice, I can't finish eating it even in three days.' (2) 这饭我吃不了，裡头净是沙子。 *Jeh fann woo chy.bu-leau, lii.tou jinq sh shatz.* 'I can't eat this rice, it's full of sand inside.', where *-leau* is a dummy complement. Again, 做不来 *tzuoh.bu-lai* is ambiguous: (1) 香港去做洋服，一个月也做不来． *Shianggaang chiuh tzuoh yangfwu, ig yueh yee tzuoh-*

*.bu-lai.* '(If you) have a suit made in Hong Kong, (you) can't have it made (and get it) here in one month.', where *-lai* is a directional complement in potential form; (2) 我只会做中國衣裳，洋服我做不来. *Woo jyy huey tzuoh Jong.gwo i.shang, yangfwu woo tzuoh.bu-lai.* 'I can only make Chinese clothes, I can't make suits.', where *-lai* is just a dummy complement. Like other complements, certain verbs with these dummy complements may have idiomatic meanings, thus making the V-R compounds proper entries in a dictionary, as: 受不了 *show.bu-leau* 'find unbearable, insufferable; 跟他谈得来 *gen ta tarn.de-lai* 'can talk (with) him,—finds him congenial'. Similarly, there is 说得(～ 不 )来 *shuo.de(～.bu)-lai* '(un)congenial'; 合得(～ 不 )来 *her.de(～.bu)-lai* 'can(not) get along together'. The use of *-lai* as dummy complement can be compared with the use of *lai* as proverb in 你不会修，讓我来. *Nii bu huey shiou, ranq woo lai.* 'You don't know how to repair it, let me do it.' However, the semantic connection here is probably only an indirect one.

(3) Minimal Potential Complement or Suffix 得 *-.de.* The verb 得 *der* 'get, obtain', as we have seen, can serve as an ordinary complement and then means 'done, completed, ready'. As such it is capable of being in the potential form: 做得得 *tzuoh-.de-der* 'can do to a finish,—can finish', 做不得 *tzuoh.bu-der* 'cannot finish'. Now instead of using one of the general dummy complements *-leau* or *-lai* to express possibility, a netural-tone *-.de* '-able' is simply attached to the main verb, forming a potential suffix. For example, *yaw.de* 'desirable'; 吃得 *chy.de* 'eatable,—taste good'; 做得 *tzuoh.de* 'can be done,—allowable'; 说得 *shuo.de* 'can be mentioned'. The verb is by no means limited to use in the passive sense. Thus *chy.de* is active in 他好了，現在吃得了. *Ta hao le, shianntzay chy.de le.* 'He is well again, he can eat (i.e., has an appetite) now.' Other cases of active meanings are: 懂得 *doong.de* 'understand'; 记得 *jih.de* 'can remember,—remember'; 认得 *renn.de* 'can recognize,—to be acquainted with'; 曉得 *sheau.de* (Yangtze basin dialects) 'know'; 免得 *mean.de* 'can avoid (doing or letting happen)'; 省得

*sheeng.de* 'can save (the trouble of doing or letting happen)'; by analogy also 懶得 *laan.de* 'too lazy to'; 难得 *nan.de* 'difficult to get to,—rarely do' (to be distinguished from 难得 *nander* 'difficult to get,—praiseworthy, good for you!'). Note that the last four forms, namely, *mean.de, sheeng.de, laan.de,* and *nan.de,* do not take nouns but verbs and S-P clauses as objects and thus behave partly like auxiliary verbs and partly like conjunctions.

That this -*.de* is not a pure suffix is seen from the fact that in the negative, an infix -*.bu-* is still inserted between the verb and -*.de-,* without, however, the full tone *der* being restored. Thus we have 吃不得 *chy.bu.de* 'uneatable'; 要不得 *yaw.bu.de* 'undesirable'; 认不得 *renn.bu.de* 'cannot recognize'; 做不得 *tzuoh.bu.de* 'must not do' or 'must not be done' ( ≠ *tzuoh.bu-der* 'cannot get finished';) 说不得 *shuo.bu.de* 'mustn't say' or 'unmentionable'; 曉不得 *sheau.bu.de* 'do not know) (Yangtze basin dial.). The following cases also have *bu* at the beginning, sometimes with a weaker potential force. Thus 不认得 *bu-renn.de* 'do not recognize' as against 认不得 *renn.bu.de* 'cannot recognize', even though for the verb 认得 *renn.de* the two may amount to the same thing for the person spoken of, though not for the speaker who uses these potential forms. As to 曉不得 *sheau-.bu.de* 'do not know', it is definitely less widespread geographically than the simpler 不曉得 *bu sheau.de.* There is only 不懂得 *budoong.de* or simply *bu-doong,* there is no °*doong.bu.de.*

The suffix -*.de* is not unlimitedly versatile, and the examples cited in this section cover most of the important cases. Some of the opposites have quite different idiomatic meanings, and some of the positive forms do not occur except as back formations from the negative. Thus, 見不得 (人) *jiann.bu.de* (*ren*) has the special meaning of 'cannot see (people) (because unpresentable or for fear of consequences)', but 不見得 *bu-jiann.de* is a denial of 'it can be seen', hence 'it is improbable that ... .'; the positive form *jiann.de,* however, is only used as a back formation in rhetorical questions like: 你怎么見得他不来? *Nii tzeem jiann.de ta bu lai?* 'How do you get the idea that he is not coming' (lit., how can see)'. In the case of 捨不得 *shee.bu.de* 'hate to part with (money or a loved one)', the positive form *shee.de* 'is willing to forego' almost approaches the negative in frequency of occurrence. Similarly, there is a very common negative form 了不得 *leau.bu.de*, lit. 'cannot end' but normally used as 'good no end,—wonderful, marvelous'—one of the rare cases where an expression in the neutral sense has acquired a regularly good sense. The positive form is now obsolete and occurs only as an apparent back formation in rhetorical questions like 这还了 得? *Jeh hair leau.de?* lit. 'Can this ever end?' equivalent, except for stylistic discrepancy, to 'Can you beat that?' with an expected negative answer, 可了不得! *Kee leau.bu.de!* The plain negative form °*bu-leau.de* does not occur.[47] But there is a V-O form 不得了 *buderleau.* lit. 'cannot get (to) an end', which, contrary to *leau.bu.de*, usually has the pejorative sense of 'no end of trouble,—what a mess!'[48] The two negative forms 怪不得

------

[47]Although the plain, nonpotential form *bu leau* does occur, as 这事 不了. *Jeh shyh bu leau.* 'This business will not end (in giving us trouble).'

[48]The contrast between *buderleau* and *leau.bu.de* is sharply brought out in a popular jingle of Chungking during World War II, which said that now we are in a quandary (*buderleau*) but in the future we will be wonderful (*leau.bu.de*). Following the four tones of Chungking 55:, 11:, 42:, and 35: ( ˥ , ˩ , ˥˩ , ˧˥ ), I made a tune for the jingle as follows:

我 是 中 華 國 民,
Ngoo syh Tzonghwa gwémin,
(Woo sh Jonghwa gwomin,

我 愛 中 華
Ngoo ngay Tzonghwa
Woo ay Jonghwa

民 國.　　　現 在　我 们 不 得 了,
Mingwé.　　Shianntzay ngoomen bwudérneau,
Mingwo.　　Shianntzay woomen buderleau,

*guay.bu.de* '(you) can't blame,—no wonder that ...' and 怨 不 得
*yuann.bu.de* '(you) can't complain,—no wonder that ...' do not
even have back formations and function as conjunctions. The
form 恨 不 得 *henn.bu.de* '(I) regret that I do not get to,—would
that I could ...' is different from any of the preceding forms, since
it does not mean 'cannot regret' but 'I regret that I cannot' and
is therefore reduced in stress pattern and function to that of an
adverb. Example:   我 恨 不 得 現 在 就 跑 了! *Woo henn.bu-
.de shianntzay jiow paole!* 'I wish I could run away now!'

(4) Lexical Potential Complements. Most potential complements are transient words formed by infixion of ordinary separable V-R compounds. A limited number of potential compounds,
however, occur either mostly or exclusively in potential form,
with idiomatic meanings. A few occur only in the negative form,
the positive being either nonexistent or available only as back
formation. For example, there is 来得(～ 不 )及 *lai.de(～.bu)-jyi*
'can(not) come so as to reach,—have (not) enough time for, will
(not) be in time for ... -ing', but no °*lai-jyi*. In the case of 说定
了 *shuo-dinqle* 'reach a decision from talking' as ordinary V-R
compound, the corresponding potential *shuo.de-dinq* is rare, but
the negative, *shuo.bu-dinq* 'cannot say for sure,—there is no telling but that ... ,—quite possibly', occurs very frequently. The
V-R compound 用着 *yonq$_0$jaur* 'get to use,—have occasion to
use' is not used very often, but *yonq.de-jaur* 'have occasion to
use' is more frequent, and *yonq.bu-jaur* 'unnecessary', 'don't have
to' is extremely frequent. There is no ° 犯着 °*fann$_0$jaur*, but
there is *fann.bu-jaur* 'cannot take the offensive so as to,—it
doesn't pay to run the risk of ... -ing', with *fann.de-jaur* occurring
in rhetorical questions. As most cases of predominantly potential

将来 我们 要 了 不 得。
Jiangnai   ngoomen   yaw   neaubwudér.
Jianglai   woomen    yaw   leaubude.)

compounds are of the directional type, we shall leave them to the next section.

    *6.6.6. Directional Complements.* There are four types of directional complements: (1) the verbs 来 *lai* 'come,—hither' and 去 *chiuh* 'go,—thither, away', as: 送去 *sonq.chiuh* 'send away'; (2) the nine verbs 上 *shanq* 'ascend,—up', 下 *shiah* 'descend,—down', 進 *jinn* 'enter,—in', 出 *chu* 'exit,—out', 起 *chii* 'rise,—up', 回 *hwei* 'return,—back', 过 *guoh* 'pass,—over', 开 *kai* 'open,—apart, away', and 拢 *loong* 'gather,—together', as: 走开！ *Tzoou-.kai!* 'Go away!'; (3) double complements formed with a type 2 followed by a type 1 complement, as: 扔过去 *rheng.guoh.chiuh* 'throw over there'; (4) verbs of motion which can form single complements but not double complements with type 1, as: 碰倒了椅子 *penq-daole yiitz* 'have knocked down a chair'.

Table 9

German Separable Prefixes and Chinese Directional Complements,
Types 1, 2, and 3

| Direction | Types 1 and 2 | German Prefix | Type 3 | German Prefix | Type 3 | German Prefix |
|---|---|---|---|---|---|---|
| ⤵ | -.lai | her- | | | | |
| ⤴ | -.chiuh | hin- | | | | |
| ↑ | -.shanq | auf- | -.shanq.lai | herauf- | -.shanq.chiuh | hinauf- |
| ↓ | -.shiah | ab- | -.shiah.lai | herab- | -.shiah.chiuh | hinab- |
| ⊕→ | -.jinn | ein- | -.jinn.lai | herein- | -.jinn.chiuh | hinein- |
| ↺→ | -.chu | aus- | -.chu.lai | heraus- | -.chu.chiuh | hinaus- |
| ↗ | -.chii | empor- | -.chii.lai | | | |
| ↶ | -.hwei | zurück- | -.hwei.lai | | -.hwei.chiuh | |
| ⟶ | -.guoh | über- | -.guoh.lai | herüber- | -.guoh.chiuh | hinüber- |
| ← → | $-_o$kai | auseinander- | $-_o$kai.lai | | | |
| → ← | -loong | zusammen- | $-_o$loong.lai | | | |

Directional complements differ from ordinary complements in that they are normally in the neutral tone except in potential form and that they do not require the suffix -.le as regularly as do ordinary complements. If these two characteristics are taken as defining differentia of directional complements, then type (4) are not directional complements except in a semantic sense.

Directional complements behave very much like German separable prefixes, as can be seen from the accompanying table of comparison.

A directional complement of types 1 or 3 can be attached to any verb that makes sense with it. Directional complements of types 2 and 4 are more restricted in scope of combination. All types make numerous idioms with verbs, especially in potential form, which will be treated later (sec. 6.6.7).

(1) Type 1: -.lai and -.chiuh. Besides being main verbs themselves, lai 'come' and chiuh 'go' as complements indicate motion toward or away from the speaker, respectively. For example, 今儿拿去, 明儿就洗来了. *Jiel na.chiuh, miengl jiow shii.lai le.* 'Today (you) take it away (to the laundry), tomorrow it will be washed (and brought) here.' Note that in the potential form, the directional complement recovers its tone, as 明儿就洗得来吗? *Miengl jiow shii.de-lai ma?* 'Can it be washed (and brought) here by tomorrow?'

(2) Type 2: -.shanq, -.shiah, -.jinn, -.chu, -.chii, -.hwei, -$_0$guoh, -$_0$kai, -loong. For comparison, we shall give examples of the nine complements of type 2 both as main verbs and as complements. While the majority of compounds with types 1 and 3 form transient words of no lexical import, the majority of compounds with type 2 complements have idiomatic meanings and are therefore lexical in nature.

(2.1) 上 *shanq* as verb 'go up, take up': 上楼 *shanq-lou* 'go upstairs'; 上枱 *shanq-tair* 'go on the stage; assume a high office'; 上油 *shanq-you* 'put in oil (gasoline or grease)'.

上 -$_0$*shanq* as complement 'up, on': 戴上帽子 *day.shanq mawtz* 'put on one's hat'; 爱上了他了 *ay.shanqle ta le* 'love up,—fall in love with him (or her)'; 吃上(了)瘾了 *chy$_0$shanq-(le) yiin le* 'eat on to a habit,—get addicted to'; 关上门 *guan-.shanq men* 'shut up the door'; 穿上新衣裳 *chuan.shanq* *shin-i.shang* 'put on new clothes'; 抹上点儿黄油 *moo.shanq deal hwangyou* 'put on some butter'.

(2.2) 下 *shiah* as verb 'go down, take down': 下水 *shiah-shoei* 'go down or put down into water'; 下獄 *shiah-yuh* 'go (down) into prison'; 下麵 *shiah-miann* 'put down (into the soup) noodles, —prepare noodles'; 下蛋 *shiah-dann* 'lay eggs'; 下海 *shiah-hae* 'go down to sea; enter the theatrical profession'.

下 -$_0$*shiah* as complement 'down': 齒下很多的錢 *liou-.shiah heen duo de chyan* 'leave behind a lot of money'.

(2.3) 進 *jinn* as verb 'enter': 進城 *jinn cherng* 'enter the city'.

進 -$_0$*jinn* as complement 'in(to)': 走進了一个花園儿 *tzoou.jinnle ig huayual* 'walk into a garden'.

Note that the L form 入 *ruh* 'enter in(to)' is much less active than *jinn*, but is still actively used in Cantonese under the cognate form *yap*. On the other hand, *jinn* in the sense of 'advance' is the only meaning recognized in L and Cantonese but is relatively restricted in Mandarin.

(2.4) 出 *chu* as verb 'go out, put or give out': 出门 *chu-men* 'go out the door'; 出事 *chu-shyh* 'comes out an event,—there is an accident'; 出卅 *chu-shyh* 'come out into the world,—to be born'; 出錢 *chu-chyan* 'put out money'.

出 -$_0$*chu* as complement 'out': 提出抗议 *tyi-chu kanqyih* 'bring out,—bring up, a protest'.

(2.5) 起 *chii* as verb 'rise'; 起床 *chii-chwang* 'get up from bed'; 起程 *chii-cherng* 'start journey'.

起 -$_0$*chii* as complement 'up': 發起一个運動 *fachii ig yunn$_0$donq* 'issue up,—initiate, a movement'.

(2.6) 回 *hwei* as verb 'return': 回家 *hwei-jia* 'return home'; 回他的信 *hwei tade shinn* 'answer his letter'.

回 -$_0$*hwei* as complement 'back': 收回成命 *shouhwei cherngming* 'gather back firm order,—rescind an order'.

(2.7) 过 *guoh* as verb 'pass': 过夜 *guoh-yeh* FB 'pass the night'; 过桥 *guoh-chyau* 'cross the bridge'.

过 -$_0$*guoh* as complement 'over': 飛过大西洋 *fei$_0$guoh Dahshiyang* 'fly over the Atlantic'. To be distinguished both from the phase complement: 'have already flown over the Atlantic' and the aspect suffix: 'have once flown over the Atlantic before' [see sec. 4.4.5 (4) and 6.6.2 (6)].

(2.8)闭 *kai* as verb 'open': 闭铺子 *kai puhtz* 'open a store'.

闭 -₀*kai* as complement 'open, apart': 站闭! *Jann-kai!* 'Stand aside!'; 闹闭了 *naw-kaile* 'fight open,—have come to an open conflict'; 说闭了 *shuo-kaile* 'say open,—call a spade a spade'; 分闭 *fen.kai* 'divide apart,—separate', to be distinguished from the subordinative compound *fenkai* ∼ *fenj kai,* as in 中日文班 分闭。*Jong- Ryhwen-ban fenkai.* 'Classes in Chinese and Japanese to be opened separately'

(2.9)拢 *loong* as verb 'come close': 拢岸 *loong-ann* 'approach shore,—moor' (S. Mand).

拢 -₀*loong* as complement 'together': 靠拢 *kaw-loong* 'lean to,—go over to the Communist side (on the part of non-Communists)'.

In paired directional V-R, usually as an adverbial phrase, the directional complements always have full tone, as 你干麻 老走出走进的? *Nii gannma lao tzoou-chu tzoou-jinn de?* 'Why are you walking in and out all the time?'; 他那么搬上搬 下的搬些什么? *Ta nemm ban-shanq ban-shiah de ban .shie sherme?* 'What is he moving up and down like that?' 那些鸟儿 飞来飞去的不走。 *Neyshie neaul fei-lai fei-chiuh de bu tzoou.* 'Those birds fly back and forth and won't go away.'

(3) Type 3: compound directional complements. As verbs, *shanq.lai, shiah.chiuh,* and so on are used mostly in the literal sense. We shall therefore dispense with giving examples of them. As double directional complements, however, they still form a fair number of lexical compounds.

(3.1)上来 *shanq.lai* 'come up': 爬上来 *par.shanq.lai* 'climb up' (spoken by person above); 端上来 *duan.shanq.lai* 'serve up (with both hands)'.

上去 *shanq.chiuh* 'go up': 爬上去 *par.shanq.chiuh* 'climb up' (spoken by person below); 迎上去 *yng.shanq.chiuh* 'meet (someone or something) coming down'; 送上去 *sonq.shanq.chiuh* 'send up'; 看上去不坏 *kann.shanq.chiuh bu huay* 'When one looks on it,—at it, it is not bad,—apparently not bad'.

(3.2) 下来 *shiah.lai* 'come down': 滚下来 *goen.shiah.lai* 'roll down'; 掉下来 *diaw.shiah.lai* 'fall (drop) down'; 他把臉一放下来说... *Ta bae lean i-fanq.shiah.lai shuo* ... 'He just let his face down,—his countenance fell, saying ... '

下去 *shiah.chiuh* 'go down': 扔下去 *rheng.shiah.chiuh* 'throw down'; 等下去 *deeng.shiah.chiuh* 'wait down (the time dimension),—continue to wait'; 过下去,住-,说-, ... *guoh.shiah-.chiuh, juh-, shuo-,* etc., 'pass (one's days) on,—live on, go on residing, go on talking', etc.

(3.3) 进来 *jinn.lai* 'come in': 引进来 *yiin.jinn.lai* 'lead in'; 拉进来 *lha.jinn.lai* 'pull in'.

进去 *jinn.chiuh* 'go in': 推进去 *tuei.jinn.chiuh* 'push in'; 滲进去 *shenn.jinn.chiuh* 'seep in'; 听进去 *ting.jinn.chiuh* 'listen in, take in,—listen to (advice)'.

(3.4) 出来 *chu.lai* 'come out': 放出来 *fanq.chu.lai* 'let out, release'; 说出来 *shuo.chu.lai* 'say out,—tell (a secret, etc.)'; 有个东西从飛机裡掉出来了。 *Yeou g dong.shi tsorng feiji-.lii diaw .chu.lai le.* 'Something has dropped out of the airplane.' (said by a person on the ground or in another plane).

出去 *chu.chiuh* 'go out': 攆出去 *nean.chu.chiuh* 'drive out, chase away'; 说出去 *shuo.chu.chiuh* 'say out,—tell (a secret, etc.) to the outside world'; ... 掉出去了 ... *diaw.chu.chiuh le* ' ... have dropped out' (said by a person in the plane); 嫁出去 *jiah.chu.chiuh* 'married off (of a girl)'; 滚出去! *Goen.chu.chiuh!* 'Roll out away,—get out of here!'; 逃出去 *taur.chu.chiuh* 'run out away,—escape'.[49]

---

[49] 史记,張丞相列传(*Shyy Jih*, Jang Cherngshianq Liehjuann), Kaiming ed., p. 0227:1, has 汉王遁出去。*Hann Wang duenn chu chiuh.* 'Hann Wang escaped out away.' This must have been one of the earliest, if not the earliest, occurrence of a compound directional complement. We have no knowledge of the stress pattern of the language of 司馬遷 Symaa Chian, but in the modern practice of reading wenyan, it is read *duenn chu chiuh*, rather than *duenn.chu.chiuh*. 汉书五行志(*Hann Shu*, Wuushyng Jyh), Kaiming ed., p. 0405:3, has 鉄銷皆飛上去。*Tieeshiau jie fei shanq chiuh.* 'Iron sparks all flew up'; also (p. 0410:2) 擊之為狗,走出去。 *Ji jy wei goou, tzoou chu chiuh.* '(They) struck it (and it) changed into a dog, and ran [sic] out away.'

(3.5) 起来 *chii.lai* 'rise, get up': 拎起来 *lhing.chii.lai* 'lift up (from top)': 举起来 *jeu.chii.lai* 'lift up (from below)'; 细起来 *koen.chii.lai* 'tie up (in a bundle)'. As directional complement, it can take the potential form, as in 举不起来 *jeu.bu-chiilai* 'cannot lift up', or be split [sec. 6.6.8 (5)], as in 举起手来 *jeu-.chii shoou .lai* 'lift up the hand'.

The form 起去 *chii.chiuh* is rare in Peiping either as a verb or as a double directional complement. It is heard more often in Southern Mandarin and some other dialects. In Peiping a later riser would be more likely to say to an earlier-rising bedmate: 你先起来! *Nii shian chii.lai!* 'You get up first!', even though the direction is away from the speaker. In Nanking one would say 起去 *chii.kih* in this case, *kih* being an alternate colloquial Nanking form for *chiuh*. There was also *-chii.chiuh* in old Mandarin, as 飞起去 *fei.chii.chiuh* 'fly (up) away'.[50] In Southern Mandarin one also hears 拿起去! *Na. chii.chiuh!* 'Take (it) away!'

(3.6) 回来 *hwei.lai* 'come back': 请回来 *chiing.hwei.lai* 'invite back'; 要回来 *yaw.hwei.lai* 'demand back (loaned article, money, etc.)', to be distinguished from the auxiliary verb plus verb construction, with a different stress-tone pattern, *chiing hwei.lai* 'please come back'; *yaw hwei.lai* 'want to come back; will come back'.

回去 *hwei.chiuh* 'go back': 缩回去 *suo.hwei.chiuh* 'shrink back'; 放回去 *fanq.hwei.chiuh* 'release back'.

(3.7) 过来 *guoh.lai* 'come over': 递过来 *dih.guoh.lai* 'hand over'; 明白过来 *ming.bair.guoh.lai* 'become understanding, clear about something (after thinking it over)'; 醒过来 *shiing-.guoh.lai* 'wake up'.

过去 *guoh.chiuh* 'go over': 转过去 *juann.guoh.chiuh* 'turn away'; 昏过去 *huen.guoh.chiuh* 'faint away'; 背过去 *bey.guoh-.chiuh* 'back away,—turn one's back away'.

Note that the occurrence of *-lai* or *-chiuh* is often determined by the nature of things, as 醒过来 *shiing.guoh.lai* 'wake up', as against 晕过去 *iun.guoh.chiuh* 'faint away', unless indeed one

---

[50]Quoted from 西遊记 (*Shiyoujih*) in *YYYJ*, 2:20 ff. (1957).

should imagine an earlier-drunken person speaking to a later-drunken person: 你 也 昏过来了. *Nii yee huen.guoh.lai le.* 'You have fainted hither, too.' or one dreamer to another in the same dream 你先醒过去. *Nii shian shiing.guoh.chiuh.* 'You wake away first (while I dream on for a while).'

(3.8) 闹来 *kai.lai* does not occur as a verb of motion. In 把车 闹 来! *Bae che kai.lai!* 'Drive the car here!' *kai* 'put in operation, operate, drive is the main verb, and this *kai.lai* has nothing to do with the double directional complement as in 打闹来 *daa.kai.lai* 'break open (a package, etc.)'; 分闹来 *fen.kai.lai* 'separate out', though in the latter cases *daa.kai* and *fen.kai* are more common than the longer forms.

As double directional complement, °闹去 °-*.kai.chiuh* does not occur.

(3.9) °拢来 °*loong.lai* does not occur as a verb. As double complement: 聚拢来 *jiuh$_0$loong.lai* 'gather together'; 靠拢来 *kaw$_0$loong.lai* 'lean close to' (S. Mand).

There is no verb °拢去 °*loong.chiuh*, nor double directional complement °$_0$*loong.chiuh*. This is simply a record of a fact and should not be inferred on the ground of contradiction in terms, since the complement -*kai.lai* also seems self-contradictory and yet is very much in existence.

(4) Type 4: Directional Complements Which Do Not Compound with -*.lai* or -*.chiuh*.—Type 4 complements are verbs of motion which, like most other verbs, can also be complements. They usually retain their tones as complements, take -*le* in actual use, but do not take either -*.lai* or -*.chiuh* after them.

The word 住 *juh* as a verb means 'live, dwell'. As a complement, with optional neutral tone, -$_0$*juh*, it indicates a state of holding fast, somewhat like the progressive-aspect suffix -*j*. Examples: 记住 *jih$_0$juh* 'keep in mind'; 繫住 *jih$_0$juh* 'tie securely'; 拿住 *na$_0$juh* 'hold fast'; 攢住 *tzuann$_0$juh* 'grasp firmly'; 挡住 *daang$_0$juh* 'screen off, hold off'; 推住 *tuei$_0$juh* 'push firmly'; 托 住 *tuo$_0$juh* 'support steadily'; 拢住 *loong$_0$juh* 'gather together securely'; 圍住 *wei$_0$juh* 'surround closely'. That the occurrence of -$_0$*juh* precludes the use of the suffix -*j* seems to make it more like a suffix. On the other hand, in all the preceding examples, the $_o juh$ can have a full tone, can be followed by -le, and can be in the potential form, thus behaving like any other ordinary complement, as: 抵住了 dii-juhle 'push against firmly'; 拿不住 na.bu-juh 'cannot hold fast'. Note that while Cantonese 住 -jüh and 緊 -kanx correspond in function quite closely to Mandarin -juh and -j, respectively, there are many intermediate cases where Cantonese -jüh translates into Mandarin -j, as Cant: 擰住! Nheng-jüh! Mand: 拿着! Naj! 'Hold fast!' In the special sense of 'stopped (in his tracks)', -$_o juh$ occurs in 把他问住了 bae ta wenn$_o$juhle 'have stumped him with a question', 把他难住了 bae ta nan$_o$juhle 'have stopped him with a difficulty,—have put him in a quandary or dilemma'.

The three complements (a) 到 $daw_1$ 'arrive', (b) 倒 $daw_2$ 'upside down', and (c) 倒 -dao 'toppled over' are to be distinguished from each other as well as from the dialectal phase complement 到 -dao.[51] Following are examples of 到 -$daw_1$, 倒 -$daw_2$, and 倒 -dao as directional complements of type 4:

(a) 倒 -$daw_1$: 拿倒了 na-dawle 'take and arrive at the destination'; 送到了 sonq-dawle 'send so as to arrive at the destination'.

(b) 到 -$daw_2$: 拿到了 na-dawle 'hold upside down'; 掛倒了 guah-dawle 'hang upside down'.[52]

(c) 倒 -dao: 拿倒了 na-daole 'take and (by accident) cause to topple over'; 打倒了 daa-daole 'knock down'.

The verb 走 tzoou 'walk' takes -.lai and -.chiuh for its type 1 directional complement, and in the paired form tzoou-lai tzoou-chiuh 'walk to and fro', but it does not combine with them to

---

[51] This dialectal phase complement, as we have seen [sec. 6.6.2 (4) ], corresponds to the Standard Mandarin phase complements (1) 着 -.jaur, (2) 到 -.daw, and (3) 見 -jiann for successful perception or attempted action. For example, 拿 到³ 了 na-daole 'go fetching and succeeds in getting at' (dial.), 找 到³ 了 jao-daole 'look for and find' (dial.).

[52] Note, however, that in wenyan this is in 3rd Tone, as in the coordinate compound 顛倒 diandao L 'topsy-turvy' and the V-O compound 倒戈 dao-ge L 'reverses the spears,—to mutiny, rebel'.

form double directional complements. As a complement of type
4, it is derived, not from the verb *tzoou* as 'walk' but from it as
'go away', as in 飛机已竟走了. *Feiji yiijinq tzooule.* 'The
plane has already left.' As complements, we have: 帽子给風
颳走了. *Mawtz geei feng gua-tzooule.* 'My hat has been blown
away by the wind.'; 他把車开走了. *Ta bae che kai-tzooule.*
'He has driven off with the car.' With figurative meaning, there
is: 唱走了音 *chanq-tzooule* in 'sing off pitch'; 鞋穿走了樣
子. *Shye chuan-tzooule yangtz.* 'The shoes have been worn out of
shape.'

The verb 跑 *pao* 'run', a slightly more lively word than *tzoou*,
has a similar, but not quite the same, range of V-R compounds.
Thus, there is 送走 *songq-tzoou* 'send away', but no °送跑 °*songq-
pao.*

The verb 掉 *diaw* 'drop, fall (from a height)' behave, as a
complement, like the German prefix *weg-* 'off', as: 擦掉了
*tsa$_o$diawle* 'wipe off', 跑掉了 *pao$_o$diawle* 'run away'; 菲菜快
炒了吃，不然就老掉了. *Jeou.tsay kuay chaole chy, buran
jiow lao.diawle.* 'The *Allium odorum* should be stir-fried right
away, otherwise it will get tough (and thus lost to you).' This
use of -$_o$*diaw* is much less frequent in Mandarin than the corresponding Wu dialect complement 脱 *t'e'* (cognate with Mandarin 脱 *tuo* 'take off, doff'). Forms like 死掉了 *syy$_o$diawle* for
*syyle* 'have died (off)' have been trying hard to become a translation borrowing from Wu into Mandarin, but so far they are
limited to speakers of Mandarin whose first dialect was Wu. As
an ordinary complement, *tuo* in 摆脱 *baetuo* 'shake free (of some
encumbrance)' is very restricted and the compound is solid.

The verb 翻 *fan* 'turn over' is used as a complement in V-R
complements like 打翻了鍋 *daa-fanle guo* 'upset the pot'. In
Cantonese, however, *fan* is used as directional complement of
type 2, equivalent to Mandarin 回 -*hwei*, German prefix *zurück-*.
Although Mandarin has 翻来掉去 *fan-lai diaw-chiuh* 'flop this
way and turn that way', there is no *fan-lai* alone, nor is it used,
as in Cantonese, as a compound directional complement after
another verb, equivalent to 回来 -.*hwei.lai.*

The verbs 摊 *tan* 'fall into a heap', 塌 *ta* 'fall to pieces', and 垮 *koa* 'collapse' can occur as complements, as: 地震把房子 震摊了, 震塌了, 震垮了。 *Dihjenn bae farngtz jenn-tanle, jenn-tale,* or *jenn-koale.* 'The earthquake has shaken down the house into a heap, to pieces, made the house collapse.' Although these verbs can themselves take compound directional complements, as 塌下末 *ta.shiah.lai* 'fall down to pieces', they cannot take -*.lai* or -*.chiuh* to form directional complements.

The verbs 散 *sann* 'scatter' and 散 *saan* 'loose, get loosened' can take -*.kai.lai* as type 3 complement, as 我的鞋带儿散开 末了。 *Woode shyedall saan.kai.lai le* (S. Mand). 'My shoestring has come loose.' But as complements they are not followed by -*.lai* or -*.chiuh,* as 是谁给弄散的? *Sh sheir geei nonq-saan de?* 'Who was it who loosened it?'; 把敌军冲散了 *bae dyi-jiun chong-sannle* 'scattered the enemy troops'. Note that, while the type 2 complement 开 -*.kai* 'apart, open' corresponds to the German separable prefix *auseinander-,* the type 4 complement 散 -*sann* 'scattered' is more like the German inseparable prefix *zer-.*

6.6.7. *Lexical Potential Directional Complements.* Having discussed directional complements, we are now in a position to take up the V-R compounds with directional complements which are only or mainly in potential form. Most of these are lexical compounds, with idiomatic meanings either instead of or in addition to the zero-grade (literal) meanings. In the following examples, if the negative form is predominant, the positive form, occurring as a back formation in questions and the like, will be given *after* the negative. Only in rare cases does a positive potential form exist to the exclusion of the negative.

Type 1, with 末 -*lai* and 去 -*chiuh.*—Under dummy potential complements [sec. 6.6.5 (2)] we have already examined cases of -*.de*(~ *.bu*)-*lai* 'can(not)'. A few lexical cases occur after the verbs *shiah* and *guoh:*

下不(~ 得)末 *shiah.bu*(~ *.de*)-*lai:* 你这么说叫他脸 上下不末。 *Nii tzemm shuo jiaw ta lean.shanq shiah.bu-lai.* 'When you talk this way, you will make him unable to get off with his face,—will embarrass him.'

下不(～﹐得)去 *shiah.bu(～.de)-chiuh:* 他那么做法，实在是下不去！ *Ta nemm tzuoh.faa, shyrtzay sh shiah.bu-chiuh!* 'When he acts that way, it's really unacceptable,—it really looks bad!'

过得(～不)来 *guoh.de(～.bu)-lai:* 这地方你过得来过不来？ *Jeh dih.fang nii guoh.de-lai guoh.bu-lai?* 'Can you get used to living here?'; 我跟他很过得来。 *Woo gen ta heen guoh.de-lai.* 'I get along very well with him.'

过得去 *guoh.de-chiuh:* 他的光景还过得去。 *Tade guang.jiing hair guoh.de-chiuh.* 'His circumstances are fairly passable,—he is fairly well off.'

过不去 *guoh.bu-chiuh:* 你是不是要跟我过不去？ *Nii sh bush yaw gen woo guoh.bu-chiuh?* 'Do you desire that you reach an impasse with me,—do you mean to make trouble with me?'

过意不去 *guoh.yih.bu-chiuh:* 我砸了他的好碗，也不要我赔，真是过意不去。 *Woo tzarle tade hao woan, yee bu yaw woo peir, jensh guoh.yih.bu-chiuh.* 'I broke his good bowl and he didn't want me to pay for it. I just can't get over it,—feel embarrassed.'

Types 2 and 3 with 上，下，起，过 *shanq, -shiah, -chii, -guoh.*

说不(～得)上 *shuo.bu(～.de)-shanq:* 这箱子我推都推不動，更说不上搬走了。 *Jeh shiangtz woo tuei dou tuei.bu-donq, genq shuo.bu-shanq ban-tzooule.* 'I can't even budge this trunk, let alone move it away.' The force of *-shanq* here is that the point does not come up to the threshold of relevance. To be distinguished from:

说不(～得)上来 *shuo.bu(～.de)-shanqlai:* 他姓什么我一时说不上来了。 *Ta shinq sherme woo ishyr shuo.bu-shanqlai le.* 'I can't recall at the moment what his name was.' The point of *-shanqlai* here is that the name does not come up to the threshold of my consciousness.

挨不(～得)上 *ai.bu(～.de)-shanq:* 他也反对？根本挨不上嘿！ *Ta yee faanduey? Genbeen ai.bu-shanq me!* 'He is opposed, too? He can't make contact on it,[53]—it's none of his business to start with!'

犯不 (～ 得) 上 *fann.bu*(～.*de*)-*shanq*: Same as 犯不 (～ 得) 着 *fann.bu*(～.*de*)-*jaur* [sec. 6.6.5 (4)].

看不 (～ 得) 上 *kann.bu*(～.*de*)-*shanq*: 这衣裳他一点儿也看不上眼。 *Jeh i.shang ta ideal yee kann.bu-shang yean.* 'This dress does not come up to her eyes,—does not interest her at all.'

装 *juang-* 'pack', 搁 *ge* or 放 *fanq-* 'place', 住 *juh-* 'dwell', 挤 *jii-* 'crowd', 容 *rong-* 'contain', 得 (～ 不) 下 -.*de*(～.*bu*)-*shiah*: 箱子太小，装不下这些东西。 *Shiangtz tay sheau, juang.bu-shiah jeh.shie dong.shi.* 'The trunk is too small; it won't hold these things.' 东西太多，装不下这箱子裡。 *Dong.shi tay duo, juang.bu-shiah jeh shiangtz.lii.* 'There are too many things, they won't go into this trunk.' 箱子太小，我装不下这些东西。 *Shiangtz tay sheau, woo juang.bu-shiah jeh.shie dong.shi.* 'The trunk is too small, I can't pack in these things.' To be distinguished from:

装得 (～ 不) 下去 *juang.de*(～ .*bu*)-*shiahchiuh*: 你看，方窟窿圆把儿，怎么装得下去？ *Nii kann, fang ku.long yuan ball, tzeem juang.de-shiahchiuh?* 'Look, square hole and round handle, how can you fit them together?' Whereas the complement -.*de*(～.*bu*)*shiah* has to do only with the capacity of the container, -.*de*(～.*bu*)-*shiahchiuh* has to do with (im)possibility, for various reasons, including shape, method of arrangement, and so on, as well as capacity.

吃得 (～ 不) 下 *chy.de*(～.*bu*)-*shiah*: 我昨儿病了吃不下，今儿吃得下了。 *Woo tzwol binq le chy.bu-shiah, jiel chy-.de-shiah le.* 'I was sick yesterday and had no appetite, today I have an appetite again.' To be distinguished from:

吃 *chy-* 'eat', 喝 *he-* 'drink', 嚥 *yann-* 'swallow' 得 (～ 不) 下去 -.*de*(～.*bu*)-*shiahchiuh*: 这饭太硬，我简直吃不下去。

---

[53]Since *ai* means also 'takes one's turn', this may have come through 'it doesn't begin to be his turn'. cf. 输不着 *luen.bu-jaur* 'It can't be his turn,—none of his business.'

*Jeh fann tay yinq, woo jeanjyr chy.bu-shiahchiuh*[54] 'This rice is too hard, I simply can't eat it down.'

禁 *jin-* 'stand, endure', 擔 *dan-* 'undertake, bear' 得 (∼ 不) 起 *-.de(∼.bu)-chii:* 出了事你擔得起嗎? *Chule shyh nii dan.de-chii ma?* 'If anything happens, will you be able to bear (up) the responsibility?'

看 *kann-* 'look', 瞧 *chyau-* 'look, glance' 得 (∼ 不) 起 *-.de(∼ .bu)-chii:* 他谁都看不起, 就看得起一个人. *Ta sheir dou kann.bu-chii, jiow kann.de-chii ig ren.* 'He can't look up at anybody,—he looks down upon everybody, (except that he) respects only one person.'

对不 (∼ 得) 起 *duey.bu(∼ .de)-chii:* 哎呀, 真对不起! *Ai.ia, jen duey.bu-chii!* 'Oh, I really can't face up (to you),— I'm so sorry!'     那我就对不起了! *Nah woo jiow duey.bu-chii le!* 'Well, then, I am sorry!' (as a threat).

穿 *chuan-* 'wear (clothes)', 戴 *day-* 'wear (hat, jewelry, etc.)', 吃 *chy-* 'eat', 喝 *he-* 'drink', 抽 *chou-* 'smoke', 住 *juh-* 'dwell', 坐 *tzuoh-* 'ride', 玩儿 *wal-* 'play', 賭 *duu-* 'gamble', 输 *shu-* 'lose', 赔 *peir-* 'pay (damage)', 買 *mae-* 'buy', 用 *yonq-* 'use' 得 (∼ 不) 起 *-.de(∼ .bu)-chii:* 绸衣裳穿不起穿布的. *Chour-i.shang chuan.bu-chii chuan buhde.* 'If you can't afford to wear silk clothes, wear cotton ones.' In the sense of 'can (not) afford to' this complement *-.de(∼ .bu)-chii* goes with any verb that makes sense with it, although the ones listed are by far the most frequent. The expression 看的 (∼ 不) 起 *kann-.de (∼ .bu)-chii* can also be used in this way, so that besides 'respects (∼ looks down upon)' it can also mean 'can(not) afford to see' (e.g., operas).

---

[54]The use of *-chiuh* rather than *-lai* here suggests that the speaker imagines the food, in going from mouth to stomach, is going away from himself; in other words, the seat of the ego is in the head and not, as is often attributed to the Chinese, in the stomach. On the other hand, one not only says 我说的话, 他听不進去. *Woo shuo de huah, ta ting.bu-jinnchiuh.* 'What I say, he doesn't take in.', but also: 他说的话, 我也听不進去. *Ta shuo de huah, woo yee ting.bu-jinnchiuh.* (and not °*ting.bu-jinnlai!*) 'What he says, I don't take in either.' It is therefore not such a simple matter to locate the ego merely on linguistic grounds.

说 *shuo-* 'talk', 打 *daa-* 'beat', 跑 *pao-* 'run', etc., 不 (～ 得 ) 过 *-bu(～.de)-guoh*:  谁也跑不过他。 *Sheir yee pao.bu-guoh ta.* 'Nobody can outrun him.' In the Wu dialects, the equivalent of *-.bu-guoh* is also used as an intensive suffix to adjectives, as: 热不过 *nye -ve'-kuh* (*reh.bu-guoh*) 'unsurpassably hot,—very hot'. But one does say in Mandarin 最好不过 *tzueyhao .bu-guoh* 'unsurpassably good,—awfully good'. It is a different construction, of course, from that of 最好不过九十分儿 *Tzuey hao bu guoh jeou.shyr-fel.* 'The best is not above (a grade of) 90%.'

苷 *goan-* 'control', ( 照 )顾 *guh-, jaw.guh-* 'take care of', 伺候 *tsy.how-* 'wait on', 忙 *mang-* 'busy about', 喂 *wey-* 'feed', 请 *chiing-* 'invite',  应酬 *yinq.chour-* 'entertain', 招待 *jau₀day-* 'receive, entertain', 教 *jiau-* 'teach', 问 *wenn-* 'ask', 审 *sheen-* 'try (at law)', ( 审 )查 *char-* 'investigate', *sheenchar-* 'investigate', etc., 得 (～ 不 )过来 *-.de(～.bu)-guohlai*:  客人太多，我应酬不过来。 *Kehren tay duo, woo yinq.chour.bu-guohlai.* 'There are too many guests, I can't entertain them all around.' This idiomatic meaning of 'back and around (a whole mass or group)' differs from the literal meaning of *guohlai* in that the latter has to do with crossing one boundary. Thus, if a mailman says 我走不过来。 *Woo tzoou.bu-guohlai.*, because a vicious dog is barking at him, he means literally he can't come across. But if it is because he has too many houses to deliver mail to, then *tzoou.bu-guohlai* means that he can't make the round in the allotted time, which is the idiomatic meaning being discussed here. The positive form 绕得过来 *raw.de-guohlai* 'can wind around' is used only in the literal sense, for example, in speaking of the length· of a package twine. The negative form *raw.bu-guohlai* can be taken either literally or in the special sense of 'cannot follow the involved logic, difficult pronunciation, etc.'

说得 (～ 不 )过去 *shuo.de(～ .bu)-guohchiuh*:  这种古怪的提议，实在说不过去。 *Jeh-tzoong guu₀guay de tyiyih, shyrtzay shuo.bu-guohchiuh.* 'Such a strange proposal really cannot be spoken and get by,—is quite unacceptable.'

Type 4 with 到, 住, 动 *-daw, -juh, -donq.*

到 -*daw*: 这事情我做（办）不到．*Jeh shyh.chyng woo tzuoh-* (or *bann-*) *.bu-daw.* 'This thing is impossible for me to do (or manage).' 想不到他会逃了？ *Sheang.bu-daw ta huey taur le?* 'Who would have thought that he would run away?' 那也好不到哪儿去． *Nah yee hao.bu-daw naal chiuh.* 'That can't be good to anywhere,—to any extent,—that won't be much better.' Similarly, with 坏... *huay* ... 'not much worse', 利害 ... *lih.hay* ... 'not much more powerful ... ', 阔... *kuoh* ... 'not much more wealthy', and so on. This does not occur in positive potential form except in rhetorical questions.

靠得（～不）住 *kaw.de(~.bu)-juh* 'can(not) be leaned on to stay, dependable, reliable'. There is no °*kaw-juh:* the usual form for 'leaning on' is *kawj.*

对得住 *duey.de-juh* 'can stay facing (someone),—have done right with, has been fair to'. 对不住 *duey.bu-juh* 'cannot stay facing (someone)'—(1) 'do (someone) wrong', (2) 'I feel remiss,—I am sorry, pardon me!' This does not, however, have the invective force which 对不起 *duey.bu-chii* sometimes has.

Idioms with 动 -*donq* 'move': As a complement, especially in potential form, the verb *donq* 'move' expresses the general idea of successful attempt. It differs from the phase complement 着 -.*jaur* for successful contact and 见 -.*jiann* for successful perception in that it expresses a successful attempt at some change or motion. Plain forms with -*donq* are much less frequent than potential forms.

搬得（～不）动 *ban.de(~.bu)-donq* 'can(not) move (so that it will budge)'; 拉... *lha.de(~.bu)-donq* 'can(not) pull it out (or loose)'; 推... *tuei.de(~.bu)-donq* 'can(not) push it (away, in, etc.)'; 拿... *na.de(~.bu)-donq* 'can(not) take it (because too heavy, stuck, etc.)'; 劝... *chiuann.de(~.bu)-donq* 'can(not) move by persuasion'; 说... *shuo.de(~.bu)-donq* 'can(not) move by talking'.

*6.6.8. Objects in V-R Compounds.* When a verb has both an object and a complement, it gives rise to various possibilities of construction. It makes a difference whether the subject or the object is the actor of the complement. In 我骂哭了他了．

*Woo mah-ku.le ta le.* 'I scolded him until he cried.', it is *ta* 'he' that cried, while in 你 做累了事可以歇ㄦ。 *Nii tzuoh-leyle shyh kee.yii shie.shie.* 'When you have worked so as to be tired, you may rest a little.', it is *nii* 'you' and not *shyh* 'work' that might be tired. One transformational difference that this makes is that the pretransitive is available if the complement belongs to the object but not if it belongs to the subject. Thus we can say 我把他罵哭了。 *Woo bae ta mah-kule.* but not °*Woo bae shyh tzuoh-leyle.*, since it is not the work that gets tired. Exceptionally, however, the force of analogy also results in apparently illogical forms. Thus, one does say 你得把饭吃饱了. *Nii deei bae fann chy-baole.* 'You must eat a full dinner.', although it is you and not the dinner that is to be filled. In fact, there is a common S-P predicate in 我酒醉饭饱. *Woo jeou tzuey fann bao.* 'As for me, the drink is drunk (adj.) and the food is full.' The use of the pretransitive *bae* is therefore not as rare as one would infer from the construction of actor-action and action-goal.

(1) V-R O. The simplest way a V-R compound can take an object is the usual verb-object order: 热死我了。 *Reh.syy woo le.* 'I am hot to death!'; 打倒帝國主义! *Daa-dao dihgwo-juuyih!* '[Strike] down (with) imperialism!'; 拍死了个蒼蝇 *pai.syyle g tsang.yng* 'swat a fly dead'; 風颳倒了花盆ㄦ。 *Feng gua-daole huaperl.* 'The wind has blown down the flowerpot.'; 吃饱了饭 *chy-baole fann* 'eat, until one is full, a meal'; 喝醉了酒 *he-tzueyle jeou* 'drink, until one is drunk, wine'; 看完了戲 *kann-wanle shih* 'watch, until the finish, a play'; 讨厭極了他了 *taoyann-jyile ta le* 'loathe extremely him,—find him an awful nuisance'; 怕極了見生人了 *pah-jyile jiann shengren le* 'fear extremely seeing strangers,—awfully afraid of seeing strangers'.

Examples with double directional complements: 買回来了三升米 *mae.hwei.laile san-sheng mii* 'bought back (home) three pecks of rice'; 送过去一份ㄦ礼 *sonq.guoh.chiuh i-fell lii* 'send over a gift'; 看出来是假的 *kann.chu.lai sh jeade* 'find out that it is false'; 車裡跳出来一个人 *che.lii tiaw.chu.lai ig ren* 'from the vehicle jumps out a man'.

Examples of potential forms are: 站不住脚 *jann.bu-juh jeau* 'cannot stand steadily (on one's) feet'; 吃不下飯 *chy.bu-shiah fann* 'cannot eat down meal,—have no appetite'; 看不見人 *kann.bu-jiann ren* 'cannot see people'; 睡不着覚 *shuey.bu-jaur jiaw* 'cannot sleep'.

The preceding V-R O constructions should be distinguished from the V-R$_{V-O}$ constructions, that is, a verb and a complement, which is itself in the form of a verb-object construction. In other words, the ICs in the former are 2 + 1, while the ICs in the latter are 1 + 2. Examples of 1 + 2 or V-R$_{V-O}$ are 扎流血了 *ja- liou-shiee le* 'prick so that blood flows'; 说翻臉了 *shuo-fan-lean le* 'talk so that the faces are turned out,—talk to a breakdown in friendly relations'; 買上当了 *mae- shanq-danq le* 'bought so as to go on the pawnshop,—got gypped in the purchase'; 冻傷風了 *donq- shang-feng .le* 'chilled so as to have caught cold'; 话又说回头了 *huah yow shuo- hwei-tour le* 'words (will have to be) said in return again,—but on the other hand'. In such cases it is usual to have a perfective suffix *-le* after the second verb, thus: *ja- lioule-shiee le,* etc.

(2) V-O V-R. Since, for reasons of frequent association and of one or both terms being bound, both V-O and V-R constructions tend to resist separation, a way of leaving both intact is to repeat the verb, first to go with the object, then with the complement: 吃飯吃完了 *chy-fann chy-wanle* 'eat meal eat to a finish,—in eating one's meal eat to a finish,—finish eating one's meal'; 睡覚睡醒了 *shuey-jiaw shuey-shiingle* 'sleep nap sleep to waking up,—wake up after sleeping'; 賭錢賭输了 *duu-chyan duu-shule* 'in gambling money, gamble until one loses,—lose in a gamble'. With potentials: 唱歌儿唱不好 *chanq-gel chanq.bu-hao* 'in singing,—cannot sing well'; 吃飯还吃得下 *chy-fann hair chy.de-shiah* 'can eat down meal,—have an appetite'; 射箭射不準 *sheh-jiann sheh.bu-joen* 'in shooting arrows, cannot shoot accurately'; 看事看不明白 *kann-shyh kann.bu-ming.bair* 'in looking at affair, cannot see clearly,—cannot see things intelligently'; 扶乩扶不灵 *fwuji fwu.bu-ling* 'in holding

onto the ouija board, cannot hold efficaciously,—cannot make the ouija board work', where 乩 -*ji* 'ouija board' is bound. For examples with compound complements we have 看书看不下去 *kann-shu kann.bu-shiahchiuh* 'cannot read down (the time dimension),—cannot read on'; 做事做不下去 *tzuoh shyh tzuoh.bu-shiahchiuh* 'cannot go on with the job'. As for the relation between the V-O and the V-R in such forms, they should be analyzed as S-P rather than V-V in series, since it is possible to insert not only an adverb but also a subject, as 吃饭早吃完了. *Chy-fann tzao chy-wanle.* 'As for eating one's meal, one has finished long ago.' 唱歌儿我唱不好. *Chanq-ge'l woo chanq.bu-hao.* 'As for singing, I can't sing well.'

(3) *bae*-O V-R. Another way of placing the object so as to have the verb and complement together is to use the pretransitive *bae*: 把他派来 *bae ta pay.lai* 'send him here'; 霜把菓子冻坏了. *Shuang bae guootz donq-huayle.* 'Frost has damaged the fruits by freezing.'; 把碗擦干了 *bae woan tsa-ganle* 'wipe the bowl clean'; 把包袱打起来 *bae bau.fu daa.kai.lai* 'open up the bundle'; 把花儿种起来! *Bae hual jonq-chii.lai!* 'Plant [up] the flower!'

(4) V-O R. If the object belongs to the verb and the complement belongs to the V-O construction as a whole, instead of the object belonging to the V-R construction as a whole, then the object will come next to the verb to form an IC in relation to the complement. In the typical case of such a construction, the V-O construction is followed by a complement of degree: 费事死了 *fey-shyh.syyle* 'spend-trouble to death,—it takes a lot of trouble'; 不懂事极了 *bu doong shyh -jyile* 'don't-understand-things to an extreme degree,—awfully unintelligent'; 怕见生人极了 *pah jiann sheng-ren -jyile* 'awfully afraid to meet strangers'. Potential forms, however, do not normally allow the insertion of an object. A few relic forms are still spoken, such as 放心不下 *fanq-shin.bu-shiah* 'cannot let the mind relax', 看他不起 *kann.ta.bu-chii* 'cannot look up to him,—look down

upon him', but these are no longer productive and split forms like *fanq.bu-shiah shin .lai* are now preferred.[55]

Compound directional complements are quite common in this construction, as: 他拿了五塊錢出来,对我说... *Ta nale wuu-kuay chyan .chu.lai, duey woo shuo ...* 'He took out five dollars and said to me ... ' Note that if *chu.lai* here were a second member of a V-V series and not a complement to *nale*, it would have full tone on *chu-* and the sentence would mean 'He took five dollars and (he) came out and said to me ... ' Further examples with compound complements: 放一勺儿酱油進去 *fanq i-shaurl jianqyou .jinn.chiuh* 'put a spoonful of soy sauce in'; 流了许多水出来 *lioule sheuduo shoei .chu.lai* 'flowed out a lot of water'; 造点儿人才出来 *tzaw .deal rentsair .chu.lai* 'build up some personnel'; 派个人出去 *pay g ren .chu.chiuh* 'dispatch a man out there'. In the last example *chu.chiuh* would be a second verb in a pivotal construction if *chu* had full tone, in which case it would mean 'dispatches a man to go out there'. It amounts to about the same thing, but would be of a different construction.

(5) Split directional complements V-R O R′. Instead of the order VO RR′, the northern dialects, as compared with the southern dialects, prefer a split order V-R O R′, though both orders are possible in both the north and the south. The split complement may be compared with the separable double German prefix, with the difference that, whereas in German the order of elements is V O RR′, the Chinese order is V-R O R′. Thus, 我拿出一本儿书来。 *Woo na.chu i-beel shu .lai.* 'I take out a book.' would be in German 'Ich nehme ein Buch heraus.', which corresponds more to *Woo na i-beel shu .chu.lai.*, also a possible form, as we have seen. Other examples of split complements are: 端上一杯茶来 *duan-shanq i-bei char .lai* 'serve up a cup of tea'; 吹進许多土来 *chuei$_0$jinn sheuduo tuu .lai* 'blow in a lot of dust'; 没看出是假的来 *mei kann.chu sh jeade .lai* 'did not see that it was a false one'; *kann.chu pohjann .lai .le* 'see a flaw'; 硬起心腸来 *yinq.chii shin$_0$charng .lai* 'harden

[55]For a fuller discussion and more examples, see Leu, *LWJyi*, 59-68.

(up) one's heart'; 举起手耒 *jeu.chii shoou .lai* 'raise (up) one's hand'; 車裡跳出一个人耒。 *Che.lii tiaw.chu ig ren .lai.* 'From the vehicle jumps out a man.'; 畄下三个小孩儿耒 *liou.shiah san g sheauharl .lai* 'leave behind three children (e.g., to a baby sitter for the evening)'. The last has somewhat different implications from *liou₀shiah san g sheauharl* 'leave behind (survived by) three children'. Actually, both meanings are possible for both forms, but with the different likelihoods as indicated. The difference is due to the usual tendency for a type 2 complement (-₀*shiah*) to have a more idiomatic meaning, and a type 3 complement (-.*shiah.lai*) to have a literal meaning.

Examples of split potential complements: 放不下心耒 *fanq.bu-shiah shin .lai* 'cannot let down one's mind,—cannot feel relaxed'; 说不出话耒 *shuo.bu-chu huah .lai* 'cannot say a word'; 听不出他闹了那么半天到底为的是什么事情耒 *ting.bu-chu ta nawle nemm banntian dawdii wey de sh sherm shyh.chyng .lai* 'cannot make out (from listening to him) what it was all about after he has made such a fuss'.

When the object in a split complement represents a place (not necessarily a place word), it is not possible to have V-RR′ O or V O RR′ as alternate forms. Thus, for 说出一个字耒 *shuo.chu ig tzyh .lai* 'say (out) a word', one can also say *shuo-.chu.lai ig tzyh* or *shuo ig tzyh .chu.lai*. But if *cherng* 'city' forms the object of *tzoou.jinn.chiuh* 'go into' it must be in the form of 走進城去 *tzoou₀jinn cherng .chiuh*. Similarly, we have 滚下山去 *goen.shiah shan .chiuh* 'roll down the hill'; 闯進屋裡去 *choang₀jinn u.lii .chiuh* 'rush into the room'; 走出门耒 *tzoou.chu men .lai* 'come out of the door'; 飛过海去 *fei₀guoh hae .chiuh* 'fly (away) over the sea'; 打回老家去 *daa₀hwei lao-jia .chiuh* 'fight back to the (lost) old homestead'. Another limitation is that the pretransitive construction is not available for objects representing locations. Thus, one can say either 拿出一本儿书耒 *na.chu i-beel shu .lai* or 把一本儿书拿出耒 *bae i-beel shu na.chu.lai* 'take out a book'; either 放下脸耒 *fanq.shiah lean .lai* or 把脸放下耒 *bae lean fanq.shiah.lai* 'let the countenance fall'; but only 拿出屋子耒

*na.chu utz .lai* 'take (it) out of the room'; 拿不出手未 *na.bu-.chu shoou .lai* 'cannot take it out of the hand,—the work is not presentable', but 把手拿出未! *Bae shoou na.chu.lai!* 'Take out (your) hand (from your pocket, etc.)!'

(6) Redundant complements V-R O RR´, V-RR´O R´, etc. A directional complement sometimes seems to occur both before and after the object. Thus, besides 送未一份儿礼 *sonq.lai i-fell lii* 'send this way a gift' and *sonq i-fell lii .lai* 'send a gift this way', there is also *sonq.lai i-fell lii .lai.* Besides the nonredundant forms:

| 拿出未一隻鵝 | *na.chu.lai* | *i-jy er* | |
|---|---|---|---|
| | 'take out here a goose' | | |
| 拿　一隻鵝出未 | *na* | *i-jy er* | *.chu.lai* |
| | 'take | a goose | out here' |
| 拿出　一隻鵝 未 | *na.chu* | *i-jy er* | *.lai* |
| | 'take out | a goose | here' |

there are also the redundant forms:

| 拿出未一隻鵝 未 | *na.chu.lai* | *i-jy er* | *.lai* |
|---|---|---|---|
| | 'take out here a goose | | here' |
| 拿出　一隻鵝出未 | *na.chu* | *i-jy er* | *.chu.lai* |
| | 'take out | a goose | out here' |
| 拿出未一隻鵝出未 | *na.chu.lai* | *i-jy er* | *.chu.lai* |
| | 'take out here a goose out here' | | |

the last being rare. (Cf. also next subsection, on *.lai* as particle.) The redundant forms do not occur with monosyllabic objects, such as in the nonexistent °*sonq.guoh.lai lii .lai,* and are more likely with long objects. Thus, a repetition of a complement or a part of it has the effect of marking off the object as an IC by a pair of parenthesis signs, as it were. This can be compared with the redundant demonstratives both before a long clause modifier and before the modified expressions, such as 那个昨儿未吃饭说我的饭不好吃的那个人 *neyg tzwol lai chy fann shuo woode fann bu haochy de neyg ren* 'that yesterday came to dinner and said my dinner was not good that man,—the man who came to dinner and said ... '. Thus, with -.*chu.lai,* we have: 怎么做得出这么没有道理的事儿出未?

*Tzeem tzuoh.de-chu tzemm meiyeou daw.lii de shell .chu.lai?* 'How is it possible to carry *out* such an unreasonable action *out*,—how can one do such an absurd thing?'

(7) Particles of purpose 来 *.lai* and 去 *.chiuh*. Another contributing factor for the redundancy is the similarity between -.*lai* and -.*chiuh* as directional complements and *.lai* and *.chiuh* as final particles (P 15 & P 16 in sec. 8.5.5 expressing purpose. From the V-V series 来打球 *lai daa chyou* 'come to play ball' there is 换了衣裳打球来 *huannle i.shang daa-chyou .lai* 'change one's clothes to play ball'. From 去買菜 *chiuh mae tsay* 'go to buy provisions' there is: 上街買菜去 *shanq-jie mae tsay .chiuh* 'go to the market (in order) to buy provisions', where the neutral tone *.lai* or *.chiuh* expresses purpose rather than direction.

The difference between *.lai* as directional complement and *.lai* as particle of purpose was once brought out in a very striking manner in a conversation in which one was misunderstood as the other. Back in the 1920's, Dr. Hu Shih told a servant to telephone Hu's cousin to come for some theater tickets left for him, saying 请他来取! *Chiing ta lai cheu!* 'Ask him to come to get (them)!', where *lai* is first verb in a V-V series, whereupon the servant said 他取来. *Ta cheu .lai.* Understanding *.lai* as a directional complement, Hu was puzzled, as that would not make sense and so said again 叫他来取! *Jiaw ta lai cheu!* 'Tell him come and get them!' And the servant said again 他说他取来。*Ta shuo ta cheu .lai.* 'He said he was going to get it.' And it was only after reflecting on the use of *.lai* as particle of purpose in the northern dialects that Hu began to understand that the *.lai* was not a directional complement but a particle, corresponding to the first verb of purpose in his own V-V series *lai cheu*.[56]

Note that the other particle of purpose *.chiuh* has an alternant *.keh* as a Peiping localism. While only the form *chiuh* is available as first verb in a V-V series and only -.*chiuh* as directional complement, the final particle of purpose has, in additional to *.chiuh*, the localism *.keh*, as 我拿了槍打獵去。*Woo nale*

---

[56]Based on a conversation shortly after the incident and confirmed in a letter to the writer in 1958.

*chiang daa-lieh .keh* 'I get (my) gun a-hunting go.' However, the form *keh* is also occasionally heard as a main verb, especially among speakers of Manchu origin.

Now, although the choice between *.lai* and *.chiuh* as particles is still much influenced by the consideration of direction, the fact that they have become particles makes it possible for full directional complement, when called for, to be used additionally. Thus, in 我写信请他派耒一位代表耒。 *Woo shiee-shinn chiing ta pay.lai i-wey daybeau .lai.* 'I wrote asking him to send here a representative here.', the last *.lai* serves both as a particle of purpose and as the second half of a pair of parenthesis signs. In other words, some of the redundant forms are usually a mixture of constructions. As extreme examples of redundancy, one could say 你想出耒了个怪主意耒, 去骗人去啊? 我也想出耒了个怪主意耒, 耒骗人耒. *Nii sheang.chu.laile g guay-jwu.yih .lai, .chiuh piann-ren .chiuh a? Woo yee sheang.chu-.laile g guay-jwu.yih .lai, .lai piann-ren .lai.* 'You have thought out a queer scheme (and go) to fool people (go)? I, too, have thought out a queer scheme (and come) to fool people (come).'

That the extra *-.lai* and *-.chiuh* cannot always be regarded as a split compound directional complement and must be explained as indicated above can also be seen from cases where omission of the object would result in a nonexistent compound directional complement. Thus, there is 送耒三封信耒 *sonq.lai san-feng shinn .lai* 'send three letter here', but no such complement as °*-.lai.lai*. Although there is both 爬上山去 *par.shanq shan .chiuh* 'climb up the hill' and 上去 *-.shanq.chiuh*, there is no ° 到去 °*-.daw.chiuh* from 住到乡下去 *juh .daw shiang.shiah .chiuh* 'live in the country [away]', where *.chiuh* is a particle.

## 6.7. Complex Compounds

*6.7.1. Structural Types.* In the preceding sections we dealt primarily with compounds in which the ICs were single morphemes, with occasional reference to certain very productive complex forms. We shall now make an over-all review of compounds of more than two morphemes, which will of course involve more possible types of structures. Since, however, there will be nothing new in the relations between the ICs, we shall not try to give all the possible types of combinations,[57] but instead illustrate a few very productive types and then take up certain special types of complex compounds and quasi-compounds.

By far the greatest number of complex compounds are subordinative compounds as regards the ICs, though each constituent in turn may be a compound of any syntactical type. Thus, in 螺旋推進器 *luoshyuan-tueijinnchih* 'snail-turn + push-advance instrument,—screw propeller', *luoshyuan* is subordinated to *tueijinnchih*, which in turn has *tueijinn* 'propel' subordinated to *chih* B 'instrument', but *tueijinn* 'push forward,—propel' is a V-R compound. In 擦皮鞋油 *tsa-pyishye -you* 'rub leather-shoe + oil, —shoe polish', *tsa-pyishye* is subordinated to *you*, while *tsa* as transitive verb has for its object *pyishye*, which in turn is a subordinative compound in which *pyi* modifies *shye*.

Besides the complex compounds involving determinatives and localizers (secs. 6.4.3 and 6.4.4), many of which are of the nature of transient words, the most productive complex compounds are three-morpheme compounds of the following types: (1) A-NN compounds, (2) AN-N compounds, (3) VO-N compounds, and (4) NNN compounds. Other types; (5) VV-N, (6) AA-N, (7) VR-N, and (8) other compounds, are much less frequent lexically.

(1) A-NN Compounds. 白皮纸 *bair-pyijyy* 'white leather-(like)-paper', 白皮鞋 *bair-pyishye* 'white shoes' (Occidental-style shoes being called *pyishye* 'leather shoes', the ICs are therefore not AN-N, but A-NN), 白木耳 *bair-muh'eel* 'white wood-ear,—an edible fungus', 紅十字 *Horng Shyrtzyh* 'Red " 十 " -Character,—Red Cross', 活地獄 *hwo-dihyuh* 'living earth-prison,—living hell', 鹹鴨蛋 *shyan-iadann* 'salt(ed) duck egg'.

(2) AN-N Compounds. 白皮书 *bairpyi-shu* 'white-cover document,—a (government) white paper', 長顆米 *charngke-mii*

---

~ 長粒儿米 *charngliell-mii* 'long-grain rice', 孤兒院 *gu'erl-yuann* 'bereft-children institution,—an orphanage', 小数点(儿) *sheaushuh-dean* (~-*deal*) 'small-number point,—decimal point', 脆皮鴨 *tsueypyi-ia* 'crisp-skin duck,—Peking (roast) duck'.

(3) VO-N Compounds. 起重机 *chiijonq-ji* 'raise-weight machine,—a crane', 防空壕 *farngkong-haur* 'defend-air trench,—air raid shelter', 分水嶺 *fenshoei-liing* 'divide-water mountain range,—watershed', 救生圈 *jiowsheng-chiuan* 'save-life ring,—life preserver', 拿手戲 *nashoou-shih* 'take-hand act,—an act one performs easily by just using the hand,—an action one is used to being successful in, one's specialty,' 顯微鏡 *sheanwei-jinq* 'reveal-tiny optical instrument,—microscope', 收音机 *shouin-ji* 'receive-sound machine,—radio (receiver)', 錄音机 *luh'in-ji* 'record-sound machine,—(disc or tape) recorder', 探海灯 *tann-hae-deng* 'probe-sea lamp,—searchlight', 探險隊 *tannshean-duey* 'probe-danger group,—an exploration group', 偷針眼 *toujen-yean* 'steal-needle eye,—a pimple on the eyelid' (so-called from the lore that one gets it for having stolen a needle), 望遠鏡 *wanqyeuan-jinq* 'gaze-distance optical instrument,—telescope'.

(4) NN-N and N-NN Compounds. We have already considered coordinate compounds, which we called polymers, consisting of long strings of constituents in coordination (sec. 6.3.3). More often, a string of nouns forms a subordinative compound of various internal substructures. The commonest type is a subordinate compound NN which modifies N in turn: 帆布鞋 *farnbuh-shye* 'sail-cloth shoes,—canvas shoes', 海岸線 *haeann-shiann* 'seashore line,—shoreline', 金鱼池 *jinyu-chyr* 'goldfish pond', 墨水筆 *mohshoei-bii* 'ink-liquid writing instrument,—(ordinary) pen'. Sometimes the first two constituents are coordinate, as 糖醋鱼 *tarngtsuh-yu* 'sugar-vinegar fish,—sweet and sour fish', 金銀島 *Jin'yn Dao* 'gold-silver island,—(translation of R. L. Stevenson's) *Treasure Island*'. The combination of N + NN is much rarer, as 糖蘋菓 *tarng-pyngguoo* 'sugar apple-fruit,—candied apple', 鸡皮膚 *ji-pyi.fu* 'chicken skin-skin,—goose flesh'.

(5) VV-N Compounds. 驱逐艦 *chiujwu-jiann* 'chase-pursue ship,—destroyer', 降落傘 *jianqluoh-saan* 'descending-dropping

umbrella,—parachute', 计算尺 *jihsuann-chyy* 'calculating-reckoning ruler,—slide rule' (also called *suannchyy* for short), 联合国 *Lianher Gwo* 'United-Combined Countries,—United Nations', 升降机 *shengjianq-ji* 'rising-descending machine,—elevator'.

(6) AA-N Compounds. 长短句 *charngdoan-jiuh* 'long-short sentences,—verse with lines of unequal lengths', also called 词 *tsyr*, 红黑帽 *hornghei-maw* 'red-black caps,—members of a magistrate's retinue in the old-style yamen, who wore red caps and black caps' (cf. Eng. 'redcap'), 酸辣汤 *suanlah-tang* 'sour-hot soup,—(any thick) soup with vinegar and pepper'.

(7) VR-N Compounds. 放大镜 *fanqdah-jinq* 'let-large optical instrument,—magnifying glass', 扩大器 *kuohdah-chih* 'expand-large instrument,—amplifier', 漂白粉 *peaubair-feen* 'bleach-white powder,—bleaching powder'.

(8) Other Compounds. SP-N: 地震仪 *dihjenn-yi* 'earthquake instrument, — seismograph', 人来疯 *renlai-feng* 'people-come madness,—show-off liveliness of children or animals before visitors'. V-NN: 炒牛肉 *chao-niourow* 'stir-fried beef'. V-AN: 拌黄瓜 *bann-hwang.gua* 'mixed yellow melon,—cucumber salad'. Apart from names of dishes the form V-AN is rare. The title *Paradise Lost* has been translated as 失乐园 *Shy Lehyuan* 'Lost Happiness-Garden', but unless the reader or hearer knows that it is the translation of *Paradise Lost*, he will certainly analyze the ICs as 2 + 1 'garden of lost happiness' rather than 'lost garden-of-happiness'.

V-VN as V-R is infrequent. An example is 洗掉色了 *shii-diawshaele* 'washed so that the color runs', where the *shii-diaw* (which could mean 'wash off' elsewhere) is not an IC here, but *diaw-shae* V-O 'lose color' is complement to *shii*.

6.7.2. *Syllabicity and Rhythm*. Syllabicity and rhythm play a very important part in wenyan, and since many compounds in the spoken language follow syntactical types in wenyan, the structure of complex compounds also depends upon these factors.

(1) 3-Syllable Compounds. With three syllables, the rhythmic type □.□ □ is always 2 + 1, as in 豆付浆 *dow.fu-jiang* 'beancurd milk', and type □ □.□ is usually 1 + 2, as in 炸

鍋巴 *jar-guo.ba* 'fried pot-sticker,—fried rice toast'. When there is no neutral tone, the 1 + 2 pattern is somewhat more frequent than 2 + 1, though both are quite common. Besides the examples given above under A-NN and AN-N, there is the pair 北平人 *Beeipyng-ren* 'Peiping person,—a native of Peiping' and 北平園 *Beei Pyngyuan* 'North Pingyuan' (Cant. *Pak Bhengyun*),—name of one of several municipal housing projects in San Francisco Chinatown named by the cardinal directions. In the names of persons, a monosyllabic surname, which is always bound, forms a compound proper name with the given name in the pattern of 1 + 2, but some families like to play with making a 2 + 1 pattern also meaningful. Thus, the name 黄家汉 *Hwang Jiahann*, which is 1 + 2, sounds, and is meant to sound, like 2 + 1: 'the Hwang-family's man'. Similarly, there are probably thousands of persons by the name of 黄种强 *Hwang Joongchyang* because, as 2 + 1, it says: 'The yellow race is strong.'

(2) 4-Syllable Compounds. By far the greatest number of 4-syllable compounds are of the type 2 + 2, in which most of the main ICs are in subordinative relation, with a variety of internal structures. Examples are: 安全火柴 *anchyuan-huoochair* 'safety matches', 百貨公司 *baehuoh-gongsy* 'hundred-goods company, —department store', 公共汽車 *gonggonq-chihche* 'public-to-gether gasoline-vehicle,—public automobile,—bus', 國際法庭 *Gwojih Faatyng* 'countries among law court,—the International Court of Justice', 航空母艦 *harngkong-muujiann* 'sailing-the-air mother-ship,—aircraft carrier', 水月電灯 *shoeiyueh diann-deng* 'water-moon electric-light,—acetylene lamp', 有声電影 *yeousheng-diannyiing* 'have-sound electric image,—sound movie'.

Of the 3 + 1 types, the 3 is more likely to be 2 + 1 than 1 + 2, since (2 + 1) + 1 still gives some of the rhythm of 2 + 2. Examples of (2 + 1) + 1 are: 自来水筆 *tzyhlaishoei-bii* 'self-coming-water pen,—fountain pen', 九龙山人 *Jeouloong Shan Ren* 'Ninedragon-Mountain Man,—pen name of a painter', 萝卜丝儿餅 *luo.bo-sel -biing* 'radish-shreds cake'. Examples of (1 + 2) + 1 are: 红十字会 *Horng-Shyrtzyh Huey* 'Red Cross Association', 染指甲草 *raan-jy.jea -tsao* 'dyeing-the fingernail grass,—balsam, touch-me-not'.

The pressure for 2 + 2 is so strong as to make any 3 + 1 compound understood as 2 + 2 if it makes sense at all, even though between the two syllables YZ in X Y Z W, Z may be a shade louder in 2 + 2 than in (1 + 2) + 1 compounds. The form 擦皮鞋油 *tsa-pyishye -you* 'rub-leather shoe oil,—polishing-shoe oil,—shoe polish' if analyzed as 2 + 2 would give *tsapyishyeyou* 'rub-leather shoe-polish' and there is no such thing, though it would be a possible compound word. Sometimes both 2 + 2 and 3 + 1 constructions for the same string of morphemes can make sense. Thus, 被選舉人 *bey-sheuanjeu -ren* is nowadays understood as (1 + 2) + 1: 'receiving-electing person,—person (to be) elected', but during the imperial days, when election was uncommon and the word *jeuren* 'second civil service examination degree' was frequently heard, it would have been understood as 2 + 2: 'jeuren who has been chosen'. In the experimental farm of Wuhan University there is, or used to be, a sign: 无肺病牛 *Wu fey binq niou* 'Without lung sick(ness) cows', which was obviously meant to be (1 + 2) + 1: 'without-lungsickness cows,—TB-free cows'; but the pressure for the 2 + 2 analysis, making it read: 'lungless sick cows', is so strong that the sign always makes passers-by smile or look puzzled.

Type 1 + 3 is rare except with certain listable versatile morphemes, often called prefixes (sec. 4.3.2), occurring in titles, terms of address, and so on. For example, 副研究員 *fuh-yanjiowyuan* 'assistant research fellow', 二表姊夫 *ell-beaujiee.fu* 'second external elder female sibling-husband,—second cousin-in-law' (where the grammatical ICs are 1 + 3, although the logical ICs are 3 + 1: 'so-and-so's husband'), 蒋委員長 *Jeang Woeiyuanjaang* 'Chiang Committee-head,—Chairman of Committee Chiang'. A bound and restricted morpheme does not compound readily with a group of three. Thus, in 1916, when my Chinese became rusty after having studied several years in America and I called my office 支编辑部 *Jy- Bian.jih-Buh* 'Branch Editorial Office' (of the periodical 科学 *Keshyue* 'Science'), the editor-in-chief 楊銓

*Yang Chyuan* promptly changed it to 编辑支部 *Bian.jih Jybuh* 'Editorial Branch Office', which, though logically less clear, made much smoother rhythm and better grammar.

(3) Longer Compounds. In compounds longer than four syllables, the much preferred rhythm is to have groups of two, with or without a remainder, according as the number of syllables is odd or even. Thus, with 5-syllable compounds, 2 + 3 is much more common than 3 + 2. There are any number of compounds like 公共汽車站 *gonggonq-chihche -jann* 'bus station', 螺旋推進器 *luoshyuan- tueijinn-chih* 'screw propeller', 國语统一筹備委員会 *Gwoyeu Toong'i Chourbey Woeiyuan Huey* 'National Language Unification Preparatory Committee',[58] but relatively few like 兂政府主义 *wu-jenqfuu -juuyih* 'without-government-ism,—anarchism', 降落伞部隊 *jianqluoh-saan -buhduey* 'parachute troops,—paratroopers'. Even when the total number of syllables is even, it would not be natural if not divided into groups of two. Thus, in the title of the periodical 考古人類学刊 *Kaoguu Renleyshyue Kan* "Bulletin of Archeology and Anthropology', the rhythm of [(2 + 2) + 1] + 1, as spoken, tends to be forced into that of (2 + 2) + 2, even though there is no such a compound as *shyuekan*. A title like ... 年刊 *Kaoguu Renleyshyue Niankan* 'Archeological and Anthropological Annual' (which it is) would sound more analyzable, but it would be longer and the combination (2 + 3) + 2 less rhythmical.

Type 3 + 3 practically never occurs as a compound. Once, looking over a row of Chinese and Japanese books stacked on the shelf, with titles in characters on their backs, I immediately spotted the Japanese books from the titles in combinations of 3 + 3 in 中國语音韵论 *Jonggwo-yeu Inyunn-luenn* 'Chinese-Language Phonology -Treatise' and 中國 语新词典 *Jong-gwo-yeu Shin-tsyrdean* 'Chinese-Language New-Dictionary', and

---

[58]Cf. headline: "England Side Captain Selection Difficulty Rumour", quoted by Sir Ernest Gowers, *The Complete Plain Words*, London: H. M. Stationery Office, 1954, p. 103; and instruction from a government guide-book:"All grantees should make sure that a protocol call to the President of your affiliated university is scheduled in your 'must-do'-before-leaving-Japan list of things." [Hyphens mine.]

the combination {1 + (2 + 2)} + 1 in   旧中國小说集
*Jiow Jonggwo-sheaushuo Jyi* 'Old Chinese Novels Collections,—
Collection of Old Chinese Novels', which a Chinese author would
rename more rhythmically, like   中國语言音韵论 *Jonggwo-*
*yeuyan Inyunn-Luenn*, etc., or, in talking about them, break them
up into phrases, such as *Jonggwo-yeu (yan) de inyunnluenn*, etc.
Now this apparent defect in the Japanese titles came from a pure
illusion on my part, arising from the habit of Chinese readers, including those who know Japanese, to read kanji in Chinese one--
character-one-syllable pronunciation instead of in Japanese, as it is
meant to be. When a Japanese author calls his book apparently
*Jonggwo-yeu Inyunn-Luenn*, he is really naming it *Chuukoku-go*
*Onin-ron* and since a long vowel or a syllable with a nasal ending
counts as two morae, the rhythm of the pattern is really not 3 +
3, but {(2 + 2) + 1} + {(2 + 2) + 2}, which is not at all the
same thing. This does not, however, imply that Japanese follows
rules of rhythm similar to Chinese in making Sino-Japanese compounds; it often does not.

  *6.7.3. Telescoped Compounds.* When the same morpheme
occurs as the last part of a first IC and the first part of a second
IC, it is usually not repeated. Thus, when the phrase 留学的
学生 *lioushyue de shyue.sheng* 'student who remains to study—
student who is studying or has studied abroad' is made into a
compound, it is not *lioushyue-shyue.sheng*, but *lioushyuesheng*.
This can be compared with English 'atomic-bomb bomber' telescoped into 'atomic bomber', except that such forms are much
more frequent in Chinese. Other examples are 东方学会 *Dong-*
*fang Shyuehuey* 'Oriental Society', 陸軍部長 *luhjiun-buhjaang*
'army department head,—minister of the army', 南京市長
*Nanjing Shyhjaang* 'Nanking City-head, Mayor of Nanking', 人
類学会 *renley-shyuehuey* 'anthropological learned society,—
society of anthropology' (cf. phrase: *renley de shyuehuey* 'man-
kind's learned societies'), 獸医院 *showiyuann* 'animal-medicine
(medical) institution,—veterinary hospital', 莱陽県誌 *Laiyang*
*Shiannjyh* 'Laiyang district district-records,—gazeteer of the district of Laiyang'. It will be noticed that the telescoping not only
makes the compounds shorter, but can often avoid the awkward

3 + 2 forms by changing them into the more rhythmic 2 + 2
forms. Telescoping, however, is not automatic or obligatory.
Thus, 山东大学⁀报 *Shandong Dahshyue Shyuebaw* 'Shan-
tung University Journal' repeats *shyue*. In the name of the periodical 清華学报 *Chinghwa Shyuebaw* 'Tsing Hua Journal',
*Chinghwa* is short for ( 國立 ) 清華大学 (*Gwolih*) *Chinghwa*
*Dahshyue* '(National) Tsing Hua University', in which *shyue*
would not be telescoped if *dahshyue* were to appear in the name.

 *6.7.4. Decompounds.* A decompound is a derived word when
a compound takes an affix and thus ceases, in its main structure,
to be a compound (Bloomfield, *Lg*, 210). Thus, *gentleman* is a
compound noun and *gentlemanly* is a decompound. The fact that
a word consists of a succession of two full morphemes and a suffix
does not necessarily make it a decompound. Thus 豆芽儿 *dowyal*
'beansprouts' is an ordinary compound, since its ICs are *dow* B
'bean' and the derived word *yal* 'sprout'. Similarly, in 樹根儿
*shuhgel* 'tree root', *shuh* F 'tree' is compounded with *gel* 'root',
which alternates, except for style, with the unsuffixed form *gen*.
But in 取灯儿 *cheudengl* 'get-light -er', the ICs are *cheudeng*
'gets light' and *-l* 'er', 'that with which to get light,—matches',
there being no such word as °*dengl*. Similarly, in 蝎虎子 *shiehuutz* BB-x 'scorpion tiger *suffix*,—that which acts as a tiger to
the scorpion,—scorpion eater,—lizard (popularly believed to eat
scorpions)', the suffix *-tz* makes a derived word of the bound compound *shiehuu-*, there being no such word as °*huutz*. Again, in
叫花子 *jiawhuatz* 'beggar', 叫化 *jiawhuah* (note change in
tone) 'calling and mendicant,—calling for alms' ends in the agent
suffix *-tz*. There is, to be sure, 花子 *huatz* 'beggar', but that
comes from the dropping of *jiaw-* through aphaeresis (sec. 6.7.6.4).
Then, through blending of *jiaw-* with the prefix *lao-*, we have the
most commonly used form 老花子 *laohuatz* for 'beggars (young
or old)'.

 In a form XYx, if XY and/or Yx occurs as a word, then it is
often uncertain what the ICs are. Thus in 電影儿 *diannyeengl*
'electric shadow *suffix*,—movie', there is a noun *yeengl* 'shadow'
as well as a noun *diannyiing*, a less informal name for 'motion

picture', so that either *diannyiing* + *l* or *diann* + *yeengl* is a possible analysis. Quite similarly, 蜡人儿 *lahrel* 'wax figure' can be analyzed either as *lahren* + *l* 'wax man *suffix*' or as *lah* + *rel* 'wax manikin'. In 電滚子 *dianngoentz* 'electric roller,—(popular term for) motor', there is no °*dianngoen* but there is *goentz* 'roller (in general)' and so *dianngoentz* is better analyzed as a compound of *diann* and *goentz*. In the V-O compound *bauyual* ← *bau-yuan-l* 'guarantee original (supply) *suffix*,—buy up what remains', there is no °*bauyuan* as a V-O compound nor °*yual* as a noun. But as one can say *baule-yual le* 'have bought up the rest' and *baude-leau yual ma?* 'Can you buy all that's left?' it should be regarded as a V-O compound, and thus different from the true decompound *cheudengl* 'matches', which cannot be so expanded.

On the whole, decompounds do not form a very productive class in Chinese.

### 6.7.5. *Literary Clichés and Exocentric Phrases*

6.7.5.1. *Literary Clichés.* When a literary expression is occasionally quoted in speech, its grammatical nature will of course fall outside the scope of the style of language we are studying, and there will be no need to analyze its grammatical structure any more than that of any dialect expression or foreign language expression which may occasionally be used in certain contexts. But if a literary expression occurs frequently in speech and if neither speaker nor hearer feels any italics or quotation marks around it, so to speak, then it should be considered a part of the language. The only thing special about it, then, is that its internal structure follows the grammar of the literary and not that of ordinary speech. In fact, this is precisely how most of the solid compounds are formed in which the parts are in ordinary syntactical relations in the literary but are no longer separable in the colloquial.

Following are some examples of literary clichés commonly used in speech, with translations (after the sign "=") in ordinary spoken form:

(a) 一面之词 *i-miann jy tsyr* = *i-fangmian (shuo) de huah* 'one side's words,—words of one of two opposing sides', as in 你不应该单凭一面之词就决定的. *Nii bu inggai dan pyng i-miann jy tsyr jiow jyuedinq de.* 'You ought not to depend only on the words of one side and decide it.'

(b) 非驢非馬 *fei liu fei maa* = (*yow*) *bush liu* (*yow*) *bush maa* 'is neither a donkey nor a horse,—nondescript', as in 这非驢非馬的办法一定会失敗的. *Jeh fei liu fei maa de bannfaa idinq huey shybay de.* 'This kind of method, which is neither one thing nor the other, will certainly fail.'

(c) 滿面春風 *maan-miann chuenfeng* = *maan-lean de chuenfeng* '(with) spring wind all over the face,—graciously, all smiles', as in 他滿面春風的欢迎他们進来。 *Ta maan-miann chuenfeng de huan'yng tamen jinn.lai.* 'With smiles all over his face, he welcomed them in.'

(d) 大庭廣众 *dah-tyng goang-jonq* (no structural equivalent in the colloquial) 'great hall wide multitude,—public place', as in 怎么可以在大庭廣众就脱起衣裳来了? *Tzeem keeyii tzay dah-tyng goang-jonq jiow tuo.chii i.shang .lai le?* 'How can (you, he, etc.) start undressing right in public?'

(e) 豈有此理? *chii yeou tsyy lii?* = *Naal yeou jeyg daw-.lii?* 'How can there be such a reason?—it is unreasonable,—ridiculous!' This expression is of special interest for two reasons. One is that it is used so often in speech that, when one writes in the literary style, it is no longer usable and one will have to go to synonymous paraphrases such as: 寧有是理乎? *Ning yeou sh lii hu?* The other point of interest is that, although the expression is in the form of an interrogative sentence, it has acquired the function of an adjective. In 做了一件豈有此理的事情 *tzuohle i-jiann chii-yeou-tsyy-lii de shyh.chyng* 'did an unreasonable thing', we could still regard the expression as a clause, since any clause can be subordinated to a following noun by introducing the particle *de*, but in 这简直太豈有此理了! *Jeh jeanjyr tay chii-yeou-tsyy-lii le!* 'This is simply too ridiculous!' the adverb of degree *tay* shows that what follows must be an adjective, or quality verb.

(f) 莫名其妙 *Moh ming chyi miaw* = 没人叫得出他的妙处 *mei ren jiaw.de-chu tade miaw.chuh* 'No one can name

its intricacy,—mysterious, incomprehensible,—to be at a loss'. This
is a full sentence, with 莫 *moh* < *mâk*, a fusion of 兮或 *miu ɣwɔk*
(Mand *wu huoh*) 'there is no one who', as subject and 名 *ming* 'to
name' as verb. (By popular etymology, the verb 名 *ming* is often
understood as *ming* 'understand' and written 明.) But as an
exocentric compound, it can be either an adjective or a transitive
verb, as in  他的作風有点儿莫名其妙。  *Tade tzuohfeng
yeoudeal moh-ming-chyi-miaw.* 'His style (of action, writing, etc.)
is a little nobody-can-name-its-mystery,—a little peculiar.', and
in  我真莫名其妙他的用意。  *Woo jen moh-ming-chyi-miaw
tade yonqyih.* 'I really can't understand his motive.'[59]

6.7.5.2. *Exocentric Phrases.* The last two examples are not
only in the literary style but are also exocentric in function. But
exocentric phrases (in the wide sense to include S-P clauses) can
also be in the ordinary colloquial form. This commonly occurs
with names of plants, plays, dishes, and the like, which, being
used as nouns, can be modified by D-M compounds. Here are
some examples:

(g) 鉄樹開花  *tiee-shuh-kai-hua* 'iron tree blossoms—name
of a plant'.

(h) 萝卜賽雪梨  *luo.bo.say-sheueli*  'radish   excels   snow
pears,—a large, crisp, turnip-like radish of Peiping and vicinity'.

(i) 炮打襄陽城  *Paw Daa Shiangyang Cherng* 'Guns Hit
Shiangyang City', name of a play or a form of firewords depicting
the incident.

(j) 薛仁貴征東  *Shiue Renguey Jeng Dong* 'Shiue Renguey
Conquers the East (Korea)', name of a novel.

All of the above can take D-M modifiers such as 一棵 *i-ke*
'a plant', 这齣 *jey-chu* 'this-(M for plays)' and 两本儿 *leang-beel*
'two volumes *or* copies'.

Of more doubtful nature are names of dishes formed with the
garnish as the apparent subject, method of cooking as the apparent verb, and the main ingredient as the apparent object, as in:

(k) 萝卜烧肉  *luo.bo-shaurow* 'turnips   cook   meat'.   Here

---

[59]For additional examples see J. Leighton Stuart, *Chinese Four-Character
Phrases*, Peiping, 1946.

*shaurow* can very well be regarded as 'cooked meat', a subordinative compound, which in turn can be modified by *luo.bo* '(with) turnips' to form a complex subordinative compound. Similarly formed are:

(l) 蛋炒飯 *dannchao-fann* 'egg-stirred rice,—stir-fried rice with eggs'.

(m) 醬爆鸡丁ㄦ *jianqbaw-jidiengl* 'sauce-splattered chicken dice'.

*6.7.6. Abbreviations and Aphaeresis*

*6.7.6.1. Abbreviation by Morphemes.* Because most Chinese morphemes are monosyllabic and most syllables are written with single characters, abbreviations usually take the form of a selection of a few key morphemes from a long string of morphemes. For example, 女子高等师范学校 *Neutzyy Gaudeeng Shyfann Shyueshiaw* 'Female-Persons Higher-Grade Teacher-Norm Learning-School,—Women's Higher Normal School' is abbreviated to 女高师 *Neugaushy*, which then looks like a compound of the form BFB with ICs 1 + 2. From 航空運输 *harngkong yuunshu* 'sail the air transportation' comes the abbreviation 空運 *kongyunn* 'air transport'. On May 3, 1963, the *Central Daily News*, Taipei, announced a 耕者有其田成果展 *Gengjee Yeou Chyi Tyan Cherngguoo Jaan* 'Exhibition of Results of the Tillers Own Their Farms (movement)'. On May 4, the same movement appeared as 耕有田 *Geng Yeou Tyan* 'Till-Own-Farms (movement)'. From 國際联盟 *Gwojih Liannmeng* 'International League,—League of Nations' comes the abbreviation 國联 *Gwolian*. The name 联合國 *Lianher Gwo* is already so short as to need no abbreviation, but the long name of 联合國教育科学文化组织 *Liangher Gwo Jiawyuh Keshyue Wenhuah Tzuujy* 'United Nations Educational Scientific Cultural Organization' is abbreviated to 联教组织 *Linjiaw Tzuujy*, as if to say 'Unit Educ Organization', which would still have more than twice as many syllables, whereas the form 'UNESCO' is more comparable in length to the Chinese abbreviation. (A more recent translation as 教科文组织 *Jiawkewen Tzuujy* 'Educ Sci Cul Organization' is longer and less rhythmical.) When 執行委員

会 *jyrshyng woeiyuanhuey* 'executive committee' is abbreviated to 執委会 *jyrwoei-huey*, then it is more comparable to the familiar 'ex com'.[60]

*6.7.6.2. Ambiguous Abbreviations.* Since abbreviation by morphemes means more than by letters, there is less chance of ambiguity than by letters, as in *NBC* (*B* for 'Biscuit' or Broadcasting'?) or *AAA* (second *A* for 'Anthropological' or 'Automobile'?). But ambiguities do occur with morpheme abbreviations, too. Thus, 北大 *Beeidah* used to mean only 國立北京大学 *Gwolih Beejing Dahshyue* 'The National Peking University', but now the newspapers refer to 北大西洋联盟组织 *Beei Dahshi Yang Lianmeng Tzuujy* 'the North Atlantic (Ocean) Treaty Organization' also as *Beeidah* 'NATO'. During World War II days, 联大 *Liandah* meant only 西南联合大学 *Shinan Lianher Dahshyue* 'the Southwestern Associated Universities' (in Kunming); now the newspapers refer to 联合國大会 *Lianher Gwo Dahhuey* 'United Nations Assembly' also as *Liandah*. In one case reported, a letter addressed to 西医ㄥ院 *Shi-i-i-yuann* 'Western Medicine Hospital' was returned to the sender with the post-office notation: "Comrade, there are too many hospitals of Western medicine in this city [Sian]; which one did you want to mail this letter to?" Actually the writer meant 西北医学院附属医院 *Shibeei Ishyueyuann Fuhshuu I-yuann* 'Northwestern Medical School Affiliated Hospital'.[61]

*6.7.6.3. Obscure Abbreviations as New Compounds.* When the full form of an abbreviation has been forgotten or when the full form and the abbreviation have acquired differences in meaning or connotation (cf. 'FBI' as compared with 'Federal Bureau of Investigation and 'GI' as compared with 'government issue'), then the abbreviation attains the status of a new compound in its own right and the tracing of the full form, though often interesting and important, should be a separate task from that of analyzing the

---

[60]For further discussions on this and related problems, see Y. R. Chao, "Graphic and Phonetic Aspects of Linguistic and Mathematical Symbols", *Proc. of Symposia in Applied Math.*, 12.78-80 of 69-82 (1961).

[61]Quoted in ZGYW, no. 63:5 (1957).

new compound as it is. Thus, the relatively new term 语文 *yeu-wen* 'language, especially considering both its sounds and its system of writing', has been abbreviated from 语言文字 *yeuyan wentzyh* 'language and writing'. But 语文问题 *yeuwen wenntyi* 'problem(s) of language (incl. writing)' is one type of problem, whereas 语言文字问题 *yeuyan wentzyh wentyi* could mean either (1) the same thing or (2) two types of problems. The phrase *wenshyue yihshuh de fuhshing* 'the flourishing again of literature and the arts' is of general application, but 文藝復兴 *Wenyih Fuhshing* is the usual term for the European Renaissance. In central Taiwan there is a bridge as well as a place called 大肚桥 *Dahduh Chyau* 'Big Belly Bridge', which is often understood to be a compound in which *Dahduh* modifies *Chyau*. But the local people know that the name is abbreviated from 大肚溪桥 *Dahduh-Shi Chyau* 'Big-Belly Creek Bridge', so that *Dahduh*, in modifying *Chyau*, is doing so as an abbreviated name of the stream.

6.7.6.4. *Aphaeretic Forms.* Sometimes a compound is abbreviated through aphaeresis, or the dropping of an initial syllable, irrespective of its being an IC or not. Thus the word for 'peanut' used to be 落花生 *luohhua-sheng* 'dropped the flowers (on the ground, then the fruit) grows,—peanuts', which among Russians who lived in China used to be called *lukashin* and is still so-called, in the *on*-form, *rakkasei* in Japanese. But many who eat the common peanut and say the word 花生 *huasheng* do not realize that an initial *luoh ~ law* 'drop' has been omitted and so the present status of the word, at the descriptive level, is simply that of an asyntactic compound. Similar to *huasheng* is the word 花子 *huatz* < 叫花子 *jiawhuatz*, which we regarded as a decompound (sec. 6.7.3). In the latter case the full form is still not obsolete and is used side by side with the aphaeretic form. An interesting lack of parallel development was in the words for 'train' and 'steamship'. When I first heard of these modern inventions, they were called 火轮车 *huooluenche* 'fire-wheel vehicle' and 火轮船 *huooluen-chwan* 'fire-wheel ship'. At one stage of the change toward abbreviation, they were called 火车 *huooche* but still *huooluen-chwan;* then finally, *huooche* and, not ° 火船 °*huoo-*

*chwan*, but 輪船 *luenchwan* (though in Cantonese it is 火船 *fox-zun*, cognate with a hypothetical °*huoochwan*). This asymmetrical change can be compared with the case of the English words 'min-ute' and 'second', which were abbreviated from *prima minuta* 'first minute (part)' and *secunda minuta* 'second minute (part)'. From the descriptive, nonhistorical point of view, *huooche* 'fire vehicle' is a vehicle which presumably derives its energy from fire, and *luenchwan* 'wheel ship' is a ship which has a lot of wheels in its machinery. A fire engine, by the way, is 救火車 *jiowhuoo-che* 'rescue-fire vehicle', homophonous with 旧火車 *jiow-huooche* 'old train', in which the ICs come out when transformed as *jiow-huoo de che* 'vehicle (with) which (one) rescues fires' and *jiow de huooche* 'a train that's old'.

# CHAPTER 7
## PARTS OF SPEECH: SUBJECTIVES

## 7.1. General Observations on Parts of Speech

*7.1.1. Parts of Speech and Form Classes.* A form class is a functional class of forms of any size. For example, 桃 *taur* B 'peach', 梨 *li* F 'pear', 桃儿 *taurl* 'peach', 雪梨 *sheueli* 'snow pear,—a white, crisp variety of pear', 很大的梨 *heen dah de li* 'very large pear', and 我昨儿買的梨 *woo tzwol mae de li* 'the pear I bought yesterday' are all of the form class of nominal expressions, but only *li*, a single-morpheme word, *taurl*, a derived word, and *sheueli*, a compound word, are words and they belong to the part of speech of nouns. In general, a part of speech is a form class whose members are words.

It is sometimes convenient to distinguish the sizes of the same form class by using terms ending in *-al* for phrases and the traditional names of the parts of speech for words. Thus, 梨 *li* 'pear' is a noun, but 剛買来的梨 *gang mae.lai de li* 'the pear just bought' is a nominal; 走 *tzoou* 'go' is a verb, but 不一定走 *bu idinq tzoou* 'not necessarily go' is a verbal. We shall use the term 'expression' when referring to a member of a form class, whether it is a word or a phrase. For example, both 吃 *chy* 'eat', a verb, and 吃东西 *chy dong.shi* 'eat food', a verbal, are verbal expressions. By another usage, however, the *-al* terms have also been used to include single words, and are then synonymous with 'expressions'.

*7.1.2. Listables and Open Classes.* Parts of speech, as well as other form classes, can sometimes be defined by enumeration without stating any common property possessed by all of its members.[1]

---

[1]This is in fact Russell's principle of abstraction, according to which the (common) property of a class of objects consists simply of the fact that the

For example, pronouns can be enumerated exhaustively in a short list. So can final particles. Nouns and verbs, on the other hand, cannot be listed within the scope of a grammar book and can only be listed in a regular lexicon. While it is logically sufficient to define classes by enumeration, it may not seem satisfactory from the point of grammar, and we shall try to state whatever common property the class may have. From the point of view of the learner of the language, however, definition by enumeration can be a very useful thing and one "gets the hang" of the thing after using the individual items in their functions, so that any general statement of a common property is only a summary and an afterthought. After all, a child learns to speak grammatically from the behavior of the individual members of the lists, even the unlistable, open classes.

*7.1.3. Listable Subclasses of Open Classes.* Sometimes a large form class contains subclasses, some of which are listable and others open. For example, under the large class of substantives, pronouns are listable, but nouns form an open class; under verbs, auxiliary verbs are listable and action verbs form an open class; under measures, individual classifiers are listable and standard units of measure, if we include names of units used in the natural sciences, form an open class. An open class, let it be understood, is not necessarily a class of an infinite number of members, but a class which cannot be handled conveniently in a descriptive grammar, but can be included in a lexicon, to which additions are often made without involving substantial change in the grammar of the language.

*7.1.4. Overlapping Classes.* When a word belongs sometimes to one part of speech and sometimes to another, there is then an overlapping of classes,[2] or, from the point of view of the word in question, it has multiple membership. Every language has a certain proportion of words with multiple membership, no matter how the parts of speech and their subclasses are set up. English is rich in cases of overlapping classes, as in 'a cut', 'to cut', 'has cut', 'he cut'; in 'water' as a mass noun, 'water(s)' as a bounded

---

objects are the members of that class. Russell observes that this might just as well be called the principle of concretion. See Bertrand Russell, *Principles of Mathematics*, Cambridge, 1903, pp. 166, 219-220.

[2]Bloomfield calls it *class-cleavage* (*Language*, 204 ff.).

noun, and 'to water' as a transitive verb. In Chinese 怪 *guay* is an adjective in 可是这很怪. *Keesh jeh heen guay.* 'But this is odd.', an adverb in 怪难看的 *guay nankann de* 'rather ugly', and a transitive verb in 别怪我! *Bye guay woo!* 'Don't find me odd,—don't blame me!'; 背 *bey* is a noun in 背上头 *bey.shanq.tou* 'on the back', a transitive verb in 背一首诗 *bey i-shoou shy* 'recite a poem' (since reciting by heart is to be done by turning one's back toward the teacher), and an adjective in 我今儿手背. *Woo jiel shoou bey.* 'I today the hand is contrary,—I have an unlucky hand today (at mahjong, dominoes, cards, etc.).' For this reason it is a common belief, or used to be, that Chinese has no parts of speech.[3] With all the ramifications of overlapping, however, the majority of Chinese words have limited functions. Thus, 鱼 *yu* 'fish' is a noun and does not behave like verbs by taking aspect suffixes to form °鱼着 , °鱼过 , °鱼了 °*yuj,* °*yu.guoh* °*yule;* nor can adverbs 更 *genq* 'still more', 最 *tzuey* 'most' function as predicative verbs in °我更. °*Woo genq.,* or °他最. °*Ta tzuey.* Verbs cannot be modified by D-M compounds to form constructions like °三斤走 °*san-jin tzoou* or °两片

---

[3]The most quoted opinion is that of the late Henri Maspero, who said: "En réalité les mots chinois ne sont ni noms ni verbes, ils sont quelque chose d'indifférenciés," "La Langue Chinoise", *Conférences de l Institut de Linguistique de l'Université de Paris,* Année 1933, Paris, 1934, p. 35. More moderate and critical views have been expressed by Bernhard Karlgren in "The Parts of Speech and the Chinese Language", *Language and Society,* Essays Presented to Arthur M. Jensen on His 70th Birthday, Copenhagen, 1961, pp. 73-78, and by Walter Simon, "Has the Chinese Language Parts of Speech?" *Trans. of the Phil. Soc.,* London, 1937, p. 99, to which Maspero replied in *Bull. de la Soc. de Ling. de Paris,* Paris, 1938, p. 209. The leading Chinese grammarian, Li Jiinshi, said, in his *GYWF* (1924), p. 24, n. 10, 凡词, 依句辨品, 離句专品. *Farn tsyr, i jiuh biann piin, li jiuh wu piin.* 'In general, the class of a word depends upon the sentence it occurs in; separated from its sentence, it has no class.', but modified his view later in *ZGYW,* no. 15 (1953), pp. 10-11, where he said 词已定類,由職顯類. *Tsyr yii dinq ley, you jyr shean ley.* 'While a word already belongs to a definite class, it is through its function that its class becomes manifest.' My present treatment is similar, though different in many details, to that of Fa-Kao Chou in *BIHP* 22:303-322 (1950).

说 °*leang-piann shuo.* The forms 一个走，一个飛。 *Ig tzoou, ig fei.* 'One walks, the other flies.' look like exceptions, but here *ig* is subject to *tzoou* and *fei*, with potential pause or pause particles, and does not modify *tzoou* and *fei*, which are still verbs here.

In general, overlapping does not occur. For example, 花 *hua* 'flower' and flowery',—blurred (of visions)' is adjective or noun, but most nouns, such as 根 *gen* 'root', are not adjectives and most adjectives, such as 熟 *shour* 'ripe', are not nouns. There is class overlap with 老 *lao* 'old' as adjective and *lao* 'all the time, always' as adverb, but most adjectives, such as 嫩 *nenn* 'tender', are not adverbs and most adverbs, such as 还 *hair* 'still', are not adjectives. If in setting up word classes for any language a grammarian should find that two of his classes overlap for a large marjority of their members, then the classification is at fault and should be so revised that most of the apparently overlapping cases can be separated, or else he should give up the original divison as being nongrammatical and do with only one class.

Balanced and Unbalanced Overlapping. The textual frequencies with which a word occurs in different parts of speech are sometimes of the same order, or balanced, and sometimes of quite different orders, or unbalanced. For example, most adjectives are not used as causative verbs, and those that are are cases of class overlap. But the relative frequencies of a word occurring as A and V are not always the same. Thus, 破 *poh* 'broken' A and *poh* 'break' Vt occur with comparable, if not equal, frequencies; on the other hand, 烂 *lann* 'pulped, decayed, corroded' A is far more common than *lann* 'corrode' Vt., so that one speaker felt it necessary to paraphrase it, for fear that the verb would be heard as an adjective, in the following sentence: 这荚子要烂了，——我的意思是说这荚子要拿那个药水烂了. *Jeh goantz yaw lann le—woode yih.sy sh shuo jeh goantz yaw na neyg yawshoei lann le.* 'This (drain) pipe should be corroded— what I mean is that this pipe should be corroded with that chemical solution.' Further examples of balanced overlapping are: 病 *binq* A 'sick', N 'sickness'; 气 *chih* N 'air', A 'angry', V 'to be angry with'; 麻 *ma* N 'hemp', A 'feel like (coarse) hemp,—numb, have the pins and needles'; 生 *sheng* A 'raw; unripe', V 'give birth to, to be born'; 鎖 *suoo* N~V 'lock'. Most dissyllabic verbs, especially the new terms, are also nouns, as: 报告 *bawgaw* N~V 'report'; 代表 *daybeau* V 'represent', N 'representative, delegate'; 抵抗 *diikanq* V 'resist', N 'resistance; 進步 *jinn$_o$buh* N ~ V 'progress'.

Further examples of unbalanced overlapping (with the class of less frequent use illustrated by sentences) are: 氷 *bing* N 'ice', A in: 这茶太氷了。 *Jeh char tay bing le.* 'This tea is too icy.', V in: 这茶还得氷一会儿. *Jeh char hair deei bing .i.hoel.* 'This tea has to be chilled a little more.'; 燙 *tanq* A 'hot', V in: 这酒得燙一燙. *Jeh jeou deei tanq .i.tanq.* 'This (rice) wine has to be heated a little.' 被单儿燙了没有？ *Beydal tanqle mei.you?* 'Have the sheets been ironed?'; 水 *shoei* N 'water', A 'watery', as in: 这块翡翠很水。 *Jeh-kuay feeitsuey heen shoei.* 'This piece of jade is very watery (translucent).'; 清楚 *ching.chuu* A 'clear', V 'to be clear about', as in: 我不大清楚他的计画. *Woo budah ching.chuu tade jih.huah.* 'I am not very clear about his plans.' (cf. 明白 *ming.bair* 'clear, to be clear about', which is a balanced case); 高兴 *gaushinq* A 'glad, pleased', V as in: 他什么缘故不高兴我了. *Ta sherm yuan.guh bu-gaushinq woo le.* 'For some reason he is displeased with me.'; 规矩 *guei.jeu* N 'rule', A as in: 这工人的活不够规矩. *Jeh gongren de hwo bu gow guei.jeu.* 'This workman's work is not sufficiently accurate.' The less frequent function is usually a later started usage. Some very recent usages are still felt as neologisms. From 意味 *yih$_o$wey* N 'meaning' there is now *yih$_o$weyj* V 'meaning-ing,—having the meaning that ... ,—meaning that ...'. From 坦白 *taanbair* A 'plain, frank', comes *taanbair* V 'tell frankly (about oneself),—confess to the authorities', which is a post-1950 usage.

It should be noted that class overlap refers only to the same word belonging to different classes and not to homophonous but different words belonging to different classes. It is obvious that 煤 *mei* N 'coal' and 没 *mei* V 'have not' are simply unrelated homophones. So are 樹木 *shuh.muh* (individual) N 'a number' and 数目 *shuh.muh* (collective) N 'trees'. But even where the written characters are the same, they may still be homophones, as in 打 *daa* V 'strike' and *daa* (an alternate form of the more frequent *dar*) M 'dozen'; 等 *deeng* V 'wait' and *deeng* M 'grade'; 才 *tsair* N 'talent' and 才 *tsair* H 'just, then and only then'. In the last two examples, the homophones are etymologically related, but at the descriptive level they are homophones and therefore not cases of overlapping classes to which the same word belongs.

*7.1.5. Marked and Unmarked Parts of Speech.* In a small minority of cases parts of speech of Chinese words are recognizable by definite markers. For example, nouns are recognizable by the nominal suffixes *-tz, -l, .tou, -.ba*, etc. (sec. 4.4.4), and verbs by the suffixes *-le, -j, .guoh*, etc. (sec. 6.4.5). But even here there is some class overlap in the suffix *-l*, as in the verbs 玩儿 *wal* 'to play', 颠儿 *dial* 'beat it' (slang for 'go away'), and 火儿了 *huol le* 'get mad' (i.e., 'become angry'). Most words, however, belong to one part of speech or another by virtue of their positions in functional frames, and the class is determined by selection, in other words, arbitrary membership. For example, 馬 *maa* 'horse' and 公式 *gongshyh* 'formula' are nouns because they occur in 三匹馬 *san-pi maa* 'three horses' and 两个公式 *leangg gongshyh* 'two formulae'; 長 *charng* and 要紧 *yawjiin* are adjectives because they occur in 長绳子 *charng sherngtz* 'long rope' and 很要紧 *heen yawjiin* 'very important'; 嘎? *Ar?* 'Huh?' ('What did you say?') and 嗯. *Ng.* 'M-hm.' ('Yes.') are interjections because they occur only in zero frames; that is, they do not occur in construction with anything else. In other words, parts of speech in Chinese are mainly distinguished syntactically; morphological markers, if any, are of only secondary importance.

*7.1.6. Full and Empty Words.* The Chinese traditional classification of full and empty words corresponds closely to the modern division of content words and function words. In discussing parts of speech, Fries cites the first stanza of the Jabberwocky:

'Twas brillig, and the slithy toves
  Did gyre and gimble in the wabe;
All mimsy were the borogoves,
  And the mome raths outgrabe.

from which he extracts the empty words or morphemes which form the framework, with its structural meanings, as follows:

'Twas———, and the————y ————s
    Did ———— and ———— in the ————;
All ————y were the ————s,
    And the ———— ————s ————.[4]

Similarly, from my translation of the above:

有一天臬裡，那些活济ㄟ的猶子

    在衕边儿倸着那么趹那么覓；

好难罒啊，那些脖若獚子；

    还有窠的猪子呕的格儿．

*Yeou i-tian beir.lii, neh.shie how.jihjide toutz*
    *Tzay wey.bial jiinj nemm gorng nemm berl;*
*Hao nansell a, neh.shie bo.rogoutz;*
    *Hair yeou mia de rhatz ow de gerl.*

With mostly nonsense full words (for which there are no characters or characters have to be made up, as indicated by subscribed dots), we can extract the empty frame:

*Yeou i-tian ————.lii, neh.shie ————de ————tz*
    *Tzay ————.bial ————j nemm ———— nemm————;*
*Hao ———— a, neh.shie ————tz;*
    *Hair yeou ————de ————tz —— de ————.*

Fries sets up for English four parts of speech proper: nouns and pronouns, verbs, adjectives, and adverbs, and then sixteen classes of function words. Without entering into the question of English parts of speech, we can observe that the division of full and empty words or morphemes in Chinese is to some extent a matter of degree. The suffixes *-de, -j, -l* and *-tz* are clearly empty morphemes, as are particles *me, ne, a,* and so on. Words like *yeou* 'has, there is', *tzay* 'to be at', and *hair* 'still, moreover' are intermediate in nature. As for 好 *hao* ... *!* 'how ... !' adverb of degree, 那么 *nemm(e)* 'so' adverb or degree or manner, 天 *-tian* 'day' measure to time, 裡 *-.lii* 'inside' localizer for place or time, and 边儿 *-.bial* 'side' localizer for place, they have fairly definite extralinguistic meanings as well as structural meanings. Similarly, directional complements 來 *-.lai* 去 *-.chiuh*, etc. have fairly "full"

---

[4]C. C. Fries, *The Structure of English*, New York, 1952, p. 70.

meanings; and we have regarded 起来 -.chii.lai as having multiple class membership, since in 飛起来 *fei.chii.lai* 'fly up' it is a directional complement [sec. 6.6.6 (3.5)] and in 哭起来了 *ku.chii.lai le* 'start to cry' it is an aspect suffix [sec. 4.4.5(3)].

What is of greater relevance in grammatical discussion is not so much whether a form has to do with content or form or whether it is full or empty, as the question whether it is one of a manageable list and how frequently it occurs. We shall then find a rather high degree of correlation between the following two types: (1) full or content words, of open classes, of low or medium frequency, mostly tonal, for example, 猪 *ju* 'pig', 蓝 *lan* 'blue', 跑 *pao* 'run', 快 *kuay* 'fast', and (2) empty or function words, of listable classes, of high frequency, mostly atonal (neutral), for example, $_0$*sh* 'is', *de* 'thereof', $_0$*tzay* 'at', 吧 *.ba* interrogative or advisative particle.

*7.1.7 Bound Parts of Speech.* We found the possibility of free, isolated utterance to be too drastic a criterion for a form to be a word and substituted for it the requirement of unlimited versatility with regard to combination with certain form classes (sec. 3.8.2). This would allow particles like *a, ba, ne,* determinatives like 哪 *neei-* 'which', 半 *bann-* 'half a', classifiers like 条 *-tyau* 'strip', 片 *-piann* 'slice', 塊 *-kuay* 'piece', and adverbs like 就 *jiow* 'then', 最 *tzuey* 'most' to be counted as words and their form classes to be parts of speech or their subclasses. This is what we shall follow below.

*7.1.8 Subdivisions and Superdivisions of Parts of Speech.* The general principle by which to decide whether to set up subdivisions or superdivisions of a certain classification is to ask whether we can make significant statements about the units that are set up. Thus, nouns can be subdivided into individual nouns, mass nouns, and so on, because individual nouns take the general individual classifier g or at most two or three other classifiers, as in 一个狗 *ig goou*, 一隻狗 *i-jy goou*, or 一条狗 *i-tyau goou* 'a dog', while mass nouns do not take g or any particular classifier, but take any of a number of quantitative measures, such as 一些水 *i-shie shoei* 'some water', 一滴水 *i-di shoei* 'a drop of water', 一杯水 *i-bei shoei* 'a cup of water', 一西〻水 *i-shishi shoei* 'one cc. of water', and many other measures. On the other hand, over and above nouns, pronouns, and so on, we can set up the larger class of substantives, because they all have their principal functions as subject or object and can be modified by adjectival expressions. Over and above adjectives and (action) verbs we can set up the larger class of predicatives, or verbs in the wider sense, because they can all function as predicates and may be modified by adverbial expressions. It is sometimes a matter of choice as to whether there is enough consistent difference to justify a subdivision or enough common property to set up larger classes.

*7.1.9 The Parts of Speech Listed.* In table 10, listing the parts of speech to be discussed, F stands for 'free', B for 'bound' F! for 'always free', -B for 'start-bound', B- for 'end-bound', and ( ) for 'lexically not numerous'. We shall discuss the subdivisions and superdivisions of these classes in the following sections.

Table 10

Parts of Speech

Substantives:

| N | Nouns | 人 | ren 'man', | | |
| | | 火 | huoo 'fire' | F | |
| Nr | Proper names | 李白 | Lii-Bor 'Li Po', | | |
| | | 约翰 | Iuehann 'John' | F | |
| Np | Place words | 廣州 | Goangjou 'Canton', | | |
| | | 梅恩 | Meien 'Maine' | F | |
| Nt | Time words | 今儿 | jiel 'today', | | |
| | | 現在 | shiantzay 'now' | F | |
| D-M | D-M compounds | 三磅 | san-banq '3 lbs.', | | |
| | | 这回 | jey-hwei 'this time' | F | |
| D | Determinatives | 三 | san- 'three', | | |
| | | 每 | meei- 'each' | (F) | B- |
| M | Measures | 片 | -piann 'slice', | | |
| | | 里 | -lii 'li' | | -B |
| L | Localizers | 裡 | -olii 'inside', | | |
| | | 上 | -.shanq 'on' | | (-B) |
| P | Pronouns | 我 | woo 'I', | | |
| | | 什么 | sherme 'what' | (F) | |

Verbs and Other Parts of Speech:

| V | Verbs (incl. A adjectives) | 吃 | chy 'eats', | | |
| | | 長 | charng 'long' | F | |
| K | Prepositions | 被 | bey 'by', | | |
| | | 从 | tsorng 'from' | | B- |
| H | Adverbs | 忽然 | huran 'suddenly', | | |
| | | 也 | yee 'also' | F | B- |
| J | Conjunctions | 那么 | nemme 'then', | | |
| | | 假如 | jearu 'if' | F | |
| P | Particles | 嗎 | ma interrog. part., | | |
| | | 啊 | a pause part. | | (-B) |
| I! | Interjections | 嘿! | Hei! 'Heh!', | | |
| | | 廿! | .Eh! 'M-hm' | | (F!) |

A substantive is a word which normally functions as the subject or as the object of a verb. Less frequently, it functions, usually with the subordinative particle *de*, as the modifier of another substantive and, still less frequently, as a nominal predicate. A substantive may be a noun, a proper name, a place or time word, a D-M compound, or a pronoun; less often it is a determinative alone, a measure alone, or a localizer alone.

## 7.2. Nouns

A noun is a substantive which can be modified by a D-M compound. Examples are: 風 *feng* 'wind', 本事 *been.shyh* 'ability', 事 *shyh* 'event; business', 东西 *dong.shi* 'thing, object', 主意 *jwu.yih* 'plan, intention'. As phrases with D-M compounds we have 这本儿书 *jey-beel shu* 'this book', 十杯酒 *shyr-bei jeou* 'ten cups of wine', 二斤盐 *ell-jin yan* 'two catties of salt'.

Nouns form an open class which occupies the major portion of the lexicon of the language. There are not only more nouns than any other part of speech, but more nouns than all the other parts of speech put together. This does not of course include the countless number of transient words which can be formed of any numeral and a measure, since dictionaries do not include transient words except as illustrative examples.

A relatively small number of nouns have overt markers, such as the suffixes *-tz, l, -.tou*, etc. and a listable number of versatile end morphemes such as 性*-shinq*, 員 *-yuan*, etc. (sec. 4.4.2). In spite of high textual frequencies of occurrence of nouns ending in *-tz* and *-l*, marked nouns form a minority of nouns even textually and a still smaller minority lexically. Most nouns are therefore recognizable as nouns syntactically in that they have the syntactical properties of substantives in general (mentioned above) and are modifiable by a D-M compound in particular.

As a negative criterion, nouns cannot be modified by monosyllabic adverbs, as 不 *bu* 'not', 也 *yee* 'also', 还 *hair* 'still', and 更 *genq* 'still more'. There are two types of apparent exceptions: (1) A noun may be a noun or some other part of speech by way of class overlap, as 光 *guang* N 'light': 很光 *heen guang* 'very smooth, very bare'; 鼓 *guu* 'drum': 太鼓[5] 了 *tay guu le* 'get too bulging (like a drum)'; 土 *tuu* N 'earth, dirt': 真土 *jen tuu* 'very rustic, uncouth'. (2) A noun may be used predicatively and an adverb may modify it, not as a noun, but as a predicate, as in: 这个人太君子人了。 *Jeyg ren tay jiuntzyyren le.* 'This man is too much of a gentleman,—leans backward to be fair.'

Nouns do not normally reduplicate to form distributives. Exceptions are 人ㄟ *renren* 'everyman'; 事ㄟ如意。*Shyhshyh ruyih.* 'Everything is as one wishes.'; 山ㄟ有老虎。*Shanshan yeou laohuu.* 'Every mountain has tigers.' The last two reduplicates are rare. As for *ren*, it is better to treat it as a case of N~ M overlap, since there is not only *renren* but also 一人 *i-ren* 'one person,—each person' or 'alone' and 每人 *meei-ren* 'each person', with *ren* as measure, as well as *ig ren* and *meeig ren*, with *ren* as noun. On other forms of reduplication in nouns, see section 4.2.

According to the nature of the D-M compound that goes with a noun, we can subdivide the class of nouns into the following

---

[5]Popularly written 凸, but it is etymologically the same morpheme as *guu* for 'drum', both descriptively and historically.

subclasses: (1) individual nouns, (2) mass nouns, (3) collective nouns, and (4) abstract nouns.

(1) Individual Nouns. Individual nouns are associated with their specific classifiers, so that in dictionaries the specific classifier must be cited under each individual noun to identify its class, somewhat like the indication of genders for languages with distinctions of gender. For example, 一張桌子 *i-jang juotz* 'a table', 兩把刀 *leang-baa dau* 'two knives', 那件事情 *ney-jiann shyh.chyng* 'that business or event', 这条河 *jey-tyau her* 'this river'. Note that the association of specific classifiers with nouns is primarily the association of words and only roughly in terms of meaning. Thus, although both 枝 *-jy*, with root meaning 'twig', and 根 (儿) *gen~gel*, with root meaning 'root', are usually described as classifiers for stick-like objects, this is only a rough guide, and both dictionaries and learners must still note with each noun which specific classifier it goes with. For example, 一根儿棍子 *i-gel guenntz* 'a rod', 一枝筆 *i-jy bii* 'a pen', and not the other way round, although both a rod and a pen are stick-like things as things. In fact, the word 枝子 *jytz* 'branch, twig' takes the general classifier *g* in preference to *gen~gel*, since most individual nouns ending in *-tz* take *g*. Even for an identical person or thing, the classifier depends upon what word is used to name him or it. Thus, if a person is spoken of as 先生 *shian.sheng* 'a gentleman', he is 一位先生 *i-wey shian.sheng*, but if simply as 人 *ren* 'a man', he is 一个人 *ig ren*. If a large extended object for sleeping on is spoken of as 'a piece of furniture', it is 一件家俱 *i-jiann jia.jiuh*, but as 'a bed' it is 一張床 *i-jang chwang*. Grammatical classifiers are therefore a matter of words and not of things. Comparing classifiers again with genders, it is somewhat like the case of the same person being referred to in German as *die Frau* but *das Weib*, or the same thing as *der Kopf* but *das Haupt*.

Some nouns take more than one kind of classifier, usually with a difference in meaning. For example, 一扇门 *i-shann men* 'a door' refers more to the door as a physical object, but *i-daw men* 'a door' refers to it as a doorway to go through. Thus, if one person says 你得走那道门。*Nii deei tzoou ney-daw men.* 'You

have to go by that door.', another person may reply 那扇门
闭 的 太 紧, 我 闬 不 闬. *Ney-shann men guan de tay jiin, woo
kai.bu-kai.* 'That door is shut too tight, I can't open it.' The
general classifier *g* is a possible alternate for almost any individual classifier. In the case of *men*, for instance, *g* can be used in
either of the sentences in place of *-daw* or *-shann*. Other examples are: 一个先生 *ig shian.sheng* 'a teacher; a physician
(dial.)'; 一位先生 *i-wey shian.sheng* 'a gentleman', 一个 太ㄗ
*ig tay.tay* 'a wife, a mistress of a household': 一位太ㄗ *i-wey
tay.tay* 'a (married) lady', 一个 小姐 *ig sheau.jiee* 'an unmarried woman': 一位小姐 *i-wey sheau.jiee* 'a young (unmarried)
lady'.

Some individual nouns have no specific classifiers and take
only the general classifier *g*. Examples are 一个贼 *ig tzeir* 'a
thief', 一个橘子 *ig jyutz* 'an orange', 一个馒头 *ig man.tou*
'a (steamed) bun', 一个问题 *ig wenntyi* 'a problem', 一个蚂
蚁 *ig maa$_0$yii* 'an ant', 一个榜样 *ig baang$_0$yanq* 'a model (to
follow)', 一个学校 *ig shyueshiaw* 'a school' or less frequently
一 家(儿) 学校 *i-jia(l) shyueshiaw* (as compared with Cantonese *iatkaan hoakhaaw*, with specific classifier 间 *-kaan*, of which
the Mandarin cognate *-jian* is limited to words for rooms and not
applicable to words for organizations or whole buildings.)

(2) Mass Nouns. Mass nouns do not have specific classifiers,
but can be modified by D-M compounds in which M is (a) a
standard measure, as in 一尺布 *i-chyy buh* 'a foot of cloth',
十磅糖 *shyr-banq tarng* '10 pounds sugar', 五加仑汽油
*wuu-jialuen chihyou* 'five gallons of gasoline'; (b) a container
measure or a temporary measure, as in 一杯茶 *i-bei char* 'a cup
of tea', 一身雪 *i-shen sheue* 'a body of snow,—snow all over
one', 一屋子烟 *i-utz ian* 'a roomful of smoke'; (c) a partitive
measure, as in 一点儿水 *ideal shoei* 'a little water', 那些酒
*ney$_0$shie jeou* 'that amount of wine', 一会儿工夫 (儿) *ihoel
gong.fu(l)* 'a moment of time'; and (d) a shape in which the mass
can be gathered, as in 一块布 *i-kuay buh* 'a piece of cloth', 两
堆土 *leang-duei tuu* 'two piles of earth', 一滩水 *i-tan shoei*
'a (shallow) pool of water,—a puddle. Mass nouns do not take the

individual classifier g, but can take any of the four kinds of measures or shapes that make sense. A further formal feature is that, between the D-M compound and the noun, one can insert an optional *de* for mass nouns but not for individual nouns. Thus, one can say either 兩磅肉 *leang-banq row* 'two pounds meat' or *leang banq de row* 'two pounds of meat', but not °*leang-wey de shian.sheng* for 'two gentlemen'.

In a minority of cases, a word may be an individual noun or a mass noun by way of class overlap. For example, 面包 *miannbau* is an individual noun in 一个面包 *ig miannbau* 'a (loaf of) bread', but a mass noun in 一塊面包 *i-kuay miannbau* 'a piece of bread' and 一片面包 *i-piann miannbau* 'a slice of bread'; 石子儿 *shyrtzeel* is an individual noun in 一个石子儿 *ig shyrtzeel* 'a pebble' and a mass noun in 一噸石子儿 *i-duen shyrtzeel* 'a ton of gravel'. (Cf. 'too many potatoes' vs. 'too much potato and too little meat'.) In the case of an individual noun used with a container measure [sec. 7.9 (5)], however, it is better not to consider it as a case of class overlap, as container measures can be applied to all sorts of individual nouns, as 一屋子人 *i-utz ren* 'a roomful of people, 一地的东西 *i-dih de dong.shi* 'a floorful of things', 一口的新名词 *i-koou de shin-mingtsyr* 'a mouthful of new terms'.

(3) Collective Nouns. A distinction should be made between (individual) nouns or measures denoting collections of things and collective nouns in the grammatical sense. Thus 团体 *twantii* 'body (of persons), organization' is an individual noun, since it occurs in 一个团体 *ig twantii* 'an organization'. Similarly, we have 一个学会 *ig shyuehuey* 'a learned society' and 两个不同的階级 *leangg butorng de jie.jyi* 'two different (social) classes'. Bound forms like -*chyun* 'group', 套 -*taw* 'set', and 隊 -*duey* 'group' are measures and not nouns, as in 一群鸟儿 *i-chyun neaul* 'a flock of birds', 一套洋服 *i-taw yangfwu* 'a set of foreign clothes,—a suit. 一隊兵 *i-duey bing* 'a group of soldiers'.

Collective nouns, on the other hand, do not take individual classifiers, but can take temporary or partitive measures. Thus,

两 位 先 生 *leang-wey shian.sheng* 'two gentlemen', but 那些
孩子们 *ney₀shie hairtz.men* 'those children'; 一 張 桌 子 *i-jang
juotz* 'a table', 四 把 椅子 *syh-baa yiitz* 'four chairs', but 一 堂
桌 椅 *i-tarng juoyii* 'a hall of tables and chairs,—a set of tables
and chairs'. An apparent exception is the expression 一位民众
*i-wey minjonq* 'one gentleman of the masses', which I once heard
in a restaurant called 民众食堂 *Minjonq Shyrtarng* 'Restaurant
of the Masses'. Although *minjonq* is a collective noun, it was used
here actually as the name of a special snack-and-tea combination,
which would, and often does, take the individual classifier 客 *keh*
'an order of' and is thus a quasi-quoted form and therefore an
individual noun.

Some collective nouns can be recognized by the suffix -*.men*,
except that the word 娘儿们儿 *niangl.mel* ( ← *niang-l* + *.men-
l*) is either (a) a collective noun, as in: 这书是写给娘儿们儿
看的。 *Jeh shu sh shiee geei niangl.mel kann de.* 'This book was
written for womenfolk to read.', or (b) an individual noun, as in
原 来 是 个 娘儿 们儿! *Yuanlai sh g niangl.mel!* 'Why, it's
a girl!' The occurrence of the suffix -*.men* in individual nouns is,
however, quite rare. (Cf. sec. 4.4.4.)

Collective nouns are also formed by compounding an individual noun with its classifier or a mass noun with a standard
measure, in that order. Thus we have 一 辆 車 *i-lianq che* 'a
vehicle'; 車辆 *chelianq* 'vehicles; traffic'. But, conversely, a noun
followed by and compounded with its measure is not necessarily a collective noun. For example, 一 茛 筆 *i-goan bii* 'a pen':
一个筆茛 (儿) *ig biigoan* (~ *biigoal*) 'a penholder', still an
individual noun. [For additional examples, see sec. 6.4.3 (4).]

Finally, collective nouns are formed by enumerating or exemplifying the individuals in the collection, as: 父母 *fuhmuu* 'parents', 桌椅板凳 *juoyii-baan.denq* 'tables, chairs, and benches,
—furniture', 亭台楼阁 *tyng-tair-lou-ger* 'pavilions, terraces, storied buildings, raised alcoves,—elaborate architecture', 風花雪
月 *feng-hua-sheue-yueh* 'winds, flower, snow, and the moon,—
lyric subjects'.

In general, collective nouns cannot take D-M compounds in

which D is a numeral other than *i* 'one'. Thus, with individual nouns one can have 一个, 两个, 三个学生 *ig, leangg, san'g shyue.sheng* 'one, two, three students' or an indefinite number 一班学生 *i-ban shyue.sheng* 'a class of students'. With a collective noun, a phrase like 三个学生们 *san'g shyue.sheng.men* is rare, but one can always say 一班学生们 *i-ban shyue.sheng-men* 'a group of students'. Since *fuhmuu* 'parents' is a collective noun, one cannot say: ° 他有两个父母。 °*Ta yeou leangg fuhmuu.*, but one can say: 他父母两个都在。 *Ta fuhmuu leangg dou tzay.* '(As for) his parents, both are living.' In Southern Mandarin the term *shanq.ren* 'upper (generation) person,—parent' is an individual noun, so that one can say *ig shanq.ren* and *leangg shanq.ren*, which is rare in the North.

(4) Abstract Nouns. Abstract nouns are nouns which can only take certain group measures 种 *-joong* 'kind', 類 *-ley* 'category', 派 *-pay* 'type, style', measure for verbs 頓 *-duenn* 'a spell, a siege', 番 *-fan* 'once over', and partitive measures as 些 *-shie* 'some', and 点儿 *-deal* 'a little', but not individual classifiers or standard measures. Although the formal features stated above coincide largely with words denoting qualities, states, and actions, it is only a rough correspondence. It goes without saying that individual and mass nouns for many concrete things also take the general and indefinite measures, but nouns for many abstractions can also be grammatically individual and mass nouns. Thus in 两个学说 *leangg shyueshuo* 'two theories' and 一个 *ig* or 一塲夢 *i-chaang menq* 'an arena of dream,—a dream', 三塲戲 *san-chaang shih* 'three plays (as performed)', the words *shyueshuo*, *menq*, and *shih* are individual nouns; in 四年工夫 *syh-nian gong.fu* 'four years' time (spent)', 用三分力量 *yonq san-fen lih.liang* 'use three-tenths of one's strength,—use a little strength', *gong.fu* and *lih.liang* are mass nouns.

Examples of abstract nouns are: 病 *binq* 'sickness' as in: 他的脾气不好是一种病。 *Tade pyi.chih bu hao sh i-joong binq.* 'That his temper is bad is a kind of sickness.'; 恩 *en* 'a kind act': 人家对他那点儿恩他老记得。 *Ren.jia duey ta ney-deal en ta lao jih.de.* 'He always remembers that little kindness

they did to him.'; 禍 *huoh* 'disaster, misfortune': 我怕你要惹
出一塲大禍来了。   *Woo pah nii yaw ree.chu i-chaang dah-
huoh .lai le.* 'I am afraid you will cause a great disaster.' (cf. V-O
form under Mc'14, p. 594); 累 *ley* 'burden': 一个人身体不好
也是一种累。 *Ig ren shentii bu hao yee sh i-joong ley.* 'When
a man has poor health, it is also a kind of burden.'; 礼 *lii* 'propriety': 礼到了，人家就不能再怪你了。 *Lii dawle, ren.jia
jiow buneng tzay guay nii le.* 'When the propriety has gotten
there,—when you have done the proper thing, then they can't
blame you any more.' On the whole, monosyllabic abstract nouns
are not very common. It is true that dissyllabic nouns or any
other parts of speech are more numerous than monosyllables, but
it is even more true of abstract nouns.

Examples of longer abstract nouns are: 成绩 *cherng$_0$ji* 'accomplishment, attainment (of a student, official, etc.)'; 道理 *daw-
.lii* 'reason, principle'; 患难 *huann$_0$nann* 'hardships, vicissitudes';
火气 *huoo.chih* 'hot temper, impatience'; 交情 *jiau.chyng*
'friendship'; 人生 *rensheng* 'life', as in: 人生如夢 *Rensheng ru
menq.* 'Life is but a dream.'; 可能性 *keenengshinq* 'possibility'.
Note that *keeneng* can also be an adjective 'possible' or an individual noun 'a possibility, a possible case' as in: 有两个可能。
*Yeou leangg keeneng.* 'There are two possibilities.' Abstract nouns
often have class overlap with other parts of speech. In the following examples the etymologically primary meaning is given first:
福气 *fwu.chih* N~A 'good luck; lucky'; 爭执 *jeng$_0$jyr* V~N
'struggle; wrangle'; 虧空 *kuei$_0$konq* V~N 'incur a deficit; deficit';
迷信 *mishinn* N~A~Vt 'superstition; superstitious; believe in
superstitiously'; 希望 *shiwanq*  V~N  'hope'; 羞耻 *shiou$_0$chyy*
N~A 'shameful; shame'.

*7.2.1. Nouns and General D-M Compounds.* In defining the
subtypes of nouns by the types of D-M compounds associated
with them, an exception should be made of the most general
forms *ig* (~*g* after verbs), *jeyg,* and *neyg,* which modify not only
individual nouns but all nouns. Thus, with the abstract noun
道理 *daw.lii* 'reason, principle', one can say: 他也说不出
(一)个道理来。 *Ta yee shuo.bu-chu (i)g daw.lii .lai.* 'He can't

give any reason, either.' With 商量 *shang.liang* V 'consult' or abstract N 'consultation', one can say: 这事情咱们得有个商量才可以决定世! *Jeh shyh.chyng tzarmen deei yeou (i)g shang.liang tsair keeyii jyuedinq è!* 'About this matter, we've got to have a consultation before we can decide, you know!' With a mass noun *jeou* 'wine', one can say: 这个酒酰,你那个酒太新了。 *Jeyg jeou shwen, nii neyg jeou tay shin le.* 'This wine is mellow, that wine of yours is too new.' Other determinatives besides *i* before *g* and other measures besides *g* after *jey-* or *ney-* are not so unrestricted, but are limited as defined above. Thus, one cannot say °*leangg shang.liang* for 'two consultations', but has to use some construction as 商量两次 *shang.liang leang-tsyh* 'consult twice'. As for the interrogative *neeig*, it is used with non-individual nouns only in contrast with *jeyg* or *neyg* in the near context, as in: 请你把那个酒给我一点儿! *Chiing nii bae neyg jeou geei woo ideal!* 'Please give me some of that wine!' 哪个? 那个啊? *Neeig? Neyg'a?* 'Which wine? That wine?' If there is no *jeyg* or *neyg* in the near context, one will have to use the usual forms of D-M for mass nouns, as in: 你要哪瓶(~哪种)酒? *Nii yaw neei-pyng (~ neei-joong) jeou?* 'Which bottle (~which kind) of wine do you want?'

## 7.3. Proper Names

Proper names are substantives which cannot be modified by D-M compounds. They can be referred to by the pronouns 他 *ta* and 他们 *tamen* as substitutes and, in common with animate nouns, can be the subject of certain verbs 拿 *na* 'take', 想 *sheang* 'think', etc., but cannot be object to 到 *daw* '(go) to', 在 *tzay* '(to be) at', as time and place words can.

We are using the term "proper name" rather than "proper noun", since we have defined nouns narrowly as modifiable by D-M compounds. On the other hand, a place name is not a proper name in the sense we are using the term, since a place is a place word, which, unlike proper names, can be object of 到 *daw*, 在 *tzay*, and so on?

Semantically, most proper names are names of persons, living or dead, real or fictitious, though by no means strictly limited to human beings. A proper name is expected to be sufficiently unique to refer to only one individual. There are, to be sure, often different individuals with the same name. But in any instance of occurrence the listener is expected to identify the individual referred to from the name without a D-M compound or any other determinative modifier. This is different from implicit definite reference implied by a preposed position in the sentence. For example, the definite reference implied by the subject position of the individual nouns *ren* in 人来了. *Ren lai le.* 'The man has come.', and *shu* in 书買的太貴了. *Shu mae de tay guey le.* 'The book has been bought at too high a price.' does not make *ren* or *shu* a proper name.

An apparent exception to the non-occurrence of D-M compounds before proper names is in such forms as: 有两个王良. *Yeou leangg Wang Liang.* 'There are two Wang Liangs.' Here *Wang Liang* stands for 两个叫王良的 *leangg jiaw Wang Liang de* 'two individuals named *Wang Liang*', thus putting *Wang Liang* in quasi-quotation, which is realized phonologically in the usual contrasting stress on *"leangg*, whereas in a sentence: 有两个黄鼠狼. *Yeou leangg hwangshuulang.* 'There are two weasels.', there will be only the normal stress on *hwangshuu'lang.*

*7.3.1. Freedom and Syllabicity in Proper Names.* Chinese proper names have various degrees of freedom according to their syllabicity and, to a lesser degree, the situational context. Monosyllables, except for special cases noted below, are always bound. Thus, if a man has a "full name" like 黄松 *Hwang Song,* you can neither call him by his 姓 *shinq*, or surname, *Hwang* nor by his 名字 *ming.tzyh* (or 名 *minq* L), or given name, *Song,* even though as ordinary words both *hwang* 'yellow' and *song* 'pine' are free words. The force of compounding between a monosyllabic surname and a monosyllabic given name is so strong that even a wife sometimes calls a husband, less frequently a husband calls a wife, by his (or her) full name. This practice is not unusual among the new generation, where, in coeducational schools, roll calls have made full surname-given name compounds items of high-frequency hearing and so schoolmates get to know each other in such forms.

Dissyllabic given names without the surname do get called in mature life, but no monosyllabic surnames or given names.

There are very few dissyllabic surnames. All of them are free. Thus, one can say: 欧陽来了，可是司徒有事耽擱了. *Ouyang lai le, keesh Sytwu yeou shyh dan.ge le.* 'Ouyang has come, but Sytwu was detained on business.', where, if the surnames were monosyllabic and if the speaker did not wish to be so formal as to use 先生 *.shian.sheng* 'Mr.' after the surname or did not know or did not feel sufficiently well acquainted to use the given name or courtesy name, he would add a colorless prefix 老 *Lao*,      thus: 老張認得路，不用去問老李了． *Lao Jang renn.de luh, buyonq chiuh wenn Lao Lii le.* 'Jang knows the way, we (or you) don't need to go and ask Lii.'

The courtesy name or 号 *haw* (known, in biographical usage, as 字 *tzyh* L) is always in modern usage dissyllabic and free. It is usually given by one's teacher or a friend in one's late teens,[6] very often with some allusive relation to one's given name. For example, 張飛 *Jang Fei* had the courtesy name of 翼德 *Yihder*, where *fei* means 'to fly', and *yihder* means 'wing virtue'. Sometimes an empty word is prefixed or suffixed to a monosyllabic given name to form a courtesy name, as 李白 *Lii Bor* (~ *Lii Bair*): *Lii Taybor* (~ *Lii Taybair*), where *tay* 'great, grand' is merely an intensifier. One of the commonest suffixes to add for such purposes is *jy* 'it' L, as 胡適 *Hwu Shyh* 'Hu Shih': 胡適之 *Hwu Shyhjy*, when *shyh* means 'to fit' and *Shyhjy* 'fit it'.[7]

Most literate men and some women have courtesy names. Sometimes a person has in addition a sobriquet or studio name, usually invented by himself, or a nickname given by others, which often takes the form of a descriptive phrase and is unlimited as to the number of syllables. For example, 梁啟超 *Liang Chiichau* (1873-1929) whose courtesy name was 任公 *Renngong*, used as his

---

[6]Von Anna Bernhardi had the ages of acquiring the given name and the courtesy name reversed in her "Chinesische Frauennamen", *Mitteil. d. Sem. f. Orient. Spr.*, Berlin, 16:1.1 (1913). In the prevailing custom, the given name is given at or soon after birth and the courtesy name much later.

[7]One of the late Dr. Hu Shih's seals had the form *Hwu Shyh Shyhjy jy yinn* 'Hu Shih Shihchih's seal', as follows:

studio name or pen name 飲氷室主人 *Yiinbing-shyh Juuren* 'Master of the Ice-Drinking Room'. Nicknames are of course not usually answered to by their owners, but sometimes they capitalize on them, as in the case of 王麻子 *Wang Matz* 'Wang the Pock-Marked', which probably started as a behind-the-back nickname, later used by himself and his descendants and successors as the famous makers of scissors in Peiping.

The tendency to treat monosyllabic proper names as bound, whether surnames or given names, is so strong that foreign monosyllabic names are usually transliterated as dissyllables in order to be mentionable alone. Thus the American name *Dean* has appeared in Chinese newspapers as 第安 *Dih'an*. Likewise, *John* is usually transliterated as 約翰 *Iuehann* (i.e., *Johan*), but *Johnson*, being dissyllabic, appears variously as 約翰孫 *Iuehannsuen*, 詹生 *Jansheng*, etc. This tendency also exists in place names, both foreign and Chinese, as illustrated below [sec. 7.4(1)].

7.3.2. *Special Uses of Monosyllabic Proper Names*

(a) In the L style most morphemes are free words, including monosyllabic proper names. Thus the name of 曹操 *Tsaur Tsau* is a compound word in modern speech, sometimes even with a neutral tone: ㄘㄠ˙ . but the dynastic histories frequently refer to the man simply as 操 *Tsau*.

(b) Monosyllables, being bound, can occur not only in the form of surname-name form of a full name, but also in subordinative compounds in which the center is a term of address. With surnames we have compounds like 王先生 *Wang .Shian.sheng* 'Mr. Wang'; with given names we have 巧姊 *Cheau Jiee* '(Older) Sister Cheau', where *Cheau* is either a monosyllabic name or a (bound) part of a dissyllabic name.

(c) In epistolary style, which in these days of writing in bairhuah still follows the L style in matters of salutation and other matters of form, the writer refers to himself either by a term of address or his given name, and if the name is a dissyllable, he often uses only one of the syllables, as a somewhat deferential form. For example, if the writer's given name is 文 *Wen*, he will refer to himself as *Wen*, with the character written off to one side, half a space to the right of the column (or below the line when one writes, Western style, from left to right). If his name is 斯文 *Sywen*, he will call himself *Sy* if he shares with his brothers (or with all siblings and/or with all cousins) the second syllable *Wen*, but *Wen* if his brothers have *Sy* in their names.

(d)  While the preceding cases are all of a marginal nature as to the independence of monosyllabic names, a special case of true free form is in the monosyllabic names used with the connotation of intimacy or endearment, as from parent to child or between husband and wife. Thus, a person with a name 斯文 *Sywen* or 瑪麗 *Maalih* 'Mary' may be called by his or her parent or by his or her spouse simply as *Sywen* or *Maalih*, but also, with connotation of intimacy or endearment, *Wen* or *Lih*. In the nature of the case this occurs much more frequently in vocative positions than in included positions as subject, object, or modifiers.

A sidelight on this usage is in the indecision on the part of Chinese residing abroad as to whether to treat a dissyllabic given name as one compound word, which it is in Chinese, or as a "first name" and a "middle name". A person with a name like *Wang Mingshan* usually has on his passport the form *Wang Ming-shan*. As he stays longer abroad, he finds life simpler to sign himself "last name" last as *Ming-shan Wang*. Then he finds that makers of directories will list him as *M. Wang*, along with a column of other M. Wangs in the telephone directory. So he decides to break up the compound into two names *Ming Shan*, with two initials. Thus he ends up with acquiring a first name of *Ming*, which his colleagues of two weeks' acquaintance in the same office will call him by. Now note the formal differences between this kind of "first name" and the monosyllabic forms with special connotations of endearment described above. When *Wang Mingshan*, ˊˊˉ  (or ˊˉˉ at conversational tempo) is known, in English, as *Ming Shan Wang*  ˉˉˋ  and called by his first name *Ming*, the name is said as an English word with the usual intonation of ˋ with a longer drawl than it had in the original 2nd tone ˊ. It has therefore neither the same form nor the same connotations as a Chinese monosyllabic free proper name. Thus, if Mr. Wang is addressed by a girl in his office as *Ming* ˋ , it is getting familiar, but he will understand that "it does not mean a thing", while if someone other than his wife or a senior member of his family

speaking in Chinese to him calls him *Ming* 丁 , he will wonder:
"Who are you to call me *Ming* 丁?"

Brothers or sisters, or all siblings together, are often numbered
as 老大 *Laodah* (not °老一 °*Lao'i*), 老二 *Lao'ell,* and so on.
These are informal proper names, used either as terms of direct
address or as designative terms. A monosyllabic surname is often
followed by a numeral to make an informal term of address, as in
王二 *Wang Ell* 'Brother Two of the Wangs'. This form is limited
to brothers only. The phrase 張三李四 *Jang San Lii Syh*
'(Brother) Three of the Jangs and/or (Brother) Four of the Liis'
has acquired the connotation of 'Smith and Jones,—anybody'.

While 老 *Lao* as a prefix has lost its meaning of 'old', 小 *sheau*
still retains its meaning of 'little' and is used in terms of address
before 二, 三 *ell, san,* etc. as in 小二 *Sheau Ell* 'Little Brother
(or Sister) Two', 小三儿 *Sheausal* 'Little Brother (or Sister)
Three', etc. Such forms are more informal than the *Lao-* forms.
But the monosyllabic forms 三儿 *Sal,* 四儿 *Sell,* etc., are used
only as terms of endearment by parents or senior members of the
family and not even between husband and wife, as other monosyllabic forms of names are.

*7.3.3. Meanings of Proper Names.* Although proper names have
connotational meanings arising from the pragmatical aspects of
their use, their lexical meanings are a different matter. Surnames
are either morphemes of the general lexicon, as 白 *Bair* 'white',
李 *Lii* 'plum' B, or from place names which no longer have any
lexical meaning, as 吳 *Wu,* 秦 *Chyn.* Given names are usually
taken from the general lexicon of the language, even though sometimes one has to go to the dictionary and find rare characters[8] in
order to have members of the clan of the same generation con-
form to a pattern of generation indicator, such as characters all
having the radical 75 木, 85 水, or 167 金. But once a name is
established, its function in the sentence is that of an index, in the
sense in which Charles S. Peirce used the term, that is, it refers

---

[8]From the legal point of view, both in China and in most other countries, a person's name is the way it is written rather than the way it is
spoken.

by pointing at the referent without meaning what the word otherwise means. Thus no contradiction is involved in saying 王培德 是个坏人。 *Wang Peirder sh g huay ren.* 'Wang Peirder is a bad man.', because neither *Wang* is said or heard as the word 'king' or is *Peirder* 'cultivate virtue' said or heard as more than identifying a person. The sentence does not sound at all paradoxical. The case of nicknames and pen names, made up with special emphasis on meaning, is somewhat different. But with usage these also tend to become ordinary proper names, like *Wang Matz* or *Yiinbing-shyh Juuren,* mentioned above.

Other aspects of proper names, such as the use of kinship terms and other terms of address as proper names, have been treated elsewhere,[9] and, as these have to do more with the cultural than with the grammatical aspects of the subject, they will not be detailed here.

## 7.4. Place Words

A place word is a substantive which can fill the following positions:

| | | |
|---|---|---|
| 在 ... | *tzay...* | 'to be at...' |
| 到 ... | *daw...* | 'arrive at...' |
| 到 ... 去 | *daw...$_0$chiuh* | 'go to...' |
| 上 ... 去 | *shanq...$_0$chiuh* | 'go to...' |
| 从 ... 来 (etc.) | *tsorng... lai* (etc.) | 'come (etc.)...from' |
| 望 ... 走 (etc.) | *wanq... tzoou* (etc.) | 'go (etc.)...toward' |

Thus, one cannot say ° 到门去 °*daw men $_0$chiuh* for 'go to the door', since *men* is a noun, nor ° 从老张到我来 °*tsorng Lao Jang daw woo lai* for 'comes from Jang to me', since *Lao Jang* is a proper name and *woo* is a pronoun. But it is all right to say 到门那儿去 *daw men.nall $_0$chiuh* 'go to the door', since *men-.nall* 'door-there,—where the door is' is a place word, and 从张 家到我这儿来 *tsorng Jang.jia daw woo.jell lai* 'come from the

---

[9]Yuen Ren Chao, "Chinese Terms of Address', *Language,* 32:217-241 (1956).

Jangs to me', since *Jang.jia* 'chez les Jangs' and *woo.jell* 'me-here, —chez moi' are place words.

Since place words are substantives, they share the general properties of substantives in occurring as subjects, as objects (to other verbs as well as to *tzay, daw*, etc.) and as attributes. For example, 还是我们这儿舒服. *Hairsh woomen.jell shu.fwu.* 'After all, our place is more comfortable.' 我看不見门背後. *Woo kann.bu-jiann menbeyhow.* 'I can't see behind the door.' 家裡的事情我不荏. *Jia.lii de shyh.chyng woo bu goan.* 'Things in the household I don't bother with.' One very frequent use of a place word as subject is to set the scene for what the predicate says, whether in the form of a verbal predicate or in the form of an S-P predicate. For example, 月亮上有人. *Yueh.liang.shanq yeou ren.* 'The moon-thereon has people,—there are people on the moon.' 鍋裡没饭了. *Guo.lii mei fann le.* 'Pot-inside has no more rice,—there is no more rice in the pot.' 我们家裡大人做事, 小的上学. *Woomen jia.lii dah.ren tzuoh-shyh, sheau de shanq-shyue.* '(In) our home, the grownups work, the young ones go to school.'

Place words can be (1) place names, (2) certain D-M compounds, (3) certain N-L compounds and other compounds involving localizers, and (4) nouns for places used as place names.

(1) Place names. We are not placing place names under proper names, since proper names cannot be objects to *tzay, daw*, etc., as place names can. Like proper names, place names have definite reference. When one says 有兩个通州. *Yeou leangg Tong.jou.* 'There are two T'ungchows.', *Tong.jou* should be regarded as quasi-quoted: 'There are two places called "T'ungchow." ', rather than as an ordinary individual noun. (Cf. *Yeou leangg Wang Liang.*, sec. 7.3.) Otherwise, place names, like proper names, cannot be modified by D-M compounds, as some other place words can. For example, in 到一个什么城?哦, 到盐湖城. *Daw ig sherm cherng? Oh, daw Yanhwu Cherng.* 'To a what kind of city? Oh, yes, to Salt Lake City.' where the first *cherng* is a place word of type 4 (see below) rather than a place name and is modifiable by the D-M compound *ig*, while *Cherng* in *Yanhwu Cherng* is part of the place name. If *ig* is in-

serted in the second sentence, it will make the place name quasi-quoted again: 'a place they call "Salt Lake City"'. Cf. 'I met a (certain) Mr. Smith.'

Syllabicity and Freedom in Place Names. Like names of persons, monosyllabic place names are bound and have to be compounded with some generic word to form a complete place word. Thus 欧罗巴 *Ouluoba* 'Europe' is free, but with the shorter form *Ou* one has to say 欧洲 *Ou.jou* 'Eu-continent,—Europe'. Similarly, 中國 *Jong.gwo* 'China-country,—China', but 日本 *Ryhbeen* 'Japan', 美國 *Meei.gwo* '(A)me(rica)-country,—America', but 美利堅合众國 *Meeilihjian Herjonqgwo* 'the United States of America'. Most of the well-known countries go by the abbreviated monosyllabic form, compounded with -.*gwo*. The relatively less frequently mentioned names of countries go by the full polysyllabic names, as in 賀蘭 *Heh.lan* (officially 荷蘭 *Herlan*) 'Holland', 挪威 *Nuouei* 'Norway', 西班牙 *Shibanya* 'Spain'. Some country names occur with comparable frequency in both forms, as 意大利 (officially 義大利) *Yihdahlih* 'Italy', somewhat less frequently 意(or 義)國 *Yih.gwo*. Names of subdivisions of countries and cities, too, have to be compounded with the generic word if they are monosyllabic, but may stand alone if polysyllabic. For example, 蘇州 *Su.jou* 'prefecture Su,—Soochow', 定県 *Dinqshiann* 'district Ting,—Ting Hsien', but 天津 *Tian.jin* (~ .*jing*) 'Tientsin', 上海 *Shanq*₀*hae* 'Shanghai', unless one wishes to say explicitly 'the municipality of' and add 市 *shyh* after it. But 沙市 *Shashyh* 'Sha-shih (Hupeh) 'has to have 市 *shyh* as a bound part of the name, since 沙 *sha* is a monosyllable. In transliterations/translations of foreign names, there is 加州 *Jiajou* 'the state of Ca(lifornia)', but 加利福尼亚 *Jialihfwuniyah* 'California', 麻省 *Masheeng* 'the province,—commonwealth of Ma(ssachusetts)', but (very formal and rare) 麻沙朱色兹 *Mashajusehtzy* 'Massachusetts'. On the other hand, foreign monosyllabic names, if not compounded with a generic word, as in 森河 *Sen Her* 'the Seine River' and 関島 *Guan Dao* 'Guam Island', have to be broken up into two syllables in the transliteration in order to stand alone, as 梅恩 *Mei'en* 'Maine', 波昂 *Bo'arng* 'Bonn'. (Cf. similar treatment of proper names, secs. 7.3.1 and 7.3.2.)

Semantically, there are place names for geographical units, political units, and various institutions regarded as places. Examples are 亚洲 *Yah$_o$jou* 'Asia', 中國 *Jong.gwo* 'China', 北边 *Beei.bian* 'the North', 山东 *Shan.dong* 'Shantung', 曲阜 *Chiufuh* '(the city of) Ch'ü-fu', 大街 *Dahjie* 'Main Street'. But in 这是一条大街。*Jeh sh i-tyau dah-jie.* 'This is a main street.', *dahjie* is a phrase with an ordinary individual noun *jie* as center, and the street in question may actually bear a different name, say, 'Market Street', and not the place name *Dah Jie*. As examples of place names of institutions, we have 在一中念书 *tzay I Jong niann-shu* 'study at First High', 在青年会做书记 *tzay Chingnian Huey tzuoh shujih* 'work as a secretary at the YMCA', 从美國領事館出来 *tsorng Meei.gwo Liing.shyhgoan chu-.lai* 'come out from the American Consulate'. The names of mountains, rivers, lakes, and to a lesser extent seas and oceans, however, usually require the localizers 上 *-.shanq*, 裡 *-.lii*, and so forth, to go with 在 *tzay*, though they can go with 到 *daw* and 从 *tsorng* without a localizer. Thus one can say 住在台山 *juh tzay Tairshan* 'lives in T'oi-shan', since *Tairshan* is the name of a city, but must say 住在泰山上 *juh tzay Tayshan.shanq* 'lives on Mount T'ai', since *Tayshan* is the name of a mountain. One can say 从太湖飞到黄河有多远? *Tsorng Tayhwu fei daw Hwangher yeou dwo yeuan?* 'How far is it to fly from (Lake) T'ai Hu to the Yellow River?' but 有个小船儿在黄河上走呐。*Yeou g sheau chwal tzay Hwangher.shanq tzoou ne.* 'There is a little boat sailing on the Yellow River.'

(2) Position Words. Position words form a listable and very versatile subclass of place words which express the relative positions of things. Examples are 裡头 *lii.tou* 'inside', 右边儿 *yow-.bial* 'the right side', 背後 *beyhow* 'the rear', 这裡 *jeh.lii* 'in here,—here', 别处(儿) *bye$_o$chuh ~ ($_o$chull)* 'elsewhere'. Like other place words, position words can be placed in the same slot as the other other substantives. For example, 底下有火。*Dii-.shiah yeou huoo.* 'Below has fire,—there is fire below.' 你在哪儿

呐? *Nii tzay naal ne?* 'You are where,—where are you?' 裡头的声音外头听不見。 *Lii.tou de sheng.in way.tou ting-.bu-jiann.* 'The sounds inside cannot be heard outside.' Position words are very often modified by other substantives expressing that to which the position is relative, as in 屋子的中间儿有張桌子 *utz de jongjiall yeou jang juotz.* 'The middle of the room has a table,—there is a table in the middle of the room.' 身上的哪儿疼? *Shen.shanq de naal terng?* 'What part of the body does it hurt,—where does it hurt?' When the relative position is in a bound form, then we have an N-L compound, as in 身上 *shen.shanq* 'body's above,—on the body', which will be discussed in paragraph (3) below.

Most position words are dissyllables, usually consisting of a specifying determinative and a suffix or a versatile end morpheme. The degree of versatility of the parts varies considerably and will be detailed in table 11 below.

(2.1) Before taking up the dissyllables, we shall first examine the few monosyllables whose occurrence is somewhat restricted. Except for the three two-morpheme position words 这儿 *jell* 'here', 那儿 *nall* 'there', and 哪儿 *naal* 'where', which have the more formal dissyllabic variants 这裡 *jeh.lii*, 那裡 *nah.lii*, and 哪裡 *naa.lii*, respectively, and should be treated as complex forms (2.2 below), the other monosyllables consist of the localizers (sec. 7.10) 上 *shanq* 'up', 下 *shiah* 'down', 前 *chyan* 'front', 後 *how* 'back', 內 *ney* 'inside' (but not 裡 *lii* 'inside'), 外 *way* 'outside', 左 *tzuoo* 'left', 右 *yow* 'right', 东 *dong* 'east', 南 *nan* 'south', 西 *shi* 'west', and 北 *beei* 'north' and occur mostly in certain fixed phrases based largely on wenyan, in which of course most morphemes are free words. Examples are 上有天堂,下有蘇杭。*Shanq yeou tiantarng, shiah yeou Su-Harng.* 'Above there is heaven, below there are Soochow and Hangchow (where pleasures and sceneries are considered heavenly).' 左也不是,右也不是。*Tzuoo yee bush, yow yee bush.* 'Neither the left nor the right is right,—there is no pleasing him.' 前不見古人,後不

見来者. *Chyan bu jiann guuren, how bu jiann laijee.* L[10] 'Before (now) one cannot see the ancients, after (now) one cannot see those to come.' 内乞怨女, 外乞曠夫. *Ney wu yuann neu, way wu kuanq fu.* L 'Inside has no complaining girls, outside has no unoccupied men,—everybody gets married.' 东張ㄑ, 西望ㄑ. *dong jang.jang, shi wanq.wanq* 'take a peek east, take a peep west,—take a look in all directions,' but there is no °南張ㄑ, 北望ㄑ. °*Nan jang.jang, beei wanq.wanq.* Even more frozen is the shorter form *dong-jang-shi-wanq,* which should be regarded as a compound functioning as a verb, as in 他东張西望了半天, 也没找着. *Ta dong-jang-shi-wanq-le banntian, yee mei jao-jaur.* 'He looked all around for a long time and did not find it either.'

Note that 裡 *lii* 'inside', synonymous with 内 *ney* 'inside' cannot be followed by a verb, as *ney* can.

In all the examples cited above, substituting dissyllables for the monosyllables by adding 头 -.*tou* 边ㄦ -.*bial,* etc. would result in a more purely modern spoken style, though it may not then sound so neat and rhythmic. For example, 上头有天堂, 底下有蘇州跟杭州. *Shanq.tou yeou tiantarng, dii.shiah yeou Su.jou gen Harng.jou.,* would be completely normal speech, but would sound quite prosaic, with a loss of rhyme and rhythm.

Besides restricted occurrences before verbs, table 11 shows the restricted occurrences of monosyllabic specifying determinatives after verbs or prepositions. An asterisk "°" means non-occurring, and forms in parentheses "( )" are rare or have specialized meanings, some of which, marked in braces "[ ]", do not even express position. The form 之中 *jy jong* L 'inside of, within, among' is not included here because it is wenyan; 之间 *jyjian* 'in between' is not included because, although it is spoken, it is a position word, in which *jian* is not a determinative but a localizer (sec. 7.10, L 13).

First, some general observations. As soon as any of the speci-

<hr />

[10]First two lines of 陈子昂, 登幽州台歌(Chern Tzyy'arng, "Deng Ioujoutair Ge").

Table 11

Monosyllabic Determinatives After Prepositions

| | | | 1<br>在<br>tzay<br>'at' | 2<br>望<br>wanq<br>'toward' | 3<br>向<br>shianq<br>'toward' | 4<br>到<br>daw<br>'to' | 5<br>从<br>tsorng<br>'from' | 6<br>以<br>yii<br>'to the...of' | 7<br>之<br>jy<br>'to (~ in)<br>the...of' |
|---|---|---|---|---|---|---|---|---|---|
| a. | 上 | shanq | 'above' | 在上 | 望上 | 向上 | * | 从上 | 以上 | 之上 |
| b. | 下 | shiah | 'below' | 在下 | 望下 | 向下 | * | 从下 | 以下 | 之下 |
| c. | 前 | chyan | 'front' | 在前 | 望前 | 向前 | * | { 从前 } | {以前 } | 之前 |
| d. | 後 | how | 'back' | 在後 | 望後 | 向後 | * | * | {以後 } | 之後 |
| e. | 內 | ney | 'inside' | {在內 } | * | 向內 | * | * | {以內 } | 之內 |
| f. | 裡 | lii | 'inside' | * | 望裡 | 向裡 | * | * | * | * |
| g. | 外 | way | 'outside' | {在外 } | 望外 | 向外 | * | * | 以外 | 之外 |
| h. | 左 | tzuoo | 'left' | (在左 ) | 望左 | 向左 | * | 从左 | * | 之左 |
| i. | 右 | yow | 'right' | (在右 ) | 望右 | 向右 | * | 从右 | * | 之右 |
| j. | 东 | dong | 'east' | (在东 ) | 望东 | 向东 | (到东 ) | (从东 ) | 以东 | 之东 |
| k. | 南 | nan | 'south' | (在南 ) | 望南 | 向南 | (到南 ) | (从南 ) | 以南 | 之南 |
| l. | 西 | shi | 'west' | (在西 ) | 望西 | 向西 | (到西 ) | (从西 ) | 以西 | 之西 |
| m. | 北 | beei | 'north' | (在北 ) | 望北 | 向北 | (到北 ) | (从北 ) | 以北 | 之北 |

fying determinatives is made into a dissyllabic position word by
the addition of -.*tou*, -.*bial*, etc., then most of the cases marked °,
( ), or [ ] become phrases with plain meaning. For example, there
is no ° 到 前 *daw chyan*, but there is 到 前 头 *daw chyan.tou* 'to
the front'; 从 东 *tsorng dong* is limited to such pairs as 从 东 到
西 *tsorng dong daw shi* 'from the east to the west': 在 外 *tzay
way* has the special meaning of 'not included', but 在 外 头 *tzay
way.tou* simply means 'is outside'. Secondly, none of these monosyllables can be preceded or followed by *de*, whereas all their
corresponding dissyllabic position words can. Thus, there is no
° 的 上 °*de shanq* or ° 上 的 °*shanq de*, but there is 书 的 上
头 *shu de shanq.tou* 'book's above,—above the book' and 上 头
的 书 *shanq.tou de shu* 'above's book,—the book above'; no ° 东
的 °*dong de* or ° 的 东 °*de dong*, but there is 东 边 儿 的 房 子
*dong.bial de farngtz* 'east's house,—the house in the east' and
房 子 的 东 边 儿 *farngtz de dong.bial* 'house's east side,—east side
of the house.' Thirdly, since 向 *shianq*, 以 *yii*, and 之 *jy* are borrowings from wenyan and are still felt as such, they combine
more readily with the monosyllables. Moreover, since 内 *ney* is
more literary than its synonym 裡 *lii*, we have 以 内 *yiiney* 'within' and 之 内 *jy ney* 'inside of', but no ° 以 裡 °*yii lii* or ° 之 裡
*jy lii*. That there is 向 裡 *shianq lii* as well 向 内 *shianq ney*
'toward the inside' is probably because *shianq* is more nearly
naturalized in speech than *yii* and *jy*.

Taking up the individual cases in the table, we note that le
在 内 *tzayney* and lg 在 外 *tzayway* have the special meanings of
'included' and 'not included', respectively. 2e ° 望 内 °*wanq ney*
is nonexisting because the styles don't mix. 5c 从 前 *tsorngchyan*
'formerly' is used only as a time word. In the spatial sense, it
will have to be 从 前 头 *tsorng chyan.tou* 'from the front', where
*chyan.tou* is a position word. Similarly, 6c 以 前 *yiichyan* 'previously' and 6d 以 後 *yiihow* 'afterwards' are time words only. 6e
以 内 *yiiney* 'inside of' and 6g 以 外 *yiiway* 'outside of' are used
more in the abstract sense with reference to lists and classes than
in the sense of spatial positions. In 6j, k, l, and m 以 东 'to the

east of', etc., an alternate form for 以 is its (original) homophone 迤 *yii* 'moves at an angle' L.

(2.2) Coming now to dissyllabic forms, we shall find that they are all free position words and, as already noted, more likely taken in the simple literal sense. We shall first tabulate the localizers in combination with suffixes resulting in position words, then note certain special position words which are in the form of compounds rather than suffixed words.

The form 1b 下头 *shiah.tou* 'below' is put in parentheses because it is more common in the Wu dialects than in Mandarin, in which the normal word for 'below' is 底下 *dii.shiah*, 'bottom-below,—under the bottom' which is a position word of the N-L type (under type 3 below.) The suffix -.*tou* in column 1 is to be distinguished from 头儿 *tourl* 'head, end' and its many extensions of meaning, since *tourl* is a noun, as in 这棍子有个很尖的头儿，头儿上有个钩子。 *Jeh guenntz yeou g heen jian de tourl, tourl.shanq yeou g goutz.* 'This stick has a sharp end; at the end there is a hook.', and from the position word 头儿 *tourl* 'end', as in 在东头儿路北 *tzay dong-tourl luh-beei* 'is at the east end, north side of the street'. There is also a Peiping localism 头儿裡 *tourl.lii* 'in front', synonymous with 前头 *chyan.tou*. The suffix 面(儿) -.*miann(-ll)* in column 3 is less common than 头 -.*tou* or 边(儿) -.*bian(-l)*,[11] as shown in the table. In column 4, the suffix 裡 -.*lii* and its nonsyllabic form 儿 -*l* [one of the three nonsyllabic homophonous suffixes, sec. 4.4.4, item (1a)] does not combine with items a to m, but with items n-p, *jeh*, *nah*, and *naa*, and their variants, resulting in the formal 这裡 *jeh.lii* 'here', 那裡 *nah.lii* 'there' and 哪裡 *naa.lii* 'where', and the less formal

---

[11]Although as root morphemes 面 *miann* means '(two-dimensional) side, face' and 边 *bian* means 'border, edge', the distinction is not usually maintained when they occur as parts of place words. The same ambivalence is of course found in English 'side', as in the following sentence from the *Daily Telegraph*: "The award was for  1 stamps showing the Queen on the one side and Windsor Castle on the other," quoted by *Punch* (March 22, 1961, p. 454) with the query: "You mean you just lick the edge?" Here a Chinese translator would probably use 一边儿 *i-bial* for 'one side'.

Table 12

Dissyllabic Position Words

| | | 1<br>头<br>-.tou<br>'end' | 2<br>边(儿)<br>-.bian(-l)<br>'side, border' | 3<br>面(儿)<br>-miann(-ll)<br>'side, face' | 4<br>裡~儿<br>-.lii~ -l<br>'in' |
|---|---|---|---|---|---|
| a. | 上 shanq 'above' | 上头 | (上边(儿)) | (上面(儿)) | * |
| b. | 下 shiah 'below' | (下头) | (下边(儿)) | (下面(儿)) | * |
| c. | 前 chyan 'front' | 前头 | (前边(儿)) | (前面(儿)) | * |
| d. | 後 how 'back' | 後头 | (後边(儿)) | (後面(儿)) | * |
| e. | 内 ney 'inside' | * | * | * | * |
| f. | 裡 lii 'inside' | 裡头 | (裡边(儿)) | (裡面(儿)) | * |
| g. | 外 way 'outside' | 外头 | (外边(儿)) | (外面(儿)) | * |
| h. | 左 tzuoo 'left' | * | 左边(儿) | (左面(儿)) | * |
| i. | 右 yow 'right' | * | 右边(儿) | (右面(儿)) | * |
| j. | 东 dong 'east' | * | 东边(儿) | * | * |
| k. | 南 nan 'south' | * | 南边(儿) | * | * |
| l. | 西 shi 'west' | * | 西边(儿) | * | * |
| m. | 北 beei 'north' | * | 北边(儿) | * | * |
| n. | 这 jeh 'this' | * | 这边(儿) | (这面(儿)) | 这裡~过儿 |
| o. | 那 nah 'that' | * | 那边(儿) | (那面(儿)) | 那裡~那儿 |
| p. | 哪 naa 'which' | * | 哪边(儿) | (哪面(儿)) | 哪裡~哪儿 |

这儿 *jell*, 那儿 *nall*, and 哪儿 *naal*. Because of the open quality of the vowel *e* in the fourth tone, *jell* has a variant *jall*, and, even more commonly, *nall* has a variant *nell*. There is no ° 内裡 °*ney.lii*, but there is 内裡 *neylii* 'the inside (intention, information)', which is a compound of synonyms in which *lii* has full tone and is not a suffix. There is of course no ° 裡 ˨ °*lii.lii*, but there is *lii* + *-l* > *lieel*, which is, however, not a position word but a noun with the diminutive suffix 儿 ( ← 兒 ) *-l* ( ← *erl*) and means 'the inside of a garment,—lining', alternating with 裡子 *liitz*.

There remain certain dissyllabic position words which have not been included in the table, since their parts do not combine actively with other parts. For the 'middle', or 'between', there are the four forms based on the localizers 中 *jong* and 间 *jian(n)*: 当中 *dangjong* 'right in the middle', 当间儿 *dangjiall* 'right at the interspace', 中间儿 *jongjiall* 'middle interspace' and 中间 *jongjian* 'middle interspace' in ascending order of formality and descending order of frequency of occurrence. For 'beside' or 'by the side (of)' there is 旁边儿 *parngbial*, which does not belong to table 12, since *-bial* is not in neutral tone and not a suffix. Synonymous with 後头 *how.tou* there is 背後 *beyhow* 'behind the back (of)', which is in the form of N-L. Besides the very general 裡头 *lii.tou* 'inside' and the more abstract 内裡 *neylii* 'inside (story, etc.)', there is also 内中 *neyjong* 'inside (story, etc.)'.

The measure 处 *-chuh* 'place, locality', as in 一处地方 *i-chuh dihfang* 'a place' forms four compounds and one reduplicate as position words: 遠处 *yeuan$_0$chuh* 'distant place', 近处 *jinn$_0$chuh* 'near place', 别处（儿） *bye$_0$chuh(-ll)* 'elsewhere', 到处（儿） *daw$_0$chuh(-ll)* 'everywhere that one reaches,—everywhere', and 处 ˨ （儿） *chuh$_0$chuh(-ll)* 'everywhere'. For example, 他现在在别处呐。 *Ta shianntzay tzay bye.chuh ne.* 'He is now elsewhere.' Because *dawchuh* already has *daw* as part of the compound and because *chuhchuh* tends to be in an advanced position in the sentence [sec. 4.2.3 (3)], they do not usually occur after *tzay*. For example, instead of 你不能在到处（～ 在 处 ˨ ）吐痰！ *Nii buneng tzay dawchuh (~ tzay chuhchuh) tuu-*

*tarn!* 'You mustn't spit everywhere!', the more usual form is *Nii buneng dawchuh* (~ *chuhchuh*) *tuu-tarn!* On the other hand, these place words occur very naturally in the subject position, as in 到处有烟. *Dawchuh yeou ian.* 'Everywhere has smoke,— there is smoke everywhere.' 处ㄟ有毛病。 *Chuhchuh yeou mau- .binq.* 'Everywhere has flaws,—there are flaws everywhere.'

Of the two-syllable combinations of the specifying determinatives, some are free place words, namely, 东南 *Dongnan* 'SE', 东北 *Dongbeei* 'NE', 西南 *Shinan* 'SW', and 西北 *Shibeei* 'NW', as in 东南有红橘子. *Dongnan yeou horng-jyutz.* 'The Southeast has red tangerines.' 别对着西北看! *Bye dueyj Shibeei kann!* 'Don't look toward the Northwest!' The following are bound, or semibound: 左上 *tzuoo-shanq* 'upper left', 左下 *tzuoo-shiah* 'lower left', 右上 *yow-shanq* 'upper right', 右下 *yow-shiah* 'lower right', as in 一直写到纸的左下角儿 *ijyr shiee daw jyy de tzuoo-shiah-jeaul* 'write straight on to the lower left corner of the paper'. One does say, to be sure, 中国 字是从右上望下写的. *Jonggwo-tzyh sh tsorng yow-shanq wanq shiah shiee de.* 'Chinese characters are written from top right-hand down.' But apart from *tsorng, wanq,* and their synonyms, those forms do not occur except in compounds and are thus semi-bound, in the sense that they occupy positions parallel to free forms, as in a paraphrase of the above with free place words: 中国字是从右边儿上头望底下写的。 *Jonggwo-tzyh sh tsorng yow.bial shanq.tou wanq dii.shiah shiee de.*

(3) N-L Compounds as Place Words. A place word may be formed with a noun, a proper name, or a pronoun as attribute, compounded with a localizer. By far the greatest number of cases are those with nouns, since nouns not only form a very large open class but almost the whole list of the localizers can go with them. Examples of N-L compounds as place words are 心裡 *shin.lii* 'in the heart (or mind)', 山上 *shan.shanq* 'on the mountain', 海外 *haeway* 'outside the seas,—overseas', 身边 *shenbian* 'on or near one's person', 手下 *shooushiah* 'under the hand,— under one's command or control, in one's possession', and so on throughout the lexicon as well as in transient compounds of no specialization of meaning.

After proper names and pronouns, however, only the general localizers 那儿 -.*nall* 'there,—where ... is' and 这儿 -.*jell* 'here,—where (I) am or (we) are' are available, the latter being limited to the speaker or persons situated near the speaker. For example, 筆记本儿也不在我这儿也 不在老三那儿，一定还在你那儿呐。 *Biijihbeel yee bu tzay woo.jell, yee bu tzay Laosan-.nall, idinq hair tzay nii.nall ne.* 'The notebook is neither at my place, nor at Third Brother's, it must still be at your place.'

Since the nature of compounds with localizers has been fully analyzed and illustrated under compounds (sec. 6.4.4) and the localizers will be listed below (sec. 7.10), we shall not go into further detail about this category of place words.

(4) Nouns for Places Used as Place Names. Nouns for places are not necessarily place words and usually need the addition of localizers to form place words, as exemplified under (3) above. Additional examples of nouns for places which are not place words are 江 *jiang* '(large) river', 河 *her* 'river', 湖 *hwu* 'lake', 城 *cherng* 'city', 路 *luh* 'road', 街 *jie* 'street', 房子 *farngtz* 'house', 大厦 *dah-shiah* '(large modern) building', 宝塔 *baotaa* 'pagoda'. Certain nouns for places, however, are used so often to refer to specific places understood by both speaker and hearer that they acquire the status of place names. Thus, one can say not only 在一个郵政局裡做事 *tzay ig youjenqjyu .lii tzuoh-shyh* 'work at a post office' and 一直走到了一个 郵政局那儿才回来 *i jyr tzoou-dawle ig youjenqjyu.nall tsair hwei.lai* 'walked straight on to a post office before coming back', where localizers -.*lii* and -.*nall* are required to make place words out of *youjenqjyu*, but also 在郵政局做事 *tzay Youjenqjyu tzuoh-shyh* 'work at the Post Office' and 走到了郵政局才回来 *tzoou-dawle You-jenqjyu tsair hwei.lai* 'walked to the Post Office before coming back', where *Youjenqjyu* is '*the* Post Office' which has a particular reference. Similar nouns which can function as place words without the addition of localizers are 家 *jia* 'home' (although not as frequent as 家裡 *jia.lii*), 学校 *shyue.shiaw* 'school', 舖子 *puhtz* 'store', 饭馆儿 *fanngoal* 'restaurant', 客厅 *kehting* 'sitting room', 饭厅 *fannting* 'dining room', 书房 *shufarng* 'study', 厨房

*chwufarng* 'kitchen', 飛机塲 *feijichaang* 'airport', 車站 *chejann* 'station', 電报(～ 话 )局 *diannbaw* (～*huah*)*jyu* 'telegraph (～ -phone) company', 教堂 *jiawtarng* 'church'.[12] Note that most of such words take the definite article in English, as in 在飛机塲 見! *Tzay feijichaang jiann!* 'See you at the airport!'

  *7.4.1 Place Words and Place Phrases:* Place Expressions. A place phrase is a phrase with a place word as center and with most of the syntactic functions of a place word. For example, 左边儿 *tzuoo.bial* 'the left side' is a place word; 谁的左边 儿 *sheirde tzuoo.bial* 'whose left' and 那位戴黑眼镜儿 的先生的左边儿 *ney-wey day hei yeanjienql de shian.sheng de tzuoo.bial* '(to) the left of the gentleman wearing dark glasses' are place phrases. Forms like 湖南 *Hwu$_0$nan* 'south of the Lake, —Hunan', 江北 *Jiangbeei* 'north of the River,—(name of region of Kiangsu to the north of the Yangtze', are place names in the form of compounds and therefore place words, where *hwu* is not any lake but refers only to 洞庭湖 *Dong$_0$tyng Hwu* 'Tungt'ing Lake,' and *jiang* is not any large river but specifically 長江 *Charng Jiang* 'the Yangtze River', and *Jiangbeei* is not any part to the north of the Yangtze but only that part which lies within the Kiangsu province. In the general sense one would use the phrase 長江以北 *Charng Jiang yiibeei* or ( 長 ) 江的北边儿 (*Charng) Jiang de beei.bial.* In general, all place expressions, whether place words or place phrases, enter into about the same syntactical positions in sentences, but differ in that phrases in relation to their constituent free words are more likely to be taken literally without lexical specialization than compound place words in relation to their bound constituents. (Cf. table 8 in chap. 6.)

  *7.4.2 Phrases with ... de$_0$dih.fang*(l) *as '(with) respect (to)'.* Besides being a noun or a place word, *dih.fang*(l) can also be the center of a place expression with the extended meaning of '(with) respect(to)', as in 在能够幫你的地方儿，他没有不幫你 的. *Tzay nenggow bang nii de dih.fangl, ta mei.yeou bu bang nii de.* 'Wherever he can help you, there is nowhere that he won't

---

  [12]Most of the examples are taken from Fred Fangyü Wang's *Chinese Dialogues,* Yale Mirror Series A5, New Haven, 1953, p. 79.

help you,—if he can be of help to you in any way, he will certainly help you.'

## 7.5. Time Words

Like place words, a time word can fill the following positions:

| 在 ... | *tzay...* | 'to be at' |
| 到 ... | *daw...* | 'reach (the time of) ...' |

but, unlike place words, cannot fill the positions:

| 到 ... 去 | *daw...$_0$chiuh* | 'go to...' |
| 上 ... 去 | *shanq...$_0$chiuh* | 'go to...' |
| 从 ... 来 (etc.) | *tsorng...lai(etc.)* | 'come (etc.)...from' |
| 望 ... 走 (etc.) | *wanq...tzoou* (etc.) | 'go (etc.)...toward' |

On the other hand, a time word can fill the following positions:

| 等 到 ... | *deeng$_0$daw...* | 'by...', 'by the time when' |
| 从...V- 起 | *tsorng...V-chii* | 'start to V from...' |

The frames 到... 為止 *daw...weijyy* 'reach...as stopping (point),—as far as' and 从... 起 *tsorng...chii* 'start from...' can be filled by both place words and time words, as well as words for quantity. For example, 到北緯二十三度半為止 *daw beeiwoei ell-.shyrsan-duh-bann weijyy* 'as far as 23½° N', 到五点為止 *daw wuu-dean weijyy* 'up to five o'clock', 到十磅為止 *daw shyr-banq weijyy* 'up to ten pounds'. The sentence 長針慢ㇲ儿的望十二点走。 *Charngjen mannmhalde wanq shyr'ell-dean tzoou.* 'The minute hand moves slowly toward twelve o'clock.', looks like an exception, but here *shyr'ell-dean* is not really a time word, since it is quasi-quoted and means the place on the dial toward which the minute hand is moving and is thus a place word and not a true time word.

Not all words expressing time are time words. Adverbs of time such as 馬上 *maa$_0$shanq* 'at once', 立刻 *lih$_0$keh* 'immediately', 隨時 *sweishyr* 'any moment', 已经 *yii$_0$jing* 'already', 已竟 *yii$_0$jing* 'already', 本来 *beenlai* 'originally, 起初 *chiichu* 'at first', 忽然 *huran* 'suddenly'—none of these can fill the positions for time words mentioned above and thus are not time words in the grammatical sense. Thus one cannot say ° 在已竟 °*tzay yiijinq* or ° 从本来 °*tsorng beenlai,* but one can say 在那会儿 *tzay ney.hoel* 'at that moment' and 从刚才起 *tsorng gangtsair chii* 'starting from a while ago.' One can also say 从以前 *tsorng yiichyan* 'from before' and 到以後 (~後来) *daw yiihow* (~ *how-lai*) 'to afterwards' (*yiihow* being limited to past time mostly).

Words for length of time, usually in the form of N-M compounds, are not time words. Thus 月 *yueh* 'month', 礼拜 *liibay* 'week',[13] 三年 *san-nian* 'three years' are not time words.

Like place words, time words can be subjects, objects, or attributes to other substantive expressions, as in 今天晴天. *Jin.tian chyngtian.* 'Today (is a) clear day.' 我一直醒到天亮. *Woo ijyr shiing daw tianlianq,* 'I stayed awake all the time till daybreak.' 将来的事情有将来的人问. *Jianglai de shyh-.chyng yeou jianglai de ren wenn.* 'For matters of the future, there will be people of the future to deal with them'. As subject, a time word often sets the scene, followed further by an S-P predicate in which (the smaller) S is the actor and P the action, as in 今天我们过年. *Jin.tian woomen guoh-nian.* 'Today we celebrate the New Year.' If there are both time and place words as subjects, the time word usually though not always precedes the place word, as in 今天海上風浪很大. *Jin.tian hae.shanq fenglang heen dah.* 'Today on the sea the wind and waves are high.' But the main topic is what decides the main subject. For example, 我们家裡今年过年，可是去年没有. *Woomen jia.lii jin.nian guoh-nian, keesh chiuh.nian mei.yeou.* 'In our house we celebrate the New Year this year, but last year we did not.', where the place word *jia.lii* is the main subject under which *jin.nian* and *chiuh.nian* are smaller subjects. (Cf. sec 2.10.7.)

Semantically, time words are words expressing the location of time on a time scale in relation to history, as for example 周朝 *Jou.chaur* 'the Chou dynasty', 一九六七 *i-jeou-liow-chi* '1967', or on a scale relative to the time of speaking, as for example

---

[13]But as a short way of saying 礼拜日 (~ 天) *Liibayryh* (~ *tian*) 'Sunday', it is a time word.

古时候儿 *guu.shyr.howl* '(in) ancient times', 明天 *ming.tian* 'tomorrow'.

In internal structure, time words are always complex, including the five monosyllables 前儿 *chyal* 'day before yesterday', 昨儿 *tzwol* 'yesterday', 今儿 *jiel* 'today', 明儿 *miengl* 'tomorrow', and 後儿 *howl* 'day after tomorrow', in which the suffix *-l* is derived from 日 *ryh* 'day'. The forms 今日 *jinryh* 'today', 明日 *mingryh* 'tomorrow', and so on, are definitely wenyan, while the forms 今天 *jin.tian*, 明天 *ming.tian*, etc., are less informal than the *-l* form and thus completely neutral in style. We shall consider (1) time names, (2) relative time words, and (3) certain N-L compounds and other compounds involving localizers.

(1) Time Names. Time names are words for historical time positions, consisting of the dynastic names and reigning titles, and other era names. Since the specific names of dynasties are always monosyllabic and not free, they are always compounded with 朝 -.*chaur* 'dynasty' to form a time word, as in 从商朝到周朝有多少年? *Tsorng Shang.chaur daw Jou.chaur yeou duo.shao-nian?* 'How many years was it from the Shang to the Chou dynasty?' But with determinatives like 前, 後, 东, 西 *chyan, how, Dong, Shi* 'former, latter, East, West', the resulting dynastic names are dissyllabic and free, as in 从西汉到东汉一共差不多有四百年. *Tsorng Shihann daw Donghann igonq chah.buduo yeou syhbae-nian.* 'From the Western to the Eastern Han it was about 400 years altogether.'

Era names in the form of reigning titles, however, are usually followed by 年间 *nianjian* 'in the years of ...' or ( 的 ) 时候儿 *(de).shyrhowl* '(in) the time of' or ( 的 ) 时代 *(de) shyrday* '(in) the era of', in order to form a time word or a time phrase. Thus, although one can say 从洪武到崇祯 *tsorng Horngwuu daw Chorngjen* 'from Hungwu (1308-1398) to Ch'ung-chen (1628-1644)', one cannot say °这瓶是在乾隆製的. °*Jeh pyng sh tzay Chyanlong jyh de.* for 'This vase was made during (the reign of) Ch'ien-lung.' If a connoisseur sees a seal 乾隆年製 *Chyanlong nian jyh* 'made in the era of Ch'ien-lung', which is of course L, he will say aloud 哦, 是乾隆年间做的. *Oh, sh Chyanlong-*

*nianjian tzuoh de.* 'I see, it was made in the time of Ch'ien-lung.',
where *Chyanlong-nianjian* is a time word of the N-L type. During
the Ming and Ch'ing dynasties, in which each emperor had only
one era name, the era names acquired the status of proper names,
with or without 皇帝 *Hwangdih* 'Emperor' after them in close
apposition, which makes them even more different from time
words.

Some time names are used in cycles, so that each of them
will be used repeatedly, and which cycle is meant will depend
upon the context. For example, in 我礼拜一到的。*Woo
Liibay'i daw de.* 'I arrived Monday.', the speaker obviously refers
to the nearest past Monday. This can be compared to the use of
common first names in English where the particular John or Mary
is to be understood from context. Following are the most common cyclic time words:

干支 *ganjy*, or combinations of the ten 天干 *tiangan* 'heav-
en's stems' with the twelve 地支 *dihjyy* 'earth's branches', forming 60 (the LCM of 10 and 12) combinations known as the sexagesimal cycle. The heaven's stems and the earth's branches are,
respectively:

| 甲 | 乙 | 丙 | 丁 | 戊 | 己 | 庚 | 辛 | 壬 | 癸 |
|----|----|----|----|----|----|----|----|----|----|
| *Jea* | *Yii* | *Biing* | *Ding* | *Wuh* | *Jii* | *Geng* | *Shin* | *Ren* | *Goei* |

and

| 子 | 丑 | 寅 | 卯 | 辰 | 巳 | 午 | 未 | 申 | 酉 | 戌 | 亥 |
|----|----|----|----|----|----|----|----|----|----|----|----|
| *Tzyy* | *Choou* | *Yn* | *Mao* | *Chern* | *Syh* | *Wuu* | *Wey* | *Shen* | *Yeou* | *Shiu* | *Hay* |

forming the years 甲子 *Jeatzyy*, 乙丑 *Yiichoou*, and so on to the
sixtieth year of the cycle 癸亥 *Goeihay*. The heaven's stems, and
less frequently the earth's branches, are also used as abstract
counters like A, B, C, D, and the earth's branches are also used
as the (double) hours of the day, the commonly used ones being
子时 *tzyyshyr* 'midnight', 午时 *wuushyr* 'noon', 上午 *shang$_0$wuu* 'forenoon, A.M.', and 下午 *shiah$_0$wuu* 'afternoon, P.M.'.
The sexagesimal combinations used to be also applied to days but
are now limited to years, the most recent cycles being from
甲子 *Jeatzyy* 1864 to 癸亥 *Goeihay* 1923 and from 1924 to
1983. A few of the cyclic combinations have acquired special

meanings from the historical events which happened in the years named and thus have become fixed, for the present generations, and no longer variable. The best known are 甲午 *Jeawuu* = 1894, the Sino-Japanese naval war, 戊戌 *Wuhshiu* = 1898, the year of the abortive reform movement, 庚子 *Gengtzyy* = 1900, the year of the Boxer Rebellion, and *Shinhay* = 1911, the year of the Republican Revolution. For example, when one says 他是在庚 子年出世的。 *Ta sh tzay Gengtzyy-nian chu-shyh de.* 'He came out into the world,—was born in the year Gengtzyy.', a hearer would at once think of 1900 rather than 1960, without knowing whether a young child or an old person is being referred to.

Since there are ten heaven's stems and the sexagesimal system of reckoning years has been used without interruption since the Shang dynasty, there is a constant relation between the heaven's stems and the last digit of dates in years A.D. (except for a delay of about a month in the New Year on the lunar calendar). A mnemonic device for memorizing the relationship at several strategic points is as follows:

| Heaven's Stem | Last Digit in Years A.D. | Mnemonic Point |
|---|---|---|
| 甲 Jea | -4 | 四 'four' |
| 乙 Yii | -5 | 乙 is "5" reversed |
| 丙 Biing | -6 | |
| 丁 Ding | -7 | 7 |
| 戊 Wuh | -8 | |
| 己 Jii | -9 | Jeou 'nine' |
| 庚 Geng | -0 | Ling 'zero' |
| 辛 Shin | -1 | 1 |
| 壬 Ren | -2 | |
| 癸 Goei | -3 | 癸 has 3 parts: ㄱ, ㄑ, and 天. |

Time names for individual years are usually in the form of a numeral (taken in the ordinal sense but without the ordinal prefix 第 *dih-*) usually compounded with 年 *nian* 'year' and, if necessary for identifying the era, modified by the name of the era. The simplest form is just the numeral, as in 我是在一八九二生

的. *Woo sh tzay i-ba-jeou-ell sheng de.* 'I was born in 1892'. 他是
四九到的美國. *Ta sh syh-jeou daw de Meeigwo.* 'It was in
'49 that he arrived in America.' In these forms one can use longer
compounds or phrases such as 一八九二年 *i-ba-jeou-ell-nian,*
西曆一八九二年        *Shilih i-ba-jeou-ell-nian* 'Western chronology year 1892', 公曆一九四九年 *Gonglih i-jeou-syh-jeou-
nian* 'General chronology 1949', or even in full numeral words
一千九百四十九年        *i-chian    jeou-bae    syhshyr-jeou-nian*
'year one thousand nine hundred forty-nine'. Note that when the
year in Chinese chronology is mentioned, the plain numeral form
cannot be used. Thus one can say 一九四九(年) *i-jeou-syh-
jeou-(nian)*, or 四九(年) *syh-jeou(-nian)*, but if it is 民國 *Mingwo* '(year of) the Republic', one must say 三十八年 *sanshyr-ba-
nian* and not 三八 *san-ba* or 三十八 *sanshyr-ba*, with or without *Mingwo* before it, while plain 三八 *san-ba* can only mean
'1938'. The first year of any era is always called 元年 *yuan-nian*
'prime-year' and *nian* cannot be omitted, since *yuan* is a bound
form.

Because of the absence of the ordinal prefix 第 *dih-* in year
names, ambiguities are possible when a cardinal interpretation of
the numeral also makes sense. Thus the form    光緒三十四年
*Guangshiuh sanshyr-syh-nian* can be either the phrase 'the thirty-
fourth year of Kuanghsu (i.e., 1908)' or the sentence 'Kuang-hsu's
reign was thirty-four years (long).' In most cases, the context will
resolve the ambiguity.

The time names for the seasons of the year are 春天 *chuen-
.tian* 'spring', 夏天 *shiah.tian* 'summer', 秋天 *chiou.tian* 'autumn',
and 冬天 *dong.tian* 'winter'. These are not D-M compounds with
measure *tian* 'day', since they do not mean 'spring days', etc.,[14]
but simply 'spring', or 'spring time', etc. For 'spring days', etc.,
one will have to use the phrases 春天(的)日子 *chuen.tian (de)
ryhtz*, etc.

---

[14]In fact, the cognate forms for 春天, 夏天, etc., are also used as
the names of the seasons in Cantonese and Foochow, in neither of which 天
means 'day'.

The names of the months are 正月 *Jeng.yueh* (sic) or 一月 *I.yueh* 'January', 二月 *Ell.yueh* 'February', and so on to 十二月 *Shyr'ell.yueh,* 'December.' These look like, but are not, N-M compounds, since *yueh* 'month' is normally not a measure, but an ordinary individual noun, taking a classifier, as in 一个月 *ig yueh* 'a month'. The names of the months are compounded of numerals, taken in the ordinal sense, with the noun *yueh*. When the Gregorian calendar was first adopted in China in 1912, a distinction used to be made between 正月 *Jeng.yueh* 'the first moon (in the lunar calendar)' and 一月 *I.yueh* 'January'. The Gregorian calendar is used more and more and the lunar calendar is becoming obsolete, and both words are at present used for 'January'.

There are two sets of time words for the days of the week. There is a religious set based on the noun 礼拜 *liibay* 'worship'. Sunday being the day of worship, it is called 礼拜日 *Lii$_o$bayryh* or 礼拜天 *Lii$_o$baytian* or simply 礼拜 *Liibay*, as in 明天礼拜了，你去做礼拜吗? *Ming.tian Liibay le, nii chiuh tzuoh liibay ma?* 'Tomorrow will be Sunday, are you going to go to Sunday service?' The other days of the week are called 礼拜一 *Lii$_o$bay'i* 'Monday', 礼拜二 *Lii$_o$bay'ell* 'Tuesday', and so on to 礼拜六 *Lii$_o$bayliow* 'Saturday'. The other set of time names for the days of the week are 星期一 *Shingchi'i* 'Monday', 星期二 *Shingchi'ell* 'Tuesday', ... 星期六 *Shingchiliow* 'Saturday', and 星期日 *Shingchiryh* or 星期天 *Shingchitian* or (less frequently than *Liibay*) simply 星期 *Shingchi* 'Sunday'. These terms are based on the fact that the sidereal month, or the real time it takes the moon to revolve around the earth, is close to 28 days, or four weeks, so that the positions of the moon among the stars are associated with days of the week, whence 星期 *shingchi* 'star-period'. Although the time words with *liibay* are Christian in derivation and those with *shingchi* are secular in origin, both sets are used by both Christians and non-Christians. The main linguistic difference now is that *Liibay'i, Liibay'ell*, etc. are slightly more colloquial and *Shingchi'i, Shingchi'ell*, etc., are slightly more formal. Thus, with the colloquial *jeyg* 'this' one can say both 这个礼拜 *jeyg liibay* and 这个星期 *jeyg shingchi* for 'this week', but with the more formal and bound 本 *been-* 'the present (one)', one can say *been-shingchi*, but, because of stylistic disparity, *been-liibay* is rare. The terms 週 *jou* 'week' and 週末 *joumoh* are L.

The words for certain days of the year are in the form of time names. These are the festivals and the beginning dates of the 24 subdivisions of the solar year[15] known as 二十四節 *ellshyrsyh-jye* or 二十四个節气 *ellshyrsyhg jye$_0$chih*. The most important festival days are 年初一 *Nianchu'i* or 大年初一 *Dahnian-chu'i* 'New Year's Day (whether on the solar or on the lunar calendar), with a more formal variant 元旦 *Yuandann*, literally 'first morning'; 端午 *Duanwuu* or 端陽 *Duan$_0$yang* or 五月節 *Wuu-.yueh-jye* 'the 5th of the 5th moon, day for the annual dragon-boat races'; and 中秋 *Jongchiou* or 八月節 *Ba.yueh-jye* 'Mid-autumn Festival, on the 15th of the 8th moon' (usually coinciding with the harvest moon). The translations of borrowed Occidental festival days, 聖诞 *Shenqdann* or 聖诞節 *Shenqdann-jye* 'Sacred-birth Festival,—Christmas', 復活節 *Fuhhwo-jye* 'Resurrection Festival,—Easter', etc., are also time names. Of the beginning dates of the twenty-four subdivisions of the solar year, only the following five are of frequent reference in everyday speech, namely: 春分 *Chuenfen* 'vernal equinox' (March 20), 清明 *Ching-$_0$ming* (April 5, day for visiting tombs of relatives and last day for flying kites), 夏至 *Shiahjyh* 'summer solstice' (June 21), 秋分 *Chioufen* 'autumnal equinox' (September 23), and 冬至 *Dongjyh* 'winter solstice' (December 21).

Within the month there are no special time names, the terms 朔 *shuoh* 'first of the (lunar) month' and 望 *wanq* '15th of

---

[15]Often erroneously regarded, both by the Chinese and, to a lesser extent, by Occidentals, as belonging to the lunar calendar, because the dates used to be given in the lunar calendar before 1912 (and consequently varied from year to year) and because in the solar calendars printed since then people have not bothered to include these more or less fixed dates of the solar year, or because of the wrong idea that they had more to do with the lunar year. In fact there has grown up the practice, especially in Taiwan, of calling the lunar calendar 農曆 *nonglih* 'the farmer's calendar', whereas the 24 sections of the (solar) year are not only suitable for the farmer's use but in some cases actually named in terms having relevance to farming.

the (lunar) month' being L only. Otherwise the days of the month are named as 初一 *chu'i* 'the 1st', 初二 *chu'ell* 'the 2nd', etc., for the lunar month and 一号 *ihaw* 'No. 1,—the 1st', 二号 *ell-haw* 'the 2nd', etc., for the solar month. From the 11th on, *chu-* is not used, polysyllabic numerals being free, but *-haw* is optional. For example, 礼拜三是八月十号，所以礼拜四是八月十一号(～八月十一). *Liibaysan sh Ba.yueh shyrhaw, suooyii Liibaysyh sh Ba.yueh shyrihaw* (or *Ba.yueh shyri*). 'Wednesday is August tenth, so Thursday is August eleventh (*or* August eleven).' As in the case of 正月 *Jeng.yueh* being used more and more for the first month in both the solar and the lunar calendars, the *chu-* forms are now also used in both calendars for the first ten days of the month, but forms ending in *-haw* are always limited to the solar calendar.

Of time names for portions of the day, the most important are 早晨 *tzao.chern*, 早.起 *tzao.chii* (≠ *tzao chii* 'get up early'), and a blend of these: 早.□ *tzao.chin*, all three meaning 'morning', 晌午 *shaang.huo* '(around) noontime', 晚上 *woan.shanq* 'evening', 夜裡 *yeh.lii* 'night', 白天 *bair.tian* 'daytime', 黑下 *hei-.shiah* 'under darkness,—night', 上午 *shanq$_0$wuu* 'A.M.', 下午 *shiah$_0$wuu* 'P.M.', 上半天 *shanq.bann.tian* 'forenoon', 下半天 *shiah.bann.tian* 'afternoon', 晚半天儿 *woan.bann.tial* (sic) 'late afternoon', 中午 *jongwuu* or 正午 *jenqwuu* 'noon', and 半夜 *bannyeh* 'midnight'.

Of the hours of the day as time names, the old-style twelve 时辰 *shyr.chern* 'double hours', named in terms of the twelve earth's branches followed by 时 *-shyr* 'time,—(double) hour, as in 子时 *tzyyshyr* 'midnight', 丑时 *chooushyr* '2 A.M.' etc., are not used much in speech except in referring to one's hour of birth, such as used in fortunetelling. Instead of the twelve *shyr.chern*, 'double hours', the modern 钟头 *jongtour* (not °*jong.tou!*) 'hours' or 小时 *sheaushyr* 'lesser *shyr(.chern)*' L is used. Both *shyr.chern* and *jongtour* are nouns for units of duration, as in 五个钟头 *wuug jongtour* 'five hours' taking the measure g. The time names for the hours are in the form of n-M N, where n is from 一 *i* 'one' to 十二 *shyr'ell* 'twelve', M is 点 *-dean* 'point (of)', and N is 钟

*jong* 'clock', for example, 六点钟 *liow-dean jong* 'six o'clock'. Although 点钟 corresponds to 'o'clock', it is not a constituent, since it is the n-M (*liow-dean*), which is in construction with *jong*. [Cf., however, 年级 *nianjyi*, sec. 6.4.3(5).] The compound 钟点 *jongdean* 'an hour, as a point of time', however, is a noun having its measure *g*, as in 你派了我的两个钟点都不方便. *Nii payle woo de leangg jongdean dou bu fangbiann.* 'Both those hours you assigned me are inconvenient.' The noun 钟 *jong* after n-*dean* can be omitted, as in 我一直等到了六点才走. *Woo ijyr deeng dawle liow-dean tsair tzoou.* 'I waited all the time until six before I left.' The measure 点 -*dean*, however, cannot be omitted after polysyllabic numerals as the measure 号 -*haw* or the prefix 初 *chu-* can be in dates. Thus, 我等到了 十一才走. *Woo deeng dawle shyri tsair tzoou.* can only mean 'I waited until the 11th (of the month).' For 'waited until eleven' one must say *deeng dawle shyri-dean.*

In time names for fractions of the hour given in terms of the measures 刻 -*keh* 'quarter', 分 -*fen* 'minute', and 秒 -*meau* 'second', the noun 钟 *jong* 'clock' is omitted even oftener than on the exact hours. Thus, 现在十点钟了. *Shianntzay shyr-dean jong le.* 'It's ten o'clock now.' and 现在十点了. *Shianntzay shyr-dean le.* 'It's ten now.' are about equally common. But in 现在十 一点五十九分五十九秒了. *Shianntzay shyri-dean wuushyrjeou-fen wuushyrjeou-meau le.* 'It's now 11:59:59.' one usually omits the 钟 *jong* at the end. Of the fractional measures of the hour, only 分 *fen* 'minute' is occasionally omitted. Thus, in 咱 们等到七点三十五(分)(钟)就走罢. *Tzarmen deeng daw chi-dean sanshyrwuu (-fen) (jong) jiow tzoou ba.* 'Let's wait until seven thirty-five and then leave.', the *jong* is usually omitted and the *fen* is about as often omitted as said. Needless to say, monosyllabic numerals being bound, a numeral under eleven must be followed by the measure, with optional 零 *ling* 'zero,—and' before them, as in 七点(零)三分 *chi-dean (ling) san-fen* 'seven o'clock (and) three minutes,—three past seven'. The measure 刻 -*keh* is now used only at exact quarters, as in 十二点三刻 *shyr'ell-dean san-keh* 'twelve o'clock and three quarters,—quarter to one'.

Formerly, at the turn of the century, one used to say things like 八点两刻十分 *ba-dean leang-keh shyr-fen* 'eight o'clock two quarters and ten minutes,—twenty minutes to nine', but now one says 八点四十（分）*ba-dean syhshyr (-fen)* 'eight o'clock forty (minutes)'. Note that minutes are counted right up to 59 except in an explicit reference as to how long it will be before the next hour, in which case one says, for instance, 八点前二十分钟 *ba-dean-chyan ellshyr-fen jong* 'twenty minutes before eight', or 还有二十分钟到八点。 *Hair yeou ellshyr-fen jong daw ba dean.* 'There will still be twenty minutes to reach eight o'clock.' Note also that the reason 钟 is not omitted in such cases is that the minutes are not points of time (time names) but lengths of time before a certain (point of) time—eight o'clock, and in n-M compounds for lengths of time the noun is not omitted, as in 我等了你两点半钟了。 *Woo deengle nii leang-dean-bann jong le.* 'I have waited for you for two and half hours.', where no time name is involved. Alternatively, one can use the noun 钟头 *jong-tour* 'hour', whose measure is g, and say 两个半钟头 *leangg-bann jongtour*.

(2) Relative Time Words. Like position words, relative time words form a short list, and can be subject, object or attribute, as in 现在有风。*Shianntzay yeou feng.* 'Now has wind,—there is wind now.', 住到明年 *juh₀daw mingnian* 'stay until next year', 今天的事情 *jin.tian de shyh.chyng* 'today's business'. Relative time words are complex in structure and most are polysyllabic, usually in the form of D-M compounds. In a very few cases there is some overlapping of time and space words. Thus, 这裡 *jeh.lii* 'in here,—here' is place word only, but 这会儿 *jey.hoel* 'this moment' is occasionally also used in the sense of 'here', whereas with the second syllable unrounded （这 □儿 *jey.hel*), it is less often used as a time word. On the other hand, 这地儿 *jey.diell* 'this place,—here' is also used in the sense of 'now'. [Cf. sec. 6.4.3(1.1).]

In general, however, position words and relative time words are quite distinct. Moreover, the specifying determinatives for time words from a different list and overlap only slightly those for place words, namely 上 *shanq*-, 下 *shiah*-, 前 *chyan*-, and 後 *how*-. The measures for time words are time measures, of course, and even the suffix 儿 -*l*, that for time words, as in 今儿 *jiel* 'today', is derived from 日 *ryh* 'day' B, while the -*l* for place words, as in 这儿 *jell* 'here', is derived, as we saw, from 裡 *lii* 'inside', which is primarily a localizer for place. They are, therefore, homophonous but different morphemes.

Most relative time words are in the form of D-M compounds, in which the determinatives and the measures combine with a high degree of, but not unlimited, versatility. It will therefore be useful to set up a table of occurrences and non-occurrences of relative time words, as we did for place words, in table 13. Note that since *jiel, miengl*, etc., are monosyllabic, they seem to act as determinatives and form D-M compounds with g, resulting in *jielg, mienglg, tzwolg, howlg, chyalg*, which are synonymous with and slightly more colloquial than the simpler *jiel, miengl*, etc.

In table 13 the determinatives are in the order of time, except for item 1 那 *nah*-～*ney*- 'that', which usually, though not necessarily, refers to the past, and m 哪 *naa*-～*neei*- 'which?', which may refer to the past, present, or future. To the measures we have added for comparison also the suffix 3 儿 -*l* 'day' and the noun 8 月 *yueh* 'month'. The measures 7 礼拜 *liibay* 'week', 10 学期 *shyuechi* 'semester', and 12 世纪 *shyhjih* 'century' are alternatively also nouns and as such can themselves take a measure 个 g. As in table 12, "°" means non-existing, "( )" means rare, and L means wenyan only. Note that the determinative a 前 *chyan*- means 'before last' or 'the previous' according to the measure that follows; for example, 前天 *chyan.tian* 'day before yesterday', but 前个月 *chyan-g yueh* 'the previous month'. Of the forms under f 这 *jeh*- ～ *jey*- 'this', 这会儿 *jeh.hoel* always means 'now', while 这天 *jey-tian* 'this day (we are talking about)' is not necessarily 'today', for which we have 今天 *jin.tian*; also, 这年 *jey-nian* 'this year (*about* which we are talking)' is not necessarily 'this year (*in* which we are talking)', for which we have 今年 *jin.nian*. With the other measures 这 *jeh*- ～ *jey*- can be taken in either sense. In order not to clutter up the table, we have not tabulated 大前天 *dahchyan.tian* or 大前儿 *dahchyal* 'day before day before yesterday', 大前年 *dahchyan.nian* 'year before year before last', 大後天 *dahhow.tian* or 大後儿 *dahhowl* 'day after day after tomorrow', 大後年 *dahhow.nian* 'year after year after next', 上と礼拜 *shanq-shanq-liibay* 'week before last', and 下と礼拜 *shiah-shiah-liibay* 'week after next'.

The determinatives 上 *shanq-* and 下 *shiah-* as applied to 学期 *shyuechi* 'semester' and 礼拜 *liibay* 'week' have certain complications. The simple form 上学期 *shanq-shyuechi* usually means 'first term (of the school year)' and is thus not a time word related to the present, but a time name; but it can also be used, though less frequently, as a relative time word in the sense of 'last semester (i.e., the semester before the present)'. Similarly, 下学期 *shiah-shyuechi* usually means 'second semester' but occasionally 'next semester'. With 一 *i*, 个 *g*, or 一个 *ig*, however, the result is always relative to the present. Thus, 上一学期 *shanq-i-shyuechi*, 上一个学期 *shanq-ig shyuechi*, or 上个学期 *shanq-g shyuechi* can only mean 'last semester', and the corresponding forms with 下 *shiah-* can mean only 'next semester'. Note particularly the skewed relationship between the four forms with zero, *i* (with *shyuechi* as M), *g*, and *ig* (with *shyuechi* as N) on the one hand and the two meanings of 'first-second' vs. 'last-next' on the other, as shown in table 14.

Table 14

**Shanq**- and **Shiah**- as Applied to **Shyuechi**

| Form Class | Zero | i | g | ig |
|---|---|---|---|---|
| | Measure | | Noun | |
| | Usually | Less often | Always | |
| **shanq**- | 'first' | 'last' | 'last' | |
| **shiah**- | 'second' | 'next' | 'next' | |

With *liibay* itself as 'week', there is no complication: 上礼拜 *shanq-liibay* with or without the insertion of *i*, *g*, or *ig* always means 'last week', and the corresponding forms with 下 *shiah-* al-

Table 13

Relative Time Words

| | 1 | 2 | 3 | 4 | 5 | 6 |
|---|---|---|---|---|---|---|
| | M | M | -x | M | M | M |
| | 天 | 日 | 儿 | 回 | 次 | 会儿 |
| | -tian | -ryh | -l | -hwei | -tsyh | -hoel |
| | 'day' | 'day' | 'day' | 'time' | 'time' | 'moment' |
| a.  前 chyan- 'before last' | 前.天 | L | 前儿 | — | — | — |
|  前 chyan- 'previous' | — | — | — | 前.回 | 前次 | 前一会儿 |
| b.  去 chiuh- 'gone, last' | * | * | * | * | * | * |
| c.  上 shanq- 'last' | * | * | * | 上.回 | 上。次 | * |
| d.  昨 tzwo- 'yester-' | 昨.天 | L | 昨儿 | * | * | * |
| e.  今 jin- 'to-, this' | 今.天 | L | 今儿 | (今回) | (今次) | * |
| f.  这 jeh- ~ jey- 'this' | 这天 | (这日) | * | 这.回 | 这.次 | 这.会儿 |
| g.  本 been- 'the current' | * | L | * | * | * | * |
| h.  明 ming- 'next' | 明.天 | L | 明儿 | * | * | * |
| i.  下 shiah- 'next' | * | * | * | 下.回 | 下.次 | * |
| j.  耒 lai- 'coming' | * | L | * | * | * | * |
| k.  後 how- 'after next' | 後.天 | L | 後儿 | (後回) | (後次) | * |
| l.  那 nah- ~ ney- 'that' | 那天 | (那日) | * | 那.回 | 那次 | 那.会儿 |
| m.  哪 naa- ~ neei- 'which?' | 哪天 | 哪ㄋ日 | * | 哪.回 | 哪.次 | 哪.会儿 |

| 7 | 8 | 9 | 10 | 11 | 12 | 13 |
|---|---|---|----|----|----|----|
| M~N | N | M | M~N | M | M~N | M~N |
| 礼拜 | 月 | 季 | 学期 | 年 | 年度 | 世纪 |
| liibay | yueh | jih | shyuechi | nian | nianduh | shyhjih |
| 'week' | 'month' | 'season' | 'semester' | 'year' | 'academic or fiscal year' | 'century' |
| — | — | — | — | 前.年 | — | — |
| 前礼拜 | 前个月 | 前一季 | 前学期 | — | * | 前一世纪 |
| * | * | * | * | 去.年 | * | * |
| 上礼拜 | 上个月 | 上一季 | 上学期 | ˙ | 上年度 | * |
| * | * | * | * | L | * | * |
| * | * | * | * | 今.年 | * | * |
| 这个礼拜 | 这个月 | 这一季 | 这个学期 | 这年 | 这个年度 | 这个世纪 |
| L | 本月 | (本季) | 本学期 | L | 本年度 | 本世纪 |
| * | * | * | * | 明.年 | * | * |
| 下礼拜 | 下个月 | 下一季 | 下学期 | 下年 | 下年度 | * |
| * | * | * | * | L | * | (L) |
| * | * | * | * | 後.年 | * | * |
| 那个礼拜 | 那个月 | 那一季 | 那个学期 | 那年 | 那个年度 | 那个世纪 |
| 哪个礼拜 | 哪个月 | 哪一季 | 哪个学期 | 哪年 | 哪个年度 | 哪个世纪 |

ways mean 'next week'. But with the individual days of the week
(for which there is no room in table 13), there is a problem of
skewed relationship between form and meaning, not with respect
to form class and meaning, but with respect to immediate constituents, or ICs. The compound 下礼拜六 *shiah-Liibayliow*, for
example, is a compound of the determinative 下 *shiah-*'next' and
the time name 礼拜六 *Liibayliow* 'Saturday', but it does not
necessarily mean '(the) next Saturday (that comes along)' and is
not applicable to the next Saturday if one is talking on Monday
of the same week. For the semantic ICs are 下礼拜 *shiah-*
*liibay* 'next week' and ( 的 礼拜 ) 六 (*de Liibay*) *liow* ' . . . 's
Saturday', so that *shiah-Liibayliow* means really *shiah-liibay de*
*Liibayliow* 'a week from Saturday'. In English, when one talks on
Saturday about 'next Saturday' there is of course no ambiguity.
When one talks on Friday, 'next Saturday' commonly still means
*shiah-*(*liibay de*) *Liibayliow* 'next (week's) Satuday'; otherwise, one
would just say 'tomorrow'. As one recedes farther and farther
back in the week, it becomes more and more ambiguous, and if one
talks on Monday about 'next Saturday' it most likely means *jeyg*
(*liibay de*) *Liibayliow* 'this week's Saturday'. Because of the
semantic ICs in Chinese being always (1) *shiah-liibay* and (2) the
numeral which names the day of the week, there is never doubt
about which week is meant, so that even if one is talking on
Monday, *shiah-Liibayliow* can only mean 'next (week's) Saturday'.
The same IC relations hold for the determinative 上 *shanq-* 'last'.
For example, talking on Sunday (which is reckoned as the seventh
and last day of the week in Chinese usage) about 上礼拜一
*shanq-Liibay'i*, it refers to the Monday thirteen days ago.

There are a number of relative time words which are not in
the form of determinatives compounded with measures or nouns
for units of time. For past time, we have 过去 *guohchiuh* 'the
past', 从前 *tsorngchyan* 'formerly', 当初 *dangchu* 'at first', 起初
*chiichu* 'at first', 起先 *chiishian* 'at first', 起头儿 *chiitourl* 'at
the start', 先头 *shiantour* 'at first', 以前 *yiichyan* 'before'. Although translated for convenience as adverbs in English, they are
substantives and can follow 从 *tsorng* 'from', including even 从前
*tsorngchyan*. For example, one can say 从从前到现在 *tsorng*

*tsorngchyan daw shianntzay* 'from former times to the present'.
The time word 起头儿 *chiitourl* is a V-O compound and can still
be used as V-O, so that one can say 这个我不会起头儿，
请你给我起个头儿。嗐！就从起头儿起头儿就是
了！*Jeyg woo bu huey chii-tourl, chiing nii geei woo chii g tourl.
Hai! jiow tsorng chiitourl chii-tourl .jiow.shle!* 'This thing I don't
know how to begin, will you begin it for me? Well, just begin
from the beginning, that's all!' The preceding time words take 从
*tsorng* 'from' but not 到 *daw* 'to'.

The three time words 近来 *jinnlai* 'recently', 刚才 *gangtsair*
'just now', and 现在 *shianntzay* 'now', as well as 这会儿 *jey-
.hoel* 'this moment', 那会儿 *ney.hoel* 'then', and 哪会儿 *neei-
.hoel* 'when?', can take both 从 *tsorng* 'from' and 到 *daw* 'to'.

For future time, we have 以後 *yiihow* 'after', 後来 *howlai*
'afterwards', and 将来 *jianglai* 'the future', which can take 到
*daw* 'to' but not 从 *tsorng* 'from'.

Note that some of the time words mentioned above refer not
so much to the time *at* which one speaks, as to the time *of* which
one speaks. Thus, 以前 *yiichyan* 'before' may refer to time before
some future as well as present or past event, and 以後 *yiihow*
'after' may refer to time after some past event; in fact 後来
*how₀lai* 'afterwards' is used more often for past than for future
events.[16]

Certain words of relative time are not relative time words in
the grammatical sense, since they function differently from time
words. Thus, although 刚才 *gangtsair* 'just now' is a time word,
its near synonyms 刚 *gang* and 刚刚 *ganggang* 'just' are not time
words since they are adverbs, preceding verbs only, and cannot
be objects of 在 *tzay* 'at', 从 *tsorng* 'from', or 到 *daw* 'to'. A few
words of relative time function as V-O constructions: 过会儿
*guoh.hoel* 'pass a moment,—after a while', 等会儿 *deeng.hoel*
'wait a moment,—after a while', 獃会儿 *dai.hoel* 'stay a moment,—after a while', 过天 *guoh.tian* 'pass days,—after a few

---

[16]On the special redundant forms 没… 以前 *mei … yiichyan* and 已竟…
以後 *yiijinq … yiihow*, see sec. 2.12.7(4).

days', 趕明儿 *gaanmiengl* 'hurry to tomorrow,—some morning'. These do not take *tzay*, etc. Because they occur mostly in first position in V-V series, they behave like adverbs, except that *deeng.hoel* and *dai.hoel* also occur as main verbs, as in 別走啊! 请 你 再 獃 会儿! *Bye tzoou a! Chiing nii tzay dai.hoel!* 'Don't go away! Please stay a while longer!'

(3) N-L Compounds as Time Words. Time words consisting of substantive-localizer compounds are similar to place words of the same type. Most localizers enter in both time words and place words, as in 飯前 *fann-chyan* 'before meal(s)', 飯後 *fann-how* 'after meal(s)', but 门前 *men-chyan* 'in front of the door', 门後 *men-how* or 门背後 *men-beyhow*[17] 'behind the door'. Even in English one hears the colloquialism 'ten minutes in front of five o'clock' and the like. As examples of time words with localizers which are common to both time and place words, we have 早上 *tzao.shanq* 'on the morning (cf. "top of the morning"),—in the morning' (dial.), 中上 *jong.shanq* 'on the mid(day),—around noon' (dial.), 晚上 *woan.shanq* 'on the evening,—in the evening', 黑下 *hei.shiah* 'under darkness,—at night', 目下 *muhshiah* 'under the eyes,—currently', 目前 *muhchyan* 'in front of the eyes,—in the immediate future', 雨前 *yeuchyan* 'before the (spring) rains,— green tea picked before the rains', 午前 *wuuchyan* 'before noon' (≠ 上午 *shanq$_0$wuu* 'forenoon', 事後 *shyhhow* 'after the event', 午後 *wuuhow* 'after noon' (≠ 下午 *shiah$_0$wuu* 'the afternoon'), 日後 *ryhhow* 'in after days,—in the future', 日裡 *ryh.lii* 'in the day', 夜裡 *yeh.lii* 'in the night', 二月裡 *Ell.yueh.lii* 'in February', 月中 *yuehjong* 'in the middle of the month', 日內 *ryhney* L 'within a few days'. The compound localizers 前後 *-$_0$chyan$_0$how*, 上下 *-$_0$shanq$_0$shiah*, and 左右 *-$_0$tzuoo$_0$yow*, all meaning 'thereabouts', are used in both time and place words,

---

[17]This analysis of the ICs as being *men* + *beyhow*, rather than *menbey* + *how*, is based on the fact that the compound is synonymous with the phrase 门的背後 *men de beyhow* 'the rear of the door', but not synonymous with 门背的後头 *menbey de how.tou* 'behind the back-side of the door'.

even though 左 *tzuoo* 'left' and 右 *yow* 'right', whether as determinatives or localizers, are limited to place words when not
occurring as a pair. For example,　我们 的 约 会 是 在 下 午
六 点 前 後（～ 上 下 ～　左 右 ）. *Woomende iuehuey sh tzay
shiahwuu liow-dean-$_0$chyan$_0$how (～ -$_0$shanq$_0$shiah ～ -$_0$tzuoo-
$_0$yow).* 'Our engagement is for 6 P.M. or thereabouts.'

　　The general localizers 那儿 -.*nall* and 这儿 -.*jell*, as in 桌 子
那儿 *juotz.nall* 'at the table', 我们这儿 *woomen.jell* 'chez
nous', are not used in time words. The localizers 内 -*ney* 'inside'
and 外 -*way* 'outside' are sometimes used in time words but more
often in place words. Thus 他 得 初 十 以 外 才 到 呐。 *Ta deei
chushyr yiiway tsair daw ne.* 'He will have to arrive beyond the
10th.' is not as common as with 初 十 以 後 *chushyr yiihow*
'after the 10th'.

　　The localizers 先 -*shian* 'before', 初 -*chu* 'beginning', 底 -*dii*
'end', and 末 -*moh* 'end' occur in time words only. Examples are
事先 *shyhshian* 'before the event', synonymous with 事 前
*shyhchyan*, 月初 *yuehchu* 'the first (days) of the month', 年初
*nianchu* 'the beginning of the year', 月 底 *yuehdii* 'end of the
month', 年底 *niandii* 'end of the year', and the translation borrowing 週末 *joumoh* 'weekend'. Note that in the spatial sense,
the compound form 底下 *dii.shiah* 'below' will have to be used
(= the dialectal form 下 头 *shiah.tou* 'below').

　　Time between is expressed by the same dissyllables as for
place between [sec. 7.4(2.2)]: 当中 *dangjong*, 当 间儿 *dangjiall*,
中 间儿 *jongjiall*, and 中间 *jongjian*, as in 在 春 分 跟 夏 至
的 中 间儿 *tzay chuenfen gen shiahjyh de jongjiall* 'between the
vernal equinox and the summer solstice'. Note, however, that the
form 之 间 *jy jian* L 'between' is used more often in time phrases
than in place phrases, so that 在 三 点 四 点 之 间 *tzay san-
dean syh-dean jy jian* 'between three and four o'clock' sounds less
stiff than 在 蘇 州 上 海 之 间 *tzay Su.jou Shanqhae jy jian*
'between Soochow and Shanghai', for which it would be more
usual to say 在 蘇 州 跟 上 海 的 当 中 *tzay Su.jou gen Shanqhae (de) dangjong* (or any of the other three synonyms of *dang-*

*jong*). The monosyllabic localizers 中 *jong* and 间 *jian* are rather restricted. We have seen its use in 月中 *yuehjong* 'middle of the month', there being no ° 年中 °*nianjong* for 'midyear'; one reason for its non-use is probably homophony with 年终 *nianjong* 'end of the year'. The highly restricted status of 中 *jong* in time words can be compared with the parallel case of place words, as in 关中 *Guanjong* 'Inside the Pass (modern Shensi)', 地中海 *Dihjong Hae* 'Within-land sea,—Mediterranean Sea'.

Time words and Time Phrases: Time Expressions. As in place expressions, the bound constituents in a time word are not always of unlimited versatility, cannot be compounded at will, and very often result in specialized meanings, while time phrases can be made up at will, usually without specialization of meaning. Thus, there is no ° 世纪底 °*shyhjih-dii* or ° 世纪末 °*shyhjih-moh* for 'fin de siècle'. With dissyllabic and thus free localizers (which are themselves place or time words) one can always make up phrases which can be taken literally, as in 十九 世纪的末年   *shyrjeou shyhjih de moh-nian* 'the end-years of the nineteenth century'.

## 7.6.  D-M Compounds

In Chapter 6 ( sec. 6.4.3), we briefly discussed compounds of determinatives and measures, or D-M compounds, as to the versatility of the parts and the specialization of the compounds. We shall now consider in greater detail D-M compounds as a part of speech. Since determinatives are listable and measures are largely listable, D and M can be defined by enumeration, and, though D-M compounds form a large number of transient words, such as 三天 *san-tian* 'three days', 十条 *shyr-tyau* 'ten strips', 两回 *leang-hwei* 'two times,—twice', and 这趟 *jey-tanq* 'this trip', they can simply be defined as subordinative compounds of D and M. But we can say more about D-M compounds than these somewhat empty, though sufficient, formulations. A D-M compound is a substantive and can enter into constructions as subject, object, or attribute, as in 三块太甜了。*San-kuay tay tyan le.* 'Three lumps will be too sweet.' 我忘了那次了。 *Woo wanqle ney-tsyh le.* 'I have forgotten that time.' 十斤的肉有十斤的价钱。 *Shyr-jin de row yeou shyr-jin de jiah.chyan.* 'Ten catties' meat has ten catties' price.' In the last example, *shyr-jin* in attributive position, marked by *de*, modifies *row* and *jiah.chyan* with different meanings of modification. Since 十斤的价钱 *shyr-jin de jiah.chyan* is synonymous, in this context, with *shyr-jin row de jiah.chyan*, the D-M compound has the function of a pronoun. D-M compounds are often used to refer to D-M N. A D-M compound does not usually modify another D-M compound, though it often does a noun. Thus 这个三年 *jeyg san-nian* 'this three-year (period)' is not as common as 这三年 *jey-san-nian* 'these three years', which is a complex D-M compound of the d-n-M type. In a relatively small number of lexical cases a determinative and a measure do not form a D-M compound but some other kind of substantive. Thus, 三条 *san-tyau*, besides being an ordinary D-M compound meaning 'three (strips of belt, rivers, etc.)', it is also a place name, as in 住在三条 *juh tzay Santyau* 'lives on Third Street', or an individual noun in 吃了一张三条 *chyle i-jang Santyau* 'has chow-ed a Three of Bamboo', where *Santyau* is a noun with its specific classifier measure 张 *-jang* for names of pieces in mahjong, domino, or card (but not chess or go) games.

*7.6.1 Complex D-M Compounds.* Before listing determinatives and measures in the succeeding sections, we shall first consider some types of complex D-M compounds with more than one determinative and/or more than one measure, as in 这十万卷书 *jeh shyr-wann-jiuann shu* 'these 100,000 fascicules of books', where *jeh* is a demonstrative determinative, *shyr-* a numeral or numerical determinative, *wann* a numerical measure, *jiuann* another measure, and *shu* a noun. In table 15, the different types of constructions are given first with one fixed series of examples, then a variety of examples for the different types. The point of the table is that not all combinations occur: for example, there is no °些人 °*shie ren* except after a demonstrative or a verb, and there is no °三人 °*san ren* except in wenyan, which is not listed here. To save space, the morphemes in the fixed forms are given in characters only: 这 *jeh* 'this, these', 三 *san* 'three', 百 *bae* '100', 个 *g* general classifier, 人 *ren* 'man, men', 找 *jao* 'look for', 些 $_o$*shie* 'some, a number of, an amount of'.

### 7.6.2. *Some Syntactical Properties of D-M Compounds.*

(1) The Place of Modifiers in D-M N Constructions. Since the D-M constructions is a compound and resists the insertion of other elements, a modifier usually comes after the M and before the N. Thus 一个好人 *ig hao-ren* 'a good man' and not °*i-hao-g ren;* 这张方桌子 *jey-jang fang-juotz* 'this square table' and not °*jey-fang-jang juotz* But when the modifier does modify the measure, then it will of course have to precede the measure, as in 一大张纸 *i-dah-jang jyy* 'a big sheet of paper', 一铁箱子 的宝贝 *i-tiee-shiangtz de bao.bey* 'an iron-chestful of treasures'. When both orders make sense and are synonymous, the advanced position of the modifier has a more lively effect. For example 一 大块石头 *i-dah-kuay shyr.tou* 'a big piece of rock' is livelier than the more matter-of-fact phrase 一块大石头 *i-kuay dah shyr.tou* 'a large rock'. When a lexical meaning is involved, then the two orders will have more than merely a stylistic difference. Thus, 抽一大口烟 *chou i-dah-koou ian* 'draws a big mouthful of smoke' ≠ 抽一口大烟 *chou i-koou dah'ian* 'draws a mouthful of opium'; 一小粒儿米 *i-sheau-liell mii* 'a small grain of rice' ≠ 一粒儿小米 *i-liell sheau$_o$mii* 'a grain of millet'.

(2) M Functioning as *i*-M. After a verb -*i* 'a' is often omitted before a measure, which is usually unstressed, while the center of the object expression is stressed, as objects usually are. For example, 来一碗汤! *Lai* $_o i_o$*woan tang!* 'Bring a bowl of soup!' is often shortened to *Lai* $_o$*woan tang!* Similarly, 说 ($_o$一)$_o$ 句话 *shuo* ($_o i$)$_o$*jiuh huah* 'say a word', 吃($_o$一)$_o$点儿点心 *chy* ($_o i$)$_o$*deal dean.shin* 'eat some refreshments'. We noted that there is a strong tendency for expressions of definite reference to be in the subject position and those of indefinite reference to be in the object position. When the latter involves the omission of 一 *i* 'a', then the postverbal position becomes obligatory, in other words, one cannot begin a sentence with M as an abbreviated form of

D-M. The only exception to this is in the Cantonese dialect, in which one can say 条绳唔够長. *Dhiu zheng° mu kaw jheung.* 'The rope is not long enough.', and 啲人重未嚟. *Ti yan joq mey lai.* 'The people have not yet come.' However, the determinative omitted here is not 一 *iat* 'a', but 嗰 *kox* 'the, those', so that the sentences translated into Mandarin will read: 那条绳子不够長. *Ney-tyau sherngtz bu gow charng.*, and 那些人还没来. *Ney$_0$shie ren hair mei lai.*, or the definite reference will simply be implied by position without *ney-tyau* and *ney$_0$shie.* Thus the apparent exception still proves the rule that the abbreviation of D-M to M is limited to postverbal expressions, since in Mandarin only *i*-M is abbreviated to M and *ney*-M (or *nah*-M) is not abbreviated as it is in Cantonese.

(3) D-M N and D-M *de* N. Under subordination (p. 273) we considered D-M as modifying N, so that 一个 *ig* 'a' modifies 人 *ren* 'man' in *ig ren*, 两碗 *leang-woan* 'two bowls' modifies 粥 *jou* 'congee' in *leang-woan jou*. Since *de* is the principal marker of modification, or subordination, can it always be inserted between D-M and N? In general measures for individuals, or classifiers, cannot take *de*, there being no ° 一个 的人 °*ig de ren* for 'a man', no ° 两枝的筆 °*leang-jy de bii* for 'two pens', and so on. With standard measures, *de* is optional, as 一升(的)米 *i-sheng (de) mii* 'a peck of rice', 几码(的)绸子 *jii-maa (de) chourtz* 'several yards of silk'. With polysyllabic unit measures, as some foreign units are, *de* is usually inserted, as in 走了十里(的)路 *tzooule shyr-lii (de) luh* 'walked ten li', but in 走了三英里的路 *tzooule san-inglii de luh* 'walked three miles', *de* is usually retained. Similarly, 打了十两(的)麻油 *daale shyr-leang (de) mayou* 'bought ten ounces of sesame oil', but 上了十加侖的汽油 *shanqle shyr-jialuen de chihyou* 'put in ten gallons of gasoline'. With the units of time 点 -*dean* 'hour', 分 -*fen* 'minute', 秒 -*meau* 'second', the only noun associated with them is 钟 *jong* '(o')clock' and no *de* is ever inserted, since *dean jong, fen jong, meau jong* are almost measures on their own account, with other nouns for time added, as in 一分钟的工夫儿 *i-fen jong de gong.ful* 'a minute's time', 一点钟的工

Table 15

Complex D-M Compounds

| Fixed Examples | | | | | | Varied Examples | | | | | | | |
|---|---|---|---|---|---|---|---|---|---|---|---|---|---|
| (V) | Dd | Dm | Mn | M | N | (V) | Dd | Dm | Mn | M | N | Romanization | Translation |
| | 这 | | | | | | 这 | | | (不行) | | Jeh (bu shyng). | 'This (won't do).' |
| | 这 | 三 | 百 | 个 | 人 | | 那 | | 两 | 千 | | | ney-leang-chian | 'those two thousand' |
| | 这 | 三 | 百 | 个 | 人 | | 前 | 二 | 十 | 年 | | | chyan-ell.shyr-nian | '20 years before'* |
| | 这 | 三 | 百 | 个 | 人 | | 那 | 五 | 百 | 枝 | 蜡 | | ney-wuubae-jy lah | 'those 500 candles' |
| | 这 | 三 | 百 | 个 | 人 | | 每 | 两 | 万 | | 兵 | | meel-leang-wann bing | 'each 20,000 soldiers' |
| | 这 | 三 | 百 | 个 | 人 | | 哪 | 几 | | 种 | | | neel-jii-joong? | 'which (several) kinds?' |
| | 这 | 三 | | 个 | 人 | | 下 | 一 | | 个 | 礼拜 | | shiah-ig liibay | 'next (one) week' |
| | 这 | | 些 | 个 | 人 | | 这 | | 些 | (够了) | | | Jey₀ shie (gow le). | 'These (will be enough).' |
| | 这 | | 些 | 个 | 人 | | 那 | | 些 | 家 | | | ney₀ shie-jia | 'those (houses, etc.)' |
| | 这 | | 些 | 个 | 人 | | 那 | | 些 | 家 | 饭馆儿 | | ney₀ shie-jia fanngoal | 'those restaurants' |
| | 这 | | 些 | 个 | 人 | | 前 | | 些 | | 时候儿 | | chyan₀ shie shyr.howl | 'some time before' |
| | 这 | | | 个 | 人 | | 哪 | | | 本? | | | neel-been? | 'which volume?' |
| | 这 | | | 个 | 人 | | 全 | | | 部 | 书 | | chyuan-buh shu | 'the whole book (work)' |
| | 这 | | | 个 | 人 | | 那 | | | | 玩意儿 | | nah wanyell | 'that toy (lit. or fig.)' |

| | | | | | Romanization | Gloss |
|---|---|---|---|---|---|---|
| | | | 五 | 十 | wuushyr | 'fifty' |
| | | | 二 | 千 两 | ell-chian-leang | '2,000 tael' |
| 三 | 百 | 人 | 几 | 万 块 钱 | jii-wann-kuay chyan | 'several 10,000 dollars' |
| 三 | 百 | 个 人 | 两 | 打 鸡子儿 | leang-dar jitzeel | 'two dozen eggs' |
| 三 | 百 | 个 人 | 半 | 天 | bann-tian | 'half a day,—long time' |
| 三 | 百 | 个 人 | 一 | 磅 肉 | 1-banq row | 'one pound of meat' |
| (找) | 些 | 个 | (拿) 些 | (去)! | (Na) .shie (.chiuh)! | 'Take some (away)!' |
| (找) | 些 | 个 人 | (买) 些 | (里)! | (Mae) .shie g(ba)! | 'Buy some!' |
| (找) | 些 | 个 人 | (问了) 些 | 谁? | (Wennle) .shie g sheir? | 'Asked whom?' |
| (找) | 些 | | (找) 些 | 绳子 | (Jao) .shie sherngtz! | 'Find some ropes!' |
| (找) | 块 | 个 | (刀) 块 | (里)! | (Chy) .kuay (ba)! | 'Eat a piece!' |
| (找) | 碗 | 个 人 | (沏) 碗 | 茶 | (chi) .woan char | 'makes a cup of tea' |

*Note that with 前 chyan- as a determinative, the expression 前 二 十 年 chyan-ell-shyr-nian is ambiguously equivalent to either (a) chyan-ig ell.shyr-nian 'a preceding or first period of 20 years' or (b) 二 十 年 前 ell.shyr-nian-chyan (with -chyan as a localizer) '20 years ago'.

夫儿 *i-dean jong de gong.ful* 'an hour's time'. In the last case there is another synonymous expression 一个钟头的工夫 儿 *ig jongtour de gong.ful*, where the presence of *g* shows that *jongtour* is a noun and not a measure. The case of the monetary units 塊 *-kuay* 'dollar', 毛 *-mau* '(unit of) ten cents', 分 *-fen* 'cent' is similar to that of time lengths, as they are closely associated with the word 錢 *chyan* 'money', so much so that 毛錢 *mauchyan* or 毛錢儿 *mauchyal* 'dime' is actually a compound noun. There still remains a difference between 兩毛錢 *leang-mau chyan* 'twenty cents (of money)' and 兩个毛錢儿 *leangg mauchyal* 'two dimes'. As with time units, no *de* is inserted between the D-M and *chyan*.

Temporary measures, and less frequently container measures as opposed to standard measures, usually take *de*, which has the effect of making explicit the use of a noun for a measure. For example, 一碗湯 *i-woan tang* 'a bowl of soup', 一杯酒 *i-bei jeou* 'a cup of wine', 兩勺儿醬油 *leang-shaurl jianqyou* 'two spoonfuls of soy sauce', since one usually measures these materials in these containers, but in 灑了一地的糖 *saale i-dih de tarng* 'spilled a floorful of sugar', 引了一厨房的螞蟻 *yiinle i-chwufarng de maa_oyii* 'attracted a kitchenful of ants', the *de* is preferred because *dih* and *chwufarng* are nouns and are only temporarily used as measures.

(4) D-M *de* as 'of' and as Reverse 'of'. In most occurrences of *de*, it can be equated to English ''s', or to 'of' with terms on both sides of 'of' reversed, so that A *de* B is 'A's B' or 'B of A'. Examples are: 一根儿三尺的棍子 *i-gel san-chyy de guenntz* 'a three-foot rod' or 'a rod of three feet', 四季的花儿都不一樣. *Syh-jih de hual dou bu iyanq.* 'The four seasons' flowers, —the flowers of the four seasons—are all different.' But with a D-M compound, the *de* usually translates into 'of' in the same order of terms. For example, 做了三个钟头的活 *tzuohle san'g jongtour de hwo* 'did three hours' work' or 'did work of three hours' length', 打了兩担的柴火 *daale leang-dann de chair.huoo* 'gathered two loads of fuel'. In general the 'of' of quantities has the same order of terms as *de*, while the 'of' of

'pertaining' has the reverse order of terms. In some cases, both uses of *de* are possible, so that the D-M *de* N is ambivalent and the order of the translated terms will be different. For example, 我 今 天 跑 了 二 十 層 的 楼. *Woo jin.tian paole ell.shyr-tserng de lou.* 'I ran twenty flights of stairs today.', which may have been one continuous ascent to the twentieth floor, ten round trips to the second floor, or any equivalent amount of stairs-run-ning, but 他 们 租 了 个 二 十 層 的 楼. *Tamen tzule g ell.shyr-tserng de lou.* 'They rented a twenty-story building,—a building of twenty stories.' Note that with measures such as 种 *-joong* 'kind, sort', 流 *-liou* 'class (of people)', and so on, the 'of' can work both ways, as in 那 一 流 的 政 客 *nah-i-liou de jenqkeh* 'that kind of politician' or 'politicians of that type'. In the case of 一 樣 ( 儿 ) *i-yanq(l)* there is an additional function as an adjective. Thus, besides 叫 了 一 樣 儿 菜 *jiawle i-yanql tsay* 'ordered a dish of food', there is also 跟 那 樣 儿 菜 完 全 一 樣 *gen ney-yanql tsay wanchyuan iyanq* 'exactly the same as the other dish', where *iyanq* 'the same' can be modified by the adverb *wanchy-uan* 'entirely'. Similarly, besides 一 共 只 兩 樣 儿 *igonq jyy leangyanql* 'two kinds altogether', but 太 兩 樣 了 *tay leangyanq le* 'too different'. On the whole, as adjectives the suffix -儿 *-l* is not used, especially with *iyanq*, while as M proper the suffix is optional. Note that only *iyanq* 'same' and *leangyanq* 'different' are adjectives. From 三 樣 ( 儿 ) *san-yanq(l)* 'three kinds' on, all forms are D-M compounds and therefore substantives, not modi-fiable by adverbs of degree.

(5) D-M N vs. N D-M. The D-M N order follows the usual order of subordinative construction, whether there is an inserted *de* or not. In the invoice or inventory style the order is reversed, as in: 方 桌 一 張 *fang-juo i-jang* 'square table(s), one', 站 灯 兩 架 *jann-deng leang jiah* 'floor lamps, two (stands)', 籐 椅 六 把 *terng-yii liow-baa* 'rattan chairs, six'. Invoices or inventories are of course not in the ordinary spoken style. But even this order can be explained in terms of normal spoken syntax. The D-M compound can be regarded as a nominal predicate to the noun as subject. In fact, in taking inventories, one person often calls out

the category (N) and another will answer with the quantity (D-M), so that the conversation may be something like this:

A. 地毯 呐 ? *Dihtaan ne?* 'How about rugs?'

B. 地毯 啊 ? *Dihtaan a?* 'Rugs?'

A. 嗯, 地毯. *Ng, dihtaan.* 'Yeah, rugs.'

B. 地毯 嘿, 地毯两条。 *Dihtaan me—, dihtaan leang-tyau.*
'Rugs—uh—rugs, two (strips).'

A. 茶几 呐 ? *Charji ne?* 'And tea tables?'

B. 茶几 四个. *Charji syh-geh.* 'Tea tables, four.'

A. 书架 *Shujiah—* 'Bookcases—'

B. 一件. *I-jiann.* 'One (article).'

and the result is an inventory all in the N D-M form. This is quite parallel with the interpretation of a full sentence as question and answer, as illustrated in the previous husband-and-wife conversation about getting the dinner ready (sec. 2.6.2).

(6) D-M D′-M′ Forms. While one D-M compound does not usually modify another D-M compound, as we have seen, two D-M compounds may occur in succession: (a) in simple coordination, as in 两个办法简直是半斤八两. *Leangg bannfaa jeanjyr sh bann-jin ba-leang.* 'The two methods are just half a pound and eight ounces,—six (of one) and half a dozen (of the other)., 这家儿那家儿的菜都贵. *Jey-jial ney-jial de tsay dou guey.* 'The dishes of this (restaurant) and that (restaurant) are both expensive.'; (b) as S-P, as in 八块ㄦ十六块。*Ba-kuay ba-kuay shyrliow-kuay.* 'Eight dollars (and) eight dollars (are) sixteen dollars.', where the two *ba-kuay* are in coordination, which in turn form the subject of *shyrliow-kuay* as nominal predicate: (c) to form vivid forms of adverbs and adjectives, as in 一句ㄦ的说 *i-jiuh-i-jiuh-de shuo* 'says (it) sentence by sentence', 三步两步的跑 *san-buh-leang-buh-de pao* 'runs two and three steps at a time', 一座ㄦ的海岛 *i-tzuoh-i-tzuoh-de haedao* 'one island after another'. When two D-M compounds in which D is a numeral are subject and predicate, the expression is often a rate, such as speed, price, and so on: 一点钟二十英里 *i-dean jong ell.shyr-Inglii* 'one hour 20 miles,—20 miles an hour', 每磅三毛钱 *meei-banq san-mau chyan* 'each pound 30

cents,—30 cents a pound', 五十塊錢一兩 *wuushyr-kuay chyan i-leang* '\$50 an ounce'. The order of the two quantities is not fixed, but is influenced by two factors: (a) Other things being equal, the denominator in the rate is usually mentioned first.[18] Thus, in the preceding example, 二十英里一点 钟 *ell.shyr-Inglii i-dean jong* is possible, such as in answer to the question: How long will it take to go 20 miles? Ans. 1 hour; but ordinarily the order is *i-dean jong ell.shyr-Inglii.* (b) The other factor is that in naming prices, the preferred order is money-thing, so that 'three for a dollar' is usually turned around into 一 塊錢三个 *i-kuay chyan san'g,* though in answer to a question as to how much three will cost, one will say 三个一塊錢 *san'g i-kuay chyan.* But even here, it is possible to displace the logical predicate to the grammatical subject by extra stress and say "*i-kuay-chyan san'g* (cf. sec. 2.5.2).

(7) D-M Compounds as Quantity Words. D-M compounds are so called because their constituents are a determinative and a measure. Since the subclasses of substantives we have described so far are defined in terms of their syntactical function rather than internal structure, there remains the possibility that a word is both a D-M compound and some of those subclasses of substantives. For reasons of convenient treatment we have set up D-M compounds as the present subsection [7.7], but they overlap with members of the other subclasses. We have, indeed, already come across a number of such cases, especially under place words, such as 南边儿 *nan.bial* 'south side,—the south' and 两头儿 *leang-tourl* 'both ends', and time words, such as 这$_0$回 *jey$_0$hwei* 'this time' and all the other forms in table 13. We noted also that some D-M compounds function as pronouns in that D-M is used as a substitute for D-M N, as in 十个梨太多了，我只要 買五个. *Shyrg li tay duo le, woo jyy yaw mae wuug.* 'Ten pears will be too many, I only want to buy five.' The common demonstrative pronouns 这个 *jeyg* 'this', 那个 *neyg* 'that', and the interrogative pronoun 哪个 *neeig* 'which', are also D-M in their make-up. But there remain a large number of D-M's, in

---

[18]Cf. the naming of fractions, sec. 7.8(3d).

fact most of those with a numeral as determinative (in other
words, n-M's), which are neither nouns, nor place words, nor time
words, nor pronouns, but quantity words. Examples are 三年
*san-nian* 'three years', 五尺 *wuu-chyy* 'five feet', 一百噸 *ibae-
duen* '100 tons'. That *nian* 'year' is a unit of time does not make
*san-nian* a time word, since one cannot say ° 在三年 °*tzay san-
nian* for 'in three years (from now)', but 三年內 *san-nian-ney*
'within three years' is a time word and 三年以內 *san-nian
yiiney* 'within three years' is a time phrase and they can take 在
*tzay* 'at' or 到 *daw* 'up to, by' before them.

Syntactically, a quantity word Q' can fill the following frames
of comparison in relation to adjectives (represented by A below):

| | | | |
|---|---|---|---|
| (a) | 比 Q A | *bii* Q A | 'A-er than Q' |
| (b) | 有 Q ( 那么 ) A | *yeou* Q (*nemm*) A | 'as A as Q' |
| (c) | 没(有) Q ( 那么 ) A | *mei* (*yeou*) Q (*nemm*) A | 'not as A as Q' |
| (d) | 不到 Q | *budaw* Q | 'less than Q' |
| (e) | 不止 Q | *bujyy* Q | 'more than Q' |
| (f) | 从 $Q_1$ 到 $Q_2$ | *tsorng* $Q_1$ *daw* $Q_2$ | 'from $Q_1$ to $Q_2$' |
| (g) | 在 Q 以上 | *tzay* Q *yiishanq* | 'above Q' |
| (h) | 在 Q 以下 | *tzay* Q *yiishiah* | 'below Q' |
| (i) | 在 Q 以外 | *tzay* Q *yiiway* | 'beyond Q' |
| (j) | 在 Q 以內 | *tzay* Q *yiiney* | 'within Q' |

As more concrete examples, we have: (a) 比一寸長 *biii-tsuenn
charng* 'longer than one inch', (b) 有十斤重 *yeou shyr-jin jonq*
'as heavy as ten catties', (c) 没一年那么長 *mei i-nian nemm
charng* 'not as long as one year', (d) 不到兩瓶 *budaw leang-
pyng* 'less than two bottles', (e) 不止十把 *bujyy shyr-baa*
'more than ten bunches', (f) 从四尺到六尺 *tsorng syh-chyy
daw liow-chyy* 'from four to six feet', (g) 在十年以上 *tzay
shyr-nian yiishanq* 'above ten years', (h) 在三岁以下 *tzay
san-suey yiishiah* 'under three years old', (i) 在一百万光年
以外 *tzay ibae-wann-guangnian yiiway* 'beyond one million
light-years', (j) 在八丈以內 *tzay ba-janq yiiney* 'within eighty
feet'. Note that while in f, quantity words can be used with 从
... 到 *tsorng ... daw*, they cannot be used with 在 *tzay* alone with-

out the addition of 以上 *yiishanq*, etc. (g, h, i, j, ) or its more literary equivalents 之上 *jy shanq*, etc. Thus, one can say 在 今年 *tzay jin.nian* 'in this year', but not ° 在兩年 °*tzay leang-nian* for 'in two years', since *jin.nian* is a time word and *leang-nian* is a quantity word. But one can say 在兩年以內 *tzay leang.nian yiiney* 'within two years', since the localizer *yiiney* makes a time phrase of the quantity word of time. For 'in two years' in the sense of 'two years from now', the expression is 兩年（以）後 *leang-nian (yii) how*, which is equally applicable to 'after two years'. In other words, there is no such distinction in Chinese, as there is in English, as that between 'after' for the past and 'in' for the future.

Like time and place words [sec. 7.5(3)], quantity words may be subordinated to the compound localizers 上下 -$_0$*shanq*$_0$*shiah* 'up or down,—thereabouts' and 左右 -$_0$*tzuoo*$_0$*yow* 'left or right, —thereabouts', as in 六尺上下 *liow-chyy*$_0$*shanq*$_0$*shiah* 'six feet or thereabouts', and 十年左右 *shyr-nian*$_0$*tzuoo*$_0$*yow* 'ten years or so'. But only time names can also take 前後 -*chyanhow* 'before or after,—thereabouts', as in 春分總是在三月二十 前後. *Chuenfen tzoongsh tzay San.yueh ellshyr chyanhow.* 'The vernal equinox is always on March 20 or thereabouts.'

## 7.7. N-L Compounds

Unlike D-M compounds, which may be place words, time words, quantity words, or pronouns, the class of N-L compounds are mostly either place words, such as 心裡 *shin.lii* 'in the heart', 'in the mind', 牆上 *chyang.shanq* 'on the wall', or time words, such as 夜裡 *yeh.lii* 'in the night', 飯前 *fann-chyan* 'before meal(s)'. Only a very limited number of N-L compounds are nouns, proper names, or pronouns. Thus, 陛下 *bihshiah* 'under the imperial steps,—Your Majesty' and 閣下 *gershiah* 'under your studio,—you, sir' are pronouns [see sec. 7.11.4 (2.6)], and 門下 *menshiah* 'under the gate,—pupil' is a noun, and 王家裡 *Wong-ka'-lii* (Soochow dial.) 'in the Wang's family,—fellow named

Wang' is a proper name. These N-L compounds are very restricted in number and always have lexical meanings.

As N-L compounds have been discussed from the point of
view of compounding (sec. 6.4.4), as place words [sec. 7.3.3(3)],
and as time words [sec. 7.5(3)], and since the localizers will be
listed below (sec. 7.10), we shall not go into further detail and
have not listed them in table 10, earlier in this chapter.


# 7.8.  Determinatives

Most determinatives (D), measures (M), and localizers (L) are
bound and monosyllabic morphemes.  Determinatives are end-
bound and measures and localizers are start-bound, forming
typically D-M and N-L compounds, whether transient or lexical.
One reason that these have been treated as parts of speech or
word classes is that most of them are of unlimited versatility in
forming transient words of no lexical import, such as 那片 *ney-
piann* 'that slice', 三课 *san-keh* 'three lessons', and 门上 *men-
.shanq* 'on the door', while special lexical cases are no more
frequent, relatively, than special idioms of phrases of free words.
Another reason is that D, M, and L, like final particles, are often
in construction with phrases as ICs. For example, in  两大箱
子的衣裳  *leang-dah-shiangtz de i-shang* 'two big trunks of
clothes', the determinative *leang* is in construction with *dah-
shiangtz* as a temporary measure. In  他住的那所房子裡
有暖气。 *Ta juh de ney-suoo farngtz.lii yeou noanchih.* 'There is
heating in the house he lives in.', the localizer -*.lii* is phonologically enclitic to the noun *farngtz,* but is not in construction with
it; for if it were, forming a place word *farngtz.lii,* then it would
not be modifiable by the D-M compound *ney-suoo,* which can
only modify nouns. It is not even in construction with *ney-suoo
farngtz,* but with the whole substantive expression with a clause
modifier *ta juh de ney-suoo farngtz.*

In the cases where a D, an M, or an L has more than one
syllable and is stressed, then it is free and often occurs without
forming D-M or N-L compounds. Thus one can say  你要多
o少? *Nii yaw duo*o*shao?* as well as  你要多o少个？ *Nii yaw*

*duo~o~shao-g?* for 'How many (presumably many) do you want?' but one can only say 你要几个? *Nii yaw jiig?* and not ° 你要 几? °*Nii yaw jii?* for 'How many (presumably a few) do you want?' With dissyllabic measures, there is usually class overlap between noun and measure; for example, 三星期 *san-shingchi* ～ 三个星期 *san'g shingchi* 'three weeks', 两对週 *leang-dueyjou* ～ 两个对週 *leangg dueyjou* 'two 24-hours', the latter perhaps with the effect of 'two 24-hourses'.

There are four kinds of determinatives: (1) demonstrative determinatives (Dd), (2) specifying determinatives (Dc), (3) numerical determinatives, or numerals (Dn), and (4) quantitative determinatives (Dq).

(1) Demonstrative Determinatives. These consist of the three forms 这 *jeh-* ～ *jey-* 'this', 那 *nah-* ～ *ney-* 'that', and 哪 *naa* ～ *neei-* 'which'.[19] They also occur free as pronouns, and their phonological variant features will be described later under pronouns [sec. 7.11.4(4)]. As bound determinatives, they are as versatile as numerals in that they compound with all classes of measures: with classifiers, as 这个 *jeyg* 'this', 那张 *ney-jang* 'that sheet', 哪省 *neei-sheeng* 'which province', and 那趟 *ney-tanq* 'that trip'. With standard measures and temporary measures, usually, though not necessarily, a numeral is inserted to form a compound determinative of the dn-M type, as 这一天 *jey-i-tian* 'this (one) day', 那一地的泥 *ney-i-dih de ni* 'that floorful of mud'.

The demonstrative determinatives form place words with localizers and the suffix *-l* ( ← localizer 裡 *-.lii*), as 在这裡 *tzay jeh.lii* 'is here' and 在这儿 *tzay jell* 'is here'.

(2) Specifying Determinatives. These are: 每 *meei-* 'each', 各 *geh-* 'the various —s', 别 *bye-* 'other, different', 另 *linq-* 'other,

---

[19]Both *nah-* and *naa-* (and their variants) used to be written with the same character 那 and the reader had to decide which it was from context. In 1924, I proposed to limit 那 to *nah-* only and to write 哪 for *naa-*, which has since become the general practice. See my 那的分化的我见 ("My View on the Differentiation of 那"), 国语月刊 (*National Language Monthly*), 2.2 (1924).

separate', 旁 *parng-* 'other', 本 *been-* 'this, the present (one)', 某 *moou-* 'a certain', 上 *shanq-* 'former, last', 下 *shiah-* 'next', 前 *chyan-* 'previous to last, previous', 後 *how-* 'after next', 今 *jin-* 'to-, this', 明 *ming-* 'next', 昨 *tzwo-* 'yester-', and 去 *chiuh-* 'last'. Of these only 每 *meei-* 'each' approaches the demonstratives in versatility, in that it combines with all except temporary measures. The determinative 各 *geh* is usually translated as 'each' but it refers to a group as a whole, as in 各國的政府 *geh-gwo de jenqfuu* 'the governments of various countries'. The possible D-M compound 各个 *gehg(eh)* 'the various individuals' occurs in wenyan but is usually avoided in speech, since it is homophonous with 个个 *g(eh)g(eh)* 'everyone', even though the latter often occurs in the form *g(eh)gehl*. [On the continued use of 各个 in writing by speakers of dialects in which 各 *geh* is pronounced in the Entering Tone, see sec. 7.11.3(3.5).] With the determinatives 別 *bye-*, 另 *linq-*, 旁 *parng-*, 本 *been-*, and 某 *moou-*, the occurrences are restricted to some of the quasi-measures and measures for verbs, as 另章 *linq-jang* 'another chapter', 某次 *moou-tsyh* 'a certain time, once'. With the insertion of 一 *-i-* 'a' they can be combined with individual measures or classifiers, as 某一件事 *moou-i-jiann shyh* 'a certain matter', except for 本 *been-*, which does not take *i*. On the occurrence of 上 *shanq-*, 下 *shiah-*, 前 *chyan-*, 後 *how-*, 今 *jin-*, 明 *ming-*, 昨 *tzwo-*, and 去 *chiuh-*, see table 13 for the time words.

(3) Numerical Determinatives. The scope of numerals as determinatives is both wider and narrower than that of numbers in the arithmetical sense. It is wider, because numerals include 几 *jii-* 'how many' or 'a few'; it is narrower, since both 二 *ell-* and 兩 *leang-* express the same number 'two', and yet behave quite differently as numerals.

Numerals are ordinarily used for cardinal numbers, while ordinal numbers are expressed by numerals preceded by 第 *dih-* '-th', resulting in prefixed determinatives, for example, 九章 *jeou-jang* 'nine chapters', but 第九章 *dihjeou-jang* 'Chapter 9'. In certain lexical compounds, however, the numeral is taken in either the cardinal or the ordinal sense. For example, in 三國

*San Gwo* 'the Three Kingdoms', 四书 *Syh Shu* 'the Four Books', 五经 *Wuu Jing* 'the Five Classics', 九章 *Jeou Jang* '(book on mathematics called) Nine Chapters', the numerals denote cardinal numbers, but in names of the months 一月 *I.yueh*, 二月 *Ell.yueh*, ... 十二月 *Shyr'ell.yueh* 'January, February, ... December' and in terms of address 二哥 *Ellge* 'Second (older) Brother', 四妹 *Syhmey* 'Fourth (younger) Sister', and so on, the numerals are taken in the ordinal sense. In some cases, a form n-M may be ambivalently either 'the nth M' or 'n M's', as 三条 *san-tyau* 'three of bamboo' (three being actually three strips on the mahjong piece) or 'Third Street', short for 第三条胡同 *dihsan-tyau hwutonq* 'the Third Lane'. In mentioning years of an era, the prefix 第 *dih-* is not used, so that 五十三年 *wuu.shyrsan-nian* may mean either 53 years or the year 53 of a certain era, and 一千九百六十五年 *ichian-jeoubae-liowshyrwuu-nian* may mean either 1965 years or A.D. 1965. On 二回 *ell.hwei* 'next time' and 两回 *leang-hwei* 'twice' see the subsection on *ell* and *leang* below.

(a) Simple Numerals. The simple numerals are: 一 *i* 'one', 二 *ell* 'two', 两 *leang* 'two', 三 *san* 'three', 四 *syh* 'four', 五 *wuu* 'five', 六 *liow* 'six', 七 *chi* 'seven', 八 *ba* 'eight', 九 *jeou* 'nine', 十 *shyr* 'ten', and 零 *ling* 'zero', the last occurring only in compound numerals and in scientific language.

In radio communications, according to information furnished me by Maurice H. Tseng, a set of noise-resistant forms have recently come into use when numerals are read off. They are shown in the table, in which it will be seen that any two of the syllables differ very clearly in vocalism, ending, and tone.

|  | 1 | 2 | 3 | 4 | 5 | 6 | 7 | 8 | 9 | 0 |
|---|---|---|---|---|---|---|---|---|---|---|
| 1st Tone | 幺 *iau* |  | 三 *san* |  |  |  | 乖 *guai* | 八 *ba* | 勾 *gou* |  |
| 3rd Tone |  | 两 *leang* |  |  | 五 *wuu* |  |  |  |  |  |
| 4th Tone |  |  |  | 四 *syh* |  | 六 *liow* |  |  |  | 洞 *donq* |

Special behavior of *i* (a 1). The morpheme *i* has three tones according to the tone of the syllable following it. A stressed *i*-M differs from an unstressed .*i*-$_0$M somewhat as English 'one' differs from 'a' and 'an', which are in fact derived from a weakened 'one'. For example, 只 喝 了 一 杯 酒 *jyy hele i-bei jeou* 'drank only one cup of wine', but 喝 了 一 杯 酒 *hele .i₀-bei jeou* 'drank a cup of wine'. When weakened still more, *i* is entirely dropped and ₀M takes the place of the D-M compound *i*-M. This, as we have seen [sec. 7.6.2(2)], occurs only after verbs, as in 得 找 个人 *deei jao g ren* 'must find a man', 跑 趟 街 *pao tanq jie* 'make a trip to town', 買 升 米 *mae sheng mii* 'buy a peck of rice'. With temporary measures and quasi-measures this omission of *i* from *i*-M after verbs is rare. The tone sandhi is as follows:

| Before | *i* has | as in |
|---|---|---|
| 1st Tone | 4th Tone | 一天 *i-tian*[20] 'a day', 一杯 *i-bei* 'a cupful' |
| 2nd Tone | 4th Tone | 一年 *i-nian* 'a year', 一回 *i-hwei* 'once' |
| 3rd Tone | 4th Tone | 一百 *ibae* '100', 一会儿 *i-hoel* 'a while' |
| 4th Tone | 2nd Tone | 一对 *'i-duey'* 'a pair', 一半儿 *iball* 'a half' |
| a pause | 1st Tone | 十一 *'shyr'i'* '11', 初一 *chu'i* '1st of month' |

In lexical compounds with stressed *i* as 'one', it does not have the tone sandhi, resulting in the 4th or 2nd Tone, but always has the 1st Tone. For example, 一 中 *I jong* 'First Middle', short for 第 一 中学 *Dih'i Jongshyue* 'First Middle School', as against 只 有 一 盅 酒 *jyy yeou i-jong (yih-jong) jeou* 'only one (small) cup of wine', where it is the usual *i*-M compound. In 一 九 一 一 *i-jeou-i-i* '1911', not only the last *i*, but the other two, are also in the 1st Tone.

The numerals *ell* and *leang* (a2). *Ell* is used as an abstract number and in compound numbers. In counting 一, 二, 三, 四 *i, ell, san, syh* 'one, two, three, four', the forms are quasi-quoted, and one can say 报 名 数 的 时 候 我 报 错 了 个 二. *Baw mingshuh de shyr.how, woo baw-tsuohle g ell.* 'When counting off, I counted a "two" by mistake.' In such cases the numbers

---

[20]For simplicity, especially in grammatical discussions, we are giving the three different morphs of the morpheme in the form of *i* (or strictly {i}, where "{}" indicates a morphophonemic notation). Some writers, for example Walter Simon, write phonemically *yih*, *yi*, and *i*, which makes it easier for beginners to read in an elementary text, but slightly complicates grammatical statements.

occur as nouns, as all quoted forms are, modifiable by *ig* or *g*, and not as numerals in the sense of numerical determinatives.

We noted that in broadcasting usage 兩 *leang* is used in calling off figures. In Shanghai, where the dialect has nasal initials for both 二 *gni²* 'two' and 五 *ng²* 'five', the vowel *i* in *gni²* being acoustically weak and the (new) Shanghai Lower Rising and Lower Going Tones being indistinguishable, telephone operators and most of the telephoning public use *liang* for 'two'. (Cf. *zwo* in telephoning in Germany, to avoid confusion of *zwei* with *drei*.)

As determinatives before measures, both *ell* and *leang* occur, as in 二斤塩 *ell-jin yan* or 兩斤塩 *leang-jin-yan* 'two catties of salt'. But *ell* and *leang* do not occur with equal versatility with all measures. There is 兩个 *leangg* 'two', but no °二个 °*ellg*,[21] there is 二十 *ellshyr* 'twenty' (*shyr* being here a measure), but no °兩十 °*leangshyr*. As a simple numeral, *leang* is used much more than *ell* on the whole. As to the choice between *ell* and *leang*, it depends mostly upon the category of the M involved. Individual measures, or classifiers, take *leang* and only rarely also *ell*, as in 兩把 *leang-baa* 'two (of knives, chairs, etc.)', 兩片 *leang-piann* 'two slices', 兩位 *leang-wey* 'two (honorific classifier)' but also 二位 *ell-wey*. Standard units take *leang*, with certain units of old standing also taking *ell*, as in 兩天 *leang-tian* 'two days', 兩磅 *leang-banq* 'two pounds', 兩成 *leang-cherng* or 二成 *ell-cherng* 'two tenths,—20%', 一塊兩毛 *i-kuay leang-mau* or 一塊二毛 *i-kuay ell-mau* 'one dollar twenty cents', 兩毛五 *leang-mau-wuu* or 二毛五 *ell-mau-wuu* 'twenty-five cents', but 兩毛 *leang-mau* and very rarely *ell-mau* 'twenty cents'. With the unit 兩 *leang* 'tael', there is only 二兩 *ell-leang* 'two taels', but no °兩兩 °*leang-leang*. In the lively reduplicate 三儿兩儿的来 *sansan-leangleangde lai* 'come in two's and three's', there is of course no *leang* as a measure involved. With quasi-measures and measures for verbs, *leang* is almost always used, as

---

[21]It is a different matter, as we have seen (sec. 6.4.3, n. 18), when a writer of the new generation, especially in familiar letter writing, writes in characters 二个 but says to himself *leangg* and which the reader also reads as *leangg*.

in 兩省 *leang-sheeng* 'two provinces', 兩课 *leang-keh* 'two lessons', 兩下儿 *leang-shiall* 'two strokes', 兩回 *leang$_0$hwei* 'twice', In 二回 *ell.hwei* 'next time', *ell* is an ordinal number. So is 二次 *ell-tsyh* in 二次革命 *Elltsyh Germinq* 'the Second Revolution (of 1913)'.

If n-M is followed by a noun or an adjective, then the use of *ell* is more likely than in n-M alone. Thus, 兩寸 *leang-tsuenn* 'two inches' is more frequent than 二寸 *ell-tsuenn*, but 二寸長 *ell-tsuenn charng* 'two inches long' is about as frequent as 兩寸長 *leang-tsuenn charng*.

In the approximate number 'two or three' followed by a measure, both *ell-san* and *leang-san* are often possible where only *leang* would be used if not followed by *san*. Thus, while there is no °二磅 °*ell-banq* for 'two pounds', one can say either 二三磅 *ell-san-banq* or 兩三磅 *leang-san banq* for 'two or three pounds'. With 十 *shyr* 'ten' as a measure, however, there is only 二三十 *ell-sanshyr* '20 or 30' and no ° 兩三十 °*leang-sanshyr*.

Like the case of *i*-M meaning 'one' when stressed, and meaning 'a(n)' when in neutral tone or shortened to $_0$M, the stressed form of 兩 *leang* followed by a measure means '(exactly) two' while .*leang*$_0$M means 'a couple of, a few' (possibly three, four, or five). For example, 今天得念兩课. *Jin.tian deei niann leang-keh.* 'We must study two lessons today'. But with .*leang*$_0$*keh*, it means 'We must study a couple of lessons today.' As in the case of .*i*$_0$M, this weak form of .*leang*$_0$M occurs only after verbs.

*Lea* and *sa* as fusions (a 2,3). The n-M compound 兩个 *leangg* has a shorter form 俩 *lea*, which is grammatically longer than the numeral *leang*, but phonologically actually shorter. One cannot say ° 要兩 °*yaw leang*, since *leang* is bound, but must say 要兩个 *yaw leangg* 'want two', but, apart from greater informality of style, this is quite synonymous with 要俩 *yaw lea*, *lea* being simply a fusion of the dissyllabic *leangg* into one syllable. Similarly *san'g* is telescoped into *sa*, so that, although one cannot say ° 我要三。 °*Woo yaw san.*, one can say 我要仨。 *Woo yaw sa.* 'I want three.' Because there is a common character

俩 for *lea,* there is a common misconception that there is something special about the number two and that, with its Radical 9, it has special reference to persons, as it appears so often in 我 们俩 *woomen lea* 'we two' in engagement and wedding announcements.[22] Actually, *lea* is grammatically quite equivalent to *leangg,* so that 俩蘋菓 *lea pynguoo* 'two apples' is just as natural as 俩学生 *lea shyue.sheng* 'two students'. That 俩先生 *lea shian.sheng* 'two teachers' or 'two gentlemen', though grammatical, does not sound so natural is because, with the respect due to persons addressed as *shian.sheng,* the measure *g* (which forms a part of *lea*) is expected to be replaced by the honorific form 位 *wey.* That *lea* and *sa* are not special comes from the fact that one also says 四 呃 *syh.e,* 五 呃 *wuu.e* as weakened forms of *syh.g(eh), wuu.g(eh)* 'four, five', since the intervocalic *g* is easily weakened into a sonorant [ γ ] and then disappears. With the low vowel *a* in 兩 *leang,* 三 *san* and 八 *ba,* the dropping of the final consonant leaves only a lengthened *a* with a centralized vocalic ending, and since such a low diphthong fits badly the rest of the phonological system, it falls into the familiar slot of a simple *a,* thus resulting in the paradoxical form of a shorter phonological shape representing a longer grammatical form.[23]

Tone sandhi of *chi* and *ba* (a 7, 8). Analogously with *i,* the numerals 七 *chi* 'seven' and 八 *ba* 'eight' appear in the 2nd Tone before 4th Tones, as in 七 个 *chig* (pron. *chyi.geh*), 八 件 *ba-jiann* (pron. *bar-jiann*). This tone sandhi is present in the speech of a slight majority of the speakers. Since those whose speech does not have this tone sandhi represent a quite large minority of the speech community, we shall, for reasons of simplicity, make no further note of this phenomenon beyond noting it here.

---

[22]It is a different matter, however, when one writes—or rather when two write— 我 们俩 个 人 for *woomen leangg ren,* where 俩 is simply an unauthorized, or at least unusual, way of writing 兩 *leang,* as it was never intended to be pronounced *woomen leag ren.*

[23]For further details see my articles 俩, 仨, 四 呃 , 八 呃 in 东 方 雑 志 (*Eastern Miscellany*), 24:12 (1927), and "A Note on *lea, sa,* etc.", *HJAS,* 1:33-38 (1936).

(b) Compound Numerals Below 100. Compound numerals being polysyllabic, they are free words, as in 他今年十七了. *Ta jin.nian shyrchi le.* 'He is seventeen this year.' The numerals from 11 to 19 are coordinate compounds of the measure 十 *shyr* 'ten' plus one of the other simple numerals: 十一 *shyr'i* '11', 十二 *shyr'ell* '12', 十三 *shyrsan* '13', and so on to 十九 *shyrjeou* '19'. If, however, one of these occurs in a larger compound of which there are hundreds, then the measure 十 *shyr* 'ten' will usually be modified by the numeral 一 *i* 'one', as in 五百一十二 *wuubae-ishyr'ell* '512', though *wuubae shyr'ell* is also possible. In mentioning years of four figures with '1' in the ten place, the insertion of *i* is often influenced by considerations of rhythm, as 一千九百一十四 *ichian jeoubae ishyr-syh* '1914', but 一千九百十四年 *ichian jeoubae shyrsyh-nian* 'the year 1914'. If the hundred place is a zero, then a following "1" in the ten place will not have *i* before the *shyr;* for example, 1016 will be spoken as 一千零十六 *ichian-ling-shyrliow.*

Another use of *i* before *shyr* is in counting things by fives, as one often does in China. A postal clerk counting a stack of postal cards will shirft their edges at an angle and bend off the edges, usually by three and two at a time and say 一五, 一十, 十五, 二十, 二十五, 三十, ... *i-wuu, i-shyr, shyrwuu, ell₀shyr, ell.shyrwuu, san₀shyr,* ... 'five, ten, fifteen, twenty, twenty-five, thirty, ...' In saying *i-wuu, i-shyr,* the *i* usually follows the usual tone sandhi and comes out in the 4th Tone. This shows that it really means 'a five, a ten', so that *wuu* in this instance is treated as a unit measure, since a stressed *i* in the first tone in the sense of 'one' is resistant to tone sandhi.

Integral multiples of ten take the form of a subordinative compound $n_0M$, in which n is one of the simple numerals and M is *shyr*. If the compound numeral thus formed is followed by another measure or a noun, *shyr* is usually in the neutral tone, as in 二十本书 *ell.shyr-been shu* '20 volumes of books', 一共三十人 *igonq san.shyr ren* '30 men altogether'. But, when final, *shyr* has an optional neutral tone, as in 不到五十 *bu daw wuu₀shyr* 'not reaching 50,—less than 50'.

The remaining numerals under 100 take the form of $n_1$.*shyr-*

$n_2$, in which the subordinative compound $n_1$.*shyr* is in turn compounded in coordination with the end figure $n_2$, forming 二十 一 *ell.shyr'i* '21', 二十二 *ell.shyr'ell* '22', and so on to 九十九 *jeou.shyr-jeou* '99'.

(c) Higher Compound Numerals. Numerals from 100 up are formed by coordination of subordinative compounds of the n-M type in which M is a power of 10, as in 三万一千四百 一十六 *sanwann ichian syhbae ishyr-liow* '31416'. In old school arithmetic, a whole series of names for powers of 10 were taught, such as 億 *yih*, 兆 *jaw*, 京 *jing*, 垓 *gai*, 无量数 *wuliang-shuh* 'immeasurable number', 恆河沙数 *Hernghersha-shuh* 'Sands-of-the-Ganges number' (of obviously Indian origin), 不可思议 *bukee-syyih* 'the inconceivable'. Of these only 兆 *jaw* was used to any practical extent, but it had the disadvantage of being ambiguously 十億 *shyr-yih* '1,000,000' or 万万 *wann-wann* '100,000,-000' and a conference of scientific organizations held during the 1930's decided to abolish it. The unit 億 *yih* also had the disadvantage of being ambiguously 十万 *shyr-wann* '100,000' or 万万 *wann-wann* '100,000,000', but with the frequent use of the (American) billion in current affairs, 億 *yih* has returned to active use with the now standarized meaning of 万万 *wann-wann*, so that a radio announcer or a simultaneous translator at the United Nations will have at the tip of his tongue such equivalences as 十億 *shyr-yih* 'one billion', 九百九十億 *jeoubae-jeoushyr-yih* '99 billion'.

The basic measures for powers of ten have always been 十 *shyr* '10', 百 *bae* '100', 千 *chian* '1,000', 万 *wann* '10,000'. Above these are multiples of 万 *wann* until the square of 万 *wann* is reached, when 億 *yih* or 万万 *wann-wann* comes in. In fact, for a time, figures were marked off by fours, so that a twelve-place number was written in three groups of four, such as 1234,5678, 9123 and read as:

| | | |
|---|---|---|
| 一千二百三十四億 | *ichian ellbae shanshyr-syh yih* | '1234 x $10^8$ |
| 五千六百七十八万 | *wuuchian liowbae chishyr-ba wann* | 5678 x $10^4$ |
| 九千一百二十三 | *jeouchian ibae ellshyr-san* | 9123 (x 1) |

which in the usual English system will have to be regrouped in four three's and read as:

| one hundred twenty-three | billion | $123 \times 10^9$ |
| four hundred fifty-six | million | $456 \times 10^6$ |
| seven hundred eighty-nine | thousand | $789 \times 10^3$ |
| one hundred twenty-three | | $123 \ (\times \ 1)$ |

As a result of foreign influence, figures are now usually marked off in groups of three, but the nomenclature is still based on the system of 一 i 'l' (or $10^0$), 万 wann '$10^4$', and 億 yih '$10^8$', as before. The older expression 万万 wannwann for '$10^8$' is spoken, as in 人口七万万 renkoou chi-wannwann 'population seven hundred million'. The unit yih '$10^8$' has not been very popular in speech, probably because of the similarity of sounds yih and i. There is, however, no chance of real ambiguity, since i is always a determinative and yih always a measure. Even when i is pronounced in the 4th Tone, as it is in 一千 i-chian 'a thousand', it cannot be 億 yih, since the order ° 億千 °yih-chian would not be possible.

   Note that within the system of 一, 十, 百, 千, 万 i,shyr, bae, chian, wann, any multiple which advances the unit to the next place must be called by the name of that place. For example, since 19 x 100 = 1900, it is never called ° 十九百 °shyrjeou-bae 'nineteen hundred', but must be called 一千九百 ichian jeoubae 'one thousand nine hundred', nor can 20,000 be called ° 二十千 °ell.shyr-chian, but must be called 二万 ellwann or 兩万 leangwann.

   If a number ends in one or more zeros, then the word expressing it will end in 十 shyr '10', 百 bae '100', 千 chian '1,000', 万 wann '10,000' or 億 yih '100,000' (not counting the obsolete forms). Such a word may function as a D-M compound of the n-M type and thus can be followed by a noun, as in 八百人 babae ren '800 men', or as a numeral and thus followed by another measure, as in 八百个人 babaeg ren '800 men'. With most nouns, the form with an additional measure is preferred. For example, 三千架飛机 sanchian-jiah feiji is preferred to

三千飛机 *sanchian feiji* for '3,000 airplanes'. Of the even tens, if 十 *shyr* is not preceded by *i* (cf. b above) and there is no larger number preceding, then it is a monosyllable and functions only as a numeral and not as a measure and must be followed by another measure if a noun follows, for example 十个人 *shyrg ren* 'ten men', while 十人 *shyr ren* is strictly wenyan, although 二十人 *ell.shyr ren* is perfectly ordinary speech.

Intermediate zeros are spoken as 零 ling, as in 一千零二十四 *ichian ling ell.shyrsyh* '1,024'. In older usage, *ling* was to be repeated as many times as there are zeros, as in 七十二万零〻八十六 *chishyr'ell-wann ling ling ba.shyrliow* '720,086', but this rule is no longer observed in speech and one *ling* serves for all consecutive intermediate zeros, except of course in telephoning, when all the figures have to be read singly. But if a telephone number is given "in full spelling", then one *ling* can still serve for two. Thus, one can say 总局两千零五 *Tzoong-jyu leangchian ling wuu* 'Main two thousand and five' as well as *ell-ling-ling-wuu* 'two-oh-oh-five'. In the former the repetition of *ling* is optional, while in the latter it is obligatory. With even hundreds it is more usual to say *bae* and *chian* instead of *ling,* as in 东局三千九百 *Dongjyu sanchian jeoubae* 'East three thousand nine hundred'. Note that it is not of the same pattern as English 'East three nine hundred'. With even thousands, the measure 号 *haw* 'number ...' is usually added, as in 西局三千号 *Shijyu sanchian-haw* 'West three thousand'. The advent of dial telephones will not render these linguistic forms obsolete, as one will still have occasion to give verbal information about telephone numbers.

(d) Fractions and Decimals. A fraction n/m is usually expressed as m 分之 n m-*fenn jy* n[24] 'm parts' n,—n out of m parts, —n m-ths', where *jy* is borrowed from the wenyan equivalent of 的 *de*. The formula being L in construction, the numerator n is free, whether polysyllabic or monosyllabic. If translated into pure

---

[24]"Taken as 'part', 分 is *fenn;* taken as 'divide' or 'division', 分 is *fen.* Both are spoken. I prefer to say *fenn* because it fits better phonologically with the dialectal cognates.

spoken syntax, a fraction like 四分之三 *syh-fenn jy san* '³/₄'
would be spoken of as 四分裡头的三分 *syh-fenn.lii.tou de
san-fenn* 'three parts within four parts', which is a quantity
phrase. The shorter and more usual form, since it is L in syntax,
can be regarded as a quantity word and a transient word of high
productivity. Thus, although the discussion of numerals has led
to fractions, the latter have turned out to be quantity words
rather than numerical determinatives.

Decimals expressed as fractions behave like fractions, as in
十分之三 *shyr-fenn jy san* 'three tenths'. When the denomin-
ator is an even power of 10 greater than ten itself, the numeral *i*
may be omitted, as in 千分之三 *chian-fenn jy san* 'three one-
thousandths' (alternatively, 一千分之三 *ichian-fenn jy san*)
or 万分之一 *wann-fenn jy i* 'one ten-thousandth' (whence
the conjunction 万一 *wann'i* '1 chance in 10,000,—if perchance, in case'). The grammatical import of this is that 百, 千,
万 *bae, chian, wann* (but not 億 *yih*) here function as numerical
determinatives, which they do not in other compounds. In this
respect, 十 *shyr* more genuinely has class overlap in being either a
determinative or a measure with complete versatility.

There is no special word or phrase for 'per cent' besides the
usual fractional form, such as 百分之五十一 *bae-fenn jy
wuushyr'i* '51 hundredths, —51%'. If it is not necessary to go
into exact hundredths, one usually speaks of 成 *cherng* or 分 *fen*
[sec.(8), Mq 87 and 88, below] and 'tenths', as in 他非得
等到十二成(~分)靠得住才敢做吶。 *Ta feideei deeng
daw shyr'ell-cherng (~ -fen) kaw.dejuh tsair gaan tzuoh ne.* 'He
must wait until he is 120% sure before he dares to do it.'

A mixed fraction is given as a coordinate construction, consisting of the integer modifying the measure, then the marker for
coordination 又 *yow* 'moreover, and, in addition', and then the
fraction, as in 十尺又百分之二十五。 *shyr-chyy yow bae-
fenn jy ell.shyrwuu* '10 feet and 25/100'. Optionally, the measure
may come last: 十又百分之二十五尺 *shyr yow bae-fenn
jy ell.shyrwuu-chyy* '10 and 25/100 feet'. Only in scientific language does one read off decimal places, as in 原子量一点儿零

ₐ 八 零 *yuantzyy-lianq i-deal-ling-ling-ba-ling* 'atomic weight 1.0080', 温度華氏九十八点儿六度 *uenduh Hwashyh jeou.shyrba-deal-liow-duh* 'temperature 98.6° F'.

When a measure follows an integer, a following decimal place (less frequently more than one place) is often read off without *yow* or fractional forms, as in 九十八度六 *jeou.shyrba-duh-liow* '98.6°'. This is in fact a special case of a general type in which $n_1$-$M_1$ $n_2$-$M_2$ is abbreviated to $n_1$-$M_1$-$n_2$, where $n_1$-$M_1$ and $n_2$-$M_2$ are in coordination, expressing addition, and $M_2$, the next smaller denomination after $M_1$, is understood. Thus, 两毛五分 *leang-mau wuu-fen* 'two dimes five cents,—25 cents' is usually spoken as *leang-mau-wuu*. One consequence of $n_1$-$M$-$n_2$ being understood as $n_1$-$M_1$ $n_2$-$M_2$ is that if the M's are powers of 10, a simple numeral after a $n_1$'M form may stand for tens, hundreds, and so on, instead of units. For example, 你欠我三百六 *Nii chiann woo sanbae-liow.* can only mean 'You owe me 360' (not '306'). Similarly, 五万八 *wuuwann-ba* means '58,000' (not '50,008').

This short form $n_1$-$M$-$n_2$ is sometimes also used with non-decimal systems of units, as in 三先令六 *san-shianling-liow* 'three shillings and sixpence, —three and six', omitting 辨士 *biannshyh* 'pence' as $M_2$. Note that this form applies only to measures and not to nouns or a noun and a measure. For example, even though the month is the next unit below the year, the word 月 *yueh* 'month' is a noun, and so 'one year and five months' cannot be expressed as °一年五 °*i-nian-wuu*, since *yueh* has to have its own measure g, as in 一年五个月 *i-nian wuug yueh*. To avoid the possible ambiguity of D-M Ḋ-Ṁ being addition or division [i.e., as a rate; cf. sec. 7.6.2(6)], addition may be made explicit by inserting 又 *yow* 'moreover', 零 *ling* 'and', or 加 *jia* 'adding', but not 跟 *gen* 'and, with'. In most contexts, however, such ambiguities do not arise, as 在这儿有一年五个月了 *tzay jell yeou i-nian wuug yueh le* 'have been here for one year and five months', 一年五个月玩儿，只七个月做事 *i-nian wuug yueh wal, jyy chig yueh tzuoh-shyh* 'play five months of the year and work only seven months'. When two

denominations are not related decimally, the coordinative marker
零 *ling* 'and' can be used even between consecutive denominations, as in 一磅零四兩 *i-banq ling syh-leang* 'one pound and
four ounces'. In the case of feet and inches, however, *ling* is not
used, as the Western foot and inch are very close to the Chinese
foot and inch, which are related decimally.

(4) Quantitative Determinatives. Intermediate between specifying determinatives and numerals, we have the quantitative
determinatives, which do not give exact numbers, but express
relative quantities or, in the case of interrogatives, unknown
quantities. They are: (a) 一 *i* (with full stress and tone sandhi) 'all',
(b) 滿 *maan* 'full', (c) 全 *chyuan* 'entire', (d) 整 *jeeng* 'whole', (e)
半 *bann* 'half', (f) 幾 *jii* 'how many?', $_o$*jii* 'a few', (g) 多 *duo* 'many'
or 'which?', (h) 多少 *duo$_o$shao* ~ *dwo$_o$shao* 'how many?' or
'many', (i) 許多 *sheuduo* 'many' or 'much', (j) 好些 *haoshie* ~
*haurshie* 'a good deal of', (k) 好多 *haoduo* 'a good many', (l) 好
幾 *haojii* 'quite a few', and (m) 很多 *heenduo* 'very many'. These
do not all behave alike before various kinds of measures, as will
be described below.

(a)    *i* 'all'. In 只要一塊錢 *jyy yaw i-kuay chyan* 'wants
only one dollar', the *i* is the stressed numeral, meaning 'one'. In
只要 ( . 一 ) . 塊布 *jyy yaw* (.*i*) .*kuay buh* 'wants only a piece
of cloth', the .*i* is unstressed and omissible and means 'a'. As a
quantitative determinative, it is stressed, but has all the usual
tone sandhi, instead of being sandhi-resistant as *i* 'one' is. In this
form, it means 'all over the, throughout the, to the whole extent
of' and is not followed by an individual measure (classifier), a
standard measure, or a measure for verbs, but by a temporary
measure or a container measure, usually followed by *de* with or
without another following noun. Examples are: 一臉的髒 *i-lean
de tzang* 'a face of dirt,—dirt all over the face', 一屋子的烟
*i-utz de ian* 'a roomful of smoke', 你看你洒的一身的！ *Nii
kann nii saa de i-shen de!* 'Look at what you've splashed all over
yourself!' 一路下雨。 *I-luh shiah-yeu.* 'It rained all the way.'
Note that in 一國的人 *i-gwo de ren* 'the people of one (or a)
country' *i* is an ordinary numeral and not the quantitative deter-

minative 'all' that is under discussion here. (Cf. 全 *chyuan* under c below.)

(b) 满 *maan* 'full'. As a quantitative determinative, *maan* is like *i* in being limited to modifying temporary measures or container measures, as in 满肚子的不高兴 *maan-duhtz de bugaushinq* 'a bosomful of displeasure', 满天的霜 *maan-tian de shuang* 'a skyful of frost', 梨花儿闹的满树的。 *Lihual kai de maan-shuh de.* 'The pear flowers are blooming all over the tree.' In fact, in all the examples under (a) and (b), *i* and *maan* are interchangeable with little difference in meaning except that *maan* says 'full' explicitly, while *i* only implies it. Quasi-measures do not combine with *maan*, there being no ° 满国 °*maan-gwo*.

(c) 全 *chyuan* 'entire'. Somewhat different from *i* and *maan*, 全 *chyuan* is used mostly with quasi-measures, as in 全国的人 *chyuan-gwo de ren* 'the people of the entire country', 全课的 生字 *chyuan-keh de shengtzyh* 'the new words of the entire lesson'. It occurs in group measures, as in 全套 *chyuan-taw* or 全 副 *chyuan-fuh* 'the entire set', and temporary measures, as in 全身子的 *chyuan-shentz de* 'over the entire body'. In the case of standard measures there is only 全年 *chyuan-nian* 'the entire year'.

(d) 整 *jeeng* 'whole'. Different from *i*, *maan*, and *chyuan*, their near synonym *jeeng* combines with most types of measures, as in 整条儿 *jeeng-tyaul* 'whole strip', 整瓶 *jeeng-pyng* 'whole bottle of', 整课 *jeeng-keh* 'whole lesson'; less often with standard measures, as in 整加仑 *jeeng-jialuen* 'whole gallon'; and not at all with measures for verbs.

(e) 半 *bann* 'half'. When used as a determinative (and not as a measure), *bann* is like *jeeng*, of which it is an antonym. It occurs with individual measures, as in 半个 *bann.g* 'half a', 半张 *bann-jang* 'half a sheet'; with standard measures, as in 半分钟 *bann-fen jong* 'half a minute', 半寸 *bann-tsuenn* 'half an inch'; with container measures, as in 半箱子 *bann-shiangtz* 'half a trunkful'; and less often with quasi-measures, as 半辈子 *bann-beytz* 'half a lifetime'. The expression 一半天 *i-bann-tian* 'in a day or so' is of the same construction as 两三天 *leang-san-tian* 'two or three days', where *i* and *bann* are coordinate determinatives compounded with the measure *tian*.

If 半 *bann-* forms a lexical compound with a word which can also be a noun, then ambiguities may arise in such expressions as 四个半音 *syhg bann-in* 'four semitones' or *syhg-bann in* 'four-and-half tones (= 9 semitones)'. There is no ambiguity in 两个半寸 *leangg bann-tsuen* 'two half-inches (= one inch)', since *tsuen* is not a noun, nor in 看了两本半书 *kannle leang-been-bann shu* 'read two and half books', since *shu* is a noun and there is no such compound as °*bann-shu*. Where such ambiguities do arise, they can usually be resolved by using suitable stresses and pauses to mark out the ICs.

(f) 几 *jii* 'how many?' or '(number) which?' and ₀*jii* 'a few'. The determinative *jii* or ₀*jii* is highly versatile and occurs with all except temporary measures, and is thus like the numerals, as in 几件? *jii-jiann?* 'how many items?', 几师? *jii-shy?* 'how many (army) divisions?', 几县? *jii-shiann?* 'how many hsien?', and 几下儿 *jii-shiall?* 'how many strokes?' As with other interrogatives, ₀*jii*, with optional neutral tone, can be taken in the indefinite sense of 'a few' and must occur after a verb or after a demonstrative, as in 有几个人 *yeou ₀jiig ren* 'there are a few people', and 那几部书 *ney ₀jii-buh shu* 'those few books'.

As a quantitative determinative, *jii* is the only one that is used much in the ordinal sense of 'number which?' or 'which-eth?', as in 几儿 *jieel* 'which day of the month?', 几月 *jii.yueh* 'what month of the year?', 西历几年 *Shilih jii-nian* 'what year of the Western chronology?', 十几世纪 *shyrjii-shyhjih* 'what century (from the 11th through the 19th)?' In 礼拜几 *liibayjii* 'what day of the week', *jii* is also used in the ordinal sense, but there it is not a determinative, since it is modified by *liibay* and is the center of the subordinative compound: 'the week's which day?'[25]

The only other quantitative determinatives used in the ordinal

---

[25]In the speech of Mandarin-speaking Chinese in America, whose Chinese usually contains many borrowings from English, one hears such expressions as 你是 nineteen-几-teen 生的? *Nii sh nineteen-jii-teen sheng de?* 'You were born in nineteen-which-teen?'

sense, but much more restrictedly than *jii*, are 多 *duo* and 多少 *duo*₀*shao* ~ *dwo*₀*shao*, as noted below.

(g) 多 *duo* 'many' or 'which?'. While *duo* is versatile as a predicate 'many, much', its use as a determinative is very restricted. The only active compounds with *duo* as a determinative are 多年 *duo-nian* 'many years' ( 多天 *duo-tian* 'many days' being rare and 多日 *duo-ryh* being L), and, in the ordinal sense, *duo.hoel* 'which moment,—when?' and 多乿 *duo.tzaan* 'which moment,—when?' As a determinative, however, the near synonym 多少 *duo*₀*shao* ~ *dwo*₀*shao* is much more versatile, as illustrated under (h) below.

(g') 几 *-jii*, 多 *-duo*, and 来 *-*₀*lai* as indefinite additions.—After multiples of 10, 100, and so on, indefinite additions are expressed by 几 *-jii*, 多 *-duo*, or 来 *-*₀*lai*, as in 十几双鞋 *shyrjii-shuang shye* 'ten-odd pairs of shoes', 这房子卖五万几呐！ *Jeh farngtz may wuu-wann-jii ne!* 'This house sells for as much as fifty and several (thousand)!' When occurring before nouns, forms ending in *-jii* and *-*₀*lai* have to be followed by measures, as in 二十几个人 *ell.shyrjiig ren* 'twenty-odd people', 三百来块钱 *sanbae*₀*lai-kuay chyan* '$300 and something'; on the other hand, forms ending in *-duo* sometimes do not require a measure, as in 一百多人 *ibae-duo ren* or 一百多个人 *ibae-duog ren* 'over 100 people'. The three forms do not cover the same range of numbers. For example, 十几个 *shyrjiig* ranges from 11 to 19, and 十多个 *shyrduog* has the same range but is more likely to be under than over 15, while 十来个 *shyr*₀*laig* includes 10 itself and rarely over 15. When *-*₀*lai* is in the neutral tone, it is sometimes weakened to *-.la*.

The remaining quantitative determinatives, from (h) to (m), are dissyllabic. Except (l) 好几 *haojii*, they are also alternatively quantity words besides being determinatives and can thus either stand alone or modify nouns without a measure. For example, besides 许多件衣裳 *sheuduo-jiann i.shang* 'many articles of clothing', one can also say 许多衣裳 *sheuduo i.shang* 'many clothes' and 買了许多 *maele sheuduo* 'has bought many, has bought a lot', whereas with monosyllabic quantitative determina-

tives, (a) to (h) and the dissyllable *haojii*, one can only say 几件
衣裳 *jii-jiann i.shang* 'several articles of clothing', but not °几
衣裳 °*jii i.shang* or °買了好几 °*maele haojii*. As determinatives those dissyllables combine with all except temporary measures.

(h) 多少 $duo_0shao$ ~ $dwo_0shao$ 'how many?' or 'many'.—
Besides the differences just mentioned, $duo_0shao$ is a near synonym of *jii* in being an interrogative when stressed and an indefinite when unstressed. But one additional difference between the
two is that with *jii* the presumed number is not more than ten,
while with $duo_0shao$ ~ $dwo_0shao$ a larger number is presumed.
For example,   这个小孩儿几岁啦? *Jeyg sheauharl jii-suey*
*l'a?* 'How old is this child?' but   那位先生有多少岁? *Ney-*
*wey shian.sheng yeou duo.shao-suey?* 'How old is that gentleman?' Another difference is that while *jii* refers to discrete numbers: 'a few, several', 多少 $duo_0shao$ ~ $dwo_0shao$ is applicable
both to discrete numbers: 'how many?' or 'many' and to non-
discrete quantities: 'how much?' or 'much'.

Note that $duo_0shao$ ~ $dwo_0shao$ as a quantitative word compounded from a pair of antonyms is quite different from the adverb-adjective construction *duo shao* ~ *dwo shao* 'how little' (or
'how few'). In a conversation about military supplies given to
China, I once heard a sentence as   能给中國多少就多少。
*Neng geei Jong.gwo duoshao* (compound of antonyms) *jiow duo-*
*shao.* 'They gave China as much as possible.', but it turned out
that the speaker had meant exactly the opposite: *Neng geei*
*Jong.gwo duo shao* (adverb-adjective) *jiow duo shao.* 'They gave
China as little as possible.', where *duoshao* as understood (since the
speaker actually took the non-neutral tone option) and *duo shao* as
meant were completely homophonous.

(i) 许多 *sheuduo* 'many, much', and

(j) 好些 *haoshie* ~ *haurshie* 'a good deal of, a lot of'
are not used as interrogatives and are applicable to both discrete
and non-discrete quantities, as in  许多根糖棍儿 *sheuduo-*
*gen tarngguell* 'many candy sticks', 许多糖 *sheuduo tarng* 'a lot
of sugar', 好些道菜 *haoshie-daw tsay* 'many courses of food',
好些饭 *haoshie fann* 'a lot of rice'.

(k) 好多 *haoduo* 'a good many', with or without a measure, is mostly limited to discrete numbers, for example, 好多人抽好多种烟。 *Haoduo ren chou haoduo-joong ian.* 'Many people smoke many kinds of smoke.', but 屋子裡有许多烟。 *Utz.lii yeou sheuduo ian* (in preference to *haoduo ian*). 'There is a lot of smoke in the room.'

(l) 好几 *haojii* 'quite a few'.—Except for not being used as an interrogative, *haojii* is quite like *jii* in combining with any measure except temporary measures and in not being free. Thus, we have 好几个 *haojiig* 'quite a few', 好几尺 *haojii-chyy* 'quite a few feet', 好几桶 *haojii-toong* 'quite a few buckets of', 好几幕 *haojii-muh* 'quite a few acts (of a play)', and 好几遍 *haojii-biann* 'quite a few times (read, said, etc.)'.

(m) 很多 *heen duo* 'very many, very much' is like *sheuduo* and *haoshie* ~ *haurshie* when used as a determinative. But while none of the quantitative determinatives cited so far, except 多 *duo*, can function also as a predicate, *heen duo* can be used, as in 这儿的雨很多。 *Jell de yeu heen duo.* 'The rain here is plentiful'. To be sure, 多少 *duo shao* ~ *dwo shao* 'how few' or 'how little' can also be used as a predicate expression, but it has little relation with the coordinative compounds of antonyms *duo$_0$shao* ~ *dwo$_0$shao* 'how much, how many, etc.'.

It would seem that 很少 *heen shao* 'very few, very little', should be similar to *heen duo*, since it is its exact antonym. But it is not a quantitative determinative and can only function as a predicate. For example, there is 椅子很少。 *Yiitz heen shao.* 'Chairs are very few.', but no °很少把椅子 °*heenshao-baa yiitz* for 'very few chairs', even though there is 很多把椅子 *heenduo-baa yiitz* 'very many chairs'. But being an adjectival phrase, it can be placed in an attributive position before nouns, as in 很少人知道 *heen shao ren jy.daw* 'few people know', or, usually with the addition of the subordinative marker *de*, as in 很少的椅子 *heen shao de yiitz* 'very few chairs'.

As free monosyllabic words, both 多 *duo* 'many, much' and 少 *shao* 'few, little' can function as predicates and, except for the very restricted use of *duo* under (g), do not function as determinatives, there being no ° 多分钟  °*duo-fen jong* for 'many minutes' or ° 少分钟  °*shao-fen jong* for 'a few minutes', for which one says 许多分钟 *sheuduo-fen jong* and 几分钟 *jii-fen jong*, respectively. Both can also function as transitive verbs, as in 这儿 多了一个人。 *Jell duole ig ren.* 'This place has an excess of one man.', 他们那儿还少一个人。 *Tamen nall hair shao ig ren.* 'They still lack one man there.' As usual, the *i* can be omitted, but then *duo g ren* and *shao g ren* are still V-O constructions and not D-M N constructions.

Table 16 summarizes the types of measures which combine with various kinds of quantitative determinatives described above. To save space, the examples are given in characters only, for most of which the romanizations and meanings have already been given in the preceding paragraphs. Those which have not been given are:

(h) 1. 本 *been* 'volumes', 5. 罐 *guann* 'jars', 7. 岁 *suey* 'years old', 8. 縣 *shiann* 'hsien', 9. 趟 *tanq* 'trips'

(i) 5. 盤 *parn* 'tray', 7. 兩 *leang* 'tael'

(j) 5. 匣儿 *shyal* 'boxes', 7. 斤 *jin* 'catties', 8. 処 *chuh* 'places', 9. 次 *tsyh* 'times'

(k) 5. 杯 *bei* 'cupfuls', 7. 里 *lii* 'li', 8. 年 *nian* 'years'

(m) 5. 碟儿 *dyel* 'dishes of', 7. 磅 *banq* 'lbs.'

As in the other tables, "°" means nonexistent, and "()" means rare. Note that since (x) 少 *shao* 'few' and (y) 很少 *heen shao* 'very few' are adjectives and not determinatives, they are starred under all the measures. For simplicity, measures 1-4 are put under one column, since they behave similarly with respect to quantitative determinatives. For details of their differences, see table 17.

## 7.9. Measures

A measure[26] is a bound morpheme which forms a D-M compound with one of the determinatives enumerated above. There are nine kinds of measures: (1) classifiers, or individual measures

---

[26]I used the term "auxiliary noun" or "AN" in *Mand Prim* and *Conc*

(Mc), (2) classifiers specially associated with V-O constructions (Mc'), (3) group measures (Mg), (4) partitive measures (Mp), (5) container measures (Mo), (6) temporary measures (Mt), (7) standard measures (Mm), (8) quasi-measures (Mq), and (9) measures for verbs (Mv).

The same morpheme sometimes serves as different kinds of measures. For example, in 刺 一 刀 *tsyh i-dau* or 扎 一 刀 *ja i-dau* 'makes a stab (with a knife)' and 剌 一 刀 *la i-dau* 'makes a slash (with a knife)', *dau* is a measure for verbs, while in 一 刀 皮 纸 *i-dau pyijyy* 'a ream of skin-paper (a kind of strong paper)', it is a standard measure. In 一 排 樹 *i-pair shuh* 'a row of trees', *pair* is a group measure, and in 一 排 步兵 *i-pair buhbing*, it could be a group measure: 'a row of infantry soldiers', but since there is such a standard measure as *pair*, it will usually be understood as 'a platoon of infantry soldiers'. In 一 口 饭 *i-koou fann* 'a mouthful of rice', *koou* is a partitive measure, but in 一 口 钟 *i-koou jong* 'a (large) bell', *koou* is a classifier.

Many of the measures are also other parts of speech, mostly nouns, which have their own measures. Thus, besides being a measure for verbs and a standard measure, 刀 *dau* is also a noun with its own classifier 把 *baa*, classifier for things with handles, as in 一 把 刀 *i-baa dau* 'a knife'. With 床 *chwang*, we have 一 張 床 *i-jang chwang* (N) 'a bed', 一床的蛇蚤 *i-chwang de geh-₀tzao* (Mt) 'a bedful of fleas', and 一床被窝 *i-chwang bey.uo* (Mc) 'a quilt'.

(1) Classifiers (Mc). Classifiers, or individual measures, have also been called numeratives or numerary adjuncts (NA), because a numeral cannot directly modify a noun except in wenyan ( 一 馬 *i maa* L instead of 一 匹 馬 *i-pi maa* 'a horse') but must be followed by an interposed classifier according to the shape, kind, or some other property associated with the noun. Each individual noun has its proper classifier: 一 棵 樹 *i-ke shuh* 'a tree', 兩把

---

*Dict.* In order to reduce the abbreviation to one letter (M) and to avoid possible confusion with the adjective-noun construction (A-N), I am now following Hockett's terminology and symbolism.

TABLE 16

Quantitative Determinatives and Measures

| As Measures / Quantitative Determinatives | 1-4 Mc Classifiers, etc. | 5 Mo Containers | 6 Mt Temporary Measures | 7 Mm Standard Measures | 8 Mq Quasi-Measures | 9 Mv Measures for Verbs | As Free Adjectives |
|---|---|---|---|---|---|---|---|
| (a) 一 1 'all' | * | 一屋子 | 一臉 | * | * | * | * |
| (b) 满 maan 'full' | * | 满肚子 | 满樹 | * | * | * | 'full' |
| (c) 全 chyuan 'entire' | 全套 | * | (全身) | (全年) | 全國 | * | 'complete' |
| (d) 整 jeeng 'whole' | 整套 | 整瓶 | 整桌子 | 整足 | (整课) | * | * |
| (e) 半 bann 'half' | 半張 | 半箱子 | * | 半寸 | (半輩子) | (半回) | * |
| (f) 几 {jii 'how many' / jii 'a few'} | 几件 | 几盒儿 | * | 几呎 | 几縣 | 几下儿 | * |
| (g) 多 duo 'many' | * | * | * | (多年) | * | * | 'many, much' |

| | | | | | | | |
|---|---|---|---|---|---|---|---|
| (h) 多少 duo shao ~ dwo.o shao 'how many?' or 'many, much' | 多少本 | 多少罐 | * | * | 多少步 | 多少縣 | 多少趟 |
| (i) 许多 sheuduo 'many, much' | 许多根 | 许多盘 | * | 许多两 | | 许多国 | 许多下儿 |
| (j) 好些 haoshie ~ haurshie 'a good deal of, a lot of' | 好些道 | 好些匣儿 | * | 好些斤 | | 好些处 | 好些次 |
| (k) 好多 haoduo 'a good many' | 好多种 | 好多杯 | * | 好多里 | | 好多年 | 好多回 |
| (l) 好几 haojii 'quite a few' | 好几个 | 好几桶 | * | 好几尺 | | 好几幕 | 好几遍 |
| (m) 很多 heenduo 'very many, very much' | 很多件 | 很多碟儿 | * | 很多磅 | | 很多国 | 很多次   'very many, very much' |
| (x) 少 shao 'few, little' | * | * | * | * | | * | *   'few, little' |
| (v) 很少 heen shao 'very few, very little' | * | * | * | * | | * | *   'very few, very little' |

刀 *leang-baa dau* 'two knives', 三头牛 *san-tour niou* 'three head of cattle'. The analogy is sometimes drawn between classifiers for nouns and genders in inflected languages. But the analogy does not go very far: There are several dozen classifiers instead of two or three genders; classifiers do not affect the form of adjectives or pronouns; and there is a general classifier 个(~ 個 ~ 箇) *geh* (abbreviated as *g*), which is applicable to all individual nouns. In the marginal case of 那个人 *neyg ren* 'that man' being referred to as 他 *ta* 'he' as against 那位先生 *ney-wey shian.sheng* 'that gentleman' being referred to as 您 *Tan* 'he', it is not so much a question of classifier as one of use of honorific or deferential pronouns, since *Tan* will also be used to refer to other terms of address such as 爸爸 *bah.bah* 'papa', 妈妈 *mha.mha* 'mama'.

Besides taking 个 *g* as an alternative classifier to other, more specific ones, some nouns have two or more specific classifiers according to variations in meaning. For example, 一扇门 *i-shann men* 'a door (the physical object)', 一道门 *i-daw men* 'a door (doorway)', 一个门 *ig men* 'a door (in either sense)'; 这本(儿) 书 *jey-been* (~ *beel*) *shu* 'this book (the thing)', 这部书 *jey-buh shu* 'this book (the work)', 这个书 *jeyg shu* 'this book (in either sense)'; 一副对子 *i-fuh dueytz* 'a pair of scrolls (written and mounted)', 一个对子 *ig dueytz* '(the text of) a couplet (whether written and mounted or only composed)'; 一块手巾 *i-kuay shoou.jin* or 一块手绢儿 *i-kuay shooujiuall* 'a handkerchief', 一条手巾 *i-tyau shoou.jin* 'a towel'.

Between a classifier and a following noun no *de* is inserted. For example, there is 这本书 *jey-been shu* 'this book', but no °这本的书 °*jey-been de shu*. The only case where *de* is used when the determinative is a numeral n and the D-M is a restrictive modifier of N, in the sense of 'n-M-ed N', as 两面儿的镜子 *leang-miall de jinqtz* 'two-faced mirror', as distinguished from 两面镜子 *leang-miann jinqtz* 'two mirrors', where *miann* is simply the classifier and has no translation. In fact, 'two double-faced mirrors' will be called 两面两面儿的镜子 *leang-miann leang-miall de jinqtz*. Again, 一本书 *i-been shu* 'a book (the thing)', 一部书 *i-buh shu* 'a book (the work)', 一部十本的书 *i-buh shyr-been de shu* 'a work of ten volumes'.

List of Classifiers. In the following list of classifiers, unless noted otherwise, any classifier may be preceded by a demonstrative or a numerical determinative and followed by the noun or nouns given as examples, and the classifier reduplicated without a determinative can be used as a distributive. For instance, "Mc 14. 盏 *jaan:* 灯 *deng* 'lamp'" means one can, unless otherwise qualified, always say 这盏灯 *jey-jaan deng* 'this lamp', 那盏灯 *ney-jaan deng* 'that lamp', 哪盏灯? *neei jaan deng?* 'which lamp?', 一盏灯 *i-jaan deng* 'a lamp', 两盏灯 *leang-jaan deng* 'two lamps', ... 几盏灯 *jii-jaan deng* 'how many or several lamps', and 盏ㄥ灯 *jaanjaan deng* 'every lamp'.

Although all the measures have meanings when they occur as nouns or in other functions, such meanings are either entered in parentheses or simply omitted in the listing, if a D-M N phrase can only be translated as D N. For example, although Mc 1 is given as "('an individual')", 一个人 *ig ren* cannot be translated as 'an individual of a man' or, in pidgin English, as 'one piece man', but simply as 'a man'. This is true of most of the classifiers, except in a few cases, such as 两头牛 *leang-tour niou* 'two head of cattle', 这件事 *jey-jiann shyh* 'this item of business', and 几件衣裳 *jii-jiann i.shang* 'several articles of clothing' (but 几件大氅 *jii-jiann dahchaang* 'several overcoats'). For the other types of measures, however, the meanings can usually be translated, as in 一幫流氓 *i-bang lioumang* 'a gang of ruffians', 五磅糖 *wuu-banq tarng* 'five pounds of sugar', and 走几步 *tzoou jii-buh* 'walk a few steps'. When a noun cited as an example is marked "(dial.)", it does not mean that the noun is dialectal, but that the use of that particular classifier with that noun is dialectal.

The following list of measures is fairly complete, though no claim is made that the list is absolutely exhaustive.

Mc 1. 个 $_0$g(*eh*) ('an individual'): 人 *ren* 'man', 问题 *wenntyi* 'problem', 学校 *shyueshiaw* 'school', 机会 *ji$_0$huey* 'opportunity'.

Mc 2. 位 *wey* (polite form for Mc 1): 先生 *shian.sheng* 'gentleman', 来賓 *laibin* 'visitor, guest'.

Mc 3. 隻 *jy* ('one of a pair'): 手 *shoou* 'hand', 鵝 *er* 'goose', 狗 *goou* 'dog', 船 *chwan* 'ship'.

Mc 4. 件 *jiann* ('item, article'): 事(情) *shyh(.chyng)* 'business, event', 东西 *dong.shi* 'thing', 傢伙 *jia.huoo* 'tool', 衣裳 *i.shang* 'garment'.

Mc 5. 枚 *mei* ('round piece'): 奬章 *jeangjang* 'medal'.

Mc 6. 朶(儿) *duoo(l)*: 花儿 *hual* 'flower', 雲彩 *yun.tsae'* 'cloud'.

Mc 7. 尊 *tzuen*: 佛像 *forshianq* 'Buddhist statue', 大砲 *dahpaw* 'cannon'.

Mc 8. 所(儿) *suoo(l)* ('place'): 房子 *farngtz* 'house', 公寓 *gongyuh* 'apartment house'.

Mc 9. 座 *dzuoh* ('seat'): 洋房 *yangfarng* 'foreign-style house', 自鳴鐘 *tzyhmingjong* 'self-singing clock, —(old term for) clock', 海島 *haedao* '(small) island', 山 *shan* 'mountain'.

Mc 10. 家(儿) *jia(l)* ('household'): 人家儿 *renjial* 'household', 鋪子 *puhtz* 'store, shop'.

Mc 11. 架 *jiah* ('framework'): 飛机 *feiji* 'airplane', 望遠鏡 *wanqyeuanjing* 'telescope', 机閞槍 *jiguanchiang* 'machine gun'.

Mc 12. 辆 *lianq*: 車 *che* 'car, vehicle'. N.B. 兩辆汽車 *leanglianq chihche* 'two automobiles'.

Mc 13. 艘 *sou* L: 軍艦 *jiunjiann* 'warship'. Use Mc 1 or 3 in speech.

Mc 14. 盞 *jaan* ('dish'): 灯 *deng* 'lamp, light'.

Mc 15. 匹 *pi*: 馬 *maa* 'horse', 騾子 *luotz* 'mule', 驢 *liu* 'donkey'.

Mc 16. 头 *tour* ('head'): 牛 *niou* 'cattle'. N.B. 兩头牛 *leangtour niou* 'two head of cattle', but 兩头蛇 *leangtour-sher* 'two-headed snake' is a compound noun with Mc 35 条 *tyau*, as in 兩条兩头蛇 *leang-tyau leangtour-sher* 'two two-headed snakes'. ≠ Mt (b) or Mq 12.

Mc 17. 口 *koou* ('opening'): 井 *jiing* 'well', 鐘 *jong* '(large) bell'. ≠ Mc′ 2, Mp 37, Mq 39, or Mv 25.

Mc 18. 封 *feng* ('envelope'): 信 *shinn* 'letter (the thing)'. Cf. 一个信 *ig shinn* 'a letter (the message as written)' and 一个 信儿 *ig shiell* 'a message (as told or heard)'.

Mc 19. 頂 *diing* ('top'): 帽子 *mawtz* 'hat', 轿子 *jiawtz* 'sedan chair'.

Mc 20. 本 ( 儿 ) *been ~ beel* ('volume'): 书 *shu* 'book (the thing)', 賬 ( 本儿 ) *janq(beel)* 'account book', 日记 *ryhjih* 'diary', 画儿 *huall* '(bound volume of) pictures'. ≠ Mq 41.

Mc 21. 床 *chwang* ('bed'): 被 ( 窩 ) *bey(.uo)* 'quilt, bedding', 被单 ( 儿 ) *beydan ~ -dal* 'bedsheet'. N.B. The noun 被窩儿 *bey'uol* 'quilt-nest,—the made-up bed (that which one gets into)' takes Mc 1.

Mc 22. 面 *miann* ('surface'): 旂 ( 子 ) *chyi(tz)* 'flag', 鏡子 *jinqtz* 'mirror', 鑼 *luo* '(flat) gong'. ≠ Mq 45.

Mc 23. 張 *jang* ('extension, sheet'): 床 *chwang* 'bed', 桌子 *juotz* 'table, desk', 凳子 *denqtz* 'stool', 椅子 *yiitz* 'chair' (dial.), 纸 *jyy* 'paper', 薄餅 *baurbiing* 'thin cake,—tortilla-like pastry'.

Mc 24. 扇 *shann* ('fan'): 门 *men* 'door (the thing)'. Cf. 一个 门 *ig men* 'a door (the thing or the doorway)'.

Mc 25. 幅 *fwu*: 画儿 *hual* 'picture, painting'.

Mc 26. 堵 *duu* ('stop up'): 墙 *chyang* 'wall (the masonry)'. Cf. 一道墙 *i-daw chyang* 'a wall (as a partition)'.

Mc 27. 把 *baa* ('takes hold'): 刀 *dau* 'knife, sword', 鍋劐子 *guochaantz* 'spatula', 斧子 *fuutz* 'axe, hatchet', 扇子 *shanntz* 'fan', 椅子 *yiitz* 'chair'. N.B. 一把剪子 or 夾鉗 *i-baa jeantz* or *jiachyan* 'A "pair" of scissors (or) pliers'. ≠ Mp 16 把 *baa(l)* 'a handful', ≠ Mv 14.

Mc 28. 牙儿 *yal* 'section': 橘子 *jyutz* 'tangerine', 橙子 *cherntz* (sic) 'orange'.

Mc 29. 瓣儿 *ball*: 花瓣儿 *huaball* 'flower petal'.

Mc 30. 根 ( 儿 ) *gen ~ gel* ('root'): 棍子 *guenntz* 'rod', 绳子 *sherngtz* 'rope, cord', 香烟 *shiang'ian* 'cigarette', 根儿 *gel* 'root'. N.B. It is possible, though not usual, to say 根儿根儿根儿 *gelgel gel* 'every root'.

Mc 31. 枝 *jy* ('branch'): 筆 *bii* 'pen, etc', 箭 *jiann* 'arrow', 槍 *chiang* 'rifle'.

Mc 32. 桿 *gaan* ('stem'): 槍 *chiang* 'rifle'.

Mc 33. 棵 *ke*: 樹 *shuh* 'tree', 草 *tsao* 'grass', 花儿 *hual* 'flower (the plant)'.

Mc 34. 莄 *goan* ('tube'): 筆 *bii* 'pen, etc.'.

Mc 35. 条 *tyau* ('strip, a length'): 蛇 *sher* 'snake', 鱼 *yu* 'fish', 狗 *goou* 'dog' (dial.), 尾巴 *yii.ba* ~ *woei.ba* 'tail', 绳子 *sherngtz* 'rope, cord', 河 *her* 'river'. N.B. 一条裤子 *i-tyau kuhtz* 'a "pair" of trousers'.

Mc 36. 道 *daw* ('way, course'): 河 *her* 'river', 桥 *chyau* 'bridge', 線 *shiann* 'line', 菜 *tsay* 'course of food', 上谕 *shanqyuh* 'edict'.

Mc 37. 顆 *ke*: 珠子 *jutz* 'pearl, bead'.

Mc 38. 粒 ( 儿) *lih* ~ *liell* 'grain': 米 *mii* 'rice', 沙子 *shatz* 'sand'.

Mc 39. 处 *chuh* ('locality'): 地方 (儿) *dih.fang(l)* 'place'.

Mc 40. 笪 *dar* (dial.): 地方 *dih.fang* 'place'.

Mc 41. 椿 *juang*: 事情 *shyh.chyng* 'event, affair'.

Mc 42. 门 *men* 'branch': 学问 *shyue₀wenn* 'learning', 科学 *ke₀shyue* 'science', 功课 *gong₀keh* 'study'.

Mc 43. 行 *harng* 'line': 買賣 *mae.may* 'trade', 本事 *been.shyh* 'skill'.

Mc 44. 部 *buh*: 书 *shu* 'book (the work or the thing)', 礼记 *Liijih* 'The Book of Rites'. Cf. Mg 31. ≠ Mq 27.

Mc 45. 篇 *pian*: 文章 *wen.jang* 'article, essay', 过秦论 *Guoh-Chyn Luenn* 'On Blaming the Ch'ins', 议论 *yih.luenn* 'discourse, theory'. ≠ Mp 22.

Mc 46. 首 *shoou*: 诗 *shy* 'poem', 歌儿 *ge'l* 'song', 月下独酌 *Yueh Shiah Dwu Jwo* 'Drinking Alone Under the Moon'.

Mc 47. 卷 *jiuann* 'volume': 期刊 *chikan* 'periodical', 东方杂诔 *Dongfang Tzarjyh* 'The Eastern Miscellany'; 'fascicule, chapter': 一卷宋史 *i-jiuann Sonq Shyy* 'a fascicule of the History of the Sungs'.

Mc 48. 期 *chi* 'issue': 雜誌 *tzarjyh* 'magazine', 纽约时报 *Neouiue Shyrbaw* 'The New York Times'.

Mc 49. 齣 *chu:* 戏 *shih* 'play, drama, opera', 空 城 计 *Kong-cherng-Jih* 'The Ruse of the Evacuated City'. Cf. Mc′ 16.

Mc 50. 幕 *muh* ('curtain'),—'an act': 话劇 *huahjiuh* 'spoken drama', 喜劇 *shiijiuh* 'comedy', 维尼思商人 *Weinisy Shang-ren* 'The Merchant of Venice'.

Mc 51. 頓 *duenn:* 飯 *fann* 'meal', 点心 *dean.shin* 'snack'. ≠ Mc′ 21 or Mv 17.

(2) Classifiers Associated with V-O (Mc′). The preceding classifiers are associated with nouns, and the resulting D-M N form occurs with comparable frequencies as subject, as object, and as attribute. The following classifiers are associated especially with verb-object constructions, but differ from measures for verbs (Mv) in that the latter are not especially associated with objects and, in the case of intransitive verbs, have no other objects at all. In the examples of verbs with objects, " ... " stands for the measure in question with a preceding determinative (with the usually omissible *i*). For example, under Mc′ 1, "说...话 *shuo ... huah*" means that 句 ₀*jiuh*, 一句 *i-jiuh*, 这句 *jey-jiuh*, and so on can be inserted. For simplicity, only the translation for the case of *i* 'a' is given. In the case of distributive reduplicates meaning 'every', since they must occur before the verbs, it will be in the order such as 句ㄥ话都说对了. *Jiuhjiuh huah dou shuo-dueyle.* 'Every sentence has been said correctly.'

Mc′ 1. 句 *jiuh* ('sentence'): 说...话 *shuo ... huah* 'say a word, —speak', 问...话 *wenn ... huah* 'asks a question'.

Mc′ 2. 口 *koou* ('mouthful'): 说...好英文 *shuo ... hao Ing'-wen* 'speak good English', 学了...標準的國语 *shyuele ... biaujoen de Gwoyeu* 'learned Standard Mandarin,—acquired a command of S. M.'. ≠ Mc 17, Mp 38, Mq 39, or Mv 25.

Mc′ 3. 手 *shoou* 'hand': 写...好字 *shiee ... hao-tzyh* 'write a good hand', 打...好牌 *daa ... hao-pair* 'play a good game of mah-jong'. ≠ Mv 19.

Mc′ 4. 筆 *bii* ('pen, etc.'): 写...好字 *shiee ... hao-tzyh* 'write a good calligraphy'. ≠ Mp 39 or Mq 14.

Mc′ 5. 票 *piaw* ('ticket'): 当...当 *danq ... danq* 'pawn a pawn-ing,—pawn something', 贖...当 *shwu ... danq* 'redeem a pawn-ing,—redeem something pawned'. ≠ Mq 36.

Mc′ 6. 屆 *jieh* 'session': 開... 会议 *kai* ... *hueyyih* 'open (or hold) a session of a conference', 召 ... 國会 *jaw* ... *gwohuey* 'convene a session of the national assembly'.

Mc′ 7. 任 *renn* 'term': 做... 总统 *tzuoh* ... *tzoongtoong* 'serve a term of the presidency', 做... 官 *tzuoh* ... *guan* 'serve a term as an official'.

Mc′ 8. 盤 *parn* 'game': 下... 棋 *shiah* ... *chyi* 'play a game of chess or go'. ≠ Mo (bb) as in 一盤棋子儿 *i-parn chyitzeel* 'a board of chessmen or go pieces (possibly in disorder)'.

Mc′ 9. 局 *jyu* 'game' L for Mc′ 8.

Mc′ 10. 桌 *juo* 'table, game': 请... 客 *chiing* ... *keh* 'entertain guests at a table', 打...牌~ 麻将 *daa* ... *pair~majianq* 'play a game of mahjong'. ≠ Mg 29 or Mt (i).

Mc′ 11. 圈 *chiuan* 'a round': 打... 牌~ 麻将 *daa* ... *pair~ majianq* 'play a round of mahjong. ≠ Mv 12.

Mc′ 12. 将 *jianq* 'four rounds' (obsolescent)': same V-O as in Mc′ 11.

Mc′ 13. 枱 *tair* ('platform'), or

Mc′ 14. 塲 *chaang* ('arena'), or

Mc′ 15. 堂 *tarng* ('hall'), or

Mc′ 16. 齣 *chu* ('exit,' 'entrance'): 唱 ...戏 *chanq* ... *shih* 'sing a (musical) play', 演... 戏 *yean* ... *shih* 'perform a play', 看 ~ 听 ...戏 *kann ~ ting* ... *shih* 'go to a show'. N.B. When the verb is 写 *shiee* or 编 *bian* 'write', only Mc′ 16 is applicable, in which case 齣 *chu* should be regarded as Mc 49, classifier of a noun 戏 *shih*, not particularly associated with two or three verbs. Mc′ 14 is also applicable to 惹 (~ 闖) ... 禍 *ree* (~ *choang*) ... *huoh* 'cause a disaster'.

Mc′ 17. 班 *ban* ('a run, flight, etc.'), or

Mc′ 18. 趟 *tanq* ('trip'): 開, 搭, 坐, 趁... 火車, 船, 飛机, 公共汽車 *kai, da, tzuoh, chenn* ... *huoochee, chwan, feiji, gonggonq-chihche* 'operate, take, ride, take ... a run of a train, a sail in a boat, a flight of an airplane, a run of a bus'.

Mc′ 19. 水 *shoei* ('water'): 洗... 衣裳 *shii* ... *i.shang* 'wash a washing of clothes'.

Mc′ 20. 炉 *lu* ('stove, kiln'): 烧... 陶器 *shau ... taurchih* 'fire a kiln of ceramics'. N.B. Unlike Mc′ 19, 火 *huoo* is rare as M [cf. sec. 4.2.3(3)].

Mc′ 21. 頓 *duenn* 'spell, session': 捱... 罵 *air ... mah* 'get a scolding', 欠...打 *chiann ... daa* 'owe a spanking,—need a spanking'. ≠ Mc 51 or Mv 17.

(3) Group Measures (Mg). Unlike classifiers, most group measures can take *de*, those which cannot being marked °*de*. Semantically, a group measure is used for a group or collection of individuals.

Mg 1. 对( 儿 ) *duey ~ duell* 'pair': 鸽子 *getz* 'pigeons', 眼睛 *yean.jing* 'eyes', 夫妻 *fuₒchi* or 夫妇 *fufuh* 'husband and wife', 耳鉗子 *eelchyantz* 'earrings'. °*de*.

Mg 2. 双 *shuang* 'pair': 眼睛 *yean.jing* 'eyes', 筷子 *kuaytz* 'chopsticks', 鞋 *shye* 'shoes', 襪子 *wahtz* 'socks, stockings' (but Mg 15 for gloves). N.B. Dialects differ in the use of Mg 1 and Mg 2 with respect to different nouns; for example, Mg 1 is used more frequently in Cantonese than in Mandarin. °*de*.

Mg 3. 打 *dar ~ daa* (translit. of) 'do(zen)': 鸡子 ( 儿) *jitzeel* '(hen's) eggs'.

Mg 4. 十 *shyr* 'ten': This is both a determinative and a measure. As a group measure, it does not take *i* 'one' except in compound numbers, in which case it is more often used as a numerical determinative than as a measure, as in 一百一十辆汽車 *ibae-ishyr-lianq chihche* '110 automobiles'. In 八十人 *bashyr ren* '80 people' *shyr* is the Mg herein considered. ° 两十 °*leang-shyr* does not occur. The form for 'twenty' is *ellₒshyr*. From Mg 4 through Mg 9, if a demonstrative determinative is used, a numeral must be inserted, as in 这一千人 *jey-i-chian ren* 'these 1,000 men', which is not true of other Mg's as 那打橘子 *ney-dar jyutz* 'that dozen of oranges', where *i* is optional. In the case of 那十个人 *ney-shyrg ren* 'those ten men', *shyr* is of course being used in its other function as a determinative. °*de*.

Mg 5. 百 *bae* 'hundred': 五百罗汉 *wuubae luoₒhann* '500 arhats'. °*de*.

Mg 6. 千 *chian* 'thousand': 三千学生 *sanchian shyue.sheng* '3,000 students'. °*de*.

Mg 7. 万 *wann* 'ten thousand': 十万兵 *shyrwann bing* '100,000 soldiers'. °*de*.

Mg 8. 億 *yih* 'hundred million': 二億居民 *ell-yih jiumin* '200,000,000 inhabitants'. For the obsolete measures 兆 *jaw*, etc., see section 7.8(3c).

Mg 9. 行 *harng* 'row, column': 字 *tzyh* 'characters', 柳樹 *leoushuh* 'willows'.

Mg 10. 身 *shen* ('body'): 洋服 *yangfwu* 'foreign clothes,—a suit'.

Mg 11. 槽 *tsaur* ('trough'): 牙 *ya* '(row of) teeth', 窗戶 *chuang.huh* '(a frame of) windows'.

Mg 12. 列 *lieh* ('train, series') L: 火車 *huooche* '(railroad) train'. °*de*.

Mg 13. 系列 *shihlieh* [transliterating translation of 'serie(s)']: 问題 *wenntyi* 'problems'.

Mg 14. 排 *pair* 'row': 子弹 *tzyydann* 'cartridges', 桑樹 *sang-shuh* 'mulberry trees'. ≠ Mg 45.

Mg 15. 副 (~ 付) *fuh* 'set': 首飾 *shoou.shyh* 'jewelry', 棋子儿 *chyitzeel* 'chessman or *go* pieces', 耳鉗子 *eelchyantz* 'earrings', 鐲子 *jwotz* 'bracelets', 手套 (儿) *shoou.taw(l)* 'gloves', 神气 *shern.chih* 'airs (that one puts on)'.

Mg 16. 套 *taw* 'set': 傢伙 *jia.huoo* 'tools', 玩意儿 *wanyell* 'toys', 把戏 *baa.shih* 'tricks'.

Mg 17. 堂 *tarng* ('hall'): 傢具 *jia₀jiuh* '(a set of) furniture'. ≠ Mc′ 15.

Mg 18. 刂儿 *darl* 'stack': 纸 *jyy* 'paper', 明信片 (儿) *ming-shinnpiann ~ -l* (sic) 'postal cards'.

Mg 19. 串 (儿) *chuann ~ chuall* 'string', or

Mg 20. 掛 *guah* '(hanging) string': 珠子 *jutz* 'pearls, beads', 佛珠 *forju* 'rosary'.

Mg 21. 幫 *bang* 'gang': 工人 *gong.ren* 'workmen'.

Mg 22. 房 *farng* 'branch (house) (of family)': 親戚 *chin.chi* 'relatives'.

Mg 23. 批 *pi* 'batch': 货 *huoh* 'goods', 学生 *shyue.sheng* 'students'.

Mg 24. 组 *tzuu* 'section, group': 人員 *renyuan* 'personnel'.

Mg 25. 窩 *uo* 'nest': 蜜蜂(儿) *mihfeng(l)* 'bees', 耗子 *hawtz* 'rats, mice'.

Mg 26. 綑 *koen* 'bundle': 柴火 *chair.huoo* 'firewood', 稻草 *dawtsao* 'hay'.

Mg 27. 羣 *chyun* 'crowd, flock, etc.': 人 *ren* 'people', 羊 *yang* 'sheep'.

Mg 28. 胎 *tai* 'litter': 小貓儿 *sheau-mhaul* 'kittens'.

Mg 29. 桌 *juo* ('table'): 菜 *tsay* '(organized set of) dishes (forming a dinner)', 酒席 *jeoushyi* 'wine spread,—formal dinner'. ≠ Mc´ 10, or Mt (i).

Mg 30. 進 *jinn* 'row': 房子 *farngtz* 'a group of rooms between courtyards, a compound'.

Mg 31. 部 *buh* 'set': 书 *shu* '(a set of) books (forming one work)'. = Mc 44 for a one-volume work. ≠Mq 27.

Mg 32. 种 *joong* 'kind, species': 东西 *dong.shi* 'things', 菜 *tsay* 'vegetable', 動物 $donq_0wuh$ 'animal'.

Mg 33. 類 *ley* 'kind, category': 东西 *dong.shi* 'things', 货物 $huoh_0wuh$ 'goods'.

Mg 34. 樣(儿) *yanq (l)* 'kind, sort': 菜 *tsay* 'cooked dish', 人 *ren* '(type of) people'.

Mg 35. 派 *pay* 'type, style': 服裝 *fwujuang* 'costume, attire', 文章 *wen.jang* 'literature'.

Mg 36. 流 *liou* ('current'), 'type, class': 人物 *renwuh* 'personages'.

Mg 37. 路 *luh* 'route': 軍隊 *jiunduey* 'troops'; 'style': 服裝 *fwujuang* 'costume, attire'.

Mg 38. 号儿 *hawl* ('number'),—'type, quality'[27]: 料子 *liawtz* 'yard goods', 蘋菓 *pynguoo* 'apples'.

---

[27]Here, as well as under Mg 32, etc., it may seem out of place to put measures with meanings like 'type, quality' under group measures of things. However, things belonging to a group usually have some property in common, so much so that it is possible in formal logic to turn around and define "property" simply as membership in a class. See sec. n.1, 7.1.2, on Bertrand Russell's principle of abstraction.

Mg 39. 师 *shy* 'division' (milit.): 人 *ren* 'men'.

Mg 40. 旅 *leu* 'brigade': 兵 *bing* 'soldiers'.

Mg 41. 团 *twan* 'regiment': 炮兵 *pawbing* 'artillery troops'.

Mg 42. 营 *yng* 'battalion': 救兵 *jiowbing* 'relief troops'.

Mg 43. 連 *lian* 'company': 娘子軍 *niangtzyyjiun* 'women soldiers'.

Mg 44. 班 *ban* 'squad': 步兵 *buhbing* 'infantry'; also 'class (in general)': 学生 *shyue.sheng* 'students'.

Mg 45. 排 *pair* 'platoon': 步兵 *buhbing* 'infantry'. ≠Mg 14.

Mg 46. 隊 *duey* 'squadron': 軍艦 *jiunjiann* 'warships'. N.B. 艦隊 *jiannduey* 'fleet' is a noun and not a measure.

(4) Partitive Measures (Mp). Partitive measures have similar formal properties to group measures except that very few of them can have distributive reduplication. Semantically, they are the opposite of group measures, and represent portions of things instead of groups of them. The opposition, however, is a matter of point of view, since the same group of individuals may also be part of a larger class. For example, Mp 1. 些 *shie* translated as 'an amount of' is Mp, while translated as 'a number of' is more like Mg, but we have put it under Mp because it does not admit numeral determinatives greater than *i* 'one'.

Mp 1. 些 *shie* 'some, an amount of, a number of': 事情 *shyh-.chyng* 'event, business, affair', 东西 *dong.shi* 'thing, article', 糧食 *liang.shyr* 'foodstuff', 麻煩 *ma.farn* 'trouble'. N.B. There is no °两些 °*leang-shie*, °三些 °*san-shie*, ...

Mp 2. 份(儿) *fenn* ~ *fell* 'portion, share': 家当 *jia$_0$danq* '(family) property', 礼 *lii* 'a gift', 錢 *chyan* 'money'.

Mp 3. 部份 *buh$_0$fenn* 'part, fraction': 人民 *renmin* 'the people', 原因 *yuan'in* 'cause', 責任 *tzer$_0$renn* 'responsibility'.

Mp 4. 半(儿) *bann* ~ *ball* 'half': 工夫 *gong.fu* 'time, duration', 力量 *lih.lianq* 'strength', 錢 *chyan* 'money'. N.B. As a determinative, 半 *bann* is the only form, whereas as Mp 4, it is either 半 *bann* or 半儿 *ball*.

Mp 5. 团(儿) *twan* ~ *twal* 'lump, mass': 泥 *ni* 'clay', 和麵 *huoh.miann* 'dough', 乱纸 *luann-jyy* 'crumpled paper'.

Mp 6. 塊 *kuay* 'lump, piece': 石头 *shyr.tou* 'rock, stone', 布

*buh* 'cloth', 雲彩 *yun.tsae* 'cloud'. Cf. Mm 43 'dollar'. N.B. The adverb 一塊儿 *ikuall* 'of one piece,—together' is a decompound, consisting of *i-kuay* 'one piece' with suffix *-l*, and has nothing to do with the D-M N phrase 一个塊儿 *ig kuall* 'a lump', with *kuall* as a noun formed, as usual, from M plus a suffix *-l* or *-tz*. The adverb 一塊堆儿 *ikuayduell* 'of one piece of a pile,—together' is also a decompound.

Mp 7. 堆 *duei* ~ *tzuei* 'pile': 土 *tuu* 'earth', 雪 *sheue* 'snow'.

Mp 8. 下子 *shiahtz* 'a containerful': 汽油 *chihyou* 'gasoline'. ≠ Mv 6.

Mp 9. 挑(子) *tiau(tz)* 'a carrying-pole load': 水菓 *shoeiguoo* 'fruit', 炭 *tann* 'charcoal'.

Mp 10. 担(子) *dann(tz)* 'a carrying-pole load': 水 *shoei* 'water', 活鱼 *hwo-yu* 'live fish'. ≠ Mm 33 '100 catties'.

Mp 11. 攢 *tswan* 'tuft, bunch': 毛 *mau* 'hair', 乱草 *luann-tsao* 'disordered grass,—weeds'.

Mp 12. 子儿 *tzeel* 'skein': 绒线 *rongshiann* 'yarn'.

Mp 13. 轴儿 *jourl* 'spool': 线 *shiann* 'thread'.

Mp 14. 绺儿 *leoul* 'strand': 头髮 *tour.fah* 'hair'.

Mp 15. 掇 *do'* (dial.) 'dab, daub': 泥 *ni* 'mud', 漆 *chi* 'paint'.

Mp 16. 把(儿) *baa(l)* 'handful, bunch': 筷子 *kuaytz* 'chopsticks', 花生 *huasheng* 'peanuts'. ≠ Mc 27 or Mv 14.

Mp 17. 捲(儿) *jeuan* ~ *jeual* 'roll': 膠片 *jiaupiann* '(photographic) film', 鋪蓋 *pu.gay* 'bedding', 纸 *jyy* 'paper'.

Mp 18. 攤子 *tantz* 'stall, mat': 舊貨 *jiow-huoh* 'second-hand goods', 水菓 *shoeiguoo* 'fruit'. Also N, as in 摆攤子(~ 儿) *bae tantz* (~ *tal*) 'sets up a (vending) stall'.

Mp 19. 灘 *tan* '(shallow) pool, puddle': 泥水 *nishoei* 'muddy water'. Also N 'a rapids'.

Mp 20. 股 *guu* ('limb'),—'stream': 热气 *reh-chih* 'hot air', 他那股劲儿 *ta ney-guu jiell* 'that mannerism of his'. ≠ Mq 37.

Mp 21. 欄 *lan* ('railing'),—'section': 新闻 *shinwen* 'news (in a paper)'.

Mp 22. 篇儿 *pial* 'sheet, leaf': 书 *shu* '(a leaf of a) book', 文章 *wen.jang* '(a leaf out of an) article or essay (of several leaves)'. ≠ Mc 45. 篇 *pian*, M for a complete article or essay.

Mp 23. 頁 ～ 葉 *yeh* 'leaf, double-page': 书 *shu* 'book', sometimes loosely used also for 'page'. N.B. In editorial and printer's usage 'page' is called 面 *miann*, which is Mq 45, since one cannot say ° 几 面 书 °*jii-miann shu*.

Mp 24. 片 *piann* 'slice': 面 包 *miannbau* 'bread', 白 雲 *bairyun* 'white cloud'.

Mp 25. 層 *tserng* 'layer, story of a building'; 雲 彩 *yun.tsae* 'cloud', 缘 故 *yuan.guh* 'reason', 楼 *lou* 'storied building', 餡 儿 *shiall* 'stuffing (in cakes, dumplings, etc.)'.

Mp 26. 重 *chorng* 'layer, row': 山 *shan* 'mountain (range)', 被 窝 *bey.uo* 'bedding', 理 由 *liiyou* 'reason'.

Mp 27. 帶 *day* 'belt, zone': 地 方 *dih.fang* 'place, locality'.

Mp 28. 截 儿 *jyel* '(a cut) section': 竹 子 *jwutz* 'bamboo'.

Mp 29. 節 儿 *jyel* 'section (between joints)': 竹 子 *jwutz* 'bamboo', 甘 蔗 *gan.jeh* 'sugar cane'.

Mp 30. 段 (儿) *duann ～ duall* 'section, (short) length': 故 事 *guh.shyh* 'story', 文 章 *wen.jang* '(paragraph of) written text'.

Mp 31. 丝 儿 *sel* 'thread, shred': 肉 *row* 'meat'.

Mp 32. 点 儿 *deal* 'a little, a few': 面 粉 *miannfeen* 'flour', 东 西 *dong.shi* 'thing', 知 谈 *jy.shyh* 'knowledge'. No °兩 *leang-* 'two', etc. ≠ 点 儿 ～ 点 子 *deal ～ deantz* 'dot, spot' N, as in 料 子 上 的 四 个 红 点 儿 *liawtz.shanq de syhg horng-deal* 'four red spots on the material'. ≠ Mq 25 or N 点 (儿) *dean ～ deal* 'dot' (the stroke " 、 " in calligraphy). ≠ Mq 26 点 *dean* '(theoretical) point'.

Mp 33. 滴 *di* 'drop': 雨 *yeu* 'rain', 药 水 (儿) *yawshoei ～ -l* '(liquid) drug', 眼 淚 (儿) *yeanley ～ -ll* 'tears'.

Mp 34. 剂 *jih* 'dose, prescription': 药 *yaw* 'medicine'.

Mp 35. 贴 *tie* (dial.), same as Mp 34.

Mp 36. 味 *wey* ('taste'), — 'serving, prescription': 葷 菜 *huentsay* 'meat dish', 麻 黄 *ma₀hwang* 'ephedra'.

Mp 37. 口 *koou* 'mouthful': 饭 *fann* 'rice', 气 *chih* 'breath of air'. ≠ Mc 17, Mc′ 2, Mq 39, or Mv 25.

Mp 38. 客 *keh* ('guest'), —'an order of': 点 心 *dean.shin* 'refreshments', 汤 麵 *tangmiann* 'soup noodles'.

Mp 39. 筆 *bii* ('pen, etc.'),—'item, unit': 欵（子）*koan(tz)* 'sum of money', 奖学金 *jeangshyuejin* 'scholarship, fellowship', 債 *jay* 'debt', 借欵 *jiehkoan* 'loan'. ≠ Mc″ 4 or Mq 14. But N.B. 一張支票 *i-jang jypiaw* 'a (money) check', with Mc 23.

(5) Container Measures (Mo). Container measures are nouns used as measures and can always take *de* before a following noun. They are like temporary measures (Mt) in being primarily nouns (with their own measures 个 *g*, etc.) and in forming an open class. They are therefore not numbered here, and the examples given for illustration are identified by letters instead of numbers. Note that in some cases (b, c, i, j, s, u, bb of the examples cited) the nouns with the suffixes *-tz* or *-l* can also occur in root form when used as a measure.

Mo (a). 盒儿 *her'l* '(small) box': 洋火 *yanghuoo* 'matches', 胭脂 *ian.jy* 'rouge'.

Mo (b). 匣（子，儿）*shya(tz ~ -l)* 'box': 首饰 *shoou.shyh* 'jewelry', 宝貝 *bao.bey* 'precious things'.

Mo (c). 箱（子）*shiang(tz)* 'case, chest, trunk': 书 *shu* 'books', 皮袍子 *pyipaurtz* 'fur coats'.

Mo (d). 架子 *jiahtz* 'rack, framework': 大氅 *dahchaang* 'overcoats', 古董 *guudoong* 'antiques'. ≠ Mc 11.

Mo (e). 书架（子）*shujiah(tz)* 'bookcase': 小说（儿）*sheaushuo(l)* 'novels'.

Mo (f). 櫃子 *gueytz* 'cabinet': 瓷器 *tsyr$_o$chih* 'chinaware', 字画（儿）*tzyhhuah ~ -ll* 'calligraphy and painting'.

Mo (g). 橱 *chwu* 'cabinet' (dial.): same as (f).

Mo (h). 抽屉 *chou$_o$tih* 'drawer': 文件 *wenjiann* 'documents, papers'.

Mo (i). 筐（子，儿）*kuang(tz ~ -l)* 'basket': 菠菜 *bo(r)tsay* 'spinach', 鲜蘑 *shianmo* 'fresh mushrooms'.

Mo (j). 篮（子）*lan(tz)* 'basket': 梨 *li* 'pears', 髒衣裳 *tzang-i.shang* 'dirty clothes'.

Mo (k). 篓子 *looutz* '(tall) basket': 炭 *tann* 'charcoal', 鲤鱼 *liiyu* 'carp'.

Mo (l). 字纸篓儿 *tzyhjyylooul* 'wastebasket': 廢纸 *feyjyy* 'waste paper'.

Mo (m). 炉子 *lutz* 'stove': 灰 *huei* 'ashes'.

Mo (n). 包 *bau* 'package': 书 *shu* 'books', 糖 *tarng* 'sugar, candy', 香烟 *shiang'ian* 'cigarettes'.

Mo (o). 袋 ~ 口袋 *day* ~ *koou.day* 'bag': 榖子 *guutz* 'grain', 干糧 *gan.liang* 'dry ration', 水泥 *shoeini* 'cement'.

Mo (p). 窝 *uo* 'nest, litter': 小貓儿 *sheau.mhaul* 'kittens'.

Mo (q). 池子 *chyrtz* 'pond': 水 *shoei* 'water'.

Mo (r). 缸 *gang* 'vat': 金鱼 *jinyu* 'goldfish', 醃白菜 *ianbairtsay* 'salted cabbage'.

Mo (s). 瓶 (子 ~儿) *pyng(tz)* ~ *pyengl* 'bottle, jar': 醋 *tsuh* 'vinegar', 花儿 *hual* 'flowers'.

Mo (t). 罐(子, 儿) *guann(tz)* ~ *guall* 'jar, can': 荔枝 *lihjy* 'litchi', 桂圓 *gueyyuan* 'longan'. N.B. 罐头 *guanntour* '(tin) can' N is less often used as Mo.

Mo (u). 罈(子) *tarn(tz)* 'urn': 酒 *jeou* 'wine'.

Mo (v). 桶 *toong* 'keg, bucket, (large) can': 汽油 *chihyou* 'gasoline'.

Mo (w). 吊子 *diawtz* 'kettle': 开水 *kaishoei* 'boiling water'.

Mo (x). 盆 *pern* 'basin, tub': 洗澡水 *shiitzao-shoei* 'bath water'.

Mo (y). 壺 *hwu* 'pot': 黄酒 *hwangjeou* 'rice wine', 茶 *char* 'tea'.

Mo (z)'. 鍋 *guo* '(cooking) pot': 麵 *miann* 'noodles'.

Mo (aa). 笼 *long* '(steaming) tier': 包子 *bautz* 'stuffed buns'.

Mo (bb). 盤(子, 儿) *parn (tz)* ~ *-l* 'tray, plate': 水菓 *shoeiguoo* 'fruit', 点心 *dean.shin* 'refreshments'. ≠ Mc′ 8.

Mo (cc). 碟儿 *dyel* 'dish, saucer': 小菜 *sheau.tsay* 'pickles, relishes'.

Mo (dd). 碗 *woan* 'bowl': 饭 *fann* 'rice'.

Mo (ee). 杯 *bei* 'cup, glass': 茶 *char* 'tea'.

Mo (ff). 盅 *jong* 'cup': 烧酒 *shaujeou* 'spirits'.

Mo (gg). 瓢 *pyau* 'spoon, ladle': 湯 *tang* 'soup'.

Mo (hh). 勺子 *shaurtz* 'spoon, ladle': 湯 *tang* 'soup'.

Mo (ii). 勺儿 *shaurl* 'spoon': 醬油 *jianqyou* 'soy sauce'.

Mo (jj). 调羹 *tyaugeng* 'spoon' (dial.). Same as (ii).

(6) Temporary Measures (mt). Temporary measures are like container measures in being primarily nouns and used directly after determinatives to measure the amount of things, but differ from them in measuring the outside extent and only rarely the inside capacities. They take *de* before a following noun more frequently than do container measures. They differ formally from the other types of measures in not allowing numerals more than *i* 'one' as determinatives, and when *i* is used it is rather the quantitative determinative (4a) in the sense of 'all over' (see sec. 7.8). Temporary measures never occur as distributive reduplicates. As in the case of container measures, the following are only examples from an open class.

Mt (a). 身 ( 子 ) *shen(tz)* 'body': 雪 *sheue* 'snow'.

Mt (b). 头 *tour* 'head': 白头髮 *bair-tour-fah* 'white hair'. ≠ Mc 16 or Mq 12.

Mt (c). 臉 *lean* 'face': 髒 *tzang* 'dirt', 汗 *hann* 'sweat'.

Mt (d). 鼻子 *byitz* 'nose': 碰了一鼻子的灰 *penqle i-byitz de huei* 'has bumped against dust all over the nose,—got rebuffed'.

Mt (e). 嘴 *tzoei* 'mouth': 粗话 *tsu-huah* 'coarse language'.

Mt (f). 肚子 *duhtz* 'stomach, abdomen': 不高兴 *bugaushinq* 'displeasure'.

Mt (g). 手 *shoou* 'hand': 疤剌 *ba.la* 'scars', 油 *you* 'grease'.

Mt (h). 脚 *jeau* 'foot': 泥 *ni* 'mud'.

Mt (i). 桌子 *juotz* 'table, desk': 剩菜 *shenq-tsay* 'leftovers', 没回的信 *mei hwei de shinn* 'unanswered letters'. ≠ Mc' 10 or Mg 29.

Mt (j). 院子 *yuanntz* 'courtyard': 樹葉子 *shuhyehtz* 'leaves'.

Mt (k). 地 *dih* 'ground, floor': 玩意儿 *wanyell* 'toys'.

Mt (l). 房頂(儿) *farngdieeng(l)* 'roof': 霜 *shuang* 'frost'.

Mt (m). 世界 *shyh.jieh* ('world'),—'all over the place': 漆 *chi* 'paint', 泥 *ni* 'mud, dirt'.

Mt (n). 事情(?) *shyh.chyng* ('event, affair, etc.'),—'all over the place': The word does not seem to make sense. The characters (not attested in any published text) are given here only for the sound. It probably is a corruption of, but occurs more frequently than, Mt (m).

(7) Standard Measures (Mm). Standard measures are measures proper. Most of them can occur in distributive reduplicates and can occur with *de*. They differ from quasi-measures in occurring with nouns, while the latter do not. The formal features for standard measures, so far as listed in table 17, look very much like those for Mc′ and Mg. The differences are, first, that Mc′ is always associated with particular V-O constructions, which standard measures are not; secondly, that standard measures can have $n_1$-$M_1$ $n_2$-($M_2$), where $M_2$ is the next smaller denomination than $M_1$, as in 六尺三（寸）*liow-chyy san-(tsuen)* 'six feet three (inches)', with omissible $M_2$, while with group measures, which are not in standard units, such forms are not possible; and thirdly, standard measures take *de* before a following noun more frequently than do Mc′ or Mg. As usual, the dissyllables do not reduplicate.

The standard measures are listable in the sense that all nontechnical units can be included in a relatively short list. Specialized terminology in the various sciences is of course outside the scope of the language under consideration. However, most units used in science are polysyllabic and thus function either exclusively or optionally as nouns rather than measures. Thus one says either 一光年 *i-guangnian* or 一个光年 *ig guangnian* for 'one light-year', just as one says 一米突 *i-miituh* or 一个米突 *ig miituh* for 'one meter', or 一米 *i-mii* but not ° 一个米 °*ig mii*.

For simplicity, only the actually spoken forms are listed here. For example, 市尺 *shyhchyy* 'municipal foot', defined as ⅓ of a meter, is included, but the theoretical 市寸 *shyhtsuenn* 'municipal inch' is hardly ever spoken and one either refers to it simply as 寸 *tsuenn* 'inch' or as fractions of the municipal foot. In the case of units with modifiers such as 英 *Ing* 'English', as in 英尺 *Ingchyy* 'English foot', and 公 *gong* 'public', as in 公斤 *gongjin* 'public catty,—kilogram', only those in actual spoken usage are included. Thus, one does speak of 英寸 *Ingtsuenn* '(English) inch', but not 英分 *Ingfen* '(English) line ($\frac{1}{10}$ inch)'.

In the case of areas named as 方 *fang-* 'square' and volumes as 立方 *lihfang-* 'cubic' followed by the unit of length, as in 方尺 *fangchyy* 'square foot' and 立方公尺 *lihfang-gongchyy* 'cubic meter', nothing new in principle is involved except the usual effect of polysyllabism and so they will not be listed. Those units with their own names such as 畝 *muu* '⅙ acre' and 加侖 *jialuen* 'gallon' will of course have to be included.

Mm 1. 尺 *chyy* '(Chinese) foot': 料子 *liawtz* '(textile) material'.

Mm 2. 寸 *tsuenn* '(Chinese) inch': 綢子 *chourtz* 'silk'.

Mm 3. 分 *fen* '¹⁄₁₀ (Chinese) inch': 氈子 *jantz* 'felt, thickness of'. N.B. Some Chinese carpenters speak of ⅛ inch as 分 *fen*, since it is quite close to ¹⁄₁₀ of a *tsuenn*. ≠ Mm 32.

Mm 4. 丈 *janq* '10 (Chinese) feet': 繩子 *sherngtz* 'rope'.

Mm 5. 里 *lii* 'li' (about a third of a mile): 路 *luh* 'road, distance', 地 *dih* 'ground, distance'.

Mm 6. 公尺 *gongchyy* 'public foot,—meter'.

Mm 7. 米(突) *mii(tuh)* 'meter'. (Similar examples of **M ~ N** apply to similar units of indigenous measures.)

Mm 8. 公寸 *gongtsuenn* 'decimeter' (rare).

Mm 9. 公分 *gongfen* 'centimeter'.

Mm 10. 生的 *shengdih* '(translit. of) centi(meter)'.

Mm 11. 公里 *gonglii* 'kilometer'.

Mm 12. 市尺 *shyhchyy* 'municipal foot, = ⅓ meter'.

Mm 13. 英尺 *Ingchyy* '(English) foot'. (The characters for English units formed by adding Rad. 30 to the Chinese units such as 呎 for 'foot', 哩 for 'mile', and so on are variously pronounced simply as *chyy, lii*, or as *Ingchyy, Inglii* (thus with two syllables to one character). To avoid ambiguity we shall not decide nor can decide on the "correct" pronunciation of these characters and limit ourselves to describing only how the foreign measures are spoken of as foreign measures.)

Mm 14. 英寸 *Ingtsuen* '(English) inch'.

Mm 15. 碼 *maa* 'yard': 尼龙 *nilong* 'nylon'. ≠ Mq 94.

Mm 16. 英里 *Inglii* 'mile'.

Mm 17. 海里 *haelii* 'nautical mile'.

Mm 18. 光年 *guangnian* 'light-year'.

Mm 19. 畝 *muu* '⅙ acre': 地 *dih* 'land', 田 *tyan* 'farm land'.

Mm 20. 頃 *chiing* '100 *muu*': 田 *tyan* 'farm land'.

Mm 21. 升 *sheng* '(Chinese dry) pint': 米 *mii* 'rice'.

Mm 22. 斗 *doou* '(Chinese) peck': 黄豆 *hwangdow* 'soybeans'.

Mm 23. 斛 *hwu* '5 (Chinese) pecks': 糧食 *liang.shyr* 'grain'.

Mm 24. 加侖 *jialuen* 'gallon': 汽油 *chihyou* 'gasoline'.

Mm 25. 品特 *piinteh* 'pint': 牛奶 *niounae* 'milk'.

Mm 26. 西 ㄟ *shishi* 'cc.': 药水 ( ㄦ ) *yawshoei ~ l* '(liquid) drug'.

Mm 27. 刀 *dau* 'knife,—cut,—ream-like unit': 纸 *jyy* 'paper'. ≠ Mv 26.

Mm 28. 疋 *pii* 'bolt': 布 *buh* 'cloth'.

Mm 29. 斤 *jin* 'catty': 肉 *row* 'meat'.

Mm 30. 两 *leang* 'tael, (Chinese) ounce': 酒 *jeou* 'wine'.

Mm 31. 錢 *chyan* 'mace' ($\frac{1}{10}$ of a tael): 銀子 *yntz* 'silver'. ≠ N 'money', ≠ N 'cash' (see Mm 45c).

Mm 32. 分 *fen* 'candareen': 金子 *jintz* 'gold'. ≠ Mm 3 or Mm 41.

Mm 33. 担 *dann* 'carrying-pole load,—100 catties': 米 *mii* 'rice'. ≠ Mp 10 (any weight).

Mm 34. 克 *keh* 'gram': 蘇打 *sudaa* 'soda'.

Mm 35. 公斤 *gongjin* 'kilogram': 煤 *mei* 'coal'.

Mm 36. 磅 *banq* 'pound': 黄油 *hwangyou* 'butter'.

Mm 37. 英两 *Ingleang* 'English mace,—ounce': 茶葉 *char-yeh* 'tea (leaves)'.

Mm 38. 噸 *duen* 'ton': 石子儿 *shyrtzeel* 'gravel'.

Mm 39. 点 *dean* 'hour'.

Mm 40. 刻 *keh* 'quarter-hour'.

Mm 41. 分 *fen* 'minute' ≠ Mm 32 or Mq 88, 99.

Mm 42. 秒 *meau* 'second': 钟 *jong* '(of the) clock'. N.B. (a) Expressions like 两点钟 *leang-dean jong* 'two hours (of the clock), are in the form D-Mm N. Since 钟 *jong* is almost the only noun which follows these standard measures, especially in the case of 点钟 *dean jong*, it is acquiring but has not quite attained the status of a compound quasi-measure, as has the compound 年级 *nianjyi* [sec. 6.4.3 (5)]. (b) Expressions like 两点钟 *leang-dean jong* are also used as time expressions: 'two o'clock', as well as 'two hours'. With the noun 钟头 *jongtour* 'hour', however, the expression 两个钟头 *leangg jongtour* means unambiguously 'two hours'. (c) The noun 钟点 *jongdean* means 'hours' in the collective sense, as in 钟点太早, 太多 *jongdean tay tzao, tay duo* 'hours too early, too many'. (d) The other time units are either quasi-measures or nouns, to be treated under (8) below.

Mm 43. 块 *kuay* 'piece,—dollar': 钱 *chyan* 'money'. N.B. (a) The denominations of money occur in various grammatical forms as measures, quasi-measures, and nouns. Sometimes the same denomination can appear in different grammatical forms. Thus, 块 *kuay* 'dollar' is a standard measure, with 钱 *chyan,* or the old-fashioned 洋钱 *yangchyan* 'foreign money,—dollar' as its noun, but in the Cantonese dialect the same unit appears as a noun, as in 一个银钱 *iatkoh ngandsin°* 'one dollar', with classifier, 个 *koh*. In the written form, since the character 块 has so many strokes, it is rarely written, and 元 *yuan* 'dollar', which is a quasi-measure (Mq 73), is used instead. (b) As in the case of the noun 钟 *jong*, which tends to be compounded with its preceding measure 点 *dean* and so on, the noun 钱 *chyan* 'money' tends to be compounded with 块 *kuay* and so on, to form compound measures, especially when followed by a noun expressing regional or national currencies. Thus, in 一块钱 *i-kuay chyan* 'one dollar', *chyan* is a noun, and in 一块美金 *i-kuay Meeijin* 'one dollar American money', *Meeijin* is a noun, but one also says 一块钱美金 *i-kuaychyan Meeijin* 'one dollar American money', in which *kuaychyan* is on the way to become a compound measure.

Mm 44. 毛 *mau* '10 cents': 钱 *chyan* 'money'. N.B. (a) This is a money unit and not a name of the dime coin, which is called 毛钱 (儿) *mauchyan ~ -l*. Thus, 两毛钱 *leang-mau chyan* '20 cents', but 两个毛钱儿 *leangg mauchyal* 'two dimes'. (b) The older and now obsolete term for this unit was 角 *jyue ~ jeau(l)* ('corner'),—'10 cents', still used, in its dialectal cognates, in the Yangtze basin. Then the Cantonese name 毫 (子) *hou(tzix)* '10 cents' was borrowed into the North in the simplified character form 毛, which the visual borrower simply read as *mau*. This confusion was strengthened by the fact that for 30 cents the Cantonese form is 三毫 (written as 三毛) *saam-hou,* where the *h* is a low-pitch glottal [h] or [ɦ] and very readily permits intersyllabic linking with the preceding *m* and thus is hardly distinguishable from *saam-mou.*

Mm 45. 分 *fen* 'cent': 錢 *chyan* 'money'. N.B. (a) Since there is a denomination 毛 *mau* '10 cents' between dollars and cents, numerals before *fen* are never greater than ten. For example, '25 cents' is not °二十五分 °*ell.shyrwuu-fen,* but 兩毛五分 *leang-mau wuu-fen* or simply *leang-mau-wuu.* (b) The copper coins for various denominations of the order of a cent are 銅子儿 *torngtzeel,* which is a noun. (c) At the turn of the century, square-holed brass coins were used and were called 錢 *chyan,* which is a noun, usually translated as 'cash', for example, 二十个錢 *ell.shyrg chyan* '20 cash'. A string of such coins formed a unit called 吊 *diaw* '(suspended) string', which is a measure, now obsolete. A string was theoretically 1,000 cash, later inflated to mean 100 cash. With the advent of the holeless copper coin, nominally equal to 10 cash, the cash was out of circulation and the word 錢 *chyan* has since been limited to the function of a noun for 'money' and is no longer a noun for a unit of money. It is a measure only as Mm 31 'mace'. (c) The wenyan for a cash is 文 *wen,* which is adopted into Cantonese in form of *man*°, which is a measure, as an alternative form to 銀錢 *ngandsin*° 'dollar', which is a noun; for example, 四文 *sey-man*°, but 四个銀錢 *seykoh ngandsin*° 'four dollars'.

Mm 46. 鎊 *banq* 'pound (sterling)': 錢 *chyan* 'money'. N.B. The other foreign money units are mostly dissyllabic and are either quasi-measures (see below) or nouns.

(8) Quasi-Measures (Mq). Quasi-measures, or autonomous measures, are measures in that they follow numerals and other determinatives directly but are unlike other measures, in that they are autonomous and do not belong to a noun or certain nouns. Hence they are marked "°" under *de* and under N in table 17. It is true that one can say, with Mq 1, 兩國的人 *leang-gwo de ren,* as one can say, with Mo (z), 兩鍋(的)飯 *leang-guo (de) fann.* But in Mq 1 it is a different kind of *de*: 'the people of the two countries', while with Mo (z), it is 'two pots of rice' and not

'rice of two pots'. In the following list of quasi-measures, no nouns are therefore given as examples. When a quasi-measure is itself alternatively also a noun, usually taking 个 *g* for its measure, it is marked " ~ N". Note that quasi-measures are autonomous only in the sense that they are not measures to a following noun. Most of them can be followed by adjectives, sometimes with an optional 那么 *nemme* 'as ... as', as in 两年那么長 *leang-nian nemm charng* 'two years long', 三站那么遠 *san-jann nemm yeuan* 'three stations away', 一指寬 *i-jyy kuan* 'one finger wide'.

Mq 1. 國 *gwo* 'country, nation'. ~ N.

Mq 2. 省 *sheeng* 'province'. ~ N. N.B. The old administrative units 府 *fuu* 'prefecture', 道 *daw* 'circuit', and 州 *jou* 'subprefecture' are obsolete, although *fuu* 'fu' and *jou* 'chow' or 'chou' still occur in the spoken forms of names of cities.

Mq 3. 州 *jou* 'state (of the U.S.A.). ~ N. This is the official equivalent for 'state', but 省 *sheeng* is almost as often used in this sense. In compounds for the names of particular states, certain preferences have become established, for example, 加州 *Jiajou* 'Ca(lifornia) state', but 麻省 *Masheeng* 'the commonwealth of 'Ma(ssachusetts)', and 纽约省 *Neouiue Sheeng* 'New York state'. Note the lack of any parallelism between the usages in Chinese and in English.

Mq 4. 県 *shiann* 'hsien, district, county'. ~ N. N.B. 城 *cherng* 'city' is a noun only and not a measure.

Mq 5. 鄉 *shiang* 'country, countryside'. The noun and place word is 鄉下 *shiang.shiah* '(down in the) country'.

Mq 6. 村 *tsuen* 'village'. The noun is 村子 *tsuentz* or 村莊 *tsuenjuang*.

Mq 7. 区 *chiu* 'locality, ward'.

Mq 8. 站 *jann* 'station'. ~ N.

Mq 9. 面(儿) *miann* ~ *-ll* 'side, face, direction', as in 四面都被包圍了 *syh-miann dou bey bauweile* 'surrounded on all four sides'. ≠ 面儿 *miall* 'powder' N, ≠ 面儿 *miall* 'facing (as opposed to lining, of garments)' N.

Mq 10. 方面 *fangmiann* 'aspect'.

Mq 11. 边(儿) *bian ~ -l* 'side', as in 两边儿都讨好 *leang-bial dou tao-hao* 'courts favor from both sides'.

Mq 12. 头(儿) *tour(l)* 'end', as in 两头進行 *leang-tour jinn-shyng* 'proceeds from both ends', 说的头ㄟ是道 *shuo de tourtour sh daw* 'talks so that every end is the (right) way,—argues point by point'. ≠ Mc 16 or Mt (b).

Mq 13. 格儿 *ger'l* 'case, partition'.

Mq 14. 筆 *bii* 'stroke'. ≠ Mc' 4, Mp 39, or N 'pen, etc.'.

Mq 15. 画(儿) *huah ~ -ll* 'stroke'.

Mq 16. 横(儿) *herng(l)* 'the stroke " 一 "'.

Mq 17. 竖(儿) *shuh ~ -ll* 'the stroke " 丨 "'.

Mq 18. 直 *jyr*, same as Mq 17.

Mq 19. 撇(儿) *piee(l)* 'the stroke " 丿 "'. ≠ N 'comma'.

Mq 20. 捺 *nah* 'the stroke " 乀 "'.

Mq 21. 挑 *tiau* 'the stroke " 丿 "'.

Mq 22. 剔 *ti* 'the stroke " ⸜ " or " ⸜ "'.

Mq 23. 鈎(儿) *gou(l)* 'the hook in strokes such as " 亅 ", " 乀 ", " ㄱ ", " ㄴ "'. ~ N.

Mq 24. 拐 *goai* 'the bend in strokes such as " ㄱ ", " ㄴ ", " ㄅ "'.

Mq 25. 点(儿) *dean ~ -l* 'the stroke " 丶 " or " . "'. ~ N. ≠ Mp 32.

Mq 26. 点 *dean* '(theoretical) point', as in 他的回答有两点。*Tade hweidar yeou leang-dean.* 'His answer had two points'. ≠ Mp 32.

Mq 27. 部 *buh* 'department, ministry (of a government)'. ≠ Mc 44 or Mg 31.

Mq 28. 司 *sy* 'division (of *buh*)'.

Mq 29. 课 *keh* 'subdivision (of *sy*)'; 'lesson', as in 上了两课 *shanq.le leang-keh* 'has taken up two lessons'.

Mq 30. 院 *yuann* ('courtyard'),—'main branches of the government', as in 五院 *wuu-yuann* 'the five yuan', 三院 *san-yuann* 'the three branches (of the American government)'; 'colleges (of a university)', as in 一个大学至少有三院。*Ig dahshyue jyhshao yeou san-yuann.* 'A university has at least three colleges.' ~ N. N.B. 大学 *dahshyue* 'university', 学院 *shyueyuann* 'college' and 学校 *shyueshiaw* (formerly 学堂 *shyuetarng*) 'school, college, university' are nouns.

Mq 31. 科 *ke* 'branch (of learning)', 'course (of study)'.

Mq 32. 系 *shih* 'department (of a college or University)'.

Mq 33. 等 *deeng* 'class, grade'.

Mq 34. 级 *jyi* 'class, steps'. N.B. (a) 等级 *deeng₀jyi* 'standing (as to official class, school class, etc.)' is a noun. (b) In forms like 一年级 *i-nian-jyi* 'first-year grade, freshman class' and 二年级 *ell-nian-jyi* 'second-year grade, sophomore class', the ICs are 2 + 1, but by back formation 年级 *nianjyi* 'standing in school or college' has become a noun, as we have already noted [sec. 6.4.3 (5)].

Mq 35. 名 *ming* 'name,—person', as in 合格的只有四名. *Herger de jyy yeou syh-ming*. 'Of those who qualify there are only four names,—persons.'[28] Cf. 他用过四个不同的名字. *Ta yonq.guoh syhg butorng de mingtz*. 'He has used four different aliases', where *mingtz* is a noun.

Mq 36. 票 *piaw* 'vote', as in 他拿了几张空白选举票，可是只能投一票。 *Ta nale jii-jang konqbair sheuanjeupiaw, keesh jyy neng tour i-piaw*. 'He took several blank ballots, but could cast only one vote.' ≠ Mc′5.

Mq 37. 股 *guu* '(stock) share'. ≠ Mp 20. The noun is *guutz*.

---

[28] Although *ming* is similar to Mc 7 尊 *tzuen*, it is not used in the usual order of n-M N in normal speech and is therefore not classed as Mc. Thus, one says 一尊菩萨 *i-tzuen pwu.sah* 'a bodhisattva', but not °三名学生 °*san-ming shyue.sheng* for 'three students', although one can say in a stiff and formal style 一名学生 *i-ming shyue.sheng*, where *i-ming* means 'a' rather than 'one'. The reverse order 学生三名 *shyue.sheng san-ming* is quite common in the inventory or invoice style. For example, in the story related to me by L.S. Yang, a late Ming-house refugee who called himself emperor escaped to Yunnan under the protection of a general there. The general's cook wrote in his account of meals served 皇帝一名 *hwangdih i-ming* 'emperor 1-*ming*', whereupon the general said 皇帝应说一尊。 *Hwangdih ing shuo i-tzuen*. 'Of emperors you should say 1-*tzuen*.' In practice, however, *tzuen* is used more with statues or portraits than with persons, secular or divine.

Mq 38. 族 *tzwu* 'tribe, clan'.

Mq 39. 口 *koou* 'mouth (to feed), (number of) persons', as in 那家有五口。 *Ney-jia yeou wuu-koou.* 'That family has five (mouths).' ≠ Mc 17, Mc' 2, Mp 37, or Mv 25.

Mq 40. 版 *baan* 'edition, printing', as in 印了五版，从来没修改过 *yinnle wuu-baan, tsornglai mei shiougae.guoh* 'has had five printings and never been revised'.

Mq 41. 册 *tseh* 'volume, pamphlet'. ≠ 本 Mc 20. For example, one can say either 这书有十本。 *Jeh shu yeou shyr-been.* or 这书有十册。 *Jeh shu yeou shyr-tseh.* for 'This work has ten volumes.', but one can only say 十本书 *shyr-been shu* and not ° 十册书 °*shyr-tseh shu* for 'ten books'. ≠ Mc 20.

Mq 42. 编 *bian* ('compile'),—'Book (I, II, etc.), Part', as in 这书一共有三编。 *Jeh shu igonq yeou san-bian.* 'This book has three parts altogether'.

Mq 43. 回 *hwei* 'chapter (of a novel)'. ≠ Mv 2.

Mq 44. 章 *jang* 'chapter'.

Mq 45. 面 *miann* 'page' (in editors' and printers' language). ≠ Mc 22. Cf. Mp 23.

Mq 46. 小節 *sheaujye* 'measure, bar (in music)'. ~ N.

Mq 47. 拍 *pai* 'beat (in music)'.

Mq 48. 板 *baan* ('clapper'),—'(principal) beat'.

Mq 49. 眼 *yean* ('eye'),—'one of the three beats indicated by touching the fingers with the thumb, following the beat with the clapper or the palm'. ≠ Mv 24.

Besides Mq 40-49, the other units having to do with language, writing, and music are Mc 20, 44-50, Mc' 1-3, Mg 9, Mp 22, 23, 29, 30, Mv 10, and the nouns 词 *tsyr* 'word (in the linguistic sense)', 词素 *tsyrsuh* 'morpheme', 言 *yan* 'word' L as in 万言书 *wannyan-shu* 'a message of 10,000 words', 字 (儿) *tzyh* ~ *tzell* 'word, character', 音 *in* 'sound, syllable, note (in music)'. All except 言 *yan*, which is L, take Mc 1. 个 *g*. The noun 词 ( 子 ) *tsyr* (*tz*) 'poem with unequal lengths of lines in fixed tonal patterns' takes Mc 46 首 *shoou*.

Mq 50. 世纪 *shyhjih* 'century'. ~ N.

Mq 51. 世 *shyh* 'one's lifetime'. (The meaning 'generation' is L only.)

Mq 52. 生 *sheng* 'one's lifetime'.

Mq 53. 輩子 *beytz* 'one's lifetime'. N.B. This is not a noun, even though it ends in *-tz*.

Mq 54. 輩 *bey* 'generation (as to seniority)', as in 他比我長兩輩. *Ta bii woo jaang leang-bey.* 'He is my senior by two generations'.

Mq 55. 代 *day* 'generation'.

Mq 56. 輪 *luen* 'cycle (of twelve years of the earth's branches)', as in 比我小兩輪 *bii woo sheau leang-luen* 'two cycles (24 years) younger than I'.

Mq 57. 年 *nian* 'year'.

Mq 58. 載 *tzae* 'year' L, used in speech only in the L-cliché 一年半載  *i-nian bann-tzae* 'a year or so'.

Mq 59. 歲 *suey* 'years old'.

Mq 60. 學期 *shyuechi* 'term, semester'. ~N.

Mq 61. 季 *jih* 'season, quarter'.

Mq 62. 月 *yueh* 'month', usually N.

Mq 63. 週 *jou* 'week', less common than Mq 64 and 65.

Mq 64. 礼拜 *liibay* 'week', usually N.

Mq 65. 星期 *shingchi* 'week', usually N.

Mq 66. 天 *tian* 'day'. 日 *ryh* 'day' is L only.

Mq 67. 夜 *yeh* 'night'.

Mq 68. 宿 *sheou* 'night'.

Mq 69. 更 *geng* ~ *jing* 'a watch of the night'.

Mq 70. 会儿  *hoel* 'moment'.

Mq 71. 陣 ( 子 ) *jenn(tz)* 'spell, a few days'.

Mq 72. 程( 子 ) *cherngtz* 'spell, a few days'.

The double hour marked by the twelve earth's branches or 时辰 *shyr.chern* is a noun. The units for hours, quarters, minutes, seconds are standard measures Mm 39, 40, 41, 42, respectively, with 钟 *jong* 'clock' as their only noun.

Mq 73. 元 ~ 圓  *yuan* ('round'),—'dollar'. This is not spoken except in reading off a written account, and the like. See Mm 43, 塊 *kuay*.

Mq 74. 换 *huann* ('exchange rate of gold to silver') as in 今
天金子五十换。 *Jin.tian jintz wuushyr-huann.* 'Today's exchange is one tael of gold to 50 tael of silver.'

Mq 75. 凩 *kai* 'ca(rat)'.

Mq 76. 先令 *shianling* 'shilling'. ~N.

Mq 77. 辨士 *biannshyh* 'pence'. ~N.

Mq 78. 法郎 *faalang* ~ *fahlang* 'franc'. ~N.

Mq 79. 方 *fang* 'franc', used by Chinese residing in France
who have mastered the uvular [ʀ] in *franc* and thus find it closer
to *fang* than with a lingual [r] or [ɹ]. It is not N or Mm; in other
words, there is no ° 一个方 °*ig fang* or ° 一方钱 °*i-fang
chyan.*

Mq 80. 马克 *maakeh* 'mark'. ~N.

Mq 81. 卢布 *lubuh* 'ruble'. ~N.

Mq 82. 卢比 *lubii* 'rupee', ~N.

There are of course many other units of money which have
their dictionary equivalents in Chinese, but, since they are not
spoken of in Mandarin-speaking communities of any size, they will
not be included here.

Mq 83. 工 *gong* '(a day's) work (of a workman)'. ~N in *ig
gong.*

Mq 84. 作 *tzuo(h)* '(a season of) work',—'a crop', as in 这儿
一年有两作。 *Jell i-nian yeou leang-tzuo.* 'There are two crops
a year here.'

Mq 85. 倍 *bey* 'double, times, -fold': N.B. 一倍 *i-bey* 'once
doubled,—twice', but 两倍 *leang-bey* is ambiguously 'twice
doubled,—four times' or, less frequently, 'two times,—twice', depending upon context. From 三倍 *san-bey* on, it is only simple
multiplication: 'three times, four times, and so on.'

Mq 86. 番 *fan* 'double, times'. In mahjong, 一番 *i-fan*, 两番
*leang-fan*, 三番 *san-fan*, 四番 *syh-fan*, etc., used to mean (2
times the score', '$2^2$,—4 times the score', '$2^3$,—8 times the score',
'$2^4$,—16 times the score, etc.', but in recent usage, *fan* is used
only as 'times', as in the second meaning of 倍 *bey*. ≠ Mv 8.

Mq 87. 成 *cherng* 'tithe, tenth', as in 九成新 *jeou-cherng shin*
'nine-tenths new'.

Mq 88. 分 *fen* '100th' or '10th', depending upon context: 有
三 分 醉 *yeou san-fen tzuey* 'as much as three-tenths drunk', 年
利 五分。*Nianlih wuu-fen.* 'The annual interest is 5%.' ≠ Mm 41
or Mq 99.

Mq 89. 厘 *li* '100th', as in 年利五厘 *Nianlih wuu-li.* 'The
annual interest is 5%'; '1000th', in context with 分 *fen*, as in 一
分 一 厘 都 不 能 錯。 *I-fen i-li dou buneng tzuoh.* 'Not a 100th
or a 1000th can be in error.'

Mq 90. 毫 *haur* '10,000th'.

Mq 91. 丝 *sy* '100,000th'. N.B. (a) Mq 90 and 91 are used
only in such idioms as 一 丝 一 毫 都 不 差。 *i-sy i-haur dou bu
cha* 'not differing by a shred or a hair' and not used as measures
otherwise. (b) Beyond 丝 *sy*, old school arithmetic also had 忽 *hu*
'negligible,—$10^{-6}$', 微 *wei* 'minute,—$10^{-7}$', 纖 *shian* 'fine,—$10^{-8}$',
沙 *sha* 'sand,—$10^{-9}$', 塵 *chern* 'dust,—$10^{-10}$', 渺 *meau* 'indiscerni-
ble,—$10^{-11}$'. Since these theoretical units were hardly ever in use
even when they were taught in school in the 1900's, their status
as Mq or other measures is not determinable. (c) Note that positive powers of 10 are group measures (Mg 4-8), whereas their
negative powers are quasi-measures (Mq 87-91).

Mq 92. 托 *tuo* 'length between finger tips with extended arms'.

Mq 93. 圍 *wei* 'circumference as measured by the extended
arms'.

Mq 94. 碼 *maa* 'span, length between extended thumb and
little finger'. ≠ Mm 15.

Mq 95. 抱 *baw* ('embrace'),—'circumference as measured by
the extended arms'.

Mq 96. 指 *jyy* 'a finger's width', less frequently, 'a finger's
length'.

Mq 97. 象 限 *shianqshiann* 'quadrant'.

Mq 98. 度 *duh* 'degree (of angle or temperature)'.

Mq 99. 分 *fen* 'minute (of angle)'. ≠ Mm 41 or Mq 88.

Mq 100. 秒 *meau* 'second (of angle)'. ≠ Mm 42.

(9) Measures for Verbs of Action (Mv). A measure for verbs
of action expresses the number of times an action takes place. It
may be a cognate object expressing the action of the verb (Mv 1-

18), or the part of the body which performs the action (Mv 19-25), or the instrument with which the action is performed (Mv 26-40). If there is another object, it follows the measure if it is a noun, as in 叫一声"妈" *jiaw i-sheng "Mha"* 'calls "Ma" once', but precedes the measure if the object is a pronoun, as 骂了他一顿 *mahle ta i-duenn* 'scolded him a spell,—gave him a scolding'. The pronoun 他 *ta* is also used in an impersonal sense, as in 睡他一觉 *shuey ta i-jiaw* 'sleep it a sleep,—just sleep (for the fun of "it")'.

Mv 1. V: The verb itself may be a measure serving as cognate object (sec. 5.4.6.1) with or without a numeral (usually *i*) as its determinative, as in 看一看 *kann.i.kann* 'take a look', whence the tentative reduplicative 看看 *kann.kann.* [Cf. sec. 4.2.3 (5).]

Mv 2. 回 *hwei.* ≠ Mq 43, and

Mv 3. 次 *tsyh* 'number of times': These two measures are mostly interchangeable, except that 回回(儿) *hweihwei ~ hwei-huel* 'every time' is more common than 次次 *tsyhtsyh.* Examples are 病过几回 *binq.guoh jii.hwei* 'have been sick several times', 没扯过一次谎 *mei chee.guoh i-tsyh hoang* 'have not once told a lie', 逃了两次 *taurle leang-tsyh* 'escaped twice'. In the lexical compounds 二回 *ell.hwei* and 二一回 *ell.i₀hwei* 'next time, by and by', *ell(.i)-* 'second, next' is taken in an ordinal sense, while 两回 *leang-hwei ~* 两次 *leang-tsyh* 'twice' are transient compounds.

Mv 4. 遍 *biann* 'once over, once through': 看 *kann* 'read', 念 *niann* 'read aloud', 说 *shuo* 'say', 查 *char* 'look up', investigate', 背 *bey* 'recite'.

Mv 5. 趟 *tanq* 'trip': 去 *chiuh* 'go there', 出...洋 *chu ... yanq* 'go abroad', 拜望 *bay.wanq* 'call on'.

Mv 6. 下儿 *shiall* 'stroke': 打 *daa* 'strike', 摸 *mho* 'feel (with the hand)', 问 *wenn* 'ask'. The form 下子 *shiahtz* is much less common in the Northern than in the other dialects.

Mv 7. 遭 *tzau* 'adventure': 走他一遭 *tzoou ta i-tzau* 'makes a trip of it as an adventure'. (Obsolescent.)

Mv 8. 番 *fan* 'once over': 说 *shuo* 'say', 劝 *chiuann* 'admonish, advise', 教训 *jiaw.shiuann* 'admonish'.  ≠Mq 86.

Mv 9. 着 *jau* ~ *juo* 'step': 做 *tzuoh* 'act', as in 你 不 该 做 那 一 着 的。 *Nii bugai tzuoh ney-i-jau de.* 'You shouldn't have taken that step'.

Mv 10. 声(儿) *sheng(l)* 'a voice': 叫 *jiaw* 'call', 言 语 *yuan.yi,* (sic) as in 请 你 言 语 一 声儿! *Chiing nii yuan.yi .i.shengl!* 'Please make a sound,—please just let (me or him) know!' 你怎么不言语啊? *Nii tzeem bu yuan.yi a?* 'Why don't you say something?'

Mv 11. 响 *sheang* 'sound': 响 三 响 *sheang san-sheang* 'sounds three times', 钟 打 了 六 响。 *Jong daale liow-sheang.* 'The clock struck six times'.

Mv 12. 圈儿 *chiual* 'a round': 转 *juann* 'revolve', 绕 *raw* 'winds'.  ≠Mc' 11. Cf. 弯儿 *ual* 'a bend' N, 圆圈儿 *yuanchiual* 'circle' N.

Mv 13. 步 *buh* 'step': 走 *tzoou* 'walk', 进 *jinn* 'advance', 迈 *may* 'step', as in 迈 三 步 *may san-buh* 'take three steps'.

Mv 14. 把 *baa* 'grip': 捏 *nhie* ‧'pinch', 掐 *chia* 'pinch', 抓 *jua* 'grasp', 拉 *lha* 'pull', 帮 *bang* 'help'.  ≠Mc 27 or Mp 16.

Mv 15. 仗 *janq* 'battle': 打 *daa* 'fight'.

Mv 16. 觉 *jiaw* 'nap': 睡 *shuey* 'sleep'. N.B. Not all cognate objects are measures. For example, 说话 *shuo-huah* 'say words,—talk' seems to be like 睡觉 *shuey-jiaw,* but while there is 睡 几 觉 *shuey jii-jiaw* 'sleep several times', there is no °说几话 °*shuo jii-huah* for 'say a few words', for which one has to use Mc' 1. 句 *jiuh* as measure.

Mv 17. 顿 *duenn* 'spell, meal': 吃 *chy* 'eat', 打 *daa* 'beat', 骂 *mah* 'scold'.  ≠Mc 51,  ≠Mc' 21, where the verb is an object.

Mv 18. 关 *guan* 'a barrier, a pass': 过 *guoh* 'pass'.  ~N with Mc 36.道 *daw,* as in 过 五 关 *guoh wuu-guan* or 过五道关 *guoh wuu-daw guan* 'go through five passes'.

Mv 19. 手(儿) *shoou(l)* ('hand'),—'act, trick': 耒 *lai* 'do', as in 可 别 再 耒 那 一 手儿! *Kee bye tzay lai ney-i-shooul!* 'Don't you try that act again!'  ≠Mc'3.

Mv 20. 脚 *jeau* '(a tread or kick of the) foot': 踩 *tsae* 'tread, step on', 踢 *ti* 'kick'.

Mv 21. 巴掌 *ba.jaang* '(a slap of the) palm': 拍 *pai* 'pat, beat', 打 *daa* 'strike, hit, clap'.

Mv 22. 拳 ( 头 ) *chyuan(.tou)* '(a hit of the) fist': 打 *daa* 'strike', 槌 *chwei* 'hammer'.

Mv 23. 拳 *chyuan* '(a single encounter of) fists (at the finger-guessing game)': 豁 *hua* 'play (such a game)'. 三拳兩勝. *San-chyuan leang-shenq.* 'In three encounters, two (scorings count as a) win.'

Mv 24. 眼 *yean* 'an eyeful, a look': 看 *kann* 'look', 瞅 *choou* 'look (less directly)', 瞟 *peau* 'ogle', 瞪 *denq* 'stare'. ≠Mq 49. N.B. There is no ° 听 一 耳 °*ting i-eel* for 'give a listening', for which Mv 1, 2, 3, 4, 6, and 10 can be used.

Mv 25. 口 *koou* 'a mouthful, a bite': 咬 *yeau* 'bite', 吃 *chy* 'eat'. ≠ Mc 17, Mc' 2, Mp 37, Mq 39, or Mv 25. N.B. Although 親嘴 *chin-tzoei* caress mouth, —kiss' is a V-O construction, *tzoei* is not a measure, so that there is no ° 親一嘴 °*chin i-tzoei* for 'give a kiss'. The measure for *chin* will be Mc 1, Mv 1, 2, 3, or 6 (but not Mv 25).

Mv 26. 刀 *dau* '(a cut of the) knife': 切 *chie* 'cut', 砍 *kaan* 'chop', 扎 *ja* or 刺 *tsyh* 'stab', 剌 *la* 'slash'. ≠ Mm 27.

Mv 27. 剪子 *jeantz* 'scissors': 絞 *jeau* 'shear, cut', 剪 *jean* 'shear, cut'.

Mv 28. 鉗子 *chyantz* 'pincers' or 'claws (of crabs, lobsters, etc.)': 夾 *jia* 'pinch'. N.B. For the instruments 夾鉗 *jiachyan* 'pliers' and 夾鑷子 *jianiehtz* 'forceps', the verb is 夾 *jia*, but the measures used with it are the general ones Mv 1, 2, 3, and 6, and not the words for the instruments.

Mv 29. 斧子 *fuutz* ~ 斧头 *fuu.tou* (the latter being more common in the Wu dialects) '(a slash with the) hatchet': 砍 *kaan* 'chop slash'.

Mv 30. 槌 ( 子 ) *chwei(tz)* '(a stroke of the) mallet, hammer': 打 *daa* 'hit'. N.B. 釘槌子 *dingchweitz* '(nail) hammer', is not a measure but a noun, and 'a stroke' in this case is Mv 6.

Mv 31. 板（子） *baan(tz)* '(a stroke of the) board': 打 *daa* 'beat, spank, slap'.

Mv 32. 鞭（子） *bian(tz)* 'whip': 打 *daa* 'beat', 抽 *chou* 'whip, lash'.

Mv 33. 棒 *banq* '(a hit with the) club': 打 *daa* 'hit'.

Mv 34. 棍（子） *guenn(tz)* '(a hit with the) rod': 打 *daa* 'hit', 杵 *chuu* 'poke'.

Mv 35. 錐子 *jueitz* '(a stab with the) awl': 錐 *juei* 'punch, stab'.

Mv 36. 針 *jen* '(a prick of the) needle': 扎 *ja* 'prick', 戳 *chuo* 'pierce' (the latter avoided by speakers of the Wu dialects, in which *chuo* is a four-letter word).

Mv 37. 箭 *jiann* '(a shot of the) arrow': 射 *sheh* 'shoot'.

Mv 38. 槍 *chiang* '(a stab with the) lance or spear': 扎 *ja* 'spears', 戳 *chuo* 'stab'.

Mv 39. 槍 *chiang* '(a shot of the) gun or rifle': 打 *daa* 'hit', 放 *fanq* 'shoot'.

TABLE 17

Types of Measures

|  | n > 1 | M | MM | 的 | N | Listable |
|---|---|---|---|---|---|---|
| (1)  Mc  Classifiers, or Individual Measures | ✓ | 个 | ( ✓ ) | * | 人 | ✓ |
| (2)  Mc´  Classifiers Associated with V–O | ✓ | 句 | ( ✓ ) | ( ) | 话 | ✓ |
| (3)  Mg  Group Measures | ✓ | 行 | ( ✓ ) | ( ) | 字 | ✓ |
| (4)  Mp  Partitive Measures | ✓ | 堆 | ( * ) | ( ) | 土 | ✓ |
| (5)  Mo  Container Measures | ✓ | 鍋 | ( * ) | ( ) | 麵 | * |
| (6)  Mt  Temporary Measures | * | 地 | * | ✓ | 东西 | * |
| (7)  Mm Standard Measures | ✓ | 尺 | ( ✓ ) | ✓ | 布 | ( ✓ ) |
| (8)  Mq  Quasi-Measures, or Autonomous Measures | ✓ | 课 | ( ✓ ) | * | * | ( ✓ ) |
| (9)  Mv  Measures for Verbs of Action | ✓ | 遭 | ( ✓ ) | * | * | ✓ |

Mv 40. 砲 *paw* '(a shot of the) gun, cannon, or firecracker': 放 *fanq* 'shoot, set off'.

In table 17 " ✓ " means 'yes', " ° " means 'no', and "(   )" means 'in most cases' or 'not absolutely'. Note that the 的 *de* is the *de* for 'of' in measures, as in 十磅的肉 *shyr-banq de row* '10 pounds of meat' and not the *de* for the pertaining 'of' as in 十磅的秤 *shyr-banq de chenq* 'a scale of 10 pounds, —a 10-pound scale', which may actually weigh 5 or 20 pounds. [Cf. sec. 7.6.2(4).]

## 7.10. Localizers

A localizer is a morpheme, for example, 上 *shanq* 'above, on', or a morpheme complex, for example, 上头 *shanq.tou* 'above, on', which forms, with a preceding subordinated substantive, such as 桌子 *juotz* 'table', a place word like 桌子上 *juotz.shanq* 'table thereon,—on the table' or a time word like 晚上 *woan.shanq* 'on the evening,—the evening'.

A simple or monomorphemic[29] localizer is always start-bound (-B), while a longer localizer can occur as a free word, it-self usually occurring as a place or time word. The latter is formed by adding to a simple localizer, for example, 外 *way* 'out-side', the suffixes 头 -.*tou* 'end' and, less often in Standard Man-darin, 边 ( ㄦ ) -.*miann* ~ -*ll* 'side' and 面 ( ㄦ ) -.*bian* ~ -*l* 'side' (table 12). By borrowing from wenyan 以 *yii* 'with' and 之 *jy* (= 的 *de*), place and time words like 以内 *yiiney* 'within, inside', 之内 *jyney* ''s inside,—inside of' can be formed and used as localizers, as in 三英里以外 (~ 之外 ) *san-Inglii yiiway* (~ *jyway*) 'outside of three miles' (table 11, cols. 6 and 7).

With the same free place word, it is possible to form a more complex place phrase or place word according as *de* is inserted and/or a stress or a neutral tone is introduced. Thus, 纸上 *jyy-*

---

[29]We do not say "monosyllabic", since the localizers -.*jell* 'here' and -.*nall* 'there' are monosyllabic but dimorphemic and yet are free as place words.

*.shanq* and 纸上头 *jyy.shanq.tou* 'on the paper' are place words, while 纸上头 *jyy shanq.tou* and 纸的上头 *jyy de shanq.tou* 'above the paper' are place phrases. There is not much difference in meaning between the word and the phrase in this and most other cases, but when it does make a difference, the closer form usually has a more specialized meaning and the looser form a more literal meaning. For example, 墙上 *chyang.shanq* or 墙上头 *chyang.shanq.tou* 'on the wall', but 墙的上头 *chyang de shanq.tou* 'above the wall'; 在政治上（头）*tzay jenqjyh.shanq (.tou)* 'in politics, politically', but 在政治的上头 *tzay jenqjyh de shanq.tou* 'above politics'; 月亮（的）那边儿 *yueh.lianq (de) ney.bial* 'that side of the moon,—the other side of the moon', but 月亮那边儿 *yueh.lianq.ney.bial* 'the side of the moon,— where the moon is'.

Note that even with a bound localizer, the substantive expression to which it is attached may be a phrase or a word. For example, 报跟书上都说. *Baw gen shu.shanq dou shuo.* 'It is said in both the newspapers and the books.', where 上 -*.shanq* goes with the phrase 报跟书 *baw gen shu*. Again, in 在一个新买的手提包裡 *tzay ig shin mae de shooutyibau .lii* 'in a newly bought handbag', the localizer -*.lii* cannot belong to the preceding noun alone, or else it would be the inside place that was newly bought and not the bag. The ICs are of course 在 *tzay* 'is at, in', and the whole place expression with 裡 -*.lii* 'inside' as center is modified by the whole long phrase before it. While this is a very common type of construction, the following modifier before 裡 -*.lii*, because of its nature as an interpolation, is relatively rare: 那一间教室也是饭堂裡的衰老的钟，敲过低沉的六响. *Nah-i-jian jiawshyh yee sh fann-tarng .lii de shuailao de jong, chiau-guoh dichern de liow-sheang.* 'The dilapidated old clock in that classroom, which was also the dining room, had struck six low, heavy strokes.'[30]

Localizers, as the term suggests, usually express the (spatial and temporal) locations (lit. or fig.) of things. Though substantive in form, they are translatable into prepositions. For this reason,

---

[30] 民气日报 (*The Nationalist Daily*), New York, April 20, 1942, p. 8.

they are also called postpositions. For example, 屋 .裡 *u.lii* 'room-interior,—in the room', 事後 *shyh-how* 'event-posterior,—after the event'.

Most of the monomorphemic localizers are also determinatives by class overlap. For example, 上 *shanq* is a determinative in 上回 *shanq.hwei* 'last time', but a localizer in 山上 *shan.shanq* 'on the mountain'; 前 *chyan* is a determinative in 前天 *chyan-.tian* 'previous day,—day before yesterday', but a localizer in 飯前 *fann-chyan* 'before meal(s)'.

Localizers are of varying, but generally very high, degrees of versatility, which is the chief reason that they are regarded as words forming a part of speech, even though bound. However, pairs of antonymous localizers often have quite different degrees of versatility; for example, the versatility of 上 *shanq* 'above' is high, but that of 下 *shiah* 'below' is low; that of 裡 *lii* 'inside' is high, but that of 外 *way* 'outside' is low.

When a localizer has optional stress, the stressed form is more likely to be restricted and does not combine with phrases, while the unstressed form is usually more versatile and can combine with either a word or a phrase. Consequently, those localizers which are never in the neutral tone are restricted in the words they are compounded with. For example, 城裡 *chernglii* 'down town': *cherng.lii* 'in the city', 一个很大的城裡 *ig heen dah de cherng .lii* 'in a very large city', but no °*ig heen dah de cherng lii*. If a stressed form is to be used with a phrase, a full two-syllable compound place word will have to be used, as 一个很大的城的裡头 *ig heen dah de cherng de lii.tou* 'the inside of a very large city'.

Localizers form a listable class. Since complex localizers are also place or time words, which have been treated under preceding sections (secs. 7.4 and 7.5), it remains only to list the simple, or monomorphemic localizers and to note their versatility, stress features, and other special properties. The only localizers longer than one morpheme listed here are 这儿 -.*jell* and 那儿 -.*nall*, which are monosyllabic. For simplicity, most of the localizers are translated as prepositions, it being understood that the place and time words of which they are centers are substantives. Sometimes, for idiomatic reasons, a different preposition is used in the illustration from the one used in translating the localizer itself, on the basis of its majority-type meaning. For example, 上 *shanq* 'on', but 天上 *tian.shanq* 'in the sky', since one does not usually say in English 'on the sky'.

L1. 上 -$_0$*shanq* 'on, above'. The stressed form usually means 'above' and is much less versatile than the neutral-tone form, usually meaning 'on': 馬上 *maashanq* 'at once', 街上 *jie.shanq* 'on the street', 櫃上 *guey.shanq* 'on the counter,—the cashier', 晚上 *woan.shanq* 'evening'.

L2. 下 -$_0$*shiah* 'below, under': 天下 *tianshiah* 'under heaven, —the world', 陛下 *bihshiah* 'under the imperial steps,—(Your ~ His ~ Her) Majesty', 目下 *muhshiah* 'under the eyes,—at the moment', 地下 *dih.shiah* 'on the ground, on the floor', 底下 *dii.shiah* 'below the bottom,—below'. In *dii.shiah*, the *sh-* is often weakened to *h* and the *a*, being in neutral tone, is weakened to *e*, so that the word is often heard as *dii.hie*. [For additional examples, see sec. 6.4.4(1).] N.B. 下 -$_0$*shiah* is rather restricted, but 底 下 *dii.shiah* is versatile.

L3. 前 -$_0$*chyan* 'front, before': 飯前 *fann-chyan* 'before meal(s)', 人前 *ren-chyan* 'in front of people,—in the presence of people', ( 他的 ) 面前 ~ 跟$_0$前 ~ 跟前儿 *(tade) miann- .chyan* ~ *gen$_0$chyan* ~ *gen$_0$cheal* 'in front of him'. N.B. 前 -$_0$*chyan* is rather restricted, but 前头 *chyan.tou* 'in front', 以前 *yiichyan* 'before (in time)', and 之前 *jychyan* 'before (in time)' are versatile.

L4. 先 -*shian* 'before (in time)': 事先 *shyh-shian* 'before the event or act'. This is very rare as a localizer, though very active as an adverb, as in 先来 *shian lai* 'comes first'. The compound form 之先 *jyshian* 'before' is more versatile, but not as frequently used as 之前 *jychyan*. The *jy*-forms are of course somewhat formal in style.

L5. 後 -*how* 'behind, after': 背後 *beyhow* 'behind the back, —the back (of someone or something)', 书後 *shuhow* 'after the book,—postface', 身後 *shenhow* 'after the person's life,—after

death', 事後 *shyh-how* 'after the event', 午後 *wuuhow* 'after
noon' (cf. 下午 *shiahwuu* 'afternoon'), 飯後 *fann-how* 'after
meal(s)'. The compound form 後头 *how.tou* is used more in the
spatial than in the temporal sense; 以後 *yiihow* and 之後 *jyhow*,
always in the temporal sense. Note that in real wenyan *jyhow* is
not so limited.

L 6. 内 *-ney* 'inside, interior': 関内 *Guanney* 'inside the
Pass' (usually referring to Shanhaikuan), 國内 *gwoney* 'in the
country' (opposite of 'abroad'), 分内 *fenn-ney* 'inside one's part,
—within one's duty'. The simple form 内 *ney* is extremely restricted. The compound forms 以内 *yiiney* and 之内 *jyney* are
more versatile, as in 在城墙以内 *tzay cherngchyang yiiney*
'be within the city walls', 三天之内 *san-tian jyney* 'within
three days'.

L 7. 裡 -₀*lii* 'inside, in': 城裡 *chernglii* 'inside the city,—
downtown', 家裡 *jia.lii* 'in the home', 这裡 *jeh.lii* 'in here,—
here', 那裡 *nah.lii* 'in there,—there', 心裡 *shin.lii* 'in the mind'.
N.B. (a) The free form 裡头 *lii.tou* 'inside' is more versatile than
the stressed bound form *-lii* 'inside', but the neutral-tone forms
*-.lii.tou* and *-.lii* are both versatile. (b) ≠ 裡子 *liitz* ~ 裡儿
*lieel* 'lining (of garments, etc.)', which are nouns. (c) The more
common spoken forms for *jeh.lii* and *nah.lii* are *jell* and *nall*, respectively, where *-.lii* is further weakened to a nonsyllabic suffix.
The corresponding interrogative form *naal* 'where' does not have
a *-.lii* form °*naa.lii*, but in reading 哪裡 or in trying to accom-
modate to speakers of other dialects, one sometimes says *naalii*
(actually ㄋ ㄚ by the usual tone sandhi), which is never used in
natural speech.[31]

L 8. 外 *-way* 'outside': 國外 *gwoway* 'outside the country,
—abroad', 郊外 *jiauway* 'outside the environment,—suburbs',
分外 *fennway* 'outside one's part,—beyond one's duty', 此外
*tsyyway* 'besides this or these', 格外 *gerway* 'outside (the usual)

---

[31]During the years of the artificial National Pronunciation from 1919 to
1932, I tried to introduce the pattern *naa.lii* ㄥ ㄧ, but it never seemed to
catch on.

categories,—particularly, especially', 紫外線 *tzyywayshiann* 'ultraviolet rays', 门外汉 *menwayhann* 'man outside the door (of the profession),—amateurish person'. The free form 外头 *way.tou,* and less commonly 外边（儿） *way.bian ~ -l* and 外面 （儿） *way₀miann ~ way.miall* are of unlimited versatility, but 外 *-way* is very restricted.

L 9. 左 *-tzuoo* 'left', and

L 10. 右 *-yow* 'right': 江左 *Jiangtzuoo* 'left side of the river, —region on the north bank of the Yangtze', obsolete, now called 江北 *Jiangbeei* (with L 17), 府右街 *Fuuyow-Jie* 'Street to the Right of the Mansion,—street name in Peiping'. The free forms 左边（儿） *tzuoo.bian ~ -l* 'the left side' and 右边（儿） *yow-.bian ~ -l* 'the right side' are of unlimited versatility, while 左 *-tzuoo* and 右 *-yow* are rather restricted.

L 11. 旁 *-parng* 'side': 道旁 *dawparng* or 路旁 *luhparng* 'roadside,—beside the road'. As a localizer, *-parng* is extremely restricted. As a specifying determinative, *parng-* '(an)other' is a little more versatile. The free form 旁边儿 *parngbial* (no neutral tone!) is of unlimited versatility, as in 桌子（的）旁边儿 *juotz (de) parngbial* 'beside the table', 廟（的）旁边儿 *miaw (de) parngbial* 'beside the temple'. N.B. In compounds like 单人旁儿 *danren-parngl* 'single-man radical （亻)', *parngl* is a noun and not a localizer.

L 12. 中 *-jong* 'middle', and

L 13. 间 *-jian* 'interspace, between': Although these are versatile localizers in wenyan, only a few relic forms remain in spoken usage, as in 其中 *chyijong* 'their middle,—among them' or. 'its middle,—inside it', 关中 *Guanjong* 'Between the Passes,—(ancient name for the region of modern) Shensi', 世间 *shyhjian* 'inside the (mundane) world', 人间 *renjian* 'among men,—among the living', 忽然间 *huranjian* 'within a sudden,—all of a sudden'.

On the free and versatile dissyllabic synonyms of 中 *jong* and 间 *jian,* namely 当中 *dangjong* 'in the middle,—middle', 当间儿 *dangjiall* 'in between,—between', 中间儿 *jongjiall* 'between', 中间 *jongjian* 'middle interspace,—between', all of which may be modified by 正 *jenq* 'right, just, exactly', as in 正当中 *jenq-dangjong* 'right in the middle', see sections 7.4(2.2) and 7.5(3).

L 14. 东 *dong* 'east'.

L 15. 南 *nan* 'south',

L 16. 西 *shi* 'west',

L 17. 北 *beei* 'north': As single-morpheme localizers, these are restricted, occurring mostly in place names, as in 关东 *Guan-dong* 'East of the Pass', 山东 *Shan$_o$dong* 'East of the mountain,—Shantung', 江南 *Jiangnan* 'South of the River,—region in lower right bank of the Yangtze', 河南 *Her$_o$nan* 'South of the (Yellow) River,—Honan', 湖南 *Hwu$_o$nan* 'South of the (Tungt'ing) Lake, —Hunan', 江北 *Jiangbeei* 'Lower Left Bank of the Yangtze', 河北 *Herbeei* 'North of the River,—Hopei', 湖北 *Hwubeei* 'North of the Lake,—Hupeh', 台北 *Tairbeei* 'Northern (part) of Taiwan, —Taipei'. In giving addresses of a house as to which side of the street it lies, the place words used are 路东 *luhdong*, 路南 *luhnan* 'east, south side of the street', and so on. The free and versatile forms are 东边（儿） *dong.bian ~ -.bial*, 西边（儿） *shi.bian ~ -l* etc., as in 房子的东边儿 *farngtz de dong.bial* 'to (or in) the east of the house'.[32] To distinguish between in and to a certain side of something, place words formed with 以（~ 迄） *yii-* can be used for 'to' and those with 部 *-buh* for 'in', as in 法國在大西洋以东， 在欧洲的西部. *Fah.gwo tzay Dahshiyang yii dong, tzay Ou.jou de shi-buh.* 'France is to the east of the Atlantic Ocean and in the west of Europe.', where it would be equally grammatical, but less precise, to say 的东边儿 *de dong.bial* 'east of' and 的西边儿 *de shi.bial* 'west of' or the sometimes spoken wenyan forms 之东 *jy dong* and 之西 *jy shi.*

L 18. 这儿 *-.jell*,

L 19. 那儿 *-.nall*: These localizers indicate the general location of whatever is expressed by the preceding substantive. Of

---

[32]In the compound 房东 *farngdong* 'landlord', *dong* is not a localizer, but a noun 'owner'.

the two, 这儿 -.*jell* refers to localities centered around the speaker, as in  我这儿 *woo.jell* 'here where I am,—at my place, chez
moi', 我们这儿 *woomen.jell* or 咱们这儿 *tzarmen.jell* 'here
where we are,—at our place, chez nous', 王先生这儿 *Wang
Shian.sheng.jell* 'here at Mr. Wang's (speaking at Mr. Wang's
place)'. 那儿 -.*nall* follows any substantive (including the first-
person pronouns), as in     书 不 在 哥ˋ那儿 , 也 不 在 他们
那儿 , 在 我 那儿 呐。 *Shu bu tzay Gege.nall, yee bu tzay ta-
men.nall, tzay woo.nall ne.* 'The book is not at Older Brother's
nor at their place, it's at my place over there.' (talking while
away from my house). A substantive other than a place word is
changed into one by adding 那儿 -.*nall* to it, but a word which
is already a place word cannot take 那儿 -.*nall*. For example,
房子那儿没樹。 *Farngtz.nall mei shuh.* 'There are no trees
where the house is.', or 我家裡没樹。*Woo jia.lii mei shuh.*
'There are no trees at my home.', but not ° 我家裡那儿...
°*Woo jia.lii.nall* ... , since 家裡 *jia.lii* is already a place word
(unless of course there is a pause after .*lii*, making *nall* a second
subject).

## 7.11. Pronouns

*7.11.1 Pronouns and Other Substitutes.* Pronouns differ from
all the other parts of speech in two important respects: (a) Instead of referring to persons or things, they refer to words or the
speaking situation. Thus, *woo* refers to the speaker, *nii* to the
person addressed, and *ta* to the person pointed at or previously
mentioned, in which case it substitutes for the expression denoting that person. (b) There are certain other words like pronouns,
but, instead of substituting for substantive expressions, they substitute for verbal or adverbial expressions. For example, in 你 不
会修这机器，让我来. *Nii buhuey shiou jeh ji.chih, ranq
woo lai.* 'You don't know how to repair this machine, let me do
it.', *lai* is a substitute for the verbal expression *shiou jeh ji.chih*
and is thus not a pronoun but a pro-verb.

For these reasons it has been found useful to set up the category of substitution or class of substitutes, cutting across the

other word classes.[33] As in all cases of cross-classification in two
or more dimensions, say with *n* classes in one dimension and *m*
classes in another, one has to make a choice whether to run
through the *n* items *m* times or the *m* items *n* times. For our
present purposes, since the subject of pronouns looms considerably larger than the other substitutes, and since a large part of
the latter is based on the same morphemes as some of the pronouns, we shall discuss both the pronouns and the other substitutes in this section, instead of farming out the few pro-verbs,
pro-adjectives, and so on, to the other parts of speech.

7.11.2. *Pronouns and Nouns.* Pronouns differ from nouns in
the following respects:

(1) They belong to a very small class of listables (see sec.
7.11.4 below), whereas nouns form an open class.

(2) They are normally not modifiable by D-M compounds.
There is 兩位先生 *leang-wey shian.sheng* 'two gentlemen', but
no ° 一位您 °*i-wey Nin* 'one you, sir'. Occasionally, however,
a D-M compound can modify a pronoun P taken in the sense of
some appearance or aspect of P, as in 有兩个我，一个我
在这儿，一个我在镜子裡。 *Yeou leangg woo, ig woo tzay
jell, ig woo tzay jinqtz.lii.* 'There are two me's, one is here, the
other is in the mirror.' The fact that *ig woo tzay jell.* cannot be
translated as 'one I am here.' is symptomatic of the non-pronom-
inal nature of *woo*, since *leangg woo* means 'two shapes like me'
and is thus of the nature of a quasi-quotation, just as in the case
of proper names modified by D-M compounds, as in *leangg Wang
Liang.* Similarly, *ig* or *g* can be used with a pronoun in the sense
of 'a person like …', as in 我当着是个生人来打门，
一看原来就是个你！ *Woo daangj sh g shengren lai daa men,
i-kann yuanlai jiow sh g nii!* 'I thought it was some stranger
knocking at the door, and when I looked, why, it was just (such
a familiar person as) you!'

(3) Pronouns are not normally modified by adjectival expressions. Only in written bairhuah does one find expressions like 一

---

[33]Bloomfield, *Language,* chap. 15; Dragunov 15(5 of Ch tr); 周法高，
中國古代语法，称代编 (Fa-Kao Chou, *Grammar of Ancient Chinese:
Substitutes*), Taipei, 1959.

个气家可归的可憐的我　　　*ig wu jia kee guei de keelian de woo* 'a poor me with no place to go home', which in traditional fiction would take some such form as 可憐我气家可归 *keelian woo wu jia kee guei* 'pity me for having no place to go home', thus making it a verb-object instead of an adjective-noun construction. Referring to the mirror-image example under (2), one can say 鏡子裡头的我是假我，鏡子外头的我才是真我呐。 *Jinqtz lii.tou de woo sh jea woo, jinqtz way.tou de woo tsair sh jen woo ne.* 'The me that's inside the mirror is an unreal me, only the me that's outside the mirror is the real me.', where we have both simple adjectives directly modifying *woo* and adjectival phrases modifying *woo* with particle *de*. But much more naturally, with less effect of word play, one would say 鏡子裡头的是我的影子，鏡子外头的才真是我呐。 *Jinqtz lii.tou de sh woode yiingtz, jinqtz way.tou de tsair jen sh woo ne.* 'What's inside the mirror is my image, only what's outside the mirror is really me.', where *jen sh* 'really is' puts the *jen* part in an adverbial position. In other words, in natural speech one would rather avoid modifying a pronoun with an adjectival expression if there is another way of saying the same thing.

(4) Pronouns, like nouns, may modify another substantive expression by addition of *de*, as in 我的书 *woode shu* 'my book', 咱们的錢 *tzarmende chyan* 'our money'. As in the case of *de* in other adjectival expressions, it can be used as a nominalizer if no modified expression follows, as in 这是你的吗? *Jeh sh niide ma?* 'Is this yours?' But, unlike nouns, a pronoun can modify (a) words of kinship or other personal relations and (b) words of spatial relationship without the addition of *de*, as in 你爸ㄣ *nii bah.bah* 'your papa', 我姊ㄣ *woo jiee.jiee* 'my older sister', 我们先生 *woo.men shian.sheng* 'our teacher', 他们前头 *ta.men chyan.tou* 'in front of them', 我後头 *woo how.tou* 'behind me'. In all these cases, insertion of *de* would make the modification more explicit, but it is not obligatory.

Note that when applied to spatial relations only free place words can be modified by pronouns without *de*. Bound localizers

(L1-L16) cannot be modified by a pronoun and form compounds as nouns can. Thus, we have 雨前 *yeuchyan* 'before the rain,—brand of green tea', 纪元前 *jihyuanchyan* 'before recording year 1,—B.C.', but not °你前 °*niichyan* for 'before you', or °他们中 °*ta.menjong* for 'among them'. But 他们当中 *ta.men dong-jong* is possible, as *dangjong* is free.

When both a personal pronoun and a D-M compound modify a noun, they occur in that order, as in 我(的)一个朋友 *woo(de) ig perng.yeou* 'a friend of mine', 你(的)那些学生 *nii (de) neyshie shyuesheng* 'those students of yours'.

Honorific and humble terms of address usually imply 'your' and 'my' in the terms, and the addition of *Ninde* or *woode*, though grammatically possible, is usually regarded as redundant and tends to lessen the intended effect of formal politeness. Thus, 令兄 *linqshiong* 'excellent older brother,—your older brother' is preferred to *Nin(de) linqshiong*, and 家父 *jiafuh* 'my father' is preferred to *woo(de) jiafuh*, except as usual, where explicit contrast is to be brought out.

(5) Phonologically, the pronouns *nii, woo, ta* and the -.*men* forms, unlike nouns, are usually unstressed (and thus in the neutral tone) when they are objects of verbs, as in 请你告送我们买点儿什么东西送他！ *Chiing .nii gaw.sonq .woo-.men mae .deal sherm dong.shi sonq .ta!* '(I) request you to tell us, buy what things to present to him,—please tell us what to buy to give to him!' The object pronoun is of course fully toned if there is contrastive stress on it, as in 可别送我们东西！ *Kee bye sonq ‖woo.men dong.shi!* 'But don't give *us* anything!' Similarly, if the pronoun *ta* occurs twice and refers to different persons, it will be stressed even in the object position, as in: 这两个人弄僵了；他不让他，他也不让他。 *Jey-leangg ren nonq-jiangle; ta bu ranq ta, ta yee bu ranq ta.* 'These two men have got into a deadlock; he won't yield to him, and he won't yield to him, either.'

(6) Pronoun objects before cognate objects.—One effect of the unstressed pronoun object is that it tends to be enclitically attached to the verb and thus precede cognate objects, if any.

Thus, we have 请了他三次 *chiingle .ta san-tsyh* 'invited him three times', but 请了三次客 *chiingle san-tsyh keh* 'invited three times guests,—gave three parties'. When there is a resultative complement, which usually resists separation from the verb, a pronoun can be inserted, but not a noun. Thus, with a pronoun, one can say either 骂他骂的很利害 *mah .ta mah de heen lih.hay* 'in scolding him, scold very severely' or, with inserted pronoun object, 骂的他很利害 *mah de .ta heen lih-.hay* 'scold him very severely'. But with a noun, one can only say 骂人骂的很利害 *mah ren mah de heen lih.hay* 'in scolding people, scold very severely' and not °骂的人很利害 °*mah de ren heen lih.hay*, unless one meant 'the scolder is very fierce', which is an entirely different type of construction. In the Jehol dialect quoted by Dragunov (p. 213; Chinese transl., p. 197) even the bound form 的慌 -*.de.huang* allows the insertion of a pronoun, as in 他恨的他慌。 *Ta henn de ta huang.* (stresses originally unmarked). 'He hates him badly.', which in Standard Mandarin would be 他恨他真恨的慌。 *Ta henn .ta jen henn.de.huang.* 'In hating him he hates badly.' [Cf. sec. 4.4.7 (5).]

*7.11.3 Pronouns and Proper Names.* Pronouns differ from proper names in being listable, while proper names belong to an open class. Pragmatically, the two are alike in referring to persons or things by pointing at them without describing them. Thus, both pronouns and proper names are said to be semantically empty.[34] Actually, pronouns and proper names are as rich in meaning as any other parts of speech. Their special pragmatical function lies in that identification of the referent is taken for granted without further description.

*7.11.4 Pronouns in Detail.*

(1) Ordinary Personal Pronouns. The ordinary personal pronouns are 我 *woo* 'I, me', 你 *nii* 'you (thou)', and 他 *ta* 'he, him, she, her, it'.

(1.1) Order and Coordination. When occurring in coordination, only the three forms *nii woo* 'you and I', *nii woo ta* 'you, I,

---

[34]See Knud Togeby, *Structure Immanente*, p. 212.

and he', and, somewhat less frequently, *woo nii ta* 'I, you, and he' are used without pauses or markers. But if pauses or markers are used between the items, then any order is possible. Thus, there is no: ° 我 他 一 塊 ㄦ 到 了. °*Woo ta ikuall dawle.* for 'I and he have arrived together.', but one can say: *Woo gen ta ikuall dawle.* If *nii* or *ta* is used twice to refer to different persons, a marker such as *gen* or/and a pause is obligatory, as in: 你 (,) 跟 你 先 末 , 你 (,) 跟 你 頂 好 等 一 会 ㄦ. *Nii(,) gen nii shian lai, nii (,) gen nii diing hao deeng i.hoel.* 'You₁ and you₂ come first, you₃ and you₄ had better wait a while.' (pointing and speaking to four different persons in turn). On the usage concerning the "A, B, and C" formula, see sec. 5.2.3.

(1.2) Plural Forms. The plural forms of personal pronouns are formed by suffixing 们 -.*men*, resulting in 我 们 *woo.men* 'we', 你 们 *nii.men* 'you', and 他 们 *ta.men* 'they', which we have been writing as *woomen, niimen, tamen* for short. Depending upon tempo and following sounds, the suffix is shortened to syllabic -*m* or, less usually, to -*me*. Before labials, -.*men* is usually shortened to -*m*, as in: 他 们 不 末. *Tam bu lai.* 'They don't come.' Note that this sentence is not homophonous with 您 不 末. *Tan bu lai.* 'He (*honorif.*) doesn't come.', where the -*n* is usually pronounced -*m* by assimilation to the following *bu*. [See sec. 1.3.9(2).] The shorter forms -*me* and -*m* for the plural ending are not written with any characters other than the full form [cf. sec. 4.4.4(5)].

(1.3) Forms of *woomen*. While *woom, niim,* and *tam* can all occur as indicated above, as dissyllables, each with syllabic *m* in the neutral tone, there are two additional forms of *woomen* which are different in their make up. One is the monosyllabic *weem*, with checked vowel *e*, pronounced [ə], and nonsyllabic ending -*m*. The other is *mm*, which is a syllabic *m* in the 3rd Tone. The form *weem* is less frequently heard than either *woom* or *mm*. It differs from *woom* in that, being one syllable, it has not only a different vocalism but also a different tone sandhi. Thus, in the tunes of the following sentences:

Woo.men bu lai.
Woo.me bu lai.
Woo.m bu lai.
Weem bu lai.

the -.*men*, -.*me*, and the syllabic -.*m* in *woo.m* all have a half-high pitch as a post-3rd Tone neutral tone normally has, whereas the -*m* as the non-syllabic ending in *weem*, being part of the $\frac{1}{2}$ 3rd Tone, remains low. Note also that the vowel is shorter and more fronted in such a checked syllable than in an open vowel such as *woo*.

The form *mm* is a familiar form, often spoken by women and children, though also used by men. It can occur in all positions, as in 这事儿我们不幹。*Jeh shell mm bu gann.* 'This (sort of thing) we don't do.' 给我们点儿茶喝！*Geei mm deal char he!* 'Give us some tea to drink!' 这是我们的。*Jeh sh mmde.* 'This is ours.'

(1.4) Restricted Uses of *ta*. The third person singular pronoun *ta* is usually equated to 'he, she, it', but as 'it' it occurs mostly in the object position, much less often in the attributive position, and very rarely as subject. Thus, 让他去罢！*Ranq ta chiuh ba!* can mean either 'Let him (~ her) go!' or 'Let it go (let the matter drop)!', but 他不在这儿。*Ta bu tzay jell.* can only mean 'He (~ she) is not here.' and not 'It is not here.' In the following sentence: 凡是听了一个消息，你得知道他的来源，才能断定他是真的还是假的。 *Farnsh tingle ig shiau.shi, nii deei jy.daw tade laiyuan, tsair neng duannding ta sh jende hairsh jeade.* 'Whenever you hear a news, you must know its source before you can judge it to be true or false.', *tade* modifies *laiyuan* and is in the neutral tone, even though *laiyuan* and not *tade* is the center of the object to the verb *jy-.daw*. In *duannding ta sh* 'judge it to be', with optional neutral tone in *ta*, we have a pivotal construction, where *ta* is the object of *duannding* and subject of *sh*.

Note that the difference between *ta* as a pronoun for animate objects and inanimate objects (with limitations of positions stated above) is a matter of the speaker's use of the word as having animate or inanimate reference and not a matter of the biological or physical nature of the referent. Not only can an animal or a supernatural being be referred to as *ta* (in any position), but, if trees and stones talk in a fable, it will be very natural to refer to such things in the subject position, as in: 北風看見那走道儿的人把袍子脱了，他就知道他输了给太陽

3. *Beeifeng kann.jiann nah tzooudawl de ren bae paurtz tuole ta jiow jydaw ta shule geei tay.yang le.* 'When the north wind saw the traveler take off his cloak, he knew that he had lost to the sun.', where *ta*, referring to the north wind, is used twice in the subject position.

What may be considered as semipersonified is the use of *ta* to refer to something which is regarded as actively affecting a person in some way. For example: 这个调儿真讨厌，他老在你腦子裡转的不停。 *Jeyg diawl jen taoyann, ta lao tzay nii naotz.lii juann de butyng.* 'What a nuisance, this tune, it keeps turning around in your head without stop.' 这局面不好。你要是不早想法子，他会越变越糟的。 *Jeh jyumiann buhao. Nii yawsh bu tzao sheang fartz, ta huey yueh biann yueh tzau de.* 'The situation is bad. If you don't do something about it in time, it will become worse and worse.'

Rather different from the fully personified *ta*, translatable as 'he' or 'she', and the semipersonified *ta* 'it', the use of *ta* in written bairhuah is completely unrestricted as to scope of reference and position in the sentence. For example: 物理学是自然科学裡的最基本的一门科学。他是本校学生的必修科之一。 *Wuhliishyue sh tzyhran keshyue.lii de tzuey jibeende i-men keshyue. Ta sh been-shiaw shyue.sheng de bihshiouke jy i.* 'Physics is a most basic science among the natural sciences. It is one of the required courses in this school.' In ordinary speech one would use *jeh* or *nah* or repeat the noun rather than use *ta* to refer to *wuhliishyue*.

On the use of *ta* as a meaningless 'mock object', see sec. 5.4.6.5.

(1.5) Restricted Uses of *ta.men.* While *ta* is frequently used for inanimate things if it is in the object position, the plural form *ta.men* is not used for inanimate things in any position, except, of course, when they are personified. When referring to more than one thing, the singular form *ta* is still the normal pronoun to use and, as stated for the case of one single thing, it is always in the object position and rather infrequently in the attributive position. For example: 这些梨烂了，最好把他扔了罢。 *Jey.shie li lannle, tzuey hao bae ta rhengle ba.* 'These pears have spoiled, better throw them ("it") away.' Even when semi-personified, and thus admitting of being placed in the subject position, reference to a plurality of things still takes the form of *ta*, rather than *ta-men*, as: 这 些 小问 题 老 接着 来, 他 把 正事 情 都 耽 搁 了。 *Jeh.shie sheau wenntyi lao jiej lai, ta bae jenq shyh.chyng dou dan.ge le.* 'These little problems keep coming, they ("it") have delayed all the important things.' This non-use of *tamen* for inanimate things is such a firmly established feature of the language that it is carried over to the learning of foreign languages. Thus, in the example about spoiled pears, a Chinese student of English will say 'These pears have spoiled, better throw it away.', thinking of the spoiled pears as 'it'. It takes from five to ten years, or never, to bring himself to say 'them' in referring to pears, even though in the object position. On the other hand, it is definitely a Westernism to say, as in a recent text for teaching beginning Chinese: 这两个字你 不细々兒的看你就 要把他 们念错了。 *Jey leangg tzyh nii bu shihshielde kann nii jiow yaw bae ta.men niann-tsuohle.* 'If you do not look closely at these two characters, you will read them wrongly,' where a Chinese speaker would normally say *.ta* instead of *ta.men* or *.ta.men*.

(1.6) The Plural Suffix *-.ta.men*. After a proper name or a term of address used as a proper name, a suffixed *-.ta.men* can be added, with the meaning of *'et alii'*. For example: 你怎么先 到 了 ？ 李四 他们 呐？ *Nii tzeem shian dawle? Lii Syh tamen ne?* 'How come you've arrived first? How about Lii Syh and so forth?' In the following example: 二姊他 们不去了，他说 他们都累了. *Elljiee tamen bu chiuh le; ta shuo tamen dou ley le.* 'Second Sister and so forth are not going; she says they are not going; she says they are all tired.', the first *tamen* stands for 'and others who were going with Second Sister', while the second *tamen* includes both Second Sister and the others of the group.[35] This use of *tamen* as *'et alii'* is quite similar to that of

---

[35]The first time I became conscious of this was when, as a child, I caught myself saying 舅々.他.们 呐？ *Jiow.jiow tamen ne?* 'What about Uncle and the rest? (Are they going with us or by another boat?)' Immedi-

什么的 *.shermde* as 'et cetera' or, more colloquially, 'and things' (cf. 'Have you seen Mary and them?' in some midwestern American dialects.) It is to be distinguished from a resumptive pronoun in apposition with a preceding noun or nouns, as in: 孩子们(,)他们都来了。*Hairtzmen(,)tamen dou laile.* 'The children, they have all come here.' 我父親跟母親，他们都很健壯。*Woo fuh.chin gen muu.chin, tamen dou heen jiannjuanq.* 'My father and mother, they are both in very good health.' This is very different from the *-.ta.men* as '*et al.*' in: 父親母親.他.们都到了。*Fuh.chin muu.chin -.ta.men dou dawle.* 'Father and Mother and others have all arrived.', where *.ta.men* means 'plus one or more persons (presumably of my parents' generation)'.

(1.7) Omission of Possessive Pronouns. In comparing pronouns with nouns (sec. 7.11.2), we noted that possessive pronouns before words of personal relationship or position words can omit the subordinative particle *de*. But possessive pronouns, with or without *de*, are dispensed with altogether if the possessor is presumed to be obvious to the hearer. In this respect Chinese is like German or French but unlike English, in which possessive pronouns are expressed even when no contrastive function is served. Examples are: 他戴上了帽子走了。*Ta day.shanqle mawtz tzooule.* 'He put on his hat and left.' 我碰了头了。*Woo penqle tour le.* 'I have bumped my head.' 你得闭着眼睛洗臉，可是得張着嘴刷牙。*Nii deei bihj yean.jing shii lean, keesh deei jangj tzoei shua ya.* 'You must wash your face with your eyes closed, but brush your teeth with your mouth

---

ately after saying this, a form which I had unconsciously learned to use, it seemed to me rather strange that *tamen* could be tagged onto the word for 'Uncle', but when I tried to say it differently, I could not think of any other way of saying the same thing short of enumerating 'and Auntie, and Cousin One, and Cousin Two, and (the whole list of persons)', since at that age I did not know such formal expressions as 其餘的人 *chyiyu de ren* 'the remaining persons', which would have been out of place anyway in such a context. Quite recently, a writer discussing this special function of *tamen* used exactly the same example *jiow.jiow tamen.* (See 沈𤆬 on 她 in *Central Daily News*, Taipei, June 2, 1965.)

open.' But with contrast, 他穿的是他的大氅，不是他自己的大氅。 *Ta chuan de sh tade dahchaang, bush ta tzyhjii de dahchaang.* 'The one he is wearing is *his* (someone else's) overcoat, not his own overcoat.'

One special use of possessive pronouns is to express impatience or disparagement. For example, to a child: 快做工课去! *Kuay tzuoh gongkeh .chiuh!* 'Hurry up and do your lesson!' is just a simple command, but with *niide* the command will have a more impatient tone. For an example of disparagement: 让他们散他们的谣言去! *Ranq tamen sann tamende yau.yan .chiuh!* 'Let them spread their rumors!', where the possessive *tamende* has the effect of making light of the effect of the rumors.

On what I call possessive objects, which can apply to both nouns and pronouns, see sections 5.3.6.5(1.1), 5.4.6.6, and 6.5.7 (4).

(2) Special Personal Pronouns

(2.1) Inclusive 'We' and Exclusive 'We'. In the pure Peiping dialect, *woomen* includes the speaker and a person or persons spoken of, but not the person spoken to, whereas *tzarmen* includes at least both the speaker and the person spoken to, with optional inclusion of additional persons. For example: 我没錢；你也没錢。咱们都是窮人。 *Woo mei chyan; nii yee mei chyan. Tzarmen doush chyong ren.* 'I have no money; you have no money. We (= you and I) are both poor people.' 你们是南方人；我们是北方人。咱们都是中國人。 *Niimen sh nanfangren; woomen sh beeifangren. Tzarmen doush Jong-.gworen.* 'You are southerners; we are northerners. We (= you people and we others) are all Chinese.' Note that while there are generally no distinctive forms for the inclusive 'we' and exclusive 'we' in English, the expression: *Let's go!* is always taken in the inclusive sense, being equivalent to 咱们走罢! *Tzar.men tzoou ba!* The form: *Let us go!* on the other hand, can be used in either sense (1) same as 'Let's go!' or (2) 'Permit us to go (don't detain us any longer)!' = 让我们走罢! *Ranq woomen tzoou ba!*

(2.2) *Woomen* as Inclusive 'We'. As a result of influence from other dialects, most of which have only one form of 'we', writers of written bairhuah mostly use *woomen* not only in both senses, but, in somewhat formal speech, such as on public occasions, whether for *woomen* or for *tzarmen*, as in: 我们今天 得下了决心, 想法子使我们的国家强盛起来。 *Woomen jintian deei shiahle jyueshin, sheang fartz shyy woomende gwojia chyangshenq .chii.lai.* 'Today we must make a resolution and try to make our country strong and prosperous.', the use of *tzarmen*, though it would be correct, it would not give the same desired pompous effect.

(2.3) *Tzarmen* as Exclusive 'We'. An opposite special usage consists in using the normally inclusive form *tzar.men* in an exclusive sense. This is in a very familiar style, especially in a good-natured argument in which the opposite side is intentionally put on my side. For example: 这饭得让咱们来请啊！ *Jeh fann deei ranq tzarmen lai chiing a!* 'Let *us* (~ me) be host(s) for this dinner, (and you should agree or have agreed with me)!'

(2.4) *Tzarmen* as 'You'. In an even more familiar style, often used in talking to children, *tzarmen* refers only to 'you', as in: 那類地 方儿咱们不去。 *Nah-ley dihfangl tzarm bu chiuh.* 'We (~ I) don't go to those places (and I advise you not to go there, either).' When a child cries, one says 咱们饿了吧？ *Tzarmen ehle ba?* 'We are hungry, aren't we?' But a Chinese medical nurse would not say to an adult patient: 'How are we today?'

(2.5) *Tzarmen, Tzarnmen, Tzarm,* and *Tzarn.* In the most common form *tzarmen*, the first syllable ends in an open vowel, with the usual central (or back) quality of an open low vowel. The form *tzar* is bound, though it occurs free in some dialects. But there is a free form *tzarn* of much less frequent occurrence than *tzarmen*, but with the same meaning of '(inclusive) we'. This, when suffixed with *-men* gives *tzarnmen*, where the final *-n* after the low vowel is very unstable and assimilates to the following *m-*, so that *tzarnmen* is actually pronounced *tzarmmen*, with a fronted *a* or, since the *n* in *an* is always much weaker than in *en* in Mandarin, it is actually pronounced with a fronted nasalized vowel [ã] or [æ̃]. The difference between *tzarmen* and *tzarnmen* is rather similar to that between *woomen* and *weem*, where the checked vowel has a more fronted quality. In frequency of occurrence, the order is *tzarmen, tzarnmen, tzarm,* and *tzarn.*

(2.6) Humble and Honorific Forms. In traditional epistolary style, there is a whole system of humble and honorific forms consisting mostly of terms of address, instead of the usual personal pronouns. In actual speech, which is our concern here, the forms are limited to a very few.

(a) For the first person, if a person wishes to be diffident and humble, he simply avoids saying *woo* as much as possible and then only in a non-subject position. For example, instead of saying: 我对於这件事有点儿怀疑。 *Woo dueyyu jeyjiann shyh yeoudeal hwaiyi.* 'I have some doubts about this thing.', it is less blunt to say: 这件事使我有点儿怀疑. *Jey-jiann shyh shyy woo yeoudeal hwaiyi.* 'This thing makes me a little doubtful.'

In public speaking a slightly humble form for referring to oneself is 兄弟 *shiong.dih* '(your) younger brother' (limited to use by men, of course) and, less frequently, 鄙人 *biiren* 'lowly person'. Another form is 本人 *beenren* 'same person', which is not particularly humble, but not quite so self-asserting as *woo.*

During the imperial days there was a humble form 小的 *sheau.di* (not -*.de*) 'the small one', used by servants in speaking to officials, but it went out of use even before the Republican Revolution of 1911.

While in epistolary style one speaks of oneself as 妹 *mey* '(your) younger sister', 男 *nan* '(your) son', or 武 *Wuu* (if it is the writer's given name or part of his given name, say, 建武 *Jiann-wuu*), a child does often refer to himself in speaking as 妹 *Mey* 'sister', 宝宝 *Bao.bao* 'Baby', and so on. This, however, is really substituting a substitute by a proper name before the children learn how to use "shifters", such as pronouns are.[36]

(b) The form 您 *Nin* as a polite or honorific form of *nii* is very commonly used in Peiping, as in 这是您的吗？ *Jeh sh Ninde ma?* 'Is this yours, sir (or madam, as the case may be)?' It is used between strangers, in addressing persons of a higher

---

[36]Otto Jespersen, *Language,* New York, 1922, pp. 123-124.

status, such as a teacher or a relative of a higher generation or even a sibling or cousin much older than oneself.

Instead of *Nin*, which is not used in the Central and Southern dialects[37] the proper term of address is used *as* the second-person pronoun, such as 王先生 *Wang .Shian.sheng* 'Mr. Wang', 爸ㄅ *Bah.bah* 'Papa', 大姨儿 *Dahyel* '(First) Auntie (on mother's side)'. It is more polite to speak of the second person as *shiang.sheng* than the same suffixed to the surname. Thus we have, in descending order of politeness:

|     |           |              |              |
| --- | --------- | ------------ | ------------ |
| (1) | 先.生       | 记得 先.生       |              |
| (2) | 王.先.生     | 记得 王.先.生     | 上次说的话吗?      |
| (3) | 王.先.生,    | 您记得您        |              |

|     |                   |                         |           |
| --- | ----------------- | ----------------------- | --------- |
| (1) | *Shian.sheng*     | *jihde Shian.sheng*     | *shanq-tsyh* |
| (2) | *Wang .Shian.sheng* | *jihide Wang .Shian.sheng* | *shuo de* |
| (3) | *Wang .Shian.sheng,* | *Nin jihde Nin*          | *huah ma?* |

all of which can be translated as: 'Sir (or Mr. Wang), do you remember what you said last time, sir?' In (3), *Wang .Shian.sheng* is used as a vocative expression and the pronoun is *Nin*. But it should be remembered that in (1) and (2), *Shian.sheng* and *Wang .Shian.sheng* are used as second-person pronouns and not as nouns or proper names; otherwise the second occurrence in each sentence would take the third-person pronoun form *ta*, thus: (1') *Shian.sheng jihde ta shanq.tsyh shuo de huah ma?* 'Does the teacher remember what he said last time?' and (2') *Wang .Shian .sheng jihde ta ... ?* 'Does Mr. Wang remember what he ... ?' in which case no honorific forms are involved at all. In this respect the Chinese honorific second-person pronoun put in the form of the term of address differs from such polite forms in the third person, as in French: *Monsieur voudrais-t-il me dire son nom?* 'Would the gentleman please give me *his* name?' which is quite different from the grammar of polite Chinese.

In most of the Central and Southern dialects, where there is no form corresponding to *Nin*, the only polite forms available are (1) and (2) or else the plain form *nii*.

*Nin* has no spoken plural form. The form 您们 is found only

---

[37]Except in Nanking, where there is a form *Niierngl* ← *nii-laorenjia*, used like *Nin* in most contexts.

in written bairhuah. The corresponding spoken form is 您二位 *Nin ell-wey* or 你们二位 *Niimen ell-wey* 'You two gentlemen (~ you two ladies ~ you one lady and one gentleman)' or 你们 几位 *niimen jii-wey* 'you several ladies and/or gentlemen', where *wey* is the honorific equivalent of the individual measure 个 *g*. In a public speech 各位 *gehwey* or 诸位 *juwey* is used either vocatively as 'Ladies and gentlemen!' or as part of a sentence as 'you ladies and gentlemen'.

The honorific or deferential forms 陛下 *Bihshiah* 'Your Majesty' and 殿下 *Diannshiah* 'Your Highness' (the crown prince) are obsolescent, as there are few occasions when the Chinese would speak in Chinese to foreign sovereigns or nobility. Between equals, the polite form 足下 *tzwushiah* 'under your feet,—you, sir' is used only in epistolary style and is wenyan. So is 阁下 *gershiah* 'under your studio,—you, sir', which, however, is actually spoken in some of the central dialects.

(c) The third person pronoun 怹 *Tan* is heard much less frequently than *Nin*, probably because the third person is not always present and thus there is less necessity for the honorific form. The plural form 怹们 *Tanmen* is even rarer, even in writing.[38]

(2.7) Gender in Pronouns as a Structural Borrowing: 他 'he', 她 'she', 牠 'it'. Borrowing of grammatical structure from one language into another is much rarer than borrowing of vocabulary items. The borrowing of distinctions of gender in personal pronouns from Western languages into Chinese is one of those conscious attempts to change linguistic usage on which much effort has been spent and only slight changes of a marginal nature have resulted. It was about the time of the 1917 Literary Revolution that writers began to differentiate the third-person pronoun 他 into 他 'he', 她 'she', and 牠 'it', the last being suggested by the form 物 *wuh* 'thing' L. Little attention was paid to the question of how these were to be pronounced, and most readers read all

---

[38]An instance of its use, four times on one page, is in 周法高, 中国 古代语法, 造句编 上 (Fa-Kao Chou, *Grammar of Classical Chinese: Syntax*), Part I, Taipei, 1961, p. 18.

three as *ta* when reading aloud. During the succeeding years I
myself tried to give some linguistic status to these differentiated
graphs by proposing the forms 他 *ta* 'he', 她 *i* 'she', and 牠 *to* 'it'.
The syllable *to* does not exist in the Peiping dialect, but in the
artificial National Pronunciation of 1919-1932, in which *o* and *e*
were different phonemes as one of the concessions to other dialects, *to* was to be the pronunciation for 牠. The existence of
these forms was partially established in two instances. One was
in my translation of *Alice's Adventures in Wonderland* where 她,
besides being noted as pronounced *i*, also rhymed with 低 *di*[39],
and 牠, besides being noted as pronounced *to*, also rhymed with
何 *hor* (in the 1919-1932 National Pronunciation).[40] The other
instance was that these pronouns were so pronounced in my 1922
series of National Language Records, Lesson 9. The existence of
these forms was only partially established because, as far as I
know, nobody has ever been known to use these differentiated
forms in their speech, so that their authenticity is more philological than linguistic.

Subsequently, when the National Pronunciation was changed
to that of Peiping,[41] the form *to* was changed to *te*, which has
some linguistic basis, since the pronoun referring to inanimate
objects would be in the object position and neutral tone, and *.ta*
would tend to be pronounced *.te* anyway.

The present usage is as follows: So far as speech is concerned, there is no differentiation of gender except that *ta* referring to inanimates tends to be pronounced *te*, as noted, not as a
result of conscious innovation, but along with *ta* referring to persons, too, when it is in the object position, as in: 別理他. *Bye
lii .ta* ( ~ *.te*). 'Don't pay any attention to him.' As for graphical
differentiation, most writers use 他 for 'he', 她 for 'she' and, now

---

[39] 趙元任翻譯, 阿麗思漫遊奇境記, (Jaw Yuanren fanyih,
*Alihsy Mannyou Chyijiing Jih*), Shanghai, 1922, p. 182.

[40]*Ibid*, p. 184.

[41]As embodied in 國音常用字彙, (*Gwoin Charngyonq Tzyhhuey*),
Shanghai, 1932, now more accessible in the form of 國音標準彙編
(*Gwoin Beaujoen Hueybian*), Taipei, 1947.

more frequently than 牠, the simpler graph 它 for 'it', all three being pronounced *ta*, or *.ta ~ .te* in the object position. I usually follow this usage when writing in Chinese, but when giving examples from spoken Chinese, as in the present book, I use only the undifferentiated 他 (except when quoting other writers), since there is only one spoken form. In some translations of the Bible the capital 'He', etc., is given as 祂, being a graphical blend of 神 and 他, presumably pronounced as 他.

(2.8) The feminine second-person pronoun is occasionally written 妳, presumably pronounced *nii*. I have seen it only in letters. It has nothing to do with 妳 as a simplified form of the rare variant graph 嬭 for 奶 *nae* 'breast; milk'. In current epistolary style, even 您们 for 'you' (plural feminine) is often seen, presumably to be pronounced *Nin.men*.

(3) General Personal Pronouns. There is a class of pronouns referring to persons which are applicable to first, second, or third persons and can be used independently or in apposition with them. They refer to 'self', 'others', 'alone', 'both', 'everyone', etc.

(3.1) Pronouns for 'Self'. The most commonly used pronoun for 'self' is *tzyhjii*, as in: 自己有錢的时候儿，就应该用 自己的錢。 *Tzyhjii yeou chyan de shyr.howl, jiow inggai yonq tzyhjiide chyan.* 'When one has money oneself, one should use one's own money.' In apposition with the ordinary personal pronouns, we have the forms *woo tzyhjii* 'I myself', *nii tzyhjii* 'you yourself', *ta tzyhjii* 'he himself', *woomen tzyhjii* 'we ourselves', and so on, as in: 你应该问～你自己。 *Nii inggai wenn.wenn nii tzyhjii.* 'You ought to ask yourself.' In apposition with other substantives we have such forms as in: 总统自己就是总指 揮。*Tzoongtoong tzyhjii jiow sh tzoong-jyyhuei.* 'The President himself is the commander-in-chief.' 我没看見老王自己， 只看見了老王的太太。 *Woo mei kann.jiann Lao Wang tzyhjii, jyy kann.jiannle Lao Wang de tay.tay.* 'I didn't see Wang himself, I only saw Wang's wife.'

There are also the more colloquial form 自各儿 *tzyhgeel* and the much less frequent 自己各儿 *tzyhjiigeel*, which, except for greater informality of style, are otherwise interchangeable with

*tzyhjii.* For example: 那个貓自各儿追自各儿的尾巴.
*Neyg mhau tzyhgeel juei tzyhgeel de yii.ba.* 'That cat chases its
own tail.' This is to be distinguished from 各自 *gehtzyh* 'each
himself, yourself, etc.', which is semi-L in style, as in: 你们应
该各自去找出路去. *Niimen inggai gehtzyh chiuh jao
chuluh chiuh.* 'You ought to find a way out each for himself.'
Being an adverb, *gehtzyh* must precede a verb and cannot be the
object of a verb as the pronoun *tzyhjii* can, as in: 你们应该
给自己想个出路. *Niimen inggai geei tzyhjii sheangg chuluh.*
'You ought to find a way out for yourselves.'

The form 己身 *jiishen* 'own person', besides occurring as L-
form in the classics, is also used for 'ego' in describing kinship relations, as for instance in a genealogical table. The form 自我
*tzyhwoo* 'self-' is not free. It occurs in such compounds as 自我
檢討 *tzyhwoo-jeantao* 'self-examination' in recent political news.
Neither *jiishen* nor *tzyhwoo* is used in everyday speech.

Taken separately, 自 *tzyh* and 己 *jii* are L forms and occur
only in bound form in compounds, of which *tzyhjii* itself is an instance. In the literary language *tzyh* as object always precedes a
verb,    as    in 自滿 *tzyhmaan*    'satisfied    with    oneself'
L, 自命不凡 *tzyhming bufarn* 'calls oneself uncommon' L. On
the other hand, *jii* can occur either before or after a verb, as
in 己所不欲，勿施於人. *Jii suoo bu yuh, wuh shy yu ren.*[42]
'What one does not want oneself, do not apply to others.'
L. 知己知彼，百戰百勝. *Jy jii jy bii, bae jann bae shenq.*
'Know your own side and know the other side, and in a hundred
battles you will win a hundred victories.' The difference between
*tzyh* and *jii* corresponds therefore approximately to that between *se*
and *soi* in French. In modern compounds, the same order is followed as in the literary language. Because of its preposed position,
*tzyh* has also acquired an attributive function and is thus often
equivalent to the prefixes *auto-* and *sui-* in foreign words, as
in 自主 *tzyhjuu* 'autonomous', 自殺 *tzyhsha* 'suicide'. Compounds with *jii* are not as productive as with *tzyh*. Examples
are 克己 *kehjii*          'subdue-oneself,—disadvantageous          to
oneself,—reasonable    (in    referring    to    a    seller's    prices    for

---

[42]*The Analects* (顏淵), XII.2.

goods)', 知己 *jyjii* 'know-self,—(1) is intimately acquainted, or (2) an intimate friend'.

(3.2) Pronouns for 'Others'. In wenyan 人 *ren*, besides being an individual noun, is also a pronoun meaning 'other(s)' as an antonym of 己 *jii*, as in 己所不欲，勿施於人. *Jii suoo bu yuh, wuh shy yu ren.*, cited above. This use of *ren* is occasionally used in modern speech, as in: 騙人騙自己. *Piann ren piann tzyhjii.* 'In fooling others, one is fooling oneself.' 自己做錯了事，不应该怪人。 *Tzyhjii tzuoh-tsuohle shyh, bu inggai guay ren.* 'When one has done something wrong oneself, one should not blame it on someone else ( ~ others).'

The forms 人.家 *ren.jia* and the post-verbal .人.家 *.ren.jia* look like plurals of *ren* in the above sense, but are actually used in both the singular and the plural sense. For example: 人家的事情咱们用不着茪。 *Ren.jia de shyh.chyng tzarmen yonq.bujiau goan.* 'Others' affairs we needn't bother about.' 人家给了你东西，你得谢ﾟ人家。 *Ren.jia geeile nii dong.shi, nii deei shieh.shieh .ren.jia.* 'When others give you something, you must thank them.'

A special use of *ren* and *ren.jia* as 'other(s)' which usually means 'someone other than I' or 'those who are other than we', is in the sense of 'someone other than you' or 'those who are other than you', and thus gets to be only a rhetorical way of saying 'I'. For example: 别拱人! *Bye goong ren!* 'Don't crowd me!' implying 'Don't crowd someone other than yourself.' 你来的那么遲，叫人家等了这么半天! *Nii lai de nemm chyr, jiaw .ren.jia deengle tzemm banntian!* 'You have come so late, you have made me (someone else than you) wait for such a long time!'

This pronoun *ren.jia* is quite different from the noun 人家ﾟ *renjial* 'household', with no neutral tone and the normal, slightly greater stress on *-jial*. As a noun, it has its specific classifier, which in this case happens to be *jia* 家, so that 'a household' takes the form 一家人家ﾟ *i-jia renjial*. Similarly, 那家人家ﾟ *ney-jia renjial* 'that household, that family'.

Another noun to be distinguished from the pronoun *ren.jia*

'other(s)' is 人 *ren* in the extended sense of 'physical, psychological, or moral quality or condition of a person', as in: 只要他(的) 人好, 聰明不聰明没関係。 *Jyy yaw ta(de) ren hao, tsong-.ming bu tsong.ming mei guan.shih.* 'So long as his (moral) personality is good, it makes no difference whether he is clever or not.' 他苦燒苦的人都糊塗了。 *Ta fa-shau fa de ren dou hwu-.du le.* 'He had such a fever that his mind was quite confused.' In talking about a cat which tried to catch the goldfish from the bowl and fell off the table, I caught myself saying, before realizing the apparent paradox, 他自己人捽下来了。*Ta tzyhjii ren shuai-.shiahlai le.* 'It in person (i.e., bodily) fell off.'
The following was said by my wife about our sick cat: 他今天 人好点儿了。 *Ta jin.tian ren hao.deal le.* 'Today its condition is better.', where it is not so much a case of personification as a case of the noun *ren* used in the sense of 'state of health or sickness'. [Cf. (3.4) below.]

With the determinative 別 *bye-* 'other' are formed the pronouns 別.人 *bye.ren* and 別.人.家 *bye.ren.jia*, which are synonymous with *ren* and *ren.jia*, but with *bye* 'other' more explicitly expressed. The only syntactical difference between *bye.ren* and the other forms for 'other(s)' is that it can be modified by (*i*) *g*, as in: 我以為是你，原来是个別人！ *Woo yiiwei sh nii, yuanlai sh g bye.ren!* 'I thought it was you, why, it was someone else!' This is, however, not sufficient reason to treat *bye.ren* as a noun instead of a pronoun, since one can also say: 我以為 是別人，原来是个你！ *Woo yiiwei sh bye.ren, yuanlai sh g nii!* 'I thought it was someone else, why, it was you!' As we saw before, the scope of applicability of *g* is much wider than for other classifiers.

(3.3) Pronouns for 'Alone'. The pronoun 一个人 $ig_o ren$ 'alone' is to be distinguished from the D-M N phrase 一个人 *ig ren* 'a person'. The form $ig_o ren$ occurs usually in apposition to another substantive, as in: 那个厨子一个人能做一桌酒 席。 *Neyg chwutz ig.ren neng tzuoh i-juo jeoushyi.* 'That cook can single-handed cook a whole banquet.' That it is not an adverb, as English *alone* can be, but is a pronoun is seen in such an example as:　一个人等了半天 就走了。　*Ig.ren deengle banntian jiow tzooule.* 'He waited alone for a long time and then left.'

A variant form which is a Peiping localism is *ireel*. In Cantonese, in which the long rising "changed tone" (pitch 25: ⌐) corresponds in most cases to the retroflex suffix 儿 *-l* in Mandarin, the form 一 个 人 *iatkohyan°* corresponds very closely in structure and meaning to *ireel* 'alone', while the phrase *iatkoh yan*, with no changed tone, corresponds to *ig ren* 'a person'.

While $ig_0ren$ or *ireel* is normally limited to application to one person alone, it is occasionally applied to more than one, especially in children's language. For example:　爸 ㇏ 出去了，就是我跟 妈一人儿在家。　*Bah.bah chu.chiuhle, jiowsh woo gen Mha ireel tzay jia.* 'Papa has gone out, just I and Ma alone are home.' (Cf. Russian *my odni* 'we ones, —we alone.')

(3.4) Pronouns for 'Both'.—Quite similar to $ig_0ren$ and *ireel* are 两个.人 $leangg_0ren$ and　俩人儿 $lea_0rel$ 'both' or 'the two', as distinguished from 两个人 *leangg ren* 'two people'. For example:　海象跟木匠，他们俩人儿慢㇏儿的跑。*Haeshianq gen Muh.jianq, tam learel mannmhald' pao.* 'The Walrus and the Carpenter, the two were running slowly.'　有一回，北風跟太陽两个人在那儿争论谁的本事大。　*Yeou i-hwei, Beeifeng gen Tay.yang leangg.ren tzay.nall jengluenn sheirde been.shyh dah.* 'Once upon a time, the North Wind and the Sun, the two were arguing who was the stronger.'

In the Wu dialects the pronouns 千子 *i'götz* 'alone' and 两家头 *leanggad'eu* 'both' do not contain the morpheme 人 *gnen*, the *Wu* cognate for *ren*. Thus, if it may seem paradoxical to say in Mandarin:　一个貓跟一个狗，他们两个人老打的不停。*Ig mhau gen ig goou, tam leangg.ren lao daa de butyng.* 'A cat and dog, the two (people) keep fighting without stopping.', it does not sound at all incongruous when *leangkadeu*, lit. 'two-family-*suffix*' is used for 'both', or when *i'kötz* is used for 'one (animal) alone'.

(3.5) Pronouns for 'All', 'Every', and 'Each'.—The pronouns for 'all' are, in descending order of frequency, 大家 *dahjia*, 大伙儿 *dahhoel*, and 大ₒ家伙儿 $dah_0jiahoel$. The pronoun *dahjia* is to be distinguished from the adjective-measure compound *dah-jia* as in 一 大 家 人 家ㄦ *i-dah-jia renjial* 'a big family', where the first *jia* is the classifier for *renjial*. These pronouns have the meaning of 'all present' or all concerned'. As for 'all' in general, it is normally expressed by the adverb *dou* 'in all cases', which can also occur concurrently with *dahjia*, etc. Examples are: 大 家 的 事 情 应 该 大 家 做。 *Dahjia de shyh.chyng inggai dahjia tzuoh.* 'The affairs of all (of a group, a family, a nation, etc.) should be done by all.' 我们大家都这么想。 *Woo.men dahjia dou tzemm sheang.* 'We all think so.'

Other forms for 'all' are the reduplicates 人 ₹ *renren* 'every-man', 个 ₹ (ㄦ) *gehgeh(l)* 'everyone' and D-M compounds 每 个 *meeig* 'each one', 每 人 *meeiren* 'each person', 各 人 *gehren* 'the various persons', 各 个 *gehgeh* 'the various individuals (of persons or things)'. In the last two forms the determinative 各 *geh* ( < kâk) is homophonous with the individual classifier 个 *geh-* in Mandarin. Consequently, the two sound exactly like 个 人 *gehren* 'an individual' and 个 个 *gehgeh* 'everyone', respectively. The words 各 人 'the various persons' and 各 个 'the various individuals' are less frequently used than their corresponding homophones. That they have not quite gone out of use must be due partly to the fact that speakers of Cantonese and Wu dialects, who speak with an accent when speaking Mandarin, use an entering tone (with -*k* for Cantonese and /-ʔ/ or [V̆] in Wu) and thus keep the distinctions alive.

On *renren* and *gehgeh(l)* as distributive reduplicates, see also section 4.2.3 (3).

(3.6) Impersonal *nii*. The second-person pronoun 你 *nii* 'you' is often used in the sense of 'one' with the same colloquial and familiar effect of *you* in English. For example: 这 种 问 题 啊，你 得 想 好 久 才 想 得 出 办 法 来 呐。 *Jey-tzoong wenntyi a, nii deei sheang haojeou tsair sheang.de-chu bann.faa lai ne.* 'About this sort of problem you (i.e., one) will have to think a long while before you (one) can find a way out.' 那 些 小 孩 子 鬧 得 叫 你 不 能 吉 心 做 事. *Neyshie sheauhairtz naw de jiaw nii buneng juanshin tzuoh-shyh* 'Those children make such a noise, it makes you ( ~ me ~ one) unable to concentrate on your ( ~ my ~ one's) work'. [On the non-use of *niide shyh* correspond- ing to 'your work' in the translation, see section 7.11.4 (1.7) above.]

(4) Demonstrative Pronouns. Pronouns referring to near and far reference usually take the form of D-M compounds, such as 这 个 *jehg* 'this individual' and 那位 *ney-wey* 'that gentlemen ( ~ lady)'.

The forms 这 *jeh* 'this' and 那 *nah* 'that' without a com- pounded measure, and their variants, are pronouns in their own right, but their occurrence is circumscribed under rather special conditions which need detailed statement.

(4.1) *Jeh*, with long, open, and therefore back vowel (Row-a, col. 3, table 2b, sec. 1.3.3), occurs as subject, as in: 这也不要 紧。*Jeh yee buyawjiin.* 'This is not important, either.' 这把我难 住了。*Jeh bae woo nan.juhle.* 'This stumps me.' 这算是这 儿最高的房子了。    *Jeh suann sh jell tzuey gau de farngtz le.* 'This is regarded as the tallest building here.' 这我不大懂。 *Jeh woo budah doong.* 'This I do not understand very well.' It does not occur as object, there being no ° 我要这。 °*Woo yaw jeh.* for 'I want this.', nor in attributive position with *de*, there being no ° 这的价钱是三毛。   °*Jeh de jiah.chyan sh san-mau.* for 'The price of this is thirty cents.' Instead, the available form in the object position and attributive position with *de* is the D-M compound 这个 *jehg*, so that *yaw jehg* 'wants this' and *jehg de jiah.chyan* 'the price of this' are possible forms.

(4.2) *Jeh-*, with checked, and therefore centralized, vowel [ə] when followed closely by *.sh* or a monosyllabic adverb. Thus, be- sides the less commonly used *jeh* under (4.1) in  这是王先生。 *Jeh .sh Wang .Shian.sheng.*, with the back vowel, 'This is Mr. Wang', one more commonly says, with a shorter and more cen- tralized vowel [ə], *Jeh.sh Wang .Shian.sheng.* Similarly, in 这就 难说了。 *Jeh jiow nan shuo le.* 'This, then, is hard to say.', there is alternation between open juncture with back vowel and close juncture with central vowel, the former with slightly more em- phasis on the subject *jeh* '(as for) this' and the latter, occurring more frequently, with no special implications and with greater frequency of occurrence.

(4.3) *Jey* is etymologically *jeh* + *i* 'this one', but is no longer limited to the singular. As a pronoun, it is like (4.1) *jeh* and (4.2) *jeh-* in occurring only as subject, as in 这是我的三本书. *Jey sh woode sanbeen shu.* 'These are my three books.', and not as object or in attributive position with *de*, there being no ° 我 不信这. °*Woo bu shinn jey.* for 'I don't believe this.' or ° 这的 结果很难预料. °*Jey de jyeguoo heen nan yuhliaw*, for 'The result of this is very hard to predict.' As with *jeh*, the substitution of a D-M compound such as *jeyg* for *jey* would change the last two examples into possible sentences.

As a pronoun, however, the form *jey* occurs much less frequently than *jeh* or *jeh-*.

On *jeh* and *jey* as determinatives, see section 7.8 (1).

(4.4) *Nah*, with long, open low vowel, like *jeh* under (4.1), occurs similarly as subject, but not as object or in attribute position with *de*. Examples are: 可是那很怪. *Keesh nah heen guay.* 'But that is odd.' 那是谁的大氅? *Nah sh sheirde dahchaang?* 'Whose overcoat is that?' 那谁都買不起. *Nah sheir dou mae.bu-chii.* 'That nobody can afford to buy.' There is no ° 我喜欢那. °*Woo shii.huan nah.* for 'I like that.' or ° 你 知道不知道那的原因 ? °*Nii jydaw bujydaw nah de yuan'in?* 'Do you know the cause of that?' In each case the substitution of the D-M compound *nahg* would make the sentence possible.

*Nah* as first subject with an S-P predicate often has the force of 'as for that', as in 那我没办法了. *Nah woo mei bann.faa le.* 'As for that, I don't know what to do about it.' Although this *nah* can be translated as 'in that case', it is more like a conjunction than an adverb [cf. sec. 7.12 (1)], since it cannot follow a subject, as in 那我就不去了. *Nah woo jiow bu chiuh le.* 'In that case, I am not going.', for which one cannot say °*Woo nah jiow bu chiuh le.*

(4.5) *Neh-*, with central checked vowel, instead of the low vowel in *nah*, occurs rather less frequently than the corresponding *jeh-*. In other words, of the following symmetrically arranged forms:

    (a) *Jeh sh Wang .Shian.sheng* (with [ɤ])
    (b) *Jeh.sh Wang .Shian.sheng* (with [ə])
    (c) *Nah sh Wang .Shian.sheng* (with [ʌ])
    (d) *Neh.sh Wang .Shian.sheng* (with [ə])
the commonest forms are, asymmetrically, (b) and (c).

(4.6) *Ney*, in analogy with *jey*, is used instead of a theoretical *nah* + *i* > °*nay*, which does not occur. Like *jey*, the independent pronoun *ney* is used less frequently than the primary form *nah* or the D-M compound *neyg*. Thus, 那ⁱ是我的帽子。*Ney sh woode mawtz.* 'That is my hat.' is less common than either: *Nah sh woode mawtz.* or: *Neyg sh woode mawtz.* Like *jey*, *ney* is also applicable to a plurality of things, as in: 那ⁱ全是我的朋友。*Ney chyuansh woode perng.yeou.* 'Those are all my friends.'

(5) Interrogative Pronouns. The interrogative pronouns are 谁 *sheir* 'who', 什么 *sherme* 'what'[43] and their variants and derived and compounded forms. All interrogative pronouns, like other interrogative forms, can also be used (a) in the indefinite sense, usually unstressed, as in 找个谁来帮ⁱ你。 *Jao g ₀sheir .lai bang.bang nii.* 'Find someone to help you a little.', and (b) in the arbitrary sense, always stressed, preposed, and followed by 也 *yee* or 都 *dou*, as in 我谁也找不着. *Woo sheir yee jao.bu-jaur.* 'I can't find anybody.'

(5.1) *Sheir* 'who' has a more formal variant *shwei*. This pronoun occurs in all positions, as in: 我也不知道谁是谁，谁跟谁好，谁是谁的朋友。*Woo yee bujydaw sheir sh sheir, sheir gen sheir hao, sheir sh sheirde perng.yeou.* 'I don't know at all who is who, who is good to whom, or who is ( ∼ are) whose friend(s).' Although *sheir* can refer to either one or more persons, plural reference can be made explicit by ₀*shie-sheir*, which is, however, limited to positions after verbs. For ex-

---

[43]We are not including 哪 *naa* 'which?' as a pronoun, as it is always bound and does not even take *sh* 'is' enclitically as 这 *jeh* 'this' and 那 *nah* 'that' do. There are in Southern Mandarin forms like 哪会 ... ? *Naa huey ... ?* or 哪能 ... ? *Naa neng ... ?* 'How can ... ?', and 哪有 [... ?] *Naa yeou ... ?* 'How can there be ... ?' in rhetorical questions. But in Northern speech it is *Naal huey ... ? Naal neng ... ? Naal yeou ... ?* etc., implying 'Where, pray, can ... ?', where *naal* is a place word.

ample: 叫些谁来帮忙呐？ *Jiaw ₀shie sheir lai bang-mang ne?* 'Whom (pl.) should one call for help?' 昨儿晚上的客人都有些谁？ *Tzuol woan.shanq de keh.ren dou yeou ₀shie sheir?* 'Who were all those guests last night?'

Like interrogatives of other parts of speech, *sheir*, always stressed, usually followed by *dou* or *yee* before a verb, can refer to 'any or every member of a class', as in: 谁都来了。*Sheir dou lai le.* 'Everyone has come.' 谁也不注意。*Sheir yee bu juhyih.* 'Nobody pays any attention to it.' 他谁的话都不信。*Ta sheirde huah dou bu shinn.* 'He doesn't believe anyone's words.' Since reference to a whole class implies definite reference, the word *sheir* must be in an earlier part of the sentence. Thus, if the last example was changed to *Ta bu shinn sheir de huah*, the *sheir* would be the ordinary interrogative 'who' and the sentence would mean 'Whose words does he not believe?', which can be either a rhetorical or a bona fide question. It is, however, possible to find *sheir* as object to a verb, provided that another verb, the main verb of the sentence, follows. For example: 你求谁也没用。*Nii chyou sheir yee meiyonq.* 'No matter whom you ask, it will be useless.' It can also occur in a compressed sentence (sec. 2.12.10), such as: 他问了谁都不知道。*Ta wennle sheir dou bujydaw.* 'No matter whom he asked, they didn't know.'

Like interrogatives of other parts of speech, *sheir*, when unstressed or in neutral tone, can be taken in an indefinite sense. It is then an indefinite personal pronoun for 'someone' or 'some (pl.)'. Examples are: 咱们走错了路了，得问₂谁才行。*Tzarmen tzoou-tsuohle luh le, deei wenn.wenn .sheir tsair shyng.* 'We have taken the wrong road, we'll have to ask somebody.' 这枝原子笔不是我的，一定是谁遗得这儿的。*Jey-jy yuantzyybii bush woode, idinq sh sheir lah de jell de.* 'This ball-point pen is not mine, it must have been left here by someone.' 他戴错了谁的帽子了。*Ta day-tsuohle sheirde mawtz le.* 'He has worn someone else's hat by mistake.', which could be a question if *sheir* received contrasting stress, in which case it would mean 'Whose hat has he worn by mistake?' As an indefinite personal pronoun, *sheir* does not occur at the beginning of a sentence. At least a word such as *sh* or *yeou* must precede it, as in: 有谁来看你来着。 *Yeou sheir lai kann nii laij.* 'There was someone who came to see you.' Here again, a contrastive stress on *sheir* would change the statement into a question: 'Who was it who·came to see you?'

In many dialects, 'who' takes the form of the D-M compound 哪个 *naag* 'which one' or its equivalent, such as 边个 *pin⁰koh* in Cantonese, where the interrogative determinative *pin⁰* is equivalent to *naa*. Some dialects use 什么人 *sherm-ren* 'what person' or its equivalent, such as 啥人 *shahgnen* in Soochow.

(5.2) *Sherme* is the interrogative pronoun for things. This is written with a variety of characters and pronounced in a variety of ways with little difference in function, except as noted below. The commonest form of characters in older books appears as 甚麼, with simplified variants of 麼 as 庅 or 么 (the latter being also a homograph of 么 *iau* 'number one' or 'number last', as in 老么 *lao'iau* 'youngest among siblings'). The form 甚 *shern* (homograph of 甚 *shenn* 'very' L) is rare and occurs only in the obsolescent phrase 姓甚名谁 *shinq shern ming shwei* 'surnamed what and named who'. More and more favored are the graphs with fewer strokes: 什麼, 什庅, 什么, or 什末, but rarely 甚末, for *sherme*, where 什 is also a homograph for 什 *shyr* 'ten', 'miscellaneous' B.

In pronunciation, the first vowel in *sherme* is the checked vowel [ə] and thus makes the following *m* part of the syllable. However, the second (neutral-tone) vowel does not drop in pitch, as it would if it formed a separate neutral-tone syllable. For this among other reasons, Hockett (Peip Phon, 255) uses the term "microsegment" for that which carries one tone, so that *sherme*, having one 2nd Tone, is a microsegment but may still be called two syllables, if the term "syllable" is used at all, but in all other cases a microsegment is the same as a syllable. The special nature of *sherme* is seen in the minimally contrasting sentences:

(a) 那是神吗？ *Nah sh shern ma?*   'Is that a god?'
(b) 那是蛇吗？ *Nah sh sher ma?*   'Is that a snake?'
(c) 那是什么？ *Nah sh sherme?*   'What is that?'
(d) 那是□么？ *Nah sh sher.me?!*   'Whatever *is* that?!'

In these four different sentences, first note that the interrogative particle 嗎, which we conventionally spell as *ma*, has its vowel neutralized into the midvowel [ə], so that *ma* is homophonous with *me*. Sentence (a), since a final *n* normally assimilates to a following *m*, so that *shern .ma* is actually pronounced *sherm .me*, differs from sentence (c) only in having a geminated *m* and a (usually) lower pitched *ma*; i.e., the last two syllables in (a) are 𝄐𝄐 , while those in (c) are 𝄐 ˈ  or simply 𝄐 as one "microsegment". Sentences (b) and (d) are completely homophonous, except that (d) is usually reinforced by a particle 呀 *ia*. In both cases, *sher* being an open syllable, it has the long back vowel [ ɤ ]. In both (b) and (d), the last two syllables have the tonal pattern of 𝄐𝄐 . The word for 'what' in (d) is not of very common use, as it occurs only in questions in which disapproval or disgust is expressed. (Cf. sec. 1.3.9.)

*Sherme* occurs freely as subject or object or as attribute. Examples are: 兌, 你 听! 什 么 响 ? *É, nii ting! Sherm sheang?* 'Say, listen! What is sounding?' 你 在 那儿 想 什 么 ? *Nii tzaynall sheang sherme?* 'What are you thinking?' [On *sherm* vs. *sherme* see sec. 4.4.7.(1).] In attributive position, it makes a difference whether *sherme* is followed by *de*. Directly modifying a nominal expression, *sherme* means 'what kind of', 'of what nature', etc., as in 什 么 书? *sherm shu?* 'what book?' 什 么 事? *sherm shyh?* 'what event, business, etc.?' 什 么 东 西 ? *sherm dong.shi?* 'what thing?' 什 么 地 方(儿) ? *sherm dih.fang(l)?* 'what place,—where?' 什 么 时 候(儿) ? *sherm ₀shyr.how(l)?* 'what time,—when?' 什 么 人 ? *sherm ren?* 'what person,—who?' On the other hand, *sherme de* is used only in the partitive sense of 'of what?', 'belonging to what?', as in: 像 个 头 啊 ? 像 个 什 么 的 头 ? *Shianq g tour a? Shianq g sherm de tour?* 'Like a head? Like the head of what?' 什么的 速 度 比 光 的 速 度 还 快 ? *Sherm de suhduh bii guang de suhduh hair kuay?* 'The speed of what is faster than the speed of light?' This interrogative and therefore stressed *sherm de?* 'of what?' is to be distinguished from the neutral-tone *.shermde*, which is semantically close to '(and) what not' but stylistically nearer to 'and so forth' or 'and things', as in: 我 们 没 事儿 幹 的 时 候儿, 常 去 散ₒ 步 , 打ₒ球,

浮儿水什么的。 *Woomen mei shell gann de .shyr.howl, charng chiuh san.san-buh, daa.daa chyou, fuh.fuh shoei .shermde.* 'When we have nothing to do, we often go for a hike, play ball, have a swim, and so forth.' 纸啊，笔啊，墨水儿啊，笔记本儿啊，什么的，我都買了. *Jyy a, bii a, mohshoel a, biijihbeel a, .shermde, woo dou maele.* 'Paper, and pens, and ink, and note-books, and things—I've bought everything.' This sentence, in which *.shermde* is part of the long subject, to which *woo dou maele* is an S-P clause predicate, is of a quite different structure from the nearly synonymous sentence 纸啊，... 笔记本儿啊，我什么都買了。 *Jyy a, ... biijihbeel a, woo "sherm dou maele.* 'Paper, ... and notebooks, I've bought everything', where *sherme* (without *de*) is stressed and is used in the sense of 'any and every-thing' (cf. below). The unstressed 'and so forth' *sherme* can also occur in an inverted order, that is, preceding the enumerated items, in which case it can be translated as 'such things as' or 'things like'. For example: 北風说：世界上的 东西没有不怕我的。什么貓啊，狗啊，花呀，草啊，他们一见了我就嚇的不得了。 *Beeifeng shuo: Shyh.jieh.shanq de donq.shi meiyeou bu pah woo de. .Sherm maw a, goou a, hua ia, tsao a, tamen i jiannle woo jiow shiah de buderleau le.* 'The North Wind said: There is not a thing in the world that is not afraid of me. Things like cats and dogs, flowers and grasses, the moment they see me, they are frightened no end.' 什么声，光，化，電，我一樣儿都不懂。 *.Sherm sheng, guang, huah, diann, woo iyanql dou bu doong.* 'Such things as acoustics, optics, chem-istry, electricity, I don't understand any of them.'

*Sherme,* with full stress and tone, is used rhetorically in retort to some word or phrase one heards and disapproves of, as in: 什么'声 光化電'？ 我不懂你说的什么？ *Sherm "sheng, guang, huah, diann"? Woo bu doong nii shuo de sherme?* 'What do you mean, "acoustics, optics, chemistry, electricity"? I don't understand what you are talking about.' If there is no good news and someone says 好消息. *Hao shiau.shi.* 'Good news.', someone else may say 什么好消息？ *Sherm hao shiau.shi?* 'What good news?' This may be a bona fide question or, with contrasting stress on *sherme,* a rhetorical question: '(Pray) what good news?!'

If a visitor who has heard about the famous California sunshine happens to arrive on a foggy day, he may ask 什么 加州的 太陽 啊？ *Sherm Jia Jou de tay.yang a?!* 'What California sun?' However, the attributive position of 'what' in the English translation of the last two examples is deceptive, since this rhetorical use of (stressed) *sherme* is not limited to the attributive position, but can occur before any expression the use of which is disapproved by the hearer. For example, if someone says 睡覚了！*Shuey-jiaw le!* 'It's time to go to bed!', someone else might retort 什么睡覚了?! 晚饭还没吃吶. *Sherm shuey-jiaw le?! Woanfann hair mei chy ne.* 'What do you mean, go to bed?! We haven't had our supper yet.' This form again is to be distinguished from the somewhat weaker form when *sherme* is followed by 叫 *jiaw* 'call, is called'. Thus, while 什么好消息？ *Sherm hao shiau.shi?!* is to be translated as 'What do you mean, good news?!', *Sherm jiaw hao shiau.shi?* is more like 'What do you mean by good news?', which can also be a rhetorical question, but in a less peremptory tone than without *jiaw* or 'by'.

A still less stressed and peremptory attributive *sherme*, somewhat like the *sherme* before enumerations, but occurring with only one item, may be translated as 'so-called', as in 说什么山珍海味哪儿有 这么樣儿香？ *Shuo .sherm shanjen-haewey naal yeou tzemmyanql shiang?* 'What mountain rarities and sea delicacies are as delicious as that?' and in 认为什么 " 指示形容词 " *rennwei .sherm "jyyshyh shyngrongtsyr"* 'to regard as so-called "demonstrative adjectives" '.[44]

The form 麻 *ma* 'what?' occurs only in the V-O compound 干麻 *gannma?* 'do what?' as in 你 干麻 吶？ *Nii gannma ne?* 'What are you doing?' From 'do what?' comes also the extended meaning 'in order to do what?', 'what for?', or 'why?', as in 你 干麻老哭？ *Nii gannma lao ku?* 'Why do you keep crying?' 他 干麻不等我 就走了？ *Ta gannma bu deeng woo jiow tzoou.le?* 'Why did he leave without waiting for me?' In some dialects, for example, in Tientsin, 麻 *ma* is simply a shorter form for *sherme* and can occur in all positions where *sherme* can. But

---

[44]Wang Lih, *Liiluenn*, I, 27 (neutral tone mine).

in Peiping, *gannma* is the only context in which *ma* occurs, and is not even ionizable. Thus, there is no °*gannj ma?* or °*gannle ma?* or °*gann.guoh ma?* When an aspect suffix is involved, the full form *sherme* is used instead of *ma*, as in  他幹过些什么？ *Ta gann.guoh .shie sherme?* 'What things has he done before?'

Like *sheir* 'who' and other interrogatives, *sherme* can be used in the indefinite sense. When unstressed, .*sherme* means 'something', and when stressed, usually followed by *dou* or *yee* 'in all cases', before a verb, means 'anything' or, in attributive positions, 'any'. For example  我想吃点儿什么。吃点儿什么呐？我什么都吃。*Woo sheang chy .deal .sherme. Chy .deal sherm ne? Woo sherm dou chy.* 'I want to eat a little something. What do you want to eat? I'll eat anything.' Just as unstressed .*sherme* can mean 'something', so can unstressed .*shermde* mean (the colloquial) 'and things', usually following a list of items ending with the particle 咧 *le* (sec. 8.5.5.P3), as in 桌子椅子咧什么的 *juotz yiitz le .shermde* 'tables, chairs, and things'.

The formula  有什么 A? *Yeou sherm* A?, where A is an adjective, is a pivotal construction meaning 'What is there that is A?' For example  那有什么希奇？ *Nah yeou sherm shichyi?* 'What is there that's unusual about that?' This being a rhetorical question, the expected answer in the negative is 那没(有)什么希奇. *Nah mei(yeou) .sherm shichyi.* 'There is nothing unusual in that.' Note, however, that the simple predicate *mei .sherme* 'there isn't anything' is always taken in the favorable sense of 'nothing is the matter with ...', as in  这个画儿倒还没什么。 *Jeyg huall daw hair mei .sherme.* 'This painting is rather there-is-nothing-wrong-with-it,—rather good.'

## 7.12. Other Substitutes

Most substitutes other than pronouns are derived from the determinatives or demonstratives 这 *jeh* 'this', 那 *nah* 'that' (and their variants), the interrogative/indefinite pronoun 什么 *sherme* 'what' and the interrogative/indefinite adverb 怎么 *tzeeme* 'how'.

(1) Pro-adverbs. The pro-adverbs 这 么 *tzemme* ~ (the more formal) *jemme* 'so, thus', 那 么 *nemme* ~ (the much rarer) *nahme* 'so, thus', 哪 么 *neeme* (there being no °*naame*) 'how', and 怎 么 *tzeeme* 'how' do not apply equally to manner and degree, nor occur with comparable frequencies. While 这 么 *tzemme* 'in this manner, to this degree (as in "this big")' and 那 么 *nemme* 'in that manner, to that degree (as in "that big")' differ as to near and distant reference, they apply equally to manner and degree. The interrogative 哪 么 *neeme* 'how' is rare and used more in Tientsin than in Peiping, where, if used at all, it is usually associated with two alternatives, as in      这 么 做 你 也 不 要 , 那 么 做 你 也 不 要 ,  你 要 哪么做 呐 ? *Tzemm tzuoh nii yee buyaw, nemm tzuoh nii yee bu yaw, nii yaw neem tzuoh ne?* 'You don't want it done this way, and you don't want it done that way; how do you want it done, then?' 哪 么 *neeme* is never used as an adverb of degree, for which 多 *duo* ~ *dwo* (with optional *-me*) is used, as in 多 么 大 *dwom dah* 'how big'. The usual interrogative/indefinite adverb of manner is 怎 么 *tzeeme* 'how', which would be the usual word to use instead of the less common 哪 么 *neeme* in the third clause in the preceding example.

The low-vowel form of the distant demonstrative 那 *nah* rarely occurs in adverbial form except in starting a sentence with *nahme* or *nah* 'in that case', which is often followed by a pause or a pause particle, thus making it a free conjunction rather than an attributive adverb. In fact, since the *me* in *nahme* is often prolonged, it is rather the particle of hesitation *me* than the adverbial suffix *-me*, which is not only short but sometimes even loses its vowel. One can in fact say either 那 嚜 *nah me—* 'in that case—uh—' or 那 呀 *nah ia—* 'in that case—uh—'. The low-vowel form of the interrogative *naa* occurs as short for *naal* 'where (pray), whence (pray)' in rhetorical questions, as in 他 哪 ( 儿 ) 会 信 你 的 话 呀 ? *Ta naa(l) huey shinn niide huah ia?* 'How would he believe in your words?!'

To the preceding *-me* forms an optional 樣 ( 儿 ) ~ ( 子 ) *-ₒyanq(l)* ~ *(tz)* may be added or substituted with no differences in function or meaning except that the longer forms sound a little more explicit and that the forms without -me or -l are slightly more formal. Thus, besides the plain 那么做 nemm tzuoh and the slightly more formal 那樣(子)做 nahyanq(tz) tzuoh 'does it that way', there are the nearly equivalent forms *nemmyanq tzuoh, nemmyanql tzuoh, nemmyanqtz tzuoh*. Those forms with 樣 yanq, however, do not modify adjectives as often as they do action verbs. For example, 这么大 tzemm dah can only mean 'this big', but 这么樣儿好 *tzemmyanql hao*, although it could be understood as 'so good', is more likely to be heard as an S-P construction: 'this way is good,—this is better'.

There is a reading pronunciation of 怎 as *tzeen*, and in pre-1900 novels one often reads 你便怎樣? which will usually be pronounced as *Nii biann tzeenyanq?* 'What will you do, then?' for which the modern equivalent would be 你就怎么(樣)呐? *Nii jiow tzeem(yanq) ne?* Actually, *tzeen* is simply a modernized reading of *tzeem*, since the older final -m has become modern -n except in the relic form 怎么 *tzeeme*. (Cf. Cantonese 怎 *timx* 'how'.)

(2) Pro-adjectives. There are no words which are primarily substitutes for adjectives. The most common substitutes for adjectives are the demonstratives 那个, usually in the form of *nahg* rather than *neyg*, and the less frequently used 这个 *jehg* or *jeyg*. 那个 *nahg* is used only predicatively, as in 这位先生很有点儿那个. *Jey-wey shian.sheng heen yeoudeal nahg.* 'This gentleman is quite that way.' (to avoid using an uncomplimentary adjective). If an adjective has been used in a near context, *nahg, nahyanq*, and so on can also be used as its substitute, as in 他弟々很奸诈，可是他自己一点儿不那个～那樣。*Ta dih.dih heen jianjah, keesh ta tzyhjii ideal bu nahg ~ nahyanq.* 'His younger brother is very crafty, but he himself is not that way at all.' As a pro-adjective, 那个 *nahg* does not occur in attributive position, as it is too easily heard as a demonstrative adjective in its own right, 那个人 *nahg ren* or *neyg ren* would simply mean 'that man' instead of 'that sort of man'. The pro-adverbs 这么 *tzemme*, etc., can be used attribu-

tively before a nominal expression, usually with the addition of *de*, as in 这么样儿的一个人 *tzemmyanql de ig ren* 'such a man', 完全不是那么一回事儿. *Wanchyuan bush nemm i-hwei shell.* 'It wasn't that sort of an affair at all,—that wasn't it at all.'

(3) Pro-verbs. Next to pronouns, the most frequently occurring substitutes are pro-verbs. The most general pro-verb is 耒 *lai*, as in 你画的不像，等我耒！ *Nii huah de bu shianq, deeng woo lai!* 'The thing (or portrait) you draw is not like it, let me do it!' In this example, the use of *lai* could be explained as being abbreviated from 耒画 *lai huah* '(let me) come and draw it'. But the use of *lai* is so generalized that it can be used to substitute for any verb, even with a direct object after it, as in 耒牌 *lai pair* as a substitute for 打牌 *daa pair* or 玩儿牌 *wal pair* 'play mahjong'. In 他不会，不能让他耒. *Ta bu huey, buneng ranq ta lai.* 'He doesn't know how, you can't let him do it.', *lai* is a pro-verb for 'do it', as it makes no sense to regard it as 'come' here.

The verbs 弄 *nonq* (*lonq* is L; *nenq* and *now* are more colloquial than *nonq*), 搞 *gao* (very recent borrowing from dial. pron. of 搅 *jeau* 'stir, churn'), and the still dialectal verb 整 *jeeng* (e.g., *ceg* in Cantonese, *tzeen* ∨ in Changsha) all have the meaning of 'do with' or the colloquial 'fix', often followed by a resultative complement, as in 弄好了 *nonq-haole* 'done well, set it right', 弄错了 *nonq-tsuohle* 'got it wrong, made a mistake about it', 搞不通 *gao.bu-tong* 'can't do it so as to get through' (said by a plumber working on a stopped-up drain or by a fellow-traveler trying to become acceptably indoctrinated). These words should, however, be regarded as ordinary verbs with a very general range of meanings rather than pro-verbs, since they do not usually substitute for some other verb, as 耒 *lai* or English 'do' does.

The commonest type of pro-verbs, however, are of the same form as most of the pro-adverbs, namely, 这么 *tzemme* 'do this', 那么 *nemme* 'do that', 怎么 *tzeeme* 'do what?' and their variants formed with -*yanq(l)* ~ (*tz*). As verbs, they can be preceded by auxiliary verbs or followed by aspect suffixes or even objects,

as 别那么呀！ *Bye nemme ia!* 'Don't do that!' 你得这么
着才行。 *Nii deei tzemmj tsair shyng.* 'You must do this before
it will do.' 他要怎么你就怎么你。 *Ta yaw tzeem nii jiow
tzeem nii.* 'He does what he pleases with you.'

Because 那个 *nahg* 'do that' is already a pro-verb, it is not
necessary to say 做那个 *tzuoh nahg* for 'do that'. In fact, the
expression *tzuoh nahg* and especially 干那个 *gann nahg* 'do
that' is often used as a euphemism or circumlocution for some
unmentioned or unmentionable verb, and, as the indirection of
such expressions wears out in time, their value deteriorates, so
that in present usage the only safe way to say 'do that' is to use
the pro-verb 那么 *nemme* and its variants.

The interrogative pronoun 什么 *sherme* 'what?' is not used as
a pro-verb. In a sentence like 你要我什么他？ *Nii yaw woo
sherm ta?* 'You want me to what him?' it is not a case of a pro-
verb, but a quasi-quoted word to be filled like a blank. The
blank happens to be in the position of the main verb in this case,
but it could occur anywhere. For example, if one fails to catch
the last word, which is an adjective, in the sentence 这消息
不很确实。 *Jeh shiau.shi bu heen chiuehshyr.* 'This news is not
very authentic.', one would ask 不很什么？ *Bu heen sherme?*
if the questioner wanted the exact word repeated. On the other
hand, if he wants the contents clarified, though he may have
heard the word he would ask 不很怎么？ *Bu heen tzeeme?*
The difference involved here will come out if one tries to translate into Chinese the uses of 'what' in the following dialogue:

"'Doesn't your wife's hiding the gun worry you?' he asked.
'No,' I said.
'It would me,' he confessed.
'It would *what* you?' I demanded.
It seemed to disturb him. '*What* would what me?' he asked
cautiously."[45]

---

[45]James Thurber, "The Psychosemanticist Will See You Now, Mr.
Thurber", *The New Yorker*, May 28, 1955, quoted in *Science* 123:3200.707
(April 27, 1956).

Here the first sentence with 'what' will come out as 那个会怎么你？ *Neyg huey tzeem nii?* and the other sentence will be 什么会怎么我？ *Sherm huey tzeeme woo?* But if the speakers were concerned, which they did not seem to be, with filling the blanks for words, then 'what' would come out as *sherme* in all three instances.

(4) Pro-sentences. Pro-sentences take the form of interjections, serving as a repetition of the utterance without repeating the actual words. In a command, it usually takes the form of 啊！ ah! spoken after the sentence and a pause, as in 别动, 啊！ *Bye donq, ah!* 'Don't move, don't!' This is different from and stronger than the same command ending with the particle 啊 *a*, as in 别动啊！ *Bye donq a!* 'Don't move!' The difference comes out more clearly when the last syllable in the command ends in an open vowel, which would need the particle 呀 *ia* to break the hiatus, whereas the interjection as pro-sentence will still be 啊 *a*, since it is preceded by a pause. Thus, we have 别怕呀！ *Bye pah ia!* 'Don't be afraid!' but 别怕, 啊！ *Bye pah, ah!* 'Don't be afraid, don't!'

After an interrogative sentence, the pro-sentence is 嘎? *ar?* with varient vocality and even nasalized vowels such as [ ɔ̃ ]. For example, 你去不去, 嘎? *Nii chiuh bu chiuh, ar?* 'Are you going? are you?' Here, again, a particle 啊 *a*, which will not have the rising tone, will be weaker than the pro-sentence, as in 你去不去啊? *Nii chiuh bu chiuh a?* 'Are you going?'

After a statement a pro-sentence will take the form of the interrogative interjection 嘎? *ar?* or the 'n'est-ce pas' type of phrase 是不是? *sh bush?* For example, 今天天气很好, 嘎? *Jin.tian tian.chih heen hao, ar?* 'Today's weather is very fine, isn't it?' 你不打算来, 是不是? *Nii bu daa.suann lai, sh bush?* 'You are not planning to come, are you?'

# 8.1 Verbs (Including Adjectives)

*8.1.1. Classification of Verbs.* We are using the term 'verb' in the wide sense of any word which can be modified by the negative 不 *bu* 'not' or 没 *mei* 'have not or did not'[1] and which can serve as the predicate or the center of a predicative expression. Verbs in this wide sense will then by synonymous with predicatives, which will then include verbs in a narrow sense as well as adjectives, since Chinese adjectives can function as predicates or centers of predicates.[2]

We shall set up the large division of transitive and intransitive verbs, not so much according as they do or do not have objects, as by the kinds of objects they have. Intransitive verbs take only cognate objects, (e) and (f) in table 18, and objects which could be reversed as "inverted subjects" [as in 下 雨 *shiah-yeu* 'drops rain': 雨 下 了 *yeu shiah le* 'rain drops' (sec. 5.4.7.2)]. Transitive verbs, on the other hand, can take any object, even when it does not make sense, as 姓 貓 *shinq Mhau* 'to be (sur)named Cat', 買 一 个 夢 *mae ig menq* 'buy a dream', it is still grammatical.

In the following classification of verbs according to the profile of environments in which they can occur, we shall set up: 1. intransitive action verbs (Vi), 2. intransitive quality verbs, or ad-

---

[1]Except that *mei* as an abbreviated form of the main verb 没 有 *mei-*₀*yeou* 'does not have' is not further modified by *bu* or *mei*.

[2]The currently common Chinese term for 'predicative' is 谓词 *weytsyr*, that for 'verb' is 动词 *donqtsyr*, and that for 'adjective' is 形容词 *shyngrongtsyr*, while that for 'predicate', which may be a word or a longer expression, is 谓语 *weyyeu*. Etymologically, 'verb' and 'predicate' would of course have equal claim to be translated as 谓 *wey* 'speak of' B.

jectives (A), 3. status verbs (Vst), 4. transitive action verbs (Vt), 5. transitive quality verbs ($V_A$), 6. classificatory verbs (Vc), 7. the verb 是 *sh*, 8. the verb 有 *yeou*, and 9. auxiliary verbs (Vx).

These may or may not be preceded by (a) 不 *bu* 'not'; (b) 没 *mei* 'have not or did not'; (c) 很 *heen* 'very' and other adverbs of degree such as 更 *genq* 'more, -er', 太 *tay* 'too (much)', 多 *duo* ~ *dwo* 'how (to what degree)', 最 *tzuey* 'most, -est'; and (d) 别 *bye* 'don't' and other auxiliary verbs such as 肯 *keen* 'to be willing to', 敢 *gaan* 'dare'; or they may be followed by (e) 三 年 *san-nian* 'three years', 兩 磅 *leang-banq* '2 lbs.', and other cognate objects of extent or degree; (f) 一 回 *i-hwei* 'once', 几 次 *jii-tsyh* 'several times', and other cognate objects of number of times; (g) a reduplicate, as in 走 ﹖ *tzoou.tzoou* 'walk a little, just walk', 说 ﹖ *shuo.shuo* 'just say a word', and other tentative aspect reduplicates; (h) 着 -*j* progressive aspect suffix '-ing'; (i) the indefinite past aspect suffix 过 -.*guoh* 'have ever ... -ed or did once before'; (j) the perfective suffix 了 -*le* '-ed, have ... -ed'; and they may or may not occur in (k) the simple command form, as in 来! *Lai!* 'Come!' or (l) in the V-not-V form of a question, as in 来 不 来? *Lai bu lai?* 'Are you coming?' These do not by any means exhaust the manifold formal properties of various types of verbs, but they will serve in combination to differentiate them by their different profiles, as shown in table 18.

*8.1.1.1. Secondary Features of Classification.* The features marked in the table with ( ) are secondary in the sense that they are present (✓) or absent (∗) under limited conditions, as noted below. The lettered paragraphs refer to the column headings in the table.

(a) The general negative adverb 不 *bu* 'not', being the defining feature of all verbs, should be marked " ✓ " for all cases. The only verb which does not normally take *bu* is 有 *yeou* 'have'. When, however, a 'not'-V-O construction is analyzed as 'not' + V-O, especially in a conditional clause, then *bu* instead of 没 *mei* can be used, as in    不 有 一 个 可 靠 的 人 幫 忙 ，
不 会 成 功 的. *Bu yeou ig keekaw de ren bang-mang, idinq bu-huey chernggong de.* 'Without having a dependable man to help,

TABLE 18

Classification of Verbs

| | (a) 不 | (b) 沒 | (c) 很 | (d) 別 | (e) 三尺 | (f) 一回 | (g) 起~ | (h) 着 | (i) 过 | (j) 了 | (k) 来！未来？ | (l) 未末？ |
|---|---|---|---|---|---|---|---|---|---|---|---|---|
| **Intransitive:** | | | | | | | | | | | | |
| 1. Action (Vi) 走 | ✓ | ✓ | * | ✓ | (✓)e | ✓ | ✓ | ✓ | ✓ | ✓ | ✓ | ✓ |
| 2. Quality (A) 大 | ✓ | (✓)b | ✓ | * | ✓ | * | * | (✓)h | (✓)i | (✓)j | (*)k | ✓ |
| 3. Status (Vst) 病 | ✓ | (✓)b | ✓ | (✓)d | (✓)e | ✓ | * | ✓ | ✓ | (✓)j | * | ✓ |
| **Transitive:** | | | | | | | | | | | | |
| 4. Action (Vt) 吃饭 | ✓ | ✓ | * | ✓ | ✓ | ✓ | (✓)g | ✓ | ✓ | ✓ | ✓ | ✓ |
| 5. Quality (V_A) 爱财 | ✓ | (✓)b | ✓ | ✓ | ✓ | ✓ | * | (*)h | ✓ | ✓ | * | ✓ |
| 6. Classificatory (Vc) 姓李 | ✓ | ✓ | * | (*)d | * | * | * | * | (✓)i | (✓)j | * | ✓ |
| 7. **sh** 是人 | ✓ | * | (✓)c | * | * | * | * | * | (✓)i | * | * | ✓ |
| 8. **yeou** 有书 | ✓ | (✓)b | ✓ | * | * | (✓)f | * | (✓)h | ✓ | ✓ | * | (*)l |
| 9. Auxiliary (Vx) 会飞 | (*)a | ✓ | ✓ | (*)d | * | * | * | * | (✓)i | * | (*)k | ✓ |

you will certainly not succeed.', although even here, most speakers and writers will still use *mei* instead of *bu*.

(b) The form 没 *mei* has two functions. One is the negative of the main verb 有 *yeou* 'has', to be discussed later (sec. 8.1.9). The other, always with neutral tone *mei.yeou*, is the auxiliary verb for 'have not ... -ed, did not ... ', and *mei* V is the negative of V-*j*, V.*guoh*, and V -*le*, as in: 别 老 站 着! *Bye lao jannj!* 'Don't be standing (there) all the time!' 我 没 老 站 着。*Woo mei lao jannj.* 'I am not standing all the time.' 你 到 过 中 國 没 有? *Nii daw.guoh Jong.gwo meiyeou?* 'Have you been to China?' 我 没 到 过。*Woo mei daw.guoh.* 'I have not been ('there).' 他 走 了 没 有? *Ta tzooule meiyeou?* 'Has he left?' 他 没 走。*Ta mei tzoou.* 'He has not.' (Note that when a form in -*le* is negated by *mei*, -*le* is usually not retained, as -*j* and -.*guoh* usually are.)

The occurrence of *mei* before 2. adjectives and 3. status verbs is limited to denial of -*le* forms, as in 小 了 三 寸 *sheaule san-tsuenn* 'have become or been made (too) small by 3 inches': 没 小 三 寸 *mei sheau san-tsuenn* 'have not become or been made (too) small by 3 inches'. Before 9. auxiliary verbs, *bu* is usually preferred to *mei* when 'have not ... -ed or did not ... ' is meant, as in 他 不 打 算 来,也 不 能 夠 来。*Ta bu daa.suann lai, yee bu nenggow lai.* 'He didn't (~ doesn't) plan to come, nor could (~ can) come.', but when one speaks with particular precision, one also says 他 没 打 算 来,也 没 能 夠 来。*Ta mei daa.suann lai, yee mei nenggow lai.* 'He didn't plan to come, nor was he able to come.'

(c) The adverbs of degree, 很 *heen* 'very', 最 *tzuey* 'most, -est', etc., modify 是 *sh* only in very restricted cases, as in 最 是 有 用 *tzuey sh yeouyonq* 'to be most certainly useful', as contrasted with 最 有 用 *tzuey yeouyonq* 'to be most useful', 很 是 一 个 问题 *heen sh ig weentyi* 'to be very much of a problem'.[3]

---

[3] 饶 继 庭 (Rau Jihtyng), in his " 很 " + 動 词 结 构 ("*Heen* + Verbal Constructions), *ZGYW*, no. 107:15-17 (1961), notes that a transitive verb with a quantified object can be modified by *heen*, even though the verb as such cannot, as in 很 写 过 几 篇 文章 *heen shiee.guoh jii-pian wen.jang*

(d) Auxiliary verbs go only in restricted cases with 3. status verbs (Vst), as in 会病 *huey binq* 'can get sick'. They occur in restricted cases with 6. classificatory verbs, as in 老八，你要姓什么都行，就是别姓王！ *Lao Ba, nii yaw shinq sherm dou shyng, jiowsh bye shinq Wang!* 'Lao Ba, you can have any name you want, only don't have the name Wang!' (because the full name would form a term of abuse). Auxiliary verbs occur more freely with 9. another auxiliary verb, as in 得会说中国话 *deei huey shuo Jong.gwohuah* 'have to be able to speak Chinese' [sec. 8.1.10(d)].

(e) Cognate objects in the form of quantity words after 1. intransitive verbs of action (Vi), as in 走两步 *tzoou leang-buh* 'walk two steps', and 3. status verbs (Vst), as in 麻了一陣 *male i-jenn* 'have felt numb for a spell', are somewhat more restricted, as compared with similar objects after 2. adjectives (A), as in 大几岁 *dah jii-suey* 'several years older', 好一百倍 *hao ibae-bey* 'one hundred times better'.

(f) Cognate objects for the number of times does not go often with 8. the verb *yeou*, as in 有过一次錢 *yeou.guoh i-tsyh chyan* 'have had money once,—wealthy once'. In the expression 有一回 *yeou i-hwei* 'there was one time,—once upon a time', *i-hwei* is a direct object and not a cognate object of *yeou*.

(g) Transitive verbs of action, when reduplicated, are reduplicated before the object, as in 看ㄜ书 *kann.kann shu* 'read books a little,—do a little reading', 拜望ㄜ朋友 *bay.wanq .bay.wanq perng.yeou* 'just make some calls on friends', except in old Mandarin, in which the reduplication sometimes comes after the object, as in 你也照顧猪八戒照顧！ *Nii yee jaw.guh Ju Bajieh ₀jaw.guh!* 'You'd better take care of Ju Bajieh a little!, and 八戒，你过来，一芯照顧你照顧！ *Bajieh, nii guoh.lai, ifa jaw.guh nii ₀jaw.guh!* 'Bajieh, you come over, so we can take care of you a little!'[4] In the case of exocentric V-O compounds

---

'has written quite a few articles', 很睡了一会儿 *heen shueyle ihoel* 'has slept for quite a while'.

[4] 西遊记, chap. 85.

used as Vt [sec. 6.5.3(1)], the whole compound can be reduplicated before the real object, as in 得注意ㄦㄦ脚底下的冰
*deei juhyih .juh.yih jeau dii.shiah de bing* 'must pay a little attention to the ice under your feet'.

(h) The aspect suffix *-j* does not normally go with 2. adjectives or 5. transitive quality verbs. In 润着呐 *kuoh jne* 'awfully
rich' and 喜欢他着呐 *shii.huan ta jne* 'like him a lot', the *jne*
is a compound phrase particle and not the progressive aspect
suffix, since it occurs after the object *ta* and is not attached to
the verb.

(i) The suffix 过 *-.guoh* for the indefinite past suffix has restricted occurrence with 2. adjectives, as in 从来没有这么
好过 *tsornglai meiyeou tzemm hao.guoh* 'it has never been so
good before';[5] with 6. classificatory verbs, as in   从小儿就没
像过他爹   *tsorngsheaul jiow mei shianq.guoh ta die* 'since
childhood has never resembled his dad'; very rarely with 7. the
verb *sh*, as in 我从来没是过谁的人。*Woo tsornglai mei
sh.guoh sheirde ren.* 'I have never been anybody's man.' [sec.
5.4.5(3)]; and rarely with 9. auxiliary verbs, as in   英文我会
说过，可是现在忘了。*Ingwen woo huey shuo .guoh, keesh
shianntzay wanqle.* 'I could once speak English, but now have
forgotten it.' Note that *-.guoh* is in construction with *huey shuo*
and not with either *huey* or *shuo*.

(j) The perfective suffix *-le* occurs with 2. adjectives and 3.
status verbs when there is a cognate object, as in   大了三寸
*dahle san-tsuenn* 'have grown (or exceeded) by 3 inches', 病了
一场 *binqle i-chaang* 'have had a siege of illness'. This is to be
distinguished from the inchoative particle *le* (P 2, sec. 8.5.5), as
in 现在大了 *shianntzay dah le* 'have become big now', when
the *le* is not a word suffix. Like *-.guoh*, the suffix *-le* also occurs
rarely with 6. classificatory verbs, as in   他姓了王才怪呐！
*Ta shinqle Wang tsair guay ne!* 'It would be awfully queer if he
were named Wang,—if his name were Wang!'

---

[5]In a speech by Hu Shih, at a concert in Taipei, January 31, 1959.

(k) The column marked " 耒 " *Lai!* 'Come!' indicates whether each type of verb does or does not occur in commands, or imperative forms. Commands occur mostly with verbs of action, namely 1. (Vi) and 4. (Vt). Forms with adjectives such as 快! *Kuay!* 'Quick!' and adjectives as commands are usually either in vivid reduplicated form, as in 好ㄗㄦ的! *Haohaulde!* 'Be good!' or 'Be careful!' or in comparative form, as in 小心点ㄦ! *Sheau.shin.deal!* 'More careful, —Be careful!' and 慢着点ㄦ! *Mannj.deal!* 'Being more slow, —Take it easy!' If someone is adjusting a picture and someone else says 高! *Gau!* 'High!' it is ambiguous, meaning either (1) 高点ㄦ! *Gau.deal!* '(Make it) higher!' or (2) 高了. *Gau le.* 'It is high now (high enough or too high).'

The verbs 7. 是 *sh* and 8. 有 *yeou* are not used in commands. The English 'Be a man!' has to be rendered as 做一个大丈夫! *Tzuoh ig day-janq₀fu!,* where *tzuoh* 'act in the capacity of' is a transitive verb of action. So is *na* 'take' in 拿几个梨! *Na ₀jiig li!* 'Have a few pears!'

The only auxiliary verbs (Vx) which are in command form are 别…! *Bye …!* 'Don't …!' and 甭…! *Berng …!* 'Don't … (because you don't need to)!'

(l) In the V-*bu*-V form of questions as applied to 8., the verb *yeou* takes the negative *mei* instead of *bu*, as noted above. Note, however, that as an auxiliary verb, the *yeou meiyeou* formula is used only in the Cantonese and Fukienese dialects and has only recently been introduced into Mandarin as a Southernism, as in 你有没有看完这部书? *Nii yeou meiyeou kann-wan jey-buh shu?* 'Have you finished reading this book?', for which the normal Northern form is 你看完了这部书（了）没有? *Nii kann-wanle jey-buh shu (le) meiyeou?,* to which a negative answer is *Meiyeou.* 'I have not.', but an affirmative answer has to be *Kann-wanle.* An answer °*Yeou.* 'I have.', though sometimes heard in Taiwan, has not yet begun to be borrowed by native speakers of Mandarin.

*8.1.1.2. Cross-Classifications of Verbs.* Some writers (e.g.,

Simon, Verb Complex, 562) recognize classes of verbs which lie outside the classes enumerated above. Those we shall treat either as their subclasses or as cutting across them in another dimension. Thus, the "post-verb" 在 *tzay* as in 住在这裡 *juh .tzay jeh.lii* 'live here' is a classificatory verb which happens to be in the position of a complement (sec 5.6.3); the "linkverb" 劝 *chiuann* as in 劝他買 *chiuann ta mae* 'advise him to buy' is a transitive verb of action which is in the position of the first verb in a pivotal construction (sec 2.13.1); the "endverbs" 去 *chiuh* and 耒 *lai* in 買东西去 *mae dong.shi .chiuh* 'go to buy things' are what we have called particles of purpose, which are always in the neutral tone [sec 6.6.8(7)]. In 给他買书 *geei ta mae shu* 'buy books for him', *geei* is used in first position in a V-V series, and is thus a preposition by class overlap with *geei* 'give' as Vt.

*8.1.2. Intransitive Verbs of Action (Vi).* Intransitive verbs of action form an open class, and the following are only examples. Although the headings are in semantic terms, most of them are paralleled by formal features, such as verbs of existence, appearance, and disappearance allowing "inverted subjects" [see sec. 8.1.2.2(4) below].

*8.1.2.1. Examples of Vi.* In the following examples the verbs are given mostly in simple root forms. Sometimes certain aspect suffixes are regularly attached in the nature of the case, such as 活着 *hwoj* 'to be living' as against 死了 *syyle* 'have died', whereas 活了 *hwole* means 'have revived', there being no °死着 *syyj*. For 'dying' one says 快死了 *kuay syyle* 'soon to die'.

(1) Verbs of Coming: Other than 耒 *lai* 'come' itself, verbs of coming are formed with verbs compounded with *lai* as a directional complement, as 上耒 *shanq.lai* 'come up', 出耒 *chu.lai* 'come out', 过耒 *guoh.lai* 'come over'.

(2) Verbs of Going: There are two simple verbs for going in the Northern dialects. In the sense of leaving a place or *s'en aller*, it is 走 *tzoou*, as in 咱们走吧! *Tzarmen tzoou ba!* 'Let's go!' In the sense of going to a place or *aller*, it is 去 *chiuh*, as in 你去不去? *Nii chiuh bu chiuh?* 'Are you going there?' This distinction is not maintained in the Central and Southern dialects,

which have other distinctions cutting across the one above. Other verbs of going are formed with *chiuh* as a directional complement, as 進去 *jinn.chiuh* 'go in', 过去 *guoh.chiuh* 'go across', and so on.

(3) Verbs for Change of Position or Motion: These are usually in compound form, with a directional complement, as in 起来 *chii.lai* 'get up' (from a sitting or lying position), 坐下来 *tzuoh.shiah.lai* 'sit down', 站起来 *jann.chii.lai* 'stand up', 躺下来 *taang.shiah.lai* 'lie down', and 停下来 *tyng.shiah.lai* 'stop'.

(4) Other Verbs of Locomotion: 走 *tzoou* 'walk', 跑 *pao* 'run', 爬 *par*, 'crawl', 滚 *goen* 'roll', 飛 *fei* 'fly', 摔 *shuai* 'fall, trip', 掉 *diaw* 'fall (through the air), drop', 落 *law ~ luoh* 'fall (of leaves, etc.), alight (of birds)', 下 *shiah* 'descend (of rain, snow, etc.)', 降 *jianq* 'descend' L, 倒 *daw* 'back (of automobiles, trains, etc.)', 流 *liou* 'flow', 出溜 *chu.liou* 'slide', 溜達 *lhiou.da* 'stroll'.

(5) Verbs of Motion: 動 *donq* 'move', 活動 *hwo.donq* 'move about actively', 走動 *tzoou₀donq* 'move about (after being laid up)', 转 *joan* 'turn (through an angle)', 转 *juann* 'revolve', also Vt 'turn (something) through an angle',[6] 扭 *neou* 'twist', 摇 *yau* 'shake, sway', 摆 *bae* 'sway', 摇晃 *yau₀huang* 'sway', 晃悠 *huang-.iou* 'sway', 抖 *doou* 'shake', 哆嗦 *duo.suo* 'tremble', 倒 *dao* 'topple, collapse', 長 *jaang* 'grow', 漲 *janq* 'expand', 缩 *suo* 'shrink'.

(6) Verbs of Existence or Static Position: 獃 *dai* 'stay', 等 *deeng* 'wait', 住 *juh* 'live, dwell', 歇 *shie* 'rest', 休息 *shiou.shi* 'rest', 躺着 *taangj* 'to be lying down', 睡着 *shueyj* 'to be lying down or sleeping', 坐 *tzuoh* 'sit', 踞着 *duenj* 'crouch', 站 *jann* 'stand', 活着 *hwoj* 'to be living', 醒着 *shiingj* 'to be awake'. Examples cited with *-j* are those in which the progressive aspect is most frequently met with.

(7) Verbs of Appearance: 生 *sheng* 'to be born', 到 *daw*

---

[6]As usual, the range of meanings of a free morpheme does not always coincide with that of the same etymon as bound or as wenyan. Thus, 转 is always *joan* in lexical compounds, whether it is turning fast or slowly, whether through a small angle or many revolutions, as in 旋转 *shyuanjoan* 'revolves', 公转, 自转 *gongjoan, tzyhjoan* 'revolution, rotation (of planets)'.

'arrive (of trains, etc., or persons)', 出現 *chushiann* 'appear'. All the verbs listed under (1) can be regarded as verbs of appearance for purposes of allowing "inverted subjects".

(8) Verbs of Disappearance: 死 *syy* 'die', 逃 *taur* 'escape', 跑 *pao* 'run away'. All the verbs of going listed under (2) can be regarded as verbs of disappearance for purposes of allowing "inverted subjects".

(9) Verbs of Vocal Action: 哭 *ku* 'cry, weep', 笑 *shiaw* 'laugh, smile', 叫 *jiaw* 'call', 嚷 *raang* 'shout', 嚷ㄥ *rhang.rang* ㄱ.ㄖ 'shout noisily' ( ≠ *raang.raang* ㄣ.ㄖ 'shout a little'), 喊 *haan* 'shout' or 'call' (dial.).

(10) Other Examples: 踌躇 *chour.chwu* 'hesitate', 進行 *jinn-shyng* 'proceed', 完 *wan* 'finish'.

Note that when one of these verbs has a tentative reduplicate, it usually takes a suffix -*l* if it is a static verb, as 歇ㄦ *shie.shiel* 'rest a little', but not if it is dynamic, as 走ㄥ *tzoou.tzoou* 'walk a little'.

*8.1.2.2. Objects of Vi.* Both intransitive and transitive verbs have objects, but intransitive verbs have only the following limited kinds of objects (cf. sec. 5.4.6.1):

(1) Cognate Objects of Quality and Number of Times (columns e and f in table 18): 哭了一天 *kule i-tian* 'cried for a whole day', 跑了几趟 *paole jii-tanq* 'ran several times'.

(2) Destinations of Verbs of Locomotion: 飛上海 *fei Shanqhae* 'fly (to) Shanghai', 開纽约 *kai Neouiue* 'sail (run, etc.) for New York', 走江湖 *tzoou jiang-hwu* 'go about among the rivers and lakes,—go adventuring', 来这儿 *lai jell* 'come here'. A Cantonism which has recently become quite well established among speakers of Mandarin is 去 *chiuh* 'go to', as in 去美國 *chiuh Meei.gwo* 'go to America', which in old style, still the commoner form, is 上(~ 到)美國去 *shanq (~ daw) Meei.gwo chiuh*.

(3) Origins After Verbs of Locomotion: In wenyan of the classical period a place word after 去 *chiuh* would denote the origin of locomotion, as in 去魯 *chiuh Luu* 'go away from the state of Luu,—leave Luu'. The verbs 上 *shanq* 'ascend' and 下

*shiah* 'descend' work both ways, and whether the object is destination or origin is determined only lexically. Thus, 上山 *shanq-shan* 'go up the mountain', 下山 *shiah-shan* 'go down (from) the mountain', 上船 *shanq-chwan* 'go on board', 下船 *shiah-chwan* 'disembark', but in old usage, when the junks were usually lower than the shore, it was 下船 *shiah-chwan* 'go (down) on board' and 上岸 *shanq-ann* 'go (up) ashore', the latter form still used. The verb 出 *chu* 'go or come out' (but not 進 *jinn* and 入 *ruh* 'enter') also works both ways, as in 出洋 *chu-yang* 'go out over the oceans,—go abroad', 出世 *chu-shyh* 'come out into the world, —be born', but 出门 *chu-men* 'go out of the door (lit.), or get married off', 出家 *chu-jia* 'go out of the family,—renounce the family to become a monk', 出院 *chu-yuann* 'go out of the hospital,—to be discharged from the hospital'. All cases of 出 *chu* and the uses of 上 *shanq* and 下 *shiah* for origin of locomotion are lexically restricted.

(4) "Inverted Subjects" of Existence: Since we have treated "inverted subjects" as grammatical objects (sec. 5.4.7.1), they are objects to Vi if the verb is intransitive, as in 讲台上坐着个美国学生。 *Jeangtair.shang tzuohj g Meei.gwo shyue.sheng.* 'On the platform sits an American student.' 地下睡着两隻狗。 *Dihshiah shueyj leang-jy goou.* 'On the floor there sleep two dogs.' But in 墙上掛着一幅画儿。 *Chyang.shang guahj i-fwu huall.* 'On the wall hangs a picture.', 掛 *guah* 'hang' had better be treated as a Vt, since one can say 掛画儿 *guah-huall* 'hang pictures', but not ° 坐学生 °*tzuoh shyue.sheng* 'sit student' or ° 睡狗 °*shuey-goou* 'sleep dog' as a V-O construction.

(5) "Inverted Subjects" of Coming and Appearance: 起了 (~ 下了) 大雾了。 *Chiile (~ shiahle) dah-wuh le.* 'There arises (~ descends) a great fog.' 来了一个客人。 *Laile ig keh.ren.* 'There has come a guest.' 跑进来了两个贼。 *Pao-jinn.laile leangg tzeir.* 'There have come in two thieves.' One can, to be sure, say 起(~ 下)雾 *chii* (~ *shiah*) *wuh* and 来客 *lai-keh* as V-O constructions, but not ° 把雾起(~ 下)了 °*bae wuh chii* (~ *shiah*) *le* or ° 把客人来了 ° *bae keh.ren laile.*

(6) "Inverted Subjects" of Going and Disappearance: The verb here often has the sense of letting or permitting things to happen, as in 跑掉了两个贼。 *Pao-diawle leangg tzeir.* 'There ran away two thieves,—two thieves got away.' 走了水了! *Tzooule shoei le!* 'There has gone away the water,—there is a fire!' 这産妇死孩子死怕了。 *Jeh chaanfuh syy hairtz syy-pahle.* 'This woman in maternity is scared of (often) having her babies die (on her).' (Leu, S & O, 218.) But in 我掉(～丢)了钱包了。 *Woo diaw (～ diou) le chyanbau le.* 'I've lost my purse.', 掉 *diaw* or 丢 *diou* should be regarded as transitive verbs, not so much because I was responsible for the loss, as because these verbs admit the pretransitive contruction 把钱包掉(～丢)了 *bae chyanbau diaw (～diou) le.* With intransitive verbs, such forms as 把个父親死了 *bae g fuh.chin syy.le* 'let his father die (on him)' are after all rare.

*8.1.2.3. Class Overlaps with Transitive Verbs and Other Parts of Speech.* Although a large percentage of verbs of action are both transitive and intransitive, the extent of overlapping is not so great as to render the division unimportant, and a dictionary should record individually cases of Vt and Vi as do the Webster's dictionaries for English verbs. This comes out clearly especially in cases where near synonyms and near antonyms do not behave alike. For example, there is 要睡好床 *yaw shuey hao chwang* 'wants to sleep in a good bed', but no °要躺好床 °*yaw taang hao chwang* for 'wants to lie on a good bed'. Therefore 睡 *shuey* is both Vt 'sleep in' and Vi 'sleep', while 躺 *taang* is only Vi 'lie'.

(1) Vi-R → Vt: An intransitive verb of action often becomes a transitive verb by being compounded with a resultative comple-ment.[7] For example, 哭哑了嗓子 *ku-yeale saangtz* 'cry one's throat hoarse', 笑疼了肚子 *shiaw-terngle duhtz* 'laugh until the stomach hurts', 跌傷了腿 *dye-shangle toei* 'fall and injure the leg', all of which admit of pretransitive constructions, such as 把嗓子哭哑了 *bae saangtz ku-yeale,* etc. It goes without

---

[7]Noted in Hwu-Wen *Tannsuoo,* from which some of the examples here have been taken.

saying that a transitive verb can remain transitive when compounded with a resultative complement, as in 打窗户 *daa
chuang.huh* 'hit the window' and 打破了窗户 *daa-pohle
chuang.huh* 'hit and break the window'.

(2) Causative Verbs: Some intransitive verbs also occur transitively in a causative sense, as in 上菜 *shanq-tsay* 'bring up,—
serve courses of dishes', 上螺丝 *shanq luo.sy* 'put on a screw',
上门 *shanq-men* 'put on,—install a door' or 'put on the board
doors (for the night in old-style shops)' (cf. 上门 *shanq-men* 'go
up to the door,—visits a house' with *men* as object of destination
after a Vi), 下蛋 *shiah-dann* 'lay (down) eggs', 下棋 *shiah-chyi*
'lay down chess (men),—play chess', 下装 *shiah-juang* 'doff costume', 起螺丝 *chii luo.sy* 'raise screw,—unscrew a screw', 出
錢 *chu-chyan* 'put out money (for some purpose)', 出米 *chu-mii*
'produce rice', 出疹子 *chu-jeentz* 'have the measles', 出汗 *chu-
hann* 'perspire', 跑馬 *pao-maa* 'race the horses', 跑狗 *pao-goou*
'race the dogs' (but 走狗 *tzoougoou* 'a running dog' and not 'walk
the dogs'), 末点儿茶！ *Lai deal char!* 'Bring some tea!' 去皮
*chiuh-pyi*[8] 'remove the skin', 飛噴射机 *fei penshehji* 'fly a jet
plane' (as against 飛巴黎 *fei Bali* 'fly Paris' with object of destination where 飛 *fei* is still Vi).

(3) Other Examples of Overlap between Vi and Vt: 等ㆍ
(儿)! *Deeng.deeng(l)!* 'Wait a little!' ( ≠ *deeng deeng* 'et cetera'
L): 等他不等？ *Deeng ta bu deeng?* 'Shall we wait for him?'
小心别摔！ *Sheau.shin bye shuai!* 'Be careful and don't fall!'
摔东西小心别打了人！ *Shuai dong.shi sheau.shin bye
daale ren!* 'When you throw things away, be careful and don't hit
anybody!' 笑 *shiaw* 'laugh, smile': 笑他 *shiaw ta* 'laugh at him'.

*8.1.3. Intransitive Quality Verbs, or Adjectives* (A). We are
treating adjectives as a species of verbs in order to emphasize the
typical function of Chinese adjectives as predicatives without requiring a verb 'to be' such as 是 *sh*, since 好 *hao* already means

---

[8]Ancient reading 去 > *cheu* for the causative verb is obsolete and 去
> *chiuh* serves for both the Vi and the causative Vt.

'to be good' as well as 'good'.[9] In Indo-European languages adjectives often have similar inflections, or at least parallel inflections, to those of nouns, and are thus more like nouns than verbs. Adjectives in Chinese, on the other hand, function readily as predicatives as well as attributive modifiers, and in the latter capacity the conditions for adjectives are almost as much circumscribed as for action verbs. For example, there is 涼水 *liang-shoei* 'cold water', but 涼手 *liang-shoou* 'cold hand' is not as common as 冰涼的手 *bing-liang de shoou* 'hand that is ice-cold' [cf. sec. 8.1.3.3(1)]. With action verbs one can say 來人 *lai-ren* 'the coming man,—messenger', and yet 去人 *chiuh-ren* for 'the going man' is rare, for which one usually says 去的人 *chiuh de ren* 'the man who goes'. On the whole, even though adjectives occupy attributive positions before substantives more readily than do verbs of action, the construction is not to be taken for granted in all cases.

*8.1.3.1.  Classifications of Adjectives.*  Apart from semantic classifications of qualities, such as physical versus mental qualities, positive versus negative qualities, and so on, which do not regularly reflect formal features, there are few formal subdivisions of adjectives which come out as classes of comparable size. We shall mention the following types of subdivisions that have been proposed.

(1) Simple and Complex Adjectives. Ju Dershi[10] divides adjectives into Type Jea ( 甲 ), Simple, and Type Yii ( 乙 ), Complex Adjectives. The former includes not only monosyllables such as 大 *dah* 'large', 紅 *horng* 'red', and 多 *duo* 'many, much', but also disyllables like 干淨 *gan.jinq* 'clean', 糊塗 *hwu.du* 'muddled', 偉大 *woeidah* 'great, grand'. The complex adjectives, on the other hand, are (1) reduplicated forms such as 小ㄓ儿 *sheaushiaul* 'tiny little', 老ㄓ实ㄓ *lao.laoshyrshy(r)* 'honest and frank', 糊哩

---

[9]Some writers regularly translate entries of Chinese adjectives in the verbal form, for example, 满 *mǎn*, 'to be full', 咸 *syán* 'be salty' (Fred F-Y. Wang, *Chinese Dialogues*, New Haven, 1953, pp. 368, 376).

[10] 朱德熙, 現代汉语形容词研究 (Ju Dershi, "Studies in Present-Day Chinese Adjectives"), *YYYJ*, 1, 83-84 of 83-111 (1956), which is so far the best treatment of Chinese adjectives.

糊塗 *hwu.lihwudu* (~ -*twu*) 'good and muddled'; (2) those with lively suffixes, as 乱哄ㄦ *luannhonghong* 'confused and noisy', 灰不溜秋 *huei.bulhiouchiou* 'drab and grayish'; (3) with intensifying prefix-like elements, as 冰涼 *bing-liang* 'ice-cold', 通红 *tong-horng* 'red through and through', 噴香 *penn-shiang* 'puffing-sweet'; and (4) forms with adverbs of degree and in coordination, as 挺好 *tiing hao* 'pretty good', 又高又大 *yow gau yow dah* 'both tall and big'.

(2) Comparative and Noncomparative Adjectives. Quite parallel with Ju's classification, apparently independently arrived at, is Malmqvist's division of adjectives into comparative and noncomparative.[11] The former includes adjectives which admit degrees of comparison, but also certain transitive verbs of quality, as in 爱財 *ay tsair* 'love wealth', which we have set up as a separate type ($V_A$). The noncomparatives are exactly the same as Ju's Type Yii, except that some of the examples given, being from a different dialect, do not occur in Northern Mandarin.

Leaving the degree of comparison of adjectives to the next subsection (sec. 8.1.3.2), we shall observe that the dichotomy of comparative and noncomparative adjectives or Type Jea and Type Yii are numerically quite unbalanced. Compared with the vast number of comparatives one can find in a dictionary, the other type is extremely limited, unless one also counts phrases (Ju's subtype 4 and Malmqvist's subtype e), such as 又高又大 *yow gau yow dah* 'both tall and big', which of course are not cases of parts of speech.

Another feature of the noncomparative or Type Yii adjectives is that they seem to fit badly the profile for adjectives we set up in table 18. The reason for that is not far to seek. The profile given there is for adjectives as a species of verbs, whose typical function is that of a predicate. Now, in the vivid forms like 慢ㄦ *mannmhal* 'good and slow' and intensified forms such as 通

---

[11]Malmqvist, Sïch'uanese, 138-140. The dialects of Szechwan are varieties of SW Mandarin, and most of what he says about grammar applies also to Northern Mandarin. Most of his examples are also usable, apart from differences in pronunciation and occurrence or nonoccurrence of certain words or phrases.

红 *tong-horng* 'red through and through', the place of adverbs of degree like 很 *heen* 'very' and 更 *genq* 'more' in column (c) is already preempted, as they are "built in" in the vivid and intensive forms. There is no ° 更通红 °*genq tong-horng* 'more red through and through' for the same reason that there is no ° 更 很红 °*genq heen horng* 'more very red'. As for expressions such as 不冷不热 *bu leeng bu reh* 'neither cold nor hot' and 非常 漂亮 *feicharng piaw.lianq* 'extremely elegant', it is the phrases as wholes which are "noncomparative", but the individual adjectives occurring in them behave just like most other adjectives. It is, however, a different matter when a comparative adverb modifies the predication, as in 他更是糊哩糊塗的了. *Ta genqsh hwu.lihwudude le.* 'He is all the more muddle-headed.' 这屋子跟那屋子一樣的亮堂ノ的。 *Jeh utz gen nah utz iyanqde lianqtarngtangde.* 'This room and that room are equally (truly) good and bright.'

(3) Another dichotomy that has often been made is that between adjectives of absolute qualities and those which admit of degrees and therefore can be modified by adverbs of degree. Dragunov (p. 898; Chinese transl., p. 161) calls the former nominal adjectives, of which 圓 *yuan* 'round', 空 *kong* 'empty', 对 *duey* 'right' are examples. Even in the context of teaching English as a school subject, one hears or reads that a thing is either round or not round, a statement is either true or false, a problem is either major or minor.[12] For the purpose of technical logic or some special science it may be, and very often is, desirable to set up certain predicatives which admit of no degrees. But so far as common and acceptable[13] usage goes, one does say 很圓 *heen yuan* 'very round', 最新 *tzuey shin* 'newest', 你真对! *Nii jen duey!* 'How right you are!'

(4) Finally, the dichotomy between attributive and predica-

---

[12]But Director William H. Pickering of NASA's jet propulsion lab says, "We don't really know how major the failure [of the moon rocket] is." *Berkeley* (Calif.) *Daily Gazette*, April 24, 1963, p. 4.

[13]Acceptable in the sense of causing no raising of eyebrows on the part of the hearer.

tive adjectives is of some grammatical importance, although here, too, the sizes of the two divisions are also quite unbalanced, as will be seen.

(a) Attributive adjectives. Under substantives we included the determinatives, some of which occur as free adjectives and can be predicates, as 多 *duo* '(are) many, (is) much'. Most of them, however, occur only before measures and a few also before nouns. Only the few which can occur before nouns but not before a pause can be regarded as exclusively attributive adjectives. This boils down to the two demonstratives 这 *jeh* 'this' and 那 *nah* 'that' and does not even include 哪 *naa* 'which', which can only be followed by measures and not nouns. Some of the specifying determinatives, to be sure, can be followed by 人 *ren* 'man', as in 每人 *meei.ren* 'each person', 别人 *bye.ren* 'other(s)', but, as we have seen, *ren* has other characteristics of pronouns and measures and is not functioning as a noun after those determinatives. Thus, exclusively attributive adjectives would form an extremely small class of two members. Since, however, *jeh* and *nah* also fit badly the profile for adjectives, it would be better to regard them still as determinatives, bound not necessarily to measures but also to nouns. It is significant that when *jeh* and *nah* occur before nouns without an intermediary measure *g*, etc., they are usually in the neutral tone and take the checked vowel [ə]. Thus it will be simpler to regard them as proclitics, or prefixes of unlimited versatility, rather than setting up a special class of exclusively attributive adjectives. This treatment also has the advantage of keeping adjectives primarily as predicatives.

(b) Predicative adjectives. A very small minority of adjectives occur exclusively or predominantly in predicative positions. Note the predicative position of the adjectives in Chinese in contrast to the attributive position in the English translation in 我们人多茶碗少，茶够了碗不够。 *Woomen ren duo char-woan shao, char gowle woan bu gow.* 'There are many of us but few teacups; we have enough tea, but not enough cups.'[14] Other examples of predominantly predicative adjectives are: 行 *shyng*

---

[14] *Phonog Course*, 80-81, quoted in Dragunov (p. 177; Chinese transl., p. 163).

'okay', 成 *cherng* 'okay', 对 *duey* 'correct', 懸 *shyuan* 'perilous' (except in 懸事儿 *shyuan-shell* 'risky business), 乏 *far* 'fatigued' (but 乏貨 *far-huoh* 'inferior goods', lit. or fig.), 诡 *goei* 'shrewd, crafty' ( 诡辩 *goeibiann* 'sophistry' is a compound and *biann* 'argues' is not a free noun). These do not modify substantives even with the addition of the subordinative particle *de*, as ° 诡 的计策 *°goei de jihtseh* for 'a shrewd plan', but one can say 很诡的计策 *heen goei de jihtseh*. (Cf. sec. 8.1.3.) In 这个 □ 东西！ *Jeyg goei-dong.shi!* 'The scoundrel!', the 诡 is usually descriptive-etymologized as 鬼 'devilish'.

*8.1.3.2 Degrees of Comparison in Adjectives.* Chinese adjectives do not have comparative or superlative forms in a morphological sense, and various degrees of comparison are expressed by adverbs and in the form of V-V series. The nearest to a suffix for the comparative degree is 一点儿 *-(.i).deal* '-er', a weakened form of *ideal* 'a little', as in 好（一）点儿 *hao.deal* ( 𠃌 ⼁ ) or *hao.i.deal* 'better' as against 只好一点儿 *jyy hao ideal* 'only a little better', the latter being a V-O construction with a cognate object of extent 2e, table 18, just like 短三寸 *doan san-tsuenn* 'short by three inches'.

Comparisons in adjectives may be made explicitly or implicitly. In 这个比那个好。 *Jeyg bii neyg hao.* 'This is better than that.', the comparison is explicit. In 还是这个好。 *Hairsh jeyg hao.* 'After all, this is good,—better.', the comparison is implicit. In the latter example, one could use a comparative form *hao(.i).deal* instead of *hao*, but there would still be no explicit comparison without 比那个 *bii neyg* 'than that'.

There are five possible degrees of comparison in adjectives: (1) equal, (2) superior, (3) inferior, (4) superlative, (5) anti-superlative, and their respective contradictories. Corresponding to these degrees are a set of somewhat sundry and irregular grammatical forms. This lack of symmetry is not surprising, since grammatical forms do not usually fit neatly the logico-mathematical notions which they express, as we shall see below.[15]

---

[15]For a general treatment of the logical psychological, and linguistic aspects of quantities, see Edward Sapir, "Grading, A Study in Semantics",

(1) Equal Degree. An equal degree is explicitly compared in the form:

x *gen* y *iyanq* A
跟　　一樣

where *gen* 'and, with' has also the less common or dialectal variants 同 *torng*, 和 *hann~hay~her;* and *iyanq* has the much less common variant 一般 *iban*. This formula is ambivalently of two different constructions as regards ICs. With *gen* as 'with', we have a V-V series, and the translation will be 'x is equally A with y.'; with *gen* as a coordinate conjunction, we have a compound subject x *gen* y and the translation will be 'x and y are equally A.' Corresponding to the first construction, the contradictory form is:

x *bu gen* y *iyanq* A. 'x is not equally A with y.'

Corresponding to the other construction, the contradictory form is:

x *gen* y *bu iyanq* A. 'x and y are not equally A.'

Here are some actual examples: 水跟火一樣危險。*Shoei gen huoo iyanq weishean.* 'Water is equally dangerous with fire.' ~ 'Water and fire are equally dangerous.' 无线電的電浪跟光一樣快。*Wushianndiann de diannlanq gen guang iyanq kuay.* 'The electric waves of the wireless are of the same speed as light.' 东西的价錢应该跟东西的价值一樣高。*Dong.shi de jiah.chyan inggai gen dong.shi de jiahjyr iyanq gau.* 'The prices of things ought to be of the same level as their values.' As examples of contradictories of equal degrees, we have 我跟他不一樣高。*Woo gen ta bu iyanq gau.* 'I and he are not equally tall.' 维他命不跟肉一樣補。*Weitaminq bu gen row iyanq buu.* 'Vitamins are not equally nourishing with meat.' (may be more, maybe less).

(1.1) Equaling Degree. Similar to, but somewhat different from, the equal degree is what might be called the equaling

in *Philosophy of Science*, 11:93-116 (1944), and in D. G. Mandelbaum, ed., *Selected Writings of Edward Sapir*, Berkeley and Los Angeles, 1949, pp. 122-149.

degree, where x approaches y from below and equals it on the scale of A. The formula is:

$$x \; yeou \; y \; A$$
有

or, more commonly,

$$x \; yeou \; y \; nemm \; A$$
有       那么

both of which may be translated as 'x is as A as y.' For example, 他 有 老 三 ( 那 么 ) 聰 明 嗎 ? *Ta yeou Lao San (nemm) tsong-.ming ma?* 'Is he as clever as Lao San?'    大 車 寬 的 有 小 車 那 么 長。 *Dah-che kuan de yeou sheau-che nemm charng.* 'The big car is as wide as the small car is long.' A variant for *yeou* is 像 *shianq* 'like', which occurs more often in subordinative clauses than in independent clauses. For example, 像 他 那 么 聰 明 的 一个人    *shianq ta nemm tsong$_o$ming de ig ren* 'a man as clever as he'. On the contradictory forms of equaling degrees, see (3) below.

(2) Superior, or Comparative, Degree. We have seen that the cognate object   一 点 儿 *ideal* 'a little', occurring after an adjective in the neutral tone, functions as a suffix for the superior degree. But its use is not obligatory either in explicit or in implicit comparison. Thus, with explicit comparison:    北 風 说 , " 我 的 本 事 比 你 ( 的 ) 大 ." *Beeifeng shuo, "Woode been.shyh bii nii(de) dah."* 'The North Wind said, "My power is greater than yours."' With implicit comparison: 到 底 是 太 陽 的 本 事 大。 *Dawdii sh Tay.yang de been.shyh dah.* 'After all, the Sun was the stronger.' In both examples, the use of *dah.i.deal* or *dah-.deal* would make the superior degree clearer, but not greater, and if *ideal* is stressed, thus forming a true cognate object, it will actually lessen the extent of superiority.

There are two forms of making explicit comparisons which are fairly common but still frowned upon by parents and teachers. One is the use of 品 *piin* for 比 *bii* 'than', as in   这 个 品 那 个 長。 *Jeyg piin neyg charng.* 'This is longer than that'. This is probably a localism as a phonetic variant of *bii*.[16] The other is a comparison between things by mentioning them in shorter forms than what is logically referred to. Thus in comparing pencils one may say 我 的 鉛筆 比 你 的 尖。 *Woode chianbii bii niide jian.* 'My pencil is sharper than yours.', or, if it is understood what is being talked about, simply, 我 比 你 尖。 *Woo bii nii jian.* 'I am sharper than you.', which often passes unnoticed if it is obvious what is meant. (Cf. sec. 2.4.1.)

The contradictory of the comparative degree is formed by putting the negative *bu* 'not' before *bii* 'than', as in 我 不 比 他 懶。*Woo bu bii ta laan.* 'I am not lazier than he.', which is a true contradictory and not a contrary, since I may be either equally lazy or more diligent. If *bu* occurs after the *bii* phrase and before the adjective, as in 这个 比 那个 不好。 *Jeyg bii neyg buhao.* 'This is worse than that.', then *bu* is part of the second V in the V-V series, forming with it a compound, since here *buhao* is not simply the contradictory of *hao*, but the contrary quality of *hao*, namely 'bad'.

Implicit comparative degree has no simple contradictory form, but has to be denied by putting 不是 *bush* 'not that' before the whole sentence. For example:

| 他们谁高？ | *Tamen sheir gau?* | 'Which of them is taller?' |
| 老二高。 | *Lao Ell Gau.* | 'Lao Ell is taller.' |
| 不，我想不是<br>老二高。 | *Bu, woo sheang bush*<br>*Lao Ell gau.* | 'No, I don't think<br>Lao Ell is taller.' |

If a simple negative was added before the adjective, it would cease to be a contradictory of the superior degree and would be a contradictory of a simple predicative adjective: 他 不 高。*Ta bu*

---

[16]I am writing the character as 品 because it is the only one to fit the sound and make some sense: 'grade' (verb or noun). Actually, I have only heard it spoken and have never seen it actually written as 品, even by writers like Lao Shee (Lao Shaw), whose writings are rich in Peiping localisms. The dissyllabic variants 比较 *biijeau* and 较比 *jiawbii* (K 29 and 30, sec. 8.2.5), on the other hand, are slightly more formal than the plain 比 *bii* (K 28).

*gau.* 'He is not tall.', whereas the denial of an implicit superior degree 他 高. *Ta gau.* 'He is taller.' should leave the possibility that both are tall men.

(2.1) Emphatic Superior Degree. The adverb 更 *genq* is sometimes equated to 'more, -er'. Actually it is used, with or without -(*.i*).*deal,* in explicit or implicit comparison, only when the superior degree is to be emphasized, though not necessarily intensified. Thus, 比 那 个 更 好 *bii neyg genq hao* 'still better than that' is said when the speaker suspects that the listener may assume that it is not better and wishes to emphasize the superior degree, though it need not be much superior. Other forms of emphatic comparative are 还 *hair,* 还 要 *hair yaw,* and 还 更 *hair genq,* all meaning 'still — -er'. In implicit comparison, however, a simple 还 *hair* is not used, since it could also mean 'rather, fairly, somewhat', as in 这 个 书 还 好. *Jeyg shu hair hao.* 'This book is fairly good.', but 比 冰 还 冷 *bii bing hair leeng* 'still colder ~ even colder than ice', in which the comparison is explicit.

(2.2) Intensive Superior Degree. When a superior degree is intensified and not merely emphasized, it takes the form of a predicative complement (sec. 5.6.4): ... ( 的 ) 多 ... *(de) duo* 'much ... er', as in     今 儿 比 昨 儿 热 , 热 ( 的 ) 多 了. *Jiel bii tzwol reh, reh (de) duo le.* 'Today is hotter than yesterday, much hotter.' The contradictory of the intensive superior degree may be formed by having the negative *bu* either before *bii* or before the predicative complement *duo,* but not before the adjective. For example, 他 不 比 我 高 的 多. *Ta bu bii woo gau de duo.* 'He is not much-taller-than-I.' or 他 比 我 高 的 不 多. *Ta bii woo gau de bu duo.* 'He is not-much taller than I.', the latter implying that he is taller, but not much. There is no ° 他 比 我 不 高 的 多. °*Ta bii woo bu gau de duo.* But if there is such compound as *bu-A* 'un-A', then we can have forms like 他 比 你 不 快 活 的 多. *Ta bii nii bukuay.hwo de duo.* 'He is much more unhappy than you.', which is simply an ordinary intensive superior degree with an adjective which happens to have a built-in negative.

A less common, though by no means rare, construction is the double intensive superior degree, in the form of iterated predicative complements. For example, 今年的雨量比去年的大的多的多。 *Jin.nian de yeuliang bii chiuh.nian de dah de duo de duo.* 'This year's rainfall is (by far) much greater than last year's.', where the first *duo* is the small predicate and the second *duo* is the main predicate.

(3) Inferior Degree. An inferior degree is not the contradictory of the superior degree or of the equal degree, but the contradictory of the equaling degree. Since the latter uses 有 *yeou*, its contradictory is 没 ( 有 ) *mei (yeou)*, as follows:

x *mei (yeou)* y (*nemm*) A.
没 （有） （那么）

which can be translated either as 'x is not so A as y' or 'x is less A than y.' For example, 我没 ( 有 )你 ( 那 么 )聪 明。 *Woo mei-(yeou) nii (nemm) tsong.ming.* 'I am not so clever as you.' or 'I am less clever than you.' Used much less often are 不如 *buru* 'not as' and 不及 *bujyi* 'not reaching', as in '不及'不如'不如'用的那么多。 *'Bujyi' buru 'buru' yonq de nemm duo.* '*Bujyi* is not used as often as *buru*.'

(4) Superlative Degree. An adjective is put in the superlative degree by being placed after 顶 *diing* 'most, -est' or 最 *tzuey* 'most, -est'. If the scope within which a superlative is to be made explicit, it usually takes the form of a noun-localizer phrase or compound, as in 天下最要紧的事 *tianshiah tzuey yawjiin de shyh* 'the most important thing in the world', 咱们当中顶年轻的 *tzarmen dangjong diing nianching de* 'the youngest among us'.

As in English, the superlative form is often used loosely in a general, absolute sense, as in 这是一位脾气最好的先生。*Jeh sh i-wey pyi.chih tzuey hao de shian.sheng.* 'This is a good-natured gentleman.' 那是一件顶麻烦的事儿。 *Nah sh i-jiann diing ma.farn de shell.* 'That is a most troublesome thing.' The use of *i*-M, as well as the English 'a' shows that the superlative form is not being used in the superlative sense.

Note that usages differ where there is a choice between the superlative and the superior degrees. Thus, in 咱们顶好

等会儿再决定罢。 *Tzarmen diing hao deeng.hoel tzay jyuedinq ba.* 'We had better wait a while before we decide.', *diing hao* could be translated as 'best', but 'better' would be better. The superior degree can also be used here, but not before the verb, as in   咱们等会儿去好 ( 点儿 )。 *Tzarmen deeng.hoel chiuh hao(.deal).* 'It would be better if we went later.'

The contradictory of the superlative degree is in the nominalized form 不是最…的 *bush tzuey … de* 'is not the most … of', as in   洛磯山不是西半球最高的山。 *Luohji Shan bush Shibannchyou tzuey gau de shan.* 'The Rocky Mountains are not the highest mountains in the Western Hemisphere.' The double adverbs 不顶 *bu diing* 'not the most' is used only in the looser type of superlatives, as in   这儿冬天不顶冷。 *Jell dong.tian bu diing leeng.* 'The winter here is not coldest,—not very cold.'

(5) Anti-superlative Degree. The formula 最 (～ 顶 ) 不 A *tzuey* (～ *diing*) *bu* A has an ambivalent construction as to the ICs. For example,  最不聪明的办法 *tzuey bu tsong.ming de bannfaa* is either 'the least wise course' or 'the most unwise course'. In most cases it makes no difference in truth value. On the whole the ICs are 1 + 2, that is, 最 (～ 顶 ) + 不 … *tzuey* (～ *diing*) + *bu* … , whether *bu* forms a compound with the following adjective or not. For example,  最不客气的说法 *tzuey bu keh.chih de shuofaa* is either 'the least-polite thing to say' or 'the most impolite thing to say'. If the lowest degree of (positive) politeness is to be implied (with 2 + 1 ICs), it will have to be paraphrased in some such form as   就算不特别客气，至少 也该对他说声再见。 *Jiow suann bu tehbye keh.chih, jyhshao yee gai duey ta shuo sheng tzayjiann.* 'Even if not specially polite,—the least (still) polite thing should in any case be to say good-by to him.'

*8.1.3.3. Adjectives in Attributive Positions.* We noted (sec. 8.1.3) that adjectives, like verbs of actions, can modify substantives under somewhat circumscribed conditions. Thus, there is 短袖子 *doan shiowtz* 'short sleeves', but no ° 短沉默 °*doan chernmoh* for 'short silence', for which it has to be 短～的沉

默 *doandoande chernmoh.*[17] The following factors influence the occurrence of attributive adjectives:

(1) Syllabicity. Leaving out of consideration cases of subordinate compounds in which either the first or the second part is always bound and the cases of trochaic compounds (with the stress pattern '□.□ ), a free monosyllabic adjective and a free monosyllabic noun can usually form a subordinative phrase. But because of the great abundance of subordinative compounds of this type, even an A-N phrase with FF parts tends to be treated as a compound, whether or not there is lexical specialization. Phonologically, the phrase 薄纸 *baur-jyy* 'thin paper' has the same stress pattern as the lexical compound 薄饼 *baurbiing* 'thin cakes,—(Chinese wheat-flour) tortillas'. Because of this, there is usually some hesitancy on the part of speakers (and writers) to make up dissyllabic A-N phrases at will and a preference for making the modification more explicit by inserting the particle *de* or changing the adjective into Type Yii (noncomparative) form and adding *de.* Thus, 涼水 *liang-shoei* 'cold water' occurs frequently, but there is less occasion to speak of 涼臉 *liang lean* 'cold face' and so it takes the form 氷涼的臉 *bing-liang de lean* 'a face that's ice-cold'. Nevertheless, it is not ungrammatical to say 別拿你那涼臉挨着人！ *Bye na nii nah liang-lean aij ren!* 'Don't touch me with that cold face of yours!' [On *ren* for 'me', see sec. 7.11.4(3.2).]

With one of the two parts longer than one syllable, especially 2 + 1 or 1 + 2, the tendency to add *de* is great, since it will

---

[17]Ju Dershi (op. cit., 87-88) states the conditions for occurrence or nonoccurrence of the A-N forms, but they are general tendencies rather than fixed rules. For example, there is 重担子 *jonq danntz* 'heavy load', but, according to Ju, ° 重箱子 °*jonq shiangtz* for 'heavy trunk', for which it has to be 很重的箱子 *heen jonq de shiangtz* 'a very heavy trunk'. But this is true only as regards relative frequencies of occurrence. To be sure, one does hear 重担子 *jonq danntz* all the time, but the other cannot be ruled out as nonoccurring or ungrammatical. For example, it is perfectly natural to say 你不累嗎，老提逴着那么个重箱子？ *Nii bu ley ma, lao di-.lhiouj nemm g jonq shiangtz?* 'Aren't you tired, carryong that heavy trunk all the time?'

balance out the rhythm better, except of course in lexical cases, which will be considered next.

(2) Lexical and Nonlexical Cases. While the direct A-N construction may or may not have a specialized meaning, as 老松 樹 *lao songshuh* 'old pine': 老朋友 *lao perng.yeou* 'old friend (friend of long standing)'. the A *de* N form always has a literal and nonlexical meaning, as in 老的朋友 *lao de perng.yeou* 'a friend who is old,—an elderly friend'. Other examples are: 香水（儿）*shiangshoei* (~ *l*) 'fragrant water,—perfume': 香的 水 *shiang de shoei* '(any) water which is fragrant'. Sometimes the A-N construction results in an exocentric compound, as in 热心 *rehshin* 'warm-heart(ed),—enthusiastic': 热的心 *reh de shin* 'a(n anatomical heart) which is warm (e.g., of a cooked duck or chicken)'; 黄河 *Hwang Her* 'the Yellow River': 黄的河 *hwang de her* '(any) river which is yellow'.

While it is outside the scope of a grammar to give more than a few examples of A-N phrases, it would nevertheless be useful to include in a dictionary those of very high frequency of occurrence, even if the lexical specialization is very slight, such as 大 街 *dahjie* 'main street', 涼水 *liang-shoei* 'cold water', 窮人 *chyong-ren* 'poor people'.

(3) Restrictive and Descriptive Functions of Adjectives. In 白纸 *bair-jyy* 'white paper' the adjective *bair* distinguishes it from 黒 *hei* 'black' and has a restrictive function, but in 黒墨 *heimoh* 'black inkstick', 酸醋 *suantsuh* '(sour) vinegar' (dial.), and 鹹塩 *shyanyan* '(salty) salt' (dial.), since most inksticks are black (in China), vinegar is always sour, and salt is always salty, the adjectives only add more description to the qualities without distinguishing them from other qualities. On the whole, descriptive adjectives such as 青天 *chingtian* 'the blue sky', do not take the particle *de* as often as restrictive adjectives, as in 黒暗的 天 *hei'ann de tian* 'a dark sky'. But this tendency is by no means an absolute rule. Thus, *de* is optional in 他老用貴纸，不肯 用便宜纸。*Ta lao yonq guey-jyy, bukeen yonq pyan.yi jyy.* 'He always uses expensive paper and won't use cheap paper.' With *de* in descriptive use: 这位糊塗的先生把自己的

岁数都忘了． *Jey-wey hwu.du de shian.sheng, bae tzyhjii de suey.shuh dou wanq.le.* 'This absent-minded gentleman has even forgotten his own age.', where *jey-wey* restricts the reference without needing the adjective *hwu.du.*

Type Yii (noncomparative) adjectives, which as we saw were mostly adjectival phrases, are usually descriptive (Ju, *op. cit.*, 83), but here, again, the rule is not absolute. For example, 我只要小儿的一块 糖，不要那么大一块。 *Woo jyy yaw sheaushiaulde i-kuay tarng, buyaw nemm dah i-kuah.* 'I only want a tiny little piece of candy, I don't want a piece that big.', where the adjectives are obviously restrictive. Sometimes the order of the D-M compound makes a difference. In 那个 疯ㄟ傻ㄟ的人又来了。 *Neyg fengfeng-shaashaa de ren yow lai le.* 'That man, who acts queerly, has come again.', the adjective is descriptive. In 疯ㄟ傻ㄟ的那个人又来了。 *Fengfeng-shaashaa de neyg ren yow lai le.* 'The man who acts queerly has come again.', it is restrictive. (Cf. sec. 5.3.6.2.)

(4) Order of Adjectives. The order $A_1A_2N$ usually implies the ICs $A_1$ + $A_2N$, as in 大黑狗 *dah hei-goou* 'big black dog, i.e., a big one among black dogs', but 黑大衣 *hei dah'i* 'black overcoat' (among overcoats of other colors). But very often the ICs are $A_1A_2$ + N, where $A_1$ and $A_2$ are in coordination, as in 甜酸排骨 *tyan-suan pairguu* 'sweet and sour ribs'. Although a big dog among black ones is logically equivalent to a black one among big dogs, since logical multiplication (conjunction of qualities) is said to be "commutative", the grammatical order of elements is usually rather circumscribed, especially, though not exclusively, in the case of compounds, such as 酸辣湯 *suanlah-tang* 'sour and (pepper) hot soup'. Even in nonlexical and phrasal constructions, there is no °红大房子 °*horng dah farngtz* any more than there is 'red large house' in English.[18] Sometimes the order can be partially explained by taking into account the speaker's intention or the nature of the qualities. For example,

---

[18]See Benjamin Whorf, "Grammatical Categories," *Language*, 21.5 (1945).

there is 细長白毛 *shih charng bair mau* 'fine long white hair (fur)', because whiteness is considered inherent in the hair, length is incidental, and fineness even more fortuitous. But as in other matters linguistic, semantic explanations only help one to remember the forms after having found out what the forms are without resort to the (not always reliable) semantic categories. In most cases, the order of adjectives is empirical, often lexical, facts. We have one order in 大寬路 *dah kuan-luh* 'big wide road', but the opposite order in 寬大的心腸 *kuandah de shincharng* 'broad and big heart,—magnanimous heart', *kuandah* being a common compound.

When the adjectives are placed in coordination by the adverbial markers 又...又 *yow ... yow* 'both ... and', with the particle *de*, then the result will be a phrase taken literally and the order is much freer, as in 又辣又酸的湯 *yow lah yow suan de tang* '(any) soup which tastes both hot and sour', 一个很聰明並且很勤儉的 学生 *ig heen tsong.ming binqchiee heen chyn.jiann de shyue.sheng* 'a very clever, moreover very hardworking student'.

When a noun is modified by a D-M compound, an adjective of Type Jea (that is, simple or comparative adjectives) must be placed after the D-M compound, as in 一个好看的女人 *ig haokann de neu.ren* 'a beautiful woman', but with Type Yii, it may usually either precede or follow, as in 一个那么好看的女人 *ig nemm haokann de neu.ren* 'a woman who is so beautiful' or 那么好看的一个女人 *nemm haokann de ig neu.ren* 'so beautiful a woman' (Ju, *op. cit.*, 86).

On the rare cases of adjectival expressions modifying personal pronouns, see section 5.3.6.5 (1.4).

*8.1.3.4. Adjectives in Predicative Positions.* As the principal predicative properties have already been exhibited in the profile for adjectives in table 18, we need only to add some predicative aspects of adjectives not included in the table, namely, (1) noncognate objects, (2) occurrence of particle *le* after adjectives, and (3) uses of *sh* before adjectives.

(1) Adjectives with Noncognate Objects. In 姊ㄥ大我三歲. *Jiee.jiee dah woo san-suey.* 'My elder sister is three years

older than I am.', *dah* not only takes the cognate object *san-suey* but also another object, similar, in position, to an indirect object, *woo*, which can be equated to 'exceeds in age'. Malmqvist (*op. cit.*, 138) regards *dah* as a member of "an extremely restricted form class," of which he cites only the example *dah* in the sentence above. Similarly one can say 我小爺々兩輩。 *Woo sheau Ye.ye leang-bey.* 'I am two generations younger than Grandpa.' Less often is 高 *gau* used in this way as 'exceeds in height', as in 老張高我三寸. *Lao Jang gau woo san-tsuenn.* 'Jang is three inches taller than I am.', and still less often is 矮 *ae* 'short (in stature)' so used. Rather than setting up such a small subclass, it will be simpler to regard these few cases as words having class overlap where the same verb is sometimes transitive and sometimes intransitive. Thus, the adjective 短 *doan* 'short' in 短一尺 *doan i-chyy* 'short by one foot' is still an adjective, with a cognate object; but in 我还短一百塊錢. *Woo hair doan ibae-kuay chyan.* 'I am still $100 short.', and in 我还短你一百塊錢。 *Woo hair doan nii ibae-kuay chyan.* 'I still owe you $100.', *doan* is a transitive verb, though used in a different way from *dah*, *sheau*, and so on. In 我並不多他一个人。*Woo binq bu duo ta ig ren.* 'I do not really find him one too many,—he is no extra bother to me.', *duo* is used in a putative sense as a transitive verb, in still another way. The methodological import of such cases is that if they are treated as class overlaps, provided there are not too many of them (sec. 7.1.4), it is a relatively simple matter to take care of in a dictionary, whereas if special classes are to be set up for the overlapping cases, then the numbers of subclasses from n main classes would approach the unwieldy number of $n^2$, since one can find isolated cases of almost any class overlapping any other, and the number $n^2$ still does not take into account words which belong to more than two classes.

(2) Occurrence of Particle *le* After Adjectives. The *le* in column j in table 18 (p. 665) is the "word" *le*, or "suffix" *le*. The "phrase" *le*, or "particle" *le* is quite a different thing. The "particle" *le* occurs after a predicative adjective in several ways, all based on the function of *le* expressing a change to something

new. One is the simple predication of a new situation, as in 昨天冷，今天暖和了。 *Tzwo.tian leeng, jin.tian noan.hwo. le.* 'Yesterday was cold, today is (has become) warm.' Here, without the *le*, the two clauses can be reversed and result in the same truth value. But with *le* added, expressing a change between yesterday and today, the order of the clauses will have to follow the time order. But with verbs of action, which can take a particle *le* for past events, it is quite all right to say 今天天晴；昨天下雨了。 *Jin.tian tian chyng; tzwo.tian shiah-yeu le.* 'Today the day is fine; yesterday it rained.', where *shiah-yeu* is a V-O construction with a verb of action in it. In the common interjection of agreement 对了！ ₀*Duey.le!*, the *le* comes from the idea 'Now you begin to be right.' (cf. the American colloquialism 'Now you're talking.'), where the *le* corresponds to 'now'. With the great frequency of occurrence, the tone on *duey* is worn out to neutrality and *.Duey.le* then becomes just a sound of assent, as distinguished from the one-word sentence 对！ *Duey!* '(That's) correct!' or '(You are) right!' Other examples of the new-situation *le* after adjectives are: 东西贵了。 *Dong.shi guey le.* 'Things are expensive now.' 他身体好了。*Ta shen.tii hao le.* 'His health is good now.' 汤冷了。 *Tang leeng le.* 'The soup has got cold.' (whether you want it so or not).

A similar use of *le* after adjectives is to express excess over some expected norm instead of a quality which was not there to begin with. In the example about 贵 *guey* 'expensive' above, the implication is that previously things were 便宜 *pyan.yi* 'cheap', but if someone buys or prices a thing too high, one could, without necessarily using any adverb like 太 *tay* 'too, excessively', simply say 这东西贵了。 *Jeh dong.shi guey le.* 'This thing is too expensive.' Similarly, to a cook: 汤鹹了。*Tang shyan le.* 'The soup is too salty.', to a waiter: 汤冷了。*Tang leeng le.* 'The soup is too cold.'; to a tailor: 袖子长了。*Shiowtz charng le.* 'The sleeves are too long.' Homophonous expressions can occur in V-R constructions, since a resultative complement will normally require *le* in any case, as in 栽缝把袖子剪短了 *Tsair.ferng bae shiowtz jean-doanle* 'The tailor has cut the sleeves too short' ~ 'The tailor has shortened the sleeves (as desired).'

Finally an adjective in the superlative with *le* implies some process of selection among possible candidates, as in 这儿的医生当中牛医生最出名了。 *Jell de i.sheng dangjong Niou I.sheng tzuey chuming le.* 'Among the physicians here Dr. Niou is the most famous.', which implies a quick mental review of all the doctors, and arriving at the conclusion about Dr. Niou. Similarly, 他自己做错了又怪人最讨厭了。 *Ta tzyhjii tzuoh-tsuohle yow guay ren tzuey taoyann le.* 'It's most annoying (among his other annoying traits) when he blames others for his own mistakes.', where the *le* is translated by the words in parentheses.

(3) Uses of 是 *sh* Before Adjectives. Since Chinese adjectives are primarily verbs, they need no verb 'to be' as predicates. But, like other verbs, adjectives can be preceded by *sh* in one of the following ways:

(a) When the adjective is nominalized by a following *de*, an optional *sh* is usually inserted before the *A-de* construction. Thus, 这瓜甜. *Jeh gua tyan.* 'This melon is sweet.', but 这瓜是甜的. *Jeh gua sh tyan de.* 'This melon is a sweet one.'

(b) When there is a contrast before two adjectives, as in 他是笨, 不是坏。 *Ta sh benn, bush huay.* 'He is stupid, not bad.'

(c) When there is assertive stress, as in 他"是傻嘓! *Ta <u>sh</u> shaa me!* 'He *is* stupid!'

(d) In the formula A *sh* A to express concession, as in 热是热, 可是不潮湿。 *Reh ₀sh reh, keesh bu chaur₀shy.* '(As for being) hot, it is hot,—it is hot, to be sure, but it is not damp.'

Note, however, that all these uses of *sh* are by no means limited to adjectives, but to other verbs as well. Thus:

(a) With nominalizing *de*: 这瓜是从哈密来的. *Jeh gua sh tsorng Hamih lai de.* 'This melon (is one that) came from Hami.' 我是去买东西的。 *Woo sh chiuh mae dong.shi de.* 'It was to buy things that I went.'

(b) For contrast with other verbs: 我是问ㄥ他, 不是罵他。 *Woo sh wenn.wenn ta, bush mah ta.* 'I was just asking him, not scolding him.'

(c) With assertive stress: 他们那儿"是卖旧货嘿！ *Tamen.nall sh may jiow-huoh me!* 'They do sell second-hand goods there!' 我"是打算去。 *Woo sh daa.suann chiuh.* 'I do intend to go there.'

(d) V *sh* V to express concession: 跑是能跑，可是一跑就累。 *Pao ₀sh neng pao, keesh i pao jiow ley.* '(One) can run all right, but as soon as (one) runs, (one) gets tired.' 到会是到会，可是不发言。 *Daw-huey ₀sh daw-huey, keesh bu fa-yan.* '(One) attends the meeting, to be sure, but does not speak (at the meeting).'

*8.1.3.5. Adjectives as Complements.* While both verbs of action and adjectives can be complements to another verb, as in 打翻了 *daa-fanle* 'knocks (with the result) turns over,—upsets' and 戴歪了 *day-uaile* 'wears (e.g., hat) crooked', most resultative complements are adjectives. The detailed treatment of complements is given in chapter 6, where a list of common complements, mostly adjectives, is given [sec. 6.6.2(2)].

*8.1.3.6. Overlaps of Adjectives with Other Form Classes.* As we have noted, adjectives may overlap another form class. Actually the commonest cases are with (1) nouns, (2) transitive verbs, and (3) adverbs.

(1) Adjectives and Nouns. When a word can be preceded by a D-M compound such as 一种 *i-joong* 'a kind of', then it is a noun by definition. Thus, 这是一种香。 *Jeh sh i-joong shiang.* 'This is a kind of fragrance.' ~ 'This is a kind of incense.' Words for tastes and colors are usually both adjectives and nouns, as 我不喜欢那种甜。 *Woo bu shii.huan ney-joong tyan.* 'I don't like that kind of sweetness.' 你分得出几种红来？ *Nii fen.de-chu jii-joong horng .lai?* 'How many kinds of red can you distinguish?' In some special cases a color word may be used either for the quality or for something with that quality. For example, 鸡子儿的白儿 *jitzeel de barl* means only 'the white of an egg', but 鸡子儿的白 *jitzeel de bair* means ambiguously 'the whiteness of an egg' or 'the white of an egg'. However, 鸡子儿的黄 *jitzeel de hwang* 'the yellowness of an

egg' is not ambiguous, since the word for 'yolk' is *hwangl*, with a suffix *-l*. In many dialects, however, no suffix is used for 'yolk', and *hwang* as noun would have the same status as *bair*. In isolated cases the noun-adjective overlap does not have to do with any special semantic category: 散 *saan* (not counting *sann* 'scatter', which is a different morpheme) 'loose, not compact': 'powdered medicine'; 小 *sheau* 'small': 'concubine'. The opposite, 大 *dah* 'the chief wife', as a noun, however, is used only in the near context of *sheau*. Cases of A-tz → N as in 矮 *ae* 'short': 矮子 *aetz* 'shorty, dwarf' are of course a matter of derivation and not of class overlap [sec. 4.4.4 (2.6)].

Sometimes, an adjective comes from a back formation in which a negative *bu* 'un-' is taken off a noun. Thus from 你这法子很不科学. *Nii jeh fartz heen bukeshyue.* 'This method of yours is very unscientific.': 我觉得很科学嘛! *Woo jyuede heen keshyue me!* 'I find it very scientific!', where *keshyue* is usually a noun 'science' and not used as an adjective except in the near context of *bukeshyue*.[19] Similarly, 规则 *guei₀tzer* 'regulation': 不规则 *buguei₀tzer* 'irregular': 很规则 *heen guei₀tzer* 'very regular', which, being of slightly older standing than *heen keshyue*, depends less upon the presence of the negative to be usable. On the other hand, 规矩 *guei.jeu* 'rule' is a word of much older standing than *guei₀tzer* and is used without restriction also as an adjective 'well-behaved' without the presence of 不规矩 *buguei.jeu* 'unruly,—bad-mannered' in the near context. In the carpentry sense of 'true' vs. 'off', the positive form of the adjective occurs even more often than the negative.

(2) Adjectives and Transitive Verbs. Many adjectives are also transitive verbs in a causative sense, that is, they tell how something is to be made so; and a few in a putative sense, that is, they indicate that something is thought or found to be so. Thus, 一碗热汤 *i-woan reh-tang* 'a bowl of hot soup', but 把汤热一热 *bae tang reh .i.reh* 'heat the soup a little'. Similarly, 烫酒 *tanq-jeou* 'hot wine' or 'heat the wine' (as one does rice

---

[19]See 王如霖 (Wang Rulin) on *bukeshyue* in ZGYW, no. 69:139 (1958).

wine); 涼 茶 *liang-char* 'cold tea' or 'cool the tea', depending upon context. (The verb 晾 *lianq* means 'expose to the air, to cool or to dry' and is not a simple causative of 涼 *liang*.)  螺丝太紧，请 你把他鬆一鬆. *Luo$_0$sy tay jiin, chiing nii bae ta song .i.song.* 'The screw is too tight, please loosen it a bit.' With *song* and *jiin* interchanged, we get 'The screw is too loose, please tighten it a bit.' Since class overlap is a matter of empirical lexical fact, it does not necessarily go by pairs of antonyms. Thus, 忙 *mang* 'busy' or 'to be busy about, occupied with', but 閒 *shyan* 'idle' and 空 *konq* 'to be unoccupied, at leisure' are not used as Vt; 明白 *ming.bair* 'clear' or 'to be clear about,—understand', but 糊塗 *hwu.du* 'muddled, confused' is adjective only; 短 *doan* 'short' or 'lack; owe' [sec. 8.1.3.4(1) above], but 長 *charng* 'long' is adjective only.

(3) Adjectives and Adverbs. There are so many cases of overlapping of adjectives with adverbs that some writers prefer to consider it one of the normal functions of adjectives to modify verbs (including other adjectives), unless there is a difference in meaning. For example, Ju Dershi (*op. cit.*, 94-96) sets up two types: Type A 靜養 *jinq-yeang* 'quietly recuperate', 橫寫 *herng-shiee* 'horizontally write', 長住 *charng-juh* 'permanently stay (at)', where the variety of adjectives so used is very wide but the verbs so modified by each of them is extremely restricted, usually to one, two, or three different verbs. Thus, with 細 *shih* 'fine', there is 細看 *shih-kann* 'look at closely', 細想 *shih-sheang* 'think over carefully', and 細說 *shih-shuo* 'talk about in detail', but with its opposite 粗 *tsu* 'coarse', there is only 粗看 *tsu-kann* 'look over casually', and no °粗想 °*tsu-sheang* or °粗說 °*tsu-shuo*. In such cases, we shall regard such lexically restricted associated adjectives and verbs as compounds. Ju's Type B includes a rather short list, which he regards as nearly exhaustive, in most of which the adverbial use has a different, though related, meaning to the adjectival use. Under this type we shall regard the words as belonging to overlapping classes of adverbs and adjectives. Ju's list is given here.[20]

---

[20]See also 傅婧, 付词跟形容词的界限问题 (Fuh Jinq, "The

| Adjectives | | Adverbs |
|---|---|---|
| 光 'bare' | 光说不做 | *Guang shuo bu tzuoh* 'merely talk without doing it' |
| 白 'white' | 白担心 | *bair dan-shin* 'worry in vain' |
| 老 'old' | 老打架 | *lao daa-jiah* 'fight constantly' |
| 直 'straight' | 直哭 | *jyr ku* 'keep crying' |
| 硬 'hard' | 硬要去 | *yinq yaw chiuh* 'inflexibly want to go,—insist on going' |
| 多 'much' | 多想～ | *duo sheang.sheang* 'think a little more' |
| 少 'little' | 少吃点儿肉！| *Shao chy .deal row!* 'Eat less meat!' |
| 遲 'late' | 遲到了 | *chyr dawle* 'arrived late' |
| 全 'complete' | 全看見了 | *chyuan kann.jiann le* 'have seen it all' |
| 晚 'late' | 晚出来一步 | *woan chu.lai i-buh* 'come out a step later' |
| 怪 'queer' | 怪好的 | *guay hao de* 'rather good' |
| 难 'difficult' | 难解决 | *nan jiee₀jyue* 'difficult to solve' |
| 準 'accurate' | 準答应 | *joen da.yinq* 'will definitely promise' |
| 快 'quick' | 快到了 | *kuay daw le* 'will soon arrive' |
| 早 'early' | 早死了 | *tzao syyle* 'died long ago' |
| 真 'real' | 真相信<br>真好！| *jen shiangshinn* 'really believe', *jen hao* 'How nice!' |

---

Problem of the Boundary between Adverbs and Adjectives"), ZGYW, no. 29 (1954), reprinted in ZGYW Tsorngshu, vol. 2, p. 162 of 160-165, Shanghai, 1956, where she sets up a table of criteria in which her group Biing gives the examples 老, 直, 白, 满, 怪, 光, 好, 快, which are all in Ju's list.

| 假 'false' | 假生气 | *jea sheng-chih* 'falsely get angry, —pretend to be angry' |
| 窮 'poor' | 窮遮騰 | *chyong je.deng* 'bum about like a poor man,—flounder in-effectively' |
| 乱 'confused' | 乱動 | *luann donq* 'move at random' |
| 干 'dry' | 干着急 | *gan jau-jyi* 'dryly worry,— worry in vain' |
| 满 'full' | 滿不在乎 | *maan butzay.hu* 'fully don't care,—quite indifferent' |
| 好 'good' | 好利害 | *hao li'.hay!* 'how powerful!' |
| 大 'great' | 大气 | *dah chih* 'greatly angry' |

In order to make the adverbial meanings clearer, we have changed most of the illustrating phrases. Ju also lists an additional use of *hao* in 好商量 *hao shang.liang* 'may very well discuss (the matter)'. However, it is better to treat *hao* as an auxiliary verb, since one can say 好不好商量？ *Hao .bu.hao shang-.liang?* 'May one discuss it?' and there is no H-*bu*-H form for asking questions like the V-*bu*-V forms. On the other hand, to the 真 *jen* 'really' in the list, we have added the exclamatory adverb 真 *jen* 'how ... !' Ju lists two words under both Type A and Type B: 直 *jyr*<sub>A</sub> 'straight': *Jyr*<sub>B</sub> 'straight on,—keep ... -ing', and 怪 *guay*<sub>A</sub> 'queer, strange': *guay*<sub>B</sub> 'pretty, rather'. As for the example Ju gives under Type A, 怪叫 *guay-jiaw*, it is doubtful whether it is ever used as a verb. In a phrase like 他一声怪叫 *ta i-sheng guay-jiaw*, it is a nominal expression 'a strange cry from him' rather than 'He cried strangely,—he made a strange cry.' With the word order *Ta guay-jiaw i-sheng*, it sounds more like written bairhuah than normal speech.

*8.1.4 Status Verbs.* Status verbs are similar to but different from quality verbs, or adjectives. The term is not to be confused with "stative verbs" used by some writers for adjectives, since Chinese adjectives are primarily verbs. Semantically, a status verb expresses the status or condition a person or thing gets into.

Since there is usually an implication of change from a different previous condition, it is often followed by the particle *le*, as in 我饿了. *Woo eh le.* 'I am ( ~ was) hungry.' 现在饱了. *Shianntzay bao le.* 'I am full now.' 他灰心了. *Ta hueishin le.* 'He has got ash-hearted,—discouraged.' 苺子塞(住)了. *Goantz sai(.juh)le.* 'The pipe is stopped up.' 现在通了. *Shianntzay tong le.* 'It goes through now,—is open now.'

8.1.4.1. *Status Verbs and Adjectives.* The profiles for status verbs and adjectives in table 18 look rather similar. But the relative frequencies of the shared features are quite different. Thus, with adjectives, the occurrence of *le* (column j) and its negative 没 *mei* (column b) is only incidental, as in 你的錶慢了. *Niide beau mannle.* 'Your watch is (too) slow.' 錶没慢. *Beau mei mann.* 'The watch did not get (too) slow.' With status verbs, *le* and *mei* are much more common, as in 饭煳了. *Fann hwule.* 'The rice is getting ( ~ has got) burned.' 没煳. *Mei hwu.* 'It wasn't burned.'

In column d 别 *bye* 'don't!' and other auxiliary verbs, especially 要 *yaw* 'will' and 会 *huey* 'will likely, might, could', occur very often with status verbs, as in 别病! *Bye binq!* 'Don't get sick!' 你的饼干儿要僵了( ~ 皮了). *Niide biinggal yaw jiangle ( ~ pyile).* 'Your crackers will get uncrisp,—soggy.' 搁得罐子裡就不会僵. *Ge de guanntz.lii jiow buhuey jiang.* 'They won't become soggy if placed in a can.' 这料子洗了不会皱. *Jeh liawtz shiile buhuey jow.* 'This material won't get wrinkled after washing.'

In column f status verbs can have cognate objects of number of times, as in 腿麻了好几回. *Toei male haojii-hwei.* .'My leg has felt numb several times.' In column i the indefinite past aspect of 过-.*guoh* is unusual with adjectives, as we saw in the case of 这么好过 *tzemm hao.guoh* 'been so good before' [sec. 8.11(i)], but it is very common with status verbs, as in 我从来没醉过. *Woo tsornglai mei tzuey.guoh.* 'I have never been drunk before.' 苏必路湖以前没全冻过. *Subihluh Hwu yiichyan mei chyuan donq.guoh.* 'Lake Superior was never frozen over before.'

*8.1.4.2. Status Verbs in Attributive Position.* Like adjectives and verbs of action status verbs can directly modify a substantive without *de* only in certain restricted lexical cases, as in 餓鬼 *ehgoei* 'hungry ghost', 皺綢 *jowchour* 'wrinkled silk—crepe', 漏斗 *lowdoou* 'leaking bushel,—funnel', 漏勺 ( 儿 ) *lowshaur(l)* 'leaking ladle,—strainer', 殭屍 *jiang₀shy* 'stiff(ened) corpse,— vampire', 散沙 *saan-sha* 'loosened sand' (simile for unorganized people); otherwise, a status verb needs a subordinative particle *de* before a substantive, as in    别用那个疼的指头！*Bye yonq neyg terng de jyr.tou!* 'Don't use the aching finger!' 他挑了两 块脆的饼干儿吃. *Ta tiaule leang-kuay tsuey de biinggal chy.* 'He chose two crisp crackers to eat.' 漏的房顶挡不了雨. *Low de farngdiing daang.bu-leau yeu.* 'A leaking roof cannot keep the rain out.'

*8.1.4.3. Status Verbs as Complements.* Because status verbs have mostly to do with something having gotten into a certain status, they occur more often as complements than do either adjectives or intransitive verbs of action. Examples are: 急瘋了 *jyi-fengle* 'worry oneself crazy', 哭啞了 *ku-yeale* 'cry oneself hoarse', 睡醒了 *shuey-shiingle* 'have slept (until) awake,— wake up', 吃饱了 *chy-baole* 'eat oneself full', 玩儿迷了 *wal-mile* 'play (until one gets) addicted', 打通了 *daa-tongle* 'strike through', 罵皮了 *mah-pyile* 'scold (until the child becomes) insensitive (to scolding)'.

*8.1.4.4. Overlapping of Status Verbs with Other Form Classes.* Status verbs sometimes have class overlapping, usually with a difference in meaning, with adjectives, verbs of action, etc. In the last examples cited, 通 *tong* can also be an adjective for 'logical, grammatical', as against 不通 *butong* 'illogical, ungrammatical', but in 鼻子不通. *Byitz bu tong.* 'The nose is stopped up', *tong* is a status verb. The status verb 皮 *pyi* 'insensitive (to discipline)' is also an adjective for 'naughty', and both are from the noun for 'skin' (whence 'tough as skin,—insensitive or naughty'). The status verb 乏 *far*, as in 我今天乏了. *Woo jin.tian far le.* 'I feel fatigued today.', is also an adjective (probably a Peip. localism) in 这便宜酒真乏. *Jeh pyan.yi jeou jen far.* 'This cheap wine is of pretty poor quality.' In 他病了。 *Ta binq le.* 'He is ( ~ has become) sick.', *binq* is a status verb; in 他有病。 *Ta yeou binq.* 'He has a sickness.', it is a noun. Since 没(有) *mei (yeou)* is either an auxiliary verb or a principal verb, 他没(有)病。*Ta mei(yeou) binq.* is ambivalently either 'He has not been sick.' or 'He has no sickness.'

8.1.5. *Transitive Verbs of Action (Vt).* Except for having a wide range of objects, transitive verbs of action have practically the same profile of syntactical properties as intransitive verbs of action, as shown in table 18.

8.1.5.1. *Objects of Transitive Verbs.*

(1) Omission of Object. We have seen (sec. 5.4.5) that the object of a transitive verb is omitted if it is in the near context. Actually, if it is implied in the situational context, no object word needs even to be present in the linguistic context. For example, if one person is washing the dishes, another may say 让我来擦 ! *Ranq woo lai tsa!* 'Let me wipe them!', even though no 碗 *woan* 'bowls' or 碟子 *dyetz* 'dishes' have been mentioned. Sometimes a V-O construction represents a general type of action and if only the verb is present, it will suggest that some specific object is omitted. For example, 别说话! *Bye shuo-huah!* 'Don't say words,—don't talk!' but 别说! *Bye shuo!* 'Don't say it!' 别吃东西 ! *Bye chy dong.shi!* 'Don't eat things,—don't eat!' but 别吃! *Bye chy!* 'Don't eat it!' 他在那儿想事情呐。 *Ta tzay.nall sheang shyh.chyng ne.* 'He is thinking about something.', but 他在那儿想呐。 *Ta tzay.nall sheang ne.* 'He is thinking about it.' Note that if the situational context is clear enough, it even takes precedence over the linguistic context. For example, when I covered my dining table with the manuscript of this book and objected to having it cleared for setting the table, my wife agreed and said 现在谁来我都不理。*Shianntzay sheir lai woo dou bu lii.* Out of context, the object of 理 *lii* would be understood as 谁 *sheir* in the first clause and the sentence would mean 'Now no matter who comes I won't pay any attention to him.' But since the talk was about the dining table, even though the word 桌子 *jwotz* itself did not appear in the near context, or even in that discourse, 理 *lii* meant and was readily understood

as 'tidy up'. It would not have made any difference if an object
他 *.ta* had been put after the verb, as it could still have referred
to either the guests or the table.

(2) Transitive Verbs in V-O Form. There are V-O phrases
and compounds of various degrees of separability and specialization. A compound of old standing is just like any other ordinary
transitive verb and is not separable or ionizable. For example,
抱怨 *baw.yuann* 'hold a grudge,—blame', as in 事情坏了别
抱怨我。    *Shyh.chyng huayle bye baw.yuann woo.* 'When
things go bad, don't blame me.' With 出版 *chu-baan* 'put out
an edition,—publish' there is both     已经出过版了    *yii.jing
chu.guoh-baan le* 'has already been published' and, recently, 出
版过一部书  *chubaan.guoh i-buh shu* 'has published a book'.
For additional examples see sections 5.4.6.4 and 6.5.3 (1).

(3) Quantified Objects in the Past. While there is no distinction of tense for verbs, whether intransitive or transitive, if there
is a quantified object and the verb refers to past action, a perfective-aspect suffix *le* is required. For example,    我昨儿買了
一件贵东西. *Woo tzwol maele i-jiann guey dong.shi.* 'I
bought an expensive article yesterday.' 他只念了三年的
大学. *Ta jyy niannle san-nian de dahshyue.* 'He had only three
years of college.' If the aspect suffix *-.guoh* for the indefinite past
is used, then it takes the place of *le*, with the special meaning of
'did or have at least once before,—ever' or in case of the negative
没...过  *mei ... -.guoh* 'never', as in 他一辈子没上过十年
的学. *Ta i-beytz mei shanq.guoh shyr-nian de shyue.* 'In his
whole life he has never been in school for (as much as) ten years.'

8.1.5.2. *Direction of Action of Transitive Verbs*

(1) "Passive Voice". We have seen that, since there is no
distinction of voice in Chinese verbs, the direction of a verb may
be outward from the subject as actor or inward toward the subject as goal (secs. 2.4.2, 2.10.7, and 5.4.7.2). If a direction inward
is to be made explicit, then the so-called "passive voice" form
with 被 *bey* is used, as in 房子被燒了. *Farngtz bey shau
le.* 'The house has been burned down.' If the agent is to be expressed, it is placed after *bey* as its object: 房子被火燒了.
*Farngtz bey huoo shaule.* 'The house has been burned by fire.'

The *bey* construction is usually limited to disposal verbs (see below), usually of unfavorable meanings. But recently, from translating foreign passive verbs, 'by', or some equivalent in a Western language, is mechanically equated to *bey* and applied to verbs of favorable meanings or verbs with no disposal implications, as in 那封信没被他收到。 *Ney-feng shinn mei bey ta shoudaw.* 'That letter has not been received by him.', which in ordinary speech would be recast as 那封信他没收到。 *Ney-feng shinn ta mei shoudaw.* '(As for) that letter he did not receive (it).' or 那封信没收到。 *Ney-feng shinn mei shoudaw.* 'That letter was not received.'

(2) "Middle Voice" Verbs. There are verbs of action the direction of which goes either way. The simplest way is to treat them as intransitive verbs of action rather than transitive verbs of action inwards, or in the passive, unless there is an agent word to make the received action explicit. For example, in 鎖被賊给开了。 *Suoo bey tzeir geei kai le.* 'The lock was opened by thieves.', *kai* 'opened' is clearly what the *suoo* 'lock' receives. But in 门已经开了。 *Men yii.jing kai le.* 'The door has already opened.', it is simpler to regard *kai* 'open' as intransitive than as a passive transitive 'opened', just like 花儿已经开了。 *Hual yii.jing kai le.* 'The flowers have already opened,—blossomed.' Similarly, 水溅得一地。 *Shoei po de i-dih.* 'Water has splashed all over the floor (not necessarily has been splashed).' 画儿掛的不正。 *Huall guah de bu jenq.* 'The picture hangs crooked (not necessarily has been hung).' 一根儿長枝子一直掛到地。 *I-gel charng jytz ijyr guah daw dih.* 'A long twig hangs right down to the ground (and has obviously not been hung there by anybody).' Sometimes the direction of action is unclear even though the grammatical form is in the simple, direct V-O form. For example, 我走不動，你扶着我！ *Woo tzoou.bu-donq, nii fwuj woo!* I am too tired to walk, please hold me for (my) support!', but 你走不動，你扶着我吧！ *Nii tzoou.bu-donq, nii fwuj woo ba!* 'You are too tired to walk, better hold me for (your) support!', where the grammatical direction of action is

*fwuj* → *woo*, 'hold me for support' but the physical directions of action in the two cases are exactly opposite to each other.[21]

Other examples of verbs of indeterminate direction are 火 滅 了. *Huoo miehle.* 'The fire has gone out ~ has been extinguished.' 國 滅 了. *Gwo miehle.* 'The country has perished ~ has been conquered.' 風 浪 平 了. *Fenglanq pyngle.* 'The storm has subsided.' 乱 平 了. *Luann pyngle.* 'The uprising has subsided ~ has been quelled.' 天 下 定 了. *Tianshiah dinqle.* 'The empire has settled down ~ has been settled.' In his preface to the *Chieh Yunn*, Luh Faayan says 吾 輩 数 人 定 則 定 矣. *Wubey shuhren dinq tzer dinq yii.* L, which translated 'nto modern speech is something like 咱 们 几 个 人 定 了 就 定 了. *Tzarmen jiig ren dinqle jiow dinqle.* '(If) the few of us decide upon it (the system of phonology), then it is decided.' The first *dinq* is a transitive verb, with the usual omission of the object, and the second *dinq* could be taken as a verb with direction inward, but more simply as an intransitive verb 'get settled,—become definite.' Sometimes, there is skewed relationship between an adjective and a transitive verb which are near synonyms, for example: 清 楚 *ching.chuu* 'clear' A, but 明 白 *ming.bair* (1) 'clear' A, (2) 'understand' Vt. In this particular instance the relation is doubly skewed, since in current written bairhuah, *ching.chuu* is also used, though still rarely, as Vt in a putative sense, as in 音 樂 学 … 使 作 曲 家 可 以 清 楚 他 们 寫 作 的 現 象 *Inyuehshyue ... shyy tzuohcheujia keeyii ching.chuu tamen shieetzuoh de shiannshianq* 'musicology can make composers understand their act of composing,' where in everyday speech one would say *doong,* or 了 解 *leaujiee,* or *ming.bair,* rather than *ching.chuu.*[22]

*8.1.5.3. Subtypes of Vt.* Various classifications of transitive verbs have been made, most of them based on semantic considerations, such as physical action: 打 *daa* 'strike, 推 *tuei* 'push', or

---

[21]See 任 銘 善 Ren Mingshann's discussion of this example in Leu, *S 与 O*, 231-232.

[22]Reported by Jean Jyhshinn in an interview with Rulan Chao, who, on being asked later, said that she had not used the word *ching.chuu* as Vt in that interview, *Jengshinn Shinwen Weekly*, April 30, 1966, p. 5.

mental action: 想 *sheang* 'think', 疑心 *yi.shin* 'suspect', etc. There is no limit to such classification, but if only formal criteria are used, the differences among transitive verbs of action are more limited.

(1) Disposal and Nondisposal Verbs. Verbs expressing disposal of something in some way have the syntactical property of admitting the pretransitive construction with 把 *bae* (sec. 5.5.4). Wang Lih calls such verbs *Chuujyh-shyh* ( 处置式 ) (*Yeufaa*, I, 160, *Outline* 105). For example, 把碗砸了 *bae woan tzarle* 'smashed the bowl', 把书念熟了 *bae shu niannshour le* 'take the book and read it well,—learn the lesson well', but not °把 月亮看見了 °*bae yueh.lianq kann.jiannle* 'take the moon and see it', since seeing or other such involuntary perception simply happens and is not disposing of something. On the other hand, one can say 把事情看清楚了! *Bae shyh.chyng kann-ching.chuule!* 'Look at the thing clearly!' since the compound verb *kann-ching.chuu* 'look at clearly' is something one can do to a thing.

(a) Examples of Disposal Verbs with 把 *bae*. 做 *tzuoh* 'do', 幹 *gann* 'do, perform', 搁 *ge* 'place', 安 *an* 'install', 動 *donq* 'move', 甩 *shoai* 'fling', 拿 *na* 'take', 打 *daa* 'strike', 切 *chie* 'cut', 弄 *nonq* 'do with, fix (in the colloquial sense)', 叠 *dye* 'fold', 摺 *jer* 'fold' (dial.), 修 *shiou* 'repair' or 'whittle (e.g., a pencil)', 归置 *guei.jyh* 'tidy up', 摩 *mo* 'rub', 刷 *shua* 'brush', 洗 *shii* 'wash', 送 *sonq* 'send', 害 *hay* 'harm', 殺 *sha* 'kill', 責備 *tzer.bey* 'reprimand', 称讚 *cheng₀tzann* 'praise', 告送 *gaw.sonq* 'tell', 忘了 *wanqle* 'forget', etc., in an open class. As we have seen (sec. 5.5.4.4), when a pretransitive is used with one of these verbs, a complement or a minimum of a suffix *le* has to be added, as in 把他殺了 *bae ta shale* 'kill him (off)'.

(b) Verbs Taking the "Passive Form" with 被 *bey*. The verbs which take 把 *bae* and those which take 被 *bey* are very much the same class except for certain verbs of perception, such as 看見 *kann.jiann* 'see', 听見 *ting.jiann* 'hear', 闻見 *wen.jiann* 'smell', 覚着 *jyuej* 'feel', as in 这消息早被他听見了。 *Jeh shiau.shi tzao bey ta ting.jiannle.* 'This news was heard by him long ago.', but not ° 他 把 这 消息 听 見 了。    °*Ta bae jeh shiau-.shi ting.jiannle.* for 'He heard this news.' But it is possible to say 你 得 把 我 的 话 听 清楚 了 ！ *Nii deei bae woode huah ting-ching.chuule!* 'You must listen to my words clearly!', since 听 *ting* 'listen' or 听清楚 *ting-ching.chuu* 'listen clearly' is a different verb from the verb of actual perception 听見 *ting-.jiann.*

(c) Verbs Taking Neither 把 *bae* nor 被 *bey*. Certain transitive verbs, not nearly as numerous as disposal verbs, but still forming an open class, take neither 把 *bae* nor 被 *bey*. Thus, from 我 茇 烧。*Woo fa-shau.* 'I develop a fever,—I have a fever.', there is no ° 我 把 烧 茇 高 了。°*Woo bae shau fa-gaule.*, nor ° 烧 被 茇 高 了。°*Shau bey fa-gaule.*, but one can say 我 的 烧 茇 的 很 高。*Woode shau fa de heen gau.* 'My fever is developed very high.' 他 害 喜 ～ 害 孩子。*Ta hay-shii～hay hairtz.* 'She is sick with child,—she has the morning sickness.' There is no °*Ta bae shii hayle.*, while *Ta bae hairtz hayle.* would mean 'She has (fatally) harmed her child.'

"Inverted subjects" of verbs of appearance and disappearance [sec. 8.1.2.1 (7 and 8)] are also non-disposal verbs. Thus, from 下 雨 *shiah yeu* 'down rain,—it rains', there is no ° 把 雨 下 了。°*Bae yeu shiahle.* or ° 雨 被 下 了。°*Yeu bey shiahle.*; from 来 碗 湯 ！ *Lai woan tang!* 'Bring a bowl of soup!', there is no ° 把 湯 来 了。°*Bae tang laile.* or ° 湯 被 来 了。°*Tang bey laile.*; and from 湖 南 出 米。*Hwunan chu-mii.* 'Hunan produces rice.', there is no ° 湖南 把 米 出 了。°*Hwunan bae mii chule.* or ° 米 被 湖南 出 了。°*Mii bey Hwunan chule.*, but one can say 米 出 在 湖南。*Mii chu tzay Hwunan.* 'Rice comes out in Hunan,—rice is produced in Hunan.'

(2) Link Verbs and Think Verbs. In 我 讓 他 来。*Woo ranq ta lai.* 'I let him come.', *ranq* is what we have called a prepivotal verb (sec. 2.13.2) and others have called a link verb,[23] to which *ta* is object, serving in turn as subject of *lai*. In verbs of the 'think, say' type, on the other hand, as in 我 想 他 一定 来。

---

[23]For example, Malmqvist, Sïch'uanese, 145-146.

*Woo sheang ta idinq lai.* 'I think he will certainly come.', *sheang* takes the whole clause *ta idinq lai* as its object. One test of the different ICs in the two constructions is the possibility of an after-thought addition of the preceding subject and verb (sec. 2.13.1). Thus, we can say 他一定來，我想. *Ta idinq lai, $_0$woo $_0$sheang.* 'He will certainly come, I think.', but not ° 他來，我讓. °*Ta lai, $_0$woo $_0$ranq.* '°Him come, I let.' For a typical list of link verbs, see section 2.13.2. Additional examples of verbs with clause objects are 以為 *yiiwei* 'take it (mistakenly) that ... ', 覺着 *jyuej* 'feel that ... , notice that ... , find that ... ', 忘了 *wangle* 'forget that ... ', 疑心 *yi.shin* 'suspect that ... ', 盼望 *pann.wanq* 'hope that ... ', 希望 *shi$_0$wanq* 'hope that ... ',[24] and 指望 *jyy-$_0$wanq* 'expect that ... '.

*8.1.5.4. Class Overlaps with Other Form Classes.* We have already seen cases of overlapping between transitive and intransitive verbs. It should be noted further that with a disposal verb, if it happens also to be an intransitive verb which can take an object of destination or origin of locomotion, the difference in both meaning and function can be brought out clearly by the use or non-use of the pretransitive form. Thus, 出 *chu* 'go out of' in 出國 *chu-gwo* 'go abroad', 出院 *chu-yuann* 'go out of the hos-pital', 出洋 *chu-yang* 'go abroad' cannot take the form ° 把國出了 °*bae gwo chule*, and so on. But with the causative Vt 出 *chu* 'produce, emit', one can say 你把气出了就舒服了。 *Nii bae chih chule jiow shu.fwu le.* 'You will feel better after you have given vent to your anger.' 病人把汗出了燒就退了. *Binqren bae hann chule shau jiow tuey le.* 'When the patient has let the perspiration out, the fever will then subside.' From 去上海 *chiuh Shanqhae* 'go to Shanghai', 走右边儿 *tzoou yow.bial* 'go by the right', one cannot say ° 把上海去了 °*bae Shanqhae chiuhle*, and so on. But with the causative Vt 去

---

[24]The verbs *pann.wanq* and *shi$_0$wanq* are used only for future events. For past events, as in 'I hope the job wasn't too difficult.', it will have to be reworded in some such form as 那事情該別太难吧? *Nah shyh.chyng gai bye tay nan ba?* 'That job had better not be too difficult, had it?'

*chiuh* 'remove', and 走 *tzoou* 'move (as a chessman)', one can say
把髒去了 *bae tzang chiuhle* 'remove the dirt' and 把卒子
走一步 *bae tzwutz tzoou i-buh* 'move the pawn one step'.

For examples of overlapping of transitive verbs of action with
adjectives, see section 8.1.3.6 (2). Other examples are 平 *pyng*
'level' A, but 把乱平了 *bae luann pyngle* 'have quelled the
uprising', with *pyng* 'level, quell' as Vt; 疼 *terng* 'it hurt . . .'
status verb, but 把孩子疼的不像樣 *bae hairtz terng de
bushianqyanq* 'love the child beyond reason', with *terng* 'feel
sympathetic pain with,—love' as Vt.

Overlaps of Vt with nouns are much less common now than
formerly, as in 火其书 *huoo chyi shu* 'fire their books' L, 水其
田 *shoei chyi tyan* 'water their fields' L. But one does say 油
(漆)房子 *you(chi) farngtz* 'paint the house', 鼓着嘴 *guuj tzoei*
'drum up one's mouth,—puff up one's mouth', 把臉背过去
*bae lean bey.guoh.chiuh* 'back away the face,—turn the face
away', where the primary meaning of 背 *bey* is 'the back' in the
anatomical sense.

   *8.1.6. Transitive Quality Verbs (V$_A$).* Transitive quality verbs
are like transitive action verbs in having an open class of objects,
but differ from them, as shown in table 18, chiefly in (c) taking
adverbs of degree 很 *heen* 'very', 太 *tay* 'too', etc., as illustrated
below, (g) having no tentative-aspect reduplicates, (h) having no
progressive aspect, there being no ° 他信着教呐. °*Ta shinnj
jiaw ne.* 'He is believing in religion.' [there is 他信教着呐.
*Ta shinn jiaw jne.* 'He believes in religion very much.', where *jne*
is a sentence particle (P 18) and not part of the verb], and (k)
having no imperative form, there being no ° 知道你自己！
°*Jy.daw nii tzyhjii!* for 'Know thyself!', which has to be paraphrased in some such way as 你应该知道你自己. *Nii
inggai jy.daw nii tzyhjii.* 'You ought to know yourself.' Moreover,
a V$_A$ does not take the pretransitive 把 *bae*, etc., there being no
° 把佛信了 °*bae For shinnle* for 'believe in Buddha'.

   (1) Quality Transitive Verbs Proper. The formal characteristics mentioned above may apply to the verbs as such or to the
V-O construction as a whole. If applicable to the verbs as such,

then property (c) about adverbs of degree will be applicable
even if the object does not immediately follow the verb. For
example, with 很怕鬼 *heen pah goei* 'very much fear ghosts,—
is very afraid of ghosts', one can say 鬼我不很怕, 可是
賊我最怕了. *Goei woo bu heen pah, keesh tzeir woo tzuey
pah le.* 'Ghosts I am not afraid of, but burglars I am most afraid
of.' Thus, 怕 *pah* can be modified by *heen* and *tzuey* and is therefore a quality transitive verb. Other examples are 貪財 *tan-tsair*
'covet wealth', 貪酒 *tan-jeou* 'to be greedy for wine', as in 財
他 不 大 貪, 可是酒他貪的很. *Tsair ta budah tan, keesh
jeou ta tan de heen.* 'He does not covet wealth very much,
but he is very greedy for wine.'; 愛 *ay* 'love', 喜欢 *shii.huan*
'like', as in 他最愛(～ 頂喜欢 )的是小兒子. *Ta tzuey ay*
(～ *diing shii.huan*) *de sh sheau-erltz.* 'The one he loves (～
likes) most is his youngest son.'; 信鬼 *shinn-goei* 'believe in
ghosts', 相信他心通 *shiangshinn tashintong* 'believe in
telepathy', as in 鬼他不大信, 可是他 心通他非常
相信. *Goei ta budah shinn, keesh tashintong ta feicharng
shiangshinn.* 'He doesn't believe much in ghosts, but he believes
very much in telepathy.'

(2) Quality V-O Phrases. There are certain V-O phrases,
usually with lexical specialization of meaning, in which the verb
does not take adverbs of degree as $V_A$'s do, but which as whole
phrases behave like $V_A$'s. For example, with 放心 *fanq-shin*
'relax mind,—feel relaxed', there is 很放心 *heen fanq-shin* 'feel
quite relaxed', but, although both *fanq* and *shin* are free, there
is no °心很放 °*shin heen fanq*. Therefore *fanq* is a transitive
action verb, and it is the V-O phrase that behaves like a quality
verb. Since a V-O construction behaves externally like an intransitive verb, a quality V-O phrase will then behave like an adjective, but internally it still admits of aspects in the verb and modifiers to the object. For example, with 省事 *sheeng-shyh* 'save
work,—save trouble', there is 很省事 *heen sheeng-shyh* 'need
very little trouble', 省了我许多事 *sheengle woo sheuduo
shyh* 'have saved me a lot of trouble'. Other examples of quality
V-O phrases are 太費事 *tay fey-shyh* 'too much spend work,—

too troublesome (to do)', 怪費心的 *guay fey-shin de* 'pretty expensive to the mind,—quite a bother', 最傷腦筋 *tzuey shang nao$_0$jin* 'most hurt the brain,—to be quite a problem'. Certain quality V-O phrases are formed with the verb 有 *yeou* 'have' and its negative 没 *mei* 'have not', as in 很有意思 *heen yeou yih.sy* 'very much have meaning,—very interesting', 太没礼貌了 *tay mei lii$_0$maw le* 'too much without courtesy, —too rude', 那么没規矩 *nemm mei guei.jeu* 'so without (proper) behavior,—so ill-mannered', 这话很有道理. *Jeh huah heen yeou daw.lii.* 'These words very much have reason,— are perfectly right.' (cf. Fr. *avoir raison*). It goes without saying that a quality V-O depends upon both the V and O, whereas V$_A$ proper of the 爱 *ay* 'love', 怕 *pah* 'fear' type are quality verbs regardless. Thus, 傷身体 *shang shen$_0$tii* 'hurt the body' is like 傷腦筋 *shang nao$_0$jin* 'to be quite a problem' cited above, but the idiomatic phrase 傷風 *shang-feng* 'get hurt (by) the wind,—catch cold' is simply an ordinary Vt-O, which one either does or does not. For 'catch a bad cold' it will have to be re-phrased in some such form as 傷風傷的很利害 *shang-feng shang de heen lihhay* '(in) catching the cold, caught it strong-ly'. Similarly, there is 很放心 *heen fanq-shin* 'feel very relaxed', but 放假 *fanq-jiah* 'let out for a vacation or holiday,—give or take a holiday' is something which one either does or does not.

There are a few V$_A$'s which form quality V-O phrases in which they have special causative functions. Thus, with 恨 *henn* 'hate', there is 非常恨他 *feicharng henn ta* 'very much hate him'. But with the pronoun 人 *ren* 'one' as object, *henn* can be used causatively as 'cause one to hate', as in 这件事真恨人！ *Jeh-jiann shyh jen henn-ren!* 'How this event makes one hate it!' Similarly, in addition to the simple meaning in 怕人 *pah-ren* 'to be afraid of people', there is the causative meaning in 那臉看了真怕人. *Nah lean kannle jen pah-ren.* 'Looking at that face really frightens one.' Likewise, 气人 *chih-ren* 'anger one,—be provoking', 惱人 *nao-ren* 'annoying'.

Quite a number of quality V-O phrases have adjective as objects, as in 吃香 *chy-shiang* 'eat the delicious,—to be in favor,

popular', 要強 *yaw-chyang* 'want to be strong,—ambitious',
貪涼 *tan-liang* 'greedy for the cool,—indulge in staying in cool
air', 怕兇 *pah-shiong* 'to be afraid of the fierce,—timid'.

(3) Quality V-O Compounds. When one or both parts in a
V-O construction are bound, the result will be a compound
word, and if it is a quality verb, it is simply an adjective. However, the V-O nature is sometimes still present when it can be
ionized. Thus, with 吃虧 *chy-kuei* 'absorb loss,—suffer loss,—
to be at a disadvantage', there is 很吃过点儿虧 *heen
chy.-guoh deal huei* 'have suffered quite a little loss', as well as
这樣太吃虧了. *Jehyanq tay chy-kuei le.* 'This way will be too
disadvantageous.'; similarly 上算 *shanq-suann* 'go into (favorable)
reckoning,—to be advantageous,—it pays' and 上当 *shanq-danq*
'go up into a trick,—to be tricked' can be modified by 很 *heen*
'very', 太 *tay* 'too', and so on, or ionized with aspect suffixes, and
so on. However, solid compounds are fully adjectives and are not
only not ionizable but can sometimes even take on vivid reduplication, as in 合式 *hershyh* 'fit the form,—suitable':  合ㄦ式ㄦ
的一身衣裳 *herhershyhshyh de i-shen i.shang* 'a perfectly
fitting suit of clothes', 像樣(ㄦ) *shiang-yanq(l)* 'resemble (the
right) shape,—in proper shape or style':  很像ㄦ樣ㄦ的
一堂傢具 *heen shianqshianqyanqyanqlde i-tarng jiajiuh*
'quite a presentable set of furniture'. Not all solid V-O compounds which behave like $V_A$'s can be so reduplicated. For example, 知趣 *jychiuh* 'know the interest (of people concerned),—
tactful' and 乞味 *wuwey* 'have no taste,—in bad taste, uncalled
for' are not reduplicable. Whether reduplicable or not, solid
quality V-O compounds are simply adjectives.

*8.1.7. Classificatory Verbs (Vc).* Classificatory verbs form a
short list, whose semantic property is that of classifying what is
expressed by the subject as being the same or in some way
classed under that of the object.[25] Their formal properties, as
shown in table 18, are that: (a) and (b) they take both the nega-

---

[25] In my *Mand Prim*, 48, the heading of classificatory verbs included
the verb 是 *sh* 'to be', which, because of its special syntactical properties,
we are now setting apart as a separate class with a unique member.

tives 不 *bu* and 没 *mei;* (c) except for Vc 7, they do not take *heen* or other adverbs of degree; (d), (g) and (k), except for Vc 5 and 6, they do not appear in simple or tentative imperative form; (e), (f), except for Vc 5 and 6, they do not take cognate objects of extent or number of times; (h), (i), (j) they do not usually take aspects suffixes *-j. -.guoh,* or *-le,* forms like 我姓了李才怪 呐! *Woo shinqle Lii tsair guay ne!* 'It would be strange if my name were Lii.' being rare. (1) They have the usual V-*bu*-V form of interrogatives. Following is the list:

V c 1: 等于 *deeng₀yu* 'to be equal to' is a recent borrowing from mathematical terminology into ordinary speech, as 三加 七等于十。 *San jia chi deengyu shyr.* 'Three plus seven is equal to ten.', 又减十就等于零 *yow jean shyr jiow deengyu ling* 'again, minus ten, equals zero'. 告送了他没听清楚就等 于没告送. *Gaw.sonqle ta mei ting-ching.chuu jiow deengyu mei gaw.sonq.* 'To have told him and not to be heard clearly is as good as not to have told him.' The negative 没等于 *mei deengyu* is rare, even referring to the past. For example, 你 说我的成绩等于零, 你看, 并没等于零嘤! *Nii shuo woode cherngji deengyu ling, nii kann, binq mei deengyu ling me!* 'You said my accomplishment was equal to nil, but look, it wasn't equal to nil, was it?' But even here, it would be more usual to use *bu* instead of *mei,* the slight difference being that *mei* emphasizes what was not so and *bu* points at the present accomplishment.

Vc 2: 叫 *jiaw* 'to be called, have the name of' takes the name as object, as in 我叫小毛茛。 *Woo jiaw Sheau Mauliang.* 'I am called Little Buttercup.' The passive form in the English translation might suggest that this is only an instance of the in-ward action of a transitive verb of action as in 事情幹完了. *Shyh.chyng gann-wanle.* 'The job is done.' That this is not the case can be seen by comparing it with (1) 我罵小毛茛. *Woo mah Sheau Mauliang.* 'I scold Little Buttercup.' and (2) 我叫 小毛茛, 小毛茛不答应. *Woo jiaw Sheau Mauliang, Sheau Mauling bu da.yinq.* 'I call Little Buttercup, but Little Buttercup doesn't answer.' Here the verbs *mah* and *jiaw* are transitive verbs of action. But when *jiaw* is translated in the passive form as 'am called', it is not so much a passive action as a classificatory equation and the direction is neither inward nor outward but more or less neutral, and the verb *jiaw* in this case can best be equated to the German *heissen*. The verb *jiaw*, then, can be either Vt or Vc by class overlap (as well as being a pretransitive, a passive agent preposition K 49, and a link verb 'to cause').

Vc 3: 姓 *shinq*, besides being a noun for 'surname, family name', is also a classificatory verb 'have the (family) name of', as in 他姓李，我姓欧阳. *Ta shinq Lii, woo shinq Ouyang.* 'His name is Lii, and my name is Ouyang.' That such sentences do not have nominal predicates is seen in the negative 他不姓李. *Ta bu shinq Lii.* 'He is not named Lii', as compared with the differently constructed sentence 他的姓不是李. *Tade shinq bush Lii.* 'His surname is not Lii.' The verb *shinq* occurs only rarely with *mei*, *-.guoh*, or *-le*. Possible examples are 我们这一族从来没姓过李，要是姓了李才怪呐！ *Woomen jey-i tzwu tsornglai mei shinq.guoh Lii, yawsh shinqle Lii tsair guay ne!* 'This clan of ours has never had the family name of Lii and it would be strange if we had had the name of Lii!' Of a woman who has married more than once, one might say 这位太ㄜ姓张姓了三年，现在又姓王了. *Jeh-way tay.tay shinq Jang shinqle san-nian, shianntzay yow shinq Wang le.* 'This lady had the (married) name of Jang for three years, and now her name is Wang again.'

Note that a monosyllabic Chinese family name is bound and is therefore either end-bound with the given name (sec. 7.3.1) or start-bound with the preceding verb *shinq*. That is why, of the following possible forms for *shinq* with a monosyllabic family name as object:

(a) V *bu* V O?      姓不姓王？    *Shinq bu shinq Wang?*
(b) V O *bu* O?      姓王不姓？    *Shinq Wang bu shinq?*
(c) V O *bu* V O?  姓王不姓王？  *Shinq Wang bu shinq Wang?*
(d) *Sh bush* V O?  是不是姓王？  *Sh bush shinq Wang?*

(c) and (d) with V and O together, are more common than (a) and (b), with the V and O ionized. The form V O *ma?* is not included here because it has a slightly more negative implication, while the four forms given above are completely noncommittal as to what the answer will be.

Do not confuse this verbal use of 姓 *shinq* with the nominal use of 名 *ming* 'given name' L, 字 *tzyh* 'courtesy name' L, 号 *haw* 'courtesy name', 号 *haw* 'sobriquet' L, etc., all of which can occur as the small subjects in S-P predicates, as in 此公名羽, 字雲長. *Tsyy gong ming Yeu, tzyh Yuncharng.* L' (About) this gentleman, the name is Yeu, the courtesy name is Yuncharng.' The colloquial equivalent for this will still take the S-P predicate construction: 这位先生名字叫羽, 号雲長。 *Jey-wey shian.sheng mingtzyh jiaw Yeu, haw Yuncharng.*, where *mingtz* takes the Vc *jiaw* and *haw* takes the nominal predicate *Yuncharng*, so that the sentence 他号雲長. *Ta haw Yuncharng.* consists of three substantives in the relation of $S_1 + (S_2$ P). To negate such a sentence, it will have to be in the form: 他不是号雲長. *Ta bush haw Yuncharng.* 'He is not such that the courtesy name is Yuncharng.', or recast as 他的号不是雲長. *Tade haw bush Yuncharng.* 'His courtesy name is not Yuncharng.', but not ° 他不号... °*Ta bu haw ...* . Only the word 姓 *shinq* has in modern speech acquired the full status of a verb, modifiable by *bu*.

Vc 4: 号称 *hawcheng* 'call-address,—to be spoken of as, known as' is usually followed by a sobriquet or some descriptive expression, as in 号称天下第一关 *hawcheng Tienshiah Dih'i Guan* 'known as the First Pass in the World', 号称打不倒 *hawcheng daa.bu-dao* 'called the un-knockout-able', 自己号称 无敵 *tzyhjii hawcheng wudyi* 'claim to be without match,— claim to be invincible'. Note that, although 号 *haw* is a noun and 称呼 *cheng.hu* can be either a noun 'term of address' or a verb 'address as', *hawcheng* is always a Vc.

Vc 5: 做 *tzuoh*[26] 'act as, to be in the capacity of' is, by class

---

[26]There have been very complicated differentiations and interdialectal borrowings of variant forms of the etymon 作 Anc. Ch. *tsâk*, resulting in 作, (Wu *tzo'*) and 做 (Wu *tzuh*), with idiomatic differences in meaning and

overlap, also Vt 'do, make'. It is Vc in the adage 读好书，说好话，做好人，行好事。 *Dwu hao-shu, shuo hao-huah, tzuoh hao-ren, shyng hao-shyh.* 'Read good books, say good words, be a good man, perform good deeds.' In fact, if the somewhat formal 行 *shyng* 'perform' were not used here, for the sake of rhetorical variation, a more usual way of saying the same thing would be 做好事 *tzuoh hao-shyh* 'do good deeds', thus showing very clearly the double function of *tzuoh* as Vc and Vt. Other examples of *tzuoh* as Vc are: 做东 *tzuoh-dong* 'being host', 做官 *tzuoh-guan* 'serve as an official', 做新娘子 *tzuoh shin-niangtz* 'being a bride', 做贼 *tzuoh-tzeir* 'act as a burglar'. In 这个可以给你做个挡子。 *Jeyg keeyii geei nii tzuoh g daangtz.* 'This can serve as a screen for you.', *tzuoh* is Vc. But it is ambiguous in 他可以给你做个挡子。 *Ta keeyii geei nii tzuoh g daangtz.* With *tzuoh* as Vc it means 'he can (himself) serve as a screen for you.', while with *tzuoh* as Vt, it means 'He can build a screen for you.' The wenyan equivalent of *tzuoh* is 为 *wei*, with the same double function, as in 为人 *wei ren* 'behave as a human being' L, but 为善 *wei shann* 'do good' L.

Vc 6: 当 *dang* 'to be in the position of, serve as', as in 当兵 *dang-bing* 'serve as a soldier', 当主人 *dang juu.ren* 'to be in the position of a host', 当伙计 *dang huoo.jih* 'serve as a waiter'. To translate the slogan 'Don't be a dish washer, buy one!' one will have to say 别当个洗碗机，买一个煞！ *Bye dang g shiiwoanji, mae ig sha!* This is to be distinguished from the causative or putative Vt 当 *danq* 'take as, regard as', as in 我拿你当好人。 *Woo na nii danq hao-ren.* 'I took you to be a good man (rightly or wrongly).' 茶可以当药。 *Char keeyii danq yaw.* 'Tea can be used as medicine.' As a 'think' verb with a clause

---

grammatical function, as in 作文 *tzuoh-wen* 'write composition (school subject)', 做人 *tzuoh-ren* 'act as a man'. There is even a compound 做作 *tzowtzuoh* 'have mannerisms'. In Mandarin, both the Entering Tone form and the Going Tone form coalesce in *tzuoh* and recently the simpler character 作 is used for both 做 and 作, thus reverting to the ancient morphemic identity, so far as Mandarin is concerned.

object, 当 *danq* usually takes the suffix -*j* and means 'think wrongly', as in 我当着你不来了。 *Woo danqj nii bu lai le.* 'I thought you weren't coming.' In this use, the majority type of Peiping pronunciation uses the 3rd Tone *daangj*, synonymous with 以为 *yiiwei* and homophonous with 挡着 *daangj* 'screening, standing in the way'.

The Vc *dang* is further to be distinguished from 当 *dang* 'to be right at', as in 当事 *dang-shyh* 'to be right on the job,—in charge of the job', 当着人前就打呵嗄 *dangj ren-chyan jiow daa ha.chy* 'yawn right in front of people'.

Both Vc 5 and Vc 6 can take aspect suffixes and in this respect behave like Vt, but, unlike disposal verbs, they cannot take pretransitives.

Vc 7: 像 *shianq* 'to be like' is in its syntactical behavior intermediate between V$_A$ and Vc in that it admits of modification by adverbs of degree, as in 陽貨很像孔子。 *Yang Huoh heen shianq Koongtzyy.* 'Yang Huoh looked very much like Confucius.', but it does not take cognate objects of extent or number of times, there being no ° 像一倍 °*shianq i-bey* for 'doubly similar' or ° 像兩次 °*shianq leang-tsyh* 'have resembled twice'.

*8.1.8. The Verb* 是 *sh 'to be'.* The nearest to the verb 是 *sh* in Western languages is the copula 'to be'.[27] We have treated the part of the predicate which comes after *sh* as its object (sec. 5.6.2), thus making *sh* a transitive verb. Although the formal properties of this verb are closest to those of the classificatory verbs, they are sufficiently different to set it apart as a one-member class, as will be seen as we go through the profile for *sh* in table 18 (sec. 8.1.1).

(a) As part of the definition of a verb, *sh* is negated by the use of *bu*, in which case *sh* is usually in the neutral tone except when specially stressed. We noted that in nominal predicates, it is not necessary to have a verb. To negate a nominal predicate, however, it must take the verbal form 不是 *bush* and not simply *bu*. For example, 这个人好人. *Jeyg ren hao-ren.* 'This man, a

---

[27] 王力,中國文法中的系词 (Wang Lih, "The Copula in Chinese Grammar"), *Tsing Hua Journal*, 12:38 (1937).

good man.' 不，他不是好人。*Bu, ta bush hao ren.* 'No, he is not a good man.'

(b) And (i) The verb *sh* rarely takes 没 *mei* as its negative. In the example 我从来没是过谁的人。 *Woo tsornglai mei sh.guoh sheirde ren.* 'I have never been anybody's man.' [secs. 5.4.5(3)], the extra stress (actually heard) is to be regarded as a way of pronouncing the quotes around *sh*, implying that someone used the word *sh* and I disapprove of it.

(c) Some adverbs of degree, 很 *heen* 'very' and 最 *tzuey* 'most', can modify *sh*, usually followed by an expression which can be modified by them without *sh*, as in 那种办法最是会出危险的。 *Ney-joong bannfaa tzuey sh huey chu weishean de.* 'Doing it that way is most likely to lead to accidents.'

(d) Auxiliary verbs are used before *sh* in rather restricted ways. There is 会是 *huey sh* 'can (possibly) be', but no °肯是 °*keen sh* for 'willing to be', for which one has to use the classificatory verb 做 *tzuoh*, as in 不肯做奴隶 *bukeen tzuoh nu₀lih* 'not willing to be a slave'. The imperative 别 *bye* 'don't' occurs only in such quasi-imperative forms as 别是出了事了吧？ *Bye sh chule shyh le ba?* 'Better not be that something had happened—was there an accident?' To say 'Don't be a slave!', either say 别做奴隶！ *Bye tzuoh nu.lih!* or 别当奴隶！ *Bye dang no.lih!* (Cf. translation of 'Don't be a dish washer!' under Vc 6 above.) With the auxiliary verb 得 *deei* 'have to', there is an unusual example from Lao Shee (Lao Shaw): 是他也得是他，不是他也得是他。 *Sh ta yee deei sh ta, bush ta yee deei sh ta.* 'If it was he, it had to be he; if it wasn't he, it had also to be he.'[28]

(e), (f), (g), (h) The verb *sh* does not take cognate object of extent or number of times and does not have a tentative aspect reduplicate or a progressive aspect, since it already has a built-in progressive meaning.

(i) On the indefinite past expressed by -*.guoh*, see (b) above.

(j) The perfective aspect applies only to *sh* as adjective [see

---

[28]Quoted in 语法小组 (Section on Grammar), ZGYW no. 35, 1955, p. 37.

(11) below], as in 是了就算了. *Shle jiow suann le.* 'When it's okay, then let it go.'

(k) There is no imperative form for *sh*. For 'Be a good man!' the verb has to be Vc 5 做 *tzuoh*, as we have seen.

(l) The interrogative form V-*bu*-V is applicable to all the uses of *sh* from (1) to (12), as detailed below.

(1) As copula, *sh* expresses equality between subject and object, as in 三加七是十. *San jia chi sh shyr.* 'Three plus seven is ten.' 明天是端陽. *Ming.tian sh Duan$_0$yang.* 'Tomorrow is the Duanyang Festival (5th of 5th moon).' 美國的京城是波士頓. *Meei.gwo de jingcherng sh Buoshyhduenn.* 'The capital of the United States is Boston.' (which, though not true, is perfectly grammatical).

(2) Subsumption under a class, or the epsilon ($\epsilon$) function, is the most common function of *sh*. The subject may be a member of a class, as in 他是回教徒. *Ta sh Hweijiawtwu.* 'He is a Moslem.', or a sub-class of a larger class, as in 松樹是常青樹. *Songshuh sh charngching.shuh.* 'The pine is an evergreen.' or 'Pines are evergreens.' If *i*-M 'a (kind of)' is used in the object, it is usually in the neutral tone and *i* is often omitted, as in 那是（一）个难题. *Nah sh (.i) g nan-tyi.* 'That's a difficult problem.' 这是（一）把刀. *Jeh sh (.i-) baa dau.* 'This is a knife.' This shows that the nominal expression after *sh* should be treated as its object rather than as the center of the predicate, with *sh* as an adverb to the predication.

(3) Predication with a more loose relation between subject and object than that of equality or subsumption is more common in Chinese than in English. A common type is predication involving size, age, and so on, in the form of a D-M compound, as in 他是十岁. *Ta sh shyr-suey.* 'He is ten years old.' 我是五尺八. *Woo sh wuu-chyy-ba.* 'I am five feet eight.', where *sh* can be omitted, with resulting nominal predicates. In the following examples, the relation expressed by *sh* is even more general: 我们是两个男孩儿一个女孩儿。 *Woomen sh leangg nanharl ig neuharl.* 'We are (such that we have) two boys and one girl.' 我是一片热心。 *Woo sh i-piann rehshin.* 'I am a lot of warm heart,—I put my whole heart into it.' 他是一

肚子的气。 *Ta sh i-duhtz de chih.* 'He is a whole bellyful of anger,—he is filled with anger.' 那孩子是古怪皮气。 *Nah hairtz sh guuguay pyi.chih.* 'That child is (of) queer temperament.'[29] All these examples can be changed into cases of nominal predicates by omitting the verb *sh*. This loose use of *sh*, as we have seen, is simply a special case of the generally loose relationship between subject and predicate (sec. 2.4.1).

(4) Existence is expressed by *sh*, usually with a place or time word as subject, as in 後头是个金鱼池。 *How.tou sh g jinyu-chyr.* '(In) the rear (there) is a goldfish pond.' 到处是水。 *Daw₀chuh sh shoei.* 'Everywhere (there) is water.' 明年是大选。 *Ming.nian sh dah-sheuan.* 'Next year (there) will be a general election.' In all such cases *sh* can be omitted, resulting in nominal predicates, but sometimes resulting in ambiguities; for example, 後头一个金鱼池 *how.tou ig jinyu-chyr* could also be a subordinative construction 'a goldfish pond in the rear'. Existence can be more explicitly expressed by 有 *yeou* 'there is', but the force of *sh* is 'there is something and that something is (the є -is) ...'.

(5) The form *sh ... de* can be used as a nominalizing specifier. For example, 他从中國来了。 *Ta tsorng Jong.gwo lai le.* 'He has come from China.', the 'he' could be anyone who happens to have (just) come from China. But 他是从中國来的。 *Ta sh tsorng Jong.gwo lai de.* 'He is one who comes from China.' implies either that he is a Chinese citizen or a resident of China or that it is from China that he has come. Other examples are 我是昨儿到的。 *Woo sh tzwol daw de.* 'It was yesterday that I arrived.' 那是他说的。 *Nah sh ta shuo de.* 'It was he that said it.' On apparently illogical sentences like 我是昨儿去看的医生。 *Woo sh tzwol chiuh kann de i.sheng.* 'I was the doctor who went to see yesterday,—It was yesterday that I went to see a doctor.', see section 5.3.6.5 (2.6) on the formula V-O *de* → V *de* O.

(6) A subject with contrasting stress can be reinforced by

[29]Samuel E. Martin has observed that this use of *sh* is carried over by Chinese speakers of English, as in 'My wife is 61, I am 58.', referring to the vintage of cars and not of the spouses.

adding a weak or neutral-tone *sh* before the verbal predicate, with or without a following nominalizing *de*. Thus, "我不去. "*Woo bu chiuh.* 'I am not going.': "我是不去(的)."*Woo $_0$sh bu chiuh (de).* '(As for) me (it) is (a case of) not going.' The contrasting stress is not necessary when both the terms contrasted are present, in which case the usually weakened or neutral tone on *sh* will have the same effect as the extra stress on the subject, as in 他的个儿是很大，不过身体不大好. *Tade gehl $_0$sh heen dah, buguoh shen.tii budah hao.* 'His build is quite big, only his health is not very good.' 人家是丰年，我是歉年. *Ren.jia sh fengnian, woo sh chiann-nian.* '(As for) them, (the year) is a bumper year; (as for) me, (the year) is a lean year.'[30]

(6.1) A special type of contrasted subject consists of a predicate prementioned as subject, then repeated in the predicate, after *sh*, resulting in a concessive form. Thus, from 我去. *Woo chiuh.* 'I am going there.', there is 我去是去. *Woo chiuh sh chiuh.* 'I am going, to be sure.'[31] implying 'so far as going is concerned, I am going, but ... '.  When a contrast is placed on a V-O construction, it need not be repeated as a whole, but on repetition after *sh* the O cannot be used alone; that is, of the forms:

> (a) V O *sh* V O
> (b) V O *sh* V
> (c) V *sh* V O
> (d) O *sh* V
> (e) °V O *sh* O

only the forms (a) through (d) are possible, but not (e). For example, (a) 吃饭是吃饭，可是不喝酒. *Chy-fann .sh chy-fann, keesh bu he jeou.* '(I, you, etc.) eat rice, to be sure, but do not drink wine.', (b) 吃饭是吃，可是 .... *Chy-fann .sh chy, keesh* ... , (c) 吃是吃饭，可是 ... . *Chy .sh chy-fann, keesh* ... , (d)

---

[30] 徐仲华，词类(Shyu Jonqhwa, *Parts of Speech*, Paoting, 1957, p. 59, quoting from 赵树理(Jaw Shuhlii).

[31] Or 'all right' in the colloquial sense, or simply in the intonation of ◡ on the key word 'going'. See *Mand Prim*, 184, and H. E. Palmer, *English Intonation*, Cambridge, England, 1922, chap. 24, pp. 82-83.

饭 是 吃 , 可 是 酒 不 喝. *Fann sh chy, keesh jeou bu he.* '(As for) rice (I, etc.) eat (it), but wine I don't drink.', but there is no °吃饭是饭 , °*Chy-fann .sh fann*, since the object *fann* is not the center of the contrasted predicate. If, however, there is a nominal predicate, then this concessive use *sh* is also available, as in 好人是好人 , 就是 不太聪明. *Hao-ren .sh hao-ren, jiowsh bu tay tsong.ming.* 'He is a good man, all right, only not too intelligent.'

(7) Contrastive predication (without concessive implication) involves no prementioning of the predicate in the subject, but can be expressed by an unstressed $_osh$ followed by the contrasting predicate, as in 他是累, 不是睏. *Ta .sh "ley, bush "kuenn.* 'He is tired, not sleepy.' 我是劝你 , 不是骂你. *Woo .sh "chiuann nii, bush mah nii.* 'I am giving you advice, not scolding you.'

(8) Assertive predicate is stressed by stressing *sh*, as in 他 "是累 , 不是 不累. *Ta "sh ley, bush buley.* 'He *is* tired, not untired.'

Under both (7) and (8) the use of *sh* makes the contrasting and assertive predication more explicit by suggesting 'He is a case of being tired', and so on. However, as we have seen, contrastive and assertive functions of predicates can be present without the use of *sh* as part of an enlarged predicate.

(9) *Sh* can introduce a clause, with the force of 'it is that … ', or in the case of *bush* 'not that … ', as in 是怎末啦 ? 是马惊了. *Sh tzeem l'a? Sh maa jingle.* 'What's happened? It was that a horse ran away,—there was a runaway horse.' 不是 我 不要末 , 是他 不让我末. *Bush woo buyaw lai, sh ta bu ranq woo lai.* 'Not that I didn't want to come, but (it was that) he didn't let me come.'

(10) The formula A 是 B 的 缘 故. A *sh* B *de $_oyuan.guh$.* looks as if it meant 'A is the reason for B.', but it actually means 'A is so, for the reason of (i.e., namely) B.' For example, 他老渴 是跑 了许多路的缘 故. *Ta lao kee sh paole sheuduo luh de $_oyuan.guh$.* 'That he is thirsty all the time is because he has trudged quite a long distance.' 地下湿是下了雨的缘故.

*Dih.shiah shy sh shiahle yeu de* ₀*yuan.guh.* 'That the ground is wet is because it has been raining.'

Similarly, the formula W 是 M 的 意 思。 W *sh M de* ₀*yih.sy.* seems to mean 'W is the meaning of M.', but it also means the reverse 'W is such that it has the meaning of (i.e., namely) M.', as in 英 文 'good' 是 好 的 意 思。 *Ingwen 'good' sh hao de yih.sy.* 'English "good" means good.' For further analysis and examples of these formulas, see section 5.3.6.5(1.1).

(11) As an adjective by way of class overlap, *sh* means 'right',[32] as in 是 的, 你 说 的 是, 你 说 的 很 是。 *Sh de, nii shuo de sh, nii shuo de heen sh.* 'Right, what you said was right, what you said was very right.' This has nothing to do with 是 你 说 的。 *Sh nii shuo de.* 'It was you who said it.' The negative 不 是 *bush* is often used nominally as 'error, mistake, fault', as in 承 认 我 的 不 是 *cherngrenn woode bush* 'admit my error', 对 他 赔 个 不 是 *duey ta peir g bush* 'apologizes to him for an offense'.

This adjectival use of *sh* 'right' is to be distinguished from the usual copula *sh* with object omitted, as in 这 是 真 花 儿 不 是 ？我 想 是。 *Jeh sh jen-hual bush? Woo sheang sh.* 'Are these real flowers? I think they are.' 陈 丹 理 在 哪 儿 ? 我 就 是。 *Chern Danlii tzay naal? Woo jiow sh.* 'Where is Chern Danlii? I am (he).'

(12) An attributive form of *sh* without the subordinative particle *de* has the meaning of 'whatever is, all', as in 是 人 都 来 了。 *Sh ren dou laile.* 'Whoever is a man has come,—everyone has come.' 是 字 典 都 查 了。 *Sh tzyhdean dou charle.* '(I) have looked (it) up in all the dictionaries.' An unusual construction with this *sh* is 比 是 花 都 好 闻 呢 *bii sh hua dou haowen ne* 'smells better than all (other) flowers'.[33]

(13) As suffix by class overlap, *sh*, always in the neutral tone, occurs in 要 是 *yawsh* 'if', 若 是 *ruohsh* 'if', 凡 是 *farnsh* 'whatever is' [as in (12) above], 都 是 *doush* 'all, in all cases', 就 是

---

[32]Cf. 'Is you is or is you ain't?' heard in a movie in the 1930's.

[33]Quoted by Wang Leaui, *Outline*, 131.

*jiowsh* 'namely' or 'even if', 只是 *jyysh* 'merely', 还是 *hairsh* 'still' or 'or (else)', 或是 *huohsh* 'or (either … or)', 可是 *keesh* 'but', 但是 *dannsh* 'but', 原是 *yuansh* 'originally', 硬是 ~ 睖 是 *yinqsh ~ lenqsh* 'simply, just, the hard fact is that … ', 横是 *herngsh* 'anyway' (< 横竖 *herngshuh* 'horizontal or vertical'). Some of them are still separable as adverb plus verbal *sh*, as in 若不是 *ruoh bush* 'if not (is)', but in most cases they are either not separable or separable with a difference in meaning, as 可 是 *keesh* 'but', 可不是吗? *Keebush ma?* 'Isn't that, though?'

(14) A form of suffixed *sh* observed by Dragunov (p. 39; Chinese transl., pp. 29-30) in some of the Shensi dialects is that of an indicator of the subject. Thus, in 这个茶不是好茶. *Jeyg char bush hao-char.* 'This tea is not good tea.', the *sh* in *bush* is simply the ordinary copula. But in 这个茶是不是好茶。 *Jeyg char-sh bush hao-char.* 'This-tea-is-such-that-it is not good tea.', the first *sh* merely makes clearer the subject function of *jeyg char*, and the verb itself is in fact the contradictory of *sh*. Dragunov does not specify whether such a *sh* is in the neutral tone in the Kansu dialect quoted, nor how frequently this occurs as compared with subjects without such a suffix. Let it be noted, however, that this *sh* is very similar to the subject with contrastive stress under (6) above and it is quite possible for the same sentence, usually with extra stress on the subject, to occur in many other dialects: "这个茶是不是好茶. "*Jeyg char.sh bush hao-char.* It is of course quite different from the sentence with the same string of morphemes in a different IC structure meaning 'Is this tea a good tea?' in which *sh.bu.sh* is the V-*bu*-V form of an interrogative sentence.

(15) A meaningless time-filler in chanting poetry is the neutral-tone *sh* often inserted between lines or at caesuras, along with other particles which do not form part of the lines, as in:

黄 河 是 遠 上 白 雲 间 啊 ——

*Hwangher .sh yeuan shanq bair yun jian a ——*
'The Yellow River goes back far among the white clouds,

♩ ♩ ♩ ♩.. ♪ ♩ ♩ ♩ ♩.
一 片 孤 城 是 万 仞 山 呕 —

*I-piann gu cherng .sh wann-reen shan ou* ——
'A waif of a lone city on a mountain of 80,000 feet'.°

While a free sprinkling of *sh* and other particles is frowned upon by serious students of poetry, it is often indulged in, especially when one is enjoying the intoning of poetry aloud.

(16) Finally, *sh* is used as a somewhat unctious reply to a command, as in 把这个拿走！— 是！ *Bae jeyg na-tzoou!—Sh!* 'Take this away!—Yes, sir or madam, as the case may be!'

Note that this interjection *sh*, often in neutral tone, though, like other interjections, often fully stressed, is not the same as the adjective *sh* 'right' [under (11) above], which can occur in the predicative sentence 是的. $_0$*Sh de.* 'That's right.' and may be used between equals. As interjections, *sh* cannot be followed by *de*.

*8.1.9. The Verb* 有 *yeou 'To Have', There Is'.*—Students of comparative philosophy have had trouble in stating the so-called problems of being in Chinese terms, since the verbs *sh* and *yeou* cover different scopes and have different grammatical behavior from the *esse* type of words. The syntactical characteristics of *yeou* are partly similar to VA and partly similar to the verb *sh*, as can be seen by examining the profile for *yeou* in table 18.

(a) and (b) The negative of *yeou* is *mei$_0$yeou* or *mei*, the latter being limited to non-final positions. The form 不 有 *bu yeou*, except in the dialect of K'unming and some other Yunnan dialects, is rare and usually does not form an IC.

(c) With adverbs of degree before *yeou*, there is the question of the scope of modification. In 最有耐性 *tzuey yeou nay-.shinq* 'most have patience,—is most patient', 很有錢 *heen yeou chyan* 'very much have money,—have a lot of money', and so on,

_____

°First two lines of 出 塞 'Going Out of the Pass', by 王 之 渙 *Wang Jyhuann* in *Tarngshy Sanbae Shoou*, Peking: Hsin Hua Book Co., fasc. 8, p. 23.

it is not possible to turn it around and say ° 耐性最有 °*nay-.shinq tzuey yeou*, ° 錢很有 °*chyan heen yeou*, as one could with transitive quality verbs ($V_A$) as in 他最爱小兒子. *Ta tzuey ay sheau erltz.* 'He loves his youngest son most.': 小兒子 他最爱。 *Sheau erltz ta tzuey ay.* 'The youngest son he loves most.' 他很相信算命。 *Ta heen shiangshinn suann-minq.* 'He believes very much in fortune-telling': 算命 他很相信。 *Suann-ming ta heen shiangshinn.* 'Fortune-telling he very much believes in.' All this goes to show that in the case of *yeou* the adverbs of degree apply really to the whole V-O constructions, while with $V_A$'s they modify the verbs as such.

(d) Most auxiliary verbs can occur with *yeou*, as in 会有 *huey yeou* or 能有 *neng yeou* 'can have' or 'there can be', 願 意有 *yuann.yih yeou* 'wish to have', 得有 *deei yeou* 'must have' or 'there has to be'. But there is no ° 肯有 °*keen yeou* for 'willing to have', or ° 别有 *bye yeou* 'don't have!', or ° 甭有 °*berng yeou* 'don't have, because you needn't have'. In Southern Mandarin a parting interviewer says 请有事! *Chiing yeou shyh!* 'Please have business,—please don't bother to see me to the door!' but this is not used in the North.

(e) and (f) The verb *yeou* does not take cognate objects of extent or number of times as such. In 有过一塲(～一次) 腥红热 *yeou.guoh i-chaang* (～ *i-tsyh*) *shinghorng-reh* 'have had a siege of (～ once had) scarlet fever', the *i*-M is a modifier of the object rather than a cognate object of the verb.

(g) There is no tentative-aspect reduplicate ° 有ㄋ °*yeou-.yeou.*

(h) The progressive form 有着 *yeouj* is beginning to appear in written bairhuah, as in 李領弟是一位有着崑曲家 学渊缘的人。 *Lii Liingdih sh i-wey yeouj Kuencheu jiashyue iuanyuan de ren.* 'Lindy Li [Mark] is a person who is possessing a source of family tradition in the art of Kuencheu.'[34] To be

---

[34] 范韵村(Fann Yunntsuen), 过丹巴登桥教崑曲 ("Across the Dumbarton Bridge to Teach Kuencheu"), 新闻天地 (*Newsdom*), serial no. 961, p. 47 (May 13, 1961).

sure, 'has' would be a more natural translation than 'is possessing', but for that matter *yeou* would also have been more natural to say than *yeouj*.

(i) and (j) The indefinite past and perfective aspects are freely applicable to *yeou*, as in 有过沙眼 *yeou.guoh shayean* 'have had trachoma before', 有了錢就花 *yeoule chyan jiow hua* 'having (got) money, then spend it'.

(k) There is no direct imperative form for *yeou*. To say 'Have patience!' one has to use an auxiliary verb, as in 你得有忍耐. *Nii deei yeou reennay.* 'You have to have patience.' To say 'Have some!' one could say, in polite form, 用一点儿! *Yonq .i.deal!* 'Use a little!' or the more informal 来一点儿! *Lai .i.deal!* or, more specifically, 吃点儿! *Chy .deal!* 'Eat some!' 喝点儿! *He .deal!* 'Drink some!' 抽点儿! *Chou .deal!* 'Smoke some!' or 拿点儿! *Na .deal!* 'Take some!'

(l) Finally, in the V-not-V form of a question, 'not' will have to be *mei* instead of *bu*, as in:

有人没有人？   *Yeou ren meiyeou ren?*
有人没有   ？   *Yeou ren mieyeou   ?*
有   没有人？ *yeou   meiyeou ren?*

all of which mean 'Is there anybody?' There is no ° 有人没？ °*Yeou ren mei?* since *mei* cannot occur finally. The form 有人没人 *yeou ren mei ren* occurs only in an indirect question as a clause, as in 我不莞有人没人. *Woo bugoan yeou ren mei ren.* 'I don't care whether there is anybody or not.'

The main uses of the verb *yeou* are to express (1) possession (in the very general sense) and (2) existence. (3) In either sense *yeou* often occurs also as a link verb. (4) By way of class overlap, *yeou* is used as an auxiliary verb, (5) as a versatile first morpheme in compounds, and (6) as an interjection, as illustrated below:

(1) In the sense of 'have, possess', *yeou* has as wide a semantic range as the English verb 'to have', as in 有父母 *yeou fuhmuu* 'have parents', 兒女 *yeou erlneu* 'have children', 没有錢 *mei.yeou chyan* 'have no money', 有債 *yeou-jay* 'have debts', 有烧 *yeou-shau* 'have a fever', 有希望 *yeou shiwanq* 'have

hope', 有办法 *yeou bann₀faa* 'have a way (to deal with it)', 有
脸 *yeou-lean* 'have face,—make a good impression all around'.

With verbs as objects, *yeou* occurs in a few fixed phrases as
有吃有穿 *yeou-chy yeou-chuan* 'have eats and wears,—have
food and clothing', 有说有笑 *yeou-shuo yeou-shiaw* 'have talks
and laughs,—to be in good spirits', 有商量 *yeou shang.liang*
'have consults,—to be open to consultation or discussion', 有救
(儿) *yeou-jiow(l)* 'have rescue', 没救(儿) mei-jiow(l) 'have no
rescue,—beyond hope', the last two probably better treated as
nominal objects, since *jiow* has an optional nominal suffix -*l*.

This possessive *yeou* is the only kind which occasionally takes
*bu* as negative, as noted above (sec. 8.1.1.1.).

A special extension of the possessive *yeou* is that of having or
attaining a certain quantity from below, which we have called
the equaling degree [sec. 8.1.3.2 (1)], as in 他有十岁。*Ta yeou
shyr-suey.* 'He is as old as ten years.' This is deceptively like
the French: *Il a dix ans.*, which should really be equated to the
neutrally stated 他十岁。*Ta shyr-suey.* 'He is ten years old.'
The negative form, as in 他没我大。*Ta mei woo dah.* 'He is
not as old as I am.' follows the usual form for inferior comparison
(pp. 907-908). 他走了有三天没有？没有，他走了没
那么久。*Ta tzooule yeou san-tian meiyeou? Meiyeou, ta tzooule
mei nemm jeou.* 'Has he been away for as long as three days?
No, he has not been away that long.'

(2) The existence *yeou* or 'there is' *yeou* occurs either in
impersonal predicative V-O sentences, as in 有雾。*Yeou-wuh.*
'There is a fog.', 有人。*Yeou-ren.* 'There is somebody,—(rest-
room) "occupied".', or in sentences with place or time expressions as subjects, usually translatable into adverbial phrases, as
天下没有那种事。 *Tianshiah mei₀yeou ney-joong shyh.*
'There is no such thing in the world.', 今儿 晚上有客。 *Jiel
woan.shanq yeou-keh.* 'There will be company tonight.' Since
the unsophisticated speaker of the language does not analyze the
word *yeou* in possessive or existential terms, if he says 有风
*Yeou-feng.* 'There is wind.', and is pressed to supply a subject by

being asked 什么 有 風？ *Sherm yeou feng?* 'What has wind?'
or 谁 有 風？ *Sheir yeou feng?* 'Who has wind?' he may make
up an answer such as 天 有 風. *Tian yeou feng.* 'The sky has
wind.' or 这儿 有 風. *Jell yeou feng.* 'This place has wind,—
there is wind here.'

(2.1) In the foregoing examples, the object is the expression
for that which exists. But the subject position is by no means
rare, as in 好人 也 有，坏人 也 有，什么 樣儿 的 人 都
有. *Hao-ren yee yeou, huay-ren yee yeou, shermyanql de ren dou
yeou.* 'Good men there are, bad men there are, all sorts of men
there are.' This predicative *yeou* can be nominalized, as usual,
by putting it between *sh* and *de*, as in 这种 事 常 有；这种
事 是 常 有 的. *Jey-joong shyh charng yeou; jey-joong shyh sh
charng yeou de.* 'This kind of thing often exists; this kind of
thing is something that often exists,—is often the case.' 那 种 错
误 是 很 会 有 的. *Ney-joong tsuohwuh sh heen huey yeou de.*
'That kind of error is something that can very well be,—is quite
a possibility.'

(2.2) By placing such *yeou de* in an attributive position before
a nominal expression, as in 有 的 人 *yeou de ren* 'men who exist,
—men who there are', it turns out to have the force of 'some',
so that 有 的 东 西 *yeoude dong.shi* is equivalent to 'some
things', 有 的 时 候儿 *yeoude shyr.howl* 'there are times,—some
of the time', the latter usually reduced to a free adverb 有 .时
.候儿 *yeou.shyr.howl* or even to *yeou.shoul* 'sometimes'. This
equating of 'some' to existence agrees quite well with the modern
post-Aristotelian treatment of particular propositions as implying
existence, which universal propositions do not.[35]

(2.3) The idiom 有 的 是 *yeou de sh* 'there is plenty' also
comes from the existential meaning of *yeou*, as in 钱 夠 不 夠？
*Chyan gow bu gow?* 'Is the money enough?' 钱 有 的 是. *Chyan
yeou de sh.* '(As for) money whatever there is (it) is (that),—

---

[35]Y. R. Chao, "Notes on Chinese Grammar and Logic", *Philosophy East
and West*, 5:31-41 (1955).

there is plenty of money.', or 有的是錢. *Yeou de sh chyan.* 'If there is anything, it is money,—there is plenty of money.' On 有的 ... 还是 *yeoude ... hairsh* 'rather than, better ... ', see sect. 8.4.2 (3.2).

(2.4) Since the particle *le* can express a change of situation, *yeou le* 'there is now (where there was not before)' can express appearance and *mei(yeou) le* 'there is no more (where there was before)' can express disappearance. For example, 有了，找着了. *Yeou le, jao₀jaurle.* 'There it is, I've found it.' 汽油完全没(有)了. *Chihyou wanchyuan mei(yeou) le.* 'The gasoline is entirely gone,—we are out of gas.'

(3) The verb *yeou* functions as a link verb in pivotal constructions both in the sense of 'have, and in the sense of 'there is'. For example, 我有朋友帮忙. *Woo yeou perng.yeou bang-mang.* 'I have friends to help.' 我没有夾鉗夾核桃. *Woo mei.yeou jiachyan jia her.taur.* 'I have no pliers to crack the walnuts with.' 有人来看你. *Yeou ren lai kann nii.* 'There is someone to see you.' 没人在家. *Mei ren tzay-jia.* 'There is nobody who is at home,—nobody home.' In the form 家裡没人. *Jia.lii mei-ren.* 'Home-inside has no person,—there is nobody at home.', the place word is the subject, followed by the *yeou* of existence. Note that *yeou* is never used in the sense of 'having (something) done'. The expression 有衣裳洗. *Yeou i.shang shii.* can only mean 'There are clothes to wash.' To say 'have the clothes washed instead of washing them oneself', it will have to be reworded as something like 拿衣裳给人洗，自己不洗 *na i.shang geei ren shii, tzyhjii bu shii* 'take the clothes to give others to wash instead of washing (them) oneself'.

(4) On the non-use of *yeou* as an auxiliary verb in the affirmative form, see Vx 44 in sect. 8.1.10.3 below.

The following functions of *yeou* are included here because they are derived from the verb *yeou*, although in these functions it is no longer a verb.

(5) As a modern prefix or as a versatile first morpheme in V-O compounds, *yeou* is either followed by a bound object or compounded with an otherwise free object with specialization of

meaning. These compounds usually translate into adjectives (or adverbs) ending in '-ful', '-ous', '-ic', '-ing', '-ed', and so on, or phrases with 'with'. Examples are: 有用 ( 处 ) *yeouyonq(.chuh)* FF 'has use,—useful', 有毒 *yeoudwu* FF 'poisonous', 有意思 *yeou-yih.sy* FF 'has meaning,—interesting', 有意 *yeouyih* FB 'has intention,—intentional(ly)', 有效 *yeoushiaw* FB 'has effect, —effective', 有限 *yeoushiann* FB 'has limit,—limited', 有限公 司 *yeoushiann gongsy* 'Co., Ltd.', 有声有色 *yeousheng-yeouseh* 'with sound and color,—with great vivacity', 有声電影 *yeou-sheng-diannyiing* '(with) sound movie'.

Similar uses of the negative of *yeou,* usually in the short form *mei-* rather than the full verbal form *mei₀yeou,* are more restricted than the affirmative. Examples of *mei* as a first morpheme in V-O compounds are: 没用 *meiyonq* 'has no use,—useless', 没准 儿 ₀*mei₀joel ...* 'there is no certainty,—there is no telling but that ... , perhaps', 没法子 *mei fartz* ～ 没法儿 *meifal* (sic) 'there is no way (out),—it can't be helped', as in 没法儿不答应他 *meifal bu da.ying ta* '(you) can't help agreeing with (～promising) him', 没什么 *mei .sherme* 'there is nothing (the matter with it),—pretty good', 没头没脑的 *mei-tour-mei-nao-de* 'without head or brain,—out of the clear blue'.

The L and therefore always bound morpheme 𠮾 *wu-* is much more versatile than the colloquial *mei* and is usually translatable into affixes '-less', 'un-', 'in-', 'a-'(privative) or phrases beginning with 'without'. Examples are: 𠮾数 *wushuh* 'countless', 𠮾线 電 *wushianndiann* 'wireless', 𠮾谓 *wuwey* 'without (anything to) speak of,—pointless', 𠮾味 *wuwey* 'tasteless,—in bad taste', 𠮾机 ( 化学 ) *wuji (huahshyue)* 'inorganic (chemistry)', 𠮾名氏 *wumingshyh* 'without name or surname,—anonymous', 𠮾条件 的 *wutyaujiannde* 'unconditional (ly)', 𠮾效 *wushiaw* 'ineffective', 𠮾缘𠮾故 *wuyuan-wuguh* 'without cause or reason', the last being a vivid reduplicate in which the compound 缘故 *yuan.guh* 'reason' is semi-ionized.

(6) Finally, *Yeou!* from the existence idea under (2.1) above, used to be the proper interjection for 'Present!' in answer to roll

calls at the civil service examinations during the imperial days. The modern equivalent, at school for instance, is 到! *Daw!* 'Here!' A similar but still clearly verbal use of the possession *yeou* is found in the exclamatory sentence ( 我 ) 有 了 ! (*Woo*) *yeou le!* 'I have it!' when a way is found out of a problem or the answer to a riddle has been guessed.

*8.1.10. Auxiliary Verbs (Vx).* Auxiliary verbs take other verbs or verbal expressions as objects instead of substantives, but differ from other transitive verbs in taking no perfective suffix *-le* before the objects and in other respects, as detailed below. They are sometimes called 'modal auxiliaries' because they usually express the semantic modes of the following verbs as distinguished from verbs which we have called resultative complements, but which others have sometimes also called auxiliary verbs. Note that Chinese Vx's do not always translate into auxiliary verbs in English. For example both 能 *neng* and its nearest equivalent in English 'can' are Vx's, but 願意 *yuann.yih* is a Vx, whereas its nearest translation 'wish (to)' is not. In fact some Chinese grammarians use the term 能願動词 *neng-yuann donqtsyr* 'the "can-wish" verbs' for auxiliary verbs. The profile of Vx's, as seen from table 18, is as follows:

(a) An auxiliary verb, like other verbs, takes *bu* for a negative. Moreover, since it has a verb for an object, the object can also be modified by *bu*. Thus from 能去 *neng chiuh* 'can go', there is 不能去 *buneng chiuh* 'cannot go', 能不去 *neng bu chiuh* 'can not-go,—is able not to go', and 不能不去 *buneng bu chiuh* 'cannot not-go,—cannot but go, cannot help going'.[36]

(b) The negative 没 *mei* applies in a restricted way to auxiliary verbs, namely Vx 1, 2, 3 (only as 'know how to'), 4, 5, 6, 7, 14, 23 (but not 24), 30, and 31. It differs from *bu*, not so much in tense, as in the noncompletion of some happening. For example, 他昨儿不能来. *Ta tzwol buneng lai.* 'He couldn't come yesterday.' describes a static situation, but with *mei* substituted for *bu*, it means that he failed to make it possible to come

---

[36]In fact, the forms Vx V, *bu* Vx V, Vx *bu* V, and *bu* Vx *bu* V are among the chief tests for Vx's used in Luh, *GTFaa*, 60.

or that things happened that prevented his coming. Similarly,
他 不 肯 告送. *Ta bukeen gaw.sonq.* 'He was unwilling to tell,
he wouldn't tell.': 他 没 肯 告送. *Ta mei keen gaw.sonq.* 'He
didn't show any willingness to tell.' 我 不 敢 试. *Woo bugaan
shyh.* 'I dare(d) not try.': 我 没 敢 试. *Woo mei gaan shyh.* 'I did
not dare to try.' 他 不 好 意 思要. *Ta buhaoyih.sy yaw.* 'He
was too shy to ask for it.': 他 没 好 意 思 要. *Ta mei hao yih.sy
yaw.* 'He didn't have the nerve to ask for it.' Some speakers,
however, prefer to use *bu* in both senses without distinction.

(c) The adverb of degree 很 *heen* 'very' applies to most but
not all auxiliary verbs, although Luh (*GTFaa*, 60) uses it as one
of the tests. The Vx's which do not take *heen* are: Vx 10, 11, 12,
20, 21, 22, 27, 28, 30, 31, 38, 39, 40, 41, 42, 43, 44, 45, 46, 47,
and 48.

(d) Auxiliary verbs can occur in succession, such as: 会要
*huey yaw* 'may (possibly) want to', 会能 *huey neng* 'may be able
to', 会怕 *huey pah* 'may be afraid to', 会肯 *huey keen* 'may be
willing to', 可以会 *keeyii huey* 'may possibly', (应) 该要 (*ing*)
*gai yaw* 'ought to have to', (应) 该可以 (*ing*) *gai keeyii* 'ought
to be able to', (应) 该会肯 (*ing*) *gai huey keen* 'it ought to be
possible to be willing to', 不会不敢不愿意去 *buhuey bu-
gaan buyuann.yih chiuh* 'cannot possibly be afraid to be unwilling to go there'. Probably many strings do not occur because
they do not make sense, as ° 肯 得 可 以 °*keen deei keeyii* 'willing to have to may'. The forms 要想 *yawsheang* and 想要
*sheangyaw*, both meaning 'wish to', are coordinate compounds
and not phrases of two Vx's. Note that the compound Vx *yawsheang* is to be distinguished from the J + Vx phrase *yaw sheang
~ yawsh sheang* 'if (one) wishes to.'

(e) Cognate objects of extent can follow the second verb and
do not belong to the auxiliary verb. Thus, in 能去三年 *neng
chiuh san-nian* 'can go there for three years', *san-nian* is the
object of *chiuh* and not of *neng*, so that it is impossible to say
°能(了)三年 °*nengle san-nian.*

(f) Cognate objects of number of times, likewise, belong to

the second verb, or to the whole phrase, rather than to the Vx alone. For example, in 肯玩儿过三次 *keen wal.guoh san-tsyh* 'has three times been willing to play' but not ° 肯过三次 °*keen.guoh san-tsyh* 'has been willing three times'.

(g), (h), (i) and (j) There is no tentative reduplicate, like ° 能 ⁊ °*neng.neng*, or progressive ° 能着 °*nengj* 'being able to' or perfective *-le* as in ° 能了去 °*nengle chiuh*. In 他早能去了. *Ta tzao neng chiuh le.* 'He was able to go long ago.', the *le* is a particle to the whole phrase. In 你会忘了. *Nii huey wanqle.* 'You will forget.', the *-le* is part of the verb *wanqle*.

(k) There is no imperative ° 能! °*Neng!* 'Be able to...!'

(l) The V-*bu*-V form of questions is applicable to all auxiliary verbs, as shown under (a).

*8.1.10.1. Differences of Vx from Similar Verbs.*

(1) Link verbs in pivotal constructions allow the insertion of a substantive as pivot, while no substantive can be inserted between Vx and V. For example, in 不叫(他)吃 他不敢吃. *Bu jiaw (ta) chy ta bugaan chy.* '(If you) don't tell (him) to eat he dare not eat.', the *jiaw chy* allows an insertion of the pivot *ta* and therefore *jiaw* is not an auxiliary verb.

(2) Think verbs, or verbs with clause objects, are not Vx's, as in 我盼望, 希望, 指望(他)来 ～ 下雨. *Woo ～ pann.wanq, shi$_0$wanq, jyy.wang (ta) lai ～ shiah-yeu.* 'I hope, hope, expect that (he) comes ～ that it rains.' Here if the subject in the clause were omitted, as in 我希望来. *Woo shi$_0$wanq lai.* 'I hope to come.', it would be quite another sentence. If the first verb were omitted it might not even make sense, as ° 我下雨. °*Woo shiah yeu.* 'I rain.'[37]

(3) Verbs of action with verbal objects [cf. sec. 5.5.3 (10)] differ from Vx's in having all the usual aspects of Vt's, which Vx's do not have. Thus, one can say 答应了走 *da.yinqle tzoou* 'have promised to go', 决定了来 *jyuedinqle lai* 'have decided to come', 继续着做 *jih$_0$shiuhj tzuoh* 'continue to do it', 準備

---

[37] 语法小组 ZGYW, no. 35, 1955.

了去 *joenbeyle chiuh* 'have made ready to go'.[38] With cognate objects, we have 打算了好久 逛華山 *daa.suannle haojeou guanq Hwashan* 'have planned a long time to visit the Hua Shan'. While a Vx can be followed by *bu*-V, a first verb 耒 *lai* or 去 *chiuh* in a V-V series cannot be followed by *bu*-V. Thus, there is no °去不说 °*chiuh bu shuo* 'go not to say it'. In 去不答 应他 *chiuh buda.yinq ta* 'go to disagree with him,—demand satisfaction from him', the whole verb *buda.yinq* is a verb of action.

(4) An adverb before a verb (H V) differs from an auxiliary verb in several respects. The V-not-V question is asked differently:

H V 还吃 不吃 ? *Hair chy bu chy?* 'Will (you) still eat?'

Vx V 能不能耒 ? *Neng buneng lai?* 'Can you come?'

The answer to such questions can be 能耒.*Neng lai.* 'I can.', or simply能.*Neng.*, but it cannot be °还.°*Hair.* 'Still.' When a concessive contrast with 是 *sh* [sec. 8.1.8 (6)] is used, a single auxiliary verb can be placed before or after *sh*, but not an adverb. For example, 他要是要耒.~他耒是要的. *Ta yaw sh yaw lai.* ~ *Ta lai sh yaw de.* 'He wants to come, to be sure.', but with an adverb, one cannot say ° 他就是就耒。°*Ta jiow sh jiow lai.* or ° 他耒是 就的。°*Ta lai sh jiow de.* It will have to be 他耒 是 就耒. *Ta lai sh jiow lai.* or 他就耒是就耒. *Ta jiow lai sh jiow lai.* 'He will come right away, to be sure.'

Adverbs with *de* and/or -*l* as marker cannot of course be auxiliary verbs, as in 偏ㄦ( 的 ) 跑了 *pianpial (de) pao le* 'ran away, of all things', 假装ㄦ( 的 )答应 *jeajuangl (de) da.yinq* 'falsely promise,—pretend to promise'.

An adverb derived from a wenyan phrase involving an auxiliary verb is 恨．不．得 *henn.bu.de* 'would that (I) could'. In the wenyan phrase in 恨不得亨而食之 *henn bu der peng erl*

---

[38]The last two first verbs were regarded as auxiliary verbs ("V pred") in Charles F. Hockett and Chaoying Fang *et al.*, *Dictionary of Spoken Chinese*, War Department Technical Manual 30-933, Washington, D.C., 1945, pp. 156, 168.

*shyr jy* '(I) regret that (I) cannot cook and eat him', *henn* is a verb with the rest of the phrase as its object, and *der* is an auxiliary verb with the rest of the phrase as *its* object. A translation into modern colloquial would be 我可惜不能把他煮了 吃了. *Woo keeshi bu.neng bae ta juule chyle.* But with *henn.bu-.de* as an adverb, the ICs are differently grouped and it modifies the verb or verbs that follow as a whole and no auxiliary verb is involved, as in 恨不得現在就走 *henn.bu.de shianntzay jiow tzoou* 'wish I could go right away', 恨不得天ㄦ去 玩ㄦ *henn.bu.de tiantial chiuh wal* 'wish I could go and play every day'.

8.1.10.2. *Overlaps of Auxiliary Verbs with Other Form Classes.* Auxiliary verbs sometimes overlap with transitive verbs of action, link verbs, and other form classes. As in other cases of overlaps, the frame in which the word occurs will determine the class, though occasionally there are ambivalent analyses. For example, in 想来 *sheang lai* 'wish to come', *sheang* is a $V_A$; in 我(很)想 你. *Woo (heen) sheang nii.* 'I miss you (a lot).' it is Vt with a nominal object; and in 我想你应该来. *Woo sheang nii inggai lai.* 'I think you ought to come.' it is a think verb, that is, a Vt with a clause object. In 不用印 *bu yonq yinn*, with Vt + N, it means 'do not use a seal (chop)'; with Vx + V, it means 'do not need to print'. Similarly, 要漿 *yaw jiang* 'want to starch' Vx + V: 'need (some) starch' Vt + N. In the following list of Vx's, the different meanings will be numbered and additional (overlapping) form classes will be marked with a "+" sign.

8.1.10.3. *Auxiliary Verbs Listed*

Vx 1. 能 *neng* (1) 'can, is able to': 这个脚麻了, 不能 動. *Jeyg jeau male, buneng donq.* 'This foot is numb and cannot move.' 能来就请来. *Neng lai jiow chiing lai.* 'Please come if you can'. In the special idiom of 不能人 *buneng ren* 'cannot be man,—to be impotent.' (less frequently in the affirmative form), it is better to regard *ren* as a verb by class overlap than to regard *neng* as Vt, with *ren* N as object. (2) 'May, to be permitted to' ( = Vx 15 可以 *kee₀yii*): 能不能走啦？ *Neng buneng tzoou l'a?* 'Can I go now?' = 可以不可以走啦 ? *Keeyii bukeeyii tzoou l'a?* 'May I go now?'

Note that the frequency of *neng* is much lower than that of English 'can', because whenever a verb has a complement, the potential V.*de*-R or V.*bu*-R form (sec. 6.6.5) is preferred, as in 看得見 *kann.de-jiann* rather than 能看見 *neng kann.jiann* 'can see'. Even when there is no complement, a dummy comple- ment [sec. 6.6.5 (2)] is sometimes added in order to use the po- tential form, for example, 動不了 *donq.bu-leau* instead of 不能 動 *buneng donq* 'cannot move', the latter more likely to be taken in sense (2) 'mustn't or shouldn't', as in the nursery rhyme 不開, 不開, 不開, 不能開! *Bu kai, bu kai, bu kai, buneng kai!* '(I) won't open, ... , can't open (the door to you, the wolf)!' But if the door gets stuck, then one says 開不開 *kai.bu-kai* or 開不 動 *kai.bu-donq.*

Vx 2. 能夠 *neng₀gow* 'can, to be able to' or 'may', probably a borrowing from one of the Southern dialects.

Vx 3. 会 *huey* (1) 'can, know how to': 会浮水 *huey fuh-shoei* 'can swim', 会说廣东话 *huey shuo Goangdonghuah* 'can speak Cantonese'. (2) 'could possibly or would probably': 这儿 不会的. *Jell buhuey de.* 'It can't happen here.', 你不会忘 了吧 ? *Nii buhuey wangle ba?* 'You won't forget, will you?'

+ V$_A$ 'has the skill or knowledge of': 会水 *huey shoei* 'know water,—can swim', 会德文 *huey Derwen* 'know German' (cf. *Können Sie Deutsch?*)

Vx 4. 要 *yaw* (1) 'want to': 我要回家。*Woo yaw hwei-jia.* 'I want to go home.' 你要幹麻 ? *Nii yaw gannma?* 'What do you want to do?' (2) 'will, going to': 要下雨了. *Yaw shiah-yeu le.* 'It's going to rain.' 要捧! *Yaw shuai!* '(You) are going to fall down!' 要坏! *Yaw huay!* 'It is going to be bad!' (said when an accident is about to happen in a split second). The negative of this near-future *yaw* is not *buyaw*, but *bu* V or *buhuey* V, with meaning (2) of Vx 3, as in 我想不下雨. *Woo sheang bu shiah- yeu.* 'I don't think it will rain.' 我不会捧. *Woo buhuey shuai.* 'I am not going to fall down.' (3) 'to be' (in comparisons): 比墨

还要黑 *bii moh hair yaw hei* 'even blacker than ink'. 英國比瑞典要小点儿。 *Ing.gwo bii Rueydean yaw sheau.deal.* 'England is smaller than Sweden.' (example adapted from Malmqvist, Sich'uanese, 167). (4) 'must, have to': 你头髮这么長不要剪了嗎? *Nii tour.faa tzemm charng buyaw jean le ma?* 'Your hair is so long, doesn't it have to be cut?' 这衣裳要洗了。 *Jeh i.shang yaw shii le.* 'These clothes must be washed.' (cf. the colloquial 'want to be washed'). Note that, since 不要 *buyaw* is not available in meaning (2), the form V-*bu*-V is not available for questions. There is 要下雨了嗎? *Yaw shiahyeu le ma?* 'Is it going to rain?' or 会下雨不会? *Huey shiah-yeu .bu.huey?* 'Will it rain?', with Vx 3(2), but no °要下雨不要? °*Yaw shiah-yeu .bu.yaw?*

+ V$_A$ 'want, desire': 要錢不要命 *yaw chyan bu yaw-minq* 'want money so much as not to want one's life', 这孩子很要好。 *Jeh hairtz heen yaw-hao.* 'This child very much wants to be good.'

+ Vt 'ask for': 要飯(儿)的 *yawfann* (~ *ll*) *de* want-rice-er,—beggar', 问他要点儿开水! *Wenn ta yaw deal kai-shoei!* 'Ask him for some boiling water!' (Cf. the more formal and peremptory 要求 *iauchyou* 'demand'.)

Some of the Vx's which are alternatively Vt's do not seem to reduplicate as readily as most Vt's do, but such reduplication is by no means excluded, as in 你问他要ㄥ看! *Nii wenn ta yaw.yaw .kann!* 'You just ask him for it and see!' With Vx 23 overlapping Vt, one can say 他没得过奖, 让他常得ㄥ奖就知道了。 *Ta mei der.guoh jeang, ranq ta charng der.der jeang jiow jy.daw le.* 'He has never got any prize; let him often get some prizes and he will know.'

Vx 5. 想 *sheang* 'wish to, desire to': 你想不想发財? *Nii sheang busheang fa-tsair?* 'Do you wish to get rich?' 他想做聖人. *Ta sheang tzuoh shenq$_o$ren.* 'He desires to be a perfect man.'

+ V$_A$ 'long for, miss': 我想你。 *Woo sheang nii.* 'I miss you.' 不应该想人家的錢. *Buinggai sheang ren.jia de chyan.* 'One ought not to covet other people's money.'

+ Vt 'think up, think of': 想法子 *sheang fartz* 'think of a way,—try', 想了个主意 *sheangle g jwu.yih* 'have thought out a plan', 想不到... *sheang.bu-daw* ... 'cannot think and reach (it), —who would have thought that ... ?'  想起来了, ... *sheang-.chii.lai le,* ... '(I) have (just) thought of it,—by the way, ... '.

+ Vt as link verb (with pivot) 'wish ... to': 我想他来. *Woo sheang ta lai.* 'I desire him to come.' 快想个人帮忙. *Kuay sheang g ren banq-mang.* 'Hurry up and think of some one to help.'

+ Vt as think verb (with clause object) 'think that, believe that': 你想要下雨吗? *Nii sheang yaw shiah-yeu ma?* 'Do you think it's going to rain?' 我想不会. *Woo sheang buhuey.* 'I don't think it will.' N.B. To believe that something is not so must be expressed by putting *bu* or *mei* in the clause and not before *sheang*. The form 不想 *bu sheang* or 没想 *mei sheang* is possible only with the other functions and meanings of *sheang* and is never used as 'I don't think that ... ' in the sense of 'I think that ... not ... '.

Vx 6. 想要 *sheangyaw*, and

Vx 7. 要想 *yawsheang* are synonymous with *sheang*, as Vx, but not as V$_A$ and Vt.

Vx. 8. 爱 *ay* 'love to, fond of ... -ing, tend to': 爱吃冰淇淋 *ay chy bingchyilin* 'love to eat ice cream', 他净爱跟人打架. *Ta jinq ay gen ren daa-jiah.* 'He just loves to get into a row with people.' 这个小孩净爱摔交. *Jeyg sheauharl jinq ay shuai-jiau.* 'This child tends to trip and fall all the time.'

+ V$_A$ 'love': 最爱小儿子 *tzuey ay sheau erltz* 'love the youngest son best', 爱国 *ay-gwo* 'love one's country, — to be patriotic'.

Vx 9. 愿.意 *yuann.yih* 'wish to, to be willing to':   我愿意现在就去. *Woo yuann.yih shianntzay jiow chiuh.* 'I wish to go right now.' 有的愿意出钱, 有的愿意出力.   *Yeou de yuann.yih chu-chyan, yeou de yuann.yih chu-lih.* 'Some are willing to contribute money and some are willing to contribute work.'

+ Vt with clause object, or think verb 'wish that': 我愿

意 你 别 那 么 样儿 聋. *Woo yuann.yih nii bye nemmyanql long.*
'I wish you were not quite so deaf.' 我 愿 意 一 年 到 头儿 是
春 天. *Woo yuann.yih i-nian daw-tourl sh chuen.tian.* 'I wish it
were spring all the year round.'

+ Vst 'pleased': 他 听 了 那 个 话 很 不 愿 意. *Ta tingle
neyg huah heen bu yuannyih.* 'When he heard that, he was
greatly displeased.' N.B. This is usually in the negative form and
usually has full tone on *-yih*.

Vx 10. 情$_o$願 *chyng$_o$yuann* 'would rather': 情$_o$願 死 , 也
不 投 降  *chyng$_o$yuann syy, yee bu tourshyang* 'would rather die
than surrender'. 不 自 由 , 情 願 死. *Bu tzyhyou, chyng$_o$yuann
syy.* '(If) not free, would rather die,—give me liberty or give me
death.', the traditional translation in wenyan being 不 自 由 ,
毋 寧 死. *Bu tzyhyou, wuning syy.*

+ Vst 'could be reconciled, would be satisfied': 只 要 不 给
他 , 你 给 了 谁 我 都 情$_o$願. *Jyyyaw bu geei ta, nii geeile sheir
woo dou chyng$_o$yuann.* 'So long as you don't give it to him, I'd
be satisfied no matter whom you give it to.'

N.B. Although 寧可 *ningkee* and 寧願 *ningyuann* are near
synonyms of Vx 10 *chyng$_o$yuann*. they are not Vx's but adverbs,
as they cannot occur in the frames Vx V *bu* Vx? or Vx *bu* Vx V?
or, in an answer, Vx, as a one-word sentence.

Vx 11. 乐意 *leh$_o$yih* 'to be glad to':    我 们 很 乐意 加入
你 们 的 团体。 *Woomen heen leh$_o$yih jiaruh niimen de twantii.*
'We are very glad to join your group.'

Vx 12. 喜 欢 *shii.huan* 'like to': 喜 欢 说话 *shii.huan shuo-
huah* 'like to talk', 喜 欢 玩儿  *shii.huan wal* 'like to play'.

+ V$_A$ 'like': 喜 欢 花儿 *shii.huan hual* 'like flowers'. Ambivalent constructions will result if a following word, usually a
dissyllable, can be either a verb or a noun, for example, 喜 欢
遊 戏 *shii.huan youshih* 'like to play games' or 'like games'.

The Wu dialect equivalent of Vx 12 is 欢喜 *hwöhii.* When
borrowed into Mand as *huan$_o$shii,* it is not used as Vx, but as
Vst, as in  心 裡 很 欢喜 *shin.lii heen huan$_o$shii* 'feel very glad'.

Vx 13. 高 兴 *gaushinq* 'high spirits,—glad to, feel like ... -ing':

高兴 不 高兴 出 去 野餐 去？ *Gaushinq bu gaushinq chu-.chiuh yeetsan .chiuh?* 'Do you feel like going out for a picnic?' 我 真 高兴 跟 你 見 面。*Woo jen gaushinq gen nii jiann-miann.* 'I am awfully glad to meet with you.'

+ V_A 'is pleased with', usually in the negative, as in 你 什 么 事 不 高兴 他 了？ *Nii sherm shyh bugaushinq ta le?* 'What was the matter that you were displeased with him?'

+ Vst 'to be glad, in good spirits': 今儿 大家 都 很 高兴. *Jiel dahjia dou heen gaushinq.* 'Everybody is in good spirits today.'

Vx 14. 肯 *keen* 'to be willing, not unwilling' (therefore less positive than Vx 9): 谁 肯 做 那 个 事儿？ *Sheir keen tzuoh neyg shell?* 'Who is willing to do that?' 骡子 不 肯 動。 *Luotz bukeen donq.* 'The mule won't move.' 不 是 不 能 也，就 是 不 肯 也！ *Bush buneng è, jiowsh bukeen è!* 'Not unable, just unwilling!'

Vx 15. 可 以 *kee_oyii* 'may, to be permitted to, it is all right to': 可 以 進 来 吧？ *Keeyii jinn.lai ba?* 'May I come in?' 怎 么 可 以 说 那 个 话 呐？ *Tzeem keeyii shuo neyg huah ne?* 'How can you say that?' Note that, although 可 *kee* is wenyan, the double negative 不 可 不 *bukee bu* 'cannot but,—must, will have to' is often used as a short form for 不 可 以 不 *bukeeyii bu*, as in 那个 戏 不 可 不 看. *Neyg shih bukee bu kann.* 'That play mustn't be not seen,—you must see that play'.

Vx 16. 许 *sheu* 'to be permitted to, may': 你 们 不 许 在 这儿 玩儿. *Niimen busheu tzay jell wal.* 'You are not permitted to play here.' 只 许 進 来，不 许 出 去。 *Jyy sheu jinn.lai, busheu chu.chiuh.* '(You) may only come in, but may not go out.'

+ Vt with pivot 'permit to': 我 不 许 你 走，你 就 不 许 走. *Woo bu sheu nii tzoou, nii jiow busheu tzoou.* 'If I don't permit you to go, then you may not go', the second *sheu* being Vx 16.

+ H 'perhaps'~ 也 许 *yeesheu*: 他 许 知道，也 许 不 知 道. *Ta sheu jy.daw, yeesheu bujy.daw.* 'Perhaps he knows, and perhaps he doesn't.' That this is an adverb and not an auxiliary verb can be seen from the fact that it cannot even be modified by *bu*, since 不许 *busheu* can only mean 'not permitted to' or 'do not permit'.

Vx 17. 准 *joen* 'to be permitted to, may': 不准抽烟 *bujoen chou-ian* 'not permitted to smoke', the usual sign being 不准吸烟 *bu joen shi-ian* 'No Smoking', where *shi* 'inhale' is L or dialectal.

准 *joen* is synonymous with Vx 16 许 *sheu*, but is not used as an adverb. There is an adverb 準[39]*joen* ∼ 一準(儿) *ijoen* (∼ -*l*) 'definitely', as in 他 準 来. *Ta joen lai.* 'He will definitely come.' Note that the negative form 没 準儿 *mei-joel* as V-O means 'there's no certainty', but as H it means 'there's no telling but that,—quite possibly'.

Vx 18. 应该 *inggai* 'ought to',

Vx 19. 该 *gai* 'ought to' + Vt 'owe' (for Vx 19 only): 还该 你 多 少 ? *Hair gai nii duoshao?* 'How much do I still owe you?', synonymous with 欠 *chiann* 'owe'.,

Vx 20. 应 当 *ingdang* 'ought to', and

Vx 21. 该 当 *gaidang* 'ought to', in descending order of frequency of occurrence: 咱们应该散会了. *Tzarmen inggai sann-huey le.* 'We ought to adjourn.' 你不该告送他的. *Nii bugai gaw.sonq ta de.* 'You shouldn't have told him.' 这该不该, 这么给他们上这个当? *Jeh gai bu gai, tzemm geei tamen shanq jeyg danq?* 'Was that what we ought to have done, to have played them such a trick?'

Vx 22. 得 '*der* (1) 'may' L: In legal language, which is mostly in wenyan, *der* has a permissive force, as in 得委托代表出席 *der woeituo daybeau chushyi* L 'may delegate a proxy to attend the meeting'. The negative 不得 *buder* 'not permitted', then, has a prohibitive force, as in 不得超过三十人 *buder chauguoh sanshyr ren* L 'must not exceed 30 men'. Just as 可 *kee* and 不可 *bukee* are not spoken but 不可不 *bukee bu* is, so are 得 *der* and 不得 *buder* not spoken, but 不得不 *buder bu* is, as in 不得不服从命令 *buder bu fwutsorng minq.linq* 'cannot

---

[39]Etymologically the same as 准, but recently differentiated graphically as well as grammatically.

but obey orders'. (2) 'get to, to be able to': 不得了 *buderleau* 'cannot get to an end,—it's awful, awfully', 没得見着他 *mei der jiann₀jaur ta* 'did not get to see him', 不得下台 *buder shiah-tair* 'cannot get down the platform,—cannot get out of a situation', 难得去看電影ㄦ *nander chiuh kann diannyeengl* 'hardly get to see a movie,—rarely go to a movie'.

+ Vt 'get, obtain': 得了一筆奖学金 *derle i-bii jeang-shyue-jin* 'got a scholarship'. 得便请你给我带个好ㄦ 给他. *Der-biann chiing nii geei woo day g haol geei ta.* 'If you get the convenience,—if convenient, please give my regards to him.' 种瓜得瓜，种豆得豆。 *Jonq gua der gua, jonq dow der dow.* 'Plant melons, and you get melons, plant beans, and you get beans,—as ye sow, so shall ye reap'.

Vx 23. 得 *deei* 'have got to, must': 我得告送你一件事. *Woo deei gaw.sonq nii i-jiann shyh.* 'I must tell you something.' 得不得带錢? *Deei budeei day chyan?* 'Do you have to take some money along?'

This auxiliary verb is etymologically and graphically the same as Vx 22. *der*, but while *der* means (1) 'may' or (2) 'to be able to', *deei* means 'must'. *Deei* differs further from *der* in being more colloquial and geographically more limited. It is less free as a word in that the form Vx V is preferred to Vx alone. For example, to the question 得不得等? *Deei budeei deeng?* 'Does one have to wait?' the answer *Deei deeng* is preferred to simply *Deei*. The negative form *budeei* occurs mostly in the V-*bu*-V form of a question and *budeei*, even with a following verb, is not nearly as frequent as its synonym 不用 *buyonq*, as in 你不得老跟 着他. *Nii budeei lao genj ta.* 'You don't have to follow him all the time.', more frequently, 你不用老跟着他. *Nii buyonq lao genj ta.* 'You needn't follow him all the time.'

N.B. There is no ° 不得不 °*budeei bu*, but there is, with Vx 22, 不得不 *buder bu* 'cannot but,—to be obliged to'. (Cf. Vx 15, 不可不 *bukee bu*.)

+ Vt 'need, take': 这个得十三天的工夫. *Jeyg deei shyrsan-tian de gong.fu.* 'This will take 13 days' work'. This is less common than *deei yaw ~ deei yonq* 'must take', of which it is a shorter form.

Vx 24. 須得ˇ *shiudeei*,

Vx 25. 必得ˇ *bihdeei*,

Vx 26. 須要 *shiuyaw*, and

Vx 27. 必須 *bihshiu* are very close synonyms, all meaning 'must needs, it is necessary to', as in 你須得ˇ(～必得ˇ～須要 ～ 必須) 先通知我们才能公佈. *Nii shiudeei* (～ *bihdeei ~ shiuyaw ~ bihshiu*) *shian tongjyy woomen tsair neng gongbuh.* 'You will have to notify us first before you can announce it.' All these auxiliary verbs are like *deei,* but more formal in style. Vx 24 and 25, having -*deei* at the end, do not occur finally. In wenyan 必 *bih* 'must' L and 須 *shiu* 'must' are free. In speech only the negative (and other compound) forms are used: 不必 *bubih* 'need not', 不須 *bushiu* 'need not'. The interrogative form °必不必 °*bih bubih* is not used, and 須不須 *shiu bushiu* as in 須不須帮他? *Shiu bushiu bang ta?* 'De we need to help him?' is much less common than 要不要 *yaw buyaw* [Vx 4(3)] and 得ˇ不得ˇ *deei budeei* in the same context.

+ V$_A$ 須 *shiu* 'need', usually written 需 instead of 須, is a free verb, as 國家最需人才的时候 *gwojia tzuey shiu rentsair de shyr.how* 'the time when the country needs human resources most'. If the word following *shiu* is either V or N by class overlap, then *shiu* may be either Vx 須 'need to' or V$_A$ 需 'need', as 不須帮助 *bushiu bangjuh* 'do not need to help (～ need to be helped)': 不需帮助 *bu shiu bangjuh* 'do not need help'. Similar ambivalence is present in *shiu* followed by 保護 *bao$_0$huh* 'protect ~ protection'.

Vx 28. 不用 *buyonq* 'need not', not used in the affirmative except in the interrogative form 用不用写張收条? *Yonq buyonq shiee jang shoutyau?* 'Do I need to write a receipt?', to which a negative answer can be 不用. *Buyong.* 'You don't need to.', but an affimative answer has to be 要. *Yaw.*, 要写. *Yaw shiee.*, or 得ˇ写一張. *Deei shiee i-jang.*, but not °用. °*Yonq.* or °用写. °*Yong shiee.*

Vx 29. 敢 *gaan* 'dare': 你 怎 么 敢 叫 我 名 字 ？ *Nii tzeem gaan jiaw woo ming.tzyh?* 'How dare you call me by (given) name?' 他 不 敢 不 照 说 的 做. *Ta bugaan bu jaw shuo de tzuoh.* 'He dare not but do as (he was) told.' 你 敢 ！ *Nii gaan!* 'I dare you (to do that)!'

Vx 30. 好 意 思 *haoyih.sy* 'has the cheek to': 他 居 然 好 意 思 吃 了 也 不 给 錢. *Ta jiuran haoyih.sy chyle yee bu geei chyan.* 'He actually had the cheek to eat without paying for it.' The negative form 不 好 意 思 *buhaoyih.sy* 'too shy to, diffident to, embarrassed to' occurs more often than the positive form, as in 不 好 意 思 收 这 么 重 的 礼 *buhaoyih.sy shou tzemm jonq de lii* 'too embarrassed to accept such a large gift'. 他 想 是 想 , 就 是 不 好 意 思 要. *Ta sheang sh sheang, jiowsh buhaoyih.sy yaw.* 'He desires it, to be sure, only he is too shy to ask.'

+ A (negative form only) 'embarrassed': 他 鬧 的 大 家 都 很 不 好 意 思. *Ta naw de dahjia dou heen buhaoyih.sy.* 'He made such a scene that everybody was embarrassed.'

Vx 31. 怕 *pah* 'to be afraid to': 怕 見 生 人 *pah jiann sheng-ren* 'afraid to meet strangers', 怕 傷 了 風 *pah shangle feng* 'afraid to catch cold', 不 怕 不 成 功 *bupah bu chernggong* 'not afraid not to succeed,—sure of succeeding'.

+ V$_A$ 'to be afraid of': 怕 鬼 *pah-goei* 'is afraid of ghosts', 怕 生 *pah-sheng* 'afraid of strangers', 怕 傷 寒 *pah shangharn* 'afraid of the typhoid', 你 最 怕 什 么 ？ *Nii tzuey pah sherme?* 'What are you most afraid of?' Also 'to be sensitive to', as 怕 吹 風 *pah chuei-feng* 'sensitive to drafts'.

+ Vt with clause object (think verb) (1) 'to be afraid that': 我 怕 他 得 了 傷 寒 了. *Woo pah ta derle shangharn le.* 'I am afraid he has got the typhoid.' (2) 'I think, perhaps': 怕 要 下 雨 了 吧 ？ *Pah yaw shiah-yeu le ba?* 'I'm afraid it's going to rain,—perhaps it's going to rain.' This *pah* is interchangeable with 恐 怕 *koong.pah.*

Vx 32. 值 得 *jyr.de* 'worth ... -ing, it pays to': 你 值 得 跑 那 么 遠 嗎 ？ *Nii jyr.de pao nemm yeuan ma?* 'Does it pay you to go that far (for it)?' 这书很值得看儿. *Jeh shu heen jyr.de kann.kann.* 'This book is quite worth reading.'

Vx 33. 懒得 *laan.de* 'to be too lazy to, won't bother with ... -ing, don't care to': 我懒得洗杯子，就这么用了. *Woo laan.de shii beitz, jiow tzemm yonq le.* 'I am too lazy to wash the cup, I'll use it as it is.' 那种人我懒得跟他说话. *Ney-joong ren woo laan.de gen ta shuo-huah.* 'I don't care to talk with that kind of person.'

Vx 34. 省得 *sheeng.de* 'save the trouble of ... -ing, will not have to': 那我就省得自己去了. *Nah woo jiow sheeng.de tzyhjii chiuh le.* 'Then I won't have to go myself.'

+ J 'in order that ... not, lest': 我躲的远儿的，省得他来麻烦我. *Woo duoo de yeuan'iualde, sheeng.de ta lai ma.farn woo.* 'I stay good and far away, so that he won't come and bother me.' In this sense, 省得 *sheeng.de* is interchangable with 免得 *mean.de*, but the latter is not used as a Vx.

Vx 35. 乐₀得~乐得儿 *leh₀der ~ lehder'l* 'would gladly, might as well': 横是不要钱，咱们乐得儿拿几个. *Herngsh buyaw chyan, tzarmen lehder'l na .jiig.* 'Since it costs no money, we might as well take a few.' 你既然是自己弄的麻烦，他们乐得丢了手不莞. *Nii jihran sh tzyhjii nonq de ma.farn, tamen lehder dioule shoou bugoan.* 'Since you got into the trouble yourself, they would gladly wash their hands of it.'

Vx 36. 不便 *bubiann* 'find it inconvenient to, would hesitate to': 你不便问他太ㄦ还在不在吧? *Nii bubiann wenn ta tay.tay hair tzay butzay ba?* 'You would hesitate to ask if his wife is still living, wouldn't you?' 也，不便. *Èh, bubiann.* 'Yes, I would.' The affirmative form is lacking, except as part of the somewhat rare V-*bu*-V form, as in 你便不便邀他一块儿来? *Nii biann bubiann iau ta ikuall lai?* 'Will it not inconvenience you to invite him to come together?' A negative answer to this could be 不便. *Bubiann.*, but an affirmative answer cannot be °便.°*Biann.* and will have to be reworded, such as 好，不要紧. *Hao, buyawjiin.* 'Okay, it doesn't matter.'

N.B. This auxiliary verb is different from the now obsolete

adverb 便 *biann,* synonymous with 就 *jiow* 'then', as in 你 便 怎 樣？ *Nii biann tzeenyanq?* = modern 你 就 怎 么 樣？ *Nii jiow tzeemyanq?* 'What, then, are you going to do about it?' 一 問 便 知。 *I-wenn biann jy.* = modern 一 问 就 知 道 了。 *I wenn jiow jy.daw le.* 'Just ask and (then) you will know.' This use of 便 *biann* as 就 *jiow* occurs in the Sung dynasty philosophical writings, the Ming and Ch'ing novels, and the early part of 20th-century written bairhuah.

Vx 37.好 *hao* (1) 'the better to, in order to, can': 我 闭 着 门, 你 们 好 進 来. *Woo kaij men, niimen hao jinn.lai.* 'I'll keep the door open, so that you can come in.' 认 识 字, 好 读 书. *Renn.shyh tzyh, hao dwu shu.* 'Learn the characters, in order (the better) to read.' 你 鬧 的 我 不 好 用功. *Nii naw de woo buhao yonq-gong.* 'You make such a noise that I cannot very well study.'

現 在 你 好 不 好 用功 啦？ *Shianntzay nii hao buhao yonq-gong l'a?* 'Can you study now?' (2) 'all right to, may' (a borrowing from Wu dial. usage): 好 不 好 出 去？ *Hao buhao chu.chiuh?* = 可 以 不 可 以 出 去？ *Keeyii.bu.kee.yii chu.chiuh?* 'May I go out?' 不 好 那 樣 子！ *Buhao nah yanqtz!* = 頂 好 別 那 樣 子！ *Diinghao bye nah yanqtz!* 'Better not act like that!' (Cf. Cantonese 唔好 *muxoo* [mhou ⌐ ↗ ] 'Better not ... !') 我 又 不 好 不 告 送 他. *Woo yow buhao bu gaw.sonq ta.* 'And I cannot very well not-tell him,—keep it from him.'

+ H (1) 'easy to': 这 事 情 好 做 不 好 做？ *Jeh shyh.chyng hao tzuoh bu hao tzuoh?* 'Is this thing easy to do?' That this is not a Vx can be seen from the answer 好做.*Hao tzuoh.* 'It is.', but not °好.°*Hao.* 'Easy.' The forms 好 做 不 好？ *Hao tzuoh buhao?* and 好 不 好 做？ *Hao buhao tzuoh?* are also rare. This is be- cause monosyllabic adverbs are bound with the following verb and are not so free as auxiliary verbs. The same is true of the negative 不好 *buhao* 'not easy' and the antony 难 *nan* 'hard to'. (2) 'good to': 好 看 *haokann* 'good to look at, good-looking', 好 吃 *haochy* 'good to eat, taste good'. The antonym of 好*hao* in this sense is not 坏*huay* 'bad', but 难*nan* or 不好 *buhao,* as in 难 看 *nankann* 'ugly', 不好看 *buhaokann* 'not good-looking,

—look bad', there being no ° 坏看 °*huay-kann* 'bad-looking'.
Because of the two meanings of 好 *hao* and 难 *nan* as adverbs,
ambiguities sometimes arise, as in 这 螃 蟹 难 吃. *Jeh parng.shieh
nan chy.* 'This crab is difficult to eat (or '. . . tastes bad?') 这 碗
饭 不好吃. *Jey-woan fann buhaochy.* 'This bowl of rice does
not taste good.' (or 'This job is not easy to do.'?) Note that with
either meaning of *hao* before an action verb, the result is an
adjectival expression.

Vx 38. 不 配 *bupey* 'not fit to, not qualified to': 他 不 配 当
先 生. *Ta bupey dang shian.sheng.* 'He is not fit to be a teacher.'
你 不 配 做 天 , 你 塌 了 吧 ! *Nii bupey tzuoh tian, nii tale
ba!* 'You don't know how to be heaven, you better collapse!'[40]
The affirmative form 配 *pey* is a back formation, occurring in
questions in the *V-bu-V* form or in rhetorical questions, as in
他 自己 淨念 錯了字儿 , 还 配 笑話 別人 嗎 ? *Ta
tzyhjii jinq niann-tsuohle tzell, hair pey shiaw.huah bye.ren ma?*
'(As) he is constantly mispronouncing words himself, would he be
qualified to laugh at others (for their mispronunciations)?'

Vx 39. 不 要 ! *Buyaw!* 'Don't!' This is a Vx for negative im-
peratives and is quite different from the negative of Vx 4 in
which *yaw* means 'want to' and so on. Thus, statement: 你 不
要 来. *Nii buyaw lai.* 'You don't want to come.', as against command: 你 不 要 来 ! *Nii buyaw lai!* 'Don't come!' Since this is an
imperative Vx, it will of course have no interrogative form.

Vx 40. 别! *Bye!* 'Don't!' This is simply a fusion, with modification, of the syllables *bu* and *yaw*, the 2nd Tone being derived
from the raised *bu* before the 4th Tone *yaw*. In some dialects the
fusion is more simple and direct, as in Soochow 覅 *fiæh* < 勿 *fe'*
+ 要 *iæh*.

Vx 41. 甭 *Berng!* 'Don't, because you don't need to'. This is a
fusion of Vx 28 不 用 *buyonq* 'need not'. It implies a much softer
command than with the more direct 别 *bye*.

Vx 42. 冇[41] *moo!* ← 唔 *mu* + 好 *xoo* 'Don't, because it is

---

[40]Late Ming dynasty ballad.

[41]This fusion is not recognized in the usual Cantonese texts, and the
character 冇 is used here only for the sound.

better not to!' [Cf. Vx 37(2).] This is the usual Cantonese negative imperative instead of the rarer blunt form 咪 *mae*. In other words, the relative frequency of *bye* to *berng* is not quite the same as that of *mae* to *moo*.

Vx 43. 没 ( 有 ) *mei($_0$yeou)* (1) 'have not, did not': 我 没 ( 有 ) 看 見 他. *Woo mei($_0$yeou) kann.jiann ta.* 'I have not seen him' ~ 'I did not see him.' (2) 'not ... -ing': 你 別 老 瞪 着 眼 睛 ! *Nii bye lao denqj yean.jing!* 'Don't be staring all the time!' 我 没 老 瞪 着 眼 睛。 *Woo mei lao denqj yean.jing.* 'I wasn't staring all the time.' The positive form for meaning (1) is not 有 *yeou*, but the perfective suffix *-le*. Therefore the V-not-V form of questions with this auxiliary verb takes the form of V-*le meiyeou* (the *-yeou* is obligatory since *mei* cannot occur finally), as in 吃 了 飯 ( 了 ) 没 有 ? *Chyle fann (le) meiyeou?* 'Have you had your meal?' (a common form of greeting). Ans. 吃 了. *Chyle.* 'Yes, I have.' or 没 有. *Meiyeou.* 'No, I haven't.' or 还 没 吶。*Hair mei ne.* 'Not yet.'

A very new borrowing from Cantonese, reinforced by the influence of the Taiwanese form of the Southern Fukien dialect, consists of the use of 有 *yeou* as the positive form of Vx 43, as in 你 有 看 見 他 没 有 ? *Nii yeou kann.jiann ta meiyeou?* 'Have you seen him?' or 'Did you see him?' This is getting to be fairly acceptable Mandarin among those in contact with Southerners. But the simple answer 有. *Yeou.* 'Yes, I have.' or 'Yes, I did.' still grates on Northern ears.

In the preceding listing, I have not included such "new terms" as 爱 好 *ayhaw* 'cherish ... -ing', 企 畵 *chiitwu* 'contrive to', 试 畵 *shyhtwu* 'scheme to',[42] which are only seen, but not heard except when one reads written bairhuah aloud.

---

[42]The last two are considered to be Vx by 梁 式 中 (Liang Shyhjong), *ZGYW*, no. 95: 213-217 (1960).

# 8.2. Prepositions (K)[43]

*8.2.1. Prepositions as a Separate Word Class.* In connection with verbal expressions in series [sec. 5.5.2 (4)], we noted that most transitive verbs occur as first verbs only occasionally and that a listable number of verbs occur as first verbs with the same order of frequency as in other positions and are thus called coverbs (hence "K")[44] or prepositions. In a few cases, they do not occur at all in other positions and are thus prepositions par excellence. But the most important properties of prepositions are that they do not, as a rule, have aspects and that they do not usually function as centers of predicates, as will be illustrated below.

Because of the transitional nature of Chinese prepositions, both in the classificatory and in the historical sense, the characterizations given above have had to be stated in circumscribed terms and cannot serve as rigorous definitions. Consequently, we are defining prepositions by enumeration.

*8.2.2. Formal Features of Prepositions*

(1) As to the lack of aspects, prepositions, as a rule, (a) do not have tentative reduplicates, (b) do not have the inchoative suffix -*.chii.lai* 'start to', (c) do not have the indefinite past aspect with -*.guoh*, (d) rarely have the perfective aspect with -*le*, and (e) have

---

[43]For a review of the conception of 介字 *jiehtzyh* or 介词 *jiehtsyr* used by Chinese grammarians, see 黎錦熙, 刘世儒, 汉语介词的新体系 (Li Jiinshi and Liou Shyhru, "A New System of Chinese Prepositions"), ZGYW, no. 56:16-24 (1957), in which the authors pointed out that it was 陈承澤 Chern Cherngtzer, who, in his 國文法草創 ("Draft for a Chinese Grammar"), 学藝 *Wissen und Wissenschaft* (1922), first regarded 之 *jy* as not being a preposition, although Li and Liou still regard its modern equivalent *de* as being one. This shows how much influence terminology has on its scope of use in spite of its avowed arbitrariness. Since *jiehtsyr* is an intermediate introducer, *jy* or modern *de* serves as an excellent introducer between related words. On the other hand, a preposition will have to be preposed and not postposed as *jy* and *de* are. For our purposes, we shall exclude *jy* and *de*, not for terminological reasons, but for the formal reason that prepositions have other syntactical properties.

[44]Charles F. Hockett and Chaoying Fang *et al., Dictionary of Spoken Chinese,* War Department Technical Manual 30-933, Washington, D.C., 1945, pp. 18-19.

the progressive aspect with -*j* only in a few cases, as listed. Where there is a great difference in meaning, we shall regard the case as one of class overlap. For example, in 比 *bii.bii* 'make a comparison', 跟这个比起来 *gen jeyg bii.chii.lai* 'start to compare with this', 跟他比过本事 *gen ta bii.guoh been.shyh* 'have once compared abilities with him', the *bii* is the action verb for 'compare' and not the preposition for 'than'. In some cases, the suffixes can be regarded as built-in parts of the meaning, as 為 *wey* or 為着 *weyj* 'for the purpose of, for the sake of', 為了 *weyle* (either = *weyj* or) 'because of'.

Since we have considered the use or non-use of aspect suffixes as a matter of degree, even prepositions which usually do not take such suffixes may in certain contexts take several of them, as cited by Shyy Jennhwa, who rightly emphasizes the total behavior of words to determine their parts of speech. Some of his examples are: 風向標的箭头正朝着南呢。 *Fengshianqbiau de jianntour jenq chaurj Nan ne.* 'The arrowhead of the weathercock is now facing the South.' 風向標 ... 已经朝了南。 *Fengshianqbiau ... yiijing chaurle Nan.* 'The ... weathercock has already been facing the South.' 这家的大门从前朝过南，後来改朝了北。 *Jey-jia de dahman tsorngchyan chaur.guoh Nan, howlai gae chaurle Beei.* 'The front door of this house faced the South once before, but afterwards was altered and has been facing the North.'[45]

(2) Prepositions do not normally serve as centers of predicates. Thus: (a) They do not often occur as the main verb. The use of 為 *wey* in 你為谁呐？我谁也不為。 *Nii wey sheir ne? Woo sheir yee bu wey.* 'What are you (doing this) for? I am not for anybody.' is rare. Similarly, 从 *tsorng* 'from' is more often used in the form 你得从这儿走。 *Nii deei tsorng jell tsoou.* 'You must go from here.' or 从上望下写！ *Tsorng shanq wanq*

---

[45] 史振曄，也谈关于介词结构作谓语 (Shyy Jennyeh, "More on Prepositional Constructions as Predicates"), ZGYW, no. 60:48 (1957). Since in all Shyy's examples 朝 *chaur* is the main verb, it would be better to cite examples like 朝着南边儿指着 *chaurj Nan.bial jyyj* 'pointing toward the South'.

*shiah shiee!* 'Write from top to bottom!' and less often in the form 你得从这儿. *Nii deei tsorng jell.* 'You must from here' (cf. Germ. *Sie müssen aus hir*). In 你得从个先生. *Nii deei tsorng g shian.sheng.* 'You have to follow a teacher.', however, *tsorng* is an action verb by class overlap. (b) In 你从不从 枟香山支？ *Nii tsorng bu tsorng Tarnshiang Shan tzoou?* 'Are you going by way of Honolulu?' *tsorng* is a preposition, to be sure, but it is better to regard it as the V-*bu*-V form of the whole V-V series, with the repetition applied to whatever happens to be the first syllable, just like 你绖不绖过枟香山？ *Nii jing-bu-jingguoh Tarnshiang Shan?* 'Are you going to pass through Honolulu?' (c) Prepositions do not form one-word sentences, even in supplementary answers to questions. In the questions given above, one cannot answer °从.°*Tsorng.* except as the verb 'follow'. To the question 你跟我去吧？ *Nii gen woo chiuh ba?* 'You are going with me?' or 你跟不跟我去？ *Nii gen bu gen woo chiuh?* 'Are you going with me?' one cannot answer simply °跟.°*Gen.* 'With.', except sometimes in children's speech. (d) Prepositions, except as part of a total V-V series, do not often follow an auxiliary verb. Forms like 只能望上，不 能望下. *Jyy neng wanq shanq, buneng wanq shiah.* 'You can only [move, look, etc.] upwards, not downwards.' are of restricted occurrence.

(3) A preposition does not usually omit its object, as an ordinary transitive verb normally does when the object is in the near context (see sec. 8.1.5.1). The exceptions are K 45 把 *bae*, 50 被 *bey*, 46(1) 给 *geei*, 34 照 *jaw*, and 1 在 *tzay*, and the wenyan prepositions 44 以 *yii*, 19 为 *wey*, 25L 因 *in*, 20 从 *tsorng*, and 47 将 *jiang*. See section 5.5.2(3) for examples of use.

*8.2.3. Functions of K-O Phrases.*[46] Some prepositions we have included in the defining list share the important features of having no aspect and occupying no predicative position but do not ever

---

[46]We are calling a preposition plus an object a 'K-O phrase' to avoid the ambiguity of 'prepositional phrase', which may be a K-O phrase or a phrase used *as* a preposition, for example, 'by means of'.

or do not primarily occur in first position in a V-V series, thus leaving the possibility of a K-O phrase being in other positions than that of the first verbal position. There are four functions which a K-O phrase may have in the sentence:

(1) As the $V_1$ expression modifying the $V_2$ expression it is of course the most important and most frequent function. With action verbs in the $V_2$ expression we have examples as 在床上 睡 *tzay chwang.shanq shuey* 'sleep in the bed', 到七点吃飯 *daw chi.dean chy fann* 'eat dinner by seven o'clock'. With other than action verbs, we have 跟他要好 *gen ta yawhao* 'to be friendly with him', 于我方便 *yu woo fang₀biann* 'convenient for me', 对人太不客气 *duey ren tay bukeh.chih* 'too im-polite to people', 離家很遠 ( ~ 近 ) *li jia heen yeuan ( ~ jinn)* 'very far from ( ~ near to) home'.

(2) A K-O phrase may modify a nominal expression with the insertion of *de* just like ordinary verbal expressions, as in 对朋 友的態度 *duey perng.yeou de tay.duh* 'attitude toward friends', 朝西的窗户 *chaur Shi de chuang.huh* 'window facing the West', 沿海的几省 *yan hae de jii-sheeng* 'the provinces along the sea', 在家的日子 *tzay jia de ryhtz* 'the days at home', 臨動身的兩个鐘头 *lin donq-shen de leangg jong-tour* 'the two hours preceding departure'. Some prepositions used in this position in English to modify a nominal expression cannot do so in Chinese without a second verbal expression. Thus, 'people from America' is not ° 从美國的人    °*tsorng Meeigwo de ren*, but 从美國来的人 *tsorng Meei.gwo lai de ren* with 来 *lai* 'come' as $V_2$; 'the story according to him' is not ° 據他 的故事 °*jiuh ta de guh.shyh*, but 據他讲的故事 *jiuh ta jeang de guh.shyh*, with 讲 *jeang* 'told' as $V_2$.

(3) K-O phrase as subject: We have treated the subject in a Chinese sentence as the expression which introduces the topic or subject matter, which may or may not be the actor, if the verb is a verb of action (see sec. 2.4.1). In most cases a Chinese S-P sentence can be translated into a straight S-P sentence in Eng-lish, as in 念书写字得要个清静的地方. *Niann-shu shiee-tzyh deei yaw g ching₀jinq de dih.fang.* 'Studying and writ-

ing need a quiet place.' But in a substantial minority of cases the translation will have to be reworded, as in 念书写字还没找到个清静的地方呐。 *Niann-shu shiee-tzyh hair mei jaodaw g ching₀jinq de dih.fang ne.* 'As for studying and writing, (one ~ I) have not yet found a quiet place.' It is in fact also possible to say in Chinese 至于念书写字，还没... *Jyhyu niann-shu shiee-tzyh, hair mei ...* , where the preposition 至于 *jyhyu* is the exact counterpart of 'as for', but with these differences: (a) While *jyhyu* is optional in Chinese, 'as for' is obligatory in English, if the subject is not the actor of the predicate; (b) with 'as for', a second subject ('one ~ I') is required in the English, whereas no additional subject is required even if 至于 *jyhyu* is used, since the whole K-O expression can be the subject. Similarly, in 关于那个问题，我还没打定主意呐。 *Guanyu neyg wenntyi, woo hair mei daa-dinq jwu.yih ne.* 'With regard to that problem, I have not yet made up my mind.', either 关于 *guanyu* or 我 *woo* or both may be omitted, but in the translation, both 'with regard to' and 'I' are obligatory. When *guanyu* is expressed, we have a K-O phrase as the main subject, with or without *woo* as a small subject. For other examples, including a comparison with the French K-O phrase *jusqu'aux enfants* as subject, see section 2.8.4.

(4) K-O phrases as complements are limited to 到 *daw*, 在 *tzay*, and 给 *geei*, all translatable as 'to' or 'at'. For example, 走到家裡 *tzoou daw jia.lii* 'go into the home', 等到天亮 *deeng daw tianlianq* 'wait until daybreak', 说到他信 *shuo daw ta shinn* 'talk until he is convinced', 借给你钱 *jieh geei nii chyan* 'lend to you money', 借钱给你 *jieh chyan geei nii* 'lend money to you', 坐在椅子上 *tzuoh tzay yiitz.shang* 'sit on the chair', 住在上海 *juh tzay Shanghae* 'live in Shanghai'. For further examples and on de as a blend of *daw* and *tzay*, see section 5.6.3. In wenyan there is a preposition 于 *hu*, which is used in complement position, but since in modern speech it occurs only in solid compounds such as 在乎 *tzay.hu* 'care about', 犹之乎 *youjyhu* 'as if', 于是乎 *yushyhhu* 'thereupon', 纯乎 *chwenhu* 'purely', we are not including 乎 *hu* in our list. The cliché 出乎

意料之外 *chu hu yihliaw jy way* 'exceed the outside of expectations,—surprising', though used in speech, is L in structure.

    *8.2.4. Meanings of Prepositions.* In connection with V-V series
(sec. 5.5.3), we gave the class meanings of the first verbal expressions. Some of them, namely (1) first in time order, (6) means to
end, and (10) action on action, do not occur typically in first
position and are not K-O phrases. The others are: (2) time when
(at or from), (3) place where (at or from), (4) interest and benefit,
(5) purpose, cause, and reason, (7) manner, instrument, (8) comparison, (9) association, and, under a separate subsection, pretransitives. For a diagrammatic summary of the meanings, see table
19, sec. 8.2.6.

    Note that for place or time arrived at, a K-O phrase occupies
the position of a complement, which is different from that of a
$V_2$ expression in a V-V series, since in a V-R construction the first
verb is the center, while in a V-V series the second verb is the
center. A formal difference is that the preposition in a complement is usually in the neutral tone and is very often compounded
enclitically with the verb. Note also that in wenyan prepositions
for 'place or time toward or at' (as well as 'arrive at') are in the
complement position and that prepositions for 'place from' or
'time from' occupy either position, as 序於劍橋 *shiuh yu
Jiannchyau* 'prefaced at Cambridge' L, colloquially: 在劍橋写
(的)序 *tzay Jiannchyau shiee (de) shiuh* 'at Cambridge written
preface', 来自何处? *lai tzyh herchuh?* 'come from where?' L,
colloquially: 从那儿来? *tsorng naal lai?* but also 自遠方来
*tzyh yeuanfang lai* 'from distant place come' L, colloquially: 从
遠地方来 *tsorng yeuan dih.fang lai,* in the same order.

    *8.2.5 List of Prepositions.* In the following list of prepositions,
we have not illustrated all their uses but refer to the sections
concerned if they are discussed elsewhere in greater detail. Class
overlaps are also not mentioned exhaustively, but only where
there may be possible confusion of functions.

    **K1.** 在 *tzay* 'at, on, in': 在劍橋上学 *tzay Jiannchyau
shanq-shyue* 'go to school at (~ in) Cambridge'. There are three
other local variant forms: *day, ai,* and *air* which could be, but
are never actually, written 待, 挨, 捱, respectively, for the sound.

These variants cannot be used in the complement position. Thus, for first position there is 他们在 (~待~挨~捱) 家裡玩儿 呐。 *Tamen tzay (~ day ~ ai ~ air) jia.lii wal ne.* 'They are playing at home.', but only 住在 (~得) 家裡 *juh.tzay (~ de) jia.lii* 'live at home'.

For specifying place or time 'on, in, before, after', and so on, the general formula is *tzay* N-L, where N-L is a place or time word or phrase, on which see section 7.10 for details.

+ Vc 'is at': 在家 *tzay-jia* 'to be at home', 在礼 *tzay-lii* 'to be at propriety,—do not smoke or drink'.

+ Vst 'to be there, to be present, to be living': 王先生不 在。*Wang .Shian.sheng bu tzay.* 'Mr. Wang is not in.' 王...不在 了。*Wang ... bu tzay le.* 'Mr. Wang is no longer there,—is deceased.'

K 2. 跟 *gen* 'with':   别跟他闹玩笑！ *Bye gen ta kai wanshiaw!* 'Don't joke with him!' This is the most frequently used 'with' or 'and' word in the North.

+ J 跟 'and':  張三跟李四是兩个人。 *Jang San gen Lii Syh sh leangg ren.* 'Jang 3 and Lii 4 are two men.' On the nonuse of conjunctions and the "A, B, and C" rule, see section 5.2.2 (4 and 5).

+ Vt 'follow':  老跟着人就不能独立了。 *Lao genj ren jiow buneng dwulih le.* 'If you are following someone all the time, you won't be able to be independent.'

K 3. 和 *hann ~ hay ~ her* 'with'. This is interchangeable with, but much less often used than, 跟 *gen*. In written bairhuah, 和, with fewer strokes than 跟, is used much more often, but then it is usually pronounced *her* (see below), which is now a rather widespread usage in reading bairhuah text.[47]

---

[47]During the 1950's the school children in Taiwan who read 和 as *her* in their textbooks were corrected by their teachers, who insisted that as preposition or conjunction it should be pronounced *hann*. Since, however, in correcting their pupils, the teachers tended to put a contrastive stress on the word being corrected: Not *woo "her nii,* but *woo "hann nii!* the result was an unnaturally stressed form of *hann.* This aroused much opposition from

+ J 'and': 就是你和我俩人在这儿。 *Jiow sh nii hann woo lea ren tzay jell.* 'Just you and I two people are here.'

The various other meanings and functions associated with the etymon written 和 are so different that they should be regarded as different morphemes under the same homograph. For details see *Conc Dict*, 35-36.

K 4. 同 *torng* 'with'.

+ J 'and'. This is the equivalent of 跟 *gen* in the Central dialects and Cantonese. It is included here because it is often borrowed by Northern speakers and occasionally found in written bairhuah. We are not counting 与 *yeu* and 及 *jyi*, which are purely wenyan words for 'with' and 'and'.

K 5. 到 *daw* (1) 'to, toward': 你到我们家来，还是我到你们家去？ *Nii daw woomen jia lai, hairsh woo daw niimen jia chiuh?* 'Will you come to our house, or shall I go to yours?' In complement position: 走到天边 *tzoou₀daw tianbian* 'go to the edge of the sky, — go as far as possible.' (2) 'by the time, till, until': 到熟了就停火． *Daw shourle jiow tyng-huoo.* 'Stop the fire when it is done.' In complement position: 一直等到天黑 *ijyr deeng daw tian hei* 'waited (straight on) until it was dark'. Note that while 'till' and 'until' are synonymous, the apparently corresponding forms 到 *daw* and 不到 *bu daw* are used in opposite senses. For example, 不到累极了他不去睡觉． *Bu daw ley-jyile ta bu chiuh shuey-jiaw.* 'Until he is awfully tired, he won't go to sleep.', but 等到累极了他才去睡觉呐． *Deeng daw ley-jyile ta tsair chiuh shuey-jiaw ne.* 'Only by the time when he is awfully tired does he go to sleep, —he won't go to sleep till he is awfully tired.'

+ Vi, Vt 'arrive (at)': 春天到了． *Chuen.tian dawle.* 'Spring

---

parents and other teachers, especially those teaching literary Chinese. Since the storm in the teacup subsided, the situation has returned to about the same as before, namely, people write 和 and pronounce it *her* in reading written bairhuah aloud, but say *gen* if they were born or lived long in the North, while if they acquired Mandarin late they may write and say 同 *torng*.

has arrived.' 我预备六点到家. *Woo yuh.bey liow-dean daw-jia.* 'I expect to reach home at six.'

K 6. 上 *shanq* 'to, toward' = K 5(1): 请你上我这儿来. *Chiing nii shanq woo.jell lai.* 'Please come to my place.'

For other uses of 上 *shanq*, see section 7.10.

K 7. 临 *lin* 'just before': 他临死都不认错. *Ta lin-syy dou bu renn-tsuoh.* 'He would not admit he was wrong even just before he died.' 你临走怎么没谢谢主人? *Nii lin-tzoou tzeem mei shieh.shieh juu.ren?* 'How come you didn't thank your host before leaving?' 临上轿扎耳朵眼儿 *lin shanq-jiaw ja eel.douyeal* 'pierce (earring) holes in the ear lobes just before getting into the nuptial sedan chair,—leave things to the last moment'. This preposition can take any action verb as object, but with nouns it is limited to a few bound forms, as in 临时 *linshyr* 'just before the time, for the time being, temporarily', 临阵脱逃 *linjenn tuotaur* 'desert just before (taking the front) position' L.

+ Vt 'to copy from a model': 临帖 *lin-tieh* 'to copy from a rubbing of calligraphy', 临吴道子 *lin Wu Dawtzyy* 'to copy from Wu Dawtzyy's painting'.

K 8. 趁 *chenn* 'riding the opportunity of, by the time of': 趁早预备! *Chenn-tzao yuh.bey!* 'Prepare while it is still early!' 趁他没走问他! *Chenn ta mei tzoou wenn ta!* 'Ask him before he leaves!' 趁机会逃吧! *Chenn ji₀huey taur ba.*' 'Let's escape while riding the opportunity,—Let's escape while we can!'

+ Vt 'ride': 你趁哪班飞机? *Nii chenn neei-ban feiji?* 'Which flight are you taking?'

K 9. 趕 *gaan* 'catching up with, by the time of': 你得趕天黑以前到. *Nii deei gaan tian hei yiichyan daw.* 'You must arrive before it is dark.' 趕暑假时候做得完吗? *Gaan shuujiah .shyr.how tzuoh.de-wan ma?* 'Can you finish by the time of the summer vacation?'

+ Vt 'drive, hurry, catch': 趕车 *gaan-che* 'drive (an animal-drawn) vehicle', 趕工 *gaan-gong* 'do rush work', 趕不上这趟

火車 *gaan.bu-shanq jey-tanq huooche* 'cannot catch this (run of the) train'.

K 10. 望[48] *wanq* 'to, toward': 望前头看 *wanq chyan.tou kann* 'look toward the front', 望左边儿倒 *wanq tzuoo.bial dao* 'fall toward the left'.

There is a Peiping usage by which this preposition is pronounced *wann* instead of *wanq* before dental, retroflex, and palatal initials. I followed this in *Mand Prim* (n. 23, p. 154), but this is probably a minority-type pronunciation. For examples see sec. 5.5.3, n. 43.

+ Vt 'look up to, gaze at': 你幹麻老望着月亮? *Nii gannma lao wanqj yueh.lianq?* 'Why are you gazing at the moon all the time?'

+ N 'hope': 我怕这事儿没望了。 *Woo pah jeh shell mei wanq le.* 'I am afraid there is no hope in this thing.'

K 11. 衝(着) *chonq(j)* (1) 'toward, facing': 别衝着人打嚏! *Bye chonqj ren daa-tih!* 'Don't sneeze facing people!' 開香檳得把瓶子衝(着)上(头)開。*Kai shiangbin deei bae pyngtz chonq(j) shanq (.tou) kai.* 'In opening champagne, you must open it with the bottle facing up.' (2) 'on behalf of, as a favor to': 我衝着你的面子才借这錢给他的。 *Woo chonqj niide mianntz tsair jieh jeh chyan geei ta de.* 'It was as a favor to you that I lent him this money.'

+ Vc 'face': 槍口一齐衝(着)外(头)。*Chiangkoou ichyi chonq(j) way (.tou).* 'All gun (muzzle)s face outwards.'

K 12. 朝(着) *chaur(j)* 'toward, facing': 朝南走 *chaur Nan*

---

[48]Usually written 往. We prefer the form 望 *wanq* < *mi̯wang*' because the preposition with the same function and meaning in both the Wu dialects and in Cantonese is [mɔː ŋ'], which is also the pronunciation for 望 as Vt 'look up to, gaze up' in those dialects. As for 往 ʿ*woang* < ʿ*ji̯wang* 'go to', it does not have the right tone for Wu and Cantonese, and not even for Mandarin. As a concession to common habit in the use of characters, I did write 往 for the preposition *wanq* in the illustrative sentence 勇往ˇ往ˋ前 *yeongwoang wanq chyan* 'bravely go toward the front' in my 國语留声片课本 (*Textbook for National Language Records*), Shanghai, 1922, p. 21A. It may have been good pedagogy, but it was bad etymology.

*tzoou* 'go toward the South,—go southward', 朝後头看ㄈ *chaur how.tou kann.kann* 'take a look toward the rear'.

+ Vc 'faces': 这窗户朝北. *Jeh chuang.huh chaur Beei.* 'This window faces North.' [cf. sec. 8.2.2 (1).]

K 13. 向 *shianq* 'toward' L: 向右看——齐! *Shianq yow kann—chyi!* 'Toward the right look—even!,—Eyes—right!' In written bairhuah, also in complement position: 走向自由的路 *tzoou shianq tzyhyou de luh* 'go toward the way to freedom'.

+ V$_A$ 向着 'to be partial to, to be on the side of': 你向着我还是向着我的仇人? *Nii shianqj woo hairsh shianqj woo de chourren?* 'Are you on my side or on the side of my enemy?' In this sense it always has the suffix *-j*.

K 14. 对(着) *duey(j)* 'facing, toward, to': 这些话是对(着)谁说的? *Jeh$_o$shie huah sh duey(j) sheir shuo de?* 'To whom were these words addressed?' 他对你并不坏也! *Ta duey nii binq bu huay è!* 'He is really not bad to you, is he?' 我对你说的都是真话. *Woo duey nii shuo de dou sh jen huah.* 'What I am saying to you is all true.' 他对人很和气. *Ta duey ren heen her.chih.* 'He is very kind to people.'

+ Vt (1) 'face, match': 倘有人害他, 你如何对他? *Taang yeou ren hay ta, nii ruher duey ta?* 'If they hurt her, how would you face them (deal with them)?',[49] *duey dueytz* 'match antithetical couplets'. (2) mix (liquids): 酒裡对水 *jeou.lii duey shoei* 'mix water in the wine'.

+ A 'correct': 对! *Duey!* 'Correct!', 对了! $_o$*Dueyle!* 'That's right!', 'Yes!'

K 15. 于 *yu* 'in, for, with regard to': 于事情没有帮助 *yu shyh.chyng mei.yeou bang$_o$juh* 'to be of no help to matters', 于身体有害处 *yu shen$_o$tii yeou hay.chuh* 'harmful to the body'.

Originally there were two different prepositions or main verbs 于 *jiu* > *yu* and 於 *.iwo* > (theoretical) *iu*, with slightly different

---

[49]From the poem 他: 思祖国也 *Ta: Sy Tzuugwo yee* 'Her: My Ancestral Country', by Hu Shih.

meanings,[50] now both *yu* in most modern dialects except Cantonese, which still maintains the distinction, though only in pronunciation. Very recently, because of lack of distinction, in sound or meaning, the simpler character 于 has been used more and more in place of 於, as for example in the present book.

While 于 *yu* is still the most general preposition in wenyan, covering about the same range as 在 *tzay*, its use in speech is limited only to the types of examples given above.

K 16. 对于 $duey_oyu$ 'in, with regard to, about': 他对于那件事情很生气. *Ta dueyyu ney-jiann shyh.chyng heen sheng-chih.* 'He was very angry about that matter.' 我对于打球一点儿没兴趣. *Woo $duey_oyu$ daa-chyou ideal mei shinq-$_o$chiuh.* 'I am not at all interested in ball games.'

K 17. 関于 $guan_oyu$ 'with regard to, about, concerning': 関于國外的情形, 他一点儿不熟悉. *$Guan_oyu$ gwoway de chyng.shyng, ta ideal bu shwu.shi.* 'About conditions abroad, he is not at all familiar.' 我只问你関于技術方面的问题. *Woo jyy wenn nii $guan_oyu$ $jih_oshuh$ fangmiann de wenntyi.* 'I am only asking you some questions concerning the technical aspects.'

K 18. 至于 $jyh_oyu$ 'as to, as for': 至于课外的活動他们就不荳了. *$Jyh_oyu$ kehway de hwodonq, tamen jiow bu goan le.* 'As for extracurricular activities, they are not concerned with them.' 至于酒錢给多少, 要看客人的高兴了. *$Jyh_oyu$ jeou.chyan geei duoshao, yaw kann keh.ren de gaushinq le.* 'As to how much to tip, it depends upon the customer's pleasure.'

N.B. As for the negative 不至于 *bujyh.yu* 'it will not come to that,—it won't be as bad as,—probably not', it is lot a preposition, but an adverb, as in 他们俩不至于打起来吧 *Tamen lea bujyh.yu daa.chii.lai ba?* 'They two will probably not get into a fight, will they?'

K 19. 为 (着 ~ 了) *wey (j~le)* 'for, for the sake of, for the

────────────
[50]See B. Karlgren, "On the Authenticity and Nature of the Tso Chuan", *Göteborg Högskolas Arsskrift*, XXXII, 3:41-49 of 1-65 (1926).

purpose of, on account of': 为国家犠牲 *wey gwojia shisheng* 'sacrifice for the country's sake'. 为着(～了) 这点儿钱不值得跑那么一趟。 *Weyj (～le) jey-deal chyan bujyrde pao nemm i-tanq.* 'For this little money, it won't be (wasn't) worthwhile to make that trip.' 为什么呐? *Wey sherm ne?* 'What for?' 为了什么呐? *Weyle sherm ne?* 'On account of what?' 为的是什么呐? *Wey de sh sherm ne?* 'What (purpose) was it for?'

K 20. 从 *tsorng,*

K 21. 打 *daa,*

K 22. 解 *jiee,* and

K 23. 起 *chii* (in descending order of frequency of use) 'from, by, by way of': 病从口入,祸从口出。 *Binq tsorng koou ruh, huoh tsorng koou chu.* 'Sickness comes in by mouth, calamity comes out by (word of) mouth' (proverb).[51] 从(～打～解～起) 这儿到那儿有多远? *Tsorng (～daa～jiee～chii) jell daw nall yeou dwo yeuan?* 'How far is it from here to there?' 从(～打～解～起)聖诞到新年有一个礼拜. *Tsorng (～daa ～jiee～chii) Shenqdann daw Shinnian yeou ig liibay.* 'From Christmas to New Year's there is one week.'

The meanings of the verbs 打 *daa* 'strike' and 解 *jiee* 'untie, explain' are so remote from 'from' that they had better be regarded as homophone-homographs of the prepositions. 起 *chii* 'rise', 'start' is close enough to be considered an overlap of the same word as preposition and verb. As preposition, however, it is less often used than any of the other 'from' words. Even less frequently used in speech is 由 *you*, which in the sense of 'from' is L. (CF. K 26 & K 55.) A blend of K22 & K23 is 且 *chiee*.

K 24. 自从 *tzyhtsorng* 'from, ever since': 自从一九零〇的庚子到最近的庚子足〇有六十年了. *Tzyhtsorng i-jeou-ling-ling de Gengtzyy daw tzuey jinn de Gengtzyy tzwu-tzwu yeou liow.shyr-nian.* 'From the *Gengtzyy* of 1900 to the

---

[51]Normally 从 *tsorng* must take a place or time word for object. But proverbs are often in a mixed L and colloquial style.

most recent *Gengtzyy* there were fully 60 years.' 自从 他 走了 以後，我 一直 老 不 放心. *Tzyhtsorng ta tzooule yiihow, woo ijyr lao bufanqshin.* 'Ever since he left, I have been worried all the time.'

K 25. 因为 *in$_0$wey* 'because of': 他 因为 什么 缘 故 不 能 来？ *Ta inwey sherm yuan.guh buneng lai?* 'For what reason couldn't he come?' 因为 重 傷風 不 能 来. *Inwey jonq-shang-feng buneng lai.* 'He couldn't come because of a bad cold.'

+J 'because': 因为 下雨了，所以 不能 打球了. *Inwey shiah-yeu le, suooyii buneng daa-chyou le.* 'Because it rained, (so) they (~ we) couldn't play ball.'

K 26. 由于 *youyu* 'due to, owing to' L. This is the wenyan equivalent of K 25 and is very rarely spoken. The exact L equivalent of 因为 *inwey* is simply 因 *in*. One does say, to be sure, 因此 *intsyy* 'for this reason', which should, however, be regarded as a compound, since neither 因 *in* nor 此 *tsyy* is used as a free word. (Cf. K 55, *you*.)

K 27. 離 ($_0$开) *li* ($_0$*kai*) '(static) from, (static) to': 这儿 離 鏡头 不够远. *Jell li jinqtour bu gow yeuan.* 'This is not far enough from the camera lens.' 現在 離($_0$开) 暑假 只一个 月了. *Shianntzay li ($_0$kai) shuujiah jyy ig yueh le.* 'It is now only one month to the summer vacation.'

+Vt     'leaves': 这小孩儿 从未没 離 (开) 过家. *Jeh sheauharl tsornglai mei li ($_0$kai).guoh jia.* 'This child has never been away from home.'

K 28. 比 *bii*,

K 29. 比 较 *biijeau*, and

K 30. 较 比 *jiawbii* (sic) (in descending order of frequency) 'than': 他 比 你 高. *Ta bii nii gau.* 'He is taller than you.'

+Vt 'compare' (limited to K 28 and K 29).

N.B. The Wuism 勝过 *shenq$_0$guoh* 'surpass,— to be better than', sometimes used in Mandarin, is used only as a predicate and not as a preposition, as in 出去 勝过 在家裡 等着. *Chu-.chiuh shenq$_0$guoh tzay jia.lii deengj.* 'Going out is better than waiting at home.'

K 31. 像 *shianq* 'like, as': 像他那么高 *shianq ta nemm gau* 'like him that tall,—as tall as he', 像我这么做 *shianq woo tzemm tzuoh* 'like I thus do,—as I do'. (Cf. the colloquial 'like I do'.)

+ V$_A$ 'to be like, resemble': 像他父親 *shianq ta fu.chin* 'resemble his father'.

K 32. 沿(着) *yan (j)* 'along': 你得沿着槽儿擦，才擦得着髒呐。 *Nii deei yanj tsaurl tsa, tsair tsa.de-jaur tzang ne.* 'You must wipe along the groove to get at the dirt.' The unsuffixed form is restricted to certain phrases, as in 沿海 *yan-hae* 'along the sea (coast)', 沿江 *yan-jiang* 'along the river', 沿岸 *yan-ann* 'along the bank', 沿街 *yan-jie* 'along the street'.

N.B. In the 4th Tone with the suffix *-l*, 沿儿 *yall* 'side' B should be considered a different morpheme complex, as in 西河沿儿 *Shi.heryall* 'West Riverside' (street in Peiping).

K 33. 順(着) *shuenn (j)* 'following along, in the direction of': 你得順着毛儿刷他。 *Nii deei shuennj maul shua ta.* 'You must brush it in the direction of the hair.' 别光順着我说话呀！ *Bye guang shuennj woo shuo-huah ia!* 'Don't just say exactly as I say!' 順那边儿走！ *Shuenn ney.bial tzoou!* 'Go along that side!'

+ Vt: 别光順着我呀！ *Bye guang shuennj woo ia!* 'Don't just follow me (in everything)!'

+ A 'favorable': 我今天的牌很順。 *Woo jin.tian de pair heen shuenn.* 'My hand (in mahjong, etc.) has been very favorable today.'

N.B. The antonym 倒着 *dawj* 'in the reverse direction' is an adverb only and does not take an object.

K 34. 照(着) *jaw (j)*,

K 35. 按(着) *ann (j)*,

K 36. 按照(着) *annjaw (j)*, and

K 37. 依照 *ijaw* 'according to' (in ascending order of formality): 你们都得照(着)[～按(着)～按照(着)～依照]一定的时刻表做事。 *Niimen dou deei jaw(j) [～ann(j)～annjaw(j)～ijaw] idinq de shyrkehbeau tzuoh-shyh.* 'You must all work according to a definite schedule.' 照規矩紅灯不能拐弯儿. *Jaw guei.jeu horng-deng buneng goai-ual* 'According to the regulations you can't turn on a red light.'

K 34 + Vt 照 *jaw* 'shine upon'; 'take (as photograph)',

K 38. 攄 *jiuh*, and

K 39. 根攄 *genjiuh* 'according to, on the basis of': 你不能（根）攄一个人的报告就决定方針. *Nii buneng (gen-) jiuh ig ren de bawgaw jiow jyuedinq fangjen.* 'You can't decide on a policy on the basis of one man's report.' 攄说取消了. *Jiuh shuo cheushiaule.* 'According to (what they) say, it has been canceled.'

+ N 'basis': 有一点儿事实上的根攄 *yeou ideal shyh-shyr.shanq de genjiuh* 'have some basis in fact'.

K 40. 憑（着）*pyng(j)*, and

K 41. 靠（着）*kaw(j)* 'on the strength of, according to': 我就憑（着）[～靠（着）]两只手过活. *Woo jiow pyng(j) [～ kaw(j)] leangj shoou guoh-hwo.* 'I make my living just by the strength of my two hands.' 憑良心说话 *pyng liang.shin shuo-huah* 'speak from conscience', 靠（着）右边儿开! *Kaw(j) yow-.bial kai!* 'Drive on the right!'

+ Vt 'lean (on)': 别靠（着）牆! *Bye kaw(j) chyang!* 'Don't lean against the wall!' 你不能靠他. *Nii buneng kaw ta.* 'You mustn't depend on him.'

K 42. 论 *luenn* 'by the': 论磅卖 *luenn banq may* 'sell by the pound'.

+ Vt 'discuss'.

K 43. 用 *yonq* 'with': 用左手写字 *yonq tzuooshoou shiee-tzyh* 'write with the left hand'.

+ Vt 'use': 用錢 *yonq chyan* 'use money', 用人 *yonq ren* 'employ people' [≠ *yonq.ren* 'employed people,—servant(s)]'.

K 44. 拿 *na* 'with': 我不会拿左手写字. *Woo buhuey na tzuooshoou shiee-tzyh.* 'I don't know how to write with my left hand.' 你得拿好话慢儿的劝他. *Nii deei na hao-huah mannmhalde chiuann ta.* 'You have to persuade him gradually with kind words.'

The wenyan equivalent of K 43 & 44 is 以 *yii* 'take, with'. It occurs bound in 所以 *suooyii* 'therewith,—therefore', 以為 *yiiwei* 'take to be,—take it that,—thought (mistakenly)'. It occurs separately only in a few L clichés, as in 以退為進 *yii tuey wei jinn* 'take retreat as (a strategem for) advance' L. We are therefore not counting it as one of the free prepositions.

+ Vt 'take, hold': 他拿了一把宝劍. *Ta nale i-baa bao-jiann.* 'He took a magic sword.' 拿稳了！ *Na-woen le!* 'Hold it steady!'

K 45. 把 *bae* ~ *bay* ~ *baa* 'taking hold of'.

+ Vt (pron. *baa* only) 'take hold of': 别老把着门！ *Bye lao baaj men!* 'Don't hold the door all the time!'

+ Mc 27 一把剪子 *i-baa jeantz* 'a (pair of) scissors' (sec. 7.9).

K 46 (1). 给 *geei* 'taking hold of'.

+ Vt 'give': 给酒錢 *geei jeou.chyan* 'give tips'.

K 47. 將 *jiang* 'taking hold of', wenyan and Cantonese (pron. *tzeung*) equivalent of K 45.

K 48. 莄 *goan* 'calling' (= K 45 when the second verb is *jiaw* 'call, name').

+ Vt 'control, take care of, take account of': 莄事務 *goan shyh*₀*wuh* 'take charge of affairs', 莄饭 *goan-fann* 'include meals', 我不莄了！ *Woo bugoan le!* 'I won't be bothered with it any more!'

K 49 (1). 叫 *jiaw* 'calling' (dial. form for K 48).

K 45-49 are the pretransitives, which introduce the object before the specific second verb. For details, see section 5.5.4.

K 50. 被 *bey* '(passive) by',

K 46 (2). 给 *geei* '(passive) by',

K 49 (2). 叫 *jiaw* '(passive) by', and

K 51. 讓 *ranq* '(passive) by' (in descending, though comparable, order of frequency): 被(~给~叫~讓) 狗咬了 *bey* ( ~ *geei* ~ *jiaw* ~ *ranq*) *goou yeaule* 'was bitten by a dog'. For further examples, see section 5.5.2 (3b).

K 52. 替 *tih* 'substituting for, in place of, for': 我不能到

会，请你替我出席吧． *Woo buneng daw huey, chiing nii tih woo chu-shyi ba.* 'I can't go to the meeting, please attend in my place.' In the Wu dialects, 替 *tih* is often used for 给 *geei* (3) below:

K 46. 给 *geei* (3) 'for, to the benefit (~harm) of': 别把这新衣裳给我弄髒了． *Bye bae jeh shin i.shang geei woo nong-tzangle.* 'Don't soil this new dress for me.' 请你给我说几句好话． *Chiing nii geei woo shuo jii-jiuh hao-huah.* 'Please say a few good words for me.'

K 53. 除（了～去）…（以外～之外） *chwu(le)* … *(yiiway ~jyway)* 'except for, outside of': 除了你以外没人会． *Chwule nii yiiway mei ren huey.* 'Nobody besides you can.' 除了逃走只有打． *Chwule taurtzoou jyy yeou daa.* 'Other than running away, the only thing is to fight.' 他除去小说以外，什么书都不看． *Ta chwuchiuh sheaushuo yiiway, sherm shu dou bu kann.* 'Other than novels he doesn't read any books.' Before a clause, *chwule ( … bu)* 'unless' or *chwule ( … tsair)* 'only if' is also used as a conjunction [secs. 2.12.7 (3) and 8.4.2 (3.2)].

K 54. 归 *guei* 'to be up to': 归谁给费？ *Guei sheir geei fey?* 'It's up to whom to give the fees?' 这事情归他苤． *Jeh shyh-.chyng guei ta goan.* 'This thing is for him to manage.'

K 55. 由 *you* 'through, for … to': 由主席召集会议． *You juushyi jawjyi hueyyih.* 'It is for the chairman to convene the meeting.'

K 56. 连 *lian* 'including, even': 连你都不懂？ *Lian nii dou bu doong?* 'Even you don't understand?' 他连你都不怕． *Ta lian nii dou bu pah.* 'He is not afraid of even you.'

K 57. 连…带 *lian … day* 'including … and … ': 他连汤带水都喝了． *Ta lian tang day shoei dou hele.* 'He drank both the soup and the water.' 连兵带将都到了． *Lian bing day jianq dou daw.le.* 'Both the soldiers and the generals have arrived.' (See sec. 2.8.4 on subject introduced by a preposition.)

8.2.6. *Schematic Table of Prepositions.* In table 19 are summarized the uses of prepositions according to meaning. In the column of diagrams, a dot represents the subject, if any; a circle, the object of the preposition; arrows represent direction of motion, facing, or action; and a broken-line circle represents the object displaced. Each meaning given is only a brief reminder of a cluster of meanings.

## 8.3  Adverbs (H)

### 8.3.1. *Formal Properties of Adverbs*

(1) Adverbs Primarily as Modifiers of Verbs.—Adverbs are attributes, or modifiers, of verbs, including adjectives, and of other adverbs, as in 先 走 *shian tzoou* 'go first', 最 美 *tzuey meei* 'most beautiful'. 不 一 定 *bu idinq* 'not necessarily'. In a string $H_1$, $H_2$, V, the ICs are $H_1 + H_2V$, rather than $H_1H_2 + V$, as in 又 大 笑 了 *yow dah-shiaw le* 'again greatly laugh,—laugh greatly again', where 又 *yow* modifies 大 笑 *dah-shiaw*, which is a verbal phrase as a whole. Similarly, 还 不 早 来 *hair bu tzao-lai* 'still not early come,—still won't come early' has the ICs $H_1 + (H_2 + H_3V)$. In 不 大 懂 *budah doong* 'do not understand very well', the ICs are $2 + 1$ because *budah* is a compound.

An adverb does not normally modify nouns. When it does, it really modifies the noun or the nominal expression as a predicate or, more questionably, as a subject. In other words, an adverb can modify the main parts of the sentence[52] rather than words or phrases as such. Examples are: 这 人 夠 朋 友 *Jeh ren gow perng.yeou.* 'This man (is) enough of a friend.' 你 简 直 傻 子 嘿! *Nii jeanjyr shaatz me!* 'You (are) simply a fool!' 那 一 定 好 消 息 ! *Nah idinq hao shiau.shi!* 'That certainly (is) good news!' 他 太 渾 蛋 了! *Ta tay hwendann le!* 'He (is) too much of a muddled egg,—a scoundrel!' (See also sec. 2.9.3 on nominal predicates.) In wenyan, we have 不 亦 君 子 乎 ? *Bu yih jiun-tzyy hu?* '(Is)n't he indeed a gentleman?' 皆 薛 居 州 也. *Jie Shiue Jiujou yee.* 'All of them are (people like) Shiue Jiujou.', where *jie*, like the colloquial 都 *dou*, is always an adverb.

As modifier of the subject, the wenyan 凡 *farn* 'all cases of' is

---

[52]The " 句 子 成 分 " (*jiuhtz cherngfenn*) of Chinese grammarians.

Table 19

SCHEMATIC TABLE OF PREPOSITIONS

| Number | Diagram | Brief Meaning | Spatio-Temporal | Other Meanings |
|---|---|---|---|---|
| 1 | ○ | 'at' | 在（~待~挨~捱） | 'in', 'on' 在 … 上（头） |
| 2–4 | ○ | 'with' | 跟、和、同 (dial.) | |
| 5–6 | ○ | 'to' | 到、上 | |
| | | 'by (the time when)' | 到 | |
| 7–9 | ○ | 'just before' | 临、趁、趕 | |
| 10–19 | ○ | 'toward' | 望、衝(着)、朝(着)、向、对(着) | 对、于、对于、闲于、至于、为(着~了) |
| 20–26 | ○→ | 'from' | 从、打、解、起、自从 | 因、为、由于 |
| 27–31 | ○↔ | '(static) from' | 離(闲) | 比、比较、较比、像 |
| 32–42 | ○ | 'along' | 沿(着)、顺(着) | 照(着)、按(着)、按照(着)、依照、据、根据、凭(着)、靠(着)、论 |

| | | | |
|---|---|---|---|
| 用, 拿 | 'by means of' | | 43–44 |
| 把, 给(1), 将, 教, 叫(1) | 'taking hold of' | | 45–49 |
| 被, 给(2), 叫(2), 让 | 'by' | | 50,46(2), 49,51 |
| 替, 给(3) | 'for' | | 52,46(3) |
| 除了, 除去, 除…以~之外 | 'except' | | 53 |
| 归, 由, 数, 连…带 | 'through' | | 54–57 |

L, as in 凡 人 皆 有 死.[53] *Farn ren jie yeou syy.* 'Men in all cases have death,—all men are mortal.' In the colloquial, 凡 人 *farnren* is an A-N compound, meaning 'mundane people' as distinguished from 仙 人 $shian_oren$ 'the immortals'. For 'All men are mortal.', one will have to say 凡 是 人 都 有 死. *Farnsh ren dou yeou syy.* 'Whoever are men in all cases have death.', where *farnsh* corresponds to the *farn* L and is an adverb to *ren* as subject. Similarly, 要 是 我 就 不 那 么 樣. *Yawsh woo jiow bu nemmyanq.* 'In my case, I wouldn't do that.', where *yawsh*, ordinarily used as an 'if' word, would be a regular conjunction in the slightly longer sentence *Yawsh woo, woo jiow bu nemmyanq.* 'If it were I, I wouldn't do that.' The similarity of the two sentences is not fortuitous, since a dependent clause in Chinese is very much like a subject, as we have seen (secs. 2.12.5 and 2.12.6). Other than full dependent clauses as adverbial expressions, an adverb modifying a nominal subject of the 凡 是 *farnsh* type is rare.

Adverbs do not modify nominal expressions as objects of verbs or of prepositions.

On adverbs modifying clauses or sentences, see below.

(2) Free Utterance of Adverbs. Adverbs do not, as a rule, form one-word sentences, even as supplementary answers to questions. The only exception among monosyllables is 不. *Bu.* 'No', which can be regarded as an interjection by class overlap. A few polysyllables are used thus, for example, 一 定 *idinq* 'definitely', 也 许 *yeesheu* 'perhaps', 並 不 *binq bu* 'not, as a matter of fact, 不 至 于 吧? *Bujyh.yu ba?* 'Probably not (as bad as that), was it?' Some polysyllabic adverbs formed from verbal expressions when used alone revert to their verbal status and are often taken more nearly in the literal sense than as adverbs. For example, 差 一 点儿 摔 *chah.ideal shuai* 'almost fell down': 摔 了 没 有?— 没 有, 差 一 点儿. *Shuaile meiyeou?—Meiyeou, chah.ideal.* 'Did you fall down?—No, but almost,' 没 準儿 会 下 雨. *Meijoel huey shiah-yeu.* 'There is no telling but that it may rain,—it will probably rain.': 会 下 雨 不 会?— 没 準儿.

---

[53]This analysis was suggested to me by Fa-Kao Chou.

*Huey shiah-yeu buhuey?—Mei joel.* 'Will it rain?—There is no telling,—there is no certainty.'

One-word adverbs as commands seem to be slightly more common than as statements. Examples are: 快! *Kuay!* 'Hurry!' 慢! *Mann!* 'Slow!' Vivid reduplicates with *de* are more common, as 慢ㄦ的! *Mannmhalde!* 'Be good and slow!' 好ㄦ的! *Haohaulde!* 'Carefully!' Very often the comparative suffix .点ㄦ -.*deal* 'a little, -er' is added in the command, as in 慢着点ㄦ! *Mannj.deal!* 'Take it slowly!' 正一点ㄦ! *Jenq.i.deal!* 'More upright!' But note that these almost always turn out to be also adjectives by class overlap. Exclusively adverbial commands are rare, for example 大声ㄦ! *Dahshengl!* 'Loudly!' or 大声点ㄦ *Dahsheng.deal!* 'Louder!' 一块ㄦ! *Ikuall!* 'Together!' (as in a class recitation). Commands like 使劲! *Shyy-jinn!* 'Use strength,—(V) hard!' 趕緊! *Gaan-jiin!* 'Hurry up!', etc., should be regarded as adverbial expressions derived from verbal expressions which revert to verbal status in commands.

(3) Adverbs as S, P, or O. Adverbs do not occur as subjects, as predicates (except predicative complements), or as objects. In 这ㄦ 有人. *Jell yeou ren.* 'This place has people,—there are people here.', *jell* is a place word, which is a substantive and not an adverb. In 等到現在 *deeng daw shianntzay* 'wait to now', *shianntzay* is a time word, therefore also a substantive.

(4) Adverbs as Complements. Adverbs do not, as a rule, occur as complements to verbs. The only exceptions are (a) 很[54] *heen* 'very', as in the predicative complement in 好的很 *hao de heen* 'good to a high degree', which is a little stronger than the weak 'very good' in 很好 *heen hao*, and (b)極 *jyi* 'extremely', as in 好極了 *hao-jyile* 'good to an extreme'. In actual use 極好 *jyi hao* is a very deliberately spoken 'extremely good', while 好極了 *hao-jyile* is a colloquial and mildly exclamatory 'awfully good'.

---

[54]Etymologically the same word as 狠 *heen* 'fierce', originally also written 很.

*8.3.2. Adverbial Phrases*

(1) V₁ **Phrases.** The most common type of adverbial phrase is that of the V₁ phrase in V-V series, as in 用心做事 *yonq-shin tzuoh-shyh* 'use the mind and do things,—work with concentration'. A special case of the V₁ phrase is that of the K-O phrase, where the V₁ is never or rarely used as an independent verb and is thus a preposition, as in 从这儿走 *tsorng jell tzoou* 'go from here', where 从这儿 *tsorng jell* is an adverbial phrase. In a few cases, the object of the preposition is omitted and the first verb itself is used as an adverb, as in 他在玩儿呐. *Ta tzay wal ne.* 'He is (a-)playing.', where an omitted 那儿 *nall* 'there', and not 玩儿 *wal* 'playing', is the object of 在 *tzay*. In fact, the more common form in everyday speech is 他在那儿玩儿呐。 *Ta tzay.nall wal ne.*, rather than the shorter form. For other cases of first verbs with omitted objects, resulting in adverbs, see section 5.5.2(3).

An adverbial phrase consisting of more than one adverb is rare, as we have seen, since the succession of H₁, H₂, V is likely to be H₁ + H₂V rather than H₁H₂ + V, and even in the latter case H₁H₂ usually forms a compound instead of a phrase.

(2) **Adverbial Phrases with Appositional ₀*Nemme*.** A V-O phrase and certain other phrases used adverbially often have an optional 那么 ₀*nemme* 'in the above manner, to the above degree, -like'. For example, in 拼命跑 *pin-minq pao* or 拼着命跑 *pinj minq pao* 'stake one's life and run,—run like mad', *pin(j) minq* is the usual V₁ expression modifying *pao*. But one can also say 拼着命那么跑 *pinj minq ₀nemm pao* 'run as if to save one's life'. Similarly, 瞪着眼睛（那么）看 *denqj yean-.jing (nemm) kann* 'stare with the eyes and look in that manner,—look with staring eyes', 手不扶着那么骑 *shoou bu fwuj ₀nemm chyi* 'hands not supporting, ride like that,—no hands', 一隻脚（那么）站着 *i-jy jeau (nemm) jannj* 'one foot, stand like that, — stand on one foot', 直着嗓子（那么）叫 *jyrj saangtz (nemm) jiaw* '(with) straight (loud) voice, shout', 半醒半睡那么说话 *bann-shiing bann-shuey ₀nemm shuo-huah* 'half awake

and half asleep -like talk,—talk as if half-awake and half-asleep'. In the last example the resumptive *nemme* is obligatory, since *bann-shiing bann-shuey* are not $V_1$-O phrases and do not modify verbs. But if the adverbial suffix *de* [sec. 5.3.6.5 (3)] is added, then *nemme* is optional. Cf. (4) below.

The resumptive $_0$*nemme* can sometimes be preceded by or replaced by *de*, as in 拼命的那么跑 *pin-minq de nemm pao* 'runs like mad'.

(3) Adverbial Phrases With or Without 在 *tzay* or 当 *dang*. We have treated place, time, and condition words as substantives. When they introduce the topic, they are the subjects. When they are the objects of 在 *tzay* 'at' or 当 *dang* 'right at', they form first verbal expressions to modify what follows. For example, 学校裡有学生。 *Shyueshiaw.lii yeou shyue.sheng.* 'School('s) inside has students,—there are students in the school.' has a place-word subject, while in the less commonly used form 在学校裡有学生。*Tzay shyueshiaw.lii yeou shyue.sheng.* '(Being) in the school there are students.', we have a V-V series in which the $V_1$ expression is a K-O phrase. Similarly, 太陽下去的时候儿停工。 *Tay.yang shiah.chiuh de .shyr.howl tyng-gong.* 'The time the sun goes down, (one) stops work.' has *shyr.howl* as subject and in 当太陽… *Dang tay.yang …* 'Right at the time the sun …' we have *dang … shyr.howl* as a $V_1$ expression. As we have noted before [sec. 2.12.7(4)], when $_0$*shyr.howl* or $_0$*dih.fang*, with or without *tzay, dang,* or the like, is in the neutral tone, then the enclosed time, place, or conditional expression acquires adverbial status.

(4) Other Adverbial Expressions Marked by *de*. On other adverbial expressions which end in the adverbial suffix *de*, see section 5.3.6.5(3.5). On the varieties of *de* and usages of the characters 的, 底, and 地, see section 4.4.6.

8.3.3. *The "H A de N" Formula.* It is common knowledge among Chinese grammarians that adjectives can as a rule directly modify nouns, as in 好人 *hao-ren* 'good man' and 红花儿 *horng-hual* 'red flower', but that as soon as an adjective is modified by an adverb, the resulting adjectival expression must be fol-

lowed by *de* before it can modify a nominal expression, as 一个
不好的人 *ig bu hao de ren* 'a not good man', 一朵很红
的花儿 *i-duoo heen horng de hual* 'a very red flower'. Similarly, *de* is required in 太舒服的日子 *tay shu.fwu de ryhtz*
'too comfortable days', 最便宜的货 *tzuey pyan.yi de huoh*
'most cheap goods,—the cheapest goods', 真利害的药 *jen lih-
.hay de yaw* 'really potent drug'. One can say 三分醉意 *san-
fen tzueyyih* 'three-tenths drunkenness', since *san-fen* is adjectival
to *tzueyyih* as noun, but must use *de* in 十分醉的人 *shyrfen
tzuey de ren* 'ten-tenths drunken person', where *shyrfen* '100%,
—completely' is adverbial to *tzuey* 'drunken'.

The following apparent exceptions are really not cases of HA
modifying a nominal expression: In 他本来坏人. *Ta beenlai
huay-ren.* 'He originally (was) a bad man.', the adverb *beenlai*
modifies the nominal predicate *huay-ren* and does not modify
the adjective *huay*. To say 'an originally bad man' a *de* will still
have to be inserted after *huay*. Similarly, in 这一定好消息.
*Jeh idinq hao shiau.shi.* 'This certainly (is) good news.', *idinq*
modifies the nominal predicate *hao shiau.shi* and not the adjective
*hao*. In 特别快车 *tehbye kuayche* 'express train', *tehbye*
'special' is adjective and *kuayche* 'fast train' is an A-N compound.
In fact, one can say 特别快车就是停的少，並不是特别
快的火车. *Tehbye kuayche jiowsh tyng de shao, binq bush
tehbye kuay de huooche.* 'The special fast-train simply stops
fewer times, it is not a specially fast train.', where the second
*tehbye kuay* is H A and therefore needs a *de* before the noun. In
the expression 不全家来。*Bu chyuanjia lai.* 'Not the whole
family (only a part of it) is coming.', the ICs are 1 + (2 + 1):
cf. 不全的家 *bu chyuan de jia* 'not a complete home (e.g.,
broken by divorce, etc.)', which follows the usual H A *de* N formula.

The somewhat arbitrary and empirical rule of AH *de* N may
be seen in a more intelligible light if we remember that adjectives
are a species of intransitive verbs. Not every intransitive verb of
action (Vi) can modify a noun without a subordinative particle *de*.

There is 逃兵 *taurbing* 'escap(ed~ing) soldier,—deserter' as well as 逃的兵 *taur de bing* 'soldier who escapes'. Similarly, 耒人 *lairen* 'com(e~ing) man,—messenger': 耒的人 *lai de ren* 'man who comes', 跑道 *paodaw* 'runway': 跑的道(儿) *pao de daw* (*l*) 'road for running' (e.g., track for races, a thief's escape route). But in general an action verb modifying a noun needs *de* if there is no specialization of meaning to make it into a compound. In A-N combinations, it is often taken for granted that any adjective, as distinguished from an action verb, can modify any noun. But this is only a difference of degree. Actually, many adjectives need *de* to modify a noun, as in 貴的糕 *guey de gau* 'expensive cake', 長的河 *charng de her* 'a long river', 寬的床 *kuan de chwang* 'a wide bed', as against 貴处 *gueychuh* '(your) esteemed locality, —your province or city', 長江 *Charng Jiang* 'Long River,—the Yangtze', 寬街 *Kuan Jie* 'Broad Street'. Thus both adjectives and action verbs directly modifying nouns form compounds with them, usually with specialized meanings. Even when there is no specialized meaning, as in 高山 *gau-shan* 'high mountain', 小國 *sheau-gwo* 'small country', it is still felt to be a compound in the sense that the adjective is no longer free to be modified by an adverb. Thus the reason that 'the smallest country' is not 最小國 *tzuey sheau gwo* is that *tzuey*, being an adverb, cannot modify the nominal compound *sheau-gwo*. But 最小的國 *tzuey sheau de gwo* is all right, because *tzuey sheau de* is a verbal expression plus *de*, which can modify a noun, quite on a par with 先耒的人 *shian lai de ren* 'the man who comes first'.[55] (Cf. also secs. 8.1.3 and 8.1.3.3.)

An interesting grammatical slip I heard was 整的草莓糕 *jeeng de tsaomei-gau* 'whole strawberry-cake', where 'whole' seems to modify the whole compound, but from the situational context it was said and understood as 'cake with whole strawberries'. When asked about it, the speaker repeated it as 整的草莓的糕 *jeeng de tsaomei de gau* 'cake of strawberries which are whole'.

---

[55]Cf. Bloomfield, 232, on 'very black bird', but not '°very blackbird'; *très sage femme*, but not °*très sage-femme*.

*8.3.4. Syllabicity and Freedom.* All monosyllabic adverbs are end-bound, except *bu*, which can be a complete answer to a question, as we have seen. As for polysyllables, mostly dissyllables, a few can be free as complete utterances, as 几乎. *Jihu.* 'Almost.', 的確. *Dyichiueh.* 'Really and truly.', but most of them are only semi-free, in the sense that they allow pauses or pause particles, but must still be followed by the words they modify. Thus, in the blanks in 这个人啊，□ □ 啊, 喜欢说话. *Jeyg ren a, — — a, shii.huan shuo-huah.* 'This man,—(ly), likes to talk.', one can fill polysyllabic adverbs such as 本来 *beenlai* 'originally', 居然 *jiuran* 'indeed', 一向 *ishianq* 'all along', 尤其 *youchyi* 'especially'. With some polysyllables, especially those which overlap with adjectives, even such pauses are not allowable, as in 他坚决(的)不去. *Ta jianjyue (de) bu chiuh.* 'He resolutely refuses to go.': 他意思很坚决. *Ta yih.sy heen jianjyue.* 'His intention is quite set.' 你得细心檢查. *Nii deei shihshin jeanchar.* 'You must examine it meticulously.': 这个人很细心. *Jeyg ren heen shihshin.* 'This man is fine-minded,—has a meticulous mind.' Those which allow pauses can usually precede the subject and thus function as conjunctions, as we shall see below (sec. 8.4). They are what Simon, Verb Complex, 560, calls clause words.

*8.3.5. Overlaps with Other Parts of Speech*

. (1) Adverbs and Adjectives. As we have noticed [sec. 8.1.3.6 (3)], so many adjectives are also adverbs that it might seem possible to treat adjectives as having as one of their functions the modifying of verbs. But since this is not true of all, or even most, adjectives, it is still better to treat these cases as class overlaps [cf. sec. 6.4.5(2)]. One test is to compare the behavior of antonyms. Thus, there is 大骂 *dah mah* 'scold greatly', 大笑 *dah shiaw* 'laugh greatly', 大吃 *dah chy* 'eat greatly,—voraciously', but there is no ° 小笑 °*sheau shiaw* or ° 小骂 °*sheau mah*, and 小吃 *sheauchy* 'little eat,—hors d'oeuvres' is a noun. But conversely, even if both antonyms occur before verbs, they can still be both adverbs and adjectives by overlap, as in 我不能多说话，多说了话睡不着觉. *Woo buneng duo shuo-huah, duo shuole-huah shuey.bu-jaur jiaw.* 'I can't talk much, if I have talked much, I can't sleep.' 我 不 能 少 睡 觉 , 少 睡 了 觉 做 不 了 事. *Woo buneng shao shuey-jiaw, shao shueyle-jiaw tzuoh-.bu-leau shyh.* 'I can't sleep little, if I sleep little, I can't work well.' Whether any given adjective is or is not an adverb by overlap is largely a lexical fact that must be recorded in the dictionary.

There is often, though not always, considerable semantic divergence between a word as adjective and as adverb. Thus 老 *lao* A 'old, aged, tough (of food texture)': H 'all the time'; 快 *kuay* A 'quick': H 'quickly' or 'soon'; 正 *jenq* A 'upright': H 'just (then)'; 早 *tzao* A 'early': H 'early' or 'long ago', as in 早 点儿起来!— 我早起来了. *Tzao.deal chii.lai!—Woo tzao chii-.lai le.* 'Get up early!—I got up long ago.'

Sometimes the occurrences of antonyms in adjectives and adverbs are quite skewed, as in the pairs 好 *hao* 'good', 坏 *huay* 'bad', 容易 *rong.yih* 'easy', 难 *nan* difficult'. Their very asymmetrical distribution of functions and meanings is shown in table 20. Thus, 容易 *rong.yih* 'easy' or 'easily'; 坏 *huay* 'bad' is never used as adverb; 好 *hao* 'good' and 难 *nan* 'difficult' are unambiguous as adjectives, but as adverbs the two words do the jobs of two pairs of antonyms, so that one could play on these words and say 螃蟹虽然好吃，可是难吃. *Parng.shieh sweiran haochy, keesh nan chy.*[56] 'Although crabs taste good, they are difficult to eat.', 螃蟹虽然不好吃，可是不难吃. *Parng-.shieh sweiran buhao chy, keesh bu nanchy.* 'Although crabs are not easy to eat, yet they taste not bad.' On 好 *hao* as the exclamatory adverb 'how ... !' and other A-H overlaps, see the list on pp. 697-698.

(2) A-V Compounds and H-V Phrases. An adjective may modify a verb in a subordinative compound, as in 小看 *sheau-*

---

[56]The differences could be indicated by different stressing, as shown in the spacing in the romanization, but it is resorted to only for fear of being misunderstood. In normal speech 'good (∼bad) to eat' and 'easy (∼hard) to eat' are completely homophonous.

Table 20

Skewed Functions of **hao** and **nan**

| A or H Modified<br>Modifier | A<br>事情 **shyh.chyng** 'thing' | H<br>吃 **chy** 'eat' |
|---|---|---|
| 好 **hao** | 好事情 'good thing' | 好吃   1. 'good to eat',<br>2. 'easy to eat' |
| 坏 **huay** | 坏事情 'bad thing' | * |
| 容易 **rong.yih** | 容易(的)事情 'easy thing' | 容易吃 'easy to eat' |
| 难 **nan** | 难事情 'difficult thing' | 难吃   1. 'tastes bad',<br>2. 'difficult to eat' |

*kann* 'small-look-at,—belittle', 白煮 *bairjuu* 'white-boiled,—plain-boiled (without seasoning)', 干炸 *ganjar* 'dry-fried (without sauce)'.

These are different from H-V phrases in that they are not expandable as the latter are (Luh, *GTFaa*, 58). Thus, 白煮 *bairjuu* 'plain-boiled' is not expandable, but the H-V phrase 白煮 *bair juu* 'boil in vain' can be expanded, as in 白那么煮了半天 *bair nemm juule banntian* 'boiled like that for a long time in vain'.

(3) Pro-verbs and Pro-adverbs. The four adverbs 这么 *tzemme* (~ *jemme*) 'so, thus, in this way', 那么 *nemme* 'so, thus, in that way', 哪么 *neeme?* 'in what way?' (rare) and 怎么 *tzeeme* 'how?' are pro-adverbs of manner or degree which are also pro-verbs by class overlap, with meanings, respectively, 'do this', 'do that', 'do what?', and 'do what?'. For examples of use, see section 7.12(3).

(4) Adverbs and Conjunctions. There is a difference between (a) adverbial conjunctions, or words which are at the same time adverbs and conjunctions, and (b) words which are sometimes adverbs and sometimes conjunctions by class overlap. In 你来我就走. *Nii lai woo jiow tzoou.* '(If) you come, I then go.', 就 *jiow* is both an adverb modifying 走 *tzoou* and a conjunction for the consequent clause. Most of the correlative adverbial conjunctions are of this kind. In class overlaps, on the other hand, the word is either an adverb or a conjunction. For example, in 他所以生气是你骂了他的缘故. *Ta suooyii sheng-chih sh nii mahle ta de yuan.guh.* 'He wherefore got angry,—the reason he was angry was that you had scolded him.',[57] 所以 *suooyii* is an adverb, modifying 生气 *sheng-chih*. But in 你骂了他，所以他生气了. *Nii mahle ta, suooyii ta sheng-chih le.* 'You scolded him, therefore he was angry.', 所以 *suooyii* is a conjunction.

The relation between cases (a) and cases (b), however, is a skewed one. Thus, in 他也来. *Ta yee lai.* 'He also comes.', 也

----

[57] 刘冠群, 说"所以" (Liou Guanchyun, "On *Suooyii*"), ZGYW, no. 55:9-10 (1957).

*yee* is an adverb, in 他 也 来 也 去. *Ta yee lai yee chiuh.* 'He both comes and goes.', 也 *yee* is an adverbial conjunction.

*8.3.6. Classification of Adverbs.* Adverbs are almost listable. But as rather different lists have been arrived at by different writers,[58] it will be better to leave the class open.

The following classes of adverbs are given in the prevailing order of precedence if there is more than one adverb occurring in succession. But the order is not at all fixed and is very much influenced by considerations of ICs, as 都 不 好 *dou bu hao* 'all not good,—all bad': 不 都 好 *bu dou hao* 'not all good (some bad)', 总 先 去 *tzoong shian chiuh* 'always go there first': 先 总 去 *shian tzoong chiuh* 'at first always go there'. Under each class we shall first give monosyllabic examples, followed by polysyllabic ones.

(1) Adverbs of Scope and Quantity

Monosyllables: 也$_1$*yee* 'also, too'; 都$_1$*dou* 'all, in all cases'; 总$_1$*tzoong* 'always, in all cases'; ( 完 )全 *(wan)chyuan* 'completely'; 再$_1$*tzay* 'more', as in 再要一个 *tzay yaw ig* 'want one more'; 还$_1$*hair* 'more', as in 还要一个 *hair yaw ig* 'want one more'; 另 ( 外 ) *linq*($_0$*way*) 'additionally'.

只 (~ 止 ~ 祇 ) *jyy* 'only'; 光 *guang* 'merely'; 就$_1$*jiow* 'only, just'; 淨 *jinq* 'merely, (doing) nothing but'; 才$_1$*tsair* 'only, no more than'; 单 *dan* 'merely'; 剛 *gang* 'just, exactly'.

Because the adverb must come immediately before the verb, if the scope refers to more than one expression which is not the verb, there is possibility of ambiguity, which may sometimes be resolved by different stressing. Thus, in 这 话 我 都 不 懂. *Jeh huah woo dou bu doong.*, if the stress is on *dou*, it refers to *jeh huah* and the sentence means 'I understand no part of this statement.', but if *woo* is stressed, it means 'Even I don't understand this statement.'[59] Again,       这 些 瓜 我 们 个ㄦ 都 尝 了. *Jehshie gua woomen gehgehl dou charngle.* (1) 'We have tasted

---

[58]For example, Luh, *GTFaa*, 56-57, has a list of adverbs proper and (57-58) a list of quasi-adverbs. Simon, Verb Complex, 568-570, has a different and longer list, subdivided into followability and/or precedability by *bu.*

[59]Example given by L. S. Yang.

every one of these melons.' or (2) 'Every one of us has tasted these melons.', where the ambiguity can only be resolved by re-wording the sentence, if not resolved by the context.

Polysyllables: 一共 *igonq* 'all together'; 总共 *tzoonggonq* 'all together'; 僅々 *jiinjiin* 'merely, no more than'; 剛々₁ *ganggang* ~ 恰々 *chiahchiah* ~ 剛好 *ganghao* ~ 恰好 *chiahhao* 'exactly'; 比较(的) *biijeau(de)* 'comparatively'; 相对的 *shiangdueyde* 'relatively'; 大约 *dahiue* 'about'; 约摸 *iuemho* 'approximately'; 大约摸儿 *dahiuemool* 'about'; 几乎 *jihu* 'almost'; 差一点儿 *chah.i₀deal* 'lack a little,—almost' ~ 差一点儿没 *chah.i₀deal mei* 'all but,—almost' (cf. 'near hit': 'near miss'); 索性 *swoo₀shinq* 'might as well, all the way'.

(2) Adverbs of Evaluation

Monosyllables: 可(是)₀ *kee(.sh)* 'however', as in 我可不许. *Woo kee bu sheu.* 'I, however, won't permit it,—as for me, I won't permit it.' 那可了不得! *Nah kee leau.bu.de!* 'Isn't that wonderful, though!'; 卻(是) *chiueh (.sh)*, same as the preceding, of which *chiueh* is really the reading pronunciation; 倒 *daw* 'contrary to (pessimistic) expectations,—rather (good, etc.)'; 偏(々儿) *pian (pian ~ -l)* 'one-sidedly,—willfully, would of all things', as in 他偏々儿挑这时候儿害起病来了. *Ta pian-pial tiau jeh shyr.howl hay.chii binq .lai le.* 'He would now of all times start to get sick.'; 就 *jiow* '(as for S, S P) then', as in 我就不这樣. *Woo jiow bu jehyang.* 'I, then, am not like this, —as for me, I am not like this.'[60] [cf. (4) below]; 还₂ *hair* 'still (in spite of reasons to the contrary),—rather', as 还好 *hair hao* 'rather good, not bad' [ch. (4) below]; 竟 *jinq* 'actually' (to one's unpleasant surprise); 也₂ *yee* (rhetorical) too', as in 見了人也不打招呼. *Jiannle ren yee bu daa-jau.hu.* 'When he meets somebody, he doesn't say hello, either.' [cf. 不亦乐乎? *bu yih leh hu?* L 'Isn't that something to be happy about?' (*The Analects*, I), and the colloquial 'That's wrong.—That's right, too!']; 都₂ *dou* 'all', as in 你们都買了些什么怪东西?

---

[60]Cf. 我则异于是. *Woo tzer yih yu shyh.* L 'As for me, I am different from this.' (*The Analects*), 微子, XVIII, 8).

*Nii.men dou maele shie sherm guay dong.shi?* 'What are all those queer things you bought?'; 硬 ( 是 ) *yinq* (*.sh*) ~ 楞 ( 是 )     *lenq* (*.sh*) 'the hard fact is ... , just', as in   没核桃夹子，硬得拿牙咬. *Mei her.taur-jiatz, yinq deei na ya yeau.* 'There is no nut-cracker, you just have to bite it with your teeth.'

Polysyllables: 幸亏 *shinq$_o$kuei* 'fortunately'; 居然 *jiuran* 'indeed' (to one's pleasant surprise); 果然 *guooran* 'actually' (favorably or unfavorably)' 其实 *chyishyr* 'as a matter of fact'; 究竟 *jioujinq* 'in the last resort, really'; 根本 *genbeen* 'fundamentally, basically'; 轧根儿 *yahgel* 'pressing to the root of the matter,— to begin with, to start with', as in   他们轧根儿就没脚. *Tam yahgel jiow mei jeau.* 'They hadn't any feet to start with.'; 简直 *jeanjyr* 'simply, downright', as in 简直要命 *jeanjyr yawming* 'simply awful'; 横是 *herng.sh* (← 横竖 *herngshuh* 'horizontal or vertical') 'anyway'; 反正 *faan$_o$jenq* 'reverse or right, —anyway'; 姑且 *gu$_o$chiee* 'tentatively'; 故意 *guh$_o$yih* ~ 成心 *cherngshin* 'purposely'. N.B. 成心 ≠ 诚心 , which is an adjective 'honest', for which the adverb is 诚心诚意的 *cherngshin-cherngyihde* 'honestly and faithfully'.

(3) Adverbs of Affirmation and Negation

Monosyllables: Simple affirmation is expressed by the verb 是 *sh* (sec. 8.1.8). Adverbs of affirmation have implications of evaluation, as shown under (2) above. Following are primarily adverbs of negation:

不 *bu* 'not'; 没 *mei* 'not' (before 有 *yeou* 'have'); 没 ( $_o$ 有 ) *mei* ($_oyeou$) 'have not' or 'did not' (see Vx 43). When applied to verbs of voluntary actions in the past, *mei* (*yeou*) is used for simple negation, while *bu* usually has the effect of 'would not', as in 他见了先生也 不站起来.  *Ta jiannle shian.sheng yee bu jann.chii.lai.* 'He saw his teacher and did not (bother to) stand up.'  他没看见他，所以没站起来。*Ta mei kann.jiann ta, suooyii mei jann.chii.lai.* 'He did not see him, and so he did not stand up.'   铃儿响了，你怎么不 去开门去？    *Liengl sheang le, nii tzeem bu chiuh kai-men .chiuh?* 'Why didn't you open the door when the bell rang?'   我没去开门，因为我 轧根儿没听见铃儿响哩. *Woo mei chiuh kai-men, inwey woo yahgel mei ting.jiann liengl sheang me.* 'I didn't open the door, because I didn't hear the bell ring in the first place.' But *bu* and *mei* are interchangeable in the greeting formula 好久没(～ 不) 見 了! *Haojeou mei (~ bu) jiann le!* 'Long time no see!'

The adverb 非(要) *fei* ($_0$*yaw*) 'insistently', however, is an adverb of strong affirmation, as in 他非要自己来。 *Ta feiyaw tzyhjii lai.* 'He insists on doing it himself.' This is really an abbreviated form of the correlative conjunctions 非...不 -.- *fei . . . bu* - . - 'not - . - unless . . . ' [sec. 8.4.2(3.2) below].

A rhetorical negative adverb is 豈? *chii?* 'how?', as in 他 豈可以对我这樣? *Ta chii keeyii duey woo jehyanq?* 'How can he do this to me?' 豈有此理? *Chii yeou tzyh lii?* 'How can there be such reason,—ridiculous!'[61] 豈敢? *Chii gaan?* 'How dare (I)?' (also used, sometimes in the XYXY reduplicated form, as an interjection in reply to a compliment).

Polysyllables: 不必 *bubih*[62] 'not necessarily, don't have to', 不如 *buru* 'not as (good as),—had better', 不妨 *bufarng* 'not hindering,—might as well', 决不 *jyuebu* 'decidedly not', 绝不 *jyuebu* 'absolutely not', 毫不 *haurbu* 'not a hair,—not a particle', 並不 *binqbu* 'really not, as a matter of fact not'. Although some of these are translated with Engish auxiliary verbs, they are adverbs, as they do not satisfy the tests for auxiliary verbs, especially in the V-not-V form of questions. The preceding are compounds in which the part other than *bu* is a bound morpheme.[63] We are not including as examples combinations like 可不 *kee bu*

---

[61]This is wenyan in form, with the demonstrative 此 *tsyy* instead of 这 *jeh*, as in 哪儿有这个道理? *Naal yeou jeyg daw.lii?* 'Whence such reason?' But the phrase is used so often in speech that it is no longer usable in wenyan, so that in an actual wenyan context it will have to be made more "L" in some such form as 寧有是理乎? *Ning yeou sh lii hu?*

[62]This is not a Vx, since it cannot occur in the form °必不必?° *bih bubih?* like 得ˇ不得ˇ? *deei bu deei?* 'must (one) ?'

[63]A partial exception must be made of 並不 *binqbu*, in which *binq*, not free in the North, is free in Southern Mandarin, as in 他並很高兴. *Ta binq heen gaushinq.* 'He is very glad, as a matter of fact.', in which read 其实 *chyishyr*, for Northern Mandarin, instead of 並 *binq*.

'however, not', 豈 不 *chii bu* 'isn't it, doesn't it', and so on, 也 不 *yee bu* 'not, either', and 不 也 *bu yee* 'not also', since these not only are not compounds but are not even constituents, since the first morpheme modifies a compound or phrase of which the second element is the beginning morpheme. Phrases or compounds with two or more negatives cancel out algebraic fashion instead of reinforcing each other as in French and Russian: 你 太 不 小 心 了. *Nii tay bu sheau.shin le.* 'You were too careless.' 我 没 不 小 心. *Woo mei bu-sheau.shin.* 'I wasn't careless.' With compounds: 这 种 人 也 不 乏 可 取 的 地 方. *Jey-tzoong ren yee buwu keecheu de dih.fang.* 'This kind of person is not without merit.' 那 未 免 太 不 讲 理 了. *Nah weymean tay bu jeang-lii le.* 'That is not without being too unreasonable,—that is being too unreasonable.'

(4) Adverbs of Time

Monosyllables: 先 *shian* 'first'; 初 *chu* 'at first, for the first time'; 乍 *jah* 'at first blush'; 早 *tzao* 'early' or 'long ago'; 才₂ *tsair* 'just now'; 才...呐 *tsair ... ne* 'then and only then, not until' (= German *erst*); 正...呐 *jenq ... ne* 'just ... -ing', as in 正 吃 饭 呐 *jenq chy-fann ne* 'is just eating dinner'; 就₃ *jiow* 'right away' or 'then' [cf. sec. 2.12.7(3)]; 便 *biann* (old Mandarin equivalent of 就₃ *jiow*); 快 *kuay* 'will soon'; 一 *i* 'once, just', as in 他 开 门 一 看, 看 见 一 个 老 头 儿. *Ta kai-men i-kann, kann.jiannle ig lao-tourl.* 'He opened the door and looked once,—took a look, and saw an old man.'; 再₂ *tzay* 'once more' (event or action considered), as in 还 要 再 来, 可 是 始 终 没 再 来 *hair yaw tzay lai, keesh shyyjong mei tzay lai* 'wanted to come again, but after all didn't come again'; 又 *yow* 'again' (actual), as in 他 说 不 再 来 了, 可 是 後 来 又 来 了. *Ta shuo bu tzay lai le, keesh howlai yow lai le.* 'He said he wasn't coming again, but afterwards he did come again.'; 还₁ *hair* 'still', as in 他 昨 儿 还 好 𝑧 儿 的, 怎 么 今 儿 病 了? *Ta tzwol hair haohaulde, tzeem jiel binq le?* 'He was (still) quite all right yesterday, how come he is sick today?' [cf. (2) above]; 重 *chorng* 'once over', as in 重 抄 *chorng chau* 'copy once over'; 老 *lao* 'all the time, continuously, always'; 总$_2$ *tzoong* 'every time, invariably, always'; 且…呐 *chiee … ne* 'incessantly, keep … -ing', as in 他且说 呐. *Ta chiee shuo ne.* 'He will keep talking'; 儜(着) *jiinj* 'all the way, keep V-ing'; 淨$_2$ *jinq* 'do nothing but V-ing'; 常(ㄗ)(ㄦ) *charng ~ charngcharng ~ charngchangl* 'often'; 晚 *woan* 'late'; 遲 *chyr* 'late'; 後 *how* 'afterwards'.

Polysyllables: 当初 *dangchu ~* 起初 *chiichu* 'at first'; 老早 *laotzao* 'long ago'; 早巳 *tzaoyii* 'already long ago'; 巳绖 *yii.jing* 'already'; 巳竟 *yiijinq* 'already' (Peip.); 本来 *beenlai* 'originally'; 向来 *shianglai ~* 一向 *ishianq* 'hitherto, all along'; 向不 *shiangbu ~* 从(来)不 *tsorng(lai)bu* 'so far never'; 曾绖 *tserng$_0$jing* 'has ~ did once before'; 近来 *jinnlai* 'recently'; 刚ㄗ$_2$ *ganggang ~* 刚才 *gangtsair* 'just now'; 暂时 *jannshyr ~* 暂且 *jann$_0$chiee* 'temporarily'; 忽然 *huran* 'suddenly'; 立刻 *lihkeh* 'immediately, at once'; 馬上 *maa$_0$shanq* 'right away'; 趕紧 *gaanjiin ~* 'hurriedly'; 时常 *shyrcharng ~* 时ㄗ *shyrshyr ~* 不时的 *bushyrde* 'from time to time'; 每ㄗ *meeimeei ~* 往ㄗ *woangwoang* 'frequently'; 再三 *tzaysan*[64] *~* 屡次 *leutsyh* 'several times'; 永遠 *yeongyeuan ~* 永久 *yeongjeou* 'forever'; 一直 *ijyr* 'constantly'; 早晚 *tzaowoan ~* 遲早 *chyrtzao ~* 早遲 *tzaochyr* 'sooner or later'; 後来 *how$_0$lai* 'afterwards'; 几时? *jii$_0$shyr?* 'when?'; 多歪? *duo.tzaan ~ dwo.tzaan?* 'when?'; 多会ㄦ? *duo.hoel? ~ dwo.hoel?* 'when?' The following should be regarded as separate adverbs: 正在 *jenq $_0$tzay* 'just at …-ing'; 早就 *tzao $_0$jiow* 'long ago'; 不老 *bu lao* 'not always', as in 不老吃东西 *bu lao chy dong.shi* 'do not always eat things (but eat some of the time)'; 老不 *lao bu* 'always not', as in 老不吃东西 *lao bu chy dong-.shi* 'never eat'. Note that *bu lao* 'not always' ≠ *bulao* 'not very' [(6) below, under Monosyllables], involving different IC structures.

(5) Adverbs of Contingency

Monosyllables: 真 *jen* 'really' [cf. (6) *jen!* 'awfully'], as in 真 信他 *jen shinn ta* 'really believe him'; 假 *jea* 'falsely, pretend to', as in 你别假笑！ *Nii bye jea shiaw!* 'Don't you pretend to

---

[64]An old reading *sann* as adverb is now obsolete.

laugh!' 準 *joen* 'definitely, surely'; 许 *sheu* 'perhaps'; 就₄ *jiow* 'then, consequently'.

Polysyllables: 一定 *idinq,* 必定 *bihdinq* 'certainly'; 实在 *shyrtzay* 'really'; 的確 *dyichiueh* 'really and truly'; 绝对 *jyue-duey* 'absolutely'; 一準(儿) *ijoen* (~*l*) 'definitely, certainly'; 没 準儿 *meijoel* 'there is no telling,—perhaps'; 不定 *buding* 'not certainly,—perhaps' (but A 'not definite' and Vt 'do not determine'): 大概 *dahgay* 'probably'; 也许 *yeesheu* 'possibly'; 几乎 *jihu* 'almost'; 差一点(没) *chah.ideal* (*mei*) 'almost' [cf. (1)].

(6) Adverbs of Degree

Monosyllables: Adverbs of degree modify adjectives but do not as a rule modify verbs of action except[65] certain V-O [see sec. 8.1.6 (2)] and V-R compounds. One can say 最傷腦筋 *tzuey shang naojin* 'most injurious to the brain,—most troublesome', 很吃虧 *heen chy-kuei* 'very much eat loss,—suffer much loss', but not ° 很吃饭 °*heen chy-fann* for 'eat much food'. With V-R one can say 更看得出来了 *genq kann.de-chulai le* 'can still better make out (by looking)', but not ° 太摔傷了 °*tay shuai-shangle* for 'injured too badly from a fall'. With adjectives, a complement will close the construction to further modification by adverbs of degree, there being no ° 最坏透了 °*tzuey huay-towle,* but with an adverb of contingency, one can say 真坏透了 *jen huay-towle* 'really bad through and through!' An adverb of degree may modify a noun, at a higher level of construction, as a nominal predicate, as in 那个人太渾蛋 了！ *Neyg ren tay hwen-dann le.* 'That man is too much of a muddy egg,—a damn fool.' 这个人夠朋友. *Jeyg ren gow perng.yeou.* 'This man is friend enough (to do me a favor, etc.).'

Following are the most important adverbs of degree:

Monosyllables: 很 *heen* 'very'; 挺 *tiing* (phon. modif. of 頂

---

[65] 李春林 (Lii Chuenlin) and 余立人 (Yu Lihren), in their 程度副 词修饰动词能不受限制吗? ("Can adverbs of Degree Modify Verbs without Limitation?"), *ZGYW,* no. 53:536 and 545 (1956), stated these exceptions in rather broad terms.

*diing* 'most') 'pretty (colloq.), rather'; 怪 *guay* 'awfully';[66] 真 (!) *jen!* 'awfully, (colloq.) real', as 真好！ *Jen hao!* 'Awfully nice!' [≠ 真 *jen* 'really' at beginning of (5) above]; 好！ *hao* (!) 'what a ... !, how ... !' as in 好大的鱼！ *Hao dah de yu!* 'What a big fish!' 好利害！ *Hao lih.hay!* 'How powerful!'; 好不利害！ *Haobu lih.hay!* 'Isn't that powerful!' (*haobu* before polysyllables only); 极 *jyi* 'extremely'; 满 *maan* 'quite, fairly' (recent borrowing from the Wu dialects); 才 ... 呐 *tsair* ... *ne* 'then and only then will it be ... ,—extremely', as in 才麻煩呐 *tsair ma.farn ne* 'extremely troublesome'; 还₃ *hair* 'rather, fairly', as in 他身体还好． *Ta shentii hair hao.* 'His health is fairly good.'; 还₄ (要) *hair (yaw)* 'still more', as in 你坏，他比你还坏． *Nii huay, ta bii nii hair huay.* 'You (think you) are shrewd, but he is even shrewder than you.'; 更 *genq* 'still more' = 还₄ *hair*; 再 *tzay* 'still more' (considered, not actual), as in 再冷一点儿我也不怕． *Tzay leeng.i.deal woo yee bu pah.* 'Even if it gets colder, I won't mind it, either.', 再好没有了． *Tzay hao meiyeou le.* 'still better there isn't,—nothing can be better,—that's just fine.'; 頂 *diing* ~ 最 *tzuey* 'most', often used also as a general intensive, as in 这是一件頂運气的事情． *Jeh sh i-jiann diing yunn-.chih de shyh.chyng.* 'This is a most fortunate thing.'; 太 *tay* 'too (excessively)'; 忒 *tuei* ~ *tei* 'too' (Peip.) (the pron. *teh* is only L or dial.); 多？ *duo* ~ *dwo*? 'how?' as in 泰山有多高？ *Tay Shan yeou dwo gau?* 'How high is Mount T'ai?'; 夠 *gow* 'sufficiently'. The following wenyan adverbs of degree are occasionally, but not very frequently, heard in speech: 甚 *shenn* 'very' L; 至 *jyh* 'most' L; 頗 *po* 'rather, quite' L; 绝 *jyue* 'exceedingly' L ( ≠ the colloq. A 'peculiar'); 较 *jiaw* 'comparatively' L.

Polysyllables: 非常 *feicharng* 'very, awfully'; 异常 *yihcharng* 'unusually'; 十分 *shyrfen* 'ten tenths,—100 per cent'; 特别

---

[66]Dragunov (208-209, Chinese transl. 192-193) notes that with these adverbs with subjective attitudes the sentence often ends in *de*, which nominalizes the situation, as in 我怪睏的，得要睡觉去了． *Woo guay kuenn de, deei yaw shuey-jiaw .chiuh le.* 'I am awfully sleepy that's-how-I-feel, I'll have to go to sleep.'

*tehbye* 'specially'; 尤其 *youchyi* 'especially'; 有点儿 *yeou₀deal* 'a little, somewhat'; 畧微 *liueh'wei* ~ 稍為 *shaowei* 'slightly'; 比較(的) *biijeau(de)* 'comparatively'; 不大 *budah* 'not very' or 'not often'; 不老 *bulao* 'not very' (borrowing from Tientsin); 过于 *guohyu* 'excessively'; 过分(的) *guohfenn(de)* 'beyond measure'; 这么 *tzemme* 'so, this (big, etc.)'; 那么 *nemme* 'so, that (big, etc.)'; 多(么)? *duo(me)* ~ *dwo(me)*? 'how?', as in 离家多么遠? *li jia dwom yeuan?* 'how far from home?'

Degrees can also be expressed by complements, as in 好極了 *hao-jyile* 'good to an extreme,—awfully good' (≠ the less exclamatory and less colloquial adverb 極 *jyi* 'extremely') or by predicative complements, as in 好的很 *hao de heen* 'good, very, —very good' and 疼的利害 *terng de lih.hay* 'it hurts badly'.

(7) Adverbs of Place. Most place expressions are either place words and phrases as in 屋裡坐 *u.lii tzuoh* 'room-inside sit,— sit in the room' or K-O phrases, with place-word objects, as in 从这儿起 *tsorng jell chii* 'start from here', 在哪儿会? *Tzay naal huey?* 'Where shall we meet?' Single adverbs of place are rather rare. Examples are: 遍 *biann* 'throughout', as in 遍查ㄧ不着 *biann char char.bu-jaur* 'looked for it everywhere and could not find it'; 哪儿? *Naal?* 'where?', as in 哪儿来的话? *Naal lai de huah?* 'Whence such words?,—No, indeed!'; 处ㄧ(儿) *chuhchuh(~ -ll)* ~ 到处(儿) *dawchuh(~ -ll)* 'everywhere', as in 到处散谣言 *dawchuh sann yau.yan* 'scatter rumors everywhere'.

(8) Adverbs of Manner

Monosyllables: 正(着) *jenq(j)* 'right side up'; 倒(着) *daw(j)* 'upside down'; 直ㄧ(着) *jyr(j)* 'straight, directly'; 反(着) *faan(j)* 'reversely, inside out', as in 这皮襖可以反穿. *Jeh pyiao keeyii faan chuan.* 'This fur jacket may be worn inside out.'; 横(着) *herng(j)* 'horizontally, across'; 竖(着) *shuh(j)* 'vertically', as in 毛筆得竖着拿. *Maubii deei shuhj na.* 'The writing brush must be held vertically.'; 白 *bair* 'in vain' (白煮 *bairjuu* 'plain-boiled' is a compound and is not expandable), as in 白(早)去 *bair (tzao) chiuh* 'go (early) in vain'; 空 *kong* 'vainly, merely', as in 空说不做 *kong shuo bu tzuoh* 'merely talk without doing it'; 大 *dah* 'greatly', as in 大笑 *dah shiaw* 'laugh greatly'.

Polysyllables: 空手 *kongshoou* 'empty-handedly'; 一塊儿 *ikuall* 'together'; 一斉 *ichyi* ~ 一起 *ichii* 'together, in unison'; 勉強 *meancheang* 'perforce, forcedly'; 大声儿 *dahshengl* 'loudly'. On vivid reduplicates of the 慢〻儿的 *mannmhalde* 'good and slowly' type, see section 4.2.4.1.

But 这么 *tzemme* 'thus, in this manner'; 那么 *nemme* 'thus, in that manner'; 怎么? *tzeeme?* 'how?'; and the rare 哪么? *neeme?* 'in what way (of two ways)?' are usually pronounced as monosyllables (*tzemm, nemm, tzeem,* and *neem*) when occurring attributively before a modified expression.

(9) Interrogative Adverbs. These, except for 可₂ *kee* for yes-or-no questions, have already appeared under the other headings: (4) 几时? *jii₀shyr?* 'when?', 多昝? *duo.tzaan* ~ *dwo.tzaan?* 'when?', 多会儿? *duo.hoel* ~ *dwo.hoel?* 'when?'; (6) 多(么)? *duo(me)* ~ *dwo(me)?* 'how, to what degree?'; (7) 哪儿? *naal?* 'where?'; (8) 怎么? *tzeeme?* 'how, in what manner?', 哪么? *neeme?* 'in what way (of two ways)?'. The adverb 可 *kee* is used more frequently in Southern Mandarin (in which it is often unaspirated and weak: *.ge*), though it is by no means a borrowing from the South. For example, 你可知道他叫什么? *Nii kee jy.daw ta jiaw sherme?* = 你知道不知道他叫什么? *Nii jy.daw bujy.daw ta jiaw sherme?* 'Do you know what he is called?' Note that with *kee* as an interrogative adverb, 他可能来? *Ta kee neng lai?* 'Can he come?' is a question; while with *keeneng* as a conjunction [sec. 8.4.2(4)], it is a statement: *Ta keeneng lai.* 'He possibly will come.', where *keeneng* as a conjunction may also precede the subject.

Interrogative adverbs, like other interrogatives, can, when specially stressed and followed by 都 *dou* or 也 *yee,* be used in the arbitrary sense of 'any', as in 他怎么也不行。*Ta tzeem yee bushyng.* 'As for him, no matter how, it won't do,—there is no pleasing him.' When unstressed an interrogative is taken in an indefinite sense, as in 来了没多久 *laile mei dwo jeou* 'has not come for any length of time', 不 怎 么 好 *bu tzeem hao* 'not good in any way,—not particularly good', 他 把 那 机 关 怎 么 一 板 就 動 起 来 了. *Ta bae neh jiguan tzeem i-ban jiow donq.chii-.lai le.* 'He somehow gave the mechanism a twist and it started to move.' The lack of symmetry between interrogative adverbs of manner and those of degree can be seen from table 21.

TABLE 21

Demonstrative and Interrogative Adverbs

| | Manner | | Degree |
| --- | --- | --- | --- |
| | One of Two | Any Number | |
| Near | 这 么 tzemme | | 这 么 tzemme |
| Far | 那 么 nemme | | 那 么 nemme |
| Interrogative | 哪 么 neeme | 怎 么 tzeeme | 多 (么) duo(me) ~ dwo(me) |
| Arbitrary | 哪 么 "neeme | 怎 么 "tzeeme | 多 (么) "duo(me) ~ "dwo(me) |
| Indefinite | * | 怎 么 $_o$tzeeme | 多 (么) $_o$duo(me) ~ $_o$dwo(me) |

# 8.4 Conjunctions

*8.4.1 Conjunctions, Prepositions, and Adverbs.* Chinese conjunctions, as we have noted before, are hardly distinguishable from prepositions or adverbs. Thus, 你 跟 他 一 块 儿 走. *Nii gen ta ikuall tzoou.* can be translated either as 'You go with him.' or 'You and he go together.' (cf. secs. 5.2.1 and 5.2.2); and in 你 假如 不 来, 我 就 不 去. *Nii jearu bu lai, woo jiow bu chiuh.* 'You if don't come, I then won't go,—if you don't come, then I won't go.', the conjunction-like words 假 如 *jearu* 'if' and 就 *jiow* 'then' occupy the typical position of adverbs, namely, between the subject and the verb (cf. sec. 2.12.6). In fact, the status of the Chinese conjunction is so uncertain that Dragunov did not even give it recognition as a separate class.

In some cases, however, it is necessary to recognize the beginnings of a new, if small, word class. Thus, in 吃 饭 跟 睡 觉

是兩件事。*Chy-fann gen shuey-jiaw sh leang-jiann shyh.*
'Eating and sleeping are two things.', if 跟*gen* is translated as
'together with', then 'Eating, together with sleeping, is two
things' or '... makes two things.' will seem too artificial, and it
will be simpler to treat 跟*gen* as a coordinate conjunction 'and'.
The same can be said of such a sentence as 理髮跟刮臉都
要.*Liifah gen gua-lean dou yaw.* 'I want both a haircut and a
shave.'

In another type of case, if a word marking the relations of
clauses and sentences cannot follow but must precede a subject,
then it must be treated as a conjunction. For example, in 他來
了，但是他太ㄜ没來. *Ta laile, dannsh ta tay.tay mei lai.*
'He came, but his wife did not.', 但是 *dannsh* is a conjunction
and cannot follow the subject 他太ㄜ *ta tay.tay.* In this respect,
the near synonym 可是 *keesh* 'however' behaves differently, since
it can either precede or follow the subject, as in 他太ㄜ可是
没來. *Ta tay.tay keesh mei lai.* 'His wife, however, did not
come.'

*8.4.2 Types of Conjunctions.* Except for a few prepositional
conjunctions, most conjunctions are adverbial conjunctions, which
serve both to join and to modify. We shall give examples of the
following types of conjunctions: (1) prepositional conjunctions; (2)
macrosyntactic conjunctions; (3) correlative conjunctions, both
(3.1)$J_1 \neq J_2$, and (3.2) $J_1 = J_2$; and (4) reduced main clauses.

(1) Prepositional Conjunctions. The prepositions K 2 跟*gen*,
K 3 和*hann~hay~*(reading pronunciation) *her*, and (the dialectal) K4 同*torng* are prepositions when regarded as 'with, together with' and conjunctions when regarded as 'and'. As we
have seen, there are relatively few cases where A *gen* B has to be
treated as necessarily a coordination of A and B. Note that these
conjunctions can only join nominal expressions and never join
verbal expressions or clauses.

(2) Macrosyntactic Use of Conjunctions. A speaker can begin
a sentence with 但是 *dannsh* 'but' after completing a previous
sentence or in commenting on something another person has said.
The occurrence of such a word is therefore dependent on something outside of the sentence in which it occurs, somewhat as

pronouns are dependent on their antecedents. Such dependence is not syntactic, but macrosyntactic.[67] But we call such use of adverbial conjunctions macrosyntactic *use* and not just macro-syntactic conjunctions as a subclass, since all conjunctions used macrosyntactically can also be used syntactically, for example, in 我 喝酒 , 但是 不 抽烟. *Woo he-jeou, dannsh bu chou-ian.* 'I drink, but don't smoke.

Some conjunctions used macrosyntactically must precede the subject (unless they join predicates, as in the last example), and are thus conjunctions proper. Besides 但是 *dannsh* 'but', other non-post-subject conjunctions are: 不过 *buguoh* 'only, but'; 並 且 *binq_{0}chiee* ~ 而且 *erl_{0}chiee* 'moreover'; 況且 *kuanq_{0}chiee* 'a fortiori'; 否則 *fooutzer* 'if not, then,—otherwise', as in 快 走 吧! 否則 你 趕 不 上 了. *Kuay tzoou ba! Fooutzer nii gaan.bu-shanq le.* 'Hurry up and go! Otherwise you won't be able to catch up.'; 例 如 *lihru* 'for example'; 比 方 *bii_{0}fang* 'for instance'.

Others whose occurrence depends upon outside sentences can either precede the subject or come between the subject and the predicate and are thus still adverbial conjunctions. 'We are not considering here pure adverbs like 就 *jiow* 'then', which *must* occur after subjects.) Examples of adverbial conjunctions are: 可 是 *keesh* 'but, however' (therefore different from 但 是 *dannsh*); 不 然 *buran* 'otherwise' (therefore different from 否則 *foutzer*), as in 不然你 ~ 你 不然 趕 不 上 了. *Buran nii ~ Nii buran gaan.bu-shanq le.* 'Otherwise you won't be able to catch up.'; 因為 *inwey* 'because'; 所以 *suooyii* 'therefore'; 因此 *intsyy* 'for this reason'; 後來 *how_{0}lai* 'afterwards'; 或是 *huohsh* ~ *hesh* 'or'; 或者 *huohjee* 'or'. On the choice of position before or after the subject, see section 2.12.6.

(3) Correlative Conjunctions. There are many pairs of cor-relative words which serve to bind clauses together into com-pound or complex sentences. Sometimes either the first or the second is adverb only and never precedes the subject, or is con-

[67]On such dependences see Z. F. Harris, "Discourse Analysis", *Language*, 28:1.15 (1952), and Viola Waterhouse, "Independent and Dependent Sentences", *IJAL*, 29:45-54 (1962).

junction only and never follows the subject. In most cases, however, the correlatives are adverbial conjunctions and can either
precede or follow. In the following examples the adverbs are
marked H, the conjunctions marked J, and the adverbial conjunctions are left unmarked. Since many of these have been discussed
in connection with composite sentences (secs. 2.11 and 2.13), we
shall do no more than mention the most important.

(3.1) Same Word Repeated: 越...越 *yueh*$_H$ ... *yueh*$_H$ ~ 愈
... 愈 *yuh* ... *yuh* 'the more ... the more', 'the ... -er, the ... -er';
也...也 *yee*$_H$ ... *yee*$_H$ ~ 又...又 *yow*$_H$ ... *yow*$_H$ 'both ... and';
也不...也不 *yee bu* ... *yee bu* 'neither ... nor'; 不...不 *bu*$_H$ ...
*bu*$_H$ '(if) not ... not, — not ... unless'; 一头儿... 一头儿 ‒‒
~ 一边儿 ... 一边儿 ‒‒ *itourl* ... *itourl* ‒‒ ~ *ibial* ... *ibial* ‒‒
'‒‒ while ...', as in 一头儿跑一头儿哭 *itourl pao itourl ku*
'(he) cries as he runs'; 或是... 或是 $_o$*huohsh* ... $_o$*huohsh* ~ .*hesh*
... .*hesh* 'either ... or'; ( 还 ) 是 ... ( 还 ) 是 ‒‒? ($_o$*hair*)*sh* ... ($_o$*hair*)-
*sh* ‒‒? [secs. 5.2.2 (4 and 5)]. On correlative clauses without the
use of conjunctions, see section 2.12.8.

(3.2) Different Words as Correlatives (see also sec. 2.12.7):
虽然 ...也~ 但是 ~ 可是 *sweiran* ... *yee*$_H$ ~ *dannsh* ~
*keesh* 'although ... yet'; 因 为... 所以 *in*$_o$*wey* ... *suoo*$_o$*yii* 'because
... therefore'; 既然...就 *jihran* ... *jiow*$_H$ 'inasmuch as ... (then)';
要是 ~ 要 ~ 假如 ~ ◯ ... 就 *yawsh* ~ *yaw*$_H$ ~ *jearu* ~
*zero* ... *jiow* 'if ... then'; ( 除 )非 ~ 除了...不 ‒‒ (*chwu*)*fei* ~
*chwule* ... *bu* ‒‒ 'not ‒‒ unless ...' 除 )非 ~ 除了...才 ‒‒
(*chwu*)*fei* ~ *chwule* ... *tsair* ‒‒ 'only if ... will then ‒‒'; 不是
... 就是 *bush* ... *jiowsh* 'if not ... then,—either ... or'; 只要...就
*jyyyaw* ... *jiow* 'so long as ... then'; 既 不... 又 不 *jih bu*$_H$ ... *yow*
*bu*$_H$ 'neither ... nor'; ‒‒ 尚且 ... 何 况 ‒‒呐? ‒‒ *shanqchiee* ...
*herkuanq*$_J$ ‒‒ *ne*? 'even ‒‒ ... , how much more will ‒‒'; 不但
... 并 且 ~ 而且 *budann* ... *binq*$_o$*chiee* ~ *erl*$_o$*chiee* 'not only ...
but also'; 宁可... 也不 *ningkee* ... *yee bu* 'would rather ... than';
与其 ~ 有的...宁可~ 不如 ~ 还是 *yeuchyi* ~ *yeoude*
... *ningkee* ~ *buru* ~ *hairsh* 'rather than ... had better'; 儘荵...
还是 *jiingoan* ... *hairsh* 'no matter if ... still'; 再~ 多...也
*tzay*$_H$ ~ *duo*$_H$ ~ *dwo*$_H$ ... *yee*$_H$ 'no matter how ... still'; 就是~

即使 ... 也 *jiowsh* ~ *jyishyyⱼ* ... *yee*<sub>H</sub> 'even if ... still'; 剛 ( ~ 才 )...就 *gang* ( ~ *tsair* ) ... *jiow* 'just as ... then'; 一 ...就 *i*<sub>H</sub> ... *jiow*<sub>H</sub> 'as soon as ... (then)'; 一个 ... ( 就 ) *ig*<sub>H</sub> ... (*jiow*<sub>H</sub>) 'with a ... (then)'. Note that in the last form *ig* is followed by a verbal expression, as in 他一个不留神 ( 就 ) 摔倒了。 *Ta ig bulioushern (jiow) shuai-daole.* 'With a not-attending,—with a moment of inattention, he fell down.'; *ig* differs from *i* also in that the second verbal expression states an actuality instead of a possibility.

The pair 一来 ..., 二来 ( ~ 二一来 ) *ilai* ..., *ell'lai* (~*ell'-ilai*) 'in the first place ..., in the second place' is often used macrosyntactically when each part of the pair begins a sentence or even a paragraph. After *ell'lai*, however, *sanlai, syhlai*, and so on are rare, for which the nominal (absolute) subject 第三層 *dihsan-tserng* 'the third layer (of reasons, factors, etc.),—in the third place', and so on will be used.

(4) Reduced Main Clauses. Most polysyllabic conjunctions can occur between subject and predicate, with or without pauses, and/or particles, or added as an afterthought, as in 他呀, 其实 啊, 不想来. *Ta ia, chyishyr a, busheang lai.* 'He, as a matter of fact, doesn't want to come.' A special type of conjunction is derived from clauses of the 'I think' type, occurring either at the beginning or at the end of the original object clause, which is now the main clause, while the original main or mother clause is reduced to a proclitic conjunction or an enclitic particle. We saw examples of these in connection with complex sentences (sec. 2.14.5). Following are further examples:

总而言之 <sub>o</sub>*tzoong* <sub>o</sub>*erl* <sub>o</sub>*yan* <sub>o</sub>*jy* 'in one word, in any case'; 这就是说 <sub>o</sub>*jeh* <sub>o</sub>*jiowsh* <sub>o</sub>*shuo* 'that is to say'; 换言之 <sub>o</sub>*huann* <sub>o</sub>*yan* <sub>o</sub>*jy* 'in other words'; 换句话说 <sub>o</sub>*huann* *.jiuh* *.huah* <sub>o</sub>*shuo* 'in other words'; 再不就 <sub>o</sub>*tzay*<sub>o</sub>*bu*<sub>o</sub>*jiow* 'or else'; 再不 ( 你就 ) <sub>o</sub>*tzay* <sub>o</sub>*bu* (*nii jiow*) 'or else (you could)'; 恐怕 <sub>o</sub>*koong*<sub>o</sub>*pah* 'I'm afraid,—perhaps'; 可能 *keeneng* 'possibly'; 光景 <sub>o</sub>*guang*<sub>o</sub>*jiing* 'as things look'; 我想 <sub>o</sub>*woo* <sub>o</sub>*sheang* 'I guess'; 苰保 <sub>o</sub>*goan*<sub>o</sub>*bao* 'I bet'; 难道 ... 不成? <sub>o</sub>*nan*<sub>o</sub>*daw* ... *.bu.cherng?* 'do you mean to say that ... ?'; 擮说 <sub>o</sub>*jiuh*<sub>o</sub>*shuo* 'according to what they say'; 谁

知道 .sheir .j'aw 'who knows but that … '; 敢情 gaan.chyng …
~ 敢子 gaantz … (written 敢則 in older texts) 'why[68] (if it isn't)
… !'; 结果 $_o$jye$_o$guoo 'as a result'; 回头 $_o$hwei$_o$tour 'by and
by'. Some of these still retain the full meaning and main clause
status when stressed, as in 谁知道他跑得哪儿去了?
Sheir jy.daw ta pao de naal chiuh le? 'Who knows where he has
gone?': 谁知道他死了！ .Sheir .j'aw ta syy le! 'Who should
have known that he died!'

# 8.5. Particles

*8.5.1. Particles, Suffixes, and Interjections.* Particles are like
suffixes and interjections in being in the neutral tone. Both particles and suffixes are start-bound, but while suffixes belong to
words, particles belong to phrases or sentences, sometimes even
with cases of overlapping classes, such as *de* in 他的书 *tade shu*
'his book', where *de* is a suffix, and in 他看的书 *ta kann de shu*
'the book he reads', where it is a particle, in construction with
the clause 他看 *ta kann*.[69] Interjections are like particles in
being in the neutral tone, but, while particles are always unstressed, interjections are usually stressed, and though without
tone, they have a variety of intonational patterns, as we shall see
later. Another difference is that particles are always bound, being
enclitic to the preceding syllable and in construction with the
whole preceding phrase, while interjections are free. In fact,
interjections are the only class of words which are never bound.[70]
Class overlapping also occurs in a few cases between particles and
interjections, as in 早点儿回来啊！ *Tzao.deal hwei.lai a!* Do

---

[68]Usually pronounced 'wy' even by those speakers of English who pronounce 'what' and 'watt' differently.

[69]In my 北京、蘇州、常州语助词的研究 ("Studies in the Par-
ticles of Peking, Soochow, and Changchow"), *Tsing Hua Journal*, 3:865-918
(1926), I followed the tradition of grouping suffixes and particles together.

[70]With the rare exception of the Wu dialect of Chintan ( 金壇 ),
which has an interjection *hhei* 'uh-huh, m-hm', as well as a *hhei.lau*, something like Mandarin 是的 *sh de* 'right, correct' and *hhei .we*, like 是的嚜
*sh de me* 'so it is'.

come back early!' where the particle *a* has a slight effect of 'do' in the translation. In  早点儿 回来 , 啊! *Tzao.deal hwei.lai, a!* 'Come back early, won't you?' the interjection *a* (the comma before which is realized as a pause and/or as a glottal stop) does not necessarily make the request stronger, but gives it the effect of a repeated request.

    8.5.2. *Phrase Particles and Sentence Particles.* Some particles occur after phrases only, as 咧 *le* in 打球咧, 下棋咧, 什么 的,他樣儿都会. *Daa-chyou le, shiah-chyi le, shermde, ta yanqyanql dou huey.* 'Playing ball, playing chess, and so forth, he can do all of them.' Others occur only as sentence particles, as 嗎 *ma* in 你知道嗎? *Nii jy.daw ma?* 'Do you know?' A few occur in either function, as in 要是走啊, 没盤費. *Yawsh tzoou a, mei parnfey.* 'If I go, I've no money to travel.', with 啊 *a* as phrase (or clause) particle, and  没盤費也得走啊! *Mei parnfey yee deei tzoou a!* 'Even without travel money, you still have to go ↗', where 啊 *a* is a sentence particle, translated by the upswing intonation on the word 'go'.

    8.5.3. *Succession and Fusion of Particles.* When particles occur in succession, the first is in construction with the preceding phrase or sentence, the succeeding one in construction with that plus the first particle, and so on in Chinese-puzzle fashion. For example, 没来呐. *Mei lai ne.* '(He) has not yet come.': 没来呐 吧? *Mei lai ne ba?* '(He) has not come yet, I suppose?' 他不 会答应你的. *Ta buhuey da.yinq nii de.* 'He won't promise you, that's the situation.': with ... *de le*, it means 'that's the situation, as it has now developed': with ... *de le ba?* it means 'that's the situation, as it has now developed, don't you think?'

    When a particle is followed by another particle beginning with a vowel, the two will fuse into one syllable, although each will still retain its function, as in 这个不能吃了. *Jeyg buneng chy le.* 'This can't be eaten any more.': 这个不能吃啦? *Jeyg buneng chy l'a?* 'This can't be eaten any more?', where 啦 *l'a* is a fusion of 了 *le* and 啊 *a*. Note that many of these fusions do not have characters to write them in and in some cases where there are characters pronounced with the fused syllable, they are

not commonly written for the fused particles. Thus, when to 快
吃罢，饭冷了！ *Kuay chy ba, fann leeng le!* 'Hurry up and
eat, your rice is getting cold!' is added the warning particle 呕
*ou* 'mind you!' we get fused particles 罢呕 *ba ou* → □ *bou* and
了呕 *le ou* → 喽 *lou*, with no character for the former and a
possible, and sometimes used, character 喽 for the latter. Thus
we get 哒 *da* ← 的啊 *de a*, 啦 *l'a* ← 了啊 *le a*, 哪 *na* ← 呐啊
*ne a*. One could write 兜 *dou* for the fusion of 的呕 *de ou*, or
耨 *nou* for 呐呕 *ne ou*, but it is never done.[71] In general, the
occurrence of characters for fusions is quite fortuitous and is of
no linguistic import, though occasionally it may be of relevance
in philological research when it concerns old fusions, such as 而
已 ,*ńźi* '*i* > 耳 '*ńźi* (read as *erl yii* and *eel* in modern wenyan),
equivalent to P 22 就是了 *jiowshle* 'that's all there is to it'.

*8.5.4. Compound Particles.* Compound particles are particles
consisting of two or more morphemes functioning as a whole in
relation to what precedes instead of separately, as successive
particles do. Thus, in 他跑着呐。 *Ta paoj ne.* 'He is running.',
the progressive aspect suffix 着 -*j* is part of the verb 跑 *pao*, while
in 他好着呐！ *Ta hao jne!* 'He is awfully good!' 着呐 *jne* is
a compound particle P 18 expressing intensity. The ambivalent
sentence 他闹着呐。 if analyzed as *Ta nawj ne.* means 'He is
making noises.', but as *Ta naw jne.* means 'He is awfully noisy.'
(See also pp. 1088-1089.)

*8.5.5. List of Particles*

P 1. 的 *de* 'such is the case': 告送了他，他会生气的。
*Gaw.sonqle ta, ta huey sheng-chih de.* 'If you tell him, he will
get angry, that's-what's-going-to-happen.'     我没省个大子儿
的。 *Woo mei sheeng g dahtzeel de.* 'I didn't save a big penny,
that's-what-I-forgot-to-do.' 你应该问ᵛ他的。 *Nii inggai wenn-
.wenn ta de.* 'You ought to have tried and asked him, that's-what-
you-should-have-done.'

---

[71]Except in my *Tsing Hua Journal* article, vol. 3 (1926), p. 910, which
of course does not count as "text".

On the use of *de* as subordinative particle to phrases and suffix to words, see sections 4.4.6 and 5.3.6.

P 2 了 *le*.

(1) Inchoative *le:* 糟了，下雨了。*Tzau le, shiah-yeu le.* 'Too bad, it's raining.' This inchoative *le* may be applied to a situation which is new or only new to the speaker. For example, it may have been raining for some time and on looking outside and realizing that it is raining, one can still say 下雨了。*Shiah-yeu le.* The situation may be something regarded as a quantity or degree attained, as in 唉呀，十一点半了！*Aiia, shyri-dean-bann le!* 'Goodness, it's (as late as) half past eleven!' 你今年四十岁了，都！*Nii jin.nian syh.shyr-suey le, dou!* 'You are this year (as old as) forty years old, even!' With adjectives, this inchoative *le* may imply an excessive degree, as in 湯鹹了。*Tang shyan le.* 'The soup is too salty.', although in a context in which the soup was at first found to be not salty enough, then 湯鹹了。*Tang shyan le.* will mean 'The soup is salty (enough) now.' 这鞋小了。*Jeh shye sheau le.* 'These shoes are (too) small.' 你写重了。*Nii shiee-chorngle.* 'You have written repetitiously.'

(2) Command in Response to a New Situation: 吃饭了！*Chy-fann le!* 'Let's eat now!' 请了！*Chiing le!* 'Please (now)!' 咱们坐了！*Tzarmen tzuoh le!* 'Let's sit down now!'

(3) Progress in Story: 後来天就晴了。*Howlai tian jiow chyng le.* 'And then the weather cleared.' 那房子就塌了。*Nah farngtz jiow ta le.* 'Then the house collapsed.' 他就说了："…" *Ta jiow shuo le: "…"* 'Then he said: "…"'

(4) Isolated Event in the Past: 我昨儿到張家吃饭了。*Woo tzuol daw Jang.jia chy-fann le.* 'I went to the Jang's for dinner yesterday.' 那天我也去听了。*Ney-tian woo yee chiuh ting le.* 'That day, I went to listen, too.' 是的，昨天他真的哭了。*Sh de, tzwo.tian ta jende ku le.* 'Yes, he really cried yesterday.'[72]

---

[72]These sentences, with *de* instead of *le*, were included in my *Tsing Hua Journal* article (p. 873) as examples of the specifying *de*. I have since noticed that in the Northern dialects, where an isolated event in the past is men-

(5) Completed Action as of the Present: 我回来了. *Woo hwei.lai le.* 'I have come back.'        我今儿早晨写了三封信了. *Woo jiel tzao.chern shieele san-feng shinn le.* 'I have written three letters this morning.' (talking before lunch time). 我教书教了四十年了. *Woo jiau-shu jiaule syh.shyr-nian le.* 'I have been teaching for 40 years.' This "sentence" *le*, as we have noted [sec. 4.4.5(1)], is different from the "word" *le*, or "suffix" *le*. In translation it usually goes into the perfect tense in English, while with the perfective-aspect suffix *le* (obligatory for quantified objects for past events), it goes into the preterit, as 我今儿早晨写了三封信. *Woo jiel tzao.chern shieele san-feng shinn.* 'I wrote three letters this morning.' (talking in the afternoon or evening). 我教了四十年的书. *Woo jiaule syh.shyr-nian de shu.* 'I taught for 40 years.' (and am now retired).

(6) Consequent Clause to Indicate Situation. While the new-situation *le* under (1) is often translatable as 'now', the *le* in a consequent clause, with or without 就 *jiow*, is often translatable as 'then', as in 那我就不走了. *Nah woo jiow bu tzoou le.* 'In that case, I won't go, then.'        你一摁门铃儿, 他就来开门了. *Nii i enn menliengl, ta jiow lai kai-men le.* 'As soon as you ring the doorbell, he will come and open the door.'

A conditional or other dependent clause may also contain a *le* [cf. sec. 2.12.7(3)], and such use of *le* was listed in *Mand Prim* (p. 194) as the 7th function of *le*. However, the *le* used in this way is not a "sentence" *le*, but a "word" *le*, and we are therefore not listing it here. The difference between the "sentence" *le* expressing consequence and the "word" *le* expressing condition can be seen (1) from the position in the sentence, as in 就来开门了 *jiow lai kai-men le* 'will come and open the door': 他开了门你就进去. *Ta kaile men nii jiow jinn.chiuh.* 'If (or when) he opens the door, you must go in.'; (2) from the dialectal forms as in Shanghai 伊来仔我就可以去哉. *Yi lez ngu ziew kooyii chih ze.* = Mand 他来了我就可以走了. *Ta*

---

tioned, as in these sentences, *le* is preferred, whereas in the Wu dialects the equivalent of *de* is preferred. See also sec. 5.3.6.5 (2.5) above.

*laile woo jiow keeyii tzoou le.* 'If (or when) he comes, then I can go.', where the "word" *le* in the dependent clause is *z* and the "sentence" *le* in the main clause is *ze* (corresponding, respectively, to 仔 *tzy* and 哉 *tze* in Soochow and 咀 *cox* and 咯 *lhoh* in Cantonese).    Similarly, 我看完仔报就去睏哉. *Ngu    köh-wöz baw ziew chih kuenq ze.* Mand    我看完了报就去睡了. *Woo kann-wanle baw jiow chiuh shuey le.* 'When I finished reading the newspaper, I went to sleep.'

(7) Obviousness: 这个你当然懂了! *Jeyg nii dangran doong le!* 'This you understand, of course!' 再好没有了! *Tzay hao meiyeou le!* 'Nothing can be better than that!' This particle often has the alternate form 咯 *lo* instead of 了 *le.* In the translation, the force of this "obviousness" *le* (~ *lo*) corresponds to an upswing in the English intonation.

P 3. 咧 *le* particle of lively enumeration: 不荛是胭脂咧, 粉咧, 锅咧, 缝纫机咧, 什么都卖. *Bugoan sh ian.jy le, feen le, guo le, ferngrennji le, sherm dou may.* 'No matter whether it's rouge, powder, pots, or sewing machines, they sell everything.' See also P 8 (10) and P 28.

P 4. 吗 *ma,* particle for yes-or-no questions: 外头下雨了 吗? *Way.tou shiah-yeu le ma?* 'Is it raining outside?' 你还打 算出去吗? *Nii hair daa.suann chu.chiuh ma?* 'Are you still planning to go out?' This form of a question contains either a slight or considerable doubt about an affirmative answer, implying a probability of less than 50%. When the question contains a negative adverb, it is a rhetorical question, suggesting a reply to the contrary, as in 你不怕老虎吗? *Nii bu pah laohuu ma?* 'Aren't you afraid of tigers?' (of course you are, or should be).

你没听见那件大新闻吗? *Nii mei ting.jiann ney-jiann dah shinwen ma?* 'Haven't you heard the big news?' Questions ending in 吗 *ma* are not quite equivalent to the V-not-V form of questions, which is completely noncommital as to the answer. Thus, in 你怕风不怕? *Nii pah feng bu pah?* 'Are you afraid of wind,—do you mind the draft?' the chance of a positive or negative answer, in the mind of the questioner, is just 50:50.

Because particles are in the neutral tone and unstressed, the low vowel *a* and the midvowel *e* are indistinguishable. However, in questions ending in 嗎 *ma* the sentence intonation is usually fairly high and ends in a slight drawl. It is therefore distinguishable from P 5 嚜 *me* below, which is always short. We are therefore transcribing 嗎 as *ma*.

Besides the usual character 嗎 for this particle, older books also use 麼～広～ 么 ～嘛～ 麻 as graphic variants.

On 嗎 *ma* as a fusion of a negative with P 8 阿 *a*, see P 11 吧 *ba* below.

P 5. 嚜～麼 , etc. *me*.

(1) Pause Particle with Hesitation: 'as for, in the case of ... well': 今天我不能, 明天嚜, 待会儿再说罢. *Jin.tian woo buneng; ming.tian me, dai.hoel tzay shuo ba.* 'I can't today; as for tomorrow, well, let's talk about it later.' 要是他不肯 嚜, 你就让他去罢. *Yawsh ta bu keen me, nii jiow ranq ta chiuh ba.* 'If he is unwilling, well, you just let it go.'

(2) Dogmatic Assertion: 'you should know', 'don't you see?': 我说是的嚜! 你就是不懂嚜! *Woo shuo sh de me! Nii jiowsh bu doong me!* 'I say it is! You just don't understand!'[73] A case may perhaps be made for differentiating (1) and (2) as two separate particles, especially as (1) is more often written 麼(or its variants) than 嚜, while (2) is almost always written 嚜.

P 6. 吶 ～ 呢 *ne*.

(1) Questions in a Context: 那么他吶? 他来不来吶?

---

[73]Because this involves a dogmatic and superior attitude on the part of the speaker, I have often found it difficult, on my field trips for dialect survey, to elicit the dialectal equivalents of this particle from the informants, who often felt diffident about assuming a dogmatic tone. I would take a pencil and say to the informant (in as near his dialect as I knew how) 'This is a pen.' 'No, this is a pencil.', he would say. 'No, it isn't.' 'Yes, it is.' And after a few times, if he got in the right mood, he would say impatiently, 是 的 嚜, 这 "是 鉛 筆 嚜! *Sh de me, jeh sh chianbii me!* 'Yes it is, it *is* a pencil!' But if the informant was a student who mistakenly thought that I had come out to teach him the standard National Language, instead of trying to learn from him, then it was often impossible to elicit the impatient, dogmatic mood of the particle 嚜 *me*.

*Nemme ta ne? Ta lai .bu .lai ne?* 'Well, then, how about him? Is he coming?' 現在咱们幹点儿什么呐? *Shianntzay tzarmen gann deal sherm ne?* 'Now what shall we do for a while?' Cf P 8.

(2) Questions with a Specific Point: 你懂了; "他懂不懂呐? *Nii doong le; "ta doong bu doong ne?* 'You understand now; does *he* understand?' 他会拉提琴; "你呐? *Ta huey lha tyi-chyn; "nii ne?* 'He can play the violin, how about *you?*'

(3) Deliberate Pause: 'as for, in the case of': 将耒的问题呐, 那就等到将耒再说. *Jianglai de wenntyi ne, nah jiow deeng daw jianglai tzay shuo.* 'As for problems of the future, they can wait until the future before we deal with them.' 錢呐, 錢用光了; 事情呐, 事情没做. *Chyan ne, chyan yonq-guangle; shyh.chyng ne, shyh.chyng mei tzuoh.* 'As for money, it is all spent; as for the business, it wasn't done.'

(4) Mild Warning: 'mind you!': 这倒很危险呐! *Jeh daw heen weishean ne!* 'This is rather dangerous, mind you!' 那不是玩儿的呐! *Nah bush wal de ne!* 'That's nothing to trifle with, mind you!'

P 7. 呐~哩 *ne*. The character 哩 is found in old novels, and the pronunciation *li* which it naturally suggests is actually used in dialects in which P 6 呢 is pronounced *ni* or *nyi*.

(1) Continued State: 'still, ... -ing': 还没到时候儿呐. *Hair mei daw shyr.howl ne.* 'It isn't time yet.' 说着话呐. *Shuoj huah ne.* 'They are talking,—line busy.'

One special form of this 呐 *ne* is a sarcastic retort, implying that things are far beyond a state assumed by the previous speaker as still existing, as in 真好玩儿! —还'好玩儿'呐?! *Jen haowal!—Hair 'haowal' ne?!* 'What fun!—You still call that fun?!' 老朋友啊!—还"老朋友"呐?! *Lao perng.yeou a!—Hair "lao perng .yeou" ne?!* 'My old friend!—What do you mean, "old friend"?!' (having betrayed me).

(2) Assertion of Equaling Degree: 'as much as': We noted [sec. 8.1.3.2 (1.1)] that the verb 有 *yeou* is used for asserting a degree as much as a certain quantity. This can be further strengthened by adding the particle 呐 *ne*, as in 有一百尺呐,

深的很呐。 *Yeou ibae-chyy ne, shen de heen ne.* 'It's as much as 100 feet, it's quite deep.'

(3) Interest in Additional Information: 他们还卖古琴呐. *Tamen hair may guuchyn ne.* 'They are even selling the ancient zither (among other exotic things).' 後院ㄦ还有个金鱼池呐. *Howyuall hair yeou g jinyu-chyr ne.* 'And there is a goldfish pond in the backyard, too (to my pleasant surprise).' 他还会扯谎呐. *Ta hair huey chee-hoang ne.* 'He can even pull lies,—tell lies (I did not expect him to be that clever).'

P 8. 啊 *a* ~ 呀 *ia*: This particle, which has many functions, has a somewhat complicated phonemics and morphophonemics. Like the other particles beginning with a vowel, namely P 9 and P 12, they link freely with the preceding consonants or vowels instead of resisting linking as full words do; when a full word nominally begins with a vowel, it usually has a velar sonorant [ γ ] or a glottal stop (cf. sec. 1.3.2), but with this linking effect before the (real) vowel there results a whole series of apparent variants of the particle 啊 *a*, some of which, because of the availability of characters for some of the resulting syllables, give the appearance of different particles, as in 耒呀 *lai* (*i*)*a*, 好哇 *hao* (*u*)*a*, 人哪 *ren* (*n*)*a*, 娘 □ *niang* (*ng*)*a*, 吃 □ *chy* (*ra*), 字 □ *tzyh* (*z*)*a*.[74] Actually, the only phonemically different shapes for the particle are 啊 *a* and 呀 *ia*, the latter occurring after open vowels, namely *a* and *e* (of which *o* is an allophone), and the former in all other cases, with automatic linking as shown above. Consequently, we shall write 耒啊 *lai a* and let the 呀 *ia* effect take care of itself, but write 我呀 *woo ia*, since here we have a real morphophonemic alternation. In the following examples we shall treat 啊 *a* and 呀 *ia* as the same particle (cf. English 'a' and 'an' as the same article).

---

[74]Li Jiinshi even invented the symbol 帀 (inverted 业) for Karlgren's apical vowels ィ ( = [ ʐ ]) and ㇉ ( = [ʑ]) so as to write the particles in the last two examples as 帀 Y . Hockett (Peip Morphoph, 77) also recognizes a gemination in *lai ia, ren na*, and so on. But to my ear it is nothing more than an effect of linking.

(1) Starting a Question: 谁啊? *sheir a?* 'Who is it?' 你 明 儿 出 去 不 出 去 啊? *Nii miengl chu.chiuh bu chu.chiuh a?* 'Are you going out tomorrow?'   这 个 包 裹 是 哪 儿 来 哟? *Jeyg bauguoo sh naal lai d'a?* 'Where did this package come from?' All these questions can be asked, more bluntly, without any particle, but the addition of 啊 *a* softens them with the effect of 'by the way', 'excuse me', 'to change the subject', and the like.

(2) Confirmation Question: This 啊 *a* is not only low, but the whole sentence is spoken low, sometimes so low as to sound breathy. It is used for asking for confirmation of a posed statement, with the effect of 'Did I hear you right?' as in 你 不 去 啊? *Nii bu chiuh a?* 'You are not going?' 这 个 啊? *Jeyg a?* 'This one, you mean?' This form of a question differs from a question with P 4 吗 *ma* in three respects: (a) While the *ma*-questions have a high pitch, the *a*-questions have a low pitch; (b) the *ma*-questions should be translated into the inverted (V-S) order in English, and the *a*-questions should be translated in the straight order (S-V), with a high intonation, in English; (c) the *ma* questions are concerned with the truth of the content ( < 50% probability), while the *a*-questions are more concerned with the confirmation of having correctly heard what has been said.

(3) Vocative Particle: 老 張 啊! *Lao Jang a!* 'Oh, Lao Jang!' 喂, 先 生 啊! *Uai, shian.sheng a!* 'Say, mister!' Like the interrogative 啊 *a* under (1), this 啊 *a* has a slightly more airy and less blunt effect than a direct address without any particle.

(4) Commands: 说 呀, 别 害 怕 呀! *Shuo ia! Bye haypah ia!* 'Say it! Don't be afraid!' 走 啊! 咱 们 都 走 啊! *Tzoou a! Tzarmen dou tzoou a!* 'Let's go! Let's all go!' This has a slightly insistent air, not as modest-toned as the advisative P 10 罢 *ba* and not as impatient as P 13 煞 *sha*.

(5) Exclamation: 小 王 啊! 你 还 没 上 床 啊 ?!    *Sheau Wang a! Nii hair mei shanq-chwang a?!* 'Little Wang! Aren't you in bed yet?!' 我 就 跑 啊, 跑 啊, 跑 啊! 跑 到 他 们 趕 不 上 就 好 啦! *Woo jiow pao a, pao a, pao a! Pao daw tamen gaan.bu-shanq jiow hao l'a!* 'I ran and ran and ran! How nice it would be if I could run until they couldn't catch up with me!'

This 啊 *a* is rather long-drawn-out and associated with a low sentence intonation. Note that this exclamatory use of 啊 *a* does not exclude its concurrent use in the other functions, such as the vocative, as in the first example.

The expletive 啊 *a* often added ad lib in chanting poetry or singing is of this nature, as in 少小離家老大回, often chanted as 少小離家—是老大回啊— *Shawsheau li jia —sh lao-dah hwei a—* 'When young and small I left home, when old and big I come back.' This is usually regarded as a mannerism, which one tends to indulge in, especially when enjoying the lines. (See also example on p. 723-4.)

(6) Impatient Statement: 我並没做錯呀! *Woo binq mei tzuoh-tsuoh ia!* 'I didn't do it wrong!' 这个非得那么做才行啊! *Jeyg feideei nemm tzuoh tsair shyng a!* 'This had to be done that way (before it would do)!' This 啊 *a* is fairly short and the pitch of the sentence is moderately high, with the force of 'you see or ought to see', expressed usually by a falling-rising intonation over the corresponding English sentence. It is less peremptory than P 5 (2) 嚜 *me*, which means 'don't you see? (and I am afraid you still don't)'. But it is stronger than the milder P 9 吔 *è*, with the force of 'of course you know (and might as well admit it)'.

(7) Reminder: 本来你也知道啊，也用不着 再说啊, ... *Beenlai nii yee jy.daw a, yee yonq.bu-₀jaur tzay shuo a* ... 'As you already know, and I don't have to say it again, ... ' This 啊 *a* has a slight rising intonation, approaching the 2nd Tone *ar*, sometimes even ending in a glottal stop. In this sense, it usually remains an open vowel instead of taking the alternate form *ia* after open vowels.[75]

(8) Warning: 这个人的话是靠不住的啊! 你别上他的当啊! *Jeyg ren de huah sh kaw.bu-juh d'a! Nii bye shanq tade danq a!* 'This man's word is unreliable, mind you! Don't you be fooled by him!' This 啊 *a* often has a slightly falling

_____
[75]Because of this different morphophonemic behavior, a case may perhaps be made for considering this *a* particle a different morpheme from the *a* ~ *ia* of P 8.

intonation or a rising-falling intonation (232:). It is slightly weaker and less explicit than the same sentence followed by the interjection 啊 *a!* with the same intonations.

(9) Pause for Hearer: 我说呀，你听啊，这位先生啊，他的话呀，你不能全信。 *Woo shuo ia, nii ting a, jey-wey shian.sheng a, tade huah ia, nii buneng chyuan shinn.* 'I say, listen, as for this gentlemen, what he says, you can't believe entirely.' 要是你还不肯啊，那我就不荄了。 *Yawsh nii hair bukeen a, nah woo jiow bu goan le.* 'If you are still unwilling, then I will just wash my hands of it.' This deliberate pause 啊 *a* is to give the hearer time to let what is said sink in, as distinguished from the hesitation pause P 5 (1) 嚜 ～ 麼 *me* to give the *speaker* time to think what to say next, and from P 6 (3) 呐 *ne* to bring up specific points for both speaker and hearer to consider.

(10) Enumeration: 什么天啊，地啊，日啊，月呀，風啊，草啊，这些字啊，都会写了。 *Sherme tian (n)a, dih (i)a, ryh (r)a, yueh ia, feng (ng)a, tsao (u)a, jeh.shie tzyh (z)a, dou huey shiee le.* 'Things like heaven, earth, sun, moon, wind, grass, these words, he can write all of them.' This particle implies more interest in the items enumerated than does P 3 咧 *le*, with which the speaker tries to impress the hearer in a condescending manner. (See also P 28.)

P 9. 世 ～ 诶 [76] *è* '(as) you know': 这樣不行世！不能就算了世！ 还得细想ぇ呐世！ *Jehyanql bushyng è! Buneng jiow suann l'è! Hair deei shih sheang.sheang.sheang n'è!* 'This won't do, you know! You can't just let it go at that! You'll still have to think it over carefully, you know!' This differs from P 5 (2) 嚜 *me* in implying that the hearer will see things right if he is

---

[76]The character 诶 (as well as 欸 for I 8 in sec. 8.6.4) was assigned by executive fiat of *Gwoin Charngyonq Tzyhhuey*, Shanghai, 1932, published under the authority of the Chinese Ministry of Education, but has never found its way in actual text, either as a particle or as an interjection (P 2-P 7). I recommend the use of the National Phonetic letter 世, which is much easier to write and much better known.

only reminded, while with 噁 *me* the hearer is definitely wrong
and has to be strongly corrected.

P 10. 吧 ~ 罷 ~ 罢 *ba*

(1) Advisative Particle:　快点儿走吧！*Kuay.deal tzoou ba!*
'Better hurry up and go!'　咱们就这么办吧！*Tzarmen jiow
tzemm bann ba!* 'Let's just do it that way!'　那个你甭给錢
了吧！*Neyg nii berng geei chyan le ba!* 'Then you won't need
to pay for that!'

(2) Suppositions as Alternatives:[77]　不给錢吧，不好意思
白拿；给錢吧，又给不起。*Bu geei chyan ba, buhaoyih.sy
bair na; geei chyan ba, yow geei.bu-chii.* 'Suppose I don't pay for
it, I am ashamed to take something for nothing; and if I am to
pay for it, I can't afford it.'

In a question like　你到底要幹什么吧？*Nii dawdii yaw
gann sherm ba?* 'What do you want to do, anyway?', the *ba* is not
P 11, but the advisative *ba* of P 10 (1) having the force of 'Tell
me, what do you … ?'

P 11. 吧 *ba:* This is counted as a separate particle from P 10,
because it is a fusion of 不啊 *bu a* → 吧 *ba*, whereas P 10 is a
reduced form of the verb 罢 *bah* 'finish'. We are listing both this
particle and P 4 嗎 *ma* separately and leave other successions and
fusions unlisted because their separate parts are no longer used
separately in the same context. In the case of 嗎 *ma*, a relic of an
older negative beginning with *m-*, one cannot say °你去 m-啊？
°*Nii chiuh m-a?* for 你去嗎？*Nii chiuh ma?* 'Are you going?'
(Supplying 没 *mei* for *m-* would result in a different sentence.)
In the case of 吧 *ba*, one cannot say ° 你去不啊？°*Nii chiuh
bu a?* Since there is no such form as ° 你去不？°*Nii chiuh bu?*
If we were describing other dialects, however, the situation with
respect to the descriptive etymology of such words might be
different. Thus, in Cantonese the equivalent of 不 *bu* is 唔 *mu* [m̩],
which easily fuses with (Cantonese) 呀 *ah* and forms 嗎 *mah*, and
therefore 嗎 *mah* need not be counted separately for Cantonese.
Again, in the dialect of Paoting, Hopei, one can say 你去不？

---

[77] Lien-Sheng Yang suggests that this may be called the "dilemma 罢".

*Nii chiuh bu?* as well as 你去吧? *Nii chiuh ba?* for 'Are you going?' Consequently 吧 *ba* for 不啊 *bu a* is a simple fusion and need not be counted as a separate particle, as it has to be for Standard Mandarin.

(1) In Yes-or-No Questions: 你知道吧? *Nii jy.daw ba?* 'Do you know?' 我告送过你了吧? *Woo gaw.sonq.guo nii le ba?* 'Have I told you before?'

(2) In Doubtful Posed Statements: This 吧 *ba* is shorter and the sentence intonation is slightly lower. Thus, with the same words as under (1), the doubtful posed statement would mean 'you know, I suppose?' and 'I told you before, or did I?'

P 12. 呕 *ou:*

(1) Warning Reminder: 不早了呕! 快走吧呕! 乜, 别忙啊, 你先问他是去不去呕! *Bu tzao l'ou! Kuay tzoou b'ou! È, bye mang a, nii shian wenn ta sh chiuh bu chiuh ou!* 'It's getting late! Hurry up and go! Say, don't be in such a hurry, ask him first if he is going there at all, you know!' This is a softer, although more urgent, warning than P 8 (8), and has the force of 'you know, and do act according to what you know!'

(2) Exclamation: This is like P 8 (5) 啊 *a*, but with more of the attitude to impress: 放学喽(  ← 了 ＋ 呕)! 咱们都回家喽! *Fanq-shyue l'ou! Tzarmen dou hwei-jia l'ou!* 'School is out! We are all going home (yippee)!' (See also the example on p. 724.)

P 13. 煞 *sha:* This is the most peremptory and impatient of the interrogative and assertive particles. It is used more frequently in Southern Mandarin and in some of the Wu dialects and therefore is less strong there than in the North. It is often heard on the stage in spoken (as against sung) dialogues.

(1) Impatient Statement: 这样不对的煞! *Jehyanq buduey de sha!* 'This is wrong, you see?!' 吃了东西得给钱煞! *Chyle dong.shi deei geei chyan sha!* 'Having eaten the things, you have to pay, you see?!'

(2) Impatient Command: 让人过去煞! 别挡着路煞! *Ranq ren guoh.chiuh sha! Bye daangj luh sha!* 'Let me [cf. sec. 7.11.4 (3.2)] pass! Don't be in the way!'

(3) Impatient Question: 你到底是怎么回事儿煞?

*Nii dawdii sh tzeem hwei shell sha?* 'What's the matter with you, anyway?'　你 怎 么 見 了 人 也 不 打 招 呼 焌 ?　*Nii    tzeem jiannle ren yee bu daa-jau.hu sha?* 'Why don't you say hello when you see people?'

P 14. 看 *.kann*: Tentative Particle 'and see':　你 问 z 他 看 ! *Nii wenn.wenn ta .kann!* 'Just ask him and see (what happens)!' 不 妨 试 一 试 看 . *Bufarng shyh .i.shyh .kann.* 'No harm to try and see.' 咱 们 最 好 去 看 z 看 .　*Tzarmen tzuey hao chiuh kann.kann .kann.* 'We better go take a look and see.' In the last example, the second 看 *kann* is a tentative reduplicate, from the cognate object *i-kann* 'a look', and the third one is the particle for 'and see what happens'.

P 15. 来 *.lai*, and

P 16. 去 *.chiuh:* These are similar to, but different from, the directional complements 来 *-.lai* and 去 *-chiuh*. For illustrations of use, see section 6.6.8 (7).

P 17. ₀来 ₀*lai* 'and': This is a pause or drawl particle in reciting in singsong style as a syllable filler:　山 後 有 个 大 绵 羊 , 你 吃 肚 来 我 吃 腸 . *Shan-how yeou g dah mianyang, nii chy duu* ₀*lai woo chy charng.* 'There is a big (dead) sheep behind the hills. You can eat the tripe and I'll eat the intestines.' (from a folk ballad). 一 个 去 ₀来 一 个 来 . *Ig chiuh* ₀*lai ig lai.* 'One goes and another comes.' P 17 is never used in reciting serious poetry. This is different from the nonsensical filler 是 *sh* (no. 15, p. 973), which is proclitic to what follows and is thus more a conjunction than a particle. While this *sh* may sound pedantic, its use is often indulged in when reading serious poetry, in which P 17, however, has no place. It would be the height of disrespect to Tu Fu (*Duh Fuu*) to read ° 車 辚 z ₀来 馬 蕭 z .　°*Jiu linlin* ₀*lai maa shiau-shiau.* 'Chariots rumble and horses neigh.'

The next eight particles, P 18-P 25, are compound particles in which the constituent morphemes are identifiable, but which function as whole particles to the sentence instead of in succession.

P 18.　着 (z) ( 的 ) 呐　~ 着 (z) ( 的 ) 哩 *j(j)* (*de*)*ne* 'very, awfully': This comes from the assertion of a quality A, in retort to a possible assertion that it is not A, that it not only *is* A but is

actually *being* A, as in  他 不 快 活 吧 ？ ——不 ，他 快 活 着 呐 ！
*Ta bu kuay .hwo ba?—Bu, ta kuay.hwo jne!* 'He is not happy, is
he?—You are wrong, he is *very* happy (lit., he is being happy)!'
他 们 俩 好 着 ㄹ 呐 ！ *Tamen lea haoj jne!* 'The two of them
are being awfully good to each other!' The longer form *haoj
jdene* is less common than the simple *hao jne*.

Note that 着 呐 *jne* is a (sentence) particle and must come
after the object if there is one, while -*j* is a (word) suffix and
must come immediately after the verb in V-O phrases or ionizable compounds, as in 别 閙 ！我 打 着 電 话 呐. *Bye naw! Woo
daaj diannhuah ne.* 'Quiet! I am telephoning.' On the other hand,
P 18 着 呐 *jne*, being a particle, must also follow the object, as
in 他 听 话 着 呐. *Ta ting-huah jne.* 'He very much listens to
words,—he is quite obedient.'

P 19. 耒 着 *.laij* 'was ... -ing':    你 昨ㄦ 晚 上 幹 麻 耒 着
？—— 我 看 電 視 耒 着. *Nii tzwol woan.shanq gannma .laij?—
Woo kann diannshyh laij.* 'What were you doing last night?—I
was watching the TV.'    那 帽 子 在 那ㄦ 掛 着 耒 着 ，怎 么
没 有 了 ？ *Nah mawtz tzay.nall guahj laij, tzeem meiyeou le?*
'The hat was hanging there, how come it's no longer there?'
While this particle usually has to do with events in the recent
past, it is by no means limited to the past. For example, one can
say    诸 葛 亮 是 哪ㄦ 的 人 耒 着 ？ *Ju.gee Lianq sh naal de
ren .laij?* 'Where did you say Ju.gee Lianq was a native of?' The
difference between (a) 你 姓 什 么 ？ *Nii shinq sherme?* and (b)
你 姓 什 么 耒 着 ？ *Nii shing sherm .laij?* is approximately that
between 'a) 'What's your name?' (with falling intonation) and (b)
'What was your name?' (with high and rising intonation).

P 20. 似 的 *.shyhde* 'as if ... ': 我 觉 着 菝 燒 似 的. *Woo
jyuej fa-shau .shyhde.* 'I feel as if I have a fever.' This particle is
often preceded by ( 好 )像 *(hao)ₒshianq* 'seems', as in 你 的 声 音
好 像 还 没 醒 呐 似 的. *Niide sheng.in haoshianq hair mei
shiing ne .shyhde.* 'Your voice sounds as if you weren't quite
awake yet.' The morpheme 似 *syh* 'resembles' L, occurring in
compounds   like 類 似 *leysyh* 'similar'   and 跟 ... 相 似 *gen* ...

*shiangsyh* 'similar to ... ', has the special form *shyh* in this compound particle 似的 *.shyhde*. It has nothing to do with the (except for stress) homophonous 是的 *sh de* 'that's right'.

P 21. 罢了 *bale* ~ *bele*, and

P 22. 就是了 *.jiowshle*. These compound particles are interchangeable in most cases, the only differences being that P 21 has a more impatient tone than P 22 and is used more in commands than in statements, and that P 21 is used more often than P 22 in the Central dialects than in the North. In Cantonese both particles are equivalent to 啫 *ce*[O]. In wenyan both are equivalent to 耳 *eel*, which, as we have seen (sec. 8.5.3), was a fusion of 而已 *erl yii*.

(1) Limitation: 'just, that's all there is to it': 不过就是问问罢了。 *Buguoh jiowsh wenn.wenn bale.* 'I was just asking, that's all.' 他不是不会，是不肯就是了. *Ta bush buhuey, sh bukeen .jiowshle.* 'He was not unable, just unwilling, that's all.'

(2) Free Permission: 'as one pleases': 让他去就是了！ *Ranq ta chiuh .jiowshle!* 'Just let it go!' 爱说什么说什么就是了！ *Ay shuo sherm shuo sherm .jiowshle!* 'Just say what you like, that's all!'

(3) Impatient Command: 'Hurry up and ... ': 快走罢了！ *Kuay tzoou bele!* 'Hurry up and go!' 答应了他就是了！ *Da.yinqle ta .jiowshle!* 'Just promise him (and be done with it)!'

P 23. 得了 [o]*derle*: '... and that will do': This is similar to P 21 and 22, but with the implication that 'that is all to make it all right'. 你买了得了。 *Nii maele derle.* 'You just buy it (and it will be all right).' This is equivalent to 好哉 *haoze* (in Shanghai), as in 儂先去好哉！ *Nung sie chih haoze.* 'You just go first (and that's all that's necessary).' = Mand 你先走得了。 *Nii shian tzoou derle.*

P 24. 的话 *de*[o]*huah* 'the case of ... ', 'the matter of ... ', 'if ... ': 要是他还不知道的话，你就不必告送他了。 *Yawsh ta hair bujydaw de*[o]*huah, nii jiow bubih gawsonq ta le.* 'If it is a matter of his not knowing it,—in case he still does not know, you need not tell him.' 你实在不肯的话，我也

不勉強你. *Nii shyrtzay bukeen de.huah, woo yee bu mean-cheang nii.* 'If you are really unwilling, I won't force you, either.'

P 25. 的时候(儿)  *de.shyr.how(l)*: 'the time of ... ', 'when ...': 去看戏的时候儿得先買票. *Chiuh kann-shih de.shyr.howl, deei shian mae piaw.* 'When you go to see a show, you must first buy a ticket.', where 的时候儿 *de.shyr.howl*, originally *de* followed by the modified noun, is now enclitic and functions as a particle which can even be omitted: 去看戏得先買票. *Chiuh kann-shih deei shian mae piaw.* 'As for going to see a show, you must first buy a ticket.' In some dialects, as we have seen (sec. 2.8.3), *de.shyr.how* is nothing but a pause particle after the subject.

P 26. 不是嗎? *.bushma?* 'Isn't it?', *'n'est-ce pas?'* This can be used alone, as an interjection, or as a particle attached to a sentence without a pause, as in    去年一冬没下雪不是嗎? *Chiuh.nian i-dong mei shiah-sheue .bushma?* 'Last year it didn't snow the whole winter, wasn't that so?'

P 27.   The Rising Ending ↗, and

P 28.   The Falling Ending ↘. These two intonational endings of phrases and sentences are of a very special morphophonemic nature. I used to treat these as part of Chinese sentence intonation, but later found it better to treat them as particles,[78] since they do not affect the intonational pattern of the whole construction, but only the voiced part of the last syllable. The only thing special about each of these two particles is that it does not have a segmental phoneme of its own, but resides parasitically on the last morpheme by prolonging it for the length of a neutral-tone syllable on which to put a rising or falling ending. The actual pitch of these rising endings is as follows:

| *After* | *Pitch* | *Graph* | | *Example* | |
|---------|---------|---------|---|-----------|---|
| 1st Tone | 556: | ⌐ 近倫敦? | *Jinn Luenduen* ↗? | 'Near London?' |
| 2nd Tone | 356: | ⌐ 不行? | *Bushyng* ↗? | 'It won't do?' |
| 3rd Tone | 2145: | ⌐ 就要走? | *Jiow yaw tzoou* ↗? | 'Go right away?' |
| 4th Tone | 513: | ↘ 我不要! | *Woo buyaw* ↗! | 'I don't want it!' |

---

[78]"The Morphemic Status of Certain Chinese Tones", *Trans. of the International Congress of Orientalists in Japan*, IV, 44-48 (1959).

The portion of the graph to the left of the vertical reference line is the tone proper; the portion to its right is the rising ending. After the neutral tone, there is a rise of a degree or two, as in 这 是 他 的 ? *Jeh sh tade* ↗? 'This is his?' The meanings of the rising ending are:

(1) Incredulity: 'Do you mean to say ... ?' In the preceding examples, all except the 4th Tone example are of this meaning.

(2) Impatience: This often has a crescendo, ending in a glottal stop. If I have refused something that someone repeatedly tries to give me, I may finally say 我 不 要 ↗! *Woo buyaw?* ↗! In trying to stop a child from playing with something he shouldn't, one may say 你 佟 玩儿ㄓㄓ, 回头 玩儿 坏了 ↗ ! *Nii jiin wal jiin wal, hweitour wal-*HUAYLE! ↗! ( ↱ ↘ ↱ ) 'You keep playing with it and by and by you will SPOIL IT!'

(3) Peremptory Command: This also may have a crescendo, ending in a glottal stop. 宝ㄗ, 别 动 那 东西 ↗ ! *Bao.bao, bye donq neh dong.*SHI ↗! 'Baby, don't touch that thing!' Here the "unstressed" syllable -.*shi* may be actually louder and higher than *dong* as a result of the superposed crescendo and the rising ending.

The pitch patterns of the falling ending P 28 ↘ are as follows:

| *After* | *Pitch* | *Graph* | | *Example* | |
|---|---|---|---|---|---|
| 1st Tone | 552: | ↘ | 有薑 | *Yeou jiang,* | 'There's ginger, |
| 2nd Tone | 352: | ↗↘ | 有糖 | *yeou tarng,* | and sugar, |
| 3rd Tone | 2141: | ⋀ | 有酒 | *yeou jeou,* | and wine, |
| 4th Tone | 5121: | ↘↗↘ | 有醋 | *yeou tsuh.* | and vinegar.' |

The 4th Tone may simply trail off without rising appreciably as 5221: ↘. When the last syllable is a neutral tone, then the falling occurs over its entire duration, as in the case of the 4th Tone, thus:

| 55: | 21: | ↘↘ | 青 的 ↘ | *ching de* ↘ | 'blue ones', |
|---|---|---|---|---|---|
| 35: | 31: | ↗↘ | 黄 的 ↘ | *hwang de* ↘ | 'yellow ones', |
| 21: | 41: | ↘↘ | 紫 的 ↘ | *tzyy de* ↘ | 'purple ones', |
| 51: | 121: | ↘↘ ⎫ | | | |
| ~ 52: | 21: | ↘↘ ⎬ | 绿 的 ↘ | *liuh de* ↘ | 'green ones' |

The functions of the falling ending are much more varied than those of the rising ending. On the whole they express a somewhat superior or condescending attitude on the part of the speaker, as when an adult talks to children. In most of the translations the English intonation has a low rising nucleus.

(1) Lively Enumeration to Impress: For examples, see the two preceding pitch patterns.

(2) Hearty Agreement: 世˘ ↘, 这樣才对 ↘! *Èè* ↘! *Jehyanq tsair duey* ↘! 'Yeah, that's right!' ('Now you are talking!')

(3) Correcting Errors: 你錯了 ↘, 先生 ↘! *Nii tsuoh le* ↘, *.shian.sheng* ↘! 'You are mistaken, (my dear) sir!' 外國人也不全是有本事的 ↘! *Way.gworen yee bu chyuan sh yeou been.shyh de* ↘! '(You should know) foreigners are not all experts!'

(4) Remonstrance: 宝ₜ ↘! 别動那东西 ↘! *Bao.bao* ↘, *bye donq neh dong.shi* ↘! 'Baby, don't touch that thing, please!' Compared with the same sentence with a rising ending ↗ (see above), this command is much softer and less peremptory, though just as firm and insistent.

(5) Reassurance: 别怕, 啊 ↘! 不要緊 ↘! *Bye pah, a* ↘! *Buyawjiin* ↘! 'Don't be afraid! That's all right!'

(6) Pretended Emotion: 唉! 真可憐 ↘! *Ai! Jen keelian* ↘! 'Ah! How pitiful!' Contrast this with the same sentence spoken with real (or life-like) emotion, which has no additional falling ending but is spoken low, with a very narrow pitch range. The two patterns are somewhat as follows:

Insincere:  ⟋ ⟍ ⌐ ⌙ ⟋
Sincere:  ⟍ ⊣ ⌙ ⌙

(7) Vocative Forms: In calling a person by name or by a term of direct address, the pitch range of the tones are narrowed, followed by P 28 ↘, as in: 二哥! *Ell Ge!* ( ⁞ ↘ ⟍ ), 老二! *Lao Ell!* ( ⁞ ⌙ ⟋ ), 三姐! *San Jiee!* ( ⁞ ⌐ ⟋ ), 小四儿! *Sheau Sell!* ( ⁞ ⌙ ↘ ), 妹ₜ! *Mey.mey!* ( ⁞ ↘ ⌐ ). Note that in vocative forms a 4th Tone or a 4th plus neutral simply trails off and does not rise and fall on the ↘ as in the other functions. Compare the vocative 先生! *Shian.sheng!* ( ⌐ ⌙ ) 'Sir!' and, the sarcastic .先.生! *.Shian.sheng!* ( .⌐ ⌙ ), under (3).

# 8.6. Interjections

*8.6.1. Interjections as Ever-Free Forms.* As we have noted, interjections are the only class of free forms which are always free, thus differing diametrically from particles, which are always bound. There are a few cases of class overlap, as 啊 *a* and 乜 *è*, but most interjections are not particles and most particles are not interjections.

*8.6.2. Phonological Features of Interjections*

(1) Interjections have no tone but have definite intonations.

(2) The segmental phonemes of interjections often go outside the range of the phonemic inventory for other classes of words. For example, the sound of sighing 唉! *hhai!* has a voiced *h*, which is not an ordinary phoneme in Mandarin (though it is in the Wu dialects).

*8.6.3. Variations and Uniformity Among Dialects and Languages.* While particles vary from dialect to dialect as much as do other items of the lexicon, interjections, along with their intonations, vary much less, not only among the dialects but even among different languages. But the arbitrary nature of interjections and their intonations is still the predominant factor in all interjections. Hence all interjections will still have to be recorded as vocabulary items.

*8.6.4. List of Interjections.*

I 1. 喂! *.Uè!* ~ *.Uai!* ~ *.Uei!* 'Hello!' (in telephoning); 'Heh, you there!' This interjection has a theoretical pronunciation *uei* used as quoted forms, as in   他 接 電 话 不 说 喂 , 只 说 这 是 李 宅. *Ta jie diannhuah bu shuo 'Uei', jyy shuo 'Jeh sh Lii jair.'* When he answers the phone he doesn't say "Hello", he just says "This is the Lii residence." '

I 2. 乜! *.Èh!* 'Yeah!', 'Uh-huh!'. This is the sound of agreement, a somewhat weaker form than the predicative sentence 对 了。 $_0$*Duey le.* or 是 的。$_0$*sh de.* 'That's right.'

I 3. 乜 ↘! *È* ↘! 'How right you are!' ''atta boy!' This eppresses agreement more effusively.

I 4. 乜ˇ! *Èè!* 'You are perfectly right at that!' This expresses hearty agreement, but in a more deliberate manner. This has a rather low tone, more like 212: than the 214: of the full 3rd Tone.

I 5. ㄝˇ ㄟ! *Èè* ㄟ! 'That's right, at last!' 'Now you are talk-ing!' This is used when something is done or said that finally meets with one's approval.

I 6. ㄝ! *È!* 'Say!' 'Look!' 'Wait a minute!' This is used when something suddenly happens, or suddenly occurs to one. It is short and, since it is in the 1st Tone with neither a rising nor a falling ending, the pitch does not drop.

I 7. ㄝˊ! *Èr!*

(1) 'That's right, as I guessed!' 'That's good, as I have always said!' This is short and sometimes ends in a glottal stop. It ex-presses satisfied self-assurance.

(2) 'What the ... ?!' 'What?!' This expresses sudden surprise, as in ㄝˊ？你 也 在 这儿 ？ *Èr?! Nii yee tzay jell?* 'What?! You here too?'

I 8. ㄟ ~ 欸.[79] *Ei.* 'Yes.'

(1) In answer to one's name.

(2) In compliance with a command.

This interjection is somewhat limited to the North. Elsewhere, I 9, I 12, I 14, etc., are used.

I 9. 嗯。.*Ng.* ~ .*M.* ~ ə̄. 'Yes.'. 'M-hm.' This is the weakest form of assent, which is little more than acknowledging 'I am listen-ing.', and therefore not so polite or respectful for use all the time without an occasional I 2 ('I agree') and I 14 ('I see'). Note that the articulation may be velar, labial, or nasal-vocalic, but not dental,—in other words, not a syllabic °*n*. This sometimes begins, like vocalic beginnings, with a glottal stop, but it does not mean 'No.', as 'Hm?m' and '?m?m' do in English, both of which, espe-cially the latter, could be understood as 'Yes.' in Chinese, being the same as I 9 repeated.

I 10. 嗄？ *Ar?* ~ ə̄r?

(1) 'Huh?', 'What did you say?' 'Beg pardon?'

(2) 'Yes, what?' (in answer to one's name).

I 11. 嗯？ *Nng?* ~ *Mm?* ~ ə̄ə̄? Puzzled surprise. Also 啊？ *Aa?* in the Central dialects.

---

[79]Not to be confused with 欵 *koan* 'funds'. See also n. 76 under p. 806.

I 12. 嗯 ↘! *Mm* ↘ *!* 'No, indeed!' Note that the pitch pattern of a 3rd Tone plus a falling ending (P 28) is 2141:, i.e., ⋏.

I 13. 啊! *.Ah!*

(1) 'Ah!' With about the same range of mild feelings as English 'Ah!'.

(2) Repeated request (sec. 8.5.1. p. 1069).

I 14. 哦～喔。 *.Oh*. 'I see'. This is explicit acknowledgment of receiving new information and is therefore more polite than I 2, which implies 'I know about the matter and I agree with you'. We are listing the character 哦 as the first choice, as it is the most commonly written, although *Gwoin Charngyonq Tzyhhuey* assigns only the character 喔 to this interjection. Note that this is a simple vowel [ ɔ ], as distinguished from English 'Oh', which is a diphthong: [ ou ].

I 15. 哦? *Or?* 'Is that so?' (surprise).

I 16. 嚄 ↗? *Oo* ↗? 'How strange?' (puzzled surprise).

I 17. 嚄 ↘! *Oo* ↘! 'So that's it!', '*Now* I understand!', 'It just dawned on me!'

I 18. 呃— *.e*— ～ 嗯 — *.Ng*—'Uh—', 'Er—' (sound of hesitation).

I 19. 哼! *.Heng* (i.e., [hə])! ～ *Hm!* 'Aha!' 'Ahem!' This implies a slightly superior attitude.

I 20. 哎! *.Ai!* 'Well!' This is something less than an actual sigh as in I 22. It is an expression of being mildly disconcerted or being resigned to a situation.

I 21. 嗳 ↘! *Ae* ↘! 'No, indeed!', 'Oh, no!' 'You shouldn't have done that!' This expresses strong but good-natured disapproval, such as on being presented with a big gift.

I 22. 唉! *.Hhai!* (i.e., [ɦ ai]) Sound of sighing.

I 23. 咳! *.Hai!* (i.e., [χai]) Expression of disapproval, said as when seeing someone put salt in the tea.

I 24. 嗬! *.He!* 'My goodness!'

I 25. 哈! *.Hha!* (i.e., [ ɦ a ]) 'Ha!' Sound of elation or satisfaction.

I 26. 哈ㄣ! *.Ha.ha!* (i.e., [haha]) 'Haha!' This is a spoken

laughter, as distinguished from real laughter on the one hand and from the onomatopoetic word 哈ィ *haha* in a sentence, which has the usual uvular initial *h* (i.e., [ χ ]).

I 27. 唷! *.Io!* 'Oh (I forgot).' This is short and in the first tone.

I 28. 哟ㄟ! *Iau* ㄟ! 'Goodness me!'

I 29 呦ㄟ! *Iou* ㄟ! Expression of amused disgust, disapproval, or being scandalized.

I 30. 哎呀! *.Ai.ia!* 'My goodness!' 'Oh!' This is the most general interjection for something, usually but not always, unpleasant that suddenly comes up.

I 31. 阿呀! *.A.ia!* Dialect form for I 30.

I 32. 哎哟! *Aiiau!* Stronger form for I 28.

I 33. 也ʔ~咦ʔ *Yee* ↗ʔ~*Èè* ↗ʔ Expression of puzzled surprise. This is usually said in commenting on a situation, while I 15 or I 16 is said in response to something said.

I 34. 呸! *Pei* ㄟ! 'Tut!' A somewhat deliberate interjection of contempt.

I 35. 啐! *Chi̯!* (Voiceless [ tɕ̥'i]) 'Tut!' This is stronger than I 34. There is a reading pronunciation *tsuei*, not actually spoken. Cf. verb 啐 *tsuey* 'spits at'.

I 36. 吁( ~ 嘘 )! *Shiu* (Voiceless [ɕy]) 'Shush!' Probably a borrowing from English.

I 37. 啡— *Pf—* (Dentilabial sound with air sucked in). Sound of being in a quandary: 'What shall I do?'

I 38. 嘖! *Tz̠!* (Voiceless dental affricate, with air sucked in).

(1) Interjection of admiration for something done neatly or looking nice.

(2) Same as I 36.

I 39. 嘖ィ! *Tz̠ Tz̠!* 'Tut tut!' 'How scandalous!' 'How awful!'

I 40. 嘶! *Ss̠!* (Voiceless dental fricative, with air sucked in).

(1) 'Brr!', 'It's cold!'

(2) 'Ouch!' Interjection of sudden pain, usually pronounced short.

(3) 'Oh, by the way, ... ' Interjection of a sudden turn of thought, also short, often breaking off in the middle of a sentence.

I 41. ㄌ˟ —*Lh*ʷ— (Voiceless *l*, with rounding toward the end, with air sucked in [ 㲃ʷ ]. Sometimes used in story-telling, when a new aspect of a character or of an incident comes up for immediate consideration, as in ㄌ˟— 还 有 一 樣ㄦ。 *Lhw—hair yeou i-yanql.* 'Hold on, there is one thing more.'

I 42. 哈 ~ 啊! *.Hha!* [ ɦa ] 'Ah!' Exclamation of elation or relief, as in 哈, 完 啦! *.Hha, wanl'a!* 'Whew, that's done!'

# SELECTED BIBLIOGRAPHY

Bach, Emmon, *An Introduction to Transformational Grammars*, New York: Holt, Rinehart and Winston, 1964.

Bloomfield, Leonard, *Language*, New York: Henry Holt, 1933.

Bolinger, Dwight L., "Linear Modification", *PMLA*, 67:1117-1144 (1952).

Boodberg, Peter A., "Some Proleptic Remarks on the Evolution of Archaic Chinese", *HJAS*, 2:333-372 (1937).

Carr, Denzel, "A Characterization of the Chinese National Language", *Bulletin de la Société Polonaise de Linguistique*, 3:38-96 (1932).

Chao, Y. R. ( 趙元任 ), 北京蘇州常州语助词的研究 "Beijing Sujou Charngjou Yeujuhtsyr de Yanjiow", *Tsing Hua Journal*, 3:865-918 (1926).

——, *Cantonese Primer*, Cambridge, Mass.: Harvard University Press, 1947.

——, "Chinese Terms of Address", *Language*, 22:212-241 (1956).

——, "Formal and Semantic Discrepancies Between Different Levels of Chinese Structure", *BIHP*, 28:1-16 (1956).

——, *Language and Symbolic Systems*, Cambridge: Cambridge University Press, 1968.

——, "The Logical Structure of Chinese Words", *Language*, 22:4-13 (1946).

——, *Mandarin Primer*, Cambridge, Mass.: Harvard University Press, 1948; Folkway Records, FP 8002.

——, "A Note on *Lea, Sa*, etc.", HJAS, 1:33-38 (1936).

——, "Notes on Chinese Logic and Grammar", *Philosophy of Science*, 2:31-41 (1955).

——, "A Preliminary Study of English Intonation (with American Variants) and Its Chinese Equivalents", *Ts'ai Yüan P'ei Anniversary Volume*, Supplement I of BIHP, 105-156 (1932).

Chao, Y. R., 現代吳语的研究 *Studies in the Modern Wu Dial-ects*, Peking: Tsing Hua University, 1928.

——, 新國语留声机片课本 *Shin Gwoyeu Lioushengpian Kehbeen*, Shanghai: Commercial Press, 1935.

——, 语言成份裡意义有气的程度问题 'Yeuyan Cherngfenn-lii Yihyih Yeou-wu de Cherngduh Wenntyi", *Tsing Hua Journal*, 2:1-17 (1961).

——, and L. S. Yang, *Concise Dictionary of Spoken Chinese*, Cambridge, Mass.: Harvard University Press, 1947.

Chern Chyongtzann ( 陈瓊瓚 ), 修饰语和名词之间的 '的'字 "Shioushyh-yeu her Mingtsyr jy-jian de 'Dih' Tzyh", *ZGYW*, 40:22-27 (1955).

*Chern Jiannmin* ( 陈建民 ), 论兼语式和一些有关句子 分析法的问题 "Luenn Jian-yeushyh her Ishie Yeouguan Jiuhtz Fenshifaa de Wenntyi", *ZGYW*, 93:101-106 (1960).

Chmielewski, Janusz, "Syntax and Word-Formation in Chinese," *Zakład Orientalistyki Polskiej Akademii Nauk, Rocznik Orientalistyczny*, xxviii, 1:107-125 (Warsaw, 1964).

Chomsky, Noam, *Aspects of the Theory of Syntax*, Cambridge: M.I.T. Press, 1965.

Chou, Fa-Kao ( 周法高 ), 古代汉语之法 Guuday Hannyeu Yeufaa, Taipei: Academia Sinica, 1959-1961; 3 vols. to date.

——, 中國语的词類 "Jonggwo-yeu de Tsyrley", *BIHP*, 22:303-322 (1950).

DeGroot, A. Willem, "Subject Predicate Analysis", *Lingua*, 6: 301-318 (1957).

*Dictionary of Spoken Chinese*, compiled by the staff of the Insti-tute of Far Eastern Languages, Yale University, New Hav-en, 1965.

Dragunov, A. A., *Issledovanija po Grammatike Sovremennogo Kitaiskogo Jazyka, Chasti Rechi*, Moscow: Akademija Nauk, 1952.

Egerod, Søren, *The Lungtu Dialect: A Descriptive and Historical Study of a South China Idiom*, Copenhagen: Einar Munks-gaard, 1956.

Emeneau, Murray B., *Studies in Vietnamese Grammar*, Berkeley and Los Angeles: University of California Press, 1951.

Frei, Henri, "The Ergative Construction in Chinese", *Gengo Kenkyu*, 31:22-50 (1956) and 32:83-115 (1957).

Fries, Charles C., *The Structure of English*, New York: Harcourt Brace, 1952.

Fuh Donghwa ( 傅东华 ), 北京音意读字的初步探讨 *Beeijing-In Yihdwu-Tzyh de Chubuh Tanntao*, Peking, 1958.

Fuh Tzyydong ( 傅子东 ), 词類的区分和辨认 "Tsyrley de Chiufen her Biannrenn", *ZGYW*, 51:11-16 (1956).

Grootaers, Willem A., "Initial 'pə' in a Shansi Dialect, a Problem in Grammar", TP, 42:36-69 (1954).

*Gwoin Biaujoen Hueybian* 國音標準彙編 Taipei, 1958.

Hall, Robert A., Jr., "A Note on Bound Forms", *Journal of English and Germanic Philology*, 45:450 (1946).

Halliday, M.A.K., "Grammatical Categories in Modern Chinese", *Transactions of the Philological Society*, 178-224 (1956).

Hartman, Lawton M., III, "The Segmental Phonemes of the Peiping Dialect", *Language*, 20:28-42 (1944).

Hockett, Charles, *A Course in Modern Linguistics*, New York: The Macmillan Company, 1959.

——, "Peiping Morphophonemics", *Language*, 26:63-85 (1950).

——, "Peiping Phonology", *JAOS*, 67:253-267 (1947).

——, "Two Models of Grammatical Description", *Word*, 10:210-234 (1954).

——, Chaoying Fang *et al.*, *Dictionary of Spoken Chinese*, War Department Technical Manual 30-933, Washington, D.C., 1945.

Householder, F. W., "Lists in Grammar", *Logic, Methodology, and Philosophy of Science: Proceedings of the 1960 International Congress*, Stanford, California: Stanford University Press, 1962, pp. 567-576.

——, "On Linguistic Primes", *Word*, 15:231-239 (1959).

Hwu Fuh ( 胡附 ) and Wen Liann ( 文鍊 ), 現代汉语之法探索 *Shiannday Hannyeu Yeufaa Tannsuoo*, Shanghai, 1955.

Hwu Jwuan ( 胡竹安 ), 動词後的'给'的词性和双 賓
语 问题  "Donqtsyr-how de 'geei' de Tsyrshinq her
Shuang-binyeu Wenntyi", *ZGYW*, 95:222-224 (1960).

Jakobson, Roman, "Why 'Mama' and 'Papa'?", *Perspectives in
Psychological Theory* (Essays in Honor of Heinz Werner),
New York: New York University Press, 1960, pp. 124-134.

Jang Showkang ( 張寿康 ), 畧论汉语 構 词法 "Liuehluenn
Hannyeu Gowtsyr-faa", *ZGYW*, 60:1-8 *(1957)*.

Jenq  Linshi  ( 郑林羲 ),  从一种统计看汉语词類 :
汉语的词儿和拼写法 "Tsorng i-joong Toongjih Kann
Hannyeu Tsyrley", *Hannyeu de Tserl her Pinshiee-faa*,
Collection I (1959), pp. 31-39.

Jespersen, Otto, *Analytic Syntax*, London:  George  Allen  and
Unwin, 1937.

——, *Language, Its Nature, Development and Origin*, New York:
Henry Holt, 1922.

Jou   Chyrming   ( 周遟明 ), 汉语的 使動性複式動词
"Hannyeu de Shyydonq-shinq Fuhshyh Dongtsyr", *YYYJ*,
2:23-59 (1957).

Ju Dershi ( 朱德熙 ),  現代汉语形容词的 研 究  "Shiannday Hannyeu Shyngrongtsyr de Yanjiow", *YYYJ*, 1:83-112
(1956).

Karlgren, Bernhard, *Etudes sur la Phonologie Chinoise*, Leyden
and  Stockholm,  1915-1926.  Authorized  Chinese  translation: 中國音韵學研究, 高本漢著, 趙元任、羅
常培、李方桂合译, Shanghai, 1948.

——, "Grammata Serica Recensa", *BMFEA*, 29:1-332 (1957).

——, "The Parts of Speech and the Chinese Language", *Language and Society* (Essays Presented to Arthur M. Jensen
on His Seventieth Birthday), (1961), pp. 73-78.

Korotkov, N. N., *et al.*, *Kitaiskij Jazyk*, Moscow:  Izadatel'stvo
Vostochnoj Literatury, 1956.

Kratochvíl, P., "Word  Classes  in  Modern  Standard  Chinese",
*Lingua*, 17:129-152 (1966).

Lackowski, Peter, "Words as Linguistic Primes", *Language*, 39:
211-215 (1963).

Leu  Jihpyng  ( 呂冀平 ) *et al.*, 汉语的主语賓语问题
*Hannyeu de Juuyeu Binyeu Wenntyi*, Peking, 1958.

Leu Shwushiang （呂叔湘）, 汉语ㄟ法论文集 *Hannyeu Yeufaa Luennwen-jyi*, Peking: Keshyue Chubaansheh, 1955.

——, 中國文法要略 *Jonggwo Wenfaa Yawliueh*, Shanghai: Commercial Press, 1947.

Li Jiinshi and Liou Shyhru （黎錦熙 and 刘世儒）, 中國语法教材 *Jonggwo Yeufaa Jiawtsair*, Peking: Wuushyrnian Chubaansheh, 1955.

Liou Fuh (= Liu Fu 刘復) and Lii Jiaruey （李家瑞）, 宋元以来俗字谱 *Sonq Yuan Yiilai Swutzyh Puu*, Shanghai: Academia Sinica, 1930.

Luh Jyhwei ( = C. W. Luh 陆志韋）, 汉语单音词ㄟ彙 *Hannyeu Dan'intsyr Tsyrhuey*, Peiping, 1936; reprinted as 北京话单音词ㄟ彙 *Beeijing Huah Dan'intsyr Tsyrhuey*, Peking, 1950, 2d printing, 1956.

——, 汉语的並立四字格 "Hannyeu de Binqlih Syh-tzyh Ger", *YYYJ*, 1:45-82 (1956).

——, 汉语的構词法 *Hannyeu de Gowtsyrfaa*, Peking: Keshyue Chubaansheh, 1964, revised ed.

Maa Yng （馬瀛）, 破音字举例 *Pohin Tzyh Jeulih*, Shanghai, 1923.

Malkiel, Yakov, "Studies in Irreversible Binominals", *Lingua*, 8: 113-160 (1959).

Malmqvist, Göran "The Syntax of Bound Forms in Sïch'uanese", *BMFEA*, 33:125-199 (1961).

Martin, Samuel E., "Problems of Hierarchy and Indeterminacy in Mandarin Phonology", *BIHP*, 29:209-229 (1958).

Mei Tsu-lin, "The Logic of Depth Grammar", *Philosophy and Phenomenological Research*, 24:97-105 (1963).

Mullie, Joseph, *The Structural Principles of the Chinese Language*, English transl. by A. C. Versichel, Peking, 1932, 2 vols.

Nida, Eugene, "The Analysis of Grammatical Constituents", *Language*, 24:168-177 (1948).

Ozaki, Yūjirō, "How Should the 'Passive Voice' in Chinese Be Treated?" *Tōhōgaku*, 20:77-87 (1960).

Pike, Kenneth S., "Taxemes and Immediate Constituents", *Language*, 19:65-82 (1943).

Pittman, Richard S., "On Defining Morphology and Syntax", *IJAL*, 25:199- (1959).

*Putong Qingshengci Huibian* ( 普通轻声词彙编 ), Peking: Shangwuh Yinnshuagoan, 1963.

Schafer, Edward H., "Preliminary Remarks on the Structure and Imagery of the Medieval Period", *TP*, 50:257-264 (1963).

Simon, Harry F., "Some Remarks on the Structure of the Verb Complex in Standard Chinese", *BSOAS*, 21:553-577 (1958).

——, "Two Substantival Complexes in Spoken Chinese", *BSOAS*, 15:327-355 (1953).

Simon, Walter, "Has the Chinese Language Parts of Speech?" *Transactions of the Philological Society*, 99-119 (1937).

Shianq Ruoh ( 向若 ), 关于'给'的词性 "Guan'yu 'geei' de Tsyrshinq", ZGYW, 92:64-65 (1960).

Shyu Jonqhwa ( 徐仲华 ), 词類 *Tsyrley*, Baodinq: Herbeei Renmin Chubaansheh, 1957.

Togeby, Knud, *Structure Immanente de la Langue Française*, Copenhagen, 1951.

Voegelin, Charles F., "Meaning Correlations and Selections in Morphology—Syntax Paradigms", *BIHP*, 29:91-111 (1957).

Wang, Fred Fang-yü, *Chinese Dialogues*, New Haven, Conn.: Yale Institute of Far Eastern Languages, 1953.

Wang, Fwutyng ( 王福庭 ), 連動式还是連谓式？ "Liandonq-shyh hairsh Lianwey-shyh?", ZGYW, 96:281-284 (1960) and 97:339-342 (1960).

Wang Hwan ( 王还 ), 说在 "Shuo Tzay", ZGYW, 56:25-26 (1957).

Wang Leaui ( 王了一 ), 汉语ㄥ法細要 *Hannyeu Yeufaa Gangyaw*, Shanghai: Shin Jyshyh Chubaansheh, 1957.

Wang Lih ( = Wang Leaui ) ( 王力 ), 古代汉语 *Guuday Hannyeu*, Peking 1962, 2 vols.

——, 中國現代语法 *Jonggwo Shiannday Yeufaa*, Shanghai, 1947, 2 vols.

Wang, William S.-Y. ( 王士元 ), "Some Syntactical Rules for Mandarin", *Proceedings of the Ninth International Congress of Linguists*, ed. H. G. Lunt, The Hague, Mouton and Co., 1964, pp. 191-202.

——, "Phonological Features of Tone", *IJAL*, 33:93-105 (1967).

Waterhouse, Viola, "Independent and Dependent Sentences", *IJAL*, 29:45-54 (1962).

Wells, Rulon S., "Immediate Constituents", *Language*, 23:81-117 (1947).

Whorf, Benjamin Lee, "Grammatical Categories", *Language*, 21: 1-11 (1945).

Wu Jinqtswen ( 吳競存 ), 论向心式 "Luenn Shianqshin-shyh", *Yeuyanshyue Luenntsorng*, Shanghai, 1957, pp. 130-148.

Wu Jyhann ( 吳之翰 ), 方位词使用情况的初步考察 "Fangwey-tsyr Shyyyonq Chyngkuanq de Chubuh Kao-char", *ZGYW*, 136:206-210 (1965).

Yang, L. S., "The Concept of Free and Bound in Spoken Chinese", *HJAS*. 11:462-469 (1949).

*Yeufaa Jeanghuah* ( 语法讲话 ), Peking, 1953.

*Yeuyanshyue Luenntsorng* ( 语言学论从 ), Shanghai: Shin Jyshyh Chubaansheh, 1957, 2 vols.

Yu Miin ( 俞敏 ), 汉语的句子 "Hannyeu de Jiuhtz", *ZGYW*, 61:7-10 (1957).

Zhongguoyhye [sic] Shidian ( 中國语学事典 ), compiled by Chūgoku Kenkyūkai, Tokyo: Kōnan Shoten, 1958.

---

[1]To save space, the notation "ff." is dispensed with wherever the reference is to more than one page.

| (2)° | 1st Tone | ba | po | shy | tai | tong | |
| | 2nd Tone | bar | por | shyr | tair | torng | |
| (3) | 1st Tone | shiuan | uan | shing | chu | chi | |
| | 2nd Tone | shyuan | wan | shyng | chwu | chyi | |
| (4) | 1st Tone | tzy | shan | jin | fei | duo | |
| | 3rd Tone | tzyy | shaan | jiin | feei | duoo | |
| (5) | 1st Tone | jiau | guei | shiue | dai | shau | |
| | 3rd Tone | jeau | goei | sheue | dae | shao | |
| (6) | 1st Tone | chiu | gai | dou | shin | fang | jiel |
| | 4th Tone | chiuh | gay | dow | shinn | fanq | jiell |
| (7) | 1st Tone | mha | nhiou | lhau | rheng | | |
| | 2nd Tone | ma | niou | lau | reng | | |
| (8) | 3rd Tone | C- | chii | goan | guoo | jiee | |
| | 3rd Tone | | yii | woan | woo | yee | |
| (9) | 4th Tone | C- | guay | jiow | chih | shuh | |
| | 4th Tone | | way | yow | yih | wuh | |

°The numbers refer to the rules of tonal spelling, pp. 29-30.